| 1 | 2 | 3 | 4 | 5 | 6 | 7 | 8 | 9 | 10 | 11 | 12 | 13 | 14 | 15 | 16 | 17 | 18 | 19 |

■ BUSINESS & SOCIETY
Ethics *and* Stakeholder Management
Sixth Edition

Archie B. Carroll
University of Georgia

Ann K. Buchholtz
University of Georgia

THOMSON
SOUTH-WESTERN

Australia · Canada · Mexico · Singapore · Spain · United Kingdom · United States

THOMSON

SOUTH-WESTERN

Business and Society: Ethics and Stakeholder Management, 6e

Archie B. Carroll and Ann K. Buchholz

Vice President/Editorial Director:
Jack W. Calhoun

Vice President/Editor-in-Chief:
Dave Shaut

Senior Publisher:
Melissa S. Acuña

Executive Editor:
John Szilagyi

Sr. Developmental Editor:
Judy O'Neill

Contributing Developmental Editors:
Susanna C. Smart
Heather Churchman

Marketing Manager:
Jacquelyn Carrillo

Manager of Technology, Editorial:
Vicky True

Technology Project Editor:
Kristen Meere

Media Editor:
Karen L. Schaffer

Production Editor:
Daniel C. Plofchan

Manufacturing Coordinator:
Doug Wilke

Art Director:
Stacey Jenkins Shirley

Production House:
Rebecca Gray

Cover and Internal Designer:
Lisa Albonetti

Cover Illustration:
Courtesy of Veer.com

Printer:
QuebecorWorld – Taunton
Taunton, MA

For permission to use material from this
text or product, submit a request online
at http://www.thomsonrights.com.
Any additional questions about permis-
sions can be submitted by email to
thomsonrights@thomson.com.

For more information
contact South-Western,
5191 Natorp Boulevard,
Mason, Ohio, 45040.
Or you can visit our Internet site at:
http://www.swlearning.com

PREFACE

Business & Society: Ethics and Stakeholder Management, Sixth Edition, employs a *stakeholder management* framework, emphasizing business's social and ethical responsibilities to both external and internal stakeholder groups. A *managerial perspective* is embedded within the book's dual themes of *business ethics* and *stakeholder management*. The ethics dimension is central because it is becoming increasingly clear that ethical or moral considerations are woven into the fabric of the public issues that organizations face. Economic and legal issues are inevitably present, too. However, these aspects are treated more thoroughly in other business administration courses.

The stakeholder management perspective is essential because it requires managers to (1) identify the various groups or individuals who have stakes in the firm or its actions, decisions, and practices, and (2) incorporate the stakeholders' concerns into the firm's strategic plans and operations. Stakeholder management is an approach that increases the likelihood that decision makers will integrate ethical wisdom with management wisdom in all that they do.

This edition went to press before complete resolution had been made on the fraud and ethics scandals that dominated the business news in the first five years of the 2000s. The Enron scandal and subsequent scandals involving such firms as WorldCom, Tyco, Arthur Andersen, Adelphia, Global Crossings, and HealthSouth have all occurred since the previous edition. Many of the trials of the CEOs and top executives of these firms are still underway, and readers are urged to keep up with these for the latest developments. The horrific attacks on the World Trade Center in New York and the Pentagon in Washington, DC, on September 11, 2001, are still in our memories, especially for their relevance to topics such as crisis management, global ethics, the business–government relationship, and impacts on both internal and external stakeholders. These major events will be with us forever, and we urge readers to keep in mind the extent to which our world is now changed as they read through the book and consider its content.

APPLICABLE COURSES FOR TEXT

This text is appropriate for college and university courses that are variously titled Business and Society; Business and Its Environment; Business and Public Policy; Social Issues in Management; Business, Government, and Society; Stakeholder Management; and Business Ethics. This book is appropriate for either a required or elective course seeking to meet the requirements of the Association to Advance Collegiate Schools of Business (AACSB International) for coverage of perspectives that form the context for business: ethical and global issues; the influence of political, social, legal and regulatory, environmental and technological issues; and the impact of diversity on organizations. The book is primarily intended for undergraduate courses, but when supplemented with other materials it would be appropriate for graduate courses. The book has proved useful in countries outside of the

United States, but the primary perspective of the book is the business and society inter-face as experienced inside the United States. Other developed countries share in many of these same relationships.

OBJECTIVES IN RELEVANT COURSES

Depending on the placement of a course in the curriculum or the individual instructor's philosophy, this book could be used for a variety of objectives. The courses for which it is intended include several essential goals, such as the following:

1. Students should be made aware of the demands that emanate from stakeholders and are placed on business firms.
2. As prospective managers, students need to understand appropriate business respons-es and management approaches for dealing with social, political, environmental, technological, and global issues and stakeholders.
3. An appreciation of ethical issues and the influence these issues have on management decision making, behavior, policies, and practices is important.
4. The broad question of business's legitimacy as an institution in a global society is at stake and must be addressed from both a business and societal perspective.
5. The increasing extent to which social, ethical, public, and global issues must be con-sidered from a strategic perspective is critical in such courses.

NEW TO THE SIXTH EDITION

This Sixth Edition has been updated and revised to reflect the most recent research, laws, cases, and examples. Material in this new edition includes:

- New research and examples throughout all the chapters
- Coverage throughout the text of the ethics scandals of the early 2000s and their influence on business, society, and organizations
- Discussion of new laws such as the Sarbanes–Oxley Act and the Alien Tort Claims Act
- New "Ethics in Practice" and "Search the Web" features in each chapter
- Forty-two end-of-text cases, which include:
  - Fourteen new cases, including cases on Martha Stewart, the pharmaceutical industry, Wal-Mart and its labor practices, violence in the workplace, "looks" dis-crimination, transgender issues, sexual harassment, Dick Grasso's compensation, and alcohol versus tobacco advertising
  - Fourteen revised and updated cases from the previous edition
- Recommended case list at the end of each chapter
- Recommended Web resources at the end of each chapter
- Favorite cases from past editions included in the *Instructor's Manual with Test Bank* so that they may be duplicated and used in class
- InfoTrac sidebars interspersed throughout all chapters that direct students to rele-vant, in-depth topics; also included are end-of-chapter references to InfoTrac's online database
- A thoroughly revised instructor's manual that includes hints for using the videos
- A glossary on the text's Web site (http://carroll.swlearning.com)

"ETHICS IN PRACTICE" FEATURE

Continuing in this Sixth Edition are in-chapter features titled "Ethics in Practice." Interspersed throughout the text, these features present actual ethical situations or dilemmas faced personally in the work experiences of our former students. These were originally written for class discussion, and most of them are real-life situations actually confronted by college students in their part-time and full-time work experiences. The students contributed these experiences on a voluntary basis, and we are pleased they gave us permission to use them. We would like to acknowledge them for their contributions to the book. Instructors may wish to use these as minicases for class discussion on a daily basis when a lengthier case is not assigned.

"SEARCH THE WEB" FEATURE

The "Search the Web" inserts in each chapter highlight an important and relevant Web page or pages that augment each chapter's text material. The "Search the Web" feature may highlight a pertinent organization and its activities or special topics covered in the chapter. These features permit students to explore topics in depth. Most of the Web sites have links to other related sites. The use of search engines to find other relevant materials is encouraged as the Web now catalogs a wealth of relevant information to the text topics and cases.

STRUCTURE OF THE BOOK

Part 1 provides an introductory coverage of pertinent business and society topics and issues. Because most courses for which this book is intended evolved from the issue of corporate social responsibility, this concept is treated early on. Part 1 documents and discusses how corporate social responsiveness evolved from social responsibility and how these two matured into a concern for corporate social performance and corporate citizenship. Also given early coverage is the stakeholder management concept.

Part 2 addresses strategic management for stakeholder responsiveness. The purpose of this part is to discuss management considerations for dealing with the issues discussed throughout the text. A strategic management perspective is useful because these issues have impacts on the total organization and have become intense for many upper-level managers. Special treatment is given to corporate public policy, issues and crisis management, and public affairs management. Some instructors may elect to cover Part 2 later in their courses. Part 2 could easily be covered after Part 4 or 5. This option would be most appropriate for those using the book for a business ethics course or who desire to spend less time on the management perspective.

Part 3 contains four chapters dedicated to business ethics topics. In real life, business ethics cannot be separated from the full range of external and internal stakeholder concerns. Part 3 focuses on business ethics fundamentals, personal and organizational ethics, business ethics and technology, and ethical issues in the global arena. External stakeholder issues are the subjects of Part 4. Vital topics here include business's relations with government, consumers, the environment, and the community.

The theme of Part 5 is internal stakeholder issues. In this part, we consider workplace issues and the key themes of employee rights, employment discrimination, and affirmative action. Owner stakeholders are also treated in Part 5. The topic of corporate governance captures most owner stakeholder concerns.

CASE STUDIES AT END OF TEXT

The 42 cases placed at the end of the book address a wide range of topics and decision situations. The cases are of varying length. Fourteen of the cases are new to the Sixth Edition; among these are some longer cases. Fourteen other cases have been updated. All the cases are intended to provide instructors and students with real-life situations within which to further analyze course issues and topics covered throughout the book. New to this edition are lists of recommended cases for each chapter. The 42 cases have intentionally been placed at the end of the text material so that instructors will feel freer to use them with any text material they desire.

Many of the cases in this book carry ramifications that spill over into several areas. Almost all of them may be used for different chapters. Preceding the cases is a set of guidelines for case analysis that the instructor may wish to use in place of or in addition to the questions that appear at the end of each case. The *Instructor's Manual with Test Bank* provides suggestions regarding which cases to use with each chapter.

Some cases from previous editions have been moved to the *Instructor's Manual with Test Bank*. If instructors wish to use some of their favorite previous cases, they may copy them and distribute them in class.

SUPPORT FOR THE INSTRUCTOR

Instructor's Manual with Test Bank (ISBN 0-324-22582-2). Prepared by Craig Van Sandt of Augustana College, the *Instructor's Manual with Test Bank* includes learning objectives, teaching suggestions, complete chapter outlines, highlighted key terms, answers to discussion questions, suggestions for using the management and organization video, case notes, and supplemental cases. The test bank for each chapter includes true/false and multiple-choice questions.

A computerized version of the test bank is also available electronically. ExamView® Pro (ISBN 0-324-11498-2), an easy-to-use test-generating program, enables instructors to create printed tests, Internet tests, and online (LAN-based) tests quickly. Instructors can enter their own questions, using the software provided, and customize the appearance of the tests they create. The QuickTest wizard permits test generators to use an existing bank of questions to create a test in minutes, using a step-by-step selection process.

PowerPoint Slides. Prepared by Deborah J. Baker, Texas Christian University, the PowerPoint presentation is colorful and varied, designed to hold students' interest and reinforce each chapter's main points. The PowerPoint presentation is only available on the Web site (http://carroll.swlearning.com).

Turner Learning/CNN, Management and Organization Video (DVD ISBN 0-324-32188-0, VHS ISBN 0-324-22585-7). Bring the newsgathering and programming power of CNN into your classroom with this VHS cassette of high-interest clips from the world's leading 24-hour global news network. Short segments—perfect for introducing key concepts—cover a range of issues, from white-collar crime, corporate fraud, outsourcing of jobs, lobbying ethics, looks discrimination, questionable marketing, biotechnology, and more. Suggestions for video usage are provided in the *Instructor's Manual with Test Bank*, making it easy to gain the most from this exceptional resource.

Web Site. A dynamic, comprehensive Web site at http://carroll.swlearning.com features an Interactive Study Center with quizzes, CNN video clips, PowerPoint slides, and InfoTrac resources. Instructors can download resources, including the *Instructor's Manual with Test Bank* and PowerPoint presentation slides.

ACKNOWLEDGMENTS

First, we would like to express gratitude to our professional colleagues in the Social Issues in Management Division of the Academy of Management, the International Association for Business and Society (IABS), and the Society for Business Ethics. Over the years these individuals have meant a lot to us and have helped provide a stimulating environment in which we could intellectually pursue these topics in which we have a common interest. Many of these individuals are cited in this book quite liberally, and their work is appreciated.

Second, we would like to thank the many adopters of the five previous editions who took the time to provide us with helpful critiques. Many of their ideas and suggestions have been used for this Sixth Edition. We give particular thanks to the reviewers of the Fifth Edition for their input and direction:

Paula Becker Alexander, Seton Hall University
Laquita C. Blockson, University of Northern Iowa
Peggy A. Golden, University of Northern Iowa
Michele A. Govekar, Ohio Northern University
Robert H. Hogner, Florida International University
Sylvester R. Houston, University of Denver
Timothy A. Matherly, Florida State University
Ira E. Wessler, Robert Morris University

We especially want to thank the reviewers for all previous editions. We tried to honor their recommendations and suggestions as time and space permitted. Their contributions have led to improvements in the text:

Steven C. Alber, Hawaii Pacific University
Peter Burkhardt, Western State College of Colorado
George S. Cole, Shippensburg University
Jeanne Enders, Portland State University
John William Geranios, George Washington University
Kathleen Getz, American University
Russell Gough, Pepperdine University
Ralph W. Jackson, University of Tulsa
David C. Jacobs, American University
Ed Leonard, Indiana University–Purdue University Fort Wayne
Kenneth R. Mayer, Cleveland State University

Douglas M. McCabe, Georgetown University
Bill McShain, Cumberland University
Harvey Nussbaum, Wayne State University
E. Leroy Plumlee, Western Washington University
Richard Raspen, Wilkes University
Dawna Rhoades, Embry-Riddle Aeronautical University
William Rupp, Robert Morris University
Robert J. Rustic, The University of Findlay
John K. Sands, Western Washington University
David S. Steingard, St. Joseph's University
John M. Stevens, The Pennsylvania State University
Diane L. Swanson, Kansas State University
Dave Thiessen, Lewis-Clark State College
Jeff R. Turner, Howard Payne University
Marion Webb, Cleveland State University
George E. Weber, Whitworth College

We would also like to express gratitude to our students, who not only have provided comments on a regular basis but who have also made this Sixth Edition relevant with the ethical dilemmas they have personally contributed, which are highlighted in the "Ethics in Practice" features that accompany many of the chapters. In addition to those students who are named in the "Ethics in Practice" features and have given permission for their materials to be used, we would like to thank the following students whose contributions carry over from the previous editions: Edward Bashuk, Adrienne Brown, Luis Delgado, Henry DeLoach, Chris Fain, Kristen Nessmith, and Angela Sanders. For the Sixth Edition, we would like to thank the following students who provided the anonymous contributions to the "Ethics in Practice" feature: Bryan Burnette, Eric Harvey, Sloane Hyatt, Jensen Mast, Luke Nelson, and Will Nimmer. Also, we thank Nicole Zielinski, Kevin Brinker, and Kimberly Patterson for their contributions.

We express grateful appreciation to all of the authors of the other cases that appear in the final section of the text. Contributing cases were Steven Brenner, Portland State University; Bryan Dennis, Idaho State University; Joe Gerard, SUNY Institute of Technology; Jill Brown and Kareem Shabana, University of Georgia; Norma Carr-Ruffino, San Francisco State University; and Julia Merren, former student. We also thank other faculty members who contributed cases for previous editions that carried forward into the Sixth Edition. At the University of Georgia, we especially want to thank our departmental staff, without whose support we would not have been able to finish the book on time. This outstanding group includes Ruth Davis, Dana Myers, and Billie West.

Finally, we wish to express appreciation to our family members and friends for their patience, understanding, and support when work on the book altered our priorities and plans.

Archie B. Carroll
Ann K. Buchholtz

ABOUT THE AUTHORS

Archie B. Carroll is professor of management and holder of the Robert W. Scherer Chair of Management and Corporate Public Affairs in the Terry College of Business at the University of Georgia. He has served on the faculty of the University of Georgia since 1972. Dr. Carroll received his three academic degrees from The Florida State University in Tallahassee.

Professor Carroll has published numerous books and articles. His research has appeared in the *Academy of Management Journal, Academy of Management Review, Business and Society, Journal of Business Ethics, Business Ethics Quarterly*, and many others.

His teaching, research, and consulting interests are in business and society, business ethics, corporate social performance, global stakeholder management, and strategic management. He is currently serving on the editorial review boards of *Business and Society, Business Ethics Quarterly, Journal of Management*, and the *Journal of Public Affairs*. He is former division chair of the Social Issues in Management (SIM) Division of the Academy of Management and a founding board member of the International Association for Business and Society (IABS). He is a Fellow of the Southern Management Association.

In 1992, Dr. Carroll was awarded the Sumner Marcus Award for Distinguished Service by the SIM Division of the Academy of Management; and in 1993, he was awarded the Terry College of Business, University of Georgia, Distinguished Research Award for his 20 years of work in corporate social performance, business ethics, and strategic planning. In 1998–1999, he served as president of the Society for Business Ethics. In 2000, he was appointed director of the Nonprofit Management and Community Service Program in the Terry College of Business. In 2003, he was awarded the Distinguished Service Award by the Terry College of Business.

Ann K. Buchholtz is an associate professor of strategic management in the Terry College of Business at the University of Georgia. She has served on the faculty of the University of Georgia since 1997. Dr. Buchholtz received her Ph.D. from the Leonard N. Stern School of Business at New York University.

Professor Buchholtz's teaching, research, and consulting interests are in the areas of business ethics, social issues, strategic leadership, and corporate governance. Journals in which her work has been published include *Business and Society, Business Ethics Quarterly, Academy of Management Journal, Academy of Management Review, Academy of Management Executive, Organization Science, Journal of Management, Business Horizons, Journal of Managerial Issues, Journal of General Management* and *Human Resource Management Review*. She serves on the editorial review boards of the *Journal of Management* and the *Journal of Managerial Issues* and the governing board of the Social Issues in Management Division (SIM) of the Academy of Management. Prior to entering academe, Dr. Buchholtz's work focused on the educational, vocational, and residential needs of individuals with disabilities. She has worked in a variety of organizations, in both managerial and consultative capacities, and has consulted with numerous public and private firms.

BRIEF CONTENTS

CONTENTS

Part 1

BUSINESS, SOCIETY, *and* STAKEHOLDERS

Chapter 1

■ THE BUSINESS *and* SOCIETY RELATIONSHIP

CHAPTER LEARNING OUTCOMES

After studying this chapter, you should be able to:

1 Characterize business and society and their interrelationships.
2 Describe pluralism and identify its attributes, strengths, and weaknesses.
3 Clarify how our pluralistic society has become a special-interest society.
4 Identify, discuss, and illustrate the factors leading up to business criticism.
5 Single out the major criticisms of business and characterize business's general response.
6 Categorize the major themes of the book: managerial approach, ethics, and stakeholder management.

For decades now, news stories have brought to the attention of the public countless social and ethical issues that have framed the business and society relationship. Much of this has been reported as some form of business criticism.

Recent criticism began with the rash of scandals first brought to light in late 2001 and continues until today. Initially, the Enron scandal came to light when the firm filed for bankruptcy. Eventually the degree of fraud impacting investors, employees, and others became known to the general public. The Enron scandal did not occur in isolation. Senior officers, banks, accountants, credit agencies, lawyers, stock analysts, and others were implicated.

The most serious indictment fell upon the accounting firm of Arthur Andersen, which eventually went bankrupt due to fraud and complicity in the Enron debacle. Scandals involving WorldCom, Global Crossing, Tyco, and Adelphia all came to light throughout 2002; analysts to this day are still trying to figure out what went wrong and why. Since that time, other corporate names have appeared in the news for committing alleged violations of the public trust or for raising questions regarding corporate ethics: Martha Stewart, Rite Aid, ImClone, HealthSouth, and Parmalat. As *Business Week* observed, "Watching executives climb the courthouse steps became a spectator sport in 2002."[1] This sport continues today.

In addition, questions have been raised about a host of other business issues and companies: the safety of SUVs, the distraction of cell phones, lawsuits against fast-food companies, questions about Firestone tires, and the use of illegal immigrants as employees. The litany of such issues could go on and on, but these examples illustrate the continuing tensions between business and society, which can be traced to specific incidents, trends, or events.

In addition to these specific incidents, many common issues carrying social or ethical implications have arisen within the relationship between business and society. Some of these general issues have included executive compensation, companies attempting to downsize pension programs, sexual harassment in the workplace, abuse of corporate power, toxic waste disposal, use of lie detectors, minority rights, AIDS in the workplace, smoking in the workplace, drug testing, insider trading, whistle-blowing, product liability, fetal protection issues, and use of political action committees by business to influence the outcome of legislation.

These examples of both specific corporate incidents and general issues typify the kinds of stories about business and society that one finds today in newspapers, magazines, television, and on the Internet. We offer these concerns as illustrations of the widespread interactions between business and society that capture the headlines almost daily.

Most of these corporate episodes are situations in which the public or some segment of the public believes that a firm has done something wrong or treated some individual or group unfairly. In some cases, major laws have been broken. In virtually all of these episodes, questions of whether business firms have behaved properly have arisen—that is, whether they have been socially responsible or ethical. Ethical questions are typically present in these kinds of situations. In today's socially conscious environment, a business firm frequently finds itself on the defensive: It finds itself being criticized for some action it has taken or failed to take. Whether a business is right or wrong sometimes does not matter. Powerful groups, aided by a cooperative media, can frequently exert enormous pressure on businesses and wield significant influence on public opinion, causing firms to take or not take particular courses of action.

In other instances, such as the general issues mentioned earlier, businesses are attempting to deal with broad societal concerns (such as the "rights" movement, discrimination in the workplace, loss of jobs to foreign countries, or violence in the workplace). Businesses must weigh the pros and cons of these issues and adopt the best postures, given the many, and often conflicting, points of view that are being expressed. Although the correct responses are not always easy to identify, businesses must respond and be willing to live with the consequences.

At a general level, we are discussing the role of business in society. In this book, we will address many of these concerns—the role of business versus the role of government in our socioeconomic system; what a firm must do to be considered socially responsible; what managers must do to be considered ethical; and what responsibilities U.S.-based firms have in an age of globalization. The issues we mentioned earlier are anything but abstract. They require immediate attention and definite courses of action, which quite often become the next subject of debate on the roles and responsibilities of business in society.

We are now over halfway through the first decade of the new millennium, and many economic, legal, ethical, and technological questions and issues about business and society continue to be debated. This period is turbulent. It has been characterized by significant changes in the economy, in society, in technology, and in global relationships. Against this ongoing turbulence in the business and society relationship, we want to discuss some ideas that are fundamental to an understanding of where we are and how we got here.

BUSINESS AND SOCIETY

This chapter will discuss some basic concepts that are important in the continuing business and society discussion. Among these concepts are pluralism, our special-interest society, business criticism, corporate power, and corporate social response to stakeholders. First, let us briefly define and explain two key terms: business and society.

Business: Defined

Business may be defined as the collection of private, commercially oriented (profit-oriented) organizations, ranging in size from one-person proprietorships (such as Aqua Linda Restaurant, Gibson's Men's Wear, and Zim's Bagels) to corporate giants (such as Johnson & Johnson, BellSouth, Coca-Cola, General Mills and UPS). Between these extremes, of course, are many medium-sized proprietorships, partnerships, and corporations.

When we discuss business in this collective sense, we refer to businesses of all sizes and in all types of industries. But as we embark on our discussion of business and society, we will, for a variety of reasons, doubtless find ourselves speaking more of big business in selected industries. Big business is highly visible. Its products and advertising are more widely known. Consequently, big business is more frequently in the critical public eye. In addition, people in our society often associate size with power, and the powerful are given closer scrutiny. Although it is well-known that small businesses in our society far outnumber large ones, the impact, pervasiveness, power, and visibility of large firms keep them on the front page much more of the time.

With respect to different industries, some are simply more conducive to the creation of visible, controversial social problems than are others. For example, many manufacturing firms by nature cause air and water pollution. Such firms, therefore, are more likely to be subject to criticism than a life insurance company, which emits no obvious pollution. The auto industry, most recently with SUVs, is a particular case in point. Much of the criticism against General Motors (GM) and the other automakers is raised because of their high visibility as manufacturers, the products they make (which are the largest single source of air pollution), and the popularity of their products (many families own one or more cars).

Some industries are highly visible because of the advertising-intensive nature of their products (for example, Johnson & Johnson, Sony, Anheuser-Busch, and Home Depot). Other industries (for example, the cigarette, toy, and food products industries) are scrutinized because of the possible effects of their products on health or because of their roles in providing health-related products (such as pharmaceutical firms).

When we refer to business in its relationship with society, therefore, we may focus our attention too much on large businesses in particular industries. But we should not lose sight of the fact that small- and medium-sized companies also are important. In fact, over the past decade, problems have arisen for small businesses because they have been subjected to many of the same regulations and demands as those imposed by government on large organizations. In many instances, however, smaller businesses do not have the resources to meet the requirements for increased accountability on many of the social fronts that we will discuss.

Society: Defined

Society may be defined as a community, a nation, or a broad grouping of people having common traditions, values, institutions, and collective activities and interests. As such, when we speak of business and society relationships, we may in fact mean business and the local community (business and Atlanta), business and the United States as a whole, or business and a specific group of people (consumers, minorities, investors).

When we refer to business and the entire society, we think of society as being composed of numerous interest groups, more or less formalized organizations, and a variety of institutions. Each of these groups, organizations, and institutions is a purposeful aggregation of people who have united because they represent a common cause or share a set of common beliefs about a particular issue. Examples of interest groups or purposeful organizations are numerous: Friends of the Earth, Common Cause, chambers of commerce, National Association of Manufacturers, People for the Ethical Treatment of Animals (PETA), and Rainforest Action Network.

SOCIETY AS THE MACROENVIRONMENT

The environment of society is a key concept in understanding business and society relationships. At its broadest level, the societal environment might be thought of in terms of a **macroenvironment**, which includes the total environment outside the firm. The macroenvironment is the entire societal context in which the organization resides. In a sense, the idea of the macroenvironment is just another way of thinking about society. In fact, early courses on business and society in business schools were sometimes (and some still are) titled "Business and Its Environment." The concept of the macroenvironment, however, evokes different images or ways of thinking about business and society relationships and is therefore useful in terms of framing or understanding the total business context.

A useful conceptualization of the macroenvironment is to think of it as being composed of four segments: social, economic, political, and technological.[2]

The **social environment**, as one component, focuses on demographics, lifestyles, and social values of the society. Of particular interest here is the manner in which shifts in these factors affect the organization and its functioning. The **economic environment** focuses on the nature and direction of the economy in which business operates. Variables of interest might include such indices as gross national product, inflation, interest rates, unemployment rates, foreign-exchange fluctuations, global trade, balance of payments, and various other aspects of economic activity. In the past decade, hyper-competition and the global economy have dominated the economic segment of the environment.

The **political environment** focuses on the processes by which laws get passed and officials get elected and all other aspects of the interaction between the firm, political processes, and government. Of particular interest to business in this segment are the regulatory process and the changes that occur over time in business regulation of various industries and various issues. Finally, the **technological environment** represents the total set of technology-based advancements or progress taking place in society. Pertinent aspects of this segment include new products, processes, and materials, as well as the states of knowledge and scientific advancement in both theoretical and applied senses. The process of technological change is of special importance here.[3] In recent years, computer-based technologies and biotechnology have been driving this segment of environmental turbulence.

Thinking of business and society relationships in terms of a macroenvironment provides us with a useful way of understanding the kinds of issues that constitute the broad milieu in which business functions. Throughout this book, we will see evidence of these turbulent environmental segments and will come to appreciate what challenges managers face as they strive to develop effective organizations. Each of the many specific groups and organizations that make up our pluralistic society can typically be traced to one of these four environmental segments; therefore, it is helpful to appreciate at a conceptual level what these segments are.

OUR PLURALISTIC SOCIETY

Our society's pluralistic nature makes for business and society relationships that are more interesting and novel than those in some other societies. **Pluralism** is a condition in which there is diffusion of power among society's many groups and organizations. The following definition of a pluralistic society is useful for our purposes: "A pluralistic society is one in which there is wide decentralization and diversity of power concentration."[4]

The key descriptive terms in this definition are *decentralization* and *diversity*. In other words, power is dispersed. Power is not in the hands of any single institution (such as business, government, labor, or the military) or a small number of groups. Many years ago, in *The Federalist Papers*, James Madison speculated that pluralism was a virtuous scheme. He correctly anticipated the rise of numerous organizations in our society as a consequence of it. Some of the virtues of a pluralistic society are summarized in Figure 1-1.

FIGURE 1-1

The Virtures of a Pluralistic Society

A Pluralistic Society...

- Prevents power from being concentrated in the hands of a few
- Maximizes freedom of expression and action and strikes a balance between monism (social organization into one institution) on the one hand and anarchy (social organization into an infinite number of persons) on the other[a]
- Is one in which the allegiance of individuals to groups is dispersed
- Creates a widely diversified set of loyalties to many organizations and minimizes the danger that a leader of any one organization will be left uncontrolled[b]
- Provides a built-in set of checks and balances, in that groups can exert power over one another with no single organization (business, government) dominating and becoming overly influential

---

SOURCES: [a]Keith Davis and Robert L. Blomstrom, *Business and Society: Environment and Responsibility*, 3d ed. (New York: McGraw-Hill, 1975), 63. [b]Joseph W. McGuire, *Business and Society* (New York: McGraw-Hill, 1963), 132.

Pluralism Has Strengths and Weaknesses

All social systems have strengths and weaknesses, and pluralism is no exception. A pluralistic society prevents power from being concentrated in the hands of a few. It also maximizes freedom of expression and action. Pluralism provides for a built-in set of checks and balances so that no single group dominates. By contrast, a weakness in a pluralistic system is that it creates an environment in which diverse institutions pursue their own self-interests, with the result that there is no unified direction to bring together individual pursuits. Another weakness is that groups and institutions proliferate to the extent that their goals tend to overlap, thus causing confusion as to which organizations best serve which functions. Pluralism forces conflict onto center stage because of its emphasis on autonomous groups, each pursuing its own objectives. In light of these concerns, a pluralistic system does not appear to be very efficient.

History and experience have demonstrated, however, that the merits of pluralism are considerable and that most people in society prefer the situation that has resulted from it. Indeed, pluralism has worked to achieve equilibrium in the balance of power of the dominant institutions that constitute the American way of life.

Multiple Publics, Systems, and Stakeholders

Knowing that society is composed of so many different semiautonomous and autonomous groups might cause one to question whether we can realistically speak of society in a broad sense that has any generally agreed-upon meaning. Nevertheless, we do speak in such terms, knowing that, unless we specify a particular societal subgroup or subsystem, we are referring to all those persons, groups, and institutions that constitute our society. This situation raises an important point: When we speak of business/society relationships, we usually refer either to particular segments or subgroups of society (consumers, women, minorities, environmentalists, youth) or to business and some system in our society (politics, law, custom, religion, economics). These groups of people or systems may also be referred to in an institutional form (business and the courts, business and Common Cause, business and the church, business and the AFL-CIO, business and the Federal Trade Commission).

Figure 1-2 displays in graphic form the points of interface between business and some of these multiple publics, systems, or stakeholders with which business has social relationships. Stakeholders are those groups or individuals with whom an organization interacts or has interdependencies. We will develop the stakeholder concept further in Chapter 3. It should be noted that each of the stakeholder groups may be further subdivided into more specific subgroups.

If sheer numbers of relationships are an indicator of complexity, we could easily argue that business's current relationships with different segments of society constitute a truly complex social environment. If we had the capacity to draw a diagram similar to Figure 1-2 that noted all the detail composing each of those points of interface, it would be too complex to comprehend. Today, managers cannot sidestep this problem, because management must live with these interfaces on a daily basis.

OUR SPECIAL-INTEREST SOCIETY

Our pluralistic society has become a **special-interest society**. That is, we have carried the idea of pluralism to an extreme in which we have literally tens of thousands of special-interest groups, each pursuing its own limited agenda. General-purpose interest organi-

FIGURE 1-2

Business and Selected Stakeholder Relationships

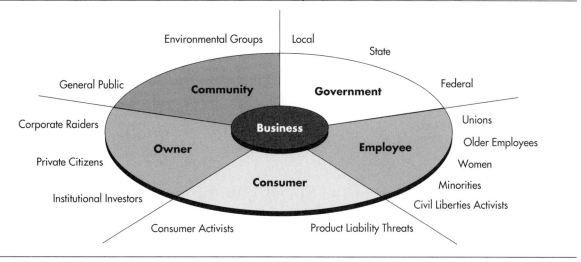

zations, such as Common Cause and the U.S. Chamber of Commerce, still exist. However, the past two decades have been characterized by increasing specialization on the part of interest groups representing all sectors of society—consumers, employees, investors, communities, the natural environment, government, and business itself. One newspaper headline noted that "there is a group for every cause." Special-interest groups not only have grown in number at an accelerated pace but also have become increasingly activist, intense, diverse, and focused on single issues. Such groups are increasingly committed to their causes.

An example of the proliferation of special-interest groups was described by the owner of a service station in Washington, DC, who watched as a debate over free markets, capitalism, and the environment brought different groups to his pumps. There were activists from the American Land Rights Association, Americans for Tax Reform, American Conservative Union, and FreeRepublic, all arriving in American-made, gas-guzzling, U.S.-flag-draped SUVs to fuel up on high octane. Counterprotestors arrived representing the U.S. Public Interest Research Group; two Greenpeace activists arrived, costumed as the Exxon Tiger and Saddam Hussein.[5]

The consequence of such specialization is that each of these groups has been able to attract a significant following that is dedicated to the group's goals. Increased memberships have meant increased revenues and a sharper focus as each of these groups has aggressively sought its narrow purposes. The likelihood of these groups working at cross-purposes and with no unified set of goals has made life immensely more complex for the major institutions, such as business and government, that have to deal with them.

BUSINESS CRITICISM AND CORPORATE RESPONSE

It is inevitable in a pluralistic, special-interest society that the major institutions that make up that society, such as business and government, will become the subjects of considerable scrutiny and criticism. Our purpose here is not so much to focus on the negative as to illustrate how the process of business criticism has shaped the major issues in the evolution of the business/society relationship today. Were it not for the fact that individuals and groups have been critical of business, we would not be dealing with this subject in a book or a course, and few changes would occur in the business/society relationship over time. But such changes have taken place, and it is helpful to see the role that business criticism has assumed in leading and bringing about change. The concept of business response to criticism will be developed more completely in Chapter 2, where we present the complete business criticism/response cycle.

Figure 1-3 illustrates how certain factors that have arisen in the social environment have created an atmosphere in which business criticism has taken place and flourished. In this chapter, we see the response on the part of business as entailing an increased concern for the social environment and a changed social contract (relationship) between business and society. Each of these factors merits special consideration.

Factors in the Social Environment

Many factors in the social environment have created a climate in which criticism of business has taken place and flourished. Some of these factors occur relatively independently, but some are interrelated with others. In other words, they occur and grow hand in hand.

SEARCH THE WEB

SPECIAL-INTEREST GROUPS

One of the most interesting and demanding pressures on the business/society relationship is that exerted by special-interest groups. Many of these groups focus on specific topics and then direct their concerns or demands to companies they wish to influence. Special-interest groups have become more numerous and increasingly activist, diverse, and focused on single issues. Unique companies, such as Good Money, Inc., that specialize in socially responsible and ethical investing, consuming, and business practices, have reason to catalog and monitor these interest groups.

One of Good Money's Web pages, "Social Investing and Consuming Activist Groups and Organizations," found at **http://www.goodmoney.com/directry_active.htm**, lists and briefly describes a few of the special-interest groups with which business must contend. Good Money's Web page contains more information about the following special-interest groups, but it catalogs many more.

- 20/20 Vision—An advocacy organization dedicated to protecting the environment and promoting peace through grassroots action.

- EarthWINS—An organization dedicated to supporting activism for the environment, peace, justice, human rights, and Native Americans.

- Environmental Defense Fund—A group that reports and acts on a broad range of regional, national, and international environmental issues.

- International Fund for Animal Welfare—An organization that promotes the just and kind treatment of animals.

- Public Interest Research Group (The PIRGs)—Groups that promote social action to safeguard the public interest.

- Rainforest Action Network—An organization whose mission is to save the world's rainforests from destruction.

FIGURE 1-3

Social Environment Factors, Business Criticism, and Corporate Response

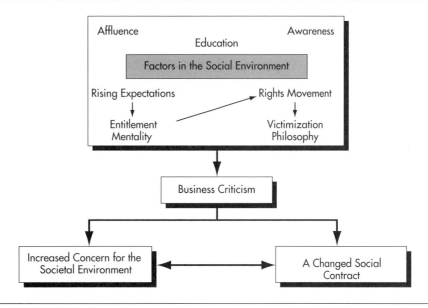

Affluence and Education. Two factors that have developed side by side are affluence and education. As a society becomes more affluent and better educated, higher expectations of its major institutions, such as business, naturally follow.

Affluence refers to the level of wealth, disposable income, and standard of living of the society. Measures of our country's standard of living indicate that it has been rising for decades. Although some Americans perceive that U.S. living standards have stopped rising, data from The Conference Board indicate that life is better for most of us now than in the past and continues to be so in spite of the recent state of the economy, which has been mixed over the past few years. The Conference Board concluded: "All told, the period 1970–1990 represents an era of substantial economic expansion and a marked improvement in the living standards of the average American." Although the expansion subsided somewhat in the late 1990s and early 2000s, The Conference Board further observed that today's young adults are living nearly twice as well off as their parents and that this improvement in American living standards will continue.[6] Per capita personal income continues to rise, and this has created a high standard of living for the U. S. citizenry, despite the fact that not everyone has shared in this prosperity.

Alongside an increased standard of living has been a growth in the average formal **education** of the populace. The U.S. Census Bureau reports that between 1970 and 2000, the number of American adults who were high school graduates grew from 55 percent to 83 percent, and the number who were college graduates increased from 11 percent to 24 percent. As citizens continue to become more highly educated, their expectations of life generally rise. The combination of affluence and education forms the underpinning for a climate in which societal criticism of major institutions, such as business, naturally arises.

Awareness Through Television.

Closely related to formal education is the high and growing level of public awareness in our society. Although newspapers and magazines are still read by only a fraction of our population, a more powerful medium—television—is accessed by virtually our entire society. Through television, the citizenry gets a variety of information that contributes to a climate of business criticism. In addition, the Internet has brought new levels of awareness in our country and around the world.

First, let us establish the prevalence and power of TV. Several statistics document the extent to which our society is dependent on TV for information. According to data compiled by the A. C. Nielsen Company, the average daily time spent viewing television per household in 1950 was 4½ hours. By 2001, Nielsen reports this figure had grown to over 7½ hours. As one writer put it: "Think about it. A typical day for an American household now divides into three nearly equal parts: eight hours of sleep, seven hours of TV, and nine hours of work or school, including getting there and back."[7] In the United States today, 98 percent of homes have color TVs, and a great majority of Americans have two or more televisions in their homes. These statistics suggest that television is indeed a pervasive and powerful medium in our society.

Straight News and Investigative News Programs.

There are at least three ways in which information that leads to criticism of business appears on television. First, there are straight news shows, such as the ubiquitous 24-hour cable news channels, the evening news on the major networks, and investigative news programs. It is debatable whether or not the major news programs are treating business fairly, but in one major study conducted by Corporate Reputation Watch, senior executives identified media criticism, along with unethical behavior, as the biggest threats to a company's reputation. Reflecting on the lessons learned from Enron, WorldCom, Tyco, and other high-profile cases of corporate wrongdoing, half the executives surveyed thought unethical behavior and media criticism were the biggest threats to their corporate reputations.[8]

The downbeat slant in reporting both business news and political news led James Fallows to write a book titled *Breaking the News: How the Media Undermine American Democracy*. Fallows skewers what media writer Howard Kurtz calls "drive-by journalism," which tends to take down all institutions in its sights.[9] Fallows goes on to argue that the media favor sizzle over substance and that they have a mindless fixation on conflict rather than truth. In this environment, business is an easy target.

Although many business leaders believe that the news media are biased against them by exaggerating the facts and overplaying the issues, journalists see it differently. They counter that business executives try to avoid them, are evasive when questioned about major issues, and try to downplay problems that might reflect negatively on their companies. The consequence is an adversarial relationship that perhaps helps to explain some of the unfavorable coverage.

Business has to deal not only with the problems of straight news coverage but also with a continuing proliferation of investigative news programs, such as *60 Minutes*, *20/20*, *Dateline NBC*, *Primetime Live*, and PBS's *Frontline* that seem to thrive on exposés of corporate wrongdoings or questionable practices. Whereas the straight news programs make some effort to be objective, the investigative shows are tougher on business. These shows are enormously popular and influential, and many companies squirm when their reporters show up on their premises complete with camera crews.

Prime-Time Television Programs.

The second way in which criticisms of business appear on TV is through prime-time television programs. Television's depiction of busi-

Some journalists have expressed concern about the results of "drive-by journalism." *Business Week* points out that while the media frequently demand high ethical standards in business, "this enthusiasm for higher professional standards . . . does not necessarily extend to ourselves." [France, Mike. *Business Week* (19 April 2004, i3879 p60).] You can read about the questionable decision to release the name of a juror in the Tyco case and the rumor that an investigative news program on Michael Jackson was scrapped in return for an exclusive interview with the Gloved One by logging on to InfoTrac College Edition at **http://www.infotrac-college.com** and keying record number A115345817.

nesspeople brings to mind the scheming J. R. Ewing of *Dallas*, whose backstabbing shenanigans dominated prime-time TV for over a decade (1978–1991) before it went off the air. More recently, the popular TV show *The Apprentice*, featuring billionaire business-man Donald Trump, has depicted aspiring business executives in often questionable roles. More often than not, the businessperson has been portrayed across the nation's television screens as a smirking, scheming, cheating, and conniving "bad guy." A vice president of the U.S. Chamber of Commerce put it this way: "There is a tendency in entertainment television to depict many businesspeople as wealthy, unscrupulous, and succeeding through less-than-honorable dealings. This is totally incorrect."[10]

Any redeeming social values that business and businesspeople may have rarely show up on prime-time television. Rather, businesspeople are often cast as evil and greedy social parasites whose efforts to get more for themselves are justly condemned and usually thwarted.[11] There are many views as to why this portrayal has occurred. Some would argue that business is being characterized accurately. Others say that the television writers are dissatisfied with the direction our nation has taken and believe they have an important role in reforming American society.[12] Apparently they think that this treatment of business will bring about change.

When Hollywood is not depicting business in a bad light on TV, it may be doing it through the movies. Dan Seligman, a writer for *Forbes*, says that a good example of this depiction was in the movie *Mission Impossible 2*, starring Tom Cruise. In this movie, Cruise plays the hero as he seeks to save the world from terrorists and pharmaceutical greed and a deadly toxin called *chimera*.[13]

Commercials. A third way in which television contributes to business criticism is through commercials. This may be business's own fault. To the extent that business does not honestly and fairly portray its products and services on TV, it undercuts its own credibility. Commercials are a two-edged sword. On the one hand, they may sell more products and services in the short run. On the other hand, they could damage business's long-term credibility if they promote products and services deceptively. According to RealVision, an initiative to raise awareness about television's impact on society, TV today promotes excessive commercialism as well as sedentary lifestyles.[14]

In three specific settings—news coverage, prime-time programming, and commercials—a strained environment is fostered by this "awareness" factor made available through the power and pervasiveness of television. We should make it clear that the media are not to blame for business's problems. If it were not for the fact that the behavior of some businesses is questionable, the media would not be able to create this kind of environment. The media, therefore, makes the public aware of questionable practices and should be seen as only one major factor that contributes to the environment in which business now finds itself.

Revolution of Rising Expectations.
In addition to affluence, formal education, and awareness through television, there are other societal developments that have fostered the climate in which business criticism has occurred. Growing out of these factors has been a **revolution of rising expectations**. This is defined as an attitude or a belief that each succeeding generation ought to have a standard of living higher than that of its predecessor and that its expectations of major institutions, such as business, should be greater also. Building on this line of thinking, one could argue that business is criticized today because society's expectations of its performance have outpaced business's ability

to meet these growing expectations. To the extent that this has occurred over the past 20 years, business finds itself with a larger problem.[15]

A **social problem** has been described as a gap between society's expectations of social conditions and the current social realities.[16] From the viewpoint of a business firm, the social problem is experienced as the gap grows between society's *expectations* of the firm's social performance and its *actual* social performance. Rising expectations typically outpace the responsiveness of institutions such as business, thus creating a constant predicament in that it is subject to criticism. Figure 1-4 illustrates the larger "social problem" that business faces today. It is depicted by the "gap" between society's expectations of business and business's actual social performance.

Although the general trend of rising expectations continues, the revolution moderates at times when the economy is not as robust. Job situations, health, family lives, and overall quality of life continue to rise. The emergence or exacerbation of social problems such as crime, poverty, homelessness, AIDS, environmental pollution, alcohol and drug abuse, and, now, terrorism are always there to moderate rising expectations.[17]

Entitlement Mentality.   One outgrowth of the revolution of rising expectations has been what has been referred to as an **entitlement mentality**. Several years ago, the Public Relations Society conducted a study of public expectations, with particular focus on public attitudes toward the philosophy of entitlement. This philosophy is the general belief that someone is owed something (for example, a job, an education, or health care) just because she or he is a member of society. The survey was conducted on a nationwide basis, and a significant gap was found between what people thought they were entitled to have and what they actually had—a steadily improving standard of living, a guaranteed job for all those willing and able to work, and products certified as safe and not hazardous to one's health.[18]

In the latter part of the first decade of the 2000s, jobs, insurance, retirement programs, and health care have become issues over which entitlement thinking has been discussed. Each of these has significant implications for the business community.

FIGURE 1-4

Society's Expectations Versus Business's Actual Social Performance

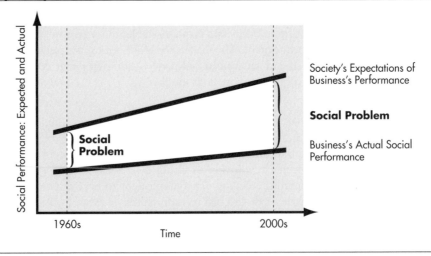

Rights Movement. The revolution of rising expectations, the entitlement mentality, and all of the factors discussed so far have contributed to what has been termed the **rights movement** that is present in society today. The Bill of Rights was attached to the U.S. Constitution almost as an afterthought and was virtually unused for more than a century. But in the past several decades, and at an accelerating pace, the U.S. Supreme Court has heard large numbers of cases aimed at establishing for some groups various rights that perhaps never occurred to the founders of our nation.[19]

Some of these rights, such as the right to privacy and the right to due process, have been perceived as generic for all citizens. However, in addition to these generalized rights, there has been activism for rights for particular groups in U.S. society. This modern movement began with the civil rights cases of the 1950s. Many groups have been inspired by the success of African-Americans and have sought progress by similar means. Thus, we have seen the protected status of minorities grow to include Hispanic Americans, Asian-Americans, Native Americans, women, the handicapped, the aged, and other groups. At various levels—federal, state, and local—we have seen claims for the rights of homosexuals, smokers, nonsmokers, obese persons, AIDS victims, and illegal immigrants, just to mention a few.

There seems to be no limit to the numbers of groups and individuals seeking "rights" in our society. Business, as one of society's major institutions, has been hit with an ever-expanding array of expectations as to how people want to be treated, not only as employees but also as owners, consumers, and members of the community. The "rights" movement is interrelated with the special-interest society we discussed earlier and sometimes follows an "entitlement" mentality among some people and within some sectors of society.

John Leo, a columnist for *U.S. News & World Report*, has argued for a moratorium on new rights.[20] He has argued that "freshly minted" rights are so common these days that they even appear on cereal boxes. He cites as an example Post Alpha-Bits® boxes, which a few years ago carried a 7-point "Kids Bill of Rights" that included one right concerning world citizenship ("you have the right to be seen, heard, and respected as a citizen of the world") and one right entitling each cereal buyer to world peace ("you have the right to a world that is peaceful and an environment that is not spoiled"). One cannot help but speculate what challenges business will face when every "goal, need, wish, or itch" is more and more framed as a right.[21]

Victimization Philosophy. It has become apparent since the early 1990s that there are growing numbers of individuals and groups who see themselves as having been victimized by society. *New York* magazine featured a cover story on "The New Culture of Victimization," with the title "Don't Blame Me!"[22] *Esquire* probed what it called "A Confederacy of Complainers."[23] Charles Sykes published *A Nation of Victims: The Decay of the American Character.*[24] Sykes' thesis, with which these other observers would agree, is that the United States is fast becoming a "society of victims."

What is particularly interesting about the novel philosophy of victimization is the widespread extent to which it is dispersing in the population. According to these writers, the victim mentality is just as likely to be seen among all groups in society—regardless of race, gender, age, or any other classification. Sykes observed that previous movements may have been seen as a "revolution of rising expectations," whereas the current movement might be called a "revolution of rising sensitivities" in which grievance begets grievance.

In such a society of victims, feelings rather than reason prevail, and people start perceiving that they are being unfairly "hurt" by society's institutions—government, business, and education. One example is worthy of note. In Chicago, a man complained to the Minority Rights Division of the U.S. Attorney's office that McDonald's was violating equal-protection laws because its restaurants' seats were not wide enough for his unusually large backside. As Sykes observes, "The new culture reflects a readiness not merely to feel sorry for oneself but to wield one's resentments as weapons of social advantage and to regard deficiencies as entitlements to society's deference."[25]

As the previous example illustrates, the philosophy of victimization is intimately related to and sometimes inseparable from the rights movement and the entitlement mentality. Taken together, these new ways of viewing one's plight—as someone else's unfairness—may pose special challenges for business managers in the future.

In summary, affluence and education, awareness through television, the revolution of rising expectations, an entitlement mentality, the rights movement, and the **victimization philosophy** have formed a backdrop against which criticism of business has grown and flourished. This does help to explain why we have an environment that is so conducive to criticism of business. In the next two subsections, we will see what some of the criticisms of business have been, and we will discuss some of the general results of such criticisms.

Criticisms of Business: Use and Abuse of Power

Few businesses have drawn as much criticism for abuses of power as Wal-Mart, even as the company wins kudos for revolutionizing distribution, spurring productivity, and fighting inflation. Is Wal-Mart the "enemy of all that's good and right in our nation"? Or is it "America's most admired company"? [Useem, Jerry. *Fortune* (8 March 2004, v149 i5 p118).] You might answer yes to the first question if you're a wage earner or live in a community whose small businesses can expect to be challenged by a new Wal-Mart. You might answer yes to the second question if you're a Wal-Mart shareholder or a price-conscious consumer. Read points on both sides by logging on to InfoTrac College Edition at **http://www.infotrac-college.com** and keying record number A113566627.

Many criticisms have been leveled at business over the years: Business is too big, it's too powerful, it pollutes the environment and exploits people for its own gain, it takes advantage of workers and consumers, it does not tell the truth, and so on. A catalog of business criticisms would be extensive. If one were to identify a common thread that seems to run through all the complaints, it seems to be business's use and perceived abuse of power. This is an issue that will not go away. In its September 11, 2000, issue, *Business Week* poses as its cover story: "Too Much Corporate Power?" In this feature article, *Business Week* presents its surveys of the public regarding business power. Most Americans are willing to acknowledge that Corporate America gets much credit for the good fortunes of the country. In spite of this, 72 percent of Americans say business has too much power over too many aspects of their lives.[26] In the October 6, 2003, issue, *Business Week* ran another cover story; this time it asked "Is Wal-Mart Too Powerful?"[27] Whether at the general level or the level of the firm, questions about business's power continue to be raised.

Some of the points of friction between business and the public, in which corporate power is identified as the culprit, include such topics as CEO pay, investor losses, mounting anger and frustration over health care and drug prices, poor airline service, HMOs that override doctors' decisions, faulty tires, in-your-face marketing, globalization, corporate bankrolling of politicians, sweatshops, urban sprawl, and low wages. Before discussing business power in more detail, we should note that in addition to the use or abuse of power, the major criticism seems to be that business often engages in questionable or unethical behavior with respect to its stakeholders.

What is **business power**? Business power refers to the ability or capacity to produce an effect or to bring influence to bear on a situation or people. Power, in and of itself, may be either positive or negative. In the context of business criticism, however, power typically is perceived as being abused. Business certainly does have enormous power, but whether it abuses power is an issue that needs to be carefully examined. We will not settle this issue here, but the allegation that business abuses power remains the central theme behind the details.

Ethics in Practice

DRINK SPECIALS?

While working as a waitress in a busy restaurant/bar, I observed a practice that was very common but appeared questionable. Often, in busy places of business, it is all too easy for employees to bend the rules and get away with it. Managers have so much on their hands that they have to trust their employees and, sadly, not everyone is trustworthy. In our restaurant, servers and bartenders were given a daily "spill sheet" on which they were supposed to record any alcoholic (and, especially, expensive) drinks that were accidentally spilled in the course of business that day.

When an employee is moving fast and dodging customers, spills are a natural occurrence, and the "spill sheet" was meant to take those accidents into account for the restaurant. When I began working there, I realized that at the end of the night not all of the spills on the list were genuine. Employees, typically bartenders because they had direct access, would serve free drinks to their friends all night and put the drinks on the spill sheet.

To accommodate large numbers of missing drinks, bartenders would serve their friends the same kind of beer all night and then claim a dropped case of that brand of beer. They could also claim a dropped liquor bottle and have enough to keep alcohol flowing for their friends. Other employees would also take responsibility for some of the spills to make the bartenders appear credible.

I was asked on several occasions to take responsibility for a fake "spill." In this way, employees used the spill sheet to their advantage instead of for its intended purpose. They would serve free drinks courtesy of "spilling" until the volume reached was just under the suspicious level. As long as a pattern was not formed, the managers never knew they were being deceived.

1. What type of ethical standards, if any, were the employees in the restaurant living by when they committed this common, but questionable action? Is the "entitlement mentality" at work here?

2. If you were an employee and you saw this situation, would you feel it should be reported or would you keep your mouth shut and let the practice continue? If you were asked to participate and take a "spill" for the team, what would you do? Why?

3. If your manager ever confronted you about some excessive spilling, would you personally feel it was more ethical to protect the other employees or tell your manager the truth?

Contributed Anonymously

Levels of Power. To understand business power, one must note that it resides at and may be manifested at several different levels. Epstein identified four such levels: the macro level, the intermediate level, the micro level, and the individual level.[28] The *macro level* refers to the corporate system—Corporate America—the totality of business organizations. Power here emanates from the sheer size, resources, and dominance of the corporate system. The *intermediate level* refers to groups of corporations acting in concert in an effort to produce a desired effect—to raise prices, control markets, dominate purchasers, promote an issue, or pass or defeat legislation. Prime examples are the airlines, cable TV companies, banks, OPEC, pharmaceutical companies, or defense contractors pursuing interests they have in common. The combined effect of companies acting in concert is significant. The *micro level* of power is the level of the individual firm. This might refer to the exertion of power or influence by any major corporation—Microsoft, Wal-Mart, Procter & Gamble, or Nike, for example. The final level is the *individual level*. This refers to the individual corporate leader exerting power—Ted Turner, Donald Trump, Michael Eisner (Disney), Carly Fiorina (Hewlett-Packard), Bill Gates (Microsoft), or Anita Roddick (The Body Shop).

The important point here is that as one analyzes corporate power, one should think in terms of the different levels at which that power is manifested. When this is done, it is not easy to conclude whether corporate power is excessive or has been abused. Specific levels of power need to be examined before conclusions can be reached.

Spheres of Power.

In addition to levels of power, there are also many different spheres or arenas in which this power may be manifested. Figure 1-5 depicts one way of looking at the levels Epstein identified and some of the spheres of power to which he was referring. *Economic power* and *political power* are two spheres that are referred to often, but business has other, more subtle forms of power as well. These other spheres include *social and cultural power, power over the individual, technological power,* and *environmental power.*

Is the power of business excessive? Does business abuse its power? Obviously, many people think so. To provide careful and fair answers to these questions, however, one must very judiciously specify which level of power is being referred to and in which sphere the power is being employed. When this is done, it is not simple to arrive at generalizable answers.

Furthermore, the nature of power is such that it is sometimes wielded unintentionally. Sometimes it is consequential; that is, it is not wielded intentionally but nevertheless exerts its influence even though no attempt is made to exercise it.[29]

Balance of Power and Responsibility.

Whether or not business abuses its power or allows its use of power to become excessive is a central issue that cuts through all the topics we will be discussing in this book. But, power cannot be viewed in isola-

---

FIGURE 1-5

Levels and Spheres of Corporate Power

Levels / Spheres	Macro Level (the business system)	Intermediate Level (several firms)	Micro Level (single firm)	Individual Level (single executive)
Economic				
Social/Cultural				
Individual				
Technological				
Environmental				
Political				

tion from responsibility, and this power/responsibility relationship is the foundation of calls for corporate social responsibility. The **Iron Law of Responsibility** is a concept that addresses this: "In the long run, those who do not use power in a manner which society considers responsible will tend to lose it."[30] Stated another way, whenever power and responsibility become substantially out of balance, forces will be generated to bring them into closer balance.

When power gets out of balance, a variety of forces come to bear on business to be more responsible and more responsive to the criticisms being made against it. Some of these more obvious forces include governmental actions, such as increased regulations and new laws. The investigative news media become interested in what is going on, and a whole host of special-interest groups bring pressure to bear. In the *Business Week* cover story cited earlier, the point was made that "it's this power imbalance that's helping to breed the current resentment against corporations."[31]

The tobacco industry is an excellent example of an industry that has felt the brunt of efforts to address allegations of abuse of power. Complaints that the industry produces a dangerous, addictive product and markets that product to young people have been escalating for years. The U.S. Food and Drug Administration (FDA) tried to assert jurisdiction over cigarettes and has been trying to rein in tobacco companies through aggressive regulation. One major outcome of this effort to bring the tobacco industry under control was a proposed $368 billion settlement, to be paid over 25 years, in which the tobacco firms settle lawsuits against them, submit to new regulations, and meet strict goals for reducing smoking in the United States. Although the industry continues to fight these measures, as it always has, it is expected that by the year 2022 tobacco's role in American society will be forever reduced.[32]

In 2002, the Congress quickly passed the Sarbanes–Oxley Act, which was designed to rein in the power and abuse that were manifested in such scandals as Enron, WorldCom, Arthur Andersen, and Tyco. Executives have been grumbling that the new law will be costly, cumbersome, and redundant, but this illustrates what happens when power and responsibility get out of balance.[33]

Business Response: Concern and Changing Social Contract

Growing out of criticisms of business and the idea of the power/responsibility equation has been an increased concern for the stakeholder environment on the part of business and a changed social contract. We previously indicated that the social environment was composed of such factors as demographics, lifestyles, and social values of the society. It may also be seen as a collection of conditions, events, and trends that reflect how people think and behave and what they value. As firms have sensed that the social environment and the expectations of business are changing, they have realized that they must change, too.

The **social contract** is that set of two-way understandings that characterizes the relationship between major institutions—in our case, business and society. The social contract is changing, and this change is a direct outgrowth of the increased importance of the social environment. The social contract has been changing to reflect society's expectations of business, especially in the social and ethical realms.

The social contract between business and society, as illustrated in Figure 1-6 on page 20, is partially articulated through:

FIGURE 1-6

Elements in the Social Contract

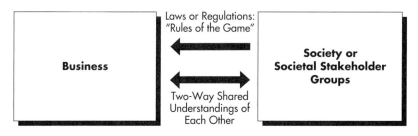

1. *Laws and regulations* that society has established as the framework within which business must operate; and,
2. *Shared understandings* that evolve as to each group's expectations of the other

It is clear how laws and regulations spell out the "rules of the game" for business. Shared understandings, on the other hand, create more confusion and room for misunderstandings. In a sense, these shared understandings reflect mutual expectations regarding each other's roles, responsibilities, and ethics. These unspoken components of the social contract represent what Donaldson and Dunfee refer to as the normative perspective on the relationship (that is, what "ought" to be done by each party to the social contract).[34]

A parallel example to the business/society social contract may be seen in the relationship between a professor and the students in his or her class. University regulations and the syllabus for the course spell out the formal aspects of this relationship. The shared understandings address those expectations that are generally understood but not necessarily spelled out formally. An example might be "fairness." The student expects the professor to be "fair" in making assignments, in the level of work expected, in grading, and so on. Likewise, the professor expects the student to be fair in evaluating him or her on course evaluation forms, to be fair by not passing off someone else's work as his or her own, and so on.

An editorial from *Business Week* on the subject of the social contract summarizes well the modern era of business and society relationships:

> *Today it is clear that the terms of the contract between society and business are, in fact, changing in substantial and important ways. Business is being asked to assume broader responsibilities to society than ever before, and to serve a wider range of human values . . . . Inasmuch as business exists to serve society, its future will depend on the quality of management's response to the changing expectations of the public.*[35]

More recently, a 2000 *Business Week* editorial commented on the new social contract by saying "Listen up, Corporate America. The American people are having a most serious discussion about your role in their lives." The editorial was referring to the recent criticisms coming out in the early 2000s about abuse of corporate power.[36] Such a statement suggests that as time continues, we will constantly witness changes in the social contract between business and society.

FOCUS OF THE BOOK

This book takes a *managerial approach* to the business and society relationship. The managerial approach emphasizes two main themes that are important today: **business ethics** and **stakeholder management**. First, let us discuss the managerial approach.

Managerial Approach

Managers are practical, and they have begun to deal with social and ethical concerns in ways similar to those they have used to deal with traditional business functions—operations, marketing, finance, and so forth—in a rational, systematic, and administratively rigorous fashion. By viewing issues of social and ethical concern from a managerial frame of reference, managers have been able to reduce seemingly unmanageable concerns to ones that can be dealt with in a rational and evenhanded fashion. Yet, at the same time, managers have had to integrate traditional economic and financial considerations with ethical or moral considerations.

A managerial approach to the business/society relationship confronts the individual manager continuously with questions such as:

- What changes are occurring or will occur in society's expectations of business that mandate business's taking the initiative with respect to particular societal or ethical problems?
- Did business in general, or our firm in particular, have a role in creating these problems?
- What impact is social change having on the organization, and how should we best respond to it?
- Can we reduce broad social problems to a size that can be effectively addressed from a managerial point of view?
- With which social and ethical problems can we act most effectively?
- What are the specific problems, alternatives for solving these problems, and implications for management's approach to dealing with social issues?
- How can we best plan and organize for responsiveness to socially related business problems?

From the standpoint of urgency in managerial response, management is concerned with two broad types or classes of social issues. First, there are those issues or crises that arise on the spur of the moment and for which management must formulate relatively quick responses. These may be either issues that management has never faced before or issues it has faced but does not have time to deal with, except on a short-term basis. A typical example might be a protest group that shows up on management's doorstep one day, arguing vehemently that the company should withdraw its sponsorship of a violent television show scheduled to air the next week.

Second, there are issues or problems that management has time to deal with on a more long-term basis. These issues include environmental pollution, employment discrimination, product safety, and occupational safety and health. In other words, these are enduring issues that will be of concern to society for a long time and for which management must develop a reasonably thoughtful organizational response. Management must thus be concerned with both short-term and long-term capabilities for dealing with social problems and the organization's social performance.

Ethics in Practice

DONATIONS FOR PROFIT

While working as the director of junior golf at a Nashville area golf course, I was put in charge of fund-raising. This task required me to spend numerous hours calling and visiting local businesses, seeking their donations for our end-of-the-summer golf tournament. After weeks of campaigning for money, I was pleased to have raised $3,000 for the tournament. The money was intended to be used for prizes, food, and trophies for the 2-day Tournament of Champions.

I notified the golf course manager of my intentions to spend the money at a local golf store to purchase prizes for the participants. Upon hearing of my decision to spend all of the contribution money on the tournament, my manager asked me to only spend $1,500. I was confused by this request because I had encouraged various companies to contribute by telling them that their money would all be spent on the children registered in the tournament. My manager, however, told me that the golf course would pocket the other $1,500 as pure profit. He said the economy has been struggling and that the course could use any extra money to boost profits.

I was deeply angered that I had given my word to these companies and now the golf course was going to pocket half the donations. Feeling that my manager was in the wrong, I went to him again, this time with an ultimatum. The money was either to be spent entirely on the tournament or I would return all of the checks personally, citing my manager's plan as the reason. In response, he said that I could spend the money anyway I desired, but he would appreciate it if I were frugal with the money. I spent it all.

1. Was my manager wrong for seeking to pocket the donation money as profit? Does it make any difference that the golf course was experiencing perilous economic times? (After all, if the course goes out of business, tournaments cannot be held at all).

2. Was I right in challenging my manager? Should I have handled this differently?

3. Do you think the companies would have felt cheated if the golf course had pocketed their donations?

Contributed by Eric Knox

The test of success of the managerial approach will be the extent to which leaders can improve an organization's social performance by taking a managerial approach rather than dealing with the issues on an ad hoc basis. Such a managerial approach will require balancing the needs of urgency with the careful response to enduring issues.

Business Ethics Theme

The managerial focus attempts to take a practical look at the social issues and expectations business faces, but ethical questions inevitably come into play. **Ethics** basically refers to issues of right, wrong, fairness, and justice, and business ethics focuses on ethical issues that arise in the commercial realm. Ethical threads run throughout our discussion because questions of right, wrong, fairness, and justice, no matter how slippery they are to deal with, permeate business's activities as it attempts to interact effectively with major stakeholder groups: employees, customers, owners, government, and the global and local communities. In light of the ethical scandals in recent years, the ethics theme resonates as one of the most critical dimensions of business and society relationships.

The inevitable task of management is not only to deal with the various stakeholder groups in an ethical fashion but also to reconcile the conflicts of interest that occur between the organization and the stakeholder groups. Implicit in this challenge is the ethical dimension that is present in practically all business decision making where stakeholders are concerned. In addition to the challenge of treating fairly the groups with which business interacts, management faces the equally important task of creating an organizational climate in which all employees make decisions with the interests of the public, as well as those of the organization, in mind. At stake is not only the firm's reputation but also the reputation of the business community in general.

Stakeholder Management Theme

As we have indicated throughout this chapter, **stakeholders** are individuals or groups with which business interacts who have a "stake," or vested interest, in the firm. They could be called "publics," but this term may imply that they are outside the business sphere and should be dealt with as external players rather than as integral parts of the business and society relationship. As a matter of fact, stakeholders actually constitute the most important elements of that broad grouping known as society.

We consider two broad groups of stakeholders in this book. First, we consider *external stakeholders*, which include government, consumers, and community members. Domestic and global stakeholders are major concerns. We treat government first because it represents the public. It is helpful to understand the role and workings of government in order to best appreciate business's relationships with other groups. Consumers may be business's most important stakeholders. Members of the community are crucial, too, and they are concerned about a variety of issues. One of the most important is the natural environment. Two other major community issues include business giving (or corporate philanthropy) and plant closings (including downsizing and sending jobs offshore). All these issues have direct effects on the public. Social activist groups representing external stakeholders also must be considered to be a part of this classification.

The second broad grouping of stakeholders is composed of *internal stakeholders*. Business owners and employees are the principal groups of internal stakeholders. We live in an organizational society, and many people think that their roles as employees are just as important as their roles as investors or owners. Both of these groups have legitimate legal and moral claims on the organization, and management's task is to address their needs and balance these needs against those of the firm and of other stakeholder groups. We will develop the idea of stakeholder management more fully in Chapter 3.

STRUCTURE OF THE BOOK

The structure of this book is outlined in Figure 1-7 on page 24.

In Part 1, titled "Business, Society, and Stakeholders," there are three chapters. Chapter 1 provides an overview of the business and society relationship. Chapter 2 covers corporate citizenship: social responsibility, responsiveness, and performance. Chapter 3 addresses the stakeholder management concept. These chapters provide a crucial foundation for understanding all of the discussions that follow. They provide the context for the business and society relationship.

Part 2 is titled "Strategic Management for Corporate Stakeholder Performance." Its two chapters address management-related topics. Chapter 4 covers strategic management and corporate public affairs. Chapter 5 deals with issues management and crisis management.

FIGURE 1-7

Organization and Flow of the Book

Business, Society, and Stakeholders

PART ONE
1. The Business and Society Relationship
2. Corporate Citizenship: Social Responsibility, Responsiveness, and Performance
3. The Stakeholder Approach to Business, Society, and Ethics

Strategic Management for Corporate Stakeholder Performance

PART TWO
4. Strategic Management and Public Affairs
5. Issues Management and Crisis Management

Business Ethics and Management

PART THREE
6. Business Ethics Fundamentals
7. Personal and Organizational Ethics
8. Business Ethics and Technology
9. Ethical Issues in the Global Arena

External Stakeholder Issues

PART FOUR
10. Business, Government, and Regulation
11. Business's Influence on Government and Public Policy
12. Consumer Stakeholders: Information Issues and Responses
13. Consumer Stakeholders: Product and Service Issues
14. The Natural Environment as Stakeholder
15. Business and Community Stakeholders

Internal Stakeholder Issues

PART FIVE
16. Employee Stakeholders and Workplace Issues
17. Employee Stakeholders: Privacy, Safety, and Health
18. Employment Discrimination and Affirmative Action
19. Owner Stakeholders and Corporate Governance

CASES

Part 3, "Business Ethics and Management," focuses exclusively on business ethics. Business ethics fundamentals are established in Chapter 6, and personal and organizational ethics are discussed in more detail in Chapter 7. Chapter 8 addresses business ethics and technology. Chapter 9 treats business ethics in the global or international sphere. Although ethical issues cut through and permeate many of the discussions in this book, this significant treatment of business ethics is warranted by a need to explore in some detail what is meant by the ethical dimension in management.

Part 4, "External Stakeholder Issues," addresses the major external stakeholders of business. In Chapter 10, because government is such an active player in all the groups to follow, we consider business/government relationships and government regulations. In Chapter 11, we discuss how business endeavors to shape and influence government and public policy. Chapters 12 and 13 address consumer stakeholders. Chapter 14 addresses the natural environment as stakeholder. Chapter 15 addresses business and community stakeholder issues, including corporate philanthropy.

In Part 5, "Internal Stakeholder Issues," employees and owners, are addressed. Chapter 16 considers employees and major workplace issues, and Chapter 17 looks carefully at the issues of employee privacy, safety, and health. In Chapter 18, we focus on the special case of employment discrimination. Chapter 19 concludes the text with a discussion of corporate governance and the management and shareholder relationship. In the past few years, we have seen many changes take place in corporate governance as a result of earlier scandals.

Depending on the emphasis desired in the course, Part 2 could be covered where it is currently located, or it could be postponed until after Part 5. Alternatively, it could be omitted if a strategic management orientation is not desired.

Taken as a whole, the book strives to take the reader through a building-block arrangement of basic concepts and ideas that are vital to the business and society relationship and to explore the nature of social and ethical issues and stakeholder groups with which management must interact. It considers the external and internal stakeholder groups in some depth.

▪ SUMMARY

The pluralistic business system in the United States has several advantages and some disadvantages. Within this context, business firms must deal with a multitude of stakeholders and an increasingly special-interest society. A major force that shapes the public's view of business is the criticism that business receives from a variety of sources. Factors in the social environment that have contributed to an atmosphere in which business criticism thrives include affluence, education, public awareness developed through the media (especially TV), the revolution of rising expectations, a growing entitlement mentality, the rights movement, and a philosophy of victimization. In addition, actual questionable practices on the part of business have made it a natural target. The ethics scandals, including Enron and post-Enron, have perpetuated criticisms of business. Not all firms are guilty, but the guilty attract negative attention to the entire business community. One result is that the trust and legitimacy of the entire business system is called into question.

A major criticism of business is that it abuses its power. To understand power, you need to recognize that it may exist and operate at four different levels: the level of the entire business system, groups of companies acting in concert, the level of the individual firm, and the level of the individual corporate executive. Moreover, business power may be manifested in several different spheres: economic, political, technological, environmental, social, and individual. It is difficult to assess whether business is actually abusing its power, but it is clear that business has enormous power and that it must exercise this power carefully. Power evokes responsibility, and this is the central reason that calls for corporate responsiveness have been prevalent in recent years. The Iron Law of Responsibility has called for greater balance in power and responsibility. These concerns have led to a changing social environment for business and a changed social contract.

▪ KEY TERMS

affluence (page 11)
business (page 5)
business ethics (page 21)
business power (page 16)
economic environment (page 6)
education (page 11)
entitlement mentality (page 14)
ethics (page 22)
Iron Law of Responsibility (page 19)
macroenvironment (page 6)
pluralism (page 7)
political environment (page 6)

revolution of rising expectations (page 13)
rights movement (page 15)
social contract (page 19)
social environment (page 6)
social problem (page 14)
society (page 6)
special-interest society (page 8)
stakeholder management (page 21)
stakeholders (page 23)
technological environment (page 7)
victimization philosophy (page 16)

▪ DISCUSSION QUESTIONS

1. In discussions of business and society, why is there a tendency to focus on large rather than small- or medium-sized firms? Have the corporate ethics scandals of the early 2000s affected small- and medium-sized firms? If so, in what ways have these firms been affected?

2. What is the one greatest strength of a pluralistic society? What is the one greatest weakness? Do these characteristics work for or against business?

3. Identify and explain the major factors in the social environment that create an atmosphere in which business criticism takes place and prospers. How are the factors related to one another?

4. Give an example of each of the four levels of power discussed in this chapter. Also, give an example of each of the spheres of business power.

5. Explain in your own words the *Iron Law of Responsibility* and the *social contract*. Give an example of a shared understanding between you as a consumer or an employee and a firm with which you do business or for which you work. Was Congress justified in passing the Sarbanes–Oxley Act in 2002 due to the business scandals of the early 2000s?

▪ RECOMMENDED CASES

Many of the end-of-text cases may be related to Chapter 1. You may wish to consider studying the following cases with Chapter 1.

Case 1. "WAL-MART: THE MAIN STREET MERCHANT OF DOOM." This case about Wal-Mart addresses and illustrates a host of business and society relationship issues. It especially introduces the topics of business power, business impact on the community, and social responsibility. In what ways has Wal-Mart's power impacted the community? Has it used its power responsibly?

Cases 2A and 2B. "THE BODY SHOP INTERNATIONAL PLC" AND "THE BODY SHOP'S ADVERTISING CAMPAIGN." These two Body Shop cases illustrate how the changing social contract has affected one major socially-conscious company. The cases also raise issues about business criticism and corporate response to criticism. In the 2B case, the issue of Anita Roddick keeping her word to her supporters is a key issue.

Cases 3A and 3B. "THE BODY SHOP'S REPUTATION IS TARNISHED" AND "THE BODY SHOP INTERNATIONAL PLC (1998–2004)." present a host of issues about corporate power, social responsibility, stakeholders, and business ethics. The case illustrates the quandary a company faces when some of its practices seem inconsistent with its stated principles.

■ WEB RESOURCES

The URLs listed here are current at the time of publication. Should any of these Web sites change, please search under the company's or organization's name for an updated address.

Better Business Bureau (BBB)
http://www.bbb.org

Business Roundtable
http://www.brtable.org

Business Week
http://www.businessweek.com

Corporate Accountability Project
http://www.corporation.org

Fortune
http://www.fortune.com

The Conference Board
http://www.conference-board.org

National Federation of Independent Businesses
http://www.nfibonline.com

Public Interest Groups
http://www.pirg.org

The Wall Street Journal
http://www.wsj.com

U.S. Chamber of Commerce
http://www.uschamber.com

 InfoTrac® College Edition   http://www.infotrac-college.com

Articles from Business Week, Fortune, *and* The Wall Street Journal *can be researched, retrieved, and read from your desktop using InfoTrac's online database.*

■ ENDNOTES

1. "The Perp Walk," *Business Week* (January 13, 2003), 86.
2. Liam Fahey and V. K. Narayanan, *Macroenvironmental Analysis for Strategic Management* (St. Paul: West, 1986), 28–30.
3. *Ibid.*
4. Joseph W. McGuire, *Business and Society* (New York: McGraw-Hill, 1963), 130.
5. "Location Is Everything," *Washington Times National Weekly Edition* (June 17–23, 2002), 6.
6. Fabian Linden, "The American Dream," *Across the Board* (May 1991), 7–10.
7. "Average American Family Watches TV 7 Hours Each Day," *Athens Banner Herald* (January 25, 1984), 23.
8. "Executives See Unethical Behavior, Media Criticisms as Threats," *Nashville Business Journal* (June 11, 2002).
9. James Fallows, *Breaking the News: How the Media Undermine American Democracy* (Pantheon Press, 1996). See also Howard Kurtz, *Hot Air: All Talk, All the Time* (Basic Books, 1997).
10. Eric Pace, "On TV Novels, the Bad Guy Sells," *The New York Times* (April 15, 1984).
11. Linda S. Lichter, S. Robert Lichter, and Stanley Rothman, "How Show Business Shows Business," *Public Opinion* (November 1982), 10–12.
12. Nedra West, "Business and the Soaps," *Business Forum* (Spring 1983), 4.
13. Dan Seligman, "Tom Cruise Versus Corporate Evil," *Forbes* (September 4, 2000), 82.
14. "Facts and Figures About Our TV Habits," (2003), http://www.tvturnoff.org.
15. Robert J. Samuelson, *The Good Life and Its Discontents: The American Dream in the Age of Entitlement, 1945–1995* (Times Books, 1996).
16. Neil H. Jacoby, *Corporate Power and Social Responsibility* (New York: Macmillan, 1973), 186–188.
17. Linda DeStefano, "Looking Ahead to the Year 2000: No Utopia, But Most Expect a Better Life," *The Gallup Poll Monthly* (January 1990), 21.
18. Joseph Nolan, "Business Beware: Early Warning Signs for the Eighties," *Public Opinion* (April/May 1981), 16.
19. Charlotte Low, "Someone's Rights, Another's Wrongs," *Insight* (January 26, 1987), 8.
20. John Leo, "No More Rights Turns," *U.S. News & World Report* (October 23, 1995), 34.
21. John Leo, "A Man's Got a Right to Rights," *U.S. News & World Report* (August 4, 1997), 15.
22. John Taylor, "Don't Blame Me!" *New York* (June 3, 1991).
23. Pete Hamill, "A Confederacy of Complainers," *Esquire* (July 1991).
24. Charles J. Sykes, *A Nation of Victims: The Decay of the American Character* (New York: St. Martin's Press, 1991).
25. *Ibid.*, 12.

26. Aaron Bernstein, "Too Much Corporate Power?" *Business Week* (September 11, 2000), 144–155.

27. "Is Wal-Mart Too Powerful?" *Business Week* (October 6, 2003).

28. Edwin M. Epstein, "Dimensions of Corporate Power: Part I," *California Management Review* (Winter 1973), 11.

29. *Ibid.*

30. Keith Davis and Robert L. Blomstrom, *Business and Its Environment* (New York: McGraw-Hill, 1966), 174–175.

31. Bernstein, 146.

32. John Carey, "The Tobacco Deal: Not So Fast," *Business Week* (July 7, 1997), 34–37; Richard Lacayo, "Smoke Gets in Your Aye," *Time* (January 26, 1998), 50; Jeffrey H. Birnbaum, "Tobacco's Can of Worms," *Fortune* (July 21, 1997), 58–60; Dwight R. Lee, "Will Government's Crusade Against Tobacco Work?" (Center for The Study of American Business, July 1997).

33. "Honesty Is a Pricey Policy," *Business Week* (October 27, 2003), 100–101.

34. Thomas Donaldson and Thomas W. Dunfee, "Toward a Unified Conception of Business Ethics: Integrative Social Contracts Theory," *Academy of Management Review* (April 1994), 252–253.

35. "The New 'Social Contract,'" *Business Week* (July 3, 1971).

36. "New Economy, New Social Contract," *Business Week* (September 11, 2000), 182.

CORPORATE CITIZENSHIP: SOCIAL RESPONSIBILITY, RESPONSIVENESS, *and* PERFORMANCE

CHAPTER LEARNING OUTCOMES

After studying this chapter, you should be able to:

1 Explain how corporate social responsibility (CSR) evolved and encompasses economic, legal, ethical, and philanthropic components.

2 Provide business examples of CSR and corporate citizenship.

3 Differentiate between corporate citizenship, social responsibility, responsiveness, and performance.

4 Elaborate on the concept of corporate social performance (CSP).

5 Provide an overview of studies relating social performance to financial performance.

6 Describe the socially responsible investing movement.

For the past three decades, business has been undergoing the most intense scrutiny it has ever received from the public. As a result of the many allegations being leveled at it— charges that it has little concern for the consumer, cares nothing about the deteriorating social order, has no concept of acceptable ethical behavior, and is indifferent to the problems of minorities and the environment—concern is continuing to be expressed as to what responsibilities business has to society. These concerns have generated an unprecedented number of pleas for corporate social responsibility (CSR). More recently, CSR has been embraced in the broader term—*corporate citizenship*. Concepts that have evolved from CSR include corporate social *responsiveness* and corporate social *performance*. Today, many business executives prefer the term *corporate citizenship* as an inclusive reference to social responsibility issues.

CSR continues to be a "front-burner" issue within the business community, and this is highlighted by the formation and growth since 1992 of an organization called

Business for Social Responsibility (BSR). According to BSR, it was formed to fill an urgent need for a national business alliance that fosters socially responsible corporate policies. In 2004, BSR reported over 1,400 business member firms, including among its membership such recognizable names as Levi Strauss & Co., Stride Rite, Ford, GM, Reebok, Honeywell, Coca-Cola, Liz Claiborne, Inc., The Timberland Co., and hundreds of others. Further, BSR publishes reports such as *Corporate Social Responsibility: A Guide to Better Business Practice* to help its member firms and the business world.[1]

In this chapter, we intend to explore several different aspects of the CSR topic and to provide some insights into what CSR means and how businesses are carrying it out. We are dedicating an entire chapter to the CSR issue and concepts that have emerged from it because it is a core idea that underlies most of our discussions in this book.

THE CORPORATE SOCIAL RESPONSIBILITY CONCEPT

In Chapter 1, we traced how criticisms of business have led to increased concern for the social environment and a changed social contract. Out of these ideas has grown the notion of corporate social responsibility, or CSR. Before providing some historical perspective, let us impart an initial view of what corporate social responsibility means.

An early view of CSR was stated as follows: "**Corporate social responsibility** is seriously considering the impact of the company's actions on society."[2] Another definition was that "the idea of social responsibility . . . requires the individual to consider his [or her] acts in terms of a whole social system, and holds him [or her] responsible for the effects of his [or her] acts anywhere in that system."[3]

Both of these definitions provide preliminary insights into the idea of social responsibility that will help us appreciate some brief history. Figure 2-1 illustrates the business criticism/social response cycle, depicting how the concept of CSR grew out of the ideas introduced in Chapter 1—business criticism and the increased concern for the social environment and the changed social contract. We see also in Figure 2-1 that the commitment to social responsibility by businesses has led to increased corporate *responsiveness* to stakeholders and improved social (stakeholder) *performance*—ideas that are developed more fully in this chapter.

As we will discuss later, some today prefer the language of "corporate citizenship" to collectively embrace the host of concepts related to CSR. However, for now, a useful summary of the themes or emphases of each of the chapter title concepts helps us see the flow of ideas accentuated as these concepts have developed:

CORPORATE CITIZENSHIP CONCEPTS

Corporate social *responsibility*—emphasizes obligation, accountability

↓

Corporate social *responsiveness*—emphasizes action, activity

↓

Corporate social *performance*—emphasizes outcomes, results

FIGURE 2-1

Business Criticism/Social Response Cycle

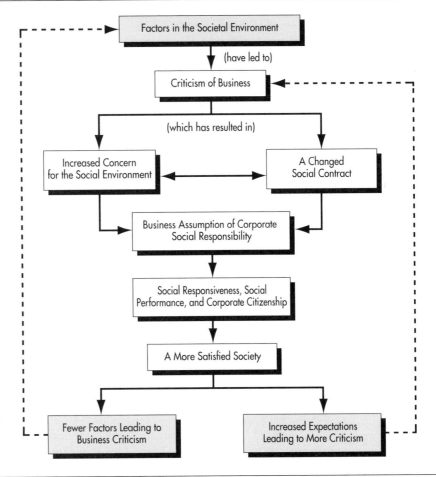

The growth of these ideas has brought about a society more satisfied with business. However, this satisfaction, although it has reduced the number of factors leading to business criticism, has at the same time led to increased expectations that have resulted in more criticism. This double effect is indicated in Figure 2-1. The net result is that the overall levels of business social performance and societal satisfaction should increase with time in spite of this interplay of positive and negative factors. Should business not be responsive to societal expectations, it could conceivably enter a downward spiral, resulting in significant deterioration in the business/society relationship. The corporate fraud scandals beginning in 2001–2002 have seriously called businesses' concern for society into question.

Historical Perspective on CSR

The concept of business responsibility that prevailed in the United States during most of our history was fashioned after the traditional, or classical, *economic model*. Adam Smith's concept of the "invisible hand" was its major point of departure. The classical view held that a society could best determine its needs and wants through the marketplace. If business is rewarded on the basis of its ability to respond to the demands of the market, the self-interested pursuit of that reward will result in society getting what it wants. Thus, the "invisible hand" of the market transforms self-interest into societal interest. Unfortunately, although the marketplace did a reasonably good job in deciding what goods and services should be produced, it did not fare as well in ensuring that business always acted fairly and ethically.

Years later, when laws constraining business behavior began to proliferate, it might be said that a *legal model* emerged. Society's expectations of business changed from being strictly economic in nature to encompassing issues that had been previously at business's discretion. Over time, a *social model* or *stakeholder model* has evolved.

In practice, although business early subscribed to the economic emphasis and was willing to be subjected to an increasing number of laws imposed by society, the business community later did not fully live by the tenets of even these early conceptions of business responsibility. As McKie observed, "The business community never has adhered with perfect fidelity to an ideologically pure version of its responsibilities, drawn from the classical conception of the enterprise in economic society, though many businessmen (people) have firmly believed in the main tenets of the creed."[4]

Modification of the Economic Model

A modification of the classical economic model was seen in practice in at least three areas: philanthropy, community obligations, and paternalism.[5] History shows that businesspeople did engage in **philanthropy**—contributions to charity and other worthy causes—even during periods characterized by the traditional economic view. Voluntary **community obligations** to improve, beautify, and uplift were evident. One early example of this was the cooperative effort between the railroads and the YMCA immediately after the Civil War to provide community services in areas served by the railroads. Although these services economically benefited the railroads, they were at the same time philanthropic.[6]

During the latter part of the nineteenth century and even into the twentieth century, **paternalism** appeared in many forms. One of the most visible examples was the company town. Although business's motives for creating company towns (for example, the Pullman/Illinois experiment) were mixed, business had to do a considerable amount of the work in governing them. Thus, the company accepted a form of paternalistic social responsibility.[7]

The emergence of large corporations during the late 1800s played a major role in hastening movement away from the classical economic view. As society grew from the economic structure of small, powerless firms governed primarily by the marketplace to large corporations in which power was more concentrated, questions of the responsibility of business to society surfaced.[8]

Although the idea of corporate social responsibility had not yet fully developed in the 1920s, managers even then had a more positive view of their role. Community service was in the forefront. The most visible example was the Community Chest movement, which received its impetus from business. Morrell Heald suggests that this was the first large-scale endeavor in which business leaders became involved with other nongovernmental community groups for a common, nonbusiness purpose that necessitated their contribution of time and money to community welfare projects.[9] The social responsibility of business, then, had received a further broadening of its meaning.

The 1930s signaled a transition from a predominantly laissez-faire economy to a mixed economy in which business found itself one of the constituencies monitored by a more activist government. From this time well into the 1950s, business's social responsibilities grew to include employee welfare (pension and insurance plans), safety, medical care, retirement programs, and so on. McKie has suggested that these new developments were spurred both by governmental compulsion and by an enlarged concept of business responsibility.[10]

Neil J. Mitchell, in his book *The Generous Corporation*, presents an interesting thesis regarding how CSR evolved.[11] Mitchell's view is that the ideology of corporate social responsibility, particularly philanthropy, was developed by American business leaders as a strategic response to the antibusiness fervor that was beginning in the late 1800s and early 1900s. The antibusiness reaction was the result of specific business actions, such as railroad price gouging, and public resentment of the emerging gigantic fortunes being made by late nineteenth-century moguls, such as Andrew Carnegie and John D. Rockefeller.[12]

As business leaders came to realize that the government had the power to intervene in the economy and, in fact, was being encouraged to do so by public opinion, there was a need for a philosophy that promoted large corporations as a force for social good. Thus, Mitchell argued, business leaders attempted to persuade those affected by business power that such power was being used appropriately. An example of this early progressive business ideology was reflected in Carnegie's 1889 essay, "The Gospel of Wealth," which asserted that business must pursue profits but that business wealth should be used for the benefit of the community. Philanthropy, therefore, became the most efficient means of using corporate wealth for public benefit. A prime example of this was Carnegie's funding and building of more than 2,500 libraries.

In a discussion of little-known history, Mitchell documents by way of specific examples how business developed this idea of the generous corporation and how it had distinct advantages: It helped business gain support from national and local governments, and it helped to achieve in America a social stability that was unknown in Europe during that period. In Ronald Berenbeim's review of Mitchell's book, he argues that the main motive for corporate generosity in the early 1900s was essentially the same as it has been in the 1990s—to keep government at arm's length.[13]

Acceptance and Broadening of Meaning. The period from the 1950s to the present may be considered the modern era in which the concept of corporate social responsibility gained considerable acceptance and broadening of meaning. During this time, the emphasis has moved from little more than a general awareness of social and moral concerns to a period in which specific issues, such as product safety, honesty in advertising, employee rights, affirmative action, environmental sustainability, ethical behavior, and global CSR have been emphasized. The issue orientation eventually gave way to the more recent focus on social performance and corporate citizenship. First, however, we can expand upon the modern view of CSR by examining a few definitions or understandings of this term that have developed in recent years.

SEARCH THE WEB

BUSINESS FOR SOCIAL RESPONSIBILITY

Businesses in growing numbers are very interested in CSR. One leading organization that companies join to advocate CSR is Business for Social Responsibility (BSR). BSR is a national business association that helps companies seeking to implement policies and practices that contribute to the companies' sustained and responsible success. BSR also operates the Business for Social Responsibility Education Fund, a nonprofit research, education, and advocacy organization that promotes more responsible business practices in the broad business community and in society. BSR runs programs on a range of social responsibility and stakeholders issues, including business ethics, the workplace, the marketplace, the community, the environment, and the global economy. To learn more about what business is actually doing in the realm of social responsibility, visit BSR's Web site at **http://www.bsr.org**.

CSR: Evolving Viewpoints

Let's now return to the basic question: What does corporate social responsibility really mean? Up to this point, we have been operating with a rather simple definition of social responsibility:

> *Corporate social responsibility is seriously considering the impact of the company's actions on society.*

Although this definition has inherent ambiguities, we will find that most of the definitions presented by others also have limitations. Part of the difficulty in deriving a definition on which we might get consensus is the problem of determining, operationally, what the definition implies for management. This poses a challenge because organizations vary in size, in the types of products they produce, in their profitability and resources, in their impact on society and stakeholders, and so on. Because of this, the ways in which they embrace and practice social responsibility also vary.

One might ask: Why is this so? Are there not absolutes, areas in which all firms must be responsible? Yes, there are, and these are expressed by those expectations society has translated into legal components of the social contract. But as we will suggest here, CSR goes beyond simply "abiding by the law" (although abiding by the law is not always simple). In the realm of activities above and beyond abiding by the law, the variables (size of the firm, types of products produced, stakeholders affected, and so on) become more relevant.

A second definition is worth considering. Davis and Blomstrom defined corporate social responsibility as follows:

> *Social responsibility is the obligation of decision makers to take actions which protect and improve the welfare of society as a whole along with their own interests.*[14]

This definition suggests two active aspects of social responsibility—*protecting* and *improving*. To protect the welfare of society implies the avoidance of negative impacts on society. To improve the welfare of society implies the creation of positive benefits for society. Like the first definition, this second characterization contains several words that are perhaps unavoidably vague. For example, words from these definitions that might permit managers wide latitude in interpretation include *seriously*, *considering*, *protect*, *improve*, and *welfare* (of society). The intention here is not to be critical of these good, general definitions but rather to illustrate how businesspeople and others become quite legitimately confused when they try to translate the concept of CSR into practice.

A third definition, by McGuire, is also quite general. But, unlike the previous two, it places social responsibilities in context vis-à-vis economic and legal objectives:

> *The idea of social responsibility supposes that the corporation has not only economic and legal obligations, but also certain responsibilities to society which extend beyond these obligations.*[15]

This statement is attractive in that it acknowledges the importance of economic objectives side by side with legal obligations while also encompassing a broader conception of the firm's responsibilities.

A fourth definition, set forth by Epstein, relates CSR to business management's growing concern with stakeholders and ethics. He asserts:

> *Corporate social responsibility relates primarily to achieving outcomes from organizational decisions concerning specific issues or problems which (by some normative standard) have beneficial rather than adverse effects upon pertinent corporate stakeholders. The norma-*

tive correctness of the products of corporate action have been the main focus of corporate social responsibility.[16]

Epstein's definition is helpful because it emphasizes the outcomes, products, or results of corporate actions for stakeholders, which are only implicit in the other definitions. Over the years, a number of different views on CSR have evolved.[17]

A Four-Part Definition of CSR

Each of the presented definitions of corporate social responsibility is valuable. At this point, we would like to present Carroll's four-part definition of CSR that focuses on the *types* of social responsibilities it might be argued that business has. Carroll's definition helps us to understand the component parts that make up CSR, and it is the definition that we will build upon in this book:

> *The social responsibility of business encompasses the economic, legal, ethical, and discretionary (philanthropic) expectations that society has of organizations at a given point in time.*[18]

Carroll's four-part definition attempts to place economic and legal expectations of business in context by relating them to more socially-oriented concerns. These social concerns include ethical responsibilities and philanthropic (voluntary/discretionary) responsibilities.

Economic Responsibilities.   First, there are business's **economic responsibilities**. It may seem odd to call an economic responsibility a social responsibility, but, in effect, this is what it is. First and foremost, the American social system calls for business to be an economic institution. That is, it should be an institution whose orientation is to produce goods and services that society wants and to sell them at fair prices—prices that society thinks represent the true value of the goods and services delivered and that provide business with profits adequate to ensure its perpetuation and growth and to reward its investors. While thinking about its economic responsibilities, business employs many management concepts that are directed toward financial effectiveness—attention to revenues, costs, strategic decision making, and the host of business concepts focused on maximizing the long-term financial performance of the organization. In the mid-2000s, the worldwide hyper-competition in business has highlighted business's economic responsibilities. But, economic responsibilities are not enough.

Legal Responsibilities.   Second, there are business's **legal responsibilities**. Just as society has sanctioned our economic system by permitting business to assume the productive role mentioned earlier, as a partial fulfillment of the social contract, it has also laid down the ground rules—the laws—under which business is expected to operate. Legal responsibilities reflect society's view of "codified ethics" in the sense that they embody basic notions of fair practices as established by our lawmakers. It is business's responsibility to society to comply with these laws. If business does not agree with laws that have been passed or are about to be passed, our society has provided a mechanism by which dissenters can be heard through the political process. In the past 35 years, our society has witnessed a proliferation of laws and regulations striving to control business behavior. A recent *Newsweek* cover story titled "Lawsuit Hell: How Fear of Litigation Is Paralyzing Our Professions" emphasizes the burgeoning role that the legal responsibility of organizations is assuming.[19] The legal aspect of the business and society relationship will be developed in more detail in later chapters.

Ethics in Practice

FEELING "USED"

While attending college, I spent a few years working at a used-textbook store. The majority of the books we sold were used books that we purchased from students, individuals, and used-book wholesalers. Sometimes when putting books out on the shelves, I would encounter books with phrases like "Instructor's Copy" or "Sample Copy—Not for Resale" printed on the covers. When I asked my boss about these books, he told me that they were free copies given out to instructors, but it was perfectly legal for us to sell the books because we had purchased them from another person. This made sense to me and satisfied my curiosity.

Later in the day, my boss showed me a pile of these sample-copy books and said that we take colored tape and cover up the areas that contain the phrases such as "Sample Copy." When I asked why we did this, he told me that although we are legally able to sell the books, the phrases sometimes discourage customers from buying these copies although the content is identical to the standard copies. I then asked how we got these books if they were instructor copies and were not supposed to be resold.

I was told that the publishing companies send free copies of books to professors to let them read and evaluate them with the hope that they will order

the book as material for their classes. We get some of these books when professors sell their sample copies to us or a used-book wholesaler, but the majority come from individuals who go around college campuses (calling themselves *book-buyers*) buying these books from professors and then selling them to a used-book store or a used-book wholesaler.

My boss also stated that because the content inside is the same, we really do not care if they are the standard copy or a sample copy and, therefore, we buy and sell these books for the same prices as the standard copies.

1. Is it a socially responsible (legal? ethical?) practice for a bookstore to purchase and then resell these books that were given out as free copies?

2. Is it an ethical practice for the bookstore to conceal the fact that these books are, indeed, instructor's or sample copies?

3. Is it an ethical practice for book-buyers to roam the halls of college campuses and buy these free books from professors who no longer want them?

4. Is it an ethical practice for professors to sell books that were sent to them as free sample copies?

Contributed Anonymously

As important as legal responsibilities are, legal responsibilities do not embrace the full range of behaviors expected of business by society. On its own, law is inadequate for at least three reasons. First, the law cannot possibly address all the topics, areas, or issues that business may face. New topics continually emerge such as Internet-based business (e-commerce) and genetically-modified foods. Second, the law often lags behind more recent concepts of what is considered appropriate behavior. For example, as technology permits more exact measurements of environmental contamination, laws based on measures made by obsolete equipment become outdated but not frequently changed. Third, laws are made by lawmakers and may reflect the personal interests and political motivations of legislators rather than appropriate ethical justifications. A wise sage once said: "Never go to see how sausages or laws are made." It may not be a pretty picture. Although we would like to believe that our lawmakers are focusing on "what is right," political maneuvering often suggests otherwise.

Ethical Responsibilities.

Because laws are important but not adequate, **ethical responsibilities** embrace those activities and practices that are expected or prohibited by societal members even though they are not codified into law. Ethical responsibilities embody the full scope of norms, standards, and expectations that reflect what consumers, employees, shareholders, and the community regard as fair, just, and in keeping with the respect for or protection of stakeholders' moral rights.[20]

In one sense, changes in ethics or values precede the establishment of laws because they become the driving forces behind the initial creation of laws and regulations. For example, the civil rights, environmental, and consumer movements reflected basic alterations in societal values and thus may be seen as ethical bellwethers foreshadowing and leading to later legislation. In another sense, ethical responsibilities may be seen as embracing and reflecting newly emerging values and norms that society expects business to meet, even though they may reflect a higher standard of performance than that currently required by law. Ethical responsibilities in this sense are often ill defined or continually under public scrutiny and debate as to their legitimacy and thus are frequently difficult for business to agree upon. Regardless, business is expected to be responsive to newly emerging concepts of what constitutes ethical practices. In recent years, ethics in the global arena have complicated things.

Superimposed on these ethical expectations emanating from societal and stakeholder groups are the implied levels of ethical performance suggested by a consideration of the great ethical principles of moral philosophy, such as justice, rights, and utilitarianism.[21]

Because ethical responsibilities are so important, we devote Part 3, composed of four chapters, to the subject. For the moment, let us think of ethical responsibilities as encompassing those areas in which society expects certain levels of moral or principled performance but for which it has not yet articulated or codified into law.

Philanthropic Responsibilities.

Fourth, there are business's voluntary/discretionary or **philanthropic responsibilities**. These are viewed as responsibilities because they reflect current expectations of business by the public. These activities are voluntary, guided only by business's desire to engage in social activities that are not mandated, not required by law, and not generally expected of business in an ethical sense. Nevertheless, the public has an expectation that business will engage in philanthropy and thus this category has become a part of the social contract between business and society. Such activities might include corporate giving, product and service donations, volunteerism, partnerships with local government and other organizations, and any other kind of voluntary involvement of the organization and its employees with the community or other stakeholders. Examples of companies fulfilling their philanthropic responsibilities, and "doing well by doing good" are many:

- Chick-fil-A, the fast-food restaurant, through the WinShape Centre Foundation, operates foster homes for more than 120 children, sponsors a summer camp that has hosted more than 21,000 children since 1985, and has provided college scholarships for more than 16,500 students.
- Merck & Co., the drug giant, supports science education in and around Rahway, New Jersey.
- IBM gives away computers and computer training to schools around the country.
- UPS has committed $2 million to a two-year program, the Volunteer Impact Initiative, designed to help nonprofit organizations develop innovative ways to recruit, train, and manage volunteers.

- Agilent Technologies supports employees' philanthropy by providing up to four hours a month of paid time off for volunteer work and helping staff members find volunteer opportunities in their communities via a central corporate database.
- Thousands of companies give away money, services, and volunteer time to education, youth, health organizations, arts and culture, neighborhood improvement, minority affairs, and programs for the handicapped.

The distinction between ethical responsibilities and philanthropic responsibilities is that the latter typically are not expected in a moral or an ethical sense. Communities desire and expect business to contribute its money, facilities, and employee time to humanitarian programs or purposes, but they do not regard firms as unethical if they do not provide these services at the desired levels. Therefore, these responsibilities are more discretionary, or voluntary, on business's part, although the societal expectation that they be provided is always present. This category of responsibilities is often referred to as good "corporate citizenship."

In essence, our definition forms a four-part conceptualization of corporate social responsibility that includes the economic, legal, ethical, and philanthropic expectations placed on organizations by society at a given point in time. Figure 2-2 summarizes the four components, society's expectation regarding each component, and examples. The implication is that business has accountability for these areas of responsibility and performance. This four-part definition provides us with categories within which to place the various expectations that society has of business. With each of these categories considered to be an indispensable facet of the total social responsibility of business, we have a conceptual model that more completely describes the kinds of expectations that society expects of business. One advantage of this model is that it can accommodate those who have argued against CSR by characterizing an economic emphasis as separate from a social emphasis. This model offers these two facets along with others that collectively make up corporate social responsibility.

The Pyramid of Corporate Social Responsibility. A helpful way of graphically depicting the four-part definition of CSR is envisioning a pyramid composed of

FIGURE 2-2

Understanding the Four Components of Corporate Social Responsibility

Type of Responsibility	Societal Expectation	Explanations
Economic	REQUIRED of business by society	Be profitable. Maximize sales, minimize costs. Make sound strategic decisions. Be attentive to dividend policy. Provide investors with adequate and attractive returns on their investments.
Legal	REQUIRED of business by society	Obey all laws, adhere to all regulations. Environmental and consumer laws. Laws protecting employees. Obey Sarbanes–Oxley Act. Fulfill all contractual obligations. Honor warranties and guarantees.
Ethical	EXPECTED of business by society	Avoid questionable practices. Respond to spirit as well as letter of law. Assume law is a floor on behavior, operate above minimum required. Do what is right, fair, and just. Assert ethical leadership.
Philanthropic	DESIRED/EXPECTED of business by society	Be a good corporate citizen. Give back. Make corporate contributions. Provide programs supporting community—education, health/human services, culture and arts, civic. Provide for community betterment. Engage in volunteerism.

four layers. This **Pyramid of Corporate Social Responsibility (CSR)** is shown in Figure 2-3.[22]

The pyramid portrays the four components of CSR, beginning with the basic building block of economic performance at the base. At the same time, business is expected to obey the law, because the law is society's codification of acceptable and unacceptable practices. In addition, there is business's responsibility to be ethical. At its most basic level, this is the obligation to do what is right, just, and fair and to avoid or minimize harm to stakeholders (employees, consumers, the environment, and others). Finally, business is expected to be a good corporate citizen—to fulfill its philanthropic responsibility to contribute financial and human resources to the community and to improve the quality of life.

No metaphor is perfect, and the Pyramid of CSR is no exception. It is intended to illustrate that the total social responsibility of business is composed of distinct components that, when taken together, make up the whole. Although the components have been treated as separate concepts for discussion purposes, they are not mutually exclusive and

FIGURE 2-3

The Pyramid of Corporate Social Responsibility

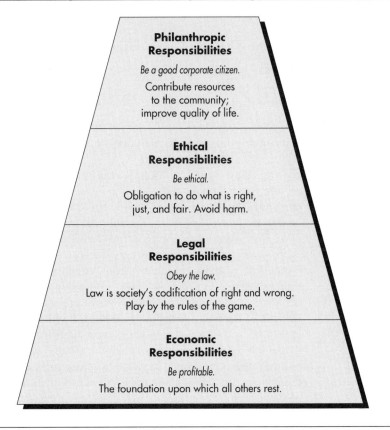

SOURCE: Archie B. Carroll, "The Pyramid of Corporate Social Responsibility: Toward the Moral Management of Organizational Stakeholders," *Business Horizons* (July–August 1991), 42. Copyright © 1991 by the Foundation for the School of Business at Indiana University. Used with permission.

are not intended to juxtapose a firm's economic responsibilities with its other responsibilities. At the same time, a consideration of the separate components helps the manager to see that the different types or kinds of obligations are in constant and dynamic tension with one another.

The most critical tensions, of course, are those between economic and legal, economic and ethical, and economic and philanthropic. The traditionalist might see this as a conflict between a firm's "concern for profits" and its "concern for society," but it is suggested here that this is an oversimplification. A CSR or stakeholder perspective would recognize these tensions as organizational realities but would focus on the total pyramid as a unified whole and on how the firm might engage in decisions, actions, policies, and practices that *simultaneously* fulfill all its component parts. This pyramid should not be interpreted to mean that business is expected to fulfill its social responsibilities in some sequential fashion, starting at the base. Rather, business is expected to fulfill all its responsibilities simultaneously.

In summary, the total social responsibility of business entails the concurrent fulfillment of the firm's economic, legal, ethical, and philanthropic responsibilities. In equation form, this might be expressed as follows:

$$\textit{Economic Responsibilities} + \textit{Legal Responsibilities} + \textit{Ethical Responsibilities}$$
$$+ \textit{Philanthropic Responsibilities}$$
$$= \textit{Total Corporate Social Responsibility}$$

Stated in more practical and managerial terms, the socially responsible firm should strive to:

- Make a profit.
- Obey the law.
- Be ethical.
- Be a good corporate citizen.

It is especially important to note that the four-part CSR definition and the Pyramid of CSR represent a stakeholder model. That is, each of the four components of responsibility addresses different stakeholders in terms of the varying priorities in which the stakeholders are affected. Economic responsibilities most dramatically impact owners/shareholders and employees (because if the business is not financially successful, owners and employees will be directly affected). When the Arthur Andersen accounting firm went out of business in 2002, employees were displaced and significantly affected. Legal responsibilities are certainly crucial with respect to owners, but in today's society the threat of litigation against businesses emanates frequently from employees and consumer stakeholders. Ethical responsibilities affect all stakeholder groups, but an examination of the ethical issues business faces today suggests that they involve consumers and employees most frequently. Because of the fraud of the early 2000s, investor groups have also been greatly affected. Finally, philanthropic responsibilities most affect the community, but it could be reasoned that employees are next affected because some research has suggested that a company's philanthropic performance significantly affects its employees' morale. Figure 2-4 presents this stakeholder view of CSR, along with a hypothetical priority scheme in which the stakeholder groups are addressed/affected by the companies' actions in that realm. The numbers in the cells are not based on empirical evidence but are only suggestive to illustrate how stakeholders are affected. Other priority schemes could easily be argued.

As we study the evolution of business's major areas of social concern, as presented in various chapters in Parts 2 and 3, we will see how our model's four facets (economic, legal,

FIGURE 2-4

A Stakeholder View of Corporate Social Responsibility

CSR Component	Stakeholder Group Addressed and Primarily Affected				
	Owners	Consumers	Employees	Community	Others
Economic	1	4	2	3	5
Legal	3	2	1	4	5
Ethical	3	1	2	4	5
Philanthropic	3	4	2	1	5

NOTE: Numbers in cells suggest one prioritization of stakeholders addressed and affected within each CSR component. Numbers are illustrative only. Do you agree with these priorities? Why? Why not? Discuss.

ethical, and philanthropic) provide us with a useful framework for conceptualizing the issue of corporate social responsibility. The social contract between business and society is to a large extent formulated from mutual understandings that exist in each area of our basic model. But, it should be noted that the ethical and philanthropic categories, taken together, more nearly capture the essence of what people generally mean today when they speak of the social responsibility of business. Situating these two categories relative to the legal and economic obligations, however, keeps them in proper perspective.

ARGUMENTS AGAINST AND FOR CORPORATE SOCIAL RESPONSIBILITY

In an effort to provide a balanced view of CSR, we will consider the arguments that traditionally have been raised against and for it. We should state clearly at the outset, however, that those who argue against corporate social responsibility are not using in their considerations the comprehensive four-part CSR definition and model presented here. Rather, it appears that the critics are viewing CSR more narrowly—as only the efforts of the organization to pursue social goals (primarily our philanthropic category). Some critics equate CSR with only the philanthropic category. Only a very few businesspeople and academics argue against the fundamental notion of CSR today. The debate among businesspeople more often centers on the kinds and degrees of CSR and on subtle ethical questions, rather than on the basic question of whether or not business should be socially responsible or a good corporate citizen. Among academics, economists and finance specialists are probably the easiest groups to single out as questioning corporate social goals. But even some of them no longer resist CSR on the grounds of economic theory.

Arguments Against CSR

Let us first look at the arguments that have surfaced over the years from the anti-CSR school of thought. Most notable has been the classical economic argument. This traditional view holds that management has one responsibility: to maximize the profits of its owners or shareholders. This classical economic school, led by economist Milton Friedman, argues that social issues are not the concern of businesspeople and that these problems should be resolved by the unfettered workings of the free-market system.[23] Further, this view holds that if the free market cannot solve the social problem, then it falls upon government and legislation to do the job. Friedman softens his argument somewhat by his assertion that management is "to make as much money as possible while conforming to the basic rules of society, both those embodied in the law and those embodied in ethical customs."[24] When Friedman's entire statement is considered, it appears that he accepts three of the four categories of the four-part model—economic, legal, and ethical. The only item not specifically embraced in his quote is the voluntary or philanthropic category. In any event, it is clear that the economic argument views corporate social responsibility more narrowly than we have in our conceptual model.

A second major objection to CSR has been that business is not equipped to handle social activities. This position holds that managers are oriented toward finance and operations and do not have the necessary expertise (social skills) to make social decisions.[25] Although this may have been true at one point in time, it is less true today. Closely related to this argument is a third: If managers were to pursue corporate social responsibility vigorously, it would tend to dilute the business's primary purpose.[26] The objection here is that CSR would put business into fields not related, as F. A. Hayek has stated, to their "proper aim."[27]

A fourth argument against CSR is that business already has enough power—economic, environmental, and technological—and so why should we place in its hands the opportunity to wield additional power?[28] In reality, today, business has this social power regardless of the argument. Further, this view tends to ignore the potential use of business's social power for the public good.

One other argument that merits mention is that by encouraging business to assume social responsibilities we might be placing it in a risky position in terms of global competition. One consequence of being socially responsible is that business must internalize costs that it formerly passed on to society in the form of dirty air, unsafe products, consequences of discrimination, and so on. The increase in the costs of products caused by including social considerations in the price structure might necessitate raising the prices of products, making them less competitive in international markets. The net effect might be to dissipate the country's advantages gained previously through technological advances. This argument weakens somewhat when we consider the reality that social responsibility is quickly becoming a global concern, not one restricted to U.S. firms and operations.

The arguments presented here constitute the principal claims made by those who oppose the CSR concept, as it once was narrowly conceived. Many of the reasons given appear logical. Value choices as to the type of society the citizenry would like to have, at some point, become part of the total social responsibility question. Whereas some of these objections might have had validity at one point in time, it is doubtful that they carry much weight today.

Arguments for CSR

Authorities have agreed upon two fundamental points: "(1) Industrial society faces serious human and social problems brought on largely by the rise of the large corporations, and (2) managers must conduct the affairs of the corporation in ways to solve or at least ameliorate these problems."[29] This generalized justification of corporate social responsibility is appealing. It actually comes close to what we might suggest as a first argument for CSR—namely, that it is in business's long-range self-interest to be socially responsi-

Business commentators concede that CSR is a thriving industry, but some consider that engaging in corporate philanthropy using income that actually belongs to shareholders is a "dubious proposition." In an article for *Fortune* (23 June 2003, v147 i12 p98+), Marc Gunther gives credit to companies such as DuPont and McDonald's for their socially responsible practices but points out that none of these policies have "paid off in a tangible way for investors." *The Economist* (U.S.) (24 January 2004, v370 i8359 p53) reports that some companies have begun to regard CSR as a "sham" and wonders if CSR has peaked. You can read both articles by logging on to InfoTrac College Edition at **http://www.infotrac-college.com** and keying record number A102931819 for the *Fortune* article and record number A112514682 for the *Economist* article.

ble. These two points provide an additional dimension by suggesting that it was partially business's fault that many of today's social problems arose in the first place and, consequently, that business should assume a role in remedying these problems. It may be inferred from this that deterioration of the social condition must be halted if business is to survive and prosper in the future.

The long-range self-interest view holds that if business is to have a healthy climate in which to exist in the future, it must take actions now that will ensure its long-term viability. Perhaps the reasoning behind this view is that society's expectations are such that if business does not respond on its own, its role in society may be altered by the public—for example, through government regulation or, more dramatically, through alternative economic systems for the production and distribution of goods and services.

It is sometimes difficult for managers who have a short-term orientation to appreciate that their rights and roles in the economic system are determined by society. Business must be responsive to society's expectations over the long term if it is to survive in its current form or in a less restrained form.

One of the most practical reasons for business to be socially responsible is to ward off future government intervention and regulation. Today there are numerous areas in which government intrudes with an expensive, elaborate regulatory apparatus to fill a void left by business's inaction. To the extent that business polices itself with self-disciplined standards and guidelines, future government intervention can be somewhat forestalled. Later, we will discuss some areas in which business could have prevented intervention and simultaneously ensured greater freedom in decision making had it imposed higher standards of behavior on itself.

Two additional arguments supporting CSR deserve mention together: "Business has the resources" and "Let business try."[30] These two views maintain that because business has a reservoir of management talent, functional expertise, and capital, and because so many others have tried and failed to solve general social problems, business should be given a chance. These arguments have some merit, because there are some social problems that can be handled, in the final analysis, only by business. Examples include a fair workplace, providing safe products, and engaging in fair advertising. Admittedly, government can and does assume a role in these areas, but business must make the final decisions.

Another argument supporting CSR is that "proacting is better than reacting." This position holds that proacting (anticipating and initiating) is more practical and less costly than simply reacting to problems once they have developed. Environmental pollution is a good example, particularly business's experience with attempting to clean up rivers, lakes, and other waterways that were neglected for years. In the long run, it would have been wiser to have prevented the environmental deterioration from occurring in the first place. A final argument in favor of CSR is that the public strongly supports it. A 2000 *Business Week*/Harris poll revealed that, with a stunning 95 percent majority, the public believes that companies should not only focus on profits for shareholders but that companies should be responsible to their workers and communities, even if making things better for workers and communities requires companies to sacrifice some profits.[31]

The Business Case for CSR

After considering both the pros and cons of CSR, most businesses today embrace the idea. In recent years, the "business case" for corporate social responsibility has been unfolding. The business case reflects why businesspeople believe that CSR brings distinct benefits or advantages to business organizations and the business community. Often, these benefits directly affect the "bottom line." The astute business guru, Michael Porter, perhaps the most listened to and respected individual today in upper-level management circles and boardrooms, has pointed out how corporate and social initiatives are intertwined. According to Porter: "Today's companies ought to invest in corporate social responsibility as part of their business strategy to become more competitive." In a competitive context, "the company's social initiatives—or its philanthropy—can have great impact. Not only for the company but also for the local society."[32]

In his book, *The Civil Corporation*, Simon Zadek has identified four ways in which firms respond to CSR pressures, and he holds that these form a composite business case for CSR. His four approaches are as follows:[33]

- *Defensive approach.* This is an approach designed to alleviate pain. Companies will do what they have to do to avoid pressure that makes them incur costs.
- *Cost-benefit approach.* This traditional approach holds that firms will undertake those activities if they can identify a direct benefit that exceeds costs.
- *Strategic approach.* In this approach, firms will recognize the changing environment and engage with CSR as part of a deliberate emergent strategy.
- *Innovation and learning approach.* In this approach, an active engagement with CSR provides new opportunities to understand the marketplace and enhances organizational learning, which leads to competitive advantage.

These approaches, taken together, build a strong business case for the pursuit of socially responsible business. Figure 2-5 summarizes the business case for CSR taken from two different sources.

Millennium Poll on Corporate Social Responsibility

As we think about the first decade of the new millennium, it is useful to consider the results of the millennium poll on CSR that was sponsored by Environics, International; the Prince of Wales Business Leaders Forum; and The Conference Board. This representative survey of 1,000 persons in each of 23 countries on 6 continents revealed how important citizens of the world felt corporate social responsibility really was. The survey revealed the following expectations that major companies would be expected to do in the twenty-first century.[34]

CORPORATE RESPONSIBILITY IN THE TWENTY-FIRST CENTURY

In the twenty-first century, major companies will be expected to do all of the following:

- Demonstrate their commitment to society's values and their contribution to society's social, environmental, and economic goals through actions.
- Fully insulate society from the negative impacts of company operations and its products and services.
- Share the benefits of company activities with key stakeholders as well as with shareholders.
- Demonstrate that the company can make more money by doing the right thing, in some cases reinventing its business strategy. This "doing well by doing good" will reassure stakeholders that the new behavior will outlast good intentions.

The survey findings suggest that CSR is fast becoming a global expectation that requires a comprehensive strategic response. Ethics and CSR need to be made a core business value integrated into all aspects of the firm.

FIGURE 2-5

The Business Case for CSR

The Top 10 Reasons Companies Are Becoming More Socially Responsible:

Reason	Percent of Respondents Agreeing
Enhanced reputation	90%
Competitive advantages	75%
Cost savings	73%
Industry trends	62%
CEO/board commitment	58%
Customer demand	57%
SRI demand	42%
Top-line growth	37%
Shareholder demand	20%
Access to capital	12%

Benefits of Social Responsibility

"How do you think companies benefit from fulfilling their social responsibilities?"
(Please choose a maximum of three alternatives. Shown here as percentages of respondents naming item.)

A better public image/reputation	75%
Greater customer loyalty	51%
A more satisfied and productive workforce	37%
Fewer regulatory or legal problems	37%
Long-term viability in the marketplace	36%
A stronger and healthier community	34%
Increased revenue	6%
Lower cost of capital	2%
No benefit	2%
Easier access to foreign markets	2%

SOURCES:

Top 10 Reasons: PricewaterhouseCoopers 2002 *Sustainability Survey Report*, reported in "Corporate America's Social Conscience," *Fortune* (May 26, 2003), S8. © PricewaterhouseCoopers LLP.

Benefits of SR: The Aspen Institute, Business and Society Program, "Where Will They Lead? 2003 MBA Student Attitudes About Business & Society" (May 2003), http://www.aspenbsp.org.

CORPORATE SOCIAL RESPONSIVENESS

We have discussed the evolution of corporate social responsibility, a model for viewing social responsibility, and the arguments for and against it. It is now worthwhile considering a concept that has arisen over the use of the terms *responsibility* and *responsiveness*. We will consider the views of several writers to develop the idea of **corporate social responsiveness**—the action-oriented variant of CSR.

A general argument that has generated much discussion over the past several decades holds that the term *responsibility* is too suggestive of efforts to pinpoint accountability or obligation. Therefore, it is not dynamic enough to fully describe business's willingness and activity—apart from obligation—to respond to social demands. For example, Ackerman and Bauer criticized the CSR term by stating, "The connotation of 'responsibility' is that of the process of assuming an obligation. It places an emphasis on motivation rather than on performance." They go on to say, "Responding to social demands is much more than deciding what to do. There remains the management task of doing what one has decided to do, and this task is far from trivial."[35] They argue that "social responsiveness" is a more apt description of what is essential in the social arena.

Their point was well made, especially when it was first set forth. *Responsibility*, taken quite literally, does imply more of a state or condition of having assumed an obligation, whereas *responsiveness* connotes a dynamic, action-oriented condition. We should not overlook, however, that much of what business has done and is doing has resulted from a particular motivation—an assumption of obligation—whether assigned by government, forced by special-interest groups, or voluntarily assumed. Perhaps business, in some instances, has failed to accept and internalize the obligation, and thus it may seem odd to refer to it as a responsibility. Nevertheless, some motivation that led to social responsiveness had to be there, even though in some cases it was not articulated to be a responsibility or an obligation. Figure 2-6 summarizes other experts' views regarding corporate social responsiveness.

Thus, the corporate social responsiveness dimension that has been discussed by some as an alternative focus to that of social responsibility is, in actuality, an *action phase* of management's response in the social sphere. In a sense, the responsiveness orientation

FIGURE 2-6

Alternative Views of Corporate Social Responsiveness

Sethi's Three-Stage Schema

Sethi proposes a three-stage schema for classifying corporate behavior: social obligation, social responsibility, and social *responsiveness*. Social responsiveness suggests that what is important is that corporations be "anticipatory" and "preventive." This third stage is concerned with business's long-term role in a dynamic social system.

Frederick's CSR_1, CSR_2, and CSR_3

CSR_1 refers to the traditional, accountability concept of CSR. CSR_2 is responsiveness-focused. It refers to the capacity of a corporation to *respond* to social pressures. It involves the literal act of responding, or of achieving a responsive posture to society. It addresses the mechanisms, procedures, arrangements, and patterns by which business responds to social pressures. CSR_3 refers to corporate social rectitude, which is concerned with the moral correctness of the actions or policies taken.

Epstein's Process View

Responsiveness is a part of the corporate social policy process. The emphasis is on the *process* aspect of social responsiveness. It focuses on both individual and organizational processes "for determining, implementing, and evaluating the firm's capacity to anticipate, respond to, and manage the issues and problems arising from the diverse claims and expectations of internal and external stakeholders."

SOURCES: S. Prakash Sethi, "Dimensions of Corporate Social Performance: An Analytical Framework," *California Management Review* (Spring 1975), 58–64; William C. Frederick, "From CSR¹ to CSR²: The Maturing of Business-and-Society Thought," Working Paper No. 279 (Graduate School of Business, University of Pittsburgh, 1978). See also William Frederick, *Business and Society*, (Vol. 33, No. 2, August 1994), 150–164; and Edwin M. Epstein, "The Corporate Social Policy Process: Beyond Business Ethics, Corporate Social Responsibility and Corporate Social Responsiveness," *California Management Review* (Vol. XXIX, No. 3, 1987), 104.

enables organizations to rationalize and operationalize their social responsibilities without getting bogged down in the quagmire of accountability, which can so easily occur if organizations try to get an exact determination of what their true responsibilities are before they take any action.

In an interesting study of social responsiveness among Canadian and Finnish forestry firms, researchers concluded that the social responsiveness of a corporation will proceed through a predictable series of phases and that managers will tend to respond to the most powerful stakeholders.[36] This study demonstrates that social responsiveness is a *process* and that stakeholder power, in addition to a sense of responsibility, may sometimes drive the process.

CORPORATE SOCIAL PERFORMANCE

For the past few decades, there has been a trend toward making the concern for social and ethical issues more and more pragmatic. The responsiveness thrust that we just discussed was a part of this trend. It is possible to integrate some of the concerns into a model of **corporate social performance (CSP)**. The performance focus is intended to suggest that what really matters is what companies are able to accomplish—the results or outcomes of their acceptance of social responsibility and adoption of a responsiveness philosophy. In developing a conceptual framework for CSP, we not only have to specify the nature (economic, legal, ethical, philanthropic) of the responsibility, but we also need to identify a particular philosophy, pattern, mode, or strategy of responsiveness. Finally, we need to identify the stakeholder issues or topical areas to which these responsibilities are manifested. One need not ponder the stakeholder issues that have evolved under the rubric of social responsibility to recognize how they have changed over time. The issues, and especially the degree of organizational interest in the issues, are always in a state of flux. As the times change, so does the emphasis on the range of social issues that business must address. This will become especially clear in Chapter 8, where we address ethics and technology.

Also of interest is the fact that particular issues are of varying concern to businesses, depending on the industry in which they exist as well as other factors. A bank, for example, is not as pressed on environmental issues as a manufacturer. Likewise, a manufacturer is considerably more absorbed with the issue of environmental protection than is an insurance company.

Carroll's CSP Model

Figure 2-7 on page 48 illustrates Carroll's **corporate social performance model**, which brings together the three major dimensions we have discussed:

1. Social responsibility categories—economic, legal, ethical, and discretionary (philanthropic)
2. Philosophy (or mode) of social responsiveness—e.g., reaction, defense, accommodation, and proaction
3. Social (or stakeholder) issues involved—consumers, environment, employees, etc.)[37]

One dimension of this model pertains to all that is included in our definition of social responsibility—the economic, legal, ethical, and discretionary (philanthropic) components.

FIGURE 2-7

Carroll's Corporate Social Performance Model

Philosophy (Mode) of Social Responsiveness

Proaction
Accommodation
Defense
Reaction

Social Responsibility

Discretionary (Philanthropic) Responsibilities

Ethical Responsibilities

Legal Responsibilities

Economic Responsibilities

Shareholders
Occupational Safety
Product Safety
Discrimination
Environment
Consumerism

Social Issues (Stakeholders) Involved

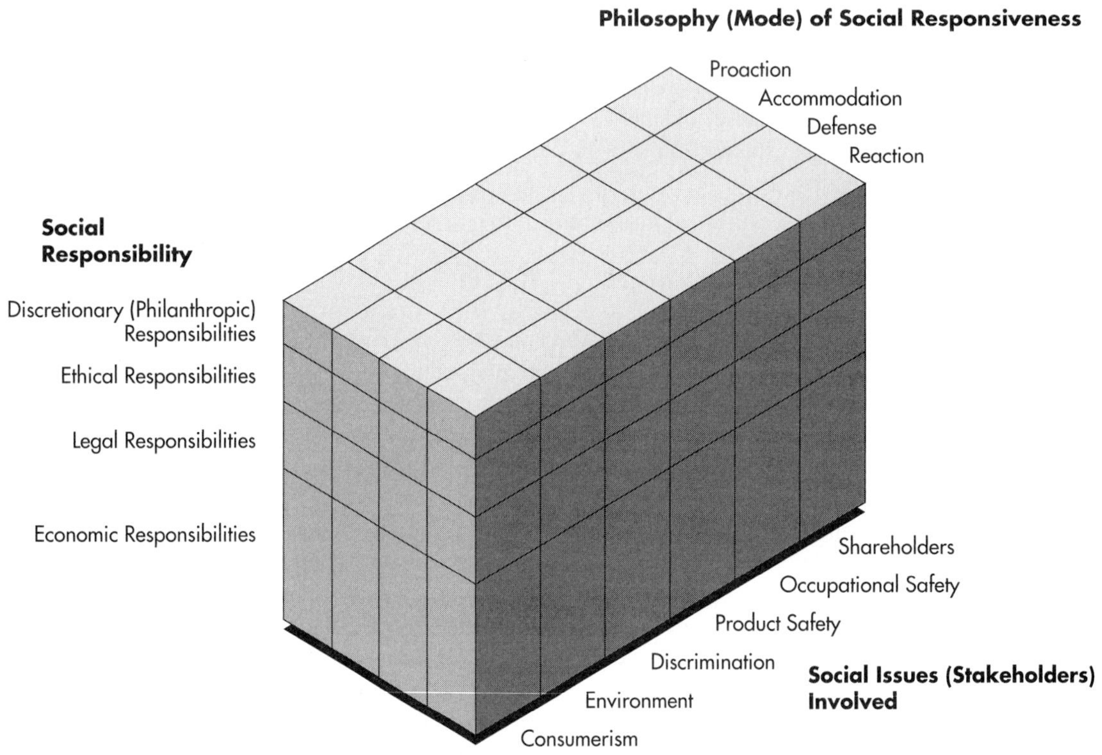

SOURCE: Archie B. Carroll, "A Three-Dimensional Conceptual Model of Corporate Social Performance," *Academy of Management Review* (Vol. 4, No. 4, 1979), 503. Reproduced with permission.

Second, there is a social responsiveness continuum. Although some writers have suggested that this is the preferable focus when one considers social responsibility, the model in Figure 2-7 suggests that responsiveness is but one additional aspect to be addressed if CSP is to be achieved. The third dimension concerns the scope of social or stakeholder issues (for example, consumerism, environment, produce safety, and discrimination) that management must address.

The corporate social performance model is intended to be useful to both academics and managers. For academics, the model is primarily a conceptual aid to perceiving the distinction among the concepts of corporate social responsibility that have appeared in the literature. What previously have been regarded as separate definitions of CSR are treated here as three separate aspects pertaining to CSP. The model's major use to the academic, therefore, is in helping to systematize the important concepts that must be taught and understood in an effort to clarify the CSR concept. The model is not the ultimate conceptualization. It is, rather, a modest but necessary step toward understanding the major facets of CSP.

The conceptual model can assist managers in understanding that social responsibility is not separate and distinct from economic performance. The model integrates economic concerns into a social performance framework. In addition, it places ethical and philanthropic expectations into a rational economic and legal framework. The model can help the manager systematically think through major stakeholder issues. Although it does not provide the answer to how far the organization should go, it does provide a conceptualization that could lead to better-managed social performance. Moreover, the model could be used as a planning tool and as a diagnostic problem-solving tool. The model can assist the manager by identifying categories within which the organization can be situated.

There have been several extensions, reformulations, or reorientations of the CSP model. Figure 2-8 summarizes some of these. Figure 2-9 on page 50 depicts Wartick and Cochran's CSP model extensions, which help to flesh out some important details.

FIGURE 2-8

Corporate Social Performance: Extensions, Reformulations, Reorientations

Wartick and Cochran's CSP Extensions

Wartick and Cochran proposed several changes/extensions to the CSP model. They proposed that the "social issues" dimension had matured into a new management field known as "social issues management." They extended the CSP model further by proposing that the three dimensions be viewed as depictng *principles* (corporate social responsibilities, reflecting a philosophical orientation), *processes* (corporate social responsiveness, reflecting an institutional orientation) and *policies* (social issues management, reflecting an organizational orientation).

Wood's Reformulated CSP Model

Wood elaborated and reformulated Carroll's model and Wartick and Cochran's extensions and set forth a reformulated model. Her new definition of corporate social performance was "A business organization's configuration of principles of social responsibility, processes of social responsiveness, and policies, programs, and other observable outcomes as they relate to the firm's societal relationships." She took this definition further by proposing that each of the three components—principles, processes, and outcomes—is composed of specific elements.

Swanson's Reorientation of CSP

Swanson elaborated on the dynamic nature of the principles, processes, and outcomes reformulated by Wood. Relying on research from corporate culture, her reoriented model links CSP to the personally held values and ethics of executive managers and other employees. She proposed that the executive's sense of morality highly influences the policies and programs of environmental assessment, stakeholder management, and issues management, carried out by employees. These internal processes are means by which organizations can impact society through *economizing* (efficiently converting inputs into outputs) and *ecologizing* (forging community-minded collaborations).

SOURCES: Steven L. Wartick and Philip L. Cochran, "The Evolution of the Corporate Social Performance Model," *Academy of Management Review* (Vol. 10, 1985), 765–766; Donna J. Wood, "Corporate Social Performance Revisited," *Academy of Management Review* (October 1991), 691–718; D. L. Swanson, "Addressing a Theoretical Problem by Reorienting the Corporate Social Performance Model," *Academy of Management Review* (Vol. 20. No. 1, 1995), 43–64. Swanson, D. L. "Toward an Integrative Theory of Business and Society: A Research Strategy for Corporate Social Performance," *Academy of Management Review* (Vol. 24. No. 3, 1999), 596–521.

FIGURE 2-9

Wartick and Cochran's Corporate Social Performance Model Extensions

Principles	Processes	Policies
Corporate Social Responsibilities	**Corporate Social Responsiveness**	**Social Issues Management**
(1) Economic	(1) Reactive	(1) Issues Identification
(2) Legal	(2) Defensive	(2) Issues Analysis
(3) Ethical	(3) Accommodative	(3) Response Development
(4) Discretionary	(4) Proactive	
Directed at:	**Directed at:**	**Directed at:**
(1) The Social Contract of Business	(1) The Capacity to Respond to Changing Societal Conditions	(1) Minimizing "Surprises"
(2) Business as a Moral Agent	(2) Managerial Approaches to Developing Responses	(2) Determining Effective Corporate Social Policies
Philosophical Orientation	**Institutional Orientation**	**Organizational Orientation**

SOURCE: Steven L. Wartick and Philip L. Cochran, "The Evolution of the Corporate Social Performance Model," *Academy of Management Review* (Vol. 10, 1985), 767.

BUSINESS'S INTEREST IN CORPORATE SOCIAL PERFORMANCE

Although there has been considerable academic research on the subject of corporate social performance over the past decade, we should stress that academics are not the only ones who are interested in this topic. Prominent business organizations and periodicals that report on social performance include *Fortune* magazine, *Business Ethics* magazine, and The Conference Board. We will discuss several of these.

Fortune's Rankings of "Most Admired" and "Least Admired" Companies

For many years now, *Fortune* magazine has conducted rankings of "America's Most Admired Companies" and has included among their "Eight Key Attributes of Reputation" the category of performance titled "Social Responsibility." The rankings are the result of a poll of more than 12,600 senior executives, outside directors, and financial analysts. In the social responsibility category, the most admired firms for 2004 were United Parcel Service (UPS), Alcoa, Washington Mutual, BP, and McDonald's.[38] In a related vein, *Fortune* also publishes "The 100 Best Companies to Work For," on an annual basis. The top companies in 2004 were J. M. Smuckers, Alston & Bird, Container Store, Edward Jones, and Republic Bancorp. It is not clear what specific impact the *Fortune* rankings have for these businesses, but surely they have some positive impact on the firms' general reputations. The important point to note here, however, is that the social responsibility category is one indicator of corporate social performance and that it was included as a criterion of admired companies by one of our country's leading business magazines.

The Conference Board's Ron Brown Award for Corporate Leadership

The Conference Board gives an annual award titled the "Ron Brown Award for Corporate Leadership." It claims to be the first presidential award to honor companies for outstanding achievements in employee and community relations.

It expects that this award will promote practices that improve business performance by supporting employees and communities. The Ron Brown Award for Corporate Leadership is presented at an annual White House ceremony, amid media coverage that ensures greater public awareness of the accomplishments being honored.

Core Principles of the Award
For a company to be eligible:

- Top management must demonstrate commitment to corporate citizenship.
- Corporate citizenship must be a shared value of the company, visible at all levels.
- Corporate citizenship must be integrated into a successful business strategy.

Key Criteria
For programs to be eligible, they must:

- Be at the "best practice" level—distinctive, innovative, and effective.
- Have a significant, measurable impact on the people they are designed to serve.
- Offer broad potential for social and economic benefits for U.S. society.
- Be sustainable and feasible within a business environment and mission.
- Be adaptable to other businesses and communities.

The winners for 2002–2003 were Fannie Mae (for employer-assisted housing initiative) and Cisco Systems (for its networking academy program).

Business Ethics Magazine Awards

For several years now, *Business Ethics* magazine has published its list of Annual Business Ethics Awards. Its winners for the year 2003 were Fastener Industries of Berea, Ohio (for employee ownership), White Dog Café of Philadelphia (for living economy), and New Belgium Brewing Co. in Ft. Collins, Colorado (for environmental excellence). The criteria used by the magazine to determine its winners include the following:[39]

Award winners should meet many (though not necessarily all) of the following criteria:

*   Be a leader in their field, out ahead of the pack, showing the way ethically.

*   Have programs or initiatives in social responsibility that demonstrate sincerity and ongoing vibrancy, and that reach deep into the company.

*   Have a significant presence on the national or world scene, so their ethical behavior sends a loud signal.

*   Be a standout in at least one area of social responsibility, though recipients need not be exemplary in all areas.

*   Have faced a recent challenge and overcome it with integrity, or taken other recent steps to show their ethical commitment is still very much alive.

Ethics in Practice

SLACKING INSTEAD OF SELLING

One summer I had a sales internship that required salespeople to make seven calls/visits to customers a day. There was no way to track whether or not these visits were actually made. Along with the seven appointments, spare time was to be used making cold calls (these calls are going to customers who have never heard of the company or have never bought anything from the company). While shadowing the salesperson, I realized he was not always going to his calls. If something came up and the customer could not meet, the salesperson would fill out the sheet as if he had actually seen the customer, leaving a very vague description of the visit. During his spare time between calls, he would shop at the local malls or even go to the golfing range. Because I was following him around, I was learning more about what shopping malls were in the area as opposed to what I needed to turn in to my boss. When I questioned him about it, seeing as how I

was concerned that I wasn't learning what to really do, he said that all the salespeople do it. He told me that everyone would get upset if I didn't do the same because my numbers and productivity would be higher than theirs, and this would make them look bad. He said it was just "how things were done" and how they had "always been done." I was torn between being their friend and fitting in or going the ethical way and doing things right.

1. What are the major ethical issues in this case?

2. What might be some of the reasons that the salespeople use to justify their activities?

3. If you were in this situation, would you participate in the activities or would you do what you think is right? Would you inform management of what is going on?

Contributed Anonymously

---

* Be profitable in the most recent year, or show a strong history of healthy profitability.
* For the Living Economy Award, be a company that is locally based, human scale, stakeholder-owned, democratically accountable, and life-serving, seeking fair profits rather than maximum profits.

Business Ethics magazine also publishes an annual volume in which it reports its "100 Best Corporate Citizens." Its goal is to "celebrate those companies that excel at serving multiple stakeholders well."[40] Among the criteria used by the panel of judges are firms:

• Having community-service programs that are employee-driven, not executive-driven
• Taking a rifle-shot rather than a shotgun approach to community service
• Encouraging employees to express their individuality
• Finding creative ways to relieve the pressures in employees' lives
• Taking a team-based approach to developing products and servicing customers
• Showing, in the end, that not even the best corporate citizens are perfect

The top five winners for 2003 were General Mills, Cummins, Inc., Intel, Procter & Gamble, and IBM. Each of these companies scored high on its social performance with respect to community, minorities and women, employees, environment, non-U.S. stakeholders, and customers.

WalkerInformation's Research

A major comprehensive study designed to measure the impact of corporate social responsibility was conducted by WalkerInformation, the twelfth largest research organization in the United States. Employing a 14-page questionnaire, WalkerInformation received responses from 1,037 heads of U.S. households (43 percent male and 57 percent female). Respondents were asked to answer questions as potential consumers, employees, or investors depending on the nature of the question. The WalkerInformation study painted a detailed account of the impact of corporate social responsibility on business firms' reputations and its relationship to stakeholder decisions to purchase from, become employed by, or invest in a particular company.[41]

In one of its questions, WalkerInformation sought to discover what the general public perceived to be the activities or characteristics of socially responsible companies. Figure 2-10 summarizes what the sample said were the top 20 activities/characteristics of socially responsible companies. The items in this listing are quite compatible with our discussion of CSR earlier in this chapter. It should be noted that most of these characteristics would be representative of the legal, ethical, and philanthropic/discretionary components of our four-part CSR definition.

WalkerInformation concluded that the public thinks CSR factors impact a company's reputation just as do traditional business factors, such as quality, service, and price. A related question on its survey pertained to the impact of social irresponsibility on firm reputation. The WalkerInformation study found that companies that are ethical and obey

---

FIGURE 2-10

Top 20 Activities/Characteristics of Socially Responsible Companies

- Makes products that are safe
- Does not pollute air or water
- Obeys the law in all aspects of business
- Promotes honest/ethical employee behavior
- Commits to safe workplace ethics

- Does not use misleading/deceptive advertising
- Upholds stated policy banning discrimination
- Utilizes "environmentally friendly" packaging
- Protects employees against sexual harassment
- Recycles within company

- Shows no past record of questionable activity
- Responds quickly to customer problems
- Maintains waste reduction program
- Provides/pays portion of medical
- Promotes energy-conservation program

- Helps displaced workers with placement
- Gives money to charitable/educational causes
- Utilizes only biodegradable/recycling materials
- Employs friendly/courteous/responsive personnel
- Tries continually to improve quality

SOURCE: WalkerInformation, 1994. Used with permission.

the law can reap rewards from CSR activities and enjoy enhanced reputations. However, those that are perceived to be unethical or that do not obey the law can do little in the way of CSR activities to correct their images. Thus, the penalties for disobeying the law are greater than the rewards for helping society.

CORPORATE CITIZENSHIP

Business practitioners and academics alike have grown fond of the term *corporate citizenship* in reference to businesses' corporate social performance. But, what does **corporate citizenship** really mean? Does it have a distinct meaning apart from the concepts of corporate social responsibility, responsiveness, and performance discussed earlier? A careful look at the concept and its literature shows that although it is a useful and attractive term, it is not distinct from the terminology we have described earlier, except in the eyes of some writers who have attempted to give it a specific, narrow meaning. If one thinks about companies as "citizens" of the countries in which they reside, corporate citizenship just means that these companies have certain responsibilities that they must perform in order to be perceived as good corporate citizens. Altman and Vidaver-Cohen say that "corporate citizenship is not a new concept, but one whose time has come."[42]

Broad Views.   *Corporate citizenship* has been described by some as a broad, encompassing term that basically embraces all that is implied in the concepts of social responsibility, responsiveness, and performance. Graves, Waddock, and Kelly, for example, define good corporate citizenship as "serving a variety of stakeholders well."[43] Fombrun also proposes a broad conception. He holds that corporate citizenship is composed of a three-part view that encompasses (1) a reflection of shared moral and ethical principles, (2) a vehicle for integrating individuals into the communities in which they work, and (3) a form of enlightened self-interest that balances all stakeholders' claims and enhances a company's long-term value.[44]

Davenport's research also resulted in a broad definition of corporate citizenship that includes a commitment to ethical business behavior and balancing the needs of stakeholders, while working to protect the environment.[45] Finally, Carroll has recast his four categories of corporate social responsibility as embracing the "four faces of corporate citizenship,"—economic, legal, ethical, and philanthropic. Each face, aspect, or responsibility reveals an important facet that contributes to the whole. He poses that "just as private citizens are expected to fulfill these responsibilities, companies are as well."[46]

Narrow Views.   At the narrow end of the spectrum, Altman speaks of corporate citizenship in terms of corporate community relations. In this view, it embraces the functions through which business intentionally interacts with nonprofit organizations, citizen groups, and other stakeholders at the community level.[47] Other definitions of corporate citizenship fall between these broad and narrow perspectives, and some refer to global corporate citizenship as well, as increasingly companies are expected to conduct themselves appropriately wherever they are doing business.

The benefits of good corporate citizenship to stakeholders are fairly apparent. But, what are the benefits of good corporate citizenship to business itself? A literature review of studies attempting to discern the benefits to companies of corporate citizenship, defined broadly, revealed empirical and anecdotal evidence supporting the following:[48]

- Improved employee relations (e.g. improves employee recruitment, retention, morale, loyalty, motivation, and productivity)
- Improved customer relationships (e.g., increased customer loyalty, acts as a tiebreaker for consumer purchasing, enhances brand image)
- Improved business performance (e.g., positively impacts bottom-line returns, increases competitive advantage, encourages cross-functional integration)
- Enhanced company's marketing efforts (e.g., helps create a positive company image, helps a company manage its reputation, supports higher prestige pricing, and enhances government affairs activities)

The terminology of corporate citizenship is especially attractive because it resonates so well with the business community's attempts to describe their own socially responsive activities and practices. Therefore, we can expect that this concept will be around for some years to come. Generally speaking, as we refer to CSR, social responsiveness, and social performance, we are also embracing activities that would typically fall under the purview of a firm's corporate citizenship.[49]

SOCIAL PERFORMANCE AND FINANCIAL PERFORMANCE

One issue that comes up frequently in considerations of corporate social performance is whether or not there is a demonstrable relationship between a firm's social responsibility or performance and its financial performance. Unfortunately, attempts to measure this relationship are typically hampered by measurement problems. The appropriate performance criteria for measuring financial performance and social responsibility are subject to debate. Furthermore, the measurement of social responsibility is fraught with definitional problems. Even if a definition of CSR could be agreed on, there still would remain the complex task of operationalizing the definition.

Over the years, studies on the social responsibility–financial performance relationship have produced varying results.[50] In one important study of this relationship, Preston and O'Bannon, examined data from 67 large U.S. corporations covering the years 1982–1992. They concluded that "there is a positive association between social and financial performance in large U.S. corporations."[51] Research by Waddock and Graves has concluded that corporate social performance (CSP) was positively associated with prior financial performance (CFP) and future financial performance.[52] In a study of the chemical industry, Griffin and Mahon found that perceptual CSP measures are "somewhat related" to the financial information. Overall, however, they found contradictory results in studies they examined.[53] Finally, a study by Roman, Hayibor, and Agle, reanalyzing the Griffin and Mahon data, concluded that the "vast majority of studies support the idea that, at the very least, good social performance does not lead to poor financial performance." They go on to say that most of the studies they reviewed indicated a positive correlation between CSP and CFP.[54]

In qualifying the research, it is important to note that there have been at least three different views, hypotheses, or perspectives that have dominated these discussions and research.

Perspective 1.   Perhaps the most popular view is built on the belief that socially responsible firms are more financially profitable. To those who advocate the concept of social performance, it is apparent why they would like to think that social performance is a driver of financial performance and, ultimately, a corporation's reputation. If it could be demonstrated that socially responsible firms, in general, are more financially successful and have better reputations, this would significantly bolster the CSP view, even in the eyes of its critics.

Perspective 1 has been studied extensively. Unfortunately, the findings of most of the studies that have sought to demonstrate this relationship have been either flawed in their methodology or inconclusive. Numerous studies have been done well, but even these have failed to produce conclusive results. In spite of this, some studies have claimed to have successfully established this linkage. For example, a study by Covenant Investment Management, a Chicago investment firm, concluded that social concern pays. This study found that 200 companies ranking highest on Covenant's overall social responsibility scale had outperformed the Standard & Poor's 500-stock index during the five years (1988–1992) studied.[55] To be considered a valid finding, however, the Covenant research would have to be subjected to careful scrutiny. Part of the problem with Perspective 1 is that positive correlations may be found, but causality is not clearly established.

Perspective 2. This view, which has not been studied as extensively, argues that a firm's financial performance is a driver of its social performance. This perspective is built somewhat on the notion that social responsibility is a "fair weather" concept; that is, when times are good and companies are enjoying financial success, we witness higher levels of social performance. In their study, Preston and O'Bannon found the strongest evidence that financial performance either precedes, or is contemporaneous with, social performance. This evidence supports the view that social–financial performance correlations are best explained by positive synergies or by "available funding."[56] The research of Waddock and Graves, cited earlier, is consistent with this finding.

Perspective 3. This position argues that there is an interactive relationship among social performance, financial performance, and corporate reputation. In this symbiotic view, the three major factors influence each other, and, because they are so interrelated, it is not easy to identify which factor is driving the process. Regardless of the perspective taken, each view advocates a significant role for CSP, and it is expected that researchers will continue to explore these perspectives for years to come. Figure 2-11 depicts the essentials of each of these views.

Finally, it should be mentioned that the "contingency" view of Husted suggests that CSP should be seen as a function of the fit between specific strategies and structures and the nature of the social issue. He argues that the social issue is determined by the expectational gaps of the firm and its stakeholders that occur within or between views of what is and/or what ought to be, and that high corporate social performance is achieved by closing these expectational gaps with the appropriate strategy and structure.[57]

A Stakeholder Bottom-Line Perspective

A basic premise of all these perspectives is that there is only one "bottom line"—a corporate bottom line that addresses primarily the stockholders', or owners', investments in the firm. An alternative view is that the firm has "multiple bottom lines" that benefit from corporate social performance. This stakeholder-bottom-line perspective argues that

FIGURE 2-11

Relationships Among Corporate Social Performance (CSP), Corporate Financial Performance (CFP), and Corporate Reputation (CR)

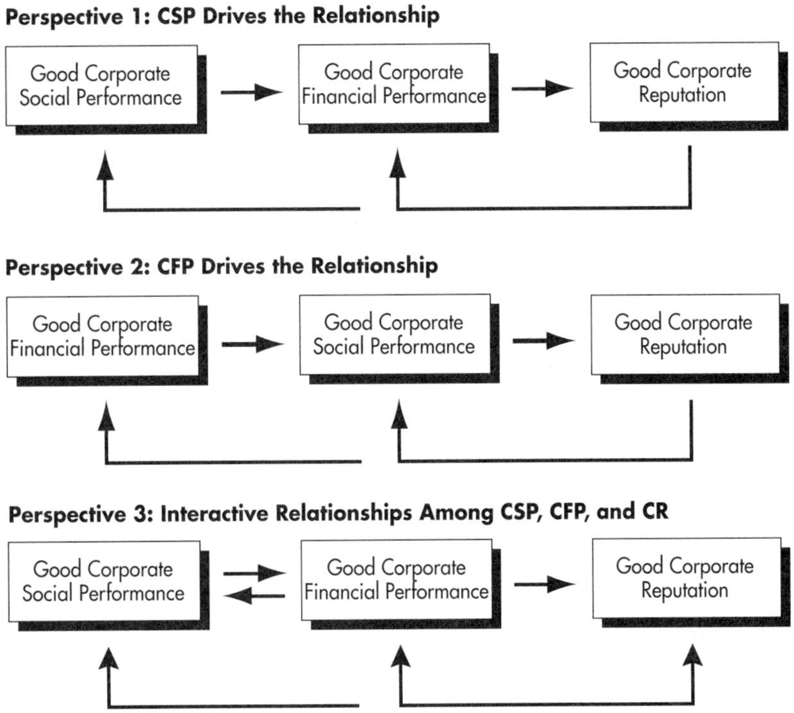

Perspective 1: CSP Drives the Relationship

Good Corporate Social Performance → Good Corporate Financial Performance → Good Corporate Reputation

Perspective 2: CFP Drives the Relationship

Good Corporate Financial Performance → Good Corporate Social Performance → Good Corporate Reputation

Perspective 3: Interactive Relationships Among CSP, CFP, and CR

Good Corporate Social Performance ⇄ Good Corporate Financial Performance → Good Corporate Reputation

the impacts or benefits of CSP cannot be fully measured or appreciated by considering only the impact of the firm's financial bottom line.

To truly operate with a stakeholder perspective, companies need to accept the multiple-bottom-line view. Thus, CSP cannot be fully comprehended unless we also consider that its impacts on stakeholders, such as consumers, employees, the community, and other stakeholder groups, are noted, measured, and considered. Research may never conclusively demonstrate a relationship between CSP and financial performance. If a stakeholder perspective is taken, however, it may be more straightforward to assess the impact of CSP on multiple stakeholders' bottom lines. This model of CSP and stakeholders' bottom lines might be depicted as shown in Figure 2-12 on page 58.

The Triple Bottom Line. A variant of the "multiple bottom line" perspective is popularly known as the **"Triple Bottom Line"** concept. The phrase *triple bottom line* has been attributed to John Elkington. The concept seeks to encapsulate for business the three key spheres of **sustainability**—*economic*, *social*, and *environmental*. The "economic bottom line" refers to the firm's creation of material wealth, including financial income and assets. The "social" bottom line is about the quality of people's lives and about equity between people, communities, and nations. The "environmental" bottom line is about protection

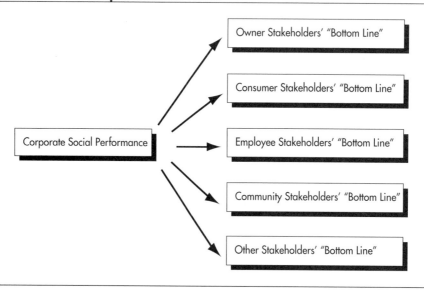

FIGURE 2-12

Relationship Between Corporate Social Performance (CSP) and Stakeholders' "Multiple Bottom Lines"

and conservation of the natural environment.[58] It may quickly be seen that these three areas are embodied in the Pyramid of CSR and represent a version of the stakeholder-bottom-line concept. At its narrowest, the term is used as a framework for measuring and reporting corporate performance in terms of economic, social, and environmental indicators. At its broadest, the concept is used to capture the whole set of values, issues, and processes that companies must address to minimize harm resulting from their activities and to create economic, social, and environmental value.[59] As a concept, it is a more detailed spelling out of the idea of corporate social performance.

As mentioned earlier, **corporate sustainability** is the goal of the triple-bottom-line approach. The goal of sustainability is to create long-term shareholder value by taking advantage of opportunities and managing risks related to economic, environmental, and social developments. Leaders in this area try to take advantage of the market's demand for sustainability products and services while successfully reducing and avoiding sustainability costs and risks. To help achieve these goals, the Dow Jones Sustainability Indexes were created to monitor and assess the sustainability of corporations.[60]

SOCIALLY RESPONSIBLE OR ETHICAL INVESTING

Special-interest groups, the media, and academics are not alone in their interest in business's social performance. Investors are also interested. The **socially responsible** or **ethical investing** movement arrived on the scene in the 1970s and has continued to grow and prosper. By the early 2000s, social investing had matured into a comprehensive investing approach complete with social and environmental screens, shareholder activism, and community investment, accounting for over $2 trillion of investments in the United States, according to the Social Investment Forum.[61]

Historically, social responsibility investing can be traced back to the early 1900s, when church endowments refused to buy "sin" stocks—then defined as shares in tobacco, alcohol, and gambling companies. During the Vietnam War era of the 1960s and early 1970s, antiwar investors refused to invest in defense contracting firms. In the early 1980s, universities, municipalities, and foundations sold off their shares of companies that had operations in South Africa to protest apartheid. By the 1990s, self-styled socially responsible investing came into its own.[62] In the 2000s, social investing is celebrating the fact that social or ethical investing is now part of the mainstream.

Socially conscious investments in pension funds, mutual funds, and municipal and private portfolios arrived at the $2.2 trillion level in 2003 and have been continuing to grow. However, managers of socially conscious funds do not use only ethical or social responsibility criteria to decide which companies to invest in. They typically consider a company's financial health before all else. Moreover, a growing corps of brokers, financial planners, and portfolio managers are available to help people evaluate investments for their social impacts.[63]

The concept of *social screening* is the backbone of the socially conscious investing movement. Investors seeking to put their money into socially responsible firms want to screen out those firms they consider to be socially irresponsible or to actively invest in those firms they think of as being socially responsible. Thus, there are negative social screens and positive social screens. Some of the *negative social screens* that have been used in recent years include the avoidance of investing in tobacco manufacturers, gambling casino operators, defense or weapons contractors, and firms doing business in South Africa.[64] In 1994, however, with the elimination of the official system of apartheid in South Africa, this was eliminated as a negative screen by many.

It is more difficult, and thus more challenging, to implement *positive social screens*, because they require the potential investor to make judgment calls as to what constitutes an acceptable or a good level of social performance on social investment criteria. Criteria that may be used as either positive or negative screens, depending on the firm's performance, might include the firm's record on issues such as equal employment opportunity and affirmative action, environmental protection, treatment of employees, corporate citizenship (broadly defined), and treatment of animals.

The financial performance of socially conscious funds shows that investors do not have to sacrifice profitability for principles. Recent evidence suggests that investors expect and receive competitive returns from social investments.[65]

It should be added, however, that there is no clear and consistent evidence that returns from socially conscious funds will equal or exceed the returns from funds that are not so carefully screened. Therefore, socially conscious funds are valued most highly by those investors who really care about the social performance of companies in their portfolios and are willing to put their money at some risk. One study concluded that there is no penalty for improved CSP in terms of institutional ownership and that high CSP tends in fact to lead to an increase in the number of institutional investors holding a given stock.[66]

The Council on Economic Priorities has suggested that there are at least three reasons why there has been an upsurge in social or ethical investing:[67]

1. There is more reliable and sophisticated research on CSP than in the past.
2. Investment firms using social criteria have established a solid track record, and investors do not have to sacrifice gains for principles.

3. The socially conscious 1960s generation is now making investment decisions.

In recent years, as more and more citizen employees are in charge of their own IRAs and 401(k)s, people have become much more sophisticated about making investment decisions than in the past. Further, more people are seeing social investments as a way in which they can exert their priorities concerning the balance of financial and social concerns.

Whether it be called social investing, ethical investing, or socially responsible investing, it is clear that social investing has "arrived" on the scene and has become a part of the mainstream. As of 2003, more than one out of every nine dollars under professional management in the United States is involved in socially responsible investing. From 1995 to 2003, socially responsible investing has grown 40 percent faster than all other professionally managed investment assets in the United States. Socially responsible investing is growing globally as well.[68] Socially conscious funds will continue to be debated in the investment community. The fact that they exist, have grown, and have prospered, however, provides evidence that the practice is a serious one and that there truly are investors in the real world who take the social performance issue quite seriously.

■ SUMMARY

Important and related concepts include those of corporate citizenship, corporate social responsibility, responsiveness, and performance. The corporate social responsibility concept has a rich history. It has grown out of many diverse views and even today does not enjoy a consensus of definition. A four-part conceptualization was presented that broadly conceives CSR as encompassing economic, legal, ethical, and philanthropic components. The four parts were presented as part of the Pyramid of CSR.

The concern for corporate social responsibility has been expanded to include a concern for social responsiveness. The responsiveness focus suggests more of an action-oriented theme by which firms not only must address their basic obligations but also must decide on basic modes of responding to these obligations. A CSP model was presented that brought the responsibility and responsiveness dimensions together into a framework that also identified realms of social or stakeholder issues that must be considered. The identification of social issues has blossomed into a field now called "issues management" or "stakeholder management."

The interest in corporate social responsibility extends beyond the academic community. On an annual basis,

Fortune magazine polls executives on various dimensions of corporate performance; one major dimension is called "Social Responsibility." A vibrant organization, Business for Social Responsibility, promises to be on the cutting edge of CSR practice. WalkerInformation has investigated how the general consuming public regards social responsibility issues. The term *corporate citizenship* has arrived on the scene to embrace a whole host of socially conscious activities and practices on the part of businesses. This term has become quite popular in the business community.

Finally, the socially responsible or ethical investing movement seems to be flourishing. This indicates that there is a growing body of investors who are sensitive to business's social and ethical (as well as financial) performance. Studies of the relationship between social responsibility and economic performance do not yield consistent results, but social efforts are nevertheless expected and are of value to both the firm and the business community. In the final analysis, sound corporate social (stakeholder) performance is associated with a "multiple-bottom-line effect" in which a number of different stakeholder groups experience enhanced bottom lines.

▪ KEY TERMS

Business for Social Responsibility (BSR) (page 30)
community obligations (page 32)
corporate citizenship (page 54)
corporate social performance (CSP) (page 47)
corporate social performance model (page 47)
corporate social responsibility (page 30)
corporate social responsiveness (page 45)
corporate sustainability (page 58)
economic responsibilities (page 35)
ethical responsibilities (page 37)

legal responsibilities (page 35)
paternalism (page 32)
philanthropic responsibilities (page 37)
philanthropy (page 32)
Pyramid of Corporate Social Responsibility (CSR) (page 39)
socially responsible or ethical investing (page 58)
sustainability (page 57)
Triple Bottom Line (page 57)

▪ DISCUSSION QUESTIONS

1. Identify and explain the Pyramid of Corporate Social Responsibility. Provide several examples of each "layer" of the pyramid. Identify and discuss some of the tensions among the layers or components.

2. In your view, what is the single strongest argument *against* the idea of corporate social responsibility? What is the single strongest argument *for* corporate social responsibility? Briefly explain.

3. Differentiate corporate social responsibility from corporate social responsiveness. Give an example of each.

4. Analyze how the Triple Bottom Line and the Pyramid of CSR are similar and different. Draw a schematic that shows how the two concepts relate to one another.

5. Discuss the interrelationships among the concepts of corporate social performance (CSP), corporate financial performance (CFP), and corporate reputation (CR). Which perspective on these relationships seems most valid to you? Explain why.

6. Does socially responsible or ethical investing seem to you to be a legitimate way in which the average citizen might demonstrate her or his concern for CSR? Discuss.

▪ RECOMMENDED CASES

Many of the end-of-text cases may be related to Chapter 2. You may wish to consider studying the following cases with Chapter 2.

Case 1. "WAL-MART: THE MAIN STREET MERCHANT OF DOOM." This case about Wal-Mart addresses and illustrates a host of business and society relationships. It especially raises the issue of a business's social responsibility to the community and its stakeholders. Is Wal-Mart a socially responsible firm or is it the "Main Street Merchant of Doom"?

Cases 2A and 2B; Cases 3A and 3B. "THE BODY SHOP INTERNATIONAL PLC." Series of four cases, all address issues related to corporate social responsibility,

corporate power, social performance, and corporate citizenship. They especially raise the issue of balancing company profits with social initiatives. Can a company claim to be a good corporate citizen and yet engage in some of the practices described in these cases? Is The Body Shop a good citizen or is the public being misled?

Case 17. "NIKE, INC." This case addresses the roles and responsibilities of a business operating at the global level. What are business's social responsibilities when doing business all over the world? How does a firm be a good corporate "world" citizen? What makes it difficult? Does Nike have a social responsibility for the subcontractors that it employs?

▪ WEB RESOURCES

The URLs listed here are current at the time of publication. Should any of these Web sites change, please search under the company's or organization's name for an updated address.

Business for Social Responsibility
  http://www.bsr.org

Business and Sustainable Development
  http://www.bsdglobal.com/tools/principles_triple.asp

Beyond Grey Pinstripes
  http:// www.beyondgreypinstripes.org/ BSR Resources
  http://www.bsr.org/BSRResources/index.cfm

Business Roundtable
  http://www.brtable.org

Business Week
  http://www.businessweek.com

Center for Corporate Citizenship Boston
  http://www.bc.edu/centers/ccc/index.html

Center on Philanthropy Indiana University
  http://www.philanthropy.iupui.edu

Corporate Accountability Project
  http://www.corporation.org

Corporate Social Responsibility Newswire
  http://www.csrwire.com

CSR Europe
  http://www.csreurope.org

Fortune
  http://www.fortune.com

Journal of Corporate Citizenship
  http://www.greenleaf-publishing.com/jcc/

The Conference Board
  http://www.conference-board.org

Public Interest Groups
  http://www.pirg.org

The Wall Street Journal
  http://www.wsj.com

U.S. Chamber of Commerce
  http://www.uschamber.com

InfoTrac® College Edition   http://www.infotrac-college.com

Articles from Business Week, Fortune, Journal of Corporate Citizenship, *and* The Wall Street Journal *can be researched, retrieved, and read from your desktop using InfoTrac's online database.*

▪ ENDNOTES

1. Business for Social Responsibility, *Corporate Social Responsibility: A Guide to Better Business Practice* (San Francisco: BSR Education Fund, 2000). BSR's Web site is http://www.bsr.org.

2. Quoted in John L. Paluszek, *Business and Society: 1976–2000* (New York: AMACOM, 1976), 1.

3. Keith Davis, "Understanding the Social Responsibility Puzzle," *Business Horizon* (Winter 1967), 45–50.

4. James W. McKie, "Changing Views," in *Social Responsibility and the Business Predicament* (Washington, DC: The Brookings Institute, 1974), 22.

5. *Ibid.*

6. See Morrell Heald, *The Social Responsibilities of Business: Company and Community, 1900–1960* (Cleveland: Case Western Reserve University Press, 1970), 12–14.

7. McKie, 23.

8. *Ibid.*, 25.

9. Heald, 119.

10. McKie, 27–28.

11. Neil J. Mitchell, *The Generous Corporation: A Political Analysis of Economic Power* (New Haven, CT: Yale University Press, 1989).

12. Ronald E. Berenbeim, "When the Corporate Conscience Was Born" (A review of Mitchell's book), *Across the Board* (October 1989), 60–62.

13. *Ibid.*, 62.

14. Keith Davis and Robert L. Blomstrom, *Business and Society: Environment and Responsibility*, 3d ed. (New York: McGraw-Hill, 1975), 39.

15. Joseph W. McGuire, *Business and Society* (New York: McGraw-Hill, 1963), 144.

16. Edwin M. Epstein, "The Corporate Social Policy Process: Beyond Business Ethics, Corporate Social Responsibility and Corporate Social Responsiveness," *California Management Review* (Vol. XXIX, No. 3, 1987), 104.

17. For a more complete history of the CSR concept, see Archie B. Carroll, "Corporate Social Responsibility: Evolution of a Definitional Construct," *Business and Society* (Vol. 38, No. 3, September 1999), 268–295.

18. Archie B. Carroll, "A Three-Dimensional Conceptual Model of Corporate Social Performance," *Academy of Management Review* (Vol. 4, No. 4, 1979), 497–505.

19. Stuart Taylor, Jr., and Evan Thomas, "Civil Wars," *Newsweek* (December 15, 2003), 43–53.

20. Archie B. Carroll, "The Pyramid of Corporate Social Responsibility: Toward the Moral Management of Organizational Stakeholders," *Business Horizons* (July–August 1991), 39–48. Also see Archie B. Carroll, "The Four Faces of Corporate Citizenship," *Business and Society Review* (Vol. 100–101, 1998), 1–7.

21. *Ibid.*

22. *Ibid.*

23. Milton Friedman, "The Social Responsibility of Business Is to Increase Its Profits," *The New York Times* (September 1962), 126.

24. *Ibid.*, 33 (emphasis added).

25. Christopher D. Stone, *Where the Law Ends* (New York: Harper Colophon Books, 1975), 77.

26. Keith Davis, "The Case For and Against Business Assumption of Social Responsibilities," *Academy of Management Journal* (June 1973), 312–322.

27. F. A. Hayek, "The Corporation in a Democratic Society: In Whose Interest Ought It and Will It Be Run?" in H. Ansoff (ed.), *Business Strategy* (Middlesex: Penguin, 1969), 225.

28. Davis, 320.

29. Thomas A. Petit, *The Moral Crisis in Management* (New York: McGraw-Hill, 1967), 58.

30. Davis, 316.

31. Cited in Aaron Bernstein, "Too Much Corporate Power," *Business Week* (September 11, 2000), 149.

32. "CSR—A Religion with Too Many Priests," *European Business Forum* (Issue 15, Autumn 2003).

33. Simon Zadek, *The Civil Corporation*. See also Lance Moir, "Social Responsibility: The Changing Role of Business," Cranfield School of Management, U.K.

34. The Millennium Poll on Corporate Social Responsibility (Environics, Intl., Ltd., Prince of Wales Business Leaders Forum, The Conference Board, 1999), http://www.Environics.net.

35. Robert Ackerman and Raymond Bauer, *Corporate Social Responsiveness: The Modern Dilemma* (Reston, VA: Reston Publishing Company, 1976), 6.

36. Juha Näsi, Salme Näsi, Nelson Phillips, and Stelios Zyglidopoulos, "The Evolution of Corporate

Responsiveness," *Business and Society* (Vol. 36, No. 3, September 1997), 296–321.

37. Carroll, 1979, 502–504.

38. Edward A. Robinson, "The Ups and Downs of the Industry Leaders," *Fortune* (March 2, 1998), 86–87. See Fortune's Web page for most recent information: http://www.fortune.com/fortune.

39. Reported in the *Business Ethics* magazine Web page: http://www.business-ethics.com.

40. Tom Klusmann, "The 100 Best Corporate Citizens," *Business Ethics* (March/April 2000), 12–16.

41. Walker Group, *Corporate Character: It's Driving Competitive Companies: Where's It Driving Yours?* (1994). See WalkerInformation's Web page: http://www.walkerinfo.com.

42. See special issue on "Corporate Citizenship," *Business and Society Review* (105:1, Spring 2000), edited by Barbara W. Altman and Deborah Vidaver-Cohen.

43. Samuel P. Graves, Sandra Waddock, and Marjorie Kelly, "How Do You Measure Corporate Citizenship?" *Business Ethics* (March/April 2001), 17.

44. Charles J. Fombrum, "Three Pillars of Corporate Citizenship," in Noel Tichy, Andrew McGill, and Lynda St. Clair (eds.), *Corporate Global Citizenship* (San Francisco: The New Lexington Press), 27–61.

45. Kimberly S. Davenport, "Corporate Citizenship: A Stakeholder Approach for Defining Corporate Social Performance and Identifying Measures for Assessing It," doctoral dissertation, The Fielding Institute, Santa Barbara, CA.

46. Archie B. Carroll, "The Four Faces of Corporate Citizenship," *Business and Society Review* (100/101, 1998), 1–7.

47. Barbara W. Altman, *Corporate Community Relations in the 1990s: A Study in Transformation*, unpublished doctoral dissertation, Boston University.

48. Archie B. Carroll, Kim Davenport, and Doug Grisaffe, "Appraising the Business Value of Corporate Citizenship: What Does the Literature Say?" Proceedings of the International Association for Business and Society, Essex Junction, VT, 2000.

49. For more on corporate citizenship, see the special issue "Corporate Citizenship," *Business and Society Review* (105:1, Spring 2000), edited by Barbara W. Altman and Deborah Vidaver-Cohen. Also see Jorg Andriof and Malcolm McIntosh (eds.), *Perspectives on Corporate Citizenship* (London: Greenleaf Publishing, 2001). Also see, Isabelle Maignan, O. C. Ferrell, and G. Tomas M. Hult, "Corporate Citizenship: Cultural Antecedents and Business Benefits," *Journal of the Academy of Marketing Science* (Vol. 27, No. 4, Fall 1999), 455–469. Also see Malcolm McIntosh, Deborah Leipziger, Keith Jones, and Gill Coleman, *Corporate Citizenship: Successful Strategies for*

Responsible Companies (London: Financial Times/Pitman Publishing), 1998.

50. See, for example, Mark Starik and Archie B. Carroll, "In Search of Beneficence: Reflections on the Connections Between Firm Social and Financial Performance," in Karen Paul (ed.), *Contemporary Issues in Business and Society in the United States and Abroad* (Lewiston, NY: The Edwin Mellen Press, 1991), 79–108; and I. M. Herremans, P. Akathaporn, and M. McInnes, "An Investigation of Corporate Social Responsibility, Reputation, and Economic Performance," *Accounting, Organizations, and Society* (Vol. 18, No. 7/8, 1993), 587–604.

51. Lee E. Preston and Douglas P. O'Bannon, "The Corporate Social–Financial Performance Relationship: A Typology and Analysis," *Business and Society* (Vol. 36, No. 4, December 1997), 419–429.

52. Sandra Waddock and Samuel Graves, "The Corporate Social Performance–Financial Performance Link," *Strategic Management Journal* (Vol. 18, No. 4, 1997), 303–319.

53. Jennifer Griffin and John Mahon, "The Corporate Social Performance and Corporate Financial Performance Debate," *Business and Society* (Vol. 36, No. 1, March 1997), 5–31.

54. Ronald Roman, Sefa Hayibor, and Bradley Agle, "The Relationship Between Social and Financial Performance," *Business and Society* (Vol. 38, No. 1, March 1999), 121. For a reply to this study, see John Mahon and Jennifer Griffin, "Painting a Portrait: A Reply," *Business and Society* (Vol. 38, No. 1, March 1999), 126–133.

55. *Chicago Tribune*, "Social Concern Pays, Study Suggests," *The Atlanta Journal* (June 7, 1993), E4.

56. Preston and O'Bannon, 428.

57. Bryan Husted, "A Contingency Theory of Corporate Social Performance," *Business and Society* (Vol. 39, No. 1, March 2000), 24–48, 41.

58. Simon Zadek, *The Civil Corporation: The New Economy of Corporate Citizenship* (London: Earthscan, 2001), 105–114.

59. "What Is the Triple Bottom Line?" (January 8, 2004), http://www.sustainability.com/philosophy/triple-bottom/tbl-intro.asp.

60. Dow Jones Sustainability Indexes, http://www.sustainability-index.com/htmle/sustainability/corpsustainability.html.

61. Philip Johansson, "Social Investing Turns 30," *Business Ethics* (January–February 2001), 12–16.

62. See, for example, Lawrence A. Armour, "Who Says Virtue Is Its Own Reward?" *Fortune* (February 16, 1998), 186–189; Thomas D. Saler, "Money & Morals," *Mutual Funds* (August 1997), 55–60; and Keith H. Hammonds, "A Portfolio with a Heart Still Needs a Brain," *Business Week* (January 26, 1998), 100.

63. See Jack A. Brill and Alan Reder, *Investing from the Heart* (New York: Crown Publishers, 1992), and Patrick McVeigh, "The Best Socially Screened Mutual Funds for 1998," *Business Ethics* (January–February 1998), 15–21.

64. William A. Sodeman, "Social Investing: The Role of Corporate Social Performance in Investment Decisions," unpublished Ph.D. dissertation, University of Georgia, 1993. See also William A. Sodeman and Archie B. Carroll, "Social Investment Firms: Their Purposes, Principles, and Investment Criteria," in *International Association for Business and Society 1994 Proceedings*, edited by Steven Wartick and Denis Collins, 339–344.

65. "Good Works and Great Profits," *Business Week* (February 16, 1998), 8.

66. Samuel B. Graves and Sandra A. Waddock, "Institutional Owners and Corporate Social Performance," *Academy of Management Journal* (Vol. 37, No. 4, August 1994), 1034–1046.

67. *Ibid.*

68. Social Investment Forum, "2003 Report on Socially Responsible Investing Trends in the U. S.," http://www.socialinvest.org.

Chapter 3

THE STAKEHOLDER APPROACH *to* BUSINESS, SOCIETY, *and* ETHICS

CHAPTER LEARNING OUTCOMES

After studying this chapter, you should be able to:

1   Define stake and stakeholder and describe the origins of these concepts.
2   Differentiate among the production, managerial, and stakeholder views of the firm.
3   Differentiate among the three values of the stakeholder model.
4   Discuss the concept of stakeholder management.
5   Identify and discuss the five major questions that capture the essence of stakeholder management.
6   Identify and discuss the concept of stakeholder management capability (SMC).
7   Describe the characteristics of a stakeholder corporation.

Life in business organizations was once simpler. First, there were the investors who put up the money to get the business started. This was in the precorporate period, so there was only one person, or a few at most, financing the business. Next, the owners needed employees to do the productive work of the firm. Because the owners themselves were frequently the managers, another group—the employees—was needed to get the business going. Then, the owners needed suppliers to make raw materials available for production and customers to purchase the products or services they were providing. All in all, it was a less complex period, with minimal and understood expectations among the various parties.

It would take many pages to describe how and why we got from that relatively simple period to the complex state of affairs we face in today's society. Many of the factors we discussed in the first two chapters were driving forces behind this societal transformation.

The principal factor, however, has been the recognition by the public, or society, that the business organization has evolved to the point that it is no longer the sole property or interest of the founder, the founder's family, or even a group of owner-investors.

The business organization today, especially the modern corporation, is the institutional centerpiece of a complex society. Our society today consists of many people with a multitude of interests, expectations, and demands as to what major organizations ought to provide to accommodate people's lifestyles. We have seen business respond to the many expectations placed on it. We have seen an ever-changing social contract. We have seen many assorted legal, ethical, and philanthropic expectations and demands being met by organizations willing to change as long as the economic incentive was still present. What was once viewed as a specialized means of providing profit through the manufacture and distribution of goods and services has become a multipurpose social institution that many people and groups depend on for their livelihood, prosperity, and fulfillment.

In a society conscious of an always-improving lifestyle, with more groups every day laying claims to their share of the good life, business organizations today need to be responsive to individuals and groups they once viewed as powerless and unable to make such claims on them. We call these individuals and groups *stakeholders*. The stakeholder approach to management is an accepted framework that is poised for further development, especially in the business-and-society arena. In the academic and business community, advances in stakeholder theory have illustrated the crucial development of the stakeholder concept.[1]

The stakeholder view was developed even further in 1996 when Britain's then Labour Party Leader Tony Blair called for an economy characterized by stakeholder capitalism as opposed to traditional shareholder capitalism. All over the world, people began rediscussing an age-old question: Whom do companies belong to and in whose interests should they be run? These discussions sharply contrasted the traditional American and British view, wherein a public company has the overriding goal of maximizing shareholder returns, with the view held by the Japanese and much of continental Europe, wherein firms accept broader obligations that seek to balance the interests of shareholders with those of other stakeholders, notably employees, suppliers, customers, and the wider "community."[2]

In terms of corporate application, Wheeler and Sillanpää have proposed a model for the "stakeholder corporation," which is discussed later in this chapter. They argued that "stakeholder inclusion" is the key to company success in the twenty-first century.[3] Walker and Marr, in *Stakeholder Power*, have presented what they consider to be a "winning plan for building stakeholder commitment and driving corporate growth."[4] In 2002, *Redefining the Corporation: Stakeholder Management and Organizational Wealth* by Post, Preston, and Sachs argued that the corporate model needs redefinition because of business size and socioeconomic power and the inaccuracy of the "ownership" model and its implications.[5] Finally, *Stakeholder Theory and Organizational Ethics* by Robert Phillips has continued to link the stakeholder approach with business ethics, a topic of central interest to us in this chapter. [6]

An outgrowth of these developments is that it has become apparent that business organizations must address the legitimate needs and expectations of stakeholders if they want to be successful in the long run.[7] Business must also address stakeholders because it is the ethical course of action to take. Stakeholders have claims, rights, and expectations that ought to be honored, and the stakeholder approach facilitates that pursuit. It is for these reasons that the stakeholder concept and orientation have become an essential part of the vocabulary and thinking in the study of business, society, and ethics.

ORIGINS OF THE STAKEHOLDER CONCEPT

The stakeholder concept has become central to understanding business and society relationships. The term *stakeholder* is a variant of the more familiar and traditional concept of *stockholders*—the investors in or owners of businesses. Just as a private individual might own his or her house, automobile, or DVD player, a stockholder owns a portion or a share of one or more businesses. Thus, a stockholder is also a stakeholder. However, stockholders are just one group of many legitimate stakeholders that business and organizations must address today to be effective.

What Is the Stake in Stakeholder?

To appreciate the concept of stakeholders, it helps to understand the idea of a stake. A **stake** is an interest or a share in an undertaking. If a group is planning to go out to dinner and a movie for the evening, each person in the group has a stake, or interest, in the group's decision. No money has yet been spent, but each member sees his or her interest (preference, taste, priority) in the decision. A stake may also be a claim. A claim is an assertion to a title or a right to something. A claim is a demand for something due or believed to be due. We can see clearly that an owner or a stockholder has an interest in and an ownership of a share of a business.

The idea of a stake can range from simply an interest in an undertaking at one extreme to a legal claim of ownership at the other extreme. In between these two extremes is a "right" to something. This right might be a legal right to certain treatment rather than a legal claim of ownership, such as that of a shareholder. Legal rights might include the right to fair treatment (e.g., not to be discriminated against) or the right to privacy (not to have one's privacy invaded or abridged). The right also might be thought of as a moral right, such as that expressed by an employee: "I've got a right not to be fired because I've worked here 30 years, and I've given this firm the best years of my life." Or a consumer might say, "I've got a right to a safe product after all I've paid for this."

As we have seen, there are several different types of stakes. Figure 3-1 on page 68 summarizes various categories or types of stakes.

What Is a Stakeholder?

It follows, then, that a **stakeholder**, is an individual or a group that has one or more of the various kinds of stakes in a business. Just as stakeholders may be affected by the actions, decisions, policies, or practices of the business firm, these stakeholders also may affect the organization's actions, decisions, policies, or practices. With stakeholders, therefore, there is a potential two-way interaction or exchange of influence. In short, a stakeholder may be thought of as "any individual or group who can affect or is affected by the actions, decisions, policies, practices, or goals of the organization."[8] This definition is quite broad, but in this way the organization or decision maker is most likely to fully explore its social and ethical responsibilities than when using a narrower definition.

FIGURE 3-1

Types of Stakes

	An Interest	A Right	Ownership
Definitions	When a person or group will be affected by a decision, it has an interest in that decision.	(1) Legal Right: When a person or group has a legal claim to be treated in a certain way or to have a particular right protected.	When a person or group has a legal title to an asset or a property.
Examples	This plant closing will affect the community. This TV commercial demeans women, and I'm a woman. I'm concerned about the environment for future generations.	Employees expect due process, privacy; customers or creditors have certain legal rights.	"This company is mine, I founded it, and I own it," or "I own 1,000 shares of this corporation."
Definitions		(2) Moral Right: When a person or group thinks it has a moral or ethical right to be treated in a certain way or to have a particular right protected.	
Examples		Fairness, justice, equity.	

WHO ARE BUSINESS'S STAKEHOLDERS?

In today's competitive, global business environment, there are many individuals and groups who are business's stakeholders. From the business point of view, there are certain individuals and groups that have legitimacy in the eyes of management. That is, they have a legitimate, direct interest in, or claim on, the operations of the firm. The most obvious of these groups are stockholders, employees, and customers. But, from the point of view of a highly pluralistic society, stakeholders include not only these groups, but other groups as well. These other groups include competitors, suppliers, the community, special-interest groups, the media, and society, or the public at large. It has also been strongly argued by Starik and others that the natural environment, nonhuman species, and future generations should be considered among business's important stakeholders.[9]

The Production, Managerial, and Stakeholder Views of the Firm

The evolution and progress of the stakeholder concept parallels the evolution of the business enterprise. In what has been termed the traditional **production view of the firm**, owners thought of stakeholders as only those individuals or groups that supplied resources or bought products or services.[10] As time passed and we witnessed the growth of corporations and the resulting separation of ownership from control, business firms began to see the need for interaction with major constituent groups if they were to be managed successfully. Thus, we witnessed the evolution of the **managerial view of the firm**. Finally, as major internal and external changes occurred in business, managers were required to undergo a revolutionary conceptual shift in how they perceived the firm and its multilateral relationships with constituent or stakeholder groups. The result was the stakeholder view of the firm.[11] In actual practice, however, some managers have not yet come to appreciate the need for the stakeholder view, but this is changing with the passage of time. Figure 3-2 depicts the evolution from the production view to the managerial view of the firm, and Figure 3-3 on page 70 illustrates the stakeholder view of the firm. The stakeholder view encompasses many different individuals and groups that are embedded in the firm's internal and external environments.

In the stakeholder view of the firm, management must perceive its stakeholders as not only those groups that management thinks have some stake in the firm but also including those groups that themselves think or perceive they have a stake in the firm. This is an essential perspective that management must take at the outset, at least until it has had a chance to weigh carefully the legitimacy of the claims and the power of various stakeholders. We should note here that each stakeholder group is composed of subgroups. For example, the government stakeholder group includes federal, state, and local government stakeholders.

FIGURE 3-2

The Production and Managerial Views of the Firm

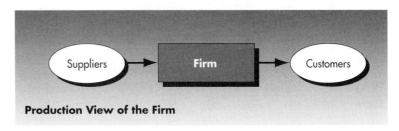

Production View of the Firm

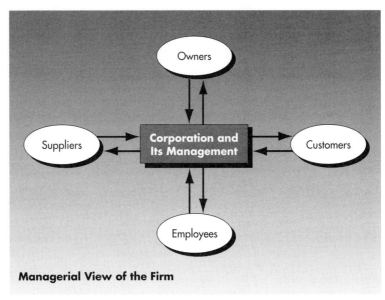

Managerial View of the Firm

FIGURE 3-3

The Stakeholder View of the Firm

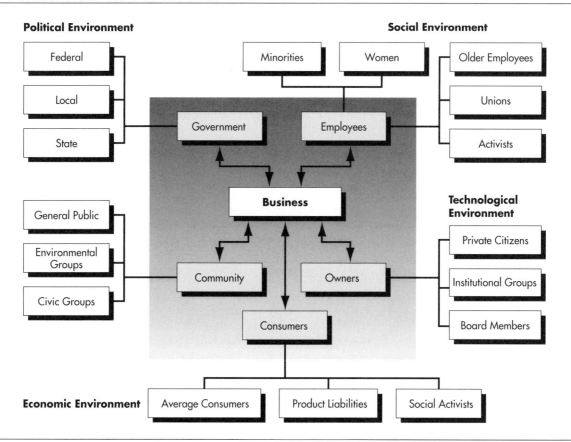

Primary and Secondary Stakeholders

Wheeler and Sillanpää have presented a useful way to categorize stakeholders. Using such categories as primary and secondary and social and nonsocial, they propose defining stakeholders as follows:[12]

Primary social stakeholders include:
- Shareholders and investors
- Employees and managers
- Customers
- Local communities
- Suppliers and other business partners

Secondary social stakeholders include:
- Government and regulators
- Civic institutions
- Social pressure groups
- Media and academic commentators
- Trade bodies
- Competitors

Primary social stakeholders have a direct stake in the organization and its success and, therefore, are influential. **Secondary social stakeholders** may be extremely influential as well, especially in affecting reputation and public standing, but their stake in the organization is more representational of public or special interests than direct. Therefore, the level of accountability to a secondary stakeholder may be lower, but these groups may wield significant power and quite often represent legitimate public concerns.[13]

Primary nonsocial stakeholders include:
- The natural environment
- Future generations
- Nonhuman species

Secondary nonsocial stakeholders include:
- Environmental interest groups (e.g., Friends of the Earth, Greenpeace, Rainforest Action Network)
- Animal welfare organizations (e.g., People for the Ethical Treatment of Animals—PETA)

It should be kept in mind that secondary stakeholders can quickly become primary ones. This often occurs by way of media or special-interest groups when the urgency of a claim (as in a boycott or demonstration) takes precedence over the legitimacy of that claim. In today's business environment, the media have the power to instantaneously transform a stakeholder's status with its round-the-clock coverage of the news. Thus, it may be useful to think of primary and secondary classes of stakeholders for discussion purposes, but we should understand how easily and quickly those categories can shift.

Core, Strategic, and Environmental Stakeholders

There are other ways to categorize stakeholders. In an alternative scheme, stakeholders are thought of as being core, strategic, or environmental. **Core stakeholders** are a specific subset of strategic stakeholders that are essential for the survival of the organization. **Strategic stakeholders** are those stakeholder groups that are vital to the organization and the particular set of threats and opportunities it faces at a particular point in time. **Environmental stakeholders** are all others in the organization's environment that are not core or strategic. One could conceptualize the relationship among these three groups of stakeholders by thinking of a series of concentric circles with core stakeholders in the middle and with strategic and environmental stakeholders moving out from the middle.[14]

Whether stakeholders are core, strategic, or environmental would depend on their characteristics or attributes, such as legitimacy, power, or urgency. Thus, stakeholders could move from category to category in a dynamic, fluid, and time-dependent fashion. This set of terms for describing stakeholders is useful because it captures, to some degree, the contingencies and dynamics that must be considered in an actual situation.

A Typology of Stakeholder Attributes: Legitimacy, Power, Urgency

Expanding on the idea that stakeholders have such attributes as legitimacy, power, and urgency, Mitchell, Agle, and Wood generated a typology of stakeholders based on these three attributes.[15] When these three attributes are superimposed, as depicted in Figure 3-4 on page 72, seven stakeholder categories result.

The three attributes of legitimacy, power, and urgency help us to see how stakeholders may be thought of and analyzed in these key terms. **Legitimacy** refers to the perceived

FIGURE 3-4

Stakeholder Typology: One, Two, or Three Attributes Present

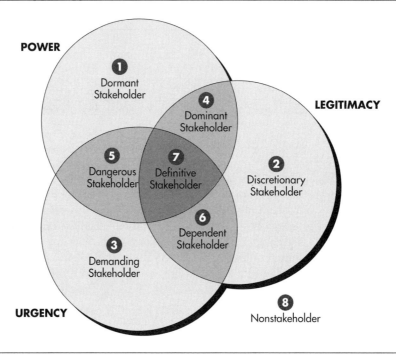

SOURCE: Reprinted with permission of Academy of Management, PO Box 3020, Briar Cliff Manor, NY 10510-8020. *Stakeholder Typology: One, Two, or Three Attributes Present* (Figure), R.K. Mitchell, B.R. Agle, and D.J. Wood, *Academy of Management Review*, October 1997. Reproduced by permission of the publisher via Copyright Clearance Center, Inc.

validity or appropriateness of a stakeholder's claim to a stake. Therefore, owners, employees, and customers represent a high degree of legitimacy due to their explicit, formal, and direct relationships with a company. Stakeholders that are more distant from the firm, such as social activist groups, competitors, or the media, might be thought to have less legitimacy.

Power refers to the ability or capacity to produce an effect—to get something done that otherwise may not be done. Therefore, whether one has legitimacy or not, power means that the stakeholder could affect the business. For example, with the help of the media, a large, vocal, social activist group such as People for the Ethical Treatment of Animals (PETA) could wield extraordinary power over a business firm. In recent years, PETA has been successful in influencing the practices and policies of fast-food restaurants regarding the treatment of chickens and cattle.

Urgency refers to the degree to which the stakeholder claim on the business calls for the business's immediate attention or response. Urgency may imply that something is critical—it really needs to get done. Or, it may imply that something needs to be done immediately, or on a timely basis. A management group may perceive a union strike, a consumer boycott, or a social activist group picketing outside headquarters as urgent.

An interesting example of a stakeholder action that illustrates both power and urgency occurred in several dozen Home Depot stores around the country. In each of the stores, strange announcements began blaring from the intercom systems: "Attention shoppers, on aisle seven you'll find mahogany ripped from the heart of the Amazon." Shocked store managers raced through the aisles trying to apprehend the environmental activists who were behind the stunt. The activists had apparently gotten the access codes to the intercoms. After months of similar antics, Home Depot bowed to the demands of the environmental group and announced that it would stop selling wood chopped from endangered forests and, instead, stock wood products certified by a new organization called the Forest Stewardship Council (FSC).[16] This newly founded group wasn't even on Home Depot's radar screen and then, all of a sudden, it had to capitulate to selling wood only certified by the FSC.

The typology of stakeholder attributes suggests that managers must attend to stakeholders based on their assessment of the extent to which competing stakeholder claims reflect legitimacy, power, and urgency. Using the categories in Figure 3-4, therefore, the stakeholder groups represented by overlapping circles (for example, those with two or three attributes, such as Categories 4, 5, 6, and 7) are highly "salient" to management and would likely receive priority attention.

SEARCH THE WEB

STAKEHOLDER THEORY

Considerable information on stakeholder theory and stakeholder management may be found in the programs and work of the Clarkson Centre for Business Ethics, Faculty of Management, University of Toronto.

Professor Max Clarkson, the Centre's major project leader, died in 1998. For more information, visit the Centre's Web site at **http://www.mgmt.utoronto.ca/CCBE**.

On this Web site, you may find resources and a comprehensive bibliography on stakeholder theory.

STRATEGIC, MULTIFIDUCIARY, AND SYNTHESIS VIEWS

One major challenge embedded in the stakeholder approach is to determine whether it should be perceived primarily as a way to better manage those groups known as stakeholders or as a way to treat more ethically those groups known as stakeholders. Goodpaster has addressed this issue by distinguishing among the strategic approach, the multifiduciary approach, and the stakeholder synthesis approach.[17]

Strategic Approach. The *strategic approach* views stakeholders primarily as factors to be taken into consideration and managed while the firm is pursuing profits for its shareholders. In this view, managers might take stakeholders into account because offended stakeholders might resist or retaliate (for example, through political action, protest, or boycott). This approach sees stakeholders as instruments that may facilitate or impede the firm's pursuit of its strategic objectives. Thus, it is an instrumental view.

Multifiduciary Approach. The *multifiduciary approach* views stakeholders as more than just individuals or groups who can wield economic or legal power. This view holds that management has a fiduciary responsibility to stakeholders just as it has this same responsibility to shareholders. In this approach, management's traditional fiduciary, or trust, duty is expanded to embrace stakeholders on roughly equal footing with shareholders. Thus, shareholders are no longer of exclusive importance as they were under the strategic approach. This view broadens the idea of a fiduciary responsibility to include stockholders and other important stakeholders.

Stakeholder Synthesis Approach.   A new, stakeholder synthesis approach is advocated by Goodpaster rather than the two previous approaches This new view holds that business does have moral responsibilities to stakeholders but that they should not be seen as part of a fiduciary obligation. Thus, management's basic fiduciary responsibility to shareholders is kept intact, but it is also expected to be implemented within a context of ethical responsibility. This ethical responsibility is business's duty not to harm, coerce, lie, cheat, steal, and so on.[18] Thus, the result is the same in the multifiduciary and stakeholder synthesis views. However, the reasoning or rationale is different.

As we continue our discussion of stakeholder management, it should be clear that we are pursuing it from a balanced perspective. This balanced perspective suggests that we are integrating the strategic approach with the stakeholder synthesis approach. We should be managing strategically and morally at the same time. The stakeholder approach should not be just a better way to manage. It also should be a more ethical way to manage.

THREE VALUES OF THE STAKEHOLDER MODEL

As an alternative to Goodpaster's strategic, multifiduciary, and stakeholder synthesis views, Donaldson and Preston have articulated three aspects or values of the stakeholder model of the firm. These three values, although interrelated, are distinct. They differentiate among the descriptive, instrumental, and normative aspects of stakeholder theory or the stakeholder model.[19]

Descriptive.   First, the stakeholder model has value because it is *descriptive*. That is, it provides language and concepts to effectively describe the corporation or organization. The corporation is a constellation of cooperative and competitive interests possessing both instrumental and intrinsic value. Understanding organizations in this way allows us to have a fuller description or explanation of how they function. The language and terms used in stakeholder theory are useful in helping us to understand organizations.

Instrumental.   Second, the stakeholder model has value because it is *instrumental*. It is useful in establishing the connections between the practice of stakeholder management and the resulting achievement of corporate performance goals. The fundamental premise here is that practicing effective stakeholder management should lead to the achievement of traditional goals, such as profitability, stability, and growth. Business school courses in strategic management often employ the instrumental model.

Normative.   Third, the stakeholder model has value because it is *normative*. In the normative perspective, stakeholders are identified by their interest in the organization whether or not the organization has any corresponding interest in them. Thus, the interests of all stakeholders are of intrinsic value. Stakeholders are seen as possessing value irrespective of their instrumental use to management. The normative view is often thought of as the moral or ethical view because it emphasizes how stakeholders *should* be regarded. Robert Phillips, in *Stakeholder Theory and Organizational Ethics*, argues that the "principle of stakeholder fairness" is the moral underpinning, or normative justification, for the stakeholder model.[20] Thus, he expounds upon the normative aspect of stakeholder thinking.

In summarizing, Donaldson and Preston assert that stakeholder theory is *managerial* in the broad sense of the term. It is managerial in the sense that it does not simply describe or predict but also recommends attitudes, structures, and practices that constitute stakeholder management. Such management necessitates the simultaneous attention to the legitimate interests of all appropriate stakeholders in the creation of organizational structures and policies.[21]

KEY QUESTIONS IN STAKEHOLDER MANAGEMENT

The managers of a business firm have the responsibility of establishing the firm's overall direction (its mission, strategies, goals, and policies) and seeing to it that these plans are carried out. As a consequence, managers have some long-term responsibilities and many that are of more immediate concern. Before the stakeholder environment became as turbulent and rapidly changing as it now is, the managerial task was relatively straightforward because the external environment was stable. As we have evolved to the stakeholder view of the firm, however, we see the managerial task as an inevitable consequence of the trends and developments we described in our first two chapters.

Stakeholder management has become important as managers have discovered the many groups that have to be relatively satisfied for the firm to meet its objectives. Without question, we still recognize the significance and necessity of profits as a return on the stockholders' investments, but we also perceive and understand the growing claims of other stakeholder groups and the success they have had in getting what they want.

The challenge of stakeholder management, therefore, is to see to it that the firm's primary stakeholders achieve their objectives and that other stakeholders are dealt with ethically and are also relatively satisfied. At the same time, the firm is expected to be profitable. This is the classic "win-win" situation. It does not always occur, but it is the appropriate goal for management to pursue to protect its long-term best interests. Management's second-best alternative is to meet the goals of its primary stakeholders, keeping in mind the important role of its owner-investors. Without economic viability, all other stakeholders' interests are lost.

With these perspectives in mind, let us approach stakeholder management with the idea that managers can become successful stewards of their stakeholders' resources by gaining knowledge about stakeholders and using this knowledge to predict and take care of their behaviors and actions. Ultimately, we should manage the situation in such a way that we achieve our objectives ethically and effectively. Thus, the important functions of stakeholder management are to describe, to understand, to analyze, and, finally, to manage.

The quest for stakeholder management embraces social, ethical, and economic considerations. Normative as well as instrumental objectives and perspectives are essential. Five major questions may be asked if we are to capture the essential information we need for stakeholder management:

1. *Who* are our stakeholders?
2. What are our stakeholders' *stakes?*
3. What *opportunities and challenges* do our stakeholders present to the firm?
4. What *responsibilities* (economic, legal, ethical, and philanthropic) does the firm have to its stakeholders?
5. What *strategies or actions* should the firm take to best address stakeholder challenges and opportunities?[22]

Who Are Our Stakeholders?

To this point, we have described the likely primary and secondary stakeholder groups of a business organization. To manage them effectively, each firm and its management group must ask and answer this question for itself: Who are our stakeholders? To answer this question fully, management must identify not only generic stakeholder groups but also specific subgroups. A generic stakeholder group is simply a broad grouping, such as employees, shareholders, environmental groups, or consumers. Within each of these generic categories there may be a few or many specific subgroups. Figure 3-5 illustrates some of the generic and specific stakeholder subgroups of a very large organization.

To illustrate the process of stakeholder identification, we will consider some events in the life of the McDonald's Corporation that resulted in their broadening significantly who were considered their stakeholders. The case study starts in the late 1990s when the social activist group PETA (People for the Ethical Treatment of Animals), which claims 700,000 members, decided it was dissatisfied with some of McDonald's practices and decided it would launch a billboard and bumper-sticker campaign against the hamburger giant.[23] PETA felt McDonald's was dragging its feet on animal welfare issues, and so PETA went on the attack. PETA announced it would put up billboards saying "The animals deserve a break today" and "McDonald's: Cruelty to Go" in Norfolk, Virginia, PETA's hometown. The ad campaign was announced when talks broke down between PETA and McDonald's on the subject of ways the company might foster animal-rights issues within the fast-food industry. Using concepts introduced earlier, PETA was a secondary social or nonsocial stakeholder and, therefore, had low legitimacy. However, its power and urgency

FIGURE 3-5

Some Generic and Specific Stakeholders of a Large Firm

Owners	Employees	Governments	Customers
Trusts	Young employees	Federal	Business purchasers
Foundations	Middle-aged employees	• EPA	Government purchasers
Mutual funds	Older employees	• FTC	Educational institutions
Board members	Women	• OSHA	Special-interest groups
Management owners	Minority groups	• CPSC	Internet purchasers
Employee pension funds	Disabled	State	
Individual owners	Special-interest groups	Local	
	Unions		

Community	Competitors	Social Activist Groups
General fund-raising	Firm A	People United to Save Humanity (PUSH)
United Way	Firm B	Rainforest Action Network
YMCA/YWCA	Firm C	Mothers Against Drunk Driving (MADD)
Middle schools	Global competition	American Civil Liberties Union
Elementary schools		Consumers Union
Residents who live close by		People for the Ethical Treatment of Animals (PETA)
All other residents		
Neighborhood associations		
Local media		
Chamber of Commerce		
Environments		

were high as it was threatening the company with a highly visible, potentially destructive campaign that was being sympathetically reported by a cooperative media.

It's not clear what all took place over the ensuing year, but it is evident that PETA's pressure tactics continued and escalated. In the fall of 2000, McDonald's announced significant changes in the demands it is now placing on its chicken and egg suppliers. McDonald's announced that its egg suppliers must now improve the "living conditions" of its chickens. Specifically, McDonald's now insists that its suppliers no longer cage its chickens wing-tip to wing-tip. Suppliers must now increase the space allotted to each hen from 48 square inches to 72 square inches per hen. Suppliers will also be required to stop "forced molting," a process that increases egg production by denying hens food and water for up to two weeks.[24]

It came out that during the ensuing year, PETA escalated its pressure tactics against the firm. PETA began distributing "unhappy meals" at restaurant playgrounds and outside the company's shareholder meeting. The kits, which came in boxes similar to McDonald's Happy Meals that it sells to children, were covered with pictures of slaughtered animals. It also depicted a bloody, knife-wielding "Son of Ron" doll that resembled the Ronald McDonald clown, as well as toy farm animals with slashed throats. One image featured a bloody cow's head and the familiar fast-food phrase "Do you want fries with that?"[25]

As a result of this example, we can see how the set of stakeholders that McDonald's had to deal with grew significantly from its traditional stakeholders to include powerful, special-interest groups such as PETA. With the cooperation of the media, especially major newspapers and magazines, PETA moved from being a secondary stakeholder to a primary stakeholder in McDonald's life.

In 2001, members of PETA and the Animal Rights Foundation of Florida (ARFF) began an attack on Burger King, similar to the attack on McDonald's. They greeted Burger King's new CEO with signs and banners reading "Burger King: King of Cruelty," while showing a video documenting the abuses that PETA hopes Burger King will put a stop to. The organizations also planned a full-page ad in *The Miami Herald*, asking the new CEO to take action to reduce the suffering of chickens, pigs, and other animals on farms that supply the company's meat and eggs. This is the latest volley in PETA's "Murder King" campaign, in which hundreds of demonstrations against Burger King have taken place in more than a dozen countries and in every U.S. state.[26] PETA has moved on and made itself an important stakeholder in many other firms, so McDonald's is not alone in having to consider this powerful stakeholder's demands.

This discussion illustrates the evolving nature of the question, "Who are our stakeholders?" In actuality, stakeholder identification is an unfolding process. However, by recognizing early the potential of failure if one does not think in stakeholder terms, the value and usefulness of stakeholder thinking can be readily seen. Had McDonald's perceived PETA as a stakeholder earlier on, perhaps it could have dealt with this situation more effectively.

Many businesses do not carefully identify their generic stakeholder groups, much less their specific stakeholder groups. This must be done, however, if management is to be in a position to answer the second major question, "What are our stakeholders' stakes?"

What Are Our Stakeholders' Stakes?

Once stakeholders have been identified, the next step is to address the question: What are our stakeholders' stakes? Even groups in the same generic category frequently have different specific interests, concerns, perceptions of rights, and expectations. Management's challenge here is to identify the nature and legitimacy of a group's stake(s) and the group's power to affect the organization. As we discussed earlier, urgency is another critical factor.

Identifying the Nature/Legitimacy of a Group's Stakes.

Let's consider an example of stakeholders who possess varying stakes. Assume that we are considering corporate owners as a generic group of stakeholders and that the corporation is large, with several million shares of stock outstanding. Among the ownership population are these more specific subgroups:

1. Institutional owners (trusts, foundations, churches, universities)
2. Large mutual fund organizations
3. Board of director members who own shares
4. Members of management who own shares
5. Hundreds of thousands of small, individual shareholders

For all these subgroups, the nature of stakeholder claims on this corporation is ownership. All these groups have legitimate claims—they are all owners. Because of other factors, such as power or urgency, these stakeholders may have to be dealt with differently.

Identifying the Power of a Group's Stakes.

When we examine power, we see significant differences. Which of the groups in the previous list are the most powerful? Certainly not the small, individual investors, unless they have found a way to organize and thus wield power. The powerful stakeholders in this case are (1) the institutional owners and mutual fund organizations, because of the sheer magnitude of their investments, and (2) the board and management shareholders, because of their dual roles of ownership and management (control).

However, if the individual shareholders could somehow form a coalition based on some interest they have in common, they could exert significant influence on management decisions. This is the day and age of dissident shareholder groups filing stockholder suits and proposing shareholder resolutions. These shareholder resolutions address issues ranging from complaints of excessive executive compensation to demands that firms improve their environmental protection policies or cease making illegal campaign contributions.

Identifying Specific Groups Within a Generic Group.

Let us now look at a manufacturing firm in an industry in Michigan that is faced with a generic group of environmental stakeholders. Within the generic group of environmental stakeholders might be the following specific groups:

1. Residents who live within a 25-mile radius of the plant
2. Other residents in the city
3. Residents who live in the path of the jet stream hundreds of miles away (some in Canada) who are being impacted by acid rain
4. Environmental Protection Agency (federal government)
5. Michigan Environmental Protection Division (state government)
6. Friends of the Earth (environmental activist group)
7. The Wilderness Society (environmental activist group)
8. Michiganians Against Smokestack Emissions (social activist group)

SEARCH THE WEB

STAKEHOLDER IDENTIFICATION AND MANAGEMENT

In a stakeholder analysis, *impact* or *power* of a stakeholder is defined as the extent to which that stakeholder is able to persuade, induce, or coerce others into following certain courses of action. There are several ways to exert such power, such as by direct authority, lobbying, or exerting a dominant market position. The power of stakeholders can be based on various sources. For a further discussion of this topic, go to **http://www.themanager.org/resources/Stakeholder%20Management.htm**.

It would require some degree of care to identify the nature, legitimacy, power, and urgency of each of these specific groups. However, it could and should be done if the firm wants to get a handle on its environmental stakeholders. Furthermore, we should stress that companies have an ethical responsibility to be sensitive to legitimate stakeholder claims even if the stakeholders have no power or leverage with management.

If we return for a moment to the McDonald's example, we would have to conclude that PETA, as a special-interest, animal welfare group, did not have a great deal of legitimacy vis-à-vis McDonald's. PETA did claim animal's rights and treatment as a moral issue, however, and thus had some general legitimacy through the concerns it represented. Unfortunately for PETA, not all of the public shares its concerns or degree of concern with these issues. However, PETA had tremendous power and urgency. It was this power, wielded in the form of adverse publicity and media attention, that doubtless played a significant role in bringing about changes in McDonald's policies.

What Opportunities and Challenges Do Our Stakeholders Present to the Firm?

Opportunities and challenges represent opposite sides of the coin when it comes to stakeholders. The opportunities are to build decent, productive working relationships with the stakeholders. Challenges, on the other hand, usually present themselves in such a way that the firm must handle the stakeholders acceptably or be hurt in some way—financially (short term or long term) or in terms of its public image or reputation in the community. Therefore, it is understandable why our emphasis is on challenges rather than on opportunities posed by stakeholders.

These challenges typically take the form of varying degrees of expectations, demands, or threats. In most instances, they arise because stakeholders think or believe that their needs are not being met adequately. The challenges also arise when stakeholder groups think that any crisis that occurs is the responsibility of the firm or that the firm caused the crisis in some way. Examples of some stakeholder crises from the late 1990s and early 2000s include:[27]

With one of the most recognizable brands in the world, Coca-Cola has plenty of opportunities and challenges. In a *Forbes* article (22 December 2003 v172 i13 p86), Paul Klebnikov examines the challenges of doing business worldwide, which often means "dealing with the devil and other questionable characters." Because the domestic market offers little opportunity for growth, Coca-Cola has little choice but to expand in foreign markets such as China, India (where high levels of pesticide were detected in locally bottled Coke), Japan, and even Uzbekistan. You can read more about Coke's global market by logging on to InfoTrac College Edition at **http://www.infotrac-college.com** and keying record number A111038480.

- *Pepsi and Coke.* It was reported in 2003–2004 that an Indian NGO (nongovernmental organization), the Centre for Science and Environment (CSE), is making life hard for these two soft drink distributors in Delhi, India. CSE tested bottles of their product and claimed they contained many times the amount of pesticides permitted by norms set by the European Union. It was even announced that the drinks would no longer be served in Indian's parliament. Both companies have continued to rebut the charges, but crises like these don't go away immediately.
- *Home Depot.* In 1998–1999, under pressure from social activist groups such as Rainforest Action Network and staged "Days of Action" by protestors, the Atlanta-based chain agreed to stop selling products made from old-growth wood. The environmentalists threatened to follow up with newspaper ads, frequent pickets, and civil disobedience if the company did not agree.

- *Boise* (an international distributor of office supplies and paper and an integrated manufacturer and distributor of paper, packaging, and building materials). In 2000, Rainforest Action Network launched a campaign to transform the entire logging industry, starting with Boise. At that time, Boise was one of the top loggers and distributors of old-growth forest products in the United States and a top distributor of wood products from the world's most endangered forests, including the tropical rainforests of the Amazon and the boreal forests of Canada. Boise was also the largest logger of U.S. public lands and the sole logging company to oppose the U.S. Forest Service Roadless Area Conservation Policy in court.

    In 2002, as a result of RAN's campaigning, Boise implemented a domestic old-growth policy, committing to "no longer harvesting timber from old-growth forests in the United States" by 2004. In 2003, to catch up with public values and meet the new marketplace standards, Boise dropped its opposition to the Roadless Policy and became the first U.S. logging and distribution company to commit to "eliminate the purchase of wood products from endangered areas."[28]

If one looks at the business experiences of the past, including the crises mentioned here, it is evident that there is a need to think in stakeholder terms to fully understand the potential threats that businesses of all kinds face on a daily basis.

Opportunities and challenges might also be viewed in terms of *potential for cooperation* and *potential for threat.* Savage and colleagues have argued that such assessments of cooperation and threat are necessary so that managers might identify strategies for dealing with stakeholders.[29] In terms of potential for threat, managers need to consider the stakeholder's relative power and its relevance to a particular issue confronting the organization. In terms of potential for cooperation, the firm needs to be sensitive to the possibility of joining forces with other stakeholders for the advantage of all parties involved.

Ross Laboratories, a division of Abbott Laboratories, was able to develop a cooperative relationship with some critics of its sales of infant formula in Third World countries. Ross and Abbott convinced these stakeholder groups (UNICEF and the World Health Organization) to join them in a program to promote infant health. Other firms, such as Nestlé, did not develop the potential to cooperate and suffered from consumer boycotts.[30]

Figure 3-6 presents a list of the factors that may increase or decrease a stakeholder's potential for threat or cooperation. By carefully analyzing these factors, managers should be able to better assess such potentials.

What Responsibilities Does the Firm Have to Its Stakeholders?

Once threats and opportunities of stakeholders have been identified and understood, the next logical question is, "What responsibilities does the firm have in its relationships with all stakeholders?" Responsibilities here could be thought of in terms of the corporate social responsibility discussion presented in Chapter 2. What economic, legal, ethical, and philanthropic responsibilities does management have to each stakeholder? Because most of the firm's economic responsibilities are principally to itself, the analysis needs to turn to legal, ethical, and philanthropic questions. The most pressing threats are typically presented as legal and ethical questions.

We should stress, however, that the firm itself has an economic stake in the legal and ethical issues it faces. For example, when Johnson & Johnson (J&J) was faced with the Tylenol poisoning incident, it had to decide what legal and ethical actions to take and

PETA has lately championed the rights of poultry being raised for fast-food companies such as KFC. At the end of 2003, PETA dropped a lawsuit it had filed against KFC to prevent KFC from claiming its poultry was handled humanely, according to *PR Week* (15 September 2003 p04). Not content to let Americans enjoy their poultry in peace, PETA suggested in early 2004 that consuming poultry products might lead to mad cow disease [*Knight Ridder/Tribune Business News* (10 February 2004)]. You can read the *PR Week* article by logging on to InfoTrac College Edition at **http://www.infotrac-college.com** and keying record number A113100454. Learn more about poultry and mad cow disease by keying record number CJ113103198.

what actions were in the firm's best economic interests. In this classic case, J&J apparently judged that recalling the tainted Tylenol products was not only the ethical action to take but also would ensure its reputation for being concerned about consumers' health and well-being. Figure 3-7 illustrates the stakeholder/responsibility matrix that

---

FIGURE 3-6

Factors Affecting Potential for Stakeholder Threat and Cooperation

	Increases or Decreases Stakeholder's Potential for Threat?	Increases or Decreases Stakeholder's Potential for Cooperation?
Stakeholder controls key resources (needed by organization)	Increases	Increases
Stakeholder does not control key resources	Decreases	Either
Stakeholder more powerful than organization	Increases	Either
Stakeholder as powerful as organization	Either	Either
Stakeholder less powerful than organization	Decreases	Increases
Stakeholder likely to take action (supportive of the organization)	Decreases	Increases
Stakeholder likely to take nonsupportive action	Increases	Decreases
Stakeholder unlikely to take any action	Decreases	Decreases
Stakeholder likely to form coalition with stakeholders	Increases	Either
Stakeholder likely to form coalition with organization	Decreases	Increases
Stakeholder unlikely to form any coalition	Decreases	Decreases

SOURCE: Grant T. Savage, Timothy W. Nix, Carlton J. Whitehead, and John D. Blair, "Strategies for Assessing and Managing Organizational Stakeholders," *Academy of Management Executive* (Vol. V, No. 2, May 1991), 64. Reprinted with permission.

FIGURE 3-7

Stakeholder/Responsibility Matrix

Stakeholders	Types of Responsibilities			
	Economic	Legal	Ethical	Philanthropic
Owners				
Customers				
Employees				
Community				
Public at Large				
Social Activist Groups				
Others				

management faces when assessing the firm's responsibilities to stakeholders. The matrix may be seen as a template that managers might use to systematically think through its various responsibilities.

What Strategies or Actions Should Management Take?

Once responsibilities have been assessed, a business must contemplate strategies and actions for dealing with its stakeholders. In every decision situation, a multitude of alternative courses of action are available, and management must choose one or several that seem best. Important questions or decision choices that management has before it in dealing with stakeholders include:

- Do we deal *directly* or *indirectly* with stakeholders?
- Do we take the *offense* or the *defense* in dealing with stakeholders?
- Do we *accommodate*, *negotiate*, *manipulate*, or *resist* stakeholder overtures?
- Do we employ a *combination of the above* strategies or pursue a *singular course* of action?[31]

It has been argued that the development of specific strategies may be based on a classification of stakeholders' potentials for cooperation and threat. If we use these two dimensions, four stakeholder types and resultant generic strategies emerge.[32] These stakeholder types and corresponding strategies are shown in Figure 3-8.

Stakeholder Type 1—the *supportive* stakeholder—is high on potential for cooperation and low on potential for threat. This is the ideal stakeholder. To a well-managed

FIGURE 3-8

Diagnostic Typology of Organizational Stakeholders

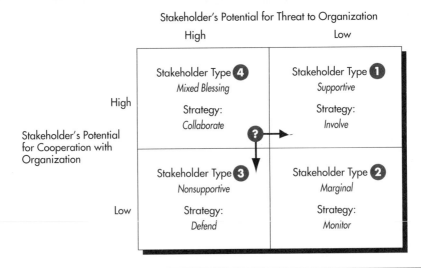

SOURCE: Grant T. Savage, Timothy W. Nix, Carlton J. Whitehead, and John D. Blair, "Strategies for Assessing and Managing Organizational Stakeholders," *Academy of Management Executive* (Vol.V, No.2 May 1991), 64. Reprinted with permission.

organization, supportive stakeholders might include its board, managers, employees, and loyal customers. Others might be suppliers and service providers. The strategy here is one of involvement. An example of this might be the strategy of involving employee stakeholders through participative management or decentralization of authority. For decades, mutual funds were the smart, safe choice for small investors. The industry had a group of supportive stakeholders. The mutual fund scandal revealed in 2003–2004, however, demonstrated that many companies in the industry were more concerned with profits, thus allowing the small investors to take a beating. The industry has damaged its supportive relationship with the small investor.

Stakeholder Type 2—the *marginal* stakeholder—is low on both potential for threat and potential for cooperation. For large organizations, these stakeholders might include professional associations of employees, consumer interest groups, or stockholders—especially those that are not organized. The strategy here is for the organization to monitor the marginal stakeholder. Monitoring is especially called for to make sure circumstances do not change. Careful monitoring could avert later problems.

Stakeholder Type 3—the *nonsupportive* stakeholder—is high on potential for threat but low on potential for cooperation. Examples of this group could include competing organizations, unions, federal or other levels of government, and the media. Special-interest groups might fall in this category. The recommended strategy here is to defend against the nonsupportive stakeholder. An example of a special-interest group that many would regard as nonsupportive is the Earth Liberation Front (ELF), a movement that originated in the Pacific Northwest. In 2003, it claimed responsibility for a string of arsons in the suburbs of Los Angeles, Detroit, and Philadelphia. ELF's attacks have targeted luxury homes and SUVs, the suburban status symbols that some environmentalists regard as despoilers of the Earth. Many such radical environmental groups have been called "eco-terrorists."[33] Such organizations do not seem interested in establishing positive, or supportive relationships, with companies and industries.

Stakeholder Type 4—the *mixed blessing* stakeholder—is high on both potential for threat and potential for cooperation. Examples of this group, in a well-managed organization, might include employees who are in short supply, clients, or customers. A mixed blessing stakeholder could become a supportive or a nonsupportive stakeholder. The recommended strategy here is to collaborate with the mixed blessing stakeholder. By maximizing collaboration, the likelihood is enhanced that this stakeholder will remain supportive.

A summary statement regarding these four stakeholder types might be as follows:[34]

> . . . *managers should attempt to satisfy minimally the needs of marginal stakeholders and to satisfy maximally the needs of supportive and mixed blessing stakeholders, enhancing the latter's support for the organization.*

The four stakeholder types and recommended strategies illustrate what was referred to earlier in this chapter as the "strategic" or instrumental view of stakeholders. But, it could be argued that by taking stakeholders' needs and concerns into consideration, we are improving our ethical treatment of them. We must go beyond just considering them, however. Management still has an ethical responsibility to stakeholders that extends beyond the strategic view. We will develop a fuller appreciation of what this ethical responsibility is in Chapters 6 through 9.

Tapping Expertise of Stakeholders.

Especially with "supportive" stakeholders, but potentially with the other categories as well, it has been argued that managers can turn

Ethics in Practice

"TAXING" QUESTIONS FOR THIS PREPARER

While in college, I worked part-time for a prominent tax preparation service. I prepared customers' taxes along with about 20 other employees at different offices. Bill had been working with the service for about three seasons, but this was my first tax season. Bill was very good at tax preparation and had a pretty good reputation. He was respected by management and seemed to do what he was asked to do.

On a few occasions, I had customers come in and want to see Bill. When I explained that Bill was not at the office that day and asked if I could assist them with any questions, they would want to wait for Bill before continuing any further. This struck me as odd because all of the files are located in the office as well as on the hard drives of the firm's computers. Any employee can assist any customer, no matter who did the actual return.

When I later asked Bill about these customers, he told me that he did a few on his own time for people that couldn't afford the company's fees. This was bothersome to me because there is no telling how many times Bill had done this and how many customers he took away from the business.

1. Who are the stakeholders in this case and what are their stakes?

2. Was it unethical for Bill to be doing these taxes on his own time?

3. Was Bill actually doing the taxes on his own time or on company time when he wasn't otherwise busy?

4. Should I have told the manager the little bit of information I knew about this situation?

Contributed Anonymously

"gadflies into allies." Yaziji has reasoned that nonprofit special-interest groups, especially nongovernmental activist organizations (NGOs), hold great promise for cooperation if managements would quit seeing them as "pests" and try to get them to join in the company endeavors.[35] He argues that these NGOs have resources such as legitimacy, awareness of social forces, distinct networks, and specialized technical expertise that can be tapped by companies to gain competitive advantage. Each of these can provide benefits for companies. Some of the resulting benefits are heading off trouble, helping to set industry standards, shaping legislation, foreseeing shifts in demands, and accelerating innovation. Such partnering with stakeholders requires a change in perspective and mentality. If it is done, however, the companies will be better prepared to deal with stakeholders in the future.

EFFECTIVE STAKEHOLDER MANAGEMENT

Effective stakeholder management requires the careful assessment of the five core questions posed here. To deal successfully with those who assert claims on the organization, managers must understand these core questions. It is tempting to wish that none of this was necessary. However, such wishing would require management to accept the production or managerial view of the firm, and these views are no longer tenable. Business today cannot turn back the clock to a simpler period. Business has been and will continue to be subjected to careful scrutiny of its actions, practices, policies, and ethics. This is the real world in which management lives, and management must accept it and deal with it. Criticisms of business and calls for better corporate citizenship have been the consequences of the changes in the business and society relationship, and the stakeholder approach to viewing the organization has become one needed response. To do less is to decline to accept the realities of business's plight in the modern world, which is increasingly global in scope, and to fail to see the kinds of adaptations that are essential if businesses are to prosper in the present and in the future.

In fairness, we should also note that there are criticisms and limitations of the stakeholder management approach. One major criticism relates to the complexity and time-consuming nature of identifying, assessing, and responding to stakeholder claims, which constitute an extremely difficult process. Also, the ranking of stakeholder claims is no easy task. Some managers continue to think in stockholder terms because this is easier. To think in stakeholder terms increases the complexity of decision making, and it is quite taxing for some managers to determine which stakeholders' claims take priority in a given situation. Despite its complexity, however, the stakeholder management view is most consistent with the environment that business faces today, and **"stakeholder thinking"** has become a necessary part of the successful manager's job.

Effective stakeholder management is facilitated by a number of other useful concepts. The following concepts—stakeholder management capability, the stakeholder corporation model, stakeholder gates of engagement, and principles of stakeholder management—round out a useful approach to stakeholder management effectiveness. Each of these will now be considered.

STAKEHOLDER MANAGEMENT CAPABILITY

Another way of thinking about effective stakeholder management is in terms of the extent to which the organization has developed its **stakeholder management capability (SMC)**.[36] Stakeholder management capability, according to Freeman, may reside at one of three levels of increasing sophistication.

Level 1—the Rational Level.
This level simply entails the company identifying who their stakeholders are and what their stakes happen to be. This is the level that would enable management to create a stakeholder map, such as that depicted in Figure 3-3. The **rational level** is descriptive and somewhat analytical, because the legitimacy of stakes, the stakeholders' power, and urgency are identified. This actually represents a beginning, or low level of SMC. Most organizations have at least identified who their stakeholders are, but not all have analyzed the nature of the stakes or the stakeholders' power. Starik has referred to Freeman's first level as the component of *familiarization* and *comprehensiveness*, because management operating at Level 1 is seeking to become familiar with their stakeholders and to develop a comprehensive assessment as to their identification and stakes.[37]

Level 2—the Process Level.
At the **process level**, organizations go a step further than Level 1 and actually develop and implement organizational processes (approaches, procedures, policies, practices) by which the firm may scan the environment and receive relevant information about stakeholders, which is then used for decision-making purposes. Typical approaches at this level include portfolio analysis processes, strategic review processes, and environmental scanning processes, which are used to assist managers in their strategic management processes.[38] Other approaches, such as issues management or crisis management (Chapter 5), might also be considered examples of

Level 2 SMC. This second level has been described by Starik as *planning integrativeness*, because management does focus on planning processes for stakeholders and integrating a consideration for stakeholders into organizational decision making.[39]

Level 3—the Transactional Level.

The **transactional level** is the highest and most developed of the three levels. This is the bottom line for stakeholder management—the extent to which managers actually engage in transactions (relationships) with stakeholders.[40] At this highest level of SMC, management must take the initiative in meeting stakeholders face to face and attempting to be responsive to their needs. Starik refers to this as the *communication* level, which is characterized by *communication proactiveness, interactiveness, genuineness, frequency, satisfaction,* and *resource adequacy*. Resource adequacy refers to management actually spending resources on stakeholder transactions.[41]

Steven Walker and Jeff Marr, in their important book *Stakeholder Power: A Winning Plan for Building Stakeholder Commitment and Driving Corporate Growth*, argue that companies should compete on the basis of intangible assets—a company's priceless relationships with customers, employees, suppliers, and shareholders. Based on their own firm's 60-year history as a pioneer in corporate reputation and market research and from case studies of organizations as diverse as LensCrafters, DHL, and Edison International, the authors offer a practical model for hardwiring stakeholder management into company strategy and reaping the rewards through continuous innovation, learning, and profitable growth.[42] Walker and Marr would subscribe to the essential nature of Level 3—the transactional level—of stakeholder management capability.

An example of Level 3 SMC is provided in the agreement reached between the Mitsubishi group and an environmentalist organization, the Rainforest Action Network (RAN), based in San Francisco. Mitsubishi agreed to curb its pollution and protect the rain forest in an agreement that was the result of five years of negotiations and meetings with RAN. The agreement would never have been possible if the two groups had not been willing to establish a relationship in which each side made certain concessions.[43]

Another example of Level 3 has been the relationship between General Motors Corp. (GMC) and the Coalition for Environmentally Responsible Economies (CERES). A little over a decade ago, these two organizations actually began to talk with one another, and the result was a mutually beneficial collaboration. The arrangement became a high-profile example of a growing trend within the environmental movement—that of using quiet discussions and negotiations rather than noisy protests to change corporate behavior. Though many positive outcomes have come from this improved stakeholder relationship, issues continue to arise that pose the potential for the two to be at odds with one another. Beginning in 2002, for example, CERES and other environmental groups have been demanding tougher governmental fuel-economy standards, while automakers such as GM have intensified their lobbying to keep existing rules in place, probably because of the popularity of high-fuel-consumption SUVs.[44]

THE STAKEHOLDER CORPORATION

Perhaps the ultimate form of the stakeholder approach or stakeholder management is the **"stakeholder corporation,"** a concept argued persuasively by Wheeler and Sillanpää. The primary element of this concept is **stakeholder inclusiveness**. The authors argue this position as follows:[45]

In the future, development of loyal relationships with customers, employees, shareholders, and other stakeholders will become one of the most important determinants of commercial viability and business success. Increasing shareholder value will be best served if your company cultivates the support of all who may influence its importance.

Advocates of the stakeholder corporation would doubtless believe in "**stakeholder symbiosis,**" which has been discussed widely by a consortium of organizations in their inaugural year activities of the Best Practices for Global Competitiveness Initiative (BPI), created and launched by the American Productivity and Quality Center, the European Foundation for Quality Management, Arthur Andersen, and Fortune Custom Projects. Stakeholder symbiosis is an idea that recognizes that all stakeholders depend on each other for their success and financial well-being.[46] Executives who have a problem with this concept would probably also have trouble becoming a part of stakeholder corporations.

STAKEHOLDER POWER: FOUR GATES OF ENGAGEMENT

Building upon these ideas, Steven Walker and Jeffrey Marr, in their book *Stakeholder Power,* have presented a practical framework for assessing the commitment level of each stakeholder group and moving them through a series of "gates."[47] It is their view that companies need to be proactive in their relationships with potential stakeholders such that these groups *desire* to be in relationships with the company. They hold that great stakeholder relationships evolve through different stages of development, and this knowledge helps management be proactive. They assert that every successful stakeholder relationship passes through four stages, which they refer to as the "four gates of engagement." These four gates include Awareness, Knowledge, Admiration, and Action. The gates are generally sequential, and each stage builds upon the previous stages.

Awareness is gate one. This means knowing that something or someone exists. This first gate seems fairly obvious. They argue, however, that there are often "hidden stakeholders" who may not be aware of the firm. These hidden stakeholders may include others, behind the scenes, who bear influence on decisions. How familiar are they with your firm? The awareness gate is similar to addressing the question "Who are our stakeholders?"

Knowledge is gate two. Developing knowledge among stakeholders addresses not only products and services but also knowledge about corporate character. This refers to the company's values, integrity, culture, and practices. At gate two, customers would see the "fit" for your product or service; employees would know your values, mission, and strategies and what the firm stands for; the community would know what you do and how you do it.

Admiration is gate three. Once a relationship has been established via awareness and knowledge, the potential for stakeholder admiration of the organization exists. To reach this stage, stakeholders must come to trust the firm. Loyalty and commitment are likely effects. Walker and Marr argue that this stage is an excellent time to "close" stakeholders—meaning to seal their trust in you by taking the next step of initiating or deepening the business relationship. This puts them into position for the final stage, which is action.

Action is gate four. By taking steps to further collaboration, the company can build partnerships that benefit both of you. At this stage, similar to SMC Level 3, you might get referrals from customers and employees, investors interested in recommending your stock or expanding their current positions, or suppliers entering into true collaboration and trust. The main implication of the "four gates" model is the need to effectively manage communications with stakeholders of all types. Management's responsibility in the model is to guide the stakeholders' progress through the gates so that strong, viable relationships may be established and maintained.[48]

This notion of stakeholder engagement is relevant to developing what Tapscott and Ticoll refer to as *The Naked Corporation*. In their recent book, they argue that there are 10 characteristics of the open enterprise and that "environmental engagement" and "stakeholder engagement" are two critical factors. Environmental engagement calls for an open operating environment: sustainable ecosystems, peace, order, and good public governance. Stakeholder engagement calls for these open enterprises to put resources and effort into reviewing, managing, recasting, and strengthening relationships with stakeholders, old and new.[49] The "open enterprise" with an emphasis on "transparency" has become crucial because of the corporate scandals of the early 2000s.

PRINCIPLES OF STAKEHOLDER MANAGEMENT

Based upon years of observation and research, a set of **"principles of stakeholder management"** has been developed for use by managers and organizations. These principles, known as "The Clarkson Principles," were named after the late Max Clarkson, a dedicated researcher on the topic of stakeholder management. The principles are intended to provide managers with guiding precepts regarding how stakeholders should be treated. Managers interested in effective stakeholder management, the transactional level of stakeholder management capability, the stakeholder corporation, and the "four gates of engagement" would quickly seek to use these guidelines. Figure 3-9 summarizes these principles. The key words in the principles suggest action words that should reflect the kind of cooperative spirit that should be used in building stakeholder relationships: *acknowledge, monitor, listen, communicate, adopt, recognize, work, avoid, acknowledge conflicts.*

STRATEGIC STEPS TOWARD SUCCESSFUL STAKEHOLDER MANAGEMENT

The global competition that characterizes business firms in the twenty-first century necessitates a stakeholder approach, both for managing effectively and managing ethically. The stakeholder approach requires that stakeholders be moved to the center of management's vision. Three strategic steps may be taken that can lead today's global competitors toward a more balanced view, which is needed in today's changing business environment.[50]

1. *Integrating stakeholder management into the firm's governing philosophy.* Boards of directors and top management groups should move the organization from the idea of "shareholder agent" to "stakeholder trustee." Long-term shareholder value will be the objective of this transition.
2. *Create a stakeholder-inclusive "values statement."* Various firms have done this. Johnson & Johnson's was called a "credo." Eastman Chemical used a "strategic intent" document. The Body Shop had a "mission statement." Regardless of what such a values statement is called, such a pledge reinforces the organization's commitment to stakeholders by way of a public statement.

FIGURE 3-9

Principles of Stakeholder Management—"The Clarkson Principles"

Principle 1	Managers should **acknowledge** and actively **monitor** the concerns of all legitimate stakeholders, and should take their interests appropriately into account in decision making and operations.
Principle 2	Managers should **listen** to and openly **communicate** with stakeholders about their respective concerns and contributions, and about the risks that they assume because of their involvement with the corporation.
Principle 3	Managers should **adopt** processes and modes of behavior that are sensitive to the concerns and capabilities of each stakeholder constituency.
Principle 4	Managers should **recognize the interdependence** of efforts and rewards among stakeholders, and should attempt to achieve a fair distribution of the benefits and burdens of corporate activity among them, taking into account their respective risks and vulnerabilities.
Principle 5	Managers should **work cooperatively** with other entities, both public and private, to ensure that risks and harms arising from corporate activities are minimized and, where they cannot be avoided, appropriately compensated.
Principle 6	Managers should **avoid altogether** activities that might jeopardize inalienable human rights (e.g., the right to life) or give rise to risks that, if clearly understood, would be patently unacceptable to relevant stakeholders.
Principle 7	Managers should **acknowledge the potential conflicts** between (a) their own role as corporate stakeholders, and (b) their legal and moral responsibilities for the interests of stakeholders, and should address such conflicts through open communication, appropriate reporting, incentive systems and, where necessary, third-party review.

SOURCE: *Principles of Stakeholder Management* (Toronto: The Clarkson Centre for Business Ethics, Joseph L. Rotman School of Management, University of Toronto, 1999), 4.

---

3. *Implement a stakeholder performance measurement system.* Such a system should be auditable, integrated, and monitored as stakeholder relations are improved. Measurement is evidence of serious intent to achieve results, and such a system will motivate a sustainable commitment to the stakeholder view.

The key to effective stakeholder management is in its implementation. After studying three companies in detail—Cummins Engine Company, Motorola, and the Royal Dutch /Shell Group—researchers concluded that the key to effective implementation is in recognizing and using stakeholder management as a core competence. When this is done, at least four indicators or manifestations of successful stakeholder management will be apparent. First, stakeholder management results in *survival.* Second, there are *avoided costs.* Third, there was *continued acceptance and use* in the companies studied. This implies success. Fourth, there was evidence of *expanded recognition and adoption* of stakeholder-oriented policies by other companies and consultants.[51] These indicators suggest the value and practical benefits that may be derived from the stakeholder approach.

▪ SUMMARY

A stakeholder is an individual or a group that claims to have one or more stakes in an organization. Stakeholders may affect the organization and, in turn, be affected by the organization's actions, policies, practices, and decisions. The stakeholder approach extends beyond the traditional production and managerial views of the firm and warrants a much broader conception of the parties involved in the organization's functioning and success. Both primary and secondary social and nonsocial stakeholders assume important roles in the eyes of management. A typology of stakeholders suggests that three attributes are especially important: legitimacy, power, and urgency.

Strategic, multifidiciary, and stakeholder synthesis views help us appreciate the perspectives that may be adopted with regard to stakeholders. The stakeholder synthesis perspective is recommended because it highlights the ethical responsibility business has to its stakeholders. The stakeholder model of the firm has three values: descriptive, instrumental, and normative. In a balanced perspective, managers are concerned with both goal achievement and ethical treatment of stakeholders.

Five key questions aid managers in stakeholder management: (1) Who are our stakeholders? (2) What are our stakeholders' stakes? (3) What challenges or opportunities are presented to our firm by our stakeholders? (4) What responsibilities does our firm have to its stakeholders? (5) What strategies or actions should our firm take with respect to our stakeholders? Effective stakeholder management requires the assessment and appropriate response to these five questions. In addition, the use of other relevant stakeholder thinking concepts is helpful. The concept of stakeholder management capability (SMC) illustrates how firms can grow and mature in their approach to stakeholder management. Stakeholder power is effected through four gates of engagement: awareness, knowledge, admiration, and action.

Seven principles of stakeholder management are helpful in guiding managers toward more effective stakeholder thinking. Although the stakeholder management approach is quite complex and time-consuming, it is a way of managing that is in tune with the complex environment that business organizations face today. The stakeholder corporation is a model that represents stakeholder thinking in its most advanced form.

▪ KEY TERMS

core stakeholders (page 71

environmental stakeholders (page 71)

legitimacy (page 71)

managerial view of the firm (page 68)

power (page 72)

primary social stakeholders (page 70)

principles of stakeholder management (page 88)

process level (page 85)

production view of the firm (page 68)

rational level (page 85)

secondary social stakeholders (page 70)

stake (page 67)

stakeholder (page 67)

stakeholder corporation (page 86)

stakeholder inclusiveness (page 86)

stakeholder management capability (SMC) (page 85)

stakeholder symbiosis (page 87)

stakeholder thinking (page 85)

stakeholder view of the firm (page 69)

strategic stakeholders (page 71)

transactional level (page 86)

urgency (page 72)

▪ DISCUSSION QUESTIONS

1. Explain the concepts of stake and stakeholder from your perspective as an individual. What kinds of stakes and stakeholders do you have? Discuss.

2. Differentiate between primary and secondary social and nonsocial stakeholders in a business situation. Give examples of each.

3. Define the terms *core stakeholders, strategic stakeholders*, and *environmental stakeholders*. What factors affect into which of these groups stakeholders are categorized?

4. Explain in your own words the differences among the production, managerial, and stakeholder views of the firm.

5. Choose any group of stakeholders listed in the stakeholder/responsibility matrix in Figure 3-7 and identify the four types of responsibilities the firm has to that stakeholder group.

6. How can a firm transition from Level 1 to Level 3 of stakeholder management capability (SMC)?

7. Is the stakeholder corporation a realistic model for business firms? Will stakeholder corporations become more prevalent in the twenty-first century? Why or why not?

▪ RECOMMENDED CASES

Many of the end-of-text cases may be related to Chapter 3. You may wish to consider studying the following cases with Chapter 3.

Case 1. "Wal-Mart: The Main Street Merchant of Doom." This case about Wal-Mart addresses and illustrates a host of stakeholder relationships. Who are Wal-Mart's stakeholders and what are their stakes? Are Wal-Mart's consumer stakeholders more important than its community stakeholders? What are the protest groups' legitimacy, power, and urgency? How should Wal-Mart engage in stakeholder management?

Cases 2A and 2B; Cases 3A and 3B. "The Body Shop International PLC." This series of four cases all address issues related to stakeholder issues and management. They especially raise the issue of balancing company profits with social initiatives. Who are The Body Shop's stakeholders and what are their stakes?

Case 24. "Firestone and Ford: The Tire Tread Separation Tragedy." This case describes the events following the outbreak of Firestone tire tread separations and the company's relationship with Ford, a company that was greatly affected by the disaster. How could these companies have managed their stakeholders and relationships better?

Case 25. "The Coffee Spill Heard 'Round the World." This case addresses the infamous coffee spill that injured an elderly woman and caused third-degree burns. Who are McDonald's stakeholders? What are their legitimacy, power, and urgency? What is McDonald's social responsibility to these stakeholders?

▪ WEB RESOURCES

The URLs listed here are current at the time of publication. Should any of these Web sites change, please search under the company's or organization's name for an updated address.

Business for Social Responsibility
http://www.bsr.org

Business and Sustainable Development
http://www.bsdglobal.com/tools/principles_triple.asp

BSR Resources
http://www.bsr.org/BSRResources/index.cfm

Business Week
http://www.businessweek.com

Caux Roundtable
http://www.cauxroundtable.org/index.html

Center for Corporate Citizenship Boston
http://www.bc.edu/centers/ccc/index.html

Center on Philanthropy Indiana University
http://www.philanthropy.iupui.edu/

ConocoPhillips Stakeholder Policies
http://www.conocophillips.com/canada/stake
holder/stake_relations.asp

Consensus Statement on Stakeholder Management
http://www.rotman.utoronto.ca/~stake/
Consensus.htm

Corporate Social Responsibility Newswire
http://www.csrwire.com

Ethical Practices in Stakeholder Relations
http://www.buseco.monash.edu.au/research/
strengths/stakeholder.php

Fortune
http://www.fortune.com

Journal of Corporate Citizenship
http://www.greenleaf-publishing.com/jcc/

jcchome.htm

The Conference Board
http://www.conference-board.org

Public Interest Groups
http://www.pirg.org

Stakeholder management
http://www.burke.com/bcsa/stakeholder_
management.htm

Stakeholder management
http://www.themanager.org/resources/
Stakeholder%20Management.htm

Trends in Stakeholder Management
http://www.navigate.co.nz/newsreti.htm

U.S. Chamber of Commerce
http://www.uschamber.com

 InfoTrac® College Edition   http://www.infotrac-college.com

Articles from Business Week, Fortune, *and the* Journal of Corporate Citizenship *can be researched, retrieved, and read from your desktop using InfoTrac's online database.*

▪ ENDNOTES

1. See, for example, Robert A. Phillips, "Stakeholder Theory and a Principle of Fairness," *Business Ethics Quarterly* (Vol. 7, No. 1, January 1997), 51–66; Sandra A. Waddock and Samuel B. Graves, "Quality of Management and Quality of Stakeholder Relations," *Business and Society* (Vol. 36, No. 3, September 1997), 250–279; Ann Svendsen, *The Stakeholder Strategy* (Berrett-Koehler Publishers, 1998); Thomas Jones and Andrew Wicks, 1999, "Convergent Stakeholder Theory," *Academy of Management Review*, (20, 1999), 404–437; and Thomas Kochan and Saul Rubinstein, "Toward a Stakeholder Theory of the Firm: The Saturn Partnership," *Organizational Science* (11:4, 2000), 367–386;

2. "Stakeholder Capitalism," *The Economist* (February 10, 1996), 23–25. See also "Shareholder Values," *The Economist* (February 10, 1996), 15–16; and John Plender, *A Stake in the Future: The Stakeholding Society* (Nicholas Brealey, 1997).

3. David Wheeler and Maria Sillanpää, *The Stakeholder Corporation: A Blueprint for Maximizing Stakeholder Value* (London: Pitman Publishing, 1997).

4. Steven F. Walker and Jeffrey W. Marr, *Stakeholder Power: A Winning Plan for Building Stakeholder Commitment and Driving Corporate Growth* (Cambridge, MA.: Perseus Publishing, 2001).

5. James E. Post, Lee E. Preston, and Sybille Sachs, *Redefining the Corporation: Stakeholder Management and Organizational Wealth* (Stanford: Stanford University Press, 2002).

6. Robert Phillips, *Stakeholder Theory and Organizational Ethics* (San Francisco: Berrett-Koehler Publishers, Inc., 2003).

7. Jeanne M. Logsdon, Donna J. Wood, and Lee E. Benson, "Research in Stakeholder Theory, 1997–1998: The Sloan Foundation Minigrant Project" (Toronto: The Clarkson Centre for Business Ethics, 2000).

8. This definition is similar to that of R. Edward Freeman in *Strategic Management: A Stakeholder Approach* (Boston: Pitman, 1984), 25.

9. Mark Starik, "Is the Environment an Organizational Stakeholder? Naturally!" *International Association for Business and Society* (IABS) 1993 Proceedings, 466–471.

10. Freeman, 5.

11. Freeman, 24–25. Also see James E. Post, Lee E. Preston, and Sybille Sachs, *Redefining the Corporation: Stakeholder Management and Organizational Wealth* (Stanford: Stanford University Press), 2002.

12. Wheeler and Sillanpää (1997), 167.

13. *Ibid.*, 168.

14. Max B. E. Clarkson (ed.), *Proceedings of the Second Toronto Conference on Stakeholder Theory* (Toronto: The Centre for Corporate Social Performance and Ethics, University of Toronto, 1994).

15. Ronald K. Mitchell, Bradley R. Agle, and Donna J. Wood, "Toward a Theory of Stakeholder Identification and Salience: Defining the Principle of Who and What Really Counts," *Academy of Management Review* (October 1997), 853–886.

16. Jim Carlton, "How Home Depot and Activists Joined to Cut Logging Abuse," *The Wall Street Journal* (September 26, 2000), A1.

17. Kenneth E. Goodpaster, "Business Ethics and Stakeholder Analysis," *Business Ethics Quarterly* (Vol. 1, No. 1, January 1991), 53–73.

18. *Ibid.*

19. Thomas Donaldson and Lee Preston, "The Stakeholder Theory of the Corporation: Concepts, Evidence, Implications," *Academy of Management Review* (Vol. 20, No. 1, 1995), 65–91.

20. Phillips (2003), 85–118.

21. *Ibid.*

22. Parallel questions are posed with respect to corporate strategy by Ian C. MacMillan and Patricia E. Jones, *Strategy Formulation: Power and Politics* (St. Paul, MN: West, 1986), 66.

23. "Animal Rights Group Aims Ad Attack at McDonald's," *The Wall Street Journal* (August 30, 1999), p. B7.

24. Marcia Yablon, "Happy Hen, Happy Meal: McDonald's Chick Fix," *U.S .News & World Report* (September 4, 2000), 46.

25. *Ibid.*, 46.

26. "News Release: Chicken and Friends Have Bone to Pick with New Burger King CEO." People for the Ethical Treatment of Animals (PETA) Web site: http://www.peta-online.org/news/0301/0301miamibk.html.

27. "Does It Pay to Be Ethical? *Business Ethics* (March/April 1997), 14. "What's Your Poison?" *The Economist* (August 9, 2003), 50. Web site of Rain Forest Action Network: http://www.ran.org/.

28. From the Web site of Rainforest Action Network: http://www.ran.org/ran_campaigns/old_growth.

29. Grant T. Savage, Timothy W. Nix, Carlton J. Whitehead, and John D. Blair, "Strategies for Assessing and Managing Organizational Stakeholders," *Academy of Management Executive* (Vol. V, No. 2, May 1991), 61–75.

30. *Ibid.*, 64.

31. MacMillan and Jones, 66–70.

32. Savage, Nix, Whitehead, and Blair, 65.

33. Seth Hettena and Laura Wides, "Eco-Terrorists Coming Out of the Wild," *USA Today* (October 3, 2003), 22A.

34. Savage, Nix, Whitehead, and Blair, 72.

35. Michael Yaziji, "Turning Gadflies into Allies," *Harvard Business Review* (February 2004), 110–115.

36. Freeman, 53.

37. Mark Starik, "Stakeholder Management and Firm Performance: Reputation and Financial Relationships to U.S. Electric Utility Consumer-Related Strategies," unpublished Ph.D. dissertation, University of Georgia, 1990, 34.

38. Freeman, 64.

39. Starik (1990), 36.

40. Freeman, 69–70.

41. Starik (1990), 36–42.

42. Steven F. Walker and Jeffrey Marr, *Stakeholder Power: A Winning Plan for Building Stakeholder Commitment and Driving Corporate Growth* (Perseus Books, 2001).

43. Charles McCoy, "Two Members of Mitsubishi Group and Environmental Activists Reach Pact," *The Wall Street Journal* (February 11, 1998), A8.

44. Jeffrey Ball, "After Long Détente, GM, Green Group Are at Odds Again," *The Wall Street Journal* (July 30, 2002), A1.

45. Wheeler and Sillanpää (1997), book cover.

46. "Stakeholder Symbiosis," *Fortune* (March 30, 1998), S2-S4, special advertising section.

47. Walker and Marr (2001), 56–65.

48. *Ibid.*

49. Don Tapscott and David Ticoll, *The Naked Corporation: How the Age of Transparency Will Revolutionize Business* (Free Press, 2003).

50. "Measurements," *Measuring and Managing Stakeholder Relationships* (Indianapolis: WalkerInformation Global Network, 1998).

51. James E. Post, Lee E. Preston, Sybille Sachs, "Managing the Extended Enterprise: The New Stakeholder View," *California Management Review* (Vol. 45, No. 1, Fall 2002), 22–25.

Part 2

STRATEGIC MANAGEMENT *for* CORPORATE STAKEHOLDER PERFORMANCE

Chapter 4

■ STRATEGIC MANAGEMENT *and* PUBLIC AFFAIRS

CHAPTER LEARNING OUTCOMES

After studying this chapter, you should be able to:

1 Explain the concept of corporate public policy and relate it to strategic management.
2 Articulate the four major strategy levels and explain enterprise-level strategy.
3 Relate the notion of social audits to strategic control.
4 Identify the major activities of public affairs departments.
5 Highlight trends with respect to the public affairs function.
6 Link public affairs with organizational characteristics.
7 Indicate how public affairs may be incorporated into every manager's job.

In this chapter and the next, we more closely examine how management has responded and should respond, in a managerial sense, to the kinds of social, ethical, and stakeholder issues developed in this book. In this chapter, we provide a broad overview of how social, ethical, and public issues fit into the general **strategic management processes** of the organization. We introduce the term *corporate public policy* to describe that component part of management decision making that embraces these issues. Finally, we discuss public affairs, or public affairs management, as the formal organizational approach companies use in dealing with these issues. The overriding goal of this chapter is to focus on planning for the turbulent social/ethical stakeholder environment, and this encompasses the strategic management process, environmental analysis, and public affairs management.

THE CONCEPT OF CORPORATE PUBLIC POLICY

The impact of the social-ethical-public-stakeholder environment on business organizations is becoming more pronounced each year. It is an understatement to suggest that this multifaceted environment has become tumultuous, and brief reminders of a few actual cases point out the validity of this claim quite dramatically. Procter & Gamble and its Rely Tampon recall, Firestone and its radial tire debacle, Ford Motor Company and its disastrous Pinto gas tank problem, and Johnson & Johnson and its tainted Tylenol capsules are *classic* reminders of how social issues can directly affect a firm's product offerings. In addition, there are many examples in which social issues have had major impacts on firms at the general management level. Exxon's catastrophic *Valdez* oil spill, Dow Corning's ill-fated silicone breast implants, and the tobacco industry's battles with the federal and state government over the dangers of its product are all examples of the impacts of top-level decisions that entail ethical ramifications. More recently, Coca-Cola's disastrous and massive recall of soft drinks in Belgium and France, its continuing controversy in India over the product's purity, and Bridgestone-Firestone's tire tread separations in a number of countries of the world and the United States provide examples of ethical issues that have dramatic implications for top executive decision makers. We would be remiss if we did not mention the scandals at such firms as Enron, WorldCom, Tyco, Adelphia, and HealthSouth, along with once-revered accounting firm, Arthur Andersen, which went out of business recently due to ethical transgressions.

What started as an awareness of social issues and social responsibility matured into a focus on the management of social responsiveness and performance. Today, the trend reflects a preoccupation with ethics, stakeholders, and corporate citizenship as we navigate the first decade of the new millennium. The term *corporate public policy* is an outgrowth of an earlier term, *corporate social policy*, which had been in general usage for over 20 years. The two concepts have essentially the same meaning, but we will use "corporate public policy" because it is more in keeping with terminology more recently used in business. Much of what takes place under the banner of corporate public policy is also referred to as *corporate citizenship* by businesses today.

Corporate Public Policy Defined

What is meant by corporate public policy?

> **Corporate public policy** *is a firm's posture, stance, strategy, or position regarding the public, social, global, and ethical aspects of stakeholders and corporate functioning.*

Later in the chapter, we will discuss how businesses formalize this concern under the rubric of **corporate public affairs**, or public affairs management. Businesses encounter many situations in their daily operations that involve highly visible public and ethical issues. Some of these issues are subject to intensive public debate for specific periods of time before they become institutionalized. Examples of such issues include sexual harassment, AIDS in the workplace, affirmative action, product safety, and employee privacy. Other issues are more basic, more enduring, and more philosophical. These issues might include the broad role of business in society, the corporate governance question, and the relative balance of business versus government direction that is best for our society.

The idea behind corporate public policy is that a firm must give specific attention to issues in which basic questions of right, wrong, justice, fairness, or public policy reside. The dynamic stakeholder environment of the past 40 years, especially the last 10 years, has necessitated that management apply a policy perspective to these issues. At one time, the social environment was thought to be a relatively constant backdrop against which the real work of business took place. Today these issues are center stage, and managers at all levels must address them. Corporate public policy is the process by which management addresses these significant concerns.

Corporate Public Policy as Part of Strategic Management

Where does corporate public policy fit into strategic management? First, let us briefly discuss strategic management. **Strategic management** refers to the overall management process that strives to position a firm relative to its market environment. A basic way in which the firm relates to its market environment is through the products and services it produces and the markets it chooses to address. Strategic management is also thought of as a kind of overall or comprehensive organizational management by the firm's top-level executives. In this sense, it represents the overall executive leadership function in which the sense of direction of the organization is decided upon and implemented.

Business process outsourcing (BPO) has become big business for three reasons, according to *The Economist* (21 February 2004 v370 i8363 p15US): Many companies doing business globally are still developing a plan for outsourcing to a location such as India, meaning the industry has great growth potential; the range of work being performed remotely is constantly expanding; and much of the global market remains untapped. But will there be a backlash against outsourcing that results in "insourcing"—taking back services that were previously outsourced? Read the current speculation by logging on to InfoTrac College Edition at **http://www.infotrac-college.com** and keying record number A113495601.

Top management teams must address many issues as a firm is positioning itself relative to its environment. The more traditional issues involve product/market decisions—the principal decision thrusts of most organizations. Other decisions relate to marketing, finance, accounting, information systems, human resources, operations, research and development, competition, and so on. Corporate public policy is that part of the overall strategic management of the organization that focuses specifically on the public, ethical, and stakeholder issues that are embedded in the functioning and decision processes of the firm. Therefore, just as a firm needs to develop policy on human resources, operations, marketing, or finance, it also must develop corporate public policy to proactively address the host of issues we have been discussing and will discuss throughout this book.

A company that concluded it needed a formal corporate public policy is Citizens Bank of Canada, a company that has been trying to build a strong reputation in the area of corporate social responsibility since it opened its doors in 1997. The bank's management concluded it needed more than the establishment of a few enlightened policies. It needed something that would set a systematic course and foundation for "doing well by doing good." Citizens' first step was the establishment of a document of guiding principles, called an *ethical policy*, which would steer the firm's practices toward its social and environmental commitments. To implement its policy and follow up on implementation, the bank created an "ethical policy compliance" unit. The initiatives of Citizens Bank illustrate the realization that companies come to regarding the need for formalized corporate public/ethics policy.[1]

A recent issue that carries with it significant strategic as well as public and ethical implications is the current trend on the part of many American firms to outsource jobs to less expensive parts of the world. Once it was just manufacturing jobs that were moved to China and other developing countries. Now, high-paying professional jobs, such as programming and accounting, are being moved to countries such as India, China, and Indonesia. The result has been a major public policy debate regarding these corporate decisions.[2]

Relationship of Ethics to Strategic Management

Although a consideration of ethics is implicit in corporate public policy discussions, it is useful to make this relationship more explicit. Over the years, a growing number of observers have stressed this point. Kenneth R. Andrews, for example, was an early pioneer for his emphasis on the moral component of corporate strategy. In particular, he highlighted the leadership challenge of determining future strategy in the face of rising moral and ethical standards. He argued that coming to terms with the morality of choice may be the most strenuous undertaking in strategic decision making. This is particularly stressful in the inherently amoral corporation.[3]

The challenge of linking ethics and strategy was moved to center stage by Freeman and Gilbert in their book, *Corporate Strategy and the Search for Ethics*. They argued that if business ethics was to have any meaning beyond pompous moralizing, it must be linked to business strategy. Their view is that we can revitalize the concept of corporate strategy by linking ethics to strategy. This linkage permits the most pressing management issues of the day to be addressed in ethical terms. They suggest the concept of enterprise strategy as the idea that best links these two vital notions, and we will examine this concept in more detail in the next section.[4]

The concept of corporate public policy and the linkage between ethics and strategy are better understood when we think about (1) the four key levels at which strategy decisions arise and (2) the steps in the strategic management process in which these decisions are embedded.

FOUR KEY STRATEGY LEVELS

Because organizations are hierarchical, it is not surprising to find that strategic management also is hierarchical in nature. That is, there are several different levels in the firm at which strategic decisions are made or the strategy process occurs. These levels range from the broadest or highest levels (where missions, visions, goals, decisions, and policies entail higher risks and are characterized by longer time horizons, more subjective values, and greater uncertainty) to the lowest levels (where planning is done for specific functional areas, where time horizons are shorter, where information needs are less complex, and where there is less uncertainty). Four key strategy levels have been documented and are important to consider: enterprise-level strategy, corporate-level strategy, business-level strategy, and functional-level strategy.

The Four Strategy Levels

The broadest level of strategic management is known as *societal-level strategy* or *enterprise-level strategy*, as it has come to be known. **Enterprise-level strategy** is the overarching strategy level that poses the basic questions, "What is the role of the organization in society?" and "What do we stand for?" Enterprise-level strategy, as we will discuss in more detail later, encompasses the development and articulation of corporate public policy. It may be considered the first and most important level at which ethics and strategy are linked. Until fairly recently, corporate-level strategy was thought to be the broadest strategy level. In a limited, traditional sense, this is true, because **corporate-level strategy** addresses what is often posed as the most defining business question for a firm, "What business(es) are we in or should we be in?" It is easy to see how **business-level strategy** is a natural follow-on because this strategy level is concerned with the question, "How should we compete in a given business or industry?" Thus, a company whose products or services take it into many different businesses, industries, or markets might need a business-level strategy to define its competitive posture in each of them. A competitive strategy might be based on low cost or a differentiated product. Finally, **functional-level strategy** addresses the question, "How should a firm integrate its various subfunctional activities and how should these activities be related to changes taking place in the various functional areas (finance, marketing, human resources, operations)?"[5]

The purpose of identifying the four strategy levels is to clarify that corporate public policy is primarily a part of enterprise-level strategy, which, in turn, is but one level of strategic decision making that occurs in organizations. Figure 4-1 illustrates that enterprise-level strategy is the broadest level and that the other levels are narrower concepts that cascade from it.

Emphasis on Enterprise-Level Strategy

The terms *enterprise-level strategy* and *societal-level strategy* may be used interchangeably. Neither of these terms is used with any degree of regularity in the business community. Although many firms address the issues that enterprise-level strategy is concerned with, use of this terminology is concentrated primarily in the academic community. This terminology arose in an attempt to describe the level of strategic thinking that an increasing number of observers believe is necessary if firms are to be fully responsive to today's complex and dynamic stakeholder environment. Many organizations today convey this enterprise or societal strategy in their missions, vision, or values statements. Others embed their enterprise strategies in codes of conduct. Increasingly, these strategies are reflecting a global level of application.

Ansoff visualized the enterprise strategy level as one in which the political legitimacy of the organization is addressed.[6] He later discussed this same concern for legitimacy using the phrase "Societal Strategy for the Business Firm."[7] Hofer and others have described the enterprise level as the societal level.

According to Freeman, enterprise-level strategy needs to be thought of in such a way that it more closely aligns "social and ethical concerns" with traditional "business concerns."[8] In setting the direction for a firm, a manager needs to understand the impact of changes in business strategy on the underlying values of the firm and the new

FIGURE 4-1

The Hierarchy of Strategy Levels

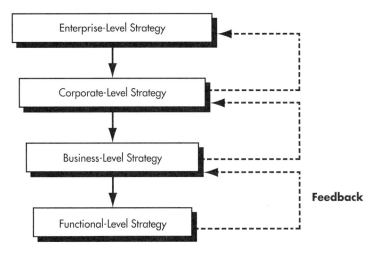

stakeholder relations that will emerge and take shape as a result. Freeman proposes that enterprise-level strategy needs to address the overriding question, "What do we stand for?"[9] Thus, at the enterprise level, the task of setting strategic direction involves understanding the role in society of a particular firm as a whole and its relationships to other social institutions. Important questions then become:

- What is the role of our organization in society?
- How is our organization perceived by our stakeholders?
- What principles or values does our organization represent?
- What obligations do we have to society at large, including the world?
- What are the implications for our current mix of business and allocation of resources?

Many firms have addressed some of these questions—perhaps only in part, perhaps only in an ad hoc way. The point of enterprise-level strategy, however, is that the firm needs to address these questions intentionally, specifically, and cohesively in such a way that a corporate public policy is articulated.

How have business firms addressed these questions? What are the manifestations of enterprise-level thinking and corporate public policy? The manifestations show up in a variety of ways in different companies—for example, how a firm responds when faced with public crises. Does it respond to its stakeholders in a positive, constructive, and sensitive way or in a negative, defensive, and insensitive way? Corporate actions reveal the presence or absence of soundly developed enterprise-level strategy. Companies also demonstrate the degree of thinking that has gone into public issues by the presence or absence and use or nonuse of codes of ethics, codes of conduct, mission statements, values statements, corporate creeds, vision statements, or other such policy-oriented codes and statements.

One company that has addressed these concerns is Borg-Warner. In a document titled "Believe It: Managing by Shared Values at Borg-Warner," Chairman James F. Bere posed and then answered these questions:

SEARCH THE WEB

ENTERPRISE-LEVEL STRATEGY IN ACTION

One of the best ways to appreciate a company's corporate public policy or enterprise-level strategy is to examine its posture on social/ethical issues. A company that is recognized recently for its corporate citizenship is Hewlett-Packard (HP). HP has been highly ranked for years as a good corporate citizen.

One way that HP presents its corporate public policy and enterprise strategy is in the form of its global citizenship policy.

A quote by Debra Dunn, senior vice president of Corporate Affairs and Global Citizenship, is insightful:

"We're working to define the role companies can and should play working in collaboration with other sectors to solve some of the fundamental problems in the world. My aspiration is that HP be viewed as a real leader in this space. A leader in forging new kinds of relationships with nonprofit organizations and governments."

To learn more about HP's commitment to global citizenship, check out its Web site: **http://www.hp.com/hpinfo/globalcitizenship/commitment.html**.

- What kind of company are we anyway?
- What does Borg-Warner stand for?
- What do we believe?

Figure 4-2 presents "The Beliefs of Borg-Warner," a document that clearly manifests enterprise-level strategy and corporate public policy.

FIGURE 4-2

The Beliefs of Borg-Warner: To Reach Beyond the Minimal

Any business is a member of a social system, entitled to the rights and bound by the responsibilities of that membership. Its freedom to pursue economic goals is constrained by law and channeled by the forces of a free market. But these demands are minimal, requiring only that a business provide wanted goods and services, compete fairly, and cause no obvious harm. For some companies, that is enough. It is not enough for Borg-Warner. We impose upon ourselves an obligation to reach beyond the minimal. We do so convinced that by making a larger contribution to the society that sustains us, we best ensure not only its future vitality, but our own.

This is what we believe.
We believe in the dignity of the individual.

However large and complex a business may be, its work is still done by people dealing with people. Each person involved is a unique human being, with pride, needs, values, and innate personal worth. For Borg-Warner to succeed, we must operate in a climate of openness and trust, in which each of us freely grants others the same respect, cooperation, and decency we seek for ourselves.

We believe in our responsibility to the common good.

Because Borg-Warner is both an economic and social force, our responsibilities to the public are large. The spur of competition and the sanctions of the law give strong guidance to our behavior, but alone do not inspire our best. For that we must heed the voice of our natural concern for others. Our challenge is to supply goods and services that are of superior value to those who use them; to create jobs that provide meaning for those who do them; to honor and enhance human life; and to offer our talents and our wealth to help improve the world we share.

We believe in the endless quest for excellence.

Although we may be better today than we were yesterday, we are not as good as we must become. Borg-Warner chooses to be a leader—in serving our customers, advancing our technologies, and rewarding all who invest in us their time, money, and trust. None of us can settle for doing less than our best, and we can never stop trying to surpass what already has been achieved.

We believe in continuous renewal.

A corporation endures and prospers only by moving forward. The past has given us the present to build on. But to follow our visions to the future, we must see the difference between traditions that give us continuity and strength, and conventions that no longer serve us—and have the courage to act on that knowledge. Most can adapt after change has occurred; we must be among the few who anticipate change, shape it to our purpose, and act as its agents.

We believe in the commonwealth of Borg-Warner and its people.

Borg-Warner is both a federation of businesses and a community of people. Our goal is to preserve the freedom each of us needs to find personal satisfaction while building the strength that comes from unity. True unity is more than a melding of self-interests; it results when values and ideals also are shared. Some of ours are spelled out in these statements of belief. Others include faith in our political, economic, and spiritual heritage; pride in our work and our company; the knowledge that loyalty must flow in many directions; and a conviction that power is strongest when shared. We look to the unifying force of these beliefs as a source of energy to brighten the future of our company and all who depend upon it.

SOURCE: Company document, Borg-Warner Corporation. For more information, check out the company Web site: http://www.bwauto.com/about.html.

Another example of enterprise-level strategy is the corporate credo of Johnson & Johnson, shown in Figure 4-3. Note that the Johnson & Johnson credo focuses on statements of responsibility by enumerating its stakeholder groups in the following sequence:

- Doctors, nurses, patients, mothers and fathers (consumers)
- Employees
- Communities
- Stockholders

Importance of Core Values.

The "**core values**" program that was implemented at the Aluminum Company of America (Alcoa) by one of its chairmen, Paul H. O'Neill, is an excellent illustration of an enterprise-level strategy. O'Neill had been chairman of Alcoa for less than three months when he began making decisions that seemed to reflect a new way of thinking at Alcoa. Four years later, it became apparent that Alcoa's six "core values" would provide the guiding direction for a new corporate conscience at the firm.[10]

The six "core values" at Alcoa were identified and articulated by O'Neill, then company president C. Fred Fetterolf, and 10 senior executives during 100 hours of discussions and reflections. The core values program, known as "Visions, Values, and Milestones," set forth a new ethics agenda built around the following six core values:

FIGURE 4-3

Johnson & Johnson Credo

Our Credo

We believe our first responsibility is to the doctors, nurses and patients, to mothers and fathers and all others who use our products and services. In meeting their needs everything we do must be of high quality. We must constantly strive to reduce our costs in order to maintain reasonable prices. Customers' orders must be serviced promptly and accurately. Our suppliers and distributors must have an opportunity to make a fair profit.

We are responsible to our employees, the men and women who work with us throughout the world. Everyone must be considered as an individual. We must respect their dignity and recognize their merit. They must have a sense of security in their jobs. Compensation must be fair and adequate, and working conditions clean, orderly and safe. We must be mindful of ways to help our employees fulfill their family responsibilities. Employees must feel free to make suggestions and complaints. There must be equal opportunity for employment, development and advancement for those qualified. We must provide competent management, and their actions must be just and ethical.

We are responsible to the communities in which we live and work and to the world community as well. We must be good citizens—support good works and charities and bear our fair share of taxes. We must encourage civic improvements and better health and education. We must maintain in good order the property we are privileged to use, protecting the environment and natural resources.

Our final responsibility is to our stockholders. Business must make a sound profit. We must experiment with new ideas. Research must be carried on, innovative programs developed and mistakes paid for. New equipment must be purchased, new facilities provided and new products launched. Reserves must be created to provide for adverse times. When we operate according to these principles, the stockholders should realize a fair return.

Johnson & Johnson

SOURCE: Reprinted with permission from Johnson & Johnson. For more information, see http://www.jnj.com/community/policies/index.htm.

1. Integrity
2. Safety and health
3. Quality of work
4. Treatment of people
5. Accountability
6. Profitability

In part, O'Neill and Fetterolf placed values at the center of their corporate culture out of deep personal religious convictions. They argued that biblical principles such as truthfulness, compassion, and stewardship should not stop at the factory gate. On another level, they said they were attempting to reshape the company into the kind of unified, harmonious enterprise that would be needed to survive and compete in the global marketplace of the future.[11]

In terms of implementation, Alcoa first began disseminating the core values to its employees. Follow-up was done with films, training seminars, and departmental meetings. Later, the company began evaluating employees to see how well they had been applying the core values in their work. Although Alcoa, like all large metal makers, has faced some tough economic times, O'Neill argued that whether business was good or bad, the firm was committed to its ethics program. O'Neill argued, "I don't think it's necessary to compromise your values to succeed economically."[12]

Another illustration of enterprise-level strategic thinking may be seen in the "Commitment to Integrity" statement articulated by The Boeing Company. This statement, presented in Figure 4-4, intends to reflect the company's values and how these values are targeted toward a vision of full customer satisfaction. Though Boeing has faced ethical challenges in recent years, it is hoped that the company will find direction in its commitment to integrity. Merck & Co., Inc., the leading pharmaceutical firm, conveys its

---

FIGURE 4-4

Commitment to Integrity

Achieving Our Vision

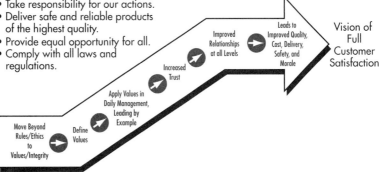

Boeing Values:
- Treat each other with respect.
- Deal fairly in all our relationships.
- Honor our commitments and obligations.
- Communicate honestly.
- Take responsibility for our actions.
- Deliver safe and reliable products of the highest quality.
- Provide equal opportunity for all.
- Comply with all laws and regulations.

Move Beyond Rules/Ethics to Values/Integrity

Define Values

Apply Values in Daily Management, Leading by Example

Increased Trust

Improved Relationships at all Levels

Leads to Improved Quality, Cost, Delivery, Safety, and Morale

Vision of Full Customer Satisfaction

---

enterprise strategy in its values statement, which is part of its mission statement. Herman Miller, maker of office furniture, reflects its enterprise strategy in its "Blueprint for Corporate Community." Herman Miller's "blueprint" lists what it believes in:

What we believe in:

- Making a meaningful contribution to our customers.
- Cultivating community, participation, and people development.
- Creating economic value for shareholders and employee-owners.
- Responding to change through design and innovation.
- Living with integrity and respecting the environment.
- A different kind of company.[13]

By 1998, Herman Miller was judged to be *Fortune*'s "most admired" major corporation in the category of social responsibility.[14] It has consistently been highly ranked.

Other manifestations of enterprise-level strategic thinking in corporations include the extent to which firms have established board or senior management committees. Such committees might include the following: public policy/issues committees, ethics committees, governance committees, social audit committees, corporate philanthropy committees, and ad hoc committees to address specific public issues. The firm's public affairs function can also indicate enterprise-level thinking. Does the firm have an established public affairs office? To whom does the director of corporate public affairs report? What role does public affairs play in corporate-level decision making? Do public affairs managers play a formal role in the firm's strategic planning?

Another major indicator of enterprise-level strategic thinking is the extent to which the firm attempts to identify social or public issues, analyze them, and integrate them into its strategic management processes. We will now discuss how corporate public policy is integrated into the strategic management process.

It is crucial that firms not only have values statements that provide guidance but that these values also "mean something." Ever since Jim Collins and Jerry Porras published *Built to Last: Successful Habits of Visionary Companies* in 1994, companies have felt they needed such statements. The authors made the case that many of the best companies adhere to a set of principles called *core values*. Core values are the deeply ingrained principles that guide all of a company's actions and decisions, and they serve as cultural cornerstones. Hewlett-Packard's well-known "HP Way" is an example.[15] Though 80 percent of today's *Fortune* 100 companies claim they have values statements that are publicly proclaimed, many of them have been debased because they are not followed. Patrick Lencioni, a management consultant, argues that companies need to make their values "mean something."[16] Lencioni argues that to be effective, companies need to "weave core values into everything." If a company's core values do not mean anything, they are hollow or empty, such as those found at Enron, and such values statements may be doing more harm than good.

In the final analysis, a firm will need to undergo a "**value shift**" if it is interested in integrating ethical and social considerations into its financially-driven strategic plans. Such a value shift, according to Lynn Sharp Paine, would require the firm to get back to basics and adopt a different kind of management than that typically practiced by companies. She argues that superior performers of the future will be those companies that can meet both the social and financial expectations of their stakeholders.[17] This is a theme we are seeking to develop in this chapter and this book.

THE STRATEGIC MANAGEMENT PROCESS

To understand how corporate public policy is but one part of the larger system of management decision making, it is useful to identify the major steps that make up the strategic management process. One conceptualization includes six steps: (1) goal formulation, (2) strategy formulation, (3) strategy evaluation, (4) strategy implementation, (5) strategic control, and (6) environmental analysis.[18] Figure 4-5 graphically portrays an expanded view of this process. Note that the environmental analysis component requires collection of information on trends, events, and issues that are occurring in the stakeholder environment and that this information is then fed into the other steps of the process. Note also that, although the tasks or steps often are discussed sequentially, they are in fact interactive and do not always occur in a neatly ordered pattern or sequence. Figure 4-5 also captures the

---

FIGURE 4-5

The Strategic Management Process and Corporate Public Policy

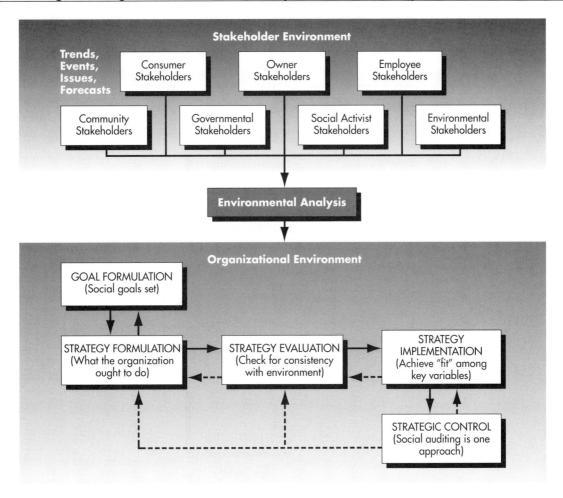

relationship between the strategic management process and corporate public policy. Figure 4-6 illustrates Andrews' four major components of strategy formulation and how "acknowledged obligations to society" fits into the step of strategy formulation.[19]

It should also be noted that strategic management may be focused on a particular aspect or core value to the business firm. An example of this would be the concept of "sustainable strategic management," as discussed at length by Ed and Jean Stead.[20] In their concept, sustainability is focused on the "triple bottom line" as discussed earlier. However, they go beyond the concern of the firm and argue that the survival and renewal of the greater economic system, social system, and ecosystem are important as well. In their concept, sustainable strategic management approaches a kind of enterprise level discussed earlier.

Social Auditing and Performance Reporting

As a management function, strategic control, the fifth step in the strategic management process, seeks to ensure that the organization stays on track and achieves its goals, missions, and strategies. Planning is not complete without control because the control function strives to keep management activities in conformance with plans.

Management control subsumes three essential steps: (1) *setting standards* against which performance may be compared, (2) *comparing* actual performance with what was planned

FIGURE 4-6

Four Components of Strategy Formulation

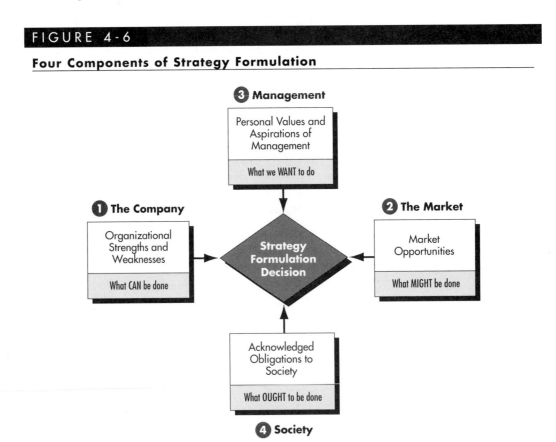

(the standard), and (3) *taking corrective action* to bring the two into alignment, if needed.[21] It has been argued that a planning system will not achieve its full potential unless at the same time it monitors and assesses the firm's progress along key strategic dimensions. Furthermore, there is a need to monitor and control the "strategic momentum" by focusing on a particular strategic direction while at the same time coping with environmental turbulence and change.[22] The social audit is a planning and control approach that is worthy of discussion within the context of strategic management. Some companies actually report their social performance relative to their standards. Others just report their social or values activities and achievements.

Development of the Social Audit.

In the context of corporate social performance or corporate public policy, the idea of a **social audit**, or **social performance report**, as a technique for providing planning and control has been experimented with for a number of years. Although the term *social audit* has been used to describe a wide variety of activities embracing various forms of social performance reporting, in this discussion it is defined as follows:

> *The social audit is a systematic attempt to identify, measure, monitor, and evaluate an organization's performance with respect to its social efforts, goals, and programs.*

Implicit in this definition is the idea that some social performance planning has already taken place. And although we talk about the social audit here as a control process, it could just as easily be thought of as a planning and control system.[23]

In the context of strategic control, the social audit could assume a role much like that portrayed in Figure 4-7 on page 110. This figure is similar to the diagram of the strategic management process and corporate public policy shown in Figure 4-5, but it is modified somewhat to focus on social goals, corporate social performance, the social audit, and the first three steps in the strategic control process.

Although the corporate social audit is not in widespread use in U.S. industry today, it continues to be advocated as an approach by which companies can integrate social concerns into strategic management. More and more today, various special-interest groups want companies to reveal their social performance results in such areas as environment, commitments to workplace conditions, fairness and honesty in dealings with suppliers, customer service standards, community and charitable involvement, and business practices in developing countries. The groups expecting this information range from social activist groups to investor groups such as mutual funds and institutional investors. The Body Shop is a company that has made widespread use of the social audit. They refer to it as *values reporting*.

Today, *social auditing, social accounting, sustainability reporting*, and *social/values reporting* are all terms used to describe the process that was once known as *social auditing*. What these processes have in common is that they make the public aware of their social and ethical results.

SEARCH THE WEB

THE BODY SHOP AND VALUES REPORTING

In the early 1990s, The Body Shop played a significant role in spearheading the move for companies to report on their social and environmental performance. When they published their first Values Report in 1995, their "sustainability reporting" was described by the United Nations Environment Programme as "trailblazing." The Body Shop received a similar accolade from them following the 1997 Values Report, which was ranked highest of all social and environmental reports globally.

For recent information on social auditing and values reporting at the Body Shop, go to **http://www.thebody shop.com/web/tbsgl/reporting_approach.jsp**.

FIGURE 4-7

The Social Audit in the Context of Strategic Control

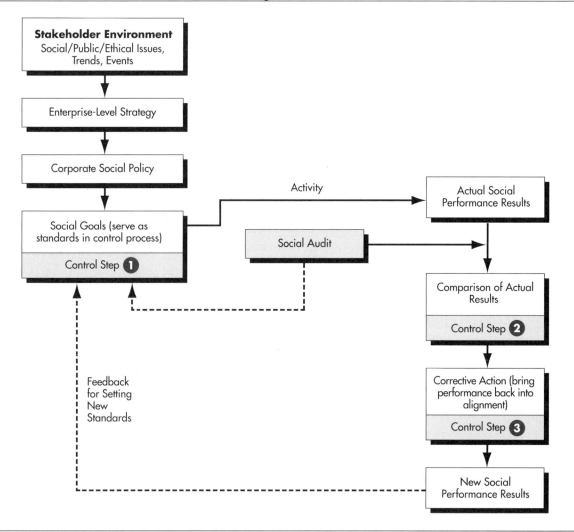

Evolution of Social Auditing and Reporting. The social audit as a concept for monitoring, measuring, and appraising the social performance of business dates back over 50 years to at least 1940.[24] In a 1940 publication of the Temporary National Economic Committee, Theodore J. Kreps presented a monograph titled "Measurement of the Social Performance of Business."[25] Another landmark in the development of social audits came in 1953 in a book by Howard R. Bowen.[26] Bowen's concept of the social audit was that of a high-level, independent appraisal conducted about every five years by a group of disinterested auditors. The auditors' report would be an evaluation with recommendations intended for internal use by the directors and the management of the firm audited.

In contrast to these earlier landmark models, the social audit as it came of age in the 1970s attempted to focus on such social performance categories as minority employment, pollution/environment, community relations, consumer issues, and philanthropic contributions. Very few companies initially undertook social audits as control mechanisms. To use a device as a control mechanism implied that there were some goals or standards against which to compare actual performance. Initially, social audits were employed by companies to examine what the company was actually doing in selected areas, appraise or evaluate social performance, identify social programs that the company thought it ought to be pursuing, or just inject into the general thinking of managers a social point of view.[27]

Social auditing fell out of favor in the 1980s. In the 1990s and early 2000s, however, there was some resurgence in interest in social performance, ethics, and values audits and reports. The company that stands out as one of the leaders in social auditing is The Body Shop. This should not be surprising inasmuch as the company's founder, Anita Roddick, once said that "Auditing shouldn't just be for accounting. A company should open its heart as well as its books."[28]

Examples of Social Auditing and Reporting.

One of the most comprehensive examples of social or ethical auditing is the process conducted by The Body Shop, the skin and hair products company. The Body Shop began its ethics audit process in the early 1990s, and the process yielded several major reports, the most complete of which was the *Values Report 1997.*[29]

This report was a 200-page volume that detailed the goals, approach, and results of the company's ethical auditing process. The volume contains the following key components of the company's corporate public policy: mission statement, founder's statement, social and ecological milestones 1995–1997, approach to ethical auditing, 1995–2000 targets, performance reports with respect to key stakeholder groups, and other reports.[30] The Body Shop's "Framework for Social Auditing and Disclosure" involves continuous improvement via the implementation of a cyclical audit loop.

One of The Body Shop's units, The Body Shop in Australia, released its own social audit via the Internet in 2001. The social audit of the Australian unit utilized a methodology based upon opinions and relevant information being gathered from stakeholder groups via interviews, facilitated group discussions, and surveys. Participants included employees, customers, suppliers, and education outreach clients. The initial audit was conducted by a consultant. Then, community and academic leaders were invited to examine the report.[31]

One additional indicator of the increasing popularity of social auditing recently is the appearance of consulting and research firms willing to help companies conduct audits. SmithOBrien Services, for example, offers as a core service the "Corporate Responsibility Audit.™" The company describes its audit as a "multidisciplinary methodology for identifying and eliminating often-overlooked negative effects of a company's operations on its stakeholders, and thus reducing legal exposure, production inefficiencies, and reputational risk."[32] The research firm WalkerInformation of Indianapolis, which provides measurement services to companies that want to know more about their impact on key stakeholder groups, also deserves mention because its service is similar to social auditing.[33] WalkerInformation's "Reputation and Stakeholder Assessment" is a comprehensive tool for measuring and managing stakeholder relationships. Through its assessment process, Walker gathers information from multiple stakeholder groups and provides the company with a "scorecard" summary of how these groups perceive or evaluate the company's reputation. Among other measures, the scorecard shows a company's reputation relative to that of the competition and of world-class leaders in other industries.[34]

One of the most significant consulting initiatives in the realm of social auditing was undertaken in 1998–1999 by the consulting firm KPMG in London, which created a social auditing consulting unit. Major clients of KPMG have included The Body Shop, Royal Dutch Shell, and Cooperative Insurance, a niche player in the British market that promotes itself as an ethical investor. The model for KPMG's social auditing was patterned after the approach developed in the book that Wheeler and Sillanpää wrote, *The Stakeholder Corporation*, referred to earlier in Chapter 3. This book lays out a detailed approach by which companies might improve their social, environmental, and financial performance by a process of inclusion and dialogue with groups both inside and outside the organization. Wheeler agrees that social auditing is "an embryonic market at the moment," but he expects the demands for the company's services to increase in the future.[35] Another excellent example of social performance reporting may be seen in the "Living our Values: Corporate Social Responsibility" report of Starbucks Coffee. This report is available online at http://www.starbucks.com/csr.

Finally, it should be mentioned that some social audits only focus on some specialized area of corporate performance such as the natural environment. Today, **environmental auditing**, as a subset of social auditing, has been very popular. Awards are even given for successful environmental auditing practices. Toward the end of 2003, for example, *Business Ethics* magazine gave its Environmental Reporting Award to Baxter Healthcare Corporation. The award was given because Baxter has played a sustained leadership role at the cutting edge of environmental auditing and reporting. Baxter was bold enough in its reporting to go beyond the typical PR and even admit when the company fell short of its ambitious goals.[36]

Motorola has always had a commitment to quality in its products and efficiency in its manufacturing processes. The company is evidently also solidly behind the principles espoused in the Global Reporting Initiative (GRI). In its latest Global Citizenship Report, Morotola claims it has met or exceeded environmental, health, and safety goals, as reporting in *PR Newswire* (18 May 2004). You can read about Motorola's achievement by logging on to InfoTrac College Edition at **http://www.infotrac-college.com** and keying record number A116740311.

Global Reporting Initiative.

One of the major impediments to the advance of effective social auditing and performance reporting is the absence of standardized measures for social reporting. Standardization is a challenge that has been undertaken by a consortium of over 300 global organizations called the **Global Reporting Initiative (GRI)**. The GRI is an extension of the U.S.-based Coalition for Environmentally Responsible Economies (CERES), which developed many of the now-accepted environmental reporting guidelines. GRI wishes that all companies would adopt its guidelines, but it is too early to determine whether this will take place. It is expected that many companies will use the standards as a kind of "best practices" document.[37] GRI's Web page states its purpose as follows:

> *The Global Reporting Initiative (GRI) is a multi-stakeholder process and independent institution whose mission is to develop and disseminate globally applicable Sustainability Reporting Guidelines. These Guidelines are for voluntary use by organisations for reporting on the economic, environmental, and social dimensions of their activities, products, and services. The GRI incorporates the active participation of representatives from business, accountancy, investment, environmental, human rights, research and labour organisations from around the world.[38]*

The GRI was established in late 1997, issued draft guidelines in 1999, revised guidelines in 2000, and by 2002 became a permanent, independent, international body with a multistakeholder governance structure involving business, accountancy, human rights, environmental, labor, and governmental organizations. U.S. companies participating include Agilent, Baxter International, Ford, Nike, GM, and Texaco.[39]

Ethics in Practice

NOT MUCH RANGE FOR THIS MANAGER

I used to work for a golf course at their driving range. The basic responsibility of my fellow employees and me was quite simple. We took money from customers, gave them a basket of golf balls to hit, made sure the supply of golf balls was adequate, and moved the tees on the driving range so there would be decent grass for the players to hit off. It was well known that everyone, including our manager, gave away free baskets of balls to family members and, occasionally, good friends. When the golf course acquired a new golf professional, the giving away of free baskets of balls was supposed to cease.

After the new golf pro had been working for a couple of months, he realized that all, or some, of the range personnel were still giving away free baskets of balls. Our manager at the time was still giving away free balls, along with all the employees, but the golf pro was not aware of this factor. The golf pro proceeded to talk to our manager and tell him that he needed to fire the employee who was continuing to give away free baskets of balls.

Because the job at the range did not require much work, everyone was laid back about the job and came in a little late almost every day. Our manager, who

was regularly late at least 15 to 30 minutes, set this trend. Within a week of the golf pro telling our manager to fire the employee who was giving away the free baskets, I noticed that the employee who had been working there for the longest time had been fired. Once this employee was gone, our manager wrote up a new set of rules and posted them in the office. The first rule was NO FREE BASKETS OF BALLS. NO EXCEPTIONS! When I read this new rule, I assumed the fired employee got caught by the golf pro giving away free baskets of balls. After I spoke with the fired employee, he told me that our manager fired him due to excessive tardiness.

1. Who, if anyone, in this case acted in an unethical manner? If they did, how?

2. Should I have told the golf pro the whole story? If I did, how would it affect the other employees and me?

3. Does the employee who was fired have a legal recourse to pursue further action?

Contributed Anonymously

As firms develop enterprise-level strategies and corporate public policies, the potential for social and ethical auditing and reporting remains high. Social auditing is best appreciated not as an isolated, periodic attempt to assess social performance but rather as an *integral part* of the overall strategic management process as it has been described here. Because the need to improve planning and control will remain as long as management desires to evaluate its corporate social performance, the need for approaches such as the social audit will likely be with us for some time, too. The net result of continued use and refinement should be improved corporate social performance and enhanced credibility of business in the eyes of its stakeholders and the public.

PUBLIC AFFAIRS

Public affairs (PA) and **public affairs management** are umbrella terms used by companies to describe the management processes that focus on the formalization and institutionalization of corporate public policy. The public affairs function is a logical and increasingly prevalent component of the overall strategic management process, which we discussed earlier. As an overall concept, public affairs management embraces corporate public policy, discussed earlier, along with **issues and crisis management**, which we consider in more detail in Chapter 5. Indeed, many issues management and crisis management programs are housed in **public affairs departments** or intimately involve public affairs professionals. Corporate public affairs also embraces the broad areas of governmental relations and corporate communications.

It is easy to get confused at this point by all the different terms that are used to describe management's efforts to address the stakeholder environment. Part of the confusion arises from the fact that companies use different titles for the same functions. For example, terms that are often used interchangeably by firms include "public affairs/external affairs," "public policy/corporate social responsibility," "corporate communications," and "public issues management/public affairs management." In addition, some companies create stand-alone public affairs departments without even addressing the strategic management issue or enterprise-level strategy.

PUBLIC AFFAIRS AS A PART OF STRATEGIC MANAGEMENT

In a comprehensive management system, which we have been describing in this chapter, the overall flow of activity would be as follows. A firm engages in strategic management, part of which includes the development of enterprise-level strategy, which poses the question, "What do we stand for?" The answers to this question should help the organization to form a corporate public policy, which is a more specific posture on the public, social, or stakeholder environment or specific issues within this environment. Some firms call this a *public affairs strategy.* Two important planning approaches in corporate public policy are issues management and, often, crisis management. These two planning aspects frequently derive from or are related to environmental analysis, which was mentioned earlier. Some companies embrace these processes as part of the corporate public affairs function. These processes are typically housed, from a departmental perspective, in a public affairs department. *Public affairs management* is a term that often describes all these components. Figure 4-8 helps illustrate likely relationships among these processes.

We will now consider how the public affairs function has evolved in business firms, what concerns public affairs departments currently face, and how public affairs thinking might be incorporated into the operating manager's job. This last issue is crucial, because public affairs management, to be most effective, is best thought of as an indispensable part of every manager's job, not as an isolated function or department that alone is responsible for the public issues and stakeholder environment of the firm.

EVOLUTION OF THE CORPORATE PUBLIC AFFAIRS FUNCTION

According to a former Public Affairs Council president, public affairs blossomed in the United States in the 1960s because of four primary reasons: (1) the growing magnitude and impact of government; (2) the changing nature of the political system, especially its progression from a patronage orientation to an issues orientation; (3) the growing recognition by business that it was being outflanked by interests that were counter to its own

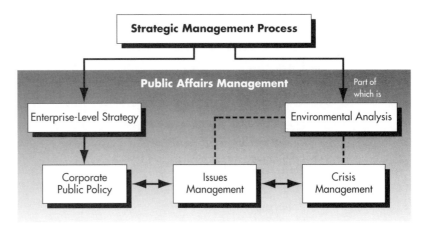

FIGURE 4-8

Relationships Among Key Corporate Public Affairs Concepts

on a number of policy matters; and (4) the need to be more active in politics outside the traditional community-related aspects, such as the symphony and art museums.[40]

Thus, the public affairs function as we know it today was an outgrowth of the social activism begun decades ago. Just as significant federal laws were passed in the early 1970s to address such issues as discrimination, environmental protection, occupational health and safety, and consumer safety, corporations responded with a surge of public affairs activities and creation of public affairs departments. Corporate public affairs departments or units, therefore, are clearly a product of the past 35 years.

Public Affairs Activities and Functions

Public affairs as a management function progressed out of isolated company initiatives designed to handle such diverse activities as community relations, corporate philanthropy and contributions, governmental affairs, lobbying, grassroots programs, corporate responsibility, and public relations. In some firms, the public relations staff handled issues involving communication with external publics, so it is not surprising that public affairs often evolved from public relations. Part of the confusion between public relations and public affairs is traceable to the fact that some corporate public relations executives changed their titles, but not their functions, to *public affairs*.

Richard Armstrong, former president of the Public Affairs Council, addressed the distinctions between **public relations (PR)** and public affairs (PA) in terms of their relative emphases, interests, and directions. He submits that the terminology is very important. The principal distinctions he has made are as follows: (1) whereas PR deals with government as one of many publics, PA professionals are experts on government, and (2) whereas PR has many communication responsibilities, PA deals with issues management and serves as a corporate conscience.[41]

Though modern public affairs may have evolved from early public relations efforts and company activities, today public affairs embraces public relations as one of its many functions.

According to a recent major survey of corporate public affairs, 64 percent of the companies surveyed included public relations in the list of activities they performed.[42]

According to the Public Affairs Council, the leading professional organization of executives who do the public affairs work of companies, its membership is composed of individuals with the following titles:[43]

- Vice presidents and senior vice presidents of
    Public affairs   Communications
    Corporate affairs   State government relations
    External affairs   Community relations and corporate foundations
    Government relations
- Heads of Washington, DC, offices
- Grassroots and PAC managers
- Legislative representatives
- Media relations directors
- Directors of international affairs
- Policy analysts
- Other public affairs staff

CURRENT PERSPECTIVES ON CORPORATE PUBLIC AFFAIRS

The Public Affairs Council, the major Washington-based professional association, has defined corporate public affairs as follows:

> *The management function responsible for monitoring and interpreting the corporation's non-commercial environment and managing the company's response to those factors.*[44]

SEARCH THE WEB

THE PUBLIC AFFAIRS COUNCIL

The Public Affairs Council (PAC) is the national organization of and for public affairs officers. It is based in Washington, DC. Members of the council are *Fortune* 500 corporations, emerging growth companies, associations, and consulting firms at the forefront of the public affairs field.

The PAC defines public affairs as the external, noncommercial activities of an organization. Some of the programs that the PAC offers include the following:

- Public affairs management
- Government affairs
- Issues management
- Community relations
- Political action committees
- Corporate communications
- Grassroots
- Corporate philanthropy
- International affairs
- Other related fields

To learn more about the Public Affairs Council, visit its Web site at **http://www.pac.org**.

This definition is quite broad and encompasses a wide assortment of activities. To appreciate what specific activities are typically included in this definition, it is useful to consider the results of a survey on the state of public affairs. This survey asked corporate respondents to indicate whether they included certain activities as parts of their public affairs function. Figure 4-9 lists the activities and the percentages of firms indicating they engaged in those activities. Government relations—federal, state, and local—heads the list, along with community relations and corporate contributions/philanthropy.[45]

Looking Out and Looking In.

Post and Kelley provide an excellent perspective on the public affairs function in organizations today. They state:

> *The public affairs function serves as a window: Looking out, the organization can observe the changing environment. Looking in, the stakeholders in that environment can observe, try to understand, and interact with the organization.*[46]

When the public affairs function is viewed in this way, it is easy to understand how Post and Kelley concluded that the "product" of the public affairs department is the smoothing of relationships with external stakeholders and the management of company-specific issues.

Buffering and Bridging.

Another important perspective on public affairs is also useful. Meznar and Nigh suggest that corporate public affairs activities can be broken into two types: activities that "buffer" the organization from the social and political environment and activities that "bridge" with that environment. They found that as organizations experienced increased environmental uncertainty, buffering and bridging increased as well. They concluded that building bridges with external environmental uncertainty was

---

FIGURE 4-9

Current Public Affairs Activities

Activity	Percent of Firms	Activity	Percent of Firms
Federal Government Relations	75	Public Interest Group Relations	51
State Government Relations	75	Educational Affairs/Outreach	44
Community Relations	71	Regulatory Affairs	43
Local Government Relations	69	Volunteer Program	41
Contributions/Philanthropy	69	Advertising	39
Grassroots	68	International Public Affairs	35
Issues Management	67	Environmental Affairs	29
Media Relations	66	Stockholder Relations	24
Political Action Committee	66	Institutional Investor	23
Public Relations	64	Consumer Affairs	17
Employee Communications	58		

SOURCE: James E. Post and Jennifer J. Griffin, *The State of Corporate Public Affairs* (Foundation for Public Affairs and Boston University School of Management, 1997), Figure 3.1. For similar data see J. J. Griffin, C.S. Fleisher, S. N. Brenner, and J. J. Boddewyn, "Corporate Public Affairs Research: Chronological Reference List," *Journal of Public Affairs* (Vol. 1, Issue 1, 2000), 9–32.

positively related to top management's philosophy.[47] Bridging is a proactive stance that is most likely to be undertaken by companies with a stakeholder orientation.

A significant challenge today for public affairs professionals is to conduct their functions in an ethical fashion. As public trends push organizations toward more transparency, there are many opportunities for questionable practices, especially in such arenas as political action, government relations, and communications. Therefore, it is encouraging to know that a code of conduct or set of ethical guidelines has been established for individuals working in public affairs. These ethical guidelines are set forth in Figure 4-10. They deserve scrutiny.

International Public Affairs Continues to Grow

It is essential at this point to provide some specific comments on international public affairs. Thirty years ago, the Public Affairs Council identified international PA as a new corporate

---

FIGURE 4-10

Ethical Guidelines for Public Affairs Professionals

The public affairs professional . . .

. . . maintains professional relationships based on honesty and reliable information, and therefore:

1. Represents accurately his or her organization's policies on economic and political matters to government, employees, shareholders, community interests, and others.

2. Serves always as a source of reliable information, discussing the varied aspects of complex public issues within the context and constraints of the advocacy role.

3. Recognizes the diverse viewpoints within the public policy process, knowing that disagreement on issues is both inevitable and healthy.

The public affairs professional . . .

. . . seeks to protect the integrity of the public policy process and the political system, and he or she therefore:

1. Publicly acknowledges his or her role as a legitimate participant in the public policy process and discloses whatever work-related information the law requires.

2. Knows, respects, and abides by federal and state laws that apply to lobbying and related public affairs activities.

3. Knows and respects the laws governing campaign finance and other political activities, and abides by the letter and intent of those laws.

The public affairs professional . . .

. . . understands the interrelation of business interests with the larger public interests, and therefore:

1. Endeavors to ensure that responsible and diverse external interests and views concerning the needs of society are considered within the corporate decision-making process.

2. Bears the responsibility for management review of public policies that may bring corporate interests into conflict with other interests.

3. Acknowledges dual obligations—to advocate the interests of his or her employer, and to preserve the openness and integrity of the democratic process.

4. Presents to his or her employer an accurate assessment of the political and social realities that may affect corporate operations.

SOURCE: The Public Affairs Council (Washington, DC), *1998 Annual Report*, 32. Reprinted with permission.

function and formed a task force to investigate it. Three points seemed to emerge time and again. First, it became obvious that more and more significant public affairs challenges and problems were occurring in the global arena, with greater impacts on the company. Second, the number of firms with effective international PA capacities was small and growing very slowly. Third, the task force found that serious internal and external challenges often made an international PA program more difficult than a domestic program.[48]

International public affairs, to function properly, must balance externally and internally focused activities. Externally, the central challenge is to manage the company's relations with various host countries where business is conducted. Requirements here include understanding and meeting host-country needs and dealing with diverse local constituencies, audiences, cultures, and governments. Internally, international PA programs must establish and coordinate external programs, educate company officials on PA techniques, and assist wherever possible the company's efforts to improve operations, activities, and image.[49] According to Post and Griffin's survey of corporate public affairs, international public affairs was found to be one of the fastest-growing new areas of public affairs activities.[50]

Competencies Needed. As international public affairs continues to grow, it is useful to think in terms of competencies that are needed in the global arena. Competencies include the knowledge, skills, and abilities that are necessary to successfully perform. Recently, Craig Fleisher, an expert on corporate public affairs, asserted that the following competencies are needed for successful international public affairs:[51]

*   *Development of intercultural competence.* This addresses how the practice of PA works in different nations.
*   *Knowing the impact of societal factors on public affairs.* For example, this includes state-to-state relations, level of economic development in different countries, and political ideologies.
*   *Understanding local public policy institutions and processes.* This entails understanding other countries' form of government, legal systems, and political culture.
*   *Nation state-specific applications of PA functions.* This includes knowing how community relations works, and all forms of stakeholder relations.
*   *Language skills.* The inability to speak multiple languages may put the PA professional at a disadvantage.
*   *Understanding global business ethics.* PA managers need to provide leadership in establishing, communicating, and maintaining ethical guidelines of companies at home and abroad.
*   *Managing international consultants, alliances, and issue partners.* Sometimes specialized assistance can only come from local experts, groups, or associations.

Continuing Research on Public Affairs

A baseline survey on the state of corporate public affairs was conducted by the Foundation for Public Affairs, and its findings were reported by James Post.[52] This survey of public affairs departments essentially supported the findings of his earlier survey but yielded a few additional trends worthy of mention.

In terms of the activities being emphasized by public affairs departments of major corporations, environmental affairs, education affairs, and grassroots activities were among the fastest-growing areas of new PA responsibility. Another important trend revealed by the survey was the reorganization of public affairs responsibilities within companies. The trend was toward more centralization of the PA function. Regarding involvement in political affairs, it had become apparent that companies were concentrating on three specific forms of corporate political involvement: visits to political officials, use of political action committees (PACs), and meetings with political candidates.[53]

The survey showed that corporate communication with various stakeholders on public policy issues had grown in recent years. It also had become apparent that there had been a shift in the past decade from separate political analysis and political action specialties within organizations toward more integrated approaches to issues management. In fact, the rise of issues management as an organizing concept in PA departments was confirmed in this survey. The growing importance of international public affairs was documented, and it was confirmed that many companies preferred to treat international public affairs as country-specific political matters that were best managed by local managers in the respective countries. Finally, it was apparent that measurement and evaluation of PA activities now were occurring in most companies surveyed.[54]

As organizations have become more sensitive to their investments in and expenditures on public affairs activities, the evaluation and measurement of public affairs management have increased. In a comprehensive study of this topic, Craig S. Fleisher found quite different approaches to evaluation and measurement taking place. He concluded that in common use were three evaluation archetypes based primarily on three factors: (1) the nature of PA evaluation policies/systems, where evaluations ranged from none to highly formalized; (2) the nature of the evaluation methods used, with methods ranging from mostly intuitive to mostly analytical; and (3) the nature of the information utilized, with information ranging from mostly objective to mostly subjective. An increasing trend toward evaluation and measurement was disclosed.[55]

Out of the focus on evaluation and measurement of public affairs activities has arisen the concept of public affairs **benchmarking**. Fleisher defines this as "an ongoing, systematic approach by which a public affairs unit measures and compares itself with higher performing and world-class units in order to generate knowledge and action about public affairs roles, practices, processes, products, services, and strategic issues that will lead to improvement in performance."[56] The concept of benchmarking had its origins in the total quality management (TQM) movement.

Findings and Trends.
To update what has been going on in the area of corporate public affairs, it is useful to look at some of the major findings of research into public affairs management. Researchers have found that various forces, perhaps most notably restructuring and downsizing driven by competitive pressures, have produced important changes. They found that there is a sharpened and expanded use of benchmarking. It has been found that nearly half the companies responding to surveys had undertaken benchmarking in the previous year. The rationales offered for this trend included mandates from the CEO and continuous self-improvement. The activities studied by way of benchmarking were most often PAC operations, issues management processes, Washington office operations, and philanthropy.[57]

Studies also have revealed that a large number of public affairs officers had reorganized their departments, partially or across the board, in recent years. Key trends seem to be (1) changes in organizational relationships, often caused by retirement and nonreplacement of previous senior public affairs staff; (2) new linkages to internal customers (e.g., in one company, each business unit has a specific PA executive assigned to service all its public affairs needs); and (3) contradictory trends in consolidation versus "disaggregation" of external public affairs functions.[58]

Other trends include use of the profit-center concept and increased attempts to measure the costs-benefits of PA efforts. PA has been seeking to contribute more to the "bottom line" by more deliberately and aggressively looking for marketing opportunities in government relations work (e.g., modifications in legislation or regulations that would increase the likelihood of government purchase of company products or services). Other trends in the use of technology include greater use of the Internet, using e-mail for company-wide alerts on breaking legislation, requiring lobbyists to use networked laptop computers, and using interactive computer systems to manage all aspects of public policy work.[59]

As a result of changes taking place in the environment of the past decade, Craig Fleisher, an expert on corporate public affairs, has proposed a "new public affairs model."[60] Fleisher proposes the new public affairs organization as one that:

1. Manages public affairs as an ongoing, year-round process, internally and externally
2. Cultivates and harvests the capability to build, develop, and maintain enduring stakeholder relationships
3. Recognizes the importance of managing the grassroots
4. Communicates in an integrated manner
5. Continuously aligns its values and strategies with the public's interests
6. Is systematically and proactively focused on helping the organization to compete

It is interesting to note that Fleisher names several nonprofit organizations as examples of organizations that have most effectively embraced these characteristics: the American Association of Retired Persons (AARP), the National Education Association, the American Medical Association (AMA), and the Christian Coalition. He says that all these organizations have achieved excellent levels of performance in the public policy marketplace through their practice of the new public affairs model.

It is becoming clear that public affairs management professionals today are keenly interested in making sure that their function continues to add value to the bottom lines of corporations. In an era of corporate downsizings and reorganizations, staff functions such as PA are quite susceptible to budget cuts by higher executives who do not see clearly how PA's performance, effectiveness, and efficiency contribute to the company's profitability and success. In keeping with this theme, it should be noted that one of the Public Affairs Council's most important handbooks is a collection of quality-oriented readings titled *Adding Value to the Public Affairs Function: Using Quality to Improve Performance*, by Peter Shafer[61] Figure 4-11 on page 122 depicts how a quality improvement program might be implemented in corporate public affairs. This theme and others are carried forward in the Public Affairs Council's handbook titled *Assessing, Managing and Maximizing Public Affairs Performance*.[62] In spite of the difficulty in measuring and assessing the contributions of public affairs, it has been argued that such measurement attempts should continue.[63]

Given the changes that have been taking place in corporate public affairs, it is useful to think about the knowledge, skills, and abilities that top public affairs officers need to have to be successful. A study of position advertisements for senior-level public affairs executives has led Fleisher to conclude that the following qualities are needed for successful public affairs management:[64]

- Established communication expertise
- Global perspective
- Integrity, credibility, and trust
- Management skills and experience
- Political and public policy insights
- Strategic thinking

FIGURE 4-11

Initiating a Quality Improvement Program in Public Affairs

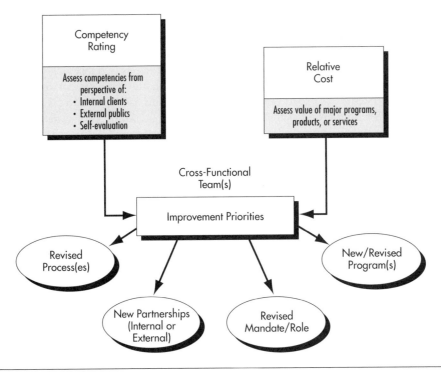

SOURCE: Peter Shafer, *Adding Value to the Public Affairs Function: Using Quality to Improve Performance* (Washington, DC: Public Affairs Council, 1994), 44.

PUBLIC AFFAIRS STRATEGY

We will not discuss the issue of **public affairs strategy** extensively, but it is useful to report the findings of a major research project that was undertaken by Robert H. Miles and resulted in the classic book titled *Managing the Corporate Social Environment: A Grounded Theory*. Because little work has been done on public affairs strategy, Miles's work deserves reference even though it cannot be thoroughly discussed. Miles's study focused on the insurance industry, but many of his findings may be applicable to other businesses.[65]

Design of External Affairs and Corporate Social Performance

Miles studied the external affairs strategies (also called *public affairs strategies*) of major insurance firms in an effort to see what relationships existed between the strategy and design of the corporate external affairs function and corporate social performance. He found that the companies that ranked best in corporate social performance had top management philosophies that were *institution oriented*. That is, top management saw the corporation as a social institution that had a duty to adapt to a changing society and thus needed a collaborative/problem-solving external affairs strategy. The **collaborative/problem-solving strategy** was one in which firms emphasized long-term relationships with a variety of external constituencies and broad problem-solving perspectives on the resolution of social issues affecting their businesses and industries.[66] Note how similar this is to the stakeholder management view and the bridge-building activity discussed previously.

Miles also found that the companies with the worst social performance records employed top management philosophies based on operation of the company as an independent economic franchise. Such philosophies were in sharp contrast with the institution-oriented perspectives of the best social performers. In addition, Miles found that these worst social performers employed an **individual/adversarial external affairs strategy**. In this posture, the executives denied the legitimacy of social claims on their businesses and minimized the significance of challenges they received from external critics. Therefore, they tended to be adversarial and legalistic.[67]

Business Exposure and External Affairs Design

On the subject of the external affairs units within firms, Miles found that a contingency relationship existed between what he called business exposure to the social environment and four dimensions of the external affairs design: breadth, depth, influence, and integration. High business exposure to the social environment means that the firm produces products or services that move them into the public arena because of such issues as their availability, affordability, reliability, and safety. In general, consumer products tend to be more "exposed" to the social environment than do commercial or industrial products.[68]

Breadth, depth, influence, and integration refer to dimensions of the external affairs unit that provide a measure of sophistication versus simplicity. Units that are high on these dimensions are sophisticated, whereas units low on these dimensions are simple. Miles found that firms with high business exposure to the social environment require more sophisticated units, whereas firms with low business exposure to the social environment could manage reasonably well with simple units.[69]

It is tempting to overgeneralize Miles's study, but we must note it as a significant finding in the realm of public affairs strategy and organizational design research. The important conclusion seems to be that a firm's corporate social performance (as well as its industry legitimacy and viability and economic performance) is a function of business exposure, top management philosophy, external affairs strategy, and external affairs design. Figure 4-12 on page 124 presents Miles's theory of corporate social performance, which remains valuable today.

Other initiatives in public relations strategy include integrating public affairs into corporate strategic planning, using strategic management audits for public affairs, building a balanced performance scorecard for public affairs, managing the corporation's reputation, and using core competencies to manage performance.[70]

| INCORPORATING PUBLIC AFFAIRS THINKING INTO ALL MANAGERS' JOBS

In today's highly specialized business world, it is easy for the day-to-day operating managers to let public affairs departments worry about government affairs, community relations, issues management, PR, or any of the numerous other PA functions. David H. Blake

FIGURE 4-12

Miles's Model of Corporate Social Performance

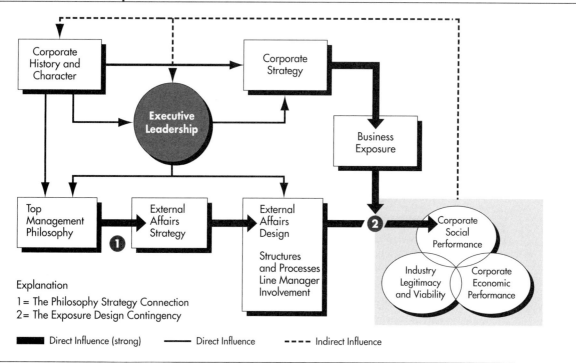

SOURCE: Robert H. Miles, *Managing the Corporate Social Environment: A Grounded Theory* (Englewood Cliffs, NJ: Prentice-Hall, Inc., 1987), 274. Reprinted with permission.

has taken the position that organizations ought to incorporate public affairs, or what we would call *public affairs thinking,* into every operating manager's job. He argues that operating managers are vital to a successful PA function, especially if they can identify the public affairs consequences of their actions, be sensitive to the concerns of external groups, act to defuse or avoid crisis situations, and know well in advance when to seek the help of the PA experts. There are no simple ways to achieve these goals, but four specific strategies may be helpful: (1) make public affairs truly relevant, (2) develop a sense of ownership of success, (3) make it easy for operating managers, and (4) show how public affairs makes a difference.[71] Each of these strategies is discussed in the following sections.

Make Public Affairs Truly Relevant

Operating managers often need help in seeing how external stakeholder factors can and do affect them. A useful mechanism is analysis of the manager's job in terms of the likely or potential impacts that her or his decisions may have on the stakeholder environment and possible developments in the environment that may affect the company or the decision maker. One procedure for doing this might be to list the manager's various impacts, the interested or affected strategic stakeholder groups, the potential actions of the groups, and the effects of the groups on jobs or the company.

Another mechanism is linking achievement of the manager's goals to public affairs. A plant manager, for example, can be shown how failure to pay attention to community groups can hinder plant expansion, increased output, and product delivery. Failure to address the affected stakeholders can be shown to be related to extensive delays as these neglected groups seek media attention or pressure local officials.

A third way to make PA relevant is to use the language of the operating manager. Instead of using the jargon of public affairs, every effort should be made to employ language and terms with which the manager is familiar. Thus, terms such as *environment* to mean *local community* and *stakeholder* to mean *employees and residents* must be used cautiously, because operating managers may not be able to fully comprehend them.[72]

Still another way to make public affairs relevant is to demonstrate to operating managers that several operations areas are affected by public affairs issues. Some of these key areas include marketing, manufacturing, and human resources. Some of the specifics in the manufacturing arena are product safety and quality, energy conservation, water pollution, air pollution, transportation, and raw materials. It is also suggested that public affairs should be linked with corporate planning.[73]

A topic of interest today to public affairs managers is that of moving jobs offshore. Many day-to-day managers are being asked to downsize their departments or to eliminate them entirely. This is a good example of a decision managers need to make that has public affairs implications and is quite relevant to today's operating managers.

Help Managers Develop a Sense of Ownership

It is helpful for operating managers to have participated in planning and goal setting and thus to have had an opportunity to develop a sense of ownership of the public affairs endeavor. Operating managers may be formally or informally enlisted in these planning efforts. At PPG Industries, Inc., operating managers have been given the responsibility for coordinating all actions concerning specific issues. As issue managers, they are asked to see to it that issue and environmental monitoring occurs, that strategy is developed, and that actions are implemented at various governmental levels.[74]

At Kroger, Inc., regional public affairs executives worked with the individual operating divisions as they have developed their business plans. A public affairs section has been included in each operating division's plan, and it is the division's plan, not the PA department's plan. As a result of these efforts, the divisions have begun to feel that they have "ownership" of the PA goals in their plans.[75] This approach seems to work much better than having PA executives simply impose goals or expectations on the operating units.

Make It Easy for Operating Managers

Operating managers have experience in meeting goals and timetables in their own realms. The PA area, however, can often appear nebulous, fuzzy, or inconclusive. Further, operating managers have neither the time for nor the interest in setting up systems or strategies for PA initiatives. This is where the PA professionals can assist them by making their tasks easier. Any procedures, data collection systems, or strategies that PA can supply should be used.

Training in public affairs can be helpful, too. Operating managers can better see the relevance and importance of PA work if carefully chosen topics are put on the agendas of their periodic training sessions. If PA effectiveness is to be monitored, measured, and made a part of performance evaluation systems, care must be taken to make sure that such systems are fair and straightforward, or at least understandable. If PA does not make a careful effort to ensure that its expectations are reasonably met, resistance, resentment, and failure will surely follow.

Show How Public Affairs Makes a Difference

Part of what professional PA staff members need to do is to keep track of public affairs successes in such a way that operating managers can see that their specific actions or efforts have led to identifiable successes for the company. A scorecard approach, whereby operating managers can see that their efforts have helped to avoid problems or prevent serious problems, is useful. The scorecard may be used to reinforce managers' efforts and to help other managers see the potential of the PA function. The scorecard should explicitly state the objectives that have been achieved, the problems that have been avoided, and the friends that have been made for the company.

Obviously, such a scorecard may be of a qualitative nature, but this is necessary in order to describe clearly what has been accomplished. Operating managers need to be shown that there are specific payoffs to be enjoyed from their public affairs efforts. It is up to the PA professionals to document these achievements. If no payoff is demonstrable from PA efforts, operating managers are likely to invest their time elsewhere.[76]

Public affairs is not just a specialized set of management functions to be performed by a designated staff. The nature of the tasks and challenges that characterize public affairs work is such that participation by operating managers is essential. It is likely that PA departments will continue to serve as the backbones of corporate organizations, but true effectiveness will require that operating managers be integrated into the accomplishment of these tasks. The mutual interdependence of these two groups—professionals and operating managers—will produce the best results.

▪ SUMMARY

Corporate public policy is a firm's posture or stance regarding the public, social, or ethical aspects of stakeholders and corporate functioning. It is a part of strategic management, particularly enterprise-level strategy. Enterprise-level strategy is the broadest, overarching level of strategy, and its focus is on the role of the organization in society. A major aspect of enterprise-level strategy is the integration of important core values into company strategy. The other strategy levels include the corporate, business, and functional levels. The strategic management process entails six stages, and a concern for social, ethical, and public issues may be seen at each stage. In the control stage, the social audit or social performance report is crucial. Environmental reporting is one popular subset of the social audit.

Public affairs might be described as the management function that is responsible for monitoring and interpret-

ing a corporation's noncommercial environment and managing its response to that environment. Public affairs is intimately linked to corporate public policy, environmental analysis, issues management, and crisis management. The major functions of public affairs departments today include government relations, political action, community involvement/responsibility, issues management, international public affairs, and corporate philanthropy. A continuing growth area is international public affairs.

In terms of public affairs strategy, a collaborative/problem-solving strategy has been shown to be more effective than one that is individualistic/adversarial. Research has shown that a firm's corporate social performance, as well as its industry legitimacy, viability, and economic performance, is a function of business exposure, top management's philosophy, external affairs strategy, and external affairs design. In addition to being viewed as a staff function, public affairs is important for operating managers. Four specific strategies for incorporating public affairs into operating managers' jobs include make it relevant, develop a sense of ownership, make it easy, and show how it can make a difference.

■ KEY TERMS

benchmarking (page 120)
business-level strategy (page 100)
collaborative/problem-solving strategy (page 123)
core values (page 104)
corporate-level strategy (page 100)
corporate public affairs (page 98)
corporate public policy (page 98)
enterprise-level strategy (page 100)
environmental auditing (page 112)
functional-level strategy (page 100)
Global Reporting Initiative (GRI) (page 112)
individual/adversarial external affairs strategy
   (page 123)

issues and crisis management (page 114)
public affairs (PA) (page 113)
public affairs department (page 114)
public affairs management (page 113)
public affairs strategy (page 122)
public relations (PR) (page 115)
social audit (page 109)
social performance report (page 109)
strategic management (page 99)
strategic management processes (page 97)
value shift (page 106)

■ DISCUSSION QUESTIONS

1. Explain the relationship between corporate public policy and strategic management.

2. Which of the four strategy levels is most concerned with social, ethical, or public issues? Discuss the characteristics of this level.

3. Identify the steps involved in the strategic management process.

4. What is a social audit? Describe how it may be seen as a tool for strategic control.

5. What is the difference between public relations and public affairs? Why has there been confusion regarding these two concepts?

6. Why do you think international public affairs is a major growth area? Give specific reasons for your answer.

7. What are the important qualities needed for public affairs officers or managers?

8. Differentiate between a collaborative/problem-solving strategy and an individual/adversarial strategy. Which seems to be more effective in corporate public affairs?

9. What are the major ways in which public affairs might be incorporated into every manager's job? Rank them in terms of what you think their impact might be.

■ RECOMMENDED CASES

Many of the end-of-text cases may be related to Chapter 4. You may wish to consider studying the following cases with Chapter 4.

Case 1. "WAL-MART: THE MAIN STREET MERCHANT OF DOOM." This case about Wal-Mart addresses and illustrates a host of business and society relationships. It especially raises the issue of a business's social responsibil-

ity to the community and its stakeholders. How should a company such as Wal-Mart integrate public issues into its strategic management? How has Wal-Mart's enterprise-level strategy been conceptualized and implemented? Would a social audit be useful to Wal-Mart? What would a corporate public affairs officer at Wal-Mart do to help the company?

Cases 2A and 2B; Cases 3A and 3B. "THE BODY SHOP INTERNATIONAL PLC." This series of four cases all address issues related to public policy, corporate social responsibility, social performance, and corporate citizenship. They especially raise the issue of balancing company profits with social initiatives. Evaluate how The Body Shop has integrated social issues into its core values and strategic management. Has The Body Shop's social auditing played an important role in its practices? Does The Body Shop need a public affairs officer? What would this person do?

Case 42. "SOCIAL REFORM OR SELF-INTEREST?" In this case, a newspaper publisher decides to become active and visible in promoting issues thinks are important to the community. His policies are not uniformly accepted. Evaluate this publisher's corporate social policy and enterprise-level strategy.

■ WEB RESOURCES

The URLs listed here are current at the time of publication. Should any of these Web sites change, please search under the company's or organization's name for an updated address.

America's Corporate Public Affairs Companies and Executives
http://www.americaslists.com/business/acpace.htm

Business for Social Responsibility
http://www.bsr.org

Business and Sustainable Development
http://www.bsdglobal.com/tools/principles_triple.asp

Business Roundtable
http://www.brtable.org

Centre for Corporate Public Affairs
http://www.accpa.com.au/default.php

Corporate Career Choices—Public Affairs
http://www.statefarm.com/careers/depts/corp_pa.htm

Corporate Accountability Project
http://www.corporation.org

Corporate Communication Institute
http://www.corporatecomm.org/research.html

Corporate Social Responsibility Newswire
http://www.csrwire.com

Council of Public Relations Firms
http://www.prfirms.org

Global Reporting Initiative
http://www.globalreporting.org

Journal of Public Affairs
http://www.henrystewart.com/journals/hspindex.htm

The Conference Board
http://www.conference-board.org

Public Affairs Council
http://www.pac.org

Public Affairs Management LLC
http://www.publicaffairsmgt.com/whatwedo.html

Public Affairs Newsletter
http://www.publicaffairsnews.com/intervie.htm

Public Interest Groups
http://www.pirg.org

Public Relations Society of America
http://www.prsa.org

Social Auditing: Determining Impact
http://www.caledonia.org.uk/socialland/social.htm

Social Auditing
http://www.neweconomics.org/gen/newways_socialaudit.aspx

Social Auditing
http://www.fpm.com/script/UK/Jun95/social.htm

The Wall Street Journal
http://www.wsj.com

U.S. Chamber of Commerce
http://www.uschamber.com

 InfoTrac® College Edition   http://www.infotrac-college.com

Articles from The Wall Street Journal *can be researched, retrieved, and read from your desktop using InfoTrac's online database.*

▪ ENDNOTES

1. Victoria Miles, "Auditing Promises: One Bank's Story," *CMA Management* (Vol. 74, No. 5, June 2000), 42–46.
2. "Software: Will Outsourcing Hurt America's Supremacy?" *Business Week* (March 1, 2004), 84–95.
3. Kenneth R. Andrews, *The Concept of Corporate Strategy*, 3d ed. (Homewood, IL: Irwin, 1987), 68–69.
4. R. Edward Freeman and Daniel R. Gilbert, Jr., *Corporate Strategy and the Search for Ethics* (Englewood Cliffs, NJ: Prentice Hall, 1988), 20. Also see R. Edward Freeman, Daniel R. Gilbert, Jr., and Edwin Hartman, "Values and the Foundations of Strategic Management," *Journal of Business Ethics* (Vol. 7, 1988), 821–834; and Daniel R. Gilbert, Jr., "Strategy and Ethics," in *The Blackwell Encyclopedic Dictionary of Business Ethics* (Malden, MA: Blackwell Publishers Ltd., 1997), 609–611.
5. Charles W. Hofer, Edwin A. Murray, Jr., Ram Charan, and Robert A. Pitts, *Strategic Management: A Casebook in Policy and Planning*, 2d ed. (St. Paul, MN: West Publishing Co., 1984), 27–29. Also see Gary Hamel and C. K. Prahalad, *Competing for the Future* (Boston: Harvard Business School Press, 1994).
6. H. Igor Ansoff, "The Changing Shape of the Strategic Problem," Paper presented at a Special Conference on Business Policy and Planning Research: The State of the Art (Pittsburgh, May 1977).
7. H. Igor Ansoff, *Implanting Strategic Management* (Englewood Cliffs, NJ: Prentice Hall, International, 1984), 129–151.
8. R. Edward Freeman, *Strategic Management: A Stakeholder Approach* (Boston: Pitman, 1984), 90.
9. *Ibid.*, 90–91. For further discussion, see Martin B. Meznar, James J. Chrisman, and Archie B. Carroll, "Social Responsibility and Strategic Management: Toward an Enterprise Strategy Classification," *Business & Professional Ethics Journal* (Vol. 10, No. 1, Spring 1991), 47–66. Also see William Q. Judge, Jr., and Hema Krishnan, "An Empirical Examination of the Scope of a Firm's Enterprise Strategy," *Business & Society* (Vol. 33, No. 2, August 1994), 167–190.
10. Laura Sessions Stepp, "Industrial-Strength Ethics, Being Tested in the Crucible of Reality," *The Washington Post National Weekly Edition* (April 8–14, 1991), 22–23.
11. *Ibid.*, 22–23.
12. *Ibid.*, 23.
13. Herman Miller Web page: http://www.hermanmiller.com.
14. Edward A. Robinson, "The Ups and Downs of the Industry Leaders," *Fortune* (March 2, 1998), 87.
15. James C. Collins and Jerry I. Porras, *Built to Last: Successful Habits of Visionary Companies* (HarperBusiness, 1994).
16. Patrick M. Lencioni, "Make Your Values Mean Something," *Harvard Business Review* (July 2002), 113–117.
17. Lynn Sharp Paine, *Value Shift: Why Companies Must Merge Social and Financial Imperatives to Achieve Superior Performance* (New York: McGraw-Hill, 2003).
18. C. W. Hofer and D. E. Schendel, *Strategy Formulation: Analytial Concepts* (St. Paul: West, 1978), 52–55. Also see J. David Hunger and Thomas L. Wheelen, *Essentials of Strategic Management* (Reading, MA: Addison-Wesley, 2000).
19. Kenneth R. Andrews, *The Concept of Corporate Strategy*, 3d ed. (Homewood, IL: Irwin, 1987), 18–20.
20. W. Edward Stead and Jean Garner Stead with Mark Starik, *Sustainable Strategic Management* (Armonk, NY: M.E. Sharpe, 2004).
21. Archie B. Carroll, *Business and Society: Managing Corporate Social Performance* (Boston: Little, Brown, 1981), 381.
22. Peter Lorange, Michael F. Scott Morton, and Sumantra Ghoshal, *Strategic Control Systems* (St. Paul, MN: West, 1986), 1, 10. Also see Hunger and Wheelen, 161–162.
23. David H. Blake, William C. Frederick, and Mildred S. Myers, *Social Auditing: Evaluating the Impact of Corporate Programs* (New York: Praeger, 1976), 3. Also see Roger Spear, "Social Audit and Social Economy" (August 8, 1998), http://www.ny.airnet.ne.jp/ccij/eng/public-e.htm.
24. Archie B. Carroll and George W. Beiler, "Landmarks in the Evolution of the Social Audit," *Academy of Management Journal* (September 1975), 589–599.
25. Theodore J. Kreps, *Measurement of the Social Performance of Business, Monograph No. 7*, "An Investigation of Concentration of Economic Power for the Temporary National Economic Committee" (Washington, DC: U.S. Government Printing Office, 1940).
26. Howard R. Bowen, *Social Responsibilities of the Businessman* (New York: Harper & Row, 1953).
27. John J. Corson and George A. Steiner, *Measuring Business's Social Performance: The Corporate Social Audit* (New York: Committee for Economic Development, 1974), 33.
28. Quoted in Jackie Blondell, "Body Language," *Australian CPA* (Vol. 71, No. 2, March 2001), 28–29.
29. The Body Shop, *Values Report 1997* (October 1997). For more information, visit the Body Shop Internet Web site at http://www.the-body-shop.com.
30. *Ibid.*
31. Jackie Blondell, *ibid.*, 29.
32. SmithOBrien Services (August 22, 1998), http://www.smithobrien.com/1Frame.html.

33. WalkerInformation, "Reputation and Stakeholder Assessment" (Indianapolis: WalkerInformation, undated).

34. *Ibid.*, 2–3.

35. Tim Watts, "Social Auditing: the KPMG UK Experience," *Australian CPA* (Vol. 69, No. 8), 46–47.

36. "Socially Responsive Business Is No Longer One-Size-Fits-All" *Business Ethics* (December 15, 2003), news release.

37. "Dow Social Reporting Raises Bar: Chemical Firm Voluntarily Releases a Lot of Negative Information," *Investor Relations Business* (March 6, 2000), 1: 12–23.

38. Global Reporting Initiative Web page: http://www.global reporting.org/about/brief.asp.

39. Global Reporting Initiative Web page: http://www.global reporting.org.

40. Craig S. Fleisher, "Evaluating Your Existing Public Affairs Management System," in Craig S. Fleisher (ed.), *Assessing, Managing and Maximizing Public Affairs Performance* (Washington, DC: Public Affairs Council, 1997), 4.

41. Richard A. Armstrong, "Public Affairs vs. Public Relations," *Public Relations Quarterly* (Fall 1981), 26. Also see Craig S. Fleisher and Natasha M. Blair, "Tracing the Parallel Evolution of Public Affairs and Public Relations: An Examination of Practice, Scholarship, and Teaching." Paper presented at The Fifth International Public Relations Research Symposium, Lake Bled, Slovenia, July 1998.

42. James E. Post and Jennifer J. Griffin, *The State of Corporate Public Affairs: Final Report* (Washington, DC, and Boston: Foundation for Public Affairs, 1997), Figure 3.1.

43. Public Affairs Council Web page: http://www.pac.org/page/WhoWeAre.shtml.

44. Public Affairs Council (Washington, DC: Public Affairs Council), 5.

45. Post and Griffin.

46. James E. Post and Patricia C. Kelley, "Lessons from the Learning Curve: The Past, Present and Future of Issues Management," in Robert L. Heath and Associates, *Strategic Issues Management* (San Francisco: Jossey-Bass, 1988), 352.

47. Martin B. Meznar and Douglas Nigh, "Buffer or Bridge? Environmental and Organizational Determinants of Public Affairs Activities in American Firms," *Academy of Management Journal* (August 1995), 975–996.

48. The Public Affairs Council, "International Public Affairs: A Preliminary Report by a PAC Task Force" (Washington, DC: Public Affairs Council, April 1983), 2. For further perspectives on international public affairs, see D. Jeffrey Lenn, Steven N. Brenner, Lee Burke, Diane Dodd-McCue, Craig S. Fleisher, Lawrence J. Lad, David R. Palmer, Kathryn S. Rogers, Sandra S. Waddock, and Richard E. Wokutch, "Managing Corporate Public Affairs and Government Relations: U.S. Multinational Corporations in Europe," in James E. Post (ed.), *Research in Corporate Social Performance and Policy*, Vol. 14 (Greenwich, CT: JAI Press, 1993), 103–108.

49. The Public Affairs Council, "Effective Management of International Public Affairs" (Washington, DC: Public Affairs Council, April 1985), 1.

50. Post and Griffin, Figure 3.2.

51. Craig S. Fleisher, "The Development of Competencies in International Public Affairs," *Journal of Public Affairs* (Vol. 3, No. 1, 2003), 76–82.

52. James E. Post and the Foundation for Public Affairs, "The State of Corporate Public Affairs in the United States: Results of a National Survey," in James E. Post (ed.), *Research in Corporate Social Performance and Policy*, Vol. 14 (Greenwich, CT: JAI Press, 1993), 79–89.

53. *Ibid.*, 81–85.

54. *Ibid.*, 85–88.

55. Craig S. Fleisher, "Public Affairs Management Performance: An Empirical Analysis of Evaluation and Measurement," in James E. Post (ed.), *Research in Corporate Social Performance and Policy*, Vol. 14 (Greenwich, CT: JAI Press, 1993), 139–163.

56. Quoted in Peter Shafer, "Benchmarking: Here's a Management Fad You Could Learn to Love," *Impact* (July/August 1994), 1–3. Also see Craig S. Fleisher, *Public Affairs Benchmarking: A Comprehensive Guide* (Washington, DC: Public Affairs Council, 1995).

57. Post and Griffin. Also see "Public Affairs: Its Origins, Its Present and Its Trends," http://www.pac.org.

58. *Ibid.*

59. *Ibid.*

60. Craig S. Fleisher, "The New Public Affairs," *Impact* (July/August 1998), 1–3.

61. Peter Shafer, *Adding Value to the Public Affairs Function: Using Quality to Improve Performance* (Washington, DC: Public Affairs Council, 1994).

62. Fleisher (1997).

63. Don C. Richards, "Corporate Public Affairs: Necessary Cost or Value-Added Asset," *Journal of Public Affairs* (Vol. 3, No. 1, 2003), 39–51.

64. Craig S. Fleisher, "The Evolving Profile, Qualifications and Roles of the Senior Public Affairs Officer," *Journal of Public Affairs* (Vol. 2, No. 2, 2002), 90–94.

65. Robert H. Miles, *Managing the Corporate Social Environment: A Grounded Theory* (Englewood Cliffs, NJ: Prentice-Hall, Inc., 1987).

66. *Ibid.*, 8.

67. *Ibid.*, 9–10, 111.

68. *Ibid.*, 2–3.

69. *Ibid.*, 11, 113.

70. Fleisher (ed.) (1997), 139–196.

71. David H. Blake, "How to Incorporate Public Affairs into the Operating Manager's Job," *Public Affairs Review* (1984), 35.
72. *Ibid.*, 36–38.
73. John E. Fleming, "Linking Public Affairs with Corporate Planning," *California Management Review* (Winter 1980), 42.
74. Blake, 38–39.
75. Jack W. Partridge, "Making Line Managers Part of the Public Affairs Team: Innovative Ideas at Kroger," in Wesley Pederson (ed.), *Cost-Effective Management for Today's Public Affairs* (Washington, DC: Public Affairs Council, 1987), 67. Also see Fleisher (1997).
76. *Ibid.*, 40–41. Also see Craig Fleisher and Darren Mahaffy, "Building the Balanced Performance Scorecard for Public Affairs," in Fleisher (1997), 152–156.

Chapter 5

ISSUES MANAGEMENT *and* CRISIS MANAGEMENT

CHAPTER LEARNING OUTCOMES

After studying this chapter, you should be able to:

1　Distinguish between the conventional and strategic approaches to issues management.
2　Identify and briefly explain the stages in the issues management process.
3　Describe the major components in the issues development process and some of the factors that have characterized issues management in actual practice.
4　Define a crisis and identify the four crisis stages.
5　List and discuss the major stages or steps involved in managing business crises.

Throughout this book, we will discuss major social and ethical issues that have become controversies in the public domain. Some have been serious events or crises that continue to serve as recognizable code words for business—Love Canal, Three Mile Island, the Tylenol poisonings, the Union Carbide Bhopal tragedy, the Exxon *Valdez* oil spill, the Coca-Cola soft drink recalls in Europe, and the Firestone/Ford tread separation controversy. In September 2001, the attacks on the Twin Towers of the World Trade Center in New York and the Pentagon presented an unprecedented crisis not only for the businesses located there but others as well. The shock waves of this terrorist attack on the symbols of global capitalism will be felt for many years to come, and the traumatic event and those that have followed have surely put the topic of crisis management back on the front burner of business's agenda. Immediately following the terrorist attacks, the Enron, WorldCom, Arthur Andersen, and other financial scandals started being reported and even today continue to represent an issue, in general, and a crisis, specifically, for many of these companies.

Other issues—employee rights, sexual harassment, product safety, food safety, workplace safety, sweatshops, bribery and corruption, smoking in the workplace, affirmative action, deceptive advertising, and so on—have not been characterized as being of crisis proportions. Nevertheless, to business these are formidable social and ethical issues that have evolved over time and that must be addressed.

Managerial decision-making processes known as **issues management** and **crisis management** are two major ways by which business has responded to these situations. These two approaches symbolize the extent to which the environment has become turbulent and the public has become sensitized to business's responses to the issues that have emerged from this turbulence. In today's environment of instantaneous and global communication, no event is too small to get noticed by everyone.

In the ideal situation, issues management and crisis management might be seen as the natural and logical by-products of a firm's development of enterprise-level strategy and overall corporate public policy, but this has not always been the case. Some firms have not thought seriously about public and ethical issues. For them, these approaches represent first attempts to come to grips with the practical reality of a threatening social environment.

Many firms have been fortunate that major crises have not materialized to stun them as they did in the Johnson & Johnson Tylenol poisonings, the Union Carbide Bhopal explosion, the Procter & Gamble Rely tampon crisis, the Dow Corning breast implant probe, the crashes of TWA Flight 800 and ValuJet Flight 592, the cyanide-tainted Sudafed capsule crisis that led to two deaths, or the attacks on the World Trade Center. Thus, they have seen what major business crises can do to companies without having experienced such crises themselves. Such firms should now be concerned with issues management and crisis management in preparing for an uncertain future.

Like all planning processes, issues management and crisis management have many characteristics in common. They also have differences, and we have chosen to treat them separately for discussion purposes. One common thread that should be mentioned at the outset is that both processes are focused on improving stakeholder management and enabling the organization to be more ethically responsive to stakeholders' expectations. Issues and crisis management, to be effective, must have as their ultimate objective an increase in the organization's social responsiveness to its stakeholders. They are also related to the extent that effective issues management may enable managements to engage in more effective crisis management. That is, some crises may be anticipated and avoided through a carefully implemented issues management initiative.

Figure 5-1 provides examples of major issue categories and specific crises that have occurred within these issue categories. A review of this figure should clearly illustrate the differences between issues and crises.

ISSUES MANAGEMENT

Issues management is a process by which organizations identify issues in the stakeholder environment, analyze and prioritize those issues in terms of their relevance to the organization, plan responses to the issues, and then evaluate and monitor the results. It is helpful to think of issues management in connection with concepts introduced in the preceding chapter, such as the strategic management process, enterprise-level strategy, corporate public policy, and environmental analysis. The process of strategic management and environmental analysis requires an overall way of managerial thinking that includes economic, technological, social, and political issues. Enterprise-level strategy

FIGURE 5-1

Issue Categories and Specific Crises Within Categories

Issue Categories

Food, Beverage, and Product Safety	Health-Related Products	Corporate Fraud and Ethics
Crises	Crises	Crises
Coke and Pepsi: India's Parliament alleged soft drinks contained pesticide residue (2004).	Banned dietary supplements androstenedione and ephedra by FDA: Crisis for dozens of pharmaceutical and vitamin firms (2004).	Enron: Scandal began with off-the-books partnerships, aggressive accounting, and allegations of fraud and bankruptcy (2001–2004).
Coke's Dasani bottled water: High levels of bromate led to recall in Great Britain (2004).	Tobacco companies: Dangerous products and advertising. Allegations of addictions and death by cancer (1990s–2004).	WorldCom: CEO Bernard Ebbers charged with massive accounting fraud (2003–2004).
Mad Cow Disease crisis: Outbreaks in Europe and Canada have created crises in sales and safety for meat industry (2001–2004).	Dow Corning: Silicone breast implants alleged to lead to serious health problems (1994).	Arthur Andersen: Implicated in Enron scandal, resulting in eventual dissolution of firm (2002).
Firestone and Ford: Tire tread separation outbreak (2001–2002).	Johnson & Johnson: Cyanide-tampering Tylenol poisonings (1982).	Tyco: CEO Kozlowski and CFO Swartz charged with corrupt practices, looting company, and tax evasion (2003–2004).
Food Lion: Supermarket chain accused by ABC-TV's *Prime Time Live* of selling spoiled meat (1992).	A. H. Robins: Dalkon Shield sales suspended when linked to pelvic inflammatory diseases resulting in spontaneous abortions (1982–1984).	Martha Stewart: Charged with securities fraud, perjury, and obstruction of justice (2003–2004).
Safeway Stores: Deli closed when health authorities alleged salmonella in sausages (1997).	Procter & Gamble: Rely tampons recalled when associated with toxic shock syndrome (1980).	Mutual fund scandal: Four companies accused of trading after markets had closed (2003–2004).
Sandhurst Farms: Orange juice recalled due to claim metal fragments found in bottle (1996).		HealthSouth: Founder and CEO Scrushy indicted on charges he cooked the books while the board stood by (2003).
Perrier Water: Suspected carcinogen benzene found in water (1994).		

and corporate public policy, on the other hand, focus on public or ethical issues. Issues management, then, devolves from these broader concepts.

Two Approaches to Issues Management

Thinking about the concepts mentioned here requires us to make some distinctions. A central consideration seems to be that issues management has been thought of in two major ways: (1) narrowly, in which public, or social, issues are the primary focus, and (2) broadly, in which strategic issues and the strategic management process are the focus of attention. Fahey has provided a useful distinction between these two approaches. He refers to (1) the conventional approach and (2) the strategic management approach.[1]

The **conventional approach** (narrowly focused) **to issues management** has the following characteristics:[2]

- Issues fall within the domain of public policy or public affairs management.
- Issues typically have a public policy/public affairs orientation or flavor.

- An issue is any trend, event, controversy, or public policy development that might affect the corporation.
- Issues originate in social/political/regulatory/judicial environments.

The **strategic management approach** (broadly inclusive) **to issues management** has evolved in a small number of companies and is typified by the following:[3]

- Issues management is typically the responsibility of senior line management or strategic planning staff.
- Issues identification is more important than it is in the conventional approach.
- Issues management is seen as an approach to the anticipation and management of external and internal challenges to the company's strategies, plans, and assumptions.

The strategic approach to issues management has also been advocated by such authorities as H. Igor Ansoff[4] and William R. King.[5] Figure 5-2 portrays strategic issues management as depicted by Ansoff. Note the "strategic" characteristics—threats/opportunities and strengths/weaknesses—that we alluded to in the preceding chapter.

At the risk of oversimplification, we will consider the principal distinction between the two perspectives on issues management to be that the conventional approach focuses on public/social issues, whereas the strategic approach is broadly inclusive of all issues. In addition, the conventional approach can be used as a "stand alone" decision-making process, whereas the strategic approach is intimately interconnected with the strategic management process as a whole. Another difference may be whether operating managers, strategic planners, or public affairs staff members are implementing the system. Beyond these distinctions, the two approaches have much in common.

Our discussion in this chapter will emphasize the conventional approach, because this book focuses on public, social, and ethical stakeholder issues. We should point out, however, that our purpose in the preceding chapter was to convey the notion that social issues ought to be seen as just one part of the broader strategic management process. There we discussed environmental analysis as a broad phenomenon. Now we emphasize social or ethical issues, although it is obvious that a consideration of these issues is embedded in a larger, more strategically focused process, such as that depicted in Figure 5-2.

Therefore, we are comfortable with both of these perspectives on issues management. We should point out that the conventional approach could be perceived as a subset of the strategic approach, although this is typically not the way companies see it. In a sense, the two approaches are highly inseparable, and it is difficult for organizations to operate effectively unless both are addressed in some way. For our purposes, however, the conventional perspective will be emphasized.

The Changing Issue Mix

The emergence in the past two decades of new "company issues management groups" and "issues managers" has been a direct outgrowth of the changing mix of issues that managers have had to handle. Economic and financial issues have always been an inherent part of the business process, although their complexity seems to have increased as international markets have broadened and competitiveness has become such an important issue. The growth of technology, especially the Internet, has presented business with other issues that need to be addressed. The most dramatic growth has been in social, ethical, and political issues—all public issues that have high visibility, media appeal, and interest among special-interest stakeholder groups. We should further observe that these issues become more interrelated over time.

FIGURE 5-2

STRATEGIC ISSUE MANAGEMENT

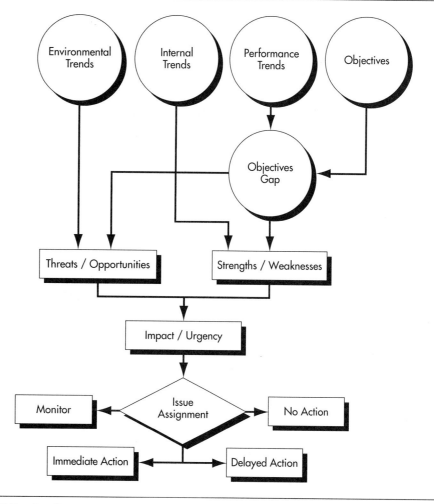

SOURCE: H. Igor Ansoff, "Strategic Issue Management," *Strategic Management Journal* (Vol. 1, 1980), 137. Reprinted by permission of John Wiley & Sons, Ltd.

For most firms, social, ethical, political, and technological issues are at the same time economic issues, because firms' success in handling them frequently has a direct bearing on their financial statuses, reputations, and economic well-being. Over time, there is a changing mix of issues and an escalating challenge that management groups face as these issues create a cumulative effect.

A Portfolio Approach.
Many firms get affected by so many issues that one wonders how they can deal with them all. One way is to see no connection between the issues; that is, issues are seen on an issue-by-issue basis. An alternative to this view is the **"portfolio approach"** advocated by Heugens, Mahon, and Wartick.[6] These researchers

maintain that experience with prior issues is likely to influence future issues and, therefore, a portfolio view is in order. Such a portfolio view provides focus and coherence to the firm's dealing with the mix of issues it faces. Issues that might show up in Royal Dutch Shell's issue portfolio, for example, might be stopping climate change, protecting biodiversity, reducing wastewater, and operating in sensitive regions. A company such as Shell might deal with hundreds of issues, but the issue portfolio helps to prioritize the company's resources. The nonadoption of certain issues into the portfolio does not signal neglect, but is part of a rational process of issues management.[7]

Issue Definition and the Issues Management Process

Before describing the issues management process, we should briefly discuss what constitutes an issue and what assumptions we are making about issues management. An **issue** may be thought of as a matter that is in dispute between two or more parties. The dispute typically evokes debate, controversy, or differences of opinion that need to be resolved. At some point, the organization needs to make a decision on the unresolved matter, but such a decision does not mean that the issue is resolved. Once an issue becomes public and subject to public debate and high-profile media exposure, its resolution becomes increasingly difficult. One of the features of issues, particularly those arising in the social or ethical realm, is that they are ongoing and therefore require ongoing responses.

Joseph Coates *et al.*, authors of *Issues Management*,[8] identify the following characteristics of an "**emerging issue**":

- The terms of the debate are not clearly defined.
- The issue deals with matters of conflicting values and interest.
- The issue does not lend itself to automatic resolution by expert knowledge.
- The issue is often stated in value-laden terms.
- Trade-offs are inherent.

John Mahon has described how complicated the question of issue definition can be in his observation about the multiple viewpoints that come into play when an issue is considered. He has noted that there are multiple stakeholders and motivations in any given management situation. Personal stakes frequently can be important factors but often are ignored or not taken into consideration. For example, some of the participants may be interested in the issue from a deep personal perspective and will not compromise or give up their positions even in the face of concrete evidence that clearly refutes them.[9] Thus, we can see that the resolution of issues in organizations is not easy.

What about the assumptions we make when we choose to use issues management? Coates *et al.* go on to say that the following assumptions are made:[10]

- Issues can be identified earlier, more completely, and more reliably than in the past.
- Early anticipation widens the organization's range of options.
- Early anticipation permits study and understanding of the full range of issues.
- Early anticipation permits the organization to develop a positive orientation toward the issue.
- The organization will have earlier identification of stakeholders.
- The organization will be able to supply information to influential publics earlier and more positively, thus allowing them to better understand the issue.

These are not only assumptions of issues management but also benefits to the extent that they make the organization more effective in its issues management process.

Model of the Issues Management Process.

Like the strategic management process that entails a multitude of sequential and interrelated steps or stages, the issues management process has been conceptualized by many different authorities in a variety of ways. Conceptualizations of issues management have been developed by companies, academics, consultants, and associations. The issues management process we will discuss here has been extracted from many of the conceptualizations previously developed. This process represents the elements or stages that seem to be common to most of those conceptualizations and consistent with the stakeholder orientation we have been developing and using.

Figure 5-3 presents a model of the issues management process as we will discuss it. It contains *planning aspects* (identification, analysis, ranking/prioritization of issues, and formulation of responses) and *implementation aspects* (implementation of responses and evaluation, monitoring, and control of results). Although we will discuss the stages in the issues management process as though they were discrete, we should recognize that in reality they may be interrelated and overlap one another.

Identification of Issues.

Many names have been given to the process of issue identification. At various times, the terms *social forecasting*, *futures research*, *environmental scanning*, and *public issues scanning* have been used. Similarly, many techniques have been employed. All of these approaches/techniques are similar, but each has its own unique

FIGURE 5-3

The Issues Management Process

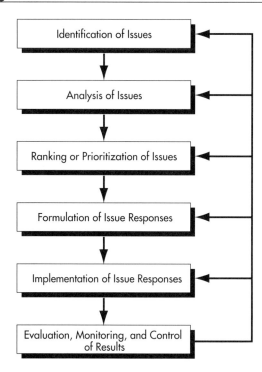

characteristics. Common to all of them, however, is the need to scan the environment and to identify emerging issues or trends that might later be determined to have some relevance to or impact on the organization.

Issue identification, in its most rudimentary form, involves the assignment to some individual in the organization the tasks of continuously scanning a variety of publications—newspapers, magazines, specialty publications, the World Wide Web—and developing a comprehensive list of issues. Often this same person, or group, is instructed to review public documents, records of congressional hearings, and other such sources of information. One result of this scanning is an internal report or a newsletter that is circulated throughout the organization. The next step in this evolution may be for the company to subscribe to a trend information service or newsletter that is prepared and published by a private individual or consulting firm that specializes in environmental or issue scanning.[11]

Two popular trend-spotting services have been (1) the author/consultant John Naisbitt, who was thrust into public recognition by his bestseller *Megatrends*, and (2) Yankelovich (formerly Yankelovich, Skelly, and White), the New York-based social research firm. For fees that range in the tens of thousands of dollars per year and more, these professionals provide firms with materials they have assembled.[12] Among the services they offer are newsletters, short weekly or monthly reports, telephone bulletins, and quarterly visits to discuss what the trends mean. Trend spotters do not claim clairvoyance, but they do say that they have less psychological resistance than their clients to seeing impending change.[13]

John Naisbitt has claimed to be different from many trend spotters. His original approach, which has been controversial, was based on the belief that trends start with isolated local events. As Naisbitt once stated, "The really important things that happen always start somewhere in the countryside. Taken together, what's going on locally is what's going on." Thus, according to Naisbitt, it is what people are doing, not what they are saying, that provides the most reliable pictures of issues. Naisbitt has continued his identification of public issues with *Megatrends 2000: Ten New Directions for the 1990s, Global Paradox, Megatrends Asia,* and *High Tech/High Touch.*[14]

Yankelovich, on the other hand, pursued a diametrically opposed strategy. Years ago, through long interviews, the company identified 35 widespread social trends, such as rejection of authority and female careerism. They then developed a survey made up of questions that assess the strengths of these trends, and each year they administer the questionnaire to 2,500 people. Yankelovich tracks the waxing and waning of these trends and claims to predict the trends' relative strengths for the next 5 years. For tens of thousands of dollars yearly, each of the service's sponsors gets the survey's results, a videocassette on the meaning of the results, a book discussing the implications of the results, and individual consulting.[15]

Futurist T. Graham Molitor, who has been a consultant on futures research, proposed that there are five leading forces as predictors of social change:[16]

- Leading events
- Leading authorities/advocates
- Leading literature
- Leading organizations
- Leading political jurisdictions

If these five forces are monitored closely, impending social change can be identified and, in some cases, predicted. Figure 5-4 presents Molitor's five leading forces, as well as

While trend spotting sounds like a field that might concentrate on predicting skirt lengths or shoe designs for next summer's fashions, it's a valuable tool for companies as varied as Hallmark, GE, and even accounting firms, according to Judith Trotsky, writing in *U.S. News & World Report* (19 April 2004 v136 i13 p4). Trotsky suggests that trends "often begin as anomalies, [as] something unusual or unique that strikes a chord." Spotting trends can involve math models, raw statistics, or right-brain intuition. You can read how various companies capitalize on trend spotting by logging on to InfoTrac College Edition at **http://www.infotrac-college.com** and keying record number A115238031.

FIGURE 5-4

Examples of Forces Leading Social Change

Leading Forces	Examples	Public Issue Realm
Events	Enron, WorldCom, Arthur Andersen	Corporate governance, fraud
	World Trade Center attacks	Security against terrorism
	Three Mile Island/Chernobyl nuclear plant explosions	Nuclear plant safety
	Bhopal explosion	Plant safety
	Earth Day	Environment
	Tylenol poisonings	Product tampering
	Love Canal	Toxic waste-environment
	Rely tampons	Product safety
	Ivan Boesky scandal	Insider trading abuses
	Thomas hearings	Sexual harassment
	Valdez oil spill	Environment
		Citizen mobilization, corporate hegemony
Authorities/Advocates	Ralph Nader	Consumerism
	Rachel Carson	Pesticides and genetic engineering
	Rev. Martin Luther King	Civil rights
	Rev. Jesse Jackson	Blacks' rights
	General Colin Powell	Volunteerism
Literature	*Global Warming* (John Houghton)	Global warming
	Unsafe at Any Speed (Ralph Nader)	Automobile safety
	Megatrends (John Naisbitt)	Issues identification
Organizations	Friends of the Earth	Environment
	Sierra Club	Environment
	Action for Children's Television (ACT)	Children's advertising
	People for the Ethical Treatment of Animals (PETA)	Animal rights
	Mothers Against Drunk Driving (MADD)	Highway safety/alcohol abuse
Political Jurisdictions	State of Michigan—Whistle-Blower Protection Act	Employee freedom of speech
	State of Delaware	Corporate governance
	States of Massachusetts, Vermont, California	Gay marriage, civil unions

examples that might be thought to illustrate his points. The attacks on the World Trade Center in New York and the Pentagon in Washington in 2001 and the wars in Afghanistan and Iraq have doubtlessly added the issue of "preparation for terrorism" to future lists of leading events portending significant social change. National security and business security are now vital issues for managers today.

Molitor is president and founder of Public Policy Forecasting, Inc. Molitor estimates that he buys 1,000 books a year to add to the 30,000 books filling his personal library. He says he scans some 60 publications each day, trying to identify trends or issues that may have implications for businesses and governments. Molitor has assembled an amazing reservoir of knowledge as he has spent four decades advising hundreds of *Fortune* 500 companies and institutions on how the world might change the next day, the next decade, even the next millennium, and how to make the most of these changes.[17]

Companies vary considerably in their willingness to spend tens or hundreds of thousands of dollars for the kinds of professional services we have described, but some rely almost exclusively on these kinds of sources for issue identification. Others use less costly and more informal means.

Though the source of all issues is the external environment, the internal perception of and managerial treatment of issues greatly affects the issue identification process. The key in issue identification is getting the people who are regularly confronted with issues in touch with top managers who can do something about them. According to Pursey Heugens, this process has two aspects. First, is **issues selling**. According to Dutton *et al.*, this relates to middle managers exerting upward influence in organizations as they try to attract the attention of top managers to issues that are salient to them and the organization.[18] The second part of this process, according to Heugens, is **issue buying**. This involves top managers adopting a more open mind-set for the issues that matter to their subordinates.[19] In short, the issue identification process is significantly affected by internal organization members and their assessments as to what is salient to the organization.

Analysis of Issues.

The next two steps in the issues management process (analysis and ranking of issues) are closely related. To analyze an issue means to carefully study, dissect, break down, group, or engage in any specific process that helps you better understand the nature or characteristics of the issue. An analysis requires that you look beyond the obvious manifestations of the issue and strive to learn more of its history, development, current nature, and potential for future relevance to the organization. William King proposed a series of key questions that focus on stakeholder groups in attempting to analyze issues:[20]

- Who (which stakeholders) is affected by the issue?
- Who has an interest in the issue?
- Who is in a position to exert influence on the issue?
- Who has expressed opinions on the issue?
- Who ought to care about the issue?

In addition to these questions, a consulting firm—Human Resources Network—proposed the following key questions to help with issue analysis:[21]

- Who started the ball rolling? (Historical view)
- Who is now involved? (Contemporary view)
- Who will get involved? (Future view)

Answers to these questions place management in a better position to rank or prioritize the issues so that it will have a better sense of the urgency with which the issues need to be addressed.

Ranking or Prioritization of Issues.

Once issues have been carefully analyzed and are well understood, it is necessary to rank them in some form of a hierarchy of importance or relevance to the organization. We should note that some issues management systems place this step before analysis. This is done especially when it is desired to screen out those issues that are obviously not relevant and deserving of further analysis.

The prioritization stage may range from a simple grouping of issues into categories of urgency to a more elaborate or sophisticated scoring system. Two examples will serve to illustrate the grouping technique. Xerox has used a process of categorizing issues into three classifications: (1) *high priority* (issues on which management must be well informed), (2) *nice to know* (issues that are interesting but not critical or urgent), and (3) *questionable* (issues that may not be issues at all unless something else happens). PPG Industries has grouped issues into three priorities: *Priority A* (critical issues that warrant executive action and review), *Priority B* (issues that warrant surveillance by the division general manager or staff), and *Priority C* (issues that have only potential impact and warrant monitoring by the public affairs department).[22]

A somewhat more sophisticated approach uses a **probability-impact matrix** requiring management to assess the *probability of occurrence* of an issue (high, medium, or low) on one dimension and its *impact on the company* (high, medium, or low) on the other dimension. In using such an approach, management would place each issue in the appropriate cell of the matrix, and the completed matrix would then serve as an aid to prioritization. As a variation on this theme, management could rank issues by considering the mathematical product of each issue's impact (for example, on a scale from 1 to 10) and probability of occurrence (on a scale from 0 to 1).

William King has provided a somewhat more elaborate issues-ranking scheme. He recommends that issues be screened on five filter criteria: strategy, relevance, actionability, criticality, and urgency.[23] Once each issue has been scored on a 10-point scale on each criterion, issues are then ranked according to their resulting point totals. Figure 5-5 illustrates this filtering/ranking process. Other techniques that have been used in issues identification, analysis, and prioritization include polls/surveys, expert panels, content analysis, the Delphi technique, trend extrapolation, scenario building, and the use of precursor events or bellwethers.[24]

Earlier we described a simple issues identification process as involving an individual in the organization or a subscription to a newsletter or trend-spotting service. The analysis and ranking stages could be done by an individual, but more often the company has

FIGURE 5-5

The Filtering and Ranking of Issues

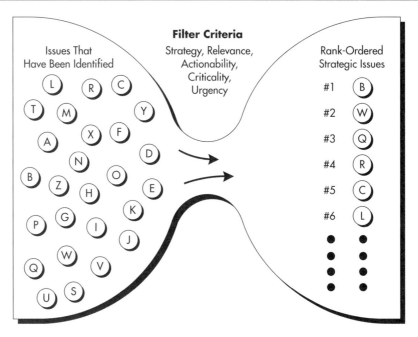

SOURCE: William R. King, "Strategic Issue Management," in William R. King and David I. Cleland (eds.) *Strategic Planning and Management Handbook* (New York: Van Nostrand Reinhold, 1987), 257. Reprinted with permission.

moved up to a next stage of formalization. This next stage involves assignment of the issues management function to a team, often as part of a public affairs department, which begins to specialize in the issues management function. This group of specialists can provide a wide range of issues management activities, depending on the commitment of the company to the process.

A number of companies have created issues management units to alert management to emerging trends and controversies and to help mobilize the companies' resources to deal with them. Firms such as Arco, Monsanto, and Sears are among those that have used such units. At Monsanto, an issues manager organized a committee of middle managers to help do the work. At Arco, the group monitored hundreds of publications, opinion polls, and think-tank reports. It then prepared its own daily publication called *Scan*, which summarized considerable data for over 500 company middle managers and top executives. The group tracked over 140 issues in all.[25]

Formulation and Implementation of Responses.

Formulation and implementation of responses are two steps in the issues management process that are combined here for discussion purposes. We should observe that the formulation and implementation stages in the issues management process are quite similar to the corresponding stages we discussed in the preceding chapter, which pertained to the strategic management process as a whole.

Formulation in this case refers to the response design process. Based on the analysis conducted, companies can then identify options that might be pursued in dealing with the issues, in making decisions, and in implementing those decisions. Strategy formulation refers not only to the formulation of the actions that the firm intends to take but also to the creation of the overall strategy, or degree of aggressiveness, employed in carrying out those actions. Options might include aggressive pursuit, gradual pursuit, or selective pursuit of goals, plans, processes, or programs.[26] All of these more detailed plans are part of the strategy formulation process.

Once plans for dealing with issues have been formulated, *implementation* becomes the focus. There are many organizational aspects that need to be addressed in the implementation process. Some of these include the clarity of the plan itself, resources needed to implement the plan, top management support, organizational structure, technical competence, and timing.[27]

Evaluation, Monitoring, and Control.

These recognizable steps in the issues management process were also treated as steps in the strategic management process in Chapter 4. In the current discussion, they mean that companies should continually evaluate the results of their responses to the issues and ensure that these actions are kept on track. In particular, this stage requires careful monitoring of stakeholders' opinions. A form of stakeholder audit—something derivative of the social audit discussed in Chapter 4—might be used. The information that is gathered during this final stage in the issues management process is then fed back to the earlier stages in the process so that changes or adjustments might be made as needed. Evaluation information may be useful at each stage in the process.

We have presented the issues management process as a complete system. In actual practice, companies apply the stages in various degrees of formality or informality as needed or desired. For example, because issues management is more important in some situations than in others, some stages of the process may be truncated to meet the needs of different firms in different industries. In addition, some firms are more committed to issues management than others.

Issues Development Process

A vital attribute of issues management is that issues tend to develop according to an evolutionary pattern. This pattern might be thought of as a developmental or growth process or, as some have called it, a life cycle. It is important for managers to have some appreciation of this **issues development process** so that they can recognize when an event or trend is becoming an issue and also because it might affect the strategy that the firm employs in dealing with the issue. Companies may take a variety of courses of action depending on the stage of the issue in the process.

One view of the issues development process holds that issues tend to follow an 8-year curve, although it is very difficult to generalize about the time frame, especially in today's world of instantaneous global communications. For the first 5 years or so of this hypothetical period, a nascent issue emerges in local newspapers, is enunciated by public-interest organizations, and is detected through public-opinion polling. According to Margaret Stroup, former director of corporate responsibility at Monsanto, the issue is low-key and flexible at this stage.[28] During this time, the issue may reflect a felt need, receive media coverage, and attract interest-group development and growth. A typical firm may notice the issue but take no action at this stage. John Mahon's view is that more issues-oriented firms may become more active in their monitoring and in their attempts to shape or help "define the issue."[29] Active firms have the capacity to prevent issues from going any further, through either effective responses to the issues or effective lobbying.

In the fifth or sixth year of the cycle, national media attention and leading political jurisdictions (for example, cities, states, countries) may address the issue. In the United States, issues managers have identified several "precursor" or bellwether states where national issues frequently arise first. Many experts think these states include California, Oregon, Florida, Michigan, and Connecticut.[30] Quite often, federal government attention is generated in the form of studies and hearings; legislation, regulation, and litigation follow. Today, it would not be uncommon for issues to mature much more quickly than the 8-year model just described. Figure 5-6 on page 146, however, presents a simplified view of what this issue development life cycle process might look like.

We should note that the stages in the process, especially the early stages, might occur in a different sequence or in an iterative pattern. Further, not all issues complete the process; some are resolved before they reach the stage of legislation or regulation. Thomas G. Marx takes the view that issues go from social expectations to political issues to legislation and finally to social control.

Illustrations of Issue Development.

Marx illustrates this evolution through two examples. First, consider the issue of environmental protection. The social expectation was manifested in Rachel Carson's book *Silent Spring* (1963); it became a political issue in Eugene McCarthy's political platform (1968); it resulted in legislation in 1971-1972 with the creation of the EPA; and it was reflected in social control by emissions standards, pollution fines, product recalls, and environmental permits in later years. The second example involves product/consumer safety. The social expectation was manifested in Ralph Nader's book *Unsafe at Any Speed* (1964); it became a political issue

FIGURE 5-6

Issue Development Life Cycle Process

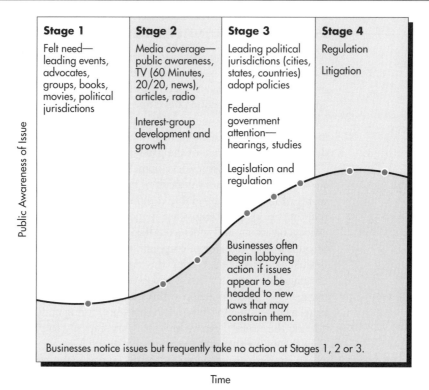

Stage 1	Stage 2	Stage 3	Stage 4
Felt need— leading events, advocates, groups, books, movies, political jurisdictions	Media coverage— public awareness, TV (60 Minutes, 20/20, news), articles, radio Interest-group development and growth	Leading political jurisdictions (cities, states, countries) adopt policies Federal government attention— hearings, studies Legislation and regulation	Regulation Litigation

Businesses often begin lobbying action if issues appear to be headed to new laws that may constrain them.

Businesses notice issues but frequently take no action at Stages 1, 2 or 3.

Public Awareness of Issue

Time

through the National Traffic Auto Safety Act and Motor Vehicle Safety Hearings (1966); it resulted in legislation in 1966 with the passage of the Motor Vehicle Safety Act and mandatory seat belt usage laws in four states (1984); and it was reflected in social control through the ordering of seat belts in all cars (1967), defects litigation, product recalls, and driver fines.[31] Both environmental protection and product/consumer safety remain as important issues today.

Finally, we are reminded by Bigelow, Fahey, and Mahon that "issues do not necessarily follow a linear, sequential path, but instead follow paths that reflect the intensity and diversity of the values and interests stakeholders bring to an issue and the complexity of the interaction among . . ." all the variables.[32] This should serve as a warning not to oversimplify the issues development process.

Issues Management in Practice

Issues management in practice today has very much become a subset of activities performed by the public affairs departments of major corporations, as noted in the previous chapter. A late 1990s survey of corporate public affairs officers of major corporations revealed that 67 percent engage in issues management functions. The percentage today is in this general arena. Furthermore, the survey revealed that there is now greater use of interdepartmental issues teams, with the public affairs department serving as coordinator and strategist but with appropriate line and staff executives charged with ultimate accountability for implementation. In practice, therefore, it can be seen that issues management does not function as a stand-alone activity but has been subsumed into a host of functions for which modern public affairs departments take responsibility.[33]

Issues management faces a serious challenge in business today. From the standpoint of the turbulence in the stakeholder environment, issues management may be needed. To become a permanent part of the organization, however, issues management will have to continuously prove itself. We can talk conceptually about the process with ease, but the field still remains somewhat nebulous even though it is struggling to become more scientific and legitimate. Managers in the real world want results, and if issues management cannot deliver those results, it will be destined to failure as a management process.

Some companies have claimed specific successes for their issues management programs. S. C. Johnson & Sons, the maker of floor waxes and other chemicals, claimed it removed environmentally chancy fluorocarbons from its aerosol sprays 3 years before federal action required the industry to do so. Sears claims it spotted the flammable-nightwear controversy early and got nonflammable goods into its stores before government action mandated it. Bank of America claimed it was alerted early by its issues managers about a practice known as "redlining" and took action to change its lending policies 2 years before Congress required banks to disclose whether they were barring all loans in certain parts of a city. According to the bank, its early action reduced its eventual cost of compliance significantly and spared it "a lot of grief and antagonism from cities and public-interest groups."[34] In the final analysis, identifiable successes such as these will be needed to ensure the future of issues management.

According to research by Pursey Heugens, companies that adopted issues management processes developed better overall reputations, better issue-specific reputations, and perform better financially in both the short and longer terms than organizations that do not practice issues management.[35] Tying issues management in with stakeholder management, Heugens also found that the most successful companies used stakeholder integration techniques in their implementation. In the current context, this meant that the firms actively sought to establish close-knit ties with a broad range of external and internal stakeholders and successfully incorporated their values and interests into management decisions.[36]

Issues Management Is a Bridge to Crisis Management

Ideally, firms use issues management to assist them in planning for and preventing crises that then require crisis management. Issues management represents careful planning that may head off impending crises. This is because many crises are embedded in issues or erupt from issues that could have been anticipated and studied in carefully designed issues management processes. Figure 5-1 illustrated the kinds of crises that may emanate from issue categories. Issues management can be seen as a form of precrisis planning. It is intended to help organizations anticipate and plan for possible crisis eruptions. Not all crises can be planned for, of course, but many can be anticipated through effective issues management programs. It has been suggested by Kate Miller that one of the most effective ways for keeping a crisis plan "living" is issues management.[37] Thus, we can see how issues and crisis management are different, but intimately related. Because of this relationship, issues management may be seen as a bridge to crisis management.

CRISIS MANAGEMENT

Crisis management as a management concept is largely a product of the past two decades. This has been the era of the megacrisis: Union Carbide's Bhopal disaster, which killed over 2,000 people in India; Johnson & Johnson's Tylenol poisonings, which resulted in numerous deaths; Procter & Gamble's Rely tampon crisis, in which that product was associated with toxic shock syndrome; and the terrifying attacks on the World Trade Center in New York, which resulted in the deaths of approximately 3,000 people. Other significant crises have included the following:

- Enron, WorldCom, Arthur Andersen, Tyco, and other companies accused of financial scandals and malfeasance.
- ValuJet's Flight 592 crashed in the Florida Everglades, killing all 110 people on board.
- Two skywalks collapsed in the Kansas City Hyatt Regency Hotel.
- TWA Flight 800 from New York to Paris crashed off the coast of Long Island.
- Schwan's ice cream company was charged as the responsible party in a salmonella outbreak in 39 states.
- Star-Kist Foods was charged with shipping rancid and decomposing tuna.
- Dow Corning was targeted in an FDA silicone breast implant probe.
- Sudafed capsules were tainted with cyanide, leading to two deaths.
- Perrier Water's benzene incident led to product recalls.
- Hurricane Andrew devastated businesses in south Florida.
- Twenty-four customers of Luby's Cafeteria in Killeen, Texas, were shot to death during a lunch-hour massacre.
- Intel's distribution of flawed Pentium chips in computers created a nightmare for the company.
- A federal building in Oklahoma City was bombed in 1995, resulting in the deaths of well over 100 persons.

SEARCH THE WEB

INSTITUTE FOR CRISIS MANAGEMENT (ICM)

ICM defines a crisis as:

"a significant business disruption which stimulates extensive news media coverage. The resulting public scrutiny will affect the organization's normal operations and also could have a political, legal, financial and governmental impact on its business."

There are four basic causes of a business crisis:

- Acts of God (storms, earthquakes, volcanic action, etc.)
- Mechanical problems (ruptured pipes, metal fatigue, etc.)
- Human errors (the wrong valve was opened, miscommunication about what to do, etc.)
- Management decisions/indecision (the problem is not serious, nobody will find out)

Most of the crises ICM has studied fall in the last category and are the result of management not taking action when they were told about a problem that eventually would grow into a crisis.

To learn more about crisis management, check out the ICM's Web site at **http://www.crisisexperts.com**.

Ethics in Practice

TYLENOL: JOHNSON & JOHNSON'S CRISIS MANAGEMENT CASE IS NOW A CLASSIC

The 1982 Tylenol poisonings is the case that put "crisis management" into the permanent management lexicon. The facts are legendary. In the fall of 1982, a murderer added 65 milligrams of cyanide to some Tylenol capsules while they were on store shelves. Seven people were killed, including three persons in one family. Johnson & Johnson (J&J), makers of Tylenol, quickly recalled and destroyed 31 million capsules at an expense of about $100 million. James Burke, the company CEO, made numerous appearances in TV ads and in news conferences notifying consumers of the actions the company was taking. Tamper-resistant packaging was quickly introduced, and the sales of Tylenol swiftly snapped back to near precrisis sales levels. The perpetrator of this crime was never found.

Many continue to hold the Tylenol case up as the classic response to a crisis. Experts argue that 'fessing up and taking corrective action quickly is the best form of crisis management. A major lesson to come out of the Tylenol crisis is that companies can take action quickly and effectively and prosper in spite of extreme adversity that befalls them.

1. Some say it was easy for J&J to take this action because the crisis did not originate within the company. Did this fact set the stage for the company's quick recovery? Would things have been different had the company been at fault?

2. How is the Tylenol case similar to or different from Ford and Firestone's linkage with dangerous tires or WorldCom, Tyco, Enron, and HealthSouth's malfeasance resulting in company leaders being accused of scheming to enrich themselves at the injury of others?

3. Was J&J really being socially responsible or were they quickly acting in their own best financial interests?

SOURCE: Eric Dezenhall, "Tylenol Can't Cure All Crises," *USA Today* (March 18, 2004), 15A. Copyright © 2004 by Dezenhall Resources.

- Coca-Cola experienced a crisis when its soft drinks were associated with illnesses in Belgium, France, and India.
- Firestone and Ford were implicated in massive tire recalls due to faulty tires causing tread separations and deaths.

It has been said by a number of observers, including Ian Mitroff, author of *Managing Crises Before They Happen*, that the Tylenol poisonings in 1982 was the case that put crisis management "on the map." That is, it was the case that marked the beginning of the new corporate discipline known as crisis management because Johnson & Johnson's voluntary recall of some 31 million Tylenol capsules was the first important example of an organization assuming responsibility for its products without being forced to do so.[38] Thus, the field of crisis management is just over 20 years old.

It should be apparent from the list of crises that there is a major distinction between issues management, discussed in the preceding section, and crisis management, the subject of this section. Issues typically evolve gradually over a period of time and represent a category of concern. Issues management is a process of identifying and preparing to respond to potential issues. Crises, on the other hand, occur abruptly. They cannot always be anticipated or forecast. Some crises occur within an issue category considered; many do not. Issues and crisis management are related, however, in that they both are concerned about organizations becoming prepared for uncertainty in the stakeholder environment.

The Nature of Crises

There are many kinds of crises. Those mentioned here have all been associated with major stakeholder groups and have achieved high-visibility status. Hurt or killed customers, hurt employees, injured stockholders, and unfair practices are the concerns of modern crisis management. Not all crises involve such public or ethical issues, but these kinds of crises almost always ensure front-page status. Major companies can be seriously damaged by such episodes, especially if the episodes are poorly handled.

What is a crisis? Dictionaries state that a **crisis** is a "turning point for better or worse," an "emotionally significant event," or a "decisive moment." We all think of crises as being emotion charged, but we do not always think of them as turning points for better or for worse. The implication here is that a crisis is a decisive moment that, if managed one way, could make things worse but, if managed another way, could make things better. Choice is present, and how the crisis is managed can make a difference.

From a managerial point of view, a line needs to be drawn between a problem and a crisis. Problems, of course, are common in business. A crisis, however, is not as common. A useful way to think about a crisis is with a definition set forth by Laurence Barton:

> *A crisis is a major, unpredictable event that has potentially negative results. The event and its aftermath may significantly damage an organization and its employees, products, services, financial condition, and reputation.*[39]

Another definition set forth by Pearson and Clair is also helpful in understanding the critical aspects of a crisis:

> *An organizational crisis is a low-probability, high-impact event that threatens the viability of the organization and is characterized by ambiguity of cause, effect, and means of resolution, as well as by a belief that decisions must be made swiftly.*[40]

According to crisis management experts quoted in Wendy Melillo's article for *ADWEEK* (13 October 2003 v44 i40 p26), Star-Kist and Heinz violated a key crisis management guideline: "Companies should always respond to a crisis in some way. . . . The classic mistake is remaining silent." Melillo explores several recent crises, including Martha Stewart's and Arthur Andersen's legal troubles, offering strategies that might have worked better in each case. Read more about the importance of crisis management in "a world of scandals" by logging on to InfoTrac College Edition at **http://www.infotrac-college.com** and keying record number A109268745.

Consider, for a moment, the case referred to earlier wherein Star-Kist Foods, a subsidiary of H. J. Heinz Co., faced a management crisis. Gerald Clay was appointed general manager of the Canadian subsidiary and was given the mandate to develop a 5-year business strategy for the firm. Just after his arrival in Canada, the crisis hit: The Canadian Broadcasting Corporation accused his company of shipping 1 million cans of rancid and decomposing tuna. Dubbed "Tunagate" by the media, the crisis dragged on for weeks. With guidance from Heinz, Clay chose to keep quiet, even as the Canadian prime minister ordered the tuna seized. The silence cost plenty. According to Clay's boss, "We were massacred in the press." The company, which used to have half the Canadian tuna market, watched revenues plunge by 90 percent. At one point, Clay's boss observed that the company's future was in doubt.[41] In the recent Firestone tire tread separation tragedy, many observers have wondered out loud whether the tire brand can be saved after the company has been ravaged by this crisis. Ford, for its part, has been fighting to save its Explorer SUV, which has been implicated in the tread separation controversy. Figure 5-7 presents a "how not to do it" case in crisis management as experienced by former New York Stock Exchange chairman, Dick Grasso. Grasso was under fire for taking $8.4 million in severance pay on top of his controversial $140 million compensation.

Being prepared for crises has become a primary activity in a growing number of companies. Part of being prepared entails knowing something about the nature of crises. Steven Fink conducted a major survey of *Fortune* 500 firms on the subject and wrote one of the first books on crisis management. Fink's survey disclosed that a staggering 89 percent of those who responded agreed that "a crisis in business today is as inevitable as

FIGURE 5-7

Crisis Management: How Not to Do It

In 2003, Dick Grasso, chairman of the New York Stock Exchange (NYSE), was under fire for his compensation level and bonuses he would receive in severance pay. Grasso was forced out under pressure on revelations that NYSE directors had agreed to give him nearly $140 million, mostly deferred compensation, and retirement pay. Supporters say he deserved this under contracts entered into. Detractors thought that this was unethical and should have been investigated further and the propriety of the compensation process be validated. Grasso was implicated in the series of controversies that raged over executive compensation and CEO malfeasance.

The news of Grasso's controversial $140 million compensation created a media firestorm. He then proceeded to make some of the same crisis and PR blunders that others had recently made, according to McCarthy and Shell, writers for *USA Today*. Instead of making things better by what he said and did, he made them worse. According to Robin Cohn, author of *The PR Crisis Bible*, he got isolated in his ivory tower and just did not realize that now was not the time to take the money. It is argued that Grasso and his team botched this crisis and that its handling may end up in PR textbooks detailing *how a crisis should not be handled*. Three big mistakes were made.

- *Minimizing the issue.* Grasso made the mistake of trying to minimize the fuss over his huge paycheck. Eric Dezenhall, crisis management expert, said, "My career has been filled with clients who want people to be thrilled about their obscene wealth. I've never succeeded."

- *Stonewalling.* Rather than giving the media as much information as possible, Grasso retreated and isolated himself and developed a bunker mentality.

- *Too little, too late.* It is possible that Grasso might have saved his job if he had performed an act of good will such as giving away some of his money to charity or agreeing to take it spread out over a period of years. It was believed, however, that he did too little, too late, and thus exited in an adverse way.

SOURCES: Gary Strauss, "Severance Pay Could Add to Grasso's Pile of Cash," *USA Today* (September 19, 2003), 6B. Michael McCarthy and Adam Shell, "Others Can Learn from Grasso's Blunders," *USA Today* (September 19, 2003), 6B.

 SEARCH THE WEB

CRISIS MANAGEMENT: THE NEW CORPORATE DISCIPLINE

An article in *Time* magazine called crisis management the "new corporate discipline." Every company today, large or small, runs the risk of a crisis. Forward-looking companies practice crisis management and either develop their own in-house crisis management programs or avail themselves of the many consulting firms that provide crisis management consulting. One consulting firm that specializes in crisis management is Lexicon Communications Corporation. Among its many services, Lexicon provides crisis management training seminars, workshops, and full-blown crisis simulations to help executives hone the skills they may need to serve on crisis management teams or to respond to the media in a crisis-filled atmosphere. To learn more about which topics might be covered in such seminars, check out the Lexicon Web site at **http://www.crisismanagement.com**.

Another major consulting firm that specializes in crisis management is The Wilson Group. Whether it's a chemical spill, a plant explosion, a plant closing, or another crisis, The Wilson Group offers personalized crisis management and media training workshops, crisis communication plans, community relations programs, and on-the-scene counsel. Part of the group's intense training includes on-camera media training for executives in a mock disaster context. To learn more about crisis management, visit The Wilson Group Web site at **http://www.wilson-group.com**.

death and taxes," but 50 percent of the executive respondents admitted that they did not have prepared crisis plans.[42] Today, more companies may be prepared for crises, but their degree of preparedness varies widely.

Types of Crises.   Situations in which the executives surveyed by Fink felt they were vulnerable to crises included industrial accidents, environmental problems, union problems/strikes, product recalls, investor relations, hostile takeovers, proxy fights, rumors/media leaks, government regulatory problems, acts of terrorism, and embezzlement.[43] Other common crises include product tampering, executive kidnapping, work-related homicides, malicious rumors, and natural disasters that destroy corporate offices or information bases.[44] Since September 11, 2001, we have had to add terrorism to this list.

Mitroff and Alpaslan have suggested that crises may be grouped into seven families:[45]

- *Economic crises* (recessions, hostile takeovers, stock market crashes)
- *Physical crises* (industrial accidents, product failures, supply breakdown)
- *Personnel crises* (strikes, exodus of key employees, workplace violence)
- *Criminal crises* (product tampering, kidnappings, acts of terrorism)
- *Information crises* (theft of proprietary information, cyberattacks)
- *Reputational crises* (rumormongering/slander, logo tampering)
- *Natural disasters* (earthquakes, floods, fires)

Of the major crises that have recently occurred, the majority of the companies reported the following outcomes: The crises escalated in intensity, were subjected to media and government scrutiny, interfered with normal business operations, and damaged the company's bottom line. As a result of the horrific attacks on the World Trade Center, companies have experienced major power shifts among executives as some bosses fumbled with their responsibilities and didn't handle the crisis well. Those bosses who handled the crisis well have garnered more responsibility while others have lost responsibilities.[46]

Four Crisis Stages

There are a number of ways we could categorize the stages through which a crisis may progress. According to Steven Fink, a crisis may consist of as many as four distinct stages: (1) a **prodromal crisis stage**, (2) an **acute crisis stage**, (3) a **chronic crisis stage**, and (4) a **crisis resolution stage**.[47]

Prodromal Crisis Stage.   This is the warning stage. ("Prodromal" is a medical term that refers to a previous notice or warning.) This warning stage could also be thought of as a symptom stage. Although it could be called a "precrisis" stage, this presupposes that one knows that a crisis is coming. According to Mitroff and Anagnos, crises "send out a repeated trail of early warning signals" that managers can learn to recognize.[48] Perhaps management should adopt this perspective: Watch each situation with the thought that it could be a crisis in the making. Early symptoms may be quite obvious, such as in the case where a social activist group tells management it will boycott the company if a certain problem is not addressed. On the other hand, symptoms may be more subtle, as in the case where defect rates for a particular product a company makes start edging up over time.

Acute Crisis Stage.   This is the stage at which the crisis actually occurs. There is no turning back; the incident has occurred. Damage has been done at this point, and it is now up to management to handle or contain the damage. If the prodromal stage is the precrisis stage, the acute stage is the actual crisis stage. The crucial decision point at which things may get worse or better has been reached.

Chronic Crisis Stage.   This is the lingering period. It may be the period of investigations, audits, or in-depth news stories. Management may see it as a period of recovery, self-analysis, or self-doubt. In Fink's survey of major companies, he found that crises tended to linger as much as two and a half times longer in firms without crisis management plans than in firms with such plans.

Crisis Resolution Stage.   This is the final stage—the goal of all crisis management efforts. Fink argues that when an early warning sign of a crisis is noted, the manager should seize control swiftly and determine the most direct and expedient route to resolution. If the warning signs are missed in the first stage, the goal is to speed up all phases and reach the final stage as soon as possible.

Figure 5-8 presents one way in which these four stages might be depicted. It should be noted that the phases may overlap and that each phase varies in intensity and duration. It is hoped that management will learn from the crisis and thus will be better prepared for, and better able to handle, any future crisis.

Poorly Managed Crises.
Other views of crises and crisis management may be taken. Gerald C. Meyers, former corporate executive and a consultant on crisis management, and others lay out the scenario for a poorly managed crisis, which typically follows a predictable pattern.[49] The pattern is as follows:

• Early indications that trouble is brewing occur.

FIGURE 5-8

Four Stages in a Management Crisis

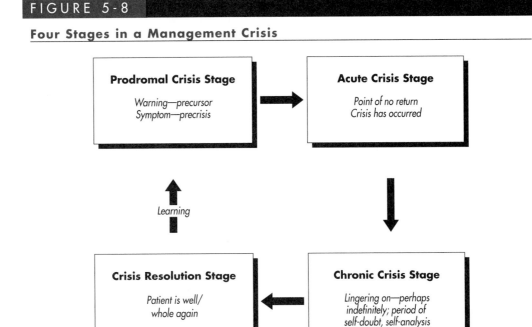

- Warnings are ignored/played down.
- Warnings build to a climax.
- Pressure mounts.
- Executives are often overwhelmed or can't cope effectively.
- Quick-fix alternatives look appealing. Hasty moves create trouble.
- Clamming-up versus opening-up options present themselves.
- Most firms choose the former.
- A siege mentality prevails.

Visualizing the attributes or pattern of a poorly managed crisis is valuable because it illustrates how not to do it—a lesson that many managers may find quite valuable.

Managing Business Crises

Fink's Three-Stage Model.   There are many suggestions for managing a crisis, although they cannot be reduced to a cookbook recipe. Steven Fink presents a simple model by arguing that there are three vital stages in crisis management:

1. *identifying* the crisis,
2. *isolating* the crisis, and
3. *managing* the crisis. All should be done quickly.[50]

Business Week's Five Practical Steps in Managing Crises.   A more complete view of crisis management holds that a series of five steps must be taken. These five steps, synthesized by *Business Week* magazine from the actual experiences of companies experiencing crises, are discussed next and are summarized in Figure 5-9.[51]

First: Identifying Areas of Vulnerability.   In this first step, some areas of vulnerability are obvious, such as potential chemical spills, whereas others are more subtle. The

---

FIGURE 5-9

Steps in Crisis Management

1. Identifying areas of vulnerability
   A. Obvious areas
   B. Subtle areas

2. Developing a plan for dealing with threats
   A. Communications planning is vital
   B. Training executives in product dangers and dealing with media

3. Forming crisis teams
   A. Vital to successful crisis management
   B. Identifying executives who can work well under stress

4. Simulating crisis drills
   A. Experience/practice is helpful
   B. "War rooms" serve as gathering places for team members

5. Learning from experience
   A. Assess effectiveness of crisis strategies
   B. Move from reaction to proaction

SOURCE: "How Companies Are Learning to Prepare for the Worst," *Business Week* (December 23, 1985), 76.

key seems to be in developing a greater consciousness of how things can go wrong and get out of hand. At Heinz, after the "Tunagate" incident, a vice president set up brainstorming sessions. He said, "We're brainstorming about how we would be affected by everything from a competitor who had a serious quality problem to a scandal involving a Heinz executive."[52] A key to identifying areas of vulnerability is "recognizing the threat." According to Watkins and Bazerman, the most skilled executives often fail at this stage because they are oblivious to emerging threats.[53]

Following are some ways that companies can identify areas of vulnerability:[54]

- *Scenario planning.* Create scenarios for crises that could occur over the next two years.
- *Risk analysis.* Estimate the probabilities and costs/benefits of estimated future events.
- *Incentives.* Reward managers for information sharing.
- *Networks.* Build formal coalitions to mobilize internal and external information suppliers.

Second: Developing a Plan for Dealing with Threats.

A plan for dealing with the most serious crisis threats is a logical next step. One of the most crucial issues is communications planning. After a Dow Chemical railroad car derailed near Toronto, forcing the evacuation of 250,000 people, Dow Canada prepared information kits on the hazards of its products so that executives would be knowledgeable enough to respond properly if a similar crisis were to arise in the future. Dow Canada also trained executives in interviewing techniques. This effort paid off several years later when an accident caused a chemical spill into a river that supplied drinking water for several nearby towns. The company's emergency response team arrived at the site almost immediately and established a press center that distributed information about the chemicals. In addition, the company recruited a neutral expert to speak on the hazards and how to deal with them. Officials praised Dow for its handling of this crisis.[55]

Richard J. Mahoney, former CEO of Monsanto Company, has offered the following *ten "Rs" for the effective handling of public policy crises.* He recommends these steps as part of an overall crisis plan:[56]

- Respond early.
- Recruit a credible spokesperson.
- Reply truthfully.
- Respect the opposition's concerns.
- Revisit the issue with follow-up.
- Retreat early if it's a loser.
- Redouble efforts early if it's a critical company issue.
- Reply with visible top management.
- Refuse to press for what is not good public policy.
- Repeat the prior statement regularly.

Some of these steps may not apply to every crisis situation, but many may be useful as part of a crisis management plan. Mahoney notes that getting an entire organization trained to deal with crises is difficult and expensive, but he paraphrases what a car repairman once said in a TV commercial: "You can pay now or pay a lot more later." Mahoney thinks that now is infinitely better for everyone.[57]

Third: Forming Crisis Teams.

Another step that can be taken as part of an overall planning effort is the formation of **crisis teams**. Such teams have played key roles in many well-managed disasters. A good example is the team formed at Procter & Gamble when its Rely tampon products were linked with the dreaded disease toxic shock syndrome. The team was quickly assembled, a vice president was appointed to head it, and after one week the decision was made to remove Rely from marketplace shelves. The quick action earned the firm praise, and it paid off for P&G in the long run.

Another task in assembling crisis teams is identifying managers who can cope effectively with stress. Not every executive can handle the fast-moving, high-pressured, ambiguous decision environment that is created by a crisis, and early identification of executives who can is important. We should also note that it is not always the CEO who can best perform in such a crisis atmosphere.

Despite the careful use of crisis teams, crises can often overwhelm a carefully constructed plan. When ValuJet's Flight 592 crashed in the Florida Everglades in 1996, for example, ValuJet flawlessly executed a 3-pronged, team-based crisis management plan calling for the company to (1) show compassion, (2) take responsibility, and (3) demonstrate that the airline learned from the crisis. Experts have said that the company handled the crisis well. However, a close look at the tragedy revealed that a series of complicating factors turned the crisis into something even more difficult than a well-scripted, perfectly executed crisis management plan could handle.[58]

Fourth: Simulating Crisis Drills.   Some companies have gone so far as to run crisis drills in which highly stressful situations are simulated so that managers can "practice" what they might do in a real crisis. As a basis for conducting crisis drills and experiential exercises, a number of companies have adopted a software package known as *Crisis Plan wRiter (CPR)*. This software allows companies to centralize and maintain up-to-date crisis management information and allows company leaders to assign responsibilities to their crisis team, target key audiences, identify and monitor potential issues, and create crisis-response processes.[59]

Fifth: Learning from Experience.   The final stage in crisis management is learning from experience. At this point, managers need to ask themselves exactly what they have learned from past crises and how that knowledge can be used to advantage in the future. Part of this stage entails an assessment of the effectiveness of the firm's crisis-handling strategies and identification of areas where improvements in capabilities need to be made. Without a crisis management system of some kind in place, the organization will find itself reacting to crises after they have occurred. If learning and preparation for the future are occurring, however, the firm may engage in more proactive behavior.[60]

Augustine's Six Stages of Crisis Management.

As an alternative to the previous steps in crisis management, Norman Augustine, former president of Lockheed Martin Corporation, distinguished among six stages of crisis management. To some extent, these overlap and embrace the steps, but it is useful to see an alternative conceptualization of the steps that should be taken in crisis management. Augustine's list begins with the idea that the crisis should be avoided:[61]

Stage 1: Avoiding the Crisis
Stage 2: Preparing to Manage the Crisis
Stage 3: Recognizing the Crisis
Stage 4: Containing the Crisis
Stage 5: Resolving the Crisis
Stage 6: Profiting from the Crisis

We should note that Pearson and Mitroff have accurately observed that effective crisis management requires a program that is tailored to a firm's specific industry, business environment, and crisis management experience. Effective crisis managers will understand that there are major crisis management factors that may vary from situation to situation, such as the type of crisis (e.g., natural disaster or human induced), the phase of the crisis, the systems affected (e.g., humans, technology, culture), and the stakeholders affected. Managers cannot eliminate crises. However, they can become keenly aware of their vulnerabilities and make concerted efforts to understand and reduce these vulnerabilities through continuous crisis management programs.[62]

Crisis Communications

An illustration of crisis management without effective communications occurred during the Jack in the Box hamburger disaster of 1993. There was an outbreak of E. coli bacteria in the Pacific Northwest area, resulting in the deaths of four children. Following this crisis, the parent company, San Diego-based Foodmaker, entered a downward spiral after lawsuits by the families of victims enraged the public and franchisees. Foodmaker did most of the right things and did them quickly. The company immediately suspended hamburger sales, recalled suspect meat from its distribution system, increased cooking time for all foods, pledged to pay for all the medical costs related to the disaster, and hired a food safety expert to design a new food-handling system. But, it forgot to do one thing: communicate with the public, including its own employees.[63]

The company's **crisis communications** efforts were inept. It waited a week before accepting any responsibility for the tragedy, preferring to point fingers at its meat supplier and even the Washington state health officials for not explaining the state's new guidelines for cooking hamburgers at higher temperatures. The media pounced on the company. The company was blasted for years even though within the company it was taking the proper steps to correct the problem. The company suffered severe financial losses, and it took at least six years before the company really felt it was on the road to recovery. "The crisis," as it is still called around company headquarters, taught the firm an important lesson. CEO Robert Nugent was quoted as saying in 1999, "Nobody wants to deal with their worst nightmare, but we should have recognized you've got to communicate."[64]

Virtually all crisis management plans call for effective crisis communications. There are a number of different stakeholder groups with whom effective communications are critical, especially the media and those immediately affected by the crisis. Many companies have failed to successfully manage their crises because of inadequate or failed communications with key stakeholder groups. Successful communications efforts are crucial to effective crisis management. It is axiomatic that *prepared* communications will be more helpful than *reactive* communications. Jonathan L. Bernstein has offered **ten steps of crisis communication** that are worth summarizing:[65]

1. Identify your crisis communications team.
2. Identify key spokespersons who will be authorized to speak for the organization.
3. Train your spokespersons.
4. Establish communications protocols.
5. Identify and know your audience.
6. Anticipate crises.
7. Assess the crisis situation.

Ethics in Practice

THE SLACKEST OF THEM ALL

During my final two years of college, I worked in a retail clothing store. There was one general manager, Chrissy, one operations manager, and five merchandise managers. Chrissy was a strict manager who followed every corporate policy and even created her own stricter rules for the store. Each merchandise manager was responsible for a department of the store, such as women's, men's, kid's, babies, and accessories.

For each department, the managers kept the displays updated, planned for biweekly shipments, and redid the "look" once a month to match the suggested layout sent from the corporate offices. The only male among the six merchandise managers was Jamie. He also happened to be the slackest of the managers. Many of the other managers and employees said the only reason he had this job was because he and Chrissy were childhood friends.

There were many strict policies to follow at this store that ranged from customer service to loss prevention. Yet, Jamie managed to break all of the policies. Here are some examples: Every night that he closed the store, he would turn off the lights at closing time to hurry the customers out of the store. When he would encounter a shoplifter, he would tell them to return the merchandise to its place while he turned his back. He would stand by the registers his entire shift instead of circulating the floor helping customers, work in his department, or perform other managerial duties. Jamie would also make the employees leave early at night even when the store was not straightened up so he could go out drinking.

Jamie engaged in all these activities on a daily basis. They were in direct violation of policies and all the employees were well aware of it. Yet nothing was ever done about it. I often wanted to say something to Chrissy to see if she ever noticed his behavior. However, I did not because of the constant rumors that Chrissy knew about his behavior, but ignored it because their friendship dated back to childhood. I could not believe Chrissy would allow this kind of behavior from a manager. She fired employees for similar actions.

1. Does this company have an "issue" or a "crisis" on its hands?

2. Is it an ethical practice to allow Jamie to slack off and not take action? Should others be allowed to slack off?

3. Should the other managers confront Chrissy for an explanation of why she tolerates this behavior from Jamie, but would fire anyone else who tried it?

4. What, if anything, would you do in this situation? Why?

Contributed by Tiffany Kemph

8. Identify key messages you will communicate to key groups.
9. Decide on communications methods.
10. Be prepared to ride out the storm.

A brief elaboration on the importance of identifying key messages that will be communicated to key groups is useful (point 8). It is important that you communicate with your internal stakeholders first because rumors are often started there, and uninformed employees can do great damage to a successful crisis management effort. Internal stakeholders are your best advocates and can be supportive during a crisis. Prepare news releases that contain as much information as possible and get this information out to all media outlets at the same time. Communicate with others in the community who have a need to know, such as public officials, disaster coordinators, stakeholders, and others. Uniformity of response is of vital importance during a crisis. Finally, have a designated "release authority" for information (point 2). The first 24 hours of a crisis can make or break the organization, and how these key spokespersons work is of vital importance to handling the crisis.[66]

Mitroff and Anagnos have stressed the importance of "telling the truth" in effective crisis communications. They argue that there are no secrets in today's society and that eventually the truth will get out. Therefore, from a practical point of view, the question is not whether the truth will be revealed but rather when that truth will become public and under what circumstances.[67] From both an ethical and a practical perspective, truth-telling is an important facet of crisis communications.

Successful Crisis Management

It is informative to conclude this chapter with an illustration of a successful crisis management case study. Earlier, we presented handling of the J&J Tylenol crisis as a success story. This success story started with the kind of phone call every company dreads—"Your product is injuring people; we're announcing it at a press conference today." Schwan's Sales Enterprises, Inc., got the call from the Minnesota Department of Health at about noon one fateful day. The Health Department reported that it had found a statistical link between Schwan's ice cream and confirmed cases of salmonella. Thousands of people in at least 39 states became ill with salmonella after eating tainted Schwan's ice cream, potentially setting the company up for a decade's worth of litigation. Instead, in a little more than a year after the outbreak, the vast majority of claims had been handled outside the legal system through direct settlements or as part of a class action in Minneapolis.[68]

Schwan's knew that its image of the smiling man in the sunshine-yellow Schwan's truck (with a Swan on the side) busily hand-delivering ice cream to grateful consumers was one of its major assets. Before the company was sure of the Health Department's findings, it halted sales and production, shut down, and invited the state health department, the Department of Agriculture, and the FDA into the plant to investigate. It also notified all its sales offices nationwide. Also, within the first 24 hours of the crisis, the company set up a hotline to answer consumer questions, contacted employees and managers to staff the hotline, prepared for a product recall, and began working with its insurer.[69]

By placing consumer safety as its number one priority, Schwan's was able to resolve the crisis much more quickly than ever would have been possible without a carefully designed crisis management plan. Whether by coincidence or preparedness, the manager of public affairs and the company's general counsel had completed a review and rewriting of the company's crisis management manual just two months before the outbreak. One vital component of the plan was a crisis management team, which went to work immediately when the news came. The crisis management team quickly set up a process for handling consumers who had been affected. The team, working with its insurance company, quickly helped customers get medical treatment and get their bills paid. Settlements to customers who suffered from salmonella symptoms included financial damages, medical expenses, and other costs, such as reimbursement for workdays missed.[70]

How did the ice cream get contaminated with salmonella? After a month's investigation that kept the Marshall, Minnesota, plant closed, it was determined that the ice cream mix supplied by a few vendors was the culprit. The mix of cream, sugar, and milk had been shipped in a tanker truck that had previously held raw, unpasteurized eggs that had the bacteria. Schwan's quietly sought and received legal damages from the suppliers but stayed focused on its customers throughout the crisis.

What did Schwan's learn from this crisis? Previously, Schwan's did not repasteurize its ice cream mix once the mix arrived at the Marshall plant. Within a few weeks of the outbreak, however, the company had broken ground to build its own repasteurization plant. The company also leased a dedicated fleet of tanker trucks to deliver the ice cream mix from the suppliers to the plant, set up a system for testing each shipment, and delayed shipping the final product until the test results were known. In summary, Schwan's planning, quick response, and customer-oriented strategy combined to retain customer loyalty and minimize the company's legal exposure.[71] It was a case of good, effective crisis management.

Undoubtedly, in the years to come, stories will be told of successful crisis management in the aftermath of the attacks on the World Trade Center in 2001 and the financial scandals of the early to mid-2000s. The United States is still uneasy about these attacks and the subsequent anthrax scares and deaths. Preparation for acts of terrorism, however, is now a vital national and business issue. Clearly, these recent events have made crisis management a priority topic in boardrooms and among managers.

▪ SUMMARY

Issues management and crisis management are two key approaches by which companies may plan for the turbulent stakeholder environment. Both these approaches are frequently found housed in a company's department of public affairs. Issues management is a process by which an organization identifies issues in the stakeholder environment, analyzes and prioritizes those issues in terms of their relevance to the organization, plans responses to the issues, and then evaluates and monitors the results. There are two approaches to issues management: the conventional approach and the strategic management approach. Issues management requires a knowledge of the changing mix of issues, the issues management process, the issues development process, and how companies might implement issues management in practice. Issues management serves as a bridge to crisis management.

Crisis management, like issues management, is not a panacea for organizations. In spite of well-intended efforts by management, not all crises will be resolved in the company's favor. Nevertheless, being prepared for the inevitable makes sense, especially in today's world of instantaneous global communications and obsessive media coverage. Whether we are thinking about the long term, the intermediate term, or the short term, managers need to be prepared to handle crises. A crisis has a number of different stages, and managing crises requires a number of key steps before, during, and after the crisis. These steps include identifying areas of vulnerability, developing a plan for dealing with threats, forming crisis teams, using crisis drills, and learning from experience. Crisis communications is critical for successful crisis management. When used in tandem, issues and crisis management can help managers fulfill their economic, legal, ethical, and philanthropic responsibilities to stakeholders.

▪ KEY TERMS

acute crisis stage (page 152)
chronic crisis stage (page 152)
conventional approach to issues management
 (page 135)
crisis (page 150)
crisis communications (page 157)
crisis management (page 134)
crisis resolution stage (page 152)
crisis teams (page 155)
emerging issue (page 138)

issue (page 138)
issue selling and buying (page 142)
issues development process (page 145)
issues management (page 134)
portfolio approach (page 137)
probability-impact matrix (page 143)
prodromal crisis stage (page 152)
strategic management approach to issues
 management (page 136)
ten steps of crisis communication (page 157)

▪ DISCUSSION QUESTIONS

1. Which of the major stages in the issues management process do you think is the most important? Why?

2. Following the approach indicated in Figure 5-1, identify a new issue category not listed in Figure 5-1. Identify several examples of "crises" that have occurred in recent years under each issue category.

3. Identify one example, other than those listed in Figure 5-4, of each of the leading force categories: events, authorities/advocates, literature, organizations, and political jurisdictions.

4. Identify a crisis that has occurred in your life or in the life of someone you know, and briefly explain it in terms of the four crisis stages: prodromal, acute, chronic, and resolution.

5. Do research on the impacts on business organizations of the attacks on the World Trade Center in New York and the scandals of the early to mid-2000s. What have been successful and unsuccessful examples of crisis management that have come out of this research? Is terrorism a likely crisis for which business may prepare? How does preparation for terrorism (which comes from without) compare with preparation for ethical scandals (which come from within)?

▪ RECOMMENDED CASES

Many of the end-of-text cases may be related to Chapter 5. You may wish to consider studying the following cases with Chapter 5.

Case 3A. "THE BODY SHOP'S REPUTATION IS TARNISHED." The Body Shop faced a crisis when an article criticizing its policies and practices was published. Identify the stages in the crisis as experienced by the company. Did the company successfully manage this crisis? Evaluate the pros and cons of its actions. Are there other steps that should have been taken?

Case 4. "FACING A FIRE." There can be few crises more severe and urgent than when a business burns down, injuring employees and destroying buildings. This is especially critical when thousands of employees are thrown out of work. What were the stages of the crisis and how was it managed at each stage? How successful was the HFS Corporation at "crisis management"? What grade would you give Hermann Singer for "crisis management"?

Case 24. "FIRESTONE AND FORD: THE TIRE TREAD SEPARATION TRAGEDY." Consumer safety and the possibility of tire separations is an "issue" that tire manufacturers and auto companies should have anticipated and been prepared for. Both Firestone and Ford experienced a crisis when the tire separations began and continued. Can you identify the crisis stages in this case? What are the ethical issues facing Firestone in this case? What are the ethical issues facing Ford? What could each have done better in handling this crisis?

▪ WEB RESOURCES

The URLs listed here are current at the time of publication. Should any of these Web sites change, please search under the company's or organization's name for an updated address.

Corporate Social Responsibility Newswire
http://www.csrwire.com

Council of Ethical Organizations
http://www.corporateethics.com

Crisis Communications
http://www.stormingmedia.us

Crisis Management: A Leadership Imperative
http://www.pfdf.org

Crisis Management Food Safety
http://www.foodsafetynetwork.ca/crisis.htm

Crisis Management Institute
http://www.cmionline.org

Crisis Management Response
http://www.bernsteincrisismanagement.com

Ethics Officers Association
http://www.eoa.org

European Crisis Management Academy
http://www.ecm-academy.nl

Institute for Crisis Management
http://www.crisisexperts.com

Nonprofit Risk Management Center
http://www.nonprofitrisk.org/mc/essentials.htm

Public Affairs Council: Issues Management
http://www.pac.org

Public Relations Society of America
http://www.prsa.org/_Resources/resources

Survive Crisis Special Interest Group
http://www.continuitycentral.com/news0767.htm

The Conference Board
http://www.conference-board.org

The Wall Street Journal
http://www.wsj.com

Wilson Group: Real World Crisis Management
http://www.wilson-group.com

InfoTrac® College Edition   http://www.infotrac-college.com

Articles from The Wall Street Journal *can be researched, retrieved, and read from your desktop using InfoTrac's online database.*

▪ ENDNOTES

1. Liam Fahey, "Issues Management: Two Approaches," *Strategic Planning Management* (November 1986), 81, 85–96.

2. *Ibid.*, 81.

3. *Ibid.*, 86.

4. H. Igor Ansoff, "Strategic Issue Management," *Strategic Management Journal* (Vol. I, 1980), 131–148.

5. William R. King, "Strategic Issue Management," in William R. King and David I. Cleland (eds.) *Strategic Planning and Management Handbook* (New York: Van Nostrand Reinhold, 1987), 252–264.

6. Pursey P.M.A.R. Heugens, John F. Mahon, Steve L. Wartick, "A Portfolio Approach to Issue Adoption," International Association for Business and Society, 2004 Annual Meeting, Jackson Hole, WY.

7. *Ibid.*

8. Joseph F. Coates, Vary T. Coates, Jennifer Jarratt, and Lisa Heinz, *Issues Management* (Mt. Airy, MD: Lomond Publications, 1986), 19–20.

9. John Mahon, "Issues Management: The Issue of Definition," *Strategic Planning Management* (November 1986), 81–82. For further discussion on what constitutes an issue, see Steven L. Wartick and John F. Mahon, "Toward a Substantive Definition of the Corporate Issue Construct," *Business & Society* (Vol. 33, No. 3, December 1994), 293–311.

10. Coates *et al.*, 18.

11. *Ibid.*, 32.

12. Myron Magnet, "Who Needs a Trend-Spotter?" Fortune (December 9, 1985), 51–56. Also see Gary Hamel and C. K. Prahalad, "Seeing the Future First," *Fortune* (September 5, 1994), 64–70.

13. Magnet, 52.
14. John Naisbitt, *Megatrends 2000: Ten New Directions for the 1990s* (New York: Morrow, 1990); *Global Paradox* (New York: Avon Books, 1994); *Megatrends Asia: Eight Asian Megatrends That Are Reshaping Our World* (New York: Simon and Schuster, 1996); and *High Tech/High Touch* (New York: Broadway Books, 1999.
15. Magnet, 56.
16. T. Graham Molitor, "How to Anticipate Public Policy Changes," *SAM Advanced Management Journal* (Vol. 42, No. 3, Summer 1977), 4.
17. Aimee Welch, "The New Futurists," *Insight* (January 15–22, 2001), 10–13.
18. J. E. Dutton, S .J. Ashford, R. M. O'Neill, E. Hayes, and E. E. Wierba, "Reading the Wind: How Middle Managers Assess the Context for Selling Issues to Top Managers," *Strategic Management Journal* (18, 1997), 407–425.
19. Pursey P. M. A. R. Heugens, "Issues Management: Core Understandings and Scholarly Development," in *Handbook of Public Affairs*, forthcoming, 2004.
20. King, 259.
21. James K. Brown, *This Business of Issues: Coping with the Company's Environment* (New York: The Conference Board, 1979), 45.
22. *Ibid.*, 33.
23. King, 257.
24. Coates *et al.*, 46.
25. Earl C. Gottschalk, Jr., "Firms Hiring New Type of Manager to Study Issues, Emerging Troubles," *The Wall Street Journal* (June 10, 1982), 33, 36.
26. I. C. MacMillan and P. E. Jones, "Designing Organizations to Compete," *Journal of Business Strategy* (Vol. 4, No. 4, Spring 1984), 13.
27. Roy Wernham, "Implementation: The Things That Matter," in King and Cleland, 453.
28. Gottschalk, 3.
29. Mahon, 81–82.
30. Gottschalk, 33.
31. Thomas G. Marx, "Integrating Public Affairs and Strategic Planning," *California Management Review* (Fall 1986), 145.
32. Barbara Bigelow, Liam Fahey, and John Mahon, "A Typology of Issue Evolution," *Business & Society* (Spring 1993), 28. For another useful perspective, see John F. Mahon and Sandra A. Waddock, "Strategic Issues Management: An Integration of Issue Life Cycle Perspectives," *Business & Society* (Spring 1992), 19–32. Also see Steven L. Wartick and Robert E. Rude, "Issues Management: Fad or Function," *California Management Review* (Fall 1986), 134–140.
33. Public Affairs Council, "Public Affairs: Its Origins, Its Present, and Its Trends," http://www.pac.org; 2001.
34. Gottschalk, 21.
35. Pursey P. M. A. R. Heugens, "Strategic Issues Management: Implications for Corporate Performance," *Business & Society* (Vol. 41, No. 4, December 2002), 456–468
36. *Ibid.*, 459.
37. Kate Miller, "Issues Management: The Link Between Organization Reality and Public Perception," *Public Relations Quarterly* (Vol. 44, No. 2, Summer 1999), 5–11.
38. Ian Mitroff, with Gus Anagnos, *Managing Crises Before They Happen: What Every Executive and Manager Needs to Know about Crisis Management* (New York: AMACOM, 2001), Chapter 2.
39. Laurence Barton, *Crisis in Organizations: Managing and Communicating in the Heat of Chaos* (Cincinnati: South-Western Publishing Co., 1993), 2. Also see Ross Campbell, *Crisis Control: Preventing & Managing Corporate Crises* (Englewood Cliffs, NJ: Prentice Hall, 1999), 11.
40. Christine M. Pearson and Judith Clair, "Reframing Crisis Management," *Academy of Management Review* (Vol. 23, No. 1, 1998), 60.
41. "How Companies Are Learning to Prepare for the Worst," *Business Week* (December 23, 1985), 74.
42. Steven Fink, *Crisis Management: Planning for the Inevitable* (New York: AMACOM, 1986).
43. *Ibid.*, 68. For further discussion of types of crises, see Ian Mitroff, "Crisis Management and Environmentalism: A Natural Fit," *California Management Review* (Winter 1994), 101–113.
44. Pearson and Clair, 60.
45. Ian I. Mitroff and Mural C. Alpaslan, "Preparing for Evil," *Harvard Business Review* (April 2003), 3–9.
46. Fink, 69. Also see Sharon H. Garrison, *The Financial Impact of Corporate Events on Corporate Stakeholders* (New York: Quorem Books, 1990); and Joe Marconi, *Crisis Marketing: When Bad Things Happen to Good Companies* (Chicago: NTC Business Books, 1997). See also Carol Hymowitz, "Companies Experience Major Power Shifts as Crises Continue," *The Wall Street Journal* (October 9, 2001), B1, and Sue Shellenbarger, "Some Bosses, Fumbling in Crisis, Have Bruised Loyalty of Employees," *The Wall Street Journal* (October 17, 2001), B1.
47. Fink, 20.
48. Mitroff and Anagnos, 2001.
49. "How Companies Are Learning to Prepare for the Worst," *Business Week* (December 23, 1985), 74–75.
50. Fink, 70.
51. "How Companies Are Learning to Prepare for the Worst," *Business Week* (December 23, 1985), 76.
52. *Ibid.*
53. Michael D. Watkins and Max H. Bazerman, "Predictable Surprises: The Disasters You Should Have Seen Coming," *Harvard Business Review* (March 2003), 3–10.

54. *Ibid.*
55. *Business Week* (1985), ibid.
56. Richard J. Mahoney, "The Anatomy of a Public Policy Crisis," *The CEO Series*, Center for the Study of American Business (May 1996), 7.
57. *Ibid.*
58. Greg Jaffe, "How Florida Crash Overwhelmed ValuJet's Skillful Crisis Control," *The Wall Street Journal* (June 5, 1996), S1.
59. Melissa Master, "Keyword: Crisis," *Across the Board* (September 1998), 62.
60. Ian Mitroff, Paul Shrivastava, and Firdaus Udwadia, "Effective Crisis Management," *Academy of Management Executive* (November 1987), 285.
61. Norman R. Augustine, "Managing the Crisis You Tried to Prevent," *Harvard Business Review* (November–December 1995), 147–158.
62. Christine M. Pearson and Ian I. Mitroff, "From Crisis Prone to Crisis Prepared: A Framework for Crisis Management," *Academy of Management Executive* (Vol. VII, No. 1, February 1993), 58–59. Also see Ian Mitroff, Christine M. Pearson, and L. Katherine Harrington, *The Essential Guide to Managing Corporate Crises* (New York: Oxford University Press, 1996).
63. Robert Goff, "Coming Clean," *Forbes* (May 17, 1999), 156–160.
64. *Ibid.*
65. Johnathan L. Bernstein, "The Ten Steps of Crisis Communications" (June 4, 2001), http://www.crisis navigator.org.
66. Richard Wm. Brundage, "Crisis Management—An Outline for Survival" (June 4, 2001), http://www.crisis navigator.org.
67. Mitroff and Anagnos (2001).
68. Bruce Rubenstein, "Salmonella-Tainted Ice Cream: How Schwan's Recovered," Corporate Legal Times Corp., http://www.cltmag.com/, June 1998.
69. *Ibid.*
70. *Ibid.*
71. *Ibid.*

Part 3

BUSINESS ETHICS *and* MANAGEMENT

Chapter 6

■ BUSINESS ETHICS FUNDAMENTALS

CHAPTER LEARNING OUTCOMES

After studying this chapter, you should be able to:

1 Describe how the public regards business ethics.
2 Define business ethics and appreciate the complexities of making ethical judgments.
3 Explain the conventional approach to business ethics.
4 Analyze economic, legal, and ethical aspects by using a Venn model.
5 Enumerate and discuss the four important ethics questions.
6 Identify and explain three models of management ethics.
7 Describe Kohlberg's three levels of developing moral judgment.
8 Identify and discuss the elements of moral judgment.

In regard to public interest in business ethics during the modern business period—approximately the past 30 years—two conclusions may be drawn. First, interest in business ethics has heightened during each of the past three decades. Second, the interest in business ethics seems to have been spurred by major headline-grabbing scandals. Certainly, there has been an ebb and flow of interest on society's part, but lately this interest has grown to a preoccupation or, as some might say, an obsession. With the ethics scandals of the early 2000s, some say this was the beginning of an "ethics industry," because there was so much to be done.

In the 1990s, there were several business ethics scandals that piqued the public's attention. It should not have come as a surprise that the U.S. Sentencing Commission in 1991 created new federal sentencing guidelines designed to deter corporate crime by creating incentives for corporations to report and accept responsibility for unlawful behavior.

One of the most visible examples of questionable ethics occurred in 1993. The NBC News show *Dateline NBC* aired a supposed exposé of exploding gas tanks in GM trucks, but NBC officials later admitted that toy rocket engines had been used as "igniters" to ensure that the staged crashes resulted in explosions for TV purposes. NBC, a unit of General Electric Co., eventually apologized for the misrepresentation and agreed to reimburse GM the roughly $2 million it had incurred investigating the NBC report. In exchange, GM agreed to drop its defamation suit against NBC.[1] To add to GE's troubles, the big story in 1994 concerned its Kidder, Peabody & Co. unit, which got embroiled in a bond-trading scandal. Kidder's government bond chief, Joseph Jett, was accused of creating $350 million in fake profits to mask losses over a several-year period. Kidder fired Mr. Jett, who denied the accusations. Jett claimed that Kidder knew about his trades and was trying to make him the fall guy. One major fallout from the scandal was the exodus of some of the firm's most successful brokers, who took with them about $2 billion in client accounts.[2]

Business ethics scandals continued through the 1990s and early 2000s. One noticeable change during this time, however, was the significant extent to which ethics, morals, and values came to characterize the general public debate concerning business in the United States. Examples of this elevated discussion include the 1992 *Newsweek* cover story titled "Whose Values?"[3] One of the most popular national best-sellers was William J. Bennett's 1993 anthology titled *The Book of Virtues: A Treasury of Great Moral Stories.*[4] In 1994, *Newsweek* featured a cover story titled "The Politics of Virtue: The Crusade Against America's Moral Decline." In this story, *Newsweek* reported the response to its poll question: "Do you think the United States is in a moral and spiritual decline?" Seventy-six percent of those responding to this national poll said "yes," whereas only 20 percent said "no."[5]

In the second half of the 1990s, many of the ethical scandals found in business involved massive charges of racial discrimination and sexual harassment. Among the well-known companies that experienced such allegations were Home Depot, Mitsubishi, Coca-Cola, and Texaco. The Texaco case involved a $196 million settlement in a class-action race discrimination lawsuit brought by employees fighting for equal pay and a chance for promotions. Bari-Ellen Roberts, lead plaintiff in the case against the oil company, revealed a dark side of corporate America in her 1998 book, *Roberts vs. Texaco: A True Story of Race and Corporate America.*[6]

Another industry that attracted widespread criticism in the late 1990s was the tobacco industry. The Food and Drug Administration's (FDA's) crackdown on tobacco, along with Congress's 1998 attempts to draft and pass landmark tobacco legislation, caused tobacco executives to begin thinking in settlement terms that would have been unthinkable in years past.[7] This issue continues today.

During the first decade of the 2000s, business ethics scandals continued in the headlines. Archer Daniels Midland (ADM) pleaded guilty to a price-fixing conspiracy that cost consumers millions in higher prices for soft drinks and detergents. ADM agreed to pay a $100 million fine. Royal Dutch Shell scrapped its plans for sinking a North Sea oil rig that environmentalists said was contaminated. They were later accused of colluding with the Nigerian government in the oppression of the Ogoni people and for failing to speak out against the execution of one of their leaders. In 2001, Bridgestone/Firestone and the Ford Motor Company were apologizing to consumers for a pattern of deadly tire failures, while blaming each other for the debacle.

The ethics scandal that has come to define modern times came to light in 2001—the Enron scandal. Enron and several of its leaders—Andrew Fastow, former CFO; Jeffrey

Skilling, former CEO; and then-CEO Kenneth Lay—were implicated in massive allegations of corporate fraud, financial misdealings, and various charges of criminal misconduct.[8] The Enron scandal unleashed an avalanche of fraud and corruption allegations and eventual bankruptcy. Today, many of the criminal trials of those indicted during this series of scandals are still underway. On the tails of the Enron scandal, the major accounting firm Arthur Andersen was implicated, and its complicity led to its eventual demise. Other scandals followed: WorldCom, Global Crossing, Tyco, Adelphia, and HealthSouth, just to mention a few. Figure 6-1 summarizes some of the major business ethics scandals that occurred beginning in 2001 that continue to the present day. Many of these companies and executives have claimed their innocence, and allegations and trials are at various stages of completion.

A couple of recent public opinion polls reveal the public's and employees' concerns about ethics in society and the workplace. According to the Barna Research Group, a 2001 poll of American adults revealed that three in four are worried about morality in the United States. This is a commentary on ethics in the United States as a nation.[9] The 2000 National Business Ethics Survey, conducted by the Ethics Resource Center in Washington, DC, revealed some specific concerns regarding the workplace. Some of the findings in this survey were revealing:

- One in eight employees feels pressure to compromise their organizations' ethics standards.
- Two-thirds of employees who feel pressure to compromise attribute this pressure to internal sources—supervisors, top management, and coworkers.

Writing a business viewpoint for *Time* (15 March 2004 v163 i11 p67), Michael Kinsley offers the suggestion that "greed is inevitable" and puts forward the notion that "greed-heads" such as Martha Stewart, Dennis Kozlowski of Tyco, and Scott Sullivan of WorldCom are actually heroes and their actions merely "a sign of the economy's robust health." Read his case for the importance of greed by logging on to InfoTrac College Edition at **http://www.infotrac-college.com** and keying record number A113985333.

FIGURE 6-1

RECENT ETHICS SCANDALS

Companies Implicated	Executives Implicated	Legal and Ethical Charges and Allegations
Enron	Andrew Fastow, Jeffrey Skilling, Kenneth Lay, Richard Causey, Ben Glissan, treasurer	Securities fraud, conspiracy to inflate profits, corrupt corporate culture
WorldCom	Scott Sullivan, CFO Bernard J. Ebbers, CEO	Accounting fraud, lying, filing false financial statements
Arthur Andersen	Entire firm; David Duncan, lead auditor for Enron	Accounting fraud, criminal charges, obstruction
Tyco	Mark Schwartz, CFO Dennis Kozlowski, CEO	Sales tax evasion, stealing through corruption, stock fraud, unauthorized bonuses and loans
Adelphia	John Rigas, sons Timothy and Michael; Michael Mulcahey; James Brown	Accounting fraud, looting the company, using it as "personal piggy bank"
Global Crossing	Gary Winnick, chairman	Misleading "swap" transactions
Dynegy	Jamie Olis, sr. dir. tax planning; Gene S. Foster; Helen C. Sharkey, accountant	Accounting fraud
HealthSouth	Richard Scrushy, CEO, fourteen former executives	Inflating earnings, maintaining false books and records, conspiracy to commit securities fraud
Boeing	Michael Sears, CFO	Unethical behavior, violating company policy, misconduct
Martha Stewart	Martha Stewart	Conspiracy, securities fraud, and obstruction of justice
Parmalat (Italy)	Calisto Tanzi, chairman and CEO, and others	Flawed corporate governance

- About one in three employees observes misconduct at work.
- The five types of misconduct observed most include lying, withholding needed information, abusive or intimidating behavior toward employees, misreporting actual time or hours worked, and discrimination.
- About one in three employees fears retaliation by management and coworkers if they report misconduct or other ethics concerns.
- Employees say that their organizations' concern for ethics is an important reason that they continue to work there.[10]

The good news is that by the time of the 2003 Ethics Resource Center's National Business Ethics Survey, employees' perceptions of their organizations' ethics were becoming more positive. Employees reported that top management was talking more about the importance of ethics, were keeping their promises more, and were modeling ethical behavior more frequently than in 2000. Observed misconduct and pressures to compromise ethics standards had declined somewhat since the 2000 survey. In spite of these positive trends, the respondents noted that vulnerabilities and challenges remained.[11]

In a survey released in early 2004 by Public Agenda, a nonpartisan opinion research organization, in a report to The Kettering Foundation, additional insights about Americans' views on business ethics were revealed. Some of the findings of Public Agenda were as follows:

- The most egregious violators of business ethics were corrupt executives who protected their own wealth while driving their companies to bankruptcy and forcing employees out of jobs.
- Greed for money and power and a weakening sense of personal values has been behind the recent ethics scandals.
- Though people are concerned about business ethics, they define it in broad terms and are especially concerned with how it has affected them—lack of job security and employee and consumer treatment.
- Many participants thought it was possible for executives to be both ethical and successful.
- The media and financial press are not regarded as vigilant watchdogs protecting the public interest.[12]

It appears that the American society of the first decade of the 2000s is clamoring for a renewed emphasis on values, morals, and ethics and that the business ethics debate of this period is but a subset of this larger societal concern. Whether the business community will be able to respond and ratchet its reputation to a new plateau remains to be seen. One thing is sure: There is a renewed interest in business ethics, and the proliferation of business ethics courses in colleges and universities, along with the revitalized interest on the part of the business community, paints an encouraging picture for the "ethics industry" of the future.

To gain an appreciation of the kinds of issues that are important under the rubric of business ethics, Figure 6-2 presents an inventory of business ethics issues compiled by the Josephson Institute of Ethics. Here we see business ethics issues categorized on the basis of stakeholder relationships. Against this backdrop, we plan to discuss business ethics, specifically, in this chapter and the next three chapters. In this chapter, we will introduce fundamental business ethics background and concepts. In Chapter 7, we will consider personal and organizational ethics. Chapter 8 addresses newly emerging technology and business ethics. Finally, in Chapter 9 our attention will turn to the international sphere as we discuss ethical issues in the global arena.

FIGURE 6-2

Examples from Inventory of Ethical Issues in Business

This checklist is designed to stimulate thought and discussion on important ethical concerns in your company and the larger business community.

For each of the following issues, indicate whether ethical problems are

5 = Very serious; 4 = Serious; 3 = Not very serious; 2 = Not a problem; 1 = No opinion.

Column I = In the business world in general   **Column II** = In your company

Employee–Employer Relations

_____ _____ Work ethic—giving a full day's work for a full day's pay
_____ _____ Petty theft (i.e., supplies, telephone, photocopying, etc.)
_____ _____ Cheating on expense accounts
_____ _____ Employee acceptance of gifts or favors from vendors
_____ _____ Distortion or falsification of internal reports
_____ _____ Cheating or overreaching on benefits (sick days, insurance, etc.)

Employer–Employee Relations

_____ _____ Sexual or racial discrimination in hiring, promotion, or pay
_____ _____ Sexual harassment
_____ _____ Invasions of employee privacy
_____ _____ Unsafe or unhealthy working conditions
_____ _____ Discouragement of internal criticism re: unfair, illegal, or improper activities
_____ _____ Unfair demands on or expectations of paid staff
_____ _____ Inadequate recognition, appreciation, or other psychic rewards to staff
_____ _____ Inappropriate blame-shifting or credit-taking to protect or advance personal careers
_____ _____ Unhealthy competition among employees about "turf," assignments, budget, etc.

Company–Customer Relations

_____ _____ Unfair product pricing
_____ _____ Deceptive marketing/advertising
_____ _____ Unsafe or unhealthy products
_____ _____ Unfair and/or legalistic handling of customer complaints
_____ _____ Discourtesy or arrogance toward customers

Company–Shareholder Relations

_____ _____ Excessive compensation for top management
_____ _____ Self-protective management policies (golden parachutes, poison pills, greenmail)
_____ _____ Mismanagement of corporate assets or opportunities
_____ _____ Public reports and/or financial statements that distort actual performance

Company–Community/Public Interest

_____ _____ Injury to the environment
_____ _____ Undue influence on the political process through lobbying, PACs, etc.
_____ _____ Payoffs, "grease," or bribes in foreign countries
_____ _____ Doing business in countries with inhumane or anti-American policies

SOURCE: Reprinted with permission © Josephson Institute of Ethics, *Ethics: Easier Said Than Done* (Vol. 2, No. 1, 1989).

THE PUBLIC'S OPINION OF BUSINESS ETHICS

The public's view of business ethics has never been very high. Anecdotal evidence suggests that many citizens see business ethics as essentially a contradiction in terms, an oxymoron, and think that there is only a fine line between a business executive and a crook. Some of the polls of people's opinions about business ethics were reported earlier. The upshot of these surveys seems to be that things are getting better, though business ethics problems continue. In spite of ups-and-downs, the consensus seems to be that we are in an era of fraud and corruption and that serious steps need to be taken to get business back on track.

Has Business Ethics Really Deteriorated?

Despite the warnings inherent in the business scandals of 2002, corporations and their officers continue to walk an ethical tightrope. In an article for *Entrepreneur* (October 2003 v31 i10 p68), Joshua Kurlantzick maintains that "little has changed in American business culture . . . because lying and dishonesty simply have become a much more accepted part of business—and of American life." Kurlantzick says that "tolerance of lying and bad behavior has seriously damaged trust in American business" and points out that to reverse this trend, society itself must change. Explore the ways society might change by logging on to InfoTrac College Edition at **http://www.infotrac-college.com** and keying record number A109403729.

Unfortunately, there is no scientific way to determine whether or not business ethics has really deteriorated. Max Ways's description of a statistical analysis (modern society's favorite kind of investigation) aimed at answering the question "How widespread is corporate misconduct?" is enlightening. He says that to describe such a project would demonstrate its impossibility. He argues that the researcher would have to count the transgressions publicly exposed in a certain period of time. Then the total number of known misdeeds would have to be correlated with the trillions and trillions of business transactions that occur daily. He concludes:

> *If we assume (recklessly) that a believable estimate of total transactions could be made, then the sum of the publicly known malfeasances almost certainly would be a minute fraction of the whole. At this point the investigator would have to abandon the conclusion that the incidence of business misconduct is so low as to be insignificant.*[13]

In fact, no such study has ever been attempted. Public opinion polls might be our best way to gather data about the current state of business ethics, but such polls are hardly definitive. The polls have reported mixed results in recent years, but we must consider some other factors that affect the public's opinions, such as media reporting and society's expectations of business's ethics.

SEARCH THE WEB

ETHICS OFFICER ASSOCIATION

What is going on in the world of business ethics? One way to find out is to check out what the Ethics Officer Association (EOA) is doing. The EOA Web site is located at **http://www.eoa.org**. The EOA is the professional association of managers of corporate ethics and compliance programs. The EOA Web site has a wealth of information about what the professional practitioners of business ethics are doing. You may find out about their mission, vision, and values. You may also see what companies belong to the EOA. It also has links to other useful business ethics Web sites.

Are the Media Reporting Ethics More Vigorously?

There is no doubt that the media are reporting ethical problems more frequently and fervently. Spurred on by the Enron and other scandals of the past few years, the media have found business ethics and, indeed, ethics questions among all institutions to be subjects of growing and sustaining interest. The Martha Stewart trial during 2003-2004 took on monumental proportions as the media turned it into the proverbial media circus that most felt exceeded its merit as a business ethics issue. Many believed that the charges against Stewart were much less severe than most of the other companies and executives summarized in Figure 6-1, but because she was an entertainment personality, the media coverage was nonstop.

Of particular interest in recent years has been the in-depth investigative reporting of business ethics on such TV shows as

60 Minutes, 20/20, Dateline NBC, Primetime Live, and *Frontline,* as well as the growing number of such programs. Such investigations keep business ethics in the public eye and make it difficult to assess whether public opinion polls are reflecting the actual business ethics of the day or simply the reactions to the latest scandals covered on a weekly basis.

Is It That Society Is Actually Changing?

We would definitely make this argument here, as we did in Chapter 1. Many business managers subscribe to this belief. W. Michael Blumenthal, one-time U.S. Secretary of the Treasury and chief executive officer of the Bendix Corporation, has been one of the leading advocates of this view. He argued:

> *It seems to me that the root causes of the questionable and illegal corporate activities that have come to light recently . . . can be traced to the sweeping changes that have taken place in our society and throughout the world and to the unwillingness of many in business to adjust to these changes.*[14]

He goes on to say, "People in business have not suddenly become immoral. What has changed are the contexts in which corporate decisions are made, the demands that are being made on business, and the nature of what is considered proper corporate conduct."[15]

Although it would be difficult to prove Blumenthal's thesis, it is an intuitively attractive one. You do not have to make a lengthy investigation of some of today's business practices to realize that a good number of what are now called unethical practices were at one time considered acceptable. Or, it may be that the practices never really were acceptable to the public but that, because they were not known, they were tolerated, thus causing no moral dilemma in the mind of the public. In spite of this analysis, one cannot help but believe that the greed by top-level business executives that has been exposed in this first decade of the new millennium has elevated the ethics issue to new heights. Executive lying has contributed to the problem. Though corporate governance has gotten better in recent years, lack of careful oversight of top echelon executives has been a problem as well. Corporate boards, in some cases, have fallen down in their duties to monitor top executive behavior, and one consequence has been the recent ethics scandals.

Figure 6-3 on page 174 illustrates how the magnitude of the ethics problem may be more detectable today than it once was, as a result of the public's expectations of business's ethical behavior rising more rapidly than actual business ethics. Note in the figure that actual business ethics is assumed to be improving but not at the same pace as public expectations are rising. The magnitude of the current ethics problem, therefore, is seen here partially to be a function of rapidly rising societal expectations about business behavior.

BUSINESS ETHICS: WHAT DOES IT REALLY MEAN?

In Chapter 2, we discussed the ethical responsibilities of business in an introductory way. We contrasted ethics with economics, law, and philanthropy. To be sure, we all have a general idea of what business ethics means, but here we would like to probe the topic more deeply. To understand business ethics, it is useful to comment on the relationship between ethics and morality.

Ethics is the discipline that deals with what is good and bad and with moral duty and obligation. Ethics can also be regarded as a set of moral principles or values. Morality is a doctrine or system of moral conduct. Moral conduct refers to that which

FIGURE 6-3

Business Ethics Today Versus Earlier Periods

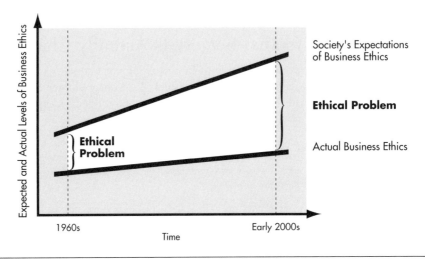

relates to principles of right and wrong in behavior. For the most part, then, we can think of ethics and morality as being so similar to one another that we may use the terms interchangeably to refer to the study of fairness, justice, and right and wrong behavior in business.

Business ethics, therefore, is concerned with good and bad or right and wrong behavior and practices that take place within a business context. Concepts of right and wrong are increasingly being interpreted today to include the more difficult and subtle questions of fairness, justice, and equity.

Two key branches of moral philosophy, or ethics, are descriptive ethics and normative ethics. It is important to distinguish between the two because they each take a different perspective. **Descriptive ethics** is concerned with describing, characterizing, and studying the morality of a people, a culture, or a society. It also compares and contrasts different moral codes, systems, practices, beliefs, and values.[16] In descriptive business ethics, therefore, our focus is on learning what is occurring in the realm of behavior, actions, decisions, policies, and practices of business firms, managers, or, perhaps, specific industries. The public opinion polls cited earlier give us glimpses of descriptive ethics—what people believe to be going on based on their perceptions and understandings. Descriptive ethics focuses on "what is" the prevailing set of ethical standards in the business community, specific organizations, or on the part of specific managers. A real danger in limiting our attention to descriptive ethics is that some people may adopt the view that "if everyone is doing it," it must be acceptable. For example, if a survey reveals that 70 percent of employees are padding their expense accounts, this describes what is taking place but it does not describe what *should* be taking place. Just because many are participating in this questionable activity doesn't make it an appropriate practice. This is why normative ethics is important.

Normative ethics, by contrast, is concerned with supplying and justifying a coherent moral system of thinking and judging. Normative ethics seeks to uncover, develop, and justify basic moral principles that are intended to guide behavior, actions, and decisions.[17]

Normative business ethics, therefore, seeks to propose some principle or principles for distinguishing what is ethical from what is unethical in the business context. It deals more with "what ought to be" or "what ought not to be" in terms of business practices. Normative ethics is concerned with establishing norms or standards by which business practices might be guided or judged.

In our study of business ethics, we need to be ever mindful of this distinction between descriptive and normative perspectives. It is tempting to observe the prevalence of a particular practice in business (for example, discrimination or deceptive advertising) and conclude that because so many are doing it (descriptive ethics), it must be acceptable behavior. Normative ethics would insist that a practice be justified on the basis of some ethical principle, argument, or rationale before being considered acceptable. Normative ethics demands a more meaningful moral anchor than just "everyone is doing it." Normative ethics is our primary frame of reference in this discussion, though we will frequently compare "what ought to be" with "what is (going on in the real world)."

In this chapter and continuing into Chapter 7, we will introduce three major approaches to thinking about business ethics:

1. Conventional approach (Chapter 6)
2. Principles approach (Chapter 7)
3. Ethical tests approach (Chapter 7)

We will discuss the conventional approach to business ethics in this chapter and the other two approaches in Chapter 7.

The Conventional Approach to Business Ethics

The **conventional approach to business ethics** is essentially an approach whereby we compare a decision or practice with prevailing norms of acceptability. We call it the conventional approach because it is believed that this is the way that conventional or general society thinks. The major challenge of this approach is answering the questions "Whose norms do we use?" in making the judgment, and "What norms are prevailing?" This approach may be depicted by highlighting the major variables to be compared with one another:

Decision or Practice ⬌ Prevailing Norms of Acceptability

There is considerable room for variability on both of these issues. With respect to whose norms are used as the basis for ethical judgments, the conventional approach would consider as legitimate those norms emanating from family, friends, religious beliefs, the local community, one's employer, law, the profession, and so on. In addition, one's conscience, or one's self, would be seen by many as a legitimate source of ethical norms. Two classic "Frank & Ernest" comic strips poke fun at the use of one's conscience. In the first, a sign on the wall reads "Tonight's Lecture: Moral Philosophy." Then it shows Frank saying to Ernest, "I'd let my conscience be my guide, but I'm in enough trouble already!" In a second comic strip, Frank says to Ernest, while they are standing at a bar, "I always use my conscience as my guide. But, fortunately, it has a terrible sense of direction." These comic strips reveal the often limiting nature of using one's conscience.

Figure 6-4 on page 176 illustrates some of the sources of norms that come to bear on the individual and that might be used in various circumstances, and over time, under the conventional approach. These sources compete in their influence on what constitutes the "prevailing norms of acceptability" for today.

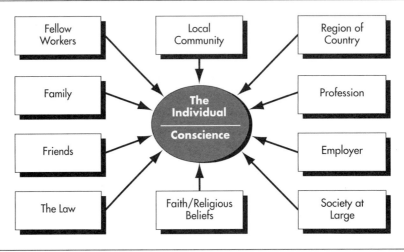

FIGURE 6-4

Sources of Ethical Norms Communicated to Individuals

In some circumstances, the conventional approach to ethics may be useful and applicable. What does a person do, however, if norms from one source conflict with norms from another source? Also, how can we be sure that societal norms are really appropriate or defensible? Our society's culture sends us many and often conflicting messages about what is appropriate ethical behavior. We get these messages from television, movies, music, and other sources in the culture. Recently, TV shows such as *Survivor* and *The Apprentice* have run episodes in which questionable ethics are depicted and sometimes celebrated. On *Survivor*, the participants are forever creating alliances and then breaking them in the interest of winning the game. *The Apprentice*, introduced in 2004, was one of the first reality shows with a business focus. Sixteen participants vie for Donald Trump's favor as they are broken into teams to compete to become Trump's "apprentice" and go to work for $250,000 on one of Trump's projects. A number of these episodes portrayed questionable ethics passed off as business-as-usual. As the women's team managed Planet Hollywood for a day, they resorted to using their sexuality to increase sales. The attractive women became "The Shooter Girls" (similar to the "Hooter" girls) and tried to sell shots to the admiring men customers, using whatever tactics worked. In one scene, while participant Amy was out on the streets trying to give away coupons, she observed "I feel like I'm pimping."[18] In other episodes, they were out on the streets of New York giving away kisses to the men who bought their products, while they flaunted their sexuality in skimpy, revealing outfits.

One of the most questionable tactics portrayed on *The Apprentice* was when the men's team was pushing to increase sales at Planet Hollywood by selling merchandise. The men's team started hawking miniature basketballs, while shouting "Get a Kwame Jackson autograph," as they had one of their own sitting at a table selling the basketballs while autographing them for buyers. They never told anyone Kwame was not a well-known NBA basketball star, but many little kids bought the basketballs anyway, thinking he was some famous star. Obviously, they had deceived many customers into thinking Kwame was an all-star. This episode created a lot of finger pointing on the show, with participants divided over the ethics of deceiving customers in this way.[19] It is just possible that an impressionable young person might see this and hundreds of other references like it and conclude that dishonesty is really the standard in business.

Another example of the conflicting messages people get today from society occurs in the realm of sexual harassment in the workplace. On the one hand, today's television, movies, advertisements, and music are replete with sexual innuendo and the treatment of women and men as sex objects. This would suggest that such behavior is normal, acceptable, even desired. On the other hand, the law and the courts are stringently prohibiting sexual gestures or innuendo in the workplace. As we will see in Chapter 18, it does not take much sexual innuendo to constitute a "hostile work environment" and a sex discrimination charge under Title VII of the Civil Rights Act. In this example, we see a norm that is prevalent in culture and society clashing with a norm evolving from employment law and business ethics.

Ethics and the Law

We have made various references to ethics and the law. In Chapter 2, we said that ethical behavior is typically thought to reside above behavior required by the law. This is the generally accepted view of ethics. We should make it clear, however, that in many respects the law and ethics overlap. To appreciate this, you need to recognize that the law embodies notions of ethics. That is, the law may be seen as a reflection of what society thinks are minimal standards of conduct and behavior. Both law and ethics have to do with what is deemed appropriate or acceptable, but law reflects society's *codified* ethics. Therefore, if a person breaks a law or violates a regulation, she or he is also behaving unethically. In spite of this overlap, we continue to talk about desirable ethical behavior as behavior that extends beyond what is required by law. Viewed from the standpoint of minimums, we would certainly say that obedience to the law is generally regarded to be a minimum standard of ethical behavior.

In addition, we should make note of the fact that the law does not address all realms in which ethical questions might be raised. Thus, there are clear roles for both law and ethics to play. It should be noted that research on illegal corporate behavior has been conducted for some time. Illegal corporate behavior, of course, comprises business practices that are in direct defiance of law or public policy. Research has focused on two dominant questions: (1) Why do firms behave illegally or what leads them to engage in illegal activities, and (2) what are the consequences of behaving illegally?[20] We will not deal with these studies of lawbreaking in this discussion; however, we should view this body of studies and investigations as being closely aligned with our interest in business ethics.

Making Ethical Judgments

When a decision is made about what is ethical (right, just, fair) using the conventional approach, there is room for variability on several counts (see Figure 6-5 on page 178). Three key elements compose such a decision. First, we observe the *decision*, *action*, or *practice* that has been committed in the workplace setting. Second, we *compare the practice with prevailing norms of acceptability*—that is, society's or some other standard of what is acceptable or unacceptable. Third, *we must recognize that value judgments are being made* by someone as to what really occurred (the actual behavior) and what the prevailing norms of acceptability really are. This means that two different people could

FIGURE 6-5

Making Ethical Judgments

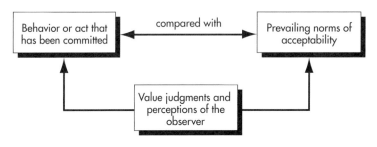

look at the same behavior or practice, compare it with their concepts of what the prevailing norms are, and reach different conclusions as to whether the behavior was ethical or not. This becomes quite complex as perceptions of what is ethical inevitably lead to the difficult task of ranking different values against one another.

If we can put aside for a moment the fact that perceptual differences about an incident do exist, and the fact that we differ among ourselves because of our personal values and philosophies of right and wrong, we are still left with the problematic task of determining society's prevailing norms of acceptability of business behavior. As a whole, members of society generally agree at a very high level of abstraction that certain behaviors are wrong. However, the consensus tends to disintegrate as we move from general to specific situations.

Let us illustrate with a business example. We might all agree with the general dictum that "You should not steal someone else's property." At a high level of abstraction (as a general precept), we probably would have consensus on this. But as we look at specific situations, our consensus may tend to disappear. Is it acceptable to take home from work such things as pencils, pens, paper clips, paper, staplers, computer discs, adding machines, and calculators? Is it acceptable to use the company telephone for personal long-distance calls? Is it acceptable to use company gasoline for private use or to pad expense accounts? Is it acceptable to use company computers for personal e-mail? What if everyone else is doing it?

What is interesting in this example is that we are more likely to reach consensus in principle than in practice. Some people who would say these practices are not acceptable might privately engage in them. Furthermore, a person who would not think of shoplifting even the smallest item from a local store might take pencils and paper home from work on a regular basis. A comic strip depicting the "Born Loser" illustrates this point. In the first panel, the father admonishes his son Wilberforce in the following way: "You know how I feel about stealing. Now tomorrow I want you to return every one of those pencils to school." In the second panel, Father says to Wilberforce, "I'll bring you all the pencils you need from work." This is an example of the classic double standard, and it illustrates how actions may be perceived differently by the observer or the participant.

Thus, in the conventional approach to business ethics, determinations of what is ethical and what is not require judgments to be made on at least three counts:

1. What is the *true nature* of the practice, behavior, or decision that occurred?
2. What are society's (or business's) *prevailing norms* of acceptability?

3. What *value judgments* are being made by someone about the practice or behavior, and what are that person's *perceptions* of applicable norms?

The human factor in the situation thus introduces the problem of perception and values and makes the decision process complicated.

The conventional approach to business ethics can be valuable, because we all need to be aware of and sensitive to the total environment in which we exist. We need to be aware of how society regards ethical issues. It has limitations, however, and we need to be cognizant of these as well. The most serious danger is that of falling into an **ethical relativism** where we pick and choose which source of norms we wish to use based on what will justify our current actions or maximize our freedom. A recent comic strip is relevant. In a courtroom, while swearing in, the witness stated, "I swear to tell the truth . . . *as I see it.*"

In the next chapter, we will argue that a principles approach is needed to augment the conventional approach. The principles approach looks at general guides to ethical decision making that come from moral philosophy. We will also present the ethical tests approach, which is more of a practical approach, in the next chapter.

ETHICS, ECONOMICS, AND LAW: A VENN MODEL

When we focus on ethics and ethical decision making, it is useful to consider the primary forces that come into tension while making ethical judgments. In Chapter 2, these were introduced as part of the 4-part definition of corporate social responsibility, and they were depicted in the Pyramid of CSR. When we are discussing a firm's CSR, philanthropy definitely enters the discussion. This is because philanthropic initiatives are the primary way many companies display their CSR in the community—through good and charitable works. In ethical decision making, however, we tend to set aside philanthropic expectations and focus on ethical expectations and, especially, those forces that primarily come into tension with ethics—economics (the quest for profits) and law. Thus, in most decision-making situations, ethics, economics, and law become the central expectations that must be considered and balanced against each other in the quest to make wise decisions.

A firm's economic, legal, and ethical responsibilities can be depicted in a Venn diagram model illustrating how certain actions, decisions, or policies fulfill one, two, or three of these responsibility categories. Figure 6-6 on page 180 presents this Venn diagram model, illustrating the overlapping potential of these responsibility categories.

In Area 1, where the decision, action, or practice fulfills all three responsibilities, the management prescription is to "go for it." That is, the action is profitable, in compliance with the law, and represents ethical behavior. In Area 2a, the action under consideration is profitable and legal, but its ethical status may be uncertain. The guideline here is to "proceed cautiously." In these kinds of situations, the ethics of the action needs to be carefully considered. In Area 2b, the action is profitable and ethical, but perhaps the law does not clearly address the issue or is ambiguous. If it is ethical, there is a good chance it is also legal, but the guideline again is to proceed cautiously. In Area 3, the action is legal and ethical but not profitable. Therefore, the strategy here would be to avoid this action or find ways to make it profitable. However, there may be a compelling case to take the action if it is legal and ethical and, thus, represents the right thing to do. Schwartz and Carroll have presented a 3-domain approach to CSR that employs a Venn diagram format such as that presented in Figure 6-6. They provide corporate examples to illustrate each section of the Venn diagram.[21]

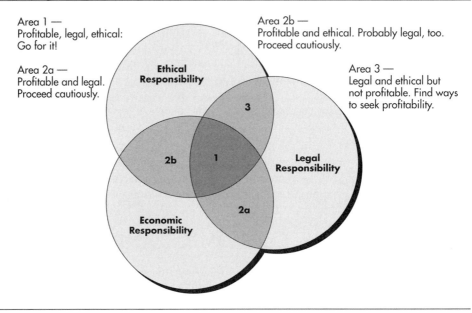

FIGURE 6-6

A Venn Diagram Model for Ethical Decision Making

Area 1 —
Profitable, legal, ethical:
Go for it!

Area 2b —
Profitable and ethical. Probably legal, too.
Proceed cautiously.

Area 2a —
Profitable and legal.
Proceed cautiously.

Area 3 —
Legal and ethical but
not profitable. Find ways
to seek profitability.

By taking philanthropy out of the picture, the ethics Venn model serves as a useful template for thinking about the more immediate expectations that society has on business in a situation in which the ethical dimension plays an important role. It illustrates clearly that many business decisions boil down to trade-offs between the influences of economics, law, and ethics.

FOUR IMPORTANT ETHICS QUESTIONS

It is also useful to provide some additional "big picture" perspectives that could legitimately be asked of ethics, in general, or of business ethics, in particular. Philosophers have concepts and terminology that are more academic, but let us approach this broad perspective, as Otto Bremer has done,[22] by starting with four apparently simple but really different kinds of questions:

1. What is?
2. What ought to be?
3. How do we get from what is to what ought to be?
4. What is our motivation in all this?

These four questions capture the core of what ethics is all about. They force an examination of *what really is* (descriptive ethics) going on in a business situation, *what ought to be* (normative ethics), how we *close the gap* between what is and what ought to be (practical question), and what our *motivation* is for doing all this.

Before we discuss each question briefly, let us suggest that these four questions may be asked at five different levels: the level of the individual (the personal level), the level of the organization, the level of the industry or profession, the societal level, and the

Ethics in Practice

ETHICS IN THE MAILROOM

To make some extra money during college, I got a part-time job in a mailroom at a rather large business. This business would send out hundreds of pieces of mail each day, all going through the mailroom. Our job as the staff of the mailroom was to package this mail to be shipped, put the proper amount of postage on it, and then take it to the post office. To put the postage on the items, we used a postage meter that was in the mailroom. The postage meter would weigh the mail and then stamp it with the correct amount of postage, and my employers would pay the postage costs in lump sums periodically throughout the year.

Occasionally my boss would run some of his personal mail along with the business mail. When I asked him if sending personal mail through the meter was basically stealing money from the company, he justified it by saying that he only used the meter to mail his bills, and he would never use it for anything over 60 cents. He also said that he had been working there

for 13 years, and he compensated for his low pay by being able to send out the occasional bill or letter. I figured that a few cents here and there would not hurt the company and looked the other way.

1. Does working for a company for 13 years justify sending out personal mail that the company pays for?

2. Does my boss's low pay justify his using company resources to send out personal mail to compensate for the low pay? After all, isn't it just "balancing things out"?

3. Did I do the right thing by looking the other way or should I have turned my boss in for stealing company money even though it was just a few cents here and there? What should I have done?

Contributed Anonymously

global or international level. By asking and then answering these questions, a greater understanding of a business ethics dilemma may be achieved.

What Is? *The Descriptive Question*

The "what is?" question forces us to face the reality of what is actually going on in an ethical sense in business or in a specific decision or practice. Ideally it is a factual, scientific, or descriptive question. Its purpose is to help us understand the reality of the ethical behavior we find before us in the business environment. As we discussed earlier when we were describing the nature of making ethical judgments, it is not always simple to state exactly what the "real" situation is. This is because we are humans and thus make mistakes when we "sense" what is happening. Also, we are conditioned by our personal beliefs, values, and biases, and these factors affect what we see or sense. Or, we may perceive real conditions for what they are but fail to think in terms of alternatives or in terms of "what ought to be." Think of the difficulty you might have in attempting to describe "what is" with respect to business ethics at the personal, organizational, industry/professional, societal, or global levels. The questions then become:

- What are your personal ethics?
- What are your organization's ethics?
- What are the ethics of your industry or profession?
- What are society's ethics?
- What are global ethics?

What Ought to Be? *The Normative Question*

This second question is quite different from the first question. It is normative rather than descriptive. It is certainly not a scientific question. The "what ought to be?" question seldom gets answered directly, particularly in a managerial setting. Managers are used to identifying alternatives and choosing the best one, but seldom is this done with questions that entail moral content or the "rightness, fairness, or justice" of a decision or practice. The "ought to be" question is often viewed in terms of what management *should do* (in an ethical sense) in a given situation. Examples of this question in a business setting might be:

- How *ought* we treat our aging employees whose productivity is declining?
- How safe *ought* we make this product, knowing full well we cannot pass all the costs on to the consumer?
- How clean an environment *should* we aim for?
- How *should* we treat long-time employees when the company is downsizing or moving the plant to a foreign country?
- *Should* we outsource certain aspects of our production to China or India even though it might mean fewer jobs at home?

At a corporate planning seminar several years ago, the leader suggested that if you are the president of a large corporation the place to start planning is with a vision of society, not with where you want to be 5 or 10 years into the future. What kind of world do you want to have? How does your industry or your firm fit into that world? An executive cannot just walk into the office one day and say, "I had a vision last night," and expect many adherents.[23] But this does not make the question or the vision invalid. It simply suggests that we must approach the "what ought to be?" questions at a more practical level. There are plenty of issues to which this question can be applied in the everyday life of a manager. Therefore, such lofty, visionary exercises are not necessary.

How to Get from What Is to What Ought to Be: *The Practical Question*

This third question represents the challenge of bridging the gap between where we are and where we ought to be with respect to ethical practices. Therefore, it represents an action dimension. It is a practical question for management. We may discuss endlessly where we "ought" to be in terms of our own personal ethics or the ethics of our firm, of our industry, or of society. As we move further away from the individual level, we have less control or influence over the "ought to be" question.

When faced with these ideas as depicted by our "ought to be" questions, we may find that from a practical point of view we cannot achieve our ideals. This does not mean we should not have asked the question in the first place. Our "ought to be" questions become goals or objectives for our ethical practices. They form the normative core of business ethics. They become moral benchmarks that help us to measure progress.

In all managerial situations, we are faced with this challenge of balancing what we *ought to do* with what we *must or can do*. The notions of Leslie Weatherhead in his book, *The Will of God*, could be adapted to our discussion here. He refers to God's intentional will, circumstantial will, and ultimate will. Looking at these concepts from a managerial or an ethics point of view, we might think in terms of what we *intend* to accomplish, what circumstances *permit* us to accomplish, and what we ultimately are *able* to accomplish. These ideas interject a measure of realism into our efforts to close the gap between where we are and where we want to be in a business ethics application.

This is also the stage at which managerial decision making and strategy come into play. The first step in managerial problem solving is identifying the problem (what "is"). Next comes identifying where we want to be (the "ought" question). Then comes the managerial challenge of closing the gap. "Gap analysis" sets the stage for concrete business action.

What Is Our Motivation? *A Question of Authenticity*

Pragmatic businesspeople do not like to dwell on this fourth question, which addresses the motivation for being ethical, because sometimes it reveals some manipulative or self-centered motive. At one level, is it perhaps not desirable to discuss motivation, because isn't it really actions that count? If someone makes a $100 contribution to a charitable cause, is it fair to ask whether the person did it (1) because she or he really believes in the cause (altruistic motivation) or (2) because she or he just wanted a tax deduction or wanted to "look" benevolent in the eyes of others (selfish motive)? Most of us would agree that it is better for a person to make a contribution rather than not make it, regardless of the motive.

Ideally, we would hope that people would be ethical because they intrinsically see that being ethical is a better way to live or manage. What kind of world (or organization) would most people prefer: one in which people behave ethically because they have selfish or instrumental reasons for doing so, or one in which they behave ethically because they really believe in what they are doing? We will accept the former, but the latter is more desirable. We will be better off in the long run if "right" managerial practices are motivated by the knowledge that there is inherent value in ethical behavior.

This can be compared to the organizational situation in which managers are attempting to motivate their workers. If a manager is interested only in greater productivity and sees that being "concerned" about employees' welfare will achieve this goal, she or he had better be prepared for the fact that employees may see through the "game playing" and eventually rebel against the manager's effort. On the other hand, employees can see when management is genuinely concerned about their welfare, and they will be responsive to such well-motivated efforts. This is borne out in practice. You can examine two companies that on the surface appear to have identical human resource policies. In one company, the employees know and feel they are being manipulated; in the other company, there is confidence that management really does care.[24] In essence, the difference is one of managements' authenticity of motive.

Although we would like to believe that managers are appropriately motivated in their quest for ethical business behavior and that motivations are important, we must continue to understand and accept Andrew Stark's observation that we live in a "messy world of mixed motives." Therefore, managers do not typically have the luxury of making abstract distinctions between altruism and self-interest but must get on with the task of designing structures, systems, incentives, and processes that accommodate the "whole" employee, regardless of motivations.[25]

THREE MODELS OF MANAGEMENT ETHICS

In attempting to understand the basic concepts of business ethics, it is useful to think in terms of key ethical models that might describe different types of management ethics found in the organizational world.[26] These models should provide some useful base points for discussion and comparison. The media have focused so much on immoral or unethical business behavior that it is easy to forget or not think about the possibility of other ethical styles or types. For example, scant attention has been given to the distinction that may be made between those activities that are *immoral* and those that are *amoral*; similarly, little attention has been given to contrasting these two forms of behavior with ethical or *moral* management.

Believing that there is value in developing descriptive models for purposes of clearer understanding, here we will describe, compare, and contrast three models or types of ethical management:

- Immoral management
- Moral management
- Amoral management

A major goal is to develop a clearer understanding of the gamut of management approaches in which ethics or morality is a defining characteristic. By seeing these approaches come to life through description and example, managers can be in an improved position to assess their own ethical approaches and those of other organizational members (supervisors, subordinates, and peers).

Another central objective is to identify more completely the amoral management model, which often is overlooked in the human rush to classify things as good or bad, moral or immoral. In a later section, we will discuss the elements of moral judgment that must be developed if the transition to moral management is to succeed. A more detailed development of each management model is valuable in coming to understand the range of ethics that leaders may intentionally or unintentionally display. Let us consider the two extremes first—immoral and moral management—and then amoral management.

Immoral Management

Using *immoral* and *unethical* as synonyms, **immoral management** is defined as a posture that not only is devoid of ethical principles or precepts but also implies a positive and active opposition to what is ethical. Immoral management decisions, behaviors, actions, and practices are discordant with ethical principles. This model holds that management's motives are selfish and that it cares only or principally about its own or its company's gains. If management's activity is actively opposed to what is regarded as ethical, this suggests that management knows right from wrong and yet chooses to do wrong. Thus, its motives are deemed greedy or selfish. According to this model, management's goals are profitability and organizational success at virtually any price. Management does not care about others' claims to be treated fairly or justly.

What about management's orientation toward the law, considering that law is often regarded as an embodiment of minimal ethics? Immoral management regards legal standards as barriers that management must avoid or overcome in order to accomplish what it wants. Immoral management would just as soon engage in illegal activity as in immoral or unethical activity.

Operating Strategy. The operating strategy of immoral management is focused on exploiting opportunities for corporate or personal gain. An active opposition to what is moral would suggest that managers cut corners anywhere and everywhere it appears useful. Thus, the key operating question guiding immoral management is, "Can we make money with this action, decision, or behavior, *regardless of what it takes*?" Implicit in this question is that nothing else matters, at least not very much. Figure 6-7 summarizes some of the major characteristics of immoral management.

FIGURE 6-7

Characteristics of Immoral Managers

- These managers intentionally do wrong.
- These managers are *self-centered* and *self-absorbed*.
- They care only about self or organization's profits/success.
- They actively oppose what is right, fair, or just.
- They *exhibit no concern* for stakeholders.
- These are the "bad guys."
- An ethics course probably would not help them.

Illustrative Cases of Immoral Management.   Examples of immoral management abound. Recently, an employee at a Toys "Я" Us store reported an experience that occurred to him at his Albuquerque store. He discovered that his manager was using the computer to alter workers' time records, secretly deleting hours to cut their paychecks and fatten his store's bottom line. The employee confronted his boss and said, "That's not exactly legal." The employee reported that his boss threatened him and told him not to talk about what he had seen.[27]

In 2004, three former executives of Computer Associates pleaded guilty to charges of securities fraud. The focus of the investigation included three high-ranking executives. In their pleas, the executives depicted a wide-ranging conspiracy to falsify the company's books and hide the falsifications from federal prosecutors. The three executives said they met to discuss the company's sales for the previous quarter and noted that the sales fell short of Wall Street's forecasts. In response, the executives decided to continue to book new sales as if they had taken place in the previous quarter. Then, to hide the backdated sales from auditors, employees of the firm deleted time stamps showing when the contracts had actually been faxed to the company. It was revealed that more than 20 percent of the company's revenue came from backdated contracts. The former chief financial officer later confessed, "I knew my conduct was wrong at the time." He faces up to 20 years in federal prison.[28]

In another case, Procter & Gamble (P&G) admitted to corporate espionage after some of its employees had rummaged through the trashcans outside the Chicago offices of Unilever, the British-Dutch Company that makes Lipton tea, Dove soap, and several brands of shampoo. Agents of P&G retrieved about 80 pages of Unilever's confidential plans. In its defense, P&G said its agents did not violate the law, but did violate the company's own ethics policies, which prohibit rummaging through garbage to acquire information on competitors. P&G agreed to pay Unilever $10 million in the spying case and agreed to an unusual third-party audit to monitor the product development and marketing plans of the company. P&G's chairman pledged that he had taken steps to ensure that the acquired material would not be used by his company.[29]

All of these are examples of immoral management where executives' decisions or actions were self-centered, actively opposed to what is right, focused on achieving organizational success at whatever the cost, and cutting corners where it was useful. These decisions were made without regard to the possible consequences of such concerns as honesty or fairness to others.

Moral Management

At the opposite extreme from immoral management is **moral management**. Moral management conforms to the highest standards of ethical behavior or professional standards of conduct. Although it is not always crystal clear what level of ethical standards prevail, moral management strives to be ethical in terms of its focus on high ethical norms and professional standards of conduct, motives, goals, orientation toward the law, and general operating strategy.

In contrast to the selfish motives in immoral management, moral management aspires to succeed, but only within the confines of sound ethical precepts—that is, standards predicated on such norms as fairness, justice, respect for rights, and due process. Moral management's motives, therefore, likely would be termed fair, balanced, or unselfish. Organizational goals continue to stress profitability, but only within the confines of legal obedience and sensitivity to and responsiveness to ethical standards. Moral management pursues its objectives of profitability, legality, and ethics as both required and desirable. Moral management would not pursue profits at the expense of the law and sound ethics. Indeed, the focus here would be not only on the letter of the law but on the spirit of the law as well. The law would be viewed as a minimal standard of ethical behavior, because moral management strives to operate at a level above what the law mandates.

Operating Strategy of Moral Management.
The operating strategy of moral management is to live by sound ethical standards, seeking out only those economic opportunities that the organization or management can pursue within the confines of ethical behavior. The organization assumes a leadership position when ethical dilemmas arise. The central question guiding moral management's actions, decisions, and behaviors is, "Will this action, decision, behavior, or practice be fair to all stakeholders involved as well as to the organization?"

Lynn Sharp Paine has set forth what she calls an "integrity strategy" that closely resembles the moral management model.[30] The **integrity strategy** is characterized by a conception of ethics as the driving force of an organization. Ethical values shape management's search for opportunities, the design of organizational systems, and the decision-making process. Ethical values in the integrity strategy provide a common frame of reference and serve to unify different functions, lines of business, and employee groups. Organizational ethics, in this view, helps to define what an organization is and what it stands for. Some common features of an integrity strategy include the following,[31] which are all consistent with the moral management model:

- Guiding values and commitments make sense and are clearly communicated.
- Company leaders are personally committed, credible, and willing to take action on the values they espouse.
- Espoused values are integrated into the normal channels of management decision making.
- The organization's systems and structures support and reinforce its values.
- All managers have the skills, knowledge, and competencies to make ethically sound decisions on a daily basis.

Each year, *Business Ethics* magazine gives its Annual Business Ethics Awards. Considering the criteria for these awards is useful, because these criteria are representative of moral management as we have been describing it. *Business Ethics'* award criteria require a company to meet many, although not necessarily all, of the following criteria:[32]

- Be a leader in the company's field, showing the way ethically.
- Sponsor programs or initiatives in responsibility that demonstrate sincerity and ongoing vibrancy, and reach deep into the company.
- Be a significant presence on the national scene, so the company's ethical behavior sends a loud signal.
- Stand out in at least one area; a company need not be perfect, nor even exemplary, in all areas.
- Demonstrate the ability to face a recent challenge and overcome it with integrity.

Note that *Business Ethics* does not expect companies to be perfect in all their actions. Likewise, the moral management model acknowledges that a firm may exhibit moral management by overcoming a challenge with integrity.

Related to moral management is moral leadership. Carroll has set forth what he refers to as the "Seven Habits of Highly Moral Leaders."[33] Borrowing from the language used by Stephen Covey in his best-selling book *The Seven Habits of Highly Effective People*,[34] these qualities would need to be so prevalent and present in the leader's approach that they become habitual as a leadership approach. Helping to further flesh out what constitutes a moral manager, the seven habits of highly moral leaders have been set forth as follows:

- They have a passion to do right.
- They are morally proactive.
- They consider all stakeholders.
- They have a strong ethical character.
- They have an obsession with fairness.
- They undertake principled decision making.
- They integrate ethics wisdom with management wisdom.[35]

Figure 6-8 summarizes the important characteristics of moral managers.

Illustrative Cases of Moral Management.   *3M Company.* An excellent example of moral management was provided by the 3M Company in an action it took in mid-2000. While conducting some blood scans of its factory workers, 3M discovered that the tests were revealing trace amounts of a chemical that 3M had made for nearly 40 years. They also found evidence that the chemical was showing up in people's bloodstreams in various parts of the United States. The chemical was perfluorooctane sulfonate

---

FIGURE 6-8

Characteristics of Moral Managers

- These managers conform to *high level of ethical or right behavior* (moral rectitude).
- They conform to high level of personal and professional *standards*.
- *Ethical leadership* is commonplace—they search out where people may be hurt.
- Their goal is to succeed but only within confines of *sound ethical precepts* (fairness, due process).
- *High integrity* is displayed in *thinking, speaking,* and *doing.*
- These managers embrace letter and *spirit* of the law. Law is seen as a *minimal* ethical level. They prefer to operate *above* legal mandates.
- They possess an acute *"moral sense"* and *moral maturity.*
- Moral managers are the "good guys."

(PFO). How the PFOs got into people's bloodstreams, whether it could pose a health risk, and what should be done about it were all questions the company had to face. Although they could not come up with answers to these questions, company executives decided to take action anyway.

On its own, 3M decided to phase out PFOs and products containing related chemicals. The most important product to be affected was Scotchgard, the company's fabric protector. Because there is no replacement chemical yet available, the company faces a potential loss of $500 million in annual sales. Given that 3M was under no mandate to act, it makes the company's actions especially noteworthy. In complimenting 3M, Carol Browner, administrator of the EPA said that "3M deserves great credit for identifying this problem and coming forward voluntarily."[36]

McCulloch. Another excellent example of moral management taking the initiative in displaying ethical leadership was provided by McCulloch Corporation, a manufacturer of chain saws. Chain saws are notoriously dangerous. The Consumer Product Safety Commission one year estimated that there were 123,000 medically attended injuries involving chain saws, up from 71,000 5 years earlier. In spite of these statistics, the Chain Saw Manufacturers Association fought mandatory safety standards. The association claimed that the accident statistics were inflated and did not offer any justification for mandatory regulations. Manufacturers support voluntary standards, although some of them say that when chain brakes—major safety devices—are offered as an option, they do not sell. Apparently, consumers do not have adequate knowledge of the risks inherent in using chain saws.

McCulloch became dissatisfied with the Chain Saw Manufacturers Association's refusal to support higher standards of safety and withdrew from it. Chain brakes have been standard on McCulloch saws since 1975 and are mandatory for most saws produced in Finland, Britain, and Australia. A Swedish company, Husqvarna, Inc., now installs chain brakes on saws it sells in the United States. Statistics from the Quebec Logging Association and from Sweden demonstrate that kickback-related accidents were reduced by about 80 percent after the mandatory installation of safety standards, including chain brakes.[37]

McCulloch is an example of moral management. After attempting and failing to persuade its association to adopt a higher ethical standard that would greatly reduce injuries, it took a courageous action and withdrew from the association. This is a prime example of moral leadership.

Merck. Another well-known case of moral management occurred when Merck & Co., the pharmaceutical firm, invested millions of dollars to develop a drug for treating "river blindness," a Third World disease that was affecting almost 18 million people. Seeing that no government or aid organization was agreeing to buy the drug, Merck pledged to supply the drug for free forever. Merck's recognition that no effective mechanism existed to distribute the drug led to its decision to go far beyond industry practice and organize a committee to oversee the drug's distribution.[38]

We should stress at this time that not all organizations now engaging in moral management have done so all along. These companies sometimes arrived at this posture after years or decades of rising consumer expectations, increased government regulations, lawsuits, and pressure from social and consumer activists. We must think of moral management, therefore, as a desirable posture that in many instances has evolved over periods of several years. If we hold management to an idealistic, 100 percent historical moral purity test, no management will fill the bill. Rather, we should consider moral those managements that now see the enlightened self-interest of responding in accordance with the moral management model rather than alternatives.

Ethics in Practice

WHAT THEY DON'T KNOW WON'T HURT THEM

During my last two years in college, I worked for an animal hospital in my hometown. In my time there, many animals passed away in their sleep or for unknown reasons. It was not uncommon. In these situations, our facility would offer the owners the service of an autopsy. An autopsy is a procedure in which the doctor would surgically open up the animal to check for any signs of what might have caused the animal's death.

Mrs. Johnson, a client of ours, brought in her dog that had unfortunately passed away while she was at work. Her dog was only five years old and the owners were not aware of any health problems. No one, including the doctor, could figure out what had caused the death of Mrs. Johnson's dog. Mrs. Johnson was asked if she would give her consent for the doctor to perform an autopsy on her dog, so maybe they would be able to answer the many questions surrounding his death.

Mrs. Johnson did not want this procedure to be done; she just wanted our facility to take care of her dog's remains. The office manager at the animal hospital told the doctor she should let the vet students, who were doing their rotations at our hospital, go ahead and perform an autopsy as a learning experiment. The office manager mentioned that the owner would never know because we were in charge of the disposal, so it wouldn't be a problem.

1. Is it ethical for the doctor to allow the vet students to perform the autopsy?

2. Should the fact that the owner would never know if the autopsy was performed affect the doctor's decision?

3. What would you do in this situation?

Contributed Anonymously

Amoral Management

Amoral management is not just a middle position on a continuum between immoral and moral management. Conceptually it has been positioned between the other two, but it is different in nature and kind from both. There are two kinds of **amoral management: intentional** and **unintentional**.

Intentional Amoral Management.
Amoral managers of this type do not factor ethical considerations into their decisions, actions, and behaviors because they believe business activity resides outside the sphere to which moral judgments apply. These managers are neither moral nor immoral. They simply think that different rules apply in business than in other realms of life. Intentionally amoral managers are in a distinct minority today. At one time, however, as managers first began to think about reconciling business practices with sound ethics, some managers adopted this stance. A few intentionally amoral managers are still around, but they are a vanishing breed in today's ethically conscious world.

Unintentional Amoral Management.
Like intentionally amoral managers, unintentionally amoral managers do not think about business activity in ethical terms. These managers are simply casual about, careless about, or inattentive to the fact that their decisions and actions may have negative or deleterious effects on others. These managers lack ethical perception and moral awareness; that is, they blithely go through their organizational lives not thinking that what they are doing has an ethical dimension

or facet. These managers are well intentioned but are either too insensitive or too self-absorbed to consider the effects of their behavior on others. These managers normally think of themselves as ethical managers, but they are frequently overlooking these unintentional, subconscious, or unconscious aspects.

Sometimes these managers may be unconscious of hidden biases that prevent them from being objective. Recently, researchers have held that many business people go through life deluded by the illusion of objectivity. Unconscious, or implicit biases, can run contrary to our consciously held, explicit beliefs.[39] Though most managers think they are ethical, sometimes even the most well-meaning person unwittingly allows unconscious thoughts and biases to influence what appears to be objective decisions. Four sources of unintentional, or unconscious, influences include implicit forms of prejudice, bias that favors one's own group, conflict of interest, and a tendency to overclaim credit.[40]

Unconscious biases have been believed to be at work among accountants in some of the recent accounting scandals. Three *structural aspects* of accounting bias include ambiguity, attachment, and approval. When ambiguity exists, people tend to reach self-serving conclusions. For example, subjective interpretations of what constitutes a deductible expense may be made in a self-serving fashion. Attachment occurs when auditors, motivated to stay in their clients' good graces, approve things they might otherwise not approve. With respect to approval, external auditors may be reviewing the work of internal auditors, and self-serving biases may become even stronger when other people's biases are being endorsed or approved, especially if those judgments align with one's own biases.[41]

In addition, three aspects of human nature may amplify unconscious biases: familiarity, discounting, and escalation. With familiarity, it is noted that people may be more willing to harm strangers (anonymous investors) than individuals they know (clients). Discounting refers to the act of overlooking or minimizing decisions that may not have immediate consequences. Finally, escalation occurs when an accountant or businessperson allows small judgments to accumulate and become large and then she decides to cover up the unwitting mistakes through concealment. Thus, small indiscretions escalate into larger ones, and unconscious biases grow into conscious corruption.[42]

Amoral management pursues profitability as its goal but does not cognitively attend to moral issues that may be intertwined with that pursuit. If there is an ethical guide to amoral management, it would be the marketplace as constrained by law—the letter of the law, not the spirit. The amoral manager sees the law as the parameters within which business pursuits take place.

Operating Strategy of Amoral Management.

The operating strategy of amoral management is not to bridle managers with excessive ethical structure but to permit free rein within the unspoken but understood tenets of the free enterprise system. Personal ethics may periodically or unintentionally enter into managerial decisions, but it does not preoccupy management. Furthermore, the impact of decisions on others is an afterthought, if it ever gets considered at all. Amoral management represents a model of decision making in which the managers' ethical mental gears, to the extent that they are present, are stuck in neutral. The key management question guiding decision making is, "Can we make money with this action, decision, or behavior?" Note that the question does not imply an active or implicit intent to be either moral or immoral.

Paine has articulated a "compliance strategy" that is consistent with amoral management. The **compliance strategy**, as contrasted with her integrity strategy, is more focused on obedience to the law as its driving force. The compliance strategy is lawyer driven and is oriented not toward ethics or integrity but more toward compliance with existing regulatory and criminal law. The compliance approach uses deterrence as its underlying assumption. This approach envisions managers as rational maximizers of self-interest, responsive to the personal costs and benefits of their choices, yet indifferent to the moral legitimacy of those choices.[43]

Figure 6-9 presents the major characteristics of amoral managers.

Illustrative Cases of Amoral Management. There are perhaps more examples of unintentionally amoral management than any other kind. When police departments first stipulated that recruits must be at least 5' 9" tall and weigh at least 180 pounds, they were making an amoral decision, because they were not considering the harmful exclusion this would impose on women and other ethnic groups who do not, on average, attain that height and weight. When companies decided to use scantily clad young women to advertise autos, men's cologne, and other products, these companies were not thinking of the degrading and demeaning characterization that would result from what they thought was an ethically neutral decision. When firms decided to do business in South Africa years ago, their decisions were neither moral nor immoral, but a major, unanticipated consequence of these decisions was the appearance of capitalistic (or U.S.) approval of apartheid.

Nestlé. Nestlé's initial decision to market infant formula in Third World countries (see Chapter 9) could have been an amoral decision. Nestlé may not have considered the detrimental effects such a seemingly innocent business decision would have on mothers and babies in a land of impure water, poverty, and illiteracy.

Video-Game Industry. It could be argued that the video-game industry has been unintentionally amoral because it has developed games that glorify extreme violence, sexism, and aggression without paying much attention to how these games impact the young people who become addicted to them. In Mortal Kombat, for example, players rip out an opponent's still-beating heart or bloody spinal cord. In Night Trap, Ninja-like

---

FIGURE 6-9

Characteristics of Amoral Managers

Intentionally Amoral Managers

These managers don't think ethics and business should "mix."

Business and ethics are seen as existing in *separate* spheres. Ethics is seen as too "Sunday schoolish."

These managers are a vanishing breed. There are very few managers like this left in the world.

Unintentionally Amoral Managers

These managers just don't consider the *ethical dimension* of decision making.

They just don't *"think ethically."*

They may lack *ethical perception* or awareness; they have no "ethics buds" that help them sense the ethical dimension.

They are well-intentioned, but morally casual or careless; may be morally *unconscious*.

Their ethical gears, if they exist, are in *neutral*.

vampires stalk minimally dressed, cowering coeds and drill through their necks with power tools. These "games" have changed significantly since Atari introduced the popular video game Pong in 1972, a digital version of Ping-Pong consisting of a square ball and two rectangular paddles.[44]

Today's video games have plenty of critics—educators, psychologists, politicians—who worry about the multitude of themes that are bloodthirsty and sexist and have foul language. About the only response from the game makers has been to introduce an age-based rating system similar to that now used in the movie industry. The game makers' view seems to be that their games are legal and harmless and that little else is left to say.

Sears.   A final useful illustration of unintentionally amoral management involves the case of Sears Roebuck and Co. and its automotive service business, which spanned much of the 1990s. Paine describes how consumers and attorneys general in 40 states accused the company of misleading consumers and selling them unneeded parts and services.[45] In the face of declining revenues and a shrinking market share, Sears' executives put into place new goals, quotas, and incentives for auto-center service personnel. Service employees were told to meet product-specific and service-specific quotas—sell so many brake jobs, batteries, and front-end alignments—or face consequences such as reduced working hours or transfers. Some employees spoke of the "pressure" they felt to generate business. Although Sears' executives did not set out to defraud customers, they put into place a commission system that led to Sears' employees feeling pressure to sell products and services that consumers did not need. Soon after the complaints against Sears occurred, CEO Edward Brennan acknowledged that management had created an environment in which mistakes were made, although no intent to deceive consumers had existed. Fortunately, Sears eliminated its quota system as a partial remedy to the problem.[46]

The Sears case is a classic example of unintentionally amoral management—a well-intentioned company drifting into questionable practices because it just did not think ethically. The company simply did not think through the impacts that its strategic decisions would have on important stakeholders.

Figure 6-10 provides a summary of the major characteristics of amoral management and the other two models that have been identified and discussed. It compares the three in terms of ethical norms, motives, goals, orientation toward the law, and operating strategy.

Two Hypotheses Regarding the Moral Management Models

There are numerous other examples of amoral management, but the ones presented here should suffice to illustrate the point. A thorough study has not been conducted to ascertain precisely what proportions of managers each model represents in the total management population. However, two possible hypotheses regarding the moral management models may be set forth.

Population Hypothesis.
One hypothesis is that the distribution of the three models might approximate a normal curve, with the amoral group occupying the large middle part of the curve and the moral and immoral categories occupying the smaller tails of the curve. It is difficult to research this question. If you asked managers what they thought they were or what others thought they were, a self-serving bias would likely enter in and you would not get an accurate picture. Another approach would be to observe management actions. This would be nearly impossible because it is not possible

FIGURE 6-10

Three Approaches to Management Ethics

Organizational Characteristics	Immoral Management	Amoral Management	Moral Management
Ethical Norms	Management decisions, actions, and behavior imply a positive and active opposition to what is moral (ethical). Decisions are discordant with accepted ethical principles. An active negation of what is moral is implied.	Management is neither moral nor immoral, but decisions lie outside the sphere to which moral judgments apply. Management activity is outside or beyond the moral order of a particular code. May imply a lack of ethical perception and moral awareness.	Management activity conforms to a standard of ethical, or right, behavior. Conforms to accepted professional standards of conduct. Ethical leadership is commonplace on the part of management.
Motives	Selfish. Management cares only about its or the company's gains.	Well-intentioned but selfish in the sense that impact on others is not considered.	Good. Management wants to succeed but only within the confines of sound ethical precepts (fairness, justice, due process).
Goals	Profitability and organizational success at any price.	Profitability. Other goals are not considered.	Profitability within the confines of legal obedience and ethical standards.
Orientation Toward Law	Legal standards are barriers that management must overcome to accomplish what it wants.	Law is the ethical guide, preferably the letter of the law. The central question is what we can do legally.	Obedience toward letter and spirit of the law. Law is a minimal ethical behavior. Prefer to operate well above what law mandates.
Strategy	Exploit opportunities for corporate gain. Cut corners when it appears useful.	Give managers free rein. Personal ethics may apply but only if managers choose. Respond to legal mandates if caught and required to do so.	Live by sound ethical standards. Assume leadership position when ethical dilemmas arise. Enlightened self-interest.

SOURCE: Archie B. Carroll, "In Search of the Moral Manager," *Business Horizons* (March/April, 1987), 8. Copyright © 1987 by the Foundation for the School of Business At Indiana University. Used with permission.

to observe all management actions for any sustained period of time. Therefore, the supposition remains a hypothesis based on one person's judgment of what is going on in the management community.

Individual Hypothesis. Equally disturbing as the belief that the amoral management style is common among managers today is an alternative hypothesis that, within the average manager, these three models may operate at various times and under various circumstances. That is, the average manager may be amoral most of the time but may slip into a moral or an immoral mode on occasion, based on a variety of impinging factors. Like the population hypothesis, this view cannot be empirically supported at this time, but it does provide an interesting perspective for managers to ponder. This perspective would be somewhat similar to the situational ethics argument that has been around for some time.

Amoral Management as a Serious Organizational Problem. With the exception of the major ethics scandals witnessed in the past few years, the more serious social problem in organizations today seems to be the group of well-intended managers who for one reason or another subscribe to or live out the amoral ethic. These are managers who are driven primarily by profitability or a bottom-line ethos, which regards economic success as the exclusive barometer of organizational and personal achievement. These amoral managers are basically good people, but they essentially see the competitive business world as ethically neutral. Until this group of managers moves toward the moral management ethic, we will continue to see American business and other organizations criticized as they have been in the past two decades.

To connect the three models of management morality with concepts introduced earlier, we show in Figure 6-11 how the components of corporate social responsibility (Chapter 2) would likely be viewed by managers using each of the three models of management morality. We illustrate in Figure 6-12 how managers using the three models would probably embrace or reject the stakeholder concept or stakeholder thinking (Chapter 3). It is hoped that these depictions of the interrelationships among these concepts will make them easier to understand and appreciate.

MAKING MORAL MANAGEMENT ACTIONABLE

The characteristics of immoral, moral, and amoral management discussed in this chapter should provide some useful benchmarks for managerial self-analysis, because self-analysis and introspection will ultimately be the way in which managers will recognize the need to move from the immoral or amoral ethic to the moral ethic. Numerous others have suggested management training for business ethics; therefore, this prescription will not be further developed here, although it has great potential. Ethics training will be discussed more fully in Chapter 7. However, until senior management fully embraces the concepts of moral management, the transformation in organizational culture that is so essential for moral management to blossom, thrive, and flourish will not take place. Ultimately, senior management has the leadership responsibility to show the way to an ethical organizational climate by leading the transition from amoral to moral management, whether this is done by business ethics training and workshops, codes of conduct, mission/vision statements, ethics officers, tighter financial controls, more ethically sensitive decision-making processes, or leadership by example.

FIGURE 6-11

Three Models of Management Morality and Emphases on CSR

Models of Management Morality	Components of the CSR Definition			
	Economic Responsibility	Legal Responsibility	Ethical Responsibility	Philanthropic Responsibility
Immoral management	✓✓✓	✓		✓
Amoral management	✓✓✓	✓✓	✓	✓
Moral management	✓✓✓	✓✓✓	✓✓✓	✓✓✓

Weighing Code:
✓ = token consideration (appearances only)
✓✓ = moderate consideration
✓✓✓ = significant consideration

FIGURE 6-12

The Moral Management Models and Acceptance or Rejection of Stakeholder Thinking (SHT)

Moral Management Model	Acceptance of Stakeholder Thinking (SHT)	Stakeholder Thinking Posture Embraced
Immoral management	SHT rejected: management is self-absorbed	SHT rejected, not deemed useful. Accepts profit maximization model but does not really pursue it.
Amoral management	SHT accepted: narrow view (minimum number of stakeholders considered)	Instrumental view of SHT prevails. How will it help management?
Moral management	SHT enthusiastically embraced: wider view (maximum number of stakeholders considered)	Normative view of SHT prevails. SHT is fully embraced in all decision making.

Underlying all these efforts, however, needs to be the fundamental recognition that amoral management exists and that it is an undesirable condition that can be certainly, if not easily, remedied. Most notably, organizational leaders must acknowledge that amoral management is a morally vacuous condition that can be quite easily disguised as just an innocent, practical, bottom-line philosophy—something to take pride in. Amoral management is, however, and will continue to be, the bane of the management profession until it is recognized for what it really is and until managers take steps to overcome it. Managers are not all "bad guys," as they so frequently are portrayed, but the idea that managerial decision making can be ethically neutral is bankrupt and no longer tenable in the society of the new millennium.[47]

DEVELOPING MORAL JUDGMENT

It is helpful to know something about how individuals, whether they are managers or employees, develop moral (or ethical) judgment. Perhaps if we knew more about this process, we could better understand our own behavior and the behavior of those around us and those we manage. Further, we might be able to better design reward systems for encouraging ethical behavior if we knew more about how employees think about ethics. A good starting point is to come to appreciate what psychologists have to say about how we as individuals develop morally. The major research on this point is **Kohlberg's levels of moral development**.[48] After this discussion, we will consider other sources of a manager's values, especially those emanating from both societal sources and from within the organization itself.

Levels of Moral Development

The psychologist, Lawrence Kohlberg, has done extensive research into the topic of **moral development**. He concluded, on the basis of over 20 years of research, that there is a general sequence of three levels (each with two stages) through which individuals evolve in learning to think or develop morally. Although his theory is not universally accepted, there is widespread practical usage of his levels of moral development, and this suggests a broad if not unanimous consensus. Figure 6-13 on page 196 illustrates Kohlberg's three levels and six stages.

FIGURE 6-13

Kohlberg's Levels of Moral Development

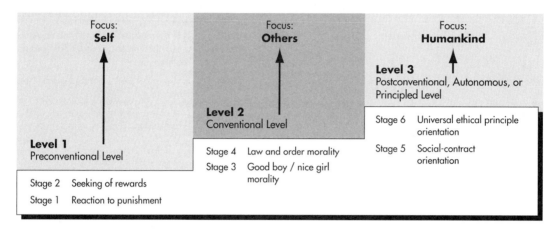

Level 1: Preconventional Level. At the preconventional level of moral development, which is typically descriptive of how people behave as infants and children, the focus is mainly on *self*. As an infant starts to grow, his or her main behavioral reactions are in response to punishments and rewards. Stage 1 is the *reaction-to-punishment stage*. If you want a child to do something (such as stay out of the street) at a very early age, spanking or scolding is typically needed. The orientation at this stage is toward avoidance of pain.

As the child gets a bit older, rewards start working. Stage 2 is the *seeking-of-rewards stage*. The child begins to see some connection between being "good" (that is, doing what Mom or Dad wants the child to do) and some reward that may be forthcoming. The reward may be parental praise or something tangible, such as candy, extra TV time, or a trip to the movies. At this preconventional level, children do not really understand the moral idea of "right" and "wrong" but rather learn to behave according to the consequences—punishment or reward—that are likely to follow.

Though we normally associate the preconventional level with the moral development of children, many adults in organizations are heavily influenced by rewards and punishments. Consequently, the preconventional level of motivation may be observed in adults as well as children and is relevant to a discussion of adult moral maturity.

Level 2: Conventional Level. As the child gets older, she or he learns that there are "others" whose ideas or welfare ought to be considered. Initially, these others include family and friends. At the conventional level of moral development, the individual learns the importance of conforming to the conventional norms of society.

The conventional level is composed of two stages. Stage 3 has been called the "*good boy/nice girl*" *morality stage*. The young person learns that there are some rewards (such as feelings of acceptance, trust, loyalty, or warmth) for living up to what is expected by family and peers, so the individual begins to conform to what is generally expected of a good son, daughter, sister, brother, friend, and so on.

Stage 4 is the *law-and-order morality stage*. Not only does the individual learn to respond to family, friends, the school, and the church, as in Stage 3, but the individual now recognizes that there are certain norms in society (in school, in the theater, in the mall, in stores, in the car) that are expected or needed if society is to function in an orderly fashion. Thus, the individual becomes socialized or acculturated into what being a good citizen means. These rules for living include not only the actual laws (don't run a red light, don't walk until the "Walk" light comes on) but also other, less official norms (don't break into line, be sure to tip the server, turn your cell phone off in restaurants). At Stage 4, the individual sees that she or he is part of a larger social system and that to function in and be accepted by this social system requires a considerable degree of acceptance of and conformity to the norms and standards of society.

Level 3: Postconventional, Autonomous, or Principled Level.   At this third level, which Kohlberg argues few people reach (and those who do reach it have trouble staying there), the focus moves beyond those "others" who are of immediate importance to the individual to *humankind* as a whole. At the postconventional level of moral development, the individual develops a notion of right and wrong that is more mature than the conventionally articulated notion. Thus, it is sometimes called the level at which moral principles become self-accepted, not because they are held by society but because the individual now perceives and embraces them as "right."

Kohlberg's third level seems to be easier to understand as a whole than when its two individual stages are considered. Stage 5 is the *social-contract orientation*. At this stage, right action is thought of in terms of general individual rights and standards that have been critically examined and agreed upon by society as a whole. There is a clear awareness of the relativism of personal values and a corresponding emphasis on processes for reaching consensus.

Stage 6 is the *universal-ethical-principle orientation*. Here the individual uses his or her conscience in accord with self-chosen ethical principles that are anticipated to be universal, comprehensive, and consistent. These universal principles (such as the Golden Rule) might be focused on such ideals as justice, human rights, and social welfare.

Kohlberg suggests that at Level 3 the individual is able to rise above the conventional level where "rightness" and "wrongness" are defined by societal institutions and that she or he is able to defend or justify her or his actions on some higher ethical basis. For example, in our society the law tells us we should not discriminate against minorities. A Level 2 manager might not discriminate because to do so is to violate the law. A Level 3 manager would not discriminate but might offer a different reason—for example, it is wrong to discriminate because it violates universal principles of human justice. Part of the difference between Levels 2 and 3, therefore, is traceable to our motivation for the course of action we take. This takes us back to our earlier discussion of motivation as one of the important ethics questions.

Our discussion to this point may have suggested that we are at Level 1 as infants, at Level 2 as youths, and, finally, at Level 3 as adults. There is some approximate correspondence between chronological age and Levels 1 and 2, but the important point should be made that Kohlberg thinks many of us as adults never get beyond Level 2. The idea of getting to Level 3 as managers is desirable, because it would require us to think about people, products, and markets at a level higher than that generally attained by conventional society. However, even if we never get there, Level 3 urges us to continually ask "What ought to be?" The first two levels tell us a lot about moral development that should be useful to us as managers. There are not many managers who consistently operate according to Level 3 principles. Sometimes a manager may dip into Level 3 on a certain issue or for a certain period of time. Sustaining that level, however, is quite challenging.

If we state the issue in terms of the question, "Why do managers behave ethically?" we might infer conclusions from Kohlberg that look like those in Figure 6-14.

Feminist Views of Kohlberg's Research.

One of the major criticisms of Kohlberg's research was set forth by Carol Gilligan. Gilligan argued that Kohlberg's conclusions may accurately depict the stages of moral development among men, whom he used as his research subjects, but that his findings are not generalizable to women.[49] According to Gilligan's view, men tend to deal with moral issues in terms that are impersonal, impartial, and abstract. Examples might include the principles of justice and rights that Kohlberg argues are relevant at the postconventional level. Women, on the other hand, perceive themselves to be part of a network of relationships with family and friends and thus are more focused on *relationship maintenance* and *hurt avoidance* when they confront moral issues. For women, then, morality is often more a matter of caring and showing responsibility toward those involved in their relationships than in adhering to abstract or impersonal principles, such as justice.

According to Gilligan, women move in and out of three moral levels.[50] At the first level, the *self* is the sole object of concern. At the second level, the chief desire is to *establish connections and participate* in social life. In other words, maintaining relationships or directing one's thoughts toward others becomes dominant. Gilligan says that this is the conventional notion of women. At the third level, women recognize their own needs and the *needs of others*—those with whom they have relationships. Gilligan goes on to say that women never settle completely at one level. As they attain moral maturity, they do more of their thinking and make more of their decisions at the third level. This level requires care for others as well as care for oneself. In this view, morality moves away from the legalistic, self-centered approach that feminists say characterizes traditional ethics.

Some recent research does not show that moral development varies by gender in the fashion described by Gilligan. However, it does support Gilligan's claim that a different perspective toward moral issues is sometimes used. Apparently, both men and women sometimes employ an impartial or impersonal moral-rules perspective and sometimes they

FIGURE 6-14

Why Managers Behave Ethically

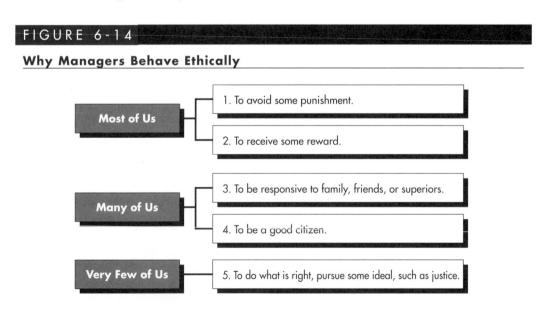

Most of Us	1. To avoid some punishment.
	2. To receive some reward.
Many of Us	3. To be responsive to family, friends, or superiors.
	4. To be a good citizen.
Very Few of Us	5. To do what is right, pursue some ideal, such as justice.

employ a care-and-responsibility perspective. This "care perspective" is still at an early stage of research, but it is useful to know that perspectives other than those found by Kohlberg are being considered.[51] More will be said about feminist theory in the next chapter.

Different Sources of a Manager's Values

In addition to considering the levels of moral development as an explanation of how and why people behave ethically, it is also useful to look at the different *sources of a manager's values*. Ethics and values are intimately related. We referred earlier to ethics as the rightness or wrongness of behavior. Ethics is also seen as the set of moral principles or values that drives behavior. Thus, the rightness or wrongness of behavior really turns out to be a manifestation of the ethical beliefs held by the individual. Values, on the other hand, are the individual's concepts of the relative worth, utility, or importance of certain ideas. Values reflect what the individual considers important in the larger scheme of things. One's values, therefore, shape one's ethics. Because this is so, it is important to understand the many different value-shaping forces that influence employees and managers.

The increasing pluralism of the society in which we live has exposed managers to a large number of values of many different kinds, and this has resulted in ethical diversity. One way to examine the sources of a manager's values is by considering both forces that originate from outside the organization to shape or influence the manager and those that emanate from within the organization. This, unfortunately, is not as simply done as we would like, because some sources are difficult to pinpoint. It should lend some order to our discussion, however.

Sources External to the Organization: The Web of Values.   The external sources of a manager's values refer to those broad sociocultural values that have evolved in society over a long period of time. Although current events (kickbacks, fraud, bribery cases) seem to affect these historic values by bringing specific ones into clearer focus at a given time, these values are rather enduring and change slowly. Quite often they emanate from major institutions or institutional themes in society.

George Steiner once stated that "every executive resides at the center of a web of values" and that there are five principal repositories of values influencing businesspeople. These five include religious, philosophical, cultural, legal, and professional values.[52]

Religious Values.   Religion has long been a basic source of morality in American society, as in most societies. Religion and morality are so intertwined that William Barclay relates them for definitional purposes: "Ethics is the bit of religion that tells us how we ought to behave."[53] The biblical tradition of Judeo-Christian theology forms the core for much of what Western society believes today about the importance of work, the concept of fairness, and the dignity of the individual. Other religious traditions likewise inform management behavior and action.

Philosophical Values.   Philosophy and various philosophical systems are also external sources of the manager's values. Beginning with preachments of the ancient Greeks, philosophers have claimed to demonstrate that *reason* can provide us with principles or morals in the same way it gives us the principles of mathematics. John Locke argued that morals are mathematically demonstrable, although he never explained how.[54] Aristotle with his Golden Rule and his doctrine of the mean, Kant with his categorical imperative, Bentham with his pain and pleasure calculus, and modern-day existentialists have shown us time and again the influence of various kinds of reasons for ethical choice. Today, the strong influence of moral relativism and postmodernism influence some people's values.

Cultural Values.   Culture, that broad synthesis of societal norms and values emanating from everyday living, has also had an impact on the manager's thinking. Modern examples of culture include music, movies, and television. The melting-pot culture of the United States is a potpourri of norms, customs, and rules that defy summarization. In recent years, it has become difficult to summarize what messages the culture is sending managers about ethics. In a recent book, *Moral Freedom: The Search for Virtue in a World of Choice*, by Alan Wolfe, the author argues that the United States, like other Western nations, is undergoing a radical revolution in morals and is now, morally speaking, a new society.[55] Wolfe thinks the traditional values that our culture has looked upon with authority (churches, families, neighborhoods, civic leaders) have lost the ability to influence people.

He goes on to say that as more and more areas of life have become democratized and open to consumer "choice," people have come to assume that they have the right to determine for themselves what it means to lead a good and virtuous life. Wolfe says that a key element in this new moral universe is nonjudgmentalism, which pushes society to suspend judgment on much immoral behavior or interpret immoral behavior as not the fault of the perpetrator. Thus, although many Americans may uphold the old virtues, in principle, they turn them into personal "options" in practice.[56] This clearly is a departure from the past, and it is probably impacting the way managers perceive the world of business. Employees, likewise, share these same perspectives and this creates challenges for managers.

Legal Values.   The legal system has been and continues to be one of the most powerful forces defining what is ethical and what is not for managers. This is true even though ethical behavior generally is that which occurs over and above legal dictates. As stated earlier, the law represents the codification of what the society considers right and wrong. Although we as members of society do not completely agree with every law in existence, there is typically more consensus for law than for ethics. Law, then, "mirrors the ideas of the entire society."[57] Law represents a minimum ethic of behavior but does not encompass all the ethical standards of behavior. Law addresses only the grossest violations of society's sense of right and wrong and thus is not adequate to describe completely all that is acceptable or unacceptable. Because it represents our official consensus ethic, however, its influence is pervasive and widely accepted.

In recent years, it has become an understatement to observe that we live in a litigious society. This trend toward suing someone to bring about justice is clearly having an impact on management decision making. Whereas the threat of litigation may make managers more careful in their treatment of stakeholders, the threat of losing tens or hundreds of millions of dollars has distorted decision making and caused many managers and companies to be running scared—never knowing what exactly is the best or fairest course of action to pursue.

Professional Values.   These include those emanating, for the most part, from professional organizations and societies that represent various jobs and positions. As such, they presumably articulate the ethical consensus of the leaders of those professions. For example, the Public Relations Society of America has a code of ethics that public relations executives have imposed on themselves as their own guide to behavior. The National Association of Realtors adopted its "Rules of Conduct" in 1913. Compliance with the code was first recommended for voluntary adoption and then made a condition of membership as long ago as 1924.[58] Professional values thus exert a more particularized impact on the manager than the four broader values discussed earlier.

In sum, several sources of values that are external to the organization come to bear on the manager. In addition to those mentioned, the manager is influenced by family, friends, acquaintances, and social events and currents of the day. The manager thus comes to the workplace with a personal philosophy that is truly a composite of numerous interacting values that have shaped her or his views of the world, of life, and of business.

Sources Internal to the Organization.

The external forces constitute the broad background or milieu against which a manager or an employee behaves or acts. They affect a person's personal views of the world and of business and help the person to formulate what is acceptable and unacceptable. There are, in addition, a number of less remote and more immediate factors that help to channel the individual's values and behavior; these grow out of the specific organizational experience itself. These internal sources of a manager's values (within the business organization) constitute more immediate and direct influences on one's behavior and decisions.

When an individual goes to work for an organization, a socialization process takes place in which the individual comes to assume the predominant values of that organization. The individual learns rather quickly that, to survive and to succeed, certain norms must be perpetuated and revered. There are several norms that are prevalent in business organizations, including

- Respect for the authority structure
- Loyalty to bosses and the organization
- Conformity to principles and practices
- Performance counts above all else
- Results count above all else

Each of these norms may assume a major role in a person who subordinates her or his own standard of ethics to those of the organization. In fact, research suggests that these internal sources play a much more significant role in shaping business ethics than do the host of external sources we considered first.

Respect for the authority structure, loyalty, conformity, performance, and *results* have been historically almost synonymous with survival and success in business. When these influences are operating together, they form a composite business ethic that is remarkably influential in its impact on individual and group behavior. These values form the central motif of organizational activity and direction.

Underlying the first three norms is the focus on performance and results. Madden referred to this as the "calculus of the bottom line."[59] One does not need to study business organizations for long to recognize that the bottom line—profits—is the sacred instrumental value that seems to take precedence over all others. "Profits now" rather than later seems to be the orientation that spells success for managers and employees alike. Respect for authority, loyalty, and conformity become means to an end, although one could certainly find organizations and people who see these as legitimate ends in themselves. Only recently are some managers and organizations starting to respond to the "multiple bottom line" or "triple bottom line" perspective introduced in Chapter 2.

| ELEMENTS OF MORAL JUDGMENT

For growth in moral judgment to take place, it is useful to appreciate the key elements involved in making moral judgments. This is a notion central to the transition from the amoral management condition to the moral management condition. Powers and Vogel have suggested that there are six major elements or capacities that are essential to making moral judgments: (1) moral imagination, (2) moral identification and ordering, (3) moral evaluation, (4) tolerance of moral disagreement and ambiguity, (5) integration of managerial and moral competence, and (6) a sense of moral obligation.[60] Each reveals an essential ingredient in developing moral judgment.

Moral Imagination

Moral imagination refers to the ability to perceive that a web of competing economic relationships is, at the same time, a web of moral or ethical relationships. Developing moral imagination means not only becoming sensitive to ethical issues in business decision making but also developing the perspective of searching out subtle places where people are likely to be detrimentally affected by decision making or behaviors of managers. This is a necessary first step but is extremely challenging because of prevailing methods of evaluating managers on bottom-line results. It is essential before anything else can happen, however.

Moral Identification and Ordering

Moral identification and ordering refers to the ability to discern the relevance or nonrelevance of moral factors that are introduced into a decision-making situation. Are the moral issues real or just rhetorical? The ability to see moral issues as issues that can be dealt with is at stake here. Once moral issues have been identified, they must be ranked, or ordered, just as economic or technological issues are prioritized during the decision-making process. A manager must not only develop this skill through experience but also finely hone it through repetition. It is only through repetition that this skill can be developed. In this ordering process, a manager may conclude that worker safety is more important than worker privacy, though both are important qualities.

Moral Evaluation

Once issues have been identified and ordered, evaluations must be made. *Moral evaluation* is the practical phase of moral judgment and entails essential skills, such as coherence and consistency, that have proved to be effective principles in other contexts. What managers need to do here is to understand the importance of clear principles, develop processes for weighing ethical factors, and develop the ability to identify what the likely moral as well as economic outcomes of a decision will be.

The real challenge in moral evaluation is to integrate the concern for others into organizational goals, purposes, and legitimacy. In the final analysis, though, the manager may not know the "right" answer or solution, although moral sensitivity has been introduced into the process. The important point is that amorality has not prevailed or driven the decision process.

Tolerance of Moral Disagreement and Ambiguity

An objection managers often have to ethics discussions is the amount of disagreement generated and the volume of ambiguity that must be tolerated in thinking ethically. This must be accepted, however, because it is a natural part of ethics discussions. To be sure, managers need closure and precision in their decisions. But the situation is seldom clear in moral discussions, just as it is in many traditional and more familiar decision contexts of managers, such as introducing a new product based on limited test marketing, choosing a new executive for a key position, deciding which of a number of excellent computer systems to install, or making a strategic decision based on instincts. All of these are precarious decisions, but managers have become accustomed to making them in spite of the disagreements and ambiguity that prevail among those involved in the decision or within the individual.

In a real sense, the *tolerance of moral disagreement and ambiguity* is simply an extension of a managerial talent or facility that is present in practically all decision-making situations managers face. But managers are more unfamiliar with this special kind of decision making because of a lack of practice.

Integration of Managerial and Moral Competence

The *integration of managerial and moral competence* underlies all that we have been discussing. Moral issues in management do not arise in isolation from traditional business decision making but right smack in the middle of it. The scandals that major corporations face today did not occur independently of the companies' economic activities but were embedded in a series of decisions that were made at various points in time and culminated from those earlier decisions. Therefore, moral competence is an integral part of managerial competence. Managers are learning—some the hard way—that there is a significant corporate, and in many instances personal, price to pay for their amorality. The amoral manager sees ethical decisions as isolated and independent of managerial decisions and competence, but the moral manager sees every evolving decision as one in which an ethical perspective must be integrated. This kind of future-looking view is an essential executive skill.

A Sense of Moral Obligation

The foundation for all the capacities we have discussed is a *sense of moral obligation* and integrity. This sense is the key to the process but is the most difficult to acquire. This sense requires the intuitive or learned understanding that moral fibers—a concern for fairness, justice, and due process to people, groups, and communities—are woven into the fabric of managerial decision making and are the integral components that hold systems together.

These qualities are perfectly consistent with, and indeed are essential prerequisites to, the free-enterprise system as we know it today. One can go back in history to Adam Smith and the foundation tenets of the free-enterprise system and not find references to immoral or unethical practices as being elements that are needed for the system to work. Milton Friedman, our modern-day Adam Smith, even alluded to the importance of ethics when he stated that the purpose of business is "to make as much money as possible while conforming to the basic rules of society, both those embodied in the law and *those embodied in ethical custom.*"[61] The moral manager, then, has a sense of moral obligation and integrity that is the glue that holds together the decision-making process in which human welfare is inevitably at stake.

Figure 6-15 summarizes the six elements of moral judgment identified by Powers and Vogel as they might be perceived by amoral and moral managers.

FIGURE 6-15

Elements of Moral Judgment in Amoral and Moral Managers

Amoral Managers	Moral Managers
Moral Imagination	
See a web of competing economic claims as just that and nothing more.	Perceive that a web of competing economic claims is simultaneously a web of moral relationships.
Are insensitive to and unaware of the hidden dimensions of where people are likely to get hurt.	Are sensitive to and hunt out the hidden dimensions of where people are likely to get hurt.
Moral Identification and Ordering	
See moral claims as squishy and not definite enough to order into hierarchies with other claims.	See which moral claims being made are relevant or irrelevant; order moral factors just as economic factors are ordered.
Moral Evaluation	
Are erratic in their application of ethics if it gets applied at all.	Are coherent and consistent in their normative reasoning.
Tolerance of Moral Disagreement and Ambiguity	
Cite ethical disagreement and ambiguity as reasons for forgetting ethics altogether.	Tolerate ethical disagreement and ambiguity while honestly acknowledging that decisions are not precise like mathematics but must finally be made nevertheless.
Integration of Managerial and Moral Competence	
See ethical decisions as isolated and independent of managerial decisions and managerial competence.	See every evolving decision as one in which a moral perspective must be integrated with a managerial one.
A Sense of Moral Obligation	
Have no sense of moral obligation and integrity that extends beyond managerial responsibility.	Have a sense of moral obligation and integrity that holds together the decision-making process in which human welfare is at stake.

SOURCE: Archie B. Carroll, "In Search of the Moral Manager," *Business Horizons* (March/April, 1987), 15. Copyright © 1987 by the Foundation for the School of Business At Indiana University. Used with permission.

■ SUMMARY

Business ethics has become a serious challenge for the business community over the past several decades. The major ethics scandals of the early 2000s have affected the public's trust of executives and major business institutions. Polls indicate that the public does not have a high regard for the ethics of managers. It is not easy to say whether business's ethics have declined or just seem to have done so because of increased media coverage and rising public expectations. Business ethics concerns the rightness, wrongness, and fairness of managerial behavior, and these are not easy judgments to make. Multiple norms compete to determine which standards business behavior should be compared with.

The conventional approach to business ethics was introduced as an initial way in which managers might think about ethical judgments. One major problem with this approach is that it is not clear which standards or norms should be used, and thus the conventional approach is susceptible to ethical relativism.

A Venn diagram model was presented as an aid to making decisions when economics, law, and ethics expectations compete with each other and are in tension. Four important ethics questions are (1) What is? (descriptive question) (2) What ought to be? (normative question) (3) How can we get from what is to what ought to be? (practical question) and (4) What is our motivation in this transition? (question of authenticity). Answering these questions helps one in an ethical analysis of a situation.

Three models of management ethics are (1) immoral management, (2) moral management, and (3) amoral management. Amoral management is further classified into intentional and unintentional categories. There are two hypotheses about the presence of these three moral types in the management population and in individuals.

A generally accepted view is that moral judgment develops according to the pattern described by Lawrence Kohlberg. His three levels of moral development are (1) preconventional, (2) conventional, and (3) postconventional, autonomous, or principled. Some have suggested that men and women use different perspectives as they perceive and deal with moral issues.

In addition to moral maturity, managers' ethics are affected by sources of values originating from external to the organization and from sources within the organization. This latter category includes respect for the authority structure, loyalty, conformity, and a concern for financial performance and results.

Finally, six elements in developing moral judgment were presented. These six elements include moral imagination, moral identification and ordering, moral evaluation, tolerance of moral disagreement and ambiguity, integration of managerial and moral competence, and a sense of moral obligation. If the moral management model is to be realized, these six elements need to be developed.

■ KEY TERMS

amoral management (page 189)

business ethics (page 174)

compliance strategy (page 191)

conventional approach to business ethics (page 175)

descriptive ethics (page 174)

ethical relativism (page 179)

ethics (page 173)

immoral management (page 184)

integrity strategy (page 186)

intentional amoral management (page 189)

Kohlberg's levels of moral development (page 195)

moral development (page 195)

moral management (page 186)

normative ethics (page 174)

unintentional amoral management (page 189)

▪ DISCUSSION QUESTIONS

1. Give a definition of ethical business behavior, explain the components involved in making ethical decisions, and give an example from your personal experience of the difficulties involved in making these determinations.

2. To demonstrate that you understand the three models of management ethics—moral, immoral, and amoral—give an example, from your personal experience, of each type. Do you agree that amorality is a serious problem? Explain.

3. Give examples, from your personal experience, of Kohlberg's Levels 1, 2, and 3. If you do not think you have ever gotten to Level 3, give an example of what it might be like.

4. Compare your motivations to behave ethically with those listed in Figure 6-14. Do the reasons given in that figure agree with your personal assessment? Discuss the similarities and differences between Figure 6-14 and your personal assessment.

5. From your personal experience, give an example of a situation you have faced that would require one of the six elements of moral judgment.

▪ RECOMMENDED CASES

Many of the end-of-text cases may be related to Chapter 6. You may wish to consider studying the following cases with Chapter 6.

Case 5. "MARTHA STEWART: FREE TRADING OR INSIDER TRADING." This case describes the actions of Martha Stewart when faced with the prospect of losing money on one of her investments. Did Martha Stewart engage in questionable practices? What were they? Were her actions personal level or organizational level? What ethical principles are applicable to Martha Stewart in this case? At what level of moral development were the parties in this case operating?

Case 6. "THE CASE OF THE KILLER PHRASES (A)." This case addresses the question of how a professor should handle a suspected cheating situation in one of his business ethics classes. What are the ethical issues in the case? Are they personal or organizational? Were the students acting morally, amorally or immorally? What ethics principles would have been valuable in helping the students and the professor think through what should have been done and what was done?

Case 8. "DOES CHEATING IN GOLF PREDICT CHEATING IN BUSINESS?" This case questions the relationship between people having one set of ethics in their personal lives and another set of ethics in their professional lives. Can one hold two different sets of ethics? Will managers who cheat in golf be able to function ethically in their professional lives? How are the two related? Evaluate all sides of this issue.

Case 10. "PHANTOM EXPENSES." How important is it for an employee to file his or her expenses correctly for business purposes? How would you respond if you were under pressure to file your expenses incorrectly to protect your colleagues? Does an employee have a greater responsibility to his or her employer or fellow employees? This case explores these issues of behaving honestly in the face of pressure to do otherwise.

▪ WEB RESOURCES

The URLs listed here are current at the time of publication. Should any of these Web sites change, please search under the company's or organization's name for an updated address.

Association for Practical and Professional Ethics
    http://www.indiana.edu/~appe

Business Ethics
    http://www.business-ethics.com

Business Week
    http://www.businessweek.com

Center for Business Ethics Bentley College
    http://ecampus.Bentley.edu/dept/cbe

Corporate Accountability Project
    http://www.corporation.org

Corporate Social Responsibility Newswire
    http://www.csrwire.com

Council of Ethical Organizations
   http://www.corporateethics.com

Ethics Officers Association
   http://www.eoa.org

Ethics Resource Center
   http://www.ethics.org

Journal of Business Ethics
   http://www.kluweronline.com/issn/0167-4544

Olsson Center for Applied Ethics,
   University of Virginia

http://www.darden.virginia.edu

The Conference Board
   http://www.conference-board.org

The Wall Street Journal
   http://www.wsj.com

Wharton Ethics Program
   http://www.wharton.upenn.edu

U.S. Chamber of Commerce
   http://www.uschamber.com

 InfoTrac® College Edition   http://www.infotrac-college.com

Articles from both Business Week *and* The Wall Street Journal *can be researched, retrieved, and read from your desktop using InfoTrac's online database.*

▪ ENDNOTES

1. "Tale of the Tape: How GM One-Upped an Embarrassed NBC on Staged News Event," *The Wall Street Journal* (February 11, 1993), A1.

2. Michael Siconolfi, "Kidder Brokers Defect Amid Scandal, Taking $2 Billion in Client Accounts," *The Wall Street Journal* (August 30, 1994), C1; Also see Terence P. Paré, "Jack Welch's Nightmare on Wall Street," *Fortune* (September 5, 1994), 40–48.

3. "Whose Values?" *Newsweek* (June 8, 1992), 19–22.

4. William J. Bennett (ed.) *The Book of Virtues: A Treasury of Great Moral Stories* (New York: Simon & Schuster, 1993).

5. "The Politics of Virtue: The Crusade Against America's Moral Decline," *Newsweek* (June 13, 1994), 30–39.

6. Bari-Ellen Roberts, with Jack E. White, *Roberts vs. Texaco: A True Story of Race and Corporate America* (New York: Avon Books, 1998).

7. Matthew Cooper, "Tobacco: Turning Up the Heat," *Newsweek* (April 13, 1998), 50–51.

8. "Corporate Scandals," *The Atlanta Journal-Constitution* (December 28, 2003), Q6–Q7.

9. "Three in Four Worried About Morality in the U.S.," *The Atlanta Journal-Constitution* (May 5, 2001), B1.

10. Joshua Joseph, "National Business Ethics Survey 2000," Web page of the Ethics Resource Center: http://www.ethics.org.

11. Ethics Resource Center, National Business Ethics Survey 2003. (Washington, DC: Ethics Resource Center, 2003), ii–iii. See: http://www.ethics.org/nbes2003/index.html

12. Steve Farkas, Ann Duffett, Jean Johnson, with Beth Syat, "A Few Bad Apples? An Exploratory Look at What Typical Americans Think About Business Ethics Today," (New York: Public Agenda, January 2004).

13. Max Ways, "A Plea for Perspective," in Clarence C. Walton (ed.) *The Ethics of Corporate Conduct* (Englewood Cliffs, NJ: Prentice Hall, 1977), 108.

14. Michael Blumenthal, "Business Morality Has Not Deteriorated—Society Has Changed," *The New York Times* (January 9, 1977).

15. *Ibid.*

16. Richard T. DeGeorge, *Business Ethics*, 4th ed. (New York: Prentice Hall, 1995), 20–21; See also Rogene A. Buchholz and Sandra B. Rosenthal, *Business Ethics* (Upper Saddle River, NJ: Prentice Hall, 1998), 3.

17. DeGeorge, *op. cit.*, 15.

18. Beth Gottfried, "The Real Thang: The Apprentice-Episode 4: Ethics Shmethics-Hollywood Gone Wild" (January 30, 2004), Go to the following Web page for updates on various TV shows, including The Apprentice: http://www.the-trades.com/.

19. *Ibid.*

20. See, for example, Melissa Baucus and Janet Near, "Can Illegal Corporate Behavior Be Predicted? An Event History Analysis," *Academy of Management Journal* (Vol. 34, No. 1, 1991), 9–36; and P.L. Cochran and D. Nigh, "Illegal Corporate Behavior and the Question of Moral Agency," in William C. Frederick (ed.) *Research in Corporate Social Performance and Policy*, Vol. 9 (Greenwich, CT: JAI Press, 1987), 73–91.

21. Mark S. Schwartz and Archie B. Carroll, "Corporate Social Responsibility: A Three-Domain Approach," *Business Ethics Quarterly* (Vol. 13, Issue 4, October 2003), 503–530.

22. Otto A. Bremer, "An Approach to Questions of Ethics in Business," *Audenshaw Document No. 116* (North Hinksey,

Oxford: The Hinksey Centre, Westminster College, 1983), 1–12.

23. *Ibid.*, 7.

24. *Ibid.*, 10–11.

25. Andrew Stark, "What's the Matter with Business Ethics?" *Harvard Business Review* (May–June 1993), 7.

26. Most of the material in this section comes from Archie B. Carroll, "In Search of the Moral Manager," *Business Horizons* (March/April 1987), 7–15; See also Archie B. Carroll, "Models of Management Morality for the New Millennium," *Business Ethics Quarterly* (Vol. 11, Issue 2, April 2001), 365–371.

27. Steven Greehouse, "Altering of Worker Time Cards Spurs Growing Number of Suits," *The New York Times* (April 4, 2004), 1.

28. Alex Berenson, "Three Plead Guilty in Computer Associates Case," *The New York Times* (April 9, 2004).

29. Julian E. Barnes, "P&G Said to Agree to Pay Unilever $10 Million in Spying Case," *The New York Times* (September 7, 2001).

30. Lynn Sharp Paine, "Managing for Organizational Integrity," *Harvard Business Review* (March–April, 1994), 106–117.

31. *Ibid.*, 111–112.

32. "Business Ethics Award Criteria," *Business Ethics* (November/December 1997), 8.

33. Archie B. Carroll, "The Moral Leader: Essential for Successful Corporate Citizenship," in Jorg Andriof and Malcolum McIntosh (eds) *Perspectives on Corporate Citizenship* (Sheffield, UK: Greenleaf Publishing Co., 2001), 139–151.

34. Stephen Covey, *The Seven Habits of Highly Effective People* (New York: Simon & Schuster, 1989).

35. Carroll (2001), *ibid.*, 145–150.

36. Joseph Weber, "3M's Big Cleanup," *Business Week* (June 5, 2000), 96–98.

37. Ray Vicker, "Rise in Chain-Saw Injuries Spurs Demand for Safety Standards, But Industry Resists," *The Wall Street Journal* (August 23, 1982), 17.

38. Business Enterprise Trust, 1994, "The Business Enterprise Trust Awards (1991 Recipients," unpublished announcement.

39. Mahzarin R. Banaji, Max H. Bazerman, and Dolly Chugh, "How (Un) Ethical Are You?" *Harvard Business Review* (December 2003), 56–64.

40. *Ibid.*

41. Max Bazerman, George Loewenstein, and Don A. Moore, "Why Good Accountants Do Bad Audits," *Harvard Business Review* (November 2002).

42. *Ibid.*

43. Paine, 109–113.

44. "Video-Game Systems," *Consumer Reports* (December 1996), 38–41.

45. Paine, 107–108.

46. *Ibid.*

47. Carroll (1987), 7–15.

48. Lawrence Kohlberg, "The Claim to Moral Adequacy of a Highest Stage of Moral Judgment," *The Journal of Philosophy* (Vol. LXX, 1973), 630–646.

49. Carol Gilligan, *In a Different Voice: Psychological Theory and Women's Development* (Cambridge, MA: Harvard University Press, 1982).

50. Manuel G. Velasquez, *Business Ethics*, 3d ed. (Englewood Cliffs, NJ: Prentice Hall, 1992), 30; See also Brian K. Burton and Craig P. Dunn, "Feminist Ethics as Moral Grounding for Stakeholder Theory," *Business Ethics Quarterly* (Vol. 6, No. 2, 1996), 136–137.

51. See, for example, Robbin Derry, "Moral Reasoning in Work Related Conflicts," in William C. Frederick (ed.) *Research in Corporate Social Performance and Policy*, Vol. 9 (Greenwich, CT: JAI Press, 1987), 25–49. See also Velasquez, 30–31.

52. George A. Steiner, *Business and Society* (New York: Random House, 1975), 226.

53. William Barclay, *Ethics in a Permissive Society* (New York: Harper & Row, 1971), 13.

54. Marvin Fox, "The Theistic Bases of Ethics," in Robert Bartels (ed.) *Ethics in Business* (Columbus, OH: Bureau of Business Research, Ohio State University, 1963), 86–87.

55. Alan Wolfe, *Moral Freedom: The Search for Virtue in a World of Choice* (New York: W.W. Norton & Co., 2001).

56. John Leo, "My Morals, Myself," *U.S. News & World Report* (August 13, 2001), 10.

57. Carl D. Fulda, "The Legal Basis of Ethics," in Bartels, 43–50.

58. H. Jackson Pontius, "Commentary on Code of Ethics of National Association of Realtors," in Ivan Hill (ed.) *The Ethical Basis of Economic Freedom* (Chapel Hill, NC: American Viewpoint, 1976), 353.

59. Carl Madden, "Forces Which Influence Ethical Behavior," in Clarence C. Walton (ed.) *The Ethics of Corporate Conduct* (Englewood Cliffs, NJ: Prentice Hall, 1977), 31–78.

60. Charles W. Powers and David Vogel, *Ethics in the Education of Business Managers* (Hastings-on-Hudson, NY: The Hastings Center, 1980), 40–45. Also see Patricia H. Werhane, *Moral Imagination and Management Decision Making* (New York: Oxford University Press, 1999).

61. Milton Friedman, "The Social Responsibility of Business Is to Increase Its Profits," *The New York Times* (September, 1962), 126 (italics added).

Chapter 7

■ PERSONAL *and* ORGANIZATIONAL ETHICS

CHAPTER LEARNING OUTCOMES

After studying this chapter, you should be able to:

1 Understand the different levels at which business ethics may be addressed.

2 Differentiate between consequence-based and duty-based principles of ethics.

3 Enumerate and discuss principles of personal ethical decision making and ethical tests for screening ethical decisions.

4 Identify the factors affecting an organization's moral climate and provide examples of these factors at work.

5 Describe and explain actions, strategies, or "best practices" that management may take to improve an organization's ethical climate.

The ethical issues on which managers must make decisions are numerous and varied. The news media tend to focus on the major ethical scandals involving well-known corporate names. Therefore, Enron, WorldCom, Tyco, Coca-Cola, Boeing, Arthur Andersen, McDonald's, Martha Stewart, and other such high-visibility firms attract considerable attention. The consequence of this is that many of the everyday, routine ethical dilemmas that managers face in medium-sized and small organizations are often overlooked.

A more typical situation for managers is to encounter day-to-day ethical dilemmas in such arenas as conflicts of interest, sexual harassment, inappropriate gifts to corporate personnel, unauthorized payments, customer dealings, evaluation of personnel, and pressure to compromise personal standards.

Unfortunately, many managers face these ethical quandaries on a daily basis but have no background or training in business ethics or ethical decision making to help them. A recent training program conducted by one of the authors illustrates this point well. The training session was in a continuing-education program, and the topic was business ethics. The 62 managers in attendance were asked how many of them had had formal business ethics training before—in college or in a company-sponsored program. Not one hand went up. This situation is changing, but it is changing slowly.

People today face ethical issues in a variety of settings, but our concerns in this chapter are personal and organizational ethics. Regarding these two, David Callahan published a high-impact book in 2004 titled *The Cheating Culture: Why More Americans Are Doing Wrong to Get Ahead*.[1] Callahan never clearly defines what "cheating" means, but synonyms that are commonly accepted in society today include *dishonest, immoral, unethical, amoral,* and *corrupt*—all terms characterizing the threats we are addressing in this chapter. He argues that we have more cheating today for four essential reasons: new pressures on people, bigger rewards for winning, temptation, and trickle-down corruption. Each of these factors influences personal and organizational ethics and thus frames the issue that needs to be addressed at these levels.

The ethics problem in business is, indeed, a serious one, and progress on this front is vital to successful business. A study of managers' desired leadership qualities was conducted by consultant and writer Lee Ellis, and he concluded that *integrity* is the quality most sought after in leaders.[2] A recently retired corporate executive, Bill George, former CEO at Medtronic, has argued that we need corporate leaders with integrity.[3] But how does one get personal integrity and, as a manager, how do you instill it in your organization and create an ethical organizational climate? These are significant challenges. How, for example, do you keep your own personal ethics focused in such a way that you avoid immorality and amorality? What principles, concepts, or guidelines are available to help you to be ethical? What specific strategies, approaches, or best practices might be emphasized to bring about an ethical culture in your company or organization?

LEVELS AT WHICH ETHICS MAY BE ADDRESSED

As individuals and as managers, we experience ethical pressures or dilemmas in a variety of settings. These pressures or dilemmas occur on different levels. These levels include the individual or personal level, the organizational level, the industry level, the societal level, and the global level. These levels cascade out from the individual to the global. Some observers believe that "ethics are ethics" regardless of whether they are applied at the personal or the organizational level. To help appreciate the types of decision situations that are faced at the various levels, however, it is worth considering them in terms of the types of issues that may arise in the different contexts.

Personal Level

First, we all experience *personal-level* ethical challenges. These challenges include situations we face in our personal lives that are generally outside the work context. Questions or dilemmas that we might face at the personal level include:

- Should I cheat on my income tax return by overinflating my charitable contributions?
- Should I tell the professor I need this course to graduate this semester when I really don't?
- Should I download music from the Internet although I realize it is someone's intellectual property?

- Should I skip out on my share of the apartment rent because I'm graduating and leaving town?
- Should I tell the cashier that she gave me change for a $20 bill when all I gave her was a $10 bill?
- Should I connect this TV cable in my new apartment and not tell the cable company?

Wanda Johnson of Savannah, Georgia, faced a personal-level ethical dilemma upon finding money. Johnson, a 34-year-old single mother of five, found temptation knocking in the form of a bagful of money that contained $120,000. Johnson, a $7.88-an-hour custodian at a local hospital, was on her lunch break when she witnessed a bag of money falling off an armored truck. Johnson could have surely used the money. She was behind in her bills and had recently pawned her television set, trying to come up with enough cash to keep the bill collectors at bay. The bag contained small bills and nobody saw her find the bag. What should she do?

Johnson later admitted that she knew she had to turn it in. After consulting with her pastor, Johnson turned in the money to the police. Johnson said that her religious upbringing had taught her what was the right thing to do. Johnson was later rewarded when SunTrust bank promised her a reward of $5,000, and she received a promise of an unspecified sum by EM Armored Car Company.[4] Would all individuals react to this ethical dilemma in the same fashion as Johnson?

Organizational Level

People also confront ethical issues at the *organizational level* (or firm level) in their roles as managers or employees. Certainly, many of these issues are similar to those we face personally. However, these issues may carry consequences for the company's reputation and success in the community and also for the kind of ethical environment or culture that will prevail on a day-to-day basis at the office. Some of the issues posed at the organizational level might include:

- Should I set high production goals for my work team to benefit the organization, even though I know it may cause them to cut corners to achieve such goals?
- Should I over report the actual time I worked on this project, hoping to get overtime pay?
- Should I overlook the wrongdoings of my colleagues and subordinates in the interest of harmony in the company?
- Should I authorize a subordinate to violate company policy so that we can close the deal and both be rewarded?
- Should I make this product safer than I'm required to by law, because I know the legal standard is grossly inadequate?
- Should I misrepresent the warranty time on this product in order to get the sale?

In August 2001, it was revealed that months before people began dying nationwide in 1998, managers at a Sara Lee Corp.-owned plant in Michigan knew they were shipping tainted hot dogs and deli meats. This was an organization-level ethical dilemma. The 1998-1999 national outbreak of listeriosis killed 15, caused six miscarriages, and sickened 101 people. Employees of the Bil Mar plant later came forward and revealed that several employees, as well as management, were aware of the contaminated meat but shipped it anyway. According to a report, a USDA worker had told a Bil Mar employee at the time that the plant was running a risk of getting into trouble if it shipped contaminated foods, but the worker said "they would never know it was our product since [listeria] has about a 2-week incubation period." Before these latest revelations, the company had pleaded guilty to a federal misdemeanor charge, paid a $200,000 fine, and made a $3 million grant to Michigan State University for food safety research.[5]

When thinking about the organizational level of ethics, the presence or absence of unethical practices goes a long way toward revealing the state of ethics that exists within that organization. To illustrate the types of unethical practices that may be evident in organizations, the results of a recent survey conducted by the Ethics Resource Center reveal what managers and employees are up against. In this survey of employees, the following were some of the types of misconduct observed and reported along with the percentage of time these items were mentioned:[6]

- Abusive or intimidating behavior toward employees (23 percent)
- Misreporting actual time or hours worked (20 percent)
- Lying to employees, customers, vendors, or the public (19 percent)
- Withholding needed information from employees, customers, vendors, or the public (18 percent)
- Discriminating on the basis of race, color, gender, age, or similar categories (13 percent)
- Stealing, theft, or related fraud (12 percent)
- Sexual harassment (11 percent)
- Falsifying financial records and reports (5 percent)
- Giving or accepting bribes, kickbacks, or inappropriate gifts (4 percent)

Each of these categories reveals the types of questionable practices that employees today face in their work lives.

Industry Level

A third level at which a manager or organization might influence business ethics is the *industry level*. The industry might be stock brokerage, real estate, insurance, manufactured homes, financial services, telemarketing, automobiles, or a host of others. Related to the industry might be the profession of which an individual is a member—accounting, engineering, pharmacy, medicine, or law. Examples of questions that might pose ethical dilemmas at this level include the following:

- Is this practice that we stockbrokers have been using for years with prospective clients really fair and in their best interests?
- Is this safety standard we electrical engineers have passed really adequate for protecting the consumer in this age of do-it-yourselfers?
- Is this standard contract we mobile home sellers have adopted really in keeping with the financial disclosure laws that have recently been strengthened?
- Is it right to pass the full airfare expense on to our clients when we are getting a discount, behind the scenes, of which they are not aware?
- Is it ethical for telemarketers to make cold calls to prospective clients during the dinner hour when we suspect they will be at home?

Not too long ago, an industry-level group of 14 Wall Street firms endorsed a set of ethical practices for the industry covering broad areas such as analysts' compensation, personal ownership of stocks by analysts, and the objectivity of reports. The action was taken by major firms such as Goldman Sachs, Merrill Lynch, and Morgan Stanley Dean Witter to counter the growing belief among many investors that Wall Street research is biased, obfuscating, or untrustworthy. The move was designed to shore up the ethical and professional standards of their investment analysts and other employees.[7] This action illustrates an industry-level problem that was addressed by the group of leading firms.

Societal and Global Levels

At the *societal and global levels*, it becomes very difficult for the individual manager to have any direct effect on business ethics. However, managers acting in concert through their companies and trade and professional associations can definitely bring about high standards and constructive changes. Because the industry, societal, and global levels are quite removed from the actual practicing manager, we will focus our attention in this chapter primarily on the personal and organizational levels. The manager's greatest impact can be felt through what he or she does personally or as a member of the management team.

An example of a major issue that companies are facing today that has industry, societal, and global ethical implications is that of moving jobs offshore—outsourcing work to less expensive regions of the world, such as China and India. In the past few years, outsourcing has included not only manufacturing jobs but increasingly it is including technical and professional jobs as well. Regarding the software industry, *Business Week* in a special 2004 article, posed the question: "Will outsourcing hurt America's supremacy?"[8] Many observers see ethical implications in business' decision to move jobs offshore to take advantage of lower labor costs.

In Chapter 9, we will deal with global ethics more specifically—a crucial topic that is increasing in importance as global capitalism comes to define our commercial world.

PERSONAL AND MANAGERIAL ETHICS

The point of departure for discussing personal and managerial ethics is the assumption that the individual wants to behave ethically or to improve his or her ethical behavior in personal or managerial situations. Keep in mind that each individual is a stakeholder of someone else. Someone else—a friend, a family member, an associate, or a businessperson—has a stake in your behavior; therefore, your ethics are important to them also. What we discuss here is aimed at those who desire to be ethical and are looking for help in doing so. All the difficulties with making ethical judgments that we discussed in the previous chapter are applicable in this discussion as well.

Personal and managerial ethics, for the most part, entails making decisions. Decision situations typically confront the individual with a conflict-of-interest situation. A conflict of interest is usually present when the individual has to choose between her or his interests and the interests of someone else or some other group (stakeholders). What it boils down to in the final analysis is answering the question, "What shall I do in this situation?"

In answering this question, more often than not it seems that individuals think about the situation briefly and then go with their instincts. There are, however, guides to ethical decision making that one could turn to if she or he really wanted to make the best ethical decisions. What are some of these guides?

In Chapter 6 we indicated that there are three major approaches to ethics or ethical decision making we would like to discuss: (1) the conventional approach, (2) the principles approach, and (3) the ethical tests approach. In Chapter 6, we discussed the conventional approach, which entailed a comparison of a decision or a practice with prevailing norms of acceptability. We discussed some of the challenges inherent in that approach. In this chapter, we discuss the other two approaches and other ethical principles and concepts as well.

Principles Approach to Ethics

The principles approach to ethics or ethical decision making is based on the idea that managers desire to anchor their decisions on a more solid foundation than the conventional approach to ethics. The conventional approach to ethics, you may recall, depended heavily on what people thought and what the prevailing standards were at the time. Several principles of ethics have evolved over the centuries as moral philosophers and ethicists have attempted to organize and codify their thinking.

This raises the question of what constitutes a principle of business ethics and how it might be applied. From a practical point of view, a principle of business ethics is an ethical concept, guideline, or rule that, if applied when you are faced with an ethical decision or practice, will assist you in taking the ethical course.[9] Principles or guidelines have been around for centuries. The Golden Rule has been around for several millennia. In the 1500-1600s, Miguel de Cervantes, the Spanish novelist and author of *Don Quixote*, uttered an important ethics principle that is still used today: *Honesty is the best policy.*

Two Types of Ethical Principles or Theories.   Moral philosophers customarily divide ethical principles or theories into two groups: teleological and deontological. **Teleological theories** focus on the *consequences* or results of the actions they produce. Utilitarianism is the major principle in this category. **Deontological theories** focus on *duties.* For example, it could be argued that managers have a duty to tell the truth when they are doing business. The ethical theory known as the *categorical imperative* formulated by Immanuel Kant best illustrates duty theory. The principle of rights and the principle of justice, two major ethics theories we will discuss, seem to be nonteleological in character.[10] Other principles, such as caring, virtue, servant leadership, and the Golden Rule reflect concerns for duty, consequences, or a combination of both.

There are many different principles of ethics, but we must limit our discussion to those that have been regarded most useful in business settings. Therefore, we will concentrate on the following major principles: utilitarianism (consequences-based), rights, and justice (duty-based). In addition, we will consider the principles of care, virtue ethics, servant leadership, and the Golden Rule—views that are also popular and relevant today. The basic idea behind the principles approach is that managers may improve their ethical decision making if they factor into their proposed actions, decisions, behaviors, and practices a consideration of certain principles or concepts of ethics. We will conclude this section with a brief consideration of how we might reconcile ethical conflicts that might arise in the use of these principles.

Principle of Utilitarianism.   Many ethicists have held that the rightness or fairness of an action can be determined best by looking at its results or consequences. If the consequences are good, the action or decision is considered good. If the consequences are bad, the action or decision is considered wrong. The **principle of utilitarianism** is, therefore, a *consequential* principle, or as stated earlier, a *teleological* principle. In its sim-

plest form, **utilitarianism** asserts that "we should always act so as to produce the greatest ratio of good to evil for everyone."[11] Another way of stating utilitarianism is to say that one should take that course of action that represents the "greatest good for the greatest number." Two of the most influential philosophers who advocated this consequential view were Jeremy Bentham (1748–1832) and John Stuart Mill (1806–1873).

The attractiveness of utilitarianism is that it forces us to think about the general welfare. It proposes a standard outside of self-interest by which to judge the value of a course of action. To make a cost-benefit analysis is to engage in utilitarian thinking. Utilitarianism forces us to think in stakeholder terms: What would produce the greatest good in our decision, considering stakeholders such as owners, employees, customers, and others, as well as ourselves? Finally, it provides for latitude in decision making in that it does not recognize specific actions as inherently good or bad but rather allows us to fit our personal decisions to the complexities of the situation.

A weakness of utilitarianism is that it ignores actions that may be inherently wrong. A strict interpretation of utilitarianism might lead a manager to fire minorities and older workers because they do not fit in or take some other drastic action that contravenes public policy and other ethics principles. In utilitarianism, by focusing on the ends (consequences) of a decision or an action, the means (the decision or action itself) may be ignored. Thus, we have the problematic situation where one may argue that the end justifies the means, using utilitarian reasoning. Therefore, the action or decision is considered objectionable only if it leads to a lesser ratio of good to evil. Another problem with the principle of utilitarianism is that it may come into conflict with the idea of justice. Critics of utilitarianism say that the mere increase in total good is not good in and of itself because it ignores the distribution of good, which is also an important issue. Another stated weakness is that, when using this principle, it is very difficult to formulate satisfactory rules for decision making. Therefore, utilitarianism, like most ethical principles, has its advantages and disadvantages.[12]

Kant's Categorical Imperative.

Immanuel Kant's **categorical imperative** is a duty-based principle of ethics, or as stated earlier, it is a deontological principle.[13] A duty is an obligation; that is, it is an action that is morally obligatory. The duty approach to ethics refers both to the obligatory nature of particular actions and to a way of reasoning about what is right and wrong.[14] Kant's categorical imperative argues that a sense of duty arises from *reason* or *rational nature*, an internal source. By contrast, the *Divine Command* principle maintains that God's law is the source of duties. Thus, we can conceptualize both internal and external sources of duty.

Kant proposed three formulations in his theory or principle. The categorical imperative is best known in the following form: "Act only according to that maxim by which you can at the same time will that it should become a universal law." Stated in clearer terms, Kant's principle is that one should act only on rules (or maxims) that you would be willing to see everyone follow.[15] Kant's second formulation, referred to as the *principle of ends*, is "so act to treat humanity, whether in your own person or in that of any other, in every case as an *end* and never as merely a means." This has also been referred to as the *respect for persons principle*.[16] This means that each person has dignity and moral worth and should never be exploited or manipulated or merely used as a means to another end.[17] The third formulation of the categorical imperative invokes the *principle of autonomy*. It basically holds that "every rational being is able to regard oneself as a maker of universal law. That is, we do not need an external authority—be it God, the state, our culture, or anyone else—to determine the nature of the moral law. We can discover this for ourselves."[18]

Kant argues that this view is not inconsistent with Judeo-Christian beliefs, his childhood heritage, but one must go through a series of logical leaps of faith to arrive at this point.[19] Like all ethical principles, Kant's principles have strengths and weaknesses and supporters and detractors. In the final analysis, it is his emphasis on duty, as opposed to consequences, that merits its treatment here. Further, the notion of universalizability and respect for persons are key ideas. The principles of rights and justice, which we discuss next, seem more consistent with the duty-based perspective than the consequences-based perspective.

Principle of Rights. One major problem with utilitarianism is that it does not handle the issue of **rights** very well. That is, utilitarianism implies that certain actions are morally right (i.e., they represent the greatest good for the greatest number) when in fact they may violate another person's rights.[20] **Moral rights** are important, justifiable claims or entitlements. Moral rights do not depend on a legal system to be valid. They are rights that we ought to have based on moral reasoning. The right to life or the right not to be killed by others is a justifiable claim in our society. The Declaration of Independence referred to the rights to life, liberty, and the pursuit of happiness. John Locke earlier had spoken of the right to property. Today we speak of human rights. Some of these are **legal rights** and some are moral rights.

The basic idea undergirding the **principle of rights** is that rights cannot simply be overridden by utility. A right can be overridden only by another, more basic or important right. Let us consider the problem if we apply the utilitarian principle. For example, if we accept the basic right to human life, we are precluded from considering whether killing someone might produce the greatest good for the greatest number. To use a business example, if a person has a right to equal treatment (not to be discriminated against), we could not argue for discriminating against that person so as to produce more good for others.[21] However, some people would say that this is precisely what we do when we advocate affirmative action.

The rights principle expresses morality from the point of view of the individual or group of individuals, whereas the utilitarian principle expresses morality in terms of the group or society as a whole. The rights view forces us in our decision making to ask what is due each individual and to promote individual welfare. The rights view also limits the validity of appeals to numbers and to society's aggregate benefit.[22] However, a central question that is not always easy to answer is: "What constitutes a legitimate right that should be honored, and what rights or whose rights take precedence over others?"

Figure 7-1 provides an overview of many of the types of rights that are being claimed in our society today. Some of these rights are legally protected, whereas others are claimed as moral rights but are not legally protected. Managers are expected to be attentive to both legal and moral rights, but there are no clear guidelines available to help one sort out which claimed moral rights should be protected, to what extent they should be protected, and which rights should take precedence over others.

In recent years, some have argued that we are in the midst of a rights revolution in which too many individuals and groups are attempting to urge society to accept their wishes or demands as rights. The proliferation of rights claims has the potential to dilute or diminish the power of more legitimate rights. If everyone's claim for special consideration is perceived as a legitimate right, the rights approach will lose its power to help management concentrate on the morally justified rights. A related problem has been the politicization of rights in recent years. As our lawmakers bestow legal or protected status upon rights claims for political reasons rather than moral reasons, managers may become blinded to

FIGURE 7-1

A Variety of Legal Rights and Claimed Moral Rights in Society Today

Civil rights	Smokers' rights
Minorities' rights	Nonsmokers' rights
Women's rights	AIDS victims' rights
Disabled people's rights	Children's rights
Older people's rights	Fetal rights
Religious affiliation rights	Embryo rights
Employee rights	Animals' rights
Consumer rights	Right to burn the American flag
Shareholder rights	Right of due process
Privacy rights	Gay rights
Right to life	Victims' rights
Criminals' rights	

which rights or whose rights really should be honored in a decision-making situation. As rights claims expand, the common core of morality may diminish, and decision makers may find it more and more difficult to balance individuals' interests with the public interest.[23]

Principle of Justice.   Just as the utilitarian principle does not handle well the idea of rights, it does not deal effectively with justice either. One way to think about the **principle of justice** is to say that it involves the fair treatment of each person. Most would argue that we have a duty to be fair to employees, consumers, and other stakeholders. But how do you decide what is fair to each person? How do you decide what each person is due? People might be given what they are due according to their type of work, their effort expended, their merit, their need, and so on. Each of these criteria might be appropriate in different situations. At one time, the view prevailed that married heads of households ought to be paid more than single males or women. Today, however, the social structure is different. Women have entered the workforce in significant numbers, some families are structured differently, and a revised concept of what is due people has evolved. The just action now is to pay everyone more on the basis of merit than needs.[24]

To use the principle of justice, we must ask, "What is meant by justice?" There are several kinds of justice. **Distributive justice** refers to the distribution of benefits and burdens. **Compensatory justice** involves compensating someone for a past injustice. **Procedural justice** refers to fair decision-making procedures, practices, or agreements.[25]

John Rawls, a political philosopher who died in 2002 at the age of 81, has been often cited as a distinguished ethicist.[26] John Rawls provides what some have referred to as a comprehensive principle of justice.[27] His theory is based on the idea that what we need first is a fair method by which we may choose the principles through which conflicts will be resolved. The two principles of justice that underlie his theory are as follows:[28]

1. Each person has an equal right to the most extensive basic liberties compatible with similar liberties for all others.
2. Social and economic inequalities are arranged so that they are both (a) reasonably expected to be to everyone's advantage and (b) attached to positions and offices open to all.

Under Rawls's first principle, each person is to be treated equally. It holds that each person should enjoy equally a full array of basic liberties.[29] The second principle is more controversial. This is often interpreted to mean that public policy should raise as high as possible the social and economic well-being of society's worst-off individuals. It is criticized by both those who argue that the principle is too strong and those who think the principle is too weak. The former think that, as long as we have equal opportunity, there is no injustice when some people benefit from their own work, skill, ingenuity, or assumed risks. Therefore, such people deserve more and should not be required to produce benefits for the least advantaged. The latter group thinks that the inequalities that may result may be so great as to be clearly unjust. Therefore, the rich get richer and the poor get only a little less poor.[30]

In developing further his second principle, Rawls imagined people gathered behind a "*veil of ignorance*," unaware of whether they, personally, were rich or poor, talented or incompetent. He then asked what kind of society would they build? He reasoned that the rule everyone would be able to agree on would be to maximize the well-being of the worst-off person, partially out of fear that anyone could wind up at the bottom.[31] This view, of course, had its critics.

Supporters of the principle of justice claim that it preserves the basic values—freedom, equality of opportunity, and a concern for the disadvantaged—that have become embedded in our moral beliefs. Critics object to various parts of the theory and would not subscribe to Rawls's principles at all. Utilitarians, for example, think the greatest good for the greatest number should reign supreme.

Principle of Caring.   It is useful to introduce the ethics of care or **principle of caring** right after our discussion of utilitarianism, rights, and justice, because the theory, frequently referred to as "feminist theory," is critical of these traditional views. These views, it has been argued, embrace a masculine approach to perceiving the world. The feminist or "care" perspective builds on the work of Carol Gilligan, whose criticisms of Kohlberg's theory of moral development were discussed in the previous chapter. Gilligan found that women often spoke in "a different voice" that was more based on responsibility to others and on the continuity of interdependent relationships.[32]

The care perspective holds that traditional ethics like the principles of utilitarianism and rights focus too much on the individual self and on cognitive thought processes. In the traditional view, "others" may be seen as threats, so rights become important. Resulting moral theories then tend to be legalistic or contractual.

Feminist theory is founded on wholly different assumptions. Feminist philosophers, for example, view the person as essentially relational, not individualistic. These philosophers do not deny the existence of the self but hold that the self has relationships that cannot be separated from the self's existence. This view emphasizes the relationships' moral worth and, by extension, the responsibilities inherent in those relationships, rather than in rights, as in traditional ethics.[33]

Feminist moral theory, therefore, emphasizes caring as opposed to justice or rights. Several writers have argued that this is consistent with stakeholder theory, or the stakeholder approach, in that the focus is on a more cooperative, caring type of relationship. In this view, firms should seek to make decisions that satisfy stakeholders, leading to situations in which all parties in the relationship gain. Robbin Derry elaborates: "In the corporate environment, there is an increasing demand for business to be attentive to its many stakeholders, particularly customers and employees, in caring ways. As organizations attempt to build such relationships, they must define the responsibilities of initiating and maintaining care. The ethics of care may be able to facilitate an understanding of these responsibilities."[34]

Ethics in Practice

WHOSE RIGHTS ARE *RIGHT*?

In 1990, the Recording Industry Association of America (RIAA) voluntarily decided to add warning labels to musical albums containing explicit lyrics. According to the RIAA, "The Parental Advisory is a notice to parents that recordings identified by this logo may contain strong language or depictions of violence, sex or substance abuse. Parental discretion is advised."

Recently, while I was working for a small record store, Aftermath Entertainment and Interscope Records released an album by Marshall Mathers, whose stage name is Eminem titled, "The Marshall Mathers LP." It contained the advisory on the front left corner in compliance with the self-adopted guidelines of the RIAA.

Upon the release of the album, many groups, including those representing gay, lesbian, and women's right, immediately cried for a recall of the album because of the slurs and messages contained within some of the songs. Women's rights groups were upset because of the extremely violent episodes describing the beatings, rapes, and murders of Mr. Mathers' wife and mother. Gay and lesbian rights groups were equally outraged at the slurs of antigay messages contained in just about every song.

Marshall Mathers has stated that messages in his albums are not to be taken seriously; they are purely for entertainment purposes. Further, he claimed the slurs contained in his album that gay and lesbian rights groups find offensive are not meant in a manner offensive only to homosexuals, but rather are slang words that degrade anyone. This argument by Mr. Mathers was defended by a description contained in the RIAA code describing which albums should be labeled with the advisory: Lyrics are often susceptible to varying interpretations. Words can have different meanings. Also, words cannot be viewed in isolation from the music that accompanies them. Lyrics when accompanied by loud and raucous music can be per-ceived differently than the same lyrics when accompanied by soft and soothing music.

This only argues for a very minor part of the issue though. The main concern arose when it became public that Interscope Records refused to release the album until certain lyrics about the shootings in 1999 at Columbine High School in Littleton, Colorado, were removed. This censoring of some of the lyrics and not others led the rights groups to believe that Interscope Records was fully aware of the impact that the lyrics would have and, in fact, chose which lyrics could be financially capitalized on, and left those on the album. The financial gains turned out to be larger than anyone expected as "The Marshall Mathers LP" became the fastest selling hip-hop album in music history.

All of this considered, the most intriguing issue that arises from this case is where the line between the artist's freedom of expression and a record company's social responsibility should lie.

1. Whose rights are more important than another's rights in a business situation such as this? How is this decision made and by whom?

2. How much responsibility concerning what is and is not appropriate for an artist to say should be decided by the recording company? By consumer demand?

3. What do you think is the record company's reasoning or logic behind protecting the rights of those associated with the Columbine shootings versus the other groups protesting in the case?

4. How do the principles of rights, justice, and utilitarianism apply in this case?

Contributed by Steve Minster

Jeanne Liedtka, on the other hand, has questioned whether organizations can care in the sense in which feminist moral theory proposes. Liedtka contends that to care in this sense, an organization would have to care in a way that is:

- Focused entirely on people, not quality, profits, or other such ideas that today use "care talk"
- Undertaken with caring as an end, not merely as a means to an end (such as quality or profits)
- Essentially personal, in that the caring reflects caring for other individuals
- Growth enhancing for the cared-for, in that the caring moves the cared-for toward the development and use of their capacities

Liedtka takes the position that caring people could lead to a caring organization that offers new possibilities for simultaneously enhancing the effectiveness and the moral quality of organizations.[35] The principle of caring offers a different perspective to guide ethical decision making—a perspective that clearly is thought provoking and valuable.

Virtue Ethics.

The major principles just discussed have been more action oriented. That is, they were designed to guide our actions and decisions. Another ethical tradition, often referred to as **virtue ethics**, merits consideration even though it is not a principle per se. Virtue ethics, rooted in the thinking of Plato and Aristotle, focuses on the individual becoming imbued with virtues (e.g., honesty, fairness, truthfulness, benevolence, nonmalfeasance).[36]

Virtue ethics is a system of thought that is centered in the heart of the person—in our case, the manager. This is in contrast to the principles we have discussed, which see the heart of ethics in actions or duties. Action-oriented principles focus on *doing*. Virtue ethics emphasizes *being*. The assumption, of course, is that the actions of a virtuous person will also be virtuous. Traditional ethical principles such as utilitarianism, rights, and justice focus on the question, "What should I do?" Virtue ethics focuses on the question, "What sort of person should I *be* or *become*?"[37]

Programs that have developed from the notion of virtue ethics have sometimes been called *character education*, because this particular theory emphasizes character development. Many observers think that one reason we have moral decline in business and society today is because we have failed to teach our young people universal principles of good character.

VF Corporation, the Josephson Institute of Ethics, and the Ethics Resource Center in Washington all have launched character education programs. Esther Schaeffer, executive director of the Character Education Partnership, has argued that character education is needed not only in schools, but in corporations as well. She holds that corporate well-being demands character and that business leaders are a vital and necessary force for putting character back into education.[38]

Virtue ethicists have brought back to the public debate the idea that virtues are important whether they be in the education of the young or in management training programs. Virtues such as honesty, integrity, loyalty, promise keeping, fairness, and respect for others are completely compatible with the major principles we have been discussing. The principles, combined with the virtues, form the foundation for effective ethical action and decision making. Whether the virtues are seen as character traits or as principles of decision making is not our major concern at this point. That they be used, whatever the motivation, is our central concern here. Business ethicists Oliver Williams and Patrick Murphy have strongly argued that the ethics of virtue in business is an idea whose time has arrived.[39]

Servant Leadership.

An increasingly popular approach to organizational leadership and thinking today is **servant leadership**. Though not an ethical principle, per se, servant leadership is an approach to ethical leadership and decision making based on the moral principle of serving others first. Can these two roles—servant and leader—be fused in one person—a manager? What are the basic tenets of servant leadership?

Servant leadership is a model of ethical management—an approach to ethical decision making—based on the idea of serving others such as employees, customers, community, and other stakeholders as the first priority. According to Robert Greenleaf, "It begins with the natural feeling that one wants to serve, to serve first." Next, a conscious choice brings one to "aspire to lead." The model manifests itself in the care taken by the leader to make sure that others' needs are being served.[40]

The modern era of servant leadership is marked primarily by the works of Robert K. Greenleaf, known today as the father of this movement. Greenleaf spent his 38-year career working for AT&T. Upon his retirement, he founded the Center for Applied Ethics, which was renamed the Greenleaf Center for Servant Leadership; it is housed in Indianapolis. Greenleaf's "second career" lasted until shortly before his death in 1990. During his time, he became influential in leadership circles as a thinker, writer, consultant, and speaker to many organizations.

In his 1977 book, *Servant Leadership*, Greenleaf gives credit to the ministry of Jesus of Nazareth as symbolically embodying the concept.[41] Though inspired by the teachings and life of Jesus, Greenleaf says he was led to crystallize his idea of servant leadership after reading Hermann Hesse's short novel, *Journey to the East*. In Hesse's story, a band of men take a mythical journey. The central figure in the story is Leo, who accompanies the party as the "servant" who does the menial chores, but who also sustains the men with his spirit and song. Leo is a person with extraordinary presence. All goes well until Leo disappears. Then the group falls into disarray, and their journey is abandoned. They can't make it without their servant, Leo.

The story's narrator, one of the party, finds Leo after some years of wandering. The narrator is taken into the Order that had sponsored the journey. There he discovers that Leo, whom he had known as "servant," was actually the titular head of the Order—its guiding spirit—a great and noble "leader." The main point Greenleaf took from this story is that the great leader is seen as servant first, and this is the key to his greatness. Leo was actually the leader all the time, but he was servant first because that was his deep internal person.

Greenleaf summarizes that the servant leader is "servant first," just as Leo was portrayed. The role begins with the natural sentiment that one first wants to serve, and then comes forth as a conscious aspiration to lead. This kind of person is distinctively different from one who is a "leader first," perhaps because of the need to gratify a power drive or acquisitiveness for material possessions. Of course, the servant-first and the leader-first are two extreme types, and there are a number of shadings and blends in between these two models. They define a useful range for thinking about leadership.

The CEO of the Greenleaf Center for Servant Leadership is Larry Spears. Spears has written several books on the topic, such as *Reflections on Leadership*. Spears has deliberated on Greenleaf's original writings for years and has culled from these writings a set of 10 key characteristics that are essential for the development of servant leaders. Each of these is worth listing because, together, they paint a portrait of servant leadership in terms of leader behaviors and characteristics. The 10 characteristics of servant leaders are as follows:[42]

- Listening
- Empathy
- Healing

- Persuasion
- Awareness
- Foresight
- Conceptualization
- Commitment to the growth of people
- Stewardship
- Building community

Each of these 10 characteristics of servant leaders is based on the ethical principle of putting the other person first—whether that other person is an employee, a customer, or some other important stakeholder. Some of these characteristics could be stated as virtues and some as behaviors. Thus, servant leadership embraces a number of the ethical perspectives discussed earlier.

Servant leadership builds a bridge between the ideas of business ethics and the ideas of leadership. Joanne Ciulla has observed that people follow servant leaders because they can trust them.[43] And, James Autry, the top-selling leadership author, argues that servant leadership is the right way, a better way of being a manager and part of organizational life. He adds, "it will enhance productivity, encourage creativity, and benefit the bottom line."[44]

The Golden Rule.   The **Golden Rule** merits discussion because of its popularity as a basic and strong principle of ethical living and decision making. A number of studies have found it to be the most powerful and useful to managers.[45] The Golden Rule—"Do unto others as you would have them do unto you"—is a fairly straightforward, easy-to-understand principle. Further, it guides the individual decision maker to behavior, actions, or decisions that she or he should be able to express as acceptable or not based on some direct comparisons with what she or he would consider ethical or fair.

The Golden Rule simply argues that, if you want to be treated fairly, treat others fairly; if you want your privacy protected, respect the privacy of others. The key is impartiality. According to this principle, we are not to make an exception of ourselves. In essence, the Golden Rule personalizes business relations and brings the ideal of fairness into business deliberations.[46]

Perhaps the reason the Golden Rule is so popular is that it is rooted in history and religious tradition and is among the oldest of the principles of living. Further, it is universal in the sense that it requires no specific religious belief or faith. Almost since time began, religious leaders and philosophers have advocated the Golden Rule in one form or another. It is easy to see, therefore, why Martin Luther could say that the Golden Rule is a part of the "natural law," because it is a moral rule that anyone can recognize and embrace without any particular religious teaching. In three different studies, when managers or respondents were asked to rank ethical principles according to their value to them, the Golden Rule was ranked first.[47]

Leadership expert John C. Maxwell published a book recently titled *There's No Such Thing as "Business" Ethics: There's Only One Rule for Making Decisions.* The one rule Maxwell advocates is the Golden Rule. According to Maxwell, there are four reasons why decision makers should adopt the Golden Rule.

1. The Golden Rule is accepted by most people.
2. The Golden Rule is easy to understand.
3. The Golden Rule is a win-win philosophy.
4. The Golden Rule is a compass when you need direction.[48]

In addition to the ethical principles and theories that we have chosen to discuss in some detail, Figure 7-2 provides a brief sketch of several ethical principles that have evolved over the years.

There is no single principle that is recommended to be always used. As one gets into each principle, one encounters a number of problems with definitions, with measurement,

---

FIGURE 7-2

A Brief Sketch of Ethical Principles

- **The Categorical Imperative:** Act only according to that maxim by which you can at the same time "will" that it should become a universal law. In other words, one should not adopt principles of action unless they can, without inconsistency, be adopted by everyone else.

- **The Conventionalist Ethic:** Individuals should act to further their self-interests so long as they do not violate the law. It is allowed, under this principle, to bluff (lie) and to take advantage of all legal opportunities and widespread practices and customs.

- **The Disclosure Rule:** If the full glare of examination by associates, friends, family, newspapers, television, etc., were to focus on your decision, would you remain comfortable with it? If you think you would, it probably is the right decision.

- **The Golden Rule:** Do unto others as you would have them do unto you. It includes not knowingly doing harm to others.

- **The Hedonistic Ethic:** Virtue is embodied in what each individual finds meaningful. There are no universal or absolute moral principles. If it feels good, do it.

- **The Intuition Ethic:** People are endowed with a kind of moral sense with which they can apprehend right and wrong. The solution to moral problems lies simply in what you feel or understand to be right in a given situation. You have a "gut feeling" and "fly by the seat of your pants."

- **The Market Ethic:** Selfish actions in the marketplace are virtuous because they contribute to efficient operation of the economy. Decision makers may take selfish actions and be motivated by personal gain in their business dealings. They should ask whether their actions in the market further financial self-interest. If so, the actions are ethical.

- **The Means-Ends Ethic:** Worthwhile ends justify efficient means—i.e., when ends are of overriding importance or virtue, unscrupulous means may be employed to reach them.

- **The Might-Equals-Right Ethic:** Justice is defined as the interest of the stronger. What is ethical is what an individual has the strength and power to accomplish. Seize what advantage you are strong enough to take without respect to ordinary social conventions and laws.

- **The Organization Ethic:** The wills and needs of individuals should be subordinated to the greater good of the organization (be it church, state, business, military, or university). An individual should ask whether actions are consistent with organizational goals and what is good for the organization.

- **The Professional Ethic:** You should do only that which can be explained before a committee of your peers.

- **The Proportionality Principle:** I am responsible for whatever I "will" as a means or an end. If both the means and the end are good in and of themselves, I may ethically permit or risk the foreseen but unwilled side effects if, and only if, I have a proportionate reason for doing so.

- **The Revelation Ethic:** Through prayer or other appeal to transcendent beings and forces, answers are given to individual minds. The decision makers pray, meditate, or otherwise commune with a superior force or being. They are then apprised of which actions are just and unjust.

- **The Utilitarian Ethic:** The greatest good for the greatest number. Determine whether the harm in an action is outweighed by the good. If the action maximizes benefit, it is the optimum course to take among alternatives that provide less benefit.

SOURCE: T. K. Das, "Ethical Preferences Among Business Students: A Comparative Study of Fourteen Ethical Principles," *Southern Management Association* (November 13–16, 1985), 11–12. For further discussion, see T. K. Das, "Ethical Principles in Business: An Empirical Study of Preferential Rankings," *International Journal of Management* (Vol. 9, No. 4, December, 1992), 462–472.

Ethics in Practice

PROMISE VERSUS LIE

During the spring, I worked in the billing department of a large organization as a student worker. All of the secretaries who worked in the billing department were close and would talk to each other about almost anything. One of the topics we enjoyed talking about the most was the office manager of the billing department and how much we would like to find another job to get away from her, because we did not like working with her. While I was working in the department, I became very close friends with the senior secretary, who worked with me in the front office.

During the same spring, my friend was offered a very prestigious job at the company. She told a few of us about having applied for the job, but she did not want us to let the office manager know that she was applying for it in case she did not get it. I was her friend, so I was not going to say anything about the situation. After a few weeks of waiting to find out if she got the job or not, she was offered the job and took it immediately. After she knew she had the new job, she told the office manager that she had been offered another job and was giving her 2 weeks' notice. All was well until the office manager came up to me one day and asked me if I had known anything about the secretary planning to leave. I was not sure what to say. I did not want to lie to the office manager, but I also did not want to break a promise I made to a good friend. What was I to do?

1. Is this ethical dilemma at the personal level or the organizational level?

2. What ethical principles are at stake in this situation?

3. What should the person who faces this ethical situation do?

Contributed by Erika Carlson-Durham

and with generalizability. The more one gets into each principle, the more one realizes how difficult it would be for a person to use each principle consistently as a guide to decision making. On the other hand, to say that an ethical principle is imperfect is not to say that it has not raised important issues that must be addressed in personal or business decision making. The major principles and approaches we have discussed have raised to our consciousness the importance of the collective good, individual rights, caring, character, and fairness.

Reconciling Ethical Conflicts.

What does a manager do when using some of the ethical principles and guidelines we have been discussing and she or he finds that there are conflicts between and among the principles? For example, what if the manager perceives that one employee's right to safety conflicts with another's right to privacy? How should this conflict be resolved? There is no unqualified way to reconcile ethical principles; however, some brief discussion may be helpful. Shaw and Barry have argued, following the ideas introduced by V. R. Ruggiero, that three common concerns must be addressed in conflict situations: obligations, ideals, and effects.[49] We will tie these concepts into our current discussion.

First, we enter into *obligations* as a part of our daily organizational lives. An example might be a verbal or written contract to which we have agreed. Principles of justice, rights, and virtue would hold that we should honor obligations. Second, as managers we might hold certain *ideals.* Such an ideal may be some morally important goal, principle, virtue, or notion of excellence worth striving for. A quest for justice, protection of rights, and balancing of individual versus group goals might be examples. Third, we are interested in the *effects*, or consequences, on stakeholders of our decisions or actions.[50] Hopefully, we can see how obligations, goals, and effects are all aspects of the ethical principles we have been discussing.

The question now arises as to how we might handle a situation wherein our obligations, goals, and effects conflict or produce mixed effects. Three rough guidelines have been proposed:[51]

1. When two or more moral obligations conflict, *choose the stronger one.*
2. When two or more ideals conflict, or when ideals conflict with obligations, *honor the more important one.*
3. When the effects are mixed, *choose the action that produces the greater good or less harm.*

These guidelines are rough because they do not precisely answer the question of which obligations or ideals should take precedence over others. However, they do give us a general approach or process for raising the issue of how such conflicts might be resolved. In the final analysis, the manager will need to consider carefully which values or obligations are more important than others.

In summary, the principles approach to ethics focuses on guidelines, ideas, or concepts that have been created to help people and organizations make wise, ethical decisions. Two ethical categories include the teleological (ends-based) and the deontological (duty-based). Both duty and consequences are important ethical concepts. In our discussion, we have treated the following as important components of the principles-based approach: utilitarianism, rights, justice, caring, virtue, servant leadership, and the Golden Rule. Such principles, or principle-based approaches, ought to cause us to think deeply and to reflect carefully on the ethical decisions we face in our personal and organizational lives. For the most part, these principles are rooted in moral philosophy and religion. On a more pragmatic level, we turn now to a series of ethical tests that constitute our third major approach to ethics.

Ethical Tests Approach

In addition to the ethical principles approach to guiding personal and managerial decision making, a number of practical **ethical tests** might be set forth, too. Whereas the principles have almost exclusively been generated by moral philosophers, the ethical tests we discuss here are more practical in orientation and do not require the depth of moral thinking that the principles do. No single test is recommended as a universal answer to the question, "What action or decision should I take in this situation?" However, each person may find one or more tests that will be useful in helping to clarify the appropriate course of action in a decision situation. To most students, the notion of a test invokes the thought of questions posed that need to be answered. Indeed, each of these tests for personal ethical decision making requires the thoughtful deliberation of a central question that gets to the heart of the matter. The answer to the question should help the decision maker decide whether the course of action, practice, or decision should be pursued from an ethical point of view.

Test of Common Sense.   With this first test, the individual simply asks, "Does the action I am getting ready to take really make sense?" When you think of behavior that might have ethical implications, it is logical to consider the practical consequences. If, for example, you would surely get caught engaging in a questionable practice, the action does not pass this test. Many unethical practices have come to light where one is led to ask whether a person really used her or his common sense at all. This test has severe limitations. For example, if you conclude that you would not get caught engaging in a questionable practice, this test might lead you to think that the questionable practice is an acceptable course of action, when in fact it is not. In addition, there may be other common-sense aspects of the situation that you have overlooked.

Test of One's Best Self.

Psychologists tell us that each person has a self-concept. Most people could construct a scenario of themselves *at their best*. This test requires the individual to pose the question, "Is this action or decision I'm getting ready to take compatible with my concept of myself *at my best*?" This test addresses the notion of the esteem in which we hold ourselves and the kind of person we want to be known as. Naturally, this test would not be of much value to those who do not hold themselves in high esteem. To those concerned about their esteem and reputation, however, this could be a powerful test.

Test of Making Something Public.

This is one of the most powerful tests.[52] It is similar to the disclosure rule defined in Figure 7-2. If you are about to engage in a questionable practice or action, you might pose the following questions: "How would I feel if others knew I was doing this? How would I feel if I knew that my decisions or actions were going to be featured on the national evening news tonight for all the world to see?" This test addresses the issue of whether your action or decision can withstand public disclosure and scrutiny. How would you feel if all your friends, family, and colleagues knew you were engaging in this action? If you feel comfortable with this thought, you are probably on solid footing. If you feel uncomfortable with this thought, you ought to rethink your position.

   The concept of public exposure is quite powerful. Several years ago, a poll of managers was taken asking whether the Foreign Corrupt Practices Act would stop bribes abroad. Many of the managers said it would not. When asked what would stop bribes, most managers thought that public exposure would be most effective. "If the public knew we were accepting bribes, this knowledge would have the best chance of being effective," they replied. This idea gives further testimony to the strength of the transparency movement that is permeating business today.

Test of Ventilation.

The idea of ventilation is to "expose" your proposed action to others and get their thoughts on it. This test works best if you get opinions from people who you know might not see things your way. The important point here is that you do not isolate yourself with your dilemma but seek others' views. After you have subjected your proposed course of action to other opinions, you may find that you have not been thinking clearly. In other words, ventilate, or share, your ethical quandary, don't keep it to yourself. Someone else may say something of value that will help you in making your decision.

Test of the Purified Idea.

An idea or action may be thought to be "purified"— that is, made right—when a person with authority says it is appropriate. Such a person might be a supervisor, an accountant, or a lawyer. The central question here is, "Am I thinking this action or decision is right just because someone with appropriate authority or knowledge says it is right?" If you look hard enough, you can find a lawyer or an accountant to endorse almost any idea if it is phrased right.[53] However, neither of them is the final arbiter of what is right or wrong. Similarly, just because a superior says an action or a decision is ethical does not make it so. The decision or course of action may still be questionable or wrong even though someone else has sanctioned it with her or his approval. This is one of the most common ethical errors people make, and they must constantly be reminded that they themselves ultimately will be held accountable if the action is indefensible.

Gag Test. This test was provided by a judge on the Louisiana Court of Appeals. He argued that a manager's clearest signal that a dubious decision or action is going too far is when you simply gag at the prospect of carrying it out.[54] Admittedly, this test can only capture the grossest of unethical behaviors, but there are some managers who may need such a general kind of test. Actually, this test is intended to be more humorous than serious, but a few might be helped by it.

None of the previously-mentioned tests alone offers a perfect way to determine whether a decision, act, or practice is ethical. If several tests are used together, especially the more powerful ones, they do provide a means of examining proposed actions before engaging in them. To repeat, this assumes that the individual really wants to do what is right and is looking for assistance. To the fundamentally unethical person, however, these tests would not be of much value.

Phillip V. Lewis conducted a 5-year study of ethical principles and ethical tests. Based on his findings, he asserted that there is high agreement on how a decision maker should behave when faced with a moral choice. He concludes:

> *In fact, there is almost a step-by-step sequence. Notice: One should (1) look at the problem from the position of the other person(s) affected by a decision; (2) try to determine what virtuous response is expected; (3) ask (a) how it would feel for the decision to be disclosed to a wide audience and (b) whether the decision is consistent with organizational goals; and (4) act in a way that is (a) right and just for any other person in a similar situation and (b) good for the organization.*[55]

Implicit in Lewis's conclusion is evidence of stakeholder theory, virtue theory, the Golden Rule, the disclosure rule, and Rawls's principle of justice.

MANAGING ORGANIZATIONAL ETHICS

To this point, our discussion has centered on principles and approaches to personal or managerial decision making. Clearly, ethical decision making is at the heart of business ethics, and we cannot stress enough the need to sharpen decision-making skills if amorality is to be prevented and moral management is to be achieved. Now we shift our attention more to the *organizational level*, where we find the context in which decision making occurs. Actions and practices that take place within the organization's culture, or climate, are just as vital as decision making in bringing about ethical business practices and results. As a result of his research, Craig VanSandt has concluded that "understanding and managing an organization's ethical work climate may go a long way toward defining the difference between how a company does and what kind of organization it is."[56]

To manage ethics in an organization, a manager must appreciate that the organization's ethical climate is just one part of its overall corporate culture. When McNeil Laboratories, a subsidiary of Johnson & Johnson, voluntarily withdrew Tylenol from the market immediately after the reports of tainted, poisoned products, some people wondered why they made this decision as they did. An often cited response was, "It's the J & J way."[57] This statement conveys a significant message about the firm's ethical work climate. It also raises the question of how organizations and managers should deal with, understand, and shape business ethics through actions taken, policies established, and examples set. The organization's moral climate is a complex entity, and we can discuss only some facets of it in this section.[58]

Figure 7-3 illustrates several levels of moral climate and some of the key factors that may come to bear on the manager as she or he makes decisions. Our focus in this section is on the organization's moral climate. Two major questions that need to be considered are (1) What factors contribute to ethical or unethical behavior in the organization? and (2) What actions or strategies might management employ to improve the organization's ethical climate?

FIGURE 7-3

Factors Affecting the Morality of Managers and Employees

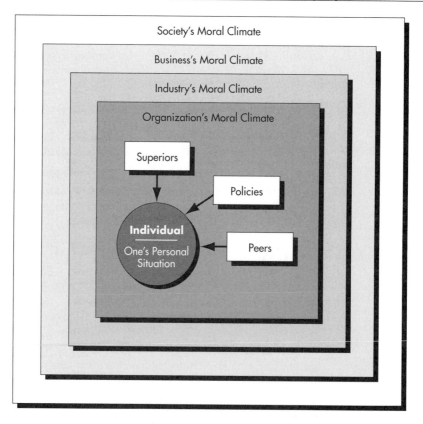

Factors Affecting the Organization's Moral Climate

For managers to be in a position to create an ethical work climate, they must first understand the factors at work in the organization that influence whether or not other managers or employees behave ethically. More than a few studies have been conducted that have sought to identify and to rank the sources of ethical behavior in organizations.

Baumhart conducted one of the earliest studies, in which he surveyed over 1,500 *Harvard Business Review* readers (executives, managers).[59] One of the questions asked was to rank several factors that the managers thought influenced or contributed to unethical behaviors or actions. The factors found in his study, in descending order of frequency of mention, were:

1. Behavior of superiors
2. The ethical practices of one's industry or profession
3. Behavior of one's peers in the organization
4. Formal organizational policy (or lack thereof)
5. Personal financial need

Brenner and Molander later replicated the Baumhart study using over 1,200 *Harvard Business Review* readers. They added one additional factor to the list: society's moral climate.[60] Posner and Schmidt surveyed over 1,400 managers, again asking them to rank the list of six factors in terms of their influence or contribution to unethical behavior.[61] Figure 7-4 presents the findings of these three landmark, baseline studies.

Although there is some variation in the rankings of the three studies, several findings are worthy of note:

1. *Behavior of superiors* was ranked as the number one influence on unethical behavior in all three studies.

FIGURE 7-4

Factors Influencing Unethical Behavior Question: "Listed below are the factors that many believe influence unethical behavior. Rank them in order of their influence or contribution to unethical behaviors or actions by managers."[a]

Factor	Posner & Schmidt Study[b] (N = 1443)	Brenner & Molander Study[c] (N = 1227)	Baumhart Study[d] (N = 1531)
Behavior of superiors	2.17(1)	2.15(1)	1.9(1)
Behavior of one's organizational peers	3.30(2)	3.37(4)	3.1(3)
Ethical practices of one's industry or profession	3.57(3)	3.34(3)	2.6(2)
Society's moral climate	3.79(4)	4.22(5)	e
Formal organizational policy (or lack thereof)	3.84(5)	3.27(2)	3.3(4)
Personal financial need	4.09(6)	4.46(6)	4.1(5)

[a] Ranking is based on a scale of 1 (most influential) to 6 (least influential).
[b] Barry Z. Posner and Warren H. Schmidt, "Values and the American Manager: An Update," *California Management Review* (Spring 1984), 202–216.
[c] Steve Brenner and Earl Molander, "Is the Ethics of Business Changing?" *Harvard Business Review* (January/February 1977).
[d] Raymond C. Baumhart, "How Ethical Are Businessmen?" *Harvard Business Review* (July/August 1961), 6ff.
[e] This item not included in 1961 study.

2. *Behavior of one's peers* was ranked high in two of the three studies.
3. *Industry or professional ethical practices* ranked in the upper half in all three studies.
4. *Personal financial need* ranked last in all three studies.

What stands out in these studies from an organizational perspective is the influence of the behavior of one's superiors and peers. Also notable about these findings is that quite often it is assumed that society's moral climate has a lot to do with managers' morality, but this factor was ranked low in the two studies in which it was considered. Apparently, society's moral climate serves as a background factor that does not have a direct and immediate impact on organizational ethics. Furthermore, it is enlightening to know that personal financial need ranked so low. What these findings suggest is that there are factors at work over which managers can exercise some discretion. Thus, we begin to see the managerial dimension of business ethics.

Pressures Exerted on Subordinates by Superiors.

One major consequence of the behavior of superiors and peers is that sometimes pressure is placed on subordinates and/or other organizational members to compromise their ethics. In an early, national study conducted by one of the authors of this text, managers were asked to what extent they agreed with the following proposition: "Managers today feel under pressure to compromise personal standards to achieve company goals."[62] It is insightful to consider the management levels of the 64.4 percent of the respondents who agreed with the proposition. The results were:

Top management: 50 percent agreed
Middle management: 65 percent agreed
Lower management: 85 percent agreed

This study revealed that the perceived pressure to compromise ethics seems to be felt most by those in lower management, followed by those in middle management. In their subsequent study, Posner and Schmidt also asked managers whether they sometimes had to compromise their personal principles to conform to organizational expectations.[63] Twenty percent of the top executives agreed, 27 percent of the middle managers agreed, and 41 percent of the lower managers agreed. In other words, the same pattern prevailed in this second study.

This coauthor's study posed another proposition: "I can conceive of a situation where you have sound ethics running from top to bottom, but because of pressures from the top to achieve results, the person down the line compromises." The pattern of findings on this proposition was similar to that of the other two findings.[64]

What is particularly troublesome about these findings is the pattern of response. It seems that the lower a manager is in the hierarchy, the more that manager perceives pressures toward unethical conduct. Although there are several plausible explanations for this phenomenon, one explanation seems particularly attractive because of its agreement with conversations this coauthor has had with various managers. This interpretation is that top-level managers do not know how strongly their subordinates perceive pressures to go along with their bosses. These varying perceptions at different levels in the managerial hierarchy suggest that higher-level managers may not be tuned in to how pressure is perceived at lower levels. There seems to be a gap in the understanding of higher managers and lower managers regarding the pressures toward unethical behavior that exist, especially in the lower echelons. This breakdown in understanding, or lack of sensitivity by top management to how far subordinates will go to please them, can be conducive to lower-level subordinates behaving unethically out of a real or perceived fear of reprisal, a misguided sense of loyalty, or a distorted concept of their jobs.

A later study of the sources and consequences of workplace pressure was conducted by the American Society of Chartered Life Underwriters & Chartered Financial Consultants and the Ethics Officer Association.[65] The findings of this study were consistent with the studies reported here and provided additional insights into the detrimental consequences of workplace pressure. Among the key findings of this study were the following:

- The majority of workers (60 percent) felt a substantial amount of pressure on the job. More than one out of four (27 percent) felt a "great deal" of pressure.
- The amount of workplace pressure has increased significantly from 5 years previously and 1 year previously. Of workers surveyed, 57 percent felt more pressure than 5 years ago, and 40 percent felt that pressure had increased in the past year.
- Nearly half of all workers (48 percent) reported that, due to pressure, they had engaged in one or more unethical and/or illegal actions during the past year. The most frequently cited misbehavior was cutting corners on quality control.
- The top five types of unethical/illegal behavior that workers reported they had engaged in over the past year in response to pressure were cutting corners on quality, covering up incidents, abusing or lying about sick days, lying or deceiving customers, and putting inappropriate pressure on others.
- The sources most commonly cited as contributing to workplace pressure were "balancing work and family" (52 percent), "poor internal communications" (51 percent), "work hours/workload" (51 percent), and "poor leadership" (51 percent).

The 2003 National Business Ethics Survey conducted by the Ethics Resource Center found that the percentage of employees reporting feeling pressure to compromise their standards has declined steadily in the past decade. They also found some other insights regarding pressure perceived:[66]

- First-line supervisors and employees were the groups most "at risk" to feel pressure.
- Organizational transitions such as mergers, acquisitions, and restructurings are associated with increased pressure of employees to compromise organizational ethics standards.
- Employees who observe ethical actions more frequently in their organization tend to feel pressure to compromise their ethical standards.
- Employees whose organizations have in place key elements of formal ethics programs feel less pressure to compromise standards.

In addition to the studies that document the extent to which managers feel pressure to perform, even if it leads to questionable activities, several actual business cases demonstrate the reality of cutting corners to achieve high production goals.

Examples of Pressure. In a glass container plant in Gulfport, Mississippi, for example, the plant manager began to fear that top management might close the aging facility because its output was falling behind those of other plants. So, the plant manager secretly started altering records and eventually inflated the value of the plant's production by 33 percent. Top management learned of this when a janitor acquired documents and reported this bogus information to company auditors. The plant manager was fired. He was not willing to discuss the matter, but his wife said her husband was under "constant pressure" to raise the plant's production and that he believed he and the other employees would have jobs as long as he was able to do so. The company's president said he had no intention of firing the plant manager for failing to meet the production goal.[67]

Another interesting case involved a big Chevrolet truck plant in Flint, Michigan. Here, three plant managers installed a secret control box in a supervisor's office so that they could override the control panel that governed the speed of the assembly line. The plant managers claimed they felt pressure to do this because top management did not understand that high absenteeism, conveyor breakdowns, and other problems were preventing them from reaching their goals. Once they began using the hidden controls, they began meeting their production goals and winning praise from their superiors. The plant managers claimed they thought top management knew that the plant managers were speeding up the line and that what the plant managers were doing was unethical. However, top management never said anything and, therefore, it was thought that the practice was accepted. The executives denied any knowledge of the secret box. The speed-up was in violation of GM's contract with the United Auto Workers' union. Once it was exposed, the company had to pay $1 million in back pay to the affected UAW members.[68]

The motive behind managers putting pressure on subordinates to perform, even at the sacrifice of their ethical standards, seems to be driven by the *"bottom-line" mentality* that places economic success above all other goals. Employees frequently find themselves making compromises as a result of the pressure coupled with the socialization process that emphasizes compliance with the authority structure, the need to conform to their superiors' wishes, and the expectation of loyalty.

Figure 7-5 presents a summary of other behaviors of superiors and/or peers that may create a questionable organizational climate.

FIGURE 7-5

Other Questionable Behaviors of Superiors or Peers

Other behaviors of one's superiors and/or peers that create a questionable organizational atmosphere include:

- **Amoral decision making.** This includes managers who themselves fail to factor ethical considerations into their actions, decisions, and behaviors. The result of this is a vacuous leadership environment.

- **Unethical acts, behaviors, or practices.** Some managers simply are not ethical themselves, and this influence wears off on others. Employees watch their superiors' behavior carefully and take cues from them as to what is acceptable.

- **Acceptance of legality as a standard of behavior.** Some managers think that if they are strictly abiding by the law they are doing the most they ought to do.

- **"Bottom-line" mentality and expectations of loyalty and conformity.** This focus places little value on doing what is right and on being sensitive to other stakeholders.

- **Absence of ethical leadership.** This is a global indicator of sorts that includes some of the other points already mentioned. In addition, management never steps out ahead of the pack and assumes a leadership role in doing what is right. This reflects an absence of moral management.

- **Objectives and evaluation systems that overemphasize profits.** If management sets unrealistic goals or does not take ethics into consideration in evaluating employees, it is creating a potentially destructive environment.

- **Insensitivity toward how subordinates perceive pressure to meet goals.** This is related to several of the previous points. Management must be constantly vigilant of the directives and expectations it is making on employees. The manager might always ask, "How might this goal, directive, or expectation be misread or misunderstood in terms of how far I want people to go to achieve it?"

- **Inadequate formal ethics policies.** Problems here might include inadequate management controls for monitoring and compliance, unreasonable reimbursement/expense policies, and the absence of a clear code of conduct.

Improving the Organization's Ethical Climate

Because the behavior of managers has been identified as the most important influence on the ethical behavior of organization members, it should come as no surprise that most actions and strategies for improving the organization's ethical climate must emanate from top management and other management levels as well. The process by which these kinds of initiatives have taken place is often referred to as "institutionalizing ethics" into the organization.[69] In this section, we will consider some of the best practices that managers have taken to improve their organizations' ethical climate. Figure 7-6 depicts a number of best practices for creating an ethical organization climate or culture. Top management leadership is at the hub of these initiatives, actions, or practices.

Top Management Leadership (Moral Management).   It has become a cliché, but this premise must be established at the outset: *The moral tone of an organization is set by top management.* This is because all managers and employees look to their bosses at the highest level for their cues as to what is acceptable practice. A former chairman of a major steel company stated it well: "Starting at the top, management has to set an example for all the others to follow."[70] Top management, through its capacity to set a personal example and to shape policy, is in the ideal position to provide a highly visible role model. The authority and ability to shape policy, both formal and implied, forms one of the vital aspects of the job of any leader in any organization. Treviño, Hartman, and Brown have referred to this aspect of becoming a moral manager as "role modeling through visible action." They continue by saying that effective moral managers recognize that they live in a fishbowl and that employees are watching them for cues about what's

FIGURE 7-6

Best Practices for Improving an Organization's Ethical Climate or Culture

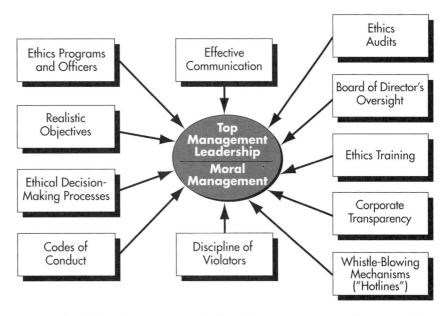

important.[71] There are ample examples of both weak and strong ethical leadership in business practice today.

Weak Ethical Leadership.   An example of weak ethical leadership (or role modeling) was found in one of the authors' consulting experiences. A situation in a small company was encountered where a long-time employee was identified as having embezzled about $20,000 over a 15-year period. When the employee was approached and questioned as to why she had done this, she explained that she thought it was all right because the president had led her to believe it was by his actions. She further explained that any time during the fall, when the leaves had fallen in his yard and he needed them raked, he would simply take company personnel off their jobs and have them do it. When the president needed cash, he would take it out of the company's petty cash box or get the key to the soft drink machine and raid its coin box. When he needed stamps to mail his personal Christmas cards, he would take them out of the company stamp box. The woman's perception was that it was all right for her to take the money because the president did it frequently. Therefore, she thought it was an acceptable practice for her as well.

Strong Ethical Leadership.   An example of positive ethical leadership may be seen in the case of a firm that was manufacturing vacuum tubes. One day the plant manager called a hurried meeting to announce that a sample of the tubes in production had failed a critical safety test. This meant that the batch of 10,000 tubes was of highly questionable safety and performance. The plant manager wondered out loud, "What are we going to do now?" Ethical leadership was shown by the vice president for technical operations, who looked around the room at each person and then declared in a low voice, "Scrap them!" According to a person who worked for this vice president, that act set the tone for the corporation for years, because every person present knew of situations in which faulty products had been shipped under pressures of time and budget.[72]

Each of these cases provides a vivid example of how a leader's actions and behavior communicated important messages to others in the organization. In the absence of knowing what to do, many employees look to the behavior of leaders for their cues as to what conduct is acceptable. In the second case, another crucial point is illustrated. When we speak of management providing ethical leadership, it is not just restricted to top management. Vice presidents, plant managers, supervisors, and, indeed, all managerial personnel share the responsibility for ethical leadership.

It has been argued that a manager's reputation for ethical leadership is founded on two pillars: perceptions of the manager as both a moral person *and* as a moral manager. Being a *moral person* is composed of three major attributes: traits, behaviors, and decision making. Important traits are stable personal attributes such as integrity, honesty, and trustworthiness. Critical behaviors—what you do, not what you say—include doing the right thing, concern shown for people, being open, and being personally moral. Decision making of the moral person needs to reflect a solid set of ethical values and principles. In this activity, the manager would hold to values, be objective/fair, demonstrate concern for society, and follow ethical decision rules.[73]

The second pillar is being a *moral manager*, a concept we developed in the previous chapter. According to researchers, moral managers recognize the importance of proactively putting ethics at the forefront of their ethical agenda. This involves three major activities. First, the moral manager must engage in *role modeling* through visible action. An emphasis is placed on visible action—action that can be witnessed by others. Second, the moral manager *communicates about ethics and values*. This is not to be done in a sermonizing way, but in a way that explains the values that guide important actions. Third,

SEARCH THE WEB

BUSINESS ETHICS AT BELLSOUTH

The Office of Ethics and Compliance at BellSouth has its own Web page. On this Web page, you can find information about ethics at BellSouth, corporate values, commitment, and ethics games and scenarios. Among the ethics scenarios, there are cases dealing with drinking on the job, attending free baseball games, bringing a pistol to work, and accepting gifts. To find out more about the Ethics Office at BellSouth, visit **http://www.ethics.bellsouth.com.**

the moral manager needs to *use rewards and discipline effectively.* This is a powerful way to send signals about desirable and undesirable conduct.[74]

In a period in which the importance of a sound corporate culture has been strongly advocated, ethical leaders must stress the primacy of integrity and morality as vital components of the organization's culture. There are many different ways and situations in which management needs to do this. In general, management needs to create a climate of moral consciousness. In everything it does, it must stress the importance of sound ethical principles and practices. A former president and chief operating officer for Caterpillar Tractor Company suggested four specific actions for accomplishing this:[75]

1. Create clear and concise policies that define the company's business ethics and conduct.
2. Select for employment only those people and firms whose characters and ethics appear to be in keeping with corporate standards.
3. Promote people on the basis of performance and ethical conduct and beliefs.
4. Company employees must feel the obligation and the opportunity to report perceived irregularities in ethics or in accounting transactions.

We should conclude by noting that the leader must infuse the organization's climate with values and ethical consciousness, not just run a one-person show. This point is made vividly clear by Steven Brenner, who observed: "Ethics programs which are seen as part of one manager's management system, and not as a part of the general organizational process, will be less likely to have a lasting role in the organization."[76] In short, ethics is about leadership as much or more than it is about programs.

Effective Communication. Management also carries a heavy burden in terms of providing ethical leadership in the area of effective communication. We have seen the importance of communicating through acts, principles, and organizational climate. We will discuss further the communication aspects of setting realistic objectives, codes of conduct, and the decision-making process. Here, however, we want to stress the importance and prevalence of communication principles, techniques, and practices.

Conveying the importance of ethics through communication includes both written and verbal forms of communication. In each of these settings, management should operate according to certain key ethical principles. Candor is one very important principle. *Candor* requires that a manager be forthright, sincere, and honest in communication transactions. In addition, it requires the manager to be fair and free from prejudice and malice in the communication. Related to this is the principle of fidelity. *Fidelity* in communication means that the communicator should be faithful to detail, should be accurate, and should avoid deception or exaggeration. *Confidentiality* is a final principle that ought to be stressed. The ethical manager must exercise care in deciding what information she or he discloses to others. Trust can be easily shattered if the manager does not have a keen sense of what is confidential in a communication.

Ethics Programs and Ethics Officers. In recent years, many companies have begun creating **ethics programs** within their organizations. Ethics programs are typically

An article in *Mondaq Business Briefing* (14 August 2003) by Sandra Doran puts corporate America on notice: "Shareholders and customers are outraged by corporate malfeasance and moral irresponsibility, and they're not going to take it any more." Doran goes on to say that because "corporate ethics is now a business imperative," it's simply good business practice for organizations in all industries to create corporate ethics programs. Read the five essential ingredients for a successful ethics program by logging on to InfoTrac College Edition at **http://www.infotrac-college. com** and keying record number A107056611.

organizational units that have been assigned the responsibility for ethics initiatives in the organization. The ethics initiatives often embrace responsibility for developing and disseminating codes of conduct, training on standards of conduct, administering some type of hotline or advice line for employees, and providing a means to report misconduct. A key finding of the 2003 National Business Ethics Survey conducted by the Ethics Resource Center was that ethics programs do make a difference. The presence of ethics programs was found to be associated with increased reporting of misconduct by employees. Employees in organizations with ethics programs also were more likely to perceive that those who violate ethics are held accountable, and in larger organizations, employees report less pressure to compromise company standards.[77]

Ethics programs are often headed by an **ethics officer** who is in charge of implementing the array of ethics initiatives of the organization. In some cases, the creation of ethics programs and designation of ethics officers have been in response to the 1991 Federal Sentencing Guidelines, which reduced penalties to those companies with ethics programs that were found guilty of ethics violations.[78] Figure 7-7 summarizes the elements that ought to exist in companies' ethics programs in order to comply with the U.S. Sentencing Commission's Organizational Guidelines. Two major benefits accrue to organizations that follow these guidelines. First, following the guidelines mitigates severe financial and oversight penalties. Second, some prosecutors are choosing not to pursue some actions when the companies in question already have sound programs in place if they follow these guidelines.[79]

Many companies started ethics programs as an effort to centralize the coordination of ethics initiatives in those companies. Many ethics programs and ethics officers initially got started with compliance issues. Only later, in some cases, did ethics or integrity become a focal point of the programs. Even today, most ethics programs and ethics officers have major corporate responsibility for both legal compliance and ethics practices, and there is some debate whether they should be called *compliance programs* or *ethics programs.*[80]

Just as ethics programs have proliferated in companies, the number of ethics officers occupying important positions in major firms has grown significantly. In fact, in 1992, ethics officers created the Ethics Officer Association (EOA) to help define their profession and its possibilities. The three major objectives of the EOA, which are consistent with the quest to improve organizations' ethical climates, are to:[81]

- Provide multiple opportunities for wider acquaintance, understanding, and cooperation among ethics officers
- Provide a structure for sharing practical approaches to specific issues of common concern
- Foster the general advancement of research, learning, teaching, sharing, and practice in the field of business ethics

By 2004, the Ethics Officers Association claimed close to 1,000 members, with over half of the *Fortune* 100 firms represented. Ethics officers in major companies provide ethics programs the best chance of succeeding and continuing to be integral parts of top management programs. Other countries around the world, such as Italy, have been exploring the creation of organizations similar to the EOA, which is headquartered in the United States.

Ethics officers have proliferated in the wake of America's recent ethical scandals.[82] Regretfully, many companies do not create ethics officer positions until they have gotten into some kind of trouble. For example, MCI has tried to rectify its problems, which grew out of the former WorldCom, by creating a new ethics officer position. MCI's new position is titled *chief ethics officer,* and this person is expected to lead MCI's ethics programs ranging from training to enforcing a revamped ethics code.[83] Another company that

---

FIGURE 7-7

Key Elements for Ethics Programs According to U.S. Sentencing Guidelines

The U.S. Sentencing Commission has identified eight key elements that companies must have in their ethics programs to satisfy the commission's regulatory review. If a company has these key elements in its ethics program, it will be dealt with less harshly should violations arise. Benefits should extend beyond compliance to ethics.

Compliance Standards. Companies are expected to have established compliance standards, which are a key part of detecting and preventing violations of the law. The development of a code of conduct is an initial step in this process. A set of ethical principles that guide decision making will strengthen these standards.

High-Level Ethics Personnel. Companies must assign compliance and ethics programs to senior executives. This person, perhaps called an *ethics officer*, must have the authority, responsibility, and resources to achieve ethics goals.

Avoidance of Delegation of Undue Discretionary Authority. Companies have a responsibility to make sure they do not delegate undue discretionary authority (e.g., access to company funds, investor information, authority to bind the company to contracts) to individuals who cannot be trusted with such authority. Someone convicted of a previous felony involving company funds would be an example. Background checks are, thus, becoming much more essential in screening employees.

Effective Communication. Standards and procedures must be effectively communicated. The company has a responsibility to make sure all personnel are aware of ethics codes, standards, policies, and practices. One major way to achieve this communication is through the conduct of ethics training programs.

Systems for Monitoring, Auditing, and Reporting. Companies are expected to have systems and procedures in place for assessing compliance. This may involve a variety of monitoring and auditing systems and reporting systems as well. In other words, companies must take reasonable steps to ensure that compliance is taking place.

Enforcement. Companies are expected to have systems in place to ensure the consistent enforcement of compliance standards. The purpose here is to make sure that everyone is following standards. A high-level executive cannot be treated differently than a low-level executive.

Detecting Offenses, Preventing Future Offenses. Once an offense has been detected, several actions need to happen. If there is an actual violation of the law, the company is expected to self-report the offense and actions taken to resolve the issue. The company needs to take further reasonable measures to prevent a similar offense from occurring in the future. The responsible person should be disciplined appropriately. Finally, the company is expected to accept responsibility for the offense as part of good corporate citizenship efforts.

Keeping Up with Industry Standards. Companies are expected, through ethics offices or programs, to keep up with industry practices and standards. This can be done by membership in national or local organizations. At the national level, an example would be the Ethics Officer Association (http://www.eoa.org). Many large cities also have their own such organizations. These organizations have as their major purpose the advancement of sound compliance and ethics programs.

SOURCES: U. S. Sentencing Commission Guidelines (http://www.ussc.gov). For further discussion, see Bruce A. Hamm, "Elements of the U. S. Federal Sentencing Guidelines" (http://www.refresher.com).

added an ethics officer position in the midst of its own scandal was Boeing Co. Boeing created a new Office of Internal Governance, which is to serve as a watchdog group responsible for ethics as well as internal audit, import-export compliance, supervision of the hiring of foreign sales consultants, and other closely regulated issues.[84] Beyond this, Boeing decided to add an additional position, that of an ethics watchdog, who would do independent monitoring of the company and would report to both the government and Boeing. This was done in an effort to get back onto good terms with the government following some previous questionable practices.[85]

Global Business Conduct Management System.   One of the latest projects of the EOA has been its feasibility study exploring the possibility of developing a global *business conduct management system* standard through the American National Standards Institute (ANSI) and the International Organization for Standardization ("ISO") process. ANSI is the U. S. standards body that is the official U. S. representative to ISO. The new standard would be designed along the lines of ISO 9004 and ISO 14004, two well-recognized management system guidelines standards in the areas of quality and environmental management, respectively. According to the EOA, the business conduct guidelines would be a single set of voluntary, internationally recognized guidelines and tools to manage organizational ethics, compliance, and business conduct programs. The guidelines would provide guidance on the design and use of a business conduct management system within an organization. The standard could then be used as a tool for any organization to use as a benchmark in measuring and demonstrating the effectiveness of its business conduct program and/or as a standard for business partners to meet.[86] As of this writing, the standard has not yet been approved. However, it is moving toward approval. If approved, the new business conduct management system could serve as a model for all organizations to follow.

Raising the Status of Ethics Officers.   One trend that has been noted by some ethics officers has been the tendency of some companies to slide the ethics officer down the organization chart so that direct access to the highest levels of organizational leadership has been decreasing. In other words, the organizational status of the ethics officer has been diminished in some organizations. Another trend has been for the focus of the ethics officer in some organizations to be "downwards," that is, spending little time working with or helping to manage the ethics of their superiors, but rather focusing on the ethics of lower-level organizational members, not senior management.[87] To reverse these trends, it has been recommended that the ethics office and the ethics officers' scope of responsibilities be enlarged to embrace the total organization, including senior management. A phrase has been developed for explaining how the ethics officers would work with their superiors. It is called "managing ethics upward."[88] In light of the rash of ethical scandals involving senior-level executives, this idea is one that has genuine value.

Two examples of how this goal might be achieved include the "bubble up" strategy and the "survey" strategy. The "bubble up" strategy would involve ethics officers using specific cases and questions that had bubbled up from the employees of the organization to meaningfully involve the senior leadership in a good faith discussion of appropriate courses of action to take. This would help senior leadership see the strong connection between their words and actions and the conduct of their employees. The "survey" strategy would necessitate that a survey be conducted of the entire population of employees, asking questions about their perceptions of the organization's ethical culture as well as their perceptions of senior leadership. Senior leadership could then be briefed on the findings and develop action plans for dealing with the results of the survey.[89] Obviously, managing ethics upward is easier to say than to do and it would need to be handled with diplomacy. Regardless, it poses a valuable idea for getting senior-level executives more involved in the ethics programs of the company.

As valuable as ethics programs and ethics officers are, there is a downside danger in their existence. By having individuals and organizational units responsible for the company's "ethics," there is some possibility that managers may come to "delegate" to these persons/units the responsibility for the firm's ethics. Ethics is everyone's job, however, and specialized units and people should not be used as a substitute for the assumption of ethical responsibility by everyone in leadership positions.

Ethics in Practice

HIGHER GOALS, MORE PRESSURE, LOWER ETHICS?

Recently, I held a position as an inside sales representative for a multinational *Fortune* 500 phone company. My job was to place unsolicited phone calls to people and convince them to switch their local and long distance calling carrier to my company. As I went through training, I was taught to "sell, sell, sell!" We were told that once we got a customer on the line, we were to not hang up unless we sold him or her a phone package.

There was also a big emphasis on meeting daily sales goals that were set by the company. As soon as I got out of training and on the phone lines, I began to encounter elderly people who had no use for the product. One day my supervisor noticed that I was not selling the product to everyone that I talked to, and she thought this was the reason I was not meeting my sales goal.

She soon asked why I did not "push" the product more. I told her that the people I was letting off the hook were too old to need anything that the company offered and that they did not even understand half of what I was talking about. She told me that I should

just sell them the product and that the customer service representatives would fix it later.

I asked my mentor what he did in these situations and he said he just tells the older people that they are getting a smaller package and then "adds on" other features without them noticing. The next time I got an elderly person on the phone, I just told her to have a nice day and then I hung up.

1. What are the ethical issues facing the company and me in this case?

2. Does this illustrate personal, organizational, or industry-level ethical issues?

3. Should I succumb to the pressure to meet company goals in these situations?

4. Is it an ethical practice for my company to continually raise goals and expect that people in my position will just "sell" and let customer service "fix" the problems?

Contributed by Joe Popkowski

Setting Realistic Objectives.   Closely related to all ethics initiatives and programs being implemented by top management is the necessity that managers at all levels set realistic objectives or goals. A manager may quite innocently and inadvertently create a condition leading to unethical behavior on a subordinate's part. Take the case of a marketing manager setting a sales goal of a 25 percent increase for the next year when a 15 percent increase is all that could be realistically expected, even with outstanding performance. In the absence of clearly established and communicated ethical norms, it is easy to see how a subordinate might believe that she or he should go to any lengths to achieve the 25 percent goal. With the goal having been set too high, the salesperson faces a situation that is conducive to unethical behavior in order to please the superior.

Fred T. Allen, a former executive, reinforces this point:

> *Top management must establish sales and profit goals that are realistic—goals that can be achieved with current business practices. Under the pressure of unrealistic goals, otherwise responsible subordinates will often take the attitude that "anything goes" in order to comply with the chief executive's target.*[90]

The point here is that there are ethical implications to even the most routine managerial decisions, such as goal setting. Managers must be keenly sensitive to the possibility of innocently creating situations in which others may perceive a need or an incentive to cut corners or do the wrong thing.

Ethical Decision-Making Processes.

Decision making is at the heart of the management process. If there is any practice or process that is synonymous with management, it is decision making. Decision making usually entails a process of stating the problem, analyzing the problem, identifying the possible courses of action that might be taken, evaluating these courses of action, deciding on the best alternative, and then implementing the chosen course of action.

Decision making at best is a challenge for management. Many decisions management faces turn out to have ethical implications or consequences. Once we leave the realm of relatively ethics-free decisions (such as which production method to use for a particular product), decisions quickly become complex, and many carry with them an ethical dimension.

Ethical decision making is not a simple process but rather a multifaceted process that is complicated by multiple alternatives, mixed outcomes, uncertain and extended consequences, and personal implications.[91] It would be nice if a set of ethical principles was readily available for the manager to "plug in" and walk away from, with a decision to be forthcoming. However, such was not the case when we discussed principles that help personal decision making, and it is not the case when we think of organizational decision making. The ethical principles we discussed earlier are useful here, but there are no simple formulas revealing easy answers.

Although it is difficult to portray graphically the process of ethical decision making, it is possible as long as we recognize that such an effort cannot totally capture reality. Figure 7-8 presents one conception of the ethical decision-making process. In this model, the individual is asked to identify the action, decision, or behavior that is being considered and then to articulate all dimensions of the proposed course of action. Next, the individual is asked to subject the course of action to what we call an *ethics screen*. An ethics screen consists of several select standards against which the proposed course of action is to be compared. The idea is that unethical actions will be "screened out" and that ethical actions will be "screened in." In the illustrated ethics screen, we reference our earlier discussion of the conventional approach (embodying standards/norms), the principles approach, and the ethical tests approach to ethical decision making. By using all or a combination of these ethical standards, it is expected that more ethical decisions will be made than otherwise.

In this model, it is left up to the individual to determine what mix of guidelines to use as the ethics screen. Normally, some combination of the guidelines contained in the screen would be helpful to the manager who truly is attempting to make an ethical decision. If the proposed course of action *fails* the ethics screen, the decision maker should not engage in the course of action but should consider a new decision, behavior, or action and submit it to this same process. If the proposed course of action *passes* the screen (the decision maker has determined it to be an ethical course of action), she or he should engage in the action, decision, or behavior and then repeat the cycle only when faced with a new ethical dilemma.

Another useful approach to making ethical decisions is to systematically ask and answer a series of simple questions. It should quickly be realized that this approach is similar to the ethical tests approach presented earlier in the chapter.

Ethics Check.

One well-known set of questions merits mention here because of its popularity in the book *The Power of Ethical Management*.[92] The "ethics check" questions are as follows:

FIGURE 7-8

A Process of Ethical Decision Making

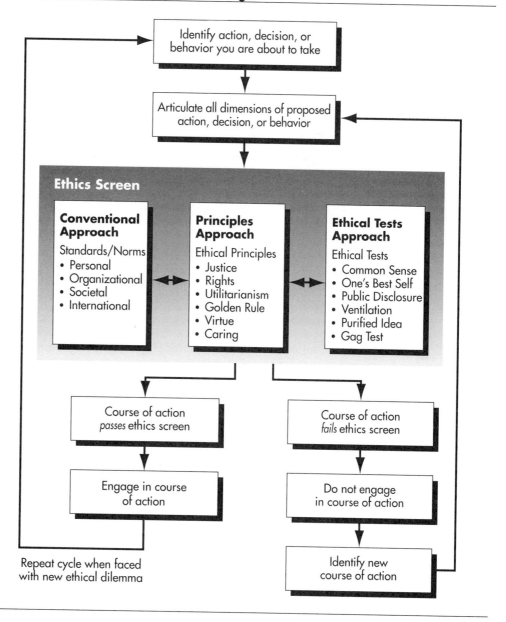

1. *Is it legal?* Will I be violating either civil law or company policy?
2. *Is it balanced?* Is it fair to all concerned in the short term as well as the long term? Does it promote win-win relationships?
3. *How will it make me feel about myself?* Will it make me proud? Would I feel good if my decision was published in the newspaper? Would I feel good if my family knew about it?

Ethics Quick Test.   Using a brief set of questions to make ethical decisions has become popular in business. For example, Texas Instruments has printed its seven-part "Ethics Quick Test" on a wallet card its employees may carry. The test's seven questions and reminders are as follows:[93]

- Is the action legal?
- Does it comply with our values?
- If you do it, will you feel bad?
- How will it look in the newspaper?
- If you know it's wrong, don't do it.
- If you're not sure, ask.
- Keep asking until you get an answer.

Sears' Guidelines.   In its Code of Business Conduct, Sears, Roebuck and Co. sets forth its five "Guidelines for Making Ethical Decisions," which are:[94]

1. Is it legal?
2. Is it within Sears' shared beliefs and policies?
3. Is it right/fair/appropriate?
4. Would I want everyone to know about this?
5. How will I feel about myself?

These sets of practical questions presented here are intended to produce a process of ethical inquiry that is of immediate use and understanding to a group of employees and managers. Note that many of the items are similar or identical to points raised earlier in the ethical tests approach. These questions help ensure that **ethical due process** takes place. They cannot tell us for sure whether our decisions are ethical or not, but they can help us be sure that we are raising the appropriate issues and genuinely attempting to be ethical.

Codes of Conduct.

Codes of Conduct.   Top management has the responsibility for establishing standards of behavior and for effectively communicating those standards to all managers and employees in the organization. One of the classic ways by which companies and ethics officers have fulfilled this responsibility is through the use of **codes of ethics**, or **codes of conduct**. Codes of ethics are a phenomenon of the past 25 years. Over 95 percent of all major corporations have them today, and the central questions in their usefulness or effectiveness revolve around the managerial policies and attitudes associated with their use.[95] Ethics codes vary considerably from company to company, but research suggests that the larger the company the more likely it is that it will have a code of conduct. Length is one attribute. Beyond length, ethics codes vary in their focus, level of detail, thematic content, and tone.[96]

A survey of corporate officers by the Ethics Resource Center, a nonprofit organization based in Washington, DC, revealed several of the *values or benefits* that business organizations received as a result of their codes of ethics. The results achieved and the percentages of executives citing the reasons give us insights into what companies really think they get from corporate ethics codes:[97]

1. Legal protection for the company (78 percent)
2. Increased company pride and loyalty (74 percent)
3. Increased consumer/public goodwill (66 percent)
4. Improved loss prevention (64 percent)

An ethics program is one step in the right direction, but a *Business Week* Online (19 February 2004) article by Amy Stone suggests that developing and distributing a code of ethics is also an essential aspect of improving an organization's ethical climate, though she admits that "it's still unclear how much good a code of conduct can do in preventing ethical lapses." Arthur Andersen, after all, had a strong ethics program and still stumbled so badly in the Enron fiasco that it went bankrupt. Read more about codes of ethics by logging on to InfoTrac College Edition at **http://www.infotrac-college.com** and keying record number A113425606.

5. Reduced bribery and kickbacks (58 percent)
6. Improved product quality (14 percent)
7. Increased productivity (12 percent)

A study by the Ethics Resource Center of the content of corporate codes found the following to be among the most frequently addressed topics in corporate codes:[98]

1. Conflicts of interest
2. Receiving gifts, gratuities, entertainment
3. Protecting company proprietary information
4. Giving gifts, gratuities, entertainment
5. Discrimination
6. Sexual harassment
7. Kickbacks
8. General conduct
9. Employee theft
10. Proper use of company assets

There have been both successes and failures reported with organizational codes of conduct, but the acid test seems to be whether or not such codes actually become "living documents," not just platitudinous public relations statements that are put into a file drawer upon dissemination. Codes may not be a panacea for management, but, when properly developed and administered, they serve to raise the level of ethical behavior in the organization by clarifying what is meant by ethical conduct and encouraging moral behavior.

A major study of the effectiveness of corporate codes found that there is a relationship between corporate codes and employee behavior in the workplace, particularly to the degree that employees perceive the codes to be implemented strongly and embedded in the organizational culture. Therefore, when codes are implemented forcefully and embedded strongly in the culture, reports of unethical employee behavior tend to be lower.[99]

A major study of corporate codes by Mark Schwartz revealed that there are a number of different ways in which employees perceive or understand codes of conduct.[100] Schwartz's research yielded eight themes or metaphors that helped to explain how codes influence behavior within organizations.

1. As a *rule book*, the code acts to clarify what behavior is expected of employees.
2. As a *signpost*, the code can lead employees to consult other individuals or corporate policies to determine the appropriateness of behavior.
3. As a *mirror*, the code provides employees with a chance to confirm whether their behavior is acceptable to the company.
4. As a *magnifying glass*, the code suggests a note of caution to be more careful or engage in greater reflection before acting.

SEARCH THE WEB

AFLAC'S CODE OF CONDUCT

A *Fortune* 500 company, AFLAC is a leading writer of voluntary insurance coverage marketed at the work site in the United States and abroad. *Fortune* magazine named AFLAC to its list of "The 100 Best Companies to Work for in America" for the fifth consecutive year in January 2003 and to its list of "America's Most Admired Companies" in the life and health insurance industry in March 2003.

According to AFLAC's CEO, Dan Amos, the company Code of Business Conduct and Ethics is a formal statement of the ethical and legal conduct, and common sense standards, that sets the tone for all of AFLAC's business activities. The goal is to conduct business in a framework of integrity of which the company can be proud.

To view AFLAC's Code of Conduct, check out the company Web page: **http://www.aflac.com**. Follow the path to *Investor Relations, Corporate Governance,* and then *Code of Conduct.*

5. As a *shield*, the code acts in a manner that allows employees to better challenge and resist unethical requests.
6. As a *smoke detector*, the code leads employees to try to convince others and warn them of their inappropriate behavior.
7. As a *fire alarm*, the code leads employees to contact the appropriate authority and report violations.
8. As a *club*, the potential enforcement of the code causes employees to comply with the code's provisions.[101]

In summary, the code metaphors provide insights into a number of ways in which codes are perceived or viewed by organizational members.

Disciplining Violators of Ethics Standards.

To bring about an ethical climate that all organizational members will believe in, management must discipline violators of its accepted ethical norms. A major reason the general public, and even employees in many organizations, have questioned business's sincerity in desiring a more ethical environment has been business's unwillingness to discipline violators. There are numerous cases of top management officers who behaved unethically and yet were retained in their positions. At lower levels, there have been cases of top management overlooking or failing to penalize unethical behavior of subordinates. These evidences of inaction on management's or the board's part represent implicit approval of the individual's behavior.

Fred Allen had argued that an organization should respond forcefully to the individual who is guilty of deliberately or flagrantly violating its code of ethics: "From the pinnacle of the corporate pyramid to its base, there can only be one course of action: dismissal. And should actual criminality be involved, there should be total cooperation with law enforcement authorities."[102]

Based on their research, Treviño, Hartman, and Brown have argued: "The moral manager consistently rewards ethical conduct and disciplines unethical conduct at all levels in the organization, and these actions serve to uphold the standards and rules."[103] The effort on the part of management has to be complete in communicating to all, by way of disciplining offenders, that unethical behavior will not be tolerated in the organization. It is management's tacit approval of violations that has seriously undermined efforts to bring about a more ethical climate in many organizational situations.

A recent, highly visible example of this point was the discharge by Boeing Co. of its chief financial officer and another senior manager for engaging in what it called unethical behavior. Michael Sears, a 34-year veteran of the industry, had been considered to be a possible successor to then chairman and CEO Phil Condit. The company said that Mr. Sears and the other senior manager had been dismissed when they tried to conceal their alleged misconduct from a team of lawyers hired by the firm to investigate their actions. At the time of the firing, the CEO said, "When we determine there have been violations of our standards, we will act swiftly to address them, just as we have today."[104] In another highly visible case, Nortel Networks, North America's largest telecommunications equipment maker, fired its chief executive officer, chief financial officer, and its controller in April 2004 for their involvement in accounting problems that had been under scrutiny. The accounting irregularities resulted in the company having to restate its earnings.[105]

Ethics "Hotlines" and Whistle-Blowing Mechanisms.

One problem that frequently leads to the covering up of unethical acts by people in an organization is that they do not know how to react when they observe a questionable practice. An effective ethical climate is contingent on employees having a mechanism for (and top management support of) "blowing the whistle" on or reporting violators. Allen has summarized this point as follows: "Employees must know exactly what is expected of them in the moral arena and how to respond to warped ethics."[106]

According to the 2003 National Business Ethics Survey, nearly two-thirds of the employees surveyed indicated that their organizations provide them with a way to report misconduct anonymously. Employees report various reasons for reporting or not reporting observed violations of ethics. Those who *did* report observations of misconduct gave the following justifications of their actions:[107]

- I thought it was the right thing to do. (99 percent)
- I felt I could count on the support of my coworkers. (76 percent)
- I believed corrective action would be taken. (74 percent)
- I believed that my report would be kept confidential. (71 percent)
- I felt I could count on the support of my supervisor or manager. (68 percent)

In this same survey, employees were asked why they did *not* report observations of misconduct. These employees gave the following reasons:[108]

- I didn't believe corrective action would be taken. (70 percent)
- I didn't trust that my report would be kept confidential. (54 percent)
- I feared retaliation from my supervisor or manager. (41 percent)
- I feared retaliation from my coworkers. (30 percent)
- I didn't know who to contact. (16 percent)

The whistle-blowing mechanism in most common use today, which typically provides for anonymous reporting, is the ethics "hotline." At both NYNEX and Northrop, for example, hotlines are used whereby employees may phone in their inquiries about the company's ethics code or report suspected wrongdoing. In one recent year, Northrop reported that about 5 percent of the company's 32,000 employees used its hotline. NYNEX also receives thousands of calls per year. At NYNEX, it was estimated that half the callers were seeking information or clarification about the corporate code, whereas only about 10 percent of the callers made allegations of wrongdoing. Ethics officers see this as a positive indication that employees are proacting and trying to head off potential problems before they occur.[109]

Hotlines can have a downside risk, however. Ethicist Barbara Ley Toffler argues that the hotlines may do harm. She suspects that many of the reported wrongdoings are false accusations and that if the company does not handle these issues carefully, it may do a lot of damage to morale.[110]

Xerox Corporation has a complaint resolution process to handle reported wrongdoings. Xerox employs a 4-step process.[111] First, the company receives and examines a complaint. The complaint, or allegation, may come from its hotline; from outside sources such as vendors, customers, or former employees; from whistle-blowers; or from law enforcement agencies. Second, the company conducts an investigation. This is completed by a team—a senior manager, legal counsel, and a human resources executive. Third, there is a management review of the team's report. Finally, step four involves the resolution. Part of the resolution is an attempt to determine why and how the reported incident occurred in the first place. Xerox thinks that the essential elements of the ethics investigation include adherence to a plan, good management communications, and a dedicated interest in ensuring a fair and impartial investigation.

In addition to hotlines for reporting wrongdoing, some companies employ toll-free numbers wherein employees may simply inquire about ethics matters. For example, the Sears Office of Ethics and Business Policy employs an "Ethics Assist" program in which employees may call about such topics as:[112]

- Interpretation of or guidance on company policy
- General ethics questions
- Code of conduct issues
- Workplace harassment/discrimination
- Selling practices
- Theft

Business Ethics Training.

For several years, there has been debate and controversy about whether managerial ethics can and should be taught. One school of thought assumes that ethics is personal, already embedded within the employee or manager and, hence, not alterable or teachable. A growing school of thought, on the other hand, argues that instruction in business ethics should be made a part of business school education, management training, executive development programs, and seminars.

Professor Kirk Hanson has been teaching business ethics for many years. Whereas he agrees with some critics who say it is tough to infuse values in university students, he also thinks that there is a legitimate role for business ethics courses. Hanson believes that we can most help the fundamentally decent, well-intentioned student. He says:

> *If we teach techniques and strategies for handling a wide variety of business decisions, we can do the same for predictable ethical decisions or challenges. Among those situations are finding a match between a person's values and those of his or her employer; managing the pushback point where one's values are tested by peers, subordinates, or superiors; handling an unethical directive from one's boss; and coping with a performance system that gives strong incentives to cut ethical corners.*[113]

In addition, in numerous organizations in the United States today, management training in business ethics is taking place. It is difficult to identify a specific percentage of firms that are providing ethics training, however. In one recent study, only 28 percent of workers studied indicated they had received ethics training in the previous 12 months.[114] In another study, more than half of the employees surveyed said their organizations provide ethics training. Further, 52 percent of this group of employees said the training was "very useful."[115]

An example of a company that has recently added ethics training is Sun Microsystems in Santa Clara, California. According to its chief compliance officer, Sun needed to go beyond it code of conduct and its business conduct office. The company was feeling pressure, especially from the recently passed Sarbanes-Oxley corporate reform law, that is increasingly holding executives responsible for what is going on in the company. At the Sun training sessions, referred to as ethics boot camps, the training is becoming more important and more intense. Sun is now requiring all managers across the globe to undergo ethics training. At the boot camp, one speaker is the company CEO. Other top managers and board members also address the employees. Most of the content is presented in small groups settings, and the executives have to wrestle with dozen of cases studies in which it was not clear what to do. Upon completion of the training courses, Sun executives and employees are given a binder that includes information on how to share what they have learned with other employees. Also, all Sun employees are now being required to take online ethics courses, offered in eight languages. As a part of the continuous training, Sun is offering refresher courses on a regular basis and has started offering conference calls in which executives in different parts of the world can discuss the ethical dilemmas they are facing and get feedback from others.[116]

What might be the purposes or objectives of ethics training? Several purposes have been suggested:

1. To increase the manager's sensitivity to ethical problems
2. To encourage critical evaluation of value priorities
3. To increase awareness of organizational realities
4. To increase awareness of societal realities
5. To improve understanding of the importance of public image and public/society relations[117]

To this list, we might add some other desirable goals:

6. To examine the ethical facets of business decision making
7. To bring about a greater degree of fairness and honesty in the workplace
8. To respond more completely to the organization's social responsibilities

Materials and formats typically used by firms in their ethics training include the following: ethics codes (as a training device), lectures, workshops/seminars, case studies, films/discussions, and articles/speeches.[118] One major firm, Lockheed Martin, introduced some humor into its ethics training by introducing the Dilbert-inspired board game, "The Ethics Challenge," for company-wide ethics training. To play the game, players (employees) move around the board by answering "Case File" questions such as, "You've been selected for a training course in Florida, and you want to go only for the vacation." Among the answers and their respective points are "Go, but skip the sessions" (0 points), "Ask your supervisor if it would be beneficial" (5 points), and, the Dogbert answer, "Wear mouse ears to work and hum 'It's a Small World After All' all day." Sessions for the company's 185,000 employees were led by supervisors, not ethics officers. Chairman of the company, Norm Augustine, kicked off the training by leading the training of those who reported to him directly.[119]

In terms of the effectiveness of ethics training, Thomas Jones discovered in his research that exposure to lengthy programs (for example, 10 weeks) resulted in significant improvements in moral development. Brief exposures to business ethics, however, yielded less encouraging results.[120] Questions remain, therefore, as to the ultimate and lasting value of superficial ethics education.

Business Roundtable Institute for Corporate Ethics.

One of the major limitations of business ethics training is that the CEO and other top-level managers have been exempted from it. All this is about to change. The Business Roundtable, an organization of CEOs, announced in 2004 that it was developing a business ethics institute targeted toward CEOs. The 150 CEOs who comprise the Business Roundtable will be involved. The institute is scheduled to be held at the Darden School at the University of Virginia. The goal of the institute is to help restore public confidence in the marketplace in light of the recent scandals in business. Through the institute, there will be research conducted, courses created, and lead executive seminars offered on business ethics. Some skeptics are wondering whether this will truly make a difference or not. Some say that CEOs are pretty set in their ways by the time they reach the pinnacle of their organizations. Optimists are withholding judgment until experience indicates whether the new institute will add value or not.[121] Regardless, it is encouraging that CEOs are finally planning to subject themselves to the same kind of training they have always wanted for their subordinates.

If ethical leadership truly begins at the top, the institute should provide a useful resource for these organization leaders.

Ethics Audits and Self-Assessments.

In increasing numbers, companies today are beginning to appreciate the need to follow up on their ethics initiatives and programs. Ethics audits are mechanisms or approaches by which a company may assess or evaluate its ethical climate or programs. **Ethics audits** are intended to carefully review such ethics initiatives as ethics programs, codes of conduct, hotlines, and ethics training programs. Ethics audits are similar to social audits discussed in Chapter 4. In addition, they are intended to examine other management activities that may add to or subtract from the company's initiatives. This might include management's sincerity, communication efforts, incentive and reward systems, and other management activities. Ethics audits may employ written instruments, committees, and employee interviews.[122]

More and more companies will assess and attempt to improve their organizations' ethical climates as instruments, methods, and services are made available for conducting such programs. An example of the resources now available include the "Business Integrity Assessment" program offered by WalkerInformation, a research company with headquarters in Indianapolis, Indiana, and offices around the world. With the methodology and instruments developed by WalkerInformation, companies may assess their ethical cultures and measure their ethics or compliance programs' effectiveness. Companies may then compare their results with national benchmark data established by Walker.[123]

Although we have not touched on all that can be done at the organizational level to improve or manage business ethics, the actions suggested represent best practices that can move management a long way toward improving the organization's ethical climate. If management takes specific steps as suggested, many behaviors or decisions that might otherwise have been questionable have a greater chance of being in line with leadership's ethical standards. Thus, ethics can be positively supervised, and managers do not have to treat value concerns as matters totally out of their influence or control. On the contrary, managers can intercede and improve the organization's ethical climate.[124]

Corporate Transparency.

One of the most recent trends toward the improvement of ethics programs is that of **transparency**. **Corporate transparency** refers to a quality, characteristic, or state in which activities, processes, practices, and decisions that take place in companies become open or visible to the outside world. The opposite of transparency is **opacity**, or an opaque condition in which activities and practices remain obscure or hidden from outside scrutiny and review.

Pressures toward transparency have come both from without and within companies. From the outside, various stakeholders such as consumers, environmentalists, government, and investors want to know more clearly what is going on within the organizations. The recent business scandals have served as an added outside force. From the inside, companies are increasingly seeing how transparency makes sense as an ethical practice. According to Pagano and Pagano in their 2003 book, *The Transparency Edge: How Credibility Can Make or Break You in Business*, a transparent management approach— "what you see is what you get" code of conduct—will increase your company's credibility in the marketplace, build loyalty, and help you gain the trust and confidence of those with whom you work.[125]

Another important recent book on transparency is titled *The Naked Corporation: How the Age of Transparency Will Revolutionize Business*, by Tapscott and Ticoll. They argue that corporate transparency, today, is not optional but inevitable. They say companies should "undress for success."[126] As companies become more open enterprises, the public and other stakeholders will come to trust them more because more will be exposed to view.

A major example that Tapscott and Ticoll point to is that of Chiquita Brands International, which in 1998 was exposed for a variety of questionable practices such as using pesticides despite an environmental agreement, secretly controlling dozens of supposedly independent banana companies, bribery, and lax security such that company boats were being used to smuggle drugs. Chiquita's reaction to this exposure was to turn the company around through a policy of corporate transparency, especially visible in its corporate social responsibility report. The CSR report began to explain the results of external audits and employee surveys, helped the company get through bankruptcy proceedings, and helped regain public trust. The authors argue a point we have made previously, that it all starts at the top. Open leadership is one of the strongest forces behind transparency.[127]

Board of Director Leadership and Oversight.

One would think that oversight and leadership of ethics initiatives by the boards of directors of businesses would be a "given." That has not been the case, however, in most instances. The primary impetus for board involvement in and oversight of ethics programs and initiatives has been the megascandals of the past five years that have impacted many major companies. This has been coupled with the passage of the 2002 Sarbanes–Oxley Act, which has overhauled federal securities laws to improve corporate governance. We will consider corporate governance in detail in Chapter 19, but here we should address the board's role in oversight of corporate ethics, one of the hottest issues in recent years.

Corporate boards, like top managers, should provide ethical leadership. SEC chair William Donaldson recently said that it is not enough for a company to profess a code of conduct. According to Donaldson, "the most important thing that a board of directors should do is determine the elements that must be embedded in the company's moral DNA."[128] In other words, strong leadership from the board and CEOs is still the most powerful force in improving the company's ethical culture.

Two specific areas covered in the Sarbanes–Oxley Act address the board's role in corporate ethics. First, companies are now required to make provisions for employees to report observed or suspected wrongdoing without fear of retaliation. Companies are now required to protect whistle-blowers, and criminal penalties may be issued to managers who ignore this provision. Companies are expected to have a formal policy that addresses such complaints, and the board should investigate all complaints and rectify issues as necessary.[129] The whistle-blowing mechanism discussed earlier is now institutionalized by law. Second, the Sarbanes–Oxley Act makes it a crime to alter, destroy, conceal, cover up, or falsify any document to prevent its use in a federal government lawsuit or proceedings. This new provision came about because of the well-publicized Arthur Andersen debacle, which involved document shredding. Document management initiatives have now become critical in companies, and one of the most debated areas is the handling of e-mails.[130] Sarbanes–Oxley has other important provisions for bringing about more effective controls and preventing fraud, but the previously mentioned items are especially important in terms of ethics oversight.

According to a recent global survey of 165 company boards conducted by The Conference Board, a growing number of boards of directors worldwide are becoming more involved in companies' ethics programs. The survey reports that although corporate scandals and Sarbanes–Oxley have been strong forces in bringing about more board involvement in ethics, other factors have motivated it as well. In the United States, general legal developments have increased board scrutiny of ethics programs, but in the United Kingdom, India, and Western Europe, "enhancement of reputation" was often cited as a reason for closer board scrutiny of corporate ethics. There is also widespread enthusiasm for training board members in ethics, but such enthusiasm does not often result in action.[131]

FROM MORAL DECISIONS TO MORAL ORGANIZATIONS

In the last two chapters, we have discussed ethical or moral acts, decisions, practices, managers, and organizations. Though the goal of ethics initiatives is to develop moral organizations, sometimes all we get are isolated ethical acts, decisions, or practices, or, if we are fortunate, isolated moral managers. Achieving the status of moral standing is a goal, whatever the level on which it may be achieved. Sometimes all we can do is bring about ethical acts, decisions, or practices. A broader goal is to create moral managers, in the sense in which they were discussed in Chapter 6. Finally, the highest-level goal for managers may be to create moral organizations. To create moral organizations, many of the best practices discussed in this chapter will need to be implemented.

The important point here is to state that the goal is to create moral decisions, moral managers, and ultimately, moral organizations while recognizing that what we frequently observe in business is the achievement of moral standing at only one of these levels. The ideal is to create a moral organization that is fully populated by moral managers making moral decisions (and practices, policies, and behaviors), but this is seldom achieved. Figure 7-9 depicts the essential characteristics of each of these levels.

FIGURE 7-9

From Moral Decisions to Moral Organizations

Moral Decision(s)

Single or isolated moral acts, behaviors, policies, practices, or decisions made by a manager or managers of an organization. These are the simplest and most basic form of achieving moral status. The principles of ethical decision making presented should assist in the development of moral decisions.

Moral Manager(s)

A manager or managers who have adopted the characteristics of moral management and this approach dominates all their decision making. These managers manifest ethical leadership and are always occupying the moral high ground. Moral managers will make moral decisions via the use of ethical principles. In addition, they will learn and use the research of ethics in organizations discussed in this chapter.

Moral Organization(s)

An organization that is dominated by the presence of moral managers making moral decisions. Moral management has become an integral part of the culture. Moral management permeates all the organization's decisions, policies, and practices. The organization uses the best practices for achieving a moral management culture. Of special importance are moral leadership provided by board of director oversight and top management leadership.

▪ SUMMARY

The subject of business ethics may be addressed at several different levels: personal, organizational, industrial, societal, and international. This chapter focuses on the personal and organizational levels.

A number of different ethical principles serve as guides to personal decision making. Ethics principles may be categorized as teleological (ends-based) or deontological (duty-based). One of the major deontological principles is the categorical imperative. Major philosophical principles of ethics include utilitarianism, rights, and justice. The Golden Rule was singled out as a particularly powerful ethical principle among various groups studied. Virtue ethics was identified as an increasingly popular concept. Servant leadership was presented as an approach to management that embraced an ethical perspective. A general method for reconciling ethical conflicts was introduced. Six practical tests were proposed to assist the individual in making ethical decisions: the test of common sense, the test of one's best self, the test of making something public, the test of ventilation, the test of the purified idea, and the gag test.

At the organizational level, factors were discussed that affect the organization's moral climate. It was argued that the behavior of one's superiors and peers and industry ethical practices were the most important influences on a firm's ethical climate. Society's moral climate and personal needs were considered to be less important. Best practices for improving the firm's ethical climate include providing leadership from management, ethics programs and ethics officers, setting realistic objectives, infusing the decision-making process with ethical considerations, employing codes of conduct, disciplining violators, creating whistle-blowing mechanisms or hotlines, training managers in business ethics, using ethics audits, adopting the concept of transparency, and board of director oversight of ethics initiatives.

The goal of ethics initiatives is to achieve a status that may be characterized not just by isolated moral decisions, but by the presence of moral managers and the ultimate achievement of a moral organization.

▪ KEY TERMS

categorical imperative (page 215)

codes of conduct (page 242)

codes of ethics (page 242)

compensatory justice (page 217)

corporate transparency (page 248)

deontological theorites/principles (page 214)

distributive justice (page 217)

ethical due process (page 242)

ethical tests (page 225)

ethics audits (page 248)

ethics officer (page 236)

ethics programs (page 235)

Golden Rule (page 222)

legal rights (page 216)

moral rights (page 216)

opacity (page 248)

principle of caring (page 218)

principle of justice (page 217)

principle of rights (page 216)

principle of utilitarianism (page 214)

procedural justice (page 217)

rights (page 216)

servant leadership (page 220)

teleological theories/principles (page 214)

transparency (page 248)

utilitarianism (page 215)

virtue ethics (page 220)

▪ DISCUSSION QUESTIONS

1. From your personal experience, give two examples of ethical dilemmas in your personal life. Give two examples of ethical dilemmas you have experienced as a member of an organization.

2. Using the examples you provided for question 1, identify one or more of the guides to personal decision making or ethical tests that you think would have helped you resolve your dilemmas. Describe how it would have helped.

3. Which is most important in ethics principles—consequences/results or duty? Discuss.

4. Assume that you are in your first real managerial position. Identify five ways in which you might provide ethical leadership. Rank them in terms of importance, and be prepared to explain your ranking.

5. What do you think about the idea of codes of conduct? Give three reasons why an organization ought to have a code of conduct, and give three reasons why an organization should not have a code of conduct. On balance, how do you regard codes of conduct?

6. A lively debate is going on in this country concerning whether business ethics can or should be taught in business schools. Do you think business ethics can and should be taught? Be prepared to explain your reasons carefully. Can top managers and board members be taught business ethics?

7. Identify and prioritize the best practices for improving the organization's ethical climate. What are the strengths and weaknesses of each?

■ RECOMMENDED CASES

Many of the end-of-text cases may be related to Chapter 7. You may wish to consider studying the following cases with Chapter 7.

Case 7. "To Hire or Not to Hire." This case addresses the issue of truth-telling and possible deception on one's job resume and application. A routine background check revealed that an applicant did not tell the truth on a job application. The manager desires to hire this employee anyway. What would you recommend to the manager and why?

Case 9. "The Travel Expense Billing Controversy." This case describes the practice that a major firm used wherein it collected discounts for travel expenses but charged its clients the full price. Is this practice justified in light of the rationale presented in the case? Was the company appropriately responding to the managers who raised issues about this practice? What is your assessment of the ethical climate in this company?

Case 10. "Phantom Expenses." How important is it that you file your expenses correctly for business purposes? How would you respond if you were pressured to file them incorrectly to protect your colleagues. How does one handle ethical issues when under pressure? This case explores these issues.

Case 11. "Family Business." This case describes the experience of a new employee who has witnessed nepotism and its consequences. What are the ethical issues in this case? Is showing favoritism to family members a justified practice? What should the new employee do and how should it be handled?

■ WEB RESOURCES

The URLs listed here are current at the time of publication. Should any of these Web sites change, please search under the company's or organization's name for an updated address.

Beard Center for Leadership in Ethics
   http://www.bus.duq.edu/Beard

Business Ethics
   http://www.business-ethics.com

Center for Business Ethics: Bentley College
   http://ecampus.Bentley.edu/dept/cbe

Center for Business Ethics: St. Thomas
   http://www.stthom.edu/cbes

Center for Public Integrity
   http://www.publicintegrity.org

United States Chamber of Commerce
   http://www.uschamber.com

Corporate Accountability Project
   http://www.corporation.org

Corporate Crime Reporter
   http://www.corporatecrimereporter.com

Corporate Social Responsibility Newswire
   http://www.csrwire.com

Council of Ethical Organizations
   http://www.corporateethics.com

Ethical Corporation Online
    http://www.ethicalcorp.com

Ethics at BellSouth
    http://www.ethics.bellsouth.com

Ethics Officers Association
    http://www.eoa.org

Ethics Resource Center
    http://www.ethics.org

Journal of Business Ethics
    http://www.kluweronline.com/issn/0167-4544

Markkula Center for Applied Ethics at Santa Clara University
    http://www.scu.edu/ethics

Olsson Center for Applied Ethics: University of Virginia
    http://www.darden.virginia.edu/olsson/index.htm

Society for Business Ethics Ethics links
    http://www.societyforbusinessethics.org/ethics.htm

The Conference Board
    http://www.conference-board.org

Transparency International
    http://www.transparency.org

Walk the Talk Company
    http://www.walkthetalk.com

Wharton Ethics Program
    http://www.wharton.upenn.edu

 InfoTrac® College Edition   http://www.infotrac-college.com

Additional information on the topics discussed in the chapter can be researched by logging onto the InfoTrac College Edition Web site.

■ ENDNOTES

1. David Callahan, *The Cheating Culture: Why More Americans Are Doing Wrong to Get Ahead* (New York: Harcourt, Inc., 2004).

2. Lee Ellis, *Leading Talents, Leading Teams* (Chicago: Northfield Publishing, 2003), 201–204.

3. Bill George, *Authentic Leadership: Rediscovering the Secrets to Creating Lasting Value* (San Francisco: Jossey-Bass, 2003).

4. Dan Chapman, "Woman Rewarded for Act of Honesty," *The Atlanta Journal-Constitution* (September 8, 2001).

5. Jennifer Dixon, "Bosses Knew Shipped Meat Was Tainted, Workers Say," *Chicago Tribune* (August 30, 2001).

6. Ethics Resource Center, *National Business Ethics Survey 2003: How Employees View Ethics in Their Organizations* (Washington, DC: Ethics Resource Center, 2003), 28. Also see http://www.ethics.org.

7. Gretchen Morgenson, "Wall Street Firms Endorse Ethics Standards for Analysts," *The New York Times* (June 13, 2001).

8. Stephen Baker and Manjeet Kripalani, "Software: Will Outsourcing Hurt America's Supremacy?" *Business Week* (March 1, 2004), 85–94. Also see "Outsourcing: Danger Ahead?" *Business Week* (March 8, 2004), 14.

9. Archie B. Carroll, "Principles of Business Ethics: Their Role in Decision Making and an Initial Consensus," *Management Decision* (Vol. 28, No. 28, 1990), 20–24.

10. John R. Boatright, *Ethics and the Conduct of Business*, 4th ed. (Upper Saddle River, NJ: Prentice Hall, 2003), 31–32.

11. Vincent Barry, *Moral Issues in Business* (Belmont, CA: Wadsworth, 1979), 43.

12. *Ibid.*, 45–46.

13. I. Kant, *Groundwork of the Metaphysic of Morals*, trans. H. J. Paton (New York: Harper and Row, 1964).

14. Victoria S. Wike, "Duty," Patricia H. Werhane and R. Edward Freeman, *The Blackwell Encyclopedic Dictionary of Business Ethics* (Malden, MA: Blackwell Publishers, Ltd, 1997), 180–181.

15. John R. Boatright, *Ethics and the Conduct of Business*, 4th ed. (Upper Saddle River, NJ: Prentice Hall, 2003), 53.

16. Scott J. Reynolds and Norman E. Bowie, "A Kantian Perspective on the Characteristics of Ethics Programs," *Business Ethics Quarterly* (Vol. 14, No. 2, April 2004), 275–292.

17. Louis P. Pojman, *Ethics: Discovering Right and Wrong* (Belmont, CA: Wadsworth, 1995), 147–148.

18. *Ibid.*, 150.

19. *Ibid.* 152–153.
20. Manuel C. *Velasquez, Business Ethics: Concepts and Cases*, 3d ed. (Englewood Cliffs, NJ: Prentice Hall, 1992), 72–73.
21. Richard T. DeGeorge, *Business Ethics*, 5th ed. (Upper Saddle River, NJ: Prentice Hall, 1999), 69–72.
22. Velasquez, 73.
23. See the following sources for a discussion of these points: David Luban, "Judicial Activism and the Concept of Rights," *Report from the Institute for Philosophy & Public Policy* (College Park, MD: University of Maryland, Winter/Spring 1994), 12–17; George F. Will, "Our Expanding Menu of Rights," *Newsweek* (December 14, 1992), 90; John Leo, "The Spread of Rights Babble," *U.S. News & World Report* (June 28, 1993), 17; and William Raspberry, "Blind Pursuit of Rights Can Endanger Civility," *The Atlanta Journal* (September 14, 1994), A14.
24. DeGeorge, 69–72.
25. *Ibid.*
26. "John Rawls," *The Economist* (December 7, 2002), 83.
27. John Rawls, *A Theory of Justice* (Cambridge, MA: Harvard University Press, 1971).
28. DeGeorge, 69–72.
29. Michael M. Weinstein, "Bringing Logic to Bear on Liberal Dogma," *The New York Times* (December 1, 2002), 5.
30. *Ibid.*, 72.
31. Weinstein, 5.
32. Robbin Derry, "Ethics of Care," in *Werhane and Freeman* (1997), 254.
33. Brian K. Burton and Craig P. Dunn, "Feminist Ethics as Moral Grounding for Stakeholder Theory," *Business Ethics Quarterly* (Vol. 6, No. 2, 1996), 133–147; See also A. C. Wicks, D. R. Gilbert, and R. E. Freeman, "A Feminist Reinterpretation of the Stakeholder Concept," *Business Ethics Quarterly* (Vol. 4, 1994), 475–497.
34. Derry (1997), 256.
35. Jeanne M. Liedtka, "Feminist Morality and Competitive Reality: A Role for an Ethic of Care?" *Business Ethics Quarterly* (Vol. 6, 1996), 179–200. See also John Dobson and Judith White, "Toward the Feminine Firm," *Business Ethics Quarterly* (Vol. 5, 1995), 463–478.
36. Alasdair MacIntyre, *After Virtue* (University of Notre Dame Press), 1981. See also Louis P. Pojman, *Ethics: Discovering Right and Wrong*, 2d ed. (Belmont, CA: Wadsworth, 1995), 160–185.
37. Pojman, 161; See also Bill Shaw, "Sources of Virtue: The Market and the Community," *Business Ethics Quarterly* (Vol. 7, 1997), 33–50; and Dennis Moberg, "Virtuous Peers in Work Organizations," *Business Ethics Quarterly* (Vol. 7, 1997), 67–85.
38. Esther F. Schaeffer, "Character Education: A Prerequisite for Corporate Ethics," *Ethics Today* (Summer 1997), 5.
39. Oliver F. Williams and Patrick E. Murphy, "The Ethics of Virtue: A Moral Theory for Business," in Oliver F. Williams and John W. Houck (eds.) *A Virtuous Life in Business* (Lanham, MD: Rowman & Littlefield Publishers, Inc., 1992), 9–27.
40. Robert K. Greenleaf, *Servant Leadership* (New York: Paulist Press, 1977).
41. *Ibid.*; See also Robert K. Greenleaf, *The Servant as Leader* (Indianapolis: Robert K. Greenleaf Center, 1991).
42. Larry C. Spears (ed.) *Reflections of Leadership* (New York: John Wiley & Sons, 1995), 4–7.
43. Joanne B. Ciulla (ed.) *Ethics: The Heart of Leadership* (Westport, CT: Praeger Publishers, 1998), 17.
44. James A. Autry, *The Servant Leader* (Roseville, CA: Prima Publishing, 2001), flyleaf.
45. Carroll (1990), 22.
46. Barry, 50–51.
47. Carroll (1990), 22.
48. John C. Maxwell, *There's No Such Thing as "Business" Ethics: There's Only One Rule for Making Decisions* (Warner Books, 2003), 24–29.
49. William Shaw and Vincent Barry, *Moral Issues in Business* (Belmont, CA: Wadsworth, 1989), 77–78; and Vincent R. Ruggiero, *The Moral Imperative* (Port Washington, NY: Alfred Publishers, 1973).
50. Shaw and Barry, 77.
51. *Ibid.*, 78.
52. Gordon L. Lippett, *The Leader Looks at Ethics*, 12–13.
53. "Stiffer Rules for Business Ethics," *Business Week* (March 30, 1974), 88.
54. Frederick Andrews, "Corporate Ethics: Talks with a Trace of Robber Baron," *The New York Times* (April 18, 1977), C49–52.
55. Phillip V. Lewis, "Ethical Principles for Decision Makers: A Longitudinal Study," *Journal of Business Ethics* (Vol. 8, 1989), 275.
56. Craig V. VanSandt, "The Relationship Between Ethical Work Climate and Moral Awareness," *Business & Society* (Vol. 42, No. 1, March 2003), 144–151.
57. Cited in John B. Cullen, Bart Victor, and Carroll Stephens, "An Ethical Weather Report: Assessing the Organization's Ethical Climate," *Organizational Dynamics* (Autumn 1989), 50.
58. For an excellent discussion, see Deborah Vidaver Cohen, "Creating and Maintaining Ethical Work Climates: Anomie in the Workplace and Implications for Managing Change," *Business Ethics Quarterly* (Vol. 3, No. 4, October 1993), 343–355. See also B. Victor and J. Cullen, "The Organizational Bases of Ethical Work Climates," *Administrative Science Quarterly* (Vol. 33,

1988), 101–125; and H. R. Smith and A. B. Carroll, "Organizational Ethics: A Stacked Deck," *Journal of Business Ethics* (Vol. 3, 1984), 95–100.

59. Raymond C. Baumhart, "How Ethical Are Businessmen?" *Harvard Business Review* (July/August, 1961), 6ff.

60. Steve Brenner and Earl Molander, "Is the Ethics of Business Changing?" *Harvard Business Review* (January/February 1977).

61. Barry Z. Posner and Warren H. Schmidt, "Values and the American Manager: An Update," *California Management Review* (Spring 1984), 202–216.

62. Archie B. Carroll, "Managerial Ethics: A Post-Watergate View," *Business Horizons* (April 1975), 75–80.

63. Posner and Schmidt, 211.

64. Carroll, 75–80.

65. American Society of Chartered Life Underwriters & Chartered Financial Consultants and Ethics Officer Association, "Sources and Consequences of Workplace Pressure: A Landmark Study," unpublished report (1997); See also Del Jones, "48% of Workers Admit to Unethical or Illegal Acts," *USA Today* (April 4–6, 1997), 1A–2A.

66. Ethics Resource Center (2003), 33.

67. George Getschow, "Some Middle Managers Cut Corners to Achieve High Corporate Goals," *The Wall Street Journal* (November 8, 1979), 1, 34.

68. *Ibid.*, 34.

69. T. V. Purcell and James Weber, *Institutionalizing Corporate Ethics: A Case History*, Special Study No. 71 (New York: The President's Association, American Management Association, 1979). See also James Weber, "Institutionalizing Ethics into Business Organizations: A Model and Research Agenda," *Business Ethics Quarterly* (Vol. 3, No. 4, October, 1993), 419–436.

70. L. W. Foy, "Business Ethics: A Reappraisal," Distinguished Lecture Series, Columbia Graduate School of Business (January 30, 1975), 2.

71. Linda Klebe Treviño, Laura Pincus Hartman, and Michael Brown, "Moral Person and Moral Manager: How Executives Develop a Reputation for Ethical Leadership," *California Management Review* (Vol. 42, No. 4, Summer 2000), 134.

72. Harvey Gittler, "Listen to the Whistle-Blowers Before It's Too Late," *The Wall Street Journal* (March 10, 1986), 16.

73. Treviño, Hartman, and Brown (2000), 128–142.

74. *Ibid.*, 133–136.

75. Lee L. Morgan, "Business Ethics Starts with the Individual," *Management Accounting* (March 1977), 14, 60.

76. Steven N. Brenner, "Influences on Corporate Ethics Programs" (San Diego, CA: International Association for Business and Society, March 16–18, 1990), 7.

77. Ethics Resource Center, *National Business Ethics Survey 2003* (Washington, DC: Ethics Resource Center, 2003), iii.

78. Susan Gaines, "Handing Out Halos," *Business Ethics* (March/April 1994), 20–24.

79. Bruce A. Hamm, "Elements of the US Federal Sentencing Guidelines," http://www.refresher.com (April 29, 2004).

80. Roy J. Snell, "Should We Call It an Ethics Program or a Compliance Program?" *Journal of Health Care Compliance* (March/April 2004), 1–2.

81. "Ethics Officer Association: Overview and Benefits" (1996), 2. The EOA office is in the Bentley College Center for Business Ethics (Waltham, MA 02154). See also http://www.eoa.org.

82. Kris Hudson, "Ethics Officers Proliferate at America's Corporations in Wake of Scandals," *Knight Ridder Tribune Business News* (February 15, 2004), 1.

83. Brian Hindo, "Teaching MCI Right from Wrong," *Business Week* (November 3, 2003), 12.

84. Andy Pasztor and J. Lynn Lunsford, "Boeing Managers Criticized in Ethics Probe," *The Wall Street Journal* (November 19, 2003), B2.

85. Andy Pasztor, "Boeing May Hire an Ethics Watchdog," *The Wall Street Journal* (May 4, 2004), A3.

86. "Business Conduct Management System Project Update," http://www.eoa.org (April 29, 2004).

87. Michael G. Daigneault, Jerry Guthrie, and Frank J. Navran, "Managing Ethics Upwards," in O.C. Ferrell, Sheb L. True, and Lou E. Pelton (eds.) *Rights, Relationships & Responsibilities* (Kennesaw, GA: Coles College of Business, Kennesaw State University, 2003), 61–69.

88. *Ibid.*, 65–69.

89. *Ibid.*, 67–69.

90. Fred T. Allen, "Corporate Morality: Is the Price Too High?" *The Wall Street Journal* (October 17, 1975), 16.

91. LaRue T. Hosmer, *The Ethics of Management* (Homewood, IL: Richard D. Irwin, 1987), 12—14.

92. Kenneth Blanchard and Norman Vincent Peale, *The Power of Ethical Management* (New York: Fawcett Crest, 1988), 20.

93. Texas Instruments, "Ethics Quick Test" (Texas Instruments Ethics Office), wallet card.

94. Sears, Roebuck and Co., *Code of Business Conduct* (1997), 2.

95. Gary Edwards, "And the Survey Said...," in Garone (ed.) (1994), 25.

96. Bruce R. Gaumnitz and John C. Lere, "A Classification Scheme for Codes of Business Ethics," *Journal of Business Ethics* (February 2004), 329.

97. *Creating a Workable Company Code of Ethics* (Washington, DC: Ethics Resource Center, 1990), VIII–1.

98. *Ethics Policies and Programs in American Business* (Washington, DC: Ethics Resource Center, 1990), 23–24.

See also W. F. Edmondson, *A Code of Ethics: Do Corporate Executives and Employees Need It?* (Itawamba Community College Press, 1990).

99. Donald L. McCabe, Linda Klebe Treviño, and Kenneth D. Butterfield, "The Influence of Collegiate and Corporate Codes of Conduct on Ethics-Related Behavior in the Workplace," *Business Ethics Quarterly* (Vol. 6, October 1996), 473.

100. Mark Schwartz, "The Nature of the Relationship Between Corporate Codes of Ethics and Behavior," *Journal of Business Ethics* (Vol. 32, 2001), 247–2001.

101. *Ibid.*, 255.

102. Allen, 16.

103. Tevino, Hartman, and Brown, op. cit., 136.

104. J. Lynn Lunsford and Anne Marie Squeo, "Boeing Dismisses Two Executives for Violating Ethical Standards," *The Wall Street Journal* (November 25, 2003).

105. Ken Benson, "Nortel Fires 3 Executives Amid Accounting Inquiry," *The New York Times* (April 28, 2004).

106. Allen, 16.

107. 2003 National Business Ethics Survey, 44.

108. *Ibid.*, 43.

109. Cited in Gaines, 22.

110. *Ibid.*, 22—23.

111. Brian R. Hollstein, "From Complaint to Resolution," in Garone (ed.) (1994), 21–22.

112. Sears Code of Business Conduct, 1997.

113. Kirk O. Hanson, "What Good Are Ethics Courses?" *Across the Board* (September 1987), 10–11.

114. "Ethics Training a Low Priority," *USA Today* (January 29, 2004), 1B.

115. *2003 National Business Ethics Survey*, 8–9.

116. Melinda Ligos, "Boot Camps on Ethics Ask the 'What Ifs?'" *The New York Times* (January 5, 2003), 12BU.

117. Ron Zemke, "Ethics Training: Can We Really Teach People Right from Wrong?" *Training HRD* (May 1977), 39.

118. *Ethics Policies and Programs in American Business* (Washington, DC: Ethics Resource Center, 1990), 34.

119. "At Last: Humor in Ethics Training," *Business Ethics* (May/June 1997), 10.

120. Thomas M. Jones, "Can Business Ethics Be Taught? Empirical Evidence," *Business & Professional Ethics Journal* (Vol. 8, 1989), 86.

121. Katherine S. Mangan, "Business Schools and Company CEOs to Create Ethics Center," *Chronicle of Higher Education* (January 30, 2004), A9. Also see Louis Lavelle and Amy Borrus, "Ethics 101 for CEOs," *Business Week* (January 26, 2004), 88.

122. Michael Metzger, Dan R. Dalton, and John W. Hill, "The Organization of Ethics and the Ethics of Organizations: The Case for Expanded Organizational Ethics Audits," *Business Ethics Quarterly* (Vol. 3, No. 1, January, 1993), 27–43. Also see S. Andrew Ostapski, "The Moral Audit," *Business and Economic Review* (Vol. 38, No. 2, January–March 1992), 17–20; and Thomas Petzinger, Jr., "This Auditing Team Wants You to Create a Moral Organization," *The Wall Street Journal* (January 19, 1996), B1.

123. WalkerInformation, "Assessing and Measuring Business Integrity" (Indianapolis, IN).

124. W. Edward Stead, Dan L. Worrell, and Jean Garner Stead, "An Integrative Model for Understanding and Managing Ethical Behavior in Business Organizations," *Journal of Business Ethics* (Vol. 9, 1990), 223—242. See also Robert D. Gatewood and Archie B. Carroll, "Assessment of Ethical Performance of Organization Members: A Conceptual Framework," *Academy of Management Review* (Vol. 16, No. 4, 1991), 667–690.

125. Barbara Pagano and Elizabeth Pagano, *The Transparency Edge: How Credibility Can Make or Break You in Business* (McGraw Hill Trade 2003).

126. Don Tapscott and David Ticoll, *The Naked Corporation: How the Age of Transparency Will Revolutionize Business* (Free Press 2003).

127. Janice Brand, "Book Review: The Naked Corporation," *Darwin Magazine* (May 4, 2004), http://www.darwin mag.com/read/writeon/column.html.

128. Quoted in Curtis C. Verschoor, "Unethical Workplace is Still with Us," *Strategic Finance* (April 2004), 16.

129. William Atkinson, "Sarbanes–Oxley Act: Not Just for Corporations," *Public Power Magazine* (March–April 2004).

130. *Ibid.*

131. The Conference Board Press Release, "Boards of Directors Getting More Involved in Companies' Ethics Programs," *PR Newswire*, (March 4, 2004).

Chapter 8

■ BUSINESS ETHICS *and* TECHNOLOGY

CHAPTER LEARNING OUTCOMES

After studying this chapter, you should be able to:

1 Identify the role that technology plays in our business lives.

2 Gain an understanding of the technological environment and the characteristics of technology that influence business ethics and stakeholders.

3 Identify the benefits and side effects of technology in business.

4 Gain an appreciation of society's intoxication with technology and the consequences of this intoxication.

5 Learn to differentiate between information technology and biotechnology and their ethical implications for the management of enterprises.

6 Identify the ethical issues involved in biotechnology and present the arguments on both sides of the issues.

We live in an age characterized by advancing technology. Each new generation experiences technological advances that were not seen by previous generations; technology is how we sustain life and make it comfortable. Technology is the core of many businesses, whether it is used to pursue new products or processes or as a means to achieve other worthwhile ends. But, technology, as many have observed, is a two-edged sword. Many positive benefits flow from technological advances. By the same token, however, many new problems or challenges are posed by advancing technology. Futurist John Naisbitt, for example, has questioned whether advancing technology has the potential to be a "liberating" or "destructive" force in society. He has said that, at best, technology supports and improves human life, and at its worst it alienates, isolates, distorts, and destroys.[1]

In either case, technology has become such a central part of doing business in the twenty-first century that it cannot be ignored. Moreover, ethical issues for business and for society have arisen as a result of technological advances. Many would argue that technology has developed at a speed that significantly outstrips the capacity of society, government, or business to grasp its consequences or ethics. In this chapter, we will explore some of these issues, knowing full well that other aspects will be mentioned in ensuing chapters as specific stakeholder groups are considered in more detail.

Consider the application of surveillance technology that was used at the 2001 Super Bowl held in Tampa, Florida. Unbeknownst to people entering Raymond James Stadium, they were unwitting participants in what might be called an "electronic police lineup." Cameras located at each entrance "taped" every face that entered the stadium. We are all familiar with camera technology, of course, so what is the big deal? Coupled with sophisticated face-recognition software, these cameras facilitated the instant measurement of the dimensions of the human face (such as the distance between eyes) and reduced each face to a numerical code. That code was then matched against the codes of known criminals and suspected terrorists that were stored in a law-enforcement database.[2]

In 2004, a new form of surveillance was in the news. Issues were raised about the camera function now built into the ubiquitous cell phones that we all carry. Private individuals were accused of looking up women's skirts by using their cell-phone cameras to take pictures while no one was noticing. This raised the issue of whether cell-phone technology has now taken away all privacy and whether new laws restricting their use should be passed. In another example, cell-phone camera technology was identified to be the source of student cheating on exams in college.

Another big issue in the realm of ethics and technology has been the revelations that employers and rental car companies have been installing global positioning systems (GPS) on vehicles and tracking people without their knowledge. In one dramatic case, a consumer filed a complaint against a car rental agency when she got her bill of $1,372.59 for two days of rental. Apparently, she had driven across the border from California to Nevada and was hit with big penalties when the rental company documented her every move while in the rental car. The woman complained that she wasn't told about the out-of-state penalty, and she wasn't told she was being tracked. One recent study revealed that one-fourth of all rental cars in the United States are equipped with tracking devices and that most consumers say they are not told.[3]

According to the president of Viisage Technology, the developer of the face-recognition software, his company was able to match 19 faces from the Super Bowl crowd to faces in the database of people with criminal records. As it turns out, no arrests were made because none of those 19 people were wanted by the police at the time, even though they all had criminal records. Was this an ethical usage of technology? The American Civil Liberties Union (ACLU) dubbed this application "Snooper Bowl." The ACLU holds that this application is just one more example of the kinds of issues that arise in the ongoing debate about the power of technology to shrink our privacy. This application may not seem too intrusive because

SEARCH THE WEB

IS TECHNOLOGY GOOD OR EVIL?

The two founders of the Institute for Business, Technology and Ethics (IBTE) come at the issue of technology from two different sides. One says that technology is good and one says that technology is evil. The two friends since the 1970s came together to create this unique, nonprofit organization that features ethics conversations regarding technology issues.

An example of the questions raised include "What are the primary ethical challenges we must face up to in the bioethics realm?" Web visitors are given the chance to share their opinions.

Visit **http://www.ethix.org** for an enlightening exploration of business and technology ethics.

it was done in a public place where expectations of privacy are low. The head of the Florida ACLU thinks that an application like this, however, is just one more step toward broad and permanent surveillance of society's members. His position was that we should first discuss a technology such as this one before using it. Further, he noted that there had been no announcement to people entering the stadium that they would be checked out in this technologically-advanced way.[4] In the cell-phone camera example, we now see how the source of privacy invasion is in the hands of private individuals. In the cheating on exams example, the technology was again used to facilitate unethical behavior. With respect to the use of GPS systems as monitoring devices, there are obviously two sides to the story.

In this chapter, we intend to explore the subject of technology and business ethics. Technology has become such an integral aspect of our work lives and consumer lives that special treatment of these topics is warranted. First, we will consider what technology means and some of its benefits and challenges. Second, we will briefly discuss the subject of ethics and technology. Finally, we will consider ethical issues connected with two major realms of technology: computers and information technology, and biotechnology.

TECHNOLOGY AND THE TECHNOLOGICAL ENVIRONMENT

Technology means many things to many people. In this chapter, **technology** will refer to the "totality of the means employed to provide objects necessary for human sustenance and comfort." It is also seen as a scientific method used in achieving a practical purpose.[5] Technology refers to all the ways people use their inventions and discoveries to satisfy their needs and desires. Since time began, people have invented and developed tools, techniques, machines, and materials to sustain life and to improve the quality of life. Sources of power have also been discovered and developed. Taken together, these technological advances have made work easier and more productive.[6] It is little surprise, therefore, that businesses have embraced and used technology as much or more than any other sector of society.

In Chapter 1, we discussed the macroenvironment of business and how this total environment was composed of a number of significant and interrelated segments such as the social, economic, political, and technological. The **technological environment**, our current topic of concern, represents the total set of technology-based advancements or progress taking place in society. Pertinent aspects of this segment include new products, processes, materials, states of knowledge, and scientific advancements in both theoretical and applied senses. The rate of change and complexity of the technological environment have made it of special interest to business today. Consider the following examples. An electronic greeting card that today plays "Happy Birthday" holds more computing power than existed in the world before 1950. One of today's home video cameras wields more processing power than the old IBM 360, the wonder machine that launched the age of mainframe computers. Computers are being used to aid scientists in comprehending the secrets of matter at the atomic level and to create amazing new materials.[7] In both information technology and the burgeoning field of biotechnology, the shape of how we are living, what products we are using, and what processes we are being exposed to are changing at an accelerating pace.

CHARACTERISTICS OF TECHNOLOGY

We have moved from a world characterized by industrial technology to one dominated by information technology and biotechnology. Whatever the technological level of advancement, there are general benefits of technology, undesirable side effects of technology, and ethical challenges inherent in technological advancements. A brief consideration of each is useful.

Benefits of Technology

Few would dispute that we as a society have benefited greatly from technology and innovation. We live better lives today as employees, consumers, and members of the community due to technology. Technology has helped us gain control over nature and to build for ourselves a civilized life. Through the ages, technology has benefited society in four main ways.[8] First, it has increased society's production of goods and services, a benefit attributable chiefly to the business sector. In the mid-1800s, people and animals were the main source of power on farms. In the early 1900s, tractors and other machines powered by gasoline and electricity became commonplace. Today, machines do virtually all the work on farms. These same kinds of results have been achieved in manufacturing, mining, and other industries; the number of products available for sale and consumption have increased appreciably.

Second, technology has reduced the amount of labor needed to produce goods and services. Not only has production increased, but productivity has also increased. This has resulted in more leisure time, which has significantly affected lifestyles. Third, technology has not only enabled greater production with a lesser amount of human labor, but it has also made labor easier and safer. Fourth, higher standards of living have been a direct result of labor-saving technology. Today in economies that have been able to take advantage of technology, people are better fed, clothed, and housed, and they enjoy more health and comfort than any other people in history. Even life expectancy has increased as a result of these other factors.[9]

Side Effects and Challenges of Technology

Technologies have benefited people in many ways. There have also been some unanticipated side effects of technology—problems or effects not anticipated before technologies were implemented. One major reason for this is that technologies were often implemented before much thought was given to possible side effects, ethical problems, or downside risks of the technologies. The automobile is a classic example. From the late 1800s to early 1900s, it was believed that automobiles would be more quiet and less smelly than horses. As more autos came into use, however, it quickly became obvious that roaring traffic noise exceeded the clatter of horse hoofs. Automobile exhaust became more toxic than the smell of horse manure. Fumes polluted the air with carbon monoxide and other impurities that threatened human health.[10] In addition, we experienced traffic jams, shortages of gasoline, and automobile accidents—some aided by cell-phone users—and "road rage."

Four categories of undesirable side effects of technology merit mention. First, there is *environmental pollution*. This ranks as one of the most undesirable side effects of technology. In spite of efforts to address this problem, most industrial nations today face significant air, water, soil, solid waste, and noise pollution. Global warming is an inevitable topic of concern today, due to technology. Second, there is *depletion of natural resources.* The rapid advance of technology continually threatens the supply of natural resources. Fuel shortages and power shortages have become a way of life. Third, there is the issue of *technological unemployment.* The most common form of technological unemployment occurs when machines take the place of humans, as we experienced in the automation phase of industrial development. Another form of technological employment is now occurring as technology jobs are being moved offshore to less expensive regions of the world. At an aggregate level, this has not been as much of a problem as once anticipated. In the short run, and to specific individuals locked into certain jobs with limited skills, however, it remains a serious threat. Fourth, there has been the *creation of unsatisfying jobs* due to technology. Many jobs in the technological world fail to give the workers a sense of accomplishment. As jobs are broken down into smaller component parts, each individual worker is further removed from the finished product that might provide a greater sense of fulfillment and pride. Monotony and boredom can easily set in when jobs are significantly shaped by certain technological processes.[11]

New technologies present many challenges to managers, organizations, and society. Foremost among the challenges is anticipating and avoiding the unwanted side effects. Some side effects cannot be forecast or overcome, of course, but much more could be done than is currently being done. Overcoming the technological determinism that seems to be driving society today would be a step in the right direction. For example, one of the most important issues today in the realm of biotechnology is that of human cloning. It is difficult to get the scientists and researchers to slow down and talk about the possible consequences (practical and ethical) of human cloning. Many of them seem driven by the technological capacities for achieving this instead of asking the important questions concerning ethics and side effects. Another challenge lies in spreading the benefits of technology. Currently, the benefits of technology are rather restricted to the developed world. The developing nations enjoy few of the benefits of technology enjoyed in the developed nations.[12] It is anticipated that as multinational corporations increasingly move to developing countries for production or exploration for resources, the opportunities for technology transfer will be greatly enhanced. This is being seen, to some extent, in the case of information and medical technology jobs being moved to India and China. The challenge, however, is to move technologies into other countries in socially responsible ways.

ETHICS AND TECHNOLOGY

To be sure, technology has many benefits for humankind. Our perspective at this juncture, however, is to raise the ethical questions that may be related to business development and use of technology. To do so does not mean that one is against technology. It simply means that one is concerned about the ethical use of and implications of technology. Like management decision making and globalization of business, the actions of the business community with respect to technology have ethical implications that should be identified and discussed. Management's goal should be to avoid immoral and amoral practices with respect to technology and to move toward a moral management posture with respect to this potent business resource.

Applying business ethics to questions involving technology is simply an extension of our discussions of business ethics up to this point. The goal of managers and businesses striving to be ethical should be to do what is right, what is fair, and to avoid harm. In making ethical judgments, the prevailing norms of acceptability regarding technology must be tested by the principles of fairness and justice, protection of rights, and utilitarianism. The goal should be to reconcile and build bridges over the gap between "what is" and "what ought to be."

With respect to the three models of management ethics, the mission should be to avoid immoral technological practices in products, processes, and applications. There is much room for abuse and misinterpretation. Technology is such a godsend for humankind that it is easy to overlook or fail to discern the ethical dimensions of decision making and application. Managers should strive to adhere to high standards of ethical behavior and policies, pay careful attention to what is legal (both that which conforms to the spirit as well as the letter of the law), and display ethical leadership in anticipating and responding to technology-related ethical dilemmas.

Two Key Issues.   There are two key ethical issues in the realm of technology that seem to drive everything. First, there is the idea of technological determinism. **Technological determinism** is the imperative that "what *can* be developed *will* be developed." When someone once asked "why do we want to put men on the moon?" the answer was always "because we *can* put men on the moon." In other words, scientists and those who work with advanced technologies are driven to push back the frontiers of technological development without consideration of ethical issues or side effects. The second important concept is that of ethical lag. **Ethical lag** is a phenomenon that has been noted. Ethical lag occurs when the speed of technological change far exceeds that of ethical development.[13] We will see throughout our consideration of technology and ethics that these two phenomena are at work.

To emphasize the ethical dimension of technology, it is useful to note how society has become obsessed with technology and its power over our lives. Only by fully understanding the magnitude of this love affair we have with technology can we focus on the ethical aspects of it and the actions that should be taken. One way to appreciate what technology is doing to us is to consider the thoughts of John Naisbitt, Nana Naisbitt, and Douglas Phillips, who recently wrote the book *High Tech/High Touch*. In this book, they discussed our current obsession with technology and described the symptoms of this obsession.[14]

Symptoms of Society's Intoxication with Technology

In *High Tech/High Touch*, Naisbitt calls upon all members of society to understand and question the place of technology in our lives. He and his colleagues argue that our world has changed from a "technologically comfortable place" into a "technologically intoxicated zone." As Naisbitt analyzes the world, he concludes that there are six symptoms of society's intoxication with technology.[15] Some of these touch upon our character as a people, and some touch upon the ethical issues business faces with technology. The six symptoms are as follows:

1. We favor the quick fix. This is true whether it relates to nutrition or religion. As we perceive a recurring void, we search for something and we want it quickly. Ironically, he says that technology promises to detoxify us—to simplify our complex lives, relieve our stress, and calm our nerves. However, this Band-Aid culture of the quick fix is ultimately an empty one. We are seduced by the promise of technology.

2. We fear and worship technology. Our behavior moves us from the extremes of worship one moment to fear the next. We accept technology, fearing that we will fall behind our competitors or coworkers. We embrace technology but then feel frustrated and annoyed when it fails to deliver.

3. We blur the distinction between what is real and what is fake. When technology can transform nature, we frequently ask "Is that real, or is that fake?" Is it authentic or simulated?

4. We accept violence as normal. Technology has made it possible for us to package violence in the form of merchandise, often spin-offs from television or movies. This violent material is often targeted at children.

5. We love technology as a toy. As affluence finances play, leisure tends toward diversion—something to fill the time. We live in a culture dominated by consumer technology, where leisure is often passively received. Electronic distractions busy us as we can't find anything worthwhile to do. The problem is that real leisure is not based on the desire to consume. It requires tranquility, patience, and attentiveness. Technology seldom delivers.

6. We live our lives distanced and distracted. The Internet, cell phones, and wireless technologies promise to connect us to the world, but when is it appropriate and when is it a distraction? Technology's bells and whistles are seductive, and they distance us and distract us.

Naisbitt's solution to this intoxication with technology is to find the right balance. That is, we need to embrace technology that preserves our humanity and reject technology that intrudes upon it. We need to know when we should push back on technology, in our work and our lives, and to affirm our humanity. We need to understand that technology zealots are as short-sighted as technology bashers. We need to question the place of technology in our lives.[16]

There is significant evidence that society is becoming concerned with the ethics of technology and the intoxication with technology that Naisbitt has so aptly described. This information should be useful for individuals as well as businesses desiring to use technology in a more ethical manner. Following are three examples of this increased societal concern. First, books are being published on the topic of ethics and technology. One example is *Practical Ethics for a Technological World* by Paul Alcorn.[17] It is encouraging to see books of this nature that attempt to bridge the gap between ethics and technology and to discuss where we are now and where we need to go. Second, special encyclopedias are being developed, such as *The Concise Encyclopedia of the Ethics of New Technologies*.[18] This encyclopedia, which is devoted to applied ethics, is one of a number that has come out in the past decade. Third, there are developing new organizations concerned about ethics and technology. One example is the nonprofit Institute for Business, Technology and Ethics (IBTE), a unique organization dedicated to exploring the mix of business, technology, and ethics. One of the major concerns of one of IBTE's founders is the unintended consequences of technology on people and how these consequences often lead to "damage control" ethics.[19]

There are a number of arenas in which specific issues of business ethics and technology might be explored. Research over the past few years reveals two broad categories of issues that now merit our consideration. Each is broad and deep, so we can only consider them in an introductory way in this chapter. Each, however, significantly touches business, either directly or indirectly. The two areas are computer-based **information technology** and **biotechnology**. Within each, there are dozens-to-hundreds of technologies that raise ethical questions. Our quest, therefore, will be to focus on the major ones that give us a representative sample of ethical issues with technology.

INFORMATION TECHNOLOGY

Computer-based information technology, or information technology (IT), as it is most often called, touches practically all businesses and stakeholders involved in those business-es. Businesses and people are either affected by technology or are directly involved in pursuits that are based on technology. We will consider them both. There are two broad areas we will discuss in this section: *electronic commerce*, or Web-based marketing, and *computer technology in the workplace*, including telecommunications. These areas overlap significantly and are interdependent, so our separation is to lend some order to the discussion.

Electronic Commerce as an Emerging Technology

Electronic commerce, often referred to as *e-commerce, e-business*, or *Web-based marketing*, is one of the most significant technological phenomena of our day. It primarily affects consumer stakeholders and competitors of the e-commerce firm. Most experts today are convinced that the Internet is rapidly reshaping the way business will be conducted around the world. Part of this is firms selling products and services online. Beyond this, companies are integrating the Internet into every aspect of their businesses.

According to Forrester Research, electronic commerce hit an estimated $6.8 trillion by 2004, with 90 percent of that coming from business-to-business sales. Consumer transactions were expected to hit $107 billion by 2003. In 2000, almost half of all adults had purchased a product online, and three-quarters of them had sought product or service information on the Internet. The pull of e-business is powerful. Companies are increasingly moving their operations to the Net. For example, after just two years, Staples, the $10.7 billion office supply retailer, boosted annual online sales to $512 million. According to one estimate, businesses will buy $2.8 billion in supplies over the Internet by 2004. Other areas of Internet growth include knowledge management and customer relationships. It is estimated that companies will spend over $10 billion to store and share their employees' knowledge over the Net by 2004, and companies are expected to invest $12.2 billion by 2004, linking customers, sales, and marketing over the Web.[20] In short, electronic commerce is a burgeoning business, and the opportunity for questionable practices arises along with this business.

Along with the growth of electronic commerce, business ethics problems have arisen as well. One major category of problems is online scams. According to Internet Fraud Watch, which is sponsored by the National Consumers League, con artists are taking advantage of the Internet's growth in popularity to bilk the unwary. During 2000, for example, the top frauds over the Internet included online auctions, general merchandise sales, Internet access services, work-at-home offers, and advance fee loans. Other scams included credit card fraud, travel and vacation scams, pyramid schemes, and bogus investment opportunities. The average dollar value consumers lose to online scams is rising as well, from an estimated $310 in 1999 to $427 in 2000.[21]

Current Issues in E-Commerce Ethics

According to Kracher and Corritore, the key current issues in e-commerce ethics are as follows:[22]

- Access
- Intellectual property

- Privacy and informed consent
- Protection of children
- Security of information
- Trust

These issues are not restricted to e-commerce. They also occur in brick-and-mortar businesses. The manifestations and scope of these issues, however, differ from that of traditional businesses. *Access* refers to the difference in computer access between the rich and the poor. *Intellectual property*, in e-commerce, is illustrated by Napster and the ethics of downloading music. *Privacy and informed consent* differ in e-commerce. An illustration is the novel ways companies place cookies on our computers without informed consent. In addition, firms such as DoubleClick collect online information and merge it with off-line information. In addition, personal information is collected online much more often than in traditional businesses. *Protection of children* is an important ethical issue, and it is illustrated in the issue of pornography. E-commerce makes porn more accessible than through traditional businesses. *Security* is such a major issue that even today some are reluctant to do business on the Web for fear their credit card numbers will be intercepted by someone not associated with the e-commerce business. Finally, *trust* is the basis for practically all business transactions, and it is especially crucial in e-commerce.[23] We will discuss some of these ethical issues in further detail.

Invasion of Privacy via Electronic Commerce

The average person encounters two forms of Internet electronic commerce: business-to-consumer transactions and business-to-business transactions. Most of us are quite familiar with business-to-consumer transactions when we do personal business on the Internet—buying products, arranging credit cards, accessing travel Web sites, and doing financial business. Employees also encounter business-to-business (B2B) transactions. B2B is anticipated to be the greatest area of e-commerce growth in the coming years. One reason for this is the rapid globalization of business. In terms of Web-based marketing to consumers, consumer stakeholders are primarily affected by such issues as database sharing, identity theft, and invasion of privacy. Invasion of privacy is a legitimate concern in all business transactions; however, the special case of electronic commerce or Web-based marketing deserves special attention because of the ease with which data can be stored and transmitted in electronic form.

One illustration of a potential invasion of privacy was that of DoubleClick, Inc., a New York-based Internet advertising company that planned to share customer information with an off-line marketing firm. Consumer advocates were up in arms that DoubleClick would betray such confidential information. Another example occurred when Toysmart.com, Inc., went out of business and offered its online customer list for sale, thus violating privacy agreements or understandings previously made with customers. Questions that arise from such situations include "What limits should there be on how online businesses use the information they gather about their customers?" "What responsibility do companies have to publicly disclose such practices?"[24]

The number one ethical issue with respect to doing business over the Internet is the question of possible invasions of consumer privacy. This is a hot topic for business executives today. According to a recent survey by The Conference Board, "e-business privacy issues" was the most discussed technology issue at Conference Board meetings.[25] In general, the consuming public is concerned as well. A survey on Internet privacy conducted by *The Wall Street Journal* and Harris Interactive revealed that 24 percent of those consumers surveyed were "very concerned" and 49 percent were "somewhat concerned" about threats to their personal privacy on the Internet. Further, about half of those surveyed indicated that concerns about privacy caused them to stop using a Web site or to forgo an online purchase.[26] Figure 8-1 summarizes some of the concerns that privacy advocates and law enforcement experts have about the Internet's threat to privacy.

Some of the technological means by which companies invade consumers' privacy include the use of cookies and spam. *Cookies* are those little identification tags that Web sites drop on our personal computer hard drives so they can recognize repeat visitors the next time we visit their Web sites. Surveys show that some consumers don't know what cookies are; others are aware of them but don't take the time to block them. According to the Pew Internet & American Life Project, only 10 percent of users set their browsers to block cookies. Part of this is due to the fact that 56 percent of Internet users didn't know what a cookie was.[27]

Many consumers interpret the receipt of *spam* as an invasion of their privacy. Opening our e-mail mailboxes only to find a few dozen unsolicited ads is aggravating, at the least, and an invasion of privacy to many. Also, some companies experiment with pulsing background ads that never go away. Interestingly, dozens of companies make programs that protect our e-mail privacy, block cookies, and filter spam and porn, but very few consumers bother to use them.[28]

One of the most serious invasion of privacy issues with respect to electronic commerce is the collection and use of personal information. Though non-Internet companies have engaged in this practice for years, everything seems magnified in the e-world

FIGURE 8-1

Ways in Which the Internet's Threat to Privacy Is the Greatest

Identity theft	Someone might use the Internet to steal your identity.
Unintentionally revealing information	You may be unintentionally revealing information about yourself as you move through cyberspace.
Lost/stolen personal information	That personal information you just provided to a Web site might be sold or stolen.
Fake Web sites	That Web site on which you just entered your credit card number and personal information may be a fake.
Government distribution of information	The government may be giving out your home address, social security number, and other personal information online.
Broadcasting information over the Internet	Companies and people who do not like you may be broadcasting your private information on the Internet.
Victim of spying— employer or spouse	Your employer or spouse may be using your computer to spy on you.
Victim of spying— strangers	Someone you do not know may be using your computer to spy on you (e.g., hackers).
Cyberstalker	You may have a cyberstalker harassing you.

SOURCE: Summarized from "Internet Insecurity," *Time*, (July 2, 2001), 46–50. For the latest news, go to the Electronic Privacy Information Center at http://www.epic.org.

in which we now live. None of us really knows how much personal information is collected, saved, swapped, or sold in e-commerce. Thousands of retailers, from department stores to catalog companies, collect and store personal information, from asking customers for their zip codes to collecting names, addresses, household income, and purchasing patterns through a store credit card. Retailers also share, exchange, and even sell their customer databases to other companies. In short, the average consumer has very little control over what is done with his or her personal data once it is collected.[29] An extreme concern is *identify theft* or tampering with one's financial accounts. Less serious is the inundation of marketing attempts, both online and off-line, that consumers are subjected to as a result of information being distributed.

Government's Involvement in Internet Privacy Protection.

The government has gotten involved in protecting consumers' privacy, and it has not all been good news. The Financial Services Modernization Act of 1999 was landmark legislation that permitted banks, insurers, and brokers to join forces. Under the law, it is now possible for consumers to get their credit cards, checking accounts, investments, home loans, and health insurance from one company. This is convenient for consumers. However, the law also empowered these companies to develop exceptionally detailed portraits of their customers just by merging files about their income, assets, debts, health, spending habits, and other personal data. Increasingly, this sensitive data is becoming a public commodity.[30]

The lawmakers who created this act were concerned about consumers' privacy, so they insisted upon some privacy protection provisions. Special-interest groups concerned about consumers' privacy wanted the law to require that companies get permission from their customers before selling personal data. This was called an "opt in" approach in which customers would have to specifically "opt in" to having their personal information used by the company for purposes beyond its original intent. At this point, however, industry lobbyists went to work and proposed an alternative approach: to allow customers to protect themselves by "opting out" from firms using their personal data. The major problem with this was that Congress did not require companies to mail the notices in a standard format or in a separate mailing.

Consequently, since 2000 and 2001, consumers have been bombarded with dozens of notices, usually stuck in an envelope bundled along with the monthly statement, frequently not being noticed or read and ending up in the trash. Even if the customer did notice the "opt out" opportunity, the offer was frequently written in legalese and set in fine print—violating just about every known guideline about how to make complex policies understandable to the average consumer. Not surprisingly, as of summer 2001 the opt-out forms were being returned only by about one in every 20 consumers. According to Mike France, a *Business Week* writer and former lawyer, some businesses interpreted this to mean that people are not really all that worked up about privacy. The real reason for the low response to the opt-out, he states, is because the notices are designed by the businesses to be ignored.[31]

Over the past several years, a number of different bills designed to protect consumer privacy on the Internet have been filed but not yet voted upon. Many of the legislators have been uncertain whether a broad privacy bill is even needed or what it should look like. Two bills were introduced in the House of Representatives. The Consumer Online Privacy and Disclosure Act and the Online Consumer Protection Act of 2001 would direct the Federal Trade Commission to set new guidelines for how information could be collected and shared on the Internet. Several other bills would prohibit businesses from sharing sensitive financial or medical information without clear permission. Privacy advocates were hoping that the Unsolicited Commercial Electronic Mail Act of 2001 would be passed and would stem the tide of spam clogging e-mail boxes. Though privacy continues to be a hot-button technology issue in Congress, many lawmakers have indicated they wanted to study the issue before throwing support behind new privacy measures.[32]

The Federal Trade Commission (FTC) is one of the primary government agencies concerned with protecting consumers' privacy today. Under the FTC Act, the commission guards against unfairness and deception. The major legislation now governing consumers' privacy include the Gramm-Leach-Bliley Act, concerned with financial privacy, and the Fair Credit Reporting Act and the Children's Online Privacy Protection Act. Figure 8-2 summarizes the FTC's privacy agenda as of 2004.

Business Initiatives.

There are a number of different ways companies might strive to protect the privacy of their customers in electronic commerce.

Ethical Leadership. First, business needs to recognize the potential ethical issues involved in electronic commerce and be committed to treating customers and all affected stakeholders in an ethical fashion. This commitment and ethical leadership undergird all other initiatives.

Privacy Policies. Companies may take the initiative with their own carefully crafted privacy policies designed to protect customers. An example of this might be a company deciding to do more than the law requires. FleetBoston Financial Corporation decided to resolve concerns regarding its use of customer financial data by adopting a new privacy policy requiring a customer's affirmative approval (an "opt in" policy) prior to the company sharing nonpublic personal information with third parties for marketing purposes. Fleet's privacy policy was a response to the New York attorney general's concern about Fleet sharing customer account information without providing full disclosure to its customers. Under Fleet's policy, the bank would not share customers' personal information without their informed, voluntary, specific, and documented consent.[33]

Chief Privacy Officers. An innovative approach to protecting consumers' privacy has been the designation of a **chief privacy officer (CPO)** in a number of major companies. Companies like American Express, Sony Corporation, Citigroup, and IBM have appointed their own privacy chiefs.[34] A recent estimate is that there are now 2,000 or more such positions around the country, and their numbers may swell in the next few years.[35] In other companies, these responsibilities are falling under the administration of a chief technology officer.

It is the primary responsibility of the chief privacy officer to keep a company out of trouble, whether in a court of law or the court of public opinion. This includes developing Internet policies, helping their companies avoid consumer litigation, creating methods of handling and resolving consumer complaints, and assessing the risk of privacy invasion of company activities and practices. Because the position is so new at most companies, these newly appointed individuals are still trying to figure out what they need to be doing. The job is a challenging one. CPOs must balance their customers' right to privacy with the employer's need for information for profit purposes.[36] Gary Clayton, CEO of the Privacy Council, said it is a new position that he expects most major businesses to have to have in the next two or three years.[37] CPOs were all the rage in the early 2000s, but the economic downturn has slowed down the movement. As the economy perks back up, CPOs, once again, have become popular.

FIGURE 8-2

Privacy Agenda of the Federal Trade Commission

The FTC is the nation's primary consumer protection champion. It plays a vital role in protecting consumers' privacy. Its recent initiatives, many of which touch upon information technology, include those listed here.

Creating a National Do-Not-Call List
Consumers who do not want telemarketers calling them can take two actions. First, they can rely on a voluntary system administered by the Direct Marketing Association. Second, they can notify each company separately. The FTC initiative provides a third way: the creation of a national do-not-call list.

Beefing Up Enforcement Against Spam
Fraudulent and deceptive spam promoting chain letters, pyramid schemes, or other kinds of get-rich-quick schemes pose significant burdens on customers. The FTC plans to increase its enforcement activities against these scams.

Helping Victims of Identity Theft
The FTC will use the data it collects from consumers to spot patterns that can help law enforcement agencies prosecute perpetrators and help businesses avoid the financial consequences of ID theft.

Stopping Pretexting
"Pretexting" is the practice of fraudulently obtaining personal financial information like account numbers and balances, often by calling banks under the pretext of being a customer. Pretexting is prohibited under the Gramm-Leach-Bliley Act.

Encouraging Accuracy in Credit Reporting and Compliance with Fair Credit Reporting Act
The FTC plans to step up its efforts to ensure that consumers are notified when information in a credit report is the reason for a denial of credit, insurance, or employment, and to ensure that all participants in the credit reporting system meet their obligations regarding accuracy of consumers' credit information.

Enforcing Privacy Promises
The FTC already has brought a number of cases to enforce the promises in privacy statements. The FTC will also investigate claims touting the privacy and security features of products.

Increasing Enforcement and Outreach on Children's Online Privacy
The FTC will continue its enforcement of the Children's Online Privacy Protection Act of 1998, as well as its business and consumer education activities.

Encouraging Consumers' Privacy Complaints
The FTC receives over 10,000 consumer complaints each week about fraudulent and deceptive business practices related to privacy. It has a toll-free phone number (1-877-FTC-HELP) and its Web site is (http://www.ftc.gov).

Enforcing the Telemarketing Sales Rules
The FTC will increase enforcement of the privacy provisions of the Telemarketing Sales Rule, especially the provisions about harassing calls and the hours during which calls are allowed.

Restricting Use of Pre-acquired Account Information
The FTC will increase its efforts to ensure that telemarketers do not use "pre-acquired account information" to bill consumers for goods or services they do not want.

Enforcing Gramm-Leach-Bliley Act (GLBA)
The GLBA of 1999 requires financial institutions to provide privacy notices to consumers, and allows consumers, with certain exceptions, to choose whether their financial institutions may share their information with third parties.

Holding Workshops
The FTC will explore holding public workshops on security issues and other ways to encourage security for personal information.

SOURCE: "Privacy Initiatives," Federal Trade Commission; http://www.ftc.gov. See also http://www.ftc.gov/donotcall; http://www.consumer.gov/idtheft; and http://www.ftc.gov/spam (May 10, 2004).

One of the latest debates is whether the CPOs will focus on *ethics* or *compliance*. Those in the ethics camp believe that CPOs need to be driven by integrity concerns and should proactively and strategically consider the privacy implications of their company's actions. Those in the compliance camp believe that CPOs should just focus on making sure the company stays out of trouble by not breaking the host of new laws it now faces. Some of these laws with privacy provisions include the Fair Credit Reporting Act, the Gramm-Leach-Bliley Act and the Sarbanes–Oxley Act. As a result of limited resources, Alan F. Westin, president of Privacy & American Business, a nonprofit organization, has concluded: "Most companies have shifted from a privacy approach that would be based on proactive steps, competitive-edge orientation and customer trust building to a narrow, legal-compliance priority."[38]

Questionable Businesses and Practices.

Several questionable businesses and practices have been made possible by electronic commerce and the use of the Internet. Three business categories that are viewed as questionable by some include Web-based pornography, Internet gambling, and Web-based music services such as Napster, MusicNet, Pressplay, and others that raise the question of the protection of intellectual property. Pornography via the Internet is just one aspect of this business. The other is the production and distribution of pornography through video rental stores and through in-room videos in hotels.[39] Many ethical questions have been raised concerning this. The Internet porn industry has become so controversial that the U.S. Supreme Court is now hearing cases as to whether the industry is violating the Child Pornography Prevention Act of 1996 and the Communication Decency Act. Song-swapping services such as Napster and several others have raised the question of the protection of intellectual property, because other people's ideas and music have been so easily acquired via the Internet. Napster has been halted and has tried to make the transition to a paid subscription service; however, other free music services are surfacing and calling into question the system's ability to protect intellectual property.[40] According to Robert Kuttner, the Internet has created situations not anticipated by previous laws for thoughtful public policy defining the public interest as well as individuals' private interests in protecting intellectual property.[41]

Two practices that have raised questions include (1) companies paying Internet search engine providers to ensure that their Web page appears early or at the top of the list when consumers do Internet searches and (2) the use of monitoring technology to monitor consumers as they use the company's products. Commercial Alert, a group founded by consumer activist Ralph Nader, asked the Federal Trade Commission to investigate online search engine companies that are concealing the impact that special fees have on Internet searches. The group asked the FTC to investigate whether eight of the Web's largest search engines (e.g., AltaVista, Lycos, AOL Time Warner, LookSmart) have been violating federal laws against deceptive advertising. The group charged that some of these search engines have abandoned their traditional, objective formulas to determine the order of the results they list and have sold the top spots to the highest bidders, without making adequate disclosures to Internet users. Apparently, to boost revenues, search engine companies have been accepting payments from businesses interested in receiving a higher ranking in certain search categories.[42] This raises an interesting question of Internet ethics: Is this an unfair advertising practice, or is this just the free-enterprise system at work?

An example of the monitoring technology occurred when an individual rented a vehicle from Acme Rent-a-Car in New Haven, Connecticut, only to find out later that he was the unwitting victim of a global-positioning-system device planted in the minivan he leased. The surveillance device recorded him speeding in three states at rates from 78 to 83 m.p.h., and each violation, digitally recorded, automatically added a $150 charge to his bill.[43]

One of the most serious problems in the realm of computer scams against consumers is the scam recently identified as "phishing." An example of this occurred when a Russian who goes by the cybername of Robotector sent an e-mail with the subject line "I still love you" to three million people. Within the message had been planted a small computer virus that, if executed, begins to record user names and passwords each time their owner visits more than 30 online banks or payment Web sites. Then, this information is secretly e-mailed back to Robotector. This technique is called "phishing" because it lures prey (computer users) with convincing bait into revealing passwords and other private data. The Anti-Phishing Working Group, an industry association, counted 1,124 such attacks in April 2004, and the number had doubled since the previous month. MessageLabs, an e-mail security company, reported an 800-fold increase in phishing attacks over a recent 6-month period.[44] The existence of these kinds of techniques points to the kinds of controversial ethical issues that arise in connection with electronic commerce.

The Workplace and Computer Technology

Whereas computer-based information technology creates ethical issues for consumer stakeholders with respect to electronic commerce and Web-based marketing, employee stakeholders also are significantly affected by technology in the workplace. We will discuss some of these issues in more detail, especially employee privacy, in Chapter 18. At this juncture, however, some brief discussion of the types of activities, technologies, and ethical issues that arise merit consideration.

Employees generally have a positive impression of the impact of technology in the workplace. A *USA Today* poll tracked employees' attitudes toward the benefits of technology in the workplace over a recent 5-year period. In four different ways, these technology users indicated increasing appreciation of the benefits of technology. They said that technology:[45]

- Expands job-related knowledge
- Increases productivity during normal work hours
- Improves communication with clients and customers
- Relieves job stress

Other benefits of technology in the workplace include improved time management, expanded professional networks, development of a competitive edge, balance of work and family needs, and increased productivity during commuting time.[46]

What are some of the technologies that are currently being used in the workplace? Following is a list that is representative of the most popular technologies being used:[47]

- Desktop computer
- Fax machine
- Answering machine
- Voice mail
- Cellular phone
- Internet
- CD-rom
- Beeper-pager
- E-mail
- Intranet/network
- Laptop computer
- Palm computer
- Videoconferencing
- Personal electronic organizer
- Robotics

How do ethical issues arise when companies use technology in the workplace? In a word—surveillance. **Surveillance** involves companies electronically watching, monitoring, or checking up on their employees. The major ethical issue, of course, is the question

Employees of large companies who sneak in visits to non-business-related Web sites during the workday or send personal e-mail messages are more at risk than ever of discovery. As reported in Fast Company [July 2004 i84 p27(2)] by Lucas Conley, companies such as Stellar Internet Monitoring can now track employee Internet use to the tenth of a second. "Such a service, it seems," Conley writes, "is not a tough sell." Today, 52% of large U.S. companies monitor employee's e-mail, and only half of employers who monitor their workers tell them they're being monitored. Are both the employers and employees "basically evil"? Find out by logging on to InfoTrac College Edition at http://www.infotrac-college.com and keying in record number A118534980.

of invasion of privacy. Employees are increasingly concerned about the extent to which their employers are monitoring their work-related activities and possibly their personal lives. Surveillance creates stress. Stress, in turn, may have a detrimental impact on performance or productivity. Thus, surveillance comes with attendant problems. It is useful to consider some of the technologies or ways that companies observe and monitor what their employees are doing on the job.

Monitoring E-Mail and Internet Usage.

The most intensely checked activities of employees are their e-mail and use of the Internet. It is little wonder why employers do this. There is evidence that employees are spending more and more of their time online in such pursuits as personal e-mail, shopping, and visiting entertainment sites. According to an American Management Association study, companies are taking these concerns seriously. They do this by checking their employees' use of these technologies. In 1996, only 35 percent of companies engaged in e-mail monitoring. By 2001, 47 percent of large companies monitored e-mail use on the job. In addition, checking up on the Web site connections employees visited grew significantly.[48]

One major reason employers check up on their employees is that inexpensive technologies are now available that enable them to do so. Most companies today do not monitor telephone calls or postal mail because it is too time-consuming and expensive to do so. However, companies can get software that monitors Internet usage for less than $10 per employee. Consequently, employee monitoring has been increasing at almost twice the rate of employees getting Net access. According to Andrew Schulman, "It's an example of the technology cart driving the policy horse."[49]

An example of the kind of e-mail abuse that plagues companies occurred when a young click-happy financial executive started using his e-mail in a way that eventually led to his dismissal, and this was not even a result of company monitoring. A 24-year-old Princeton graduate moved to Seoul, South Korea, to begin his new assignment for his employer. After being there only a few days, he began to send e-mails to his friends back home in the United States, boasting of his sexual exploits and lavish lifestyle. He sent this message to 11 of his buddies in his former New York office. The message ended up being forwarded to thousands of people on Wall Street and eventually was forwarded to his bosses at his new employer. The young executive was given the option of resigning or being dismissed.[50]

An example of a company monitoring employee e-mail illustrates the kinds of ethical issues that may arise as a consequence of monitoring.

> *Man goes to Doctor for a checkup and a battery of tests. Doctor gets results and sends them via e-mail: Man has a life-threatening disease. Meanwhile, Man's company monitors his e-mail simply to ensure he uses it only for work. Technology officer reads Man's e-mail and blabs to coworkers about Man's diagnosis. Human resources gets involved. CEO gets called in, sees very expensive lawsuit looming. Health insurance company finds out about Man's problem, considers dropping coverage. Big problems for Man. Big problems for Company.*[51]

According to Joe Murphy, managing director of Interactive Integrity, the Internet has introduced enormous compliance risk and ethical issues for companies. There is the potential for sexual harassment, improper contact with competitors, people using chat rooms, pornography, and employees sending out proprietary information over the Net. Technology, therefore, has shifted the burden onto companies to monitor the workplace.[52]

In spite of the potential invasion of privacy issues, companies are monitoring employees' e-mail and Internet usage as never before. Some of the ways in which this is being done include:[53]

- Developing policies prohibiting the Internet for personal use
- Using monitoring software
- Restricting Web site access
- Restricting hours of access

Companies are not only monitoring employee use, but taking actions as well. In a Saratoga Institute/Websense survey of 224 companies, 64 percent said they have disciplined employees for misusing the Net, and one-third fired employees for it.[54] In one of the most dramatic incidences to date, in 2004, Mike Soden, CEO of the Bank of Ireland, resigned from his £1 million-a-year position after he was discovered to be viewing pornographic Web sites on his company's computer. In a routine sweep of company Internet use, it was found that he had breached the company policy by viewing Web sites of what he called an "adult nature." Soden said he felt he had to resign because the policy was his in the first place.[55]

Monitoring of employee activities has not been limited to their use of computers and the Internet. Increasingly, it is being reported that employers are monitoring employees' whereabouts and use of time through global positioning systems. GPS tracking devices permit employers to keep track of employee automobile use; already, companies have been installing such systems and disciplining employees for abusing their work time.[56] Like all issues involving technology, there are two sides of the ethical arguments as to whether such practices are acceptable.

Other Technology Issues in the Workplace

Surveillance extends beyond companies monitoring e-mail and Internet usage. In addition to these activities, other forms of surveillance include monitoring faxes, using video cameras in the workplace, drug testing, doing online background checks, logging photocopies, and recording phone calls. Each of these poses privacy implications that must be considered from an ethical perspective.

The world of security via computers and technology entered a new era on September 11, 2001, as a result of the terrorist attacks on the World Trade Center in New York and the Pentagon in Washington, DC. People's attitudes about privacy changed somewhat as they realized that heightened security checks are needed to guard against terrorist attacks. These added security measures have begun in public institutions (airports, government buildings, large entertainment venues), and they are spilling over into the employment arena as companies become more cautious about their own security. There is already evidence that some use of face-recognition technology, "active" badges that track where you are, and other such technology-driven security measures have landed squarely in the workplace.

Ethical Implications of Cell-Phone Use.
Although e-mail and the Internet most often create ethical problems in the workplace, the use of company-sponsored cell phones by employees represents one of the fastest growing technologies with significant ethical and legal implications. To many, use of a cell phone is a private matter, and most

seem to want to keep it that way. Because companies now make cell phones available to their employees, however, this issue spills over into the business arena and becomes a business ethics topic.

A case occurred in March 2000 that dramatically illustrated this point. As reported in *The Wall Street Journal*, Jane Wagner, a San Francisco-based attorney, was working the kind of fast-paced day that is becoming increasingly common. Ms. Wagner was toting up billable hours on her cell phone for her employer while driving to a scheduled 10 P.M. meeting with a client. This was typical for Ms. Wagner—continuing to make business calls on her cell phone while driving home. This night was out of the ordinary, however. As she talked, her car swerved and struck a 15-year-old who was walking on the shoulder of the road, throwing her fatally-injured body down an embankment. Ms. Wagner later said she didn't even realize she had hit someone. She said it wasn't until morning when she was watching the news while dressing for work that she realized what she had done. She turned herself in and pleaded guilty to hit and run—a felony. The victim's family was seeking $30 million in damages from Ms. Wagner's employer.[57]

A trend with huge implications for employers is the growing number of employees—salespeople, consultants, lawyers, ad executives, and others—who are using cell phones while driving and chalking up sales or billable hours. Sixty-eight percent of the general population say they use a cell phone while driving,[58] and, surely, the percentage is higher among employees. Plaintiffs are increasingly claiming that the employer is partly to blame because it presses employees to work long hours from distant locations, often encouraging them to use cell phones without setting safety guidelines. Research is increasingly documenting the dangers of cell-phone use while driving. A 2004 study by an insurance company found that chatty drivers suffered slower reaction times, took longer to stop, and missed more road signs than drivers who were legally drunk. A new term has already been coined for accidents caused by cellphone-using drivers—DWY—Driving While Yakking.[59]

In another major court case, a New York investment banking firm was sued for damages in federal court by the family of a motorcyclist killed when one of its brokers, using a car phone, ran a red light and struck him. Plaintiffs claimed that employer pressure to contact clients after hours contributed to the tragedy, and the company settled the suit for $500,000. They did not admit any wrongdoing, but wanted to avoid a jury trial.[60]

Cases such as the two described here—both linked to technology, the cell phone—should raise red flags for employers. Few companies have the needed policies on cell-phone use at this time. In addition to cell phones, as wireless or mobile Net access gains in popularity, the same applies to this use of technology. It appears that as high-tech tools extend the workplace into every nook and corner of life, companies have been leaving the responsibility entirely up to the employees. These cases are tragic examples of what can happen when employees, using technology, become too distracted, pressured, or overfocused on their work.[61] These applications of technology in the workplace raise significant ethical issues for business now and in the future.

Unethical Activities by Employees Related to Technology.   In most of the instances described to this point, the employer has had responsibility for the use of technology and its implications. There is a final area that should be mentioned: questionable activities that are the responsibility of the employee. These activities have been aided by computer technologies. In a major study of workers, the following percentages of workers surveyed said they had engaged in this unethical activity during the previous year:[62]

- Created a potentially dangerous situation by using new technology while driving—19 percent
- Wrongly blamed an error the employee made on a technological glitch—14 percent
- Copied the company's software for home use—13 percent
- Used office equipment to shop on the Internet for personal reasons—13 percent
- Used office equipment to network/search for another job—11 percent
- Accessed private computer files without permission—6 percent
- Used new technologies to intrude on coworkers' privacy—6 percent
- Visited porn Web sites using office equipment—5 percent

Company Actions. Companies have many options for addressing the kinds of ethical issues described to this point. A major survey of *Fortune 500* nonmanagement employees revealed that management should define ethical computer use for employees. Options for doing this include company management making these decisions, using the Information Systems Society's code of ethics, and involving employees and users in a collaborative attempt to decide computer ethics. Only about one-half of those surveyed indicated that company guidelines were written and well-known.[63]

The technology we have discussed to this point is computer-driven. Therefore, guidelines for employee computer use would help in many of the arenas described. Several professional societies also offer guidelines for computer use. The Computer Ethics Institute has set forth what it calls its "Ten Commandments of Computer Ethics." These commandments are interesting and useful, and they are summarized in Figure 8-3.

BIOTECHNOLOGY

The twentieth century's revolution in information technology is merging with the twenty-first century's revolution in biotechnology. Indeed, Walter Isaacson has labeled the 2000s as the "biotech century."[64] The seeds for this revolution were spawned in 1953

FIGURE 8-3

Ten Commandments of Computer Ethics

The Computer Ethics Institute has set forth the following ten commandments of computer ethics. These should prove useful to employees and employers alike.

- Thou shalt not use a computer to harm other people.
- Thou shalt not interfere with other people's computer work.
- Thou shalt not snoop around in other people's computer files.
- Thou shalt not use a computer to steal.
- Thou shalt not use a computer to bear false witness.
- Thou shalt not copy or use proprietary software for which you have not paid.
- Thou shalt not use other people's computer resources without authorization or proper compensation.
- Thou shalt not appropriate other people's intellectual output.
- Thou shalt think about the social consequences of the program you are designing.
- Thou shalt always use a computer in ways that ensure consideration and respect for your fellow humans.

SOURCE: Reid Goldsborough, "Computers and Ethics," *Link-Up* (Vol. 17, No. 1, January/February 2000), 9.

when James Watson blurted out to Francis Crick how four nucleic acids could pair to form the self-copying code of a DNA molecule. Now, we are poised for the most significant breakthrough of all time—deciphering the human genome, the 100,000 genes encoded by 3 billion chemical pairs in our DNA. Among other achievements, this accomplishment will lead to the next medical revolution, which will not only increase the natural life span of healthy human beings but will also help to conquer cancer, grow new blood vessels, block the growth of blood vessels in tumors, create new organs from stem cells, and certainly much more.[65]

The field of biotechnology carries with it significant implications for business and for business ethics. In fact, it is spawning a new industry—the biotechnology industry. According to Dr. Alison Taunton-Rigby, president and CEO of Aquila Biopharmaceuticals, Inc., a public life sciences company based in Massachusetts, biotechnology involves "using biology to discover, develop, manufacture, market, and sell products and services."[66] The biotech industry today consists of several small entrepreneurial start-up companies funded largely by venture capitalists, along with 10 to 20 larger, more established companies. Most of the applications of biotechnology will be in health care, the pharmaceutical industry, and agriculture.[67]

Bioethics

A field called **bioethics** has emerged that deals with the ethical issues that are embedded in the use of biotechnology. As new biotech products are developed, thorny ethical issues will undoubtedly arise. In the medical field, for example, you may soon be able to determine the genetic makeup of your baby well before birth. Does this mean that those who control the technology have power over the population? Does it mean that people who can spend the money on customizing their baby's genetic makeup will in turn create an underclass of the genetically less fortunate?[68] These are just some of the ethical issues that arise as we think about their implications in the commercial sphere.

Recently, the question arose regarding the federal government's role in funding stem cell research. One of the actions President George W. Bush took was to appoint a bioethicist, Dr. Leon Kass, to chair a presidential council on bioethics. Dr. Kass was trained both as a doctor and a biochemist before entering the field of bioethics. According to some, he is obsessed with the downside of biological research.[69] Kass has been quoted as saying "Where you have technologies that touch so deeply on the nature of our humanity, [decisions about their use] shouldn't be left to a kind of technological fatalism and free markets." Though Kass does not intend to serve as the nation's bioethics cop, "The task that's been assigned to us," he says, "is not to make arrests and catch scientists. The task is to clarify the issues, to lift the public understanding of the human and moral significance of doing what we're doing."[70]

By 2004, much of the fanfare concerning the President's Council on Bioethics had been eclipsed by the attacks on the World Trade Center and the wars in Afghanistan and Iraq. As new members were being selected for the council in 2004, the issue some called the "politicization of bioethics" hit the headlines. The questions surrounding the appointment of conservatives versus liberals to the council have raised the inevitable issue of political influence in discussions of bioethics. Dr. Kass has received criticism for his careful, methodical views by some, but others have supported him, saying that we should move slowly on bioethical issues. According to one member of the President's Council, Gilbert Meilaender, if the White House has politicized bioethics, it has not occurred in the manner some charge. Meilaender believes that the critics just want to keep bioethics out of the public debate and to keep it in the private domain of a small group of experts. He believes that whereas the experts do have a role, a broader, public discussion of these issues will better illumine them and result in better decisions.[71]

On the business front, some biotechnology companies have adopted the idea of bioethics to guide them in their decision making. A question is being continually raised, however, of whether bioethical decision making is really taking place or whether the companies are using the bioethicists for public relations purposes. Companies such as Geron have pioneered the idea of a corporate bioethics advisory board. When the Jones Institute for Reproductive Medicine began its research on human embryos, it talked up the idea of panels of bioethicists. It has been observed that many companies are savvy enough to know that the greatest single obstacle to utilizing their new technologies is the potential for public backlash.[72]

According to William Saletan, who has written extensively about bioethics, the primary tool bioethicists use is *proceduralism*. This involves elaborate protocols being established that ensure that certain classical worries, such as informed consent, are not violated. The focus, in other words, is being sure that appropriate procedures are being followed rather than on the actual ethical content of the decisions. The worry continues, however, over whether corporate executives and scientists are deceiving their own consciences by focusing on the *how* rather than the *why*, on the *means* rather than the end.[73]

Both critics and supporters say that the use of bioethicists lends companies an air of credibility. The real question is this: Can they really be objective if they are on a company's payroll? Supporters say "yes," that they function like a newspaper ombudsperson who gets paid by the paper to criticize coverage and prevent potential conflicts. Detractors say "no," there's no way around at least the appearance of a conflict of interest if money is changing hands. A real danger is that the participation of bioethicists may be interpreted as a stamp of approval.[74]

Charles Colson has observed that "the biotech revolution has surged forward as the defining issue of this new century. On the one hand, it holds out great promise for medical advances enhancing life and health for all humankind. On the other, it raises unprecedented ethical issues." He goes on to conclude that "the biotech revolution is moving like a steamroller, fueled by huge potential profits, crushing everything— including moral restraint—in its path."[75] We may be too early into the biotechnology revolution to know whether this will turn out to be the case; however, it is important to raise the question of the balance between costs and benefits early on.

It is useful to consider two broad realms of biotechnology to appreciate what each represents in terms of challenges in business ethics: **genetic engineering** and **genetically modified foods (GMFs)**. Genetic engineering, primarily of humans, and genetic engineering of agricultural and food products are both part of genetic science. For discussion, however, we will separate them from one another.

Figure 8-4 on page 278 summarizes a list of several nonprofit bioethics organizations that may be found on the Web.

Genetic Engineering

Two major areas of genetic engineering, or genetic science, seem to capture the public's imagination today. One is stem cell research, and the second is cloning. Both pose huge and interesting challenges for business and business ethics.

FIGURE 8-4

Web Sites of Nonprofit Bioethics Organizations

Bioethics is such an expansive topic that there are many different organizations, especially public action organizations, that provide information regarding specific topics via the World Wide Web. Some of these include the following:

American Society for Bioethics and Humanities (http://www.asbh.org)
The American Society for Bioethics and Humanities (ASBH) is a professional society of more than 1,500 individuals, organizations, and institutions interested in bioethics and humanities. This Web site, established in January 1998, is intended initially to serve as a source of information about ASBH for members and prospective members. It also will serve as a resource for anyone interested in bioethics and humanities by providing a group of additional online resources and links to aid in finding other related information through the Internet.

The GE Food Alert Campaign Center (http://www.gefoodalert.org)
This is a Web page sponsored by the Center for Food Safety. It primarily focuses on genetically engineered foods and issues related to this topic.

National Coalition for Patient Rights (http://www.nationalcpr.org)
This is a nonprofit organization comprised of medical professionals and private citizens focused on confidentiality in health care and privacy legislation.

Do No Harm: The Coalition of Americans for Research Ethics (http://www.stemcellresearch.org)
This organization is a national coalition of researchers, health care professionals, bioethicists, legal professionals, and others dedicated to the promotion of scientific research and health care that does no harm to human life.

The Council for Responsible Genetics (http://www.gene-watch.org)
The council fosters debate on social, ethical, and environmental implications of new genetic technologies. The council publishes "GeneWATCH," a national bulletin on the implications of biotechnology. The site contains testimony presented to the U.S. Congress and position papers, and functions as a legislative clearinghouse.

Bioethics.net (http://www.bioethics.net)
This Web page is quite extensive. It hosts the *American Journal of Bioethics Online* and the Center for Bioethics at the University of Pennsylvania. It has a special section on bioethics for beginners as well as a special section on cloning and genetics.

National Human Genome Research Institute (http://www.nhgri.nih.gov)
This Web site describes the Ethical, Legal, and Social Implications (ELSI) Research program. This program supports basic and applied research that identifies and analyzes the ethical, legal, and social issues surrounding human genetics research. The ELSI Research program currently is the largest federal supporter of bioethics research, with an annual budget of over $12 million.

Stem Cell Research. **Embryonic stem cells**, the basic building blocks that are the progenitors of all other cells, were isolated in 1998 by scientists at the University of Wisconsin. Stem cells are the raw materials upon which a human body is built. Since their isolation, stem cell research has been proliferating around the world. Though the United States has historically been the world leader in biotechnology, some experts say the United States has fallen behind other countries as debate over ethical implications has slowed progress.[76] According to a member of the President's Council on Bioethics, the debate over stem cell research centers on one basic moral question: the moral status of a human embryo—the product of sperm and egg—and what constitutes a human being.[77]

Stem cells come from embryos, and they may be obtained in three ways: frozen embryos, fresh embryos, or cloned embryos. Spare frozen embryos may come from fertility clinics, having been donated by infertile couples who no longer need them for pregnancy. Most ethical guidelines recommend research only on these. Fresh embryos are those that have been specially created for research, usually in a fertility clinic. Embryos can also be created by cloning human cells. In fact, in an example of how stem cell research is outrunning public policy, a Massachusetts company used cloning technology to create human embryos that would yield the cells that might give rise to tissues that would be perfect matches for patients. This technique, known as *therapeutic cloning*, has been the subject of intense debate in Congress, which has been considering legislation to ban such research.[78] The value of stem cells is that they offer the greatest hope for developing treatments for diseases such as cancer, Alzheimer's, Parkinson's disease, and juvenile diabetes.[79] Further, stem cells may be grown into tissues for transplanting into patients who need them for nerve cells, bone cells, or muscle cells.[80]

Throughout much of 2001, President Bush considered the arguments for and against the federal government funding research using stell cells. After much debate, the president decided to proceed, but cautiously. His announced decision was to allow federal government funding for research only on stem cells that have already been harvested. By allowing federally-sponsored research only on existing stem cell lines, where "the life-and-death decision had already been made," the president was able to draw a line on stem cell research that most of the public supported.[81]

By 2004, public support for expanded stem cell research was being backed by voters in a number of key states.[82] In spring 2004, more than 200 House members from both parties signed a letter to President Bush, urging him to broaden his policy on stem cell research, though few expected changes to be made in an election year.[83] Beyond this, California and New Jersey have embarked on their own laws to authorize the cloning of human eggs to create stem cells; the legislatures of seven other states are considering similar bills of their own.[84] In 2004, former president Ronald W. Reagan died after living with Alzheimer's disease for a decade. His wife, Nancy Reagan, had been speaking out for years, advocating expanded stem cell research. Mrs. Reagan was quoted as saying, "Ronnie's long journey has finally taken him to a distant place where I can no longer reach him. Because of this, I'm determined to do whatever I can to save other families from this pain."[85]

Most of the ethical debate over stem cell research has occurred in the public arena, not business. One gets the distinct impression that businesses are ready to move forward once the societal debate begins to show some clarity. A real danger in the debate over the use of embryonic stem cells is the almost irresistible tendency to treat them as "property" ripe for commercial exploitation. The interested parties are not isolated individuals. The beneficiaries are not just the sick, the aged, or the prematurely infirm. Research universities seeking funding and prestige will benefit; pharmaceutical companies seeking new products and investors will benefit; the government has a stake as the United States races with other countries to market therapies for degenerative diseases.[86] The pharmaceutical industry is one of the best illustrations of how companies are already moving on research. In 2004, it was reported that companies such as Johnson & Johnson, Eli Lilly, Abbott Laboratories, Schering, and Wyeth were conducting regenerative research using adult stem cells.[87]

The irony of Nancy Reagan's support of stem-cell research in the name of Ronald Reagan, who held staunch pro-life views, has not escaped political pundits. One Republican aide called the suggestion that a new act in favor of stem-cell research be named for Reagan "unbelievably shameless." Nancy Reagan, however, has joined a diverse bipartisan group that includes Orrin Hatch and Ted Kennedy in support of a new act. Read the current information on stem-cell research and its political ramifications by logging on to InfoTrac College Edition at http://www.infotrac-college.com and keying in record number A118178356.

Cloning.

Stem cell research is well underway. Now, **cloning** is forcing itself into the news. Some scientists say human cloning is a distant project; however, according to some reports, Americans are already lining up to freeze the DNA of their dead loved ones, including pets and racehorses. Several different groups have claimed they are attempting to clone a human being. It is said that the Raelians, a weird but rich and scientifically sophisticated sect from Canada, are trying to "recreate" a dead child at a secret location in the United States.[88]

Actually, there are at least two debates surrounding cloning and genetic science. First, there is the issue of cloning human beings. Second, there is the issue of cloning animals and plants and using genetics to identify and fight diseases. This second quest is currently the primary focus of science. But, it is the fascination with duplicating human beings that arouses the most debate and fear. Surveys in the United States have shown that as many as 90 percent of Americans are against human cloning; in 22 other countries around the world and four U.S. states, human cloning has been declared illegal. In Japan, legislation banning human cloning became effective in June 2001.[89]

Science fiction has portrayed people interested in human cloning as crazed, power-hungry, profit-seeking individuals who exist on the fringes of society. Recently, however, the stuff of fantasy has taken on a new life. In March 2001, a group of controversial scientists—an Italian fertility specialist, an American fertility researcher, and an Israeli biotechnologist—started to tinker with cells in the laboratory and claimed they would have a human clone by 2003.[90] Also in 2001, the FDA cracked down on a group in the United States who had a secret lab where they were trying to clone a human being. Officials believe the lab was set up by Clonaid, a company billed in 1997 as the world's first human cloning company. Other groups have also stated they are trying to clone human beings.[91] In 2004, it was announced in Seoul, Korea, that South Korean scientists had produced the first human cloned embryo.[92]

Another variation of cloning is known as **therapeutic cloning**. Therapeutic cloning uses the same laboratory procedures as reproductive cloning, but its aim is not procreation but rather the creation of a source of stem cells whose properties make them a possible source of replacement tissue for a wide range of degenerative diseases. Opponents of therapeutic cloning are opposed to the creation and destruction of human life for utilitarian ends. In addition, opponents fear the exploitation of women, especially in poor countries, for their eggs. On the other side of the issue, supporters want to give therapeutic cloning a chance because of its possible health advantages.[93]

The possibility of therapeutic cloning has raised nightmare scenarios in the minds of some. The chemicals in the human body were once estimated to be worth 89 cents. Now, however, according to the authors of a provocative, and some would say shocking, new book, body parts in people and in corpses may be worth millions. In *Body Bazaar: The Market for Human Tissue in the Biotechnology Age*, Lori Andrews and Dorothy Nelkin talk optimistically about the commercialization of the human body in pursuit of new pharmaceuticals, organ transplants, and genetic research on individuals alive or dead. The book has ethicists again asking important questions: Do individuals have "rights" to their blood and tissue? Should body parts be bought and sold? Whose body is it, anyway?[94]

Andrews and Nelkin write that "whole businesses are developing around the body business. Companies have sprung up, for example, to make commercial products out of corpses' bones. Some grind up the bones into powder that, when sprinkled on broken live bones, will help them mend." They argue that body parts from the living and the dead are gold mines for pharmaceutical research. Some of the authors' writings raise provocative ethical questions that business must face: Who owns the rights to a corpse? What ethical considerations need to be evaluated when a researcher seeks to do genetic testing on long-deceased individuals? What are the ethical considerations associated with the morbid practice of using human body parts as a means of "expression"? Apparently, an artist in Germany routinely purchases corpses, plasticizes the body parts, and reassembles them, leaving flaps of skin open to display the anatomy. Does this practice debase the sanctity of the human body?[95]

Where does cloning lead? For many, the difficulties arise when biotechnologists leap from stopping diseases to adding advantages—enhancing the genes that make you more intelligent or more musical. According to William Galston, "The species should be how we *are*, not how we *might be*." In *Remaking Eden*, Lee Silver, a Princeton biologist, foresees the possibility of a two-class system, with the rich, genetically-enhanced "GenRich" class lording it over the poorer, inferior "Naturals."[96] The ethical implications of such potential futures for business are mind-boggling.

In a further insight into where cloning may be heading, a 2001 cartoon by Tom Toles depicted a man in an office sticking his head into the office copier; off to the side, there were cloned copies of him coming out of the machine. A sign on the wall stated, "July 2018. The ethical debate, part 2,473,561," and the question posed beneath the cartoon read: "Should employees be allowed to use the office cloning machine for personal business?"

There are currently no federal laws against cloning in the United States. The 2001 restrictions against federally funded stem cell research, however, have curtailed movement because federal funding is often needed for advancement. In a 2002 report on cloning, however, the President's Council on Bioethics proposed a 4-year moratorium on therapeutic cloning and an outright ban on reproductive cloning.[97]

Genetic Testing and Profiling.

One of the most significant areas of potential questionable application of biotechnology is **genetic testing**. Genetic testing flows from genetic profiling. It is said that someday each of us will have a DNA chip that contains all our genetic information. There are positives associated with this. It will help each person manage his or her own personal health risks. It will also help a physician predict how well a patient will respond to various therapies. Future drugs will be developed using genetic information so that the therapy will be coupled with the DNA information. However, **genetic profiling** also provides a perfect means for identifying a person and thus raises questions of privacy and possible discrimination based on genetic factors.[98]

In May 2001, the U.S. Equal Employment Opportunity Commission (EEOC) settled its first court action challenging the use of workplace genetic testing under the Americans with Disabilities Act of 1990 (ADA). The EEOC had sought an injunction against Burlington Northern Santa Fe Railway (BNSF) to end genetic testing of employees who filed claims for work-related injuries based on carpal tunnel syndrome. According to the EEOC, the company's genetic testing program was carried out without the knowledge or consent of its employees, and at least one worker was threatened with termination for failing to submit a blood sample for a genetic test.[99] Under the settlement, BNSF also agreed that it would not analyze blood it had previously obtained, nor would it retaliate against employees who opposed the testing. According to the EEOC, "Our swift action in this case allows Burlington Northern employees to continue to work free of retaliation and future invasions of privacy."[100]

In 2003, the U.S. Senate passed a bill designed to prevent discrimination against persons based on predictive genetic information. The issue then moved on to the House of Representatives, and the bill has not yet been made into law. The proposed bill, the Genetic Information Nondiscrimination Act of 2003, would prohibit employers from using genetic information when making hiring, firing, promotion, or job assignment decisions. Also, employers would have to treat any genetic information in the same way that they treat other confidential information. Opponents to this legislation say that this law targets a problem that does not exist and that except for the Burlington Northern case, genetic profiling has not been a significant workplace issue. In addition, opponents argue that the issues addressed in the proposed legislation are already contained in the Health Insurance Portability and Accountability Act of 1996.[101]

Genetically Modified Foods

Another major category of biotechnology that carries important ethical implications for business is the topic of genetically modified foods. This is especially the case for the multi-billion-dollar agribusiness industry. Many wholesalers and retailers, however, are also involved in the distribution of genetically modified foods. Genetically modified foods (GMFs) are also commonly referred to as *genetically engineered foods (GEFs)*. Extreme critics call them "Frankenfoods," calling attention to the parallels with the mythical character Frankenstein. The world today seems to be divided into those who favor GMFs and those who fear them. Also, a significant number of consumers are simply not informed enough to know but are quick to offer their gut-reaction opinions, usually based on fear rather than facts. Because no one seems to have been "hurt" by GMFs, there is a lot of wild speculation as well as apathy or indifference at work in judging the ethics and implications of GMF.

Scant information is available to the public as to the actual safety or lack of safety of these products because field-testing is continuing. According to L. Val Giddings, vice president for food and agriculture at the Biotechnology Industry Organization, "There is still not so much as a single, solitary sniffle or headache positively linked to their consumption."[102] A British research panel concluded in 2003 that there is no evidence that GM crops now in commercial cultivation are more dangerous to human health than conventional foods.[103] Therefore, the debate seems to hinge on whether the pros or cons of GMFs will win out as the arguments are presented. Beyond that, many people have opinions concerning whether the products or ingredients produced by genetically engineering agricultural products are dangerous or should be more strenuously regulated. In the absence of convincing evidence as to their safety, the major debate seems to be on the degree to which products that contain genetically modified ingredients should be labeled.

Two events introduced the U.S. public's attention to the topic of genetically modified foods. The first was the discovery in September 2000 that genetically engineered animal corn—*potentially* harmful to humans—was found in Taco Bell taco shells. Later it showed up in Safeway Inc.'s house-brand taco shells. The genetically engineered corn, called *Starlink*, is a product that was altered to make it resistant to pests. It contains a foreign protein that is probably safe for human consumption but has some of the chemical characteristics of a human allergen, a term for substances that can trigger anything from a mild allergic reaction to a fatal case of shock. Animal feed, of course, is not supposed to get into the human food supply whether it is genetically modified or not. The event apparently happened by accident, but it represents a case where special tracking of biotech crops might have allowed the industry to identify the corn and remove it.[104]

The second event has been the publicity on the almost universal objection to GMFs in Europe, especially in the European Union (EU). Vocal European objections to GMFs have been around for 3 to 5 years. For the past 3 years, the European Union has banned new bioengineered seeds and crops while it writes laws to govern the sale and distribution of biotech products. A major consequence for U.S. corn growers is that they have been shut out of markets worth about $200 million a year. In Europe, polls show that a majority of people believe that products made from genetically modified organisms (GMOs) are hazardous to their health.[105]

Though public opinion in Europe seems to be squarely in opposition to GMOs, there is some recent (2004) evidence that even the European Union will begin to permit the sale of genetically modified foods as long as they meet new, strict labeling standards. The new EU regulations require that consumers will need to be notified when a product contains as little as 0.9 percent genetically modified ingredients. In further steps, the EU will require that farmers and food packagers "track" the ingredients from farm to store and that Europe will soon lift a 6-year ban on testing new bioengineered crops for cultivation on European soil.[106] In Great Britain, the government has also recently granted permission for a strain of GM maize to be grown commercially as cattle feed.[107]

Americans have been growing and consuming genetically modified foods for years, especially foods such as herbicide-tolerant soybeans and pest-repellent corn, with little evidence of apparent risks to human health or the environment. The U.S. FDA, however, continues to investigate some small number of claims that such consumption has generated allergic reactions.[108]

To date there have been virtually no actual reports of specific health risks of GMOs to consumers. Their safety is a hotly debated topic in scientific and environmental circles, but public opinion polls in the United States find that the issue has yet to ignite much interest or concern among the public at large. According to a nationwide Gallup poll conducted in summer 2001, Americans' basic reaction to the use of biotechnology in agriculture and food production is slightly positive. In this poll, a bare majority, 52 percent, said they support this application; a similar number, 53 percent, are doubtful it poses a serious health hazard to consumers. Opposition to GMOs hovers around one-third of those surveyed.

In general, the poll found that awareness of biotechnology applications remains low but that confidence in the food supply remains high. Will there be a consumer backlash against biotechnology in food production when the public becomes more familiar with it? According to the Gallup poll, familiarity does not seem to breed concern. The poll found that the heaviest opposition and concern about biotech foods are among lower-income and less-educated Americans; those with college degrees and high incomes are the most likely to support the technology and to deny it has serious health hazards.[109]

In spite of public approval or indifference, evidence of some reservations continues. In 2004, for example, Monsanto Co. bowed to resistance from the U. S. food industry and decided not to introduce its new bioengineered wheat. For now, at least, it will not commercialize a type of wheat that can tolerate exposure to its Roundup herbicide, a trait that would make it easier for farmers to chemically kill weeds without harming the wheat itself.[110] Monsanto has met resistance in the past. For example, the company shelved its bug-resistant potato partially because fast-food giants such as McDonald's did not want its French fries caught up in the biotech debate.[111]

In related developments, the debate over whether meat or milk from cloned animals should be sold continues. In the fall of

---

SEARCH THE WEB

RISKS AND BENEFITS OF GENETICALLY MODIFIED FOODS (GMFs)

The appearance of GMFs in the marketplace has resulted in considerable public debate, scientific discussion, and media coverage. A variety of ecological and human health concerns have been raised with the new advances made possible by genetic modification. Do you have a position in the debate? Do you want to learn more about GMFs?

This Web page forum is sponsored by SCOPE (Science Controversies On-Line Partnerships in Education). This Web site has a range of learning resources about GMFs. Among the resources are position papers, commentaries, a reference database, e-mail lists, and other curriculum projects. Check out this site and think about the implications for business ethics.

To learn more about the benefits and risks of GMFs, visit
http://scope.educ.washington.edu/gmfood

2003, the FDA released a report saying that cloned animals pose no greater risk to human health than normally bred animals. This is the first time that a regulatory agency has said that such animals are safe to eat, and it increases the likelihood that the FDA will lift its voluntary ban on the sale of meat, milk, and food products made from cloned animals. Balancing this position, the Center for Science in the Public Interest claims that that evidence is in short supply and that the FDA risk assessment made numerous assumptions that the public may not make.[112]

Labeling. One of the most frequently discussed issues with respect to GMFs is the topic of labeling. Many consumer activists think that, at a minimum, foods that contain genetically engineered contents ought to be labeled as such. The Consumer Federation of America Foundation, for example, has issued a report recommending mandatory labeling and other ways to improve U.S. biotech food regulations. To date, the Food and Drug Administration has not required labeling of GMFs. The FDA has deliberated new rules wherein biotech companies would have to meet with federal regulators before putting a new product on the market, but they would not require special product labels. The FDA has been working on the new guidelines in an attempt to reassure consumers that GMFs are safe. Further, the agency plans to offer guidelines for companies that choose to use labels on a voluntary basis.[113]

In spite of inaction on the part of the FDA, the labeling issue will not go away. Proponents of mandatory labeling argue that the consumer has a right to full disclosure about product contents and that the consumers' right to safety argues that such knowledge should be available to them. Related to this, one of the hottest trends in food marketing is the *non-GMO label*, which stands for "nongenetically modified organisms." Just a few years ago, this was unknown in the United States. Now, however, it is popping up frequently as companies attempt to take strategic advantage of their products that do not contain GMOs. The non-GMO label is now being seen on hundreds of products ranging from pasta, produce, and breakfast cereals to frozen entrees, condiments, and beverages. Industry executives believe this is a fast-growing market segment and, though labels are not mandatory, some consumer segments are attracted to this product feature.

Opponents of mandatory labeling for GMFs argue that there is no evidence that the products have any health hazards and that being required to carry a "genetically engineered" label would stigmatize the food products and raise issues of safety where none exist. They support their argument by pointing to the fact that the FDA has concluded that GMFs are "substantially similar" to conventional foods and thus do not need to be labeled or tested for safety.

The issues of safety and labeling of GMFs are not likely to go away. Special-interest groups on both sides of the debate continue to be active in advocating their points of view. The agribusiness industry continues to argue that the foods are safe and that mandatory testing and labeling are not necessary. Consumer activists, however, have brought together environmentalists, organic farmers, chefs, and religious leaders, and they continue to make the case for rigorous safety testing and labeling.[114] To be sure, all consumer stakeholders are potentially affected by the outcome of these debates, so it is likely that they will continue into the near future.

■ SUMMARY

Business use of technology today is so dramatic that the topic merits a separate chapter. In this chapter, basic concepts such as technology and the technological environment were introduced and defined. The benefits and side effects or hazards of technology were discussed. The symptoms of society's intoxication with technology were outlined. Questions regarding the ethics of technology were raised in two broad domains: information technology and biotechnology.

In the realm of information technology, the category with the most widespread current impact in business, topics included electronic commerce, invasion of privacy via e-commerce, government's involvement in Internet privacy invasion, and business initiatives. Questionable practices and uses of technology were raised, including particular industries such as the porn industry, Internet gambling, and Web-based music services. Computer technology in

the workplace, one of the most significant areas of application, has been used for monitoring e-mail and employee movement, as well as Internet usage and other forms of surveillance. Questions regarding the ethics of new technologies such as cell phones were also raised.

The field of biotechnology was discussed with respect to social and ethical implications. A key topic in this sphere included the new field of bioethics. Two arenas of biotechnology were identified and discussed—that of genetic engineering, to include a discussion of stem cell research, cloning, and genetic testing and profiling; and the general domain of genetically modified foods. It is anticipated that the debate over food safety and labeling will continue for years as different interest groups raise questions about the appropriateness and safety of genetically modified foods.

■ KEY TERMS

bioethics (page 276)
biotechnology (page 263)
chief privacy officer (CPO) (page 268)
cloning (page 279)
electronic commerce (page 264)
embryonic stem cells (page 278)
ethical lag (page 262)
genetic engineering (page 277)
genetic profiling (page 281)

genetic testing (page 281)
genetically modified foods (GMFs) (page 277)
information technology (page 263)
surveillance (page 271)
technological determinism (page 262)
technological environment (page 259)
technology (page 259)
therapeutic cloning (page 280)

■ DISCUSSION QUESTIONS

1. Are there any benefits or negative side effects of technology in business that have not been mentioned in this chapter? Discuss.

2. Do you agree that society is intoxicated with technology? Does this pose special problems for business with respect to the ethics of technology? Will such intoxication blind people to ethical considerations?

3. Do you think business is abusing its power with respect to invasion of privacy of both consumers and employees? What about surveillance? Which particular practice do you think is the most questionable?

4. Is it an exaggeration to question the ethical implications for business of cell phone use? Discuss both sides of this issue.

5. Do you think genetically modified foods raise a legitimate safety hazard? Should government agencies such as the FDA take more action to require safety testing? What about warning labels? Do you think warning labels would unfairly stigmatize GMFs and make consumers question their safety? Is this fair to the GMF industry?

▪ RECOMMENDED CASES

Many of the end-of-text cases may be related to Chapter 8. You may wish to consider studying the following cases with Chapter 8.

Case 12. "JUST BETWEEN FRIENDS: P2P VS. IP." Downloading music from the Internet has become a widespread practice. Is this an acceptable practice because it is giving consumers what they want? Does this practice illustrate piracy of someone else's intellectual property? What role does technology play in this practice. If it is technologically feasible, is it ethical? Where do you draw the line and how?

Case 13. "THIS LITTLE PIGGY: SHOULD THE XENO-PIG MAKE IT TO MARKET?" This case addresses the question of xenotransplantation—the transfer of living cells, tissue, and organs from one species to another, such as from a pig to a human for medical purposes. Is this a case of technological determinism? Should companies be permitted to continue this practice? Is this an ethical practice? Do the benefits outweigh the risks? What ethical principles support or refute this practice?

Case 14. "TOXIC TACOS: THE CASE OF GENETICALLY MODIFIED FOODS." This case explores the issue of genetically modified foods (GMFs). Should we use GMFs because technology has made them available? What are the ethical issues embedded in the controversy over GMFs? Is it acceptable to use GMFs for animals? For humans? If you were crafting policy for GMFs, what would you recommend? What ethical concepts help you decide?

▪ WEB RESOURCES

The URLs listed here are current at the time of publication. Should any of these Web sites change, please search under the company's or organization's name for an updated address.

American Society for Bioethics & Humanities
http://www.asbh.org

Bioethics
http://www.bioethics.net

Computer Ethics Institute
http://www.cpsr.org/program/ethics/cei.html

Council for Responsible Genetics
http://www.gene-watch.org

Corporate Social Responsibility Newswire
http://www.csrwire.com

Council of Ethical Organizations
http://www.corporateethics.com

Ethics Resource Center
http://www.ethics.org

GE Food Alert Campaign Center
http://www.gefoodalert.org

Institute for Business, Technology & Ethics
http://www.ethix.org

International Society for Ethics and Information Technology
http://csethics.uis.edu/inseit

National Human Genome Research Institute
http://www.genome.gov/

National Reference Center for Bioethics
http://www.georgetown.edu/research/nrcbl/bioethics/index.htm

NIH Bioethics Resources on the Web
http://www.nih.gov/sigs/bioethics

Online Privacy Alliance
http://www.privacyalliance.org

President's Council on Bioethics
http://www.bioethics.gov

U.S. Food and Drug Administration
http://www.fda.gov

 InfoTrac® College Edition   http://www.infotrac-college.com

Additional information on the topics discussed in the chapter can be researched by logging onto the InfoTrac College Edition Web site.

■ ENDNOTES

1. John Naisbitt, Nana Naisbitt, and Douglas Phillips, *High Tech/High Touch: Technology and our Search for Meaning* (Nicholas Brealey Publishing Co, 1999).
2. Jay Bookman, "Technology in Your Face," *Atlanta Journal-Constitution*," D1.
3. "Beware of Rental Car Tracking Devices," (http://www.kron4.com, April 29, 2004.
4. *Ibid.*
5. *Webster's Ninth New Collegiate Dictionary* (Springfield, MA: Merriam-Webster, Inc., 1983), 1211.
6. "Technology," *The World Book Encyclopedia* (Chicago: World Book , Inc., 1988), 76.
7. Richard L. Daft, *Management*, 5th ed. (New York: The Dryden Press, 2000), 75.
8. "Technology," *The World Book Encyclopedia*, 77–78.
9. *Ibid.*, 78–79.
10. *Ibid.*, 79.
11. *Ibid.*, 80.
12. *Ibid.*, 80–81.
13. Beverly Kracher and Cynthia L. Corritore, "Is There a Special E-Commerce Ethics?" *Business Ethics Quarterly* (Vol. 14, Issue 1, January 2004), 77.
14. Naisbitt, Naisbitt, and Phillips (1999).
15. John Naisbitt, "High Tech, High Touch," *Executive Excellence* (Vol. 16, No. 12, December 1999), 5ff.
16. *Ibid.* Also see Stephen Goode, "Naisbitt Questions the Future of Technology," *Insight* (June 11, 2001), 37–38.
17. Paul A. Alcorn, *Practical Ethics for a Technological World* (Upper Saddle River, NJ: Prentice Hall), 2001.
18. Ruth Chadwick (ed.), *The Concise Encyclopedia of the Ethics of New Technologies* (Academic Press, 2001).
19. Sandy Reed, "The Ethics of Technology: This Group Looks at Issues for the Next Millennium," *Infoworld* (Vol. 21, Issue 42, October 18, 1999), 79ff.
20. "E-Biz: Down But Hardly Out," *Business Week* (March 26, 2001), 126–130; See also Internet Fraud Watch, http://www.fraud.org/
21. "The Dot Con," *Blink* (Summer 2001), 7.
22. Beverly Kracher and Cynthia L. Corritore, "Is There a Special E-Commerce Ethics?" *Business Ethics Quarterly* (January 2004), 71–94.
23. *Ibid.*, 78–82.
24. "Putting the Ethics in E-Business," *Computerworld* (Vol. 34, No. 45, November 6, 2000), 81ff.
25. "Executives Note Hot Business Topics," *USA Today* (July 26, 2001), 1B.
26. "Exposure in Cyberspace," *The Wall Street Journal* (March 21, 2001), B1.
27. "Privacy Options Are a Blur," *USA Today* (April 10, 2001), 3D.
28. *Ibid.*
29. Donna De Marco, "What's in a Name?" *Insight* (July 30, 2001), 30–31.
30. Mike France, "Why Privacy Notices Are a Sham," *Business Week* (June 18, 2001), 82–83.
31. *Ibid.*, 83.
32. Jason Anders, "Congress Is Wasting No Time in Effort to Address Major Issues Raised by Web," *The Wall Street Journal* (February 27, 2001), B13C.
33. "Privacy Win," *Multinational Monitor* (March 2001), 29.
34. Michelle Kessler, "Position of Privacy Officer Coming into Public Eye," *USA Today* (November 30, 2000), 1B.
35. Jared Sandberg, "The Privacy Officer," *The Wall Street Journal* (July 16, 2001), R10. Also see Steve Ulfelder, "CPOs: Hot or Not?" *Computerworld*, (March 15, 2004), 40.
36. *Ibid.*
37. Kessler, *ibid.*
38. Ulfelder, 40.
39. Timothy Egan, "Technology Sent Wall Street into Market for Pornography," *The Wall Street Journal* (October 23, 2000), A1, A20.
40. Jefferson Graham, "As Napster Shuts, Others Carry the Tune," *USA Today* (July 12, 2001), 3D.
41. Robert Kuttner, "Sorry, But the New Economy Demands New Regulations," *Business Week* (July 30, 2001), 23.
42. "Consumer Group Says Search Engines Use Deceptive Advertising," *The Wall Street Journal* (July 17, 2001), B7. See also Margaret Mannix, "Search Me, Please," *U.S. News & World Report* (July 30, 2001), 37.
43. Margaret Carlson, "Someone to Watch over Me," *Time* (July 16, 2001).
44. Jeremy Wagstaff, "Gone Phishing: Web Scam Takes Dangerous Turn," *Wall Street Journal Europe*, May 28, 2004, A5.
45. Darryl Haralson and Sam Ward, "Technology's Positive Impact," *USA Today* (October 22, 2001), 1B.
46. Amanda Mujica, Edward Petry, and Dianne Vickery, "A Future of Technology and Ethics," *Business and Society Review* (Vol. 104, Number 3, 1999), 279–290.
47. *Ibid.*, 280.
48. "Big Bro Is Eye-ing Your E-Mail," *Business Week* (June 4, 2001), 30.
49. Janet Kornblum, "The Boss Is Tracking Moves of a Third of Online Workers," *USA Today* (July 10, 2001), 3D.

50. Andrew Ross Sorkin, "An E-Mail Boast to Friends Puts Executive out of Work," *The New York Times* (May 22, 2001).

51. John Galvin, "The New Business Ethics: Cheating, Lying, Stealing—Technology Makes It Easy, Get Used to It." *Smartbusinessmag.com* (June 2000), 86.

52. *Ibid.*, 88.

53. "Keeping Tabs on Employees Online," *Business Week* (February 19, 2001), 16.

54. John Galvin, 88.

55. Gary Duncan, "Bank Chief Caught Out by Routine Surveillance," *The Times* (May 31, 2004), 19.

56. Charles Forelle, "On the Road Again, But Now the Boss Is Sitting Beside You," *The Wall Street Journal* (May 14, 2004), A1.

57. Sue Shellenbarger, "Should Employers Play a Role in Safe Use of Cellphones in Cars?" *The Wall Street Journal* (July 18, 2001), B1.

58. "Driving and Dialing," *Business Week* (July 23, 2001), 16.

59. Trish Worron, "Cellphones Don't Ring My Chimes," *The Toronto Star* (January 2004).

60. Shellenbarger, B1.

61. *Ibid.*

62. Mujica, Petry, and Vickery, 286.

63. Thomas Hilton, "Information System Ethics: A Practitioner Survey," *Journal of Business Ethics* (December 2000), 279–284.

64. Walter Isaacson, "The Biotech Century," *Time* (January 11, 1999), 42–43.

65. *Ibid.*

66. Alison Taunton-Rigby, "Bioethics: The New Frontier" (Waltham, MA: The Sears Lectureship in Business Ethics, Center for Business Ethics, Bentley College, April 19, 2000), 7.

67. *Ibid.*, 7–8.

68. Maggie Biggs, "In Implementing Emerging Technology, We May Face Thorny Ethical Problems," *Infoworld* (October 16, 2000), 106.

69. "Leon Kass, Philosopher-Politician: The President's Choice for Bioethicist-in-Chief," *The Economist* (August 18, 2001), 25.

70. Bret Stephens, ". . . And the President's New Ethicist," *The Wall Street Journal* (August 14, 2001), A14.

71. Gilbert Meilaender, "The Politics of Bioethics; In Defense of the Kass Council," The Weekly Standard (April 12, 2004). Also see James L. Merriner, "Bush's Bioethics Chief Takes a Licking, Unfairly," *Chicago Sun-Times* (March 19, 2004), 51.

72. "Bioethics: Wanna Buy a Bioethicist?" *Christianity Today* (October 1, 2001), 32–33.

73. *Ibid.*

74. Nell Boyce, "And Now, Ethics for Sale," *U.S. News & World Report* (July 30, 2001), 18–19.

75. Charles Colson, "The New Tyranny: Biotechnology Threatens to Turn Humanity into Raw Material," *Christianity Today* (October 1, 2001), 128.

76. Kerry Capell, "At Risk: A Golden Opportunity in Biotech," *Business Week* (September 10, 2001), 85–87.

77. John Heys, "University Hosts Forum on Ethics of Stem Cell Research," *Knight Ridder Tribune Business News* (March 4, 2004), 1.

78. Sheryl Gay Stolberg, "Company Using Cloning to Yield Stem Cells," *The New York Times* (July 13, 2001).

79. Tim Friend, "The Stem Cell Hard Sell," *USA Today* (July 17, 2001), 6D.

80. Rick Weiss, "Which Life Matters More?" *The Washington Post National Weekly Edition* (July 23–29, 2001), 31.

81. Nancy Gibbs and Michael Duffy, "We Must Proceed with Great Care," *Time* (August 20, 2001), 12–23.

82. "Survey: Expanded Stem Cell Research Backed by Strong Majority of Voters in 18 States," *PR Newswire* (April 26, 2004).

83. Debra Rosenberg and Claudia Kalb, "Stem Cells: A Bipartisan Push for More Lines," *Newsweek* (May 17, 2004), 10.

84. Margot Roosevelt, "Stem Cell Rebels," *Time* (May 17, 2004), 49.

85. "Strong Plea from a Strong Lady," *CBS News.Com*, May 10, 2004.

86. Kenneth Woodward, "A Question of Life or Death," *Newsweek* (July 9, 2001), 31.

87. Arlene Weintraub, "Biotech Frontier: Repairing the Engines of Life," *Business Week* (May 24, 2004), 99–106.

88. "Special: America's Next Ethical War," *The Economist* (April 14, 2001), 21–24.

89. "After Darwin, Ethics Again," *Far East Economic Review* (March 22, 2001), 40–41.

90. "Science and Technology: Cloning Around," *The Economist* (March 17, 2001), 79–80.

91. Nell Boyce and David Kaplan, "The God Game No More," *U.S. News & World Report* (July 9/July 16, 2001), 20–21.

92. Nicholas Wade, "Human Cloning Marches On, Without U.S. Help," *The New York Times* (February 14, 2004), 12 WK.

93. "Pregnant Pause," *The Economist* (January 22, 2004).

94. Quoted in Elizabeth M. Whelan, "Biomedical Prostitution?" *Insight* (May 28, 2001), 27.

95. *Ibid.*

96. "America's Next Ethical War," *The Economist* (April 14, 2001), 2122.

97. Wade (2004), 12.

98. Taunton-Rigby, 18–19.

99. "Genetic Discrimination," *Multinational Monitor* (May 2001), 30.

100. "EEOC Settles Genetics Suit with Burlington Northern," *The Wall Street Journal* (April 19, 2001), B10.

101. Mark Hoffman, "Genetic Bias Legislation Not Needed, Some Say," *Business Insurance* (October 20, 2003), 4.

102. L. Val Giddings, "No: These Crops Pass Multiple Tests Before Approval and Are a Boon to the World's Hungry," *Insight* (August 6, 2001), 43.

103. "Genetically Modified Food: In a Stew," *The Economist* (July 26, 2003), 10.

104. Paul Raeburn, "After Taco Bell: Can Biotech Learn Its Lesson?" *Business Week* (November 6, 2000), 54.

105. William Drozdiak, "Look for the European Union Label," *The Washington Post National Weekly Edition* (April 16–22, 2001), 20.

106. Scott Miller, "EU's New Rules Will Shake Up Market for Bioengineered Food," *The Wall Street Journal* (April 16, 2004), A1.

107. "GM Farming: Frankenfood Approved," *The Economist* (March 13, 2004), 57.

108. *Ibid.*

109. Lydia Saad, "Biotech Food Remains Fairly Obscure to Most Americans," The Gallup Organization Poll Analysis (August 6, 2001); http://www.gallup.com.

110. Scott Kilman, "Monsanto Drops Plans for Now to Make Bioengineered Wheat," *The Wall Street Journal* (May 11, 2004), A2.

111. *Ibid.*

112. Elizabeth Weise, "Cloned Food Gets Closer to Market," *USA Today* (October 31, 2003), 5A.

113. "FDA Developing GM Food Guidelines; New Rules Fall Short of Label Requests," *Chemical Market Reporter* (January 22, 2001), 13.

114. For an interesting discussion of the environmentalists' viewpoint, see Jonathan Rauch, "Will Frankenfood Save the Planet?" *The Atlantic Monthly* (October 2003), 103–108.

Chapter 9

ETHICAL ISSUES *in the* GLOBAL ARENA

CHAPTER LEARNING OUTCOMES

After studying this chapter, you should be able to:

1 Identify and describe the concepts of internationalization and globalization of business.
2 Summarize the arguments for and against globalization.
3 Explain the evolving role of and problems with multinational corporations in the global environment.
4 Recognize the major ethical challenges of operating in the multinational environment.
5 Describe ISCT and the concepts of hypernorms and moral free space.
6 Discuss strategies for improving global ethics.
7 Enumerate international rights and moral guidelines for improving business operations in the global sphere.

The rise of global business as a critical element in the world economy is one of the most significant developments of the past 50 years. This period has been characterized by the rapid growth of direct investment in foreign lands by the United States, by countries in Western Europe, by Japan, and by other industrialized countries as well. In the United States, domestic issues have been made immensely more complex by the escalating international trend. At the same time, the internationalization of business has created unique problems of its own. It no longer appears that international markets can be seen as opportunities that may or may not be pursued. Rather, international markets now are seen as natural extensions of an ever-expanding marketplace that must be pursued if firms are to remain competitive. Only recently has there been evidence of a backlash against global business. The attacks on the World Trade Center on September 11, 2001, the most shocking development to date, have been seen by many as an attack on global capitalism, especially that practiced by the United States. This event likely will modify in yet unseen ways the practice of global business and its ramifications for business ethics.

Peter Drucker has termed the expanded marketplace the **transnational economy**. He goes on to say that, if business expects to establish and maintain leadership in one country, it must also strive to hold a leadership position in all developed markets worldwide. This apparent need helps explain the worldwide boom in transnational investments.[1] One early definition of this transnational or global economy was as follows: trade in goods, a much smaller trade in services, the international movement of labor, and international flows of capital and information.[2] In recent years, we have seen the globalization trend continue, but its critics continue to oppose many of these efforts. In the United States, for example, arguments over the outsourcing of jobs to lesser developed countries has become a subject of national debate.

The complexity introduced by the transnational economy and the internationalization of business is seen clearly in cases in which ethical issues arise. At best, business ethics is difficult when we are dealing with one culture. Once we bring two or more cultures into consideration, it gets extremely complex. Managers have to deal not only with differing customs, protocol, and ways of operating but also with differing concepts of law and notions of what is acceptable or unacceptable ethical behavior. All of this is then exacerbated by the fact that world political issues become intertwined. For example, what might be intended as an isolated corporate attempt to bribe an official of a foreign government, in keeping with local custom, could explode into major international political tensions between two or more countries.

THE NEW, NEW WORLD OF INTERNATIONAL BUSINESS

We have traversed through several different eras in the internationalization of business since the post-World War II decade (1945–1955). There have been the Growth Years (1955–1970), the Troubled Years (1970–1980) and the New International Order (1980-present), according to one international business expert.[3] The New, New World of international business and business ethics can be said to have begun in the fall of 1999. At that time, the World Trade Organization (WTO) was meeting in Seattle, and there were massive demonstrations and protests outpouring into the streets. The WTO talks collapsed as 50,000 protestors rioted, expressing extreme hostility and violence toward the idea of global business.[4] This backlash against globalism continued with massive demonstrations in Washington, DC, in April 2000, Prague in the fall of 2000, Quebec in April 2001, Genoa during the summer of 2001, and Cancun during 2003. On a lesser scale, it continued through the G8 meeting of world leaders in Sea Island, Georgia, in the summer of 2004, though the protests were moderated.

If this backlash against global business represented one of the defining moments in the New, New World of international business, the second defining moment had to be the terrifying attacks on the World Trade Center in New York City and the Pentagon in Washington on September 11, 2001, resulting in massive death and destruction. A number of observers have claimed that the hostile attacks against the twin towers of the World Trade Center represented an attack on America's leading role in global business and all it stands for. Though it is hard to know whether this is a valid interpretation, many feel that it is and, in any event, this horrific incident marks a moment in time when world trade and commerce will never be the same or be seen in the same light. This significant act of mass murder and destruction will doubtless change global business and will inevitably impact the related concerns of global business ethics and global corporate citizenship.

First, it is helpful to consider again what global business really means. Second, it is useful to briefly consider some of the sentiments behind the continuing protests against globalism, because this new reality of world attitudes and questions being raised about global capitalism cannot be ignored.

Concepts of Global Business

There are a number of different terms used to describe the trends in global business over the past several decades. Some of the more prominent ones include internationalization, globalization, globalism, and global capitalism. Countless businesses today have become internationalized but not necessarily globalized. **Internationalization** may be thought of as a "process by which firms increase their awareness of the influence of international activities on their future and establish and conduct transactions with firms from other countries."[5] Some of the characteristics of internationalization include exporting, acting as licensor to a foreign company, establishing joint ventures outside the home country with foreign companies, and establishing or acquiring wholly owned businesses outside the home country.[6]

In contrast, the terms **globalism** or **globalization** suggest the economic integration of the globe. Globalization refers to "global economic integration of many formerly national economies into one global economy."[7] This is made possible by free trade, especially by free capital mobility, and by easy or uncontrolled migration. Whereas internationalization simply recognizes that nations increasingly rely on understandings among one another, globalization is the "effective erasure of national boundaries for economic purposes."[8] Though these are technical distinctions that are helpful to be aware of, it is not always clear when people talk about globalization whether they are just using it as another term for internationalization of business or seeing it as global economic integration. Sometimes observers are just referring to global capitalism, which is the system of free movement of resources around the world. Obviously, true globalization is an extreme status that has not yet been achieved, but one that many hold as an ultimate aspiration.

According to *Business Week*, globalization today is a term that has come to encompass everything from "expanded trade" and "factories shifting around the world" to the "international bodies that set the rules for the global economy" (i.e., World Trade Organization, International Monetary Fund and the World Bank).[9] For our purposes, *Business Week*'s broad concept of globalism or globalization probably fits best. It encompasses both internationalization and trends toward globalization, and invokes the roles of the major international organizations. We should remember, however, that we often need to probe deeply to figure out how someone is using these terms, for they may mean different things to different people.

Continuing Backlash Against Globalization

We stated earlier that there has been an evident backlash against globalization that has been most apparent since the protests in Seattle in the fall of 1999 against the activities of the World Trade Organization (WTO). The protestors at the Seattle meeting have been described in various ways. They have been identified as a peculiar meld of extreme left-ists and rightists, trade unionists, radical environmentalists, and self-appointed representatives of civil society insisting on saving the poor people of developing countries from economic development.[10] They have also been described as a visible coalition between labor and environmentalists—"teamsters and turtles"—as one sign said, as well as other key constituencies, such as human rights activists.[11] In short, they are special-interest groups committed to halting the expansion of global capitalism and trade.

The backlash against globalization that began in Seattle has been perpetuated at a number of important, global meetings since then. After Seattle came the meeting of the IMF and the World Bank in Washington, DC, in April 2000. These organizations were accused by environmental and antipoverty groups of inflicting misery and poverty on developing nations. Next came the European meeting of the IMF and World Bank in Prague in the fall of 2000, and a meeting of the heads of state of 34 nations in Quebec City in April 2001 to discuss a hemispheric free-trade zone.

The height of protest and destruction came in Genoa, Italy, in the summer of 2001 at the G8 Summit meeting of the eight wealthiest countries in the world. There were at least 2 days of violent riots that resulted in death and destruction. The violence at the G8 Summit shocked the world. One positive outcome of the Genoa meetings was an exposure of and split within the antiglobalization ranks between those who want to peacefully reform global capitalism and the anarchists who want to destroy it.

Other protest meetings were planned for Washington, DC, in September 2001, but these meetings were postponed in the aftermath of the attacks on the World Trade Center and the Pentagon. Protestors promised to continue their opposition at future meetings, saying that the attacks in New York and Washington were a direct result of U.S. foreign policy and that only an end to global capitalism would ensure safety for all.[12] Surely, there was more behind the terrorism than opposition to global business, but this is how it was seen by many.

The controversy surrounding globalization has continued in meetings of international bodies. In recent years, the breakdown of trade talks in Cancun in 2003 is one of the most significant examples. Many poor countries were counting on the WTO's Fifth Ministerial Conference in Cancun, Mexico, to improve the status of poor countries relative to developed countries, but the talks failed and were closed when it was apparent progress was not being made.[13] One analyst held that the trade talks failed "because of intransigence and brinkmanship by both rich and poor countries; because of irresponsible and inflammatory behavior by NGOs; and because of the deeply flawed decision-making system of the WTO itself."[14] Another analyst, Lori Wallich, director of Public Citizen's Global Trade Watch, said the trade talks failed because the really important issues were never discussed. Wallich said, "No one is calling for an end to trade or trade rules. But what will those rules be, and who will write them?"[15] This seems to be at the center of the controversy that aligns the rich nations against the poor.

Two recent issues have heightened sensitivities, especially in the United States, toward globalization: the trend toward the outsourcing of jobs to less-developed nations, and the 10-year birthday of NAFTA.

In the past few years, no other single issue has heightened debate over globalization in the United States more than the trend toward companies moving jobs offshore. First, it was manufacturing jobs. Recently, is has been technical jobs including higher paying white-collar jobs in the information technology industry. Economists and social scientists on both sides of this issue are debating it continuously, but public opinion polls show that **outsourcing** (also called **offshoring**) jobs abroad is unpopular. In an April 2004 *Harris/USA Today* poll, for example, 68 percent of Americans said that the outsourcing of jobs abroad was bad for the economy.[16] This opinion has been registered in spite of the jobs data, which show little impact on aggregate job losses being attributed to the off-shoring trend.[17] During difficult economic times, it is not surprising that public opinion may begin to see the negatives more clearly than the positives, and this has definitely happened with the outsourcing of jobs to other countries.

The second major issue to bring the subject of globalization into renewed debate was the 2004 10-year anniversary of the passage of the **North American Free Trade Agreement (NAFTA)**. NAFTA, passed in 1994, brought under one canopy three significantly different economies—the wealthy United States, the middle-class Canada, and striving Mexico. According to one observer, the pain of NAFTA has been felt most in the Midwest, where manufacturing jobs have been lost to Mexico and Canada, and are now being lost to China and other developing countries. It is believed that NAFTA-related job losses have been amplified by other jobs lost to globalization and that NAFTA has become the "symbol of all of that pain."[18] It is apparent that the concern over moving jobs offshore and the anniversary of NAFTA have fueled antagonism toward globalization in recent years.

The New, New World of globalization is one in which the pros and cons of globalization are now back on the table for consideration and discussion. Many observers think globalization is inevitable; an opposing group thinks a form of "globophobia" has set in. The debate on globalization is likely to continue for some time.

The Center for the Study of American Business recently published a major report on the pros and cons of globalization. They argued that on one side we see the "globalists," who strongly advocate open markets with private firms moving freely across the globe. They believe that investors, consumers, employees, and environmentalists are better off due to globalization. On the other side are the "antiglobalists," who have taken to the streets to protest the expansion and greed of corporate global enterprises. They believe that globalization is responsible for the destruction of local environments and emerging economies, abuses of human rights, the undermining of local cultures, and the sovereignty of nation-states.

The antiglobalists also decry the power of international bodies, notably the World Trade Organization, the International Monetary Fund, and the World Bank.[19] Figure 9-1 on page 296 summarizes some of these two groups' views on globalization as it affects consumers, workers, the environment, developing nations, and human rights. It should be clear from these pros and cons that globalization has significant ethical issues embedded in it for stakeholders.

Against this backdrop of the New, New World of business that we now find ourselves in, we can consider some of the ongoing ethical challenges faced by **multinational corporations (MNCs)** as they do business in the global sphere.

In an article in The Nation (2 February v278 i4 p10), Eric Alterman gives a concise history of NAFTA on the occasion of its tenth anniversary, reminding us that "elite media opinion was virtually unanimous in favor of the treaty." Ten years on, Alterman suggests, the most successful aspect of the treaty is the leverage it gave U.S. corporations over their workers. Faced with the threat of their jobs going over the border, U.S. workers were forced to back down on demands for better pay or working conditions. Nor has the treaty improved working conditions in Mexico. Read more about NAFTA's impacts by logging on to InfoTrac College Edition at http://www.infotrac-college.com and keying in record number A118178356.

MNCS AND THE GLOBAL ENVIRONMENT

Not all problems of operating in a global business environment are attributable to MNCs. However, MNCs have become the symbolic heart of the problem because they represent the prototypical international business form. Whereas in 1962 almost 60 percent of the largest corporations in the world were U.S.–based, it has been assumed for years that they were the major targets of the antiglobalization movement. In modern times, American

FIGURE 9-1

The Pros and Cons of Globalization

		Globalists	Antiglobalists
Impact On:	Consumers	Open markets allow for free trade of goods and services, lower costs, greater efficiency. Lower prices, greater variety of goods and services, rising living standards.	Benefits the wealthy and further impoverishes the poor. Widening wealth gap worldwide. Harmful to low-income consumers.
	Employees	Faster economic growth; higher wages; more employment; improved working conditions.	Globalism places profits above people—depressing wages, displacing workers, undermining workers' rights.
	Environment	Global capitalism means rapid economic growth, resources necessary to clean up environments, development of more efficient CO_2-reducing technologies, protection of ecosystems; pollution reduction.	Results in exploitation and destruction of ecosystems in name of corporate greed. Ignores adverse impacts on environments. More pollution, especially carbon dioxide. Exacerbated global warming.
	Developing Nations	Open markets, cross-border investments are keys to national economic development. Higher standards of living, better working conditions, cleaner environments.	Global capitalism, world trade bodies, world financial institutions conspire to keep developing nations in debt, destroys local economies, further impoverishes peoples.
	Human Rights	Free and open markets create cultures/institutions supporting rule of law and free expression. Spreads economic/political freedom to far corners of world (e.g., Taiwan and South Korea).	In blind pursuit of profits, global corporations ignore abuses of human rights, including political and religious oppression, false imprisonment, torture, free speech, abuses of workers, especially women and children.

SOURCE: Summarized from Robert Batterson and Murray Weidenbaum, *The Pros and Cons of Globalization* (St. Louis: Center for the Study of American Business, January 2001), 3–12.

MNCs are no longer dominant. Today, only 185 of 500 of the largest MNCs in the world are U.S.–based. The European Union has 126 and Japan has 108. Further, MNCs of developing countries, such as Mexico's Cemex, are sprouting up.[20] The size of the MNCs is another reason they are highlighted. According to *Global, Inc.*, only 47 of the 100 largest "economies" of the world are now nation-states. The other 53 are MNCs. For example, Exxon Mobil Corp., the world's largest company in terms of sales, has annual revenues that exceed the gross domestic product (GDP) of all but 20 of the world's 220 nations.[21]

Changed Scope and Nature of MNCs

Over the years, both the scope and the nature of MNCs have changed. In the early 1900s, the United Fruit Company was growing bananas in Central America and achieving a degree of notoriety for its "invasion" of Honduras. Another wave of MNCs was in the extractive industries (oil, gas, gems). Today, financial institutions, chemical companies, pharmaceutical companies, manufacturers, and service firms represent the kinds of enterprises that may be found operating in the global business environment.

The investment of U.S.–based MNCs has been phenomenal over the past three decades or more, growing to well into the hundreds of billions of dollars. We should also note that the most challenging situation for MNCs is when they are operating in so-called emerging nations, developing countries, or **less-developed countries (LDCs)**, where charges of exploitation and abuse of power seem more plausible. These situations are ripe for charges of capitalist imperialism in struggling economies, and they are often cited by the antiglobalists.

Underlying Challenges in a Multinational Environment

There are at least two underlying and related challenges or problems as firms attempt to operate in a multinational environment. One problem is *corporate legitimacy* as the MNC seeks a role in a foreign society. The other problem is the fundamentally *differing philosophies* that may exist between the firm's home country and the host country in which it seeks to operate.[22] These two challenges set the stage for examining how ethical problems arise in the global environment.

Corporate Legitimacy. For an MNC to be perceived as legitimate in the eyes of a host country, it must fulfill its social responsibilities. As we discussed earlier, these include economic, legal, ethical, and philanthropic responsibilities. Larger firms, in particular, are seen as outsiders, and the expectations on them are greater than on smaller, less visible firms. Further, the similarities and differences between the cultures of the two countries affect the perceived legitimacy. For example, an American firm operating in Canada is not likely to experience major problems. An American or a Western firm operating in Iraq, however, could be perceived as quite alien.[23] Differences between the values and lifestyles of managers who live in the two countries could pose serious legitimacy problems. If a host country finds the lifestyles or values repugnant—as many LDCs may well find the materialistic lifestyles and values of managers from advanced economies — legitimacy may be difficult to achieve.

Another, perhaps more basic, barrier to achieving legitimacy is the inherent conflict that may exist between the interests of the MNC and those of the host country. The MNC is seeking to *optimize globally*, while host governments are seeking to *optimize locally*. This may pose little difficulty for an MNC operating in a developed country, where macroeconomic or regulatory policies are sophisticated and appropriate. But it may pose serious problems in the LDCs, where there is often the perception that MNCs are beyond the control of local governments. In these latter situations, especially, it is not uncommon to see the local government impose various control devices, such as indigenization laws requiring majority ownership by locals, exclusion of foreign firms from certain industries, restrictions on foreign personnel, or even expropriation.[24]

Part of the reason MNCs have difficulty achieving legitimacy is a reaction to the real or perceived conflicts between the interests of the firm and those of the host country or government that place the MNC in a "no-win" situation. If the MNC tries to bring in the latest labor-saving technology, this may conflict with the perceived need for labor-creating technology in high-unemployment-prone LDCs. If the MNC repatriates large parts of its profits, this may be seen as depriving the local economy of new wealth. If the MNC reinvests the profits locally, this may be perceived as furthering its control over the economy. If the MNC pays market rate wages, this may be seen as exploiting labor with low wage rates. If the MNC pays a premium for labor, this may be seen as skimming the cream of the local labor supply and thus hurting local businesses that cannot afford to pay a premium. Consequently, whatever it does, the MNC is a convenient target for criticism from some faction or stakeholders. In this sometimes hostile environment, legitimacy can be both elusive and fleeting—difficult to get and even harder to keep.[25]

Differing Philosophies Between MNCs and Host Countries.

Closely related to the legitimacy issue is the dilemma of MNCs that have quite different philosophical perspectives from those of their host countries. The philosophy of Western industrialized nations, and thus their MNCs, focuses on economic growth, efficiency, specialization, free trade, and comparative advantage. By contrast, LDCs, for example, have quite different priorities. Other important objectives for them might include a more equitable income distribution or increased economic self-determination. In this context, the industrialized nations may appear to be inherently exploitative in that their presence may perpetuate the dependency of the poorer nation.[26]

These philosophical differences build in an environment of tension that sometimes results in stringent actions being unilaterally taken by the host country. During the 1970s, for example, the environment for MNCs investing in LDCs became much more harsh. Some of these harsh actions initiated by the host countries included outright expropriation (as occurred in the oil industry) and creeping expropriation (as occurred in the manufacturing industries when foreign subsidiaries were required to take on some local partners). Other restrictions included limits on profits repatriation.[27] As a result of the dilemmas that the MNCs face, it is easy to understand why philosopher Richard DeGeorge has argued that "First World MNCs are both the hope of the Third World and the scourge of the Third World."[28]

Thus, MNCs increasingly find themselves in situations where their very legitimacy is in question and their philosophical perspective is radically different from that of their host countries. Added to this are the normal problems of operating in a foreign culture with different types of governments, different languages, different legal systems, diverse stakeholders, and different social values. One could well argue that ethical challenges are built into this environment. MNCs are attempting to bridge the cultural gaps between two peoples; yet, as they attempt to adapt to local customs and business practices, they are assailed at home for not adhering to the standards, practices, laws, or ethics of their home country. Indeed, these pose ethical dilemmas for MNCs. Figure 9-2 graphically depicts the dilemma of MNCs caught between the characteristics and expectations of their home country and those of one or more host countries.

Other MNC-Host Country Challenges

Globalization is "one of the most powerful and pervasive influences on nations, businesses, workplaces, communities, and lives at the end of the 20th century," according to Rosabeth Moss Kanter, in *World Class: Thriving Locally in a Global Economy.*[29] Recent research suggests that global issues are at the forefront of CEOs' agendas. According to Richard Cavanagh, president and CEO of The Conference Board, a hot topic has been "navigating the management maze of globalization."[30] As part of this, challenges facing business have been significant in the social values and ethics arenas.

FIGURE 9-2

The Dilemma of the Multinational Corporation

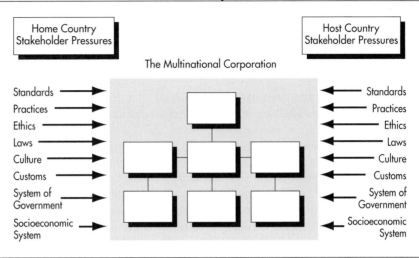

There are so many issues characterizing the challenges between MNCs and host countries that it is almost impossible to draw limits on them. However, we must limit our focus in this chapter. Before discussing a few select ethical issues in the next section, we will first attempt at least to identify what some of these broader challenges are. The issues we will touch on include the cultural aspects of global business, business/government interactions in global operations, management and control of resources in global operations, and, finally, exploration of global markets.[31]

Facing Cultural Differences.

It has been argued that the most significant reason why MNC managers fail is their inability to cope with the foreign cultural environment. Managers and companies experience culture shock when they are faced with cultures and languages that are significantly different from their own. Culture becomes one of the most critical make-or-break factors in successful multinational corporate operations. Culture, customs, language, attitudes, and institutions vary from country to country, and these differences pose sometimes insurmountable obstacles to success for MNCs. Sometimes it is difficult to differentiate a cultural issue from an ethical issue in this environment.

Business and Government Differences.

Beyond the differences that stem from cultural variables, the interaction of the business and government sectors poses challenges for MNC executives. Depending on the region of the world and industry under consideration, the extent of the business/government interactions may vary widely. In worldwide financial services, for example, heavy regulation was typical until the 1980s, when deregulation began in the United States and spread to other countries as well. Deregulation came fast to world banking, yet now some re-regulation is occurring.

Government continues to be very important in some countries. "Japan, Inc.," for example, refers to the close-knit relationship between the Japanese government and the private sector. By contrast, government and business are more at arm's length in the United States. In Korea, government has always been influential, and only in recent years has the banking sector been privatized. In Europe, government has been intimately involved in business and banking from time to time. The European Union thinks differently about the government's role in antitrust regulation than that found in the United States. Many key industries have been nationalized in Great Britain, depending on which political party is in power.[32]

Management and Control of Global Operations.

Two issues are worthy of mention here. One issue is *organizational structure and design*, and the other issue is *human resource management*. MNCs must employ a multiplicity of organizational approaches in their markets. This is in significant part due to host government regulations. MNC management becomes complex when the firm licenses in Country A, has joint ventures in Country B, and countertrades in Country C. In each environment, the firm faces different organizational challenges. A second major topic that needs to be mentioned is the proper use of human resources. In the arena of staffing, a question arises concerning the tactical use of home versus host country nationals. Use of each implies different costs and benefits for the firm. Other critical human resource issues include selection and training.[33]

Exploration of Global Markets.

A final topic in this section is the exploration of global markets as a vital MNC-host country challenge. Although U.S. MNCs dominated world markets for a period of time, this is no longer the case. Today, we have a world of intense competition among firms all over the globe. In the past 20 years, there has been a remarkable resurgence, not only from Japan and the European economies but from some other countries as well (e.g., China, Korea, Latin America). One major issue in this general topic is the question of strategic alternatives that may be used by MNCs considering expansion into new foreign markets. Various strategies involving products and promotions are possible. Relevant factors in such strategic planning include the product function or need satisfied, conditions of product use, consumers' ability to buy, and communications strategy.[34]

Another major issue surrounds the pursuit of developing Third World markets. Marketing concepts for Asia, Africa, and some countries in Latin America may differ markedly from those we have become accustomed to in the United States. This category of issue is quite important in connection with our discussion of global ethics, because less-developed countries pose significant temptations to MNCs to exploit and cut corners. International expert Richard D. Robinson suggests that we need to be sensitive to the long-run national interests of such countries. He advocates three levels of sensitivity. First, management of MNCs should be sensitive to the need to *modify or redesign products* so that they will be appropriate for their intended markets. An example of this was a truck manufacturer that modified its truck design to accommodate the rough roads, extreme heat, and high elevations found in Turkey. Second, management must be sensitive to the *impacts of products*, especially in terms of their impacts on the long-term interests of non-Western markets. For example, luxury products and those of a fundamentally labor-saving nature would not necessarily be appealing under all circumstances to a development-conscious foreign government. Third, MNC managers should be sensitive to the extent to which their *products are politically vulnerable*. Products that are politically vulnerable may lead to labor agitation, public regulation (for example, price fixing and allocation quotas), nationalization, or political debates. Examples of products that in the past have led to political debates and action include sugar, salt, kerosene, gasoline, tires, and medicines.[35]

The need to be sensitive to marketing in other countries provides an appropriate transition to our discussion of ethical issues in the global business environment. It should be clear from this discussion that ethical issues or conflicts might easily arise from cultural conditions that are not anticipated by the MNCs. Further, even though we will examine in more detail such visible issues as marketing practices, plant safety, questionable payments, and sweatshops in cheap-labor factories in developing countries, we should be ever vigilant of the fact that ethical dilemmas can also arise in such realms as operations management, financial management, labor relations, and global strategic management.

ETHICAL ISSUES IN THE GLOBAL BUSINESS ENVIRONMENT

For many companies, most of the ethical problems that arise in the international environment are in the same categories as those that arise in their domestic environments. These ethical issues reside in all of the functional areas of business: production/operations, marketing, finance, and management. These issues concern the fair treatment of stakeholders—employees, customers, the community, and competitors. These issues involve product safety, plant safety, advertising practices, human resource management, environmental problems, and so on.

The ethical problems seem to be somewhat fewer in developed countries, but they exist there as well. The ethical difficulties seem to be worse in underdeveloped countries, LDCs, or developing countries because these countries are at earlier stages of economic development and typically do not have a legal infrastructure in place to help protect their citizenry. This situation creates an environment in which there is a temptation to adhere to lower standards, or perhaps no standards, because few government regulations or activist groups exist to protect the stakeholders' interests. In the LDCs, the opportunities for business exploitation and the engagement in questionable (by developed countries' standards) practices are abundant.

We will discuss some prominent examples of ethical problems in the multinational sphere to provide some appreciation of the development of these kinds of issues for business. We will discuss two classic ethical issues that have arisen with regard to questionable marketing and manufacturing safety practices. Then, we will discuss the issue of labor or human rights abuses often found in "sweatshops" (the use of cheap labor in developing countries)—a topic that has dominated international business discussions for the past decade. Next, we will consider the special problems of corruption, bribery, and questionable payments, which have been ethical issues in the United States for over 30 years. From these examples, we should be able to develop an appreciation of the kinds of ethical challenges that confront MNCs and others doing business globally.

Questionable Marketing and Plant Safety Practices

A classic example of a questionable marketing practice is the now-infamous infant formula controversy that spanned most of the 1970s, continued into the 1980s and 1990s, and remains an issue today. The plant safety issue is best illustrated by examining the Union Carbide Bhopal crisis that began in late 1984 and continued into the 1990s and is not

Ethics in Practice

AN INNOCENT REVELATION?

For a couple of years, I worked as an assistant manager at a gas station in my hometown of Randers, Denmark. The location of the station was perfect, and this was proven every day by long lines and big sales. The way the job was scheduled was that the person on duty would always manage the station single-handedly, standing behind the desk, running the cash register. Every day, several thousand dollars was secured in the gas station's safe. Six people worked the gas station—all around the age of 18. The key to the safe was hidden in the back, and only the employees and the manager knew the hiding place. The manager would take the money stored in the safe and deposit it at the local bank every third day, but one week this action was postponed a couple of days because of a holiday. Therefore, a large sum of money was accumulating at the station. One employee was aware of this fact and revealed it to her friends. At the same time, she agreed to tell about the hiding place for the key, and within a few days her friends broke into the station, found the key, and stole $17,000 to $19,000.

The employee and her friends had figured that the insurance company would pay for my manager's loss and therefore all parties would be satisfied, except for the insurance company, who, they thought, would not really be affected by the loss. They claimed, "Everybody knows how rich these insurance companies are."

The bottom line of this story was that the insurance company did not pay, because the key was hidden in the same room where the safe was kept.

The ethical question in this story is this. If you knew that no one would discover the employee's irresponsible decision to tell about the hidden key, and that the insurance company would reimburse the manager, would you also have done the same thing if you had received a fairly big portion of the money? In this case, I assume that the insurance company could easily afford the reimbursement, which means that all parties should be satisfied (and you would get a little richer).

1. What is the ethical problem in this case? Is it a situation unique to business in Denmark?

2. If the employee's decision to tell about the hidden key was never discovered, could her action somehow be justified as just an innocent revelation? Why or why not? Identify the ethical principles involved here.

3. Imagine that the employee's revelation was never discovered. Would you have chosen to do as she did if we assume that the manager got reimbursed? Many of us pay a lot of money in insurance premiums, so why not get a little back?

Contributed by Anders Braad

---

completely resolved today. These issues are important because they illustrate the endless problems companies can face as a result of mistakes made in global business ethics.

Questionable Marketing: The Infant Formula Controversy. The **infant formula controversy** is a classic in illustrating the ethical questions that can arise while doing business abroad. We will briefly refer to James Post's observations about this now-classic case.[36] For decades, physicians working in tropical lands (many of which were LDCs) realized that there were severe health risks posed to infants from bottle feeding as opposed to breast feeding. Such countries typically had neither refrigeration nor sanitary conditions. Water supplies were not pure, and, therefore, infant formula mixed with this water contained bacteria that would likely lead to disease and diarrhea in the bottle-fed infant. Because these LDCs are typically poor, this condition encourages mothers to overdilute powdered formula, thus diminishing significantly the amount of nutrition the

infant receives. Once a mother begins bottle-feeding, her capacity for breast-feeding quickly diminishes. Poverty also leads the mother to put in the bottle less expensive substitute products. These products, such as powdered whole milk and cornstarch, are not acceptable substitutes. They are nutritionally inadequate and unsatisfactory for the baby's digestive system.

By the late 1960s, it was apparent that in the LDCs there was increased bottle-feeding, decreased breast-feeding, and a dramatic increase in the numbers of malnourished and sick babies. Bottle-feeding was cited as one of the major reasons. The ethical debate began when it was noted that several of the infant formula companies, aware of the environment just described, were promoting their products and, therefore, promoting bottle-feeding in an intense way. Such marketing practices as mass advertising, billboards, radio jingles, and free samples became commonplace. These promotional devices typically portrayed the infants who used their products as healthy and robust, in sharp contrast with the reality that was brought about by the conditions mentioned.

One of the worst marketing practices entailed the use of "milk nurses"—women dressed in nurses' uniforms who walked the halls of maternity wards urging mothers to get their babies started on formula. In reality, these women were sales representatives employed by the companies on a commission basis. Once the infants began bottle-feeding, the mothers' capacity to breast feed diminished.[37]

Although several companies were engaging in these questionable marketing practices, the Swiss conglomerate Nestlé was singled out by a Swiss social activist group in an article published in 1974 entitled "Nestlé Kills Babies." At about the same time, an article appeared in Great Britain entitled "The Baby Killers."[38] From this point on, a protracted controversy developed with Nestlé and other infant formula manufacturers on one side and a host of organizations on the other side filing shareholder resolutions and lawsuits against the company. Among the groups that were actively involved in the controversy were church groups such as the National Council of Churches and its Interfaith Center on Corporate Responsibility (ICCR), UNICEF, the World Health Organization (WHO), and the Infant Formula Action Coalition (INFACT). Nestlé was singled out because it had the largest share of the world market and because it aggressively pushed sales of its infant formula in developing countries, even after the World Health Organization developed a sales code to the contrary.[39]

In 1977, INFACT and ICCR organized and led a national boycott against Nestlé that continued for almost 7 years. More than 70 American organizations representing churches, doctors, nurses, teachers, and other professionals participated in the boycott. These groups mounted an international campaign aimed at changing these objectionable marketing practices in the LDCs.[40] In 1984, after spending tens of millions of dollars resisting the boycott, Nestlé finally reached an accord with the protesters. The company agreed to four changes in its business practices:

1. It would restrict the distribution of free samples.
2. It would use Nestlé labels to identify the benefits of breast-feeding and the hazards of bottle-feeding.
3. It promised to help ensure that hospitals would use its products in accordance with the WHO code.
4. It agreed to drop its policy of giving gifts to health professionals to encourage them to promote infant formula.

The protesters, in return, agreed to end their boycott but to continue monitoring Nestlé's performance.[41]

The infant formula controversy continued through the 1980s and well into the 1990s. In 1991, Nestlé (which controlled more than 40 percent of the worldwide market) and American Home Products (which controlled about 15 percent of the worldwide market) announced that after decades of boycotts and controversy, they planned to discontinue the practice of providing free and low-cost formula to developing countries.

With this action—its most aggressive ever—Nestlé attempted to quell the protracted criticism that it had defied WHO's marketing restrictions by dumping huge quantities of baby formula on Third World hospitals. The distribution of supply had been a lingering concern in the infant formula controversy. Until this announcement, Nestlé had supplied formula on a request basis but over the next several years planned to distribute formula only on a request basis to children "in need," as outlined in the WHO guidelines. The pledges by Nestlé and American Home Products, the world's two biggest infant formula makers, were regarded as a watershed in the bitter infant formula controversy.[42]

The infant formula controversy has been rich with examples of the actions and power of social activist groups and governments and the various strategies that might be employed by MNCs. For our purposes, however, it illustrates the character of questionable business practices by firms pursuing what might be called normal practices were it not for the fact that they were being pursued in foreign countries where local circumstances made them questionable.[43] The infant formula controversy also illustrates the endurance of certain ethical issues, particularly in the global arena.

The AIDS crisis, especially in Africa, has put an interesting twist on the infant formula debate. Some now say that UNICEF, the U.N. agency charged with protecting children, today may be indirectly responsible for thousands of African babies being infected with the deadly AIDS virus. AIDS has entered the picture since the early boycotts of Nestlé and others, and it was discovered that HIV-infected mothers could transfer the disease through breast-feeding to their own children. In response to this problem, Nestlé and formula maker Wyeth-Ayerst Labs say they stand ready to donate tons of free formula to the infected women. However, UNICEF has refused to give the green light to these gifts. Nestlé claims it has gotten desperate requests from African hospitals for free formula, but the company will not act without UNICEF's approval because it does not want to renew the boycott against the company. The executive director of UNICEF, meanwhile, has said that she doesn't believe Nestlé and the other infant formula providers have a particular role to play in the AIDS crisis. She thinks they should just comply with the WHO code.[44]

Critics of Nestlé continue beyond the AIDS issue. In 2004, the allegation is that Nestlé is now trying to market infant formula to Hispanic mothers in the United States to boost their share of this $3 billion market. The major question seems to be whether companies such as Nestlé should market baby formula to low-income immigrant mothers, many in California, when health experts and government officials maintain that breast-feeding is healthier and saves in terms of long-term health care costs. A spokeswoman for Nestlé says that the product is being marketed with a fully bilingual label so that Hispanic mothers can make an informed choice.[45]

According to a report released in 2004 by the International Baby Food Action Network, it is argued that Nestlé continues to market its infant feeding products in ways that are putting children all over the world at risk.[46] With the AIDS crisis and marketing in the United States to low-income mothers complicating the controversy, it is apparent that no easy solutions are available.

Plant Safety and the Bhopal Tragedy.
The Union Carbide **Bhopal tragedy** in late 1984 brings into sharp focus the challenges of multinationals operating in a for-

eign, particularly less-developed, environment. The legal issues surrounding this event have not yet been totally resolved and may not be for years to come in spite of agreements reached. On December 3, 1984, a leak of methyl isocyanate gas caused what many have termed the "worst industrial accident in history." The gas leak killed more than 2,000 people and injured 200,000 others. The tragedy has raised numerous legal, ethical, social, and technical questions for MNCs.[47] Observers who have studied this tragedy say the death toll and destruction are many times greater than the "official" numbers indicate.

Interviews with experts just after the accident revealed a belief that the responsibility for the accident had to be shared by the company and the Indian government. According to Union Carbide's own inspector, the Bhopal plant did not meet U.S. standards and had not been inspected in over 2 years. The Indian government allowed thousands of people to live very near the plant, and there were no evacuation procedures.[48]

Many different questions have been raised by the Bhopal disaster. Among the more important of these issues are:[49]

1. To what extent should MNCs maintain identical standards at home and abroad regardless of how lax laws are in the host country?
2. How advisable is it to locate a complex and dangerous plant in an area where the entire workforce is basically unskilled and where the populace is ignorant of the inherent risks posed by such plants?
3. How wise are laws that require plants to be staffed entirely by local employees?
4. What is the responsibility of corporations and governments in allowing the use of otherwise safe products that become dangerous because of local conditions? (This question applies to the infant formula controversy also.)
5. After reviewing all the problems, should certain kinds of plants be located in developing nations?

At the heart of these issues is the question of differing standards in different parts of the world. This dilemma arose in the 1970s, when American firms continued to export drugs and pesticides that had been restricted in the United States. Pesticides, such as DDT and others that had been associated with cancer, were shipped to and used in LDCs by farmers who did not understand the dangers or the cautions that were needed in the use of these products. Not surprisingly, poisonings occurred. In 1972, hundreds to thousands of Iraqis died from mercury-treated grain from the United States. In 1975, Egyptian farmers were killed and many made ill by a U.S.–made pesticide. Asbestos and pesticide manufacturing plants that violated American standards were built in several countries. These companies typically broke no laws in the host countries, but many experts are now saying that the Bhopal tragedy has taught us that companies have a moral responsibility to enforce high standards, especially in developing countries not yet ready or able to regulate these firms.[50]

One major problem that some observers say contributed to the Bhopal explosion and, indeed, applies to MNCs generally is the requirement that firms be significantly owned by investors in the host country. Union Carbide owned only 50.9 percent of the Bhopal, India, subsidiary. It has been observed that this situation may have reduced Union Carbide's motivation and/or capacity to ensure adequate industrial and environmental safety at its Bhopal plant, mainly by diluting the degree of parent control and reducing the flow of technical expertise into that plant. If developing countries continue to insist on a dilution of MNC control over manufacturing plants, this may also diminish the MNC's motivation and incentive to transfer environmental management and safety competence.

Another major problem highlighted by the Bhopal explosion was the fact that the people of developing countries are often unaware of the dangers of new technology. As one expert observed, countries such as India have not "internalized the technological culture."[51] On the one hand, the LDCs want technology because they see it as critical to their economic development, but their ability to understand and manage the new technology is in serious doubt.

The complexity and tragedy of the Bhopal explosion case for its victims, the Indian government, and Union Carbide are attested to by the fact that this issue is still unresolved even today. In 1989, Union Carbide extricated itself from relief efforts by agreeing to pay the Indian government $470 million to be divided among victims and their families. By 1993, courts had only distributed $3.1 million of this sum. The overburdened government relief programs in India have been mired in mismanagement and corruption. It has been observed that virtually every level of the relief bureaucracy in India is rife with corruption. Government officials demanded bribes from illiterate victims trying to obtain documents required for the relief money. Doctors have taken bribes from victims to testify in their court cases, and unscrupulous agents have fished for bribes by claiming they could get victims' cases expedited on the crowded docket. Claims courts that would determine final compensation for victims were not set up until 1992—8 years after the gas leak. Lawyers and officials say it could be another 20 years before this case is settled.[52]

According to more recent information put out by Dow Chemical, which bought Union Carbide in 2001, the gas that leaked from the plant was formed when a disgruntled employee, apparently bent on spoiling a batch of the gas, added water to a storage tank. The company said it took moral responsibility for the incident despite its being an act of sabotage. Union Carbide subsequently sold its 50.9 percent interest in Union Carbide India Limited and donated the proceeds from the sale to a trust to build a hospital in Bhopal.[53]

Even today the Union Carbide tragedy continues to haunt Dow Chemical over two decades after the accident. Survivors of the accident and their supporters continue to push Dow to pay as much as $1 billion in additional damages for what they claim are unmet medical bills and toxic-cleanup.[54] In 2004, led by a small group of socially responsible investment funds, activists continued to push Dow Chemical to provide further disclosure on potential legal and financial risks associated with the Union Carbide explosion. Dow continues to argue that the $470 million settlement it paid in 1989 resolves its outstanding liabilities.[55] Current Web pages (http://www.bhopal.org, http://www.bhopal.net, http://www.bhopal.com) show that the Bhopal tragedy continues to be of deep concern, even toward the end of the first decade of the twenty-first century.

The lessons from the Bhopal disaster are many and will continue to be debated. In companies around the globe, the Bhopal disaster has sparked continued controversy in the debate about operating abroad. To be sure, ethical and legal issues are central to the discussions. What is at stake, however, is not just the practices of businesses abroad but also the very question of the presence of businesses abroad. Depending on the final outcome of the Union Carbide debacle, MNCs may decide that the risks of doing certain types of business abroad is too great.

Sweatshops, Human Rights, and Labor Abuses

No issue has been more prominent since the early 1990s in the global business ethics debate than the MNCs' use and abuse of women and children in cheap-labor factories in developing countries. The major players in this controversy, large corporations, have highly recognizable names—Nike, Wal-Mart, Gap, Kmart, Reebok, J. C. Penney,

SEARCH THE WEB

UNITED STUDENTS AGAINST SWEATSHOPS

United Students Against Sweatshops (USAS) is an international student movement of campuses and individual students fighting for sweatshop free-labor conditions and workers' rights. USAS believes that university standards should be brought into line with those of its students, who demand that their school's logo be emblazoned on clothing made in decent working conditions. There are currently over 180 student chapters of USAS in the United States and Canada. For more information about USAS's goals and activities and about sweatshops, generally, visit the Web site at **http://www.studentsagainst sweatshops.org**.

and Disney—to name a few. The countries and regions of the world that have been involved are also recognizable—Southeast Asia, Pakistan, Indonesia, Honduras, Dominican Republic, Thailand, the Philippines, and Vietnam. Sweatshops have not been eliminated in the United States, either.[56]

Though **sweatshops**, characterized by child labor, low pay, poor working conditions, worker exploitation, and health and safety violations, have existed for decades, they have grown in number in the past few years as global competition has heated up and corporations have gone to the far reaches of the world to lower their costs and increase their productivity. A landmark event that brought the sweatshop issue into sharp focus was the 1996 revelation by labor rights activists that part of Wal-Mart's Kathie Lee Collection, a line of clothes endorsed by then-prominent U.S. talk-show host Kathie Lee Gifford, was made in Honduras by seamstresses slaving 20 hours a day for 31 cents an hour. The revelation helped turn Gifford, who was unaware of where the clothes were being made or under what conditions, into an anti-sweatshop activist.[57] The Nike Corporation has also become a lightning rod for social activists concerned about overseas manufacturing conditions, standards, and ethics. A major reason for this has been the company's high visibility, extensive advertising, and expensive shoes, as well as the stark contrast between the tens of millions of dollars Nike icon Michael Jordan earned and the $2.23 daily wage rate the company's subcontractors paid their Indonesian workers.[58]

Critics of MNC labor practices, including social activist groups, labor unions, and grassroots organizations, have been speaking out, criticizing business abusers and raising public awareness. These critics claim certain businesses are exploiting children and women by paying them poverty wages, working them to exhaustion, punishing them for minor violations, violating health and safety standards, and tearing apart their families. Many of these companies counter that they offer the children and women workers a superior alternative. They say that, although their wage rates are embarrassing by developed-world standards, those rates frequently equal or exceed local legal minimum wages, or average wages. They further say that, because so many workers in LDCs work in agriculture and farming, where they make less than the average wage, the low but legal minimums in many countries put sweatshop workers among the higher-paid workers in their areas.[59] According to a recent study conducted by economists, it was found that MNCs generally paid more, often a lot more, than the wages offered by locally owned companies. In one study, it was found that affiliates of U.S. MNCs pay a wage premium that ranges from 40 percent to 100 percent higher than the local average pay in low-income countries.[60]

The sweatshop issue has been so prominent in the past few years that, to improve their situations or images, many criticized companies have begun working diligently to improve working conditions, further joint initiatives, establish codes of conduct or standards for themselves and their subcontractors, conduct social or ethical audits, or take other steps. In 1996, former-President Clinton, with Kathie Lee Gifford, was instrumental in helping to establish the **Fair Labor Association (FLA)**, (http://www.fairlabor.org), an organization of clothing firms, unions, and human-rights groups focused on the worldwide elimination of sweatshops. Its members, which include L. L. Bean, Nike, Liz Claiborne, Nicole Miller, and Reebok, were encouraged by a survey showing that three-quarters of America's shoppers would pay higher prices for clothes and shoes bearing "No Sweat" labels.

More recently, there have been a number of proposals aimed at eliminating or improving sweatshops. Some proposals call for clothing firms and their contractors to impose a code of conduct that would prohibit child labor, forced labor, and worker abuse; establish health and safety regulations; recognize workers' right to join a union; limit the workweek to 60 hours (except in exceptional business circumstances); and insist that workers be paid at least the legal minimum wage (or the "prevailing industry wage") in every country in which garments are made. Under such proposals, the garment industry would also create an association to police the agreement.[61]

These proposals have some drawbacks, however. For example, the legal minimum wage in many developing countries is below the poverty line. In addition, the "prevailing industry wage" could prove to be a convenient escape clause. Some groups are also concerned that the task force has, in effect, sanctioned 60-hour working weeks and that it will still allow 14-year-olds to work if local laws do. Another big issue will be monitoring the agreements abroad. For example, Liz Claiborne alone has 200 contractors in over 25 countries. Furthermore, in some countries, like the Philippines, Malaysia, Thailand, and Vietnam, sweatshops go to great lengths to hide their business dealings by "fronting" businesses using false documents to "prove" they pay minimum wages and by intimidating workers to keep quiet.[62]

Another initiative to improve sweatshop conditions was organized by the **Council on Economic Priorities (CEP)**, a New York public-interest group. The CEP, with a group of influential companies, introduced a new scheme called Social Accountability 8000, or SA8000, which was designed to piggyback on the ISO8000 quality-auditing system of the International Standards Organization (ISO), now used in over 80 countries.[63]

The SA8000 initiative, launched in the fall of 1997, involved a broad spectrum of U.S. and foreign companies, such as Avon, Sainsbury, Toys 'Я' Us, and Otto Versand, which owns Eddie Bauer, plus such labor and human-rights groups as KPMG-Peat Marwick and SGS-ICS. The current standards for SA8000 are now administered by an organization called **Social Accountability International**. The new, official standard may be found at http://www.sa-intl.org, but a summary follows:

1. *Child Labor:* No workers under the age of 15; minimum lowered to 14 for countries operating under the ILO Convention 138 developing-country exception; remediation of any child found to be working
2. *Forced Labor:* No forced labor, including prison or debt bondage labor; no lodging of deposits or identity papers by employers or outside recruiters
3. *Health and Safety:* Provide a safe and healthy work environment; take steps to prevent injuries; regular health and safety worker training; system to detect threats to health and safety; access to bathrooms and potable water
4. *Freedom of Association and Right to Collective Bargaining:* Respect the right to form and join trade unions and bargain collectively; where law prohibits these freedoms, facilitate parallel means of association and bargaining
5. *Discrimination:* No discrimination based on race, caste, origin, religion, disability, gender, sexual orientation, union or political affiliation, or age; no sexual harassment

SEARCH THE WEB

SWEATSHOPS

Sweatshops in developing or underdeveloped countries are another vital international business ethics topic. To review current activities in this arena, visit the Sweatshop Watch Web site at **http://www.sweatshopwatch.org**.

6. *Discipline:* No corporal punishment, mental or physical coercion, or verbal abuse
7. *Working Hours:* Comply with the applicable law but, in any event, no more than 48 hours per week with at least one day off for every 7-day period; voluntary overtime paid at a premium rate and not to exceed 12 hours per week on a regular basis; overtime may be mandatory if part of a collective bargaining agreement
8. *Compensation:* Wages paid for a standard workweek must meet the legal and industry standards and be sufficient to meet the basic need of workers and their families; no disciplinary deductions
9. *Management Systems:* Facilities seeking to gain and maintain certification must go beyond simple compliance to integrate the standard into their management systems and practices.[64]

There are two options for companies interested in using the SA8000 standard: (1) certification to SA8000, and (2) involvement in the Corporate Involvement Program (CIP).

1. *Certification to SA8000:* Companies that operate production facilities can seek to have individual facilities certified to SA8000 through audits by one of a number of accredited certification bodies. Since the SA8000 system became fully operational in 1998, there are certified facilities in 30 countries on 5 continents and across 22 industries.
2. *SA8000 Corporate Involvement Program:* Companies that focus on selling goods or that combine production and selling can join the SA8000 Corporate Involvement Program (CIP). The CIP is a 2-level program that helps companies evaluate SA8000, implement the standard, and report publicly on implementation progress.

    * *SA8000 Explorer (CIP Level One):* Evaluate SA8000 as an *ethical sourcing tool* via pilot audits.
    * *SA8000 Signatory (CIP Level Two):*
        * Implement SA8000 over time in some or all of the supply chain through certification.
        * Communicate implementation progress to stakeholders via SAI-verified public reporting.[65]

In addition to the initiatives by such industry organizations as the Fair Labor Association and Social Accountability International (SA8000), it is important to highlight some of the efforts by individual companies to address the issues surrounding sweatshops. A number of companies have developed *global outsourcing guidelines* and codes and have made important strides in attempts at self-monitoring of their production facilities in less-developed countries. Companies such as Nike, adidas-Salomon (formerly adidas), Levi Strauss & Co., and the Gap are notable examples.[66]

In the spirit of transparency, Gap, Inc., released a 40-page report in 2004 that offered an unusual look at its factory conditions abroad. Gap's report revealed that the working conditions at many of its 3,000 factories worldwide are far from perfect. The Gap report documented a wide variety of workforce violations at plants making its clothing but revealed even worse conditions at plants vying to win Gap contracts. Some of the details revealed in the report were quite specific. The company found that 10 percent to 25 percent of its factories in China, Taiwan, and Saipan were using psychological coercion or verbal abuse. More than 50 percent of the factories visited in sub-Saharan Africa ran machinery without proper safety devices. As a result, the company revoked contracts with 136 factories in 2003 because of severe or persistent violations. Critics of sweatshops said they were pleased with the move toward greater openness. A representative from the Interfaith Center on Corporate Responsibility in New York described the report as a "major step forward."[67] Gap's strategy may motivate a number of other companies to be more forthright about their factories overseas.

Sweatshops and labor abuses sharply contrast the "haves" and the "have-nots" of the world's nations. Consumers in developed countries have benefited greatly by the lower prices made possible by cheap labor. It remains to be seen how supportive those consumers will be if prices rise because MNCs improve wage rates and conditions in LDCs. The MNCs face a new and volatile ethical issue that is not likely to go away. Their profits, public image, and reputations may hinge on how well they respond. The MNCs must handle a new dimension in their age-old quest to balance shareholder profits with the desires of expanded, global stakeholders who want better corporate social performance.

Alien Tort Claims Act and Human Rights Violations.

Looking beyond possible human rights violations in sweatshops, claims that companies may have violated the human rights of foreign nationals may come back to haunt firms that have been accused of more serious human-rights abuses. What is at stake is the U.S. courts' interpretation of an obscure piece of legislation known as the **Alien Tort Claims Act (ATCA)**. Though researchers cannot determine why Congress passed this little-known act of 1789, today it is the centerpiece of a controversy that may have widespread implications for American firms operating abroad. An interesting development has been recent efforts to use ATCA to sue transnational companies for violations of international law in countries outside the United States. The ATCA allows foreign individuals to sue U.S. firms in U.S. courts for their actions abroad. If these suits are allowed to proceed, the ATCA could become a powerful tool to increase corporate accountability around the globe.[68]

Current cases under adjudication in the United States are of interest to U.S.–based MNCs because they are increasingly being named as defendants in alien tort cases for doing business in countries with repressive governments. Some of the lawsuits allege that the companies are aiding and abetting human-rights abuses of various host governments.[69] In 2004, for example, a federal judge refused to throw out claims that ChevronTexaco might be liable for human-rights violations at a Nigerian oil platform operated by one of its subsidiaries. ChevronTexaco had been accused of sanctioning fatal attacks by the military, which had been hired to provide security for the company in 1998 and 1999. Other companies facing similar charges include Unocal Corporation and ExxonMobil Corporation.[70] If upheld in these applications, the ATCA could represent a devastating level of legal and financial liability for U.S.–based MNCs engaged in global business. Suddenly, what were once human-rights ethical issues could become significant legal issues. We know from the Nestlé and Bhopal cases that these crises are not quickly resolved. These are definitely cases to be carefully watched.

Corruption, Bribery, and Questionable Payments

Corruption, bribes, and questionable payments occurred for decades prior to the 1970s. It was in the mid-1970s, however, that evidence of widespread questionable corporate payments to foreign government officials, political parties, and other influential persons became widely known. Such major corporations as Lockheed, Gulf Oil, Northrop, Carnation, and Goodyear were among those firms admitting to such payments. Huge sums of money were involved. Gulf, for example, admitted paying $4.2 million to the political party of Korean President Park. Gulf also created a subsidiary in the Bahamas that was then used as a conduit for unlawful political contributions. Lockheed acknowledged payments of $22 million, mostly to officials in the Middle East.[71]

One of the most notorious cases was that of Lockheed giving $12.5 million in bribes and commissions in connection with the sale of $430 million worth of Tri-Star airplanes to All Nippon Airways. The president of Lockheed defended the payments, claiming that it was common practice and it was expected to give bribes in Japan. The news of the payments rocked Japan more than it did the United States, because Prime Minister Kakuei Tanaka and four others were forced to resign and stand trial. Prince Bernhard of the Netherlands was also disgraced because of his involvement with Lockheed.[72] Another important point made about this case was that Lockheed did not offer a bribe, but rather the Japanese negotiator demanded it. This point raises the continuing question in matters of this kind: "Are those who accede to bribery equal in guilt to those who demand bribes?"[73]

Corruption in international business continues to be a major problem. It starts with outright bribery of government officials and the giving of questionable political contributions. Beyond these, there are many other activities that are corrupt: the misuse of company assets for political favors, kickbacks and protection money for police, free junkets for government officials, secret price-fixing agreements, and insider dealing, just to mention a few. All of these activities have one thing in common. They are attempts to influence the outcomes of decisions wherein the nature and extent of the influence are not made public. In essence, these activities are abuses of power.[74]

Though one seldom hears an official definition of corruption, such synonyms as dishonesty, sleaze, fraud, deceit, and cheating are typically assumed. Corruption comes in many forms, some petty and some grand. Though incalculably lucrative to a few, corruption is hugely damaging in terms of its effects on stakeholders. It corrodes the rule of law, the legitimacy of government, the sanctity of property rights, and incentives to invest and accumulate. Corruption also is a drag on a country's growth. One study said that the country of Columbia's GDP would rise by about 20 percent if corruption there fell.[75] A major problem, of course, is that those who benefit from corruption most will resist attempts to curb it and often these are politicians in the decision-making roles.

Bribes, more than any other form of corruption, have been the subject of continuing debate, and they merit closer examination. Bribes, of course, are illegal and unethical, but it is informative to consider the arguments that have been set forth for and against them.

Arguments For and Against Bribery.
Arguments typically given in favor of permitting bribery include the following: (1) they are necessary for profits in order to do business; (2) everybody does it—it will happen anyway; (3) it is accepted practice in many countries—it is normal and expected; and (4) bribes are forms of commissions, taxes, or compensation for conducting business between cultures.

Arguments frequently cited against giving bribes include (1) bribes are inherently wrong and cannot be accepted under any circumstances; (2) bribes are illegal in the United States and, therefore, unfair elsewhere; (3) one should not compromise her or his own beliefs; (4) managers should not deal with corrupt governments; (5) such demands, once started, never stop; (6) one should take a stand for honesty, morality, and ethics; (7) those receiving bribes are the only ones who benefit; (8) bribes create dependence on corrupt individuals and countries; and (9) bribes deceive stockholders and pass on costs to customers.[76]

The costs of bribes and other forms of corruption are seldom fully understood or described. Several studies suggest the economic costs of such corrupt activities. When government officials accept "speed" money or "grease payments" to issue licenses, the economic cost is 3 to 10 percent above the licensing fee. When tax collectors permit underreporting of income in exchange for a bribe, income tax revenues may be reduced by up to 50 percent. When government officials take kickbacks, goods and services may

The difference between bribing officials and greasing palms is a fine line that Ronald S. Cruse, founder of Logenix International, must walk constantly in his business of "moving goods into tough places." Keeping this business running can be a matte of finding out who's in a position to provide the right information or perform the timely service—such as the Moscow cleaning lady who "rearranged" scheduling petitions in Cruse's favor. Get a glimpse of how business is conducted in lawless nations by logging on to InfoTrac College Edition at http://www.infotrac-college.com and keying in record number A104004187.

Ethics in Practice

I LOVE MY JOB—JUST DON'T ASK HOW I GOT IT!

Last spring, one of my very close friends graduated with an MBA. She interviewed with many companies during her last semester at school. However, there was no job. After graduating, she decided to apply to other companies. At one of the companies, she got preselected and then selected for the final round of interviews. After the final interview was conducted, she was informed that a decision would be mailed to her within the next 6 weeks.

My friend's father happened to know the general manager of this company. When there was no reply for almost 5 weeks, my friend's father decided to speak with the general manager. The general manager checked with the human resources department and informed my friend's father that his daughter had not been short-listed and, therefore, was not being considered in the final list of applicants for a position.

About 5 days later, my friend's father called the general manager again, but this time for something else. He had decided to offer a bribe to this friend, the general manager, in order to get his daughter the job. Bribing high-ranking managers to secure employment is an accepted practice in my country. A sum of money was mutually agreed upon, and my friend's father personally delivered the cash to the general manager. Within the next 4 weeks, she was offered the management trainee position.

After working there for a month, my friend told me this whole story and how glad she was that her father had done all this for her. She loved her job and said that she couldn't have been happier anywhere else. She also told me not to mention this to anyone because it would harm her family's reputation. Bribing is an accepted practice in my country, but not out in the open.

1. Is it ethical to give or take bribes just because everybody does it and it is an accepted practice in one's country?

2. If bribery is an accepted practice, why did the friend want to keep this quiet?

3. Should employees be hired on the basis of merit or according to how much they can bribe to secure a job?

4. If you had been in my friend's place, would you have accepted the job?

Contributed by Radhika Sadanah

---

be priced 20 to 100 percent higher to them. In addition to these direct economic costs, there are many indirect costs—demoralization and cynicism and moral revulsion against politicians and the political system. Due to bribery and corruption, politicians have been swept from office in Brazil, Italy, Japan, and Korea.[77] In 2004, at least four major, well-known companies were under investigation for alleged bribery: Titan Corp., Cargill, Monsanto, and Airbus.

The Foreign Corrupt Practices Act.

Many of the payments and bribes made by U.S.–based MNCs were not illegal prior to the passage of the 1977 Foreign Corrupt Practices Act (FCPA). Even so, firms could have been engaging in illegal activities depending on whether and how the payments were reported to the IRS. With the passage of the FCPA, however, it became a criminal offense for a representative of an American corporation to offer or give payments to the officials of other governments for the purpose of getting or maintaining business. The FCPA specifies a series of fines and prison terms that can result if a company or management is found guilty of a violation.[78] The legislation was passed not only for ethical reasons but also out of a concern for the image of the United States abroad.

Over its history, the FCPA has been controversial. The law does not prohibit so-called **grease payments**, or minor, facilitating payments to officials, for the primary purpose of getting them to do whatever they are supposed to do anyway. Such payments are commonplace in many countries. The real problem is that some forms of payments are prohibited (for example, bribes), but other payments (for example, grease payments) are not prohibited. The law is sometimes ambiguous on the distinctions between the two.[79] To violate the FCPA, payments (other than grease payments) must be made corruptly to obtain business. This suggests some kind of *quid pro quo*. The idea of a corrupt *quid pro quo* payment to a foreign official may seem clear in the abstract, but the circumstances of the payment may easily blur the distinction between what is acceptable "grease" (e.g., payments to expedite mail pickup or delivery, to obtain a work permit, to process paperwork) and what is illegal bribery. The safest strategy for managers to take is to be careful and to seek a legal opinion when questions arise.

Figure 9-3 summarizes some of the key features of the antibribery provisions of the FCPA. Figure 9-4 on page 314 presents a basic distinction, with examples, between bribes (which are prohibited) and grease (or facilitating) payments (which are not prohibited) based on the FCPA.

Bribery Trends: The Growing Anticorruption Movement. As we move toward the end of the first decade of the new millennium, corruption and bribery in global business continue to be vital topics. With significant increases in global competition, free

---

FIGURE 9-3

Key Features of the Antibribery Provisions of the Foreign Corrupt Practices Act

- In general, the FCPA prohibits American companies from making corrupt payments to foreign officials for the purpose of obtaining or keeping business.
- The Department of Justice is the chief enforcement agency, with a coordinate role played by the Securities and Exchange Commission (SEC).
- The FCPA's antibribery provisions extend to two types of behavior: (1) making bribes directly and (2) making bribes through intermediaries.
- Applies to any individual firm, officer, director, employee, or agent of the firm and any stockholder acting on behalf of the firm.
- The person making or authorizing the payment must have a corrupt intent, and the payment must be intended to induce the recipient to misuse his official position to direct business wrongfully to the payer or to any other person.
- Prohibits paying, offering, promising to pay, or authorizing to pay or offer, money or anything of value.
- The prohibition extends only to corrupt payments to a foreign official, a foreign political party or party official, or any candidate for foreign political office, or anyone acting in an official capacity.
- Prohibits corrupt payments through intermediaries.
- An explicit exception is made to the bribery provisions for "facilitating payments" for "routine governmental action."
- The following criminal penalties may be imposed: firms are subject to a fine of up to $2 million; officers, directors, stockholders, employees, and agents are subject to a fine of up to $100,000 and imprisonment for up to five years. Fines imposed on individuals may not be paid by the firm.

SOURCE: "Foreign Corrupt Practices Act Antibribery Provisions," U.S. Department of Justice, http://www.osec.doc.gov/ogc/occic/fcparev.html.

FIGURE 9-4

Bribes Compared to Grease Payments

Definitions	Examples
Grease Payments	
Relatively small sums of money given for the purpose of getting minor officials to: • Do what they are supposed to be doing • Do what they are supposed to be doing faster or sooner • Do what they are supposed to be doing better than they would otherwise	Money given to minor officials (clerks, attendants, customs inspectors) for the purpose of expediting. This form of payment helps get goods or services through red tape or administrative bureaucracies.
Bribes	
Relatively large amounts of money given for the purpose of influencing officials to make decisions or take actions that they otherwise might not take. If the officials considered the merits of the situation only, they might take some other action.	Money given, often to high-ranking officials. Purpose is often to get these people to purchase goods or services from the bribing firm. May also be used to avoid taxes, forestall unfavorable government intervention, secure favorable treatment, and so on.

markets, and democracy over the past decade, this comes as no surprise. Three developments in the past decade are worthy of mention. Each has contributed to what some have called a growing **anticorruption movement**.

Transparency International.   First, a new special-interest group was founded in Berlin in 1993—**Transparency International (TI)**—modeled after the human-rights group Amnesty International. TI has established itself as the world's foremost anticorruption lobby. It maintains over 90 national chapters run by local activists and compiles an annual corruption rating using surveys of businesspeople, political analysts, and the general public. Using various color shades to represent labels varying from "least corrupt" to "most corrupt" on a map of the world, TI's **Corruption Perception Index (CPI)** depicts countries in various ways. In the Corruption Perception Index of 2003, the least corrupt countries were identified as Finland, Iceland, Denmark, New Zealand, Singapore, and Sweden. Out of the countries ranked, the United States was ranked 18th least corrupt, tied with Ireland. The most corrupt nations as of 2003, according to the CPI, were Myanmar, Paraguay, Haiti, Nigeria, and Bangladesh.[80] Undoubtedly, TI hopes and expects that public exposure to its corruption ratings will bring pressure to bear on countries and companies to become less corrupt.

Peter Eigen, chairman of Transparency International (TI), spoke on the launch of the TI Corruption Perceptions Index 2003: "The new CPI points to high levels of corruption in many rich countries as well as poorer ones, making it imperative that developed countries enforce international conventions to curb bribery by international companies, and that private businesses fulfill their obligations under the OECD Anti-Bribery Convention, namely to stop bribing public officials around the world." But, he continued, "nine out of ten developing countries score less than 5 against a clean score of 10 in the TI CPI 2003. Their governments must implement results-oriented programmes to fight corruption, but they also urgently require practical help tailored to the needs of their national anticorruption strategies."[81]

In addition to the CPI, Transparency International also publishes what it calls the **Bribe Payers Index (BPI)**. The Bribe Payers Index ranks leading exporting countries in terms of the degree to which international companies with their headquarters in those countries are likely to pay bribes to senior public officials in key emerging market economies. In that sense, the BPI measures the supply side of bribery in the countries where the bribes are paid. Countries are ranked on a mean score from the answers given by respondents to the statement: "In the business sectors with which you are most familiar, please indicate how likely companies from the following countries are to pay or offer bribes to win or retain business in this country."[82]

A new and related index to that of Transparency International is the **Public Integrity Index**, the centerpiece of the Global Integrity report, issued by The Center for Public Integrity. The Public Integrity Index is a quantitative scorecard of governance practices in each country. The Public Integrity Index assesses the institutions and practices that citizens can use to hold their governments accountable to the public interest. This index does not measure corruption itself, but rather the opposite of corruption: the extent of citizens' ability to ensure their government is open and accountable. The Public Integrity Index ranks countries as strong, moderate, weak, or very weak on holding government accountable to its citizens.[83]

OECD Antibribery Initiatives.   A second development in the growing anticorruption movement is a new antibribery treaty and initiatives that the 29 industrialized nations of the Organization for Economic Cooperation and Development (OECD) and five other countries agreed to in late 1997.[84] The OECD member nations agreed to ban international bribery and to ask each member to introduce laws patterned after the U.S. FCPA in its country. The main thrust of the treaty was to criminalize bribes to foreign officials who have sway over everything from government procurement contracts and infrastructure projects to privatization tenders.

The OECD Convention to combat bribery went into effect on February 15, 1999. The convention makes it a crime to offer, promise, or give a bribe to a foreign public official in order to obtain or retain international business deals. A related text effectively puts an end to the practice of according tax deductibility for bribe payments made to foreign officials. The convention commits 34 signatory countries, including all the world's biggest economies, to adopt common rules to punish companies and individuals who engage in bribery transactions. By the end of 2003, 35 countries had submitted their plans to combat bribery.[85] It may be some years to come before the Antibribery Convention is fully implemented. However, the OECD represents a significant initiative in the global battle to eliminate corruption from commercial transactions.

Individual Country Initiatives.   In addition to OECD antibribery initiatives, some individual countries have begun antibribery campaigns on their own. A case in point is the efforts initiated in Mexico under the leadership of President Vicente Fox. In 2001, Fox appointed a new anticorruption czar. The first such czar, Francisco Barrio, a former governor of Chihuahua state in northern Mexico, is responsible for unearthing corruption and federal spending irregularities in a country with a long history of both. In a pilot undercover program started in 2001, Barrio's office discovered that public servants in seven Mexican cities were charging and pocketing the equivalent of $100 apiece, in addition to regular fees, to issue driver's licenses. Barrio stated that corruption cannot be eradicated in Fox's 6-year term, but the government can lay the foundation for reducing it on all levels.[86] The experience of Mexico tells us how hard it is to eliminate corruption. Corruption is widespread and deeply rooted in countries like Mexico. According to Transparency International, the average Mexican household pays an estimated 7 percent of its annual income on bribes for public service.[87] Those in the know report mixed reports with the antibribery initiatives in Mexico, but others give the president and the country credit for addressing the issue.[88]

By 2004, several other countries had reported attempts to clean up corruption. In Russia, President Vladimir Putin created an anticorruption coalition to start cleaning up his country. Putin admitted that Western investment would not pour into Russia without major improvements in governance and in the fight against corruption.[89] A startling development has been the efforts to fight corruption in Malaysia. There, the government has created an Anticorruption Agency to investigate and combat corruption. In 2004, they arrested two prominent businessmen and a sitting cabinet member on charges of corruption. Prime Minister Abdullah Ahmad Badawi believes the initiative has encouraged foreign investors, though he has received many criticisms for the programs his government has begun.[90]

The best way to deal with bribes seems to be to stem the practice before it starts. A major paradox is that the very people who often benefit from illicit payments—the politicians—are the ones who must pass the laws and set the standards against bribes and corruption in the first place. Another factor is that bribes and corruption, whenever possible, need to be exposed. Public exposure, more than anything else, has the potential to bring questionable payments under control. This means that practices and channels of accountability need to be made public.[91] The Corruption Perception Index and Bribe Payers Index should help in this regard. Beyond these steps, managers need to be able to see that such activities are no longer in their best interests. Not only do bribes corrupt the economic system, but they corrupt business relationships as well and cause business decisions to be made on the basis of factors that ultimately destroy all the institutions involved. In a sense, the new OECD treaty indicates that member nations now understand this important point. It will not eliminate bribery, but it does represent a significant step toward reducing bribery and bringing it under control.

We have by no means covered all the areas in which ethical problems reside in the global business environment. The topics treated have been major ones subjected to extensive public discussion. Examples of other issues that have become important recently and will probably increase in importance include the issues of international competitiveness, protectionism, industrial policy, political risk analysis, outsourcing, and antiterrorism. These issues are of paramount significance in discussions of business's relations with international stakeholders. Other issues that include an ethical dimension are national security versus profit interests, the use of internal transfer prices to evade high taxes in a country, mining of the ocean floor, and harboring of terrorists. Space does not permit us to discuss these issues in detail.

Other Global Ethics Issues

Many other ethical issues that MNCs face could be discussed, but space does not permit an exhaustive discussion of these issues. A couple of additional topics should be mentioned, however, because they help to characterize the difficulties associated with global business in the 2000s. As a result of the acts of terrorism evident in recent years, doing business abroad in certain countries has become more difficult and, indeed, dangerous. Kidnappings, murder, and violence against businesspeople abroad, particularly in troubled nations, are making it harder to find workers willing to subject themselves to these threats. The kidnapping and killing of Paul Johnson, Jr., in Saudi Arabia during the summer of 2004 will deter some from taking these kinds of jobs. In spite of these threats, many do accept the risks of working abroad in unsettled countries.

Peter Singer, in a new book titled *Corporate Warriors*[92], says "whether it's Columbia or Saudi Arabia or Iraq, there are always some people willing to bear those risks."[93] Even though this may be true, it will still be incumbent upon MNCs to take actions to secure the safety of those working abroad. The recent instability and violence are expected to have at least three effects on the operations of companies in some of the dangerous countries. Workers will expect higher pay to adjust for the risk-reward trade-off. Companies will face higher insurance premiums to cover workers and their assets. Higher security costs will doubtless follow.[94] MNCs will perceive an added ethical responsibility toward their employees and stakeholders while doing business in dangerous countries.

A related issue is the problem of companies deciding to continue doing business in rogue nations even though the government has prohibited it. The term *rogue nations* was first used in the 1990s to describe nations that were considered to pose a threat to the United States. In the 2000s, the term was broadened to include countries that share a number of attributes, among them countries that brutalize their own people and squander their natural resources, display no regard for international law, threaten their neighbors and callously violate international treaties, reject basic human values, and sponsor terrorism around the globe.[95] According to a *CBS News* special report titled "Doing Business with the Enemy," there are U.S. companies that are helping to drive the economies of rogue countries like Iran, Syria, and Libya, which have sponsored terrorists.[96] Though U.S. law bans American companies from doing business with rogue nations, several companies such as Halliburton, Conoco-Phillips, and General Electric have found ways to continue doing business in these countries. Apparently, the law does not apply to foreign or offshore subsidiaries as long as they are run by non-Americans.[97]

A major concern with respect to these companies is that large institutional investors, such as pension funds, own stock in many of the companies and, therefore, are indirectly supporting their business ventures. According to the CBS report, just about anyone with a 401(k) pension plan or mutual fund has money invested in companies that are doing business in these rogue nations.[98]

These issues will continue to be ethical issues for global business in the years to come. As the public becomes more aware of companies doing business in rogue nations, it is expected that heightened pressure will be placed on these companies to discontinue such ventures. Meanwhile, this is just one of among many other ethical issues that are shaping global business today.

IMPROVING GLOBAL BUSINESS ETHICS

The most obvious conclusion to extract from the discussion up to this point is that business ethics is more complex at the global level than at the domestic level. The complexity arises from the fact that a wide variety of value systems, stakeholders, cultures, forms of government, socioeconomic conditions, and standards of ethical behavior exists throughout the world. Recognition of diverse standards of ethical behavior is important, but if we assume that firms from developed countries should operate in closer accordance with developed countries' standards than with those of LDCs, the strategy of ethical leadership in the world will indeed be a challenging one. Because the United States, and hence U.S.–based MNCs, have played such a leadership role in world affairs—usually espousing fairness and human rights—U.S. firms have a heavy responsibility, particularly in underdeveloped countries and LDCs. The power-responsibility equation also argues that U.S. firms have a serious ethical responsibility in global markets. That is, our larger sense of ethical behavior and social responsiveness derives from the enormous amount of power we have.

In this section, we will first discuss the challenge of honoring and balancing the ethical traditions of a business's home country with those of its host country. We will do this primarily through a discussion of Enderle's four global types and an application of Donaldson and Dunfee's Integrative Social Contracts Theory (ISCT). Next, we will discuss Laczniak and Naor's four recommended courses of action for conducting business in foreign environments: (1) Develop worldwide codes of conduct, (2) factor ethics into global strategy, (3) suspend activities when faced with unbridgeable ethical gaps, and (4) develop periodic "ethical impact statements."[99]

In addition, Donaldson has set forth 10 fundamental international rights that are based on the principle of rights discussed in Chapter 7. These are worthy of consideration, as are DeGeorge's seven "moral guidelines" that provide guidance for MNCs.

Balancing and Reconciling the Ethics Traditions of Home and Host Countries

Perhaps one of the greatest challenges that face businesses operating in foreign countries is achieving some kind of reconciliation and balance in honoring both the cultural and moral standards of their home and host countries. Should a business adhere to its home country's ethical standards for business practices or to the host country's ethical standards? There is no simple answer to this question. The diagram presented in Figure 9-5 frames the extreme decision choices businesses face when they consider operating globally.

At one extreme is a position some might call **ethical imperialism**. This position argues that the MNC should continue to follow its home country's ethical standards even while operating in another country. Because U.S. standards for treating employees, consumers, and the natural environment are quite high relative to the standards in many less-developed countries, it is easy to see how managers might find this posture appealing.

As reliance on foreign factories has soared in recent years and harsh conditions have been documented by the media, an increasing number of companies, such as Levi Strauss; Nordstrom, Inc.; Wal-Mart; and Reebok, have espoused higher standards for foreign factories that cover such issues as wages, safety, and workers' rights to organize.[100] These standards more nearly approximate U.S. views on how such stakeholders ought to be treated than some host country's views. Such higher standards could be seen by foreign countries, however, as the United States attempting to impose its standards on the host country—thus the name "ethical imperialism" for one end of the continuum.

At the other extreme in Figure 9-5 is a position often called **cultural relativism**. This position is characterized by foreign direct investors such as MNCs following the host country's ethical standards. This is the posture reflected in the well-known saying, "When in Rome, do as the Romans do." This position would argue that the investing MNC should set aside its home country's ethical standards and adopt the ethical standards of the host

FIGURE 9-5

Ethical Choices in Home Versus Host Country Situations

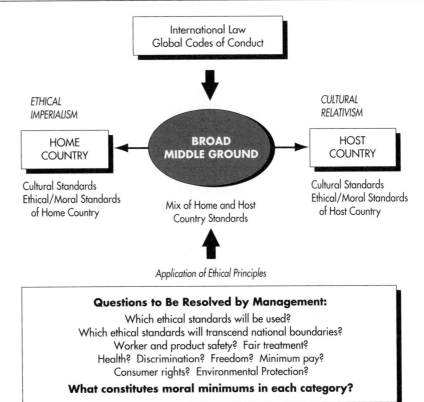

country. For example, if Saudi Arabia holds that it is illegal to hire women for most managerial positions, the investing MNC would accept and adopt this standard, even if it counters its home country's standards. Or, if the host country has no environmental protection laws, this position would argue that the MNC need not be sensitive to environmental standards.

As Tom Donaldson has argued, cultural relativism holds that no culture's ethics are better than any other's and that there are, therefore, no international rights or wrongs. If Thailand tolerates the bribery of government officials, then Thai tolerance is no worse than Japanese or German intolerance. If Switzerland does not find insider trading morally repugnant, then Swiss liberality is no worse than American restrictiveness.[101] Most ethicists find cultural relativism to be a case of moral or ethical relativism and, therefore, an unacceptable posture for MNCs to take.

Presented in Figure 9-5 is a series of questions management needs to ask to help it determine its stance on home versus host country ethics. Depending on the issue (e.g., health versus minimum pay), companies may be more or less compelled to follow their home country's ethics. Key questions that must be posed and answered include: Which ethical standards will be used? Which ethical standards will transcend national boundaries? What constitutes moral minimums with respect to each category of ethical issue?

A Typology of Global Types.   George Enderle, an international business expert, has observed and categorized at least four different types of global firms with respect to their use of home versus host country ethical standards:[102]

- Foreign country type
- Empire type
- Interconnection type
- Global type

Foreign Country Type.   This type of firm conforms to local customs and ethics, assuming that the ethical standards of the host country are adequate and appropriate. This approach represents moral or cultural relativism.

Empire Type.   This type of company applies its domestic or home country standards without making any serious adaptations to the host country. These companies export their values in a wholesale fashion, often disregarding the consequences. An example would be Great Britain in India and elsewhere prior to 1947. This approach represents ethical imperialism.

Interconnection Type.   These companies regard the international sphere as differing significantly from the domestic sphere in that their interconnectedness transcends national identities. An example of this would be states engaging in commercial business in the European Union or NAFTA. In this type, the entire concept of national interests is blurred. Companies don't try to project a national identity.

Global Type.   This type of business firm abstracts from all regional differences. These firms view the domestic or home standards as not relevant or applicable. With this type, the nation-state may be seen as vanishing as only global citizenry applies.

SEARCH THE WEB

GLOBAL CODES OF CONDUCT

Over the years, various groups interested in international business ethics have developed a number of different guidelines or codes of conduct for conducting business in the global arena. "Principles & Codes for Socially Responsible Business Practices" at **http://www.goodmoney.com/directry_codes.htm**, the Web site developed by Good Money, a company focused on socially responsible investing, has an excellent listing of select global guidelines. These important and interesting guidelines include:

- *Caux Round Table: Principles for Business*—designed to set a world standard against which business behavior can be measured.

- *CERES Principles*—formerly the Valdez Principles, the CERES Principles are for environmentally sound global business practices.

- *Declaration of a Global Ethic*—a code to address the crises in the global economy, ecology, and politics.

- *The MacBride Principles*—a corporate code of conduct for U.S. companies doing business in Northern Ireland.

- *The Maquiladoras Standards of Conduct*—drafted for companies doing business in the Maquiladores of Mexico.

- *Principles for Global Corporate Responsibility*—drafted by three interfaith organizations from Canada, the United States, and the United Kingdom for transnational corporations.

The purpose of identifying each of these types is to illustrate the various mixtures or combinations of home and host country standards that a business operating in the global sphere might adopt.

Integrative Social Contract Theory (ISCT).

Integrative Social Contract Theory (ISCT), according to Donaldson and Dunfee, is an approach to navigating cross-national cultural differences.[103] Two key concepts in this theory are the notions of *hypernorms* and *moral free space*. They explain these two concepts by depicting a series of concentric circles representing the core norms held by corporations, industries, or economic cultures. At the center are **hypernorms**, which are transcultural values. They include, for example, fundamental human rights or basic prescriptions common to most major religions. The values they represent are by definition acceptable to all cultures and all organizations.

Moving out from the center of the concentric circles, next would be **consistent norms**. These values are more culturally specific than those in the center, but are consistent with hypernorms and other legitimate norms. The next circle is **moral free space**. Here, one finds norms that are inconsistent with at least some other legitimate norms existing in other economic cultures. These norms could be in mild tension with hypernorms, though they may be compatible with them. These are strongly held cultural beliefs in particular countries. Finally, in the outer circle are **illegitimate norms**. These are norms that are incompatible with hypernorms. An example of this might be the practice of exposing workers to unacceptable levels of carcinogens.

Donaldson and Dunfee then use these different levels of norms to comment on Enderle's four types of corporations. Regarding the foreign country type, they say that nothing limits the free moral space of the host country. Thus, if a host country accepts government corruption and environmental degradation, then so much the worse for honest people and environmental integrity. Both the global and empire types succeed in avoiding the fierce relativism of the foreign country type, but may fall prey to the opposite problem. Because each of these has its own set blueprint of right and wrong, each may suffocate the host country's moral free space and leave no room for legitimate local norms. The empire type exhibits a version of moral imperialism; the global type may impose its home country morality on a host culture, thus imposing its version of a global morality on the host country.[104]

According to Donaldson and Dunfee, only the interconnection type satisfies ISCT by acknowledging both universal moral limits (hypernorms) and the ability of communities to set moral standards of their own (moral free space). This type balances better than the others a need to retain local identity with the acknowledgment of values that transcend individual communities; thus, it manages to balance moral principles with moral free space in a more convincing way than in the other three models.[105]

In summary, ISCT uses the principles of moral free space and adherence to hypernorms as a balanced approach to navigating global international waters. While honoring hypernorms, companies do not have to simply adopt a "do in Rome as the Romans do" philosophy. But, they do need to be sensitive to the transcultural value implications of their actions. In turn, the concept of moral free space makes them ever vigilant of the need to precede judgment with an attempt to understand the local host country culture. The result, of course, is the very real probability that moral tension will be an everyday part of doing business in the global sphere.[106]

It may sound like a simplistic solution to say that the MNC needs to operate in some broad middle ground where a mix of home and host country ethical standards may be used. The challenge for managers will be to determine what mix of ethical standards should be used and how this decision should be made. As mentioned earlier, managers will need to ask themselves which moral standards are applicable in the situations they face. Use of ethical principles such as those articulated in the previous chapters—rights, justice, utilitarianism, and the Golden Rule—still apply. Managers will need to decide which ethical standards should transcend national boundaries and thus represent hyper-norms: safety? health? discrimination? freedom? Managers will need to decide what will represent their moral minimums with respect to these and other issues. It would be nice to think that international laws and global codes of conduct will make these decisions easier. Though some are available, it is doubtful that such guidelines will be easily applicable. In the interim, managers will need to be guided by the ethical concepts at their disposal, possibly with help from some of the approaches to which we now turn.

Four Strategies for Improving Global Business Ethics

There are four major strategies or categories of action that would help MNCs conduct global business while maintaining an ethical sensitivity in their practices and decision making. We will now discuss these and use them to help organize suggested strategies and actions that have been made by a number of experts.

Global Codes of Conduct. There are two ways of thinking about global codes of conduct. First, there are specific corporate global codes that individual companies have developed. Second, there are global codes or guidelines that have been developed by various international organizations. Each of these deserves some consideration.

Corporate Global Codes. In Chapter 7, we discussed codes of conduct, and that discussion applies in the global sphere as well. While operating in the global sphere, MNCs have been severely criticized for operating with divergent ethical standards in different countries, thus giving the impression that they are attempting to exploit local circumstances. A growing number of MNCs, such as Chiquita Brands International, Caterpillar Tractor, Allis Chalmers, Johnson's Wax, and Rexnord, have developed and used codes geared to worldwide operations.[107]

One of the first and most well known of the corporate global codes was that of Caterpillar Tractor Company, issued by the chairman of the board, titled "A Code of Worldwide Business Conduct." The code went into considerable detail and had major sections that covered the following vital areas: ownership and investment, corporate facilities, relationships with employees, product quality, sharing of technology, accounting and financial records, different business practices, competitive conduct, observance of local laws, business ethics, relationships with public officials, and international business. The purpose of the code was clearly set forth in its introduction:

> *This revised "Code of Worldwide Business Conduct" is offered under the several headings that follow. Its purpose continues to be to guide us, in a broad and ethical sense, in all aspects of our worldwide business activities. Of course, this code isn't an attempt to prescribe actions for every business encounter. It is an attempt to capture basic, general principles to be observed by Caterpillar people everywhere.*[108]

Other companies do not have comprehensive codes addressing their international operations but rather codes containing sections that address foreign practices. For example, in its *Standards of Business Conduct*, Northrop Grumman Corporation dedicates a whole section to the subject of "International."[109] In its "International" section, the code begins as follows:

> *Employees and consultants or agents representing the company abroad or working on international business in the United States should be aware that the company's Values and Standards of Conduct apply to them anywhere in the world. Less than strict adherence to laws and regulations that apply to the company's conduct of international business would be considered a compromise of our Values and Standards of Conduct.[110]*

The code then goes on to specifically address topics such as export controls, the Foreign Corrupt Practices Act, and laws of other countries.

An example of a global code of conduct aimed specifically at improving workplace standards and workers' standards of living was implemented the late 1990s by Mattel, Inc., the $4.5 billion toy manufacturer. According to Jill E. Barad, then Mattel chairperson and CEO, "We are as concerned with the safety and fair treatment of the men and women who manufacture our products as we are with the safety and quality of the products themselves, and our new Global Manufacturing Principles demonstrate our strong commitment to that philosophy."[111]

With offices in 36 countries and products being marketed in 150 nations around the world, Mattel is a classic example of the kind of MNC that needs, and can benefit from, a global code of conduct.

Global Codes and Standards Set by International Organizations. In addition to individual corporate codes, there are a number of international organizations that have developed global codes or standards that they hope companies will adopt and follow. Some of these codes focus on one specific issue; many provide standards across a number of issue areas. Figure 9-6 on page 324 summarizes brief information about some of the more prominent of these external standards.

Ethics and Global Strategy.

The major recommendation here is that the ethical dimensions of multinational corporate activity should be considered as significant inputs into top-level strategy formulation and implementation.[112] Carroll, Hoy, and Hall have argued even more broadly that corporate social policy should be integrated into strategic management.[113] At the top level of decision making in the firm, corporate strategy is established. At this level, commitments are made that will define the underlying character and identity that the organization will have. The overall moral tone of the organization and all decision making and behaviors are set at the strategic level, and management needs to ensure that social and ethical factors do not get lost in the preoccupation with market opportunities and competitive factors.

If ethics does not get factored in at the strategic formulation level, it is doubtful that ethics will be considered at the level of operations where strategy is being implemented. Unfortunately, much current practice has tended to treat ethics and social responsibility as residual factors. A more proactive stance is needed for dealing with ethical issues at the global level. Strategic decisions that may be influenced by ethical considerations in the global sphere include, but are not limited to, product/service decisions, plant location, manufacturing policy, marketing policy and practices, and human resources management policies.

A useful illustration of ethics being factored into strategic decision making is provided by Levi Strauss & Co. Because Levi Strauss operates in many countries and diverse

FIGURE 9-6

Global Standards or Codes of Conduct Developed by International Organizations

		Brief Description
Code, Standard, Guideline	Caux Principles	Issued in 1994 by the Caux Round Table, comprised of senior business leaders from Europe, Japan and North America. An aspirational set of recommendations for corporate behavior that seeks to express a worldwide standard for ethical and responsible corporate behavior. Principles address the social impact of company operations on the local community and respect for rules and ethics.
	Global Reporting Initiative	Revision issued in 2000 by the Coalition of Environmentally Responsible Economies (CERES), including nongovernmental agencies, corporations, consultancies, accounting organizations, business associations, academics and others. GRI is an international reporting standard for voluntary use by organizations reporting on the economic, environmental, and social dimensions of their activities, products, and services.
	Global Sullivan Principles	Proposed in 1999 by the late Rev. Leon Sullivan. These are aspirational standards developed with the input of several multinational corporations. The principles include directives on labor, ethics, and environmental practices of multinational companies and their business partners.
	OECD Guidelines for Multinational Enterprises	Revised in 2000, the guidelines are recommendations addressed by governments to MNEs and are voluntary principles and standards. Governments adhering to the guidelines encourage the companies operating within the countries to observe the guidelines wherever they operate. The 2000 revisions strengthen the guidelines in human rights and environmental issues.
	Principles for Global Corporate Responsibility: Benchmarks	Revised in 1998 by the Interfaith Center on Corporate Responsibility [U.S.], Taskforce on the Churches and Corporate Responsibility [Canada], and Ecumenical Council for Corporate Responsibility [UK]. The Principles are designed to provide a "model framework" through which stakeholders can assess corporate codes of conduct, policies, and practices related to CSR expectations. The standards contain 60 principles and benchmarks to be used in assessing company performance.
	UN Global Compact	Issued in 1999 by the United Nations. Formally launched in 2000. A set of nine principles that include specific standards that endorsing companies would commit to enact.

SOURCE: Summarized from *Comparison of Selected CSR Standards* (San Francisco: Business for Social Responsibility, November 2000), 10-11. For more details, see this publication. Each of these organizations has its own Web site.

cultures, it reasoned that it must take special care in selecting its contractors and the countries where its goods are produced in order to ensure that its products are being made in a manner consistent with its values and reputation. In the early 1990s, therefore, the company developed a set of *global sourcing guidelines* that established standards its contractors must meet. As examples, their guidelines banned the use of child and prison labor. They stipulated certain environmental standards. Wages must, at minimum, comply with the law and match prevailing local practice. By factoring these ethical considerations into its strategic decisions, Levi argued that it receives important short- and long-term commercial benefits.[114]

Another example of a company integrating ethical concerns into its corporate strategies is that of Starbucks Coffee Co., the Seattle-based firm. In an innovative pilot program announced in 1998, Starbucks planned to pay a premium above market price for coffee, with the bonus going to improve the lives of coffee workers. The initial payments would be made to farms and mills in Guatemala and Costa Rica, which would co-fund health care centers, farm schools, and scholarships for farm workers' children. Starbucks's incentive program was part of a larger "Framework for Action," its plan for implementing its code of conduct, created in 1995.[115] By 2004, Starbucks had implemented a full-fledged fair-trade coffee program. Starbucks' Fair Trade certification program increases farmers' incomes through forming cooperatives and linking them directly to coffee importers— coffees are guaranteed a minimum price, allowing farmers a more sustainable way of life.[116]

Suspension of Activities.
An MNC may sometimes encounter unbridgeable gaps between the ethical values of its home country and those of its host country. When this occurs, and reconciliation does not appear to be in sight, the MNC should consider suspending activities in the host country. For example, years ago IBM and Coca-Cola established a precedent for this activity by suspending their activities in India because of that country's position on the extent of national ownership and control.[117] These companies no longer have this policy.

Also, Levi Strauss undertook a phased withdrawal from China, largely in response to human-rights concerns, and suspended sourcing in Peru because of concerns about employee safety. It later lifted the suspension because conditions had improved.[118] More recently, companies have pulled out of Burma (now also called Myanmar) due to human-rights violations. In a fight against corruption, Procter & Gamble even closed a Pampers diaper plant in Nigeria rather than pay bribes to customs inspectors.[119]

Suspension of business in a foreign country is not a decision that can or should be taken too hastily, but it must be regarded as a viable option for those firms that desire to travel on the higher moral road. Each country is at liberty to have its own standards, but this does not mean that U.S. firms must do business in that country. What does ethical leadership mean if it is not backed up by a willingness and an ability to take a moral stand when the occasion merits?

Ethical Impact Statements and Audits.
MNCs need to be constantly aware of the impacts they are having on society, particularly foreign societies. One way to do this is to periodically assess the company's impacts. Companies have a variety of impacts on foreign cultures, and ethical impacts represent only a few of these. The impact statement idea probably derived, in part, from the practice of environmental impact statements that the U.S. Environmental Protection Agency pioneered in the early 1970s. These statements are similar to the corporate social audit, a concept discussed in Chapter 4. *Social auditing* is "a systematic attempt to identify, analyze, measure (if possible), evaluate, and monitor the effect of an organization's operations on society (that is, specific social groups) and on the public well-being."[120] **Ethical impact statements** would be an attempt to assess the underlying moral justifications for corporate actions and the consequent results of those actions. The information derived from these actions would permit the MNCs to modify or change their business practices if the impact statement suggested that such changes would be necessary or desirable.

One form of ethical impact assessment is some firms' attempts to monitor their compliance with their companies' global ethics codes. For example, Mattel developed an independent audit and monitoring system for its code. Mattel's monitoring program was headed by an independent panel of commissioners who selected a percentage of the company's manufacturing facilities for annual audits. In one audit, for example, Mattel terminated its relationship with three contractor facilities—one in Indonesia for its inability to confirm the age of its employees and two in China for refusing to meet company-mandated safety procedures.[121] Today, Mattel continues its auditing of compliance to its code of conduct through its Global Manufacturing Principles.[122]

Fundamental International Rights

One major approach to doing business ethically in the global sphere has been for companies to adhere to various sets of international rights or moral guidelines. Thomas Donaldson set forth 10 fundamental international rights that he argues should be honored and respected by all international actors, including nation-states, individuals, and corporations. He argues that these rights serve to establish a "moral minimum" for the behavior of all international economic agents. Donaldson's 10 fundamental rights are as follows:[123]

1. The right to freedom of physical movement
2. The right to ownership of property
3. The right to freedom from torture
4. The right to a fair trial
5. The right to nondiscriminatory treatment (freedom from discrimination on the basis of such characteristics as race and gender)
6. The right to physical security
7. The right to freedom of speech and association
8. The right to minimal education
9. The right to political participation
10. The right to subsistence

Such a list of rights is somewhat general and still leaves considerable room for interpretation. However, the list serves to establish a beginning point for MNCs as they contemplate what responsibilities they have in international markets. These rights are similar to hypernorms in our earlier discussion. Today, the U. N. Global Compact (see Figure 9-6) sets forth a series of rights and responsibilities that reflect many of these concerns. The Global Compact asserts nine principles with respect to human rights, labor standards, and the environment.[124]

Seven Moral Guidelines for Global Business

Another way of looking at what MNCs should be doing in the global sphere is the recommendation that they follow certain moral guidelines in their operations. According to Richard DeGeorge, a business ethicist, MNCs should apply seven moral guidelines in their international operations.[125] Some of these are rather straightforward and general, but they do summarize a useful perspective that might well improve MNC operations in the global sphere. Like the principles of rights stated earlier, these moral guidelines are similar to the hypernorms discussed earlier.

- MNCs should do no intentional, direct harm.
- MNCs should produce more good than bad for the host country.
- MNCs should contribute by their activities to the host country's development.
- MNCs should respect the human rights of their employees.
- MNCs should pay their fair share of taxes.

- To the extent that local culture does not violate moral norms, MNCs should respect the local culture and work with it, not against it.
- MNCs should cooperate with the local government in the development and enforcement of just background institutions (for example, the tax system and health and safety standards).

DeGeorge does not present these seven guidelines as a panacea. He does suggest that if they were brought to bear on the dilemmas that MNCs face, the companies could avoid the moral stings of their critics. The spirit of these seven guidelines, if adopted, would go a long way toward improving MNC-host country relations.

Like the other lists presented, these guidelines can serve only as general principles for managers who are aspiring to make ethical decisions in the global arena. They do, however, provide the consensus thinking of a host of stakeholder representatives as to the responsibilities of international corporations.

■ SUMMARY

Ethical dilemmas pose difficulties, in general, for businesses, and those arising in connection with doing business in foreign lands are among the most complex. The current period is characterized by an increasing antiglobalization sentiment, and the attacks on the World Trade Center and subsequent acts of terrorism have created an unstable global environment. A cursory examination of major issues that have arisen in global business ethics over the past several decades shows that they rank right up there with the most well-known news stories. The infant formula controversy, the Bhopal tragedy, corruption and bribery, concern about human rights and sweatshops, and the exploits of MNCs in Third World countries have all provided an opportunity for business critics to assail corporate ethics in the international sphere. These problems arise for a multiplicity of reasons, but differing cultures, value systems, forms of government, socioeconomic systems, and underhanded and ill-motivated business exploits have all been contributing factors. The possible applications of the Alien Tort Claims Act (ATCA) to U. S.–based MNCs raises to a new level of urgency the actions, decisions, and policies of these firms in foreign lands.

The balancing of home and host country standards using Integrative Social Contracts Theory, global codes of conduct, the integration of ethical considerations into corporate strategy, the option of suspending activities, the use of ethical impact statements, and the adherence to international rights and moral guidelines offer some hope that global business can be better managed. Despite the recent terrorist attacks, current trends point to a growth in business activity in the transnational economy, and though there is some evidence of a backlash against globalization, these issues will become more rather than less important in the future. Indeed, it could easily be argued that business's greatest ethical challenges in the future will be at the global level.

■ KEY TERMS

■ DISCUSSION QUESTIONS

1. Drawing on the notions of moral, amoral, and immoral management introduced in Chapter 6, categorize your impressions of (a) Nestlé, in the infant formula controversy and (b) Union Carbide, in the Bhopal tragedy.

2. As an MNC seeks to balance and honor the ethical standards of both the home and host countries, conflicts inevitably will arise. What criteria do you think managers should consider as they try to decide whether to use home or host country ethical standards?

3. Explain ISCT and the concepts of hypernorms and moral free space. Provide an example of each. What dif-

ficulties would a manager encounter in applying these concepts?

4. Differentiate between a bribe and a grease payment. Give an example of each.

5. Using Donaldson's fundamental international rights, rank what you consider to be the top five of the 10 rights. Explain your ranking.

6. Of DeGeorge's seven moral guidelines, identify which single guideline you think is of most practical value for an MNC. Give a brief explanation of your choice.

■ RECOMMENDED CASES

Many of the end-of-text cases may be related to Chapter 9. You may wish to consider studying the following cases with Chapter 9.

Case 15. "SOMETHING'S ROTTEN IN HONDO." This case addresses the question of a company that is located on the border of the United States and Mexico. The case involves smokestack emissions that drift over the border into the country of Mexico. The manager is considering moving the plant to Mexico where it can avoid U. S. clean air restrictions. What ethical responsibilities does the company have to the city of Hondo, which it may be leaving? What responsibilities does the company have to Mexico?

Case 16. "GLOBAL (IN)EQUALITY? THE MERRILL LYNCH SEX BIAS CASE." Our global business world has introduced new issues not faced in the past. One of these

issues is executive and employee compensation. Should executives working in different parts of the world be paid equally? This case provides a springboard for discussing this and related global management issues.

Case 17. "NIKE, INC." This case addresses the roles and responsibilities of a business operating at the global level. What are business's social and ethical responsibilities when doing business all over the world? How does a firm be a good corporate "world" citizen? What are the global ethical issues facing Nike? Is the use of "sweatshops" a defensible practice? Is the idea of a "living wage" that would apply to all countries a feasible practice? Does Nike have responsibility for the practices and policies of its subcontractors?

■ WEB RESOURCES

The URLs listed here are current at the time of publication. Should any of these Web sites change, please search under the company's or organization's name for an updated address.

Alien Tort Claims Act
http://www.globalpolicy.org/intljustice/atca/atcaindx.htm

Bhopal Express
http://www.bhopalexpress.com/facts.html

Bhopal.Org
http://www.bhopal.org/welcome2.html

Caux Roundtable
http://www.cauxroundtable.org

Center for Public Integrity
http://www.publicintegrity.org

Co-op America Sweatshops
http://www.sweatshops.org

Corporate Social Responsibility Newswire
http://www.csrwire.com

CorpWatch
http://www.corpwatch.org

Council of Ethical Organizations
http://www.corporateethics.com

Dow Chemical Company Bhopal
http://www.dow.com/environment/debate/d15.html

Ethics Resource Center
http://www.ethics.org

Foreign Corrupt Practices Act
http://www.usdoj.gov/criminal/fraud/fcpa.html

Globalization.com
http://www.globalization.com

Global Policy Forum
http://www.globalpolicy.org/intljustice/atca/atcaindx.htm

Global Reporting Initiative
http://www.globalreporting.org

Global Sullivan Principles
http://globalsullivanprinciples.org/principles.htm

Human Rights Watch
http://www.hrw.org

Infact
http://www.infact.org

Infact Canada
http://www.infactcanada.ca/Nestle_Boycott_May31_04.htm

International Campaign for Justice in Bhopal
http://www.bhopal.net/index.php

International Labour Organization
http://www.ilo.org

OECD Guidelines Multinational Enterprises
http://www.oecd.org

Society for Business Ethics Links
http://www.societyforbusinessethics.org/ethics.htm

Students Against Sweatshops Canada
http://opirg.sa.utoronto.ca/groups/sweatshops/sas-c.html

Transparency International
http://www.transparency.de

United Nations Global Compact
http://www.unglobalcompact.org

United Students Against Sweatshops
http://www.studentsagainstsweatshops.org

World Trade Organization
http://www.wto.org

 InfoTrac® College Edition   http://www.infotrac-college.com

Additional information on the topics discussed in the chapter can be researched by logging onto the InfoTrac College Edition Web site.

▪ ENDNOTES

1. Peter F. Drucker, "The Transnational Economy," *The Wall Street Journal* (August 25, 1987), 38. See also T. S. Pinkston and Archie B. Carroll, "Corporate Citizenship Perspectives and Foreign Direct Investment in the U.S.," *Journal of Business Ethics* (Vol. 13, 1994), 157–169.

2. Paul Krugman, cited in Alan Farnham, "Global—Or Just Globaloney?" *Fortune* (June 27, 1994), 97–98.

3. Richard D. Robinson, "Background Concepts and Philosophy of International Business from World War II to the Present," in William A. Dymsza and Robert G. Vambery (eds.), *International Business Knowledge: Managing International Functions in the 1990s* (New York: Praeger, 1987), 3–4.

4. "The Meaning of Seattle," *Multinational Monitor* (December 1999), 5. See also Ernesto Zedillo, "Globaphobia," *Forbes* (March 19, 2001), 49.

5. Paul Beamish, Allen Morrison, Philip Rosenzweig, and Andrew Inkpen, *International Management: Text and Cases* (Boston: Irwin McGraw Hill, 2000), 3.

6. *Ibid.*, 3.

7. Herman E. Daly, "Globalization and Its Discontents," *Philosophy & Public Policy Quarterly* (Vol. 21, No. 2/3, Spring/Summer 2001), 17.

8. *Ibid.*, 17.

9. "Backlash Behind the Anxiety over Globalization," *Business Week* (April 24, 2000), 38.

10. Ernesto Zedillo, "Globaphobia," *Forbes* (March 19, 2001), 49.

11. *Ibid.*, "The Meaning of Seattle"(1999), 5.

12. Michael Elliott, "Death in Genoa," *Time* (July 30, 2001), 22–23; "After the Genoa Summit: Picking Up the Pieces," *The Economist* (July 28, 2001), 50; "Confronting Anti-Globalism," *Business Week* (August 6, 2001); Yaroslav Trofimov, "Antiglobalization Campaigners Vow to Carry Out Protests This Month," *The Wall Street Journal* (September 14, 2001), A8.

13. Martin Khor, "The Collapse at Cancun: A Frontline Report on the Failed WTO Negotiations," *Multinational Monitor* (October 2003), 25–29.

14. "The WTO Under Fire," *The Economist* (September 20, 2003), 26–28.

15. Lori Wallach, "Trade Secrets," *Foreign Policy* (January/February 2004), 70–71.

16. "Outsourcing Jobs Abroad Unpopular," *USA Today* (April 27, 2004), 1A.

17. Christopher Swann, "Jobs Data Show Little Impact from Offshoring," *Financial Times* (June 10, 2004), 42. For a debate on this issue, see Timothy Aeppel, "Offshore Face-Off," *The Wall Street Journal* (May 10, 2004), R6. Also see Brink Lindsey, "Ten Truths About Trade: Hard Facts About Offshoring, Imports, and Jobs," *Reason* (July 2004), 25–31.

18. Tim Weiner, "Free Trade Accord at Age 10: The Growing Pains Are Clear," *The New York Times* (December 27, 2003), A1.

19. Robert Batterson and Murray Weidenbaum, *The Pros and Cons of Globalization* (St. Louis: Center for the Study of American Business, January 2001), i.

20. George Melloan, "Feeling the Muscles of the Multinationals," *The Wall Street Journal* (January 6, 2004), A19.

21. *Ibid.* See Medard Gabel and Henry Bruner, *Global, Inc.* (New York: The New Press, 2003).

22. John Garland and Richard N. Farmer, *International Dimensions of Business Policy and Strategy* (Boston: Kent Publishing Company, 1986), 166–173.

23. *Ibid.*, 167–168.

24. *Ibid.*, 169.

25. *Ibid.*, 170–171.

26. *Ibid.*, 172.

27. *Ibid.*

28. "Ethical Dilemmas of the Multinational Enterprise," *Business Ethics Report*, Highlights of Bentley College's Sixth National Conference of Business Ethics (Waltham, MA: The Center for Business Ethics at Bentley College, October 10 and 11, 1985), 3. See also Richard T. DeGeorge, *Competing with Integrity in International Business* (New York: Oxford University Press, 1993).

29. Rosabeth Moss Kanter, *World Class: Thriving Locally in the Global Economy* (New York: Simon & Schuster, 1995).

30. Michael L. Wheeler, "Global Diversity: Reality, Opportunity, and Challenge," *Business Week* (December 1, 1997), special section.

31. James C. Baker, John C. Ryans, Jr., and Donald G. Howard, *International Business Classics* (Lexington, MA: Lexington Books, 1988), 73–367.

32. *Ibid.*, 127–138.

33. Baker, Ryans, and Howard, 245–246.

34. *Ibid.*, 314–315.

35. Richard D. Robinson, "The Challenge of the Underdeveloped National Market," in Baker, Ryans, and Howard, 347–356.

36. James E. Post, "Assessing the Nestlé Boycott: Corporate Accountability and Human Rights," *California Management Review* (Winter 1985), 115–116.

37. *Ibid.*, 116–117.

38. Rogene A. Buchholz, William D. Evans, and Robert Q. Wagley, *Management Response to Public Issues* (Englewood Cliffs, NJ: Prentice Hall, 1985), 80.

39. *Ibid.*, 81–82.
40. Oliver Williams, "Who Cast the First Stone?" *Harvard Business Review* (September–October, 1984), 155.
41. "Nestlé's Costly Accord," *Newsweek* (February 6, 1984), 52.
42. Alix M. Freedman, "Nestlé to Restrict Low-Cost Supplies of Baby Food to Developing Nations" and "American Home Infant-Formula Giveaway to End," *The Wall Street Journal* (February 4, 1991), B1.
43. For further discussion, see S. Prakash Sethi, *Multinational Corporations and the Impact of Public Advocacy on Corporate Strategy: Nestlé and the Infant Formula Case* (Boston: Kluwer Academic, 1994).
44. Alix M. Freedman and Steve Stecklow, "As Unicef Battles Baby-Formula Makers, African Infants Sicken, " *The Wall Street Journal* (December 5, 2000).
45. Miriam Jordan, "Nestle Markets Baby Formula to Hispanic Mothers in U. S.," *The Wall Street Journal* (March 4, 2004), B1.
46. "Boycott Updates," (May 31, 2004), http://www.infact canada.ca/InfactHomePage.htm.
47. Stuart Diamond, "The Disaster in Bhopal: Lessons for the Future," *The New York Times* (February 5, 1985), 1. See also Russell Mokhiber, "Bhopal," *Corporate Crime and Violence* (San Francisco: Sierra Club Books, 1988), 86–96.
48. Stuart Diamond, "Disaster in India Sharpens Debate on Doing Business in Third World," *The New York Times* (December 16, 1984), 1.
49. *Ibid.*, 1.
50. *Ibid.*
51. Thomas M. Gladwin and Ingo Walter, "Bhopal and the Multinational," *The Wall Street Journal* (January 16, 1985), 1.
52. Molly Moore, "In Bhopal, a Relentless Cloud of Despair," *The Washington Post National Weekly Edition* (October 4–10, 1993), 17.
53. "The Bhopal Tragedy," *Around Dow: Special Commemorative Issue*, 41 (undated).
54. Jim Carlton and Thaddeus Herrick, "Bhopal Haunts Dow Chemical," *The Wall Street Journal* (May 8, 2003), B3.
55. David Bogoslaw, "Dow Chem Faces Hldr Proposal on Bhopal Risk at Annual Mtg," *The Wall Street Journal* (May 13, 2004).
56. Mark Clifford, Michael Shari, and Linda Himelstein, "Pangs of Conscience: Sweatshops Haunt U.S. Consumers," *Business Week* (July 29, 1996), 46–47. See also Keith B. Richburg and Anne Swardson, "Sweatshops or Economic Development?" *The Washington Post National Weekly Edition* (August 5–11, 1996), 19.
57. "Stamping Out Sweatshops," *The Economist* (April 19, 1997), 28–29.
58. Clifford, Shari, and Himelstein, 46.
59. *Ibid.*
60. Ronald Baily, "Sweatshops Forever," *Reason* (February 2004), 12–13.
61. *The Economist* (April 19, 1997), 28.
62. *Ibid.*
63. Aaron Bernstein, "Sweatshop Police: Business Backs an Initiative on Global Working Conditions," *Business Week* (October 20, 1997), 39.
64. Details may be found at http://www.sa-intl.org.
65. http://www.cepaa.org/SA8000/SA8000.htm#sa8000 Overview (2004).
66. Laura P. Hartman, Denis G. Arnold, Richard E. Wokutch (eds.), *Rising Above Sweatshops: Innovative Approaches to Global Labor Challenges* (Westport, CT: Praeger Publishers, 2003).
67. Amy Merrick, "Gap Offers Unusual Look at Factory Conditions," *The Wall Street Journal* (May 12, 2004), A1.
68. "Alien Tort Claims Act," Global Policy Forum, http://www.globalpolicy.org/intljustice/atca/atcaindx.htm.
69. Warren Richey, "When Can Foreigners Sue in U.S. Courts?" *Christian Science Monitor* (March 30, 2004).
70. Bloomberg News, "Judge Refuses to Halt Suit Against ChevronTexaco Unit," *The New York Times* (March 27, 2004), B2.
71. Dwight R. Ladd, "The Bribery Business," in Tom L. Beauchamp (ed.), *Case Studies in Business, Society and Ethics* (Englewood Cliffs, NJ: Prentice Hall, 1983), 251.
72. "Airbus's Secret Past," *The Economist* (June 14, 2003), 55.
73. Richard T. DeGeorge, *Business Ethics* (New York: Macmillan, 1982), 53.
74. Bruce Lloyd, "Bribery, Corruption and Accountability," *Insights on Global Ethics* (Vol. 4, No. 8, September 1994), 5.
75. "Fighting Corruption," *The Economist* (April 29, 2004).
76. Ian I. Mitroff and Ralph H. Kilmann, "Teaching Managers to Do Policy Analysis: The Case of Corporate Bribery," *California Management Review* (Fall 1977), 50–52.
77. "The Destructive Costs of Greasing Palms," *Business Week* (December 6, 1993), 133–138. See also Henry W. Lane and Donald G. Simpson, "Bribery in International Business: Whose Problem Is It?" (Reading 12) in H. W. Lane, J. J. DiStefano, and M. L. Maznevski (eds.), *International Management Behavior*, 4th ed. (Oxford: Blackwell Publishers, 2000), 469–487.
78. Ladd, 256.
79. Garland and Farmer, 183.
80. Transparency International, "2003 Corruption Perception Index," http://www.transparency.org.
81. http://www.transparency.org/pressreleases_archive/2003/2003.10.07.cpi.en.html

82. http://www.transparency.org/cpi/2002/bpi_faq.en.html#what

83. http://www.publicintegrity.org/ga/ii.aspx

84. Paul Deveney, "34 Nations Sign Accord to End Bribery in Deals," *The Wall Street Journal* (December 18, 1997), A16.

85. http://www.oecd.org

86. Susan Ferriss, "Chihuahua Watchdog: Anti-Corruption Czar in Mexico Has Hands Full," *The Atlanta Journal-Constitution* (September 23, 2001), B6.

87. David Luhnow and José de Córdoba, "A Tale of Bribes and Romance Roils Mexican Politics," *The Wall Street Journal* (June 23, 2004), A1.

88. Tina Rosenberg, "The Taint of the Greased Palm," *The New York Times Magazine* (August 10, 2003), 33.

89. Paul Starobin and Catherine Belton, "Cleanup Time: The Kremlin Is Launching a Major Attack on Corruption," *Business Week* (January 14, 2002), 46–47.

90. Leslie Lopez, "Anticorruption Campaign Has Malaysia Buzzing," *The Wall Street Journal* (February 26, 2004), A8.

91. Lloyd, 5.

92. P. W. Singer, *Corporate Warriors: The Rise of the Privatized Military Industry* (Cornell University Press, 2003).

93. Quoted in Rick Hampson, "Many Accept Risks of Working Overseas," *USA Today* (June 21, 2004), 13A.

94. *Ibid.*

95. "United States Policy Toward Rogue Nations: Introduction," *E-notes* (June 24, 2004), http://www.enotes.com/united-states/1263.

96. "Doing Business with the Enemy," *CBS News.com* (January 25, 2004), http://www.cbsnews.com.

97. *Ibid.*

98. *Ibid.*

99. Gene R. Laczniak and Jacob Naor, "Global Ethics: Wrestling with the Corporate Conscience," *Business* (July–September 1985), 3–10.

100. G. Pascal Zachary, "Levi Tries to Make Sure Contract Plants in Asia Treat People Well," *The Wall Street Journal* (July 28, 1994), A1.

101. Tom Donaldson, "Global Business Must Mind Its Morals," *The New York Times* (February 13, 1994), F-11. See also Tom Donaldson, "Ethics Away from Home," *Harvard Business Review* (September–October, 1996).

102. George Enderle, "What Is International? A Typology of International Spheres and Its Relevance for Business Ethics," paper presented at annual meeting of International Association for Business and Society, Vienna, Austria, 1995, as quoted and described in Tom Donaldson and Thomas W. Dunfee, "When Ethics Travel: The Promise and Peril of Global Business Ethics," *California Management Review* (Vol 41, No. 4, Summer 1999), 48–49.

103. Donaldson and Dunfee, op. cit.

104. *Ibid.*

105. *Ibid.*

106. *Ibid.*

107. Laczniak and Naor, 7.

108. "A Code of Worldwide Business Conduct," in Frederick D. Sturdivant (ed.), *The Corporate Social Challenge: Cases and Commentaries* (Homewood, IL: Richard D. Irwin, 1985), 159–169.

109. Northrop Grumman, Standards of Business Conduct (September 2001). To access the company's Web site, go to http://www.northgrum.com/.

110. *Ibid.*, 10–11.

111. "Mattel, Inc. Launches Global Code of Conduct," unpublished press release (November 20, 1997). See also "Global Manufacturing Principles" (1997), 1–11.

112. Laczniak and Naor, 7–8.

113. Archie B. Carroll, Frank Hoy, and John Hall, "The Integration of Corporate Social Policy into Strategic Management," in S. Prakash Sethi and Cecilia M. Falbe (eds.), *Business and Society: Dimensions of Conflict and Cooperation* (Lexington, MA: Lexington Books, 1987), 449–470.

114. Robert D. Haas, "Ethics in the Trenches," *Across the Board* (May 1994), 12–13.

115. "Starbucks Pays Premium Price to Benefit Workers," *Business Ethics* (March/April 1998), 9.

116. Starbuck's policies may be accessed at http://www.starbucks.com/ourcoffees.

117. Laczniak and Naor, 8.

118. Haas, 12.

119. "The Short Arm of the Law," *The Economist* (March 2, 2002), 63–65.

120. David H. Blake, William C. Frederick, and Mildred S. Myers, *Social Auditing: Evaluating the Impact of Corporate Programs* (New York: Praeger, 1976), 3.

121. Mattel press release, November 20, 1997.

122. See the following Web site for information: http://www.mattel.com/about_us/Corp_Responsibility/cr_global.asp.

123. Thomas Donaldson, *The Ethics of International Business* (New York: Oxford University Press, 1989), 81.

124. See the following Web site: http://www.unglobalcompact.org.

125. Richard T. DeGeorge, "Ethical Dilemmas for Multinational Enterprise: A Philosophical Overview," in Hoffman, Lange, and Fedo (eds.), 39–46. See also Richard T. DeGeorge, *Business Ethics*, 5th ed. (Englewood Cliffs, NJ: Prentice Hall, 1999), Chapters 18–20; and Richard T. DeGeorge, *Competing with Integrity in International Business* (New York: Oxford University Press, 1993).

Part 4

EXTERNAL STAKEHOLDER ISSUES

Chapter 10

■ BUSINESS, GOVERNMENT, *and* REGULATION

CHAPTER LEARNING OUTCOMES

After studying this chapter, you should be able to:

1 Articulate a brief history of government's role in its relationship with business.

2 Appreciate the complex interactions among business, government, and the public.

3 Identify and describe government's nonregulatory influences, especially the concepts of industrial policy and privatization.

4 Explain government regulation and identify the major reasons for regulation, the types of regulation, and issues arising out of deregulation.

5 Provide a perspective on privatization versus federalization, along with accompanying trends.

The depth, scope, and direction of government's involvement in business has made the business/government relationship one of the most hotly debated issues of modern times. Government's role, particularly in the regulation of business, has ensured its place among the major stakeholders with which business must establish an effective working relationship if it is to survive and prosper.

Business has never been fond of government's having an activist role in establishing the ground rules under which it operates. In contrast, public interest has been cyclical, going through periods when it has thought that the federal government had too much power and other periods when it has thought that government should be more activist. Ronald Reagan came into office in 1980, when the public was growing somewhat weary of an active federal role. Throughout the 1980s, the federal government played less and less of a role, especially in terms of monitoring and regulating business. It was not without reason, therefore, that in late 1989 *Time* magazine ran a cover story entitled "Is Government Dead?"[1] The "Reagan Revolution" of an inactive federal government had left the public with a desire for government to become active again. It was against this backdrop that George Herbert Walker Bush was elected president in 1988.

During the first Bush administration (1988–1992), the country witnessed a growth in the rate of federal government spending that exceeded that of the Reagan years. The Clinton administration advocated a more activist role for the government in international politics and social concerns, while launching other initiatives to control federal spending. As the economy rebounded in the early 1990s, the peace dividend bore fruit, and cost-cutting initiatives took hold, the rate of government spending slowed dramatically. Total government spending went from 20.4 percent of GDP in 1990 to 17.6 percent in 2000, the lowest level since 1948.[2]

The George W. Bush administration came into office on a platform of a reduced role for federal government, but the attack on the World Trade Center changed everything. As the title of a *Business Week* article said, "Suddenly Washington's Wallet Is Open."[3] Repercussions of the attack, such as the bailout of the troubled airline industry, potential relief for other distressed industries, the increase in military spending, and the federalization of airport security expanded dramatically both government spending and governmental intervention in business activities. According to Harvard Business School professor Rosabeth Moss Kanter, "We have lived through a decade of increasing prosperity and an assumption that it could continue no matter what and that the government should get out of the way. Now that's over."[4] By the end of 2003, the Office of Management and Budget (OMB) was projecting a 2004 budget deficit of over $480 billion (in spite of a record $237 billion surplus in fiscal year 2000).

In this chapter, we will examine the relationship between business and government, although the general public will assume an important role in the discussion as well. A central concern in this chapter is the government's role in influencing business. Exploring this relationship carefully will provide an appreciation of the complexity of the issues surrounding business/government interactions. From the prospective manager's standpoint, one needs a rudimentary understanding of the forces and factors that are involved in these issues before one can begin to talk intelligently about strategies for dealing with them. Unfortunately, more is known about the nature of the problem than about the nature of solutions, as is common when dealing with complex social issues. In the next chapter, we will discuss how business attempts to influence government and public policy.

A BRIEF HISTORY OF GOVERNMENT'S ROLE

In the early days of the United States, the government supported business by imposing tariffs to protect our fledgling industries. In the second half of the 1800s, government gave large land grants as incentives for private business to build railroads. Several railroads had grown large and strong through mergers, and people began to use them because their service was faster, cheaper, and more efficient. This resulted in a decline in the use of alternative forms of transportation, such as highways, rivers, and canals. Many railroads began to abuse their favored positions. For example, a railroad that had a monopoly on service to a particular town might charge unfairly high rates for the service. Competitive railroads sometimes agreed among themselves to charge high but comparable rates. Higher rates were charged for shorter hauls, and preference was shown to large shippers over smaller shippers.

Public criticism of what were perceived as abusive practices led to the passage of the Interstate Commerce Act of 1887, which was intended to prevent discrimination and abuses by the railroads. This act marked the beginning of extensive federal government regulation of interstate commerce. The act created the Interstate Commerce Commission, which became the first federal regulatory agency and a model for future agencies.[5]

Many large manufacturing firms and mining firms also began to abuse consumers during the late 1800s. Typical actions included the elimination of competition and the charging of excessively high prices. During this period, several large firms formed organizations known as *trusts*. A trust was an organization that brought all or most competitors under a common control that then permitted them to eliminate most of the remaining competitors by price-cutting, an act that forced the remaining competitors out of business. Then, the trusts would restrict production and raise prices. As a response, Congress passed the Sherman Antitrust Act in 1890, which became the first in a series of actions intended to control monopolies in various industries. The Sherman Act outlawed any contract, combination, or conspiracy in restraint of trade, and it also prohibited the monopolization of any market. In the early 1900s, the federal government used the Sherman Act to break up the Standard Oil Company, the American Tobacco Company, and several other large firms that had abused their economic power.[6]

The Clayton Antitrust Act was passed in 1914 to augment the Sherman Act. It addressed other abusive practices that had arisen. It outlawed price discrimination that gave favored buyers preference over others and forbade anticompetitive contracts whereby a company would agree to sell only to suppliers who agreed not to sell the products of a rival competitor. The act prohibited an assortment of other anticompetitive practices. Also in 1914, Congress formed the Federal Trade Commission, which was intended to maintain free and fair competition and to protect consumers from unfair or misleading practices.[7]

Another great wave of regulation occurred during the Great Depression and the subsequent New Deal of the 1930s. Significant legislation included the Securities Act of 1933 and the Securities and Exchange Act of 1934. These laws were aimed at curbing abuses in the stock market, stabilizing markets, and restoring investor confidence. Significant labor legislation during this same period signaled government involvement in a new area. Several examples were the 1926 Railway Labor Act, the 1932 Norris–LaGuardia Act, and the 1935 Wagner Act.

During the New Deal period in the 1930s, government also took on a new dimension in its relationship with business, actively assuming responsibility for restoring prosperity and promoting economic growth through public works programs. In 1946, this new role of government was formalized with the passage of the Full Employment Act.

Prior to the mid-1950s, most congressional legislation affecting business was economic in nature. After that time, legislation was concerned largely with the quality of life.[8] Several illustrations of this include the Civil Rights Act of 1964, the Water Quality Act of 1965, the Occupational Safety and Health Act of 1970, the Consumer Product Safety Act of 1972, the Warranty Act of 1975, and the Americans with Disabilities Act of 1990. Recently, issues of national security have taken the forefront: Key examples of this are the USA Patriot Act of 2001 and the Homeland Security Act.

Just as the areas in which government has chosen to initiate legislation have changed, the multiplicity of roles that government has assumed has increased the complexity of its relationship with business. Several of the varied roles that government has assumed in its relationship with business are worth looking at because they suggest the influence, interrelationships, and complexities that are present.[9] These roles indicate that government:

1. Prescribes the rules of the game for business
2. Is a major purchaser of business's products and services
3. Uses its contracting power to get business to do things it wants
4. Is a major promoter and subsidizer of business
5. Is the owner of vast quantities of productive equipment and wealth
6. Is an architect of economic growth
7. Is a financier
8. Is the protector of various interests in society against business exploitation
9. Directly manages large areas of private business
10. Is the repository of the social conscience and redistributes resources to meet social objectives

After examining and assessing these various roles, one can perhaps begin to appreciate the crucial interconnectedness between business and government and the difficulty both business and the public have in fully understanding (much less prescribing) what government's role ought to be in relation to business.

THE ROLES OF GOVERNMENT AND BUSINESS

We do not intend to philosophize in this chapter on the ideal role of government in relation to business, because this is outside our stakeholder frame of reference. However, we will strive for an understanding of current major issues as they pertain to this vital relationship. For effective management, government, as a stakeholder, must be understood.

The fundamental question underlying our entire discussion of business/government relationships is, "What should be the respective roles of business and government in our socioeconomic system?" This question is far easier to ask than to answer, but as we explore it, some important basic understandings begin to emerge.

The issue could be stated in a different fashion: Given all the tasks that must be accomplished to make our society work, which of these tasks should be handled by government and which should be handled by business? This poses the issue clearly, but there are other questions that remain to be answered. If we decide, for example, that it is best to let business handle the production and distribution roles in our society, the next question becomes "How much autonomy are we willing to allow business?" If our goals were simply the production and distribution of goods and services, we would not have to constrain business severely. In modern times, however, other goals have been added to the production and distribution functions: for example, a safe working environment for those engaging in production, equal employment opportunities, fair pay, clean air, safe products, employee rights, and so on. When these goals are superimposed on the basic economic goals, the task of business becomes much more complex and challenging.

Because these latter, more socially oriented goals are not automatically factored into business decision making and processes, it often falls on government to ensure that those goals that reflect concerns of the public interest be achieved. Thus, whereas the marketplace dictates economic production decisions, government becomes one of the citizenry's designated representatives charged with articulating and protecting the public interest.

A Clash of Ethical Belief Systems

A clash of emphases partially forms the crux of the antagonistic relationship that has evolved between business and government over the years. This problem has been termed "a clash of ethical systems." The two ethical systems (systems of belief) are the **individualistic ethic of business** and the **collectivistic ethic of government**. Figure 10-1 summarizes the characteristics of these two philosophies.[10]

The clash of these two ethical systems partially explains why the current business/government relationship is adversarial in nature. In elaborating on the adversarial nature of the business/government relationship, Jacoby offered the following comments:

> *Officials of government characteristically look upon themselves as probers, inspectors, taxers, regulators, and punishers of business transgressions. Businesspeople typically view government agencies as obstacles, constraints, delayers, and impediments to economic progress, having much power to stop and little to start.*[11]

The business/government relationship not only has become adversarial but also has been deteriorating. The goals and values of our pluralistic society have become more complex, more numerous, more interrelated, and, consequently, more difficult to reconcile. The result has been increasing conflicts among diverse interest groups, with trade-off decisions becoming harder to make. In this process, it has become more difficult to establish social priorities, and consensus has in many cases become impossible to achieve.[12]

Social, Technological, and Value Changes

As we attempt to understand why all this has happened, it is only natural to look to changes in the social and technological environments for some explanations. According to Daniel Bell, since World War II four major changes have had profound impacts on American society in general and on the business/government relationship in particular. First, out of local and regional societies a truly national one has arisen.[13] Second, we have seen a "communal society" arise, characterized by a great emphasis on public goods and the internalization of external costs. Third, the revolution of rising expectations has brought with it the demand for "entitlements"—good jobs, excellent housing, and other amenities. Fourth, a rising concern has emerged for an improved "quality of life."[14]

In addition to these, six other societal value changes have shaped the course of business/government relations. These are the youth movement, the consumer protection movement, the ecology movement, the civil rights movement, the women's movement, and the egalitarian movement.[15]

In a sense, this last movement—the egalitarian movement—embraces all of the others, because it represents an effort to create an equitable balance of all facets of what is good in life in the United States. Thus, the value changes that have taken place "have multiplied the

---

FIGURE 10-1

The Clash of Ethical Systems Between Business and Government

Business Beliefs	Government Beliefs
• Individualistic ethic	• Collectivistic ethic
• Maximum concession to self-interest	• Subordination of individual goals and self-interest to group goals and group interests
• Minimizing the load of obligations society imposes on the individual (personal freedom)	• Maximizing the obligations assumed by the individual and discouraging self-interest
• Emphasizes inequalities of individuals	• Emphasizes equality of individuals

number of political decisions that have to be made relative to the number of decisions made in markets."[16] To the extent that these political decisions affect business—and they do to a great extent—we can understand the basic conflict arising once again in a clash between individualist and collectivist belief systems. Government's responses to changes taking place in society have put it in direct opposition to business in terms of both philosophy and mode of operation. Although one might argue that this clash of belief systems is not as severe today as it once was, the basic differences still serve to frame the positions of the two groups.

INTERACTION OF BUSINESS, GOVERNMENT, AND THE PUBLIC

This section offers a brief overview of the influence relationships among business, government, and the public. This should be helpful in understanding both the nature of the process by which public policy decisions are made and the current problems that characterize the business/government relationship. Figure 10-2 illustrates the pattern of these influence relationships.

One might rightly ask at this point, "Why include the public? Isn't the public represented by government?" In an ideal world, perhaps this would be true. To help us appreciate that government functions somewhat apart from the public, it has been depicted separately in the diagram. In addition, the public has its methods of influence that need to be singled out.

Government/Business Relationship

Government influences business through regulation, taxation, and other forms of persuasion that we will consider in more detail in the next section. Business, likewise, has its approach-

---

FIGURE 10-2

Interaction Among Business, Government, and the Public

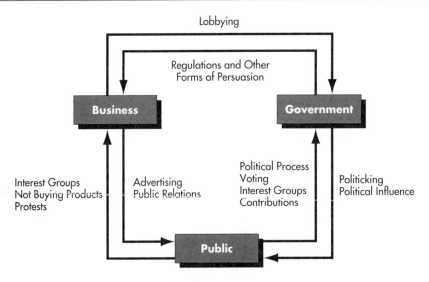

es to influencing government, which we will deal with in Chapter 11. Lobbying, in one form or another, is business's primary means of influencing government.

Public/Government Relationship

The public uses the political processes of voting and electing officials (or removing them from office) to influence government. It also exerts its influence by forming special-interest groups (farmers, small business owners, educators, senior citizens, truckers, manufacturers, and so forth) to wield more targeted influence. Government, in turn, uses politicking, public policy formation, and other political influences to have an impact on the public.

Business/Public Relationship

Business influences the public through advertising, public relations, and other forms of communication. The public influences business through the marketplace or by forming special-interest groups (for example, American Association of Retired Persons, Friends of the Earth, American Civil Liberties Union) and protest groups.

Earlier we raised the question of whether government really represents the public. This question may be stated another way: "Who determines what is in the public interest?" In our society, determining the public interest is not a simple matter. Whereas government may be the official representative of the public, we should not assume that representation occurs in a straightforward fashion. As we saw in Figure 10-2, the public takes its own initiatives both with business and with government. The three major groups, therefore, are involved in a dynamic interplay of influence processes that determine what is currently considered to be in the public interest.

Our central concern in this chapter is with government's role in influencing business, and we now turn our attention to that topic. Here we will begin to see more clearly how government is a major stakeholder of business. Government's official priority is in representing the public interest as it sees and interprets the public's wishes. But, like all large bureaucratic organizations, government also takes on a life of its own with its own goals and agenda.

GOVERNMENT'S NONREGULATORY INFLUENCE ON BUSINESS

Recognizing that in 2004 the federal government's budget went over the $2.2 trillion mark, we can begin to appreciate the magnitude of the effect government has on all institutions in society. We will limit our treatment to the federal government's influence on business, but we must remain mindful of the presence and influence of state and local governments as well.

Broadly speaking, we may categorize the kinds of influence government has on business as *nonregulatory* and *regulatory*. In the next major section, we will focus on government regulation, but in this section let us consider the wide range of nonregulatory influences that government has on business.

Two major issues merit consideration before we examine some of the specific policy tools or mechanisms government uses to influence business. These two major issues are (1) industrial policy and (2) privatization. Industrial policy is concerned with the role that our government plays in the world of international trade, and privatization zeroes in on the question of whether current public functions (for example, public education, public transit, social security, fire service) should be turned over to the private (business) sector. Both of these issues have important implications for the business/government relationship. They are both important, because they seem to come into and out of popularity on a fairly regular basis.

Industrial Policy

Important initial questions include, "What does industrial policy mean, and why has it become such a hotly debated issue?" An **industrial policy** may be defined as follows: "Any selective government measure that prevents or promotes changes in the structure of an economy."[17]

This very broad definition by itself does not give us enough focus to understand the concept. Let us elaborate. One school of thought thinks of industrial policy as some variation of the British model, wherein government provides help for older, declining industries. Therefore, when steel company executives in the United States argue for tax breaks and tariffs that would enable them to survive and compete with foreign competition, they are asking for an industrial policy.[18]

Another school of thought is exemplified by Robert Reich in his book *The Next American Frontier*, wherein he argues for a national industrial policy that attempts to identify winning (or sunrise) industries and foster their growth. As for losing (or sunset) industries, industrial policy would have as its goal redirecting resources into growth fields.[19]

Variations on these themes could yield a variety of industrial policy schools of thought. Five schools of thought that give us insights into industrial policy include the following: the accelerationists, the adjusters, the targeters, the central planners, and the bankers.[20] The **accelerationists** would try to pinpoint industries that promise to become strong international competitors and position them to move rapidly into world markets. Their goal would be to accelerate changes already signaled by the marketplace. The **adjusters** would offer adjustment assistance to declining industries in return for commitments that they would slim down, modernize, and help their employees relocate and train for new skills and jobs.

The **targeters** would target a select group of sectors or industries (for example, high tech, agriculture, energy, finance, health care equipment) to be turned into engines for growth. The **central planners** would advocate growth-oriented macroeconomic policies that would come close to comprehensive planning. Finally, the **bankers** would advocate a federally backed industrial development bank that would provide "patient capital"— money that could be sunk into a high-risk venture for 5 to 10 years or longer.

The debate over industrial policy became more active upon publication of Reich's *The Next American Frontier* in 1983 and the realization of our drab economic performance during the 1979–1982 period, when the United States lost significant ground to Japan as the world leader in industrial expansion. Many experts saw the very survival of the U.S. economy at stake in the face of subsidized foreign competition from Japan and other industrialized countries. Indeed, in 1987 a trade confrontation arose between the United States and Japan over the significant trade imbalances arising out of these issues.

During the Reagan (1980–1988) and first Bush (1988–1992) administrations, the notion of industrial policy was not looked upon with great favor. Both of these administrations advocated a free-market posture rather than government activism via industrial policy. President Clinton, however, supported several actions that typify an active industrial policy. For example, the Clinton administration took an activist stance in promoting the Internet by creating a Framework for Global Electronic Commerce. This framework outlined key principles for supporting the evolution of electronic commerce, identified where international efforts were needed, and designated the U.S. governmental agencies responsible for leading the effort. They did this because businesses were wary of becoming involved in the then-new Internet because they were unsure of the legal environment, and they feared government regulation and taxation would stifle Internet commerce.[21]

The George W. Bush administration entered office intending to follow in the early Reagan and Bush administrations' footsteps by adopting a free-market posture and minimizing government intervention. However, the events of September 11, 2001, changed that for the foreseeable future. Even politicians who were the staunchest of free-market advocates altered their views on the size of government after the World Trade Center was attacked. "Three words sum up my approach: Whatever it takes," said Representative J. D. Hayworth (R–Arizona), who was part of a group of conservative legislators who had previously tried (and failed) to pass a constitutional amendment for a balanced budget.[22] Time has shown that prediction to be true. In 2002, the *Federal Register*, a record of proposed and enacted regulations, contained 75,606 pages of new rules, the highest page count recorded by any presidential administration in history.[23]

Arguments for Industrial Policy

Proponents of an industrial policy (more active role of government in the business sector) cite a variety of reasons for supporting it. First, of course, is the declining or threatened competitiveness of the United States in world markets. A second argument is the use of industrial policy by other world governments, including Germany, Britain, France, and Italy. A third major argument is that the United States already has an industrial policy, but it is the haphazard result of unplanned taxes, tariffs, regulatory policies, and research and development policies. Our current system has been called an ad hoc industrial policy because the United States has, in fact, intervened in many specific industries as emergencies have arisen.

After the attack on the World Trade Center in 2001, the crippled airline industry requested bailouts of about $24 billion. Congress passed a bailout program of $15 billion— $5 billion in immediate cash assistance and $10 billion in loan guarantees.[24] Other affected industries soon made requests as well. There is a long history of government stepping in to rescue industries in distress. In 1971, the Lockheed Corporation received $250 million in loan guarantees from Congress. In 1976, the federal government merged seven failing Northeast railroads and then spent about $7 billion to keep the combined entity afloat. In 1979, the Chrysler Corporation received up to $1.5 billion in loan guarantees. Finally, Congress addressed the Savings and Loan Crisis of 1989 by closing more than 1,000 S&Ls at a cost of $124 billion.[25]

Some government interventions have been unqualified successes. Chrysler paid off its loan 7 years early, and the government received a profit of $350 million. Others, however, have been fraught with problems. The Lockheed bailout was rocky from the start. When it was revealed that Lockheed had paid foreign bribes, the government ousted two top executives and proceeded to give Lockheed activities very close scrutiny.[26]

Arguments Against Industrial Policy

Critics of industrial policy also have significant reasons for their views. Critics say that government interference reduces the market's efficiency. How do you keep politics out of what ought to be economic decisions? Some politicians, as well as experts, think the United States should focus on rescuing steel and other "sunset" industries. Others argue we ought to promote emerging "sunrise" industries, such as breakthrough products in high technology.

Those who oppose industrial policy say that foreign success with it has been highly variable. Japan, for example, has had as many failures as successes with its government's development agency, Ministry of International Trade and Industry (MITI). MITI is generally credited with helping to build Japan's computer, semiconductor, and steel industries, but efforts to promote the aluminum-refining, petrochemical, shipping, and commercial aircraft industries were viewed as failures.[27] One economist, Gary Saxonhouse, reports that Japanese support for research and development is less than that in the United States. He says that less than 2 percent of non-defense business research and development is financed by government in Japan, compared with 22 percent in the United States.[28] Further, Japan's favorable industrial policies (*keiretsu*), combined with lifetime employment, are ill suited to surviving economic recessions: The Japanese business system has produced too few entrepreneurial risk-takers.[29]

Finally, attempts at forming an industrial policy have been criticized as being irrational and uncoordinated and composed largely of "voluntary" restrictions on imports, occasional bailouts for near-bankruptcy companies, and a wide array of subsidies, loan guarantees, and special tax benefits for particular firms and industries. Thus, such efforts have constituted an industrial policy by default.[30] One could argue that the United States is incapable of developing a successful and planned industrial policy, given its experience and the composition of the public policy process that has characterized past decision making.

There is an ebb and flow of interest in the concept of industrial policy depending on which administration is in office and what is happening in the external environment. Many of the problems that initially started the current debate are still with us. New problems have arisen to add further complexity to the issue. Industrial policy is a powerful nonregulating approach by government to influence business that is certain to be a topic of debate for years to come.

Privatization

Privatization, generally speaking, refers to the process of "turning over to" the private sector (business) some function or service that was previously handled by some government body.[31] More than $700 billion in assets have been privatized worldwide, with emerging economies accounting for almost 40 percent of that.[32] Privatization is an integral part of the twenty-first century strategies of both developed and developing countries, with the intent being to capture both the discipline of the free market and a spirit of entrepreneurial risk-taking.[33]

To understand privatization, we need to differentiate two functions government might perform: (1) producing a service and (2) providing a service.[34]

Producing Versus Providing a Service. A city government would be providing a service if it employed a private security firm to work at the coliseum during the state

SEARCH THE WEB

To Privatize or Not to Privatize

The Reason Public Policy Institute (RPPI) sponsors a Web site devoted to the issue of privatization (**http://www.privati zation.org**). In it, they provide research and analysis, reports, and recommendations on how to streamline government through privatization. The nonpartisan group has worked closely with Democratic and Republican officials as well as a range of federal agencies. Their monthly newsletter *Privatization Watch* and their *Annual Privatization Report* provide information on the latest in privatization efforts around the globe.

Although there have been rumblings for several years about when—not if, but when—the nation's Social Security system will be bankrupted by payouts to the populous Baby Boomer generation, politicians haven't dared to tackle the issue head-on. Now it seems that the groundwork for privatizing this well-established public fund is being laid, as discussed in Money magazine (1 March 2004 v33 i3 p25). Penelope Wang suggests that the Bush administration's proposal for tax-free savings accounts is "a Trojan Horse for Social Security." Read her thoughts on privatization by logging on to InfoTrac College Edition at **http://www.infotrac-college.com** and keying record number A113100454.

basketball playoffs. This same city government would be producing a service if its own police force provided security at the same basketball tournament. The federal government would be providing medical care to the aged with a national Medicare program. The "production" of medical care would be coming from private physicians. The government would be providing and producing medical care if it employed its own staff of doctors, as, for example, the military does. The terminology can be very confusing, but the distinction must be made, because sometimes government provides a service (has a program for and actually pays for a service) and at other times it also produces a service (has its own employees who do it).[35]

The Privatization Debate.

Proponents of privatization in both the United States and Europe suggest that the functions of entire bureaucracies need to be contracted out to the private sector. They maintain that government at all levels is involved in thousands of businesses in which it has no real comparative advantage and no basic reason for being involved. They also argue that publicly owned enterprises are less efficient and less flexible than competitive private firms.[36] Opponents of privatization contend that there are certain activities that cannot be safely or effectively handled by the private sector. They point to the **federalization** of airport security (the return of airport security to the government sector) following the attack on the World Trade Center.

Privatization efforts are always undertaken with the hope that they will lead to improvements in efficiency and overall performance. In some cases, these hopes are realized but in many they are not. On average, a privatized firm's performance improves, but there is considerable variance in postprivatization performance among individual firms.[37] This variance is likely caused by differences in the ways that firms implement privatization programs. The nature of top management, the functioning of the board, and the strategic actions the firms undertake will all contribute to the likelihood of a privatization strategy's success.[38]

These two issues—industrial policy and privatization—are largely unresolved. As a result, they continue to be discussed and debated. As we have seen, the success of these efforts is largely dependent on their context—both the environments in which they are adopted and the ways in which they are implemented. It is clear that both industrial policy and privatization will have significant implications for the business/government relationship for years to come.

We now return to our discussion of the ways in which government uses various policies and mechanisms for influencing business.

Other Nonregulatory Governmental Influences on Business

Government has a significant impact on business by virtue of the fact that it has a large payroll and is a *major employer* itself. At all levels, government employs millions of people who, as a consequence of being government employees, see things from the government's perspective. Government is also in the position of being a standard-setter: For example, the 8-hour workday began in the federal government. After a decade of emphasis on the private sector, the role of government has begun to expand in response to the attack on the World Trade Center: Bailouts of troubled industries, increased defense spending, a shift of R&D money toward defense purchases, and higher spending on the social safety net all give government a larger role in the U.S. economy.[39]

Government is one of the largest *purchasers* of goods and services produced in the private sector. Some key industries, such as aerospace, electronics, and shipbuilding, are very dependent on government purchasing. Government can exert significant influence over the private sector by its insistence that minorities be hired, depressed areas be favored, small businesses be favored, and so on. Changes in government policy can dramatically change a firm's business environment.[40] For some firms in narrow markets, such as defense, the government dominates and controls whether or not those firms have a good year—indeed, whether or not they survive at all.[41]

Government influences the behavior of business through the use of *subsidies* in a variety of ways. Generous subsidies are made available to industries such as agriculture, fishing, transportation, nuclear energy, and housing and to groups in special categories, such as minority-owned enterprises and businesses in depressed areas. Quite often these subsidies have special qualifications attached.

Government also influences business, albeit indirectly, by virtue of its *transfer payments*. Government provides money for social security, welfare, and other entitlement programs that totals hundreds of billions of dollars every year. These impacts are indirect, but they do significantly affect the market for business's goods and services.[42]

Government is a major *competitor* of business. Organizations such as the TVA compete with private suppliers of electricity; the Government Printing Office competes with private commercial publishers and printing firms; and the United States Postal Service competes with private delivery services. In areas such as health, education, recreation, and security, the competition between government and private firms runs the gamut of levels—federal, state, and local.

Government loans and *loan guarantees* are sources of influence as well. Government lends money directly to small businesses, housing providers, farmers, and energy companies. Often such loans are made at lower interest rates than those of private competitors. Loan guarantee programs, such as the one provided to Chrysler, is another way in which government's influence is felt.[43]

Taxation, through the Internal Revenue Service, is another example of a government influence. Tax deductibility, tax incentives, depreciation policies, and tax credits are tools that are all at the disposal of the government. A critical example of the government's taxing power occurred when a "luxury tax" was added as a minor part of the government's deficit reduction package in the early 1990s. This new luxury tax ended up virtually crippling the boat-building industry. It led to massive layoffs and adversely affected dozens of related industries. Ironically, the luxury tax resulted in lower tax revenues than those industries had produced.[44]

Monetary policy, although it is administered through the Federal Reserve System, can have a profound effect on business. Although the Federal Reserve System is technically independent of the executive branch, it often responds to presidential leadership or initiatives.

Finally, *moral suasion* is a tool of government.[45] This refers to the government's attempts, usually through the president, to "persuade" business to act in the public interest by taking or not taking a particular course of action. These public-interest appeals might include a request to roll back a price hike, show restraint on wage and salary increases, or exercise "voluntary" restraints of one kind or another. When New York Mayor Rudy

Airlines may initially have welcomed deregulation as beneficial to their industry, but deregulation has been something of an ordeal for both airlines and their customers. In a *Fortune* article (22 March 2004 v149 i6 p108), Paul Lukas writes that "deregulation turned what had been a relatively staid industry topsy-turvy." Big airlines suddenly had to compete with low-cost airlines, and consumers experienced even more overcrowding and the inconvenience of scheduling flights via the new deregulated "hub-and-spoke" route system. The 9/11 disaster hit the airline industry, already weakened by deregulation, especially hard. Read Lukas's in-depth exploration of the importance to commerce of the airline industry by logging on to InfoTrac College Edition at **http://www.infotrac-college.com** and keying record number A114020119.

Giuliani exhorted businesses to reopen, customers to return to buying, and tourists to return to New York City after the attacks on the World Trade Center, he was exerting moral suasion.

GOVERNMENT'S REGULATORY INFLUENCES ON BUSINESS

In many ways, government regulation has been the most controversial issue in the business/government relationship. Government regulation has affected virtually every aspect of how business functions. It has affected the terms and conditions under which firms have competed in their respective industries. It has touched almost every business decision ranging from the production of goods and services to packaging, distribution, marketing, and service. Most people agree that some degree of regulation has been necessary to ensure that consumers and employees are treated fairly and are not exposed to unreasonable hazards and that the environment is protected. However, they also think that government regulation has often been too extensive in scope, too costly, and inevitably burdensome in terms of paperwork requirements and red tape.

Some analysts feel the problem is worse today than it has ever been. In a 2003 article entitled "America's Regulatory Mess," *The Economist* suggested that an increase in political funding from business has led to increased political interference in regulatory policy. Corporate donors want results from the politicians they support.[46] Another problem is the change in the nature of the regulatory issues. According to Robert Litan of the Brookings Institution, deregulation of the trucking and airline industries involved government stepping out of the way: This was welcomed by industry. However, deregulation of the telecom and electrical utility industries in the 1990s was not welcomed by industry incumbents. Regulators had to devise a form of managed competition that involved the setting of pricing, the creating of access, and so forth, which brought about elaborate rule books.[47]

Regulation: What Does It Mean?

Generally, **regulation** refers to the act of governing, directing according to rule, or bringing under the control of law or constituted authority. Although there is no universally agreed-upon definition of federal regulation, we can look to the definition of a federal regulatory agency proposed years ago by the Senate Governmental Affairs Committee.[48] It described a federal regulatory agency as one that:

1. Has decision-making authority
2. Establishes standards or guidelines conferring benefits and imposing restrictions on business conduct
3. Operates principally in the sphere of domestic business activity
4. Has its head and/or members appointed by the president (generally subject to senate confirmation)

5. Has its legal procedures generally governed by the Administrative Procedures Act

The commerce clause of the U.S. Constitution grants to the government the legal authority to regulate. Within the confines of a regulatory agency as outlined here, the composition and functioning of regulatory agencies differ. Some are headed by an administrator and are located within an executive department—for example, the Federal Aviation Administration (FAA). Others are independent commissions composed of a chairperson and several members located outside the executive and legislative branches— such as the Interstate Commerce Commission (ICC), the Federal Communications Commission (FCC), and the Securities and Exchange Commission (SEC).[49]

Reasons for Regulation

Regulations have come about over the years for a variety of reasons. Some managers probably think that government is just sitting on the sidelines looking for reasons to butt into their business. There are several legitimate reasons why government regulation has evolved, although these same businesspeople may not entirely agree with them. For the most part, however, government regulation has arisen because some kind of **market failure** (failure of the free-enterprise system) has occurred and government, intending to represent the public interest, has chosen to take corrective action. We should make it clear that many regulations have been created primarily because of the efforts of special-interest groups that have lobbied successfully for them. The governmental decision-making process in the United States is characterized by congressional regulatory response to the pressures of special-interest groups as well as to perceived market failures.

Four major reasons or justifications for regulation are typically offered: (1) controlling natural monopolies, (2) controlling negative externalities, (3) achieving social goals, and (4) other reasons.

Controlling Natural Monopolies.
One of the earliest circumstances in which government felt a need to regulate occurred when a natural monopoly existed. A **natural monopoly** exists in a market where the economics of scale are so great that the largest firm has the lowest costs and thus is able to drive out its competitors. Such a firm can supply the entire market more efficiently and cheaply than several smaller firms. Local telephone service is a good example, because parallel sets of telephone wires would involve waste and duplication that would be much more costly.

Monopolies such as this may seem "natural," but when left to their own devices could restrict output and raise prices. This potential abuse justifies the regulation of monopolies. As a consequence, we see public utilities, for example, regulated by a public utility commission. This commission determines the rates that the monopolist may charge its customers.[50]

Related to the control of natural monopolies is the government's desire to intervene when it thinks companies have engaged in anticompetitive practices. A recent example of this was the Justice Department's investigation of the Microsoft Corporation case in which the company was accused of anticompetitive trade practices. The U.S. Court of Appeals in a mixed ruling overturned an initial court ruling, recommending that Microsoft be split in two. The appeals court reprimanded the judge for publicly criticizing Microsoft but upheld the finding of fact that the Windows operating system constitutes a monopoly in the PC market and that Microsoft violated the Sherman Antitrust Act with its marketing tactics. Microsoft would bundle new features into their Windows operating system as a way of breaking into new markets. They then designed their operating system so that it worked more smoothly with Microsoft products than with others—giving it a clear and, according to the courts, unfair marketing advantage.[51] A *Business Week* editorial opined, "The courts should insist that Windows is a common carrier that must be open to all competitors, much like phone lines and cable. . . . Microsoft must accept the legal finding that it is a monopoly. As such, it has an obligation to open its operating system to competitors. If it does, it should be able to do the very thing it says is essential to its future—bundle new features into Windows that consumers want."[52]

Controlling Negative Externalities.

Another important rationale for government regulation is that of controlling the **negative externalities** (or spillover effects) that result when the manufacture or use of a product gives rise to unplanned or unintended side effects on others (other than the producer or the consumer). Examples of these negative externalities are air pollution, water pollution, and improper disposal of toxic wastes. The consequence of such negative externalities is that neither the producer nor the consumer of the product directly "pays" for all the "costs" that are created by the manufacture of the product. The "costs" that must be borne by the public include an unpleasant or a foul atmosphere, illness, and the resulting health care costs. Some have called these **social costs**, because they are absorbed by society rather than incorporated into the cost of making the product.

Preventing negative externalities is enormously expensive, and few firms are willing to pay for these added costs voluntarily. This is especially true in an industry that produces an essentially undifferentiated product, such as steel, where the millions of dollars needed to protect the environment would only add to the cost of the product and provide no benefit to the purchaser. In such situations, therefore, government regulation is seen as reasonable, and even welcomed, because it requires all firms competing in a given industry to operate according to the same rules. By forcing all firms to incur the costs, regulations level the competitive playing field.

Just as companies do not voluntarily take on huge expenditures for environmental protection, individuals often behave in the same fashion. For example, automobile emissions are one of the principal forms of air pollution. But how many private individuals would voluntarily request an emissions control system if it were offered as optional equipment? In situations such as this, a government standard that requires everyone to adhere to the regulation is much more likely to address the public's concern for air pollution.[53]

Achieving Social Goals.

Government not only employs regulations to address market failures and negative externalities but also seeks to use regulations to help achieve certain **social goals** it deems to be in the public interest. Some of these social goals are related to negative externalities in the sense that government is attempting to correct problems that might also be viewed as negative externalities by particular groups. An example of this might be the harmful effects of a dangerous product or the unfair treatment of minorities resulting from employment discrimination. These externalities are not as obvious as air pollution, but they are just as real.

Another important social goal of government is to keep people informed. One could argue that inadequate information is a serious problem and that government should use its regulatory powers to require firms to reveal certain kinds of information to consumers. Thus, the Consumer Product Safety Commission requires firms to warn consumers of potential product hazards through labeling requirements. Other regulatory mandates that address the issue of inadequate information include grading standards, weight and size information, truth-in-advertising requirements, product safety standards, and so on. A prime example of recent labeling requirements can be seen on canned goods and other products at the grocery store. Most canned goods now carry a "Nutrition Facts" label that provides consumer information on calories, fat content, and quantities per serving of sodium, cholesterol, carbohydrates, proteins, and vitamins.

Other important social goals that have been addressed include preservation of national security (deregulation of oil prices to lessen dependence on imports), considerations of fairness or equity (employment discrimination laws), protection of those who provide essential services (farmers), allocation of scarce resources (gasoline rationing), and protection of consumers from excessively high price increases (natural gas regulation).[54]

Other Reasons.   There are several other reasons for government regulation. One is to control **excess profits**. The claim for regulation here would be aimed at transferring income for the purposes of economic fairness. For example, as a result of the Arab oil embargo between 1973 and 1980, oil stocks went up suddenly by a factor of 10. One argument is that the extra profits collected by these producers are somehow undeserved and the result of plain luck, not wise investment decisions. So, in situations such as this in which profits are drastically, suddenly, and perhaps undeservedly increased, an argument has been made for government regulation.[55]

Another commonly advanced rationale for regulation is to deal with **excessive competition**. The basic idea behind this rationale is that excessive competition will lead to prices being set at unprofitably low levels. This action will force firms out of business and ultimately will result in products that are too costly because the remaining firm will raise its prices to excessive levels, leaving the public worse off than before.[56]

Types of Regulation

Broadly speaking, government regulations have been used for two central purposes: achieving certain economic goals and achieving certain social goals. Therefore, it has become customary to identify two different types of regulation: economic regulation and social regulation.

Economic Regulation.   The classical or traditional form of regulation that dates back to the 1800s in the United States is **economic regulation**. This type of regulation is best exemplified by old-line regulatory bodies such as the Interstate Commerce Commission (ICC), which was created in 1887 by Congress to regulate the railroad industry; the Civil Aeronautics Board (CAB), which was created in 1940; and the Federal Communications Commission (FCC), which was established in 1934 to consolidate federal regulation of interstate communications and, later, radio, telephone, and telegraph.

These regulatory bodies were designed primarily along industry lines and were created for the purpose of regulating business behavior through the control of or influence over economic or market variables such as prices (maximum and minimum), entry to and exit from markets, and types of services that can be offered. It is estimated that the industries subject to economic regulations by federal and state agencies accounted for about 10 percent of the gross national product.[57]

In the federal regulatory budget today, the major costs of economic regulation are for (1) finance and banking (e.g., Federal Deposit Insurance Corporation and Comptroller of the Currency), (2) industry-specific regulation (e.g., Federal Communications Commission and Federal Energy Regulatory Commission), and (3) general business (e.g., Department of Commerce, Department of Justice, Securities and Exchange Commission, and Federal Trade Commission).[58]

Later we will discuss deregulation, a trend that has significantly affected the old-line form of economic regulation that has dominated business/government relations for the past 100 years.

Social Regulation. The 1960s ushered in a new form of regulation that for all practical purposes has become what regulation means to modern-day business managers. This new form of regulation has come to be known as **social regulation**, because it has had as its major thrust the furtherance of societal objectives quite different from the earlier focus on markets and economic variables. Whereas the older form of economic regulation focused on markets, the new social regulation focuses on business's impacts on people. The emphasis on people essentially addresses the needs of people in their roles as employees, consumers, and citizens.

Two major examples of social regulations having specific impacts on people as employees were (1) the Civil Rights Act of 1964, which created the Equal Employment Opportunity Commission (EEOC) and (2) the creation of the Occupational Safety and Health Administration (OSHA) in 1970. The goal of the EEOC is to provide protection against discrimination in all employment practices. The goal of OSHA is to ensure that the nation's workplaces are safe and healthful.

An example of major social regulation protecting people as consumers was the 1972 creation of the Consumer Product Safety Commission (CPSC). This body's goal is to protect the public against unreasonable risks of injury associated with consumer products. An example of a major social regulation to protect people as citizens and residents of communities was the 1970 creation of the Environmental Protection Agency (EPA). The goal of EPA is to coordinate a variety of environmental protection efforts and to develop a unified policy at the national level.

Figure 10-3 summarizes the nature of economic versus social regulations along with pertinent examples.

FIGURE 10-3

Comparison of Economic and Social Regulations

	Economic Regulations	Social Regulations
Focus	Market conditions, economic variables (entry, exit, prices, services)	People in their roles as employees, consumers, and citizens
Industries Affected	Selected (railroads, aeronautics, communications)	Virtually all industries
Examples	Civil Aeronautics Board (CAB) Federal Communications Commission (FCC)	Equal Employment Opportunity Commission (EEOC) Occupational Safety and Health Administration (OSHA) Consumer Product Safety Commission (CPSC) Environmental Protection Agency (EPA)
Current Trend	From regulation to deregulation; however, problems with deregulation could reverse that trend	Stable—No significant increase or decrease in agencies

Whereas the older form of economic regulation was aimed primarily at companies competing in specific industries, the newer form of social regulation addresses business practices affecting all industries. In addition, there are social regulations that are industry specific, such as the National Highway Traffic Safety Administration (automobiles) and the Food and Drug Administration (food, drugs, medical devices, and cosmetics). Figure 10-4 summarizes the major U.S. independent regulatory agencies along with their dates of establishment. In addition to these, we should remember that there are several regulatory agencies that exist within executive departments of the government. Examples of this latter category include the following:

FIGURE 10-4

Major U.S. Regulatory Agencies

Agency	Year Established
Interstate Commerce Commission*	1887
Federal Reserve System (Board of Governors)	1913
Federal Trade Commission	1914
International Trade Commission	1916
Federal Home Loan Bank Board**	1932
Federal Deposit Insurance Corporation	1933
Farm Credit Administration	1933
Federal Communications Commission	1934
Securities and Exchange Commission	1934
National Labor Relations Board	1935
Small Business Administration	1953
Federal Maritime Commission	1961
Council on Environmental Quality	1969
Cost Accounting Standards Board	1970
Environmental Protection Agency	1970
Equal Employment Opportunity Commission	1970
National Credit Union Administration	1970
Occupational Safety and Health Review Commission	1971
Consumer Product Safety Commission	1972
Commodity Futures Trading Commission	1974
Council on Wage and Price Stability	1974
Nuclear Regulatory Commission	1974
Federal Election Commission	1975
National Transportation Safety Board	1975
Federal Energy Regulatory Commission	1977
Office of the Federal Inspector for the Alaska Natural Gas Transportation System	1979
Transportation Security Administration	2001

*Terminated in 1995. Replaced by the Surface Transportation Board.

**Terminated in 1939. Functions were reassigned to various housing agencies until 1955, when it was redesignated as an independent agency.

Ethics in Practice

To Comply or Not to Comply with the Government Regulation

Every summer and Christmas vacation for the past 4 years, I have worked in the maintenance department of Gilman Paper Company. Working there to help finance my college education, I have been exposed to many questionable practices. One of the most prominent problems is the adherence to safety regulations.

OSHA (Occupational Safety and Health Administration) requires that a vessel-confined-space entry permit be filled out before a person enters the confined area and that a "sniffer" (a device used to detect oxygen deficiencies and other harmful or combustible gases) be present and operational whenever a person is inside. A confined space is defined as any area without proper air ventilation and/or an area more than 5 feet deep. For example, tanks and pits are confined spaces.

Anytime a person enters or leaves a confined space, the person is required to place her or his initials on the entry permit. This is for the physical protection of the worker and the liability protection of the company. If workers are seen violating this policy, they can be reprimanded or fired on the spot.

In my many experiences with these confined spaces, I have observed on numerous occasions that these policies are not broken by the workers, but by the supervisors. It is their responsibility to obtain these permits and sign them, as well as obtain the use of a sniffer. Sometimes the supervisors and the workers will forget that we are working in a confined space and thus forget the permit and sniffer. When someone has realized that we are in a confined space, however, the supervisors have often asked us to initial the permit at various places as if the permit had been there all along.

When we work for extended periods of time in these areas, the sniffer's batteries often go dead as well. Instead of following regulations and leaving the area until a new sniffer can be obtained, the supervisors often tell employees to stay, declaring, "The air is fine. You don't need a sniffer!"

My problem is this: Should I sign these permits when I know it is dishonest, or should I do the "right" thing and let OSHA know that this regulation is being broken time and time again? After all, I'm not even a full-time employee, so who am I to cause trouble?

1. Who are the stakeholders in this case, and what are their stakes?

2. What should I have done in this situation? Is this regulation important, or is this just more government "red tape"? Should I have just "gone along to get along" with the supervisors?

Contributed by Dale Dyals

Agency	Department
Food and Health Administration	Health and Human Services
Antitrust Division	Justice
Drug Enforcement Administration	Justice
Occupational Safety and Health Administration	Labor
Federal Highway Administration	Transportation

The latest wave of government regulation is responding to events that have shaken the economy. Regulations have begun to focus on issues of national security in response to the World Trade Center attacks. In particular, the collection, protection and dissemination of information has been impacted. In addition, new economic regulations have addressed issues of corporate accountability in the wake of the Enron and WorldCom scandals. Most notably, the Sarbanes–Oxley Act (SOA) set extensive new reporting procedures and requirements for firms listed on U.S. stock exchanges. The act also institutes severe penalties for firms that fail to comply.

The SOA is emblematic of the dilemma of regulation. On one hand it is an effective response to a serious problem, the lack of investor confidence in the wake of the Enron and WorldCom scandals. As with all regulation, however, it presents additional burdens for firms. A recent survey found that auditing and reporting compliance costs, for firms with revenues under $1 billion, has increased 130 percent.[59] New listings of foreign firms on U.S. exchanges have dropped precipitously and one fifth of U.S. public companies are considering going private because of the cost of regulatory compliance.[60] The SOA is discussed in more detail in Chapter 19.

Issues Related to Regulation

It is important to consider some of the issues that have arisen out of the increased governmental role in regulating business. In general, managers have been concerned with what might be called "regulatory unreasonableness."[61] We could expect that business would just as soon not have to deal with these regulatory bodies. Therefore, some of business's reactions are simply related to the nuisance factor of having to deal with a complex array of restrictions. Other legitimate issues that have arisen over the past few years also need to be addressed.

To be certain, there are benefits of government regulation. Employees are treated more fairly and have safer work environments. Consumers are able to purchase safer products and receive more information about them. Citizens in all walks of life have cleaner air to breathe and cleaner water in lakes and rivers where they go for recreational purposes. These benefits are real, but their exact magnitudes are difficult to measure. Costs resulting from regulation also are difficult to measure. The **direct costs** of regulation are most visible when we look at the number of new agencies created, aggregate expenditures, and growth patterns of the budgets of federal agencies responsible for regulation. There were 14 major regulatory agencies prior to 1930, over 2 dozen in 1950, and 57 by the early 1980s. The most rapid expansion came in the 1970s.[62]

In addition to the direct costs of administering the regulatory agencies, there are **indirect costs** such as forms, reports, and questionnaires that business must complete to satisfy the requirements of the regulatory agencies. These costs of government regulation get passed on to the consumer in the form of higher prices. There are also **induced costs**. The induced effects of regulation are diffuse and elusive, but they constitute some of the most powerful consequences of the regulatory process. In a real sense, then, these induced effects have to be thought of as costs. Three effects are worthy of elaboration.[63]

1. *Innovation is affected.* When corporate budgets must focus on "defensive research," certain types of innovation do not take place. To the extent that firms must devote more of their scientific resources to meeting government requirements, fewer resources are available to dedicate to new product and process research and development and innovation. One industry affected in this way is the drug industry. Economists estimate that stringent FDA regulations seriously hinder innovation in the drug industry. The consequences are a slowed pace and a decreased number of new drugs arriving on the marketplace for consumer use.
2. *New investments in plant and equipment are affected.* To the extent that corporate funds must be used for regulatory compliance purposes, these funds are diverted from more productive uses. One estimate is that environmental and job safety requirements diminish by one-fourth the potential annual increase in productivity.

It should also be pointed out that uncertainty about future regulations has an adverse effect on the introduction of new products and processes.[64]

3. *Small business is adversely affected.* Although it is not intentional, most federal regulations have a disproportionately adverse effect on small firms. Large firms have more personnel and resources and are therefore better able to get the work of government done than are small firms. In one study of small business owner-managers, responses were solicited as to what they expected of government. Out of a list of nine choices, tax breaks for small firms was listed first and relief from government regulation was a close second.[65] More than any other group, small business seems to feel keenly affected by government regulation.

The frustrations of many small business owners and managers about government regulation are conveyed by Frank Cremeans's experience. On one single day, as owner of Cremeans Concrete & Supply Co. in Ohio, he was visited by officials from four separate federal and state regulatory agencies. They dropped in unannounced on his concrete business on the same day in January. The four agencies were the EPA, OSHA, the local health department, and the mine-inspection agency. Mr. Cremeans said he could not believe it. He had to drop everything and spend the entire day dealing with the officials' demands.[66]

DEREGULATION

Quite frequently, trends and countertrends overlap with one another. Such is the case with regulation and its counterpart, **deregulation**. There are many reasons for this overlapping, but typically they include both the economic and the political. From an economic perspective, there is a continual striving for the balance of freedom and control for business that will be best for society. From a political perspective, there is an ongoing interplay of different societal goals and means for achieving those goals. The outcome is a mix of economic and political decisions that seem to be in a constant state of flux. Thus, in the economy at any point in time, trends that appear counter to one another can coexist simultaneously. These trends are the natural result of competing forces seeking some sort of balance or equilibrium.

This is how we can explain the trend toward deregulation that evolved in a highly regulated environment. Deregulation represents a counterforce aimed at keeping the economy in balance. It also represents a political philosophy that was prevailing during the period of its origin and growth.

Deregulation may be thought of as one kind of regulatory reform. But, because it is unique and quite unlike the regulatory reform measures discussed earlier, we will treat it separately. Deregulation has taken place primarily with respect to economic regulations, and this, too, helps to explain its separate treatment.

Purpose of Deregulation

The basic idea behind deregulation has been to remove certain industries from the oldline economic regulations of the past. The purpose of this deregulation, or at least a reduced level of regulation, has been to increase competition with the expected benefits of greater efficiency, lower prices, and enhanced innovation. These goals have not been uniformly received, and it is still undecided whether deregulation works as a method of maximizing society's best interests. Figure 10-5 outlines the airline industry's experience with 25 years of deregulation.

Trend Toward Deregulation

When the trend toward deregulation began in the 1980s, most notably exemplified in the financial industry, the telecommunications industry, and the transportation (trucking, airline, railroad) industry, it represented business's first major redirection in 50 years.[67] The result seemed to be a mixed bag of benefits and problems. On the benefits side, prices fell in many industries, and better service appeared in some industries along with increased numbers of competitors and innovative products and services.

Several problems arose also. Although prices fell and many competitors entered some of those industries, more and more of those competitors were unable to compete with the dominant firms. They were failing, going bankrupt, or being absorbed by the larger firms. Entry barriers into some industries were enormous and had been greatly underestimated. This has been shown to be the case in airline, trucking, railroad, and long-distance telephone service.[68] Most dramatically, the savings and loan industry crisis, which resulted in an unprecedented $124 billion bailout by the U.S. government, has been generally attributed to deregulation.

Another problem that developed was that key industries became dominated by a few firms. This trend was obvious in transportation, where the major railroad, airline, and trucking companies boosted their market shares considerably during the 1980s. The top six railroads went from about 56 percent of market share to about 90 percent during this time. The top six airlines went from about 75 percent of market share to about 85 percent. The top 10 trucking firms went from about 38 percent of market share to about 58 percent. Prior to its breakup, AT&T enjoyed about an 80 percent share of the domestic market and a virtual monopoly in the huge toll-free, big-business, and overseas markets.[69]

FIGURE 10-5

25 Years of Airline Deregulation: 1978–2003

October 24, 1978, was a watershed in aviation history. On that date, President Jimmy Carter signed the Airline Deregulation Act, and the world of aviation changed forever. The Civil Aeronautics Board no longer had the power to determine pricing and set the routes. The industry quickly filled with new carriers and new routes, and the country club atmosphere soon shifted to cutthroat competition. The average U.S. airfare dropped from about $140 in 1977 to $60 in 2000 (in constant 1983 dollars). As a result, the number of U.S. airline passengers nearly tripled from 220 million in 1977 to 650 million in 2000.

For major airlines, the impact of deregulation was not so positive. Deregulation prompted the entry of the first no-frills airline, People Express, which drove prices down, making it hard for the larger firms to compete. Many airlines went bankrupt or were absorbed by others. Even heavyweights like Eastern and PanAm tottered until they both went bankrupt in 1991. Problems for large airlines remained, as US Airways and United filed for bankruptcy protection and American Airlines, the largest U.S. carrier, barely avoided filing. Today, discounters like Southwestern, AirTran, and Jet Blue keep the pressure on to lower prices in the metropolitan airports. Travelers who use smaller airports still pay higher prices.

SOURCE: Richard Newman, "Deregulation Was Good for Travelers, Hard on Airlines," *The Record*, Hackensack, NJ (December 7, 2003).

Dilemma with Deregulation

The intent of deregulation was to deregulate the industries, thus allowing for freer competition. The intent was not to deregulate health and safety requirements. The dilemma with deregulation is how to enhance the competitive nature of the affected industries without sacrificing the applicable social regulations. This is the second major problem with deregulation that needs to be discussed. Unfortunately, the dog-eat-dog competition unleashed by economic deregulation can force many companies to cut corners in ways that endanger the health and/or safety of their customers. This pattern, which seems to occur in any deregulated industry, was apparent in the trucking industry.[70]

Trucking Industry. To survive in a deregulated industry, many truckers delayed essential maintenance and spent too many hours behind the wheel. According to some industry experts, as many as one-third of the long-haul drivers turned to illegal drugs to help them cope with the grueling hours on the road. Others turned to alcohol. Statistics showed a sharp increase in the number of truck accidents from 1980 to 1986, and roadside inspections in one year turned up serious problems in 30 to 40 percent of the trucks inspected.[71]

Time and technology have helped to improve safety records. In the trucking industry, routine drug testing of drivers began in the late 1980s and alcohol testing began in 1995. Radar detectors were disallowed in 1993, while reflective striping became required. Most importantly, state motor vehicle departments became linked by nationwide license database. This stopped drivers from the common practice of holding multiple-state drivers's licenses and simply using another when ticketed for unsafe driving.

Overall, the trend toward deregulation continues globally. Around the world, industries that were once considered public goods are now being opened to market forces.

Telecommunications Industry. Since the breakup of AT&T in 1984, telephone rates have been cut in half, and aggressive competitors, such as MCI and Sprint, have moved quickly to adopt fiber optic cable and other service improvements.[72] The Telecommunications Act of 1996 did not always achieve its promise of lower rates and better service. In fact, after the act's inception, thousands of rural phone subscribers were without phone service. Before the act, cross-subsidization (urban subscribers and major long-distance carriers paid extra) ensured universal service. Although the new law proposed a new subsidy system, legal battles slowed its implementation.[73] In contrast, business and urban customers were the first beneficiaries of the new broadband services.[74]

Electric Utilities. Beginning in 1996, various states passed electric restructuring initiatives, and Congress considered a range of bills all geared to bring competition to the electric utilities. As had been true with telephone deregulation, consumers were expected to save money, but those savings were considered to have inherent trade-offs.[75] Power companies had traditionally provided special programs to aid the community and people in need. As was true of telephone companies, these programs were financed by spreading the cost over the customer base. The main concern with deregulation was that only those programs that could be used to enhance image or advertising were expected to remain.[76]

Eventually it became apparent that the problem was not going to be fair distribution of the money that would be saved. Instead, in the state of California, the problem became how to distribute the losses—$35 billion in excess costs that occurred over an 18-month period. In the words of *The Wall Street Journal*, "Given that mistakes can prove so costly, is electricity-market restructuring worth the risk?"[77]

The jury is still out on the question of deregulation. Was it a bad strategy or a good strategy implemented badly? The problems with electricity deregulation in California are partly a function of the industry. Electricity is a unique commodity in that it can't really be stored, so there isn't much surplus power available. This was exacerbated when utilities were encouraged to sell most of their generating plants and then use the spot market to buy power. Had other decisions been made differently, such as fixing prices, setting capacity, providing consumer choices, and preparing for the unexpected, the debacle might have been avoided.[78]

▪ SUMMARY

Business cannot be discussed without considering the paramount role played by government. Although the two institutions have opposing systems of belief, they are intertwined in terms of their functioning in our socioeconomic system. In addition, the public assumes a major role in a complex pattern of interactions among business, government, and the public. Government exerts a host of nonregulatory influences on business. Two influences with a macro orientation include industrial policy and privatization. A more specific influence is the fact that government is a major employer, purchaser, subsidizer, competitor, financier, and persuader. These roles permit government to affect business significantly.

One of government's most controversial interventions in business is direct regulation. Government regulates business for several legitimate reasons, and in the past two decades social regulation has been more dominant than economic regulation. There are many benefits and various costs of government regulation. A response to the problems with regulation has been deregulation. However, bad experiences in key industries such as trucking, airlines, savings and loans, banks, and utilities have caused many to wonder whether the government has gone too far in that direction.

The attack on the World Trade Center has made the public more comfortable with government's having a role in the private sector. Talk of privatization has been replaced with talk of federalization. Uncertainty stemming from the events of September 11, 2001, is likely to push public opinion away from risk-taking inherent in privatization for awhile, but the pendulum will swing back as it always has.

▪ KEY TERMS

accelerationists (page 342)

adjusters (page 342)

bankers (page 342)

central planners (page 342)

collectivistic ethic of government (page 339)

deregulation (page 355)

direct costs (page 354)

economic regulation (page 350)

excess profits (page 350)

excessive competition (page 350)

federalization (page 345)

indirect costs (page 354)

individualistic ethic of business (page 339)

induced costs (page 354)

industrial policy (page 342)

market failure (page 348)

natural monopoly (page 348)

negative externalities (page 349)

privatization (page 344)

regulation (page 347)

social costs (page 349)

social goals (page 349)

social regulation (page 351)

targeters (page 342)

■ DISCUSSION QUESTIONS

1. Briefly explain how business and government represent a clash of ethical systems (belief systems). With which do you find yourself identifying most? Explain. With which would most business students identify? Explain.

2. Explain why the public is treated as a separate group in the interactions among business, government, and the public. Doesn't government represent the public's interests? How should the public's interests be manifested?

3. What is regulation? Why does government see a need to regulate? Differentiate between economic and social regulation. What social regulations do you think are most important, and why? What social regulations ought to be eliminated? Explain.

4. Outline the major benefits and costs of government regulation. In general, do you think the benefits of government regulation exceed the costs? In what areas, if any, do you think the costs exceed the benefits?

5. What are the trade-offs between privatization and federalization? When would one or the other be more appropriate? What problems might you foresee?

■ RECOMMENDED CASES

Many of the end-of-text cases may be related to Chapter 10. You may wish to consider studying the following cases with Chapter 10.

Case 4. "FACING A FIRE." This case addresses the relationship of a business owner to the community in which his business has operated for many years. After 90 years in business, HFS Corporation has suffered a devastating fire. The owner is nearing retirement. If he takes the insurance money and closes the plant, the town will be devastated. If he opts to rebuild instead, he will face huge challenges at a time when he should be able to relax and enjoy the fruits of many years of labor. What should he do?

Case 15. "SOMETHING'S ROTTEN IN HONDO." This case addresses the social responsibilities of a plastics plant that employs a substantial portion of the residents of Hondo, a small town in Texas. George, the plant supervisor, has been given the choice between either scheduling the plant's high smokestack emissions at night to circumvent EPA guide-lines or relocating the plant to Mexico where EPA guidelines don't apply. Should George facilitate the emissions to retain jobs for the community? Do the jobs that will be retained in Hondo compensate for the dirtier air that Hondo will have? Does it even matter because the Mexico location is only 15 miles away and so the emissions from Mexico are likely to still affect Hondo?

Case 18. "TELEPHONE DEREGULATION: THE PRICING CONTROVERSY." This case explores the impact of the 1996 Telecommunications Act, which required local telephone providers to lease any or all of their network components to their new competitors at prices set by the Federal Communications Commission (FCC). Is it appropriate for the FCC to set the prices? Is it fair to require the local telephone providers to lease their components to their competitors? What might happen if the locals were allowed to set their own prices? What is the appropriate role for government to play in this situation?

■ WEB RESOURCES

The URLs listed here are current at the time of publication. Should any of these Web sites change, please search under the company's or organization's name for an updated address.

Airline safety
http://www.airsafe.com

Budget watchers
http://www.ombwatch.org

Business Roundtable
http://www.brtable.org

Business Week magazine
http://www.businessweek.com

Cato Institute
http://www.cato.org

The Economist
http://www.economist.com

Fortune magazine
http://www.fortune.com

All government information
http://www.firstgov.gov

Privatization Web site
http://www.privatization.org

Regulation magazine
http://www.cato.org/pubs/regulation/about.
html

Regulations Web site
http://www.regulations.gov

 InfoTrac® College Edition   http://www.infotrac-college.com

Articles from both Business Week *and* Fortune *can be researched, retrieved, and read from your desktop using InfoTrac's online database.*

■ ENDNOTES

1. "Is Government Dead?" *Time* (October 23, 1989).
2. Michael J. Mandel, "Rethinking the Economy," *Business Week* (October 1, 2001), 28–33.
3. Paul Magnusson, "Suddenly, Washington's Wallet Is Open," *Business Week* (October 1, 2001), 34.
4. Mandel, 30.
5. "Antitrust Laws," The World Book Encyclopedia, Vol. 1 (Chicago: World Book, 1988), 560; See also "The Interstate Commerce Act," Vol. 10, 352–353.
6. *Ibid.*
7. *Ibid.*
8. Alfred L. Seelye, "Societal Change and Business-Government Relationships," *MSU Business Topics* (Autumn 1975), 5–6.
9. George A. Steiner, *Business and Society*, 2d ed. (New York: Random House, 1975), 359–361.
10. L. Earle Birdsell, "Business and Government: The Walls Between," in Neil H. Jacoby (ed.), *The Business–Government Relationship: A Reassessment* (Santa Monica, CA: Goodyear, 1975), 32–34.
11. Jacoby, 167.
12. *Ibid.*, 168.
13. For a view somewhat counter to this, see Kevin Phillips, "The Balkanization of America," *Harper's* (May 1978), 37–47.
14. Daniel Bell, "Too Much, Too Late: Reactions to Changing Social Values," in Jacoby, 17–19.
15. Seelye, 7–8.
16. Jacoby, 168.
17. Arthur T. Denzau, "Will an 'Industrial Policy' Work for the United States?" (St. Louis: Center for the Study of American Business, Washington University, September 1983), 1.
18. *Ibid.*, 2.
19. Robert B. Reich, *The Next American Frontier* (New York: Penguin Books, 1983).
20. "Industrial Policy: Is It the Answer?" *Business Week* (July 4, 1983), 55–56.
21. Anonymous, "The Clinton Administration's Framework for Global Electronic Commerce: Executive Summary" (July 1, 1997," *Business America* (Vol. 119, No. 1, January 1998), 5–6.
22. Mandel, 30.
23. Clyde Wayne Crews, "Ten Thousand Commandments: An Annual Snapshot of the Federal Regulatory State," (Cato Institute: Washington, DC), cited in "Under Bush, Federal Regulators Are Breaking Records," *The Economist* (July 26, 2003), 57–58.
24. Magnusson, 34; http://www.cnn.com.
25. Michael Arndt, "What Kind of Rescue?" *Business Week* (October 1, 2001), 36–37.
26. *Ibid.*
27. Monroe W. Karmin, "Industrial Policy: What Is It? Do We Need One?" *U.S. News & World Report* (October 3, 1983), 47.
28. Robert J. Samuelson, "The New (Old) Industrial Policy," *Newsweek* (Mary 23, 1994), 53.
29. Hiroyuki Tezuka, "Success as the Source of Failure? Competition and Cooperation in the Japanese Economy," *Sloan Management Review* (Vol. 38, No. 2, March 1997), 83–93.
30. Ira C. Magaziner and Robert B. Reich, *Minding America's Business: The Decline and Rise of the American Economy* (New York: Vintage Books, 1983), 255.
31. Ted Kolderie, "What Do We Mean by Privatization?" (St. Louis: Center for the Study of American Business, Washington University, May 1986), 2–5.
32. Ravi Ramamurty, "A Multilevel Model of Privatization in Emerging Economies," *Academy of Management Review* (July 2000), 525–550.
33. Shaker A. Zahra, R. Duane Ireland, Isabel Gutierrez, and Michael A. Hitt, "Privatization and Entrepreneurial

Transformation: Emerging Issues and a Future Research Agenda," *Academy of Management Review* (July 2000), 509–524.

34. Kolderie, 2–5.
35. *Ibid.*, 3–5.
36. Steve Coll, "Retooling Europe," *The Washington Post National Weekly Edition* (August 22–28, 1994), 6–7.
37. Alvaro Cuervo and Bélen Villalonga, "Explaining the Variance in the Performance Effects of Privatization," *Academy of Management Review* (July 2000), 581–590.
38. *Ibid.*, 581–590.
39. Magnusson, 30.
40. Richard Reed, David J. Lemak, and W. Andrew Hesser, "Cleaning Up After the Cold War: Management and Social Issues," *Academy of Management Review* (Vol. 22, No. 3, July 1997), 614–642.
41. Murray L. Weidenbaum, *Business, Government and the Public*, 3d ed. (Englewood Cliffs, NJ: Prentice Hall, 1986), 5–6.
42. *Ibid.*, 6–8.
43. *Ibid.*
44. Alan Keyes, "Why 'Good Government' Isn't Enough," *Imprimis* (Vol. 21, No. 10, October 1992), 2.
45. *Ibid.*, 10–11.
46. "America's Regulatory Mess," *The Economist* (July 26, 2003), 57–58.
47. *Ibid.*
48. *Congressional Quarterly's Federal Regulatory Directory*, 5th ed. (1985–1986), 2.
49. *Ibid.*, 2–3.
50. *Ibid.*, 9.
51. "Microsoft: Time to Change," *Business Week* (July 16, 2001), 100.
52. *Ibid.*, 100.
53. *Congressional Quarterly's Federal Regulatory Directory*, 5th ed. (1985–1986), 10–11.
54. *Ibid.*, 12.
55. Stephen Breyer, *Regulation and Its Reform* (Cambridge, MA: Harvard University Press, 1982), 21–22.
56. *Ibid.*, 31–32.
57. Weidenbaum (1986), 178–179.
58. Melinda Warren, "Federal Regulatory Spending Reaches a New Height: An Analysis of the Budget of the U.S. Government for the Year 2001." (St. Louis, Missouri: Center for the Study of American Business, June 2000); derived from the budget of the U.S. government.
59. Jeff Thain, "Sarbanes–Oxley: Is the Price Too High? *The Wall Street Journal* (May 27, 2004), A20.

60. *Ibid.*
61. Graham K. Wilson, *Business and Politics: A Comparative Introduction* (Chatham, NJ: Chatham House, 1985), 39.
62. Murray L. Weidenbaum, *Costs of Regulation and Benefits of Reform* (St. Louis: Center for the Study of American Business, Washington University, November 1980), 3; See also Murray Weidenbaum and Melinda Warren, *It's Time to Cut Government Regulations* (St. Louis: Center for the Study of American Business, Washington University, February 1995).
63. *Ibid.*, 12–14.
64. *Ibid.*, 12.
65. James J. Chrisman and Fred L. Fry, "How Government Regulation Affects Small Business," *Business Forum* (Spring 1983), 25–28.
66. Brent Bowers and Udayan Gupta, "To Fight Big Government, Some Join It," *The Wall Street Journal* (November 11, 1994), B1. See also Robert Samuelson, "The Regulatory Juggernaut," *Newsweek* (November 7, 1994), 43.
67. "Deregulating America," *Business Week* (November 28, 1983), 80–89.
68. "Is Deregulation Working?" *Business Week* (December 22, 1986), 50–55.
69. *Ibid.*, 52.
70. Frederick C. Thayer, "The Emerging Dangers of Deregulation," *The New York Times* (February 23, 1986), 3.
71. Kenneth Labich, "The Scandal of Killer Trucks," *Fortune* (March 30, 1987), 85–87.
72. Robert J. Samuelson, "The Joy of Deregulation," *Newsweek* (February 3, 1997), 39.
73. Fred Vogelstein, "A Really Big Discount," *U.S. News & World Report* (February 2, 1998), 39–40.
74. Alex J. Mandl, "Telecom Competition Is Coming (Sooner Than You Think," *The Wall Street Journal* (January 26, 1998), A18.
75. Glenn Hodges, "Deregulating Electricity," *The Washington Post* (April 6, 1997), C1.
76. Patricia Irwin, "Why Deregulation Is Inevitable," *Electrical World* (Vol. 21, No. 7, July 1997), 62–63.
77. Rebecca Smith, "The Lessons Learned: California Has Taught Us a Lot About the Dos and Don'ts of Deregulation," *The Wall Street Journal* (September 17, 2001), R4.
78. *Ibid.*, R4.

Chapter 11

■ BUSINESS INFLUENCE *on* GOVERNMENT *and* PUBLIC POLICY

CHAPTER LEARNING OUTCOMES

After studying this chapter, you should be able to:

1 Describe the evolution of corporate political participation.

2 Differentiate among the different levels at which business lobbying occurs.

3 Explain the phenomenon of political action committees (PACs) in terms of their historical growth, the magnitude of their activity, and the arguments for and against them.

4 Define coalitions and describe the critical role they now assume in corporate political involvement.

5 Discuss the Bipartisan Campaign Reform Act and other issues surrounding campaign financing.

6 Outline the principal strategic approaches to political activism that firms are employing.

As our previous discussion of industrial policy showed, government is a central stakeholder of business. Government's interest, or stake, in business is broad and multifaceted, and its power is derived from its legal and moral right to represent the public in its dealings with business.

Today, because of the multiple roles it plays in influencing business activity, government poses significant challenges for business owners and managers. Government not only establishes the rules of the game for business functions but also influences business in its roles as competitor, financier, purchaser, supplier, watchdog, and so on. Opportunities for business and government to cooperate in a mutual pursuit of common goals are present to some extent, but the major opportunity for business is in developing strategies for effectively working with government in such a way that business's own objectives are achieved. In doing this, business has the responsibility of obeying the laws of the land and of being ethical in its responses to government expectations and mandates. To do otherwise raises the specter of abuse of political power. As the regulatory environment has become more intense and complex and as other changes have taken place in society, businesses have had little choice but to become more politically active.

Attempts by business to influence government are a major and accepted part of the public policy process in the United States. The U.S. political system is driven by the active participation of interest groups striving to achieve their own objectives. The business sector is, therefore, behaving in a normal and expected fashion when it assumes an advocacy role for its interests. Other groups, whether they be labor organizations, consumer groups, farmers' groups, doctors' organizations, real estate broker organizations, military groups, women's rights organizations, environmental groups, church groups, and so on, all strive to pursue their special interests with government. Today's pluralism necessitates that all of these groups seek to influence government. The public interest in this special-interest-driven process is that some semblance of a balance of power be maintained and that the activities and practices of these organizations remain legal and ethical.

CORPORATE POLITICAL PARTICIPATION

Political involvement is broadly defined as participation in the formulation and execution of public policy at various levels of government. As decisions about the current and future shape of society and the role of the private sector shift from the marketplace to the political arena, corporations, like all interest groups, find it imperative to increase their political involvement and activity.[1]

Historically, companies entered into debates in Washington only on an issue-by-issue basis and with no overall sense of a purpose, goal, or strategy. Companies also tended to be reactive; that is, they dealt with issues only after the issues had become threats. This approach became obsolete as the kinds of changes we have described began to occur. Today, success in Washington is just as important as success in the marketplace. Just as business has learned that it must develop competitive strategies if it is to succeed, it has learned that political strategies are essential as well.[2]

A Lesson Learned

Special-interest politics have become the way in which most legislation is passed, and even a corporate giant like Microsoft had to learn to be an active and effective player. Microsoft opened its first lobbying office in 1995, 20 years after the company was founded. The office had only one staff person, Jack Krumholtz, a 33-year-old lawyer with no real Washington experience and no secretary. He wasn't given a cushy office with a view of the Potomac. Instead, he had an office in the Microsoft federal sales office, across from a suburban shopping mall and seven miles from downtown DC.[3] Another lobbyist described the Microsoft command post as "Jack and his Jeep," because the Jeep was the only downtown location Krumholtz had available.[4]

After the U.S. Justice Department brought an antitrust case against Microsoft, the company began to realize its isolationist policy wasn't working. In addition to increasing its political giving, the company retained a cadre of well-connected lobbyists and public relations officials to present its case to legislators and the public.[5] A *Business Week* article showed Microsoft pulling out all the stops. Krumholtz and his colleagues moved to a modern building on Dupont Circle. The in-house staff had grown to 14, and they had scores of high-powered help on retainer. They gave millions to both parties in the 2000 presidential election, hired both Bush and Gore advisers as lobbyists, and became the ninth largest "soft money" corporate donor in the United States. They ran national ad campaigns featuring a "warm and fuzzy" Bill Gates and touting their multimillion-dollar charity campaign. Think tanks that supported their interests received major donations; those that espoused views counter to theirs were cut off. They even farmed out legal work to most of the law firms in DC so that most of the lawyers in town would be constrained from working for their competitors.[6] In 2004, after years of struggling with antitrust cases both domestic and abroad, Microsoft positioned one of its top lawyers to chair the American Bar Association's antitrust section, a group that has significant influence over the development of antitrust policy and law.[7]

These efforts have met with some success. A court-ordered breakup of Microsoft was overturned in appeals court. This was followed by an agreement with the Justice Department that settled the antitrust charges. However, the calm was short-lived as 2004 opened with a flurry of attacks on Microsoft's competitive practices. Urged on by Massachusetts, the only state to hold out on the settlement, the appeals court, at this writing, is set to rule on whether the settlement sanctioned Microsoft adequately.[8] Following close on the heels of the appeals court is the European Commission, which is due to rule on charges that Microsoft exploited its monopoly with its media-player software and is dominating the market in larger "server" computers.[9] At the same time, Japan fair trade officials raided the Japanese unit of Microsoft on suspicion of antitrust violations.[10] Many observers charge that Microsoft has no one to blame but itself for its problems with government agencies. An editorial in *The Economist* opined, "Microsoft's exploitation of its monopoly will continue as long as the monopoly itself does" and "a break-up of Microsoft is the only remedy that would have any impact on its conduct."[11] The editors of *eWeek* added, "Microsoft should move as far as possible from business model of yesteryear and focus on improving its products without locking out competitors."[12] Microsoft's market dominance may be less of an issue when open-source software such as Linux is further developed. Currently, Japan and South Korea are trying to entice China into joining a project to boost research on Linux.[13]

Microsoft learned the hard way that political involvement is not optional. In response, they continue to employ a range of activities to promote their interests. To appreciate more fully the participation of business in the process of public policy formation in the United States, it is necessary to understand the approaches that business uses to influence the government stakeholder. We will focus only on the following major approaches: (1) lobbying, (2) PACs, (3) coalition building, and (4) political strategy. At this point, our perspective will be largely descriptive as we seek to understand these approaches, their strengths and weaknesses, and business's successes and failures with them. At the same time, however, we must be constantly vigilant of possible abuses of power or violations of sound ethics.

Business Lobbying

Lobbying is the process of influencing public officials to promote or secure the passage or defeat of legislation. Lobbying is also used to promote the election or defeat of candidates for public office. Lobbyists are intensely self-interested. Their goals are to promote legislation that is in their organizations' interests and to defeat legislation that runs counter to their organizations' interests. Business interests, labor interests, ethnic and racial groups, professional organizations, and those simply pursuing ideological goals they believe to be in the public interest are lobbying at the federal, state, and local levels. Our focus is on business lobbying at the federal level, although we must remember that this process is also occurring daily at the state and local levels.

H. R. Mahood defines lobbying as the professionalization of the art of persuasion.[14] Lobbying serves several purposes. It is not just a technique for gaining legislative support or institutional approval for some objective such as a policy shift, a judicial ruling, or the modification or passage of a law. Lobbying may also be directed toward the reinforcement of established policy or the defeat of proposed policy shifts. Lobbying also targets the election or defeat of national, state, and local legislators. A lobbyist may be a lawyer, a public relations specialist, a former head of a public agency, a former corporate executive, or a former elected official. In this sense, there is no typical lobbyist.[15] It is clear, however, that more and more businesses, as well as other special-interest groups, are turning to lobbyists to facilitate their involvement in the public policy process. A cartoon depicts the increasing stature of lobbyists. The teacher asks the class, "Who runs America?" She then gives her students the following choices: "the President, the Supreme Court, or Congress?" An astute class member responds, "Lobbies."[16]

Organizational Levels of Lobbying

The business community engages in lobbying at several organizational levels. At the broadest level are **umbrella organizations**, which represent the collective business interests of the United States. The best examples of umbrella organizations are the Chamber of Commerce of the United States and the National Association of Manufacturers (NAM). Out of these have grown organizations that represent some subset of business in general, such as the Business Roundtable, which was organized to represent the largest firms in America, and the National Federation of Independent Businesses (NFIB), which represents smaller firms.

At the next level are **trade associations**, which are composed of many firms in a given industry or line of business. Examples include the National Automobile Dealers Association, the National Association of Home Builders, the National Association of Realtors, and the Tobacco Institute. Finally, there are individual **company lobbying** efforts. Here, firms such as IBM, BellSouth, Ford, and Delta Airlines lobby on their own behalf. Typically companies use their own personnel, establish Washington offices for the sole purpose of lobbying, or hire professional lobbying firms or consultants located in Washington or a state capital. An example of company lobbying was given previously in Microsoft's lesson learned. Figure 11-1 depicts examples of the broad range of lobbying and political-interest organizations used by businesses.

We will now discuss lobbying in greater detail, beginning with the use of professional lobbyists.

Professional Lobbyists.   Lobbyists, sometimes derisively referred to as "influence peddlers," operate under a variety of formal titles and come from a variety of backgrounds. Officially, they are lawyers, government affairs specialists, public relations consultants, or public affairs consultants. Some are on the staffs of large trade associations based in Washington. Others represent specific companies that have Washington offices dedicated to the sole purpose of representing those companies in the capitol city. Still others are professional lobbyists who work for large law firms or consulting firms in Washington that specialize in representing clients to the lawmakers.

FIGURE 11-1

Examples of the Range of Lobbying Organizations Used by Businesses

Broad Representation: Umbrella Organizations

- Chamber of Commerce of the United States
- National Association of Manufacturers (NAM)
- Business Roundtable
- National Federation of Independent Businesses (NFIB)
- State Chambers of Commerce
- City Chambers of Commerce

Midrange Representation: Trade and Professional Associations and Coalitions

- National Auto Dealers Association
- National Association of Realtors
- American Petroleum Institute
- American Trucking Association
- National Association of Medical Equipment Suppliers
- Tobacco Institute
- Health Benefits Coalition
- United States Telecom Association

Narrow/Specific Representation: Company-Level Lobbying

- Washington and State Capital Offices
- Law Firms Specializing in Lobbying
- Public Affairs Specialists
- Political Action Committees (PACs)
- Grassroots Lobbying
- Company-Based Coalitions
- Former Government Officials

The lobbying consultant in Washington frequently is a former government official. Some are ex-congressional staff members or ex-members of Congress. Others are former presidential staff assistants or other highly placed government officials. Many of these individuals are legally prohibited from discussing private business matters with anyone in the White House for one year after leaving office. However, one year is a relatively short apprenticeship for people who will likely increase their former salaries manyfold. Examples of former government officials who left public positions to represent private interests include Michael Deaver (former Reagan deputy chief of staff), Richard Allen (former national security adviser), Jody Powell (former White House press secretary), and Robert Dole (former U.S. senator). George K. Mueller was the Air Force's deputy acquisition chief when he resigned after 30 years of service to join the board of Lockheed Martin.[17] Two more 30-year veterans, David Heebner and John M. Keane, joined General Dynamics after retirement.[18] At this writing, Rep. Billy Tauzin of Louisiana, chief architect of the new Medicare prescription drug law, has received a lucrative job offer to lobby for the pharmaceutical industry: Pundits suggest that he will have already earned his salary because the Medicare bill is expected to provide windfall profits for drug makers.[19]

What do business lobbyists accomplish? Lobbyists offer a wide range of services that include drafting legislation, creating slick advertisements and direct-mail campaigns, consulting, and, most important, getting access to lawmakers. Access, or connections, seems to be the central product that the new breed of lobbyist is selling—the returned phone call, the tennis game with a key legislator, or the golf outing with the Speaker of the House. With so many competing interests in Washington today, the opportunity to get your point across in any format is a significant advantage. Lobbyists also play the important role of showing busy legislators the virtues and pitfalls of complex legislation.[20] Figure 11-2 summarizes some of the various activities that business lobbyists accomplish for their clients.

Grassroots Lobbying.

In addition to lobbying directly through the use of professional lobbyists, firms use what is called **grassroots lobbying**, which refers to the process of mobilizing the "grassroots"—individual citizens who might be most directly affected by legislative activity—to political action. Grassroots lobbying is also used actively by trade associations and the umbrella organizations. The better corporate grassroots lobbying programs usually arise in companies whose leaders recognize that people are a firm's most potent political resource. Although people cannot be directed or required to become politically involved, they can be persuaded and encouraged.

Trade associations often use grassroots support by asking their members to contact their representatives. They also organize rallies, target mail campaigns, develop instant advertisements, and use computerized phone banks.[21] However, the grassroots response must be genuine, or at least appear to be genuine. The old techniques of phony "**astroturf lobbying**" no longer hold much sway: Hundreds of phone calls or thousands of identical postcards that arrive on the same day are rarely effective.[22]

Some organizations and trade associations have created fake groups that appear to be grassroots but are largely created and funded by an organization or trade association. Recently, a group called "Americans for Technology Leadership (ATL)" funded polls that concluded the American public was not very interested in the Microsoft antitrust case. Then when 19 state attorneys general were considering what remedy to seek, ATL funded another poll that found that the public wanted their state's attorneys general to devote their attention to other issues, not the Microsoft case.[23] ATL also hired telemarketers to make

FIGURE 11-2

What Business Lobbyists Do for Their Clients

- Get access to key legislators (connections)
- Monitor legislation
- Establish communication channels with regulatory bodies
- Protect firms against surprise legislation
- Draft legislation, slick ad campaigns, direct-mail campaigns
- Provide issue papers on anticipated effects of legislative activity
- Communicate sentiments of association or company on key issues
- Influence outcome of legislation (promote helpful legislation, defeat harmful legislation)
- Assist companies in coalition building around issues that various groups may have in common
- Help members of Congress get reelected
- Organize grassroots efforts

unsolicited calls to people, asking them if they would send a letter to Congress to demand that Justice drop the antitrust case. The telemarketer would offer to draft and mail the letter to the person's congressperson for them—they simply needed to give permission for their name to be used. What is ATL? It is a group designed to develop grassroots support for Microsoft: It is funded by Microsoft and has few dues-paying members.[24] The Internet has now made it possible to not only create fake groups but also manufacture fake consumers. With the heavy use of listservers in a variety of arenas, corporations can now invent people to log on and record messages that show no indication of the company for which they are working.[25]

Grassroots lobbying has become one of the most frequently used and most effective techniques both for individual firms and for associations and coalitions. A few examples of successful grassroots lobbying efforts at the company level are helpful in understanding its power. During the debate over the North American Free Trade Agreement (NAFTA), Ford Motor Co. as well as other automakers tapped into a network of 32 top automobile suppliers and their employees to drum up letters and telephone calls to Capitol Hill in support of the trade pact. The company also called on its 5,000 dealers for grassroots lobbying support.[26] NAFTA was subsequently passed. More recently, credit unions across the nation employed grassroots lobbying to urge congressional support of H. R. 1151—the Credit Union Membership Access Act, which relaxes credit union membership requirements. In addition to eliciting the traditional onslaught of petitions and personal letters, thousands of credit union members lobbied their lawmakers directly on Capitol Hill.[27] These efforts undoubtedly led to the landslide vote in which the House passed the bill.

The technology revolution has ushered in **cyberadvocacy** as a new form of grassroots campaigning. Computers and the Internet have made communication infinitely easier. Books and consulting services have sprung up to assist organizations in using the Internet to both amass grassroots support and enable grassroots supporters to contact their legislators. There is a danger with the use of e-mail. According to Stella Anne Harrison of the Juno Advocacy Network, "Blanket e-mail messages can be equated with spam—unwarranted and irrelevant overload of e-mail messages that can be ignored. However, targeted and specific e-mails are another matter." She recommends that advocates include their name and home address so that legislators will know they are hearing from their constituents."[28]

Trade Association Lobbying.

Most major companies are members of *trade associations* that lobby on their behalf. A trade association is an organization that represents firms in a specific industry. The association receives its funds from firms in the industry that join and pay dues. According to the *Encyclopedia of Associations*, which lists all the registered national and international associations, there were over 22,000 registered in the United States in 2004. Of these, nearly 4,000 were classified as "Trade, Business, and Commercial."[29]

Lobbying at the association level is frequent today. One recent successful experience worth noting was the pharmaceutical industry's success at blocking Congress's efforts to impose price controls and allow the importation of less expensive drugs. The Pharmaceutical Research and Manufacturers of America (PhMRA) spent $8.5 million to defeat the importation component of the Medicare prescription drug benefit bill passed in 2003. Individual companies also spent millions, including Eli Lilly & Co. ($2.2 million), Bristol-Meyers Squibb Co. ($2.6 million), and Johnson & Johnson ($2.2 million). The pharmaceutical industry as a whole spent $29 million in lobbying in 2003, which was more than any other

The cost of drugs in the United States is a hot issue. While many Americans feel forced to buy drugs in Canada to maintain their budgets, the U.S. government, strongly supported by the pharmaceutical industry, is attempting to shut down that pipeline. In an article for *Time* (2 February 2004 v163 i5 p44), Donald L. Bartlett and James B. Steele reveal that the pharmaceutical industry profits greatly from its lobby, which has more than 600 lobbyists: "more than one for every member of Congress." But there is dissension in government ranks: A number of states and cities have begun to consider buying drugs directly from Canada to control costs for their employees. Find out why drugs cost Americans so much as well as arguments for and against stopping importation by logging on to InfoTrac College Edition at **http://www.infotrac-college.com** and keying record number A113530510.

sector.[30] This level of spending is likely to continue as the states, in 2004, mounted a campaign to develop their own importation plans aimed at keeping drug prices down.[31] Furthermore, another federal drug importation bill is due to be introduced again in Congress. Given the pharmaceutical industry's army of lobbyists and millions in lobbying expenditures, Representative Bernie Sanders (I–Vermont) believes it stands little hope of passing.[32] The pharmaceutical industry hired 675 lobbyists from 138 different firms in 2002, representing seven lobbyists for each U.S. senator, and spent a record $91.4 million.[33]

Trade associations sometimes find themselves in the undesirable role of battling with each other in their attempts to lobby Congress. An example of these types of battles occurred between the credit union and the banking industries regarding the scope of services credit unions should be permitted to supply. Credit unions argued that they provide services to individuals and small businesses that are shunned by traditional banks. They contended that they should be able to expand the services they provide to this generally underserved population. Banks countered that credit unions enjoy an unfair competitive advantage by virtue of their exemptions from both taxes and the Community Reinvestment Act (CRA) obligations required of banks and thrifts. They maintained that large, multiple-employer credit unions should be subject to the same taxes, CRA rules, and safety requirements as banks. Ultimately, the House passed H. R. 1151—the Credit Union Membership Access Act, which relaxed restrictions on credit union membership.[34]

Umbrella Organizations.

The umbrella organizations are associations, too. But unlike a trade association, an umbrella organization has a broad base of membership that represents businesses in several different industries of various sizes. Historically, the two major umbrella organizations in the United States have been the Chamber of Commerce of the United States and the National Association of Manufacturers. Two other prominent organizations include the Business Roundtable and the National Federation of Independent Businesses. Each of these groups has political action as one of its central objectives.

Chamber of Commerce of the United States.

The national Chamber of Commerce was founded in 1912 as a federation of businesses and business organizations. In addition to firms, corporations, and professional members, the Chamber has thousands of local, state, and regional chambers of commerce; American chambers of commerce abroad; and several thousand trade and professional associations. Its diversity of membership shows why it is referred to as an umbrella organization.

Historically, the U.S. Chamber of Commerce had been a legislative powerhouse in its ability to influence public policy. Its power gradually waned over the years.[35] When Thomas Donohue became the Chamber president, he promised to awaken the "sleeping giant, missing in action from many important battles." In 2003, after five years as president and CEO, Donohue is credited for the Chamber's being revitalized in "money, members and influence."[36] One tactic he has used to great success is to dispense favors to individual businesses that might not want their company name associated with lobbying efforts. Wal-Mart, DaimlerChrysler, and American Council of Life Insurers, among others, each contributed $1 million to a campaign to help elect judges known for being friendly to business. From 2000 to 2003, the Chamber spent over $150 million to further this goal.[37]

National Association of Manufacturers (NAM).

NAM describes itself as "America's oldest and largest national broad-based industrial trade association."[38] It represents 14,000 members. Although the membership of NAM has historically been tilted toward the larger smokestack industry firms, it now includes 10,000 small and medium-sized firms as well as 350 member associations. The membership of NAM encompasses every industrial sector and all 50 U.S. states.[39]

These are not easy times for NAM: The 2002–2003 manufacturing recovery has been the slowest on record with over 2 million jobs lost.[40] A 2003 study by NAM showed how costs unrelated to production, such as corporate tax rates, employee benefits, tort litigation, regulatory compliance, and energy, add about 22 percent to U.S. manufacturer's unit labor costs.[41] As Jerry Jasinowski, president of NAM, told a 2004 members' gathering, "people don't care about manufacturing, and they're unaware of the cost issues we face."[42] In addition to economic problems, NAM is facing anger from their small and mid-sized member firms that believe NAM is more concerned with the needs of the global companies.[43] One problem is that the concerns of small firms often differ from those of the larger, global players. One particular point of contention is the issue of free trade. The large firms tend to be free-trade advocates, a stance with which NAM agrees; however, the small firms are increasingly desirous of protection.[44]

Business Roundtable. Formed in 1972, the Business Roundtable is often regarded as an umbrella organization, although it has a restricted membership. It is an association of chief executive officers of leading corporations with a combined workforce of more than 10 million employees in the United States and $3.7 trillion in revenues.[45] Long regarded as a sleeping giant, former chairman John T. Dillon and current president John Castellani turned the organization into a "lobbying juggernaut."[46] The renewed vigor has led to increased membership with Hewlett-Packard, Ford Motor, and IBM returning as members.[47]

The Business Roundtable is different from most groups, such as the Chamber of Commerce and NAM, in the extent of participation by the chief executive officers. The Roundtable is not designed to push narrow issues that benefit narrow interests. Instead, the Roundtable selects concerns based on "the impact the problem will have on the economic well-being of the nation." Working in task forces on specific issues, the Business Roundtable is committed to "advocating public policies that ensure vigorous economic growth, a dynamic global economy, and the well-trained and productive U.S. workforce essential for future competitiveness."[48]

National Federation of Independent Businesses (NFIB). During the end of the twentieth century, the growth of small businesses came to dominate the business news. It should not be surprising, therefore, that the NFIB, as a small business association, also came into a position of power. We might think of the NFIB as an umbrella organization for smaller businesses. In the most recent edition of the Power 25 Lobbying Groups compiled for *Fortune* magazine, the NFIB ranked third overall and tops in business organizations for clout.[49]

One of the best ways to appreciate the NFIB's newfound power is to describe its success at grassroots lobbying.[50] The NFIB made its mark by strong and successful lobbying against former President Clinton's health care plan. The plan called for "employer mandates" requiring most employers to pay for their employees' health insurance. The NFIB and its 600,000 foot soldiers went to work in a grassroots lobbying campaign that eventually defeated the employer mandates proposal and helped stall the overall health care plan. More than anything else, the small business lobby showed that it had become a dominant player in the Washington public policy arena.

COALITION BUILDING

A noteworthy and growing mechanism of political involvement in the public policy process is the creation and use of **coalitions** to influence government processes. A coalition is formed when distinct groups or parties realize they have something in common that might warrant their joining forces, at least temporarily, for joint action. More often than not, an issue that various groups feel similarly about creates the opportunity for a coalition.

Coalition formation has become a standard practice for firms interested in accomplishing political goals or influencing public policy. If a company or an association wants to pass or defeat particular legislation, it needs to seek the support of any individual or organization that has a similar position on the issue.[51] Coalitions enable members to share their resources and pool their energies when they confront difficult issues. Coalitions also are used because they enable a company to push for its own agenda without necessarily having its name attached to the campaign.[52]

Because coalitions tend to form around issues, an astute political strategist could analyze past, present, and likely future coalitions so that coalition behavior could be anticipated and managed. To do this, MacMillan and Jones[53] recommend the following steps:

1. *Manage the sequence in which issues are addressed.* This kind of control can dictate priorities and emphasis and result in the proper channeling of effort to suit the organization's interests.
2. *Increase the visibility of certain issues.* By doing this, the strategist can focus attention in such a way that her or his goals are met.
3. *Unbundle issues into smaller subissues.* The strategist may be able to successfully reach her or his goals by slowly but surely accomplishing one small step at a time. The net result may be more success for the entirety.

SEARCH THE WEB

OPEN SECRETS

The Center for Responsive Politics is a nonpartisan, nonprofit research group based in Washington, DC, that tracks the flow of money in politics and assesses its impact. The Center's goal is to create "a more educated voter, an involved citizenry, and a more responsive government." Support for the Center comes from a combination of foundation grants and individual contributions. They will accept no contributions from businesses or labor unions. Their Web site (**http://www.opensecrets.org**) is filled with information regarding the role of money in the political process. By law, candidates are required to disclose contributions from any individuals who give them more than $200 and any PACs or political committees. Visitors to the Web site can find out who made political contributions from their own or any zip code (and to whom they made them). They can also search various issues and find out who is giving money, and to whom, to ensure that their interests prevail. The Web site also offers information regarding federal election law and other related issues. Visitors to the site can sign up for their "Money in Politics Alerts"—weekly e-mail messages that highlight special-interest legislation on Capitol Hill, "who is giving the money and who is getting it."

One high-profile example of coalition building around a specific issue is the Coalition for Economic Growth and American Jobs. Backers of this coalition included the U.S. Chamber of Commerce, the Business Roundtable, the American Bankers Association, the National Association of Manufacturers, and scores of other trade groups and individual companies. Recognizing that the issue of business outsourcing was evolving into a hot button for the 2004 elections, they have joined to fight the growing number of state and federal initiatives aimed at keeping jobs at home and restraining globalization.

POLITICAL ACTION COMMITTEES

To this point, our discussion of lobbying has focused primarily on interpersonal contact and powers of persuasion. We now turn our attention to **political action committees (PACs)**, the principal instruments through which business uses financial resources to influence government. PACs should be thought of as one facet of lobbying. However, because they have become such an influential phenomenon, they deserve separate treatment in this text.

Evolution of PACs

PACs have been around for years, but their influence has been most profoundly felt in the past two decades. This is perhaps because the bottom line in politics, as well as in business, is most often measured in terms of money—who has it, how much they have, and how much power they are able to bring to bear as a result. This has often been referred to as the **Golden Rule of Politics**: "He who has the gold, rules."[54]

Business PACs appeared on the scene in the early 1970s as a direct result of the 1974 amendments to the Federal Election Campaign Act (FECA). Under this law, organizations of like-minded individuals (such as business, labor, and other special-interest groups) may form together and create a PAC for the purpose of raising money and donating it to candidates for public office. PACs may contribute $5,000 per candidate per election—primary, runoff, general, or special. There are no aggregate limits on how much a PAC may contribute to numerous candidates. The $5,000 limit is less restricting than that placed on individuals, who are limited to donating $2,000 per federal candidate per election.[55]

At the start of 2004, 3,868 PACs were officially registered with the Federal Election Commission.[56] This represents a decline from the more than 4,000 PACs that were registered in 2001. Corporate PACs were the largest subgroup with 1,538 committees.[57] In the 2000 elections, PAC contributions to the House and Senate totaled $200 million, with another $200 million going to national parties as well as candidates for local and state offices.[58] From the 1996 to the 2000 presidential elections, soft money raised by Democrats and Republicans nearly doubled.[59] These numbers do not include the substantial "soft money" contributions that are not tied to a particular candidate but directly influence a candidate's campaign. However, the passing of the Bipartisan Campaign Reform Act (BCRA), commonly known as *McCain-Feingold*, has changed the rules regarding soft money and thus the way that PACs will operate in subsequent elections. Figure 11-3 on page 374 shows the top 10 PAC contributors to federal candidates.

Arguments for PACs

Not surprisingly, those who support PACs are primarily those who collect and donate the money (for example, the business community) and those who receive the money (many

FIGURE 11-3

Top 10 PAC Contributors to Federal Candidates (2003–2004)

PAC	Total Amount	Democratic Percent	Republican Percent
National Association of Realtors	$1,329,700	52%	47%
Wal-Mart Stores	$1,250,500	16%	84%
Association of Trial Lawyers	$1,041,499	91%	9%
National Association of Home Builders	$996,500	39%	61%
Laborer's Union	$964,250	81%	19%
Carpenters and Joiners Union	$927,500	61%	39%
International Brotherhood of Electrical Workers	$922,700	96%	4%
National Auto Dealer's Association	$918,100	30%	70%
United Parcel Service	$907, 685	30%	70%
Machinists/Aerospace Workers	$902,000	98%	1%

SOURCE: The Center for Responsive Politics (http://www.opensecrets.org). Based on data released by the FEC on Monday, February 9, 2004.

members of Congress and candidates for office). Businesses see PACs as a positive and constructive way to participate in the political process. They see PACs as a reasonable means by which business, labor, and other interest groups may organize their giving. They argue that business giving is offset by labor giving and by the multitude of other special-interest groups that also have formed PACs.

Many of the congressional recipients of PAC contributions also advocate PACs. There is less uniformity of support among Congress than among the business community, however. One reaction from our elected officials is resentment at the suggestion that they can be bought. The larger problem seems to be the growing dependency of politicians on PAC money to get elected. In general, members of Congress seem to support the idea of PAC contributions, because their campaign financing has become increasingly dependent on it. With each passing year, however, the need for reform of PAC laws became more apparent to many politicians.

Arguments Against PACs

Some of the most vocal opposition to PACs and the role they are playing comes from current and past members of Congress themselves. Veteran lawmakers like Paul Simon (D–Illinois) and Bill Bradley (D–New Jersey) cited the perpetual need to chase money as a major factor in why they left office.[60] The frustrations of many members of Congress are summed up in the comments of former senator Robert Dole (R–Kansas): "When these political action committees give money, they expect something in return other than good government. It is making it much more difficult to legislate. We may reach a point where if everybody is buying something with PAC money, we can't get anything done." He worries about differing treatment of the rich and the poor: "Poor people don't make campaign contributions. You might get a different result if there were a Poor-PAC up here."[61] Dole's point is borne out by a *Money* article. In it, Ann Reilly Dowd estimated the price that special-interest contributions exact on the average household. According to a recent Progressive Policy Institute study, U.S. taxpayers paid $47.7 billion for corporate tax breaks

Ethics in Practice

INFLUENCING LOCAL GOVERNMENT

My friend runs a small Atlanta chemical company that produces alum. Alum is used for many purposes, including water purification, and the company had a contract with Fulton County for this use for many years. In all the years they had this contract, they received it through open bidding. This was the case every renewal year until this year, when they were again the low bidder. A larger company based in the North with a division in Georgia was awarded the contract, even though its bid was about 3 percent higher. This would have been acceptable if there had been a quality or delivery problem in the past, but this had never been the case.

My friend met with a former county commissioner to seek advice about, and reasons for, this situation. The commissioner believed that there was an under-the-table agreement and advised my friend to sue the county and its purchasing manager. The problem is that the contract is relatively small and the lawsuit would almost certainly cost more than the contract.

1. Is filing a lawsuit the best way for this chemical company to influence the county commission? What options does the company have?

2. Do companies now have to lobby local or other governments to get business? Do they need to make PAC contributions? Bribes or kickbacks?

3. What action should this small chemical company take?

Contributed by Jack Rood

and subsidies, costing the average household about $483. Import quotas for sugar, textiles, and other goods totaled another $110 billion, with a total cost per household of $1,114. The average U.S. household was expected to pay $1,600 for legislation that protects corporations and the wealthy.[62] Although some of these tax breaks and subsidies are certain to be sound policy and would be implemented with or without financial motivation, Dowd raises an interesting point. Certainly many of those tax breaks, subsidies, and quotas can be traced back to the coffers of PACs.

PACs and the Vote-Buying Controversy.

Many studies have been done to calculate correlations between PAC giving and congressional voting. The major problem is that correlations do not necessarily prove causation. But correlations do appear convincing and are used by PAC critics to fullest advantage. Several political analysts have been able to conduct studies using more sophisticated statistical techniques than simple correlation. These studies have been able to control variables, such as party ideology and past voting records, in an effort to determine what independent effects the contributions have.

The results of these studies have been mixed. Some find strong support, others find no support, and a third group has mixed or marginal findings.[63] These mixed results have been attributed to the contexts of the situation, and so researchers have subsequently looked for contingencies that might explain the differences. In a 2003 study, Jeffrey Cohen and John Hamman explored the affect of PAC contributions on the regulation of cable television. In support of their hypotheses, they found that PAC contributions were more influential when given to House candidates than to Senate candidates. They explain it in two ways: The more frequent elections of House members make them more susceptible to campaign financing concerns, and the smaller size of the House constituencies (as opposed to the

Senate constituencies) means House members have fewer interest groups with which they must contend. Similarly, they found that PAC money was more influential when issues were at the smaller interest-group level, and its importance became diluted when issues moved to the broader arena of the entire House or Senate.[64]

Center for Public Integrity Study.

A 2003 study released by the Washington-based Center for Public Integrity reported that up to $8 billion in contracts was awarded to more than 70 U.S. companies for work in Afghanistan and postwar Iraq over a 2-year period. Most of these companies were established political players in Washington, with employees or board members who had close ties to both parties through the executive branch, members of Congress, or the highest levels of the military. These companies have contributed nearly $49 million to national political campaigns and parties since 1990. Of the 14 largest contactors receiving the largest awards, 13 employ former government officials or persons with close ties to the government. These top 14 gave nearly $23 million in political contributions from 1990 to 2003.[65]

PAC contributions appear to be most effective when certain conditions prevail.[66] These conditions include the following:

1. *When the issue is less visible.* PAC funds are more likely to be effective while the issue being debated is less visible—that is, not yet in the full glare of public and media scrutiny.
2. *During the early stages of the legislative process.* When agenda setting and subcommittee work are being done, the public, the press, and "watchdog" groups are not as attentive.
3. *When the issue is narrow, specialized, or unopposed.* PAC contributions are more effective on specialized or unopposed issues than on broad national issues.
4. *When PACs are allied.* When "PACs travel in packs" and work together, they can wield considerable power.
5. *When PACs adapt lobbying techniques to their contribution strategies.* Successful PACs also employ grassroots lobbying with contributions.

PACs and Campaign Financing

Because PAC money is easy to come by, it is clear why PACs have so much influence with their contributions. When this fact is combined with the ever-escalating sums of money that legislators need to get and stay elected, the result is quite powerful. The increasing dependency on PAC contributions is driven partly by the rising costs of getting elected and partly by the ease of getting PAC money. The cost of getting elected has skyrocketed. For the 1992 elections, Democrats and Republicans raised a combined $507.9 million. That number increased to $1,236 million in 2000—a 243 percent increase in only 8 years.[67]

Not only has the dependency on PAC money become a serious problem, but it is also growing increasingly evident that most of the money is going to incumbents. Common Cause, a citizen's lobby, studied the giving patterns of PACs. In the 2000 election, according to Common Cause research, PACs contributed $8 to House incumbents for every $1 given to challengers, and $6 to Senate incumbents for every $1 given to challengers. According to Common Cause president and CEO Scott Harshberger, "This system is a gravy train for members of Congress—and a meal ticket for special interests, many of whom want something in return." Given this advantage, it is not surprising that 98 percent of House incumbents and 82 percent of Senate incumbents won their reelection bids in the 2000 election.[68]

Citizen lobby groups and a growing number of legislators are becoming alarmed at the effects of PACs. The general public, too, distrusts PACs and considers them harmful to the nation's political process. S. Prakash Sethi and Nobuaki Namiki found that the negative reactions toward PACs were independent of socioeconomic and demographic factors, political ideology, and party affiliation. In a national survey, they found that (1) 17.6 percent of the respondents felt PACs were a good thing, (2) 43.1 percent felt PACs were a bad thing, (3) 35.6 percent believed PACs had a great deal of influence, and (4) 45.8 percent thought PACs had some influence. Sethi and Namiki concluded that "business must undertake substantive and communications-related measures to improve public perception of PAC activities if it is to maintain societal legitimacy in its involvement in the political process."[69] Figure 11-4 describes the case of Enron, an extreme example of using political contributions to negative advantage.

The Hard Facts About Soft Money. The **Bipartisan Campaign Reform Act (BCRA)**, which went into effect on November 6, 2002, represents "the most sweeping change of the U.S. campaign finance system in a quarter century."[70] The purpose of this legislation was to remove the influence of **soft money** on candidates running for national office. Soft money is a contribution made to political parties instead of to political candidates. Soft money contributions were unregulated prior to the law and were often used to run "issue ads" just prior to an election. In contrast, law already regulated **hard money**, donations made directly to the candidates. The act banned soft money and prevented special-interest groups from airing "issue ads" in the period prior to an election, while raising the limits for hard money donations. Shortly after the passage of the BCRA, several groups challenged the law's constitutionality in court. Odd bedfellows such as the AFL-CIO, the

FIGURE 11-4

Circumvention as a Government Influence Strategy

Enron's bankruptcy was the first in a wave of corporate scandals that decimated public confidence in U.S. corporations. However, the bankruptcy was just the tip of the iceberg. A study by the Citizens for Tax Justice Watchdog Group (http://www.ctj.org) found that although Enron paid no taxes in 2002, they received a $278 million tax rebate on a tax break from stock options cashed in by employees. The study also found that Enron paid no taxes in four of the five years from 1996 to 2000, during which time the company collected $381 million in tax refunds. This report underscores the importance of reading footnotes. Enron's financial reports show that the company paid millions of dollars in taxes in recent years. However the footnotes tell another story. Enron used its off-shore subsidiaries and stock-option decisions to reduce its U.S. taxes to zero. Some of the taxes in the financial reports were paid to foreign governments and other taxes were deferred. These tax savings show why it was quite easy for Enron to provide about $6 million in contributions to federal candidates and parties from 1990 to 2002. Over the last decade, 71 senators and 186 House members took political contributions from Enron. Enron isn't the only corporation to avoid tax payments. Citizens for Tax Justice conducted a study of half the *Fortune* 500 companies and found that 24 owed no taxes in 1998, 13 owed no taxes in 1997, and 16 owed no taxes in 1996.

Avoiding taxes is not the only way that firms circumvent government regulations. A 2004 edition of the news show *60 Minutes* reported that major U.S. corporations were doing business with rogue nations. U.S. law bans virtually all commerce with countries like Iran, Syria, and Libya that have sponsored terrorists. However, three *Fortune* 500 firms—Halliburton, Conoco-Phillips, and General Electric—were identified in the report as doing business in Iran and Syria. The law contains a loophole that these firms utilized: It does not apply to any foreign or offshore subsidiary that is run by non-Americans.

SOURCE: David Ivanovich, "Investigators: Enron Taxes 'Eye-Popping,'" *Houston Chronicle* (February 13, 2004); *60 Minutes* (January 25, 2004), http://www.cbsnews.com; Citizens for Tax Justice, http://www.ctj.org.

American Civil Liberties Association, the U.S. Chamber of Commerce, and the National Rifle Association claimed the law violated their right to free speech. In May 2003, a federal court found the soft money ban to be unconstitutional and allowed political parties to raise soft money again while setting restrictions on the airing of issue ads. This was immediately appealed to the Supreme Court. On September 8, 2003, the Supreme Court upheld the soft money and issue ad restrictions of the BCRA in a 5-4 ruling.

Although the new law represents a significant step forward in campaign financing, problems still remain. As Republican lobbyist Ron Kaufman said, "Campaign cash is like the Pillsbury Doughboy. You push it in one place and it pops out in another."[71] Soft money is still pouring in as Democrat and Republican strategists set up new groups to take the place of the political parties. Some worry that these groups will be less accountable than the political parties were prior to the law's inception.[72] These nonprofit organizations, known as **527s** for the section of the tax code that governs their activities, are allowed to raise and spend soft money on campaigns. The Federal Election Commission imposed limits on their use of soft money but opted not to shut them down: New formal regulations for these groups are being developed at this writing.[73]

Another means by which firms are able to get around campaign financing reform is the act of **bundling**, the collection of individual donations that are then delivered to the candidate in a lump sum. Typically a senior executive will host a fund-raising event and invite high-level employees to attend and donate up to the $2,000 limit. Executives may be given lucrative bonuses with the implicit understanding that they will make the maximum contribution. Bundling is not new, but it has reached new heights in the 2004 presidential election and has made the financial industry George Bush's biggest backer. As of January 26, 2004, nearly eight months before the presidential election, the financial industry had raised $9.5 million for the Bush campaign in small checks of up to $2,000 that were bundled for contribution. The influence of campaign financing reform on the practice of bundling is clear: In the 2000 election, 42 percent of the Bush war chest came from individual contributions, but in the 2004 election 98 percent of the contributions were from individuals. Clearly, one unintended consequence of campaign financing reform has been to shift the burden for political contributions from corporations to their employees.[74]

Strategies for Political Activism.   We have discussed some of the principal approaches by which business has become politically active—lobbying, PACs, and coalitions. To be sure, there are other approaches, but these are the major ones. In our discussion, we have unavoidably made reference to the use of these approaches as part of a strategy. To develop the idea of strategy for political activism, it is important to understand that managers must not only identify useful approaches but also address when and under what conditions these various approaches should be used or would be most effective. We do not want to carry this idea too far, because it is beyond the scope of this book. On the other hand, some discussion of strategies for political activism is necessary to help us fulfill our stakeholder frame of reference. As managers devise and execute political strategies, it is useful to see their initiatives as factors in their development of stakeholder management capabilities.

John Mahon has argued that organizations, having experienced failures and surprises in the political and social arenas, are expanding their strategic vision and action by developing strategies for coping with a rapidly changing social and political environment. Mahon asserts that the purpose of political strategy is "to secure a position of advantage regarding a given regulation or piece of legislation, to gain control of an idea or a move-

Despite bipartisan efforts to control campaign spending, special interests continue to find ways to buy influence for their candidates. Two strategies were particularly useful in circumventing campaign finance reform restrictions in the 2004 elections. Democrats made particularly strong use of 527s to create a shadow democratic party that could circumvent financing restrictions, while Republicans focused more on bundling, i.e., combining small individual contributions so that the aggregate donations are large enough to buy political influence. An article in *Business Week* (12 April 2004 i3878 p32) shows how both strategies have thwarted the goal of campaign finance reform by simply creating a new breed of fat cat donors who finesse the campaign finance reform laws to raise more money than ever before. Read more about those fat cat donors by logging on to InfoTrac College Edition at **http://www.infotrac-college.com** and keying record number A115066437.

ment and deflect it from the firm, or to deal with a local community group on an issue of importance."[75] Often such strategies are exercised in arenas beyond the regulatory/legislative scene. In pursuing political strategy, two major approaches or strategies are desirable: (1) keeping an issue off the public agenda and out of the limelight and (2) helping to define the public issue. If the company cannot do the first, which is a strategy of containment, it should strive for the second, which allows the firm to exercise some control in shaping the issue. If both of these approaches fail, the company will need to pursue a coping strategy.[76]

At this point, it is useful to consider several other ideas about political strategy: the regulatory life cycle approach, contingency approaches, and corporate political entrepreneurship.

Regulatory Life Cycle Approach

Several fairly sophisticated attempts to link corporate political strategies with key issues or variables have been set forth. Arieh Ullman has developed a relationship between the **regulatory life cycle** and the use of political strategies. He argues that there are various stages in the regulatory life cycle—formation, formulation, implementation, administration, and modification—that require or demand that the firm adjust its political strategy contingent on the stage that an issue has reached. He concludes, for example, that capturing key bureaucrats is meaningful only in the later stages, whereas corporate grassroots campaigns are advantageous only during the early stages.[77]

Contingency Approaches

Similarly, Gerald Keim and Carl Zeithaml have developed a **contingency approach** of corporate political strategy and legislative decision making. Their model considers two major variables: (1) the number of salient issues in a legislative district and (2) the amount of information a legislator possesses concerning voter preferences on these issues. Keim and Zeithaml then argue that knowledge of these two contingencies is useful in the selection of effective corporate political strategies for specific issues. If the corporation can identify the set of legislators who will be the key to important decisions, then the task is (1) to determine the salience of the issue under consideration to each legislator's constituency and (2) to identify the expected position(s) of voters on the issue. This will permit a prediction of the probable position of each legislator and facilitate the company's selection of an appropriate political strategy (for example, lobbying, constituency building, or making campaign contributions through a PAC).[78]

S. Prakash Sethi proposes that the political activities (campaign financing, direct lobbying, coalition building) of a company are contingent on (1) the various modes of corporate responses the firm determines are appropriate for the environment in which it finds itself, (2) its internal corporate conditions, and (3) its anticipated political risks. The three modes a firm may find itself in are (1) the defensive mode, (2) the accommodative mode, and (3) positive activism.[79]

The **defensive mode** is characterized by a situation in which a company sees its objectives as completely legitimate, thinks that anyone opposing these objectives is an adversary, and generally operates by itself in the political arena. The major company goal in this situation is to maintain the status quo in terms of political climate, legislative makeup, and regulatory environment. The strategies suggested are typically ad hoc and reactive. In this mode, of course, the firm would see the external environment and internal corporate conditions as conducive to such a defensive posture.[80]

The **accommodative mode** is one in which the firm thinks its political objectives are contingent on its ability to co-opt other groups to its viewpoint. Here the firm is willing to form coalitions that are likely to become the norm. This mode does not require a radical departure from traditional goals and strategies but is more responsive and adaptive to a changing political environment and structure. The accommodative mode would appear to be minimally required in today's environment.

Positive activism is a mode in which the focus moves from responding to external pressures to the initiation and development of a national agenda and a more progressive role in the public policy process. Firms become active leaders for social and political change rather than just responding to external factors. This mode is proactive in nature, and its goal is to anticipate and shape future events.[81]

In today's environment, it could be argued that the politically successful firm needs at least to take an accommodative mode and ideally to adopt a positive activism mode. There may be situations in which the defensive mode would still be appropriate, but these situations are rapidly fading from the scene. For the firm or industry that finds itself in an increasingly competitive environment, positive activism should be the strategy of choice. Furthermore, it is the strategy that is most compatible with innovative, aggressive, and professional management that understands the broader role of business in society and what it takes to be successful today.

■ SUMMARY

A new political landscape took root on September 11, 2001. An administration that entered office with a platform of reduced government intervention began to take part in corporate bailouts and federalization of services that were once in the private sector. A weak economy entered a recession, and items that were once at the forefront of the legislative agenda were shelved to deal with issues that arose with the World Trade Center tragedy. Record surpluses have been replaced by record deficits, and a nation once at peace is now a nation at war. In this environment, corporate political participation has taken on renewed importance.

The arrival of the Bipartisan Campaign Reform Act (BCRA) has created a dramatic change in the ways that

companies will be able to influence candidates and political parties. Nevertheless, lobbying and corporate political contributions will remain a permanent part of the political landscape. Business advocating for its interests is an important part of maintaining the balance of power needed in a pluralistic society. For a true balance of power to be maintained, however, businesses must advocate in a way that is both ethical and legal. The BCRA was a response to valid concerns that the use of soft money gave business and other advocates disproportionate power in the political process. As new excesses develop, new regulations will come to address the problems they present. That is the ongoing "back and forth" that characterizes the political process.

■ KEY TERMS

▪ DISCUSSION QUESTIONS

1. Explain lobbying in your own words. Describe the different levels at which lobbying takes place. Why is there a lack of unity among the umbrella organizations?

2. What is a PAC? What are the major arguments in favor of PACs? What are the major criticisms of PACs? In your opinion, are PACs a good way for business to influence the public policy process? What changes would you recommend for PACs?

3. Explain the regulatory life cycle approach to political activism. Differentiate it from contingency approaches.

4. Discuss the Bipartisan Campaign Reform Act and its likely effect on future elections. What further types of campaign financing reform would you recommend?

5. Discuss efforts by companies to circumvent governmental regulations. Is the use of legal loopholes ethical?

▪ RECOMMENDED CASES

Many of the end-of-text cases may be related to Chapter 11. You may wish to consider studying the following cases with Chapter 11.

Case 19. "THE CALA REPORT: LOBBYING ETHICS." This case is about fake grassroots organizations, also known as shell groups. These organizations are named to sound as if they arise from a consumer movement (e.g., Citizens for a Sound Economy) when they actually are formed and funded by businesses. Is it ethical for corporations to hide their pro-business agendas behind consumer-oriented names? Should they be required to have names that reflect their funding source (after all there is nothing wrong with business lobbying for business)? Should there be some requirement of disclosure? If so, what would you require?

Case 21. "WHEN SPIRITS COLLIDE: LIQUOR VS. BEER." This case describes the lobbying battle between the liquor and beer industries. When Diageo purchased Smirnoff, it became a liquor firm large enough to effectively challenge the political power of Anheuser-Busch. Diageo worked to strengthen the liquor industry lobbying group DISCUS, which began to argue against the differential treatment that liquor and beer receive in taxes and advertising. Is DISCUS right in arguing that liquor is no different from beer? Should liquor and beer be treated differently? Is it ethical for an industry group to lobby for ways to facilitate the selling of more alcohol?

Case 22. "THE NEW TOBACCO FIGHT." This case describes the efforts of advertising industry lobbying groups to strike down a proposal that would further limit tobacco advertising. The advertising industry is concerned about not only losing the revenues they generate from tobacco but also the right to advertise whatever other products might be targeted next. Would fatty foods or alcohol soon follow? Is it ethical for the advertising industry to fight for the right to advertise tobacco? Would more curbs on tobacco advertising be appropriate? Would more curbs on advertising other products be appropriate? Where do you draw the line?

■ WEB RESOURCES

The URLs listed here are current at the time of publication. Should any of these Web sites change, please search under the company's or organization's name for an updated address.

Business Roundtable
http://www.brt.org

Business Week magazine
http://www.businessweek.com

Center for Public Integrity
http://www.publicintegrity.org

Center for Responsive Politics
http://www.opensecrets.org

Citizens for Tax Justice
http://www.ctj.org

Common Cause
http://www.commoncause.org

Federal Election Commission
http://www.fec.gov

Fortune magazine
http://www.fortune.com

Health Benefits Coalition
http://www.hbcweb.com

National Association of Manufacturers
http://www.nam.org

National Federation of Independent Business
http://www.nfib.org

Public Citizen
http://www.citizen.org

Center for Public Integrity
http://www.publicintegrity.org

U.S. Chamber of Commerce
http://www.uschamber.org

The Wall Street Journal
http://www.wsj.com

InfoTrac® College Edition   http://www.infotrac-college.com

Articles from Business Week, Fortune, *and* The Wall Street Journal *can be researched, retrieved, and read from your desktop using InfoTrac's online database.*

■ ENDNOTES

1. S. Prakash Sethi, "Corporate Political Activism," *California Management Review* (Spring 1982), 32.

2. David B. Yoffie and Sigrid Bergenstein, "Creating Political Advantage: The Rise of the Corporate Political Entrepreneur," *California Management Review* (Fall 1985), 124. See also John F. Mahon, "Corporate Political Strategy," *Business in the Contemporary World* (Autumn 1989), 50–62.

3. Jeffrey H. Birnbaum, "Microsoft's Capital Offense," *Fortune* (February 2, 1998), 84–86.

4. Dan Carney, "Microsoft's All-Out Counterattack," *Business Week* (May 15, 2000), 103–106.

5. Hanna Rosin, "Mining Microsoft," *New Republic* (June 8, 1998), 12–13. See also Jeffrey H. Birnbaum, 84–86.

6. Carney, 103–106.

7. Ted Bridis, "Microsoft Lawyer to Be on Antitrust Panel," http://www.findlaw.com (February 5, 2004).

8. *Ibid.*

9. "Déjà Vu All Over Again," *The Economist* (January 31, 2004), 14–15.

10. Yuri Kageyama, *Authorities Raid Microsoft Unit* (Associated Press), http://www.findlaw.com (February 26, 2004).

11. *The Economist* (2004), 15.

12. "Microsoft Must Move On," *eWeek* (Vol. 21, Issue 1), 32.

13. Kageyama (2004).

14. H. R. Mahood, Interest Group Politics in America (Englewood Cliffs, NJ: Prentice Hall, 1990), 52.

15. *Ibid.*, 53–54.

16. Dick Lochner, editorial cartoon, *U.S. News & World Report* (September 19, 1983), 63.

17. Renae Merle, "Recruiting Uncle Sam," *Washington Post* (February 19, 2004), E1.

18. *Ibid.*

19. "The Glint of the Revolving Door," *The New York Times* (February 5, 2004).

20. Evan Thomas, "Peddling Influence," *Time* (March 3, 1986), 27.

21. Jane M. Keffer and Ronald Paul Hill, "An Ethical Approach to Lobbying Activities of Businesses in the United States," *Journal of Business Ethics* (September 1997), 1371–1379.

22. Jeffrey H. Birnbaum, "Washington's Power 25," *Fortune* (December 8, 1997), 145–158.

23. Carney, 103–106.

24. Dan Carney and Richard S. Dunham, "Outreach, Microsoft Style," *Business Week* (July 23, 2001), 47.

25. George Monbiot, "The Fake Persuaders: Corporations Are Inventing People to Rubbish Their Opponents on the Internet," *The Guardian* (May 14, 2002).

26. Peter H. Stone, "Learning from Nader," *National Journal* (June 11, 1994), 1342–1344.

27. Kristin Gilpatrick, "Sound Your Horn," *Credit Union Management* (May 1998), 10–11.

28. Stella Anne Harrison, "The Internet, Cyberadvocacy, and Citizen Communication," *Vital Speeches of the Day* (June 21, 2001).

29. *Encyclopedia of Associations* (Detroit, MI: Gale Research, Inc., 2004).

30. "Drug Firms Spend Millions to Battle Importation Plan," *The Wall Street Journal* (October 13, 2003), A15.

31. Cyril T. Zaneski, "Lawmakers Rally in Washington for Liberalized Prescription Drug Import Policy," *The Baltimore Sun* (February 25, 2004) 1.

32. *Ibid.*

33. http://www.citizen.org

34. Jeffrey Marshall, "Credit Union Battleground Shifts," *US Banker* (April 1998), 10–11. See also Jill Wechsler, "Employers, Healthcare Industry Lash Back at White House, Congress," *Managed Healthcare* (February 1998), 8.

35. Nancy E. Roman, "Chamber of Commerce Hires New Lobbyists to Counter Unions," *Washington Times—National Weekly Edition* (January 11, 1998), 10. See also Douglas Harbrecht, "Chamber of Commerce Battle Cry—Kill All the Lawyers," *Business Week* (March 2, 1998), 53.

36. John D. Schulz, "Leading the Charge," *Traffic World* (June 16, 2003), 1.

37. Robert Lenzner and Matthew Miller, "Buying Justice," *Forbes* (July 21, 2003), 64.

38. http://www.nam.org

39. *Ibid.*

40. *Ibid.*

41. Tom Grasson, "Let's Create a Pro-Manufacturing Environment," *American Machinist* (January 2004), 10.

42. Timothy Aeppel, "Manufacturer's Group Comes to Capitol Hill to Gain Support," *The Wall Street Journal* (February 12, 2004), A9.

43. *Ibid.*

44. *Ibid.*

45. http://www.brt.org

46. Louis Jacobson, "The Roundtable's Turnaround," *National Journal* (June 28, 2003), 2120.

47. *Ibid.*

48. http://www.brt.org

49. Jeffrey H. Birnbaum "Washington's Power 25," *Fortune,* (May 28, 2001), 95.

50. Susan Headden, "The Little Lobby That Could," *U.S. News & World Report* (September 12, 1994), 45–48.

51. Gerald D. Keim, "Foundations of a Political Strategy for Business," *California Management Review* (Spring 1981), 45.

52. For examples of collaboration, see the following articles: Anonymous, "Employers Seek Court Review of OSHA Compliance Program," *Business Insurance* (January 26, 1998), 1–2; John S. McClenahon, "The Dragon and the Bull (Market)," *Industry Week* (September 1, 1997), 82–86; Steven Brostoff, "Employers Back GOP Push for Medicare Market Reforms," *National Underwriter* (October 23, 1995), 33; the Health Benefits Coalition 2001 Web site, http://www.hbcweb.com.

53. Ian C. MacMillan and Patricia E. Jones, *Strategy Formulation: Power and Politics*, 2d ed. (St. Paul, MN: West, 1986), 68.

54. Larry J. Sabato, "PAC-Man Goes to Washington," *Across the Board* (October 1984), 16.

55. http://www.fec.gov

56. "FEC Issues Semi-Annual Federal PAC Count" (February 2, 2004), http://www.fec.gov.

57. *Ibid.*

58. Ginsberg (2001); the U.S. Federal Elections Commission maintains a Web site with current and historical information about candidates, parties, and PACs. The address is http://www.fec.gov.

59. The Center for Responsive Politics (http://www.opensecrets.org).

60. Ann Reilly Dowd, "Look Who's Cashing In on Congress," *Money* (December 1997), 128–138.

61. *Ibid.*

62. *Ibid.*

63. F.R. Baumgartner and B.O. Leech, *Basic Interests: The Importance of Interest Groups in Politics and Political Science*, (Chicago: University of Chicago Press, 1995) cited in Jeffrey E. Cohen and John A. Hamman, "Interest Group PAC Contributions and the 1992 Regulation of Cable Television," *The Social Science Journal* (2003), 357–369.

64. Cohen and Hamman, 357–369.

65. http://www.publicintegrity.org

66. Sabato, 23.

67. Center for Responsive Politics (2001), "Campaign Finance Reform," http://www.opensecrets.org.

68. "Incumbents Enjoy Huge Fundraising Advantage," (November 14, 2000, press release), http://common cause.org.

69. S. Prakash Sethi and Nobuaki Namiki, "The Public Backlash Against PACs," *California Management Review* (Spring 1983), 133.

70. http://www.opensecrets.org

71. Jeffrey H. Birnbaum, "The New Soft Money: Campaign Finance Reform Didn't Kill Big Political Donations, It Just Changed the Rules of the Game," *Fortune* (October 27, 2003).

72. Alan Murray, "Political Capital: Forget Theory—Finance Law Fails to Work in Practice," *The Wall Street Journal* (December 23, 2003), A4.

73. Jeanne Cummings, "U.S. Limits Advocacy Groups But Stops Short of Tougher Rules," *The Wall Street Journal* (February 19, 2004), A4.

74. Caren Chesler, "Buttonholed! Are Wall Street Employees Pressured by Bosses to Give?" *Investment Dealer's Digest* (February 2, 2004).

75. John F. Mahon, "Corporate Political Strategy," *Business in the Contemporary World* (Autumn 1989), 50–62.

76. *Ibid.*

77. Arieh A. Ullman, "The Impact of the Regulatory Life Cycle on Corporate Political Strategies," *California Management Review* (Fall 1985), 140–154.

78. Gerald D. Keim and Carl P. Zeithaml, "Corporate Political Strategy and Legislative Decision Making: A Review and Contingency Approach," *Academy of Management Review* (Vol. 11, No. 4, 1986), 828–843.

79. S. Prakash Sethi, "Corporate Political Activism," *California Management Review* (Spring 1982), 41.

80. *Ibid.*

81. *Ibid.*

Chapter 12

CONSUMER STAKEHOLDERS: INFORMATION ISSUES *and* RESPONSES

CHAPTER LEARNING OUTCOMES

After studying this chapter, you should be able to:

1 Recite the consumer's Magna Carta and explain its meaning.

2 Chronicle the evolution of the consumer movement.

3 Identify the major abuses of advertising and discuss specific controversial advertising issues.

4 Enumerate and discuss other product information issues that present problems for consumer stakeholders.

5 Describe the role and functions of the FTC.

6 Discuss the strengths and weaknesses of regulation and self-regulation of advertising.

How important are consumers as stakeholders? According to management expert Peter Drucker, there is only one valid definition of business purpose: to create a customer.[1] Of course, retaining that customer is essential, too. In *The Loyalty Effect*, Frederick Reichheld showed that small increases in customer retention rates can lead to dramatic increases in profits.[2] Clearly, businesses must create and retain customers if they are to succeed in today's competitive marketplace. It is not surprising therefore, that **customer relationship management (CRM)** has become the mantra of marketing.[3] Customer relationship management is "the ability of an organization to effectively identify, acquire, foster, and retain loyal profitable customers."[4] With CRM guiding businesses in their customer relations, one would expect consumers to be pleased, or at least satisfied, with the way they have been treated. Unfortunately, that hasn't been the case. The consumer is still "often ignored"[5] and, in practice, CRM has been said to be "an awful lot of bland talk and not a lot of action."[6]

A 2003 national survey by Customer Care Measurement and Consulting (CCMC) found that 45 percent of the individuals surveyed had a serious consumer problem or complaint in the past year and that 60 to 70 percent of those having complaints became enraged at the way the company handled the problem.[7] It is not surprising, therefore, that in a recent survey 45 percent of CEOs conceded that their corporations did not deserve the loyalty of their customers.[8] It is true that the American Customer Satisfaction Index is on the rise, up 1.2 percent in 2003; however, it measures the quality of goods and services rather than the way the customer is treated.[9] Taken together, these statistics seem to indicate that although product and service quality has improved, the treatment of customers has deteriorated. This can have serious consequences for competitiveness. In a 2-year study of customer loyalty, Frederick Reichheld tested a variety of survey items and found that one simple question was the best measure of customer loyalty: "Would you recommend this product/service to a friend?"[10] He found that, in most industries, the answer to that question correlated with the growth rates among competitors.[11]

The issue of business and the consumer stakeholder is at the forefront of discussions about business and its relationships with and responsibility to the society in which it exists. Products and services are the most visible manifestations of business in society. For this reason, the whole issue of business and its consumer stakeholders deserves a careful examination. We devote two chapters to it. In this chapter, we focus on the evolution and maturity of the consumer movement and product information issues—most notably, advertising. In Chapter 13, we consider product issues, especially product safety and liability, and business's response to its consumer stakeholders.

THE CONSUMER MOVEMENT

The basic expectations of the consumer movement can be found in the "**consumer's Magna Carta**," or the four basic consumer rights spelled out by President John F. Kennedy in his "Special Message on Protecting the Consumer Interest."[12] Those rights included the right to safety, the right to be informed, the right to choose, and the right to be heard.

The **right to safety** is concerned with the fact that many products (insecticides, foods, drugs, automobiles, appliances) are dangerous. The **right to be informed** is intimately related to the marketing and advertising function. Here the consumer's right is to know what a product really is, how it is to be used, and what cautions must be exercised in using it. This right includes the whole array of marketing: advertising, warranties, labeling, and packaging. The **right to choose**, although perhaps not as great a concern today as the first two rights, refers to the assurance that competition is working effectively. The fourth right, the **right to be heard**, was proposed because of the belief of many consumers that they could not effectively communicate to business their desires and, especially, their grievances.[13]

Although these four basic rights do not embody all the responsibilities that business owes to consumer stakeholders, they do capture the fundamentals of business's social responsibilities to consumers. Consumers today want "fair value" for money spent, a product that will meet "reasonable" expectations, full disclosure of the product's (or service's) specifications, a product/service that has been truthfully advertised, and a product that is safe and has been subjected to appropriate product safety testing. Consumers also expect that if a product is too dangerous it will be removed from the market or some other appropriate action will be taken.

For decades, there have been outcries that business has failed in these responsibilities to consumers, leaving them often neglected or mistreated.[14] The roots of consumer activism date back to 1906, when Upton Sinclair published *The Jungle*, his famous exposé of unsanitary conditions in the meat-packing industry.[15] The contemporary wave of consumer activism, however, started to build in the late 1950s, took form in the 1960s, matured in the 1970s, and continues even today, although in a different form. The following definition of **consumerism** captures the essential nature of the consumer movement:

> *Consumerism is a social movement seeking to augment the rights and powers of buyers in relation to sellers.*[16]

Henry Assael elaborates by saying that consumerism is a "set of activities of independent consumer organizations and consumer activists designed to protect the consumer. Consumerism is concerned primarily with ensuring that the consumer's rights in the process of exchange are protected." He also clarifies that it is somewhat misleading to use the term *consumer movement* unless we understand it to mean the conglomeration of the efforts of many groups rather than the efforts of any single unified organization of consumers.[17]

Although the consumer movement is often said to have begun with the publication of Ralph Nader's criticism of General Motors in *Unsafe at Any Speed*,[18] the impetus for the movement was actually a complex combination of circumstances. With respect to consumerism, Philip Kotler asserted:

> *The phenomenon was not due to any single cause. Consumerism was reborn because all of the conditions that normally combine to produce a successful social movement were present. These conditions are structural conduciveness, structural strains, growth of a generalized belief, precipitating factors, mobilization for action, and social control.*[19]

Figure 12-1 presents the five overarching lessons Consumers Union president Jim Guest has taken from the consumer's movement today.

FIGURE 12-1

Lessons from the Consumers Movement

One year after taking office as the President of Consumers Union, Jim Guest gave a speech to the Consumer Federation of America's Consumer Assembly. In it, he listed five "overarching lessons" he derived from the abuses of consumer trust that had occurred in the marketplace. The following are those lessons:

1. Although the consumer movement has had a strong impact, it is still absolutely essential for achieving a fair and just marketplace for all consumers.
2. Effective public oversight is needed where
   a. Corporations lack the incentives to regulate their own behavior responsibly
   b. Health, safety and other special concerns are an issue.
3. Our product safety net and consumer protection infrastructure have serious holes. For public watchdogs to be effective, they must receive necessary resources, authority, and public support.
4. The consumer movement must intensify the fight for affordable goods and services, fair financial practices, and a fair chance at a decent standard of living. Government must provide for those who do not have a fair chance at a decent standard of living. Too many consumers still cannot afford the basic necessities.
5. In the U.S., consumers must curb the wasteful overconsumption that threatens the environment.

In the closing of this talk "from one consumer organization to another," Guest described the movement as being in a time of both crisis and opportunity. Much has been achieved but there is still a very long way to go, with very serious and real problems remaining to be resolved.

SOURCE: Remarks by Jim Guest, President, Consumers Union of U.S., Inc., "Consumers and Consumerism in America Today," *Consumer Assembly of the Consumer's Federation of America* (March 15, 2002).

Ralph Nader's Consumerism

We cannot overstate the contribution that Ralph Nader made to the birth, growth, and nurturance of the consumer movement. Nader arrived on the scene 40 years ago, but he is still the acknowledged father of the consumer movement. In 1985, friends and admirers of Ralph Nader gathered with him to celebrate the 20th anniversary of his auto safety exposé, *Unsafe at Any Speed*. The impact of this book cannot be overstated. His book not only gave rise to auto safety regulations and devices (safety belts, padded dashboards, stronger door latches, head restraints, air bags, and so on) but it also created a new era—that of the consumer. Nader, personally, was thrust into national prominence.

Unsafe at Any Speed criticized the auto industry, generally, and General Motors, specifically. Nader objected to the safety of the GM Corvair, in particular. GM could not figure out what motivated Nader, so in 1966 it hired a couple of detectives to trail and discredit him. GM denied that it had used women as "sex lures" as part of its investigation. However, the company did apologize to Nader at a congressional hearing and paid him $480,000 for invasion of his privacy.

Nader put his money to work and built an enormous and far-reaching consumer protection empire. His legions of zealous activists became known as "Nader's Raiders."

Nader and the consumer movement were the impetus for consumer legislation being passed in the 1970s. The 1980s, however, did not turn out to be a consumer decade. One observer noted how uncontroversial Nader had become and posited that it was not only because of the climate of the times but also because most of the significant gains that were to be made had been made.[20] In the late 1980s, however, Nader began what *Business Week* dubbed his "second coming." Nader successfully campaigned to roll back car insurance rates in California and to squelch a congressional pay raise. These victories vaulted him to a prominence he had not enjoyed in years.[21] In 2000, Nader ran as the Green Party candidate for U.S. president with a campaign that focused on establishing a viable third party, attacking corporate wealth, and protecting the environment. He was unsuccessful in his goal of getting 5 percent of the total popular vote so that the Green Party would be eligible to receive federal matching funds in the 2004 presidential election. In the process, however, he raised the ire of Democrats, labor leaders, feminists, and environmentalists who characterized him as a "spoiler" for tipping the election to George W. Bush.[22] When he announced a second run for the presidency in February 2004, the Green Party disavowed him, and a poll found that two-thirds of Americans did not want him to run again.[23]

Consumer complaints did not disappear with the advent of Ralph Nader's activism. On the contrary, they intensified. Someone once said that Nader made consumer complaints respectable. Indeed, consumer complaints about business proliferated. It is impossible to catalog them all, but Figure 12-2 lists examples of the major problems consumers worry about in terms of business's products and services.

FIGURE 12-2

Examples of Consumer Problems with Business

- The high prices of many products
- The poor quality of many products
- The failure of many companies to live up to claims made in their advertising
- The poor quality of after-sales service
- Too many products breaking or going wrong after you bring them home
- Misleading packaging or labeling
- The feeling that it is a waste of time to complain about consumer problems because nothing substantial will be achieved
- Inadequate guarantees and warranties
- Failure of companies to handle complaints properly
- Too many products that are dangerous
- The absence of reliable information about various products and services
- Not knowing what to do if something is wrong with a product you have bought

Consumerism in the Twenty-First Century

Many groups make up the loose confederation known as the consumer movement. The power held by consumers is not the result of organized group lobbying—instead, its efforts are at the grassroots level. Grassroots activism of consumers has never been stronger. In England, a relatively small group of disgruntled consumers brought the country to a halt by protesting the price of gas. They set up blockades that emptied roads, closed schools, and caused panic buying in supermarkets. The Internet has made it easier for consumer groups to respond to issues more quickly and more forcefully. It makes it possible to not only inform consumers of concerns that have arisen but also to rally the troops to take action. This is of special concern for global companies whose interests are far-flung. According to Cordelia Brabbs of *Marketing*, "Global companies find themselves under the watchful eye of their customers. If they fail to behave impeccably at all times, they risk finding their misdemeanors broadcast on a high-speed information network."[24]

Before we consider more closely the corporate response to the consumer movement and the consumer stakeholder, it is fruitful to look in more detail at some of the issues that have become prominent in the business/consumer relationship and the role that the major federal regulatory bodies have assumed in addressing these issues. Broadly, we may classify the major kinds of issues into two groups: **product information** and the product itself. As stated earlier, in this chapter we focus on product information issues such as advertising, warranties, packaging, and labeling. The next chapter will focus on the product itself. Throughout our discussion of products, the reader should keep in mind that we are referring to services also.

SEARCH THE WEB

THE BETTER BUSINESS BUREAU

The Better Business Bureau (BBB) maintains a Web site that provides useful information for both business and individual consumers (**http://www.bbb.org**). Funded by member businesses, the purpose of the BBB is to "promote and foster the highest ethical relationship between businesses and the public." To further that goal, the BBB's Web site provides a variety of helpful resources, such as business and consumer alerts, consumer buying guidelines, and business publications. Web site visitors can file complaints online, obtain reports on businesses or charities, or locate the BBB serving their local communities. Although the BBB is best known for its work as a watchdog organization, it also acknowledges organizations that exemplify the best in marketplace ethics. Information about past and present BBB Torch Award winners is available on the BBB Web site.

PRODUCT INFORMATION ISSUES

Why have questions been raised about business's social and ethical responsibilities in the area of product information? Most consumers know the answer. Companies understandably want to portray their products in the most flattering light. However, efforts to paint a positive portrait of a product can easily cross the line into misinformation regarding the product's attributes. Consumers Union (CU), an independent, nonprofit testing and information organization, exists to protect consumers' interests. They conduct independent tests of products and report their findings in their print and online editions of *Consumer Reports (CR)*.[25] "Selling It" is a segment of *Consumer Reports* that is designed to "memorialize the excesses in the world of marketing." The following items were reported in 2004:

- Croyden House Instant Soup's label says it "tastes like homemade chicken soup," but then goes on to add that there is no chicken in it. However, as *CR* notes, it's only likely to taste homemade to you if the main ingredient in your homemade soup is pregelatinized tapioca starch.[26]
- Those blue bits you might see in Hungry Jack Blueberry Pancake and Waffle Mix are not blueberries. They are "bits of dextrose, partially hydrogenated soybean and cottonseed oil, bleached wheat flour, cellulose gum, blue and red coloring and other stuff that doesn't grow on a berry bush."[27]
- Blastobutter popcorn promises to "blast your taste buds into oblivion," but there is no butter anywhere to be found. Instead it contains partially hydrogenated vegetable oil and natural and artificial flavors.[28]

These cases are actual examples of the questionable use of product information. It is not clear whether the firms that created the aforementioned communications were intending to deceive, but one might reasonably conclude that some effort to mislead might have been present. Whether the motive was there or not, business has a legal responsibility, and an ethical responsibility, to fairly and accurately provide information on its products or services.

The primary issue with product or service information falls in the realm of advertising. Other information-related areas include warranties or guarantees, packaging, labeling, instructions for use, and the sales techniques used by direct sellers.

Advertising Issues

The debate over the role of advertising in society has been going on for decades. Most observers have concentrated on the economic function of advertising in our market system, but opinions are diverse as to whether advertising is beneficial or detrimental as a business function. Critics charge that it is a wasteful and inefficient tool of business and that our current standard of living would be even higher if we could be freed from the negative influence of advertising. These critics argue that advertising raises the prices of products and services because it is an unnecessary business cost whose main effect is to circulate superfluous information that could better and more cheaply be provided on product information labels or by salespeople in stores. The result is that significant amounts of money are spent that produce no net consumer benefit.[29] In response, others have claimed that advertising is a beneficial component of the market system and that the increases in the standard of living and consumer satisfaction may be attributed to it. They argue that, in general, advertising is an efficient means of distributing information because

---

Ethics in Practice

WHERE ARE MY SLIPPERS?

For the past 6 months, I have been working as a tele-sales accounts manager for a manufacturer of bedroom slippers. The firm had recently opened the telesales department, on a trial basis, to reach smaller retailers whose sales volumes were not large enough to attract the attention of the regional field representatives. Traditionally, the busiest time for the firm is the period from September to December, when retailers are ordering the inventories they want to have on hand for the Christmas shopping season. Last year, the number of orders coming in was unexpectedly heavy and the lead time needed to ship the orders was nearly a month. Unless the order was placed by the end of November, it was unlikely that the customer would have the merchandise on its shelves by Christmas.

However, the department manager encouraged us to take the late orders and promise delivery by Christmas, even though we knew that the merchandise wouldn't be delivered until early January. Most likely, the retailers wouldn't have wanted the merchandise if they had known the actual delivery date. Our manager's reasoning for this practice was that we needed to boost our department's sales revenue to ensure that upper management saw our department as a success at the end of the trial period. In other words, our jobs could be on the line. Also, each order that we may have lost meant a smaller commission check.

1. How would you characterize the practice our firm engaged in?

2. Were the jobs of all the people associated with the telesales department more important than ethical principles?

3. Should I have followed my manager's orders and gone along with what I thought was a deceptive marketing practice? Is the practice all that bad if there is some chance we could deliver on time?

Contributed by David Alan Ostendorff

---

there is such an enormous and ever-changing array of products about which consumers need to know. Advertising is an effective and relatively inexpensive way to inform consumers of new and improved products.[30]

It has been argued that even uninformative advertising still tells consumers a lot. Advertising heavily, even if vaguely, helps attract shoppers to retail stores through a kind of they-must-be-doing-something-right logic. The increased traffic then enables the retailer to offer a wider selection of goods, raising the incentive to invest in cost-reduction technologies such as computerized inventory, modern warehouses, and quantity discounts, thus further lowering marginal costs. The advertising can promote efficiency, even if it provides no hard information, by signaling to consumers where the big-company, low-price, high-variety stores are. Economists have argued that retail juggernauts such as Wal-Mart, Home Depot, and Circuit City have taken advantage of this phenomenon. Viewed in this way, advertising is seen as a net plus for society because it tends to lower prices and increase variety.[31]

The debate over whether advertising is a productive or wasteful business practice will undoubtedly continue. As a practical matter, however, advertising has become the lifeblood of the free-enterprise system. It stimulates competition and makes available information that consumers can use in comparison buying. It also provides competitors with information with which to respond in a competitive way and contains a mechanism for immediate feedback in the form of sales response. So, despite its criticisms, advertising does provide social and economic benefits to the American people.

With the thousands of products and their increasing complexity, the consumer today has a real need for information that is clear, accurate, and adequate. **Clear information** is that which is direct and straightforward and on which neither deception nor manipulation relies. **Accurate information** communicates truths, not half-truths. It avoids gross exaggeration and innuendo. **Adequate information** provides potential purchasers with enough information to make the best choice among the options available.[32]

Whereas providing information is one legitimate purpose of advertising in our society, another legitimate purpose is persuasion. Most consumers today expect that business advertises for the purpose of persuading them to buy their products or services, and they accept this as a part of the commercial system. Indeed, many people enjoy companies' attempts to come up with yet another interesting way to sell their products. It is commonplace for people to talk with one another about the latest interesting or clever advertisement they have seen. Thus, awards for outstanding or interesting advertisements have appeared on the scene. Awards for bad advertisements have become popular also. Nevertheless, there is evidence that the public may be losing its patience. A 2004 survey by Yankelovich Partners, a market research company, found that 60 percent of the survey respondents have a more negative opinion of advertising than they did two years earlier, 61 percent believe the practice has spun out of control, and 69 percent are attracted to products that would help them avoid commercials altogether.[33]

Ethical issues in advertising usually arise as companies attempt to inform and persuade consumer stakeholders. The frequently heard phrase "the seamy side of advertising" alludes to the economic and social costs that derive from advertising abuses, such as those mentioned earlier in the chapter, and of which the reader is probably able to supply ample personal examples.

Advertising Abuses.

William Shaw and Vincent Barry have identified four types of advertising abuses in which ethical issues reside. These include situations in which advertisers are ambiguous, conceal facts, exaggerate, or employ psychological appeals.[34] These four types cover most of the general criticisms leveled at advertising.

Ambiguous Advertising.   One of the more gentle ways that companies deceive is through **ambiguous advertising**, in which something about the product or service is not made clear because it is stated in a way that may mean several different things.

There are several ways in which an ad can be made ambiguous. One way is to make a statement that leaves to the viewer the opportunity to infer the message by using **weasel words**. These are words that are inherently vague and for which the company could always claim it was not misleading the consumer. An example of a weasel word is "help." Once an advertiser uses the qualifier "help," almost anything could follow, and the company could claim that it was not intending to deceive. We see ads that claim to "help us keep young," "help prevent cavities," or "help keep our houses germ free." Think how many times you have seen expressions in advertising such as "helps stop," "helps prevent," "helps fight," "helps you feel," "helps you look," or "helps you become."[35] Other weasel words include "like," "virtually," and "up to" (for example, stops pain "up to" 8 hours). The use of such words makes ads clearly ambiguous. Other vague terms that are ambiguous include "big" savings, "low" prices, "mild" cigarettes, and "sporty" cars.

Another way to make an ad ambiguous is through use of legalese, or other excessively complex and ambiguous terminology. In "Selling It," *Consumer Reports* provides the following paragraph that was included in a department store's advertising:

Ambiguous advertising has helped to launch and protect the "natural" dietary supplements industry, which sells millions of dollars per year of remedies for health challenges such as the common cold, flagging energy, and obesity, to name a few. Since 1984, when the Kellogg Company claimed that All-Bran cereal could reduce the risk for cancer, "the English language has been stretched to its limits in the attempt to link products to health benefits," according to Michael Specter's article in *The New Yorker* (2 February 2004 p064). You can read what Specter learned about dietary supplements by logging on to InfoTrac College Edition at **http://www.infotrac-college.com** and keying record number A112866560.

Items indicated on sale or referencing a comparative former or future price represent reductions from former or future offering prices (with or without actual sales) at Kohl's or at a competitor of the item or of comparable merchandise. Intermediate markdowns may have been taken. Clearance merchandise is excluded from entire stock categories herein.[36]

Concealed Facts. A type of advertising abuse called **concealed facts** refers to the practice of not telling the whole truth or deliberately not communicating information the consumer ought to have access to in making an informed choice. Another way of stating this is to say "a fact is concealed when its availability would probably make the desire, purchase, or use of the product less likely than its absence."[37] This is a difficult area, for few would argue that an advertiser is obligated to tell "everything," even if that were humanly possible. For example, a pain reliever company might claim the effectiveness of its product in superlative terms without stating that there are dozens of other products on the market that are just as effective. Or, an insurance company might promote all the forms of protection that a given policy would provide without enumerating all the situations for which the policy does not provide coverage.

Few of us honestly expect business to inform us of all the facts. As consumers, it is up to us to be informed about factors such as competitors' products, prices, and so on. Ethical issues arise when a firm, through its advertisements, presents facts in such a selective way that a false belief is created. Of course, judgment is required in determining which ads have and have not created false beliefs. This makes the entire realm of deceptive advertising a challenge. In a humorous vein, a burrito restaurant in a college town ran a newspaper ad with "FREE BEER" in large block letters; underneath in small letters were the words "will not be served." No one accused this company of unlawful deception; however, not all instances of concealed facts are considered benign.

An increasingly popular form of concealed advertising is **product placement**, the practice of embedding products in movies and TV shows. Product placements are everywhere. The judges in *American Idol* drink from Coke cups, and the "green room" in which contestants wait is now the "Coke Red Room."[38] Regis Philbin calls "his friends at AT&T" on *Who Wants to Be a Millionaire*, and agent Sydney Bristow makes calls from her Nokia phone as she hops into a Ford on *Alias*. On *Everybody Loves Raymond*, Ray Barone followed his wife in a supermarket and crashed into a display of Ragu Express Meals, knocking them all down.[39] The pharmaceutical industry also uses a variation of product placement that could best be described as **spokesperson placement**, in which celebrities like Lauren Bacall, Rob Lowe, and Kathleen Turner are paid to tout the benefits of specific drugs without disclosing that they are paid to do so.[40] In another variation, termed **plot placement**, sponsors have paid to make their products part of the plotline of a TV show. Revlon played an important part in the plotline of ABC's *All My Children*; Avon was integrated into the plotline of NBC's *Passions*.[41] These forms of advertising are a response to the "TiVO effect." The popularity of digital video recorders (DVRs) such as TiVO has lessened the time that consumers spend watching commercials. The fact that DVRs make it easy and convenient for TV watchers to zap through commercials has advertisers looking for new ways to make customers take notice.[42] Even advertising stalwarts like Coca-Cola, with its advertising budget of more than $300 million per year, are planning to rely less on traditional ads and more on product placement in DVDs and video games.[43]

In September 2003, Commercial Alert filed a petition with the FTC and the FCC to require concurrent, conspicuous, and clear disclosure of product placement ads. However the Freedom to Advertise Coalition, a coalition of advertising and media organizations,

SEARCH THE WEB

COMMERCIAL ALERT

Commercial Alert (**http://www.commercialalert.org**) is a national nonprofit organization dedicated to protecting children and communities from commercialism. Their Web site provides details about the myriad ways in which commercialism is infusing daily life in the United States and offers recommendations for citizen action. Their efforts have led to several successes:

* Alcohol ads planned for NBC were stopped.

* AOL Time Warner's plan to put commercials on *CNN Student News* was ended.

* The proposal to name Boston subway stops was rescinded.

* N2H2, a Web filter that tracked the movement of schoolchildren on the Internet and sold the information to private companies and the Pentagon, dropped out of schools.

attacked the proposal as an unconstitutional violation of artistic freedom. They say that the suggestion of "pop-up" disclosures, as the product placement occurs, will make television virtually unwatchable. They say the current rules, which permit product placement as long as the commercial relationship is disclosed, are time tested and adequate.[44] At this writing, the commissions have yet to respond.

Another recent concern has been the way in which some search engines incorporate advertising into their Web sites. Commercial Alert filed a formal complaint with the FTC, naming Alta Vista, AOL Time Warner, Direct Hit Technologies, iWon Inc., LookSmart Ltd., Microsoft Corporation, and Terra Lycos S. A. The complaint addressed two forms of Web advertising in search engines: paid placement and paid inclusion. With paid placement, ads are outside the editorial content in another box or a sidebar. With paid inclusion, advertising is within the actual search results. Commercial Alert charged that the practice of allowing companies to pay to have their products and services listed "high" is not disclosed to the consumer by these companies. In contrast, Google clearly labels its paid placements as "sponsored links" (and has no paid inclusions); therefore, Google was not included in the complaint.[45] In 2002, the FTC asked search engines to be "clear and conspicuous" in their listings of paid placements. Google remained the only search engine that fully met the FTC recommendations.[46] Figure 12-3 details the approaches search engines use, including those described in the Commercial Alert complaint.

Exaggerated Claims. Companies can also mislead consumers by exaggerating the benefits of their products and services. **Exaggerated claims** are claims that simply cannot be substantiated by any kind of evidence. An example of this would be a claim that a pain reliever is "50 percent stronger than aspirin" or "superior to any other on the market."

One kind of exaggeration is known as **puffery**, a euphemism for hyperbole or exaggeration that usually refers to the use of general superlatives. Is Budweiser really the "King of

FIGURE 12-3

Search Engine Practices

Pure Search	Paid Placement	Paid Inclusion
Search engines create an index from searching Web pages. The listing of pages from the index is based on multiple criteria.	Advertisers bid against each other to be displayed for a specific phrase (e.g., adjustable bed).	Companies pay to have their sites channeled directly to the search engine.
Results are ranked based on the criteria (and can change from day to day).	Paid placement results are near the unpaid results, but they are distinguishable due to different coloring or a label such as "sponsored links."	Search companies say the process is fair, but a 2003 *Business Week* analysis showed that paid sites rise to the top more than those that are unpaid.
Sites that are listed or visited do not give the search engine money.	Sites pay for each time a person clicks on them (typically 10 cents to $10).	Sites pay for each time a person clicks on them (typically 15 to 75 cents).

SOURCE: Ben Elgin, "Web Searches: The Fix Is In," *Business Week* (October 5, 2003), 89–90.

Beers"? Is Wheaties the "Breakfast of Champions"? Normally, a claim of general superiority fits squarely into puffery and is allowable. However, companies walk a fine line when engaging in puffery. They need to be certain that no direct comparison is being made. According to attorney D. Reed Freedman, "In 2000, it is no longer enough to take comfort in making the same kinds of claims that have been made in an industry for some time. Those (marketers) making aggressive claims need to consider ways a reasonable consumer will interpret those claims, and marketers need to be able to prove every interpretation that is reasonable."[47]

Most people are not too put off by puffery, because the claims are so general and so frequent that any consumer would know that the firm is exaggerating and simply doing what many do by claiming their product is the best. It has been argued, however, that such exaggerated product claims (1) induce people to buy things that do them no good, (2) result in loss of advertising efficiency as companies are forced to match puffery with puffery, (3) drive out good advertising, and (4) generally result in consumers losing faith in the system because they get so used to companies making claims that exceed their products' capabilities.[48]

Psychological Appeals. In advertising, **psychological appeals** are those designed to persuade on the basis of human emotions and emotional needs rather than reason. There is perhaps as much reason to be concerned about ethics in this category as in any other category. One reason is that the products can seldom deliver what the ads promise (i.e., power, prestige, sex, masculinity, femininity, approval, acceptance, and other such psychological satisfactions).[49] Another reason is that psychological appeals can stir emotions in a way that is manipulative and appears designed to take advantage of difficult situations.

After the tragic events of September 11, 2001, some companies with regular print contracts put messages of condolence where their ads would have run. When President Bush and Mayor Rudy Giuliani urged Americans to get back to work and to life as normal, businesses used the opportunity to suggest to customers that buying their product or using their service was the patriotic thing to do. A plastic surgery practice announced, "In keeping with the spirit of President Bush's message to return to business, we are continuing our monthly seminars." Former Labor Secretary Robert Reich called this practice "market patriotism" and said it was "a strange kind of sacrifice: Continue the binge we've been on for years."[50]

After September 11, many advertising campaigns were reworked with psychological appeals that sounded a patriotic theme. General Motors adopted "Keep America Rolling" as its new slogan for selling cars. The New York Sports Club gym offered discount rates and appealed to consumers to take on memberships to "Keep America Strong." In the backdrop of Tommy Hilfiger ads, the stars and stripes were waving. Flags were also emblazoned across the chests of Ralph Lauren models and in department store displays. Many questioned the appropriateness of using patriotism to sell products. "It's just gross to sell your products on the graves of these victims and their families," said Bob Garfield of *Advertising Age*. "[These are] heinous marketing programs built around the nation's emotions in this tragedy."[51] The issue arose again in the 2004 presidential election when George W. Bush used images of September 11 in political ads. Some of the relatives of victims of the tragedy expressed outrage, while others found it appropriate. Opinions about the appropriateness of these ads will vary, but one thing is clear: Advertisers walk a fine line when using psychological appeals, particularly at a time of tragedy.

Specific Controversial Advertising Issues. We have considered four major kinds of deceptive advertising—ambiguous advertising, concealed facts, exaggerated claims, and psychological appeals. There are many other variations on these themes, but these are sufficient to make our point. Later in this chapter, we will discuss the FTC's attempts to keep advertising honest. But even there we will see that the whole issue of what constitutes deceptive advertising is an evolving and amorphous concept, particularly when it comes to the task of proving deception and recommending appropriate remedial action. This is why the role of business responsibility is so crucial as business sincerely attempts to deal with its consumer stakeholders in a fair and honest manner.

Let us now consider seven specific advertising issues that have become particularly controversial in recent years: comparative advertising, use of sex and women in advertising, advertising to children, advertising of alcoholic beverages, cigarette advertising, health and environmental claims, and ad creep.

Comparative Advertising. One advertising technique that has become controversial and threatens to affect advertising negatively, in general, is **comparative advertising**. This refers to the practice of directly comparing a firm's product with the product of a competitor. Some examples are Coke versus Pepsi, Whopper versus Big Mac, Sprite versus 7-Up, and Avis versus Hertz. A recent example is the fierce battle that raged between Pizza Hut and Papa John's. When Pizza Hut ran an ad daring the customer to find a better pizza, Papa John's ran taste tests. When Papa John's ran ads claiming to have the freshest sauce, Pizza Hut ran a full-page ad describing Papa John's sauce as cooked, concentrated, and canned and extolling the popularity of its own pan pizza. When Pizza Hut sent its employees punching bags with a Papa John's logo, Papa John's ran TV commercials ridiculing the move. In a particularly stunning move, Papa John's brought out Frank Carney, one of the founders of Pizza Hut but a current owner of 53 Papa John's franchises, to declare he found a better pizza at Papa John's.[52]

At one time, the idea of naming your competitor or competitor's product in an ad was taboo in the United States. For years, the television networks did not allow it, so companies had to be content with referring to their competition as "the other leading brand" or "Brand X." In about 1972, the FTC began to accept the direct comparison approach, because it thought this approach would provide more and better information to the consumer. The networks cooperated by lifting their ban. Thus, the United States entered the new era of comparative advertising. Due to the supportive attitude of the European Union, companies in Western Europe have also been warming to the practice.[53]

Whether out of pride or general business interest, more and more companies are fighting back when they think the competition has gone too far. Companies may take their adversaries to court, before the FTC, or before voluntary associations, such as the National Advertising Division of the Council of Better Business Bureaus, that attempt to resolve these kinds of disputes. A recent example is Procter & Gamble (P&G): They faced five lawsuits in 13 months when they began mounting aggressive comparison campaigns. Kimberly-Clark sued P&G over an ad that made fun of Huggies, its diaper product.[54] Other lawsuits came from Georgia-Pacific, Playtex Products, and Johnson & Johnson. Most recently, Colgate-Palmolive sued the company over a commercial that showed a woman having difficulty with a product resembling its White Strips brand of tooth whitener.[55]

Comparative advertising is an issue that will not be going away. Internationally, the move has been toward freeing up restrictions on the practice. It is now commonplace in the United Kingdom, where complaints about competitors using comparative advertising increased from 171 complaints in 2000 to 799 complaints in 2002.[56] The European

Union has warmed to the practice.[57] Furthermore, countries like New Zealand, where trademark legislation once made it illegal to use a competitor's trademark in an ad, are now easing restrictions to follow the global trend.[58]

There can be good reasons to launch comparative, ads but they do come at a cost. Even A.G. Lafley, chief executive of P&G, has expressed concern: "Frankly, from a consumer's standpoint, I think it begins to undermine industry credibility." So when does it make sense? Robert Howell, European president of McCann-Erickson, says that market leaders should not engage in it. It can make the company look like a bully.[59] Bruce Buchanan suggests that there are several questions that should be asked by both those who are victims of comparative ads and those who are contemplating using them. For example, were consumers actually asked to compare one brand with another? Was the sample of consumers representative of product users? Could the consumers in the study really discriminate between the products being compared?[60] Questions such as these are essential if companies are to develop sound research methods on which to base comparative ads. To do otherwise is to invite criticism from the public and competitors alike.

Use of Sex in Advertising.   The use of sex in U.S. advertising was one of the burning ethical issues in the past. It took front stage in the early 1970s when several women's groups were offended by a series of television commercials sponsored by National Airlines. In 1971, National introduced its provocative "I'm Cheryl, Fly Me" advertising campaign. The airline followed that campaign with a commercial that showed female flight attendants looking seductively at the viewers, saying "I'm going to fly you like you've never been flown before."[61] The issue sparks less controversy today. Sexual references and innuendos in advertising have become commonplace. Says consumer behavior professor Bruce Stern. "We're moving into an arena that we are becoming numb to things that would have offended us a few years ago."[62]

A recent survey conducted by Market Facts for *American Demographics* found that 31 percent of the population is offended by the use of sex in advertising. Moreover, 61 percent said they are less likely to buy a product that is sold through the use of sex in advertising, while only 26 percent are more likely.[63] Even where offense is not taken, sex does not necessarily sell. The irrelevant use of sex can take attention away from the product or service being sold.[64] Some major fashion designers are moving away from sex in their 2004 campaigns: Most notably, Abercrombie and Fitch terminated their sexually explicit catalogue not because of any offense taken but because they failed to lure customers.[65]

Advertising to Children.   A hotly debated issue over the past several decades has been advertising to children, specifically on television. A typical weekday afternoon or Saturday morning in America finds millions of kids sprawled on the floor, glued to the TV or staring at the computer. American children, ages 2 to 17, watch an average of 25 hours of television, play 7 hours of video games, and do 4 hours of Internet surfing in a week.[66] By some estimates, children may watch as many as 40,000 commercials in a year.[67]

Children are the consumers of the future, and so companies are eager to get their foot in the door and develop some brand loyalty. This was taken to a new level when merchandisers began to instill brand loyalty in the adults children would eventually become. "Cool Shopping Barbie" had her own personal toy MasterCard, with a cash register that has the MasterCard logo and a terminal through which Barbie can swipe her card to make a purchase. According to William F. Keenan of Creative Solutions, an advertising and marketing agency, "M&M says that [if you] set the brand by age seven, they will favor the brand into adulthood. One of the smartest places to plant marketing seeds in the consumer consciousness is with kids."[68] This is particularly troubling given the findings of a 2004 task force of the American Psychological Association (APA). They found that children under the age of eight do not have the cognitive development to understand persuasive intent, making them easy targets.[69]

In 1990, the Children's Television Act was passed. This act prohibited the airing of commercials about products or characters during a show about those products or characters and limited the number of commercial minutes in children's shows. Critics say the FCC created weak rules to enforce the act, thereby sending the message that it was not taking the legislation seriously. Part of the act required stations and networks to schedule educational programs for children.[70] Of course, much has changed since that act was passed. With the rise of the Internet has come a new way for firms to advertise to children. More than two-thirds of the children and teen Internet sites rely on advertising for their revenue. Banner ads were not successful in reaching children, and so these Internet sites have employed games, e-mail, and wireless technology in creative ways. For example, Nabisco's Candystand.com boasts a very popular golf game with Lifesaver holes.[71]

In 1974, a Children's Advertising Review Unit (CARU) of the National Advertising Division of the Council of Better Business Bureaus was established to respond to public concerns. CARU revised its "Self-Regulatory Guidelines for Children's Advertising" in 1997. Figure 12-4 summarizes seven basic principles from those guidelines.

FIGURE 12-4

Principles of Advertising to Children

Seven Basic Principles Underlie CARU's Guidelines for Advertising Directed to Children Under the Age of 12:

1. Advertisers should always take into account the level of knowledge, sophistication, and maturity of the audience to which their message is primarily directed. Younger children have a limited capacity for evaluating the credibility of information they receive. They also may lack the ability to understand the nature of the information they provide. Advertisers, therefore, have a special responsibility to protect children from their own susceptibilities.
2. Realizing that children are imaginative and that make-believe play constitutes an important part of the growing-up process, advertisers should exercise care not to exploit unfairly the imaginative quality of children. Unreasonable expectations of product quality or performance should not be stimulated either directly or indirectly by advertising.
3. Products and content that are inappropriate for use by children should not be advertised or promoted directly to children.
4. Recognizing that advertising may play an important part in educating the child, advertisers should communicate information in a truthful and accurate manner and in language understandable to young children with full recognition that the child may learn practices from advertising that can affect his or her health and well-being.
5. Advertisers are urged to capitalize on the potential of advertising to influence behavior by developing advertising that, wherever possible, addresses itself to positive and beneficial social behavior, such as friendship, kindness, honesty, justice, generosity, and respect for others.
6. Care should be taken to incorporate minority and other groups in advertisements in order to present positive and pro-social roles and role models wherever possible. Social stereotyping and appeals to prejudice should be avoided.
7. Although many influences affect a child's personal and social development, it remains the prime responsibility of the parents to provide guidance for children. Advertisers should contribute to this parent-child relationship in a constructive manner.

SOURCE: Children's Advertising Review Unit. Reprinted with permission of the Council of Better Business Bureaus, Inc., copyright 2003. Council of Better Business Bureaus, Inc., 4200 Wilson Blvd., Arlington, VA 22203. World Wide Web: http://www.bbb.org.

The function of the CARU guidelines is to delineate those areas that need particular attention to help avoid deceptive advertising messages to children. The basic activity of CARU is the review and evaluation of child-directed advertising in all media. When advertising to children is found to be misleading, inaccurate, or inconsistent with the guidelines, CARU seeks changes through the voluntary cooperation of advertisers. In 1997, CARU developed guidelines for interactive electronic media (e.g., Internet and online services). These guidelines were developed with the cooperation and input of teleprogram producers, television representatives, telephone companies, and government agencies, together with the CARU Academic Advisory Panel and the CARU Business Advisory Panel.[72]

Although CARU is self-regulatory, they are able to use some teeth when necessary. When CARU evaluated the lilromeo.com Web site of UMG records, they found substantial violations of both CARU's guidelines and the Federal Children's Online Privacy Protection Act (COPPA). When UMG Recordings refused to cooperate, CARU referred the case to the Federal Trade Commission (FTC). The FTC entered a consent decree and imposed $400,000 in fines.[73]

Advertising of Alcoholic Beverages.   Special issues about advertising to adults also exist. One that has become quite controversial in recent years is advertising of alcoholic beverages on television. In 1996, Seagram & Sons broke a 48-year voluntary ban on advertising hard liquor on television. The company argued that a standard serving of hard liquor contained the same amount of alcohol as beer or wine, and advertising is allowed for those products.[74] DISCUS (the Distilled Spirits Council of the United States) then rewrote its "Code of Good Practice" to allow member distillers to advertise on radio and television. Although networks and cable TV moved quickly to ban the ads, the Seagram decision created a groundswell for change in all possible directions. Beer and wine sellers tried to distance themselves from the distilled-spirits industry in the hope of returning to the old arrangement, where they were free to advertise but makers of spirits were not. Advertisers positioned themselves between the two industries, hoping simply to avoid a ban.[75] Of course, television is no longer the only option now available. The hard liquor industry has turned to the Internet, using games, videos, and chat rooms to attract consumers. In one of the more elaborate sites, Absolut Vodka of Sweden allows customers to make their own films, view ads, and even peel orange rind off a bottle to reveal Absolut Mandrin.[76]

Hard liquor is not the only concern. Ralph Nader's Commercial Alert organization targeted Anheuser-Busch for its use of a variety of cartoon characters in its campaigns. They cite a KidCom market study that shows that the Budweiser frogs were American children's "favorite ads," just as the tobacco-smoking "Joe Camel" had been their favorite ad some years ago.[77] In November 2003, David Boles III filed a class-action lawsuit charging that several prominent liquor companies negligently targeted children in their advertising. Then, in February 2004, the two largest U.S. brewers, Anheuser Busch and Miller Brewing Co., were charged with enticing children as part of a cynical marketing strategy. These lawsuits are widely considered to be test cases for future litigation.[78]

Cigarette Advertising.   No industry has been under greater attack than the cigarette industry for its products and its marketing and advertising practices. As a *Time* magazine article concluded, cigarette makers are "under fire from all sides."[79] Two particularly important issues dominate the current debate about cigarette advertising. First, there is the general opposition to promotion of a dangerous product. As Louis Sullivan, former U.S. Secretary of Health and Human Services, put it, "Cigarettes are the only legal product that when used as intended cause death."[80] The second issue concerns the ethics of the tobacco industry's advertising to young people and to less-educated consumer markets.

An example of the latter concern was when R.J. Reynolds (RJR) was publicly taken to task by several consumer groups for its Joe Camel campaign. One frequently cited study appeared in the *Journal of the American Medical Association*. In this study, it was found that more than half the children age 3 to 6 were able to match the Joe Camel logo with a photograph of a cigarette. Six-year-olds were almost as familiar with Joe Camel as they were with a Mickey Mouse logo.[81] Perhaps one of the strongest indicators of the success of the Joe Camel ad campaign was the statistic of smoking among the youth market. From the time the Joe Camel mascot was introduced in 1987 to its discontinuation in 1997, Camel's share of the under-18 market soared from 0.5 to 33 percent, according to data supplied by a coalition of health groups. The market share among smokers age 18 to 24 increased from 4.4 to 7.9 percent. In 1997, the FTC ruled 3 to 2 that the Joe Camel ads violated the law by targeting children under 18, and asked RJR to remove the cartoon from any venue where a child might see it. RJR canceled the ad campaign.[82] Shortly after that, the government asked Philip Morris to retire the Marlboro man.[83]

Although Joe Camel is gone, the issue of advertising to young people remains. As an *Advertising Age* editorial opined, "Nobody said doing the right thing was always easy, but the folks at Philip Morris Co. could help write the book on how to do the right thing the wrong way when it comes to youth smoking." The company distributed 125 million free book covers with the theme "Reflect Confidence—Think Don't Smoke" to students from kindergarten through high school age. The covers feature colorful graphics and include both the surgeon general's warning and the name of Philip Morris. With the colorful graphics, the surgeon general's warning, and the copyright credit, the covers look "alarmingly like a colorful pack of cigarettes," says the magazine.[84]

There was some hope the issue of tobacco advertising to children would be less of a problem as time went by. After the 1998 tobacco settlement, the companies assumed voluntary restrictions on their advertising, promising to not advertise in magazines that were read by children. However problems remain. RJR Reynolds was fined for violating that settlement by advertising in magazines such as *InStyle*, *Spin*, and *Hot Rod*.[85] The European Union (EU) has taken stronger steps to curb the problem. EU health ministers agreed to outlaw tobacco advertising in newspapers, radio, and the Internet. The ban goes into effect in August 2005.[86]

Health and Environmental Claims.   Always under criticism are an assortment of advertising and labeling practices that entail product claims related to health and environmental safety. One major reason that these issues have come to the forefront is the renewed enforcement activities of the Food and Drug Administration (FDA), the Federal Trade Commission (FTC), and state attorneys general in cracking down on misleading claims. Since the health- and environmentally conscious 1990s, these issues have taken on major importance. Given consumers' desires for products that are healthful and protect the environment, it is not too surprising that these issues have gained so much attention.

Because health and environmental claims attract customers, marketers are tempted to tout claims that aren't really there. Nutrition bars have a $1 billion yearly market that has attracted a variety of companies. The FDA contacted 18 nutrition bar makers about their nutritional claims. The *Los Angeles Times* reported that a test of nutrition bars found that 60 percent of the bars tested failed to live up to their claims. Consumerlab.com tested 30 nutrition bars for levels of fat, sodium, and carbohydrates, among other ingredients. According to the lab, 18 of the bars were found to underreport those things that dieters try to avoid; only 12 bars reported accurately. Seven bars contained two to three times the amount of sodium they reported; four bars contained more saturated fat. Half of the products tested contained more carbohydrates than their label indicated.[87]

In 2003, the FTC investigated KFC's claims that their original recipe fried chicken has less fat than a Burger King Whopper and can work well in a low carbohydrate diet.[88] This is but one in an array of efforts by companies to portray their foods as being healthier than they are. One way of concealing a food's fat, carbohydrate, and calorie content is to be creative with the definition of a single serving. Many products that appear to be packaged as single servings are actually labeled as if they contain multiple servings. For example, an individual Stouffer's Chicken Pot Pie is labeled as being two servings, and a package of Maruchen's Oriental Ramen Noodles is two servings as well. Many consumers do not realize that they must double the calorie content listed for these products if they eat the entire package.[89]

Diet products are often offenders in this category. Marketers of the Enforma System settled FTC charges of deceptive advertising by agreeing to pay $10 million in consumer redress. They were accused of making false claims about their products, "Fat Trapper" and "Exercise in a Bottle." The product had been promoted through infomercials that featured former baseball player Steve Garvey. The claims made included, "Lose weight without dieting," "Eat anything that you want," and "Permanently blocks fat so it can't be absorbed by your body." In addition to the payout, the final order set stipulations about the company's future activities.[90] A 2003 FTC study of 300 weight-loss ads concluded that 40 percent of the ads made at least one false statement.[91] The commission warned media companies that their newspapers, magazines, and television stations that ran the ads were part of the problem and that they might take legal action against the media outlets along with providers of the products or services. However, by the end of 2003 the FTC issued a statement that media outlets were running fewer "clearly false" ads and that they would continue with the voluntary restrictions. They issued new guidelines for judging the veracity of weight loss ads.[92]

Another major controversial advertising practice is companies claiming that their products and/or their product packages are environmentally friendly or safe. DuraLube agreed to pay $2 million in consumer redress for what the FTC found were, among other things, unsubstantiated claims of being environmentally friendly. The FTC had previously charged a half-dozen other motor oil additive manufacturers, including STP and Valvoline. Along with the performance claims, the FTC found DuraLube's environmental claims regarding emission reduction and lack of chlorinated compounds to be unsubstantiated. In addition, DuraLube had claimed inaccurately that the product was tested by the EPA. In addition to the $2 million settlement, DuraLube was required to visit their distributors to notify them of the FTC order and replace all labels and packaging.[93]

Ad Creep. **Ad creep** refers to the way that advertising can increasingly be found everywhere one looks. It is generally estimated that people see about 3,000 ads each day. According to Jim Twitchell, author of *Twenty Ads That Shook the World*, the problem of ad creep is only going to get worse. He believes that the average person is exposed to about 5,000 ads each day, and the last time one could go an entire day without seeing an ad was probably about 1915. "That's nothing compared to what you'll see in the next 10 years," says Twitchell. "We're already putting them on the floor tiles in grocery stores, on worksheets in home economics classes, on video screens in shopping carts. Eventually, we could see ads on stoplights or in drinks with bubbles that will bring you a message from their sponsor."[94] Ads have also gone to places that once were not considered acceptable for advertisements. School buses, textbooks, doctor's offices, and historical monuments have all been festooned with advertisements. A flowerbed on 23rd Street in Manhattan carries the Old Navy logo, and the city of Sacramento has its corporate sponsorship campaign called "Capital Spirit." The traditional term for advertising that is located in nontraditional places is *ambient*, but *ad creep* reflects both the way the ads have grown and the way people often feel about its creators.[95]

A variety of factors contribute to ad creep. A declining network TV audience and increased dispersion from cable and Internet outlets combine with soaring network television rates to make it difficult to blanket the population with an advertising message. The advent of digital video recorders such as TiVo has made it easier for viewers to speed through ads without watching them. Furthermore, ad creep just generates more ad creep because people become numb to messages in traditional places and so unique new venues are sought—just to get the consumer's attention.[96] An example of the lengths advertisers go to get a person's attention can be found in Britain. A London ad agency has begun to recruit university students to wear brand logos on their foreheads for about GBP 4.20 ($6.83) an hour. The logos are temporary tattoos—wearers are allowed to shower but not rub their foreheads. John Carver, cofounder of Cunning Stunts Limited, thought up the idea as a way of getting around the many restrictions on cigarette advertising. Of course, only "suitably hip" foreheads need apply.[97]

These seven controversial advertising methods are simply the tip of the iceberg. Issues have been raised about the marketing of pharmaceutical drugs directly to patients through magazine and television ads. These ads encourage patients to ask their doctor for the prescription drug, to the frustration of doctors everywhere. Concerns have also been raised about the marketing of guns and ammunition, particularly in family stores like Wal-Mart and Kmart. Channel One, a television station that beams educational programming to schools across the country, has been sharply criticized for its commercials, which students end up watching along with the educational programming. Audiences everywhere have bemoaned the inclusion of commercials in the preview clips as they are captive audiences, unable to change the channel. There is no end to the list of concerns about the advertising practices undertaken today. Astute businesspeople must tread carefully to make certain they don't cross the line where their customers become more annoyed with their practices than attracted to their products.

Warranties

From the glamorous realm of advertising, we now proceed to the less glamorous issues of warranties. **Warranties** were initially used by manufacturers to limit the length of time they were expressly responsible for products. Over time, they came to be viewed by consumers as devices to protect the buyer against faulty or defective products. Most consumers have had the experience of buying a hair dryer, a stereo, a computer, a refrigerator, an automobile, a washing machine, a chain saw, or any of thousands of other products only to find that it did not work properly or did not work at all. That's when warranties and guarantees take center stage.

The law recognizes two types of warranties—implied and express. An **implied warranty** is an unspoken promise that there is nothing significantly wrong with the product and that the product can be used for the purpose intended. An **express warranty** is explicitly offered at the time of the sale. The nature of express warranties can range from advertising claims to formal certificates and be oral or written.

The passage of the Magnuson-Moss Warranty Act of 1975 helped to clarify the nature of warranties for consumers. This act was aimed at clearing up a variety of misunderstandings about manufacturers' warranties—especially whether a **full warranty** was in effect or whether certain parts of the product or certain types of defects were exclud-

Ethics in Practice

THE "LIFETIME" OF A BACKPACK

For the past few years, I have been working at a sporting goods store that sells high-quality backpacks. One day I was working at the customer counter, ringing up sales and responding to queries. A man came in with a backpack that had obviously seen a great deal of life. It was torn and worn from years of heavy use. He gave it to me and said that he was returning it so that we could make good on the backpack's "Lifetime Guarantee." The backpack is of high quality and the well-known manufacturer prominently displays the guarantee in its advertising materials.

I explained to the customer that the "lifetime guarantee" does not mean that he can return the backpack after any amount of use. The guarantee is not for *his* lifetime but, instead, it is for the *lifetime of the backpack*. I then explained that, according to the manufacturer, the lifetime of a backpack is considered to be about 4 years.

The customer became irate. He said that the wording of the guarantee was purposely deceptive and that one shouldn't have to read the fine print, or visit the company's Web site, to determine what the guarantee really means. Then he threw the backpack in my face and stormed out, leaving his backpack

behind. I thought he was being incredibly rude, so I followed him out to the parking lot to tell him so. We talked about the situation, and I explained that the information has always been available on the Web site. He questioned why he should be expected to double-check a company's Web site before buying a product. We parted cordially.

After he left, I thought about his upset and his argument. Was the customer right? Did the wording of the guarantee deceive him? If it is a 4-year warranty—why not say that? If it is deception, to what extent am I complicit? Should I warn customers about the meaning of the guarantee even if that information is likely to steer them to other products, and perhaps other stores? To whom am I most responsible?

1. Is the "lifetime guarantee" deceptive advertising?

2. Does an employee of the store have a responsibility to warn customers?

3. Does the store have a responsibility to clarify the guarantee?

4. If you were in this position, what would you do?

Contributed Anonymously

ed from coverage, resulting in a **limited warranty**. Also at issue was whether or not the buyer had to pay shipping charges when a product was sent to and from the factory for servicing of a defect.[98] It set standards for what must be contained in a warranty and the ease with which consumers must be able to understand it. If a company, for example, claims that its product has a full warranty, it must contain certain features, including repair "within a reasonable time and without charge."[99] The law holds that anything less than this unconditional assurance must be promoted as a limited warranty.

With the rise of e-commerce, warranties have become an important issue. Companies find that warranties or guarantees are essential when marketing by mail. The internationalization of commerce that has resulted from the Internet has presented new challenges. International e-commerce has been largely unregulated, but Scott Nathan, an attorney who specializes in e-commerce law, warns that those days are soon over. Although warranties present challenges whenever international commerce occurs, Nathan explains that the "speed 'n' ease" factor heightens the warranty problems. "Because of the lack of international law governing warranties," says Nathan, "be prepared to defend the performance of your polka dot widgets in a foreign court."[100]

Of course, if companies simply offer complete satisfaction, with no fine print, the warranty problem is not such a problem. Few companies accomplish this, but one prime example is L.L. Bean, whose guarantee says, "Our products are guaranteed to give 100 percent satisfaction in every way. Return anything purchased from us at any time if it proves otherwise. We will replace it, refund your purchase price or credit your credit card, as you wish. We do not want you to have anything from L.L. Bean that is not completely satisfactory."[101]

Packaging and Labeling

Abuses in the packaging and labeling areas were fairly frequent until the passage of the Federal Packaging and Labeling Act of 1967. The purpose of this act was to prohibit deceptive labeling of certain consumer products and to require disclosure of certain important information. This act, which is administered by the Federal Trade Commission, requires the FTC to issue regulations regarding net contents disclosures, identity of commodity, and name and place of manufacturer, packer, or distributor. The act authorizes additional regulations when necessary to prevent consumer deception or to facilitate value comparisons with respect to declaration of ingredients, slack filling of packages, "downsizing" of packaging, and use of "cents off" designations. The act gives the FTC responsibility for consumer commodities and cosmetics, which are regulated by the Food and Drug Administration.[102] As we mentioned in an earlier section, the packaging and labeling issue is drawing renewed interest because of health and environmental claims.

Other Product Information Issues

It is difficult to catalog all the consumer issues in which product information is a key factor. Certainly, advertising, warranties, packaging, and labeling constitute the bulk of the issues. In addition to these, however, we must briefly mention several others. Sales techniques in which direct sellers use deceptive information must be mentioned. Other laws that address information disclosure issues include the following:

1. *Equal Credit Opportunity Act*, which prohibits discrimination in the extension of consumer credit
2. *Truth-in-Lending Act*, which requires all suppliers of consumer credit to fully disclose all credit terms and to permit a 3-day right of rescission in any transaction involving a security interest in the consumer's residence (for example, in the case of home equity loans)
3. *Fair Credit Reporting Act*, which ensures that consumer-reporting agencies provide information in a manner that is fair and equitable to the consumer
4. *Fair Debt Collection Practices Act*, which regulates the practices of third-party debt-collection agencies

THE FEDERAL TRADE COMMISSION

We have discussed three main areas of product information—advertising, warranties, and packaging/labeling. Both the FTC and the FDA are actively involved in these issues. It is important now to look more closely at the federal government's major instrument, the FTC, for ensuring that business lives up to its responsibilities in these areas. Actually, the FTC has broad and sweeping powers, and it delves into several other areas that we will refer to throughout the book. The Consumer Product Safety Commission and the Food and Drug Administration are major regulatory agencies, too, but we will consider them more carefully in the next chapter, where we discuss products and services more specifically.

Some history and evolution of the FTC will be helpful in gaining a better appreciation of government activism and its relationship to the political parties in power in Washington at various points in time. The FTC is one of the oldest of the federal agencies charged with responsibility for overseeing commercial acts and practices. It was created in 1914, originally as an antitrust weapon, and was broadened in 1938 to permit the agency to pursue "unfair or deceptive acts or practices in commerce."[103]

Two major activities of the FTC are (1) to maintain free and fair competition in the economy and (2) to protect consumers from unfair or misleading practices. The FTC may issue cease and desist orders against companies it believes to be engaging in unlawful practices. The firms must then stop such practices unless a court decision sets aside the order. The FTC also issues trade regulation guides for business and conducts a wide variety of consumer-protection activities.[104] In the arena of possible deceptive advertising practices, the FTC monitors advertising and may ask advertisers for proof of their claims. If the FTC decides an ad is false or misleading, it may order the advertiser to withdraw the ad or run "corrective" advertising to inform the public that the former ads were deceptive. Advertisers also may be fined for violating an FTC order.[105]

Over the years, Congress has given the FTC enforcement responsibility in a variety of consumer-related fields, including the important Truth-in-Lending, Fair Packaging and Labeling, Fair Credit Reporting, and Equal Credit Opportunity Acts. Congress gave the FTC broad powers out of fear that any specification of a list of prohibitions might lead business to reason that it could do anything not on the list. Figure 12-5 presents an overview statement of the vision, mission, and goals of the FTC. The FTC's Bureau of Consumer Protection has the following major divisions: advertising practices, credit practices, enforcement, marketing practices, and service industry practices.

FIGURE 12-5

Role of the FTC

Vision, Mission, and Goals

The Federal Trade Commission enforces a variety of federal antitrust and consumer-protection laws. The commission seeks to ensure that the nation's markets function competitively and are vigorous, efficient, and free of undue restrictions. The commission also works to enhance the smooth operation of the marketplace by eliminating acts or practices that are unfair or deceptive. In general, the commission's efforts are directed toward stopping actions that threaten consumers' opportunities to exercise informed choice. Finally, the commission undertakes economic analysis to support its law enforcement efforts and to contribute to the policy deliberations of the Congress, the executive branch, other independent agencies, and state and local governments, when requested.

In addition to carrying out its statutory enforcement responsibilities, the commission advances the policies underlying the congressional mandates through cost-effective, nonenforcement activities, such as consumer education.

SOURCE: Federal Trade Commission, http://www.ftc.gov.

Early Activism of the FTC

The FTC actually did relatively little from 1941 to 1969, a period Thomas G. Krattenmaker called the "decades of neglect." But 1970 to 1973 were the "years of promise" for the FTC.[106] The agency became "activist" when President Richard Nixon appointed Miles Kirkpatrick chairman. Kirkpatrick and his staff of eager young lawyers put the FTC on the map, so to speak, and the agency became so aggressive that it created "an escalating struggle" between itself and business.[107] The source of the struggle was the FTC's zealousness, its fuzzy and broad powers, its lack of consistency in its own administration, and its concept of what constitutes proper business conduct.

The FTC's activism continued when Michael Pertschuk became chairman in 1977. His directorship spanned the late 1970s and early 1980s and encompassed the "kid-vid" period that we discussed earlier in this chapter. Although many of the controversial initiatives preceded his appointment, he became identified with all of them. Yet Pertschuk was accurately identified with the initiatives, because for 12 years prior to his chairmanship he was staff director and chief counsel for the Senate Commerce Committee. He had nurtured and drafted practically all the major consumer legislation that was passed, including the Magnuson-Moss Warranty Act. Unfortunately, Pertschuk developed a reputation for being antibusiness. This hurt his relationship with the business community so much that he never overcame it.[108]

Less Active Years of the FTC

Succeeding Pertschuk as chairman was James C. Miller III, appointed by President Reagan. As do so many agencies upon the election of a new administration, the FTC shifted its focus to the Reagan approach to regulation. Miller was dubbed by some in the press as Reagan's "deregulation czar," and he took the FTC off into another, less active direction. Miller characterized the FTC's activism on behalf of consumers during the 1970s as "excesses" and embarked on a course that was much more in keeping with the Reagan doctrine.[109] The same general approach to regulation continued under Miller's successor, Daniel Oliver. Miller and Oliver gained reputations as deregulators who willingly slashed the FTC's budget and staff.

The FTC Reasserts Itself in the 1990s

After almost a decade of Reagan-era deregulation that saw the FTC's workforce cut in half and its enforcement efforts greatly reduced or redirected, the FTC began reasserting itself in the early 1990s. Its chairperson became Janet D. Steiger, and under Steiger the FTC came back to life. It did not return to its heyday of the 1970s, but through a series of highly visible cases it reasserted itself. According to one observer, the FTC started looking more like the FTC of the pre-Reagan administration rather than the seemingly toothless agency it became in the 1980s.[110]

Among the high-profile cases the FTC pursued in the 1990s, it won headlines by cracking down on Nintendo, the video-game maker, for price fixing; moving in on "900" telephone numbers for advertisements aimed at children; and accusing major colleges and Capital Cities-ABC for conspiring to limit the market for televised college football games.[111]

In another initiative, the FTC took action against shoemakers who claimed their shoes are "Made in USA" when, in fact, some are "assembled" in the United States but include some imported components and materials. This was a significant action against New

Balance and Hyde Athletic Industries, who had touted the "Made in USA" claim. Although most would agree that the integrity of a "Made in USA" label is important, many agree that the increasingly global economy makes 100 percent U.S. content unreachable. A spokesman for Toyota Motor Sales USA, Inc., has said, "If you applied the FTC standard to our industry, there's no such thing as an American car."[112]

In April 1995, Robert Pitofsky, a specialist on trade regulation and antitrust law, became the chairman of the FTC. Pitofsky's appointment signaled a shift in focus for the agency. Although advertising and other marketing issues were still pursued, antitrust battles moved to the front burner. In June 1998, the FTC issued an antitrust complaint against Intel Corporation, alleging that the company withheld important technology information from competing vendors.[113] Pitofsky's reign as chairman characterized one of the most activist eras of the FTC.

The FTC in the Twenty-First Century

Timothy Muris was sworn in as new FTC chairman on June 4, 2001. He brought with him experience in three areas of the agency, having previously served as assistant director of the Planning Office (1974–1976), director of the Bureau of Consumer Protection (1981–1983), and director of the Bureau of Competition (1983–1985). The FTC's transition from the Pitofsky to the Muris administration was characterized by continuity rather than conflict. In an address to the American Antitrust Institute, Muris said that the areas in which he agreed with Pitofsky far outnumbered the areas in which they differ.[114]

An accomplishment of the Muris administration that has made a significant difference in the quality of consumers' lives is the National Do-Not-Call Registry. The registry opened to consumers in June 2003 and forbids telemarketers from calling consumers who sign up with the registry. The FTC also instituted a requirement that all companies placing marketing calls have their information available for consumer's caller id systems. Consumers can then report companies that make calls in violation.[115] The FTC has shown a preference for working in consort with business where possible but also a willingness to enact fines and penalties when firms are unable to police themselves.

SELF-REGULATION IN ADVERTISING

Cases of deceptive or unfair advertising in the United States are handled primarily by the FTC. In addition to this regulatory approach, however, self-regulation of advertising has become an important business response, primarily in the past two decades. Under the regulatory approach, advertising behavior is controlled through various governmental rules that are backed by the use of penalties. **Self-regulation**, on the other hand, refers to the control of business conduct and performance by business itself rather than by government or by market forces.[116]

Types of Self-Regulation

Business self-regulation of advertising may take on various forms. One is **self-discipline**, where the firm itself controls its own advertising. Another is **pure self-regulation**, where the industry (one's peers) controls advertising. A third type is **co-opted self-regulation**, where the industry, of its own volition, involves nonindustry people (for example, consumer or public representatives) in the development, application, and enforcement of norms. A fourth type is **negotiated self-regulation**, where the industry voluntarily negotiates the development, use, and enforcement of norms with some outside body (for example, a government department or a consumer association). Finally, a fifth type is **mandated self-regulation** (which may sound like a contradiction of terms), where the industry is ordered or designated by the government to develop, use, and enforce norms, whether alone or in concert with other bodies.[117]

The National Advertising Division's Program

The most prominent instance of self-regulation in the advertising industry is the program sponsored by the National Advertising Division (NAD) of the Council of Better Business Bureaus, Inc. The NAD and the National Advertising Review Board (NARB) were created in 1971 by the American Advertising Federation, the American Association of Advertising Agencies, the Association of National Advertisers, and the Council of Better Business Bureaus to help sustain high standards of truth and accuracy in national advertising.

The NAD initiates investigations, determines issues, collects and evaluates data, and makes the initial decision as to whether it can agree that an advertiser's claims are substantiated. When the NAD is unable to agree that substantiation is satisfactory, the advertiser is asked to undertake modification or permanent discontinuance of the advertising. If the NAD fails to resolve a controversy, appeal can be made to the NARB, which has a reservoir of over 50 men and women representing national advertisers, advertising agencies, and the public sector. The chairman of the NARB selects an impartial panel of five members for each appeal. The parties involved submit briefs expressing their views for discussion at an oral hearing, after which the panel issues a public report.[118]

It is useful to conclude this chapter by providing insights into how the three types of moral manager models, introduced in Chapter 4, would view consumer stakeholders. Therefore, Figure 12-6 presents a brief statement as to the likely orientations of immoral, amoral, and moral managers to this vital stakeholder group.

FIGURE 12-6

Three Moral Management Models and Their Orientations Toward Consumer Stakeholders

Model of Management Morality	Orientation to Consumer Stakeholders
Immoral Management	Customers are viewed as opportunities to be exploited for personal or organizational gain. Ethical standards in dealings do not prevail; indeed, an active intent to cheat, deceive, and/or mislead is present. In all marketing decisions—advertising, pricing, packaging, distribution—the customer is taken advantage of to the fullest extent.
Amoral Management	Management does not think through the ethical consequences of its decisions and actions. It simply makes decisions with profitability within the letter of the law as a guide. Management is not focused on what is fair from the perspective of the customer. The focus is on management's rights. No consideration is given to ethical implications of interactions with customers.
Moral Management	Customers are viewed as equal partners in transactions. The customer brings needs/expectations to the exchange transaction and is treated fairly. Managerial focus is on giving the customer fair value, full information, fair guarantee, and satisfaction. Consumer rights are liberally interpreted and honored.

■ SUMMARY

Among stakeholder groups, consumers rank at the top. In a consumption-driven society, business must be especially attentive to the issues that arise in its relationships with consumers. It is a paradox that consumerism arose during the very period that the business community discovered the centrality of the marketing concept to business success. The consumer's Magna Carta includes the rights to safety, to be informed, to choose, and to be heard. Consumers expect more than this, however, and thus the consumer movement, or consumerism, was born. Ralph Nader was the father of this movement and made consumer complaining respectable.

Product information issues compose a major area in the business/consumer stakeholder relationship.

Foremost among these is advertising. Many issues have arisen because of perceived advertising abuses, such as ambiguity, concealed facts, exaggerations, and psychological appeals. Specific controversial spheres have included, but are not limited to, comparative advertising, use of sex and women in advertising, advertising to children, advertising of alcoholic beverages, advertising of cigarettes, health and environmental claims, and ad creep. Other product information issues include warranties, packaging, and labeling. The major body for regulating product information issues has been the FTC. The FDA and the state attorneys general have become active as well. On its own behalf, however, business has initiated a variety of forms of self-regulation.

■ KEY TERMS

accurate information (page 392)

ad creep (page 401)

adequate information (page 392)

ambiguous advertising (page 392)

clear information (page 392)

comparative advertising (page 396)

concealed facts (page 393)

consumerism (page 387)

consumer's Magna Carta (page 386)

co-opted self-regulation (page 407)

customer relationship management (CRM) (page 385)

exaggerated claims (page 394)

express warranty (page 402)

full warranty (page 402)

implied warranty (page 402)

limited warranty (page 403)

mandated self-regulation (page 408)

negotiated self-regulation (page 408)

plot placement (page 393)

product information (page 389)

product placement (page 393)

psychological appeals (page 395)

puffery (page 394)

pure self-regulation (page 407)

right to be heard (page 386)

right to be informed (page 386)

right to choose (page 386)

right to safety (page 386)

self-discipline (page 407)

self-regulation (page 407)

spokesperson placement (page 393)

warranties (page 402)

weasel words (page 392)

■ DISCUSSION QUESTIONS

1. In addition to the basic consumer rights expressed in the consumer's Magna Carta, what other expectations do you think consumer stakeholders have of business?

2. What is your opinion of the consumerism movement? Is it "alive and well" or is it dead? Provide evidence for your observations.

3. Give an example of a major abuse of advertising from your own observations and experiences. How do you feel about this as a consumer?

4. With which of the kinds of controversial advertising issues are you most concerned? Explain.

■ RECOMMENDED CASES

Many of the end-of-text cases may be related to Chapter 12. You may wish to consider studying the following cases with Chapter 12.

Case 20. "DTC: THE PILL PUSHING DEBATE." This case addresses the pharmaceutical industry's practice of promoting medicine directly to consumers with the expectation that consumers will then ask their doctors for the medicine. What are the problems this practice can create? The practice is legal but is it ethical? Should it be allowed? Who are the stakeholders in this situation and how would you balance their competing concerns?

Cases 21 and Case 22. "WHEN SPIRITS COLLIDE" AND "THE NEW TOBACCO FIGHT." These two cases both explore products that some people use and enjoy, other people might like to see outlawed, and about

which many people feel ambivalent. This can create a variety of ethical dilemmas when these products are advertised and promoted. If you were charged with regulating those industries, what restrictions (if any) would you place on their advertising and promotion?

Case 23. "BIG PHARMA'S MARKETING TACTICS." This case describes a variety of questionable advertising and promotion tactics used by the pharmaceutical industry. These range from promotional gifts for med students and doctors to misleading pricing, kickbacks, and other financial lures. How do you balance the right of pharmaceutical companies to promote their wares with the added social responsibility inherent in selling medicine? If you were able to set limits on pharmaceutical advertising, where would you draw the line?

■ WEB RESOURCES

The URLs listed here are current at the time of publication. Should any of these Web sites change, please search under the company's or organization's name for an updated address.

American Psychological Association
http://www.apa.org

Better Business Bureau
http://www.bbb.org

Business Week magazine
http://www.businessweek.com

Children's Advertising Review Unit
http://www.caru.org

Commercial Alert
http://www.commercialalert.org

Consumer.gov
http://www.consumer.gov

Consumer Reports
http://www.consumerreports.org

Federal Trade Commission
http://www.ftc.gov

Fortune magazine
http://www.fortune.com

Public Citizen
http://www.citizen.org

The Wall Street Journal
http://www.wsj.com

 InfoTrac® College Edition   http://www.infotrac-college.com

Articles from Business Week, Fortune, *and* The Wall Street Journal *can be researched, retrieved, and read from your desktop using InfoTrac's online database.*

▪ ENDNOTES

1. Peter F. Drucker, *Management: Tasks, Responsibilities, Practices* (New York: Harper & Row, 1973), 61.

2. Frederick F. Reichheld, *The Loyalty Effect* (Cambridge, MA: Harvard Business School Press, 1996).

3. Russell S. Winer, "A Framework for Customer Relationship Management," *California Management Review* (Summer 2001), 89–105.

4. "The Customer Is Often Ignored," *Marketing Week* (September 27, 2001), 3.

5. Camilla Ballesteros, "Don't Talk About CRM; Do It," *Marketing Week* (September 27, 2001) 49.

6. *Ibid.*

7. Don Oldenburg, "Seller Beware: Customers Are Mad as Hell, *Washington Post* (September 9, 2003), C10.

8. Strativity Group, Inc., Worldwide Survey of 165 Executives, March–November 2003, cited in *Business Week* (March 8, 2004), 14.

9. Oldenburg, C10.

10. Frederick F. Reichheld, "The One Number You Need to Grow," *Harvard Business Review* (December 2003), 46–54.

11. *Ibid.*

12. Robert J. Holloway and Robert S. Hancock, *Marketing in a Changing Environment*, 2d ed. (New York: John Wiley & Sons, 1973), 558–565.

13. *Ibid.*, 565–566.

14. Robert O. Herrmann, "Consumerism: Its Goals, Organizations, and Future," *Journal of Marketing* (October 1970), 55–60.

15. Ruth Simon, "You're Losing Your Consumer Rights," *Money* (Vol. 25, No. 3, 1996), 100–111.

16. Philip Kotler, "What Consumerism Means for Marketers," *Harvard Business Review* (May–June 1972), 48–57.

17. Henry Assael, *Consumer Behavior and Marketing Action*, 3d ed. (Boston: Kent, 1987), 667.

18. Ralph Nader, *Unsafe at Any Speed* (New York: Grossman Publishers, 1965).

19. Kotler, 50. Kotler states that these conditions were proposed by Neil J. Smelser, Theory of Collective Behavior (New York: The Free Press, 1963).

20. Robert J. Samuelson, "The Aging of Ralph Nader," *Newsweek* (December 16, 1985), 57.

21. Rich Thomas, "Safe at This Speed," *Business Week* (August 22, 1994), 40; Douglas Harbrecht and Ronald Grover, "The Second Coming of Ralph Nader," *Business Week* (March 6, 1989), 28.

22. Paul Magnusson, "The Punishing Price of Nader's Passion," *Business Week* (November 20, 2000), 44.

23. Gary Fields, "Leading the News: Nader to Run for President Again; Democrats Fear a Reprise of 2000," *The Wall Street Journal* (February 23, 2003) A3.

24. Cordelia Brabbs, "Web Fuels Consumer Activism," *Marketing* (September 21, 2000), 23.

25. http://www.consumerreports.org

26. "Selling It: Goofs, Glitches, Gotchas," *Consumer Reports* (January 2004), 63.

27. *Ibid.*

28. *Ibid.*

29. William Leiss, Stephen Kline, and Sut Jhally, *Social Communication in Advertising* (Toronto: Methuen, 1986), 13.

30. *Ibid.*

31. Rob Norton, "How Uninformative Advertising Tells Consumers Quite a Bit," *Fortune* (December 26, 1994), 37.

32. William Shaw and Vincent Barry, *Moral Issues in Business*, 4th ed. (Belmont, CA: Wadsworth, 1989), 389–414.

33. Stuart Elliott, "A Survey of Consumer Atttitudes Reveals the Depth of the Challenge that the Agencies Face," *The New York Times* (April 14, 2004), C8.

34. *Ibid.*, 403.

35. *Ibid.*, 404.

36. "Selling It," *Consumer Reports* (October 2001), 63.

37. Shaw and Barry, 389–414.

38. Dean Foust and Brian Grow, "Coke: Wooing the TV Generation," *BusinessWeek Online* (March 1, 2004).

39. Brian Steinberg and Suzanne Vranica, "Prime-Time TV's New Guest Stars: Products," *The Wall Street Journal* (January 12, 2004), B1.

40. Melody Patterson, "Heartfelt Advice: Hefty Fees," *The New York Times* (August 11, 2002).

41. Joe Flint and Emily Nelson, "All My Children Gets Revlon Twist—First Came Product Placement Now TV 'Plot Placement' Yields ABC a Big Ad Buy," *The Wall Street Journal* (March 15, 2002); Leslie Ryan, "Passions Product Pitch; NBC, Avon Weave New Cosmetics Line into Soap Opera's Story," *Television Week* (July 28, 2003).

42. Ronald Grover, Tom Lowry, Gerry Khermouch, Cliff Edwards, and Dean Foust, "Can Mad. Ave. Make Zap-Proof Ads?" *Business Week* (February 2, 2004), 36–37.

43. *Ibid.*

44. Darryl Nirenberg, News Release of the Freedom to Advertise Coalition, (November 12, 2003), http://www.commercial alert.org.

45. http://www.commercialalert.org

46. *Ibid.*

47. James Heckman, "Puffery Claims No Longer So Easy to Make," *Marketing News* (February 14, 2000), 6.

48. Eli P. Cox, "Deflating the Puffer," *MSU Business Topics* (Summer 1973), 29.

49. Shaw and Barry, 406–407.

50. Ann Gerhart, "The Patriotic Pitch: Buy, America, Buy," *The Washington Post* (October 11, 2001), C1.

51. *Ibid.*

52. Dennis Berman and Robert McNatt, "Louisville's Pizza Sluggers," *Business Week* (May 4, 1998), 6.

53. Robert Gray, "Fighting Talk," *Marketing* (September 20, 2001), 26–27.

54. *The Wall Street Journal* (November 26, 2003), B1.

55. "P&G Is Settling Disputes on Ads As Suits Pile Up," *The Wall Street Journal* (November 26, 2003), B1.

56. "Should Comparing Be Left to the Consumer?" *Marketing Week* (December 4, 2003), 25.

57. Robert Gray, "Fighting Talk," *Marketing* (September 20, 2001), 26–27.

58. Jo Stafford, "Comparative Advertising—Getting It Right NZ Is About to Make It Easier to Compare Apples with Apples," *AdMedia* (March 2003), 14.

59. *Marketing Week* (December 4, 2003), 25.

60. Bruce Buchanan, "Can You Pass the Comparative Ad Challenge?" *Harvard Business Review* (July–August 1985), 106.

61. *Time* (June 24, 1974), 76.

62. Hillary Chura, "Spirited Sex; Alcohol Ads Ratchet Up the Sex to Woo Jaded Customers," *Advertising Age* (July 9, 2001), 1.

63. John Fetto, "Where's the Lovin'?" *American Demographics* (February 2001), 10–11.

64. Herbert Jack Rotfeld, "Misplaced Marketing Gardening, Pizza, Tacos, Truck Parts and Fake Jewelry: Misuse and Misdirection of Sex in Advertising," *Journal of Consumer Marketing* (Volume 20, Number 3, 2003), 189–191.

65. Jacob Bernstein, "Fashion's Miss Modesty: Designers Drop Raunchy in Favor of the Demure," WWD: *Women's Wear Daily* (February 13, 2004), 1–2.

66. D.A. Gentile and D. A. Walsh, "A Normative Study of Family Media Habits," *Applied Developmental Psychology* (January 28, 2002), 157–178.

67. V. C. Strasburg, "Children and TV Advertising: Nowhere to Run, Nowhere to Hide," *Journal of Developmental Behavioral Pediatrics* (2001), 185–187.

68. "Barbie Gets Her First Credit Card," *Credit Card Management* (January 1998), 6–8.

69. http://www.apa.org

70. Ellen Edwards, "Television's Problem Child," *The Washington Post National Weekly Edition* (June 20–26, 1994), 22.

71. Ellen Neuborne, "For Kids on the Web, It's an Ad, Ad, Ad, Ad World," *Business Week* (August 13, 2001), 108–109.

72. For information on the Better Business Bureau (BBB) and its programs, refer to http://www.bbb.org. The BBB's Web site contains the complete text of the self-regulatory guidelines.

73. http://www.caru.org/news/2004/lilromeo2.asp

74. Kirk Davidson, "Look for Abundance of Opposition to TV Ads," *Marketing News* (January 6, 1997), 26–28.

75. Alicia Mundy, "The Bar Will Soon Open," *Media Week* (January 27, 1997), 26–28.

76. Hillary Chura, "Drinking In the Internet," *Advertising Age* (September 3, 2001), 16.

77. http://www.commercialalert.org

78. Christopher Lawton, "Lawsuits Allege Alcohol Makers Target Youths," *The Wall Street Journal* (February 5, 2004), B1.

79. Gallagher, 41. See also "Tobacco: Does It Have a Future?" *Business Week* (July 4, 1994), 24–29.

80. Gallagher, *ibid.*

81. Eben Shapiro, "FTC Staff Recommends Ban of Joe Camel Campaign," *The Wall Street Journal* (August 11, 1993), B1.

82. Ira Teinowitz, "FTC's Camel Case Hinges on Ad's Power over Kids," *Advertising Age* (June 2, 1997), 4, 45.

83. Judann Pollack and Ira Teinowitz, "With Joe Camel Out, Government Wants the Marlboro Man Down," *Advertising Age* (July 14, 1997), 3, 34.

84. "Blown Cover," *Advertising Age* (September 11, 2000), 34.

85. Lisa Girion and Myron Levin, "R.J. Reynolds Fined for Ads Aimed at Teens: Tobacco: Judgment of $20 Million for Magazine Pitches Is First Financial Penalty for Violation of 1998 National Settlement," *Los Angeles Times* (June 7, 2002), C1.

86. Adrian Cox, "EU Backs Partial Tobacco Ad Ban," *Los Angeles Times* (December 3, 2002) C13.

87. Benedict Carey, "Nutritional Analysis of Bars Reveals Discrepancies," *Los Angeles Times* (November 5, 2001), S2.

88. Anna Wilde Mathews and Brian Steinberg, "FTC Examines Health Claims in KFC's Ads," *The Wall Street Journal* (November 19, 2003), B1.

89. Sherri Day, "The Smoke and Mirrors of Food Labeling," *The New York Times* (November 15, 2003), B1.

90. http://www.ftc.gov

91. Ryan J. Foley, "Trade Commission Eases Its Stance on Diet-Aid Claims," *The Wall Street Journal* (December 9, 2003), D4.

92. *Ibid.*

93. "DuraLube, Motor-Up Settle FTC Charges," FTC Press Release (March 29, 2000), http://www.ftc.gov.

94. Charles Pappas, "Ad Nauseum," *Advertising Age* (July 10, 2000), 16–18.

95. Carrie McLaren, "Ad Creep," *Print* (November/December 2000), 102–107.

96. *Ibid.*

97. Erin White, "Ad Agency Aims to Turn Heads into Billboards," *The Wall Street Journal* (February 11, 2003).

98. "The Guesswork on Warranties," *Business Week* (July 15, 1975), 51; "Marketing: Anti-Lemon Aid," *Time* (February, 1976), 76.

99. *Ibid.*

100. Amy Zuckerman, "Order in the Courts?" *World Trade* (September 2001), 26–28.

101. http://www.llbean.com

102. http://www.ftc.gov

103. "The Escalating Struggle Between the FTC and Business," *Business Week* (December 13, 1976), 52.

104. "Federal Trade Commission," *The World Book Encyclopedia*, Vol. 7 (Chicago: World Book, Inc., 1988), 68.

105. "Advertising," *The World Book Encyclopedia*, Vol. 1 (Chicago: World Book, Inc., 1988), 78.

106. Thomas G. Krattenmaker, "The Federal Trade Commission and Consumer Protection," *California Management Review* (Summer 1976), 94–95.

107. *Business Week* (December 13, 1976), 52–59.

108. Tolchin and Tolchin, 147–149.

109. James C. Miller III, "Revamping the Federal Trade Commission" (St. Louis: Center for the Study of American Business, December, 1984), 3.

110. Mark Potts, "What's Gotten into the FTC?" *The Washington Post National Weekly Edition* (June 17–23, 1991), 32.

111. *Ibid.*

112. Michael Oneal, "Does New Balance Have an American Soul?" *Business Week* (December 12, 1994), 86–87.

113. Detailed information on FTC activities is available on the FTC's Web site at http://www.ftc.gov.

114. http://www.ftc.gov

115. http://www.ftc.gov

116. J. F. Pickering and D. C. Cousins, *The Economic Implications of Codes of Practice* (Manchester, England: University of Manchester Institute of Science and Technology, Department of Management Sciences, 1980), 17. Also see J. J. Boddewyn, "Advertising Self-Regulation: Private Government and Agent of Public Policy," *Journal of Public Policy and Marketing* (1985), 129.

117. *Ibid.*, 135.

118. http://www.bbb.org

Chapter 13

CONSUMER STAKEHOLDERS: PRODUCT *and* SERVICE ISSUES

CHAPTER LEARNING OUTCOMES

After studying this chapter, you should be able to:

1 Describe and discuss the two major product issues: quality and safety.

2 Explain the role and functions of the Consumer Product Safety Commission and the Food and Drug Administration.

3 Enumerate and discuss the reasons for the growing concern about product liability and differentiate strict liability, absolute liability, and market share liability.

4 Outline business's responses to consumer stakeholders to include total quality management (TQM) programs, and Six Sigma.

Although product information is a pivotal issue between business and consumer stakeholders, product and service issues such as quality and safety occupy center stage. The quest to improve product and service quality has been driven by the demands of a competitive marketplace and an increasingly sophisticated consumer base. With product safety, an additional driving force has been the threat of product liability lawsuits and the damage they can wreak to both the balance sheet and the reputation.

The Ford Motor Company provides a notable example of the havoc that can result from product quality and safety problems. At the end of 2001, Ford CEO Jacques Nasser departed the post after 2 years in the position. His tenure had been tumultuous. Product quality problems had plagued the launches of new products, even before the problems with Firestone-brand tires hit the news in August 2000. The tire problems were eventually traced to production problems at a Bridgestone/Firestone plant, but the tire maker's accusations against Ford, coupled with the high number of Ford recalls on other vehicles, made the Ford image easier to tarnish.[1] According to J.D. Power and Associates, the company went from the best in car quality among Detroit automakers to the worst in just 3 years. Ford's profits plunged 11 percent, double the decline of the other U.S. automakers.[2] Of course the decline was not only due to product quality and safety: Unsuccessful diversification attempts were a factor as well. However, for a company that once boasted "Quality Is Job One," the decline in the J.D. Power ranking must have been a bitter pill to swallow. The fall of 2001 was a difficult time for all car companies, but the host of problems Ford faced, beyond the falling economy, made it even more difficult for them to weather the storm. As *Newsweek* commented, "This hasn't been easy for Ford, which just 2 years ago was revered as America's best automaker."[3] By 2003, Ford had improved by 18 percent in initial quality, a laudable achievement except in comparison to the 25 percent by which the industry average had improved.[4] This shows how problems with quality and safety can linger for firms, even after credible efforts to improve operations are mounted.

In this chapter, we will limit our discussion to product quality and safety issues. In connection with safety, we consider the product liability issue and the calls for tort reform. The Consumer Product Safety Commission and the Food and Drug Administration are also discussed. Finally, we will discuss business's response to consumer stakeholders regarding the issues introduced both in Chapter 12 and in this chapter.

TWO CENTRAL ISSUES: QUALITY AND SAFETY

The two central issues we are concerned with in this chapter represent the overwhelming attention that has been given to product and service issues over the past decade: quality and safety. Of course, quality and safety are not separate concepts—safety is one aspect of quality. Its importance, however, merits separate attention.

The Issue of Quality

There are several particularly important reasons for the current obsession with product quality. First, a concern for quality has been driven by the fact that the average consumer household has experienced a rise in family income and consequently demands more. With both adults often working outside the home, consumers become more demanding of a higher lifestyle. In addition, no one has surplus time to hang around repair shops or wait at home all day for service representatives to show up. This results in a need for products to work as they should, to be durable and long lasting, and to be easy to maintain and fix. The Internet has also made it possible for customers to communicate with other customers about their satisfaction, or dissatisfaction, with a product. A *Time*/CNN survey showed that consumers were less interested in technical innovation and attractive designs than they were in the product's ability to function as promised, its durability, and its ease of maintenance and repair.[5] A survey of households by Walker Research found that quality ranked first, price ranked second, and service ranked third among a list of factors consumers felt impacted a firm's reputation and their own purchasing decisions.[6]

Closely related to rising household expectations is the global competitiveness issue. Businesses now compete in a hypercompetitive landscape in which multinational strategies have given way to global strategies, and the solutions that once worked, no longer will.[7] As firms jockey for position in these hypercompetitive markets, they vie to attract customers by increasing the value of the product or service. Value is quality divided by price: A Sears Craftsman spark-plug wrench that sells for $19.99 is expected to be of proportionally higher quality than a spark-plug wrench sold at Wal-Mart for $4.95. To increase value, firms try to provide higher quality than their competitors for the same price, offer the same quality at a lower price, or some combination of the two. Each time a competitor raises the quality and/or lowers the price, other competitors scramble to catch up and the bar is raised.[8] The greater the competition, the more firms will be jockeying for position and the more often the bar will be raised. Firms that aren't continually improving their quality are certain to be left behind. The aforementioned story about Ford shows how quickly, in this highly competitive atmosphere, a well-respected company can derail.

It should be emphasized that our discussion of quality here includes service as well as products. We have clearly become a service economy in the United States, and poor quality of service has become one of the great consumer frustrations of all time. Still there is reason for hope. The University of Michigan's 2003 American Customer Satisfaction Index showed an improvement in customer satisfaction after years of decline. According to Professor Claus Fornell, who conducted the survey, "We've still got a ways to go but companies are trying harder because sales are harder to come by."[9]

On the front line of the new economy, service—bold, fast, imaginative, and customized—is now the ultimate strategic business imperative. Consumers today seem to swap horror stories about poor service as a kind of ritualistic, cathartic exercise. Consider the following examples: repeated trips to the car dealer; poor installation of refrigerator ice makers, resulting in several visits from repair people; returned food to the supermarket, resulting in brusque treatment; fouled-up travel reservations; poorly installed carpeting; no clerk at the shoe department of your favorite department store—and on and on. Shoddy service comes at a price. One study showed that 54 percent of the people interviewed would lose all loyalty to a company that had rude or unhelpful staff: One in 10 said they would walk away if a company did not seem to listen.[10]

There are at least eight critical dimensions of product or service quality that must be understood if business is to respond strategically to this factor.[11] These eight dimensions include (1) performance, (2) features, (3) reliability, (4) conformance, (5) durability, (6) serviceability, (7) aesthetics, and (8) perceived quality. *Performance* refers to a product's primary operating characteristics. For an automobile, this would include such items as handling, steering, and comfort. *Features* are the "bells and whistles" of products that supplement their basic functioning. *Reliability* reflects the probability of a product malfunctioning or failing. *Conformance* is the extent to which the product or service meets established standards. *Durability* is a measure of product life. *Serviceability* refers to the speed, courtesy, competence, and ease of repair. *Aesthetics* is a subjective factor that refers to how the product looks, feels, tastes, and so on. Finally, *perceived quality* is a subjective inference that the consumer makes on the basis of a variety of tangible and intangible product characteristics. To address the issue of product or service quality, a manager must be astute enough to appreciate these different dimensions of quality and the subtle and dynamic interplays among them.

An important question is whether quality is a social or an ethical issue or just a competitive factor that business needs to emphasize to be successful in the marketplace. Manuel Velasquez proposes three ethical theories based on the concept of duty that informs our understanding of the ethical dimensions of quality: (1) **contractual theory**, (2) **due care theory**, and (3) **social costs view**. The contractual theory focuses on the contract between the firm and the customer. Firms have a responsibility to comply with the terms of the sale, inform the customer about the nature of the product, avoid misrepresentation of any kind, and not coerce the customer in any way. The due care theory focuses on the relative vulnerability of the customer, who has less information and expertise than the firm, and the ethical responsibility that places on the firm. Customers must depend on the firm providing the product or service to live up to the claims about it and to exercise due care to avoid customer injury. The third view, social costs, extends beyond contractual theory and due care theory to suggest that, if a product causes harm, the firm should pay the costs of any injury even if the firm had met the terms of the contract, exercised all due care, and taken all reasonable precautions. This perspective serves as the underpinning for strict liability and its extension into absolute liability, which we will discuss shortly.[12]

The Issue of Safety

Business clearly has a duty to consumer stakeholders to sell them safe products and services. The concept of safety, in a definitional sense, means "free from harm or risk" or "secure from threat of danger, harm, or loss." In reality, however, the use of virtually any consumer product or service entails some degree of risk or some chance that the consumer may be harmed by the product or service.

In the 1800s, the legal view that prevailed was *caveat emptor* ("let the buyer beware"). The basic idea behind this concept was that the buyer had as much knowledge of what she or he wanted as the seller and, in any event, the marketplace would punish any violators. In the 1900s, *caveat emptor* gradually lost its favor and rationale, because it was frequently impossible for the consumer to have complete knowledge about manufactured goods.[13] Today, manufacturers are held responsible for all products placed on the market. We have a weak version of *caveat vendor* "let the seller take care."[14]

Through a series of legal developments as well as changing societal values, business has become significantly responsible for product safety. Court cases and legal doctrine now hold companies financially liable for harm to consumers. Yet this still does not answer the difficult question, "How safe are manufacturers obligated to make products?" It is not possible to make products totally "risk free"; experience has shown that consumers seem to have an uncanny ability to injure themselves in novel and creative ways, many of which cannot be anticipated. The challenge to management, therefore, is to make products as safe as possible while at the same time making them affordable and useful to consumers. Figure 13-1 presents the top 10 ways companies can avoid product recalls.

FIGURE 13-1

Top 10 List of Safety Principles

1. Build safety into product design.
2. Do product safety testing for all foreseeable hazards.
3. Keep informed about and implement latest developments in product safety.
4. Educate consumers about product safety.
5. Track and address your products' safety performance.
6. Fully investigate product safety incidents.
7. Report product safety defects promptly.
8. If a defect occurs, promptly offer a comprehensive recall plan.
9. Work with the Consumer Product Safety Council (CPSC) to make sure your recall is effective.
10. Learn from mistakes—yours and others'.

SOURCE: Speech given by former CPSC Commissioner Ann Brown to the Defense Research Institute, a national organization of product liability attorneys, challenging industry to implement a "Top 10 List" of safety principles aimed at reducing product defects that lead to recalls.

Ethics in Practice

To Check or Not to Check the Chicken?

Over the Christmas break, I went back to work at a fast-food restaurant where I had been working since high school. The restaurant sold lots of chicken sandwiches. We were supposed to measure the temperature of the chicken every hour to make sure that it was below 40 degrees (I assume in response to the incident in which a few people died as a result of bacteria formed in warm meat). That responsibility was assigned to whoever was battering the chicken at the time. All that the person had to do was stick a thermometer in the chicken, measuring the bottom, middle, and top until the digital read stayed at a single temperature for about 10 to 15 seconds. The whole process took a few minutes at most. This information was then sent to the restaurant's home office every day.

Unfortunately, not everyone would keep up with taking the temperatures. As an assistant manager, I was responsible for making sure the temperatures were checked, but it was difficult when I had other things to do. For instance, if I were at the register, I could not leave the customers to go back and make sure the batterer was taking the temperatures. At the end of the shift, I would sometimes see a sheet of paper with few or no temperatures noted on it. The store manager would have been upset had he known that I was making up temperatures I did not know to be true, but he would have been even more upset if there had been no temperatures on the sheet at all. He would just make up the numbers himself before he sent them off to the home office, with all the temperatures, of course, below 40 degrees. I have even seen the store manager make up temperatures when he was battering chicken and had forgotten to check the temperatures on the hour.

1. What is the ethical issue in this case? Is it product quality, product safety, or deceptive practices?

2. What responsibilities does the restaurant have to consumers in this situation?

3. As an assistant manager, what should I have done about this situation?

Contributed by Jason Greene

Today the public is concerned about a variety of hazards, such as the rise in genetically modified food, the dangers of living near toxic waste dumps or nuclear plants, the threat of anthrax, and so on. Food scares, both real and imagined, have occupied much of the public's attention. Although they occur everywhere, consumers in the European Union have been especially hard hit. The discovery of cancer-causing dioxin in Belgian food products caused many countries to temporarily halt imports from Belgium. Then, Coca-Cola recalled 2.5 million bottles of soft drinks that originated in two Belgian factories after children who drank it complained of stomachaches, nausea, and headaches. Bovine spongiform encephalopathy (BSE), or "mad cow" disease, precipitated a crisis for beef farmers throughout Europe. Beef consumption dropped by 27 percent in the 15 member states of the European Union, with Greece reporting a 50 percent drop. In 2001, foot-and-mouth disease delivered a staggering blow to an industry that was already reeling.[15] Food safety has even affected international trade. Japan discontinued all U.S. beef imports after the United States experienced an incident of mad cow disease in December 2003. The Bush administration resisted Japan's call for the United States to institute testing procedures comparable to those used in Japan, where all cattle are tested for disease at slaughter. Prior to the outbreak, the United States had tested one out of every 1,700 cattle.[16] Creekstone Farms Premium Beef is constructing a testing facility to be able to meet Japan's stipulations and restore sales to Japan. This move puts it at odds with an administration and an industry that both argue the testing is unnecessary.[17]

Manufacturing is another industry for which product safety is of paramount concern. Manufactured products create hazards not only because of unsafe product design but also as a result of consumers being given inadequate information regarding the hazards associated with using the products. Consequently, it is not surprising in product liability claims to find that the charges are based on one or more of several allegations. First, it may be charged that the product was improperly manufactured. Here the producer failed to exercise due care in the product's production, and this failure contributed directly to the accident or injury. Second, if the product was manufactured properly, its design could have been defective in that alternative designs or devices, if used at the time of manufacture, may have prevented the accident. Third, it may be charged that the producer failed to provide satisfactory instructions and/or warnings and that the accident or injury could have been prevented if such information had been provided. Fourth, it may be charged that the producer failed to foresee a reasonable and anticipated misuse of the product and warn against such misuse.[18] To appreciate the "big picture" of dangerous products, it should be noted that the Consumer Product Safety Commission keeps track of injuries treated in hospital emergency rooms and has identified the following categories of consumer products as being the most frequently associated with hospital-treated injuries (in order of prevalence):[19]

1. Sports and recreational activities and equipment
2. Home structures and construction materials
3. Home furnishings and fixtures
4. Housewares
5. Personal use items
6. Home workshop apparatus, tools, and attachments
7. Packaging and containers for household product
8. Toys

Whether we are dealing with consumer products, where there is potential for harm as a result of accidents or misuse, or with food products, where not-so-visible threats to human health may exist, the field of product safety is a significant responsibility and a growing challenge for the business community. It seems that no matter how careful business is with respect to these issues, the threat of product liability lawsuits has become an industry unto itself and becomes intimately linked with discussions of product safety. Therefore, we will now turn our attention to this vital topic.

Product Liability.   Product liability has become a monumental consumer issue in the United States for several reasons.

Reasons for the Growing Concern About Product Liability.   First, product liability has become such a major issue because of the sheer number of cases where products have resulted in illness, harm, or death. Second, the United States has become an increasingly litigious society. More and more U.S. citizens sue when faced with situations about which they are unhappy.

Closely paralleling the rise in the number of lawsuits in the United States has been the growing size of the financial awards given by the courts. Perhaps the path-breaking award in the product liability category was the $128.5 million awarded in 1978 in the case of a 19-year-old who at age 13 was severely injured. He was riding with a friend in a Ford Pinto that was struck from behind. The Pinto's gas tank ruptured, and the passenger compartment was filled with flames that killed his friend and severely burned him over 90 percent of his body. The badly scarred teenager underwent more than 50 operations. Ford was required by the jury to pay $666,280 to the dead driver's family and to pay the survivor $2.8 million in compensatory damages and $125 million in punitive damages.[20] The Pinto case was the beginning, but the awards have grown since then. The average jury award went from $520,000 in 1993 to $1,200,000 in 2002, an increase of 130 percent.[21]

It has been estimated that litigation's cost to society is over $200 billion per year, more than half of which goes to legal fees and costs, some of which could be spent to hire more teachers, police officers, and fire fighters. The cost of litigation to companies has been said to represent approximately 30 percent of a stepladder's price, 50 percent of a football helmet, and 95 percent of the price of a childhood vaccine. The problem is largely confined to the United States. In a year when DuPont had nearly 5,000 personal injury lawsuits inside the United States, they had fewer than 20 outside the United States. Although half the company's sales come from overseas, 95 percent of the company's legal costs come from the United States.[22]

Since the Pinto case, multimillion-dollar lawsuits have become commonplace. Some major companies have been hit so hard by lawsuits that they have filed for protection under Chapter 11 of the federal bankruptcy law. One famous example of this is the Johns Manville Corporation, which faced an avalanche of asbestos-related lawsuits that totaled 16,500 suits demanding over $12 billion.[23] Another well-known case is that of A. H. Robins, which filed for protection after facing over 5,000 product liability lawsuits in which women charged that its Dalkon Shield, an intrauterine contraceptive device, had injured them.[24] Dow Chemical, the principal manufacturer of silicone breast implants, entered Chapter 11 in 1995.[25] The strategy continues today. In April 2001, W. R. Grace & Co. filed for bankruptcy protection to shield it from asbestos-related claims.[26] In March 2004, however, the court tired of delays and refused to allow Grace a sixth extension of the proceedings.[27] Other companies encountering large lawsuits have included Union Carbide, with its poison gas explosion in Bhopal, India; Dow Chemical, with its Agent Orange defoliant; and Bridgestone/Firestone, with its defective tires. Figure 13-2 shows several recent top jury awards.

The experience of Wyeth Corp. reveals the other side of the product liability debate. Committed to paying users of their diet-drug cocktail fen-phen who had sustained heart damage, Wyeth has been overwhelmed by many more claims than they expected. As reported by Amy Barrett in *Business Week* (24 May 2004 i3884 p88), Wyeth's terms of settlement "spawned an army of lawyers, doctors, and others" who recruited patients in a process that Wyeth now believes led to fraudulent claims. Years after removing the drugs from the market, Wyeth sees no end to the litigation in sight. Read more by logging on to InfoTrac College Edition at **http://www. infotrac-college.com** and keying record number A116864816.

FIGURE 13-2

Top Jury Verdicts

Jury Award	Defendant	Case	Final Outcome
$28,000,850,000	Philip Morris, Inc.	Awarded to Betty Bullock, a 64-year-old woman with lung cancer, who blamed Philip Morris for her tobacco addiction due to company's failure to warn her of smoking risks	Court reduced verdict to $28 million.
$11,863,600,000	ExxonMobil Corp.	Company found to have violated lease agreements with the State of Alabama to extract natural gas from underwater fields	Case is on appeal.
$10,100,529,196	Philip Morris, Inc.	Company found to have claimed its Marlboro Light and Cambridge Light cigarettes were lower in tar and nicotine than regular cigarettes	An appeal is pending.
$4,931,000,000	General Motors	Awarded to plaintiffs who were severely burned when the fuel tank of a 1979 Chevrolet Malibu exploded during a collision	Court reduced verdict to $1.1 billion. GM is appealing.
$3,006,000,000	Philip Morris, Inc.	Damages awarded for the cancer of long-time smoker Richard Boeken	Court reduced award to $100 million.

SOURCE: Stuart Taylor, Jr., and Evan Thomas, "Civil Wars," *Newsweek* (December 15, 2003), 48. From *Newsweek*, December 15, 2003, © 2003 Newsweek, Inc. All rights reserved.

Our final reason for product liability becoming such an issue is the doctrine of **strict liability** and the expansion of this concept in the courts. As we mentioned previously, the social costs view of product quality underlies the concept of strict liability and its extensions. In its most general form, the doctrine of strict liability holds that anyone in the value chain of a product is liable for harm caused to the user if the product as sold was unreasonably dangerous because of its defective condition. This applies to anyone involved in the design, manufacture, or sale of a defective product. Beyond manufacturing, courts have ruled against plaintiffs from a broad array of functions, such as selling, advertising, promotion, and distribution.[28] For example, the Department of Transportation (DOT) holds warehouses liable for violations of hazardous materials regulations even when the warehouse relied on information provided by the customer (the depositor) when documenting the shipment.[29] In other words, there is no legal defense for placing on the market a product that is dangerous to a consumer because of a known or knowable defect, unless the strict liability is imposed by a statute that allows for an argument of due diligence.[30] To prove due diligence, a company must take every possible precautionary step possible and follow all industry standards.

Extensions of the Strict-Liability Rule.   Courts in several states and certain countries have established a standard that is much more demanding than strict liability. This concept is called **absolute liability**. The ruling that established this concept was handed down by the New Jersey Supreme Court in *Beshada v. Johns Manville Corporation* (1982). The plaintiffs in the Beshada case were employees of Johns Manville and other companies who had developed asbestos-related diseases as a result of exposure in the workplace.[31] The court ruled in this case that a manufacturer could be held strictly liable for failure to warn of a product hazard, even if the hazard was scientifically unknowable at the time of manufacture and sale. Therefore, a company cannot use as its defense the assurance that it did its best according to the state of the art in the industry at that time. Under this ruling, the manufacturer is liable for damages even if it had no way of knowing that the product might cause a problem later. This has led to what *The Wall Street Journal* terms the "asbestos tort blob," named for the movie blob that devours everything in its path. More than 100,000 asbestos lawsuits were filed in 2003, more than in any single previous year.[32]

Although the United States has been rightly termed the litigation nation, other countries struggle with the issue as well. For example, the Supreme Court of India upheld the absolute liability of a common carrier, in this case Patel Roadways Ltd., for goods destroyed by fire. The court ruled that, in the case of damage or loss, it is not necessary for the plaintiff to establish negligence.[33] Similarly, leading charities in Great Britain are pressuring the prime minister to institute a system of strict financial and legal liability before genetically modified crops can be introduced there.[34]

The absolute-liability rule frequently involves cases involving chemicals or drugs. For example, a drug producer might put a drug on the market (with government approval) thinking that it is safe based on current knowledge. Under the doctrine of absolute liability, the firm could be held liable for side effects or health problems that develop years, or even decades, later. The result is that a large amount of uncertainty is injected into the production process.[35] Furthermore, the company's association with the damaging product may be tenuous at best. Forty years ago, Crown Cork and Seal, Inc., had a brief connection with Mundet Cork Company, a maker of cork-lined bottle caps. Unfortunately for Crown Cork and Seal, Mundet also owned a small insulation company. Crown Cork's $7 million investment in Mundet has led to thousands of asbestos-related claims filed against it and over $350 million in asbestos-related payments to date.[36]

Another extension of strict liability is known as **market share liability**. This concept evolved from **delayed manifestation cases**—situations in which delayed reactions to such products appear years later after consumption of, or exposure to, the product.[37] Market share liability was derived from the California case in which a group of women with birth defects claimed that the defects had been caused by the drug DES, which their mothers had taken while pregnant years earlier. The women could not name the company that had made the pills their mothers had taken. But in 1980 the California Supreme Court upheld a ruling that the six drug firms that made DES would be held responsible in proportion to their market shares of DES sales unless they could prove that they had not made the actual doses the women had taken.[38] When this verdict was reached, the business press expressed alarm about the potential impact of the decision. Their concern, however, was premature. With very few exceptions, market share liability has been rejected in subsequent non-DES cases and in second-generation DES cases. DES was uniquely suited to that defense because it was a generic product, the entire industry used the same formula, and it was marketed and promoted generically by all industry members. Efforts to apply the concept to cases involving asbestos products, blood products, breast implants, DPT vaccines, polio vaccines, multipiece tire rims, lead-based paints, and benzene all failed.[39]

Product Tampering and Product Extortion.   Two other concerns that have contributed to the product liability discussion are *product tampering* and *product extortion*. The most well-known cases involved Tylenol in the 1980s—first in 1982, when seven Chicago people died from taking tainted Extra Strength Tylenol capsules, and again in 1986, when cyanide-laced bottles of Tylenol were found in New York and one woman died. James Burke, chairman of Johnson & Johnson, characterized the case as "terrorism, pure and simple."[40] In response to these and other incidents, firms began to employ tamper-evident packaging. Although improvements in packaging have slowed the rate of pharmaceutical product tampering, they have not stopped it. In 2000, two Australian pharmaceutical manufacturers received extortion threats. The extortionists are believed to have bought over-the-counter analgesics, poisoned them with strychnine, and returned them to the shelves. Four people were hospitalized, and nationwide product recalls cost the firms millions of dollars.[41]

Adulterated and poisoned products stretch beyond pharmaceuticals. After the September 11 attacks, product tampering concerns centered on anthrax and the possible ways it could be used for extortion and terror. When attorneys at Stoel Rives in Portland, Oregon, mailed 50,000 cards in envelopes with bumpy seeds, some recipients became so scared they dialed 911. Publisher's Clearinghouse mailed packages of powdered detergent to customers, causing alarm in the process.[42] Now that the furor over mail has subsided, attention has shifted to ways in which terrorists might tamper with the food supply. Since the September 11 attacks, food companies have spent hundreds of millions of dollars to upgrade security, institute employee background checks, and install lights and video cameras.[43]

Product Liability Reform.   The problems discussed up to this point have combined to generate calls from many groups for **product liability reform**, also known as **tort reform**. However, not everyone agrees that reform is needed. On one side are business groups, medical associations, local and state governments, and insurance companies that want to change the system that they claim gives costly and unfair advantage to plaintiffs in liability suits. On the other side are consumer groups and trial lawyers who defend the current system as one that protects the constitutional rights of wrongfully injured parties.[44]

The business community's criticisms of the current system illustrate some of the aspects of the controversy. Currently, we have a patchwork of state laws. Business wants a uniform federal code. Business also argues for no punitive damages unless the plaintiff meets tougher standards of proof because meeting government standards is no defense in most states. Business thinks it should have an absolute shield against punitive damages for drugs, medical devices, and aircraft that meet government regulations. Finally, business wants victorious plaintiffs to be able to recover damages only to the extent that defendants are liable.[45] On the other side of the issue are consumer and citizen groups and others who support the current system and say the critics of the product liability laws have exaggerated the problems. These supporters of the current system point out that some of the most infamous injuries inflicted on consumers were remedied mainly through lawsuits, not regulatory action. Examples include the Dalkon Shield, a contraceptive device that made thousands of women infertile; the Pinto's exploding gas tank; the damage to workers exposed to asbestos; and many lesser-known cases.[46] According to Ralph Nader, trial lawyers are "all that is left to require wrongdoers to be held accountable."[47]

Perhaps the controversy played out most dramatically in the experience of Rick Santorum, the Republican senator from Pennsylvania. Santorum has been a vocal advocate of tort reform, sponsoring several pieces of legislation that would limit claimants' options in cases of medical malpractice, including a bill that would have capped noneconomic damages at $250,000. He also consistently voted against the Patient Bill of Rights, which would grant patients the right to sue their HMOs. However, when his wife experienced back and leg numbness after a visit to a chiropractor, she sued for $500,000 and Santorum testified on her behalf, claiming that the injury would keep her from assisting in his campaign for reelection. A jury subsequently awarded her $350,000. A judge reduced the award to $175,000, and the parties eventually settled out of court.[48] Like the Santorums, most people want to limit the cost of litigation to society without limiting our ability to sue when we believe we have been wronged; in other words, we want to have our cake and eat it too.

Philip K. Howard, author of *The Collapse of Common Good* (2002), is a leading voice for tort reform. He helped to found Common Good (http://www.cgood.org), an organization devoted to reforming the legal system. Common Good's claim to be a bipartisan effort is supported by an advisory board that includes George McGovern and Newt Gingrich, representatives of both ends of the political spectrum. Rather than advocating caps on damages, Common Good argues for a reform of the system of jurisprudence, removing education and health care claims from the court system. Cases would be settled by committees of professionals that would be able to differentiate frivolous suits from those with merit. Howard argues that this would limit the overall cost of litigation to society without putting limits on the judgments awarded to those with valid claims. In spite of the bipartisan support, Howard is not without detractors. Ralph Nader and the Association of Trial Lawyers (http://www.atlanet.org) contend that Howard favors defendants at the expense of plaintiffs.[49]

The debate over product liability law is likely to continue unabated. Business claims the current system is inherently inefficient, raises the costs of litigation, and imposes a hidden tax on consumers because it inhibits innovation and dampens competitiveness. Consumer groups argue that the current system has forced companies to make safer products and listen to their customers. Studies show that both sides have valid arguments: The laws have spurred some safety improvements, but they have also hampered innovation.[50] It is expected that product liability will remain a vital issue and that as businesses increasingly internalize the notion of product safety, the entire business/consumer relationship will be well served.

We now consider two major government agencies that are dedicated to product safety: the Consumer Product Safety Commission and the Food and Drug Administration.

CONSUMER PRODUCT SAFETY COMMISSION

The **Consumer Product Safety Commission (CPSC)** is an independent regulatory agency that was created by the Consumer Product Safety Act of 1972. CPSC works to reduce the risk of injuries and deaths from consumer products by:[51]

1. Developing voluntary standards with industry
2. Issuing and enforcing mandatory standards
3. Banning consumer products if no feasible standard would adequately protect the public
4. Obtaining the recall of products or arranging for their repair
5. Conducting research on potential product hazards
6. Informing and educating consumers through the media, state and local governments, private organizations, and by responding to consumer inquiries

The CPSC points with pride to the 30 percent reduction in the rates of death and injury caused by consumer products since the agency's inception.[52] Figure 13-3 presents examples of voluntary safety standards developed by the CPSC.

FIGURE 13-3

CPSC: Development of Voluntary Standards

Voluntary Safety Standards			
Indoor Air Quality Hazards	**Children's Product Hazards**	**Fire/Electrical Hazards**	**Other Hazards**
Carbon Monoxide (CO) Detectors. Includes new alarm requirements based on both CO concentration and exposure time.	Bunk Beds. Includes provisions to prevent the collapse of the mattress and its foundation, as well as provisions to prevent entrapment or strangulation in the bunk bed's structure.	National Electrical Code. Provides added GFCI protection around household sinks, requires GFCI protection for spas and hot tubs, and adds a requirement that heat tapes be safety certified.	Automatic Garage Door Openers (two revisions). Includes cautionary labeling on the risk of entrapment.
Formaldehyde in Particleboard and Formaldehyde in Hardwood and Decorative Plywood (two standards). Specifies allowable formaldehyde emissions.	Drawstrings on Children's Clothing. Four months after CPSC presented evidence of dangers to children, manufacturers voluntarily removed drawstrings from existing children's clothing and promised that new clothing would be manufactured with safer alternatives, such as Velcro and snaps.	Handheld Hair Dryers. Includes requirements for polarized plugs, cautionary labeling on the risk of use near water, and protections from electrocution when immersed, whether the unit is turned on or off.	Above Ground/Onground Swimming Pools. Provides recommended barrier requirements (within an appendix to the standard) to prevent child drownings.

SOURCE: U.S. Consumer Product Safety Commission, http://www.cpsc.gov.

The CPSC was created at the zenith of the consumer movement as a result of initiatives taken in the late 1960s. President Lyndon Johnson established a National Commission on Product Safety in 1968, and this commission recommended the creation of a permanent agency. The commission justified its recommendation by its finding that an estimated 20 million Americans were injured annually by consumer products. President Richard Nixon, who took office while the proposed agency was still being debated, supported the agency's creation, but not as an independent agency. Congress gave the agency an unusually high degree of independence and required that it open its proceedings to the public to address the often-heard criticism of regulatory agencies that they become captives of the industries they regulate. Congress's intent was to keep business at arm's length and to involve consumers as primary participants in the agency's decision making.[53]

The CPSC experienced ups and downs as various administrations came into office. The agency grew in the 1970s, became controversial in the late 1970s, and was significantly reduced in power after the 1980 election of Ronald Reagan as president. The Reagan years of the CPSC (1980–1988) were marked by drastic budget cuts, massive staff reductions, and eventual paralysis of the agency. The agency survived several attempts to dismantle it. As one indication of the downturn it took during the Reagan years, its budget steadily declined from $40.6 million in 1980 to $32.6 million in 1988 before experiencing an upturn.[54]

Like most of the regulatory agencies in the post-Reagan environment, the CPSC began demonstrating renewed activism in the 1990s. Much of this was due to the longest serving chairperson in CPSC history, Ann Brown, who took charge in 1994 and resigned in November 2001. During Brown's tenure, funding for the agency increased by over 25 percent; civil penalty amounts increased 2,500 percent. Each year, CPSC announced an average of over 300 product recalls. Upon leaving the agency, Brown formed Safer America for Everyone (SAFE), a nonprofit organization dedicated to promoting consumer health and safety. Brown was known for pursuing voluntary cooperation with industry. During her tenure, the agency agreed to five times as many voluntary standards as mandatory.[55]

In June 2001, President Bush selected Mary Gall to serve as the chair and commissioner of the CPSC. Two months later, Congress rejected the nomination in a strict party-line vote. Democrats charged that Gall, who was known for having a "hands-off" regulatory philosophy, placed the interests of business over the safety of consumers. Gall favored industry self-regulation and consumer responsibility over government intervention. Republicans and the White House derided the vote as "pure partisan politics." They pointed to the fact that Gall was appointed by then-President Clinton and confirmed by Congress with her current philosophy.[56] In April 2002, former New Mexico attorney general Harold Stratton was nominated and subsequently confirmed by Congress. Although a believer in free markets, he assured skeptics that he would shut down businesses if necessary to get unsafe products off the market.[57] Stratton's tenure to date has both pleased and angered his critics. Just four days after taking the reins, Stratton imposed a $1 million fine on General Electric for fire-prone dishwashers.[58] However in November 2003, Stratton cast the deciding vote to drop the demand that Daisy recall 7.5 million BB guns. The Daisy lawsuit was filed by Stratton's predecessor, Ann Brown, in response to at least 15 deaths and 171 serious injuries stemming from a defect that caused BBs to be lodged in the magazine even when it appeared to be empty. About 80 percent of the deaths and injuries involved children under the age of 16. The CPSC agreed to a settlement requiring Daisy to post larger safety warnings and mount a 5-year education campaign, a settlement the commission had rejected twice before. The settlement was opposed by the commission staff, who felt any settlement should include corrective action to repair the defect. In a scathing dissent, commission member Thomas H. Moore said, "Bottom line is that we are not the business protection agency."[59]

The CPSC continues to play an important role in protecting consumers from unsafe products. The CPSC remains the only clearinghouse available for consumers who have safety concerns with the 15,000 products under its care, and it is the only mechanism available for recalling unsafe products. Figure 13-4 presents some of the challenges facing the new CPSC commissioner.

FOOD AND DRUG ADMINISTRATION

The **Food and Drug Administration (FDA)** grew out of experiments with food safety by one man—Harvey W. Wiley—chief chemist for the Agricultural Department in the late 1800s. Wiley's most famous experiments involved feeding small doses of poisons to human volunteers. The substances fed to the volunteers were similar to those found in food preservatives at the time. The volunteers became known as the "Poison Squad," and their publicity generated a public awareness of the dangers of eating adulterated foods. The Food and Drug Act of 1906 was a direct result of the publicity created by Wiley's experiments. The act was administered by Wiley's Bureau of Chemistry until 1931, when the name "Food and Drug Administration" first was used. The Food and Drug Act called for the protection of the public from potential health hazards presented by adulterated or mislabeled foods, drugs, cosmetics, and medical devices. Later laws for which the FDA became responsible included the Food, Drug, and Cosmetic Act of 1938; the Public Health Service Act of 1944; the 1968 Radiation Control for Health & Safety Act; the Fair Packaging and Labeling Act of 1966; and the 1984 Drug Price Competition and Patent Restoration Act. In response to these and other major laws, the FDA regulates foods, drugs, cosmetics, and medical devices found in interstate commerce.[60] Figure 13-5 on page 428 provides the mission of the FDA as defined by the FDA Modernization Act of 1997.

FIGURE 13-4

Holes in the Product Safety Net

Consumers Union, an organization devoted to public safety, has identified four problems confronting the Consumer Product Safety Commission.

Lack of Compliance	Companies are required to report known or suspected product safety problems, but many fail to do so. Lack of sufficient resources has limited the commission's ability to police the companies.
Limited Public Access to Key Information	Unlike other agencies, the commission can't release information about a product (unless it's deemed an 'imminent hazard') before sending the information to the manufacturer for comments and waiting up to 20 days for an answer. Other agencies (e.g., EPA, FDA, NHTSA, and OSHA) do not have this restriction.
Inadequate Consumer Notification	Recalls depend on wide distribution of information. Product warranty cards are the best way to obtain customer names and addresses, but many customers don't fill them out because manufacturers also ask invasive personal questions.
Insufficient Funding	Although its responsibilities have grown over the past 20 years, the CPSC staff has been cut by a third and its budget has been cut by more than half, adjusted for inflation.

SOURCE: Jim Guest, "Holes in Our Product Safety Net," *Consumer Reports* (October 2001), 7. © 2001 by Consumers Union of the U.S., Inc. Yonkers, NY 10703-1057, a nonprofit organization.

FIGURE 13-5

The Mission of the Food and Drug Administration

1. To promote the public health by promptly and efficiently reviewing clinical research and taking appropriate action on the marketing of regulated products in a timely manner

2. With respect to such products, protect the public health by ensuring that foods are safe, wholesome, sanitary, and properly labeled; human and veterinary drugs are safe and effective; there is reasonable assurance of the safety and effectiveness of devices intended for human use; cosmetics are safe and properly labeled; public health and safety are protected from electronic product radiation

3. Participate through appropriate processes with representatives of other countries to reduce the burden of regulation, harmonize regulatory requirements, and achieve appropriate reciprocal arrangements

4. As determined to be appropriate by the Secretary, carry out paragraphs (1) through (3) in consultation with experts in science, medicine, and public health, and in cooperation with consumers, users, manufacturers, importers, packers, distributors, and retailers of regulated products

SOURCE: http://www.fda.gov.

The powers of the FDA were expanded as a result of other laws and amendments. The 1958 Delaney Amendment to the Food, Drug, and Cosmetic Act was especially notable. The Delaney Amendment requires the FDA to ban any food or color additive that has been shown to cause cancer in laboratory test animals. In 1962, amendments were passed to require drug manufacturers to prove the effectiveness as well as the safety of their products before marketing them. In addition, the FDA was authorized to order the withdrawal of dangerous products from the market. In 1976, Congress passed legislation requiring the regulation of complex medical products and diagnostic devices.

The FDA resides within the Health and Human Services Department and engages in three broad categories of activity: analysis, surveillance, and correction. Throughout most of the 1980s, the themes emphasized were the cutting of bureaucratic delays and red tape, the speeding up of agency decisions, and the elimination of unnecessary regulation. A major blow to the agency occurred during the 1980s, when it was disclosed that four FDA employees were accused of taking cash payoffs and illegal gifts from a major generic drug company in return for favored treatment. Major challenges the FDA faced early in the first Bush administration included the AIDS epidemic, regulation of medical devices, food safety, fat substitutes, nutritional labeling, and over-the-counter drug review.[61] In 1991, under new commissioner David Kessler, the FDA embarked on an aggressive crackdown on deceptive product labels, which created a fair amount of controversy. In early 1991, the FDA targeted two highly visible products and companies to make its point. It seized Procter & Gamble's Citrus Hill "Fresh Choice" orange juice and, a few days later, Ragu "Fresh Italian" pasta sauce, the nation's leading tomato sauce brand. In both cases, the FDA forced the companies to remove the term "fresh" from their products because they thought the companies were inaccurately applying that term to their products.

The point of the FDA was clear. It was no longer going to pursue the practice, which had become commonplace throughout the 1980s, of companies suspected of violations stretching out negotiations with the agency for years while engaging in an endless back-and-forth exchange of proposals and counterproposals. The FDA was reasserting itself as an agency that was planning to take swift action against violators. In addition to the two cases cited, the FDA sent warning letters to the manufacturers of Listerine, Plax, and Viadent mouthwash brands; Weight Watchers and Kraft brands cholesterol-free mayonnaise; and

Ethics in Practice

SHOULD A COMPANY STOP THIS DEVIANT CONSUMER BEHAVIOR?

During my senior year, I was working for a major retail store. What struck me the most about this experience was how easily customers could bring back used merchandise and get refunds. A good example might be "Super Bowl Fever." People came to the store and bought the largest TV sets just to watch the Super Bowl on the weekend. Then, they returned and requested full refunds for the TV sets on the following Monday morning. Furthermore, I was amazed by the fact that some customers asked the store for full refunds without receipts, and the merchandise not only was used but in some cases had been used for several months. However, on many occasions the customers got their money back right away, or checks would be sent to them if they didn't have their receipts with them.

1. What exactly do businesses owe consumers? Is this not an example of taking consumer satisfaction to ridiculous lengths?

2. Is this an ethical practice on the part of consumers? Does a company "owe" customers this degree of satisfaction?

3. What actions, if any, should such a retail store take to control this practice?

Contributed Anonymously

Fleischmann's reduced-calorie margarine, among other products. The agency thought that these manufacturers had made claims that misrepresented the features of their products.[62]

There is perhaps no other regulatory body that has become more controversial in recent years than the FDA. Under David Kessler's leadership, the FDA aggressively and zealously pursued companies it felt were out of compliance with government regulations or were taking advantage of consumers. Supporters of the FDA applauded it for relentlessly pursuing violators. In 1997, Dr. Kessler resigned and Dr. Jane Henney, vice president of research for the University of New Mexico, was nominated to be his successor.[63] Having served under both Bush and Clinton, Henney enjoyed bipartisan credentials. However, her tenure as deputy to Dr. Kessler raised red flags for Senate Republicans who found Republican Kessler overly quick to regulate and overly slow to approve treatments and devices.[64] After contentious debate, Henney was confirmed. During her tenure in office, the "abortion pill," RU486, was approved. When the Bush administration entered office, Henney handed in her protocol resignation, which was accepted shortly thereafter, effectively firing her. Although significant lobbying to retain her occurred, she was not able to duplicate the feat of Republican David Kessler, who had been retained by the Democratic Clinton administration after being appointed by the first Bush administration. Observers felt that her failure to block the approval of RU486 doomed her reappointment.[65] Mark McClellan became the head of the FDA in late 2002 but was tapped to head Medicare just 15 months later in March 2004. In his short tenure, McClellan drew praise for streamlining the approval process for new drug therapies—something at which the FDA had been quite bad. McClellan's deputy, Les Crawford, became acting commissioner and remains so at this writing.[66]

The new commissioner will inherit a host of challenges at the FDA. Traditionally, the FDA has been concerned primarily with the effectiveness of drugs. Now a movement is growing to involve the FDA in the regulation of the dietary supplement industry.

Although the FDA did in fact ban ephedra, "after 16,000 adverse-event reports . . . that linked the adrenaline-like stimulant to heart attack, stroke and death," the FDA still has its work cut out in trying to control dietary supplement manufacturers, according to a *Forbes* article (19 April 2004 v173 i8 p78) by Nathan Vardi. Maintaining that their products are perfectly safe when used correctly, manufacturers have refused to pay claims against them and have resorted to strategies such as declaring bankruptcy to avoid prosecution. Find out more about the purveyors of "poison pills" by logging on to InfoTrac College Edition at **http://www.infotrac-college. com** and keying record number A114875039.

Proponents of greater controls argue that the FDA cannot allow unsafe products, such as ephedrine, to reach the marketplace, especially since dietary supplements are rife with potential for abuse. Opponents contend that the FDA is simply tightening its grip on vitamin vendors to protect the powerful pharmaceutical industry.[67] In response to the popularity of the Atkins and South Beach Diets, the FDA is working on clarifying the definition of carbohydrates and evaluating the glycemic index as a measure of food nutrition.[68] Other hot topics on which the FDA is working include mercury in fish, mad cow disease, imported drugs, bioterrorism, counterfeit drugs, and online purchases of medication.[69]

BUSINESS'S RESPONSE TO CONSUMER STAKEHOLDERS

Business's response to consumerism and consumer stakeholders has varied over the years. It has ranged from poorly conceived public relations ploys at one extreme to well-designed and implemented programs like total quality management (TQM) and Six Sigma at the other. The history of business's response to consumers parallels its perceptions of the seriousness, pervasiveness, effectiveness, and longevity of the consumer movement. When the consumer movement first began, business's response was casual, perhaps symbolic, and hardly effective. Today, the consumer movement has matured, and formal interactions with consumer stakeholders have become more and more institutionalized. Business has realized that consumers today are more persistent than in the past, more assertive, and more likely to use or exhaust all appeal channels before being satisfied. Armed with considerable power, consumer activists have been a major stimulus to more sincere efforts on behalf of business to provided consumers with a forum. These efforts have included the creation of toll-free hot lines, user-friendly Web sites, and consumer service representatives. Programs like total quality management and Six Sigma have become the strategic responses. These responses merit brief consideration.

Total Quality Management Programs

SEARCH THE WEB

THE AMERICAN SOCIETY FOR QUALITY

The American Society for Quality (ASQ)'s mission is to make "quality a global priority, an organizational imperative, and a personal ethic." Founded in 1946, ASQ provides a range of resources for those who seek to improve themselves and their world. Their Web site (http://www.asq.org) is a compendium of resources for improving quality and a source of links to other quality initiatives.

Total quality management (TQM) has many different characteristics, but it essentially means that all of the functions of the business are blended into a holistic, integrated philosophy built around the concepts of quality, teamwork, productivity, and customer understanding and satisfaction.[70] Figure 13-6 depicts one useful view of the principles, practices, and techniques of TQM. It should be noted that the customer, or consumer stakeholder, is the focus of the process.

A vital assumption and premise of TQM is that the customer is the final judge of quality. Therefore, the first part of the TQM process is to define quality in terms of customer expectations and requirements. Figure 13-7 on page 432 presents several different popular definitions of quality and their strengths and weaknesses.

Customer expectations and requirements are then converted to standards and specifications. Finally, the entire organization is realigned to ensure that both conformance quality

FIGURE 13-6

Principles, Practices, and Techniques of Total Quality Management

	Customer Focus	**Continuous Improvement**	**Teamwork**
Principles	• Paramount importance of customers • Providing products and services that fulfill customer needs; requires organization-wide focus on customers	• Consistent customer satisfaction can be attained only through relentless improvement of processes that create products and services	• Customer focus and continuous improvement are best achieved by collaboration throughout an organization as well as with customers and suppliers
Practices	• Direct customer contact • Collecting information about customer needs • Using information to design and deliver products and services	• Process analysis • Reengineering • Problem solving • Plan/do/check/act	• Search for arrangements that benefit all units involved in a process • Formation of various types of teams • Group skills training
Techniques	• Customer surveys and focus groups • Quality function deployment (translates customer information into product specifications)	• Flowcharts • Pareto analysis • Statistical process control • Fishbone diagrams	• Organizational development methods, such as the nominal group technique • Team-building methods (e.g., role clarification and group feedback)

SOURCE: James W. Dean, Jr., and David E. Bowen, "Management Theory and Total Quality: Improving Research and Practice Through Theory Development," *Academy of Management Review* (Vol. 19, No. 3, July 1994), 395.

(adherence to standards and specifications) and perceived quality (meeting or exceeding customer expectations) are achieved.[71] It is clear in TQM that "delighted customers" is the overarching goal of management's efforts.[72]

Opportunities for recognition have helped to propel quality efforts. In the United States and the rest of the industrialized world, the Malcolm Baldrige Award, ISO 9000, and the Deming Quality Award have enhanced the reputations of firms that undertake quality initiatives and complete them successfully. However, TQM became the buzzword of the 1980s, and many of its slogans, such as "Getting it right the first time" became viewed as clichés. It is against that backdrop that other tools developed, such as just in time (JIT) and business process reengineering (BPR). Many were concerned about a TQM shortcoming, as described by Phil Crosby, a leading TQM consultant: "TQM never did anything to define quality, which is conformance to standards."[73] The need for a more rigorous definition of quality was part of the appeal of Six Sigma, which we will describe briefly.

Six Sigma

Six Sigma is a development in total quality management that has become a way of life for many corporations. Basically, Six Sigma is a heading under which is grouped a body of methodologies and techniques. Scarcely a week goes by without a major corporation adopting Six Sigma as a way of improving quality and reducing costs.[74] Dow, DuPont, Sony, Honeywell, Nokia, GlaxoSmithKline, and Raytheon are but a few of the major corporations relying on the Six Sigma methodology. According to Jack Welch, former CEO of GE, "[Six Sigma—the Breakthrough Strategy] is the most important initiative GE has ever taken. . . . it is part of the genetic code of our future leadership."[75] Although some

FIGURE 13-7

Strengths and Weaknesses of Quality Definitions

Definition	Strengths	Weaknesses
Excellence	• Strong marketing and human resource benefits • Universally recognizable—mark of uncompromising standards and high achievement	• Provides little practical guidance to practitioners • Measurement difficulties • Attributes of excellence may change dramatically and rapidly • Sufficient number of customers must be willing to pay for excellence
Value	• Concept of value incorporates multiple attributes • Focuses attention on a firm's internal efficiency and external effectiveness • Allows for comparisons across disparate objects and experiences	• Difficulty extracting individual components of value judgment • Questionable inclusiveness • Quality and value are different constructs
Conformance to Specifications	• Facilitates precise measurement • Leads to increased efficiency • Necessary for global strategy • Should force disaggregation of consumer needs • Most parsimonious and appropriate definition for some customers	• Consumers do not know or care about internal specifications • Inappropriate for services • Potentially reduces organizational adaptability • Specifications may quickly become obsolete in rapidly changing markets • Internally focused
Meeting and/or Exceeding Expectations	• Evaluates from customer's perspective • Applicable across industries • Responsive to market changes • All-encompassing definition	• Most complex definition • Difficult to measure • Customers may not know expectations • Idiosyncratic reactions • Prepurchase attitudes affect subsequent judgments • Short-term and long-term evaluations may differ • Confusion between customer service and customer satisfaction

SOURCE: Carol. A. Reeves and David A. Bednar, "Defining Quality: Alternatives and Implications," *Academy of Management Review* (Vol. 19, No. 3, July 1994), 437.

deride Six Sigma as "TQM on steroids," it has brought new commitment and energy to the quest for quality in the new millennium. It is even said to have brought "more prominence to the quality world than it has enjoyed since the glory days of the mid-1980s."[76]

Motorola first developed Six Sigma, and Allied Signal later experimented with it, but most observers believe that GE perfected it. *Sigma* is a statistical measure of variation from the mean; higher values of sigma mean fewer defects. The six-sigma level of operation is 3.4 defects per million. Most companies operate around the four-sigma level, i.e., 6,000 defects per million. Corporations adopting the program must develop "black belts," i.e., people specifically trained to fill sponsorship roles, provide assistance, and see the program through. They must also find "champions" at senior levels of management who are committed to shepherding the program when needed.[77]

One of Six Sigma's strengths has been the clarity of the process and the steps companies must take to adopt it. However, Six Sigma is more than a toolbox with clear instructions. The program also represents a philosophy that stresses the importance of customers as well as careful measurement. Six Sigma practitioners look for facts rather than opinions, and they believe in fixing the process rather than the product.[78] Of course, these underlying principles are the foundation of TQM and most other quality efforts. The basis for all of these is the satisfaction of the consumer. Figure 13-8 outlines a consumer-stakeholder satisfaction model.

FIGURE 13-8

A Consumer-Stakeholder Satisfaction Model

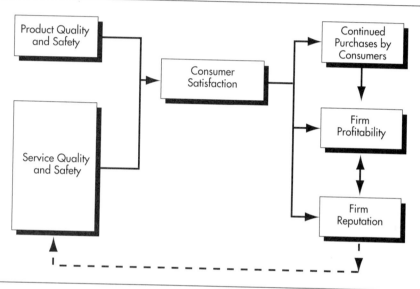

▪ SUMMARY

Consumer stakeholders have become concerned with product quality and safety, largely because businesses have failed to meet their needs reliably on these two fronts. The situation has been the same with both manufacturing and services. One major challenge has been to identify and understand all the different dimensions of the quality issue. Today, quality may mean performance, features, reliability, conformance, durability, serviceability, aesthetics, perceived quality, or some combination of these dimensions.

An extremely important legal and ethical issue has been the consumer's right to safety. Product safety has become one of the most crucial consumer issues for firms. The product liability crisis has been an outgrowth of business's lack of attention to this issue. Other factors

contributing to the product liability crisis have been the sheer number of harmful-product cases, our increasingly litigious society, the growing size of financial awards given by the courts, and rising insurance rates. A major consequence of these phenomena has been cries for tort reform. Product tampering and product extortion have also become safety-related issues. In recent years, the health and safety issues related to foods, drugs, and medical devices have propelled the Consumer Product Safety Commission and the Food and Drug Administration into prominent roles.

Quality improvement initiatives like TQM and Six Sigma have not solved all the problems. However, they and other techniques have the potential for addressing the problems in a significant way if they are properly formulated and implemented. In addition to these specific responses, a consumer focus and orientation needs to permeate management decision making if the concerns of consumers are to be handled effectively. In today's business environment, consumers have many choices. Consequently, companies have no alternative but to internalize the consumer focus if they are to succeed.

▪ KEY TERMS

absolute liability (page 422)

Consumer Product Safety Commission (CPSC) (page 425)

contractual theory (page 417)

delayed manifestation cases (page 423)

due care theory (page 417)

Food and Drug Administration (FDA) (page 427)

market share liability (page 423)

product liability reform (page 423)

Six Sigma (page 431)

social costs view (page 417)

strict liability (page 422)

tort reform (page 423)

total quality management (TQM) (page 430)

▪ DISCUSSION QUESTIONS

1. Identify the dimensions of quality. Give an example of a product or service in which each of these characteristics is important.

2. What ethical theories can help us to better understand the issue of quality? Discuss.

3. Identify the principal reasons why we have a product liability crisis. Have any reasons been omitted? Discuss.

4. Differentiate the doctrine of strict liability from the doctrines of absolute liability and market share liability. What implications do these views have for the business community and for future products and services that might be offered?

5. Given the current business and consumer climate, what do you anticipate the future to be for the CPSC and the FDA? What role does politics play in your answer?

▪ RECOMMENDED CASES

Many of the end-of-text cases may be related to Chapter 13. You may wish to consider studying the following cases with Chapter 13.

Case 14. "TOXIC TACOS: THE CASE OF GENETICALLY MODIFIED FOODS." This case offers an opportunity to explore a situation where it is not clear whether the safety of the consumer is being compromised. There are strong opinions on each side of the issue. The even split in the European Union is an example of the divisiveness the issue can create. In this contentious environment, managers must decide what role, if any, genetically modified foods will have in their operations. Who is right—the advocates or the opponents of genetically modified foods? What are the implications of choosing one side or the other?

Case 24. "FIRESTONE AND FORD: THE TIRE TREAD SEPARATION TRAGEDY." In this case, Ford and Firestone must respond when deaths and injuries result from defective Firestone tires on Ford SUVs. The case describes the litigation that resulted and the reactions from both of the companies. Is one of the companies more at fault than the other? What responsibility for the situation does the NHTSA bear? Who are the stakeholders and how have they been impacted? What recommendations would you make to address what has happened and to minimize the likelihood of its happening again?

Case 25. "THE COFFEE SPILL HEARD 'ROUND THE WORLD." This case provides lesser-known details of the well-known story of a woman who sued McDonald's after a coffee spill left her with third-degree burns. Similar incidents that have occurred since that first instance are covered, too. The question arises as to how a company can balance consumer preferences and consumer safety when the two are in conflict. Was the jury decision appropriate? What would you recommend to McDonald's?

■ WEB RESOURCES

The URLs listed here are current at the time of publication. Should any of these Web sites change, please search under the company's or organization's name for an updated address.

American Society for Quality
http://www.asq.org

Association of Trial Lawyers
http://www.atlanet.org

Business Week magazine
http://www.businessweek.com

Common Good
http://www.cgood.org

Consumer Product Safety Commission
http://www.cpsc.gov

Food and Drug Administration
http://www.fda.gov

Fortune magazine
http://www.fortune.com

 InfoTrac® College Edition   http://www.infotrac-college.com

Articles from both Business Week *and* Fortune *can be researched, retrieved, and read from your desktop using InfoTrac's online database.*

■ ENDNOTES

1. Terril Yue Jones, "Ford Board Deposes CEO Nasser," *Los Angeles Times* (October 30, 2001), 3: 1.
2. Keith Naughton, "Ford's Perfect Storm," *Newsweek* (September 17, 2001), 48.
3. *Ibid.*
4. Gary Witzenburg, "Ford's Quality Battle," *Automotive Industries* (June 2003), 32–33.
5. Janice Castro, "Making It Better," *Time* (November 13, 1989), 78–80; See also "Quality: How to Make It Pay," *Business Week* (August 8, 1994), 54ff.
6. Walker Research, "Reputation and Social Performance Assessment Study" (Indianapolis: Walker Research, August 1994), 17.
7. Michael Harvey, Milorad M. Novicevic, Timothy Kiessling, "Hypercompetition and the Future of Global Management in the Twenty-First Century," *Thunderbird International Review* (September/October 2001), 599–616.
8. Rajaram Veliyath and Elizabeth Fitzgerald, "Firm Capabilities, Business Strategies, Customer Preferences, and Hypercompetitive Arenas," *Competitiveness Review* (Vol. 10, 2000), 56–82.
9. Jane Spencer and Reed Albergotti, "Customer Satisfaction Index Climbs," *The Wall Street Journal* (February 18, 2004), D2.
10. "Customers Turned Off by Poor Service Levels," *Marketing Week* (March 5, 1998), 11.
11. David A. Garvin, "Competing on the Eight Dimensions of Quality," *Harvard Business Review* (November–December 1987), 101–109.
12. Manuel G. Velasquez, *Business Ethics: Concepts and Cases* (Prentice Hall: Upper Saddle River, NJ, 2002), 335–344.
13. Yair Aharoni, *The No Risk Society* (Chatham, NJ: Chatham House Publishers, 1981), 62–63.
14. Velasquez, 348.
15. Douglas Herbert, "Food Frights Mount in Europe," CNN.com (March 13, 2001).
16. Scott Kilman, "Beef Firm Plans Mad Cow Tests in Challenge to U.S. Standards," *The Wall Street Journal* (February 27, 2004), B4.
17. *Ibid.*
18. E. Patrick McGuire, "Product Liability: Evolution and Reform" (New York: The Conference Board, 1989), 6.
19. "2000 Report of the Consumer Products Safety Commission to the United States Congress," http://www.cpsc.gov.
20. "Ford's $128.5 Million Headache," *Time* (February 10, 1978), 65.
21. Stuart Taylor and Evan Thomas, "Civil Wars," *Newsweek* (December 15, 2003), 42–53; Robert P. Hartwig, "Whatever Happened to Tort Reform?" *National Underwriter* (November 20, 2000), 31–33.
22. Earnest W. Deavenport, Jr., "Profound Opportunities: Profound Threats," *Vital Speeches of the Day* (May 1, 1997), 428–430.

23. Andrew Hacker, "The Asbestos Nightmare," *Fortune* (January 20, 1986), 121.

24. Francine Schwadel, "Robins and Plaintiffs Face Uncertain Future," *The Wall Street Journal* (August 23, 1985), 4.

25. David J. Morrow, "Implant Maker Reaches Accord on Damage Suits," *The New York Times* (July 9, 1998), A1.

26. Kristine Henry, "Chapter 11 Fails to Hurt Grace Much," *The Sun* (July 26, 2001), 2C.

27. Soma Biswas, "No Grace for Grace," *The Deal.com* (March 24, 2004), 1.

28. Fred W. Morgan and Karl A. Boedecker, "A Historical View of Strict Liability for Product-Related Injuries," *Journal of Macromarketing* (Spring 1996), 103–117.

29. Ann Christopher, "Avoiding a Hazardous Violation," *Warehousing Management* (August, 2001), 20.

30. Kerry Powell, "Liability Language: Know the Difference Between Strict and Absolute," *On-Site* (March 2004), 46.

31. Terry Morehead Dworkin and Mary Jane Sheffet, "Product Liability in the 1980s," *Journal of Public Policy and Marketing* (1985), 71.

32. "The Asbestos Blob, Cont.," *The Wall Street Journal* (April 6, 2004), A16.

33. "Business Line: India Supreme Court Ruling on Damage Liability of Common Carrier," *Businessline* (June 30, 2000), 1.

34. "Charities Appeal to Blair to Stop Use of GM Crops in Britain," *Third Sector* (March 10, 2004), 2.

35. Roger Leroy Miller, "Drawing Limits on Liability," *The Wall Street Journal* (April 4, 1984), 28.

36. Natalie Kosteini, "Top Court Reverses Crown Asbestos Ruling," *Philadelphia Business Journal* (February 23, 2004).

37. Dworkin and Sheffet, 69.

38. Clemens P. Work, "Product Safety: A New Hot Potato for Congress," *U.S. News & World Report* (June 14, 1982), 62.

39. Edward J. Schoen, Margaret M. Hogan, Joseph S. Falcheck, "An Examination of the Legal and Ethical Public Policy Consideration Underlying DES Market Share Liability," *Journal of Business Ethics* (Vol. 24, 2000), 141–163.

40. "Tampering with Buyers' Confidence," *U.S. News & World Report* (March 3, 1986), 46.

41. Damien Thomlinson, "Drug Extortion Highlights Risks," *Business Insurance* (June 26, 2000), 33–37.

42. Dean Foust, Brian Grow, and Sheridan Prasso, "Evolution of the Envelope," *Business Week* (November 5, 2000), 14.

43. Thomas Lee, "Food Service Is on Front Line of Terror War," *St. Louis Post-Dispatch* (September 23, 2002), 8.

44. Peter Waldman and Eileen White, "Battle Rages over Damages, Insurance Rates: States Are Debating Sweeping Changes in Tort Laws," *The Wall Street Journal* (April 15, 1986), 5; See also R. J. Samuelson, "Lawyer Heaven," *The Washington Post National Weekly Edition* (June 27–July 3, 1994), 28.

45. Michele Galen, "The Class Action Against Product Liability Laws," *Business Week* (July 29, 1997), 74.

46. Richard D. Haley, "Don't Let the Rogues off the Hook," *ENR* (May 4, 1998), 89; Robert Kuttner, "How Tort Reform Will Hurt Consumers," *San Diego Union Tribune* (June 24, 1994), B7. See also Jerry Phillips, "Attacks on the Legal System: Fallacy of Tort Reform Arguments," *Trial* (February, 1992), 106–110.

47. Taylor and Thomas, 47.

48. Ben White, "For a Senate Champion of Malpractice Limits, a Controversy Close to Home" *Washington Post* (December 25, 1999), A10;; Jack Torry, "Santorum's Wife Wins Lawsuit," *Pittsburgh Post-Gazette* (December 11, 1999). Christopher Snowbeck, "Santorum Doubts Filibuster on Malpractice Bill Will End," *Pittsburgh Post-Gazette* (July 9, 2003), A7.

49. Taylor and Thomas, 42–53. Philip K. Howard, *The Collapse of the Common Good: How America's Lawsuit Culture Undermines Our Freedom* (New York: Ballantine, 2002).

50. "The Defects in Product-Liability Laws," *Business Week* (July 29, 1991), 88.

51. Information about the Consumer Product Safety Commission is available at the CPSC Web site: http://www.cpsc.gov.

52. "2000 Annual Report to Congress," Consumer Product Safety Commission, http://www.cpsc.gov.

53. "Consumer Product Safety Commission," *Federal Regulatory Directory*, 6th ed. (Washington, DC: Congressional Quarterly, 1990), 46–47.

54. *Ibid.*, 48–54.

55. "U.S. Consumer Product Safety Commission Chairman, Ann Brown, Resigns," CPSC Press Release (November 1, 2001), http://www.cpsc.gov.

56. "Bush's Safety Chief Choice Is Rejected," *St. Louis Post Dispatch* (August 3, 2001), A2.

57. Caroline E. Mayer, "Bush Nominee Puts Safety First," *Washington Post* (April 26, 2002), E1.

58. Jayne O'Donnell, "New Safety Chief to Announce GE Fine," *USA Today* (August 8, 2002), 3B.

59. Caroline E. Mayer, "Safety Panel Drops Recall Order to Maker of BB Guns," *Washington Post* (November 15, 2003), E1.

60. "Food and Drug Administration," *Federal Regulatory Directory* (Washington, DC: Congressional Quarterly, 1990), 297.

61. *Ibid.*

62. Malcolm Gladwell, "A Fresh Approach at the FDA," *The Washington Post Weekly Edition* (May 13–19, 1991), 32.

63. "Woman in the News: Jean Ellen Henney: For FDA an Old Hand," *The New York Times* (June 24, 1998), A16.

64. Richard S. Dunham, "New Trials at the FDA," *Business Week* (June 1, 1998), 50.

65. James G. Dickinson, "Henney Fired, RU-486 Approved Torpedoed Retention," *Medical Marketing and Media* (March 2001), 32.

66. Sara Calabro, "Reshuffle Won't Disrupt FDA, Pitt Says," *PRWeek* (March 8, 2004), 4.

67. Kathleen Deoul and Bruce Silverglade, "Q: Is the Food and Drug Administration Overregulating the Dietary Supplement Industry," *Insight* (August 12, 2002), 40–43.

68. Sarah Ellison, "The Good, the Bad, and the High Glycemic," *The Wall Street Journal* (November 24, 2003), B1.

69. http://www.fda.gov

70. K. Ishikawa, *What Is Total Quality Control?* (Milwaukee, WI: Quality Press, 1985).

71. Lawrence A. Crosby, "Measuring Customer Satisfaction," in E. E. Scheuing and W. F. Christopher (eds.), *The Service Quality Handbook* (New York, AMACOM, 1993), 392.

72. A. Blanton Godfrey and E. G. Kammerer, "Service Quality Vs. Manufacturing Quality: Five Myths Exploded," *The Service Quality Handbook*, 5.

73. Ron Basu, "Six Sigma to Fit Sigma," *IIE Solutions* (July 2001), 28–33.

74. Michael Hammer and Jeff Godling, "Putting Six Sigma in Perspective," *Quality* (October 2001), 58–62.

75. The Six Sigma Academy Web site, http://www.6-sigma.com.

76. Hammer and Godling, 58.

77. Basu, 28–33.

78. *Ibid.*

Chapter 14

■ THE NATURAL ENVIRONMENT *as* STAKEHOLDER

CHAPTER LEARNING OUTCOMES

After studying this chapter, you should be able to:

1 Discuss why natural environment issues are complex.

2 Describe eight major natural environment issues.

3 Describe the NIMBY environmental problem.

4 Discuss the roles that business and government play in environmental issues.

5 Explain the concept of environmental ethics.

We shall never understand the natural environment until we see it as a living organism. Land can be healthy or sick, fertile or barren, rich or poor, lovingly nurtured or bled white. Our present attitudes and laws governing the ownership and use of land represent an abuse of the concept of private property. . . . Today you can murder land for private profit. You can leave the corpse for all to see and nobody calls the cops.

Paul Brooks, *The Pursuit of Wilderness* (1971)

A BRIEF INTRODUCTION TO THE NATURAL ENVIRONMENT

Similar to other broad terms, **environment** means many things to many people—trees in the backyard, a family's favorite vacation spot, a mare and her colt in a pasture, a trout stream in the mountains, earth and the other planets and space objects in our solar system.

This chapter was coauthored by Mark Starik of George Washington University and Ann K. Buchholtz of the University of Georgia.

This chapter focuses on the natural environment—specifically, what it is, why it is important, how it has become a major concern, and what businesses and other organizations have done both to and for it. This chapter identifies what we mean when we use the term *environment* and why it has become one of the most significant societal issues of our time. We will also describe the variety of responses human organizations, including businesses, have developed to address this issue. Throughout the chapter, we will emphasize two themes: that humans are a part of their natural environment and that the environment itself, as well as the issues and human responses related to it, are extremely complex, defying simple analyses.

To assist you in making business environmental decisions in the future, we will present facts and figures, some of which will be technical and scientific, related to environmental issues and responses. These facts and figures are included to help you understand the complexities involved in the business and public environmental issues of today. Because of the influence of business, government, and environmental interest groups and individuals, these and many other technical terms and concepts are discussed in the media and, increasingly, in business and society texts. Environmental literacy, whether for wise business, government, or individual decision making, requires, at minimum, some rudimentary knowledge. Without at least some basic technical information, would-be stakeholder managers abdicate their responsibility to make prudent choices potentially crucial to the survival of their organizations, as well as to the survival of humans and other species in the natural environment. We call your attention to Figure 14-1, which presents definitions of a few of the most important environmental terms that might be helpful to you now and in the future.

THE IMPACT OF BUSINESS UPON THE NATURAL ENVIRONMENT

SEARCH THE WEB

ENVIROLINK

To interact effectively with environmental stakeholders, managers must educate themselves about environmental movement issues. Hundreds of organizations and Web sites deal with the natural environment. One particularly valuable Web site is EnviroLink Network, a grassroots environmental community located at **http://www.envirolink.org**. EnviroLink is a nonprofit organization that unites hundreds of organizations and volunteers around the world with millions of people in more than 150 countries. EnviroLink states that it "is dedicated to providing you with the most comprehensive, up-to-date environmental resources available." To learn more about EnviroLink's purposes, news, library, services, and awards, and such topics as sustainable business, animal rights, the green marketplace, and green living, visit this interesting and comprehensive Web site.

Unfortunately, businesses have played a major role in contributing to natural environment pollution and depletion. Virtually every sector of business in every country is responsible for consuming significant amounts of materials and energy and causing waste accumulation and resource degradation. For instance, forestry firms and companies that process raw materials, such as uranium, coal, and oil, have caused major air, water, and land pollution problems in their extraction, transportation, and processing stages. Manufacturing firms, such as those in steel, petrochemicals, and paper products, have long been identified as major sources of air and water pollution. However, most major industry sectors contribute significant levels of pollution.

Although manufacturing and operations processes are the most visible contributors to air, water, and land pollution, virtually every other department within a business potentially plays some role in affecting the natural environment. Research labs and engineering departments, for instance, could be producing their own nonnegligible amounts of environmental contaminants and often forwarding to their manufacturing departments products they have designed that are toxic and nonrecyclable. Finance departments, using inadequate accounting department

---

FIGURE 14-1

Glossary of Important and Helpful Environmental Terms

Environment	Broadly, anything that is external or internal to an entity. For humans, the environment can include external living, working, and playing spaces and natural resources, as well as internal physical, mental, and emotional states.
Carrying Capacity	The volume of and intensity of use by organisms that can be sustained in a particular place and at a particular time without degrading the environment's future suitability for that use. A resource's carrying capacity has limits that need to be respected for continued use.
Entropy	A measure of disorder of energy, indicating its unavailability for recycling for the same use. Energy tends to break down into lower quality with each use. For instance, a kilowatt of electricity, once it is produced and consumed, can never be used as electricity again and, if stored, will allow far less than 1 kilowatt to be consumed.
Ecosystem	All living and nonliving substances present in a particular place, often interacting with others.
Niche	The role an organism plays in its natural community, including what it eats and the conditions it requires for survival. Habitats and niches are interrelated concepts.
Cycle	The continuous looplike movement of water, air, and various nutrients, such as nitrogen, phosphorous, and sulfur, through the environment. Such cycles can be impaired in performing their evolutionary roles, such as purification and sustenance, by excessive human-caused pollution and depletion.
Threshold	The point at which a particular phenomenon, previously suppressed, suddenly begins to be activated. For instance, when a population's carrying capacity threshold is exceeded, the population tends to decrease or even crash as a result of increased morbidity and mortality.
Pollution	The existence of material or energy that has gone through a transformation process and is perceived as unwanted or devalued in a particular place at a particular time.
Irreversibility	The inability of humans and nature to restore environmental conditions to a previous state within relevant time frames. Human environment-related actions that appear irreversible are the destruction of a rainforest or wilderness area and the extinction of a species.
Sustainability	The characteristic of an entity, such as an economic or environmental system, that is related to its ability to exist and flourish over an acceptably long period of time.

data, could be recommending decisions based on short-term criteria that have not incorporated the full costs to the environment of potentially damaging projects. Human resources departments could be neglecting to incorporate environmental concerns in their personnel recruitment, selection, and development decisions, potentially advancing individuals within the organization who do not share the organization's environmental values. Finally, marketing departments could be advertising and selling environmentally dubious products and services, with or without their customers' knowledge of this fact.

Of course, every coin has two sides. The power and productivity of business, which have been the source of so much environmental damage, can also be used to support the environment and mitigate the harm that was previously caused. Later in this chapter, we will introduce you to businesses that are good stewards of the environment. First, however, we will go into more detail about the range of issues facing the natural environment.

NATURAL ENVIRONMENT ISSUES

The latest wave of environmentalism has paralleled a growing public perception that global environmental problems are severe and worsening with time. The following are eight key global natural environment problems:

- Ozone depletion
- Global warming
- Solid and hazardous wastes
- Fresh water quantity and quality
- Degradation of marine environments
- Deforestation
- Land degradation
- Endangerment of biological diversity

We will discuss each of these environmental problems briefly to give the reader a sense of the complexity and urgency with which these issues are increasingly viewed.

Ozone Depletion

Ozone is an oxygen-related gas that is harmful to life near the earth's surface but is vital in the stratosphere in blocking dangerous ultraviolet radiation from the sun. In 1985, NASA scientists observed a huge decrease in ozone over Antarctica. They then discovered a "hole" in the ozone layer that had grown as large as the North American continent. Their measurements showed that the flow of ultraviolet light had increased directly under the ozone hole. This phenomenon was attributed to human-produced chemicals—chlorofluorocarbons (CFCs), used in refrigeration, and halons, used in fire extinguisher systems, as well as other ozone-depleting chemicals. In 1987, the international community enacted strict controls on the use of these gasses through the United Nations Montreal Protocol. Scientists reported that the joint effort may be succeeding—and that the ozone hole may repair itself over the next 50 years. Charles Kolb, an atmospheric research specialist and president of Aerodyne, noted, "We're all feeling very proud of the fact that we identified the problem and then the international community responded."[1] However a rift in the international community has now formed. In 2004, the Bush administration requested that an exemption be given for methyl bromide because they were concerned that U.S. strawberry farmers would not be able to compete effectively with Mexican farmers if they were unable to use that chemical.[2] Ironically, U.S. backpedaling on the global warming issue has been credited with facilitating the European Union's success in lowering emissions ahead of schedule because the U.S. change in policy increased the availability to the EU of chemicals that substitute for ozone depleting substances.[3]

Global Warming

According to a number of reputable sources, the earth's atmosphere is in danger of heating up. According to *Fortune*, the possibility of a swift and radical change in climate is so sufficiently real that the Pentagon's strategic planners are actively developing responses to various scenarios.[4] The **greenhouse effect**—that is, the prevention of solar heat absorbed by our atmosphere from returning to space—is expected to precipitate a rate of warming that is unprecedented in the last 10,000 years.[5] The burning of fossil fuels bears the primary responsibility (75 percent) for this phenomenon, with changes in land use, such as deforestation, accounting for the rest. In 2001, United Nations scientists predicted that temperatures would rise from 1.4 degrees C to 5.8 degrees C.[6] These recent temperature increases are about half of the entire warming of the earth that has occurred in the last 10,000 years. Scientists have determined that climate change has led to changes in about 100 physical and 450 biological processes. Higher temperatures are melting the permafrost in the Russian

The Bush administration rejected the Kyoto Protocol that aimed to try to control global warming, but the European Union is taking seriously its responsibility to control carbon dioxide. The bottom line for European industries? "Pollution now has a price." The issue of carbon pollution is "no longer just for 'green nerds,'" Karen Lowry Miller quotes a London energy broker as saying, in her article in *Newsweek International* (7 June 2004 p41). Read more about how European nations intend to control "carbon" by logging on to InfoTrac College Edition at http://www.infotrac-college.com and keying record number A117536871.

Arctic, causing the foundations of 5-story apartment buildings to slump. Floods, storms, and heat waves are becoming more extreme throughout the world. The schedule of environmental changes has also been disrupted. Rivers freeze later in the winter and melt earlier in the spring. Trees flower earlier, insects emerge faster, and bird lay eggs sooner. Glaciers are melting, causing the global mean sea level to rise. The rate of climate change expected over the next 100 years is unprecedented in human history.[7] Both the severity and the effects of these shifts are unknown, as is the adaptability of ecosystems and living species, including humans, to these effects. We do not yet know if we have crossed a threshold beyond which many of these projected effects will begin to be more substantially, perhaps threateningly, realized. Figure 14-2 shows the increase in greenhouse gas emissions from the United States from 1996 to 2002. Sinks are the opposite of emissions in that they absorb carbon dioxide, and so the emissions figure accounts for the ameliorating effect of sinks.

Solid and Hazardous Wastes

The residents, businesses, and institutions of the United States produced more than 229 million tons of municipal solid waste in 2001. This is approximately 4.4 pounds of waste from each person each day and represents an increase of more than 60 percent over the 2.7 pounds per person per day that was produced in 1960. Figure 14-3 on page 444 shows the trend in municipal waste generation from 1960 to 2001. Although the amount of municipal waste generated in the United States is remarkable, it would be even worse had 68 million tons of material not been diverted away from landfills and incinerators through recycling in 2001.[8] Figure 14-4 on page 444 shows the more than twelve-fold increase in recycling that occurred from 1960 to 2001.

FIGURE 14-2

U.S. Greenhouse Gas Emissions and Sinks

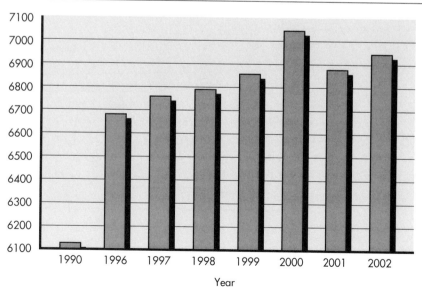

SOURCE: United States Environmental Protection Agency (2004).

FIGURE 14-3

Trends in Municipal Solid Waste Generation 1960–2001

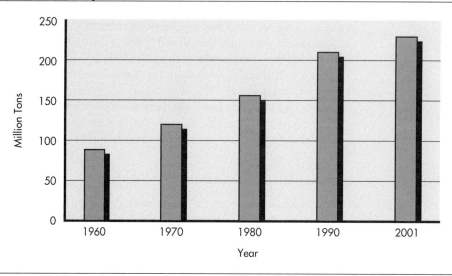

SOURCE: United States Environmental Protection Agency (2004).

FIGURE 14-4

Increase in Recycling Rate 1960–2001

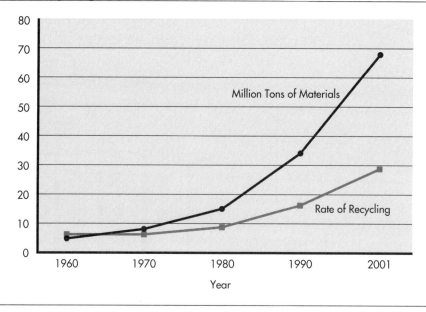

SOURCE: United States Environmental Protection Agency (2004).

About 90 percent of the global wastes considered hazardous—that is, those requiring special handling to protect humans and the environment—is produced in industrialized countries.[9] Exposure to these wastes in the environment, whether in air, water, food or soil, has been shown to cause cancer, birth defects, and a host of other problems.[10] As a result of tightening site controls in some areas, hazardous wastes are sometimes being transported away from their sources, both legally and illegally, often to sites with weaker controls.[11] Another concern is the toxicological effects of a number of new chemicals coming onto the market. Because they are new, we know less about their effects and the measures needed to protect human health and the environment from them.[12]

Fresh Water Quality and Quantity

Municipal sewage, industrial wastes, urban runoff, agricultural runoff, atmospheric fallout, and overharvesting all contribute to the degradation of the world's oceans and waterways. So too do dam sedimentation, deforestation, overgrazing, and overirrigation. Although water pollution is a global issue, consider just the effects of businesses and cities in the United States. Over one-third of our rivers, lakes, and estuaries are not safe for swimming and fishing, and not able to provide a healthy habitat for fish and other water-dependent wildlife. Over 40 percent of the nation's waterways are considered so polluted as to be in violation of the Clean Water Act, and yet millions of pounds of dangerous pollution and toxic chemicals are legally dumped into U.S. rivers, lakes, and coastal waters each year.[13] The Public Interest Research Group attributes the violations to lax government enforcement, resulting from budget cuts and a drop in employees dedicated to enforcement.[14]

Because global fresh water is unequally distributed, supplies are already overtaxed in shortage areas, reducing the quality of fresh water available for necessary human purposes. The associated results have been drought, desertification, and water-borne diseases in the developing world, as well as river, lake, bay, and accessible groundwater contamination on a large scale in developed countries. These water-shortage areas include rapidly shrinking water tables in China, the loss of two-thirds of the Aral Sea in the former Soviet Union, and the overappropriation of about half the rivers in the American West.[15] By the year 2025, two-thirds of the world's population may be living in countries under water stress conditions.[16]

Degradation of Marine Environments

Many of the same factors that affect fresh water have an impact on the marine environments. Each year, trillions of gallons of sewage and industrial waste are dumped into marine waters. These and other pollutants, such as oil and plastics, have been associated with significant damage to a number of coastal ecosystems, including salt marshes, mangrove swamps, estuaries, and coral reefs. The result has been local and regional shellfish bed closures, declining fish populations, seafood-related illnesses, and reduced shoreline protection from floods and storms.[17] Toxic and nutrient runoffs are resulting in algae blooms; trawling is destroying the sea floor; and climate change is warming the waters, causing coral reefs to die. Add to this the fact that fleets are currently 40 percent larger than the ocean can sustain, and it is no surprise that about one-third of the major commercial fish are in decline.[18]

The twentieth century saw a great deal of migration to the western regions of the United States; though arid, the West had rainfall enough to support population growth. But the drought that began in the West in 1999 shows no signs of abating. As reported by Faye Flam [*Knight Ridder/ Tribune News Service* (15 March 2004 pK1024)], scientists now speculate that the twentieth century was unusually wet and that the drought now underway is actually more typical of the region. What does water temperature in the North Atlantic have to do with the drought? Find out by logging on to InfoTrac College Edition at http://www. infotrac-college.com and keying record number CJ114264694.

Deforestation

Although humans depend on forests for building materials, fuel, medicines, chemicals, food, employment, and recreation, the world's forests can be quickly depleted by a variety of human factors. **Deforestation** adds to soil erosion problems and is a major cause of the greenhouse effect. Felled trees are no longer able to absorb carbon dioxide and are sometimes burned for land clearing and charcoal, thereby releasing rather than absorbing carbon dioxide. Moisture and nutrient ecosystem cycles can also be severely damaged in deforesting activities, negatively affecting adjacent land and water ecosystems. Deforestation is a problem for developed and developing countries alike. A conservation group, American Forests, studied the financial impact of deforestation in the greater Baltimore-Washington, DC, area and assessed the economic impact of its consequences.[19] Trees slow the movement of storm water and reduce the risk of flooding. The study showed that deforestation in Baltimore-Washington resulted in a 19 percent decrease in storm water flow. Replacing the storm water flow capabilities of these trees with engineered systems such as reservoirs would cost over a billion dollars. The dwindling tree canopy also made it more difficult to remove approximately 9.3 million pounds of pollutants from the air. The cost of air quality control to make up for this loss would be about $24 million over 24 years.[20] Tropical deforestation is also the main reason that 25 percent of the world's primates could disappear by 2030.[21] Fortunately, there is some good news on this front. The Food and Agriculture Organization (FAO) of the United Nations reported that there are strong indications of a slowdown in the rate of deforestation. From 1980 to 1990, deforestation took place at an estimated loss of 15.5 million hectares per year. A recent report, however, indicated a reason for hope. In the last decade, there has been a 10 percent slowdown in the rate of tropical deforestation.[22]

Land Degradation

Another disturbing environmental issue that human populations face is land degradation. According to the United Nations' Environment Programme, degradation includes such different multiple facets as desertification, deforestation, overgrazing, salinization, and alkalization. Soil acidification, urban sprawl, and soil sealing, or industrial soil contamination, are part of land degradation as well.[23] According to the U.N. Millennium Declaration, "nearly 2 billion hectares of land, an area about the combined size of Canada and the United States, is affected by human-induced degradation of soils, putting the livelihoods of nearly one billion people at risk. Each year an additional 20 million hectares of agricultural land either becomes too degraded for crop production, or becomes lost to urban sprawl."[24] Although many of these land degradation problems are regionalized in Third World countries, developed nations, too, have experienced land productivity difficulties. The global problem of land degradation affects about 60 percent of Africa and Asia, 11 percent of Europe, and 8 percent of North America.[25] As the population of the world continues to grow, the problems created by the loss of productive soil will only increase.

Endangerment of Biological Diversity

Throughout most of time, species lived an average of one million years, with species dying out at the rate of about one specie per million years. The current rate of species extinction is about 100 to 1,000 times greater than that.[26] Furthermore, not only is the extinction rate soaring, but the birthrate of new species is also declining.[27] In addition to the depletion of large mammal species, such as the elephants and black rhinos of Africa, and birds such as the California condor and mosquito-catcher, there are some 20,000 endangered species of animals around the world, many of which are in trouble because of overhunting and poaching. Ecosystem and habitat destruction through agricultural and urban development activities and, of course, pollution have put at risk not only wildlife, but many species of very beneficial plants as well. Up to half of all human medicines are derived from plants, and yet, in especially productive areas such as the world's rain forests, excesses in individual and organizational activities are responsible for significant and tragic ecosystem and species degradation.

Other Environmental Issues

In addition to these eight major environmental issues, other concerns have arisen around the world that appear to threaten human health and other aspects of the natural environment. **Air pollution**, both outdoors and indoors, often rates high in concern according to public opinion polls. An estimated 50 million children in developing countries suffer from chronic coughing because of smog.[28]

In addition to causing human health problems, ambient air pollution is also responsible for a condition called **acid rain**, which has caused a variety of significant negative impacts on the natural environments of several countries. Acid rain is precipitation containing harmful amounts of nitric and sulfuric acids formed when fossil fuels are burned. It can be wet (e.g., rain, fog) or dry (e.g., dust) precipitation. The damage from this fossil fuel-caused problem has been blamed for sterilizing up to 80 percent of the lakes and streams in Norway, damaging 64 percent of British forests, and destroying more than 40 percent of the coniferous forests in central Switzerland.[29] Acid rain has caused significant deterioration of both the natural environment and human structures in other areas of the world, including Pennsylvania; Nova Scotia; Agra, India; Tokyo; Central Africa; and Sao Paulo, Brazil.[30] The acid rain problem appears to be moving. Sulfur emissions, a major cause of acid rain, are down 40 percent in the United States but are expected to triple in Asia by 2010.[31]

Indoor air pollution is another environmental problem that is becoming an increasing concern, primarily in industrialized countries. Asbestos was used as an insulator in schools and other buildings in the United States for many years but has been identified as causing asbestosis, an incurable lung disease afflicting those who inhale asbestos fibers. Other serious indoor air pollutants include radon, tobacco smoke, formaldehyde, pesticide residues, and perchloroethylene (associated with dry cleaning). Certain construction materials and other household products, such as some paints, carpeting, and gas furnaces, are primarily responsible for these contaminants, which are associated with a variety of human health problems from nausea to cancer.[32]

A third environmental problem is **energy inefficiency**, or the wasting of precious nonrenewable sources of energy. Nonrenewable energy sources, such as coal, oil, and natural gas, were formed millions of years ago under unique conditions of temperature, pressure, and biological phenomena (hence the term *fossil fuels*). Once these are depleted, they will apparently be gone forever. In addition, because these fuels are not equally distributed around the world, they are the cause of significant power imbalances worldwide, with associated armed conflicts that are typically disastrous for both humans and the natural environment in general.[33]

Part of the answer to the nonrenewability problem is to use as little as possible of these energy sources through implementation of sound energy conservation practices. In addition, shifting to renewable energy sources, such as solar, wind, hydroelectric, and biomass forms of energy, is an increasingly attractive option for both industrial and agricultural societies. Several technologies for tapping these renewable, low-polluting energy sources are becoming economically competitive with nonrenewable sources.[34, 35] However, even though proponents argue that solar and wind power are ready for mass utilization, half of the electricity in the United States comes from nonrenewable and highly polluting coal.[36] Another environmental problem, which is interconnected with those mentioned earlier, deserves special attention because of its potential for harm: the production of **toxic substances**, whether as constituents of intended end-products or as unwanted by-products. Toxic substances, defined by the EPA as chemicals or mixtures that may present unreasonable risks of injury to health or to the environment,[37] can include pesticides, herbicides, solvents, fuels, radioactive substances, and many other potential candidates. Whether or not they are considered waste materials, toxic substances can have significant negative impacts on humans and on the natural environment in general. The problem with materials such as benzyl chloride, hydrogen cyanide, and methyl isocyanate is that very small amounts are incompatible with living tissue, destroy cell functions, and eventually cause total system shutdown.[38]

Although extreme care may be exercised if society decides it needs to manufacture such substances, which is a questionable prospect, two problems remain. First, we are not always aware of the effects, especially the long-term and interactive effects, of exposure to the thousands of chemicals that are produced each year. The EPA, for instance, has no long-term health effects information on most of the 70,000 chemicals it has listed. Of greatest concern are 10,000 to 14,000 high-volume chemicals for which little to no data exists.[39] Even in those instances where the toxicity of a chemical is known and the chemical is banned for sale in a country, such as the pesticide DDT in the United States, the substance can still be manufactured in that country and exported, only to return when products that have been exposed to these substances are imported.

Second, toxic substances can be associated with industrial accidents, causing unforeseen widespread biological damage. The 1984 Bhopal, India, chemical plant leak; the 1986 Chernobyl nuclear power plant meltdown in the former Soviet Union; and the 1989 Exxon *Valdez* 11-million-gallon oil spill in Alaska are three well-known environmental disasters involving toxic substances. Not so well-known are the 14,000 oil spills that are reported each year.[40] Although the Exxon *Valdez* spill covered 1,300 miles of Alaskan shoreline and was as wide as three football fields, that spill was only 53rd in the rankings of worldwide oil spills.[41] Even still, its impact continues. A 2003 study reported that the *Valdez* spill continues to wreak havoc on the marine life in Prince William Sound 14 years following the spill.[42]

Three types of pollution that recently have received less attention than they once did are *radon, noise pollution*, and *aesthetic pollution*. Radon is a radioactive gas that has been found in an increasing number of residential structures resulting from the natural radioactive decay of certain substances either found in the soil or used in construction materials. After tobacco smoking, radon has been identified as the leading cause of lung cancer in the United States.[43] Noise pollution can exist anywhere unwanted sounds are heard, but it most often results from operation of heavy machinery within limited areas. Factories, construction sites, and airports are frequently identified as noise pollution areas. Severe noise pollution can cause hearing impairment in humans and habitat disruption for other species. Aesthetic pollution occurs when visual tastes are violated and typically center around construction, signage, and land appearance. Commercial building facades, outdoor billboards, and litter were significant local issues in the past. We mention these pollution sources to illustrate that environmental issues change with time and can vary from place to place, arguing for a flexible approach to environmental management.

RESPONSIBILITY FOR ENVIRONMENTAL ISSUES

Problems such as smog, toxic waste, and acid rain can be described as "wicked problems"—that is, problems with characteristics such as interconnectedness, complexity, uncertainty, ambiguity, conflict, and societal constraints.[44] Affixing responsibility for such messy situations is problematic, because solutions to wicked problems are seldom complete and final and, therefore, credit for these solutions is seldom given or taken. *Chlorofluorocarbons*, or *CFCs*, for example, were once thought to be safe alternatives to other, more toxic refrigerants, which is why these ozone destroyers are so ubiquitous in our society's technologies.

The NIMBY Problem

One example of this question of responsibility is the **NIMBY**, or "Not In My Back Yard," phenomenon. This acronym, which can be found on bumper stickers and conference agendas and in newspaper articles, college courses, and many other communication vehicles, is the human denial of responsibility for the misuse of the environment. One example of NIMBY is the community that uses ever-increasing amounts of electricity but decides it does not want a power plant that produces electricity to locate nearby. Another is a company that generates increasing amounts of waste but is unwilling to pay the full cost of proper disposal. Essentially, NIMBY is an attitude/behavior set based on avoidance or denial of responsibility. When applied to the field of environmental management, NIMBY spells big trouble.

The obvious difficulty with the NIMBY syndrome is that the entities (human individuals, organizations, or both) causing environmental pollution or degradation are not identified as the sources of the problem, and therefore no action is taken to reduce the problem. The NIMBY phenomenon avoids or denies the root cause of the damage and addresses only the symptoms with an attitude of nonresponsibility characterized by an approach of "I'll create an environmental problem, but I want to have as little as possible to do with solving it." One popular cartoon characterizing the NIMBY problem pictures a stream of polluting, honking cars passing along a highway in front of a huge billboard that reads "Honk if you love the environment!"

Environmental Ethics

Nature itself is a polluter and destroyer. The earth's core is continually polluting many bodies of water and airsheds with a full range of toxic heavy metals. The Mount St. Helens volcano eruption unleashed significant levels of air pollution on the state of Washington. Species have been going extinct since life evolved as, in a continuous cycle of life and death, nature acts as its own destroyer. Given this fact, what does absolute human environmental sensitivity mean? Humans must consume at least some plants and water to survive. If humans and their organizations need to pollute and destroy at least some of nature for their survival, what is the relative level of degradation that is ethical? Do nonhuman species have any "rights," and, if so, what are they, and how can they be

Ethics in Practice

GOING DOWN THE DRAIN

I worked at a small business that used cars in their daily deliveries. To save money, the brothers who owned the business would conduct most of their own maintenance on the vehicles. As a result, they would periodically be involved in doing tune-ups, changing oil, and other such activities. One day I noticed that the brothers would pour the old motor oil down the drain rather than take it for recycling. This troubled me because I knew how greatly old oil can add to the degradation of the environment. I brought up the subject with them and they laughed it off. They told me that, as a small business, they did not have the time or the money to be concerned with the "niceties" of life. We discussed it several times, and they made it clear they would not change their ways.

I didn't know what to do. I liked this job. The location was perfect and the people were nice (in every other way). I wanted to keep working there until I finished school. However, I felt that I shared in the responsibility for the damage caused by the oil if I knew it was happening and did nothing about it. If I reported it to someone, I knew they'd know the report came from me. What could I do?

1. Is NIMBY involved here? If so, in what way?

2. Do you share in the responsibility for negative action when you know it is happening and say nothing?

3. What would you do if you were in that position?

Contributed Anonymously

reconciled with human rights? Concerning human rights and the environment, how do we assess the claims of indigenous cultures to the use of their respective environments? Is there any connection between the domination of humans by humans (for example, the domination of one nation, race, or gender by another) and the domination of nature by humans? This latter question is especially central to several schools of environmental ethical thought, including social ecology, ecofeminism, and environmental justice.

Whose standards will determine what is or is not ethical? Public opinion seems to be on the side of the environment. In a 2003 Gallup poll, 61 percent of respondents said they were active in or sympathetic to environmental causes. However, how much the public will do itself or insist that governments and businesses do to protect the environment is still an unanswered question. How clean do the air and water need to be, and how much is the public willing to pay to meet these standards? As in our earlier discussion of business ethics, values play a major role and can be highly variable in breadth and depth across perspectives, situations, and time.

What are some environmental values (or **green values**)? According to one source associated with the "green" movement, many environmentalists hold four beliefs as fundamental values: (1) life on earth should continue; (2) human life on earth should continue; (3) natural justice should be done; and (4) nonmaterial qualities of life are worth pursuing.[45] "Overall the Green goal is to allow everyone the opportunity to live a fulfilling life, caring and sharing with each other, future generations and other species, while living sustainably within the capacities of a limited world."[46]

Following the ethical models discussed in Chapters 6 and 7, other environmental issues can be added to develop a better idea of what environmental ethics is and how it can be practiced. Kohlberg's model of moral development, for instance, can be used to identify environment-related attitudes and behaviors by developmental level. At the preconventional (infant) level in environmental ethics, humans and human organizations can be perceived as being concerned only with self or with their own species and habitats. A conventional (adolescent) level might entail some appreciation of nature, but only when and where such appreciation is commonplace or "in." A postconventional (adult) environmental ethic might include more mature attitudes and behaviors that are more universal (including all species and habitats), of greater duration (including unborn generations), and more consistent (if we humans have a right to survive as a species, why don't all species have that right?). Similarly, the moral principle of utilitarianism—the greatest good for the greatest number—could be expanded in environmental ethics to the greatest good for the greatest numbers of species and ecosystems. The Golden Rule could read, "Do unto other species as you would have them do unto you." Finally, the "Best Self" ethical test could include the question, "Is this action or decision related to the natural environment compatible not only with my concept of myself at my best but also with my concept of myself as a human representing my species at its best?"

Values matter, but they may not provide enough constraints on human action. Without controls in place to limit the ways in which individuals and corporations exploit natural resources, a phenomenon called the **tragedy of the commons** is likely to occur.[47] A "commons" is a plot of land available to all. When the commons is large enough to accommodate the needs of everyone, no problems occur. However, as herders continue to add animals to their herds, the carrying capacity of the commons becomes strained. It is in the self-interest of each herder to allow the animals to graze, even though the cumulative grazing will inevitably destroy the commons. The analogy of a "commons" can be applied to the environment as a whole as well as its many constituent parts. One need only look at the situation with public parks to see how unconstrained use can damage a shared resource. As Garrett Hardin points out in his classic article on the tragedy of the commons in the environment, constraints must also be placed on the use of the commons (i.e., our environment) because in the absence of constraints, self-interest is likely to lead individuals and organizations to behave in ways that will not sustain our shared resources.[48]

Environmental ethics is an important and intriguing subtopic of business ethics and is gaining attention in both academics and business. However, the prudent business environmentalist is advised to guard against becoming self-righteous in terms of either personal or organizational environmental ethics. The concept of "ecological correctness" is a very slippery issue (because both nature and humans and their technology are so varied around the planet and are constantly changing). It can even be an obstacle to those who might wish to become more environmentally sensitive but are put off by a "more-ecological-than-thou" attitude.

To return to the question of who sets environmental norms, the answer may be similar to the question of who sets society's norms—We all do, in part. This analysis implies that, as in ethical questions in general, the best approach to environmental ethics may be to practice tolerance, to see the world through others' perspectives, and to continue to question one's own environmental values as well as those of others.

THE ROLE OF GOVERNMENTS IN ENVIRONMENTAL ISSUES

As we mentioned earlier, governments have played major roles in environmental issues since the inception of such issues. Governments have procured, distributed, and developed habitable lands and other resources; protected, taxed, and zoned natural environment-based areas; and, more recently, exercised regulatory control over how those environments could be used. In this section, we'll look at how governments in the United States have dealt with environmental challenges and then identify what has been done in several other countries and at the international level.

Responses of Governments in the United States

Although the U.S. federal government has influenced environmental policy since at least 1899, with its permit requirement for discharge of hazardous materials into navigable waters, the major entrance of the U.S. government into environmental issues occurred in 1970 with the signing of PL 91-190, the *National Environmental Policy Act (NEPA)*. The second section of this act spells out its purposes: "To declare a national policy which will encourage productive and enjoyable harmony between man and his environment; to promote efforts which will prevent or eliminate damage to the environment and biosphere and stimulate the health and welfare of man; and to enrich the understanding of the ecological systems and natural resources important to the Nation."[49]

In addition to establishing these broad policy goals, this legislation requires federal agencies to prepare **environmental impact statements (EISs)** for any "proposals for legislation and other major federal action significantly affecting the quality of the human environment." Environmental impact statements are reports of studies explaining and estimating the environmental impacts of questionable practices and irreversible uses of resources and proposing detailed, reasonable alternatives to these practices and uses.

Business is affected by the NEPA in several ways. First, the federal government pays private consultants to conduct tens of billions of dollars worth of EISs each year. Second, because the federal government is the largest landholder in the United States, private businesses wishing to secure licenses and permits to conduct timber, grazing, mining, and highway, dam, and nuclear construction operations likely will be parties to the preparation of EISs. Third, private businesses working under federal government contracts are typically obliged to participate in EIS preparation. Fourth, the NEPA has been used as a model by many state governments, and therefore businesses heavily involved in significant state and local government contracts are likely to be involved in the EIS process.

Also in 1970, the U.S. **Environmental Protection Agency (EPA)** was created as an independent agency to research pollution problems, aid state and local government environmental efforts, and administer many of the federal environmental laws. These laws can be categorized into three areas—air, water, and land—even though a specific problem of pollution and/or degradation, such as acid rain, often involves two or more of these categories.

Air Quality Legislation.   The key piece of federal air quality legislation, called the **Clean Air Act**, was significantly amended in 1990. The overall approach of this act is similar to that used in other areas of federal regulation, such as safety and health legislation, in that standards are set and timetables for implementation are established. In the Clean Air Act, there are two kinds of standards: primary standards, which are designed to protect human health, and secondary standards, which are intended to protect property, vegetation, climate, and aesthetic values. The EPA has set primary standards (based on health effects) and secondary standards (based on environmental effects) for a variety of air pol-

SEARCH THE WEB

THE EPA

Laws and regulations are major tools for protecting the environment. The U.S. Environmental Protection Agency (EPA) is the primary regulatory body in the United States with responsibility for administering the country's major environmental laws. The mission of the EPA is to protect human health and to safeguard the natural environment—air, water, and land—upon which life depends. For a review of the latest information on regulations and proposed rules, codified regulations, laws, and current legislation, visit the EPA's Web site at **http://www.epa.gov**.

lutants, including lead, particulates, hydrocarbons, sulfur dioxide, and nitrogen oxide. Businesses that directly produce these substances, such as electric utilities, and those whose products when used cause these substances to be produced, such as automobiles, must reduce their emissions to these standard levels within a certain time frame.[50, 51]

State governments are responsible for filing plans with the EPA on how these standards will be met. Depending on the business and the pollution emitted, firms invest in various state-of-the-art control technologies to meet these standards. For instance, the 1990 Clean Air Act required coal-burning electric power plants to cut their acid rain-related sulfur dioxide emissions roughly in half by the year 2000, and so many utilities installed new scrubbers and electrostatic precipitators or began using lower-sulfur coal.

One controversial concept in the Clean Air Act is the **emissions trading** (i.e., "bubble") concept. This approach is intended to reduce a particular pollutant over an entire industrial region by treating all emission sources as if they were under one bubble. Thus, a business can increase its emissions of sulfur dioxide in one part of a plant or region if it reduces its sulfur dioxide pollution by as much or more in another part of the plant or region. In addition, and as an extension of this bubble concept, businesses that reduce their emissions can trade these rights to other businesses that want to increase their emissions. Proponents of the bubble concept and emissions credit trading hail these policies as "free market environmentalism," whereas opponents ridicule them as "licenses to pollute." Some firms (especially utilities) have taken advantage of the concepts, while other firms (such as 3M) have refused to use their credits to pollute further, in effect "retiring" their credits so that no other firm can use their credits to produce more pollution. In 1993, the EPA began holding auctions of emissions allowances.

In a controversial move, the Bush administration has proposed a "Clear Skies Initiative" as a replacement for the Clean Air Act. The proposed law, which is bogged down in Congress at this writing, would include an emission trading system and tougher standards for nitrogen oxide, sulfur dioxide, and mercury. However, environmentalists consider the Clear Skies proposal to be more lenient than the Clean Air Act it is designed to replace. Democrats are pushing the EPA to regulate carbon dioxide, a move the Bush administration opposes.[52]

Water Quality Legislation. U.S. government involvement in water quality issues has followed a pattern similar to that of air quality issues. The **Clean Water Act** (also known as the Federal Water Pollution Control Act) was passed in the early 1970s with broad environmental quality goals and an implementation system, involving both the federal and state governments, designed to attain those goals. The ultimate purpose of the Clean Water Act was to achieve water quality consistent with protection of fish, shellfish, and wildlife and with safe conditions for human recreation in and on the water. The more tangible goal was to eliminate discharges of pollutants into navigable waters, which include most U.S. rivers, streams, and lakes. These goals were to be accomplished through a pollution permit system, called the National Pollutant Discharge Elimination

System, which specifies maximum permissible discharge levels, and often timetables for installation of state-of-the-art pollution control equipment. Another act—the *Marine Protection, Research, and Sanctuaries Act* of 1972—sets up a similar system for control of discharges into coastal ocean waters within U.S. territory. A third water quality law administered by the EPA, the *Safe Drinking Water Act* of 1974, establishes maximum contaminant levels for drinking water.[53, 54]

In 2004, Wal-Mart was ordered to pay $3.1 million in fines due to Clean Water Act violations resulting from excessive storm water runoff at 24 of its construction sites in nine states.[55] The company has also agreed to improve runoff control at its over 200 construction sites. The settlement with the EPA and the Justice Department charges Wal-Mart with failing to get permits, failing to institute a runoff control plan, and failing to install discharge controls. Runoff is a serious environmental problem because the dirt and sediment it carries into waterways can kill fish and destroy habitats. The runoff can also carry pesticides, chemicals, solvents, and other toxic substances.[56]

Land-Related Legislation.   Land pollution and degradation issues differ from air and water quality issues, because land by definition is far less fluid and therefore somewhat more visible than air and water and is more amenable to local or regional problem-solving approaches. Consequently, the U.S. federal government, in the *Solid Waste Disposal Act* of 1965, recognized that regional, state, and local governments should have the main responsibility for nontoxic waste management. The EPA's role in this area is limited to research and provision of technical and financial assistance to these other government levels. However, a 1976 amendment to this act, called the *Resource Conservation and Recovery Act*, set up a federal regulatory system for tracking and reporting the generation, transportation, and eventual disposal of hazardous wastes by businesses responsible for creating these wastes.

Concerning toxic wastes, however, the U.S. government has staked out a much larger role for itself. The 1976 **Toxic Substances Control Act** requires manufacturing and distribution businesses in the chemical industry to identify any chemicals that pose "substantial risks" of human or other natural environment harm. This act also requires chemical testing before commercialization and the possible halting of manufacture if the associated risks are unreasonable. Because there are over 70,000 chemicals already in use in the United States and more than 1,000 new chemicals introduced every year, the EPA has prioritized the substances that must be tested to focus on those that might cause cancer, birth defects, or gene mutations.

The other major U.S. government activity in toxic wastes is known as **Superfund**, or, more formally, the Comprehensive Environmental Response, Compensation, and Liability Act of 1980 (CERCLA). Superfund is an effort to clean up more than 2,000 hazardous waste dumps and spills around the country, some dating back to the previous century. Funded by taxes on chemicals and petroleum, this program has established a National Priorities List to focus on the most hazardous sites, and places legal and financial responsibility for the proper remediation of these sites on the appropriate parties. In addition, CERCLA also requires that unauthorized hazardous waste spills be reported and can order those responsible to clean up the sites.

One of the most important amendments to the Superfund law, the *Emergency Planning and Community Right-to-Know Act* of 1986, requires manufacturing companies to report to the federal government annually all of their releases into the environment of any of more than 500 toxic chemicals and chemical compounds. These reports are accumulated and made available to the public (at http://www.epa.gov/triexplorer) with the intention that an informed public will pressure manufacturers to reduce these toxic releases.[57, 58]

The Superfund celebrated its 20th anniversary in 2000. The program's list of accomplishments included over 6,400 actions taken; 757 Superfund sites with all cleanup construction completed; and private parties settlements at a value of over $18 billion.[59] By 2004, however, serious concerns were being raised. According to a report by the U.S. Public Interest Group, the Bush administration cut the rate of cleanups by 50 percent even though one in four Americans live within four miles of a Superfund site.[60]

Endangered Species.   The U.S. government's role in the natural environment is not restricted to activities of the EPA. Although this agency and the major laws it administers are the most visible, nearly every major department in the federal government has some actual or potential impact on environmental quality. Two agencies with major impacts are the U.S. Interior Department's Fish and Wildlife Service and the Commerce Department's National Marine Fisheries Act: They administer the 1973 **Endangered Species Act (ESA)**. This federal law assigns the responsibility of preventing harm to species considered "endangered" (that is, facing extinction) or "threatened" (likely to become endangered). As of January 31, 2001, 1,244 U.S. species were listed, of which 508 were animals and 736 were plants.[61] Whereas protection of species sometimes means moving them to safe areas when their original habitats have been destroyed by human activities, it often involves prevention of these activities, such as mining, construction, and fishing, before such habitat deprivation occurs. This restriction of business activities can be expected to continue as the extinction rate for nonhuman species climbs, resulting in sometimes intense political conflicts between business interests and environmental groups.[62] Some environmentalists argue that the Endangered Species Act has been weakened under the Bush administration.[63] They point to the fact that an average of 9.5 species has been added each year under the Bush administration, compared to 65 each year under the Clinton administration and 50 each year under the George H. W. Bush administration. Only half the acreage recommended has been designated as critical habitat, and important decision-making powers have been taken away from Fish and Wildlife Services and given to agencies with competing priorities.[64]

International Government Environmental Responses

Although the United States is the focus of many environmental issues as a result of its high profile in causing and responding to environmental problems, the global nature of many natural environment issues has meant that international institutions have also played important roles. Certainly, one international institution that has led the way in identifying global environmental problems and in working toward their resolution has been the *United Nations Environment Programme (UNEP)*. Since its creation in 1972, this agency has been at the forefront in each of the eight major environmental areas mentioned in the preceding chapter. As early as 1977, UNEP was studying the ozone problem and began to lay the groundwork for the 1987 **Montreal Protocol**, in which most of the CFC (chlorofluorocarbon) producing and consuming nations around the world agreed to a quick phase-out of these ozone-destroying substances. As a result, the worldwide consumption of ozone-depleting substances declined nearly 75 percent from 1994 to 2001. UNEP reports that an estimated 1.5 million cases of melanoma will have been averted by the year 2060, thanks to the Montreal Protocol.[65]

UNEP is also funding research and assisting in information exchange on the protection and more sustainable use of international waters. The Global Waters Assessment will examine the problems surrounding shared transboundary waters, develop scenarios on the future condition of the world's water, and analyze various policy options. UNEP is also the driving force behind efforts to initiate global sound management of hazardous chemicals. They were an integral part of the Rotterdam Convention, which requires that countries give explicit informed consent before hazardous chemicals cross their borders. UNEP also works to protect the world's biological diversity. Through their efforts, the elephant has been brought back from the brink of extinction.[66]

OTHER ENVIRONMENTAL STAKEHOLDERS

Environmental Interest Groups

Perhaps no force in today's society is more responsible for the "greening" of nations around the world than the many environmental interest groups making up what has come to be known as "the environmental movement." This collection of nonprofit membership and think-tank organizations has been credited with moving the world's governments and businesses, as well as publics, in the direction of environmental responsibility through a host of activities, including demonstrations, boycotts, public education, lobbying, and research.

The history of the environmental movement is instructive. Whereas a few U.S. groups (The National Audubon Society, the Izaak Walton League, and the Sierra Club) were formed in the early 1900s during the first green wave of the century, many of the largest national and international environmental groups, such as the Environmental Defense Fund (now called Environmental Defense), Greenpeace, and the National Resources Defense Council were created during the second environmental wave, during the late 1960s and early 1970s. Since that time, all of these groups and hundreds of other smaller, more locally focused environmental organizations have grown in size and clout. It was the century's third wave of environmentalism, beginning in the late 1980s, however, that gave many of these groups the power and legitimacy to become credible players in environmental policy making around the globe.

Environmental interest groups have been instrumental in significantly influencing business environmental policy in this third wave. For example, Environmental Defense coresearched and coplanned a comprehensive waste reduction plan with McDonald's Corporation, with the ultimate goal of reducing corporate waste by 80 percent. Other outcomes of relationships between environmental interest groups and business stakeholders have included corporate selection of environmental group representatives for corporate boards and top management positions, mutual participation in environmental "cleanup" projects, and corporate donations of time and money to environmental groups for their environmental conservation programs. This trend toward cooperation between otherwise adversarial groups is a characteristic of the third environmental or green wave that sets this wave apart from the two previous environmental eras. The former chairman of the Sierra Club identified three types of major U.S. environmental organizations based on this criterion of cooperation with business. He labeled groups characterized by confrontational behaviors as "radicals," groups that seek pragmatic reform through a combination of confrontation and cooperation as "mainstreamers," and groups that avoid confrontation and are more trusting of corporations as "accommodators."[67]

One group that would fall into the radical camp is the Rainforest Action Network (RAN). RAN has been particularly successful in getting large corporations to change their ways. The ways in which RAN has accomplished their goals are described in Figure 14-5. RAN is a small organization, with a budget of only $2.4 million and a staff of just 25. Nevertheless, they have managed to get the attention of big business in a way that the larger, more established environmental organizations have never managed. They have been described as a mosquito in a tent, "just a nuisance when it starts, but you can wake up later with some serious welts."[68]

A new category that is taking on increased importance is **ecoterrorists**. Ecoterrorists are not included under the radical designation described earlier. Radical groups favor confrontation, but ecoterrorists employ violent acts that involve real or threatened damage to people or property to attempt to achieve their goals. The FBI estimates that there have been about 600 acts of ecoterrorism in the United States, with losses totaling nearly $50 million.[69] More than 20 states have passed ecoterrorism laws that increase the penalties for vandalism, arson, and trespassing when ecoterrorism is involved.[70] Debate has arisen over whether the new laws are too severe. Jeff Luers, who was 22 years old, received a sentence of 23 years for setting three pickup trucks on fire at a Chevrolet dealership in Eugene, Oregon.[71] Opponents point out that in 1998 an Oregon firefighter received three years for endangering 120 firefighters by setting 30 forest fires in an effort to earn overtime pay. At this writing, the Ecoterrorism Act of 2004 (HR 4454) is working its way through the U.S. House of Representatives.

Green Consumers, Employees, and Investors

In addition to environmental groups, businesses are paying more attention to the latest green wave because of at least three other stakeholder groups: green consumers, green employees, and green investors. So-called green consumers are actual and potential customers of retail firms, usually in the industrialized countries, who express preferences for

FIGURE 14-5

The Mosquito in the Tent Strategy

Street Theater	During the holiday season, RAN carolers sang "Oil Wells" to the tune of "Jingle Bells" in front of the Citigroup headquarters on Park Avenue. RAN obtained the access code to the Home Depot intercom and announced to shoppers that they should step carefully because the wood on Aisle 13 had been ripped from the Amazon Basin and there might be blood on the floors.
Celebrity Endorsements	The night before Citigroup's annual shareholder meeting, RAN began airing commercials showing Ed Asner, Susan Sarandon, Darryl Hannah, and Ali MacGraw cutting up their Citibank credit cards.
Coalitions	RAN doesn't go it alone. They work with other environmental organizations, socially responsible investors, liberal philanthropists, and even sympathetic insiders (which is how they got the Home Depot access code).
Internet Organizing	RAN uses the Internet to both launch their own initiatives and support those of other groups.

SOURCES: Marc Gunther, "The Mosquito in the Tent," *Fortune* (March 31, 2004), 158–162; Lisa Gerwitz, "It's Not Easy Being Green," *Deal.com* (March 8, 2004), 1.

458 *Part4*   ExternalStakeholderIssues

products, services, and companies that are perceived to be more environment friendly than other competitive products, services, and firms. Marketing research firms in these countries have identified a range of green consumerism on the basis of the strengths of these preferences and reported consumer purchases. Roper Starch's *Green Gauge Report* identifies "light green" consumers (a.k.a. "greenback greens") as those who are more likely to support the environment through purchases than volunteer action.[72] They are a sought-after segment of the market—young, well-paid, highly educated, Internet savvy, predominately female, and mostly professional or white-collar employees.[73] Experts expect an increase in green consumers over the next 15 to 25 years as Generation Y (those born between 1977 and 1994) assume positions of responsibility.[74] Nearly 100 percent of the Y generation received environmental education in school, as opposed to 19 percent of the adults in general. As a result, they have been shown to be much more likely to spend money for environmentally friendly products than their parents were.[75]

A second stakeholder group with which most businesses are concerned is green employees. Although the popular press has not focused as much attention on green employees as it has on green consumers, there is evidence that employees are playing a major role in promoting environmentalism at work. In addition to union and general employee environmental concerns with plant, warehouse, and office safety and health, employees in many companies have assisted management in going beyond these tradition-

---

SEARCH THE WEB

LIVING "THE OTHER LOW-CARB LIFE"

Corporations and countries are not alone in their capacity to stem the impact of global warming. Many individuals have begun to make a commitment to the "carbon neutral" life. The carbon neutral movement is composed of individuals and organizations that have made a commitment to tracking and paying for the CO_2 that they spend. For example, environmental consultant Guy Dauncey tallies his annual carbon spending when he tallies his taxes. He found that his personal activities caused 13.5 tons of carbon emissions. The going rate for carbon is $10 a ton, and so he made arrangements to do $135 of work for the Solar Electric Light Fund, a group that helps African villagers to use solar power instead of kerosene.

The carbon neutral movement boasts some big names. The Rolling Stones, Coldplay, and the Matthew Good Band have all held carbon neutral concerts. They do this by calculating their carbon emissions and then compensating for them by investing in green projects. The climate change disaster film *The Day After Tomorrow* is said to be the first carbon neutral major

movie. The flying, driving, and cooking required for the film generated 10,000 tons of CO_2. Director Roland Emmerich balanced the account by spending $200,000 on tree planting. Some companies, such as Stonyfield Farm yogurt and Shaklee nutritional products, carry assurances of carbon neutrality. It is also possible to book a carbon neutral flight or have carbon neutral groceries delivered to your home.

Dauncey uses **http://www.chooseclimate.org** to calculate how much carbon his activities use. On this Web site, you can calculate the greenhouse warming effect of any flight and explore alternative forms of transportation. Another Web site, **http://www.climateStar.org**, provides a "carbon footprint" calculator and a range of information on global warming along with ways in which individuals can become involved in the issue.

SOURCE: Danylo Hawaleshka, "The Other Low-Carb Life," *Maclean's* (June 21, 2004), 54.

al concerns into areas such as pollution prevention, recycling, energy and environmental audits, and community environmental projects. Successful "Green Teams" have been operating at such diverse businesses as Goldman Sachs, Ace Hardware, Eastman Kodak, and Apple Computer.[76] Green employees want their workplaces to reflect their environmental values. According to Jon Whiteman of Vishay Siliconix, "There's pressure from everyone from the janitor to the CEO to make sure that we're doing our part. It's almost like running for office—you've got to make sure you're doing something for everyone."[77]

Another important business stakeholder involved in environmental issues is the green investor. Similar to investors interested in advancing social causes, individuals and organizations sometimes want to "put their money where their environmental values are" by identifying and utilizing financial instruments that are associated with environmentally oriented companies. A growing number of mutual funds, stock and bond offerings, money market funds, and other financial instruments have included environmental components in recent years. In just the first two months of 2004, 51 shareholder resolutions were filed that dealt with energy and environment issues.[78] The resolutions address concerns that range from toxic emissions to recycling and waste to nuclear power plants. About half, however, deal with the issue of climate change. According to Meg Voorhes, director of the Investor Responsibility Research Center, climate change has emerged in the last three years as the most widespread concern.[79] Some of the nation's largest investors are among those filing resolutions, including pension fund managers representing public employees in Connecticut, New York state, Maine, and New York City.[80]

In her book *Vanishing Borders*, Hilary French argues that companies with strong environmental management are likely to outperform those companies that have environmental liabilities.[81] According to French, new communications technologies enable groups of investors to mount coordinated campaigns against companies with questionable practices. She calls for an increase in the quality and quantity of environmental reporting by companies.[82] Baxter Health Care is an exemplar of the environmental reporting French seeks. Baxter won the 2003 Environmental Reporting Award from *Business Ethics* for the clear environmental goals they set as well as the honesty with which they report their results.[83]

After the Exxon *Valdez* oil spill, several environmental, labor, and social investor groups formed an organization called CERES and developed a preamble and a set of 10 policy statements called the "Valdez Principles" (later renamed the **CERES Principles**). These principles have been advanced as models for businesses to express and practice environmental sensitivity. Excerpts from these principles are listed in Figure 14-6 on page 460. Companies that have endorsed the principles include American Airlines, Bank of America, Coca-Cola, General Motors, Polaroid Corporation, and Sunoco.[84]

BUSINESS ENVIRONMENTALISM

The 3M Company is one of the best known multinational companies to have adopted a comprehensive, beyond-compliance, environmental policy and program. Begun in 1975, 3M's Pollution Prevention Pays program was a multiproduct, multiprocess approach to manufacturing. In its first year alone, through product reformulation, process modification, equipment redesign, and waste recycling, 3M prevented 73,000 tons of air emissions and 2,800 tons of sludge. They also saved more than $700 million for the company by reducing various pollutants at their sources. The company gives the credit (and financial

FIGURE 14-6

Ceres Principles

By adopting these principles, we publicly affirm our belief that corporations have a responsibility for the environment by operating in a manner that protects the earth. We believe that corporations must not compromise the ability of future generations to sustain themselves. We will update our practices constantly in light of advances in technology and new understandings in health and environmental science. In collaboration with CERES, we will promote a dynamic process to ensure that the Principles are interpreted in a way that accommodates changing technologies and environmental realities. We intend to make consistent, measurable progress in implementing these Principles and to apply them to all aspects of our operations throughout the world.

1. Protection of the Biosphere: We will reduce and make continual progress toward eliminating the release of any substance that may cause environmental damage to the air, water, or earth or its inhabitants. We will safeguard all habitats affected by our operations and will protect open spaces and wilderness, while preserving biodiversity.

2. Sustainable Use of Natural Resources: We will make sustainable use of renewable natural resources, such as water, soils, and forests. We will conserve nonrenewable natural resources through efficient use and careful planning.

3. Reduction and Disposal of Waste: We will reduce and where possible eliminate waste, through source reduction and recycling. All waste will be handled and disposed of through safe and responsible methods.

4. Energy Conservation: We will conserve energy and improve the energy efficiency of our internal operations and of the goods and services we sell. We will make every effort to use environmentally safe and sustainable energy sources.

5. Risk Reduction: We will strive to minimize the environmental, health, and safety risks to our employees and the communities in which we operate through safe technologies, facilities, and operating procedures, and by being prepared for emergencies.

6. Safe Products and Services: We will reduce and where possible eliminate the use, manufacture, or sale of products and services that cause environmental damage or health or safety hazards. We will inform our customers of the environmental impacts of our products or services and try to correct unsafe use.

7. Environmental Restoration: We will promptly and responsibly correct conditions we have caused that endanger health, safety, or the environment. To the extent feasible, we will redress injuries we have caused to persons or damage we have caused to the environment and will restore the environment.

8. Informing the Public: We will inform in a timely manner everyone who may be affected by conditions caused by our company that might endanger health, safety, or the environment. We will regularly seek advice and counsel through dialogue with persons in communities near our facilities. We will not take any action against employees for reporting dangerous incidents or conditions to management or to appropriate authorities.

9. Management Commitment: We will implement these Principles and sustain a process that ensures that the Board of Directors and Chief Executive Officer are fully informed about pertinent environmental issues and are fully responsible for environmental policy. In selecting our Board of Directors, we will consider demonstrated environmental commitment as a factor.

10. Audits and Reports: We will conduct an annual self-evaluation of our progress in implementing these Principles. We will support the timely creation of generally accepted environmental audit procedures. We will annually complete the CERES Report, which will be made available to the public.

SOURCE: CERES, http://www.ceres.org.

rewards) for these environmental successes to its employees, who have developed more than 4,500 subprojects under this program.[85] 3M scientists received the Heroes of Chemistry Award in 1997 for developing 3M HFEs as a CFC replacement. By the year 2000, 3M had cut its volatile organic air emissions by 85 percent, its releases to water by 80 percent, its solid wastes by 20 percent, and its waste generation by 35 percent.[86] It's not surprising, therefore, that in 2003 3M won the *Business Ethics* Award for Environmental Excellence. In the 1970s, 3M focused on reducing emissions. In 2004, the company is factoring environmental awareness into all stages of the product's life cycle. Their "Lifecycle Management" program is designed to minimize environmental impact from the product design to customer use and disposal. The *Business Ethics* award acknowledges 3M's "sustained commitment, innovation, and substantial impact in three decades of environmental stewardship."[87]

The makers of Stonyfield Yogurt have adopted a Climate Change Initiative. Through it, they have reduced their energy use and associated greenhouse emissions by more than 25 percent per pound of product they sell. They accomplished this by retrofitting lights, recovering and reusing hot water, and upgrading equipment. They also created offsets for the carbon dioxide their production process produces by investing in forests, renewable fuels, and fuel switching. They also play a strong role in consumer education through messages on their product packaging, e.g., "Let's put a lid on global warming." For their environmental efforts, they won a 2000 Renew America award for environmental sustainability.[88] As mentioned earlier in the chapter, they are one of a growing number of carbon neutral products.

Small businesses, too, are promoting green products and services. Smaller companies can serve as excellent incubators for new environmentally friendly processes because their size makes them more manageable. The Tunweni Brewery in Tsumeb, Namibia, was the site of the first commercial application of the Zero Emissions Research Initiative (ZERI). They recovered fibers from the spent grain through the cultivation of mushrooms, used earthworms to feed on the leftover protein, and used "waste" streams to farm fish as part of the initiative.[89] Ecotech Autoworks in McLean, Virginia, was one of the first green auto repair shops in the United States. Ecotech recycled all car fluids, especially CFC-containing air-conditioning fluid, and used recycled auto parts at customer request. This then-innovative service used recycled-tire shop floor mats and carbon monoxide-absorbing hanging spider plants, and offered a full range of environmental magazines in the customer waiting room.[90] Now environmentally friendly auto shops are available throughout the United States, and programs have been created to assist other auto repair shops to follow in the green vein.

The greening of business is a global phenomenon. Toyota campaigned to produce a solar-powered car, while Mitsubishi pursued its Malaysian rain forest reforestation effort—the environmental credit card of the Daiei Supermarket Group. This program, which was designed by two well-known Japanese environmental groups, allowed grocery consumers who use these cards to direct 0.5 percent of their grocery bills to any of 20 different environmental causes.[91] PlanetBound, a Tokyo-based firm specializing in Internet-based environmental communication, established the Eco500 project. In it they studied the Web sites of the world's largest corporations in an effort to gauge the importance that companies in diverse industry sectors and markets place on communicating a commitment to environmental responsibility and conservation. On the top of the list was the electronics giant, NEC: It was the only firm to be accorded a full 100 points for its Web site. Multiple firms, however, received a score of zero.[92]

Business environmentalism is also blossoming on the European continent. Europe is deeply divided on the environmental front. The Nordic countries, Germany and the Netherlands, have stringent regulations and a strong concern for the environment. At the opposite extreme are the former Soviet Union and Eastern Bloc countries, which are facing severe environmental damage from years of neglect and little money with which to effect a solution. Other European countries lie somewhere in between. In an effort to address this problem, Western environmental ministers are being paired with their Eastern counterparts and are working together to address the challenge of Eastern Bloc pollution. With the Greens gaining political momentum and Western European consumers willing to pay a premium for green products and services, environmental issues are certain to occupy Europe's businesses for many years to come.[93]

Environmental and Financial Performance

The prudent future business manager will likely ask, "Although protecting the earth may be a good reason to practice environmental management, will it pay off on the bottom line?" There are many anecdotes about firms making money from their environmental programs. One example is the experience of Lightolier, Inc., a Massachusetts lighting fixture manufacturer, which retrofitted its gas boiler to use 20,000 gallons of its otherwise-wasted hydraulic oil, saving $40,000, which paid for the investment in less than one year.[94] In her book *Lean and Green: Profit for Your Workplace*, Pamela Gordon describes 20 situations in which corporations enhanced their profits through sound environmental management. Savings came not only from cost reduction but also through avoiding litigation and liability, while enhancing reputation and sales.[95] In the semiconductor industry, environmentally proactive firms such as Intel Corp. and Advanced Micro Devices have been shown to outperform competitors who are not as environmentally oriented. In another study, Miles and Covin showed that being a good environmental steward enhances a firm's reputation that benefits a firm's marketing and its subsequent financial performance.[96]

Although **cost-benefit analysis** has been used in other areas, especially those related to public and private capital budgeting and investment, it has also received an extraordinary amount of attention in natural environmental policy decisions. For instance, most environmental impact statements, which are required by the National Environmental Policy Act, have one or more cost-benefit analyses as the basis for many of the environmental decisions resulting from these studies. The idea behind cost-benefit analysis is that, in a rational planning situation, an organization wants to ensure that an environmental project is worth the investment. Costs are totaled and compared with overall benefits. If benefits are sufficiently greater than costs, the project is given the go-ahead; if not, it is shelved, revised, or scrapped. Decision makers in many dam projects, other water reclamation projects, and land development projects in the United States have utilized cost-benefit analysis to determine the value of these environment-oriented projects. Environmental groups can use cost-benefit analysis to further their agenda for change. As previously discussed, the Rainforest Action Network has been able to get large corporations to make dramatic changes in the way they do business. Essentially, they do this by changing the cost-benefit equation. By upping the cost of environmental negligence, RAN tilts the business calculus, making it more likely that firms will find the results of a cost-benefit analysis indicate that an improvement in environmental performance is warranted.

Companies around the world are beginning to adopt the **triple bottom line (TBL)**, reporting that covers not only economic performance but also social and environmental. The idea behind the TBL is that it will force corporations to focus not only on financial performance but also on the ways in which the company either adds to or detracts from society and the environment.[97] A 2003 commentary in the *CPA Journal* suggested that U.S. firms would benefit if the SEC would require TBL reporting. Socially responsible firms would benefit from the exposure their activities would receive just as irresponsible firms would be forced to own up to their failings.[98] Although the SEC is unlikely to adopt the requirement any time soon, the voluntary use of TBL as a reporting framework continues to grow.

Systematic Business Responses to the Environmental Challenge

Various management approaches are available for use in selecting or constructing an environmental strategy. These include several management approaches that were discussed in more general terms in earlier chapters and a few that are specific to natural environment issues. In the first group are crisis management, issues management, and stakeholder management. Because these topics were addressed more fully in Chapters 4 and 5, only their applicability to environmental management will be discussed here. In the second group of decision-making tools are sustainability and strategic environmental management, which will be discussed more fully in this chapter.

Generic Management Decision-Making Tools.

Managers can use crisis management in the environmental area by focusing on two factors: prevention and contingency plans. As can be seen in the Exxon *Valdez* case, Exxon, Alyeska, and the federal and state governments apparently did not pay enough attention to preventing the 1989 Alaskan oil spill disaster or to implementing the inadequate contingency plan to recover the oil once it had been spilled. Although some attention had been paid to the vulnerability of the Alaskan natural environment to a small oil spill, this appears to have been understated and generally ignored. That either Exxon or Alyeska assessed its own vulnerability to a spill of any size appears doubtful. Finally, the lack of coordination between the two companies in immediately addressing the spill indicated a response plan that was only a paper tiger, never really put into practice. Had the businesses and governments followed basic crisis management principles, including vulnerability assessments and simulation drills, the outcome might have been different for both of these organizations and for Prince William Sound.

Issues management can be employed to track public interest in natural environment issues and to develop and implement plans to attempt to ensure that the scope of environmental problems is minimized and that the firm develops effective responses at each stage in the life cycles of environmental issues. Environmental issues can be developed as part of the environmental impact statement process or as part of the strategic planning macroenvironmental analysis process.

Similarly, stakeholder management applies to environmental management in that environmental stakeholders and their stakes can be identified, including the environmental public, environmental regulators, environmental groups, and various entities (human and nonhuman) across the entire natural environment. The follow-up stages of stakeholder management—that is, planning for and interacting with stakeholders—can then be conducted, so that each important environmental stakeholder is given adequate attention after it is identified.

Although crisis management, issues management, and stakeholder management can be used as generic approaches to environmental management, there are other, more targeted management approaches that are consistent with a proactive approach to environmental management. These are sustainability and strategic environmental management.

Sustainability.

There are many definitions of sustainable business. For our purposes, we will borrow from the World Commission on Environment and Development to define sustainable business as "business that meets the needs of the present without compromising the ability of future generations to meet their own needs."[99] The focus of sustainability is the creation of a good quality of life for both current and future generations of humans and nonhumans by achieving a balance between economic prosperity, ecosystem viability, and social justice.[100] The concept is akin to walking lightly on the earth, taking only what is needed and leaving behind enough for future generations to have access to the same resources.

Paul Dolan, the former president of Fetzer Vineyards, is often referred to as the "Sustainability Guru."[101] Dolan had spent decades in the wine business by the time he became president of Fetzer Vineyards in 1992. He had just read *The Ecology of Commerce* by Paul Hawken: The book gave shape to his future plans. "It suddenly became apparent to me that sustainability was the way," said Dolan. "And because wine speaks from a different platform than other products, we could be a leader. We could help change agriculture."[102]

Dolan may not have changed agriculture yet but he has certainly changed the wine industry. Sustainability is now an industry buzzword. A voluntary self-assessment tool, "Code of Sustainable Wine Growing Practices," has been developed by the California Association of Winegrape Growers and the Wine Institute. Half of California's wineries and 40 percent of grapes grown have gone through the nearly 500-page self-assessment. The movement also has spread to the state of Washington where it has been embraced.[103] Today Fetzer is the largest grower of organic grapes in the United States. It has one label, Bonterra, which uses only organic grapes. The 2,000 other acres that Fetzer farms are organic or in transition. The company is also encouraging its contract growers to adopt organic growing.[104] Fetzer now recycles 97 percent of their waste. According to Dolan, ""We don't have waste baskets anymore. When you finish a meal, you have either a paper basket, a plastic basket, a metal basket, or a scrap food basket—it's gotta fit in one of those."[105]

In April 2004, Dolan stepped down from Fetzer vineyards and formed a partnership to purchase a small Mendocino County winery, Parducci Cellars. Parducci was just certified as an organic processor and Dolan plans to take 30 acres of Syrah and old vine Petite Syrah and farm and certify them organic. He also has written a book, *True To Our Roots: Fermenting a Business Revolution*, in which he outlines six principles of Fetzer Vineyard's way of doing business. These six principles of sustainable success are listed in Figure 14-7.

Strategic Environmental Management.   The final managerial approach to addressing the business environmental challenge presented here is a well-known organization effectiveness tool that has been adapted by the authors to assist managers in devel-

---

FIGURE 14-7

Six Principles of Sustainable Success

1. Your business is part of a much larger system.
2. The culture of your business is determined by the context you create for it.
3. The soul of a business is found in the hearts of its people.
4. True power is living what you know.
5. You can't predict the future, but you can create it.
6. There is a way to make an idea's time come.

SOURCE: Paul Dolan, *True to Our Roots: Fermenting a Business Revolution* (New York: Bloomberg Press, 2003).

oping and implementing overall approaches to natural environment issues. This model is called **Strategic Environmental Management (SEM)** and is presented as one way in which organizations can readily respond to their environmental challenges and integrate a wide range of responses for environmental effectiveness.

As can be seen in Figure 14-8, this method uses the McKinsey 7S framework, in which seven typical organizational components necessary for success are identified and integrated, and several green suggestions are given for each "S." Businesses can build environmental components into their superordinate goals, strategies, structures, and so on, in order to develop an overall organizational environmental response. Superordinate goals can include an emphasis on environmental protection in a company's mission state-

FIGURE 14-8

Strategic Environmental Management (SEM)

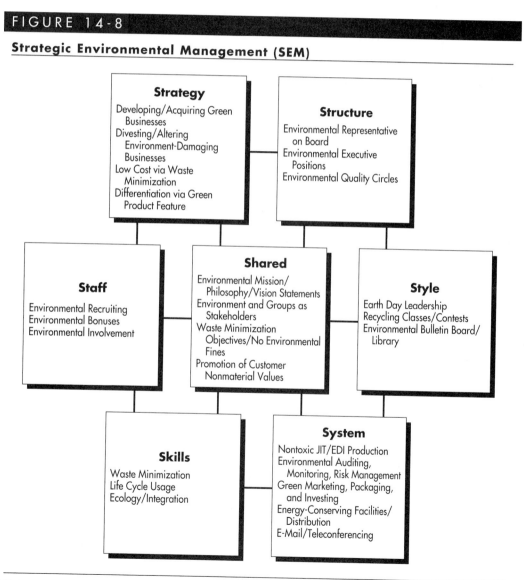

SOURCE: M. Starik and A. B. Carroll, "Strategic Environmental Management: Business as if the Earth Really Mattered," *Proceedings of 1991 International Association for Business and Society*, Sundance, UT (March 22–24, 1991), 28.

ment, for instance, whereas one of its strategies can be developing or acquiring environmentally sensitive businesses. The key to using this model is for managers to identify opportunities for developing environmental responses in each of the S categories and to ensure that each of these responses is compatible with the others.

Using this approach, the environmental manager can incorporate concern for the environment and take environmentally sensitive actions in all organization departments and at all organizational levels. For instance, the shared value of waste minimization can translate into the low-cost strategy, enhanced by environmental quality circles structures, energy-conservation systems in manufacturing facilities, and environmentally skilled staff personnel who are motivated by incentives for meeting personal environmental objectives and by managers exhibiting an environmentally sensitive style. As mentioned in the previous chapters, each organizational department can play a role in the organization's interaction with the natural environment. Research and development departments can work with manufacturing personnel to alter their products and processes to limit pollution and depletion. Finance and accounting personnel can develop effective environmental auditing systems and cost out the potential for environmentally damaging projects, with the aim of reducing this cost as much as possible. Human resources managers can begin to incorporate environmental concerns in their recruitment and training programs, attempting to build an "environmental culture" in the organization. Marketers can identify their customers' "real needs," as opposed to their frivolous (and potentially environmentally damaging) desires for products and services, and adjust their distribution systems in transportation, packaging, and labeling so as to promote environmental sensitivity. This strategic environmental management approach is similar to both the concept of industrial ecology, which "requires that an industrial system be viewed not in isolation from its surrounding systems, but in concert with them,"[106] and the international environmental management standard called **ISO 14000**, which includes organizational environmental objectives, issues, policies, systems, and documentation aimed at "continued improvement of the environmental management process, leading to improvement in environmental performance."[107]

The limitations of the SEM approach are similar to those of the McKinsey 7S model itself, including a decidedly internal orientation (nonorganization stakeholders and forces are not explicitly emphasized) and a potential for much complexity. The prudent manager, once again, is advised to remember these weaknesses and to supplement this method with others mentioned in this section. The stakeholder management approach, with its external focus, might be a good match for the more internal SEM focus. Indeed, an eighth "S" that could be added to this model is "stakeholders," which could include environmentally oriented suppliers, customers, investors, and regulators, as well as the natural environment itself.

THE FUTURE OF BUSINESS: GREENING AND/OR GROWING?

The salient environmental question we all may need to address in the future: "How much is enough?" A common business and, indeed, public policy goal in most human societies has been economic growth. Typically, businesses and societies have needed increasing amounts of either materials or energy, or both, to achieve that economic growth. Limits on growth, similar to limits on human reproduction, at either the macro or micro level, have not been widely popular. One potential problem with unrestrained economic growth worldwide is that, unless technology or people change significantly within a generation, environmental problems can change in degree from significant to severe.

World population is projected to continue to increase, potentially requiring greater demands on food and fuel resources. Both industrialized and less-industrialized nations may contribute to this dilemma. The West and Japan continue to use increasing amounts of materials and energy to maintain highly consumptive lifestyles, whereas the rest of the world continues to use these developed nations as models for their own development. Two pressing questions are (1) Can the earth support a high-consumption Western lifestyle for an increasing world population? and, if not, (2) What are the implications for business and how should business managers respond?

■ SUMMARY

We have explored a variety of environmental challenges and several actual and potential responses to these challenges. What themes appear to be woven throughout this chapter that can be especially helpful to prospective managers? First, many scientists, policy makers, public-interest groups, individuals, and businesses recognize that the natural environment is crucial for human survival and that a number of complex and interconnected human-induced activities may be threatening this environment. Problems such as human deforestation, pollution, and expanding populations are potentially endangering non-human species and ecosystems and reducing the quality of human life. Individuals and their organizations, including businesses, have been found to be directly or indirectly responsible for this situation.

Second, there are significant differences of opinion on how these problems will develop in the future and, of course, what should be done to resolve them. Individuals and organizations, including businesses, concerned about reducing environmental degradation should adopt a flexible and prudent approach to keeping themselves informed and taking actions, no matter how small, in the direction of "walking lightly on the earth." A minimum baseline of not increasing human-caused pollution and depletion may be a potential starting point for consensus building and environmental consciousness.

■ KEY TERMS

acid rain (page 447)

air pollution (page 447)

CERES Principles (page 459)

Clean Air Act (page 452)

Clean Water Act (page 453)

cost-benefit analysis (page 462)

deforestation (page 446)

ecoterrorists (page 457)

emissions trading (page 453)

Endangered Species Act (ESA) (page 455)

energy inefficiency (page 447)

environment (page 439)

environmental impact statements (EISs) (page 452)

Environmental Protection Agency (EPA) (page 452)

green values (page 450)

greenhouse effect (page 442)

indoor air pollution (page 447)

ISO 14000 (page 466)

Montreal Protocol (page 455)

NIMBY (page 449)

ozone (page 442)

Strategic Environmental Management (SEM) (page 465)

Superfund (page 454)

toxic substance (page 448)

Toxic Substances Control Act (page 454)

tragedy of the commons (page 451)

triple bottom line (TBL) (page 462)

■ DISCUSSION QUESTIONS

1. What is the natural environment?
2. What are several of the most important environmental issues now receiving worldwide attention?
3. What are some of the causes of environmental pollution and depletion?
4. What is the future outlook for the natural environment?
5. Who has responsibility for addressing environmental issues?
6. How can ethics be applied in response to environmental issues?
7. What are some examples of business environmentalism and decision models for addressing environmental concerns?
8. Should businesses and societies continue to focus on unlimited economic growth?

■ RECOMMENDED CASES

Many of the end-of-text cases may be related to Chapter 14. You may wish to consider studying the following cases with Chapter 14.

Case 26. "THE HUDSON RIVER CLEANUP AND GE." For over 30 years, GE dumped PCBs into the Hudson River. This dumping was legal at the time but led to the upper Hudson River becoming the largest Superfund site in history. The EPA charged GE with cleaning up the site and paying the costs. Is it right for a company to incur massive cleanup costs when their activities were legal within the regulations that existed at that time? Who should be responsible for the cleanup? GE? The EPA? New York? What should be done now?

Case 27. "SAFETY? WHAT SAFETY?" This case is about a company that is building a new manufacturing plant and must make decisions that will affect the extent to which their waste treatment facilities will meet environmental standards. The industry standards are currently more stringent than the federal standards, and their competition only meets the federal standards. To design a new plant that would meet the industry standards would put this company at a cost disadvantage, and so the managers have decided to build a plant that will only meet federal standards. Assistant Controller Kirk is deeply troubled by this decision. Who are the stakeholders in this case and how would you rank their competing claims? What should a company do when the most socially responsible action will put it at a competitive disadvantage?

Case 28. "LITTLE ENOUGH OR TOO MUCH?" Bryan was recently hired by a chemical company to oversee production of a new plant. Because a regulator granted the company a release to dump more chemicals, the company has opted not to build a new process into the design. Bryan is upset because he finds the decision both wrong and shortsighted. It is wrong because of the impact on the environment and shortsighted because the company may be in trouble in the future for releasing more chemicals. Is Bryan right? When regulators give a company leeway the company does not need, should the company still use it?

■ WEB RESOURCES

The URLs listed here are current at the time of publication. Should any of these Web sites change, please search under the company's or organization's name for an updated address.

CERES
   http://www.ceres.org
Choose Climate
   http://www.chooseclimate.org
ClimateStar
   http://www.climatestar.org

EnviroLink
   http://www.envirolink.org
Environmental Protection Agency
   http://www.epa.gov
Greenpeace
   http://www.greenpeace.org
National Parks Conservation Association
   http://www.npca.org
National Park Foundation
   http://www.nationalparks.org

Rainforest Action Network
    http://www.ran.org
Sierra Club
    http://www.sierraclub.org

United Nations Environment Programme
    http://www.unep.org
U.S. Public Interest Research Group
    http://www.uspirg.org

 InfoTrac® College Edition   http://www.infotrac-college.com

Additional information on the topics discussed in the chapter can be researched by logging onto the InfoTrac College Edition Web site.

▪ ENDNOTES

1. R. Cooke, "Scientists Report Gains in Protecting Ozone Layer May Be Paying Off," *Seattle Times* (March 4, 2001), A13.
2. Jeffrey Frankel, "Bush's Spectacular Failure," *The International Economy* (Spring 2004), 22–28.
3. Tom Naess, "The Effectiveness of the EU's Ozone Policy," *International Environmental Agreements: Politics, Law and Economics* (Vol. 4, No. 1, 2004), 47.
4. David Stipp, "Climate Collapse: The Pentagon's Weather Nightmare," *Fortune* (January 26, 2004).
5. N. Wilkes, "Global Warming Will Be Greater Says U.N.," *Professional Engineering* (January 31, 2001).
6. *Ibid.*
7. United Nations Environmental Programme (2004), http://www.unep.org/themes/climatechange.
8. These statistics were found on the EPA Web site, http://www.epa.gov.
9. W. H. Corson (ed.), *The Global Ecology Handbook* (Boston: Beacon Press, 1990), 247.
10. *United Nations Environmental Programme* (2004), http://www.unep.org/themes/climatechange.
11. *Ibid.*
12. *Ibid.*
13. Public Interest Research Group, Clean Water Fact Sheet (2004), http://uspirg.org/uspirg.asp?id2=5191&id3=USPIRG&.
14. G. Hess, "Significant Number of Facilities in Violation of Clean Water Act," *Chemical Market Reporter* (February 28, 2000), 25.
15. S. Postel, "Saving Water for Agriculture" in L. R. Brown *et al.*, *State of the World*, 1990 (New York: Norton, 1990), 49.
16. "Commission on Sustainable Development Holds First of Four Dialogues," Press release from the United Nations (April 24, 2000).
17. Corson, 137.
18. E. Linden, "Condition Critical," *Time—Special Edition on How to Save the Earth* (Spring 2000), 18–24.
19. "What Tree Loss Costs," *The Futurist* (August/September 1999).
20. *Ibid.*
21. E. Check, "The Silence of the Woods," *Newsweek* (November 13, 2000), 65.
22. "FAO: Strong Indications for Slowdown in Deforestation," Press release from the United Nations (August 8, 2000), 1.
23. UNEP Strategy on Land Use and Soil Conservation (2004), http://www.unep.org/pdf/UNEP-strategy-land-soil-03-2004.pdf.
24. *Ibid.*
25. *Ibid.*
26. E. Wilson, "Vanishing Before Our Eyes," *Time—Special Edition on How to Save the Earth* (Spring 2000), 29–34.
27. *Ibid.*
28. "The Battle for Planet Earth," *Newsweek* (April 24, 2000) 51–53.
29. J. Seager (ed.), *The State of the Earth Atlas* (New York: Simon & Schuster, 1990), 110.
30. J. Naar, *Design for a Livable Planet* (New York: Harper & Row, 1990), 101.
31. "The Battle for Planet Earth," 53.
32. Environmental Protection Agency, *Meeting the Environmental Challenge* (Washington, DC: USGPO, December 1990), 11.
33. J. Mathews, "Acts of War and the Environment," *The Washington Post* (April 8, 1991), A17.
34. T. W. Lippman, "Future of Wind Power Gets a Lift," *The Washington Post* (November 17, 1991), H1.
35. T. Coffin (ed.), "A Look at Alternative Energy," *The Washington Spectator* (Vol. 16, No. 18, 1991), 1–3.
36. "The Battle for Planet Earth," 53.
37. Environmental Protection Agency, *Glossary of Environmental Terms and Acronym List* (Washington, DC: U.S. EPA, 1989), 18.
38. Naar, 38.
39. Naar, 39.
40. "Responding to Oil Spills" (2001), http://www.epa.gov.
41. "Ten Years After the Spill," *Newsweek* (March 29, 1999).
42. Gerald Karey, "Exxon Spill Still Having Impact," *Platt's Oilgram News* (December 22, 2003), 4.
43. Environmental Protection Agency (1990), 10.

44. R. O. Mason and I. I. Mitroff, *Challenging Strategic Planning Assumptions* (New York: Wiley, 1981), 12–13.

45. S. Irvine and A. Pouton, *A Green Manifesto* (London: Optima, 1988), 14–16.

46. *Ibid.*, 16.

47. Garrett Hardin, "The Tragedy of the Commons," *Science* (Volume 162, 1968), 1243–1248.

48. *Ibid.*

49. Public Law 91–190 (1969), 42 U.S.C. Section 4331 *et seq.*

50. T. McAdams, Law, *Business, and Society*, 3d ed. (Homewood, IL: Irwin, 1992), 779–783.

51. O. L. Reed, *The Legal Environment of Business* (New York: McGraw-Hill, 1987), 697–703.

52. John J. Flalka, "Bush to Unveil Air-Pollution Rule; Administration Is Hoping Proposal Will Polish Image, Boost Its Clear Skies Act," *The Wall Street Journal* (April 15, 2004), A6.

53. McAdams, 784–787.

54. Reed, 704–706.

55. "Wal-Mart Stores, Inc.: U.S. Imposes $3.1 Million Fine for Clean Water Act Violations," *The Wall Street Journal* (May 13, 2004), 1.

56. *Ibid.*

57. McAdams, 788–792.

58. Reed, 709–712.

59. http://www.epa.gov/superfund/action/20years (2001).

60. http://www.pirg.org

61. http://endangered.fws.gov (2001).

62. *Ibid.*

63. Juliet Eilperin, "Endangered Species Act Sapped?" *The Washington Post* (July 4, 2004), A1.

64. *Ibid.*

65. UNEP Achievements (2004), http://www.unep.org.

66. *Ibid.*

67. M. E. Kriz, "Shades of Green," *National Journal* (July 28, 1990).

68. Mark Gunther, "The Mosquito in the Tent, *Fortune* (March 31, 2004), 158–162; Lisa Gerwitz, "It's Not Easy Being Green," *Deal.com* (March 8, 2004), 1.

69. Brad Knickerbocker, "New Laws Target Increase in Acts of Ecoterrorism," *Christian Science Monitor* (November 26, 2003), 2.

70. Karen Charman, "The U.S. Goes on Green Alert," *OnEarth* (Fall 2003), 8.

71. *Ibid.*

72. R. Gardyn, "Saving the Earth, One Click at a Time," *American Demographic* (January 2001), 30–33.

73. *Ibid.*

74. *Ibid.*

75. *Ibid.*

76. J. Makower, "Green Teams," *The Green Business Letter* (November 6, 1991), 1.

77. B. Mueller, "Distributors Help with Green Efforts," *Purchasing* (December 22, 2000), 73–76.

78. Barnaby J. Feder, "Funds Want Oil Companies to Report on Climate," *The New York Times* (February 27, 2004), C3.

79. *Ibid.*

80. *Ibid.*

81. H. French, *Vanishing Borders* (New York: W. W. Norton & Co., 2000).

82. *Ibid.*

83. http://www.business-ethics.com/annual.htm

84. CERES (2001), http://www.ceres.org.

85. *3M's Pollution Prevention Pays: An Initiative for a Cleaner Tomorrow* (St. Paul, MN: 3M Company, 1991).

86. CEO's Message (2001), http://www.3M.com.

87. http://www.business-ethics.com/annual.htm

88. Stonyfield Farm (2001), http://www.stonyfield.com.

89. European Eco-Efficiency Initiative (EEE) (2001), http://www.wbcsd.org.

90. J. Saddler, "Going for the Green," *The Wall Street Journal* (November 22, 1991), R13.

91. D. Porter, "A Greening Corporate Image—Japan Business Survey," Advertising supplement to *The Wall Street Journal* (September 23, 1991), B12.

92. Eco500, http://www.eco500.com.

93. A. Sains, "Seeing Green," *Europe* (February 2001) 16–24.

94. M. M. Hamilton, "Generating Profit from the Waste Up," *The Washington Post* (April 12, 1995), F1.

95. P. Gordon, Lean and Green: *Profit for Your Workplace* (San Francisco: Berrett Koehler, 2001).

96. M. Miles and J. Covin, "Environmental Marketing: A Source of Reputational, Competitive, and Financial Advantage," *Journal of Business Ethics* (February 2000), 299–311.

97. http://www.sustainablebusiness.com/info/aboutus.cfm

98. Daniel Tschopp, "It's Time for Triple Bottom Line Reporting," *The CPA Journal* (December 2003), 11.

99. http://www.sustainability.com/philosophy/what-is-sustainable-development.asp

100. W. Edward Stead and Jean Garner Stead with Mark Starik, *Sustainable Strategic Management* (Armonk, NY: M. E. Sharpe, Inc., 2004).

101. David Eddy, "Sustainability Guru," *American Fruit Grower* (June 2004), 10.

102. *Ibid.*, 10.

103. *Ibid.*

104. *Ibid.*

105. Marjorie Kelly, "Using Conversation to Change the World," *Business Ethics* (Winter 2003), 21.

106. T. E. Graedel and B. R. Allenby, *Industrial Ecology* (Englewood Cliffs, NJ: Prentice Hall, 1995), 9.

107. J. B. Charm, "Joel Charm on ISO 14000," *Environment Today* (Vol. 6, No. 1, 1995), 22.

Business *and* Community Stakeholders

When we speak of a community, we usually mean the immediate locale—the town, city, or state—in which a business resides. In our modern age of global business, instantaneous communication, and speedy travel, however, the region, the nation, or even the world can become the relevant community. From Mad Cow Disease in Europe to the AIDS epidemic in Africa, and from Tiananmen Square in China to the September 11th World Trade Center tragedy in New York City, businesses are affected by events throughout the world. Traditional geographic boundaries have been eclipsed by communications technology and high-speed travel. The business community now encompasses the entire world.

When we think of business and its community stakeholders, two major kinds of relationships come to mind. One is the positive contribution business can make to the community.

Examples of these positive contributions include volunteerism, company contributions, and support of programs in education, culture, urban development, the arts, civic activities, and other health and welfare endeavors. On the other hand, business can also cause harm to community stakeholders. It can pollute the environment, and it can put people out of work by outsourcing or closing a plant. Business can abuse its power and exploit consumers and employees.

In this chapter, we will concentrate on community involvement and corporate philanthropy as community stakeholder issues. In addition, we will discuss the topic of outsourcing and business or plant closings as community stakeholder concerns. This discussion should provide us with an opportunity to explore both the positive and the detrimental effects that characterize business/community relationships. We will begin with the positive.

In addition to being profitable, obeying the law, and being ethical, a company may create a positive impact in the community by giving in basically two ways: (1) donating the time and talents of its managers and employees and (2) making financial contributions. The first category, **community involvement**, manifests itself in a wide array of voluntary activities in the community. The second category involves corporate philanthropy or business giving. We should note that there is significant overlap between these two categories, because companies quite frequently donate their time and talents and give financial aid to the same general projects. First, we will discuss community involvement and the various ways in which companies enhance the quality of life in their communities.

COMMUNITY INVOLVEMENT

Perhaps one of the most compelling arguments for increased community involvement is offered by J. Michael Cook, retired chairman and chief executive officer (CEO) of Deloitte & Touche:

> We have an absolutely enormous stake in the communities where our people live and work. If we have good educational systems, good safety, and good activity programs for young people, we're going to be much more effective in attracting and retaining quality people.[1]

Therefore, business must—not only for a healthier society, but also for its own well-being—be willing to give the same serious consideration to human needs that it gives to its own needs for production and profits. Robert Cushman, former president of the Norton Company, enumerates six reasons for business involvement in the community:[2]

1. Businesspeople are efficient problem solvers.
2. Employees gain satisfaction and improved morale from involvement in community programs.
3. A positive image in the community facilitates hiring.
4. Often a company gains prestige and greater acceptance in a community when it gets actively involved.
5. Social responsibility in business is the alternative to government regulation.
6. Business helps itself by supporting those institutions that are essential to the continuation of business.

Business involvement in the community can be enlightened self-interest. Businesses are in a position to help themselves in the process of helping others. This dual objective of business clearly illustrates that making profits and addressing social concerns are not mutually exclusive endeavors. Other rationales for business involvement in community affairs provide moral

Jennifer Comiteau addresses the issue of how businesses help themselves when helping others in an article for *ADWEEK* (29 September 2003 v44i38 p24). She cites studies that show "Americans would likely switch to a brand associated with a good cause if price and quality were similar" and then explores ways that a number of corporations—PNC, American Express, AT&T, and Lee—have donated money and employee time to various causes. Read more about how "do-gooders do better" by logging on to InfoTrac College Edition at **http://www.infotrac-college.com** and keying record number A108477963.

justification, beyond that of enlightened self-interest. For example, utilitarianism has been used to support corporate giving, with arguments that improvement of the social fabric creates the greatest good for the greatest number. This need not contradict the mandates of self-interest, because the corporation is one of the community members that will benefit.[3] Although justifications for corporate involvement in the community can be made from various perspectives, one thing is clear: Business has a public responsibility to build a relationship with the community and to be sensitive to its impacts on the world around it.

This point is driven home by the introduction to an Eli Lilly *Community Service Report:*

> *As Lilly touches the lives of people worldwide, we recognize that we have a particular responsibility to be a good corporate citizen of the communities in which we operate and to help preserve the environment for the generations to come. The commitment to good corporate citizenship reflects the fundamental concern of the company and its foundation for the well-being of people and the quality of life. It is a way to share Lilly's success, to invest in the future, and to give back to society. It is an integral part of the company's mission.*[4]

Volunteer Programs

One of the most pervasive examples of business involvement in communities is a volunteer program. Corporate volunteer programs reflect the resourcefulness and responsiveness of business to communities in need of increasing services. There are numerous examples of corporations making a difference in communities through volunteer activities. The Longaberger Company has a 5-year commitment to the American Cancer Society to make and sell "Horizon of Hope" baskets, stuffed with breast cancer literature. Miller Brewing holds a "day of caring" during which the entire company gives up its time for community projects in Milwaukee. Philip Morris/Kraft employees can champion the charity of their choice and, after employees give 50 hours of service, the company contributes $1,000 to that charity. American Express employees are also encouraged to champion the charity they choose: The company's Global Volunteer Action Fund then provides grants of up to $1,000 for individuals and $2,500 for teams. MONY employees volunteer during their lunchtime one day a week to read to local elementary school students. Through its Volunteer Incentive Award, MONY makes 100 donations to employees who volunteer a minimum of 5 hours per 6-month period at the nonprofit of their choice.[5]

The potential results of these efforts are limitless. By joining with a community-based effort, General Electric (GE) helped convert the closed Benjamin Franklin High School in East Harlem to a center for science and mathematics. In addition to providing enrichments that made the school comparable to the best schools in the country, GE arranged for its employees to become mentors and tutors to the students. The rate of college-bound students at the school became one of the highest in the city and that program became the starting point of GE's award-winning College Bound initiative.[6]

Communities obviously benefit from such volunteer programs, but how do companies benefit from employee volunteerism? Business for Social Responsibility details a variety of benefits, which include:[7]

- Improving employee skills and training
- Encouraging employee teamwork
- Developing leadership skills
- Developing the local labor pool
- Recruiting and retaining employees
- Improving corporate reputation

America's Promise.

When Secretary of State Colin Powell, then retired chairman of the Joint Chiefs of Staff, was asked what represented the greatest threat to the United States, he said, "The threat is young people who are disengaged from American life, who don't believe in the American dream."[8] Although Powell's words relate to the United States, the same situation is playing out in economically developed countries throughout the world. For this reason, service to youth has always been a priority for business. The profile of that service has never been higher than when then-President Clinton and General Powell convened an all-star "Summit on Service" to attack the problem of disadvantaged and disenchanted youth. The guest list included President and Mrs. Clinton; Vice President Gore; all the living former presidents, except Ronald Reagan (who was represented by his wife, Nancy); celebrities like Oprah Winfrey and John Travolta; governors; mayors; clergy; and scores of CEOs. The purpose of the summit was to secure commitments from corporations and civic leaders to work together to fulfill five promises to the nation's children. These promises are (1) caring adults, (2) safe places and structured activities, (3) a healthy start for a healthy future, (4) marketable skills, and (5) opportunities to give back through service to one's community. The price of admission to this summit was a specific commitment to help at-risk youth.[9]

Since its inception, the **America's Promise** Alliance has grown to more than 400 national partners including corporations, foundations, youth-serving organizations, and federal and state agencies, along with more than 400 local efforts.[10] Corporate partners provide financial, in-kind, and human resources to help the organization achieve its mission. Figure 15-1 presents a selection of the commitments received and illustrates the range of activities in which companies can and have become involved.

Resource-Based Giving.

The increasingly competitive global environment has heightened pressure for efficiency in all areas, including community service. A key goal of corporate community service is to get the most good possible from each dollar spent on giving. Companies often find that they can achieve the greatest good by providing services that fit their resources and competencies. LensCrafters provides vision care because it can do so more efficiently and effectively than can a business that does not specialize in eye care. Similarly, VH1 works with music and musicians on a daily basis, so they are able to use their access to expertise and resources to support music education in the public schools.

Resource-based giving involves assessing a firm's resources and competencies and determining where sharing those resources and competencies would accomplish the most good. In the aftermath of the attack on the World Trade Center, rescue workers were using cell phones around the clock in a situation where they couldn't afford to have a dead battery but didn't have the time or electricity to recharge phones. Electric Fuel Corporation donated 500 Instant Power cell phone chargers and batteries to keep the

---

SEARCH THE WEB

A CHARITY FOR CHARITIES

Business Community Connections (**http://www.bcconnect ions.org.uk**) is a charity devoted to helping other charities forge connections with business. Based in the United Kingdom, Business Community Connections provides a free online resource to enable nonprofit organizations to gain support from business in a range of forms, including cash donations, sponsorship, employee volunteers, and gifts in-kind. They also disseminate research on the business community partnership. On a local level, they provided training courses and set up partnerships between like-minded organizations.

FIGURE 15-1

Examples of Commitments Made to America's Promise—The Alliance for Youth

Company	Community Service Commitment
Financial Resources	
Ford Motor Company Fund	Invested $5 million in the development and implementation of *Promise Stations*, an online gathering place where people share information, ideas, events, and other resources supporting children and youth.
Sears, Roebuck, and Co.	Awarded grants to help strengthen Communities of Promise.
MBNA	Made a $2 million commitment to help strengthen America's Promise's operational efforts.
In-Kind	
Sappi Fine Paper	Provides America's Promise with paper used to print the Promise Letter and the Annual Report.
GTECH	Installs After School Advantage (ASA) computer centers in existing after-school programs across the country. Each center includes approximately $25,000 worth of customized software and technology equipment.
Microsoft	Provided $480,000 for software to help America's Promise address the digital divide.
Human Resources	
Starwood Hotels and Resorts	Launched company-wide community service initiative, which encourages employees to volunteer their time in efforts to improve the communities in which they work.
Wachovia	Employees have volunteered more than 2.4 million hours since 1997, serving in schools as literacy tutors, mentors, and parent volunteers. They have committed 3 million additional hours of employee volunteer involvement by the end of 2004, giving each employee 4 hours per month of paid time away from work.
CVS/pharmacy	Offers job shadowing and internship opportunites to introduce young people to the pharmacy industry. Local CVS pharmacies also work with community organizations.

SOURCE: America's Promise—The Alliance for Youth Fact Sheet (2004).

phones working. With their head office located in lower Manhattan, only a 10-minute walk from the scene of the tragedy, they were able to hand over their entire inventory to the rescue effort.[11] In another example of resource-based giving, Aerial Communications of Minneapolis and St. Paul donated wireless phones and air time to crime-prevention block clubs throughout the twin cities.[12] Wireless communications companies have contributed to public safety and education throughout the country by donating the equipment and air time nonprofit organizations cannot afford. Information technology (IT) firms have found their capabilities to be in great demand. Because many nonprofits are technologically behind, the skills and resources of technology-based firms can make significant differences in nonprofit operations. IT workers have given their time to causes as diverse as the Mount Washington weather observatory in New Hampshire, the Berkeley Symphony in California, and the Edmondson Youth Outreach Center in Omaha, Nebraska.[13]

Drug companies have also found they can accomplish more by drawing on their specific resources. In conjunction with the World Health Organization (WHO), SmithKline

Beecham has launched a 20-year, $1.7 billion program to eradicate elephantiasis, a disease that affects about 120 million people in Asia, South America, and Africa. The plan is to give annual doses of albendazole to the 1.1 billion people worldwide who are at risk of infection by the disease. To accomplish its goal, SmithKline will donate several billion doses of the drug, as well as technical assistance and health-education support. Similarly, Merck has worked with WHO to provide free ivermectin to treat patients with river blindness in Africa, and it will help support the elephantiasis project by donating ivermectin for clinical trials to determine the drug's ability to treat elephantiasis when used jointly with albendazole.[14]

Managing Community Involvement

For discussion purposes, we are separating our treatment of managing community involvement from that of managing corporate philanthropy. It should be kept in mind, however, that in reality this separation is impossible to achieve because there are significant overlaps between these two areas. Corporate philanthropy involves primarily the giving of financial resources. Community involvement focuses on other issues in the business/community relationship, especially the contribution of managerial and employee time and talent. This section addresses these broader community issues; a later section of this chapter deals with the more specific issue of managing corporate philanthropy.

Business Stake in the Community.
When one speaks with corporate executives in the fields of community and civic affairs and examines community affairs manuals and other corporate publications, one sees a broad array of reasons why companies need to keep abreast of the issues, problems, and changes expressed as community needs. One central reason is directly related to self-interest and self-preservation. For example, companies usually have a significant physical presence in the community and want to protect that investment. Issues of interest to them are zoning regulations, the threat of neighborhood deterioration, corporate property taxes, the community tax base, and the availability of an adequately trained workforce.[15]

A second major reason companies need to stay abreast of community needs and problems is that certain issues involve direct or indirect benefits to them. Examples of such issues include health services, social services, community services, the physical environment, the appearance of the community, and the overall quality of life. A third reason has to do with the company's reputation and image in the community. For example, companies want to be thought of as responsible corporate citizens by residents, employees, and competitors. Companies may have expertise that can help solve community problems, and they want to build a reserve of community goodwill.[16]

Development of a Community Action Program.
The motivation for developing a **community action program** is evident when one considers the stake a firm has in the community. Likewise, the community represents a major stakeholder of business. Therefore, business has an added incentive to be systematic about its relationship with the community. The four steps in developing a community action program, as articulated by the Norton Company, provide a useful framework for approaching the community from a managerial frame of reference.[17]

These four steps are

1. Knowing the community
2. Knowing the company's resources
3. Selecting projects
4. Monitoring projects

These steps may be beneficial whether the company is considering specific community projects or is attempting to build a strong, long-term relationship with community stakeholders.

Knowing the Community.   A key to developing worthwhile community involvement programs is knowing the community in which the business resides. This is a research step that requires management to assess the characteristics of the local area. Every locale has particular characteristics that can help shape social programs of involvement. Who lives in the community? What is its ethnic composition? What is its unemployment level? Are there inner-city problems or pockets of poverty? What are other organizations doing? What are the really pressing social needs of the area? What is the community's morale?

Knowledge of community leadership is another factor. Is the leadership progressive? Is the leadership cohesive and unified, or is it fragmented? If it is fragmented, the company may have to make difficult choices about the groups with which it wants to work. If the community's current approach to social issues is well led, "jumping on the bandwagon" may be all that is necessary. If the community's leadership is not well organized, the company may want to provide an impetus and an agenda for restructuring or revitalizing the leadership.

Knowing the Company's Resources.   Effective addressing of various community needs requires an inventory and assessment of the company's resources and competencies. What is the variety, mix, and range of resources—personnel, money, meeting space, equipment, and supplies? Many companies are willing to give employees time to engage in and support community projects. This involvement may be in the form of managerial assistance, technical assistance, or personnel. Wide spectra of abilities, skills, interests, potentials, and experience exist in most organizations. To put any of these resources to work, however, it is necessary to know what is available, to what extent it is available, on what terms it is available, and over what period of time it is available.

Selecting Projects.   The selection of community projects for company involvement grows out of the matching of community stakeholders' needs with company resources. Frequently, because there are many such matches, the company must be selective in choosing among them. Sometimes companies develop and refine policies or guidelines to help in the selection process. These policies are extremely useful, because they further delineate areas in which the company may be involved and provide perspective for channeling the organization's energies. Frank Koch has spelled out guidelines for developing a strategy for community involvement.[18] The following list summarizes some of these guidelines.

- Community involvement must be planned and organized with the same care and energy that are devoted to other parts of the business.
- Community projects should meet the same measure of cost-effectiveness as that applied to investments in research, marketing, production, or administration.
- The corporation should capitalize on its talents and resources. Those responsible should get involved in things they understand. The company should look at social problems that affect its realm of operations.

- Employees should be involved in community programs. The programs should focus on some of the things that affect and interest those employees.
- The corporation should get involved in the communities it knows, the people it knows best, and the needs that have the best chance of being fulfilled and are important goals of the community.
- Corporate policy should allow continuing support of established causes while new initiatives are being sought.
- The best kind of support is that which helps others help themselves.

Policies and guidelines can go a long way toward rationalizing and systematizing business involvement in the community. Such policy statements should be developed and articulated throughout the organization to help provide a unified focus for company efforts.

An excellent example of a community project that was carefully chosen and is likely to meet most of the guidelines discussed here is the Ronald McDonald House sponsored by McDonald's Corporation. These houses, which annually provide shelter and solace for half a million people whose children are seriously ill, were begun in 1974. By 2004, there were 240 such houses in 25 countries. McDonald's employs the same pattern in all the communities in which the houses are located. Each is operated by a nonprofit corporation and is staffed by volunteers, except for a paid manager. Each house is located near a hospital that treats children, and families are charged a nominal amount if they can afford it and nothing if they cannot. The families may remain for as long as their children are undergoing treatment.[19]

Monitoring Projects. Monitoring company projects involves review and control. Follow-up is necessary to ensure that the projects are being executed according to plans and on schedule. Feedback from the various steps in the process provides the information management needs to monitor progress. In later chapters, we will elaborate on the managerial approach to dealing with various social issues. The guidelines previously listed, however, provide some insights into the development of business/community stakeholder relationships. As we stated earlier, community involvement is a discretionary or philanthropic activity in our corporate social performance model. The costs are significant but the potential returns, for both the corporation and the community, are great. Just as other business functions, it should be carefully managed. The Center for Corporate Citizenship at Boston College has developed a set of seven management practices, processes, and policies that represent a global standard of excellence in community involvement. These are listed in Figure 15-2.

Community Involvement of Foreign-Based Firms

Another indication of the growing sophistication with which companies are developing relationships with communities is the community involvement policies and practices of foreign-based business firms that have located in the United States. It has been extensively documented that foreign direct investing in the United States and its communities is a growing phenomenon.[20] Some observers have questioned the social consequences of foreign direct investment. It is not surprising, therefore, that researchers have sought to ascertain the extent to which these firms are becoming good "corporate citizens."

Foreign-owned companies doing business in the United States were surveyed to discover their community involvement perspectives and practices.[21] Among this group of firms, it was found that:

- Eighty-one percent had community involvement policies.

FIGURE 15-2

Standards of Excellence in Corporate Community Involvement

Standard 1: Leadership
Senior executives demonstrate support, commitment, and participation in community involvement efforts.

Standard 2: Issues Management
The company identifies and monitors issues important to its operations and reputation.

Standard 3: Relationship Building
Company management recognizes that building and maintaining relationships of trust with the community is a critical component of company strategy and operations.

Standard 4: Strategy
The company develops and implements a strategic plan for community programs and responses that is based on mutual issues, goals, and concerns of the company and the community.

Standard 5: Accountability
All levels of the organization have specific roles and responsibilities for meeting community involvement objectives.

Standard 6: Infrastructure
The company incorporates systems and policies to support, communicate, and institutionalize community involvement objectives.

Standard 7: Measurement
The company establishes an ongoing process for evaluating community involvement strategies, activities, and programs and their impact on the company and the community.

SOURCE: Center for Corporate Citizenship at Boston College, http://www.bc.edu/corporatecitizenship.

- Seventy-one percent reported that community expectations were a "very important" or "moderately important" part of their business plans.
- Their corporate giving levels and patterns approximated those of domestic companies.
- Over half reported being satisfied with their companies' community programs, but a significant number—39 percent—felt they should be more involved in their communities.

In terms of their motivations for community involvement, the foreign direct investors gave reasons very similar to those of U.S. executives[22]—namely:

- They felt a moral obligation to be involved (61 percent).
- They were responding to community expectations (56 percent).
- They felt that community involvement strengthened their corporate image (56 percent).
- They felt they were acting in enlightened self-interest (50 percent).

In interviews, these executives stated that if community involvement was done well, it allowed the business to become an accepted and valued member of society, which was good for its image with customers, employees, governments, and the wider community. Although their involvement was dominated by cash giving, the foreign-based companies had initiated other community programs, such as employee volunteerism and sponsorship (e.g., arts or sports events).[23]

In another study of the "corporate citizenship" practices and viewpoints of foreign direct investors, Pinkston and Carroll reported that these investors had "corporate citizenship orientations" that were quite similar to those of U.S.–based firms. They concluded that, based on these findings, there was little cause for concern over the increasing foreign presence in the United States. Foreign direct investors want to "fit in," and they perceive involvement with community stakeholders as a vital and integral part of that process.[24]

CORPORATE PHILANTHROPY OR BUSINESS GIVING

The word *philanthropy* comes from the Greek "*philien*," which means "to love," and "*anthropos*," which means "mankind."[25] Thus the dictionary defines **philanthropy** as "a desire to help mankind as indicated by acts of charity; love of mankind."[26] One more restricted contemporary usage of the word "philanthropy" is "business giving." In this section, we will concentrate on the voluntary giving of financial resources by business. One problem with the dictionary definition is that the motive for the giving is characterized as charitable, benevolent, or generous. In actual practice, it is difficult to assess the true motives behind businesses'—or anyone's—giving of themselves or their financial resources.

To be sure, people value the philanthropy of the business sector. A 2004 "Issue Brief" by Business for Social Responsibility cites studies that show the positive impact that corporate philanthropy can have on a firm's reputation. For example, a Cone, Inc., study found that 84 percent of those surveyed factor a company's commitment to social issues into a decision of which businesses they want in their community. Furthermore, 77 percent looked at social commitment when selecting an employer, and 66 percent considered social commitment when making investment decisions. Similarly a 2002 WalkerInformation study that was commissioned by the Council on Foundations found that corporate citizenship leads to more positive stakeholder attitudes toward the corporation and that these improved attitudes have positive performance consequences. For example, employees remain with the company longer, customers continue to make purchases from the company, and community leaders value the company as a neighbor.[27]

SEARCH THE WEB

WHO GIVES TO WHOM?

The Foundation Center is an independent, nonprofit information clearinghouse that collects, organizes, analyzes, and disseminates information on foundations, corporate giving, and related subjects. The center publishes the National Directory of Corporate Giving, which provides information on more than 2,900 corporate philanthropic programs, detailing more than 1,900 corporate foundations and more than 990 direct-giving programs. A wealth of information on corporate philanthropy and related topics can be found on the Foundation Center's Web site at **http://www.fdncenter.org**.

A Brief History of Corporate Philanthropy

Business philanthropy of one kind or another can be traced back many decades. It was in the 1920s that the most significant effort to "translate the new social consciousness of management into action" emerged in the form of organized corporate philanthropy.[28] Before World War I, steps had been taken toward establishing systematic, federated fund-raising for community services. The early successes of the YMCA, the war chests, welfare federations, Community Chests, colleges and universities, and hospitals provided impetus for these groups to organize their solicitations. The business response to the opportunity to help community needs was varied. At one extreme, large enterprises such as the Bell Telephone system, with branches, offices, and subsidiaries in thousands of communities, contributed to literally thousands of civic and social organizations. Smaller

---

Ethics in Practice

TUGGING THE HEART OR TWISTING THE ARM?

While working for a large corporation, I received numerous e-mails telling me of the large charitable contribution fund in which the company participates. All employees were highly encouraged to attend a town-hall meeting where other employees and managers spoke of how the fund had affected their lives and showed videos of the good work the fund had done. Top executives traveled to the town-hall meetings to promote the campaign and encourage 100 percent employee participation. They told us to ask our fellow employees if they had contributed yet. They wanted to reach a goal of $1 million and believed that everyone should be able to contribute. Furthermore, all managers were expected to contribute. There was even documentation on the company's intranet Web site with guidelines for how much to give. Although the company claims all donations (or lack thereof) are anonymous and have no effect on promotions or job performance ratings, many wondered if that was entirely true. This was not the first company to

strongly encourage me to contribute to its fund drive and I doubt it will be the last.

1. Why do companies participate in charitable fund programs? Is it for societal recognition, to aid a worthy cause, or is it some combination? If different firms differ in their motivation—why might that be so?

2. Is it ethical for a company to solicit voluntary charitable contributions from employees? Can they be truly voluntary? If so, how should these campaigns be designed and implemented? Where would you draw the line?

3. If companies no longer participate in charitable fund campaigns, what would be the repercussion for the charities? Does that affect your answer?

4. If you worked in this company, what would you do? Why? If you choose to contribute, what would be your driving motivation?

Contributed by Melissa S. Magoon

---

firms, such as the companies in small mill towns of North Carolina, supported schools, housing projects, religious activities, and community welfare agencies with a degree of enthusiasm that exceeded most nineteenth-century paternalism.

Corporate giving in the period from 1918 to 1929 was dominated by the Community Chest movement. In the period from 1929 to 1935, there was an attempt to allow business to deduct up to 5 percent of its pretax net income for its community donations. The years 1935 to 1945, marked by the Great Depression and World War II, did not show an expansion of business giving. The period from 1945 to 1960 saw new horizons of corporate responsibility, and the period since about 1960 can truly be called a period in which social responsibility has flourished and gone beyond simple corporate giving. But because we are focusing on corporate contributions to the community, we will exclude those broader endeavors that began in the 1960s. The debate continues about whether businesses should give away money and, if so, how much they should give.

Another debate arose over proposed federal legislation that would have required companies to disclose which charities they support and how much money they give. Although companies are required to disclose the money they give through foundations because of the tax benefits derived from the foundation's tax-exempt status, companies need not disclose direct donations. This has renewed the age-old debate about the role of business in society. Proponents of disclosure contend that the money belongs to the shareholders and they alone have the right to determine where it will go. Representative Paul Gillmor (R-Ohio) said that he introduced the disclosure bill, which was cosponsored by Representative Michael G. Oxley (R-Ohio) and Representative Thomas Manton (D-New York), because he had sat on corporate boards and observed executives distributing corporate assets to their pet charities while ignoring shareholders. Gillmor's concern was shared by law professors such as Charles M. Elson of Stetson University, who argued that philanthropy often only serves to glorify corporate managers and that, unless the philanthropy clearly benefits the company, it represents a waste of corporate assets. A few nonprofits, such as the American Red Cross, also agreed that disclosure would be good public policy. Surprisingly, the National Society of Fundraising Executives even supported disclosure, arguing that it would help the image of philanthropy, which has been hurt by scandals in recent years.[29] This broad-based support notwithstanding, most corporations and nonprofits had expressed concern that disclosure would have a chilling effect on corporate donations. Their arguments include that charitable giving is a business decision, that it would provide competitors with information about a firm's strategy, that it might incite controversy with special-interest groups, and that the paperwork would become an administrative burden.[30] In March 2000, the corporate accountability bill was withdrawn by Representative Gillmor.

The issue resurfaced in the wake of the Enron and WorldCom accounting scandals, when there were revelations about corporations giving large donations to corporate officers' pet causes. For example, Enron gave large donations to a hospital chaired by a member of its audit committee. This concern was factored into the reform legislation developed to enhance corporate accountability. The House developed a bill that included a requirement for corporations to report contributions to a nonprofit organization if any of the corporation's directors or members of their immediate family are members of that nonprofit's board. This would have applied to contributions over $10,000 made by the corporation or any officer of the corporation in the last five years, as well as any other activity that provides a "material benefit" to the nonprofit, including lobbying. This House bill passed as did a Senate version, and so a conference committee met to work out the differences between the two bills. The result, of course, was the Sarbanes–Oxley Act of 2002, which did not contain the philanthropy disclosure requirements from the original House bill.[31]

In spite of this setback, calls for transparency in corporate giving continue. Allegations have arisen that some philanthropic dollars have found their way to terrorist organizations. Corporate philanthropy must now follow the stipulations of the USA Patriot Act and Executive Order No. 13224. They ask that grant makers obtain detailed personal information about the organization's board and senior staff at all the grantee's locations as well as names of all of the organization's subcontractors when grants are being made in areas designated as areas of concern. They also ask that these names be checked against a number of nonconsolidated official lists of people and organizations associated with terrorist activities. In addition, funders are expected to identify all institutions with which the organization has banking relationships and evaluate those institutions with respect to money-laundering laws. According to the Committee to Encourage Corporate Philanthropy (http://www.corphilanthropy.org), many corporations are considering cutting back their giving programs in the affected areas because of concerns about liability and the cost of the additional administrative burdens implied by the guidelines.[32]

Another issue that has added to the calls for transparency is a concern that nonprofits are being set up to get around the campaign financing laws regarding "soft money" contributions. For example, the National Committee for Responsive Philanthropy (NCRP) and Common Cause have filed complaints with the IRS and the House Ethics Committee that House Majority Leader Tom DeLay (R–Texas) is using a nonprofit organization for political purposes. They charge that Delay's charity, "Celebrations for Children," provides a way for high-end donors to buy access to Delay and other prominent politicians. According to NCRP executive director Rick Cohen, the charity "evades campaign financing laws through political fundraising disguised as charity." Corporations are under no obligation to report their charitable giving nor to report what that giving has bought them in terms of access to politicians.[33]

Giving to the "Third Sector"—The Nonprofits

According to philanthropist John D. Rockefeller III, business giving is necessary to support what has been called the **third sector**—the nonprofit sector. The first two sectors—business and government—receive support through profits and taxes. The third sector (which includes hundreds of thousands of churches, museums, hospitals, libraries, private colleges and universities, and performing arts groups) depends on philanthropy for support. Philanthropy gives these institutions the crucial margin that assures them of their most precious asset—their independence.[34]

Why Do Companies Give? Perhaps it would be more worthwhile to know why companies give to charitable causes rather than to know how much they give. There are several ways to approach this question. We get initial insights when we consider the five categories of corporate contributions programs identified by the National Directory of Corporate Charity, as shown in Figure 15-3.[35] The motivations that are reflected in these categories range from pure self-interest to a desire to practice good corporate citizenship by supporting both traditional and innovative programs in the community.

Saiia, Carroll, and Buchholtz found that corporate giving managers believe their firms are becoming more strategic in their giving and that top managers are requiring greater strategic accountability in their corporate giving programs. They also found that firms that are more "exposed" to the environment, i.e., more open and vulnerable to the environment, are more likely to engage in strategic philanthropy.[36] In another study, Fry, Keim, and Meiners found that corporate contributions are motivated by profit considerations that influence both advertising expenditures and corporate giving. They concluded that

FIGURE 15-3

Categories of Corporate Contributions Programs

1. *The Nondonor*—This is a firm for which no evidence of charitable giving was found.

2. *The "What's in It for Us" Donor*—With this firm, most contributions relate to the company's direct interest or to the welfare of its employees.

3. *The "Company President Believes in Art Support" Donor*—With this firm, most contributions relate to the company's direct interest, employees' welfare, or management's interest.

4. *The "We Are a Good Citizen" Donor*—Here a substantial portion of the company's giving provides support for traditional nonprofit institutions.

5. *The "We Care" Donor*—Here some funds go to newer organizations and established organizations that deal with nontraditional issues.

corporate giving is a complement to advertising and is, therefore, a profit-motivated expense.[37] This perspective can certainly be supported by observing Philip Morris. In a year when they donated $75 million to charitable causes, they spent $100 million on advertising to publicize them.[38]

As economic pressures and increased international competitiveness force companies to be more careful with their earnings, we should not be surprised to see the profit motive coexisting with loftier goals in corporate contributions programs. In a subsequent section of this chapter, we show that philanthropy can be "strategic," which means that corporate giving can be aligned with the firm's economic or profitability objectives.

To Whom Do Companies Give?

During the course of any budget year, companies receive numerous requests for contributions from a wide variety of applicants. Companies must then weigh both quantitative and qualitative factors to arrive at decisions regarding the recipients of their gifts. By looking at the beneficiaries of corporate contributions, we can estimate the value business places on various societal needs in the community.

Data on corporate contributions show that business giving is distributed among five major categories of recipients in the following order of emphasis: (1) education, (2) health and human services, (3) civic and community activities, (4) culture and the arts, and (5) other or unspecified. These emphases, which The Conference Board measures on a regular basis, show a remarkable stability over time.[39] A brief discussion of each of these five categories will help explain the nature of business's involvement in philanthropy.

Education. Most of the corporate contributions in this category have gone to higher education—colleges and universities. The major educational recipients have been capital grants (including endowments), unrestricted operating grants, departmental and research grants, scholarships and fellowships, and employee matching gifts. Also included in this category are contributions to educational groups (for example, the United Negro College Fund and the Council for Financial Aid to Education) and to primary and secondary schools.

As we noted earlier, business's most frequently reported reason for supporting higher education has been to increase the pool of trained personnel. This has obvious credibility, because higher education institutions do, indeed, form the resource base from which business fills its managerial and professional positions. Although contributions to educational institutions rank high in business giving, companies do not always give blindly and expect nothing in return. Over the years, there has been some controversy about whether business should give to educational institutions that do not support the free enterprise values so important to business. The basic issue has been whether support of education should be "with strings attached" or "without strings attached."

Those who argue that business should give to education without strings attached think that attempts to dictate to educational institutions will create conflict between the institutions and industry. Louis W. Cabot, former chairman of the board of Cabot Corporation, argued that it is neither wise nor advantageous for business to limit its gifts to institutions that support free enterprise. His belief is that the corporate self-interest criterion is both illusory and dangerous. It is illusory in that it calls for sweeping generalizations about faculty members; it is dangerous because it tends to discourage all educational giving. He believes, in addition, that if a company genuinely wants to help education function with maximum effectiveness, it should support schools as a whole rather than try to control the use of its funds. On the other side of the issue have been those who think business ought to be more selective in its giving. Robert H. Malott, former chairman of the board of FMC Corporation, argued that corporate self-interest ought to serve as a guide for business giving to education. Malott is especially concerned about corporations giving financial support to schools and colleges that teach the views of radical economists and others who want government to grow at the expense of free enterprise.[40]

Unfortunately, there are no data to tell us which of these extreme positions is the most effective; they represent opposite philosophical postures. A philosophy tempered with the belief that managers should exercise some discretion over their corporate giving to education and at the same time serve the company's self-interest would achieve economic and social goals simultaneously.

Health and Human Services.   The major reason that health and welfare is one of the largest categories of business giving is the huge amount donated to such federated drives as the United Way. Dating back to the Community Chest movement, business has traditionally cooperated with federated giving mechanisms. Money given to federated drives usually goes directly to assist various agencies in a local community. Great public pressure is placed on businesses to support actively such federated campaigns, and so it is not surprising that this category is one of the largest beneficiaries. Business hopes, just as the community does, that such consolidated efforts will lend some order to the requests of major recipients in the community that business has chosen to support.[41]

In addition to federated drives, major recipients in this category include hospitals, youth agencies, and other local health and welfare agencies. Hospitals represent an obviously important need in most communities. They receive financial support for capital investments (new buildings and equipment), operating funds, and matching employee gifts. Youth agencies include such groups as the YMCA, YWCA, Boy Scouts, Girl Scouts, and Boys and Girls Clubs. Because a great part of the turmoil in the United States during the late 1960s and early 1970s had its source in the dissatisfaction of young people, many of whom were antagonistic toward large corporations, it is quite logical for business to include youth as a prominent part of its health and welfare contributions. Dreyer's Grand Ice Cream, Inc., focuses its philanthropic activities on youth to enable those youth to "develop individual initiative and talent in order for them to become contributing members of their communities and caretakers of the communities' values for the next generation."[42]

Civic and Community Activities.   This category of business giving represents a wide variety of philanthropic activities in the community. The dominant contributions in this category are those given in support of community improvement activities, environment and ecology, nonacademic research organizations (for example, the Brookings Institution, the Committee for Economic Development, and the Urban League), and neighborhood renewal.

General Mills saw the importance of community involvement when the nickname of Minneapolis went from the "City of Nice" to "Murderapolis." General Mills executives hired a consultant to analyze crime data and found that Hawthorne, just five miles from the company headquarters, was one of the city's most violent neighborhoods. In what became known as the "Hawthorne Huddle," they worked with residents, community leaders, politicians, and law enforcement to identify strategies for improvement. General Mills devoted thousands of employee hours and $2.5 million to ridding Hawthorne of its problems. The murder rate fell 32 percent and robberies fell 56 percent. Dilapidated houses were rebuilt and a new elementary school was built over bulldozed crack houses.[43]

Corning, Inc., is more than the biggest employer in Corning, New York. It is also a benefactor, landlord, and, some say, social engineer. In the past, Corning, New York, has been a company town, with Corning, Inc., being involved in providing affordable housing, day-care facilities, and new business development. Now, its efforts are more focused. The company plans to convert a remote, insular town into a place that will appeal to professionals. Its goal is to turn Corning into a town that offers social options for young singles, support for new families, and cultural diversity for minorities. Among its activities, Corning bought the run-down bars in one section of town because they did not fit in with the company's redevelopment plans. Employing a $5,000 payment and continuous lobbying, the firm got the dump owner to move. Corning is even trying to develop a region that will be less dependent on its company headquarters and its 15 factories. The company also purchased and revitalized an auto racetrack and convinced a supermarket chain to locate there. Corning continuously works to attract new business to the region, and it built the local Hilton Hotel, the local museum, and the city library.[44] In 2003, *Fortune* magazine ranked Owens Corning fifth in the building materials, glass category, in its list of America's Most-Admired Companies.[45]

Culture and the Arts.   American companies donated a total of $1.56 billion to arts organizations in 2001, according to a survey by the Business Committee for the Arts. This represents a one-third increase over the total of gifts in 1997 before adjusting for inflation. Two of the most prominent organized efforts on the part of business to support the arts are the Business Committee for the Arts (BCA) and the Arts and Business Council. Formed in the mid-1960s, the BCA is a private nationwide group that was designed to "unite corporate money with artistic need." The Arts and Business Council was also formed in the mid-1960s and initially focused on the New York area. Both organizations now have affiliates throughout the United States.[46]

It is interesting to consider why business gives to the arts. Companies seem to gain none of the direct benefits that they receive from their donations to education. As with other philanthropic categories, businesses claim various motives for their giving. There are those who argue altruistically that the reason for business's largesse is that it recognizes that art contributes to the kinds of vitality and creativity that are important to society. Alessandro DiGuisto, director of the Deutsche Bank America's Foundation, argues that giving to the arts is essential to maintaining healthy communities and consistent with DB's corporate commitment to community revitalization.[47] On the other hand, there are business executives who argue that support for the arts has been at least in part a reflection of self-interest. Paul H. Eliker, former president of SCM Corporation, contends that companies give to the arts in order to gain recognition or visibility and for general image building.[48] He claims that the great patrons of the Renaissance—the Medici's and Pope Julius II—supported culture and the arts for much the same reason: to associate themselves with the grandeur of the times.

Recipients of business donations to the arts are not likely to turn down such contributions because the givers' motives may not be purely altruistic. Business giving, whatever the intent, does benefit the giver and the receiver, as well as the general public.

Managing Corporate Philanthropy

As performance pressures on business have continued and intensified, companies more and more have had to turn their attention to managing corporate philanthropy. Early on, managers did not subject their contributions to the same kinds of rigorous analysis given to expenditures for plants and equipment, inventory, product development, marketing, and a host of other budgetary items. This began to change in the early 1980s because cutbacks in federal spending on charitable causes created an increasing need for contributions by business. At the same time, however, the economy was struggling through its worst recession in 50 years. Demands that business become more competitive became the authoritative view on corporate survival. It became increasingly clear that business had to reconcile its economic and social goals, both of which were essential.[49]

By 2001, the growth of corporate giving had slowed once again. *Business Week* offered several explanations. The recession in 1991 caused executives to cast a sharper eye on philanthropy expenditures. After cutting philanthropy in the early 1990s, many executives never returned to their old level of giving because fierce competition and the inability to raise prices made it more difficult. Mergers and acquisitions also slowed the rate of giving. The National Committee for Responsive Philanthropy surveyed 124 corporations and found that only one of 46 companies involved in a merger would increase their giving over the previous year's level. The study didn't ask whether giving would decrease. Finally, cause marketing had moved many contributions to the marketing budget, making it harder to assess the true level of corporate giving.[50]

In the two weeks following the attack on the World Trade Center, corporations gave over $120 million to relief funds: This was an unprecedented level of corporate giving.[51] According to a 2003 survey by the Chronicle of Corporate Philanthropy, however, corporate giving then declined.[52] Of course, it is always difficult to know the true impact of these numbers, because some of the corporate proceeds that go to nonprofits are not included in philanthropy figures.[53] The volunteer programs previously discussed are not included in calculations of philanthropy dollars. In addition, cause-related marketing is generally deemed a marketing expense and so does not necessarily contribute to the official tally of a company's charitable giving.[54]

Public Purpose Partnerships.

As a broad response to this growing need to reconcile financial and social goals, both of which were deemed by business to be desirable and necessary, the concept of public purpose partnerships evolved.[55] A public purpose partnership occurs when a for-profit business enters into a cooperative arrangement with a nonprofit organization for their mutual advantage. Businesses see in public purpose partnerships the opportunity for simultaneous achievement of economic and philanthropic objectives. An example of a public purpose partnership is the one between 3M Company and the University of Minnesota. The 3M Company gave $1 million to the MBA program at Minnesota. Rather than just give the money and run, 3M officials formed a committee with university officials to discuss how the two organizations could work together. This was seen as a smart move on 3M's part, because about 15 percent of its employees are alumni/alumnae of the university.[56]

Another major example of a public purpose partnership involved the McDonald's Corporation and Georgia Institute of Technology (Georgia Tech) entering into a multi-million-dollar sponsorship and marketing partnership. The arrangement called for McDonald's to give Georgia Tech $5.5 million to complete the financing of the $12.5 million renovation of its Alexander Memorial Coliseum. As part of the agreement, the building in which Georgia Tech basketball games are played was named the McDonald's Center. In addition, the McDonald's name was placed on the basketball court and on tickets and program covers for all coliseum events. The deal included other signage, advertising, and promotional elements. Although the partnership was actually formed between

McDonald's and the Georgia Tech athletic association, McDonald's representatives said they thought it could lead to other interactions and arrangements in academic and research-related activities.[57]

In 2002, the Clorox Company formed a partnership with the East Bay Community Foundation. Community foundations are nonprofit organizations that specialize in evaluating nonprofit organizations and responding to requests for funding. Clorox knew that the knowledge and expertise that the East Bay Community Foundation had in knowing local nonprofit organizations would help them to better manage their philanthropic funds. This would help to further their goal of improving the quality of life in Oakland, California, and its surrounding communities, the area in which Clorox is based.[58]

Public purpose partnerships take on many different forms. Two of the most important are strategic philanthropy and cause-related marketing. Other partnership options include sponsorships, vendor relationships, licensing agreements, and in-kind donations.[59] We will consider strategic philanthropy and cause-related marketing in detail.

Strategic Philanthropy.   **Strategic philanthropy** is an approach by which corporate giving and other philanthropic endeavors of a firm are designed in a way that best fits with the firm's overall mission, goals, or objectives. This implies that the firm has some idea of what its overall strategy is and that it is able to articulate its missions, goals, or objectives. One goal of all firms is profitability. Therefore, one requirement of strategic philanthropy is to make as direct a contribution as possible to the financial goals of the firm. Philanthropy has long been thought to be in the long-range economic interest of the firm. Strategic philanthropy simply presses for a more direct or immediate contribution of philanthropy to the firm's economic success.

An important way in which philanthropy can be made strategic is to bring contribution programs into sharper alignment with business endeavors. This means that each firm should pursue those social programs that have a direct rather than an indirect bearing on its success. Thus, a local bank should logically pursue people-oriented projects in the community in which it resides; a manufacturer might pursue programs having to do with environmental protection or technological advancement.

A third way to make philanthropy strategic is to ensure that it is well planned and managed rather than handled haphazardly and without direction. When a program is planned, this implies that it has clearly delineated goals, is properly organized and staffed, and is administered in accordance with certain established policies. Figure 15-4 presents *Business for Social Responsibility*'s recommendations for best practices in the implementation of a philanthropy program.

Strategic philanthropy must find the place of overlap where the philanthropy provides both social and economic benefits. In a recent *Harvard Business Review* article, Michael Porter and Mark Kramer argued that few companies have effectively taken advantage of the competitive advantage corporate philanthropy can provide. They consider strategic philanthropy to be a myth—simply semantics that help companies to rationalize their contributions. To be truly strategic, philanthropy must be congruent with a company's competitive context, which consists of four interrelated elements: factor conditions, demand conditions, the context for strategy and rivalry, and related and supporting industries.[60]

Factor conditions are the available inputs for productions. Porter and Kramer point to DreamWorks as an example of a company that uses strategic philanthropy to effectively improve its factor conditions. They created a program that provides training to low-income and disadvantaged youth in the skills needed to work in the entertainment indus-

FIGURE 15-4

Implementation of an Effective Strategic Philanthropy Program

An effective strategic philanthropy program should incorporate the following practices:
1. Integrate philanthropy into strategic goals and company mission.
2. Connect philanthropy with other community involvement programs.
3. Budget appropriately for philanthropy.
4. Ensure effective program infrastructure.
5. Formalize policies and guidelines for funding.
6. Involve employees in philanthropy-related activities.
7. Incorporate stakeholder communication.
8. Develop long-term business/nonprofit partnerships.

SOURCE: BST Staff, "BSR Issue Briefs: Philanthropy," Business for Social Responsibility, http://www.bsr.org.

try. Of course the societal benefits of an improved educational system are clear. While providing these social benefits, DreamWorks also enhances the labor pool from which they can draw. This not only strengthens the company but the industry as a whole, as well.[61] The General Mills example of improving the community surrounding their headquarters also addresses factor conditions by improving the general quality of life and the local infrastructure. The partnership previously mentioned between 3M and the University of Minnesota also addresses factor conditions by addressing the training that business students receive.

Demand conditions are concerned with the nature of the company's customers and the local market. Philanthropy can influence the local market's size and quality. Porter and Kramer point to Apple's long-held policy of donating computers to public schools. By introducing young people and their teachers to computers, Apple expands their market. They also increase the sophistication of their customer base, which benefits a differentiated product like Apple sells.[62] Similarly, Burger King focuses its philanthropic efforts on highly focused programs to help students, teachers, and schools.[63] This program enhances name recognition in its target population of consumers.

The context for strategy and rivalry can also be influenced by strategic philanthropy. Porter and Kramer point to the many corporations that support Transparency International as examples of firms using philanthropy to create a better environment for competition. Transparency International's mission is to deter and disclose corporate corruption around the world. The organization measures and publicizes corruption while pushing for stricter codes and enforcement. By supporting Transparency International, corporations are helping to build a better competitive environment—one that rewards fair competition.[64]

Related and supporting industries can also be strengthened through strategic philanthropy, thereby enhancing the productivity of companies. American Express provides an excellent example of a firm that uses philanthropy to strengthen its related and supporting industries. For almost 20 years, American Express has funded travel and tourism academies in secondary schools. The program trains teachers, supports curriculums, and provides both summer internships and industry mentors. It now operates in 10 countries, works with more than 3,000 schools, and has more than 120,000 students enrolled. A strong travel industry translates into important benefits for American Express.[65]

Finally, in his book titled *Corporate Social Investing*, Curt Weeden details the importance of selecting the right corporate giving manager to oversee philanthropic activities. First, the giving manager should be no more than one executive away from the CEO or chief operating officer (COO), with both a title and a level of compensation that reflect her or his position in the hierarchy. That person should have basic business skills as well as a solid knowledge of the profit-and-loss activities of the company. In addition, the giving manager should be aware of and interested in the nonprofit sector. Last, the giving manager must have the respect of fellow executives and the ability to be an effective company representative.[66]

Now let us turn our attention to a special kind of philanthropy that has become quite prevalent in recent years: cause-related marketing.

Cause-Related Marketing.

There is some debate as to whether or not cause-related marketing is really philanthropy. Porter and Kramer argue that it is marketing and nothing more.[67] However, because cause marketing represents a close linkage between a firm's financial objectives and corporate contributions, we will discuss it here. Stated in its simplest form, cause-related marketing is the direct linking of a business's product or service to a specified charity. Each time a consumer uses the service or buys the product, a donation is given to the charity by the business.[68] Cause-related marketing has, therefore, sometimes been referred to as "quid pro quo strategic philanthropy."

The term **cause-related marketing** was coined by the American Express Company to describe a program it began in 1983 in which it agreed to contribute a penny to the restoration of the Statue of Liberty every time one of its credit cards was used to make a purchase. The project generated $1.7 million for the statue restoration and a substantial increase in usage of the American Express card.[69] Since that time, companies have employed this same approach to raise millions of dollars for a wide variety of local and national causes.

Recently, cause-related marketing has given way to a new concept, **cause branding**. Cause branding represents a longer term commitment than cause marketing. It also is more directly related to the firm's line of business and their target audience. Avon Products, Inc., is a recognized leader in cause branding. Their target audience is women, and so they have developed an array of programs to raise awareness of breast cancer, a disease that mostly affects women. The company raises money for programs that provide low-income women with education and free screening. Avon sells products featuring the pink ribbon that is worn for breast cancer awareness and then donates proceeds from these products to nonprofit and university programs.[70]

The move to cause branding is likely to be successful as a marketing tool. A Cone/Roper *Cause-Related Trends Report: Evolution of Cause Branding* showed that 61 percent of consumers felt companies should make cause branding part of their regular business.[71] Moreover, 83 percent of Americans feel more positively disposed toward companies that support a cause about which they care, and 76 percent of consumers are more likely to select the more socially responsible brand when price and quality are equal. The benefits do not apply only to consumers: Employees react to cause branding as well. In companies with cause programs, 87 percent of employees indicate they feel strong loyalty, while only 67 percent feel strong loyalty in firms that do not have cause programs.[72] The findings of the 2000 Cone/Roper Executive Study show that cause branding strengthens internal corporate cultures and has a dramatic influence on employee pride, morale, and loyalty.[73]

For an example of how successful cause-related marketing can be, you need look no further than the shelves of your local grocery store for Newman's Own products. The company that began "as a lark" for Paul Newman now boasts annual sales of $190 million, and its profits are donated to a number of worthy causes. An article in *PR Week (US)* (2 February 2004 p10) points out that in fact "Newman's Own was involved in cause-related marketing before the term even existed." So successful is the brand's image that McDonald's recently chose Newman's Own salad dressings for a new line of healthy-choice salads. Read more about Newman's Own by logging on to InfoTrac College Edition at **http://www.infotrac-college.com** and keying record number A112722067.

Proponents of cause-related marketing argue that everyone involved in it comes out a winner. Business enhances its public image by being associated with a worthy cause and increases its sales at the same time. Nonprofit organizations get cash for their programs as well as enhanced marketing and public visibility made possible by business's expertise.

Critics of cause-related marketing suggest that there are issues that make the approach controversial. For nonprofit organizations that participate, one issue is the "taint of commercialism" that cause-related marketing may bring. The direct link between the nonprofit organization and the product being marketed may appear to be a promotional effort on the part of the nonprofit organization, and some may see this as compromising the organization's altruistic image. Other critics fear that if cause-related marketing becomes widespread, it could undermine the very basis of philanthropy. Still others fear that some corporations may use cause-related marketing as a substitute for, rather than a supplement to, regular corporate contributions. The consequence of this would be a zero net increase in the amount of funds available.[74]

Global Philanthropy.

Formal international philanthropy efforts are now part of global business strategies. Companies among the top 10 global contributors state that their contributions go where they have operations as well as a strong presence. In general, giving programs tend to focus on infrastructure needs, education, the environment, and health care. Some companies, such as IBM and Merck & Co., donate large quantities of product, especially to undeveloped countries.[75]

One recent example of global philanthropy involves firms that do business in sub-Saharan Africa, a region where AIDS has killed 17 million people and infected 25 million more. These companies have seen the disease take a devastating toll on their employees. They often must train two people for the same job so that they will be prepared if the employee or a family member becomes ill. Frequent absences, caused by the disease, are the norm. In response, companies such as Chevron, Coca-Cola, and the Ford Motor Company have undertaken sweeping initiatives to address the problem.[76]

Chevron provides AIDS education, psychological counseling, and free medical facilities for its employees. Although employees do not have access to retroviral treatments, they have had success using available antibiotics to treat the opportunistic infections so common with AIDS. Coca-Cola also sponsors 2-day AIDS seminars, provides condoms in all restrooms, and makes health coverage available for all employees. It provides AIDS benefits based on reasonable and customary allowances. The Ford Motor Company also promotes education and prevention while providing health coverage. It takes a three-pronged approach that includes programs for the employees, joint efforts with other employers, and a community outreach program.[77]

Executives claim several advantages of global contributions programs,[78] including:

- An improved corporate image
- A boost in market penetration
- Improved personal relations
- Improved government relations

Executives also note, however, that it can be difficult to administer programs in some cultures that do not place a high priority on voluntary activity. In addition, getting information about the impacts of their programs is difficult. As previously mentioned, it is expected that global philanthropy will continue to be an integral and growing part of corporate contributions programs. As long as companies continue to generate revenues and profits abroad, involvement in these countries and their communities will continue.[79]

THE LOSS OF JOBS

We now shift our focus to the issue of job loss from outsourcing and business and plant closings. In the preceding sections, we considered the ways in which business firms might have positive, constructive, and creative impacts on community stakeholders. Firms can also have detrimental impacts on communities. We see a most pervasive example of such negative effects when mass job layoffs occur because jobs are moved overseas or when a business or plant closes and its management does not carefully consider the community stakeholders affected.

Twenty years ago, the recession of the early 1980s provided a major catalyst for business and plant shutdowns. Some of the affected companies were in declining industries; some had outdated facilities or technology; some moved to less unionized regions of the country; some sought access to new markets; some were victims of the merger/acquisition frenzy; and many were victims of global competition. For most of the 1990s, plant closings were not as prevalent but outsourcing became more common. As we entered the new millennium, however, an economic recession brought the problem of closings back to the forefront. The sharp decline in the technology sector resulted in the sudden closing of dotcoms and other technology-based firms. The attack on the World Trade Center put industries, such as airlines, hospitality, travel, and tourism, into distress. In 2004, outsourcing emerged as a main concern as a source of job loss. The issue was so prevalent in people's minds that it became a major subject of debate in the 2004 presidential election. We will address the issue of outsourcing first and then take a more in-depth look at business and plant closings.

Outsourcing

The word **outsourcing** refers to the use of outside resources to accomplish a task that was once done in-house. At the macro level, the term is used to refer to the use of international resources to accomplish a task that was once done domestically.

The problems created by outsourcing aren't new. The current challenges have arisen because new technologies such as high-speed data links and the Internet have made it possible for white-collar work to be done overseas where labor is cheaper. In the late nineteenth century, the advent of railroads had just as transforming an effect. A writer for Scribner's in 1888 said that life had changed more in the past 75 years than it had since Julius Caesar, "and the change has chiefly been made by railways."[80] Railroads destroyed industries and whole towns, in addition to jobs. There was no longer a need for icehouses or local meatpacking plants and so they closed. While new markets opened for U.S. grain, cotton farmers lost market share to cheaper Egyptian and Indian cotton. Steamboat towns faded, and struggling farmers began to resent their dependence on the wealthy railroads.[81]

Thirty years ago, concerns over outsourcing were focused on blue-collar occupations, primarily factory workers, and it was mostly a problem in the United States. Today it affects blue- and white-collar workers alike, and its influence is felt in industrial nations around the globe. According to estimates from the McKinsey Global Institute, offshore outsourcing will increase by 30 to 40 percent a year for the next five years.[82] The issue of outsourcing is a hot potato in the political arena. When the Bush administration's chief economist, N. Gregory Mankiw, told reporters what most economists believe, that outsourcing was "a good thing," a political uproar ensued.[83]

The fact that white-collar workers are now losing their jobs has given the issue new momentum. Information technology workers have been particularly hard hit. The work of a programmer who makes $80,000 in the United States can be done by a programmer who makes $11,000 in India or $8,000 in Poland and Hungary.[84] This represents huge savings for firms dealing with global competition. In spite of the savings involved, however, outsourcing is not a panacea for companies. Some are finding that cost savings are lessened by the problems that develop from shipping jobs overseas. Capital One ended a contract for a 250-person call center in New Delhi. They found that workers would boost their sales by offering unauthorized lines of credit.[85] Similarly, Dell brought a tech support center back to the United States after customers complained of thick accents and poor service.[86] In spite of these glitches, however, outsourcing is a trend that will continue. For companies that compete in the global arena, ignoring these potential cost savings is difficult to do.

Most economists argue that international competition boosts productivity and the long-term benefits of outsourcing will outweigh the short-term losses. They point to the difference in gains in productivity between manufacturing, which has dealt with outsourcing for decades, and the previously more protected service sector, which is new to the phenomenon. With higher costs, U.S. manufacturing was forced to be more productive or go under. From 1954 to 2004, productivity in the U.S. service sector rose by 47 percent while manufacturing's productivity rose 330 percent in the same time period.[87] Proponents of outsourcing also argue that the predictions of job loss are overstated. They say they are gross estimates, not net, meaning that they fail to take into account the jobs that will be gained.[88] Prior debates over free trade support this point. During the 1990s, some feared the passage of NAFTA would create a "giant sucking sound" as jobs left the United States. However, many would say that tens of millions of new jobs were created instead.[89]

Of course, the creation of new jobs is of little consolation if you are the person whose job has disappeared. It is true that outsourcing contributes to productivity, but that productivity comes at the expense of workers. After all, if gains in productivity make it possible for one worker to do the job of two, then only that one worker will be hired and the second worker will have to look for other work. Those second workers don't always land on their feet. In the United States, more than 4 million workers have exhausted their unemployment benefits without finding other work: The U.S. economy has not had such a prolonged decline in jobs since the Depression of the 1930s.[90] As Institute for International Economics productivity expert Martin Baily notes, for the predicted benefits of outsourcing to occur people have to move into jobs that will pay them enough so that they can pay for the cheap imports.[91] Just as with business and plant closings, which we'll discuss later, the company has a responsibility to ascertain that outsourcing is the only option. If it is, the company's responsibility then shifts to doing everything possible to minimize outsourcing's negative impact on the workers involved.

Business and Plant Closings

There is no single reason for business and plant closings. Figure 15-5 on page 494 provides a window into the extent of impact that many communities are experiencing: It is a listing of some of the plant closings that happened in one small area, western North Carolina, in a matter of months and the reasons given for the action. Each job lost had a serious impact on the displaced worker, and each of these closings presented major

FIGURE 15-5

Selected Western North Carolina Business and Plant Closings and Their Reasons

Date	Product	Jobs Lost	Reason
January 2004	Fuses	290	Economic conditions
January 2004	Office furniture	480	Economic conditions
January 2004	Furniture	351	Economic conditions
December 2003	Yarn spinning/carding	53	Consolidation
November 2003	Electrical switches	313	Moving jobs to Mexico
October 2003	Milling	625	Foreign competition
September 2003	Lingerie	77	Foreign competition
September 2003	Electronic accessories	139	Outsourcing
September 2003	Furniture	506	Foreign competition
July 2003	Industrial thread	228	Foreign competition
May 2003	Auto parts	350	Moving jobs to Mexico

SOURCE: Mark Barrett, "Burnsville Yarn Plant Closing; 163 Workers Get Pink Slip," *Citizen-times.com* (March 1, 2004).

challenges for the communities in which they occurred. In the aggregate, these closings present a major challenge for a state as workers cannot look to the neighboring town for employment if those plants and businesses are closing, too.

Although the right to close a business or plant has long been regarded as a management prerogative, the business shutdowns of the past two decades—especially their dramatic effects—have called attention to the question of what place rights and responsibilities business has in relation to employee and community stakeholders. The literature of business social responsibility and policy has documented corporate concern with the detrimental impact of its actions. Indeed, business's social response patterns over the past 20 years have borne this out. Management expert Peter Drucker has suggested the following business position regarding social impacts of management decisions:

> *Because one is responsible for one's impacts, one minimizes them. The fewer impacts an institution has outside of its own specific purpose and mission, the better does it conduct itself, the more responsibly does it act, and the more acceptable a citizen, neighbor, and contributor it is.*[92]

The question is raised, therefore, whether business's responsibilities in the realm of plant closings and their impacts on employees and communities are any different from the host of responsibilities that have already been assumed in areas such as employment discrimination, employee privacy and safety, honesty in advertising, product safety, and concern for the environment. From the perspective of the employees affected, their role in plant and business closings might be considered an extension of the numerous employee rights issues.

Of the executives who have spoken out on this issue, several have indicated that there is an obligation to employees and to the community when a business opens or decides to close. As D. Kenneth Patten, former president of the Real Estate Board of New York, once stated:

> *A corporation has a responsibility not only to its employees but to the community involved. It's a simple question of corporate citizenship. Just as an individual must conduct himself in a way relating to the community, so must a corporation. As a matter of fact, a corporation has an even larger responsibility since it has been afforded even greater advantages than the individual. Just as a golfer must replace divots, a corporation must be prepared at all times to deal with hardships it may create when it moves or closes down.*[93]

Others have also argued that there is a moral obligation at stake in the business-closing issue. In an extensive consideration of plant closings, philosopher John Kavanagh has asserted that companies are not morally free to ignore the impact of a closing on employees and the community. His argument is similar to those that have been given on many other social issues—namely, that business should minimize the negative externalities (unintended side effects) of its actions.[94]

Business essentially has two opportunities to be responsive to employee and community stakeholders in shutdown situations. It can take certain actions before the decision to close is made and other actions after the decision to close has been made.

Before the Decision to Close Is Made.

Before a company makes a decision to close down, it has a responsibility to itself, its employees, and its community to thoroughly and diligently study whether the closing is the only option available. A decision to leave should be preceded by critical and realistic investigations of economic alternatives.

Diversification.   Sometimes it is possible to find other revenue streams to help the company cope with the slim margins of manufacturing. SRC Holdings was making only 2 to 3 percent a year but needed a profit of 4 percent to compete effectively. SRC chief executive John P. Stack explains, "We took our manufacturing discipline into the service sector to develop new sources of revenue. . . . Without creating these other businesses, we couldn't have survived. Manufacturing has very slim margins but if a company innovates the margins can be incredible."[95]

The Wisconsin-based Menasha Corporation is also drawing upon its expertise in manufacturing. They developed labels embedded with computer chips that use radio frequency identification technology (RFID) with the intent of making RFID capability a business they can spin off or a service they can sell.[96] Mike Johnson, a company spokesman, said "It's totally new for us; an Internet I.T. play that uses intellectual capital from our manufacturing to create a new stream of revenue we can plow back into the factory."[97] Menasha will need it: The company laid off 112 of its 5,300 workers in 2003.[98]

New Ownership.   After a careful study has been made, it may be concluded that finding new ownership for the plant or business is the only feasible alternative. Two basic options exist at this point: (1) find a new owner or (2) explore the possibility of employee ownership.[99] A company has an obligation to its employees and the community to try to sell the business as a going unit instead of shutting down. This is often not possible, but it is an avenue that should be explored. Quite often, the most promising new buyers of a firm are residents of the state who have a long-term stake in the community and are willing to make a strong commitment. Ideally, local organizations and the government will be able to offer incentives to companies willing to bring jobs to the areas.

For example, when the Grumman Olson facility closed in Lycoming County, Pennsylvania, several parties joined together to bring jobs back to the area. The local chamber of commerce worked with the state to develop an incentive package that included job creation tax credits and customized job training at the local college. Specialized

Vehicles Corporation (SVC) bought the facility, promising to offer jobs first to the displaced workers of Grumman Olson.[100]

Employee Ownership.   The idea of a company selling a plant to the employees as a way of avoiding a closedown is appealing at first glance. Hundreds of U.S. companies with at least 10 workers are **employee owned**. Most of these arrangements are the results of last-ditch efforts to stay in business. Such national firms as General Motors, National Steel, Sperry Rand, and Rath Packing Co. have sold plants to employees—plants that otherwise would have been closed.

The experiences of many of these firms have not been extremely favorable, however.[101] In numerous cases, employees have been forced to take significant wage and benefit reductions to make the business profitable. In other cases, morale and working conditions have not been satisfactory under the new method of ownership and management.

In a rather dramatic case, negotiators worked out an agreement whereby the employees of National Steel's Weirton, West Virginia, mill would purchase the mill. The new company, Weirton Steel, became what was then the nation's largest employee-owned enterprise, as well as its eighth-largest producer of steel. Experts gave the mill a surprisingly good chance of succeeding, although Weirton's workers had to take a pay cut of about 32 percent. The mill's union president argued, "Thirty-two percent less of $25 an hour is a whole lot better than 100 percent of nothing."[102]

In 1990, however, as demand sank for the steel sheet it produced, Weirton Steel found itself in the unenviable position of actually having to lay off some of its employee-owners. By 1991, Weirton had eliminated 1,000 of its 8,200 jobs, had furloughed another 200 workers, and had plans to cut 700 more jobs. After a decade as owners of the company, Weirton employees became extremely frustrated and angry that employee ownership did not guarantee them that they would not lose their jobs. One employee posed the question many were asking: "How can we be laid off if we own the company?" The reality of the situation, however, is that even an employee-owned company must take whatever actions are necessary if it is to remain solvent and profitable. One of the major pitfalls of worker ownership is that it does not rewrite the laws of capitalism—the bottom line is still the bottom line.[103] In 2004, Weirton sold its assets to the Cleveland-based International Steel Group. Weirton CEO D. Leonard Wise commented, "There's a great comfort in knowing that steelmaking will continue in Weirton. . . . It's quite difficult for smaller mills to survive these days. Therefore, as part of ISG, one of the nation's largest steelmakers, Weirton will have a greater chance of surviving given the worldwide consolidation of steel companies."[104]

In 2001, 10 years after Weirton Steel learned that employee ownership is not a protection against difficult times, United Airlines found themselves in a similar situation. In 1994, United Airlines became America's largest employee-owned corporation. In one of the nastiest and most prolonged corporate battles ever, shareholders of UAL Corp., the parent of United Airlines, awarded employee groups 55 percent of the company's stock in exchange for a $4.9 billion bundle of wage and productivity concessions. U.S. labor leaders hailed this new arrangement in worker control as a model alternative to the way companies usually battle to control costs. Labor Secretary Robert Reich, whose department facilitated the deal, asserted: "If United is successful, this will be a major landmark in American business history." But the success of the new firm was by no means ensured, because the airline has been buffeted for over a decade by infighting among employee groups, repeated forays by outside potential buyers, and takeover attempts.[105] From the beginning, there were problems with workers who resented taking pay cuts in exchange for loans to buy 55 percent of United's common stock and flight attendants whose union opted not to join the ESOP because of concerns about the pay cuts involved and other policies. Problems began in 2000, when the airline pilots conducted a slowdown during contract negotiations. Then the machinists' union threatened to strike, and United took them to court.[106] By 2001, when the attack on the World Trade Center shook the airline industry, the ESOP had ended and United was in no better position than firms without employee owners. In 2002, United filed for bankruptcy.[107]

Some critics argue that United Airlines failed as an employee-owned enterprise because workers thought employee ownership would mean they no longer needed to be concerned about labor-management issues. Research has shown that employee ownership can provide a firm with competitive advantage; for employee ownership to work, however, it is critical that employees believe they have a part to play in leading the company. A positive owner-ship culture provides employees with access to information, the power to exert influence, a sense of fairness, and a feeling of ownership and entrepreneurship.[108] It should be noted, however, that the period following the terrorist attacks of 2001 were difficult for all large airlines and so that limits the inferences one can make about the impact that employee own-ership had on United.

After the Decision to Close Is Made.
There are a multitude of actions that a business can take once the decision has been made that a closedown or relocation is unavoidable. The overriding concern should be that the company seriously attempt to mitigate the social and economic impacts of its actions on employees and the communi-ty. Regardless of the circumstances of the move, some basic planning can help alleviate the disruptions felt by those affected. There are several possible actions that management can take,[109] including:

- Conducting a community-impact analysis
- Providing advance notice to the employees/community
- Providing transfer, relocation, and outplacement benefits
- Phasing out the business gradually
- Helping the community attract replacement industry

Community-Impact Analysis. If management is responsible for its impacts on employ-ees and the community, as Drucker stated, a thorough community-impact analysis of a decision to close down or move is in order. The initial action should be to identify realisti-cally those aspects of the community that would be affected by the company's plans. This would entail asking several questions,[110] such as:

- What groups will be affected?
- How will they be affected?
- What is the timing of initial and later effects?
- What is the magnitude of the effect?
- What is the duration of the impact?
- To what extent will the impact be diffused in the community?

Once these questions have been answered, management is better equipped to modify its plans so that negative impacts can be minimized and favorable impacts, if any, can be maximized.

Advance Notice. One of the most often discussed responsibilities in business- or plant-closing situations is the provision of advance notice to workers and communities. The national advance-notice law is called the **Worker Adjustment and Retraining Notification Act (WARN)**. WARN requires those firms employing 100 or more workers to provide 60 days' advance notice to employees before shutting down or conducting substantial layoffs. With WARN, the United States joined many other nations in mandating advance notice of shutdowns. Canada requires 1 to 16 weeks, depending on the case. Great Britain requires 60 to 90 days, depending on the case, and Japan requires "sufficient advance notice."[111]

The advantages of advance notice accrue primarily to the affected employees and their communities. Workers are given time to prepare for the shutdown both emotionally and financially. Advance notice makes it easier for employees to find new jobs, because research has shown that employees have an improved chance at reemployment while they are still employed. Advance notice is motivational in that, once one joins the ranks of the unemployed, there is a tendency to coast until benefits start to be exhausted. Also, the company is in a better position to provide references, retraining, or counseling during the advance-notice period.[112]

The disadvantages of advance notice—particularly long-term advance notice— accrue principally to the business firm. Once word leaks out in the community, financial institutions may be reluctant to grant credit, customers may become worried about items purchased or promised, and the overall level of business activity may decline rapidly. One of the major disadvantages of a lengthy notice is the task of motivating workers who know they are going to lose their jobs. Declines in employee morale, pride in work, and productivity can be expected. Absenteeism may increase as workers begin to seek other employment. In addition, there is the likelihood of vandalism, pilferage, and neglect of property as employees lose interest or attempt to strike back against the employer.[113]

In 2001, a New York-based software developer was sued by its employees: They charged that the company tried to disguise mass layoffs as individual firings to avoid having to comply with the advance notice required by WARN. There is a fine line between staggering employee layoffs legally and doing it to avoid the notice requirements of WARN. Courts try to determine what employers knew at the time of the layoffs. If they deem that the employers knew they would be laying off more than 50 employees at a time, the firm is considered to be in violation of WARN. Employees who sue successfully under WARN may get back pay and benefits for up to 60 days. The penalty for not giving adequate notice is $500 per day. The only acceptable reasons for not providing a 60-day notice are (1) action being taken by the employer, which, if successful, would have postponed or eliminated the need for layoffs, (2) unforeseen business circumstances that the employer could not reasonably have foreseen, and (3) natural disasters.[114]

Transfer, Relocation, and Outplacement Benefits.   Enlightened companies are increasingly recognizing that the provision of separation or outplacement benefits is in the long-range best interest of all parties concerned. Everyone is better off if disruptions are minimized in the lives of the firm's management, the displaced workers, and the community. Outplacement benefits have been used for years as companies have attempted to remove redundant or marginal personnel with minimum disruption and cost to the company and maximum benefit to the individuals involved. Now these same benefits are being used in business and plant closings.

Gradual Phase-Outs.   Another management action that can significantly ameliorate the effects of a business shutdown is the gradual phasing out of the business. A gradual phase-out buys time for employees and the community to adjust to the new situation and to solve some of their problems.

In 2003, after the semiconductor industry took a deep downturn, Sony Electronics found it necessary to close its plant in San Antonio. They let their employees go in phases as they gradually wrapped up their customer orders. Affected workers were given 60 days' notice. This did not come as a surprise because, as one worker noted, "It was fairly well-known that the company was sick for a quite a while."[115] When asked about worker reactions, one employee said, "There were a few who were upset but some of them actually requested to be included in Phase 1 (job cuts). They wanted to get their severance packages and get on with their lives."[116] Sony provided workers with severance pay based on years on the job. They also extended benefits packages, outplacement services, and job transfers, where possible, to other Sony plants in the United States. Each departing worker also received a DVD player.[117]

Helping to Attract Replacement Industry.   The principal responsibility for attracting new industry falls on the community, but the management of the closing firm can provide cooperation and assistance. The closing company can help by providing inside information on building and equipment characteristics and capabilities, transportation options based on its experience, and contacts with other firms in its industry that may be seeking facilities. Helping the community attract replacement industry has the overwhelming advantage of rapidly replacing large numbers of lost jobs. Also, because attracted businesses tend to be smaller than those that closed, this strategy enables the community to diversify its economic base while regaining jobs.[118]

Survivors—The Forgotten Stakeholders.

When job losses occur, attention is understandably placed on the workers who lose their employment and the many repercussions that loss holds for them. Their needs must come first because they bear the brunt of the impact. However, those who retain their jobs—whether they are the remaining employees at a downsized plant or the workers at a plant that survived consolidation—are in need of support as well. Survivors are likely to evidence a variety of negative actions, perceptions, and behaviors. These include depression, guilt, stress, uncertainty, decreased loyalty, and lower enthusiasm.[119] Firms must attend to these concerns of survivors if they are to emerge stronger after job cuts. They can do this by providing:[120]

1. Emotional support—assuring employees that they are important
2. Directional support—communicating the direction the company is going and the employees' place in that journey
3. Tactical support—presenting new goals and objectives for the employees
4. Informational support—answering all questions about the layoff and future plans

One of the most important actions a firm can take when providing informational support is to answer employees' questions clearly and completely. Michael Fox, senior vice president of Ogilvy Public Relations, has worked with firms that are conducting layoffs. He says, "You've got a good chance at preserving loyalty and lessening anxiety if you've always been pretty open and transparent with information. Tell (remaining employees) how the decision was made, the layoffs were based on performance reviews, or longevity or the loss of a big customer. If a decision seems arbitrary or unclear, it will only make resentment worse."[121] It is also important that the survivors believe the laid off employees were treated well. When United Technologies paid for a year of college courses for laid off employees, the remaining employees felt better about staying on the job.[122]

We are only just beginning to define the stakes and stakeholders involved in the plant-closing issue, the impacts that business closings have on employees and communities, the public's reaction to the problem, and types of corresponding actions that management might take. From observations of other social issues that have received the kind and degree of attention that business closings have, it seems to be necessary for businesses to take positive steps if they are to be responsive to their employees and communities and if further state and federal legislation is to be avoided. Business closings and their adverse consequences are issues that business will be well advised to address in the future, lest yet another public problem culminate in new laws or another knotty regulatory apparatus.

■ SUMMARY

Community stakeholders are extremely important to companies. Companies may have positive impacts on their communities in two basic ways: donating the time and talents of managers and employees (volunteerism) and making financial contributions. Because business has a vital stake in the community, it engages in a variety of community projects. Community action programs are a key part of managing community involvement. Important components of such efforts include knowing the company's resources, selecting projects to pursue, and monitoring corporate efforts.

Business also contributes to community stakeholders through philanthropy. The third sector, or nonprofit sector, depends on business's support. Companies give for a variety of reasons—some altruistic, some self-interested. Major recipients of business giving include education, health and welfare, civic activities, and culture and the arts. As companies have attempted to manage their philanthropy, two major types of public purpose partnerships have been emphasized: (1) strategic philanthropy, which seeks to improve the overall fit between corporate needs and charitable programs, and (2) cause-related marketing, which tightens the linkage between a firm's profits and its contributions. Cause-related marketing represents a unique joining of business and charity with the potential for great benefit to each. Global philanthropy has recently become an important trend.

Just as firms have beneficial effects on community stakeholders, they can have detrimental effects as well. Business or plant closings are a prime example of these detrimental effects. Plant closings have a pervasive influence in the sense that a multitude of community stakeholders—employees, local government, other businesses, and the general citizenry—are affected. There is no single reason why these closings have occurred, but among the major reasons are economic conditions, consolidation of company operations, outmoded technology or facilities, changes in corporate strategy, and international competition.

Before management makes the decision to close a facility, it has a responsibility to itself, its employees, and the community to study thoroughly whether closing is the only or the best option. Finding a new owner for the business and pursuing the possibility of employee ownership are reasonable and desirable alternatives. After the decision to close has been made, possible actions include community-impact analysis; giving advance notice; providing transfer, relocation, or outplacement benefits; phasing out operations gradually; and helping the community attract replacement industry. Finally, the needs of survivors must be met as the firm continues operations. Companies have an added incentive to be responsive to the business-closing issue, because state and federal governments are closely watching the manner in which firms are handling this problem. Companies that are sensitive to community stakeholders will want to fashion socially responsive postures in dealing with their stakeholders.

■ KEY TERMS

America's Promise (page 474)

cause branding (page 490)

cause-related marketing (page 490)

community action program (page 476)

community involvement (page 472)

employee owned (page 496)

outsourcing (page 492)

philanthropy (page 480)

resource-based giving (page 474)

strategic philanthropy (page 488)

third sector (page 483)

Worker Adjustment and Retraining Notification Act (WARN) (page 498)

■ DISCUSSION QUESTIONS

1. Outline the essential steps involved in developing a community action program.

2. Explain the pros and cons of community involvement and corporate philanthropy, provide a brief history of corporate philanthropy, and explain why and to whom companies give.

3. Differentiate among public purpose partnerships, strategic philanthropy, cause-related marketing, and cause branding. Provide an example of each that is not discussed in the text.

4. Identify and discuss briefly what you think are the major trade-offs that firms face as they think about outsourcing or plant closings. When substantial lay-offs are involved, what are firms' responsibilities to their employees and their communities?

5. In your opinion, why does a business have a responsibility to employees and community stakeholders in a business-closing decision? Enumerate what you think are the major reasons.

■ RECOMMENDED CASES

Many of the end-of-text cases may be related to Chapter 15. You may wish to consider studying the following cases with Chapter 15.

Case 1. "THE MAIN STREET MERCHANT OF DOOM." This case addresses a company's responsibility to a community in which it conducts its business. Critics charge that Wal-Mart drives out competitors with extremely low prices, ruining the community's downtown and sometimes even raising prices once competitors are no longer there. Are the critics right? What changes should Wal-Mart make, if any?

Case 4. "FACING A FIRE." This case addresses the relationship of a business owner to the community in which his business has operated for many years. After 90 years in business, HFS Corporation has suffered a devastating fire. The owner is nearing retirement. If he takes the insurance money and closes the plant, the town will be devastated. If he opts to rebuild instead, he will face

huge challenges at a time when he should be able to relax and enjoy the fruits of many years of labor. What should he do?

Case 29. "BETASERON (A)." This case addresses the challenges faced by Berlex when it develops the first drug that could reduce the frequency and severity of relapses for people with multiple sclerosis (MS). The FDA expedited the drug's approval but manufacturing restrictions meant that only from 12,000 to 20,000 would be able to receive the drug in its first year. At least 100,000 people with the devastating disease would be eligible for treatment, but it would be three years until they could all receive the drug. MS is highly unpredictable, and so there is no way to know who will need it more. How should Berlex handle its distribution? Who should receive the drug first and what should they do about those who are unable to pay the drug's high price?

▪ WEB RESOURCES

The URLs listed here are current at the time of publication. Should any of these Web sites change, please search under the company's or organization's name for an updated address.

America's Promise
http://www.americaspromise.org

Arts and Business Council, Inc.
http://www.artsandbusiness.org

Business for Social Responsibility
http://www.bsr.org

Business Committee for the Arts, Inc.
http://www.bcainc.org

Business Week magazine
http://www.businessweek.com

Center for Corporate Citizenship
http://www.bc.edu/centers/ccc

Committee to Encourage Corporate Philanthropy
http://www.corphilanthropy.org

Fortune magazine
http://www.fortune.com

The Foundation Center
http://www.fdncenter.org

National Committee for Responsive Philanthropy
http://www.ncrp.org

OMB Watch
http://www.ombwatch.org

Points of Light Foundation
http://www.pointsoflight.org

Public Service Advertising Research Center
http://www.psaresearch.com

Ronald McDonald House
http://www.rmhc.org

InfoTrac® College Edition   http://www.infotrac-college.com

Articles from both Business Week *and* Fortune *can be researched, retrieved, and read from your desktop using InfoTrac's online database.*

▪ ENDNOTES

1. Carole Schweitzer, "Corporate Assets," *Association Management* (January 1998), 30–37.
2. *Community Action Manual* (Worcester, MA: Norton Company, April 1978), 1–2.
3. Bill Shaw and Frederick Post, "A Moral Basis for Corporate Philanthropy," *Journal of Business Ethics* (October 1993), 745–751.
4. *Community Service* (2001), http://www.lilly.com.
5. Jeff Barbian, "The Charitable Worker," *Training* (July 2001), 50–55.
6. Paul Ostergard and Benjamin R. Barber, "Should Corporations Be Praised for Their Philanthropic Efforts?" *Across the Board* (May/June 2001), 44–53.
7. http://www.bsr.org
8. Jonathan Alter, "Powell's New War," *Newsweek* (April 28, 1997), 28.
9. *Ibid.*, 28–34.
10. http://www.americaspromise.org (2004).
11. "Electric Fuel Donates 500 Instant Power™ Chargers and Batteries to Keep New York Rescue Workers' Cellphones Working," *PR Newswire* (September 17, 2001).
12. "Safety First," *Wireless Review* (March 15, 1998), 14.
13. Loretta W. Prencipe, "Volunteer for Adventure," *Network World* (June 8, 1998), 62.
14. Clive Cookson, "Drug Group in Bid to Wipe Out Elephantiasis," *Financial Times* (January 27, 1998), 5.
15. Kathryn Troy, *Studying and Addressing Community Needs: A Corporate Case Book* (New York: The Conference Board, 1985), 1.
16. *Ibid.*
17. *Community Action Manual*, 1–2.
18. Frank Koch, "A Strategy for Corporate Giving and Community Involvement," *Management Review* (December 1977), 7–13.
19. http://www.rmhc.com (2004).
20. Tammie S. Pinkston and Archie B. Carroll, "Corporate Citizenship Perspectives and Foreign Direct Investment in the U.S.," *Journal of Business Ethics* (Vol. 13, 1994), 157–169.

21. David Logan, *Community Involvement of Foreign-Owned Companies* (New York: The Conference Board, 1994), 7.
22. *Ibid.*, 16.
23. *Ibid.*, 15.
24. Pinkston and Carroll, 168–169.
25. Cecily Railborn, Antoinette Green, Lyudmila Todorova, Toni Trapani, and Wilborne E. Watson, "Corporate Philanthropy: When Is Giving Effective," *The Journal of Corporate Accounting and Finance* (November/December 2003), 47–54.
26. *Webster's New World Dictionary* (Cleveland: World Publishing Company, 1964), 1098.
27. http://www.bsr.org
28. Morrell Heald, *The Social Responsibilities of Business: Company and Community 1900–1960* (Cleveland: Case Western Reserve University Press, 1970), 112.
29. Adam Bryant, "Companies Oppose Disclosure of Details on Gifts to Charity," *The New York Times* (April 3, 1998), A1.
30. *Ibid.*
31. OMB Watch, "Corporate Disclosure Bill Goes to President Without Philanthropy Disclosure Requirements," (July 26, 2002), http://www.ombwatch.org.
32. http://www.corphilanthropy.org
33. OMB Watcher, "More Complaints Filed Against Congressman DeLay," (April 5, 2004); Press release (November 20, 2003), National Committee for Responsive Philanthropy.
34. John D. Rockfeller III, "In Defense of Philanthropy," *Business and Society Review* (Spring 1978), 26–29.
35. Sam Sternberg, *National Directory of Corporate Charity* (San Francisco: Regional Young Adult Project, 1984), 14.
36. David Saiia, Archie Carroll, and Ann Buchholtz, "Does Philanthropy Begin at Home? The Strategic Motivation Underlying Corporate Giving Programs," Presented at the 2001 Academy of Management Conference, Washington, DC.
37. Louis W. Fry, Gerald D. Keim, and Roger E. Meiners, "Corporate Contributions: Altruistic or For-Profit?" *Academy of Management Journal* (March 1982), 94–106.
38. Michael E. Porter and Mark R. Kramer, "The Competitive Advantage of Corporate Philanthropy," *Harvard Business Review* (December 2002), 57–68.
39. Anne Klepper, *Corporate Contributions, 1991* (New York: The Conference Board, 1992), 6, 9, 14.
40. Robert H. Malott, "Corporate Support of Education: Some Strings Attached," *Harvard Business Review* (July–August 1978), 133–138.
41. For an interesting study of workplace giving, see Melissa A. Berman, *The Future of Workplace Giving* (New York: The Conference Board, 1994).
42. Dreyer's Philanthropy Mission Statement, http://www.dreyersinc.com.
43. Michelle Conlin and Jessi Hempel, "The Corporate Donors," *Business Week* (December 1, 2003).
44. Keith H. Hammonds, "Corning's Class Act," *Business Week* (May 13, 1991), 68–76. See also Leslie Goff, "Corning: Those Who Live in Glass Houses . . .," *Computerworld* (May 25, 1998), S9–S10.
45. http://www.fortune.com
46. http://www.bca.org; http://www.artsandbusiness.org
47. "Community Impact Through the Arts," *Arts and Business Quarterly Online* (Spring 20004), http://www.artsandbusiness.org.
48. Paul H. Eliker, "Why Corporations Give Money to the Arts," *The Wall Street Journal* (March 31, 1978), 15.
49. James J. Chrisman and Archie B. Carroll, "Corporate Responsibility: Reconciling Economic and Social Goals," *Sloan Management Review* (Winter 1984), 59–65.
50. Christopher Schmitt, "Corporate Charity: Why It's Slowing," *Business Week* (December 18, 2000), 164–166.
51. Louis Lavelle, "Giving as Never Before," *Business Week* (October 1, 2001), 10.
52. Ian Wilhelm, Corporate Giving Takes a Dip," *Chronicle of Philanthropy* (July 24, 2003).
53. Schmitt, 164–166.
54. Curt Weeden, *Corporate Social Investing* (San Francisco: Berret Koehler, Inc., 1998), 4–6.
55. Public purpose partnerships are discussed in Richard Steckel and Robin Simons, *Doing Best by Doing Good* (New York: Dutton Publishers, 1992).
56. Andrew E. Serwer, "Company Givers Get Smart," *Fortune* (August 22, 1994), 16.
57. "Happy Deal for Tech: McDonald's Sponsorship to Finance Coliseum Facelift," *The Atlanta Journal* (January 19, 1995), C1–C2.
58. http://www.bsr.org
59. Steckel and Simons.
60. Porter and Kramer, 57–68.
61. *Ibid.*
62. *Ibid.*
63. http://www.burgerking.com
64. Porter and Kramer, 57–68.
65. *Ibid.*
66. Weeden (1998), 202–205.
67. Porter and Kramer, 57–68.
68. Patricia Caesar, "Cause-Related Marketing: The New Face of Corporate Philanthropy," *Business and Society Review* (Fall 1986), 16.
69. Martin Gottlieb, "Cashing In on a Higher Cause," *The New York Times* (July 6, 1986), 6-F.
70. Michelle Wirth Fellman, "Cause Marketing Takes a Strategic Turn," *Marketing News* (April 26, 1999), 4–8.
71. Peggy Bernstein, "Philanthropy, Reputation Go Hand in Hand," *PR News* (January 17, 2000). 1–8.
72. 1999 Cone/Roper Cause-Related Trends Report.

73. Public Service Advertising Research Center: http://www.psaresearch.com.

74. Caesar, 17–18. Also see Richard Steckel and Robin Simons, *Doing Best by Doing Good* (New York: Dutton Publishers, 1992), Chapter 6, "Cause-Related Marketing."

75. Anne Klepper, *Global Contributions of U.S. Corporations* (New York: The Conference Board, 1993), 6–7.

76. Judy Greenwald, "Employers Confront AIDS in Africa," *Business Insurance* (July 23, 2001) 15–22.

77. *Ibid.*

78. Klepper (1993), 6–7.

79. *Ibid.*

80. Bob Davis, "Wealth of Nations: Finding Lessons of Outsourcing in Four Historical Tales," *The Wall Street Journal* (March 29, 2004), A1.

81. *Ibid.*

82. Daniel W. Drezner, "The Outsourcing Bogeyman," *Foreign Affairs* (May/June 2004), http://www.foreignaffairs.org.

83. Jonathon Weisman, "Bush, Adviser Assailed for Stance on Offshore Jobs," *The Washington Post* (February 11, 2004), A4.

84. Dale Kasler, "Outsourcing Reaps Winners, Losers in U.S. Economy," *The Sacramento Bee* (April 26, 2004).

85. Brad Stone, "Should I Stay or Should I Go," *Newsweek* (April 19, 2004), 52–53.

86. *Ibid.*

87. Daniel Altman, "A More Productive Outsourcing Debate," *Business 2.0* (May 2004), http://www.business2.com.

88. Daniel W. Drezner, "The Outsourcing Bogeyman," *Foreign Affairs* (May/June 2004), http://www.foreignaffairs.org.

89. *Ibid.*

90. Jodie T. Allen, "Maybe We Could All Deliver Pizza. . ." *The Washington Post* (March 7, 2004), B1.

91. Ibid.

92. Peter F. Drucker, *Management: Tasks, Responsibilities, Practices* (New York: Harper & Row, 1974), 327–328.

93. Quoted in "A Firm's Obligations: To Employees, Community," *The Atlanta Journal* (September 19, 1977), 4-C.

94. John P. Kavanagh, "Ethical Issues in Plant Relocation," *Business and Professional Ethics Journal* (Winter 1982), 21–33.

95. Susan Diesenhouse, "To Save Factories, Owners Diversify," *The New York Times* (November 30, 2003), 5.

96. *Ibid.*

97. Ibid

98. *Ibid.*

99. Archie B. Carroll, "When Business Closes Down: Social Responsibilities and Management Actions," *California Management Review* (Winter 1984), 131.

100. Vincent J. Matteo, "The Chamber View," *Williamsport Sun-Gazette* (July 7, 2003), 2.

101. Terri Minsky, "Gripes of Rath: Workers Who Bought Iowa Slaughterhouse Regret That They Did," *The Wall Street Journal* (December 2, 1981), 1.

102. "A Steel Town's Fight for Life," *Newsweek* (March 28, 1983), 49.

103. Maria Mallary, "How Can We Be Laid Off If We Own the Company?" *Business Week* (September 9, 1991), 66.

104. "Weirton Steel to Sell Assets to ISG Following Judge's Decision," Weirton Steel Press announcement (April 22, 2004), http://www.weirton.com.

105. Kenneth Labich, "Will United Fly?" *Fortune* (August 22, 1994), 70–78.

106. Suzanne Cohen, "United Airlines ESOP Woes," *Risk Management* (June 2001), 9.

107. Greg Schneider, "Owner Role Always Tense for United Employees," *The Washington Post* (December 10, 2002), E1.

108. Cohen, 9.

109. Carroll, 132.

110. Grover Starling, *The Changing Environment of Business* (Boston: Kent, 1980), 319–320.

111. Paul D. Staudohar, "New Plant Closing Law Aids Workers in Transition," *Personnel Journal* (January 1989), 87–90.

112. Robert B. McKersie, "Advance Notice," *The Wall Street Journal* (February 25, 1980), 20.

113. *Ibid.*

114. Loretta W. Prencipe, "Impending Layoffs Need Warning," *Info World* (April 9, 2001), 15.

115. Greg Jefferson, "Sony Lays Off 120 Workers, Moves Closer to Closing San Antonio Plant," *San Antonio Express-News* (August 8, 2003), 1.

116. *Ibid.*

117. *Ibid.*

118. Cornell University Workshop Report, 28–30.

119. Suzanne M. Behr and Margaret A. White, "Layoff Survivor Sickness," *Executive Excellence* (November 2003), 18.

120. *Ibid.*

121. "Survivor Guilt: How the Corporate Ax Affects Remaining Employees," *PR News* (March 12, 2001), 1.

122. *Ibid.*

Part 5

INTERNAL STAKEHOLDER ISSUES

Chapter 16

EMPLOYEE STAKEHOLDERS *and* WORKPLACE ISSUES

CHAPTER LEARNING OUTCOMES

After studying this chapter, you should be able to:

1 Identify the major changes that are occurring in the workforce today.

2 Outline the characteristics of the new social contract between employers and employees.

3 Explain the employee rights movement and its underlying principles.

4 Describe and discuss the employment-at-will doctrine and its role in the employee's right to not to be fired.

5 Discuss the right to due process and fair treatment.

6 Describe the actions companies are taking to make the workplace friendlier.

7 Elaborate on the freedom-of-speech issue and whistle-blowing.

Society's changing values are having a great impact on the workplace. Although external stakeholders such as government, consumers, the environment, and the community continue to be major facets of business's concern for the social environment, considerable attention is now being given to employee stakeholders—their status, their treatment, their rights, and their satisfaction. This should come as no surprise when it is considered that most adults spend the bulk of their daytime hours at work.

The development of employee stakeholder rights has been a direct outgrowth of the kinds of social changes that have brought other societal issues into focus. The history of work has been one of steadily improving conditions for employees. Today's issues are quite unlike the old bread-and-butter concerns of higher pay, shorter hours, more job security, and better working conditions. These expectations still exist, but they have given way to other, more complex workplace trends and issues.

In the new millennium, two major themes or trends seem to be characterizing the modern relationship between employees and their employers. First, we will discuss the dramatic changes that have been occurring in the workplace. Prominent here will be our discussion of a newly evolving **social contract** between organizations and workers that is quite different from any such contract of the past. This new social contract is being driven by global competition. Second, we will consider a continuation of a trend toward more expansive employee rights. These two trends are interrelated, and we will describe how the changes in the workplace have precipitated a renewal in the employee rights movement.

Because these topics are so extensive, we dedicate two chapters to employee stakeholders and workplace issues. In this chapter, we discuss some of the workplace changes that have been taking place, the emerging social contract, and the employee rights movement. Three employee rights issues, in particular, are treated here: the right to not be fired without just cause, the right to due process and fair treatment, and the right to freedom of speech in the workplace. In Chapter 17, we will continue our discussion of employee rights by examining the related issues of the rights of employees to privacy, safety, and health. These two chapters should be considered a continuous discussion of employee stakeholders wherein economic, legal, and ethical responsibilities are all involved in their treatment.

THE NEW SOCIAL CONTRACT

Thirty years ago, employees stayed in the same job at the same company for years, and those companies rewarded that loyalty by offering job stability, a decent wage, and good benefits.[1] Today's typical worker has had nine jobs by the age of 30.[2] The workforce of today is more mobile, less loyal, and more diverse. Their trust in their employers has eroded over the past 20 years to the point where, as shown in a recent survey, only 38 percent of employees surveyed feel their employer is committed to them.[3] Individual identity has become uncoupled from the firm at which a person works.[4] These workforce changes have contributed to a newly emerging social contract between employers and employees. CEOs and factory workers alike know that their jobs are vulnerable, and so they have come to view themselves as free agents, working for the highest bidder.[5] As a result, today's employees aren't looking for a promise of lifetime employment. Instead, they are seeking competitive pay and benefits coupled with opportunities for professional growth. They want employers who provide them with opportunities, recognize their accomplishments, and communicate openly and honestly.[6]

What is driving the collapse of the old social contract and the emergence of the new? John A. Challenger, CEO of executive outplacement firm Challenger, Gray and Christmas, points to several forces that brought about systemic changes in the past 20 years, ultimately resulting in the business environment of today.[7] These forces include:

1. Globalization
2. Technology and automation
3. Deregulation of protected industries
4. Shareholder activism

These forces led to a new social contract that places on employees more responsibility for their own success and prosperity in the employment relationship. Job security, compensation, and advancement depend on what the employee is contributing to the organization's mission. Challenger notes that the change is demonstrated by a change in terminology:

What once was termed "personnel" is now called "human resources" and sometimes even "human capital." Businesses expect to leverage their human resources, just like any other resources, in a way that maximizes firm performance.[8] Thus, the notion of "adding value" to the organization has become a crucial factor: The bottom line is productivity. Figure 16-1 presents some of the characteristics of the old and new social contracts.

The forces that have changed the business environment bring new challenges for employers and employees alike. Employers have a need for workers with knowledge and the skill to provide it. To that end, employers have instituted a wide range of training programs and tuition reimbursement programs to keep their employees on the cutting edge of the changing environment.[9] Even in the midst of a recessionary environment, training expenditures as a percentage of payrolls continue to rise.[10] **Outplacement**, assistance provided to employees whose employment has been terminated, is also an important responsibility of the ethical firm in the new environment.

The forces also have implications for employees beyond the increased expectation of adding value to the firm. In particular, technology has blurred the boundaries between work and home. As John Challenger opined:

> *We cannot get away from work even when we are not there. Since the film* 2001: A Space Odyssey *debuted more than three decades ago, we have been wondering when computers would become human or superhuman. What sneaked up on us was the opposite: Human beings are becoming increasingly electronic. We carry our cell phones, beepers, fax machines, e-mail, portable CD players, and laptops—our offices—with us at all times.*[11]

Satellite technology means there is now no place where workers can count on getting away from work. The commute to and from work once provided downtime, but that is no longer true. The only place one can count on being out of reach is on an airplane as it takes off and lands, thanks to federal regulations.[12] Due to the forces of technology, globalization, and increased competition, attaining work/life balance is increasingly

---

FIGURE 16-1

The Changing Social Contract Between Employers and Employees

Old Social Contract	New Social Contract
Job security; long, stable career and employment relationships	Few tenure arrangements; jobs constantly "at risk"; employment as long as you "add value" to the organization
Life careers with one employer	Fewer life careers; employer changes common; careers more dynamic
Stable positions/job assignments	Temporary project assignments
Loyalty to employer; identification with employer	Loyalty to self and profession; diminished identification with employer
Paternalism; family-type relationships	Relationships far less warm and familial; no more parent-child relationships
Employee sense of entitlement	Personal responsibility for one's own career/job future
Stable, rising income	Pay that reflects contributions; pay for "value added"
Job-related skill training	Learning opportunities; employees in charge of their own education and updating
Focus on individual job accomplishments	Focus on team building and projects

Search the Web

All Is Fair?

Workplace Fairness (**http://www.workplacefairness.org**) is a nonprofit organization dedicated to promoting workplace policies and practices that support fairness in the workplace. The site is allied with the National Employment Lawyers Association. Listed as one of *PC Magazine*'s top 100 sites you can't live without, the Web site provides access to information on a wide range of issues relating to employee rights. Recent employment-related news articles can also be accessed from this Web site.

more difficult at a time when having a balance between work and home is becoming of increased importance to employees. Technology is both a help and a hindrance. Although technology makes it easier for employees to get out of the office and be at home, that same technology makes it difficult for employees to be completely at home without interference from work. This creates a new collection of challenges as the social contract between employers and employees evolves.

It is difficult to say whether the new social contract is bad or good. More than anything else, it represents an adaptation to the changing world and changing business circumstances. In some respects, workers may prefer the new model. Whatever turns out to be the case, we can expect free agent employees to be more proactive about their work environments than the loyal employees of the past once were. So it is clear that employee stakeholders' expectations of fair treatment will continue to rise, and we will continue to see the employee rights movement continue to grow.

THE EMPLOYEE RIGHTS MOVEMENT

To appreciate the background of employee rights issues (especially the rights of freedom of speech and due process), it is useful to consider the underlying public sector/private sector dichotomy that organizations in society face. The public sector is subject to constitutional control of its power. The private sector generally has not been subject to constitutional control because of the concept of **private property**. The private property notion holds that individuals and private organizations are free to use their property as they desire. As a result, private corporations historically and traditionally have not had to recognize employee rights because society honored the corporation's private property rights. The underlying issues then become why and to what extent the private property rights of business should be changed or diluted.

Although Americans have enjoyed civil liberties for nearly two centuries, these same rights have not always been afforded by many companies, government agencies, and other organizations where Americans work. David W. Ewing states the matter quite strongly:

> *Once a U.S. citizen steps through the plant or office door at 9 A.M., he or she is nearly rightless until 5 P.M., Monday through Friday. The employee continues to have political freedoms, of course, but these are not the significant ones now. While at work, the important relationships are with bosses, associates, and subordinates. Inequalities in dealing with these people are what really count for an employee.*[13]

Although there are growing exceptions to Ewing's rather strong statement, it does call attention to the importance of the issue. Ewing goes on to state, "The employee sector of our civil liberties universe is more like a black hole, with rights so compacted, so imploded by the gravitational forces of legal tradition, that, like the giant black stars in the physical universe, light can scarcely escape."[14]

A brief comment on the role of labor unions is appropriate here. In general, although labor unions have been quite successful in improving the material conditions of life at

Ethics in Practice

MANAGER'S MAKESHIFT

It is Holland Flowers's mission to deliver fresh and innovative floral designs. To achieve this, Holland Flowers hires creative university students from the local area. The company feels it is important to make every possible attempt to work around the students' schedules.

John Smith was a delivery driver for Holland Flowers and a university student. Before accepting the position with Holland Flowers in August 1994, John requested several days off the week prior to Christmas. December is a very busy time at Holland Flowers. To accommodate the increase in business, Holland Flowers hires seasonal employees. That year, the owner's son, Bob, was one of the seasonal employees. Bob was to work with John and the other drivers. The week prior to Christmas, the owner informed John that Bob was sick and unable to work. Subsequently, the owner told John he was to work that week, even though, before John was hired, they had agreed that John would be off. Reluctantly, John agreed to work.

The following night, John was downtown when he saw Bob with a drink in his hand and appearing quite healthy. John approached Bob, questioning his sickness and absence from work. Bob denied his illness, acting as if being the owner's son meant he could be off when he wanted.

John was furious, because the owner had previously stressed that Holland Flowers was built on honest working relationships. John felt that this incident went against the principles on which the company was founded. John no longer felt respect for the owner or Holland Flowers; instead, he felt lied to and betrayed. John called the owner that night and informed him of his feelings. Because the owner offered no defense, John felt he could no longer work for Holland Flowers, and he resigned.

1. Did the management of Holland Flowers behave unethically with respect to employee treatment in this case?

2. Was John right in questioning the owner's employee practices?

3. If you were John, what action would you have taken in this dilemma?

Contributed by Christopher Lockett

work—pay, fringe benefits, and working conditions—they have not been as interested in pursuing civil liberties. Unions must be given credit, however, for the gains they have made in converting what were typically regarded as management's rights or prerogatives into issues in which labor could participate. It should be noted, moreover, that labor unions seem to be disappearing from the business scene. In 1953, union representation reached its highest proportion of the private employment workforce, at 36 percent.[15] By 2003, the proportion of union members in the private sector had fallen to 8.2 percent.[16] Although the public sector union rate has held steady since 1983, it is not expected to have a significant impact on the kinds of employee rights we are discussing here.

The Meaning of Employee Rights

Before we consider specific employee rights issues, it is useful to discuss briefly what the term **employee rights** means. A lawyer might look at employee rights as claims that may be enforced in a court of law. To many economists as well, rights are only creations of the law. More generally, however, employee rights might refer to legitimate and enforceable claims or privileges obtained by workers through group membership that entitle or protect them in specific ways from the prevailing system of governance. In this light, employee rights are seen as individuals' legitimate and enforceable claims to some desired treatment, situation, or resource.[17]

Richard Edwards has argued that employee or workplace rights serve to provide workers with either (1) desired outcomes or (2) protection from unwanted outcomes. He also asserts that these rights find their source in law, union contracts, or employers' promises. Rights provided by law are called **statutory rights**. These rights include, for example, those rights established by the Civil Rights Act of 1964 (at a national level) or by Massachusetts' "right-to-know" law (at the state level), which grants production workers the right to be notified of specific toxic substances they may be exposed to in the workplace. Union contracts, by contrast, provide workers with rights established through the process of **collective bargaining**. Examples of these rights are seniority preferences, job security mechanisms, and grievance procedures.[18]

Employer promises are the third source of employees' rights categorized by Edwards. He calls these employer grants or promises **enterprise rights**. Typical examples of such enterprise rights might include the right to petition beyond one's immediate supervisor, the right to be free from physical intimidation, the right to a grievance or complaint system, the right to due process in discipline, the right to have express standards for personnel evaluation, the right to have one's job clearly defined, the right to a "just-cause" standard for dismissal, the right to be free from nepotism and unfair favoritism, and so on.[19]

It is clear that these enterprise rights, as construed by Edwards, are provided and justified by management on the basis of several different criteria. In some cases, these rights simply extend beyond what the organization is required to do by law. In other situations, they address issues that are not covered by law. In either case, these rights are sometimes justified on the basis of customs and practices that may be necessary for the firm to remain competitive (and thus are economically justified). In addition, the rights are sometimes afforded on the basis of some normative ethical principle or reasoning (for example, "This is the way workers ought to be treated"). In this situation, the ethical principles of justice, rights, and utilitarianism, as well as notions of virtue ethics, may be employed as rationales.

In this connection, management may provide the employee rights as part of an effort to display moral management, as discussed in Chapter 6. To illustrate this point further, Figure 16-2 characterizes how moral managers, as well as amoral and immoral managers, might view employee stakeholders.

To summarize, employee rights may be afforded on the basis of economic, legal, or ethical sources of justification. In a limited number of cases, companies even use philanthropic arguments as the bases for providing employee rights or benefits. For example, some companies have justified day-care rights and benefits to employees on philanthropic grounds. For purposes of our discussion here, however, we will concentrate on legal and ethical bases for considering employee rights. In all these discussions, moreover, we take the perspective of organizations blending ethical wisdom with management wisdom.

The job-related rights that are mentioned often enough to merit further discussion here include (1) the *right not to be fired without just cause*; (2) the *right to due process and fair treatment*; and (3) the *right to freedom, particularly freedom of expression and freedom of speech*. In Chapter 17, we will consider the rights to privacy, safety, and health in the workplace.

FIGURE 16-2

Three Models of Management Morality and Their Orientations Toward Employee Stakeholders

Model of Management Morality	Orientation Toward Employee Stakeholders
Moral Management	Employees are a human resource that must be treated with dignity and respect. Employees' rights to due process, privacy, freedom of speech, and safety are maximally considered in all decisions. Management seeks fair dealings with employees. The goal is to use a leadership style, such as consultative/participative, that will result in mutual confidence and trust. Commitment is a recurring theme.
Amoral Management	Employees are treated as the law requires. Attempts to motivate focus on increasing productivity rather than satisfying employees' growing maturity needs. Employees are still seen as factors of production, but a remunerative approach is used. The organization sees self-interest in treating employees with minimal respect. Organization structure, pay incentives, and rewards are all geared toward short- and medium-term productivity.
Immoral Management	Employees are viewed as factors of production to be used, exploited, and manipulated for gain of individual manager or company. No concern is shown for employees' needs/rights/expectations. Short-term focus. Coercive, controlling, alienating environment.

THE RIGHT NOT TO BE FIRED WITHOUT CAUSE

In an article for *Workforce Management* (November 2003 v82 i12 p16), Alan L. Rupe reports on how *not* to fire employees with a number of horror stories from the "bad-firing files"—firings so poorly handled it's no wonder employee rights are such a growing issue. After rehearsing the wrongdoing of other managers, he supplies tips for making terminations as easy and honorable as possible for both employers and employees. Read the horror stories by logging on to InfoTrac College Edition at **http://www.infotrac-college.com** and keying record number A111218788.

A **"good cause norm,"** the belief that employees should only be discharged for good reasons, prevails in the United States today. This belief persists in spite of the fact that most U.S. employees can be fired for any reason, or for no reason, as long as the firing is not discriminatory. Mark Roehling evaluated 13 studies of the good cause norm and found that the studies showed the norm to be widely held in a variety of situations, with respondents including undergraduate and graduate students as well as both blue- and white-collar workers.[20] Roehling suggests that the norm is held because of fundamental dignity and respect concerns.[21] Belief in the good cause norm stands in direct opposition to the employment-at-will doctrine, which many employers believe is their right. With these contradictory views being held by employer and employee, one can easily see why many disputes occur.

Employment-at-Will Doctrine

The central issue in the movement to protect workers' jobs surrounds changing views of the **employment-at-will doctrine**. This doctrine is the long-standing, common-law principle that the relationship between employer and employee is a voluntary one and can be terminated at any time by either party. Just as employees are free to quit a company any time they choose, this doctrine holds that employers can discharge employees for any reason, or no reason, as long as they do not violate federal discrimination laws, state laws, or union contracts. What this doctrine means is that if you are not protected by a union contract (the vast majority of the workforce is not) or by one of the discrimination laws, your employer is free to let you go anytime, for any reason. Most private employees in the United States are in an at-will employment relationship.[22]

The employment-at-will doctrine is being eroded by court decisions, however. The courts have ruled with increasing frequency that employers have responsibilities to employees that, from the standpoint of fairness, restrict management's former prerogative to fire at will. Terms that have been added to the vocabulary of employment relationships include *unjust dismissals* and *wrongful discharge*.

Three broad categories of issues that illustrate the legal challenges now arising in regard to employment-at-will discharges are (1) public policy exceptions, (2) contractual actions, and (3) breach of good faith actions.

Public Policy Exceptions.

For a wide variety of reasons, the courts are beginning to hold that employees who previously were unprotected from unjust firings are now so protected. One emerging major exception to the long-standing employment-at-will doctrine is known as the **public policy exception**. This exception protects employees from being fired because they refuse to commit crimes or because they try to take advantage of privileges to which they are entitled by law.[23] The courts have held that management may not discharge an employee who refuses to commit an illegal act (participation in a price-fixing scheme, for example). In one case, a company had to reinstate an X-ray technician who had been fired for refusing to perform a medical procedure that, under state law, could be performed only by a physician or registered nurse. Another public policy exception is that employees cannot be dismissed for performing public obligations, such as serving on a jury or supplying information to the police. Increasingly, the courts are protecting whistle-blowers—those who report company wrongdoings—from being fired. We will further discuss the case of whistle-blowers later in the chapter.

There have been so many claims of public policy exceptions in recent years that most courts have had to establish standards for employee plaintiffs. A plaintiff is a person who brings a lawsuit before a court of law. For example, a fired employee must specify a "clear public policy mandate," embodied in a statute, regulation, or court decision, that allegedly has been violated by her or his discharge. In addition, the employee plaintiff must show a direct causal linkage between that public policy and the discharge.[24] However, the implied existence of public policy actions is increasingly being accepted by state courts as a basis for successful employee lawsuits.[25] Today 43 out of 50 states recognize public policy exceptions.[26]

Contractual Actions.

The courts are also more frequently protecting workers who they believe have contracts or **implied contracts** with their employers. The courts are holding employers to promises they do not even realize they have made. For example, statements in employee handbooks or personnel manuals, job-offer letters, and even oral assurances about job security are now being frequently interpreted as implied contracts that management is not at liberty to violate.[27] One employee was protected because he proved in court that he was told, "Nobody gets fired around here without a good reason." Another quoted a line in an employee handbook that read, "You will not be fired without just cause."[28] Still another employee successfully argued that, when the company had used the term *permanent employee* to mean an employee who had worked beyond the 6-month probationary period, it had implied continuous employment. The implied contract exception is recognized by 38 states.[29]

Ethics in Practice

ROWDY RECRUITING

Last summer, I interned for a large company. The economy was strong, and so a large part of the company's time and money were put toward recruiting. The overwhelming majority of the company's employees were under the age of 30 and so young, energetic employees, who had recently been through the hiring process, did most of the recruiting. One Thursday night, I was asked to join a group of our employees and a young prospect for dinner. The idea was to take the recruit out for a night on the town and entertain him on his first night in our city. The next morning he was scheduled to meet with a partner at 8 A.M. for the first of many interviews.

At 7 P.M. sharp, we met the recruit, Mike, in the lobby of the hotel where he was staying. My first impression was that Mike was very nervous about dining with such a large group of our workers. When we arrived at the restaurant, the waiter handed us a wine list. As usual, we ordered a few bottles of wine for the table. When Mike refused our offer of a drink, my manager assured him it was okay. He consented and started in for a long night of alcohol consumption. We hopped from the restaurant to several bars in an upscale area of the city. Eventually, it was way past our bedtime, and we had all surpassed our limit. So we walked Mike back to his hotel and reminded him that we would be back to meet him bright and early in the morning.

Early Friday morning, my manager and I pushed our way through the revolving door of the hotel that we had just exited a few hours earlier. Though we were both feeling a bit hung over, we put on a smile and acted very professional. After a few minutes, the elevator door opened and Mike stumbled out. As he approached us, we noticed the lack of color in his face and wondered what kind of impression he would make in his interviews. As I reached out my hand to shake his, Mike turned his head and vomited on the floor of the hotel. After getting himself together, Mike began apologizing profusely. At that point, my manager informed Mike that he would no longer be interviewing with our company. I was shocked! All of us stayed out too late and had too much fun. Why would my manager punish Mike for something we had all done and even encouraged him to do?

1. Did the manager behave unethically with respect to treatment of the recruit? Does the fact that the recruit initially turned down the wine and the manager encouraged him to drink it affect your answer?

2. Do the rights of recruits differ from the rights of employees? If so, how?

3. If you were the manager, what action would you have taken in this situation? How would you handle Mike? Would you do anything to lessen the likelihood of this happening again?

Contributed Anonymously

Breach of Good Faith Actions. The courts also recognize that employers are expected to hold themselves to a standard of fairness and good faith dealings with employees. This concept is probably the broadest restraint on employment-at-will terminations. The **good faith principle** suggests that employers may run the risk of losing lawsuits to former employees if they fail to show that unsatisfactory employees had every reasonable opportunity to improve their performance before being fired. The good faith principle is recognized by 11 states: These are Alabama, Alaska, Arizona, California, Delaware, Idaho, Massachusetts, Montana, Nevada, Utah, and Wyoming.[30] The major implication of the good faith principle for companies is that they may need to introduce systems of disciplinary measures or grievance-type review procedures for employees.[31] We will discuss such due-process mechanisms later in the chapter.

Management's Response to Employees' Job Claims

With respect to employees' job claims, management needs to be aware of two important points: (1) It is now appropriate stakeholder management policy to treat workers fairly and to dismiss them only for justifiable cause, and (2) the law today increasingly protects workers who do not get fair treatment. Therefore, management has an added incentive not to get embroiled in complex legal entanglements over wrongful discharges. Four specific actions that management might consider in dealing with this issue[32] include the following:

1. *Stay on the right side of the law.* It is management's responsibility to know the law and to obey it. This is the clearest, best, and most effective position to take. The company that conducts itself honestly and legally has the least to fear from disgruntled employees.

2. *Investigate any complaints fully and in good faith.* Well-motivated complainers in organizations are likely to report problems or concerns to someone within the company first. Therefore, employee complaints about company activities should be checked out. If there is substance to the problem, management has time to make corrections internally, with a minimum of adverse publicity.

3. *Deal in good faith with your employees.* Honor commitments, including those made in writing and those that employees have a reasonable right to expect as matters of normal policy, behavior, and good faith. Employees continue to win court cases when it is determined that their companies have acted in bad faith.

4. *When you fire someone, make sure it is for a good reason.* This is the best advice possible. Also make sure that the reason is supported by sound records and documentation. Effective performance appraisals, disciplinary procedures, dispute-handling procedures, and employee communications are all keys to justifiable discharges. Management needs to be attentive to abusive or retaliatory firings that are supported by thin technicalities. If the need arises to fire someone, it should not be difficult to document sound reasons for doing so.

Before an employee is terminated, wisdom suggests that management should ask the supervisor, "If you had to appear before a jury, why would you say the employee should be discharged?" Management should also ask the supervisor if the action being taken is consistent with other actions and whether the employee was aware that certain conduct would result in discharge. Finally, management should assume that litigation might result from the firing and that the supervisor making the decision to fire might not be with the company when the case goes to court. Therefore, documentation for each event leading to the termination should be assembled immediately.[33]

Effective stakeholder management suggests that organizations seriously consider their obligations to employee stakeholders and their rights and expectations with respect to their jobs. Not only are the courts increasingly affording employees greater job protection, but evolving notions of ethical treatment are increasingly expanding employees' job rights as well. Companies that are aspiring to emulate the tenets of the moral management model will need to reexamine continuously their attitudes, perceptions, practices, and policies with respect to this issue.

THE RIGHT TO DUE PROCESS AND FAIR TREATMENT

One of the most frequently proclaimed employee rights issues of the past decade has been the right to due process. Basically, **due process** is the right to receive an impartial review of one's complaints and to be dealt with fairly. In the context of the workplace, due process is thought to be the right of employees to have decisions that adversely affect them be reviewed by objective, impartial third parties.

One major obstacle to the due-process idea is that to some extent it is seen to be contrary to the employment-at-will principle discussed earlier. It is argued, however, that due process is consistent with the democratic ideal that undergirds the universal right to fair treatment. It could be argued that, without due process, employees do not receive fair treatment in the workplace. Furthermore, the fact that the employment-at-will principle is being eroded by the courts might be taken as an indication that this principle is basically unfair. If this is true, the due-process concept makes more sense.

Patricia Werhane, a leading business ethicist, contends that, procedurally, due process extends beyond simple fair treatment and should state, "Every employee has a right to a public hearing, peer evaluation, outside arbitration, or some other open and mutually agreed-upon grievance procedure before being demoted, unwillingly transferred, or fired."[34] Thus, we see due process ranging from the expectation that employees be treated fairly to the position that employees deserve a fair system of decision making.

Sometimes the employee is treated unfairly in such a subtle way that it is difficult to know that unfair treatment has taken place. What do you do, for example, if your supervisor refuses to recommend you for promotion or permit you to transfer because she or he considers you to be exceptionally good at your job and doesn't want to lose you? How do you prove that a manager has given you a low performance appraisal because you resisted sexual advances? The issues over which due-process questions may arise can be quite difficult and subtle.

Only in the past 30 years have some leading companies given special consideration to employees' rights to due process. Historically, managers have had almost unlimited freedom to deal with employees as they wished. In many cases, unfair treatment was not intentional but was the result of inept or distracted supervisors inflicting needless harm on subordinates.[35] It can also be easily seen how amoral managers may have failed to provide employees with acceptable due process and fair treatment. By failing to institute alternative ways to resolve disputes, the managers lost an opportunity to avoid the time, energy, and money that is often lost in protracted administrative and judicial processes.[36]

Due Process

David Ewing, an authority on the question of employee civil liberties, has argued that employee due process should be regarded as but one part of a set of clearly defined rights, and a means of protecting employees from discharge, demotion, or other penalties imposed when they assert their rights. He goes on to enumerate the main requirements of a due-process system in an organization:[37]

1. It must be a procedure; it must follow rules. It must not be arbitrary.
2. It must be sufficiently visible and so well-known that potential violators of employee rights and victims of abuse are aware of it.
3. It must be predictably effective.
4. It must be institutionalized—a relatively permanent fixture in the organization.
5. It must be perceived as equitable.
6. It must be easy to use.
7. It must apply to all employees.

Ewing has gone on to define corporate due process in the following way:

> *A fair hearing procedure by a power mediator, investigator, or board with the complaining employee having the right to be represented by another employee, to present evidence, to rebut the other side's charges, to have an objective and impartial hearing, to have the wrong corrected if proved, to be free from retaliation for using the procedure, to enjoy reasonable confidentiality, to be heard reasonably soon after lodging the complaint, to get a timely decision, and so forth.*[38]

Ewing's concept of corporate due process represents a formal ideal, and it is doubtful that many corporate due-process systems meet all his requirements. However, there are many due-process systems or mechanisms in use by companies today as they strive to treat their employees fairly. In the next section, we will briefly discuss some of these approaches.

Alternative Dispute Resolution

There are several ways companies can and do provide due process for their employees. The approaches described here represent some of the **alternative dispute resolution (ADR)** methods that have been employed over the past 30 years.

Common Approaches. One of the most often-used mechanisms is the **open-door policy**. This approach typically relies on a senior-level executive who asserts that her or his "door is always open" for those who think they have been treated unfairly. Another approach has been to assign to a human resources department executive the responsibility for investigating employee grievances and either handling them or reporting them to higher management. Closely related to this technique is the assignment of this same responsibility to an assistant to the president.[39] From the employee's standpoint, the major problems with these approaches are that (1) the process is closed, (2) one person is reviewing what happened, and (3) there is a tendency in organizations for one manager to support another manager's decisions. The process is opened up somewhat by companies that use a **hearing procedure**, which permits employees to be represented by an attorney or another person, with a neutral company executive deciding the outcome based on the evidence. Similar to this approach is the use of a management *grievance committee*, which may involve multiple executives in the decision process.

The Ombudsman. An innovative due-process mechanism that has become popular for dealing with employee problems is the use of a corporate **ombudsman**, also known as *ombud* or *ombudsperson*. "Ombudsman" is a Swedish word that refers to one who investigates reported complaints and helps to achieve equitable settlements. The ombudsman approach has been used in Sweden since 1809 to curb abuses by government against individuals. In the United States, the corporate version of the ombudsman was first experimented with in 1972, when the Xerox Corporation named an ombudsman for its largest division. General Electric and the Boeing Vertol division of Boeing were quick to follow.[40]

The ombudsman's task is quite different from that of the human resources manager. Hiring, firing, setting policy, and keeping records are all the responsibility of the human resources department; the ombudsman does none of these.[41] The ombudsman in contrast is formally and officially neutral and promises client confidentiality.[42] The human resources employees represent the corporation and do not promise confidentiality.

Deborah Cardillo, Eastman Kodak corporate ombudsman since 1995, says that employees "want to handle their situation themselves, but they're stuck. The ombudsman's job is to get them unstuck. A great deal of what we do is explain to employees how their complaints or allegations can be dealt with and make it easier [for employees] to go through the formal system if they wish."[43] Currently, there are organizational ombuds at about 500 large companies, universities, and colleges, and that number is expected to rise.[44] The Sarbanes–Oxley Act, which was prompted by high-profile scandals such as Enron and WorldCom, contains a lesser known provision that encourages employees to report wrongdoing and prohibits corporate retaliation against those employees.[45] Ombuds can handle the concerns of employees who believe they have witnessed wrongdoing and do so in a way that keeps the problem from getting out of hand.[46]

The Peer Review Panel.

The **peer review panel** is another due-process mechanism currently under use at several large companies. Control Data Corporation (CDC) was one of the pioneers in the use of the peer review process. Over 30 years ago, Control Data was one of the first nonunion companies in the United States to introduce an employee grievance system. It was a system whereby an aggrieved employee could appeal all the way up the chain of authority through six management levels. The company tried to make the system work, but many times the grievance either died because of the cumbersome process or was "kicked upstairs" for some higher level of management to handle. Rulings in favor of the worker were rare. The company determined that this approach was not fair, and so it added a peer review process to the system.[47]

Eastman Kodak has made good use of the peer review concept. From 2002 to 2004, about 700 Kodak employees were involved in the program. Kodak hoped that peer review would ease the transition as it dealt with a planned workforce reduction of 4,500 to 6,000 people.[48] As Ann Reesman, general counsel of the Equal Employment Advisory Council, puts it, "The benefit of using peer review rather than some external decision maker is that the peer review panel is well-versed in the company culture and how the company operates."[49] Also, peers tend to find decisions handed down by peers to be trustworthy.[50]

Managers on the losing side sometimes complain because they think that outsiders are deciding on local issues about which they are not intimately knowledgeable. The company's position is that a manager not only has to convince herself or himself and local superiors that a personnel action is right but also must have it deemed as right against a companywide policy. The success of the system depends on (1) its having the clear support of top management for fair treatment of employees and (2) its being seen as a permanent fixture. The people who operate the peer review system must have sufficient respect and stature to make the process credible in the eyes of even the most authoritarian line manager.[51] This is especially important because peer review has no professional community to provide standards or procedural guidelines.[52]

The trend toward using ADR is growing with no end in sight. This growth is spurred partly by the time and money saved by avoiding costly litigation. Brown & Root, a Houston-based construction and engineering firm, estimates that its legal fees have dropped 30 to 50 percent since employing ADR, and 70 to 80 percent of the firm's cases are now settled within 8 weeks (40 percent within a month). Further, the proportion of adverse settlements and the size of the judgments are no different from when they went through the court system.[53] A survey conducted by Cornell University, the Foundation for the Prevention and Resolution of Conflict, and Price Waterhouse LLP showed that most *Fortune* 1000 corporations have used some form of ADR. Of these, 81 percent found ADR to be "a more satisfactory process" than litigation, while 59 percent indicated that ADR "preserves good relationships."[54] Marc Lampe applies feminist ethical theory as a theoretical basis for stakeholder theory and finds that alternative dispute resolution is preferable to the adversarial strategies that preceded it.[55]

Concerns have recently been expressed that employers are beginning to require new hires to sign contracts waiving their right to sue the firm and accepting pre-dispute **mandatory arbitration** as the alternative. Arbitration is a process where a neutral party resolves a dispute between two or more parties and the resolution is binding. In mandatory arbitration, the parties must agree to arbitration prior to any dispute occurring. Critics of this practice argue that this robs employees of their right to due process. They say that the structure of mandatory arbitration favors the organization and not the employee. Supporters contend that the arbitration process is just as fair as a jury trial while costing much less in time and money. At this writing, the courts appear to have generally upheld mandatory arbitration, but Congress is considering the Civil Rights Act of 2004, which would ban it.[56]

It is unclear what the future holds for employee due process. As Ewing has indicated, "Due process is a way of fighting institutionalized indifference to the individual—the indifference that says that productivity and efficiency are the goals of the organization, and any person who stands in the way must be sacrificed."[57] Increasingly, companies are learning they must acknowledge due process to be not only an employee right but also a sound and ethical management practice in keeping with the wishes and expectations of employees.

FREEDOM OF SPEECH IN THE WORKPLACE

Henry Boisvert was a testing supervisor at FMC Corp., makers of the Bradley Fighting Vehicle. The Bradley was designed to transport soldiers around battlefields and, when necessary, "swim" through rivers and lakes. When Boisvert tested the Bradley's ability to move through a pond, he found it filled quickly with water. He wrote the Army a report of his findings but was told by FMC supervisors that the report would never be sent. When Boisvert refused to sign a falsified report of his test results, he was fired.[58]

About the same time that Boisvert was discovering the Bradley's inability to swim, Air Force Lieutenant Colonel James Burton found additional problems with the fighting machine. When hit by enemy fire, the Bradley's aluminum armor melted and filled the inside of the vehicle with poisonous fumes. After 17 years of development and $14 billion for research and prototypes, the Bradley was unfit for warfare. Burton uncovered tests of the Bradley that were rigged by filling the gas tanks with water and the ammunition with noncombustible sand, making it impossible for the Bradley to explode. He also fought an attempt to transfer him to Alaska. After persevering to successfully force changes in the Bradley, Burton was forced to take early retirement as the officers who tried to stop his investigation were promoted.[59]

For most whistle-blowers, the story ends here, but Boisvert and Burton prevailed in their fights to fix the Bradley. After a 12-year legal battle, Boisvert received one of the largest damage awards that had ever been seen in a federal case, well over $300 million. During the trial, evidence emerged about employees using putty to fix cracks in the machine while vehicles to be selected for random inspection were marked with "X"s and worked on more carefully than the rest.[60] Burton's story also ends happily. Congress mandated that the Bradley be tested under the supervision of the National Academy of Sciences, using conditions that resembled true battlefield combat. As a result of these tests, the Bradley was redesigned and used successfully during the Persian Gulf War.

SEARCH THE WEB

HELP FOR WHISTLE-BLOWERS

The National Whistleblower Center (**http://www. whistle blowers.org**) is a "nonprofit educational and advocacy organization committed to environmental protection, nuclear safety, civil rights, government accountability and protecting the rights of employee whistleblowers." The center has successfully established many of the most important precedents protecting employee whistle-blowers throughout the United States and has revolutionized the protection afforded them.

The Web site has a wide variety of resources related to whistle-blowing. Included among them are a whistle-blower law library, a list of whistle-blower resources, model whistle-blower laws, and sources of whistle-blower protection. In addition to educating the public, they provide counseling to whistle-blowers nationwide and support for precedent-setting litigation.

Burton wrote a successful book about his experiences, *The Pentagon Wars*, which subsequently became an HBO movie.[61] It is impossible to estimate how many soldiers' lives were saved by the courage and persistence of these two men.

In 2004, the courage of another whistle-blower in the military drew worldwide attention when he made the abuse of Iraqi detainees at Abu Ghraib Prison in Baghdad public. Spec. Joseph M. Darby, a reservist in the 372nd Military Police Company, placed an anonymous note under a supervisor's door. In it, he described the sexual and physical abuse that was occurring in the prison. He subsequently came forward with a sworn statement. Photographs that later documented this abuse shocked the world.[62] Society's ambivalent attitude toward whistle-blowers is evidenced in Darby's sister-in-law's comment, "The news has been using the word 'whistle-blower,' which to me sounds like a bad thing."[63] His family stopped talking to the media due to concern about a backlash.[64]

Unfortunately, the family has reason for concern: Some whistle-blowers' stories lack happy endings. Studies of whistle-blowers have found that many experience negative outcomes such as losing their jobs. Many end up taking prescription medicine to ease the stress, while others even contemplate suicide.[65] Nevertheless, the willingness to challenge management by speaking out is typical of a growing number of employees today, and these individuals are receiving increasing amounts of protection from the courts.

Whistle-Blowing

As stated earlier, the current generation of employees has a different concept of loyalty to and acceptance of authority than that of past generations. The result is an unprecedented number of employees "blowing the whistle" on their employers. A **whistle-blower** has been called a "muckraker from within, who exposes what he [or she] considers the unconscionable practices of his [or her] own organization."[66]

What constitutes whistle-blowing? For our purposes, we define a whistle-blower as "an individual who reports to some outside party [for example, media, government agency] some wrongdoing [illegal or unethical act] that he or she knows or suspects his or her employer of committing." An alternative but similar definition of whistle-blowing is provided by Miceli and Near, two experts on the subject, who characterize it as "the disclosure by organization members [former or current] of illegal, immoral, or illegitimate practices under the control of their employers, to persons or organizations that may be able to effect action."[67]

Thus, there are four key elements in the whistle-blowing process: the whistle-blower, the act or complaint the whistle-blower is concerned about, the party to whom the complaint or report is made, and the organization against which the complaint is made.[68] Although our definition indicates that whistle-blowing is done to some outside party, there have been many cases where "internal whistle-blowers" have simply reported their concerns to members of management and yet have been treated as though they had gone to outside parties.

What is at stake is the employee's right to speak out in cases where she or he thinks the company or management is engaging in an unacceptable practice. Whistle-blowing is contrary to our cultural tradition that an employee does not question a superior's decisions and acts, especially not in public. The traditional view holds that loyalty, obedience, and confidentiality are owed solely to the corporate employer. The emerging view of employee responsibility holds that the employee has a duty not only to the employer but also to the public and to her or his own conscience. Whistle-blowing, in this latter situation, becomes a viable option for the employee should management not be responsive to expressed concerns. Figure 16-3 depicts these two views of employee responsibility.

Most whistle-blowers seem to be engaging in these acts out of a genuine or legitimate belief that the actions of their organizations are wrong and that they are doing the right thing by reporting them. They may have learned of the wrongful acts by being requested or coerced to participate in them, or they may have gained knowledge of them through observation or examination of company records. The genuinely concerned employee may initially express concern to a superior or to someone else within the organization.[69] Other potential whistle-blowers may be planning to make their reports for the purpose of striking out or retaliating against the company or a specific manager for some reason. In a survey of studies of whistle-blowers, however, Near and Miceli found the latter to be uncommon. Whistle-blowers were

FIGURE 16-3

Two Views of Employee Responsibility in a Potential Whistle-Blowing Situation

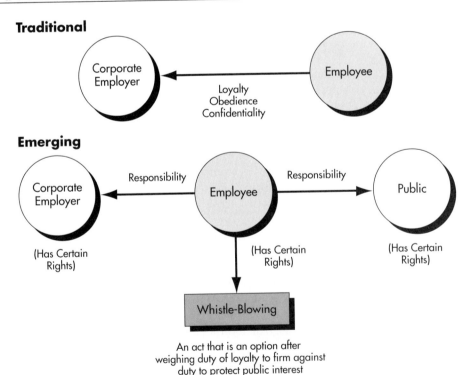

Traditional

Corporate Employer ← Loyalty / Obedience / Confidentiality — Employee

Emerging

Corporate Employer ← Responsibility — Employee — Responsibility → Public

(Has Certain Rights)   (Has Certain Rights)   (Has Certain Rights)

Whistle-Blowing

An act that is an option after weighing duty of loyalty to firm against duty to protect public interest on average more highly paid, with higher job performance than inactive observers. They were more likely to hold supervisory or professional status, and they have both the role responsibility to report wrongdoing and the knowledge of channels for doing so.[70]

The *Time* Persons of the Year for 2002 were three women who fit Near and Miceli's description. The women they named "The Whistle-blowers" were former Enron vice president Sherron Watkins, who wrote a memo to Enron CEO Kenneth Lay, warning of improprieties in the firm's accounting methods; FBI staff attorney Colleen Riley, who told FBI director Robert Mueller about the bureau's having ignored the Minneapolis field office's pleas that they investigate Zacarias Moussaoui, now indicted as a September 11 co-conspirator; and WorldCom's vice president of internal audit, Cynthia Cooper, who told the board that the company had hidden $3.8 billion in losses in falsified books.[71] According to *Time*, these women of "ordinary demeanor but exceptional guts and sense" risked their jobs, health, privacy, and sanity to bring about sea changes in their industries.[72] Some have argued that the designation of whistle-blower is incorrect because they are internal whistle-blowers. Dan Ackerman of *Forbes* writes in *The Wall Street Journal*, "A whistleblower is someone who spots a criminal inside a bank and alerts the police. That's not Sherron Watkins. What she did was write a memo to the bank robber (Mr. Lay) suggesting he was about to be caught and warning him to watch out."[73] Whatever one's opinion of the nature of their disclosures, it is hard to argue their impact on the business psyche. The media coverage of their high-profile cases is likely to have contributed to a dramatic rise in public awareness of and interest in whistle-blowing. For example, whistle-blower suits filed with the Office of Special Counsel grew from 380 in fiscal year 2001 to 555 in fiscal year 2002, an increase of 46 percent.[74]

Figure 16-4 identifies a checklist for whistleblowers to follow.

Consequences of Whistle-Blowing

What happens to employees after they blow the whistle? Unfortunately, whistle-blowers are often not rewarded for their contributions to the public interest. Although they are

---

FIGURE 16-4

A Checklist to Follow Before Blowing the Whistle

The following things should be considered before you blow the whistle :

1. Is there any alternative to blowing the whistle? Make sure you have tried to remedy the problem by reporting up the normal chain of command and have had no success.
2. Does the proposed disclosure advance public interest rather than personal or political gain? Don't act out of frustration or because you feel mistreated.
3. Have you thought about the outcomes of blowing the whistle for yourself and your family? Be prepared for the possibility of disapproval from friends, family and fellow workers.
4. Have you identified the sources of support both inside and outside the organization on which you can rely during the process? Make sure you know your legal rights and have enlisted the help of others.
5. Do you have enough evidence to support your claim? Even more evidence is needed if you plan to remain anonymous.
6. Have you identified and copied all supporting records before drawing suspicion to your concerns? Remember to keep a factual log both before and after blowing the whistle.

SOURCES: Department of Human Services, Victoria, Australia (http://www.dhs.vic.gov.au/whistleblowers/checklist.htm). *Business Week* (December 16, 2002), (http://www.businessweek.com/magazine/content/02_50/b3812095.htm), The Government Accountability Center, (http://www.whistleblower.org/getcat.php?cid=32), Kenneth K. Humphreys, "A Checklist For Whistleblowers To Follow," *Cost Engineering* (October 2003), 14.

now more likely to get some form of protection, whistle-blowers in general have sometimes paid dearly for their actions. Short of firings, various types of corporate retaliation have been taken against whistle-blowers,[75] including:

- More stringent criticism of work
- Less desirable work assignments
- Pressure to drop charges against the company
- Heavier workloads
- Lost perquisites (for example, telephone and parking privileges)
- Exclusion from meetings previously attended

One example of what can happen to whistle-blowers as a consequence of their actions is the case of James Alderson. James Alderson had been the chief financial officer of the North Valley Hospital for 17 years when Quorum, a former division of HCA, took over management of the hospital. Quorum created a second set of books and told Alderson to use these secret books to report higher than average expenses to the government for reimbursement. Knowing this would be both illegal and unethical, Alderson refused and five days later he was fired. After learning that other Quorum hospitals were cooking the books, too, Alderson went to Washington and talked to the U.S. Department of Justice. He took documentation of the false claims being filed with him. Eventually he sued Quorum and HCA under the federal False Claims Act. In 2001, HCA paid a total of $840 million, consisting of $745 million in civil damages and $95 million in criminal penalties. They later paid another $881 million to settle all remaining fraud charges and other overpayment claims against the company. In June 2003, the final settlement agreement between HCA and the U.S. Department of Justice was approved—13 years after Alderson was fired. The government received $1.5 billion from those payments, thanks to the efforts of Alderson and other whistle-blowers involved.[76]

There aren't many hospitals in Whitefish, Montana, so Alderson was forced to leave Whitefish to find work in hospital finance. For the next 10 years, Alderson tried to earn a living while continuing to gather evidence. Federal officials had told him that he needed evidence that the practices at North Valley were widespread, and the collection of that evidence was his responsibility. Building that evidence consumed Alderson's time and money. In addition to the financial drain, Alderson had made many personal sacrifices from missing his son's football games to not being at his mother's side when she died.[77] Alderson and his wife Connie kept a low profile. According to Connie, it was just like being in the witness protection program, "the only difference is that we weren't receiving any protection or money to keep us going."[78] Their low profile ended in 1998 when the television show *60 Minutes* did a profile of Alderson. Alderson then became a pariah in the health care industry. Says Alderson, "Even though I had a major impact in reducing health care fraud by $10 billion annually, I had one hospital CEO tell me to my face that I had ruined the industry and that I had given it a black eye."[79]

Under the False Claims Act, whistle-blowers receive 15 to 25 percent of the proceeds from any settlement that the government joins. Alderson comments, "I won't deny that money provided an incentive, but it was only part of the motivation. What Quorum and HCA were doing was wrong, and it took me 13 years and my career to prove it. Fortunately, I received enough money from the settlement to retire."[80] However, Connie Alderson says, "Knowing what I know now and knowing how long it's been, I'm not sure I would have agreed to pursuing the case. I don't think any amount of money is going to take care of what we've been through."[81]

Other famous cases of whistle-blowing include Ernest Fitzgerald, the Air Force employee who blew the whistle on billions of dollars in cost overruns at Lockheed, and Roger Boisjoly, who tried to halt the launch of the space shuttle *Challenger* because of frozen O-rings. Both of these whistle-blowers were fired.[82]

Although whistle-blowers frequently do get fired, as public policy increasingly sides with them and their courageous stances, other corporate actions are becoming possible. One encouraging episode is the case of Mark Jorgensen, who was employed at Prudential Insurance Co. of America.[83] Jorgensen was a manager of real estate funds for Prudential. He thought he was just being an honest guy when he exposed fraud he saw occurring in his company. His world then began to fall apart. He was abandoned by his boss, who had once been his friend. His colleagues at work began to shun him. Company lawyers accused him of breaking the law. Jorgensen, who was once a powerful and respected executive in the firm, began to hide out at the local library because he had been forbidden to return to his office. His long and successful career appeared to be dwindling to a pathetic end. Finally, he was fired.

Unlike most whistle-blowers, however, Jorgensen received a phone call from the company chairman, Robert Winters, who wanted to meet with Jorgensen to tell him some startling news: The company now believed him and wanted to reinstate him. Further, the company wanted to force out the boss he had accused of falsely inflating the values of funds that he managed. The turnabout was attributed to Jorgensen's persistence in fighting all odds in his quest to justify his convictions. Coming to the realization that Jorgensen had been right in his allegations all along, Prudential found itself in an unusual situation in business today—siding with the whistle-blower it had fought for months and eventually had fired. The company offered to reinstate Jorgensen in his job, but he elected instead to move on to another company. Prudential paid him a sizable amount to settle his lawsuit.[84] Although we do not read about many stories that end this way, it is encouraging to know that there are some stories that have happy endings. Speaking of endings (that may or may not be happy), Figure 16-5 on page 526 shows Hollywood's treatment of whistle-blowers.

Government's Protection of Whistle-Blowers

Just as employees are beginning to get some protection from the courts through the public policy exception to the employment-at-will doctrine, the same is true for whistle-blowers. The federal government was one of the first organizations to attempt to protect its own whistle-blowers. A highlight of the **1978 Civil Service Reform Act** was protection for federal employees who expose illegal, corrupt, or wasteful government activities. Unfortunately, this effort has had only mixed results.[85] It is difficult to protect whistle-blowers against retaliation because so often the reprisals are subtle. An added boost for federal employees came in 1989, when Congress passed the Whistle-Blower Protection Act and the president signed it into law. The effect of this act was to reform the Merit System Protection Board and the Office of General Counsel, the two offices that protect federal employees.[86]

The **Michigan Whistle-Blowers Protection Act of 1981** became the first state law designed to protect any employee in private industry against unjust reprisals for reporting alleged violations of federal, state, or local laws to public authorities. The burden was placed on the employer to show that questionable treatment was justified on the basis of proper personnel standards or valid business reasons.[87] The Michigan act spurred similar

FIGURE 16-5

Whistle-Blowers Get the Hollywood Treatment

Movie	Stars	Story	Inspiration
Serpico (1973)	Al Pacino (title role)	Frank Serpico is a nonconformist "hippie cop" in New York City who tries to report graft and corruption to his superiors. When they don't listen, he goes to *The New York Times*.	Based on Peter Maas's book, the movie tells a true story from Serpico's perspective. In the true story, another whistle-blower (David Durk) played a critical role, which is downplayed in the movie.
The China Syndrome (1979)	Jack Lemmon Jane Fonda Michael Douglas	Reporter (Fonda), cameraman (Douglas), and whistle-blower (Lemmon) team to expose unsafe practices in the nuclear energy industry.	Although the story is fiction, it is inspired by real events that occurred at the Browns Ferry and Dresden II reactors. Just days after the film's release, the most serious nuclear accident in U.S. history occurred at Three Mile Island.
Silkwood (1983)	Meryl Streep (title role) Kurt Russell Cher Craig T. Nelson	Whistle-blowers try to expose unsafe practices at an Oklahoma nuclear parts factory. A worker becomes contaminated.	Based on the true story of Karen Silkwood, who was a chemical technician at the Kerr-McGee plutonium fuels production plant in Crescent, Oklahoma. As a union member and activist, she was critical of plant safety.
The Insider (1999)	Russell Crowe Al Pacino Christopher Plummer	Successful scientist is fired from major tobacco company for taking a principled stand. *60 Minutes* is due to report the story, but they cave to corporate pressure.	Based on a *Vanity Fair* article, "The Man Who Knew Too Much." The movie tells the true story of Jeffrey Wigand, who was fired from Brown & Williamson tobacco company.

laws in other states. Those that have explicit statutory protection for whistle-blowers include California, Connecticut, Delaware, Florida, Hawaii, Louisiana, Maine, Michigan, Minnesota, Montana, New Hampshire, New Jersey, New York, North Carolina, Ohio, Oregon, Rhode Island, Tennessee, and Washington.[88] Some states (and the District of Columbia) consider whistleblowing to be a public policy exception to the employment-at-will doctrine. These include: Alaska, Arizona, Arkansas, California, Colorado, Connecticut, Florida, Hawaii, Idaho, Illinois, Indiana, Iowa, Kansas, Kentucky, Louisiana, Maine, Maryland, Massachusetts, Michigan, Minnesota, Missouri, Montana, Nebraska, Nevada, New Hampshire, New Jersey, New Mexico, North Carolina, North Dakota, Ohio, Oklahoma, Oregon, Pennsylvania, Rhode Island, Tennessee, Texas, Vermont, Virginia, Washington, West Virginia, Wisconsin and Wyoming.[89] In 2003, California passed SB 777, which provides significant new protection to whistle-blowers. Among other protections, the bill expands coverage to applicants as well as employees. It shifts the burden of evidence to the employer, adding civil penalties of up to $10,000 for any violations. It also sets up a whistle-blower hotline in the Attorney General's office. Employers are required to display a list of the whistle-blower protections and the hotline number.[90]

Most state courts have recognized a public policy exception, and therefore whistle-blowers have some limited protection. The normal remedy for wrongful discharge of employees is reinstatement with back pay, with some sympathetic juries adding compensatory damages for physical suffering.[91] The problem with most laws intended to protect whistle-blowers is that they were quite spotty. Some state and federal laws, such as environmental, transportation, health, safety, and civil rights statutes, have provisions that protect whistle-blowers from retaliation, but relatively few states had provisions that protect private sector employees, and these provisions vary widely in their nature and protection coverage.

This crazy quilt of whistle-blower protections made it very difficult for employees to safely shed light on corporate wrongdoing. In some states, whistle-blowers could be fired at will; in other states, they would have to sort through a bewildering assortment of statutes to determine what, if any, protection existed. However, that all changed when the Sarbanes–Oxley Act was passed in 2002.

Sarbanes–Oxley Whistle-Blower Protections

Tom Devine, Government Accounting Project (GAP) legal director, described the Sarbanes–Oxley Act as a "lunar landing in terms of strengthening corporate responsibility to shareholders and employees alike. This is a landmark breakthrough in corporate accountability and a legal revolution for corporate freedom of speech."[92] Sarbanes–Oxley makes whistle-blowing much easier. Whistle-blowers only need to make a disclosure to a supervisor, law enforcement agency, or congressional investigator that could have a "material impact" on a company's stock price. The Labor Department then bears responsibility for investigating any complaints of the whistle-blower being terminated, demoted, or harassed.[93] The protections Sarbanes–Oxley provides include:[94]

*   Comprehensive coverage for all employees of publicly traded companies
*   Comprehensive protection for any form of discrimination or harassment
*   Any corporate conduct that could threaten shareholder value
*   Timely responses through administrative investigations, temporary relief, and due process hearings
*   The right to a jury trial if an administrative ruling is not received within 180 days
*   Lessened burden of proof on the employee
*   Compensatory damages and judicial fees
*   Criminal felony penalties of up to 10 years for retaliation
*   Audit committees required to have procedures for responding to complaints

While acknowledging vast improvement, some critics still feel that the act did not go far enough. Only employees of publicly held firms are covered, and so employees of privately held firms still have limited protection. Also the law does not provide the financial incentives found in the False Claims Act.

False Claims Act

A provocative piece of federal legislation that was passed to add an incentive for whistle-blowers in the public interest is the **False Claims Act**. The False Claims Act has *qui tam* (Latin shorthand for "he who sues for the king as well as himself") provisions that allow employees to blow the whistle about contractor fraud and share with the government in any financial recoveries realized by their efforts. It dates back to the Civil War, when the Army wanted to find and prosecute profiteers who sold the same horse twice or sold boxes of sawdust while claiming they were guns. Citizens were permitted to sue on the government's behalf and receive 50 percent of the recovery. In 1943, Congress reduced the potential payout dramatically, and so it was seldom used.[95] The act was revised in 1986 to make recoveries easier to obtain and payouts more generous, thereby encouraging whistle-blowing against government contractor fraud.[96] The 1986 act grew out of outrage in the mid-1980s over reports of fraud and abuse on the part of military contractors, such as $600 toilet seats and country club memberships billed to the government.[97]

What is particularly controversial about the False Claims Act is the magnitude of the financial incentives that individual employees may earn as a result of their whistle-blowing efforts. The law allows individuals to be awarded as much as 15 to 25 percent of the proceeds in cases where the government joins in the action, and from 25 to 30 percent of the proceeds in actions that the government does not join.[98] Thus, there are millions or even tens of millions of dollars of incentives available to whistle-blowers who successfully win their suits against private contractors, thus allowing the government to get back huge sums, too.[99] HCA, the Tennessee-based health care provider, had the top two government settlements, $731 million in December 2000 and $631 million in June 2003 for a total of more than $1.5 billion.[100]

As a result of the False Claims Act, whistle-blowing against abuse of government by private companies is enjoying a renaissance. The Justice Department is recovering record sums, and whistle-blowers are becoming millionaires. John Phillips, a prominent public-interest lawyer in Los Angeles who helped persuade Congress to strengthen the False Claims Act in 1986, is enjoying a bustling law practice. His target companies have included GE, Teledyne, and National Health Laboratories.[101] He also was involved in the HCA settlements listed earlier.[102]

As of this writing, the False Claims Act has returned nearly $12 billion to the federal government.[103] The act continues to evolve as it is tested by legislation and the court. In 2003, the Supreme Court ruled unanimously that municipalities are "persons" under the False Claims Act and can be held liable for damages and penalties from submitting a false claim to the federal government. States are considered co-sovereign, and so they are not liable under the FCA; however municipalities are corporations, and so the court found that they should be treated like any other incorporated entity under the act.[104]

Given the introduction of Sarbanes–Oxley and the strength of the False Claims Act, it is clear that whistle-blowing will remain a major concern for the private sector. This necessitates careful thought and action on the part of company management as they contemplate how to respond to whistle-blowers and to whistle-blowing situations.

In 2003, a suit was filed against Bell Helicopter under the False Claims Act, according to *Knight Ridder/Tribune News Service's* Bob Cox (12 December 2003 pK3371), by a former Bell employee. The whistle-blower alleged that Bell delivered helicopters "with damaged, potentially hazardous components, billed the government for work that wasn't performed, and that employees improperly approved aircraft ready for flight." Bell denied the charges, suggesting the whistleblower was merely a disgruntled employee. Read more about the lawsuit by logging on to InfoTrac College Edition at **http://www.infotrac-college.com** and keying record number CJ111222754.

Management Responsiveness to Potential Whistle-Blowing Situations

How can an organization work with its employees to reduce their need to blow the whistle? Kenneth Walters[105] has suggested five considerations that might be kept in mind:

1. The company should assure employees that the organization will not interfere with their basic political freedoms.
2. The organization's grievance procedures should be streamlined so that employees can obtain direct and sympathetic hearings for issues on which they are likely to blow the whistle if their complaints are not heard quickly and fairly.
3. The organization's concept of social responsibility should be reviewed to make sure that it is not being construed merely as corporate giving to charity.

4. The organization should formally recognize and communicate respect for the individual consciences of employees.
5. The organization should realize that dealing harshly with a whistle-blowing employee could result in needless adverse public reaction.

Companies are learning that whistle-blowing can be averted if visible efforts are made on the part of management to listen and be responsive to employees' concerns. One specific approach is the use of an ombudsman, which we discussed earlier, as a due-process mechanism. The ombudsman can also be used to deal with employee grievances against the company. The Corporate Ombudsman Association, which includes such firms as Anheuser-Busch, Control Data, McDonald's, and Upjohn, even goes so far as to prepare training materials that include likely whistle-blowing scenarios. According to one report, the national grapevine among corporate ombudsmen is constantly buzzing with rumors of front-page scandals that they have averted. The companies that have put money into such programs say they are well worth the investment.[106]

Whether or not an ombudsman is used, management should respond in a positive way to employee objectors and dissenters. At a minimum, companies that want to be responsive to such employees[107] should engage in the following four actions:

1. *Listen*. Management must listen very carefully to the employee's concern. Be particularly attentive to the employee's valid points, and acknowledge them and show that you have a genuine respect for the employee's concerns. It is recommended that you attempt to "draw out the objector's personal concerns."
2. *Delve into why the employee is pursuing the complaint or issue*. Determining the objector's motives may give you important insights into the legitimacy of the complaint and how it should best be handled.
3. *Look for solutions that will address the interests of both the objector and the company*.
4. *Attempt to establish an equitable means of judging future actions*. Objective tests or criteria that are agreeable to both sides are superior to perseverance or negotiation as a means of resolving an impasse.

In a related set of recommendations, *Business Week* and The Conference Board have set forth four key components of a model whistle-blower policy.[108] These four recommended actions are as follows:

1. *Shout it from the rooftops*. The company should aggressively publicize a reporting policy that encourages employees to bring forward valid complaints of wrongdoing.
2. *Face the fear factor*. Employee fear may be defused by directing complaints to someone outside the whistle-blower's chain of command.
3. *Get right on it*. The complaint should be investigated immediately by an independent group, either within or outside the company.
4. *Go public*. The outcomes of investigations should be publicized whenever possible so that employees can see that complaints are taken seriously.

The desire of employees to speak out is increasingly becoming a right in their eyes and in the eyes of the courts as well. This being the case, management needs to assess carefully where it stands on this vital issue. It is becoming more and more apparent that respecting an employee's right to publicly differ with management may indeed serve the longer-term interests of the organization. We should also remember, however, that companies need and deserve protection from employees who do not perform as they should.

■ SUMMARY

Employee stakeholders today are more sensitive about employee rights issues for a variety of reasons. Underlying this new concern are changes in the social contract between employers and employees. Central among the growing employee rights issues that are treated in this chapter are the right not to be fired without just cause, the right to due process and fair treatment, and the right to freedom of speech.

The basis for the argument that we may be moving toward an employee's right not to be fired is the erosion by the courts of the employment-at-will doctrine. More and more, the courts are making exceptions to this long-standing common-law principle. Three major exceptions are the public policy exception, the idea of an implied contract, and breach of good faith. Society's concept of what represents fair treatment to employees is also changing.

The right to due process is concerned primarily with fair treatment. Common approaches for management responding to this concern include the open-door policy, human resource specialists, grievance committees, and hearing procedures. The ombudsman approach is becoming more prevalent, and recently the peer review panel seems to have become a popular due-process mechanism. Thanks to the passage of the Sarbanes–Oxley Act, whistle-blowers in the private sector now enjoy some of the protections once accorded only to public sector employees. Managers should be genuinely attentive to employees' rights in this realm if they wish to avert major scandals and prolonged litigation. A stakeholder approach that emphasizes ethical relationships with employees would ordain this attention and concern.

■ KEY TERMS

1978 Civil Service Reform Act (page 525)
alternative dispute resolution (ADR) (page 518)
collective bargaining (page 512)
due process (page 516)
employee rights (page 511)
employment-at-will doctrine (page 513)
enterprise rights (page 512)
False Claims Act (page 527)
good cause norm (page 513)
good faith principle (page 515)
hearing procedure (page 518)
implied contracts (page 514)

mandatory arbitration (page 520)
Michigan Whistle-Blowers Protection Act of 1981 (page 525)
ombudsman (page 518)
outplacement (page 509)
open-door policy (page 518)
peer review panel (page 519)
private property (page 510)
public policy exception (page 514)
social contract (page 508)
statutory rights (page 512)
whistle-blower (page 521)

■ DISCUSSION QUESTIONS

1. Rank the various changes that are occurring in the workplace in terms of their importance to the growth of the employee rights movement. Briefly explain your ranking.

2. Explain the employment-at-will doctrine, and describe why it is being eroded. Do you think its erosion is leading to a healthy or an unhealthy employ-

ment environment in the United States? Justify your reasoning.

3. In your own words, explain the right to due process. What are some of the major ways management is attempting to ensure due process in the workplace?

4. If you could choose only one, which form of alternative dispute resolution would be your choice as the

most effective approach to employee due process? Explain.

5. How do you feel about whistle-blowing now that you have read about it? Are you now more sympathetic or less sympathetic to whistle-blowers? Explain.

6. What is your assessment of the value of the False Claims Act? What is your assessment of the value of the whistle-blower protections under the Sarbanes–Oxley Act?

■ RECOMMENDED CASES

Many of the end-of-text cases may be related to Chapter 16. You may wish to consider studying the following cases with Chapter 16.

Case 11. "FAMILY BUSINESS." This case is about Jane, the newly-hired head of payroll at a family-owned business. Jane soon discovers that her boss is giving his brother easier and higher commission-paying work than the other service technicians receive. Is it appropriate for a family member to receive preferential treatment in a family firm? Alternatively, is it unfair for some service technicians to receive better assignments than others?

Case 31. "WAL-MART AND ITS ASSOCIATES: EFFICIENT OPERATOR OR NEGLECTFUL EMPLOYER?" This case about Wal-Mart addresses the increasing criticisms about Wal-Mart as an employer and its treatment of its employees. Issues raised include working off the clock, sexual discrimination, and the use of illegal immigrants. Is Wal-Mart just being efficient or is it unjust? Is this just a reflection of the changing social contract at work? What should Wal-Mart do?

Case 32. "'DEAD PEASANT' LIFE INSURANCE: SMART BUSINESS OR POOR ETHICAL PRACTICE?" This case is about corporate-owned life insurance policies (COLIs), also nicknamed "Dead Peasant" policies, that are taken out on rank and file employees. These policies are usually taken out without the employee's knowledge or consent and are actively marketed by the insurance industry. Are companies that take out COLIs simply engaging in good business practices, finding investment income wherever it exists? Or, as critics suggest, is there something wrong or even ghoulish about it?

■ WEB RESOURCES

The URLs listed here are current at the time of publication. Should any of these Web sites change, please search under the company's or organization's name for an updated address.

American Civil Liberties Union
http://www.aclu.org

Business Week
http://www.businessweek.com

Fortune
http://www.fortune.com

Government Accountability Project
http://www.whistleblower.org

National Whistleblower Center
http://www.whistleblowers.org

National Workrights Institute
http://www.workrights.org

The Ombudsman Association
http://www.ombuds-toa.org

U.S. Department of Labor
http://www.dol.gov

The Wall Street Journal
http://www.wsj.com

Worker Rights Consortium
http://www.workersrights.org

Workplace Fairness
http://www.workplacefairness.org

InfoTrac® College Edition   http://www.infotrac-college.com

Articles from Business Week, Fortune, *and* The Wall Street Journal *can be researched, retrieved, and read from your desktop using InfoTrac's online database.*

■ ENDNOTES

1. Diane Lewis, "Out in the Field: Workplace Want Loyal Workers? Then Help Them Grow," *Boston Globe* (July 15, 2001), H2.
2. Michelle Conlin, "Job Security, No. Tall Latte, Yes," *Business Week* (April 2, 2001), 62–64.
3. Lewis, H2.
4. John Challenger, "Establishing Rules for the New Workplace," *USA Today* Magazine (November 2002), 30–34.
5. *Ibid.*
6. Lewis, H2.
7. Challenger, 30–34.
8. *Ibid.*
9. *Ibid.*
10. "Despite Economy, Companies Spent More on Training in '02," *HR Focus* (February 2004), 8–9.
11. Challenger, 30.
12. Challenger, 30–34.
13. David W. Ewing, *Freedom Inside the Organization: Bringing Civil Liberties to the Workplace* (New York: McGraw-Hill, 1977), 3.
14. *Ibid.*, 5.
15. Leo Troy, The End of Unionism: An Appraisal (St. Louis: Center for the Study of American Business, Washington University, September 1994), 1–2.
16. Bureau of Labor Statistics, "Union Member Summary" (January 21, 2004), http://www.bls.gov/news.release/union2.nr0.htm.
17. Richard Edwards, Rights at Work (Washington, DC: The Brookings Institution, 1993), 25–26.
18. *Ibid.*, 31–33.
19. *Ibid.*, 33–35.
20. Mark V. Roehling, "The 'Good Cause Norm' in Employment Relations: Empirical Evidence and Policy Implications," *Employee Responsibility and Rights Journal* (September 2002), 91–104.
21. *Ibid.*
22. Tara J. Radin and Patricia H. Werhane, "Employment-At-Will, Employee Rights, and Future Directions for Employment," *Business Ethics Quarterly* (April 2003), 113–130.
23. T. J. Condon, "Fire Me and I'll Sue: A Manager's Guide to Employee Rights" (Alexander Hamilton Institute, 1984–1985), 4. Also see John D. Rapoport and Brian L. P. Zevnik, *The Employee Strikes Back!* (New York: Collier Books, 1994).
24. Linda D. McGill, "Public Policy Claims in Employee Termination Disputes," *Employment Relations Today* (Spring 1988), 46–47.
25. Axel R. Granholm, *Handbook of Employee Termination* (New York: John Wiley & Sons, 1991), 21. Also see Ronald M. Green, *The Ethical Manager* (NY: Macmillan, 1994), Chapter 5, "Employee Rights."
26. Jeffrey A. Williamson and Brian H. Kleiner, "New Developments Concerning the Covenant of Good Faith and Fair Dealing," *Management Research* News (2003), 35–41.
27. Andrew M. Kramer, "The Hazards of Firing at Will," *The Wall Street Journal* (March 9, 1987), 22. Also see Rapoport and Zevnik.
28. Richard Greene, "Don't Panic," *Forbes* (August 29, 1983), 122.
29. Williamson and Kleiner, 35–41.
30. *Ibid.*
31. Granholm, 24–25.
32. Condon, 12.
33. Kramer, 22.
34. Patricia H. Werhane, *Persons, Rights and Corporations* (Englewood Cliffs, NJ: Prentice Hall, 1985), 110.
35. Ewing, *Freedom Inside the Organization* (1977), 10.
36. Kay O. Wilburn, "Employment Disputes: Solving Them out of Court," *Management Review* (March 1998), 17–21. See also Marc Lampe, "Mediation as an Ethical Adjunct of Stakeholder Theory," *Journal of Business Ethics* (May 2001), 165–173.
37. Ewing, *Freedom Inside the Organization* (1977), 11.
38. David W. Ewing, *Justice on the Job: Resolving Grievances in the Nonunion Workplace* (Boston: Harvard Business School Press, 1989), 324.
39. Ewing, *Harvard Business Review* (1977).
40. "Where Ombudsmen Work Out," *Business Week* (May 3, 1976), 114–116.
41. Carolyn Hirschman, "Someone to Listen," *HR Magazine* (January 2003), 46–50.
42. *Ibid.*
43. *Ibid.*
44. *Ibid.*
45. Jonathan A. Segal, "The Joy of Uncooking," *HR Magazine* (November 2002), 52–57.
46. Hirschman, 46–51.
47. Fred C. Olson, "How Peer Review Works at Control Data," *Harvard Business Review* (November–December 1984), 58.
48. Margaret M. Clark, "Jury of Their Peers," *HR Magazine* (January 2004), 54.
49. *Ibid.*
50. *Ibid.*
51. Olson, 58, 64.

52. Cynthia F. Cohen, "Justice and Peer Review Systems: A Framework for Analysis," *Journal of Collective Negotiations in the Public Sector* (1999), 83–92.
53. Wilburn, 17–21.
54. Elaine McShulski, "ADR Gains Overwhelming Acceptance," *HR Magazine* (November 1997), 22.
55. Lampe, 165–173.
56. http://www.civilrights.org
57. Ewing, *Freedom Inside the Organization* (1977), 172–173.
58. Lee Gomes, "A Whistle-Blower Finds Jackpot at the End of His Quest," *The Wall Street Journal* (April 27, 1998), B1.
59. Robert P. Lawrence, "Go Ahead, Laugh at Army's Expense," *The San Diego Union-Tribune* (February 27, 1998), E12.
60. Gomes, B1.
61. Lawrence, E12.
62. Elizabeth Williamson, "One Soldier's Unlikely Act," *The Washington Post* (May 6, 2004), A16.
63. Williamson, A16.
64. *Ibid.*
65. Marcy Mason, "The Curse of Whistleblowing," *The Wall Street Journal* (March 14, 1994), A14.
66. Charles Peters and Taylor Branch (eds.) *Blowing the Whistle: Dissent in the Public Interest* (New York: Praeger, 1972), 4.
67. Marcia P. Miceli and Janet P. Near, *Blowing the Whistle: The Organizational and Legal Implications for Companies and Employees* (New York: Lexington Books, 1992), 15.
68. Janet P. Near and Marcia P. Miceli, *The Whistle-Blowing Process and Its Outcomes: A Preliminary Model* (Columbus, OH: The Ohio State University, College of Administrative Science, Working Paper Series 83–55, September, 1983), 2. See also Miceli and Near, 1992.
69. Nancy R. Hauserman, "Whistle-Blowing: Individual Morality in a Corporate Society," *Business Horizons* (March–April 1986), 5.
70. Janet P. Near and Marcia P. Miceli, "Whistleblowing— Myth and Reality," *Journal of Management* (1996 Special Issue), 507–526.
71. Richard Layco and Amanda Ripley, "Persons of the Year," *Time* (December 30, 2002), 32.
72. *Ibid.*
73. Dan Ackerman, "Whistleblower?" *The Wall Street Journal* (December 24, 2002), A10.
74. Amelia Gruber, "Whistleblower Volume Rises," *Government Executive* (September 2003), 16.
75. Janet P. Near, Marcia P. Miceli, and Tamila C. Jensen, "Variables Associated with the Whistle-Blowing Process," (Columbus, OH: The Ohio State University, College of Administrative Science, Working Paper Series 83–11, March 1983), 5.
76. Grover L. Porter, "Whistleblowers: A Rare Breed," *Strategic Finance* (August 2003), 51–53.
77. Kurt Eichenwald, "He Blew the Whistle, and Health Giants Quaked," *The New York Times* (October 18, 1998), 1.
78. Porter, 52.
79. Porter, 53.
80. *Ibid.*
81. *Ibid.*
82. Joan Hamilton, "Blowing the Whistle Without Paying the Piper," *Business Week* (June 3, 1991), 138.
83. Kurt Eichenwald, "He Told. He Suffered. Now He's a Hero," *The New York Times* (May 29, 1994), 1-F.
84. *Ibid.*
85. Joann S. Lublin, "Watchdog Has Hard Time Hearing Whistles," *The Wall Street Journal* (October 17, 1980), 30.
86. Radelat, 20.
87. Alan F. Westin, "Michigan's Law to Protect the Whistle Blowers," *The Wall Street Journal* (April 13, 1981), 18. Also see Daniel P. Westman, *Whistle Blowing: The Law of Retaliatory Discharge* (Washington, DC: The Bureau of National Affairs, 1991); Robert L. Brady, "Blowing the Whistle," *HR Focus* (February 1996), 20.
88. http://www.whistleblowerlaws.com/protection.htm
89. *Ibid.*
90. http://www.consumerwatchdog.org
91. Michael W. Sculnick, "Disciplinary Whistle-Blowers," *Employment Relations Today* (Fall 1986), 194.
92. http://www.whistleblower.org
93. Paula Dwyer, Dan Carney, Amy Borrus, Lorraine Woellert, and Christophe Palmeri, "Year of the Whistleblower," *Business Week* (December 16, 2002), 106–110.
94. http://www.whistleblower.org
95. Todd Wilkinson, "After Eight Years, An Insider Gets His Reward," *Christian Science Monitor* (July 24, 2001), 1.
96. Miceli and Near (1992), 247.
97. Andrew W. Singer, "The Whistle-Blower: Patriot or Bounty Hunter?" *Across the Board* (November 1992), 16–22.
98. Alfred G. Feliu, *Primer on Individual Employee Rights* (Washington, DC: The Bureau of National Affairs, Inc., 1992), 194–195.
99. Scott Hensley, "Settling Fraud Charges," *Modern Healthcare* (March 3, 1997), 28.
100. "The Top 100 False Claims Act Settlements: A Report to the National Press Club," *Corporate Crime Reporter* (December 30, 2003).
101. Richard B. Schmitt, "Honesty Pays Off: John Phillips Fosters a Growing Industry of Whistle-Blowing," *The Wall Street Journal* (January 11, 1995), A1.

102. http://www.whistleblowers.com

103. "The Top 100 False Claims Act Settlements: A Report to the National Press Club," 3.

104. http://journalism.medill.northwestern.edu/docket

105. Kenneth D. Walters, "Your Employees' Right to Blow the Whistle," *Harvard Business Review* (July–August 1975), 161–162.

106. Michael Brody, "Listen to Your Whistle-Blower," *Fortune* (November 24, 1986), 77–78.

107. David W. Ewing, "How to Negotiate with Employee Objectors," *Harvard Business Review* (January–February 1983), 104.

108. Lisa Driscoll, "A Better Way to Handle Whistle-Blowers: Let Them Speak," *Business Week* (July 27, 1992), 36.

Chapter 17

■ EMPLOYEE STAKEHOLDERS: PRIVACY, SAFETY, *and* HEALTH

CHAPTER LEARNING OUTCOMES

After studying this chapter, you should be able to:

1 Articulate the concerns surrounding the employee's right to privacy in the workplace.

2 Identify the advantages and disadvantages of polygraphs, integrity tests, and drug testing as management instruments for decision making.

3 Discuss the right to safety and the right to know, and summarize the role and responsibilities of OSHA.

4 Elaborate on the right to health in the workplace, with particular reference to violence in the workplace, smoke-free workplaces, family-friendly workplaces, and AIDS.

Employee stakeholders are concerned not only with the issues we discussed in the preceding chapter but also with several other issues. These other issues should be thought of as extensions of the concept of employee rights developed in Chapter 16. In this chapter, we are concerned with the employee's rights to privacy, safety, and a healthy work environment.

The right to privacy primarily addresses the psychological dimension, whereas the rights to health and safety primarily address the physical dimension. The status of an employee's right to privacy in the workplace today is ill defined at best. Constitutional protection of privacy, such as the prohibition of unreasonable searches and seizures, applies only to the actions of government, not to those of private sector employers. From a legal standpoint, the meager amount of privacy protection that exists, as with so many employee rights, is a collection of diverse statutes that vary from issue to issue and from state to state. Hence, there is a genuine need for management groups to impose ethical thinking and standards in this increasingly important area.

Employee rights to safety and health are issues of rising intensity, too. In today's workplace, whether in a manufacturing facility or an office complex, workers are exposed to hazards or risks of accidents or occupational diseases. If the normal hazards of work were not enough, the phenomenon of violence in the workplace should cause management to pay serious attention to this threat to workplace peace and stability.[1] Workplace violence incidents, coupled with concerns about terrorism, have made safety in the workplace a major concern of employees today. Other workplace health issues include smoking in the workplace and the implications of AIDS. Management also has to be aware of the need for family-friendly workplaces, with particular attention given to what legal rights employees have under the Family and Medical Leave Act (FMLA).

To reiterate a point we made in the preceding chapter, the distinction between the issues discussed there and those discussed here is made for discussion purposes. With that in mind, let us continue our consideration of social and ethical issues that have become important to employee stakeholders in recent years. If managers are to be successful in dealing with employees' needs and treating them fairly as stakeholders, they must address these concerns now and in the future.

RIGHT TO PRIVACY IN THE WORKPLACE

The employee restroom was once a place that employees could go to escape the watchful eye of management. Now with the introduction of "Hygiene Guard," a system developed by Net/Tech International, managers can make sure that employees are following proper hygiene on every bathroom trip. If an employee fails to wash properly, sensors on the soap dispensers and faucets make the employee's badge flash and put a black mark on the employee's file in the main computer.[2] Technological developments such as this have made it simpler and less expensive to conduct various types of surveillance—not only in public but also in the workplace. In turn, workplace monitoring has grown and with it come new ethical considerations. "**Privacy in the workplace** is largely illusory," says Ellen Bayer, the AMA's human resources practice leader.[3] As such, privacy has become a "hot button" issue for businesses.[4]

There are no clear legal definitions of what constitutes privacy or invasion of privacy, but everyone seems to have an opinion on when it has happened to them. Most experts say that privacy means the right to keep personal affairs to oneself and to know how information about one is being used.[5] Patricia Werhane, a business ethicist, opts for a broader definition. She says that privacy includes (1) the right to be left alone, (2) the related right to autonomy, and (3) the claim of individuals and groups to determine for themselves when, how, and to what extent information about them is communicated to others.[6] *Wired Magazine* asked a panel of privacy experts to rank the largest publicly held firms on their treatment of employee privacy. Figure 17-1 shows *Wired Magazine*'s rankings of the five best and five worst firms.[7]

Defining privacy in this way, however, does not settle the issue. In today's world, achieving these ideals is extremely difficult and fraught with judgment calls about our own privacy rights versus other people's rights. This problem is exacerbated by the increasingly computerized, technological world in which we live. We gain great efficiencies from computers and new technologies, but we also pay a price. Part of the price we pay is that information about us is stored in dozens of places, including federal agencies (the Internal Revenue Service and the Social Security Administration), state agencies (courts and motor

FIGURE 17-1

Wired Magazine's Ranking of Privacy at Work

The Best		The Worst	
1. IBM	Had the first formal privacy policy in the 1960s. Today IBM requires its health care partners to eliminate social security numbers as identification for patients.	1. Eli Lilly	Started doing background checks on contract workers after 9/11. Conducts even more stringent checks on full-time employees.
2. HP	Has six guardians who report to chief privacy officer (CPO) and protect employee privacy. Staff must complete special training to handle personnel files.	2. Wal-Mart	Hit with multiple lawsuits for improper search and surveillance. Managers were wired to tape conversations with co-workers.
3. Ford	Uses more stringent European Union privacy standards. Has special procedures to shield HR data from hackers and investigators.	3. New York Times Co.	Sued by staff physician who said she was fired for refusing to release medical information without employee consent. Times argued staff physician is not bound by confidentiality—and won.
4. Baxter Healthcare	Created an in-house version of "Safe Harbor," the stringent rules agreed upon by the United States and the European Union. Has 35 "privacy liaisons" charged with keeping the program on course.	4. Burlington Northern Santa Fe	Demanded genetic testing to refute worker's compensation claims. Employees sued and 36 workers shared a $2.2 million settlement.
5. Sears	Bans the use of social security numbers on any public identification, such as employee badges, in stores nationwide.	5. Hilton Hotels	Has history of leaking sensitive personnel information. Also employs computer monitoring, hidden cameras and background checks, as do many hotels.

SOURCE: Dustin Goot, "Ranking Privacy at Work." Originally published in *Wired* Magazine (October 2003). Copyright © 2003 by Conde Nast Publications, Inc. Reprinted by permission. All Rights Reserved.

vehicle departments), and many local departments and businesses (school systems, credit bureaus, banks, life insurance companies, and direct-mail companies).

In the realm of employee privacy, which is our central concern here, the following five important issues stand out as representative of the major workplace privacy issues:

1. Collection and use of employee information in personnel files
2. Use of the polygraph, or lie detector, in making employee decisions
3. Integrity testing
4. Drug testing
5. Monitoring of employee work, behavior, conversations, and location by electronic means

There are other issues that involve protection or invasion of privacy, but the five listed here account for the majority of today's concerns. Therefore, they merit separate consideration.

Collection and Use of Employee Information by Employers

The collection, use, and possible abuse of employee information is a serious public policy issue that warrants scrutiny. Today's government databases, with various agencies mixing and matching data, form a cohesive web of information on individual citizens. The **Privacy Act of 1974** set certain controls on the right of the government to collect, use, and share data about individuals. These restrictions were relaxed in 2001 when the

USA Patriot Act was signed into law in response to the attack on the World Trade Center towers. Although many people express concern that the Patriot Act gives the government too much latitude, restrictions still remain on how the government can collect, use, and share personal data. In contrast, very few laws protect the privacy of individuals in the workplace as monitoring of employees in the workplace grows.[8] A 2002 American Management Association (AMA) survey found that 77.7 percent of major U.S. companies record and review employee behavior: That is double the percentage of companies that did it in 1997.[9]

The necessity for guidelines regarding the collection of information became abundantly clear when the EEOC sued Burlington Northern Santa Fe Corp. for conducting secret genetic tests on workers who filed carpal tunnel syndrome claims. The tests came to light when one of the workers, Gary Avery, went to a mandatory medical exam as a follow-up to his successful carpal tunnel surgery. His wife Janice, a registered nurse, became suspicious when he was asked to give seven vials of blood. She later was told that the blood was for tests to determine whether her husband had a genetic trait that made him susceptible to carpal tunnel syndrome.[10] Burlington Northern ended up paying $2.2 million to settle the charges.[11]

Although there are still few guidelines for the collection of information, new guidelines have been developed for the way that collected information is handled. In 2001, the federal Department of Health and Human Services (HHS) issued final rules, establishing privacy standards in health care. When the standards were introduced, then-President Clinton described the new privacy standards as making "medical records much easier to see for those who should see them and much harder to see for those who shouldn't." Health care providers are expected to release the minimum amount of information necessary to meet the purpose of the disclosure. Health information is not to be used for nonhealth purposes—such as disclosures to employers to make personnel decisions, or to financial institutions—without explicit authorization from the patient.[12] Those employers that sponsor group health plans are subject to the privacy rule's regulations.[13] Indeed, even those employers that are not covered entities under the privacy rule will likely be held to a similar standard. The Americans with Disabilities Act (ADA), which is discussed later in Chapter 18, requires employers to protect the confidentiality of applicant and employee medical information, while also making it illegal to base employment decisions on a medical condition that does not affect the employee's ability to perform the essential functions of the job.

The overriding principle that should guide corporate decision making in regard to the collection and use of employee information is that companies should only collect that information from employees that is absolutely necessary and only use it in ways that are appropriate. Companies should be careful not to misuse this information by employing it for purposes for which it was not intended. Another important principle is that the employer should understand that information collected from employees is not a commodity to be exchanged, sold, or released in the marketplace.[14] Thus, the release of information to a landlord, credit grantor, or any other third party without the employee's consent may be regarded as an invasion of privacy.[15] A final important principle pertains to employees' access to information about themselves in company personnel files or other record-keeping systems. Employees should have some way of knowing what information is being stored about them, and they should have the opportunity to correct or amend inaccurate information.[16]

Ethics in Practice

ARE YOU A GOOD LIAR?

My last two years of high school were spent working part-time at a country club as a cart boy. One day I was told that $10,000 had been stolen from the golf shop the previous day and that all the employees would have to take a polygraph (lie detector) test that day. Being one of the few employees with keys to the shop and knowledge of the alarm code, I felt I would be a natural target for scrutiny. I wondered about the accuracy of those tests.

I decided to prove my innocence by telling the truth. During the test, after answering a few simple questions, I expected to be asked one question about the missing money. Instead, I was asked if I had ever stolen anything in my life, if I had ever done drugs on the job, and if I had stolen anything from the country club. I admitted that I had taken soft drinks from the beverage cart and discarded golf balls off the used cart—actions that many people do not consider stealing.

As a result, I was called into the Head Pro's office and rebuked for taking club property—I nearly lost my job. Should I have tried to cheat the lie detector test? It turns out the thief was never caught.

1. What are the ethical issues in this situation?

2. Did the club have the right to pose questions that were unrelated to the issue at hand?

3. What would you have done if you had been in this position? Why?

Contributed by Shaun M. Bank

Use of the Polygraph

In the invasion-of-privacy arena, few topics have generated as much controversy as the use of the **polygraph**, or lie detector, in business. The following brief scenario typifies the type of employee experience that led to the **Employee Polygraph Protection Act (EPPA)** of 1988, which banned most private sector uses of the lie detector. A polygraph machine was perched on a makeshift table in a tiny storage area. The examiner, hired by the employer, connected electrodes to 28-year-old Sandra Kwasniewski and then started interrogating her. "Have you ever shoplifted anything? Whom do you live with? Where does your boyfriend live? What are your dating practices? Do you drink?" Ms. Kwasniewski, manager of a gas station convenience store in the eastern United States, maintained that nothing had been stolen or even reported missing, but two days after the lie detector test she was fired.[17]

The notion of a "lie detector," historians tell us, is nothing new. The Bedouins of Arabia knew that certain physiological changes, triggered by guilt and fear, occurred when a person lied. The outstanding change they observed was that a liar would stop salivating. They developed a simple test in which a heated blade was passed across the tongue of a suspected liar. If innocent, the suspect would be salivating normally and the tongue would not be burned; if the person was lying, the tongue would be scorched. The ancient Chinese used dry rice powder. Someone suspected of lying was forced to keep a handful of rice powder in the mouth. If the powder was soggy when it was spat out, the truth was being told; if it was dry, the person was lying.[18]

Critics of today's lie detectors may well argue that the modern devices are not much more advanced than these ancient techniques. The polygraph machine, as it is known today, was developed by John Larson in 1929, although others trace it to an earlier date. It measures changes in blood pressure, respiration, and perspiration, sometimes called *galvanic skin response*. The theory behind polygraphy is that the act of lying causes stress, which in turn is manifested by observable physiological changes. The examiner, or machine operator, then interprets the subject's physiological responses to specific questions and makes inferences about whether or not the subject's answers indicate deception.[19]

Although the 1988 Employee Polygraph Protection Act banned most uses of the lie detector by private employers, it is still being used today because many employers and their applicants are exempt. Polygraphs may still be used by private employers that provide security services, protection of nuclear facilities, shipment or storage of radioactive or toxic waste, public water supply facilities, public transportation, precious commodities, or propriety information. Also, employers that manufacture, distribute, or dispense controlled substances may use polygraph tests for some of their positions. Government employers are also exempt from the prohibitions on polygraph testing. The federal government may also use polygraph tests for private consultants or experts under contract to various government departments, agencies, or bureaus.[20] When the U.S. Congress passed a law mandating that polygraphs be used on up to 20,000 Department of Energy workers, angry workers wrote letters of protest and wore buttons that said "Just say no to polygraphs."[21] One year later, the FBI announced that it would require 500 employees with access to confidential data to take the controversial test.[22] It is important to note, as he wrote from the prison cell, that Aldrich Ames passed the polygraph test with flying colors while selling U.S. secrets to Russia.[23]

Because lie detectors are still legal in very restricted circumstances, it is useful to know what are seen as their strengths and weaknesses. Proponents of lie detectors argue that employers have a right to protect their property and that lie detectors are more reliable and less expensive than alternatives. They cite the polygraph industry's claim of 95 to 100 percent accuracy in detecting deception. Proponents further argue that although employees and job applicants may sacrifice some privacy, a properly administered test gathers only information the company has a legitimate right to know.[24] Critics of lie detectors cite studies indicating inaccurate diagnoses in 50 percent of the cases. Critics also object to testing that entails broad probes into certain zones of privacy that are strictly personal and not related to the job. Examples of these personal zones include workers' sexual practices, union sympathies, finances, and political and religious beliefs.[25]

The issue of lie detection is unlikely to go away as new technologies are created. Research is progressing on the use of magnetic resonance imaging brain scans (MRIs) to separate truth from fiction.[26] Other scientists are exploring the use of voice pattern technology to develop a machine to do what a polygraph once did.[27] Still others are putting their efforts into lie detector glasses that can assess truthfulness, as well as anxiety and love.[28] As these new technologies for lie detection develop, new protections for employees will be needed to address them.

Integrity Testing

As criticism grew concerning the use of lie detectors, many companies anticipated an eventual elimination of lie detector use and began experimenting with **integrity tests** (also known as *honesty tests*). David Nye dubbed this type of test the "son of the polygraph."[29] There is a certain irony in this title, because integrity tests are already being subjected to the same kinds of criticisms that led to severe restriction of lie detector testing.

Robert J. Grossman explores the pervasive problem of embezzling—the "five-finger bonus"—in an article for *HRMagazine* (October 2003 v48 i10 p38). He describes the three factors that encourage employees to embezzle company funds: Motivation + opportunity + rationalization. Grossman suggests that integrity testing, while not foolproof, can be a "very good indicator" of a possible motivation problem. To read this in-depth discussion of corporate embezzlement and how to control it, log on to InfoTrac College Edition at http://www.infotrac-college.com and key record number A109136215.

Ethics in Practice

GIVE ME WHAT I WANT OR I'LL TELL THE PRESIDENT!

Place yourself in the role of a personnel director for a bank. It is company policy that neither personnel files nor copies of files are to leave the personnel office. The director of accounting and computer services is due to give his employees their yearly employee evaluations and has sent a memo to your secretary requesting copies of his employees' evaluations from the previous year. Your secretary shows you the memo. You are upset that the director would send such a memo to your secretary, because he should be aware of the policy concerning employee files.

So, you decide to call the director and tell him that he is welcome to read the evaluations of his employees from the previous year in the personnel office. He tells you that he does not have the time to come to personnel and read the files and that he will speak to the president of the bank about this issue. The working relationship between you and

the director has been addressed by the president before, and she has told the two of you that you need to be able to work out problems such as this between yourselves.

The dilemma is whether you should go against company policy in an effort to avoid another lecture from the president, and let the director take the copies of the evaluations to his office, or adhere to the bank's policy on protection of employee privacy.

1. What are the main ethical dilemmas in this situation?

2. Should you report the director's threat to step over you to the president?

3. What would you do in this situation?

Contributed by Leah Herrin

A study by the U.S. Office of Technology Assessment was conducted, and the findings were reported in a report titled *Truth and Honesty Testing*. The report suggested four reasons why employers were using integrity tests:[30]

1. To stem employee theft
2. To avoid "negligent hiring" suits
3. To screen employees cost-effectively
4. To replace polygraphs, which were banned by the EPPA

The format of an integrity test can be paper and pencil, computer survey, in-store kiosk, telephone interactive voice response, or an interactive Web page.[31] An integrity test typically poses 80 to 90 statements with which the employee or applicant is asked to agree or disagree. Some test questions are framed as yes-or-no and multiple-choice options. Examples include, "Would you tell your boss if you knew of another employee stealing from the company?" and "What percent of employee thieves are never caught?" and "What is the dollar value of cash or merchandise you have stolen from past employers?"[32] The tests can be customized to the needs of the company. Whereas one company might want to test for honesty and nonviolence, another might want to test for drug avoidance and turnover.[33]

Integrity tests are quick to administer, easy to grade, and cost only $6 to $15 each. This compares favorably with lie detector tests, which cost $25 to $75 each. Perhaps integrity tests have attracted less attention than polygraphs because they seem less intrusive or intimidating than lie detector tests, in which the examinee is hooked up to wires and sensors. The integrity test comes across more as a red-tape item or a job application to be filled out than as an interrogation.[34]

Faced with the elimination of the polygraph, companies wanted to find a substitute, and integrity tests seemed to be a convenient alternative. Critics of integrity tests claim they are intrusive and invade privacy by the nature of their inquiries. Critics also say that they are unreliable and that employers use them as the sole measure of the fitness of an applicant. Even when these tests are properly administered, opponents charge that employers end up rejecting many honest applicants in their efforts to screen out the dishonest ones. Management and testing companies claim the tests are very useful in weeding out potentially dishonest applicants. They claim that each question asked has a specific purpose. They also argue that hiring by "gut feeling" is problematic, and integrity tests provide a more objective assessment.[35]

Psychologists disagree widely on the validity and effectiveness of integrity tests. The American Psychological Association issued a report accepting the concept of integrity testing as superior to most other preemployment tests but noting that test publishers' accountability and documentation needed serious improvement.[36] One problem is that the test publishers and users themselves have done much of the research. A major U.S. retailer used integrity tests in 600 of their 1,900 locations to reduce turnover and shrinkage. After one year, they saw inventory shrinkage fall by more than 35 percent in the stores that used the test while it rose by 10 percent in the stores that did not. Even though turnover was not a goal of the test administration, they noted a 13 percent decrease in turnover at stores that did use the test and a 14 percent increase in turnover at stores that did not.[37]

Integrity tests are subject to the same kinds of legal and ethical hurdles that affected polygraph and drug tests. The Civil Rights Act (discussed in Chapter 18) makes it unlawful for any test to have a particularly negative impact on a protected subgroup. One integrity test, the Reid Report, has had 23 legal challenges. Administrators at Reid London House report that the EEOC or relevant state human rights agency found for each case that there was no probable cause to believe the test had disparate impact.[38] From the Americans with Disabilities Act (ADA) perspective, medical examinations can only be given to after a conditional offer of employment has been made. The EEOC has ruled that integrity tests are not medical examinations and so they can be given to applicants: Psychological examinations are only considered medical if they provide evidence of a mental disorder.[39] Most states apply the federal laws to selection tools. However, Massachusetts and Rhode Island have extended the polygraph statutes to integrity tests. In Massachusetts, integrity tests are against the law, while in Rhode Island they cannot be used as the primary basis for an employment decision.[40]

Although legal issues will be resolved on a case-by-case basis, the ethical issues surrounding integrity tests are likely to remain. A test that will identify many of those who would behave unethically at a cost to the firm will also yield "false positives," people labeled as unethical who would have been good employees. In statistics, this is called a **type 1 error**, finding an innocent person to be guilty. In contrast, a **type 2 error** finds a guilty person to be innocent. The nature of testing is such that a decrease in one type of error leads to an increase in the other. In other words, the more strictly a test is used to rule out any person who would be guilty of unethical behavior, the more innocent people will be judged unethical. It is important, therefore, that integrity tests be used judiciously and that they not be the primary criterion on which employment is based.

Drug Testing

Drug testing is an umbrella term intended to embrace drug and alcohol testing and employer testing for any suspected substance abuse. The issue of drug testing in the workplace has many of the same characteristics as the lie detector and integrity test issues. Companies say they need to do such testing to protect themselves and the public, but opponents claim that drug tests are not accurate and invade the employee's privacy.

For many years, companies did not conduct widespread testing of workers or job applicants for drug abuse. The reported reasons for their reluctance[41] included the following:

- Moral issue/privacy
- Inaccuracy of tests
- Negative impact on employee morale
- Tests show use, not abuse
- High cost
- Management, employee, and union opposition

In the past decade, however, this began to shift. In 1987, fewer than 25 percent of employers surveyed had drug-testing programs. By 1993, 85 percent of the companies surveyed by the American Management Association reported having drug-testing programs.[42] However, by the year 2001, the last year the survey was conducted, the tide had turned again: The percentage of firms using drug tests had dropped to 67 percent.[43] The cost of drug testing in a slow economy played a large part in the decrease.[44] It clearly wasn't due to a decrease in drug use. In their semiannual Drug Testing Index, Quest Diagnostics found that drug use in the U.S. workforce had climbed to 4.6 percent: The increase was driven largely by an increase in the use of amphetamines.[45]

Arguments for Drug Testing.
Proponents of drug testing argue that the costs of drug abuse on the job are staggering. The consequences range from accidents and injuries to theft, bad decisions, and ruined lives. The greatest concern is in industries where mistakes can cost lives—for example, the railroad, airline, aerospace, nuclear power, and hazardous equipment and chemicals industries. Edwin Weihenmayer, vice president at Kidder, Peabody, a New York-based investment banking firm, believes that drug testing is essential in his industry, "where the financial security of billions of dollars is entrusted to us by clients."[46] Thus, the primary ethical argument for employers conducting drug tests is the responsibility they have to their own employees and to the general public to provide safe workplaces, secure asset protection, and safe places in which to transact business.

Arguments Against Drug Testing.
Opponents of drug testing see it as both a due-process issue and an invasion-of-privacy issue. The due-process issue relates to the questionable accuracy of drug tests. Although one test manufacturer claims a 95 percent accuracy rate, some doctors disagree. For example, Dr. David Greenblatt, chief of clinical pharmacology at Tufts New England Medical Center, claims that "false positives can range up to 25 percent or higher. The test is essentially worthless."[47] In addition, some legal experts argue that, even if the tests were foolproof, they would still be an invasion of employee privacy. They claim that tests represent an unconstitutional attempt on the part of companies to control employees' behavior at home, because the tests can yield positive results days and even weeks after at-home drug use.[48]

Many legitimate questions arise in the drug-testing issue. Do employers have a right to know if their employees use drugs? Are employees performing on the job satisfactorily? Obviously, some delicate balance is needed, because employers and employees alike have legitimate interests that must be protected. This issue is a fairly new one for business, but it is apparent that it will not go away. Therefore, if companies are going to engage in some form of drug testing, they should think carefully about developing policies that not only will achieve their intended goals but also will be fair to the employees and minimize invasions of privacy. Such a balance will not be easy to achieve but must be sought. To do otherwise will guarantee decreased employee morale, more and more lawsuits, and new government regulations.

Guidelines for Drug Testing. If management perceives the need to conduct a drug-testing program to protect other stakeholders, it should carefully design and structure the program so that it will be minimally intrusive of employees' privacy rights. The following guidelines[49] may be helpful.

- Management should not discipline or fire someone for refusing to take a drug test because the results of such tests are inconclusive.
- Drug tests should typically be used only when there is legitimate suspicion of abuse by an employee or work group.
- The focus of testing should be on-the-job performance rather than off-the-job conduct.
- Employees should be informed of methods used and results obtained and given the chance to rebut the test findings.
- If an employee's status is going to be affected by the outcome of a drug test, a confirmatory test should be conducted.
- All tests should be conducted in such a way that the dignity and privacy of the employee are respected and honored.

Obviously, there are exceptions to these guidelines, and there are other guidelines that might be used. The major point is that management needs to think through its policies and their consequences very carefully when designing and conducting drug-testing programs.

State and Federal Legislation. Some states and cities have enacted or are considering laws to restrict workplace drug testing. Generally, these laws restrict the scope of testing by private and public employers and establish privacy protections and procedural safeguards. The laws do not completely ban drug testing but typically restrict the circumstances (for reasonable cause, for example) under which it may be used. States that have passed drug-testing laws include Florida, Vermont, Iowa, Minnesota, Montana, Maine, Connecticut, Rhode Island, and North Carolina. These states restrict drug testing to reasonable suspicion and place limits on the disciplinary actions employers may take. Other states are considering such legislation. This patchwork of incongruous state laws complicates drug testing for employers.[50]

At the federal level, the **Americans with Disabilities Act (ADA)** must be considered, because the definition of disability applies to drug and alcohol addiction. The ADA prohibits companies from giving applicants medical exams before they extend those applicants conditional offers of employment. Prehire drug tests, however, are permitted. Philadelphia employment lawyer Jonathan Segal advises employers to extend conditional offers before drug testing, because an innocent question on a drug test could easily become a medical question. He recommends conducting the drug test immediately after making the conditional offer and then waiting until the test results are back before beginning employment. An employer who wishes to fire or refuse to hire someone with an alcohol or a drug addiction must show that the employee poses a direct threat to others. Furthermore, if a person loses a job opportunity because of an inaccurate failed drug test, the company has committed an ADA offense by basing an action on the perception of a disability.[51]

It is worth noting some of the categories of employees that the federal government now requires be tested for on-the-job drug and alcohol use. The government requires both random alcohol and drug tests each year for 25 percent of transportation workers in such safety-sensitive jobs as trucking, aviation, railroads, and pipelines. Before, only random drug testing was required. In addition, the federal government requires drug and alcohol testing on mass-transit workers and expanded testing on intrastate truckers and bus drivers.[52] Quest International found that this group of employees remained steady in their level of drug use at 2.5 percent, an all-time low since 1998 and nearly half the level found in the general population.[53]

Employee Assistance Programs.

One of the most significant strategies undertaken by corporate America to deal with the growing alcohol- and drug-abuse problem in the workplace has been **Employee Assistance Programs (EAPs)**. EAPs originated, for the most part, in the 1940s, 1950s, and 1960s to deal with alcoholism on the job.[54] By the 1990s, EAPs had extended into other employee problem areas as well, such as compulsive gambling, financial stress, emotional stress, marital difficulties, aging, legal problems, AIDS, and other psychological, emotional, and social difficulties. The term **broad brush EAP** was created to describe this more comprehensive model.[55] In 2004, a major concern of EAPs was the impact of troop deployments in the Middle East on employees. This affected not only those deployed but also their family and friends. EAPs focused on providing resources to assist them in dealing with the stress.[56]

EAPs represent a positive and proactive step companies can take to deal with these serious problems. EAPs are designed to be confidential and nonpunitive, and they affirm three important propositions: (1) Employees are valuable members of the organization, (2) it is better to help troubled employees than to discipline or discharge them, and (3) recovered employees are better employees. It is encouraging that in an era when employees are increasingly exerting their workplace rights, enlightened companies are offering EAPs in an effort to help solve their mutual problems. More information on EAPs can be found at the Employee Assistance Program Association Web site at http://www.eap-association.org.[57]

Monitoring Employees on the Job

In the old days, supervisors monitored employees' work activities by peeking over their shoulders and judging how things were going. Next came cameras and listening devices whereby management could keep track of what was going on from remote locations. With the advent of computers, workers and civil liberties activists are concerned about the use of technology to gather information about workers on the job.[58] These concerns are well founded. In 2001, the last year they conducted their workplace monitoring survey, the American Management Association (AMA) found that 82 percent of mid- to large-sized firms participate in some type of **employee monitoring**. In some cases, the method is passive, such as video cameras in a lobby. However the vast majority, 78 percent, used more active means of monitoring their workers, such as recording their phone calls or voice mail, reading their computer files, or videotaping them. The level of active monitoring has doubled in only three years—from 35 percent in 1997 to 78 percent in

2001.[59] Clearly, employer monitoring of employees has become the norm in businesses today. The consequence is that millions of workers are laboring under the relentless gaze of electronic supervision.

What Can Be Monitored?

According to the AMA survey, 63 percent of companies monitor their employees' Internet connections; 47 percent store and then review their employees' e-mail. Nearly one in four firms use keyword searches to review their employees' e-mail. The most commonly used search was for words with explicit sexual content or scatological language (70.2 percent). Firms also search the e-mail using names of current employees (18.3 percent), names of clients (16.3 percent), names of vendors and suppliers (14.4 percent), and names of former employees (13.5 percent). Of the firms surveyed, 43 percent monitor telephone numbers called and time spent on the phone; 38 percent use video surveillance.[60] Monitoring telephone conversations is a significant arena for electronic eavesdropping, with workers in telecommunications, mail-order houses, airline reservations, and brokerage firms being hit especially hard. Not only do supervisors frequently listen in on their conversations, but computers also gather and analyze data about their work habits.

As was discussed in Chapter 8, the introduction of new technologies creates new opportunities for surveillance by employers. For example, the advent of global positioning system (GPS) technology has made it possible for worker location to be monitored. In December 2003, snowplow operators in Massachusetts marched outside the state capitol to protest a new requirement that they carry cell phones with GPS receivers. As independent contractors, they feared the highway department would use the technology to squeeze their payments unfairly.[61] UPS is planning to include GPS capability on the next generation of delivery scanners that drivers use to record pickups and deliveries.[62] Camera phones also present the possibility of becoming a new tool for employers to use. Some companies have already moved to ban them from the workplace due to fear of corporate espionage.[63]

Along with many Third World countries, the United States offers few protections for the privacy of employees in the workplace. The only federal level of privacy protection in the United States is the **Electronic Communication Privacy Act (ECPA) of 1986**. The interception or unauthorized access of a wire, oral, or electronic communication is illegal under this act unless it is covered by one of the statutory exceptions or required by government compulsion. One of the statutory exceptions is the business use exception: The act does not apply if the interception or access occurs as part of the "ordinary course of business." The act also does not apply if the person gives consent. An employee working at a place that has disclosed that it will do monitoring is considered to have given implicit consent. With these broad exceptions, it is not surprising that the ECPA has been ineffective in regulating the monitoring of employees in the workplace.[64] The one clear protection is that employers may not listen to phone conversations that are purely personal; however, they can monitor a conversation for the time required to determine that the call is personal.[65] States that have introduced some form of legislation to require employers to give employees notice of their electronic monitoring activities include New Jersey, Massachusetts, California, Illinois, Minnesota, and Alaska.[66] Only Connecticut has a law in place—it requires employers to give notice before engaging in electronic monitoring.[67]

Efforts to enact a U.S. law specifically geared toward workplace privacy have always been stymied. In 1993, Senator Paul Simon (D–IL) introduced the Privacy for Consumers and Workers Act. The measure would have established use limitations as well as a standard

SEARCH THE WEB

GUARDING PERSONAL PRIVACY

Privacy.Org is the site where you can find daily news, information, and initiatives on privacy. This Web page is a joint project of the Electronic Privacy Information Center (EPIC) and Privacy International. Based in Washington, DC, EPIC is a public interest research center that focuses public attention on emerging civil liberties issues and works to protect privacy. Based in London with an office in Washington, DC, Privacy International serves as a watchdog on surveillance by governments and corporations. The website (**http://www.privacy.org**) offers a range of news, tools, resources, and links to other privacy-related Web sites throughout the world.

for notice and access to information. However, the bill never left its committee.[68] Representative Charles Canady (R–FL) and Senator Charles Schumer (D–NY) introduced the Notice of Electronic Monitoring Act (NEMA) in 2000. Efforts were underway to reach a bipartisan bill, but they came to a halt when September 11 occurred.[69]

Effects of Being Monitored. Invasion of privacy is one major consequence of employee monitoring. Another is unfair treatment. Employees working under such systems complain about stress and tension resulting from their being expected and pressured to be more productive now that their efforts can be measured. The pressure of being constantly monitored is also producing low morale and a sense of job insecurity in many places. Employees have good reason to be concerned. According to the 2001 AMA survey, 27 percent of the firms fired employees who misused office e-mail or Internet connections; 65 percent administered some sort of punishment for those offenses.[70]

Policy Guidelines on the Issue of Privacy

As we have discussed various privacy issues, we have indicated steps that management might consider taking in an attempt to be responsive to employee stakeholders. Frederick S. Lane III, a law and technology expert and author of *The Naked Employee: How Technology Is Compromising Workplace Privacy*, offers an "Employee Privacy Bill of Rights" that sets forth guidelines for developing privacy policies and procedures that uphold the dignity of the employee. To preserve employee rights, firms should:

1. Obtain informed consent from employees and applicants before acquiring information about them.
2. Disclose the nature of any surveillance that will occur.
3. Set controls so as to avoid casual and unauthorized spread of information.
4. Limit the collection and use of medical and health data to that which is relevant to the job.
5. Require reasonable suspicion before doing drug tests.
6. Respect and preserve the boundary between work and home.

As a final recommendation, we set forth four policy guidelines that touch on several of the issues we have discussed. Robert Goldstein and Richard Nolan[71] assert that organizations should:

1. *Prepare a* **privacy impact statement**. This would require the firm to analyze the potential privacy implications to which all systems (especially computerized ones) should be subjected.

2. *Construct a comprehensive privacy plan.* The purpose of such planning would be to ensure that the necessary privacy controls are integrated into the design of a system at the very beginning.
3. *Train employees who handle personal information.* Be sure they are aware of the importance of protecting privacy and the specific procedures and policies to be followed.
4. *Make privacy a part of social responsibility programs.* Companies need to acknowledge that they have an internal responsibility to their employees and not fail to consider this when designing and implementing corporate social efforts.

Business's concern for protection of the privacy of its employees, customers, and other stakeholders is a growing business. It is not surprising, therefore, that a new form of corporate executive came on the horizon. **Chief privacy officers (CPOs)** are high-ranking executives responsible for monitoring and protecting the private information held by firms. The 2000-2003 economic slump meant few CPOs were hired. "Over the last few years, the economy made it hard to bring people in except in industries where CPOs were mandated," says Herman Collins, CEO of Privacy Leaders, an executive search firm that specializes in privacy professionals.[72] When the economy rebounds and firms begin to address the new laws and regulations that impact privacy, more focus on the hiring of CPOs is likely.

WORKPLACE SAFETY

Workplace safety has taken on new importance for today's worker. According to a 2004 SHRM/CNNfn survey, 62 percent of employees find feeling safe at work to be "very important." That figure is nearly double the 36 percent who found it to be very important in 2002.[73] "Terrorist warnings in the U.S. and the wars in the Middle East have put employees' concerns for safety at the forefront," said Susan R. Meisinger, CEO of SHRM, "It's a priority for all employers to do all they can to create and maintain a safe workplace."[74]

The main law that protects the safety and health of workers is the Occupational Safety and Health Act. This act requires the Secretary of Labor to set safety and health standards that protect employees and their families. Every private employer who engages in interstate commerce is subject to the regulations promulgated under this act.[75] The federal agency that is responsible for overseeing the safety and health of America's workers is the **Occupational Safety and Health Administration (OSHA)**. Figure 17-2 shows OSHA's mission.[76] OSHA's overarching goals for its 2003–2008 strategic management plan are:

- Reduce occupational hazards through direct intervention.
- Promote a safety and health culture through compliance assistance, cooperative programs, and strong leadership.
- Maximize OSHA's effectiveness and efficiency by strengthening its capabilities and infrastructure.

We will begin by examining the workplace safety problem and the right-to-know laws that have evolved from it. We'll then study OSHA's rocky history and its current situation. We'll last look at the issue of workplace violence, which is a serious con-

SEARCH THE WEB

EXPLORING OSHA

The Occupational Safety and Health Administration (OSHA) has a Web site that serves as a clearinghouse for information about employee safety and health on the job (http://www.osha.gov). On this site are OSHA manuals, continually updated statistics and inspection data, hazard information bulletins, and OSHA directives.

OSHA's Mission

OSHA's mission is to assure the safety and health of America's workers by setting and enforcing standards; providing training, outreach, and education; establishing partnerships; and encouraging continual improvement in workplace safety and health.

Our Services
OSHA and its state partners have approximately 2100 inspectors, plus complaint discrimination investigators, engineers, physicians, educators, standards writers, and other technical and support personnel spread over more than 200 offices throughout the country. This staff establishes protective standards, enforces those standards, and reaches out to employers and employees through technical assistance and consultation programs.

The Public We Serve
Nearly every working man and woman in the nation comes under OSHA's jurisdiction (with some exceptions such as miners, transportation workers, many public employees, and the self-employed). Other users and recipients of OSHA services include: occupational safety and health professionals, the academic community, lawyers, journalists, and personnel of other government entities.

Service Improvement Plan
OSHA is determined to use its limited resources effectively to stimulate management commitment and employee participation in comprehensive workplace safety and health programs.

Surveying Our Public
At OSHA, we are dedicated to improving the quality of our efforts and know that to be successful we must become an agency that is driven by commitment to public service. The first step is for OSHA to listen and respond to its customers. Accordingly, we conducted a survey to learn more about what employers and employees think of OSHA's services.

Because workplace inspections are one of OSHA's principal activities and because voluntary efforts to improve working conditions ultimately depend on strong enforcement, our survey focused primarily on the inspection process. We asked a random sample of employees and employers who had recently experienced an OSHA inspection what they thought of the inspection in particular, and of OSHA's standards and educational and other assistance activities in general.

Service Standards
We based OSHA's new standards for public service on what we learned from the survey, from meetings with employee and employer groups, and from focus group discussions with workers from many plants and industries across the country.

Our public service improvement program will be an ongoing one. We will continue to gather information on the quality of our performance in delivering services in areas not included in this year's survey, particularly in the construction sector. Next year, too, we plan to learn more about public response to our assistance and consultation programs.

SOURCE: http://www.osha.gov (2004).

cern in today's workplace. We'll then turn to issues of health, specifically AIDS and smoking in the workplace, and then end with a discussion of the family-friendly workplace.

The Workplace Safety Problem

Two events stand out as forerunners of the workplace safety problem. The first event ranks among the landmark cases on job safety. In Elk Grove Village, Illinois, Film Recovery Systems operated out of a single plant that extracted silver from used hospital x-ray and photographic film. To extract the silver, the employees first had to dump the film into open vats of sodium cyanide and then transfer the leached remnants to another tank. On February 10, 1983, employee Stefan Golab staggered outside and collapsed, unconscious. Efforts to revive him failed, and he was soon pronounced dead from what the local medical examiner labeled "acute cyanide toxicity."[77]

An intensive investigation by attorneys in Cook County, Illinois, revealed a long list of incriminating details: (1) Film Recovery workers seldom wore even the most rudimentary safety equipment, (2) workers were laboring in what amounted to an industrial gas chamber, and (3) company executives played down the dangers of cyanide poisoning and removed labeling that identified it as poisonous. The prosecutors took action under an Illinois homicide statute that targets anyone who knowingly commits acts that "create a strong probability of death or serious bodily harm." Three executives at Film Recovery Systems—the president, the plant manager, and the foreman—were convicted of the murder of Stefan Golab and sentenced to 25 years in prison. Their convictions marked the first time that managers had been convicted of homicide in a corporate matter such as an industrial accident.[78] The Film Recovery Systems case marked a new era in managerial responsibility for job safety. A variety of other prosecutions of managers have followed the Film Recovery Systems case. What this clearly signals is not only that employees have a moral right to a safe working environment but also that managers face prosecution if they do not ensure that employees are protected.

The second event was the dramatic and catastrophic poisonous gas leak at the Union Carbide plant in Bhopal, India, in 1984. The death toll topped 2,000, and tens of thousands more were injured. People around the globe were startled and shocked at what the results of one major industrial accident could be. Lawsuits sought damages that quickly exceeded the net worth of the company.[79] In 1991, India's Supreme Court upheld a $470 million settlement that Union Carbide had already paid, and it lifted the immunity from criminal prosecution that it had granted the company in 1989. The name "Union Carbide" became inextricably linked with the Bhopal Disaster. In 2001, Union Carbide became a wholly owned subsidiary of Dow Chemical.

Of course, not all hazards can be anticipated. The 2001 attack on the World Trade Center was a shock and surprise to the world. Shortly after the tragedy occurred, many were wondering what the impact would be on Morgan Stanley, one of the world's biggest brokerages and investment firms. The company was the largest tenant in the World Trade Center, with about 3,700 employees in two of the towers. Amazingly, fewer than 10 of their employees were among the missing, and only about 50 reported being injured. Company officials credit the evacuation procedures that Morgan Stanley developed after the 1993 bombing of the World Trade Center with saving so many of their employees' lives. The security staff used megaphones to keep people moving despite announcements over the building's public address system that instructed people to return to work. They moved their employees down the smoke-filled stairs (some more than 70 flights) and away from the twin towers. The earlier 1993 incident had alerted them to their vulnerability, and they took the steps necessary to protect the health and safety of as many of their employees as possible.[80] In a world where the unexpected is to be expected, this is the type of preparedness all workplaces should emulate.

Right-to-Know Laws

Prompted by the Union Carbide tragedy in Bhopal and other, less dramatic industrial accidents, workers have demanded to know more about the thousands of chemicals and

Ethics in Practice

HOW ETHICAL VALUES VARY

During my Christmas break, I was employed at ABC Company, a caulk manufactory located in a small town. Jim Wilson, who had little or no education, was employed in the shipping department at ABC. He was also trained as a blender in case someone in the Blending Department quit, went on vacation, or was fired. Luis Alberto, who was about 58 years old, was also employed at ABC Company, as a packer. Basically, a packer operates a machine that fills the cartridges with caulk, seals the tubes, and finally places either 12 or 24 10-ounce cartridges in a box. Luis's education did not range beyond an eighth-grade level. Luis's daughter-in-law was also employed at ABC, as a chemist in the lab. She spoke up when Luis's employment situation was on the line. She even told management when it was time to consider giving Luis an increase in his earnings.

Prior to the Christmas holiday break, the hired blender quit. Knowing how hard the position was to fill, Jim was told it was a permanent position. Jim was told by his supervisor, "Jim, you can't get another job anywhere in town because you don't have a high school diploma and you can't read, so you are up the creek if you don't take this position." Nothing was mentioned to Luis about the position. Luis's daughter-in-law made sure that the supervisor kept the opening notice out of Luis's sight. Knowing the dangers of that particular job, she thought it was in his best interest not to be made aware of it. It seems as if Jim Wilson had to do all the dirty work in the plant without being able to say anything.

1. How is ethics involved in this situation at the ABC Company?

2. If ethics is involved, what procedures should be implemented?

3. What are Jim's alternatives? What should he do? Why?

4. If you observed this situation with respect to employees as stakeholders, what would you do? Why?

Contributed by Mystro Whatley

hazardous substances they are being exposed to daily in the workplace. Experts argue that employers have a duty to provide employees with information on the hazards of workplace chemicals and to make sure that workers understand what the information means in practical terms. Since the early 1980s, many states have passed **right-to-know laws** and expanded public access to this kind of information by employees and even communities.[81] Although the states took the initiative on the right-to-know front, OSHA followed suit. In 1983, OSHA created a Hazard Communication Standard, which took effect in 1985. This standard requires covered employers to identify hazardous chemicals in their workplaces and to provide employees with specified forms of information on such substances and their hazards. Specifically, manufacturers, whether they are chemical manufacturers or users of chemicals, must take certain steps to achieve compliance with the standard.[82] These steps include the following:

1. Update inventories of hazardous chemicals present in the workplace.
2. Assemble material safety data sheets (MSDSs) for all hazardous chemicals.
3. Ensure that all containers and hazardous chemicals are properly labeled.
4. Provide workers with training on the use of hazardous chemicals.
5. Prepare and maintain a written description of the company's hazard communication program.

6. Consider any problems with trade secrets that may be raised by the standard's disclosure requirements.
7. Review state requirements for hazard disclosure.

In addition to the right-to-know laws, employees have certain workplace rights with respect to safety and health on the job that OSHA provides by law. As in our discussion of the public policy exceptions to the employment-at-will doctrine in the preceding chapter, it should be clear that workers have a right to seek safety and health on the job without fear of punishment or recrimination. Figure 17-3 spells out employee responsibilities and rights under OSHA.

The History of OSHA

OSHA was formed in 1971. From the very beginning, OSHA was troubled by the sheer size of its task—to monitor workplace safety and health in millions of workplaces with only several thousand inspectors.[83]

Nitpicking Rules.   In its early years, OSHA added to its troubles by promulgating rules and standards that seemed quite trivial when compared with the larger issues of health and safety. It was not until 1978 that OSHA decided to purge itself of some of these nitpicking rules. In one example, a telephone company was instructed that it could only provide linemen with "belts that have pocket tabs that extend at least $1\frac{1}{2}$ inches down and 3 inches back of the inside of the circle of each D-ring for riveting on plier or tool pockets . . . . There may be no more than four tool loops on any belt."[84] Such nuisance rules and standards created serious credibility problems for OSHA. Although at least 928 such rules were rescinded in 1978, many times that number remained on the books.

Spotty Record.   Over the years, OSHA's record has been spotty. In one year in the mid-1980s, injuries, illnesses, and deaths in the workplace began to climb again after several years of decline.[85] There were numerous reasons for this reversal, and not all of them could be attributed to OSHA. During the recession of the early 1980s, companies sharply reduced their spending on health and safety. With the economic recovery, many employers hired inexperienced workers, which further contributed to rising accident statistics. Further, the Reagan administration deemphasized the writing and enforcement of safety rules, and employers put greater emphasis on competitiveness, often at the expense of safety and health.[86]

FIGURE 17-3

Employee Responsibilities and Rights Under OSHA

- Each employee shall comply with the standards, rules, regulations and orders.
- Employees shall use safety equipment, personal protective equipment, and other devices and procedures provided or directed by the agency and necessary for their protection.
- Employees shall have the right to report unsafe and unhealthful working conditions to appropriate officials.
- Employees shall be authorized official time to participate in the activities.

SOURCE: http://www.osha.gov (2004).

Ethics in Practice

OSHA's Surprise Visit

During the summers, Mark Price worked at a local manufacturing plant in Reddog, Georgia. One hot and busy July day, Willie Truit and Mark received a call from the plant manager's secretary authorizing them to dispose of a batch of monomers, which are a type of hazardous waste. The order was to remove them from the inspector's sight. Willie and Mark bagged them up and threw them in the dumpster, but Mark kept asking why they were doing this. Improper disposal of hazardous materials usually results in heavy fines. This violation would have resulted in a fine of about $20,000.

Mark asked Willie what he thought would happen if they decided not to do what they were told. Willie said that they were working in an employment-at-will state and failure to do what they were authorized to do would definitely result in termination. The OSHA inspector asked Mark if he had been trained in han-

dling hazardous waste. He also asked if Mark had been told to do things that he normally didn't engage in while working. Not wearing the proper clothing and disposing of the material improperly could result in danger to both Willie and Mark. It could also endanger whoever came into contact with the material not disposed of properly.

1. If Mark chose not to perform the task he was told, how could he have protected his job? Could he have lost his job because he was working in an employment-at-will situation?

2. What would you have done if you had been caught in this ethical dilemma?

3. How would you have responded to the OSHA inspector's questions?

Contributed by Mystro Whatley

A Rejuvenated OSHA.   Like so many of the federal agencies we have discussed (FTC, FDA, CPSC), OSHA experienced a new boost of energy and enthusiasm in the post-Reagan period of the late 1980s and early 1990s. The renewed energy came at an appropriate time, because in 1988 the Bureau of Labor Statistics announced that injury rates had been increasing since about 1983. Officials admitted that a part of this increase could be attributed to more accurate reporting.

With a new administrator and an increased budget, OSHA began taking significant actions against high-visibility employers. However, OSHA continued to suffer from what it claimed to be a budget and staff that were inadequate for the job that Congress and the public expected it to do. One observer pointed out that the EPA's budget was more than 21 times that of OSHA. In some states, too, there were conflicts between OSHA and state inspectors as to who had responsibility for workplace safety. In 1991, a major accident in North Carolina illustrated this point. A fire in a poultry-processing plant led to the deaths of 25 workers. This occurred because the plant's management kept the emergency exits padlocked to deter pilfering. Employees said there were no fire exits, no sprinkler system, and no fire drills. It was discovered that no government agency had conducted a safety inspection at that plant for 11 years. Some blamed state authorities; others blamed OSHA.[87] One thing is clear: There simply are not enough inspectors to handle all businesses, and therefore a heavy responsibility falls on business for safety in the workplace.

In 1995, OSHA turned to negotiated rule-making to develop standards for industry. Efforts at conciliation continued as Charles Jeffress, a former OSHA administrator who was known as an effective conciliator, took over the agency. OSHA's efforts at reform have been criticized by labor leaders who feel that OSHA is more concerned with its own operation than with the safety and health of workers. Even the Chamber of Commerce has expressed concern that OSHA is putting more energy into improving its tarnished image than in reducing injuries and illness. Although the need for OSHA is evident, the way in which OSHA can meet that need most effectively has yet to be found.[88] In fiscal year 2004, OSHA had an authorized staff of only 2,220, including 1,123 inspectors. The agency's appropriation was $457.5 million.[89]

Questions about OSHA remain today. There are some who think OSHA has done a credible job. In its own defense, OSHA presents statistics about its overall effectiveness. OSHA claims that workplace fatalities have been cut by more than 60 percent and occupational injury and illness rates by 40 percent from 1971 to 2004.[90] However, a recent expose by the David Barstow of *The New York Times* paints a far bleaker picture. Barstow found that from 1982 to 2002, OSHA investigated 1,242 incidents of employee death for which OSHA determined the death occurred because the employer had "willful safety violations."[91] In 93 percent of these cases, OSHA declined to seek prosecution. Even the more than 70 of those employers who were repeat violators were rarely prosecuted. This reluctance to prosecute persisted even when the victims were teenagers, the violation caused multiple deaths, and administrative judges determined there was "willful wrongdoing."[92]

OSHA helped 202 firms reduce their incident's designation from "willful" to "unclassified," which virtually guarantees there will be no prosecution.[93] Why do they do this? "A simple lack of guts and political will," said John T. Phillips, a former regional OSHA administrator.[94] Barstow identified 2,197 deaths for which employers were fined $106 million in civil OSHA fines and jail sentences that *totaled* fewer than 30 years. Twenty of those 30 years were from a North Carolina chicken plant fire that killed 25 people. In contrast, WorldCom paid $750 million for misleading investors. In one year alone (2001), the prison sentences obtained by the EPA totaled 256 years.[95]

In spite of the negative press it has received, few hold out hope for substantive change in the near future at OSHA. Industry observers find OSHA's current agenda to be modest at best, with the status quo expected to dominate.[96] Peg Seminario, AFL-CIO director of occupational safety and health, says OSHA is not undertaking any "significant rule-making" and added that any new rules proposed are not likely to be promulgated under the Bush administration.[97]

Workplace Violence

One other issue is becoming a major problem and posing challenges to management—escalating violence in the workplace. "Top Security Threats," a recent survey of *Fortune* 1000 companies, shows the seriousness of the problem. Corporate security managers rated **workplace violence** as their number one concern. The Workplace Violence Research Institute reports that each workday an estimated 16,400 threats are made, 723 workers are attacked, and 43,800 are harassed. Each year, according to OSHA, more than 1,000 workers are victims of homicide at work. Each year, too, according to the U.S. Department of Justice, there are approximately 2 million assaults and threats of violence. Furthermore, one in four full-time workers has been harassed, threatened, or attacked, and coworkers account for most of the harassment.[98] A 2003 study of 280 internal workplace violence incidents showed that the majority of the perpetrators were current employees (43.6 percent) while former employees constituted 22.5 percent. The other perpetrators had relationships with the company or its employees: 22.5 percent involved domestic violence that was brought into the workplace, and 12.5 percent had a client relationship with the company.[99]

As one writer astutely observed, "Violence has crept from city to suburb, from dim alley to sunny schoolyard. It was only a matter of time before its malevolent shadow darkened the workplace."[100] Another observer concluded that "Workplace violence is the new poison of corporate America."[101]

Who Is Affected?

Approximately 2 million U.S. workers are victims of workplace violence every year.[102] Although no one is immune from workplace violence, some workers are at increased risk. According to OSHA, the workers who are more likely to experience workplace violence include:[103]

- Workers who exchange money with the public
- Workers who deliver passengers, goods, or services
- Workers who work alone or in small groups
- Workers who work late at night or very early in the morning
- Workers who work in community settings or homes where they have extensive contact with the public
- Workers who work in high-crime areas

The workers who are direct targets of the violence are not the only people affected. Not only are the family and friends of the victims impacted, but those employees in the workplace who escaped the violence also experience long-term effect. These survivors often spend years dealing with the after-effects.[104] Many fear returning to work and some never do. They will often play the event over in their minds, unable to forget what happened. Victoria Spang is a marketing director who hid in the personnel office when a client of her law firm came in with assault weapons, killing eight people and wounding six. "No one ever forgets. You'd walk by people's cubicles, and they would keep pictures of the victims up. It's a moment in life you'll always remember."[105]

Corporate image can also suffer long-term effects. The term *going postal* is a thorn in the side of the U.S. Postal Service. It became part of the lexicon after a series of post office shootings. The phrase continues even after a study commissioned by the post office found that postal workers are no more likely to commit violence than employees in other professions.[106]

Companies Respond.

How are companies responding to this new kind of workplace hazard? Experts on workplace violence emphasize the importance of anticipating these crises and formulating specific procedures through which employees can report potential trouble so companies can respond. Some firms have decided to fold workplace violence into an already existing department that oversees other personnel matters. Others have decided to take a more proactive strategy. The U.S. Postal Service, for example, has trained a 9-person intervention team to be deployed to post offices if tensions get high. It is also striving to screen potential employees more carefully and encourage existing employees to use a hotline to report hot-tempered workers they perceive to be dangerous.[107] DuPont's Personal Safety Program is a comprehensive workplace protection program that includes counselors, workshops, and a 24-hour hotline. Both DuPont and the U.S. Postal Service claim success with their programs.[108] Figure 17-4 on page 556 lists OSHA's recommendations for what employers can do to protect their employees from workplace violence.

FIGURE 17-4

OSHA's Recommendations for Preventing Workplace Violence

The best protection employers can offer is to establish a zero-tolerance policy toward workplace violence against or by their employees. The employer should establish a workplace violence prevention program or incorporate the information into an existing accident prevention program, employee handbook, or manual of standard operating procedures. It is critical to ensure that all employees know the policy and understand that all claims of workplace violence will be investigated and remedied promptly. In addition, employers can offer additional protections such as the following:

1. Provide safety education for employees so they know what conduct is not acceptable, what to do if they witness or are subjected to workplace violence, and how to protect themselves.

2. Secure the workplace. Where appropriate to the business, install video surveillance, extra lighting, and alarm systems and minimize access by outsiders through identification badges, electronic keys, and guards.

3. Provide drop safes to limit the amount of cash on hand. Keep a minimal amount of cash in registers during evenings and late-night hours.

4. Equip field staff with cellular phones and hand-held alarms or noise devices, and require them to prepare a daily work plan and keep a contact person informed of their location throughout the day. Keep employer-provided vehicles properly maintained.

5. Instruct employees not to enter any location where they feel unsafe. Introduce a "buddy system" or provide an escort service or police assistance in potentially dangerous situations or at night.

6. Develop policies and procedures covering visits by home health-care providers. Address the conduct of home visits, the presence of others in the home during visits, and the worker's right to refuse to provide services in a clearly hazardous situation.

SOURCE: "Workplace Violence," *OSHA Fact Sheet*, http://www.osha.gov.

Effective stakeholder management necessitates that companies address the growing problem of workplace violence. Companies have only recently started to put safety measures into place, but such measures will become more important in the future. Programs that deal with crises, and long-range efforts to bring about safer workplace environments, will be essential.

THE RIGHT TO HEALTH IN THE WORKPLACE

As the public became more health conscious, it was not surprising that companies in the United States became much more sensitive about health issues. In efforts to control runaway health costs, which are rising an estimated 10 percent per year, these companies took drastic steps, some of which have become controversial. Two controversial issues of health in the workplace—smoking and AIDS—merit special attention. Like other issues we have examined, these issues have employee-rights, privacy, and due-process ramifications.

Smoking in the Workplace

The issue of **smoking in the workplace** began in the 1980s in the United States. The idea that smoking ought to be curtailed or restricted in the workplace is a direct result of the growing antismoking sentiment in society in general. Much of the antismoking sentiment crystallized in 1984, when U.S. Surgeon General C. Everett Koop called for a smoke-free society. In 1986, he proclaimed that smokers were hurting not only themselves but also the nonsmoking people around them, who were being harmed by secondary, or passive, smoke in the air they breathed. Koop argued that the evidence "clearly documents that nonsmokers are placed at increased risks for developing disease as the result of exposure to environmental tobacco smoke."[109] To substantiate his point, a National Academy of Science study estimated that in one year, passive smoke was responsible for 2,400 lung cancer deaths in the United States.[110]

Evidence of the need to control smoking in the workplace continues to mount. A 2001 study reported in *Occupational Health and Environmental Medicine* studied nonsmokers in Scotland who worked around colleagues who smoked. Adjusted for age, height, gender, and socioeconomic status, the results showed that lung function was significantly impacted by the amount of secondhand smoke in the workplace. Workers exposed to the highest levels of smoke were three times more likely to have decreased lung function.[111] According to the American Lung Association, a smoking employee costs the firm at least $1,000 each year in extra direct and indirect health care costs. In addition, employees have been offered workers' compensation, unemployment, and disability payments for illness and loss of work resulting from secondhand smoke.

Corporate Responses. Although companies did not act until considerable public sentiment against smoking had developed, they have now quickly moved to adopt policies that restrict smoking. Firms are becoming increasingly aware of the costs—higher insurance expenses and higher absenteeism—of having smokers on staff. One explanation for business's initial hesitation to address smoking in the workplace was offered by the executive director of New Jersey's chapter of GASP (Group Against Smoking Pollution), a nonprofit advocacy organization. She said that there are three stages in most smoking policies. First, managers are very apprehensive. Second, the program goes over more smoothly than they anticipated. Finally, managers are flooded with positive responses from their employees.[112]

The Current Population Survey (CPS) conducted surveys of smoking in the workplace. Between 1992 and 1993, less than half of the survey's respondents said that smoking was restricted in public areas or their workspace at the office. By 1996, more than 63 percent reported smoke-free environments at work. In 2000, the Centers for Disease Control and Prevention (CDC) surveyed working adults in 17 states and the District of Columbia to determine the level of smoke in their work environments. They found that 92.3 percent of adults reported that their workplace had a policy regulating smoking in public, common, or working areas. Adults with a high school education or greater were more likely to have a smoke-free environment. The CPS and CDC data are not directly comparable, but the trend toward more smoke-free work environments is clear, particularly for those with a high school education or greater.[113]

A 2002 study illuminated a second benefit of smoke-free workplaces. Although they have been designed to protect workers from the effects of environmental tobacco smoke, there is now evidence they also support smokers in quitting. Caroline M. Fichtenberg and Stanton A. Glantz reviewed the findings of 26 studies of smoking in the workplace.[114] They found that in smoke-free workplaces the percentage of workers who smoke drops by about 4 percent. Smokers in those workplaces reduce their smoking by about three cigarettes a day. These two effects make for a combined reduction of 29 percent in cigarette use. For the United States to achieve an equivalent reduction through taxation, the cigarette tax would have to be as high as $3 per pack. The authors also studied smoke-restricted workplaces (e.g., where a designated smoking lounge might be provided) and found the impact was muted significantly, with only about half the impact on smoking prevalence and use. Interestingly, the findings of this study have been known to the tobacco industry for some time. The authors cite tobacco industry studies with the same finding. They cite a 1992 Phillip Morris internal memo, which said, "Milder workplace restrictions have much less impact on quitting rates [than totally smoke-free workplaces] and very little impact on consumption."[115]

AIDS in the Workplace

Medical breakthroughs have yielded dramatic improvements in the treatment of **acquired immune deficiency syndrome (AIDS)**. Although death rates have declined, AIDS remains one of the top causes of death for Americans between the ages of 25 and 44, the age range of half the workforce.[116] Peter J. Petesch, former cochair of the U.S. Centers for Disease Control and Prevention's Business Responds to AIDS/Labor Responds to AIDS (BRTA/LRTA) program, says that we are now in a "new era of complacency" that is undeserved, given that the number of new AIDS cases is on the rise. That fact along with public initiatives that encourage people to know their HIV/AIDS status means that AIDS will continue to be an important issue for employers.[117]

Corporate Responses.   When AIDS first appeared in the early 1980s, the business community was unsure of its responsibilities to employees who were diagnosed with the disease. In 1986, the Justice Department ruled that some employers could legally fire employees diagnosed with AIDS if the employers' motive was to protect other workers.[118] In March 1987, however, that judgment was reversed when the Supreme Court ruled that people with contagious diseases were protected by the same law that protected handicapped workers from workplace discrimination, the Rehabilitation Act of 1973.[119] With the passage of the Americans with Disabilities Act (ADA), AIDS became a recognized and covered disability.[120]

Some evidence exists that corporate AIDS programs are on the decline. In a 2002 survey by the National AIDS Fund (NAF), 22 percent of companies indicated they had AIDS awareness programs, down 6 percent from the 28 percent who had programs in 1992.[121] This apparent complacency may come at a cost as more lawsuits are filed. In one of the first lawsuits to be filed by the EEOC on behalf of a person with AIDS, a Chicago man successfully sued his employer, Nippon Express, for AIDS discrimination. The company was accused of giving meaningless work to the employee with AIDS, taking away his telephone and forbidding coworkers from speaking with him. According to the 6-year Nippon employee, workers belittled him and made cruel comments about his condition. The settlement called for Nippon Express to pay $160,000 in damages, to donate $25,000 to AIDS research, and to provide management employees with training as to how to deal with a person who has been diagnosed with AIDS or HIV.[122] In 2004, the EEOC determined there was reasonable cause to believe that Cirque de Soleil had discriminated against an acrobat who was fired because he was HIV positive. The circus has agreed to rehire the acrobat and to draft an antidiscrimination policy that protects the rights of all HIV-positive athletes to perform, but settlement has not been reached at this writing. Another case of a McDonald's employee who claims he was pressured to quit because of his illness is still pending on appeal. In 2001, a common pleas court awarded Russell Rich $5 million in damages, but the verdict was overturned in 2003 by an appeals court that found McDonald's did not get a fair trial and ordered the case retried.[123]

Eastman Kodak is a company with an effective HIV/AIDS policy. Since 1988, the company has offered general HIV/AIDS education and awareness programs, as well as specific training for managers who must deal directly with HIV-related issues. The company indicated it would tolerate no discrimination in its workplace and would terminate any employee who violates the company's HIV/AIDS policy.[124] Following is a quote from an Eastman Kodak employee who was diagnosed with HIV/AIDS. The quote was taken from the company's training manual:

> *At first I was shaken, scared, afraid that my whole life had come apart. The stigma of HIV/AIDS was on my life and I didn't know what to do or who to tell or even who to trust . . . . My mind was a mess. But I met a lady, Lydia Casiano, who I felt very comfortable with. She works in the Human Relations Department at Kodak. She assured me of Kodak's policy of privacy and told me my job is still secure! . . . This year I've received a raise and have been given opportunities to improve myself and my workplace. We have given training classes to all [division] employees and I've told everyone about this condition. Today I work in an HIV friendly atmosphere because of the efforts made by the management and workforce of Kodak.[125]*

Other organizations known for their HIV/AIDS programs include IBM, Levi Strauss & Co., the National Basketball Association (NBA), and Polaroid.[126]

Companies with operations in developing countries can be especially impacted by AIDS in the workforce. The AIDS epidemic has now surpassed the bubonic plague in the 1300s and influenza epidemic of 1917. According to UNAIDS, 40 million people around the world are now infected with HIV.[127] Researchers from the Boston University School of Public Health's Center for International Health calculated the cost of AIDS to a corporation, the cost of prevention and treatment of employees, and the benefits that prevention and treatment can achieve. They found that the benefits of prevention and treatment outweigh the costs, making them pay off financially for most companies.[128] The bottom line was that actions that were good for public health proved to also be good for business as well.

A cooperative program called Business Responds to AIDS (BRTA) was established as a joint initiative of the U.S. Centers for Disease Control and the business sector. They provide a variety of resources to help companies develop policies to deal effectively with HIV/AIDS in the workplace. BRTA recommends that, at minimum, organizations develop comprehensive programs that contain five key components,[129] as follows:

1. Workplace policy
2. Training (for managers, supervisors, and union leaders)
3. Employee education
4. Family education
5. Community involvement

What should be the corporate response to employee stakeholders on the AIDS issue? Companies should be sensitive to the needs of their employees who develop AIDS. In addition, companies should sponsor educational programs so that all workers can understand that AIDS cannot be transmitted by casual contact. Management will never be able to overcome fear and hostility if it does not engage in a thorough and ongoing educational program.[130]

Companies also need to be extremely sensitive to the privacy and due-process aspects of AIDS, and thus it is very important that companies adopt policies for dealing with AIDS cases before they arise. Managers need to be trained and educated in how to handle AIDS cases. Policies on AIDS should not be developed in an ad hoc, spur-of-the-moment fashion but as part of an overall strategy for dealing with workplace health and safety, privacy, and employee rights.

A decade ago, the Rwandan civil war cost the lives of an estimated 1 million people. The impact of this conflict on Rwandan industry, such as the local Heineken brewery, was devastating: more than half the brewery's staff were either killed or forced to flee the country. Heineken is determined to face the next regional disaster, the epidemic of HIV/AIDS, by taking positive steps to protect their workforce. Silvia Sansoni reports in *Forbes* (3 February 2003 v171 i3 p064) that Heineken has guaranteed antiretroviral drug coverage to its staff in Africa as well as their immediate dependents. Read about Heineken's commitment to its labor force by logging on to InfoTrac College Edition at http://www.infotrac-college.com and keying record number A96558374.

The Family-Friendly Workplace

Employees are increasingly less willing to spend every waking hour at work and are more committed to having time to spend at home with family. Two recent studies document this trend. One found that family time was the most important work/life priority for 82 percent of men and 85 percent of women, ages 20 to 39.[131] Another found that 90 percent of working adults felt they did not spend enough time at home with their families.[132] Many observers believe that the terrorist attacks of September 11 led many people to reevaluate their lives and priorities.[133] As a result, companies are searching for more and more ways to help employees achieve **work/life balance**, which is defined as "a state of equilibrium where the demands of a person's personal and professional life are equal."[134]

Although programs to support employee work/life balance are good business with pay-offs in employee recruitment and retention, many companies claim that they are looking out for the mental and psychological health of their employees. Whether it be for altruistic or business reasons, workplaces today are becoming more family friendly. By using this term, we are repeating a catchall phrase that refers to a host of policies and programs that today's companies have been putting into place. According to the Society for Human Resources (SHRM) 2003 Benefits Survey, the percentage of firms providing **family-friendly** benefits has continued to increase.[135] They found that the top five family-friendly benefits (and the percentage of firms offering them) are:[136]

1. Dependent care flexible spending accounts (71 percent)
2. Flextime (55 percent)
3. Family leave above required leave of the Family and Medical Leave Act (39 percent)
4. Telecommuting on a part-time basis (34 percent)
5. Compressed workweeks (31 percent)

Although not everyone thinks that companies are becoming as family friendly as they are claiming to be, it is clear that workers are talking more and more about the importance of family-friendly policies, and many leading companies are responding. With the growth in the numbers of women, single parents, and two-paycheck couples in the workforce, it seems that corporate support for families, many of whom are stressed out from their busy lives, is on the growth curve. This is further complicated by the changing nature of what constitutes a family. A 2002 study found that segments of society are subject to unique work/life balance pressures but receive less support. Typically, work/life balance studies and programs have focused on employed men and women who raise their children with spouses or partners. Often forgotten are single-earner mothers and fathers, single and childless employees with significant elder-care responsibilities, grandparents raising their grandchildren, and blended families with children from both partners' other marriages.[137]

It is in the context of organizations becoming more "friendly" on their own that we want to discuss a law aimed at health-related issues in the workplace—the Family and Medical Leave Act.

Family and Medical Leave Act.
The **Family and Medical Leave Act (FMLA)** was made into law in 1993. This act was designed to make life easier for employees with family or health problems.

Under the FMLA,[138] employees are granted the following rights:

- An employee may take up to 12 weeks of unpaid leave in any 12-month period for the birth or adoption of a child or for the care of a child, spouse, or parent with a serious health condition that limits the employee's performance.
- Employees must be reinstated in their old jobs or be given equivalent jobs upon returning to work; the employer does not have to allow employees to accrue seniority or other benefits during the leave periods.
- Employers must provide employees with health benefits during leave periods.
- Employees are protected from retaliation in the same way as under other employment laws; an employee cannot be discriminated against for complaining to other people (even the newspapers) about an employer's family leave policy.

Employers also have rights under the FMLA.[139] These rights include the following:

- Companies with fewer than 50 workers are exempt.
- Employers may demand that employees obtain medical opinions and certifications regarding their needs for leave and may require second or third opinions.
- Employers do not have to pay employees during leave periods, but they must continue health benefits.
- If an employee and a spouse are employed at the same firm and are entitled to leave, the total leave for both may be limited to 12 weeks.

The FMLA has not necessarily been easy to implement, however, because of special and technical key definitions of such terms as *serious health condition, medical certification, reasonable prior notice,* and *equivalent position.*[140] The FMLA institutionalizes at the federal level the employee's right to unpaid leave for health and family reasons. However, more than 35 states had their own leave laws before the FMLA was passed. Therefore, many companies have had experience in facing some of the difficult cases that could arise from the implementation of this law. In addition to the complex legal environment for employee issues that many companies already face, the FMLA promises to bring new challenges on a continuing basis.[141]

A 2001 study by the Department of Labor showed that the corporate views on the FMLA are mixed—still generally positive but with a downward trend that merits concern. The good news is that 87.6 percent of the businesses responding found that the FMLA had either a positive effect or no effect on business productivity, profitability, or growth. However, that's down from 92.5 percent of those surveyed in 1995. The paperwork is becoming an increasing burden. In 1995, only 24 percent found the paperwork at least somewhat difficult. That increased to 38 percent in 2001.[142] The increased concern with the paperwork may be because companies have had seven years of experience with employees taking the leave and that has unearthed some problems with its complexities.

In summary, the FMLA has not been the major problem that many envisioned, and it has accomplished much good. However, relieving the paperwork burden it places on business is important if it is to continue to provide workers with the opportunity to fulfill their family responsibilities without sacrificing their careers. Various efforts to pass additional family-friendly workplace legislation have been stymied by partisan conflict. The eventual outcome of the efforts to streamline and clarify the FMLA is certain to influence the direction corporate policies will take.

■ SUMMARY

Critical employee stakeholder issues include the rights to privacy, safety, and health. These issues should be seen as extensions of the issues and rights outlined in Chapter 16.

With the development of new technologies, workplace privacy has increasingly become a serious workplace issue. The level of concern surrounding workplace privacy is evidenced by the frequency with which it has been a topic in the print and broadcast media. As Barbara Walters warned employees in a segment of ABC News's *20/20*, "Your time is theirs and what you do on their computer or their phone is their business." The news magazine showed examples of truck drivers being monitored by satellite so closely that the company knew when, where, and how fast they drove, as well as how much gas they still had in their tanks. In another segment, companies were shown hiring undercover operators to watch and sometimes test their employees. Last, the news magazine explained why e-mail and voice mail can be monitored, even after messages are deleted. This wealth of available technology presents new challenges for companies as they weigh the importance of knowing their workers' activities against the importance of maintaining trust and morale.

Of equal, if not more, importance to employee stakeholders are the issues of workplace safety and health. The workplace safety problem led to the creation of OSHA. In spite of its difficulties, OSHA is still the federal government's major instrument for protecting workers on the job. State-promulgated right-to-know laws, as well as federal statutes, have been passed in recent years to provide employees with an added measure of protection, especially against harmful effects of exposure to chemicals and toxic substances. However, existing laws and regulations only deal with known problems. As the world changes, so do the threats to worker health and safety. Since the World Trade Center tragedy, the threat of terrorism has made many companies reassess operations as basic as their mail rooms. Other unexpected threats to worker health and safety are certain to occur and will represent new challenges for managers.

Other major health issues in the current business/employee relationship are AIDS and workplace violence. AIDS has become the most serious health issue that business or our society has ever faced. However, violence in the workplace is exacting a heavy toll, and businesses must be responsive. Smoking in the workplace and the need for employees to take family leave also impact the work environment. Wise managers will now begin to develop policies for dealing with these issues, as well as their privacy and due-process implications.

■ KEY TERMS

acquired immune deficiency syndrome (AIDS (page 558)

Americans with Disabilities Act (page 544)

broad brush EAP (page 545)

chief privacy officer (CPO) (page 548)

drug testing (page 542)

Electronic Communication Privacy Act (ECPA) of 1986 (page 546)

Employee Assistance Programs (EAPs) (page 545)

employee monitoring (page 545)

Employee Polygraph Protection Act (EPPA) (page 539)

Family and Medical Leave Act (FMLA) (page 560)

family-friendly (page 560)

integrity tests (page 540)

Occupational Safety and Health Administration (OSHA) (page 548)

polygraph (page 539)

Privacy Act of 1974 (page 537)

privacy impact statement (page 547)

privacy in the workplace (page 536)

right-to-know laws (page 551)

smoking in the workplace (page 556)

type 1 error (page 542)

type 2 error (page 542)

work/life balance (page 560)

workplace violence (page 554)

USA Patriot Act (page 538)

▪ DISCUSSION QUESTIONS

1. In your own words, describe what privacy means and what privacy protection companies should give employees.

2. Enumerate the strengths and weaknesses of the polygraph as a management tool for decision making. What polygraph uses are legitimate? What uses of the polygraph are illegitimate?

3. What are the two major arguments for and against integrity testing by employers? Under what circumstances could management most legitimately argue that integrity testing is necessary?

4. How has technology affected workplace privacy? What are the implications for the social contract between firms and their employees?

5. How has the World Trade Center tragedy affected workplace privacy? What are the long-term implications of that?

6. Which two of the four guidelines on the issue of privacy presented in this chapter do you think are the most important? Why?

7. Identify the privacy, health, and due-process ramifications of violence in the workplace and AIDS.

▪ RECOMMENDED CASES

Many of the end-of-text cases may be related to Chapter 17. You may wish to consider studying the following cases with Chapter 17.

Case 34. "VIOLENCE IN THE WORKPLACE: WHO IS TO BLAME?" This is the case of a man with a history of difficulty getting along in the workplace who often ended up in confrontations with coworkers. He then went on a shooting rampage, killing one supervisor and wounding others. The organization was later sued for not doing enough to prevent the attack. Could the organization have prevented this attack? To what level can an organization be held responsible when violence in the workplace occurs?

Case 35. "PIZZA REDLINING: EMPLOYEE SAFETY OR DISCRIMINATION?" This case addresses the issue of redlining, the practice of not delivering goods and servic-

es to areas that are perceived to be dangerous. Some cities have passed laws against redlining. Companies argue that these laws endanger their employees. Others argue that redlining is discrimination. Should redlining be outlawed?

Case 36. "AFTER-EFFECTS OF AFTER-HOURS ACTIVITIES: THE CASE OF PETER OILER." This case addresses the issue of after-hours activities and the extent to which an employer has a right to limit what an employee does in his or her time off. Peter Oiler is an exemplary employee who likes to wear women's clothes in his private time. When word of this got out, Winn-Dixie fired him from his job as a trucker. Was this a just firing or did the company overstep its bounds? What influence should a company be able to have over what an employee does in his or her private life?

▪ WEB RESOURCES

The URLs listed here are current at the time of publication. Should any of these Web sites change, please search under the company's or organization's name for an updated address.

American Civil Liberties Union
http://www.aclu.org

CDC Business Responds to AIDS
http://www.hivatwork.org

Employee Assistance Program Association
http://www.eap-association.org

National AIDS Fund
http://www.aidsfund.org

National Association of Working Women (9 to 5)
http://www.9to5.org

National Workrights Institute
http://www.workrights.org

Privacy.Org
   http://www.privacy.org

Privacy Rights Clearinghouse
   http://www.privacyrights.org

Workplace Fairness
   http://www.workplacefairness.org

 InfoTrac® College Edition   http://www.infotrac-college.com

Articles from The Wall Street Journal *can be researched, retrieved, and read from your desktop using InfoTrac's online database.*

▪ ENDNOTES

1. Asra Q. Nomani, "Murder in Workplace Is a Major Part of the Latest Death-on-the-Job Statistics," *The Wall Street Journal* (August 11, 1994), A4.

2. Frederick S. Lane, III, *The Naked Employee* (New York: AMACOM, 2003).

3. A. Scott, "No Privacy in the Workplace," *The Internal Auditor* (June 2001), 15–16.

4. "Privacy: The New Minefield," *HR Focus* (April 2001), 1–13.

5. "Big Brother, Inc., May Be Closer Than You Think," *Business Week* (February 9, 1987), 84.

6. Patricia H. Werhane, *Persons, Rights, and Corporations* (Englewood Cliffs, NJ: Prentice Hall, 1985), 118.

7. "Ranking Privacy at Work," *Wired Magazine* (October 2003), http://www.wired.com.

8. Laura Pincus Hartman, "The Rights and Wrongs of Workplace Snooping," *Journal of Business Strategy* (May/June 1998), 16–19.

9. Judy D. Holmes, "Will Big Brother Cause Your Company to Be Sued?" *Law, Investigations, and Ethics* (July/August, 2003), 39–44.

10. Steve Bates, "Science Friction," *HR Magazine* (July 2001), 34–44.

11. Joanne Wojcik, "Wired into Workplace Privacy," *Business Insurance* (September 15, 2003), 28.

12. Dana J. Domone, "Health Care Privacy Rules Released," *Workspan* (March 2001), 62–64.

13. *Ibid.*

14. Jolie Solomon, "As Firms' Personnel Files Grow, Worker Privacy Falls," *The Wall Street Journal* (April 19, 1989), B1.

15. Joseph R. DesJardins, "Privacy in Employment," in Gertrude Ezorsky (ed.), *Moral Rights in the Workplace* (Albany, NY: State University of New York Press, 1987), 133.

16. Solomon, B1.

17. Raymond Bonner, "Lie Detectors as Corporate Tools," *The New York Times* (February 13, 1983), 4F.

18. Kenneth F. Englade, "The Business of the Polygraph," *Across the Board* (October 1982), 21–22.

19. James H. Coil III and Barbara Jo Call, "Congress Targets Employers' Use of Polygraphs," *Employment Relations Today* (Spring 1986), 23.

20. David E. Terpstra, R. Bryan Kethley, Richard T. Foley, and Wanthanee Limpaphayom, "The Nature of Litigation Surrounding Five Screening Devices," *Public Personnel Management* (Spring 2000), 43–54.

21. Andrea Widener, "DOE Lab Employees Protest New Law Mandating Polygraph Tests," *Contra Costa Times* (November 8, 2000).

22. Diana Ray, "Can They Fool the Polygraph?" *Insight* (July 2–9, 2001), 18–19.

23. *Ibid.*

24. Kenneth A. Kovach, "The Truth About Employers' Use of Lie Detectors," *Business and Society Review* (Spring 1995), 65–69.

25. Ray, 17.

26. Philip Ross, "Mind Readers," *Scientific American* (September 2003), 74.

27. Linda Stern, "We Know You're Lying," *Newsweek* (November 17, 2003), E4.

28. R. Colin Johnson, "Lie-Detector Glasses Offer Peek at Future of Security," *Electronic Engineering* (January 19, 2004), 1.

29. David Nye, "Son of the Polygraph," *Across the Board* (June 1989), 21.

30. Alfred G. Feliu, *Primer on Individual Employee Rights* (Washington, DC: The Bureau of National Affairs, 1992), 211–212.

31. David W. Arnold and John W. Jones, "Who the Devil's Applying Now?" *Security Management* (March 2002), 85–88.

32. Feliu, 211–212.

33. David W. Arnold and John W. Jones, 85–88.

34. Ed Bean, "More Firms Use Attitude Tests to Keep Thieves off the Payroll," *The Wall Street Journal* (January 27, 1987), 41.

35. Gregory M. Lousig-Nont, "Seven Deadly Hiring Mistakes," *Supervision* (April 2003), 18–19.

36. Bean, 41.
37. David W. Arnold and John W. Jones, 85–88.
38. *Ibid.*
39. *Ibid.*
40. *Ibid.*
41. "Why Firms Don't Test for Drugs," *USA Today* (February 18, 1987), 7B.
42. Anne Newman, "Drug-Testing Firms Face Pluses, Minuses in New Rules," *The Wall Street Journal* (March 15, 1994), B4.
43. Kris Maher, "The Jungle," *The Wall Street Journal* (April 13, 2004), B4.
44. Maria M. Perotin, "High Cost Prompts Many Companies to Faze Out Drug Screening," *Fort Worth Star Telegram* (March 24, 2003), 1.
45. http://www.questdiagnostics.com.
46. Michael Waldholz, "Drug Testing in the Workplace: Whose Rights Take Precedence?" *The Wall Street Journal* (November 11, 1986), 39.
47. "The Many Tests for Drug Abuse," *The New York Times* (February 24, 1985), F17.
48. *Ibid.*
49. Curtis J. Sitomer, "Privacy and Personal Freedom: Balancing the Trade-Offs," *The Christian Science Monitor* (December 3, 1986), 33.
50. John Fay, *Drug Testing* (Boston: Butterworth-Heinemann, 1991), 22. Also see John D. Rapoport and Brian L. P. Zevnik, *The Employee Strikes Back!* (New York: Collier Books, 1994), 91–93; William C. Martucci and Jeffrey M. Place, "Drug Testing in the Private Sector Workplace," *Employment Relations Today* (Summer 1999), 93–102.
51. Jane Easter Bahls, "Dealing with Drugs: Keep It Legal," *HR Magazine* (March 1998), 104–116.
52. Newman, B4.
53. http://www.questdiagnostics.com.
54. Sarah F. Mulladay, "The Champion Paper Company EAP and Major Issues for Employee Assistance Programs in the 1990s—Managed Care and Aging," *Employee Assistance Quarterly* (Vol. 6, No. 3, 1991), 37–50.
55. Eileen Smith, "How to Choose the Right EAP for Your Employee," *Employee Benefit News* (November 1, 2000).
56. http://www.eap-association.org
57. *Ibid.*
58. Hartman, 16.
59. A. Scott, "No Privacy in the Workplace," *The Internal Auditor* (June 2001), 15–16.
60. *Ibid.*
61. Charles Forelle, "On the Road Again, But Now the Boss Is Sitting Beside You," *The Wall Street Journal* (May 14, 2004), 1.
62. *Ibid.*
63. John P. Mello, Jr., "Camera Phones a Flashpoint of Concern," *Boston Works* (April 11, 2004), G7.
64. Nancy J. King, "Electronic Monitoring to Promote National Security Impacts Workplace Privacy," *Employee Responsibilities and Rights Journal* (September 2003), 127–147.
65. *Ibid.*
66. http://www.workrights.org
67. http://www.epic.org/privacy/workplace
68. *Ibid.*
69. http://www.workrights.org
70. A. Scott, 15–16.
71. Robert C. Goldstein and Richard L. Nolan, "Personal Privacy Versus the Corporate Computer," *Harvard Business Review* (March–April 1975), 62–70.
72. Steve Ufelder, "CPOs: Hot or Not?" *Computerworld* (March 15, 2004), 40.
73. "Employees More Concerned with Feeling Safe at Work," SHRM press release (April 29, 2004), http://www.shrm.org.
74. *Ibid.*
75. The Legal Information Institute, http://www.law.cornell.edu/topics/workplace_safety.html.
76. http://www.osha.gov
77. Joseph P. Kahn, "When Bad Management Becomes Criminal," *Inc.* (March 1987), 47.
78. David R. Spiegel, "Enforcing Safety Laws Locally," *The New York Times* (March 23, 1986), 11F.
79. "Union Carbide Fights for Its Life," *Business Week* (December 24, 1984), 52–56.
80. "By the Numbers Operation at Morgan Stanley Finds Its Human Side," *The New York Times* (September 16, 2001), section 3, 8; "War on Terrorism: The Victims—Snapshot of the Briton Who Became an American Hero, Seconds Before Death," *The Independent* (September 27, 2001), 3.
81. James T. O'Reilly, "What's Wrong with the Right to Know?" *Across the Board* (April 1985), 24.
82. Peter A. Susser, "Chemical Hazard Disclosure Obligations," *Employment Relations Today* (Winter 1986–1987), 301–302.
83. "Now OSHA Must Justify Its Inspection Targets," *Business Week* (April 9, 1979), 64.
84. "OSHA's Nitpicking Rules Die," *Athens Banner Herald* (November 24, 1978), 5.
85. Robert L. Simison, "Job Deaths and Injuries Seem to Be Increasing After Years of Decline," *The Wall Street Journal* (March 18, 1986), 1, 25.
86. *Ibid.*, 1.
87. Scott Bronstein, "They Treated Us Like Dogs, Say Workers at Plant Where 25 Died," *The Atlanta Journal* (September 5, 1991), A6.
88. Lisa Finnegan, "Reform and Reinvention," *Occupational Hazards* (July 1998), 67–68.
89. http://www.osha.gov
90. Information on OSHA and its activities is available on the OSHA Web site at http://www.osha.gov.

91. David Barstow, "U.S. Rarely Seeks Charges for Deaths in Workplace," *The New York Times* (December 22, 2003), A1.
92. *Ibid.*
93. *Ibid.*
94. *Ibid.*
95. *Ibid.*
96. "What Do OSHA & Congress Have in Store for 2004?" *IOMA's Safety Director's Report* (February 2004), 3–4.
97. *Ibid.*, 3.
98. "Violence in the Workplace Still Number One Security Threat for Fortune 1000 Corporate Security Managers," *Business Wire* (April 3, 2001).
99. Larry J. Chavez, "Benefits That Can Help Prevent Employee Violence," *Employee Benefit Plan Review* (August 2003), 6–8.
100. Tom Dunkel, "Hazardous Duty," *The Atlanta Journal* (October 2, 1994), Q1, Q3.
101. *Ibid.*, Q1.
102. "Workplace Violence," *OSHA Fact Sheet* (2002), http://www.osha.gov.
103. *Ibid.*
104. Stephanie Armour, "Companies, Survivors Suffer Years After Violence at Work," *USA Today* (July 9, 2003), 3A.
105. *Ibid.*, 3A.
106. *Ibid.*
107. Tom Dunkel, Q3.
108. *Ibid.*, Q3.
109. Otto Friedrich, "Where There's Smoke," *Time* (February 23, 1987), 23.
110. Lois Therrien, "Warning: In More and More Places, Smoking Causes Fines," *Business Week* (December 29, 1986), 40.
111. "Risk of Smoking in Workplace," *Chemist & Druggist* (August 18, 2001), VIII.
112. Dexter Hutchins, "The Drive to Kick Smoking at Work," *Fortune* (September 15, 1986), 43.
113. Alison Stein Wellner, "Editor's Note: Smoke Signals," *Forecast* (January 2001), 12.
114. Caroline M. Fichtenberg and Stanton A. Glantz, "Effect of Smoke-Free Workplaces on Smoking Behaviour: Systematic Review," *British Medical Journal* (July 2002), 188–194.
115. *Ibid.*, 191.
116. Peter J. Petesch, "Dealing with HIV/AIDS in the Workplace," *Expert Perspectives* (August 2003), http://www.hivatwork.org.
117. *Ibid.*
118. "AIDS in the Workplace," *Newsweek* (July 7, 1986), 62.
119. "A Victory for AIDS Victims," *Newsweek* (March 16, 1987), 33.
120. Susan K. Adler, "HIV/AIDS in the Workplace," *Occupational Health and Safety* (May 1995), 79–80.
121. Jay Greene, "Employers Learn to Live with AIDS," *HR Magazine* (February 1998), 96–101.
122. David Mendell, "Settlement Is Reached in AIDS Bias Lawsuit," *Chicago Tribune* (July 30, 1998), 8.
123. "Consumer Products Brief—McDonald's Corp.: Defendant's Victory Overturned," *The Wall Street Journal* (October 13, 2003), 1.
124. Greene, 96–101.
125. *Ibid.*
126. *Ibid.* For additional information on HIV/AIDS, visit the Society for Human Resource Management (SHRM) Web site at http://www.shrm.org.
127. Sydney Rosen, Jonathon Simon, Jeffrey R. Vincent, William MacLeod, Matthew Fox, and Donald M. Thea, "AIDS Is Your Business," *Harvard Business Review* (February 2003), 80–87.
128. *Ibid.*
129. Cited in Romuald A. Stone, "AIDS in the Workplace: An Executive Update," *Academy of Management Executive* (August 1994), 57.
130. "Business Should Help Battle AIDS," *Business Week* (March 23, 1987), 174; "Why AIDS Policy Must Be a Special Policy," *Business Week* (February 1, 1993), 53–54; and "Managing AIDS," *Business Week* (February 1, 1993), 48–52.
131. Nancy R. Lockwood, "Work/Life Balance: Challenges and Solutions," *HR Magazine* (June 2003), S1.
132. *Ibid.*
133. *Ibid.*
134. *Ibid.*
135. Lockwood, S1.
136. *Ibid.*
137. Saroj Parasuraman and Jeffrey Greenhaus, "Toward Reducing Some Critical Gaps in Work-Family Research," *Human Resource Management Review* (Autumn 2002), 299–312.
138. Rapoport and Zevnik, 229–230.
139. *Ibid.*, 230–232.
140. *Ibid.*
141. Sally Roberts, "FMLA's Effects Weighed; Employers Cite Paperwork as Onus," *Business Insurance* (January 15, 2001), 3. See also Kevin Sweeney, "Studies Yield Conflicting Views on FMLA Success," *Employee Benefit News* (March 1, 2001).
142. *Ibid.*

Chapter 18

■ EMPLOYMENT DISCRIMINATION *and* AFFIRMATIVE ACTION

CHAPTER LEARNING OUTCOMES

After studying this chapter, you should be able to:

1 Chronicle the U.S. civil rights movement and minority progress for the past 50 years.

2 Outline the essentials of the federal discrimination laws, particularly Title VII of the Civil Rights Act of 1964.

3 Provide two different meanings of discrimination and give examples of how each might be committed.

4 Elaborate on issues in employment discrimination relating to race, color, national origin, sex, age, religion, and disability.

5 Identify different postures with respect to affirmative action, explain the concept of reverse discrimination, and provide an overview of the Supreme Court's decisions on affirmative action.

A particular subgroup of employee stakeholders is made up of those whose job rights are protected by federal, state, and local laws against discrimination. In the previous two chapters, we considered employee rights issues that affect virtually everyone in the workplace. In this chapter, we concentrate on that group of stakeholders whose rights are protected by discrimination laws. In general, these **protected groups** include minorities, women, older people, people with disabilities, and people with religious affiliations that might affect their conditions of employment. Many of the issues we treat in this chapter have grown out of the general notion that employees have certain workplace rights that ought to be protected.

To complicate matters, there is a group of observers who think that legitimate protective status is giving way to victim status as increasing numbers of people set forth their claims that they too should have their rights as employees protected by law. Charles Sykes argues that we have become a "society of victims" with growing numbers of employees asserting claims for protected status.[1] Sykes is not alone. According to Paul Hollander, "the ideology of victimhood is so strong in the United States today that not only does it induce people to claim victimhood where none exists, it has created a climate in which such inventions, no matter how false, are seen as true on a higher level than 'mere' facts."[2] It is within this context in which claims to be protected by law are proliferating that we embark on this discussion of employment discrimination and affirmative action. We must always remember that the civil rights movement, which effectively started it all, was quite legitimate and long overdue.

Federal antidiscrimination laws date back to the U.S. Constitution—in particular, the First, Fifth, and Fourteenth Amendments, which were designed to forbid religious discrimination and deprivation of employment rights without due process. There were also the Civil Rights Acts of 1866, 1870, and 1871, which were based on these amendments. However, none of these acts was ever effective. Most authorities agree that the Civil Rights Act of 1964 was the effective beginning of the employee protection movement, particularly for those special groups that we will be discussing in this chapter.

Civil rights issues among protected groups are highly debated and controversial. Although there is basic acceptance of the idea of groups' workplace rights being protected, the extent of this protection and the degree to which governmental policy should go to accelerate the infusion of minorities, women, and others into the workforce and into higher-paying jobs remain topics of considerable debate. To explore these and related issues, we will cover the following major topics in this chapter: the civil rights movement and minority progress; federal laws that protect against employment discrimination; the meaning of discrimination; a variety of issues related to employment discrimination; and, finally, affirmative action in the workplace.

THE CIVIL RIGHTS MOVEMENT AND MINORITY PROGRESS

It would take volumes to trace thoroughly the historical events that led ultimately to passage of the first significant piece of civil rights legislation in the modern period—the Civil Rights Act of 1964. William Glueck and James Ledvinka have provided a brief analysis of these events. They have argued that the act grew out of conflict that had been apparent for years but that erupted in the 1950s and 1960s in the form of protests and boycotts.[3]

Civil Rights in the 1950s and 1960s

Behind the American dream had historically been the belief that merit rather than privilege was the means of getting ahead. Equal opportunity was everyone's birthright. Blacks and other minorities, however, had not shared fully in this American dream. In the 1950s and 1960s, the disparity between American ideals and American realities became quite pronounced and evident for minorities. Americans became aware of it, not because they suddenly awoke to the realization that equal opportunity was not available to everyone, but because of individuals who had the courage to stand up for their rights as U.S. citizens.

It began on December 1, 1955, when Mrs. Rosa Parks, a black department store worker, was arrested for refusing to yield her bus seat to a white man. Out of that previously unthinkable act grew yet another—a bus boycott by blacks. One of the leaders of the boycott was a young minister, Dr. Martin Luther King, Jr. After the bus boycott came years of demonstrations, marches, and battles with police. Television coverage depicted scenes of civil rights demonstrators being attacked by officials with cattle prods, dogs, and fire hoses. Along with the violence that grew out of confrontations between protestors and authorities came the stark awareness of the economic inequality between the races that existed in the United States at that time.[4]

Unemployment figures for blacks were double those for whites and higher still among nonwhite youth. Blacks accounted for only 10 percent of the labor force but represented 20 percent of total unemployed and nearly 30 percent of long-term unemployed. In 1961, only about one-half of black men worked steadily at full-time jobs, whereas nearly two-thirds of white men did so. Against this backdrop of blacks and other minorities being denied their share in the American ideal of equal opportunity in employment, it should have been no surprise that Congress finally acted in a dramatic way in 1964.[5]

The 1970s: The Women's Movement Begins

The women's movement began in the 1970s. Women's groups began to see that the workplace situation was little better for women than for blacks and other minorities. Despite the fact that the labor participation rate for women was growing, women were still occupying low-paying jobs. Women were making some small inroads into managerial and professional jobs, but progress was very slow. Women, for the most part, were still in the lower paying "women's jobs," such as bank teller, secretary, waitress, and laundry worker.[6]

At first, in the early 1970s, blacks were making strong gains in employment and earnings. From the 1973–1975 recession on, however, rampant unemployment among blacks was discouraging. By the end of the 1970s, the unemployment rate was about 12 percent for blacks, compared with 5 percent for whites.

The 1980s: Gains Are Made

In the 1980s, the circumstances of blacks and women improved, but women, in general, made greater progress in the workplace than blacks. From 1983 to 1986, the unemployment rate for all whites fell from 8.4 percent to 6.1 percent. During this same time, the unemployment rate for blacks fell from 19.5 percent to 15.1 percent. For women, it fell from 6.9 percent to 5.4 percent.[7] From these statistics we can see that unemployment represented a major problem for blacks but was not a major problem for women. Indeed, the unemployment rate for blacks remained more than twice that of whites.

As the mid- to late 1980s arrived, inequality in the workforce remained a serious problem. Blacks continued to have lower participation rates in the workforce, and undoubtedly some of this was traceable to racial discrimination. Women did not have the labor participation rate problem of blacks but continued to sense that they were being excluded from higher-paying managerial jobs. Also problematic were pay inequities between men and women, and between whites and blacks, performing essentially the same jobs.

By the end of the 1980s, the progress of blacks—or, as many people prefer to be called, African-Americans—was mixed. There were notable gains on the education front, but the incomes of blacks continued to trail those of whites. In 1990, nearly 80 percent of blacks age 35 to 44 had completed 4 years of high school, compared with 63 percent in 1980. For the same period, 89 percent of whites completed high school, compared with 80 percent in 1980. In terms of college attendance, the rate for black females steadily increased from 24 percent in 1970 to 31 percent in 1988. For black males, the percent attending college declined from 29 percent in 1970 to 25 percent in 1988. The poverty rate for black Americans in 1990 remained virtually the same as it had been for the past 20 years—nearly one-third.[8]

The 1990s: Some Progress, But Problems Remain

As the century drew to a close, 28 percent of blacks still lived in poverty, compared to 11 percent of whites.[9] Although 12.9 percent of the employees in private companies were African-American, only 5.3 percent held managerial jobs.[10] Despite these problems, gains were being made at the highest levels of the corporate sector. According to Richard Parsons, president of Time Warner and one of the United States' most powerful black executives:

> *People of color are achieving corporate positions that their parents could never have dreamed of reaching, and in unprecedented numbers. Is this trend sweeping the land? No. Are there still problems? Yes. But there's no question that the group of black leaders in business is stronger than ever.*[11]

The following incident illustrates the irony inherent in the experiences of African-Americans in the workplace. In 1994, six Texaco employees filed a class-action lawsuit charging racial discrimination in hiring practices and workplace treatment. In 1996, when a tape of Texaco executives surfaced containing racial slurs directed at employees, as well as evidence that the executives were planning to shred incriminating documents and withhold information from the plaintiff's lawyers, they settled the suit for $115 million.[12] When news of the tape became public, an activist friend called New York State Comptroller Carl McCall, the first African-American to be elected to statewide office in New York, and asked him to join a picket line at the company's headquarters. McCall replied, "When you own 1 million shares of stock, you don't have to picket." McCall oversaw a public pension fund that is one of the largest in the country and one of the few that is managed by an individual rather than by a committee. He simply called Texaco Chairman Peter Bijur to express his concern. Bijur then continued to update McCall regularly on the progress of Texaco's diversity plan.[13]

The Twenty-First Century: New Challenges Arise While Old Problems Remain

One of the most significant issues in the new millennium has been the changing workforce composition. In 1995, Federated Department Store's diversity initiative covered two groups, women and minorities. By 2001, it covered 26 groups including seniors, the disabled, homosexuals, the devout, atheists, marrieds, and singles. This proliferation of protected groups has raised concerns that the still-prevalent problem of racism will shift to the back burner. According to Lisa Willis Johnson, diversity chair for the Society of Human Resource Management (SHRM), "Race was the sacrificial lamb to launch diversity and make it palatable to corporate America."[14] Relegation of race to a back burner would be a serious mistake: Racial harassment suits have risen dramatically in the past 10 years. Racist graffiti, pictures, jokes, and epithets have all been used to harass and intimidate people of color. One of the most vile forms of racial harassment is the hangman noose, a symbol of lynching. The EEOC handled 25 "noose" cases in the year 2000 and the first 6 months of 2001; that represents more cases in 18 months than had been seen in the previous 10 years.[15]

As the numbers and percentages of workers protected by discrimination laws continue to increase, following current trends, civil rights issues will continue to be front-burner topics. Operating against these trends has been a growing sentiment against affirmative action. The challenge for business will be to assimilate an increasingly diverse workforce while adopting a posture on affirmative action that does not engender additional resentful reactions on the part of the majority.

An indispensable way to understand the changing public policy with respect to employment discrimination is to examine the evolution of federal laws prohibiting discrimination. Once we have a better appreciation of the legal status of protected groups, we can more completely understand the complex issues that have arisen with respect to the evolving meaning of discrimination and its relationship to related workforce issues—in particular, affirmative action.

FEDERAL LAWS PROHIBITING DISCRIMINATION

This section provides an overview of the major laws that have been passed to protect workers against discrimination. We will concentrate our treatment on legislation at the federal level that has been created since the 1960s. We will discuss issues arising from the various forms of discrimination in more detail later in this chapter. We should keep in mind that there are a host of state and local laws that address many of these same topics, but space does not permit their consideration here. Our purpose in this section is to provide an overview of antidiscrimination laws and the major federal agencies that enforce those laws.

Title VII of the Civil Rights Act of 1964

Title VII of the Civil Rights Act of 1964, as amended, prohibits discrimination in hiring, promotion, discharge, pay, fringe benefits, and other aspects of employment on the basis of race, color, religion, sex, or national origin. Title VII was extended to cover federal, state, and local employers and educational institutions by the Equal Employment Opportunity Act of 1972. This amendment to Title VII also gave the Equal Employment Opportunity Commission (EEOC) the authority to file suits in federal district court against employers in the private sector on behalf of individuals whose charges had not been successfully conciliated. In 1978, Title VII was amended to include the Pregnancy Discrimination Act, which requires employers to treat pregnancy and pregnancy-related medical conditions the same as any other medical disability with respect to all terms and conditions of employment, including employee health benefits.[16] Figure 18-1 on page 572 presents an overview of Title VII's coverage.

SEARCH THE WEB

THE EEOC

The Web site of the U.S. Equal Employment Opportunity Commission (EEOC) is a good source for updated information about employment discrimination and litigation (**http://www.eeoc.gov**). Visitors can find enforcement statistics, a technical assistance program, and information on how to file a charge of discrimination.

FIGURE 18-1

Title VII of the Civil Rights Act of 1964

EMPLOYMENT discrimination based on race, color, religion, sex, or national origin is prohibited by Title VII of the Civil Rights Act of 1964.

Title VII covers private employers, state and local governments, and educational institutions that have 15 or more employees. The federal government, private and public employment agencies, labor organizations, and joint labor-management committees for apprenticeship and training also must abide by the law.

It is illegal under Title VII to discriminate in:

- Hiring and firing;
- Compensation, assignment, or classification of employees;
- Transfer, promotion, layoff, or recall;
- Job advertisements;
- Recruitment;
- Testing;
- Use of company facilities;
- Training and apprenticeship programs;
- Fringe benefits;
- Pay, retirement plans, and disability leave; or
- Other terms and conditions of employment.

Under the law, pregnancy, childbirth, and related medical conditions must be treated the same as any other nonpregnancy-related illness or disability.

Title VII prohibits retaliation against a person who files a charge of discrimination, participates in an investigation, or opposes an unlawful employment practice.

Employment agencies may not discriminate in receiving, classifying, or referring applications for employment or in their job advertisements.

Labor unions may not discriminate in accepting applications for membership; classifying members; referrals; training and apprenticeship programs; and in advertising for jobs. It is illegal for a labor union to cause or try to cause an employer to discriminate. It is also illegal for an employer to cause or try to cause a union to discriminate.

SOURCE: *Information for the Private Sector and State and Local Governments: EEOC* (Washington: Equal Employment Opportunity Commission), 6-7.

Age Discrimination in Employment Act of 1967

This law protects workers 40 years old and older from arbitrary age discrimination in hiring, discharge, pay, promotions, fringe benefits, and other aspects of employment. It is designed to promote employment of older people on the basis of ability rather than age and to help employers and workers find ways to meet problems arising from the impact of age on employment.

Like the provisions of Title VII, the **Age Discrimination in Employment Act (ADEA)** does not apply where age is a **bona fide occupational qualification (BFOQ)**— a qualification that might ordinarily be argued as being a basis for discrimination but for which a company can legitimately argue that it is job related and necessary. Neither does the act bar employers from differentiating among employees based on reasonable factors other than age.[17]

Equal Pay Act of 1963

As amended, this act prohibits sex discrimination in payment of wages to women and men who perform substantially equal work in the same establishment. Passage of this landmark law marked a significant milestone in helping women, who were the chief victims of unequal pay, to achieve equality in their paychecks.[18] Figure 18-2 summarizes other details of the **Equal Pay Act of 1963**.

Rehabilitation Act of 1973, Section 503

This law, as amended, prohibits job discrimination on the basis of a handicap. It applies to employers holding federal contracts or subcontracts. In addition, it requires these employers to engage in affirmative action to employ the handicapped, a concept we will discuss later in this chapter. Related to this act is the Vietnam Era Veterans Readjustment Assistance Act of 1974, which also prohibits discrimination and requires affirmative action among federal contractors or subcontractors.[19]

Americans with Disabilities Act of 1990

The most significant labor and employment statute to be enacted in 15 years was the 1990 **Americans with Disabilities Act (ADA)**. Although it was passed in July 1990, this act became effective for most businesses in July 1992, after the Equal Employment Opportunity Commission had published preliminary regulations for its implementation. The ADA prohibits discrimination based on physical or mental disabilities in private places of employment and public accommodation, in addition to requiring transportation systems and communication systems to facilitate access for the disabled. The ADA

FIGURE 18-2

Equal Pay Act of 1963

The EQUAL PAY ACT prohibits employers from discriminating between men and women on the basis of sex in the payment of wages where they perform substantially equal work under similar working conditions in the same establishment. The law also prohibits employers from reducing the wages of either sex to comply with the law.

A violation may exist where a different wage is paid to a predecessor or successor employee of the opposite sex. Labor organizations may not cause employers to violate the law.

Retaliation against a person who files a charge of equal pay discrimination, participates in an investigation, or opposes an unlawful employment practice also is illegal.

The law protects virtually all private employees, including executive, administrative, professional, and outside sales employees who are exempt from minimum wage and overtime laws. Most federal, state, and local government workers also are covered.

The law does not apply to pay differences based on factors other than sex, such as seniority, merit, or systems that determine wages based upon the quantity or quality of items produced or processed.

Many EPA violations may be violations of Title VII of the Civil Rights Act of 1964, which also prohibits sex-based wage discrimination. Such charges may be filed under both statutes.

SOURCE: *Information for the Private Sector and State and Local Governments: EEOC* (Washington: Equal Employment Opportunity Commission), 9.

is modeled after the Rehabilitation Act of 1973, which applies to federal contractors and grantees.[20] The basic provision of the ADA are detailed in Figure 18-3.

Essentially, the ADA gives individuals with disabilities civil rights protections similar to those provided to individuals on the basis of race, sex, national origin, and religion. The ADA applies not only to private employers but also to state and local governments, employment agencies, and labor unions. Employers of 15 or more employees are covered.

The ADA prohibits discrimination in all employment practices, including job application procedures, hiring, firing, advancement, compensation, training, and other terms, conditions, and privileges of employment. If a person's disability makes it difficult for that person to function, firms are expected to make *reasonable accommodations* if they do not represent an *undue hardship* for the firm. The act covers qualified individuals with disabilities. Qualified individuals are those who can perform the *essential functions* of the job.[21] The definition of essential function is sometimes difficult to determine. Golfer Casey Martin applied to the PGA for permission to ride a cart in PGA tournaments when other players were walking the course. Much controversy ensued over whether walking the golf course was an essential function of playing professional golf. The Supreme Court subsequently ruled that he could use a cart because providing the cart was a reasonable accommodation and his use of the cart would not fundamentally alter the game.

The definition of disability includes people who have physical or mental impairments that substantially limit one or more major life activities, such as seeing, hearing, speaking, walking, breathing, performing manual tasks, learning, caring for oneself, and working.[22] Uncertainty over the definition of "disability" sent the ADA to the courts for clarification.

FIGURE 18-3

The Americans with Disabilities Act

Title I of the Americans with Disabilities Act of 1990, which took effect July 26, 1992, prohibits private employers, state and local governments, employment agencies, and labor unions from discriminating against qualified individuals with disabilities in job application procedures, hiring, firing, advancement, compensation, job training, and other terms, conditions, and privileges of employment. An individual with a disability is a person who:

- Has a physical or mental impairment that substantially limits one or more major life activities;
- Has a record of such an impairment; or
- Is regarded as having such an impairment.

A qualified employee or applicant with a disability is an individual who, with or without reasonable accommodation, can perform the essential functions of the job in question. Reasonable accommodation may include, but is not limited to:

- Making existing facilities used by employees readily accessible to and usable by persons with disabilities;
- Job restructuring, modifying work schedules, reassignment to a vacant position;
- Acquiring or modifying equipment or devices; adjusting or modifying examinations, training materials, or policies; and providing qualified readers or interpreters.

An employer is required to make an accommodation to the known disability of a qualified applicant or employee if it would not impose an "undue hardship" on the operation of the employer's business. Undue hardship is defined as an action requiring significant difficulty or expense when considered in light of factors such as an employer's size, its financial resources, and the nature and structure of its operation.

An employer is not required to lower quality or production standards to make an accommodation, nor is an employer obligated to provide personal use items such as glasses or hearing aids.

SOURCE: *EEOC Fact Sheet* (Washington: Equal Employment Opportunity Commission).

In June 1998, the Supreme Court decided that the definition of "disability" included both major and minor impairments. Under this ruling, the ADA applies to disabilities as diverse as HIV, diabetes, cancer, dyslexia, and bad backs.[23] In 2003, however, the Equal Employment Opportunity Commission (EEOC) issued enforcement guidance that restricts the definition of a disability. They ruled that an *impairment* is a *disability* only if it "substantially limits one or more of the employee's **major life activities**."[24] Major life activities include speaking and interacting with others, learning, thinking, concentrating, and working.[25]

In 2004, the Supreme Court upheld an individual's right to sue under the ADA. Paraplegic and confined to a wheelchair, George Lane was ordered to appear in a court with no ramps or elevators leading to the second floor. He could not climb the steps and so he crawled up the stairs to comply with the order. When he was ordered to appear in court a second time, Lane refused to crawl or be carried. He was subsequently arrested for failing to appear in court. He charged the state of Tennessee with discrimination and sued for $100,000. When the Supreme Court upheld his right to sue, it was seen as an indication that the high court was disinclined to let states' rights arguments prevail over civil rights.[26]

The ADA quickly became a controversial law. In the early years following the act's passage, news reports were filled with stories of frivolous lawsuits and outrageous abuses of the protections offered by the ADA. Many fear these abuses created a backlash against people with disabilities. Kathi Wolfe, a Virginia writer with a visual handicap, recalls having an able-bodied writer tell her, "With the ADA, I'll bet editors are scared to reject your stuff. They'd be afraid you'd sue them." In another instance, a drugstore clerk said to Wolfe, "Please don't sue us because we don't have Braille signs." Knowing that two-thirds of severely disabled individuals remain unemployed despite the ADA, Wolfe wonders if the ADA has made employers more hesitant than ever to hire individuals with disabilities.[27]

Although the stories of ADA excess remain, the evidence supporting them is thin. In a "Dateline" report for NBC News, John Hockenberry tracked down several well-known "legends of the ADA," including a 400-pound subway worker who sued for being denied a conductor's position because he could not fit in the cab, a man who had a deep-seated need to bring a gun to work, and a dentist whose disability would not let him stop grabbing women. Hockenberry found that the first two cases were thrown out by the EEOC and that, in the third case, the dentist never actually sued because he was self-employed and so was never fired. The difficulty these cases had in getting past the EEOC appears to be typical. Hockenberry found that of the 90,000 complaints received by the EEOC, only 250 had ended up in court.[28] Of the cases that make it to court, few are won by the plaintiffs. The American Bar Association (ABA) reviewed more than 1,200 ADA cases and found that employers won 92 percent of the cases decided by a judge and 86 percent of the cases decided by the EEOC. Don Donaldson, risk manager at the Jacksonville (FL) Port Authority, said "The survey findings to me are not surprising because I've been monitoring developments and trends on this issue . . . if employers make reasonable accommodations to disabled workers, then the courts would likely rely on common sense and rule in the employer's favor."[29]

Donaldson's remarks help to explain why the ADA found a high level of support in a Louis Harris survey of corporate employers. These corporate executives, 81 percent of whom had modified their offices since the ADA went into effect, estimated the average cost of accommodation as $223 per disabled employee. About half of the executives (48 percent) said the ADA increased their costs a little, 82 percent reported no change in costs, and 7 percent reported that their costs increased "a lot." Most of the executives said the ADA should be strengthened or kept as it is; only 12 percent felt it should be weakened or repealed.[30] The executives' assessments of the ADA seem to be on target. A 2003 study by the American Bar Association found that employers won 94.5 percent of the ADA discrimination court cases and 78.1 percent of the administrative cases. As the study says, the ADA "as interpreted by the courts creates difficult obstacles for the plaintiff to overcome."[31] They must now have a disability that impairs a major life activity while still being able to perform the essential functions of the job.[32]

Civil Rights Act of 1991

In 1990 and 1991, civil rights bills were debated in Congress. The proposed bills were aimed primarily at restoring and strengthening civil rights laws and interpretations that banned discrimination in employment, many of which had been overturned by earlier U.S. Supreme Court rulings.

Finally, a bill, with some modifications, was introduced as the **Civil Rights Act of 1991**. Throughout 1991, a partisan debate between Democrats and Republicans continued on the proposed civil rights legislation. Supporters of the legislation argued that it would not mandate hiring quotas, but detractors believed that quotas would be necessitated in its implementation.

The Civil Rights Act of 1991 was passed. The primary objective of the 1991 civil rights act was to provide increased financial damages and jury trials in cases of intentional discrimination relating to sex, religion, race, disability, and national origin. Under Title VII, monetary awards were limited to such items as back pay, lost benefits, and attorney fees and costs. The new act permitted both compensatory and punitive damages to be awarded. In addition, charges of unintentional discrimination will be more difficult for employers to defend, because the act shifts the burden of proof back to the employer. Initial amounts of compensatory and punitive damages an employee could receive were set at $50,000 to $300,000. The 1991 act also altered parts of several Supreme Court decisions that had once been considered to be management victories.[33]

The laws we have just discussed constitute the backbone of federal efforts to prevent employment discrimination. Several executive orders issued by the president of the United States also prohibit discrimination. However, because these executive orders also contain provisions for affirmative action, we will discuss them during our treatment of affirmative action later in this chapter.

Equal Employment Opportunity Commission

As the major federal body created to administer and enforce job bias laws, the **Equal Employment Opportunity Commission (EEOC)** deserves special consideration. Several other federal agencies also are charged with enforcing certain aspects of the discrimination laws and executive orders, but we will restrict our discussion to the EEOC because it is the major agency.

The EEOC has five commissioners and a general counsel appointed by the president and confirmed by the Senate. The 5-member commission is responsible for making equal employment opportunity policy and approving all litigation the commission undertakes. The EEOC staff receives and investigates employment discrimination charges/complaints. If the commission finds reasonable cause to believe that unlawful discrimination has occurred, its staff attempts to conciliate the charges/complaints. When conciliation is not achieved, the EEOC may file lawsuits in federal district court against employers. Private employers may be sued under Title VII, but only the Justice Department may sue a state or local government for a violation of Title VII.[34]

To provide some appreciation of the kinds of discrimination cases handled by the EEOC, Figure 18-4 presents a breakdown of the job-bias claims filed with the EEOC from 1991 to 2003. Overall, job discrimination complaints fell in 2003 after hitting the highest level since 1995 in 2002. The EEOC attributed the 2002 spike in complaints to a variety of factors including the September 11 attacks in 2001 (discrimination because of national origin rose 13 percent), an aging population, a more diverse workforce and a weak economy.[35] In spite of the 1-year decline, discrimination claims in 2003 were at the second highest level in eight years.[36]

Like other federal regulatory bodies we have discussed, such as the EPA, FTC, and OSHA, the EEOC has had mixed success over the years. Its fortunes, successes, and failures have been somewhat dictated by the times, the administration in office, and the philosophy and zeal of its chairperson. During the late 1970s, the business community thought that the EEOC was on a "witch-hunt," looking for violations so it could punish business for its past wrongs.[37] In the 1980s, the Reagan administration responded to these concerns when it (1) eliminated the use of minority hiring goals and timetables used by employers to correct racial and ethnic disparities, (2) largely abandoned class-action lawsuits that relied on statistical evidence to prove widespread discrimination at large companies, and (3) yielded the EEOC's once-dominant role on civil rights initiatives to the Justice Department.[38] When former President Clinton took office in 1992, the EEOC stepped up enforcement of business discrimination laws. Among the crackdown's targets were unsettled discrimination lawsuits against major employers, polluters who dump their muck in minority neighborhoods, banks whose loan departments redline poor areas, and

FIGURE 18-4

Discrimination Claims Filed with the EEOC (1991–2003)

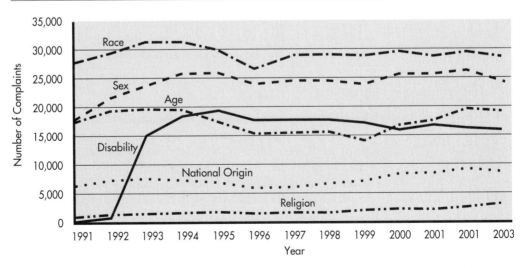

SOURCE: Data from the U.S. EEOC (http://www.eeoc.gov).

other forms of day-to-day discrimination.[39] The renewed effort, combined with a broadened mandate, resulted in an upsurge of cases. In fiscal year 1991, there were 63,898 new cases. By fiscal year 1994, there were 91,189 new cases. This increase in the number of new cases coincided with a reduction in staffing levels, which were at an all-time low. These combined trends resulted in a backlog of cases, which peaked at 110,000. Through an influx of capital from Congress, overall efficiency improvements, and efforts to use alternative dispute resolution (ADR), the backlog decreased by 45 percent and stood at a little over 61,000 in 1998.[40] The George W. Bush administration nominated Cari Dominguez, who spearheaded the "Glass Ceiling Report" for the Labor Department in 1991, to chair the EEOC. She was unanimously confirmed. At the top of her list of priorities is the concept of "proactive prevention" of discrimination and discriminatory situations. She emphasizes partnering and strategic alliances, including with associations of professionals, to achieve this goal.[41]

EXPANDED MEANINGS OF DISCRIMINATION

Over the years, it has been left to the courts to define the word *discrimination*, because it was not defined in Title VII. Over time, it has become apparent that two specific kinds of discrimination have been identified. These two kinds are known as disparate treatment and disparate impact.

Disparate Treatment

Initially, the word *discrimination* meant the use of race, color, religion, sex, or national origin as a basis for treating people differently or unequally. This form of discrimination became known as unequal treatment, or **disparate treatment**. Examples of disparate treatment might include refusing to consider blacks for a job, paying women less than men for the same work, or supporting any decision rule with a racial or sexual premise or cause.[42] According to this common-sense view of discrimination, the employer was allowed to impose any criteria so long as they were imposed on all groups alike.[43] This view of discrimination equated nondiscrimination with color-blind decision making. In other words, to avoid this kind of discrimination, it meant that all groups or individuals had to be treated equally, without regard for color, sex, or other characteristics.[44]

Disparate Impact

Congress's intent in prohibiting discrimination was to eliminate practices that contributed to economic inequality. What it found was that, although companies could adhere to the disparate treatment definition of discrimination, this did not eliminate all of the economic inequalities it was intended to address. For example, a company could use two neutral, color-blind criteria for selection—a high school diploma and a standardized ability test. Blacks and whites could be treated the same under the criteria, but the problem arose when it became apparent that the policy of equal treatment resulted in unequal consequences for blacks and whites. Blacks were less likely to have high school diplomas, and blacks who took the test were less likely than whites to pass it. Therefore, a second, more expanded idea of what constituted discrimination was thought to be needed.

The Supreme Court had to decide whether an action was discriminatory if it resulted in unequal consequences in the *Griggs v. Duke Power Company* case.[45] Duke Power had required that employees transferring to other departments have a high school diploma or pass a standardized intelligence test. This requirement excluded a disproportionate number of minority workers. The court noted that there were nonminorities who performed satisfactorily and achieved promotions though they did not have diplomas. The court then reached the groundbreaking conclusion that it was the consequences of an employer's actions, not the employer's intentions, that determined whether discrimination had taken place. If any employment practice or test had an adverse or differential effect on minorities, then it was a discriminatory practice. An unequal impact, or **disparate impact**, as this new kind of discrimination came to be known, simply meant that fewer minorities were included in the outcome of the test or the hiring or promotion practice than would be expected by their numerical proportion. The court also held that a policy or procedure with a disparate impact would be permissible if the employer could demonstrate that it was a business- or job-related necessity. In the *Duke Power* case, for example, a high school diploma and good scores on a general intelligence test were not shown to have a clearly demonstrable relationship to successful performance on the job under consideration.[46]

The concept of "unequal impact" is quite significant, because it runs counter to so many traditional employment practices. There are many other examples. The minimum height and weight requirements of some police departments have unequal impact and have been struck down by courts because they tend to disproportionately screen out women, Orientals, and Hispanics.[47] The practice of discharging employees who have had their wages garnished to pay off debts has also been struck down, because it falls heavily on minorities.[48] Several Supreme Court rulings have addressed the issue of the kind of evidence needed to document or prove discrimination. Typically, if a member of a minority group does not have a success rate at least 80 percent that of the majority group, the practice may be considered to have an adverse impact.[49] When this **four-fifths rule** is triggered, the firm will not necessarily be found guilty of having a disparate impact. It will be incumbent upon the firm, however, to show the selection practice is job related and necessary for the business.[50]

With at least two different ways in which to commit discrimination, managers have to be extremely careful, because practically any action they take could possibly have discriminatory effects. Figure 18-5 summarizes the characteristics of disparate treatment and disparate impact.

FIGURE 18-5

Two Kinds of Employment Discrimination

Definition 1 Disparate Treatment	Definition 2 Disparate Impact
Direct discrimination	Indirect discrimination
Unequal treatment	Unequal consequences or results
Decision rules with a racial/sexual premise or cause	Decision rules with racial/sexual consequences or results
Intentional discrimination	Unintentional discrimination
Prejudiced actions	Neutral, color-blind actions
Different standards for different groups	Same standards, but different consequences for different groups

SOURCE: James Ledvinka and Vida G. Scarpello, *Federal Regulation of Personnel and Human Resources Management*, 2d ed. (Boston: PWS-Kent, 1991), 48.

ISSUES IN EMPLOYMENT DISCRIMINATION

We have identified the essentials of the major laws on discrimination and traced the evolution of the concept of discrimination. Now it is useful to discuss briefly the different issues that are related to the types of discrimination we have discussed. It is also important to indicate some of the particular problems that have arisen with respect to each of the different issues.

Issues of Racial Discrimination

In spite of its place as one of the first forms of discrimination to be the focus of civil rights legislation, racial discrimination remains a problem in workplaces in the United States and throughout the world. Although racial discrimination is always hurtful, the nature of its form and impact has been different for people of different races.

The Two Nations of Black America.   In a recent essay for the *Brookings Review*, Henry Louis Gates, Jr., describes the present day as the "best of times and the worst of times" for the African-American community. Gates, the W.E.B. Dubois Professor of the Humanities and chairman of the Department of Afro-American Studies at Harvard University, profiles the "two nations of Black America" that are separated by money, power, and education:

SEARCH THE WEB

MEASURE YOUR ATTITUDES

Project Implicit (**https://implicit.harvard.edu/implicit**) is a collaborative effort between researchers at Harvard University, the University of Virginia, and the University of Washington. It contains a variety of tests that you can take to assess your feeling about a range of topics including age, race, color, gender, politics, sexuality, weight, disability, and religion. These "Implicit Association Tests" (IATs) have one thing in common—they are designed to examine thoughts and feelings that are beyond your conscious control. The tests do this by asking you to associate concepts such as "good" and "bad" with pictures, symbols, or words that reflect the concepts being tested. The researchers suggest that you take a sample test from the demonstration side and then read the information available on the IAT, because it will make more sense after you have experienced a test.

When you enter the Web site, you will have a choice between "Demonstration" and "Research." The demonstration side allows you to sample the tests, choosing which one(s) you would like to take. You may be asked to complete an optional survey, but you can proceed without completing it. If you enter the research side, you can become a participant in the studies. Throughout the Web site, you can obtain background information about the purpose of the project, the scientists who designed it, and the nature of the tests administered.

The range of studies should provide you with an opportunity to think about topics that are very important to you or unique issues that you have not had the occasion to tackle in the past. The expressed goals of Project Implicit are to provide a safe and secure virtual environment to investigate psychological issues and, at the same time, provide visitors and participants with an engaging educational experience.

We have the largest black, middle class in our history and the largest black underclass. In 1990, 2,280,000 black men were in prison, or probation, or parole, while 23,000 earned a college degree. That's a ratio of 99 to 1 compared with a ratio of 6 to 1 for white men.[51]

The two nations are reflected in the attitudes of black professionals toward corporate America. In a *Fortune* poll, most blacks indicated that they felt discrimination was still common in the workplace. However, more than two-thirds felt optimistic about the future of their careers. *Fortune* called the combination of optimism and skepticism a "post-Texaco hangover."[52]

There is no shortage of statistics to support Gates's argument that these are the "worst of times." To commemorate the 30th anniversary of the Kerner Commission Report, which warned that the nation was "moving toward two societies, one black and one white—separate and unequal," the Eisenhower Foundation prepared a monograph titled, "The Millennium Breach." In it, the authors decried the economic status and racial divide of the inner city. They found that in a time of "full employment," unemployment in the inner city is at crisis levels. Racial minorities were shown to suffer disproportionately from child poverty, which increased more than 20 percent during the 1980s. In fact, in 1998 the U.S. child poverty rate stood at four times the average of most Western European countries.[53]

What is surprising to many people is the wealth of statistics that supports Gates's arguments that these are the "best of times." The number of blacks going to college grew from 14.2 percent in 1970 to 44.2 percent in 1990. Black men in technical jobs earn almost as much as white men, while college-educated black women earn more than their college-educated white counterparts. College-educated black men are about equally likely as college-educated white men to hold managerial positions, and college-educated black female managers and executives earn 10 percent more than their white counterparts. The trends among youth also show more promise for the future. In 1970, the workforce contained five times as many black high school dropouts as black college graduates. Now, the percentage of black students dropping out is only 5 percent, not far from the 4 percent reported for white students. Smoking among black high school seniors has dropped precipitously, from 24.9 percent in 1977 to 4.1 percent in 1993. In comparison, white high school seniors had only a 7.5 percent decline during the same period (from 28.9 to 21.4 percent).[54]

Perhaps the best way to gauge progress is to compare it to 1954, when *Brown v. Board of Education* opened up educational opportunities for blacks and other minorities. According to the U.S. Bureau of Labor Statistics, blacks and other minorities recorded a 9.9 percent jobless rate in 1954, 80 percent higher than that for all workers. In 2002, blacks and other minorities had a 9.2 percent jobless rate, which was 60 percent greater than the rate for all workers.[55] Although some improvement is indicated, it is a paltry gain for 40 years of united effort.

The two nations can exist simultaneously, because the same glass may be half-full or half-empty, depending on your perspective. For example, the educational achievements of black students provide both good and bad news. In 1990, the good news was that the number of 17-year-old blacks who were able to read at an adept level had doubled from 1970 figures. The bad news was that only 20 percent were able to read at that level in 1990, while 48 percent of all American students measured could.[56] Why does the public assume the bad news is true and find the good news surprising? Although most poor people in the United States are white, the media has tended to focus on blacks when covering stories about poverty. Martin Gilens, a political scientist, studied 4 years of stories from major magazines and 5 years of news-show broadcasts on the major networks. Of the

Hugh R. Morley writes in an article distributed by *Knight Ridder/Tribune Business News* (27 February 2003 pITEM03058023) about a study to find the "Best Companies for African-Americans." The study, conducted by Family Digest magazine, identified some surprising choices, including Denny's and Johnson & Johnson, both firms that have had legal problems involving racial discrimination. The study looked at hiring policies, number of African-Americans on the corporate board, and level of charitable giving to black community groups, among other criteria. Find out what other companies are making a solid effort to be "a great place to work for all people" by logging on to InfoTrac College Edition at http://www.infotrac-college.com and keying record number CJ98156676.

poor people in the United States, 29 percent were black, but all the news magazines portrayed the majority of the poor as black, ranging from 53 percent at *U.S. News & World Report* to 66 percent at *Newsweek.* At the three major television networks, 65.2 percent of the people portrayed as poor in the news were black. The only time blacks were underrepresented was when stories were about the more sympathetic working poor or elderly. Although 42 percent of poor African-Americans work, only 12 percent were portrayed as "working poor" in the media. Similarly, 8 percent of poor black Americans are elderly, but less than 1 percent of the people portrayed as elderly poor were black.[57]

A 2004 letter to Randy Cohen's "The Ethicist" column in *The New York Times Magazine* underscores the difficulties that remain for African-Americans today, irrespective of their level of achievement. An African-American male was looking for Web programming work. When he used his first name on his resume, a name that identified his ethnicity, he received relatively few calls for interviews. He began to use his middle name on his resume and found that he got more interviews.[58] This man's experience underscores the challenges facing African-Americans today. Those who develop professional skills and achieve a higher level of education still cannot count on their credentials opening the same doors the credentials would open for other workers in the marketplace.

In summary, although many blacks are succeeding and moving ahead, poverty hangs over many others, and much media coverage gives the appearance that progress is not being made. Civil rights leaders, politicians, and academics debate fiercely the causes of and possible solutions to the problem. Even black leadership is fractured into at least two camps—those who hold that lingering racism and cramped economic opportunities are the problem and those who say that racism is not the only critical factor.[59] Those who cite racism as the root cause have no difficulty finding support for that argument: Half the black respondents in a 2004 poll said they had experienced some form of discrimination in the month preceding the poll.[60] Those who say racism is not the only factor point to the valorization of the ghetto culture and the need for blacks to take the initiative and break the cycle of poverty. At a 2004 celebration of the fiftieth anniversary of the *Brown v. Board of Education* decision, comedian Bill Cosby sparked controversy by saying that "lower economic people are not holding up their end in this deal."[61] Although this dispute is unlikely to be settled soon, there is one thing on which all parties seem to agree: The role that business could and should play remains at the forefront of this debate and is likely to be there for the foreseeable future.

The Case of Hispanics. The word *Hispanic* fails to capture the diversity in this population. It is a term created by the government and first used in the 1980 census to categorize people from Latin America or Spain. Hispanics are the only major minority group to be classified by the language they speak. They can be black (Cuba's population is 58 percent black), Asian (Peru's former President Fujimori is 100 percent Japanese), or any of a variety of races. Accordingly, many people prefer to be described as Latino (which includes people from Portugal) or as coming from their country of origin (e.g., of Puerto Rican descent).[62]

The growth rate among Hispanics in the United States is one of the most dramatic in U.S. history. The 2000 census identified a Hispanic population of 35.3 million, representing one out of eight Americans and greater than the entire population of Canada. This is a 58 percent increase from the 22.4 million Hispanics 10 years before. For the first time, more people identify themselves as Hispanic (35.3 million) than identify themselves as black (34.7 million), making Hispanics the largest minority recorded by the

U.S. census. However, 1.7 million people identify themselves as partly black and partly another race and some Hispanic people are black so the difference in sizes of the groups is largely definitional.[63]

A strong work ethic is characteristic of the Hispanic population. Originally centered in a few big metropolitan areas, thousands of Hispanics have moved to small factory towns and suburban areas for employment. Workforce participation among Hispanic males is the highest of any measured group at 80 percent, with many becoming entrepreneurs. Those living in poverty use welfare less often than poor blacks or poor whites. In spite of this level of participation and success in the workforce, many Hispanics are still working in low-wage jobs. Discrimination remains a critical problem.[64] In the 2003 "National Survey of Latinos," 31 percent of the 3,000 Hispanics polled said that they or someone close to them had experienced job discrimination in the past five years; 14 percent had experienced the discrimination themselves.[65]

Asian Image of Model Minority.

Asian-Americans have a problem that is unique to U.S. minority groups, a stereotype that may be too positive. Aggregate data about educational achievement, occupational distribution, annual household income, and other indicators of success show that Asian-Americans, particularly East Asian-Americans and Asian Indian immigrants and descendants of immigrants from Confucian countries like China, Japan, or Korea, have outperformed other minority groups and achieved a level of success comparable to that of white workers. As a result, the popular press, many pundits, and various policy makers have argued that Asian-Americans represent an ideal that should be emulated by other minorities (i.e., Asian-Americans are the "Model Minority").[66]

Recently, scholars in various disciplines, including Asian-American studies, have refuted this characterization. They argue that aggregated data hide the impact of such critical factors as highly selective immigration policies, high numbers of hours worked, and high numbers of individuals per household. When these critics have disaggregated the data used to support the Model Minority characterization, they have found a bimodal distribution. One group of well-educated, higher paid Asian-American professionals does well until they reach the glass ceiling; the other group is low skilled, low paid, and generally disadvantaged.[67]

A major report by the Commission on Civil Rights concluded, "Anti-Asian activity in the form of violence, vandalism, harassment, and intimidation continues to occur across the nation."[68] Asian-Americans have started relying more on the courts to battle discrimination and hate crimes. This seemed to signal a growing realization by Asian-Americans that their past reluctance to apply pressure through the legal system has placed them at a disadvantage.[69]

A 2004 study showed that although Asians comprise 4.4 percent of the U.S. population, they account for only 1 percent of *Fortune* 500 board members. The study was commissioned by the Committee of 100, an organization of prominent Chinese Americans; they note that the underrepresentation on *Fortune* 500 boards has occurred in spite of the fact that Asian Americans are wealthier and better educated than whites and other minority groups. Wilson Chu, a Dallas lawyer who directed the study, comments, "There's a negative perception of Asians out there. People may view them as smart people, but not as leaders."[70]

It has been argued that many of the problems of Asian-Americans stem from their image as a model minority, which embraces discipline, hard work, and education. This image has a downside, because quiet achievement can be interpreted as passivity. The

Asian-American response to this had been to avoid confrontation and simply work harder, but groups like the Committee of 100 are beginning to change that. The presence of Asian-Americans will continue to grow, and so their treatment in the workplace will be an issue for years to come.

Issues of Sex Discrimination

Issues surrounding sex discrimination are quite different from issues involving race, color, and national origin. Statistics show that women are flooding the job market, boosting economic growth, and helping to reshape the economy dramatically. Although many believe that the gap between men's and women's incomes has closed since the civil rights activism of the 1960s, the facts say otherwise. In 2003, *The New York Times* reported that women were still making only 77.5 percent of the wages earned by men.[71]

The major issues for women today include (1) getting into professional and managerial positions and out of traditional female-dominated positions, (2) achieving pay commensurate with that of men, (3) eliminating sexual harassment, and (4) being able to take maternity leave without losing their jobs. Some progress is being made on most of these fronts.

Moving into Professional/Managerial Positions.
The 2003 Catalyst Census found that women are making modest progress moving into formerly male-dominated professional and managerial jobs. However, concerns remain about a glass ceiling that prohibits women from reaching the top levels of corporate management. Women represented 13.6 percent of the corporate officers in the *Fortune* 500 in 2003. This is an increase from 9.6 percent in 1995. In 2003, 25 *Fortune* 500 companies had no women on the board, a decrease from the 96 companies that had no women directors in 1995. Only 11 companies had 25 percent or more women directors in 1995. That number increased to 54 by 2003. The majority (89.2 percent) of *Fortune* 500 firms had at least one woman on the board.[72]

A recent study asked *Fortune* 1000 male CEOs and senior-level female executives for their views on why glass ceilings exist. Their views differed. The male CEOs blamed the glass ceiling on the women's lack of experience and time "in the pipeline." The female executives disagreed sharply, citing an exclusionary corporate culture as the reason for women's lack of advancement to senior positions. They described a corporate playing field that was not level due to negative preconceptions and stereotypes. Despite their differences about the causes of the glass ceiling, the male CEOs and female executives agreed that both individuals and the organization are responsible for creating positive organizational changes.[73]

Pay Equity.
Pay equity can be approached from two directions: equal pay and comparable worth. Equal pay argues that workers doing the same job should receive the same pay, irrespective of gender. As previously mentioned, women earn about three-fourths of what men earn. Some have tried to explain the discrepancy by arguing that these statistics include women who lost both time and experience through extended maternity leave. However, the Bureau of Labor Statistics shows that only 5.1 percent of women take more than a week off beyond regular vacation time (for any reason), while 3.3 percent of men do the same.[74] A 2003 General Accounting Office (GAO) study controlled for external

factors such as women working less, leaving the workforce for longer periods of time, and working at lower paying jobs. They found that women still earned significantly less than men. "After accounting for so many external factors, it seems that still, at the root of it all, men get an inherent annual bonus just for being men," said Representative Carolyn B. Maloney (D–New York).[75]

A 2001 study from the Economic Policy Institute evaluates this issue by studying highly accomplished new media workers in New York City. They found that female Internet workers were earning, on average, $10,000 less per year than comparable male workers. According to Rosemary Batt, a coauthor of the study, "Along gender lines, the new economy doesn't seem to be very different from the old economy."[76]

The causes of this inequity are complex, involving both conscious and unconscious bias. A 2003 series of studies, however, has cast light on a behavioral factor that may be contributing to the problem—women's hesitation to negotiate. The first study found a significant difference in starting salaries among Carnegie Mellon MBA graduates. The starting salaries of female students were almost $4,000 (7.6 percent) lower than those of the male students because the women had tended to accept the first salary offer. Only 7 percent of women negotiated the salary offer while 8 times as many men (57 percent) asked for more.[77] The authors then conducted a follow-up experiment in which, after playing a word game, subjects were given $3 of the "$3 to $10" they were promised for participating. The experimenter said, "Here's $3. Is $3 OK?" The men outnumbered the women nine to one in saying it's not okay and asking for more money.[78] In the last study, the authors conducted an Internet survey of 291 people's negotiation behavior. For men, the most recent negotiation was 2 weeks earlier; for women, it was 4 weeks earlier. The second most recent negotiation for men was 7 weeks earlier, for women, it was 24 weeks earlier. Finally, when asked when they expected to negotiate next, the men expected to negotiate in 1 week; for women, it was in 4 weeks. These findings indicate that men not only negotiate more often, but they also perceive more of their situations as possible negotiations.[79] The authors suggest that these findings are driven by two factors. First, women are socialized not to negotiate from a young age. The message they receive is to place the interests of others before their own. Second, the same negotiation behavior for which men are rewarded can result in penalties for women. Behavior that in men is considered "assertive" is often perceived in women as being "pushy." The authors put forth the following recommendations for managers to close the pay gap:[80]

- Let women employees know that they should and must ask for what they want.
- Tell women employees about the benefits of negotiation.
- When men and women have comparable achievement, give them comparable raises.
- Knowing that women's style is less assertive, don't leave them out of things.
- Audit your and the firm's record for advancing women employees.
- Don't let the squeaky wheel get the grease—create a situation where equal performance receives equal rewards.

A 2003 study in the *Journal of Applied Psychology* sheds additional light on the pay gap. Being a woman is not the only source of discrepancy: Simply working with women can lead to a lower salary for both men and women. Managers who work with more women, whether the women are subordinates or peers, have lower salaries than managers who work with mostly men. These findings held true across a variety of industries.[81] "This is a hidden phenomenon that affects both men and women managers," says Cheri Ostroff, one of the study's authors.[82] For each 10 percent increase of women in the workplace, the managers' pay decreased by about $500. Those who managed a group composed completely of women were paid $9,000 less than those who managed a group divided evenly between men and women.[83] Clearly the gender gap in pay is a complex issue with a variety of causes. Addressing it will require an equally complex set of solutions.

Comparable worth presents a controversial solution to the pay-equity problem. From this perspective, workers doing different jobs should receive the same pay if those different jobs have equal inherent worth, i.e., contribute equally to the firm's performance. As previously discussed, the Equal Pay Act requires that people holding equal positions receive equal compensation. Despite the act's existence, however, the pay of men and women remains disparate, due largely to the wage effects of labor market segregation, whereby jobs traditionally held by women pay less than their requirements or contributions might indicate. The persistent disparity between men's and women's median incomes has led some legal scholars and women's advocates to recommend comparable worth.[84] Advocates of comparable worth argue that differences in seniority and education cannot explain the fact that women generally earn only about three-fourths of what men do. They argue that certain jobs are paid less just because they are traditionally held by women. Opponents of comparable worth counter that it is not pragmatic to apply comparable worth to the private sector, because the private sector lacks the public sector's civil service categories, which are fixed by legislation.[85] Their arguments are supported by a 2001 study that showed that inherent job worth is a subject that is difficult to measure reliably and accurately.[86] The only recent attempt to institute a system of comparable worth has been in one state, New York. The New York State Fair Pay Act specifically disallows a defense that inequitable wage rates match the prevailing market; this effectively creates a system consistent with comparable worth. The Fair Pay Act was passed by the State Assembly in April 2002 but died in a State Senate committee for the fifth year in a row due to intense business lobbying and partisan opposition.[87]

Sexual Harassment.

A 2002 survey, sponsored by the Employment Law Alliance, found that 21 percent of women and 7 percent of men have been sexually harassed at work. In a related finding, 20 percent of the respondents said they were aware of a romantic supervisor/subordinate relationship at work, and 54 percent said supervisors are likely to retaliate if a subordinate rejects their romantic overtures.[88]

It is difficult to document fully the extent to which **sexual harassment** has become a major issue in American business today. With the increasing number of women in the workforce, however, it is understandable why sexual harassment has become a much-debated issue. Sexual harassment has been a high-profile issue ever since 1991, when Supreme Court nominee Clarence Thomas was accused of sexual harassment by Anita Hill, a former employee of the EEOC. The country witnessed days of televised hearings over the issue, and the event created a springboard for many women to come forward and publicly claim that they had been sexually harassed by coworkers in the past. The country was divided in its opinion of whether Hill had actually been sexually harassed by Thomas 10 years earlier, and Thomas was eventually confirmed to a seat on the highest court. The Thomas hearings were a watershed event for sexual harassment. The hearings catapulted sexual harassment into the limelight, just as the explosion at the Union Carbide plant in Bhopal, India, and the massive oil spill from the Exxon *Valdez* made workplace safety and environmental issues, respectively, national concerns.

Data from the EEOC report an escalating number of sexual harassment complaints. In 1986, 2,052 complaints were filed. By 2003, there were 13,566 sexual harassment complaints.[89] Although the number of complaints in 2003 is still high, it is a decrease from the 15,889 complaints lodged in 1997.[90] With this background, let us now consider what Title VII and the EEOC have to say about sexual harassment as a type of sex discrimination.

The EEOC defines sexual harassment in the following way:

> *Unwelcome sexual advances, requests for sexual favors, and other verbal or physical conduct of a sexual nature constitute sexual harassment when submission to or rejection of this conduct explicitly or implicitly affects an individual's employment, unreasonably interferes with an individual's work performance, or creates an intimidating, hostile, or offensive work environment.*

Implicit in this definition are two broad types of sexual harassment. First is what has been called *quid pro quo* harassment. This is a situation where something is given or received for something else. For example, a boss may make it explicit or implicit that a sexual favor is expected if the employee wants a pay raise or a promotion. Second is what has been referred to as *hostile work environment* harassment. In this type, nothing is given or received, but the employee perceives a hostile or offensive work environment by virtue of uninvited sexually oriented behaviors or materials being present in the workplace. Examples of this might include sexual teasing or jokes or sexual materials, such as pictures or cartoons, being present in the workplace.

To clear up common misconceptions, the EEOC indicates that sexual harassment can occur in a variety of circumstances that include but are not limited to the following:[91]

- The victim as well as the harasser may be a woman or a man. The victim does not have to be of the opposite sex.
- The harasser can be the victim's supervisor, an agent of the employer, a supervisor in another area, a coworker, or a nonemployee.
- The victim does not have to be the person harassed but could be anyone affected by the offensive conduct.
- Unlawful sexual harassment may occur without economic injury to or discharge of the victim.
- The harasser's conduct must be unwelcome.

Figure 18-6 on page 588 lists the kinds of experiences women are typically talking about when they say they have been sexually harassed.

Meritor Savings Bank v. Vinson. Prior to 1986, sexual harassment was not a specific violation of federal law. In a landmark case, however, the Supreme Court ruled in 1986 in *Meritor Savings Bank v. Vinson* that sexual harassment was a violation of Title VII. In this case, the court ruled that the creation of a "hostile environment" through sexual harassment violates Title VII, even in the absence of economic harm to the employee or a demand for sexual favors in exchange for promotions, raises, or the like. Remedies made available to the victims at that time included back pay, damages for emotional stress, and attorney fees.[92] We should reiterate that sexual harassment can be committed by women against men or by individuals of the same sex.

Harris v. Forklift Systems. The stage was set for another major Supreme Court ruling (*Harris v. Forklift Systems*) in 1993 in what many were hoping would more clearly define what constituted sexual harassment. The court agreed to hear the case of a Tennessee woman, Teresa Harris, who claimed her boss (at Forklift Systems) made sexual remarks about her clothing, asked her to retrieve coins from his pants pockets, and once joked about going to a motel "to negotiate your raise." The lower courts had

FIGURE 18-6

Examples of Sexual Harassment Complaints

- Being subjected to sexually suggestive remarks and propositions
- Being sent on unnecessary errands through work areas where men have an added opportunity to stare
- Being subjected to sexual innuendo and joking
- Being touched by a boss while working
- Coworkers' "remarks" about a person sexually cooperating with the boss
- Suggestive looks and gestures
- Deliberate touching and "cornering"
- Suggestive body movements
- Sexually oriented materials being circulated around the office
- Pornographic cartoons and pictures posted or present in work areas
- Pressure for dates and sexual favors
- Boss's cruelty after sexual advances are resisted
- A boss rubbing employee's back while she is typing

NOTE: It should be noted that these are "complaints." Whether each item turns out to be sexual harassment or not in the eyes of the law is determined in an official hearing or trial.

thrown out her lawsuit, arguing that she had only been offended and had not suffered any "severe psychological injury."[93]

The Supreme Court overturned the lower courts and ruled that employers can be forced to pay damages even if the workers suffered no proven psychological harm. Justice Sandra Day O'Connor, who wrote the court's unanimous decision, said that employees can be awarded damages as long as their work "environment would reasonably be perceived, and is perceived, as hostile or abusive."[94]

Another key part of the Supreme Court's ruling addressed the question of "from whose perspective is sexual harassment to be judged?" Historically, the courts had used the common-law concept of a "reasonable man." A 1991 appeals court ruling had argued that the standards of a "reasonable woman" should prevail when women charged harassment. In *Harris v. Forklift Systems*, however, the Supreme Court argued that a "reasonable person" standard would prevail and that it would more appropriately focus on the conduct, not the victim.

Finally, the Supreme Court's ruling on the question of "what constitutes sexual harassment" was less than definitive. Again, Justice O'Connor wrote:

> *Whether an environment is "hostile" or "abusive" can be determined only by looking at all the circumstances. These may include the frequency of the discriminatory conduct; its severity; whether it is physically threatening or humiliating, or a mere offensive utterance; and whether it unreasonably interferes with an employee's work performance.*[95]

Title IX and Sexual Harrassment. Many people do not realize that Title IX offers protection against sexual harassment in a way that is essentially similar to Title VII. Title IX, the law that bans sex discrimination at schools receiving federal funds, is best known in its sports context for the formula that determines if schools are providing women with fair opportunities to play sports. Many people do not realize that schools can be sued for monetary damages under Title IX for knowingly allowing sexual harassment to take

Ethics in Practice

MATTERS OF THE HEART

During a recent summer, I worked at the liquor store of my best friend's stepfather. Sometimes during work hours, there would be just the two of us in the store. On numerous occasions, he made sexual comments to me about my body. He would also "accidentally" brush up against the front of me. Once he called me into his office to show me graphic pictures of girls in a pornographic magazine and asked why I had not posed for one. He seemed consumed with the female anatomy. The obvious ethical question forced me to choose between my friendship with the girl I had grown up with and my self-respect, which was severely restricted at that job. A temporary hold on my ideals won out over losing the best friend I had ever had.

1. Has sexual harassment taken place in this case, or is it just my imagination?

2. What would you have done in this situation?
   a. Continued this job without confronting the owner
   b. Quit and acted as if nothing had happened
   c. Confronted the owner to see if anything changed
   d. Other (Describe)

Contributed Anonymously

place. There are four parts to the burden of proof: (1) The school must be aware of the sexual harassment; (2) The school must fail to take steps to stop it; (3) The harassment must deny access to an educational opportunity; and (4) The harassment must take place in an educational setting.[96]

At this writing, three women have filed federal lawsuits under Title IX in a highly publicized case against the University of Colorado. The women allege that Colorado fostered an atmosphere hostile to women in its football program by allowing parties for recruits at which there was an expectation of sexual favors. These cases are unique in that they involve different alleged perpetrators, different alleged victims, and recruiting parties from different years. The women's attorneys argue that university officials were made aware of the nature of the recruiting parties and did not address the problem. The outcomes of these cases are expected to impact the ways in which universities respond to sexual harassment complaints.[97]

In 1998, Mitsubishi Motors agreed to make a record $34 million payment to settle a sexual harassment case involving female factory workers at a plant in Illinois. One year earlier, Mitsubishi had made a reported $9.5 million payment to settle a separate lawsuit with similar charges.[98] It is not surprising, therefore, that a survey by the National Association of Independent Insurers found that insurers offering sexual harassment coverage have begun writing more policies and seeing more claims.[99] Clearly, companies are taking a two-pronged approach to sexual harassment, adopting policies that discourage harassment while protecting themselves from the financial costs that can result from sexual harassment lawsuits.

The huge number of sexual harassment claims that took place in the 1990s has lessened, but the number of claims remains high. Recent Supreme Court rulings underscore the importance of companies' being diligent in their efforts to discourage harassing behavior. For example, the Supreme Court ruled that employers may be held liable even if they did not know about the harassment or their supervisors never carried out any threatened job actions.[100] Clearly, employers must develop comprehensive programs to protect their employees from harassment.

When businesses develop comprehensive and clear programs to prevent sexual harassment, they are legally rewarded. The Supreme Court recently ruled that good faith efforts to prevent and correct harassment is one prong of an "affirmative defense" companies can employ when charged with harassment. The second prong is proving the employee failed to take advantage of opportunities the firm provided for correction or prevention.[101]

Pregnancy Discrimination.

For some time, maternity leave has been an issue for women. In 1987, the Supreme Court upheld a California law that granted pregnant workers 4 months of unpaid maternity leave and guaranteed that their jobs would be waiting for them when they returned. Justice Thurgood Marshall argued, "By taking pregnancy into account, California's statute allows women, as well as men, to have families without losing their jobs."[102]

The **Pregnancy Discrimination Act of 1978**, an amendment to Title VII, requires employers to treat pregnancy and pregnancy-related medical conditions the same as any other medical disability with respect to all terms and conditions of employment. Until recently, however, few women felt protected by this law. Although the EEOC had been empowered to protect women against discrimination in pregnancy, it was not until 1991 that it won a significant case that caught the public's attention. In 1991, after 13 years of litigation, the EEOC announced a $66 million settlement by which AT&T would compensate 13,000 employees for job discrimination during pregnancy. The settlement came as a result of AT&T discriminating against women by restricting their leaves beyond that permitted by law.[103] As a result of the Pregnancy Discrimination Act, the concept of maternity leave is now outdated. In fact, companies are advised to make sure they do not have "maternity leave" policies. By using the term "maternity leave," companies imply that maternity is somehow different from other temporary disabilities.[104]

Pregnancy discrimination continues to present problems. According to EEOC statistics, pregnancy discrimination charges filed over the past five years have shown a steady increase with the total claim count rising from 3,385 in 1992, to 4,649 in 2003.[105] It is speculated that some of the increase may have been due to demographics, with aging baby boomers starting families while a majority of them work. Another cause may be corporate downsizing as employers are forced to get more work out of fewer people. They may see pregnant employees as unreliable—no longer able to work long hours and, after the child is born, the first to run home when baby gets sick.[106] The Family and Medical Leave Act has helped, but pregnancy discrimination remains an important issue.

Fetal Protection Policies.

In 1991, a new form of sex discrimination was identified as the Supreme Court ruled that **fetal protection policies** constituted sex discrimination. The decisive case was *UAW v. Johnson Controls, Inc.* Johnson Controls, like a number of other major firms, developed a policy of barring women of childbearing age from working in sites in which they, and their developing fetuses, might be exposed to such harmful chemicals as lead. Johnson Controls believed it was taking an appropriate action in protecting the women and their unborn children from exposure to chemicals. In 1984, a class-action lawsuit was brought against Johnson Controls by eight current and former employees and the United Auto Workers (UAW) union, who argued that the policy was discriminatory and illegal under Title VII of the Civil Rights Act. A U.S. district court ruled in the company's favor, and the Chicago-based U.S. Court of Appeals for the Seventh Circuit affirmed that decision. In 1991, however, the U.S. Supreme Court reversed the appellate court, arguing that the policy was on its face discriminatory and that the company had not shown that women were more likely than men to suffer reproductive damage from lead.[107]

Even though the Supreme Court ruled that injured children, once born, would not be able to bring lawsuits against the company, several experts think it likely that such lawsuits will indeed be filed in the future. One expert said, "A mother can waive her own right to sue, but she can't waive the right of a child to bring suit. So, 5 or 10 years down the line you might see children born with cognitive disabilities, and they could independently sue businesses." The UAW does not dispute this possibility and asserts that it should provide a major impetus for companies to make workplaces safer.[108]

A Corporate Response to Sexual Discrimination.

By 2004, Wal-Mart was facing several lawsuits alleging sexual discrimination and wage violations. The glare of public scrutiny took a toll on the firm's image. The National Organization of Women (NOW) had designated Wal-Mart as a "Merchant of Shame" for sex discrimination in pay, promotion, and compensation and exclusion of insurance coverage for women's contraception.[109] They cited the following as being among the facts that motivated their action:[110]

- Women employed at Wal-Mart make an average of $1.16 per hour less than men, and are promoted at a much slower rate than men.
- Women sales associates make an average of $15,000 per year—at least $1.00 per hour less than the retail industry average.
- More than three out of five Wal-Mart workers cannot afford the company's health insurance.

In response to these concerns, Chief Executive H. Lee Scott announced new diversity initiatives at the 2004 shareholders' meeting.[111] Wal-Mart will cut top executives' bonuses if the company does not meet its diversity goal, which is to promote women and minorities in proportion to the number that apply for management positions. Scott says that this move is evidence that Wal-Mart is serious about making meaningful change. "This is not something where we stand on the stage and we say we're going to try," said Scott.[112]

Although they did not provide specifics, they said they would also increase the wages of some workers, and no worker's pay would be reduced.[113] Wal-Mart also created a Compliance Office with 140 staff to make certain the company follows its rules and procedures and continues to make progress toward its goals.

Other Forms of Employment Discrimination

Much of the attention surrounding employment discrimination has focused on racial and sexual discrimination. There are, however, other important forms of discrimination that represent critical issues for business today. It is important for managers to understand the many forms that discrimination can take in an increasingly diverse workforce and where courts currently stand on those issues.

Age Discrimination.

Issues surrounding discrimination on the basis of age are increasing with each year. In the case of age discrimination, the aging of 76 million baby boomers caused a rise in the cost of age discrimination lawsuits. Although race, sex and, more recently, disability discrimination result in a greater number of lawsuits (see Figure 18-4), the settlement costs and jury awards for age discrimination suits have historically been substantially higher. Over a 10-year period, age discrimination plaintiffs were awarded an average of $219,000, compared to $147,799 for race discrimination, $106,728 for sex discrimination, and $100,345 for disability discrimination.[114]

Although the awards for age discrimination have been higher on average, they are not obtained easily. One typical type of age discrimination involves older workers, some only in their 40s, being laid off to save money because younger workers can be paid less. Many companies get around this by requiring workers, to receive severance packages, to sign waivers of their right to sue. Although a 1998 Supreme Court decision protected older workers by setting some conditions on those waivers, a 1993 Supreme Court decision made it much more difficult to prove that age discrimination was the cause of a layoff. One employment law attorney is quoted as saying that his firm is agreeing to take fewer age bias cases, not because there is less bias occurring but because age discrimination cases are notoriously hard to win.[115] After a review of age discrimination in the workplace, Sheldon Steinhauser concluded:

> *American firms can no longer afford to tolerate cultures of negativity toward older workers. Nearly 16 million Americans age 55 and over are working or seeking work. This number will increase drastically as the baby boomer generation ages. Further, trends in pension benefits, potential changes in Social Security, better health and fitness, and higher education levels will keep many of these people working longer. And they will all be covered by workplace laws banning age discrimination. Employers that fail to wake up to age discrimination and age bias in the workplace could collectively spend millions, perhaps even billions, of dollars in court-imposed fines, punitive damages, and legal fees. Executives need to take action now to minimize wrongful termination complaints and lawsuits in the future.[116]*

The problem of age discrimination is not going away. A 2004 survey by Execunet, a career networking and job search service, found that 82 percent of senior executives believed age discrimination was a serious problem in the workplace of today. That's an increase from the 78 percent who felt that way in 2001. Even more telling is the fact that 94 percent of the respondents, who are almost all in their 40s and 50s, felt that they had been the victim of age discrimination at some time. Specifically, they felt that age had taken them out of the running for a particular job.[117]

In 2004, the Supreme Court tackled a particularly challenging question regarding reverse age discrimination. The case stemmed from a collective bargaining agreement between General Dynamics and the United Auto Workers (UAW) that allowed the company to eliminate health benefits for future retirees while grandfathering in those who were 50 years of age or older at the time of the agreement. Dennis Cline was between 40 and 50 years old when the agreement occurred, so he would not be eligible for the benefits. He joined with other employees in the same age range to bring an action before the EEOC. The EEOC's efforts to get the parties to settle informally failed, and so the employees sued General Dynamics in federal district court. The district court dismissed the case, saying that the ADEA did not protect the younger from the older. The Sixth Circuit Court of Appeals reversed the district court, saying that the ADEA prohibits discrimination against any individual because of age. General Dynamics appealed to the Supreme Court, and they agreed to hear the case because different district courts had come to different conclusions on this issue. The EEOC filed a "friend of the court" brief in favor of the employees. Ultimately, the Supreme Court reversed the Sixth Circuit Court, saying that the ADEA does not prohibit favoring the old over the young.[118]

Ethics in Practice

IS RELIGION ALLOWED IN THE WORKPLACE?

For 6 months, I worked as a receptionist at a local doctor's office that employed about 30 people. The owner and head practitioner was a member of a religious cult. During business hours, everything seemed normal for a doctor's office of this size, but during the 2-hour lunch break, all of the employees had to go upstairs and go "on course." These mandatory courses encompassed everything from communication skills to office efficiency. They were all designed by a man who founded the religious cult of which my boss was a member. Granted that they were business teachings, other staff members and I felt that these teachings were heavily weighted with religious undertones.

For example, one of the most important keys to these lessons was that you had to understand every word. After every exercise we were individually tested to make sure that we knew all of the words. Most of the words that I didn't understand could not be found in the dictionary, because they came straight from the man's religious teachings. Whenever I questioned my boss about a word, it usually led into a long discussion about the cult leader's works, and I would have to read paragraphs out of the religious teachings to "fully understand" the meaning. To me, it felt as though I was being brainwashed, and from then on I scheduled my university classes during this course time.

My dilemma was this: Did the doctor have the right to insist that we submit to such "teachings," which made us uncomfortable?

1. Is any form of discrimination or harassment taking place in this case?

2. What ethical issues arise in this case?

3. If you were faced with this dilemma, what action would you take?

Contributed by Allison Grice

Around the world, Muslim women wear the hijab (headscarf) as a sign of modesty. The wearing of the hijab has lately become an issue in European countries, heartland America, and even the "happiest place on earth," Walt Disney World. Henry Pierson Curtis writes in an article distributed by *Knight Ridder/Tribune News Service* (21 May 2004 pK5246) that a Muslim woman has filed a religious discrimination suit against Disney, claiming she lost her job because she refused to remove her hijab. Read more about this first-ever challenge of the Disney dress code by logging on to InfoTrac College Edition at http://www.infotrac-college.com and keying record number CJ116987181.

Religious Discrimination.   Religious discrimination is a relatively new issue in the workplace, but it is one that is growing quickly. In the last decade, religious discrimination complaints have jumped 75 percent, from 1,449 in 1993 to 2,532 in 2003.[119] In contrast, racial discrimination charges have decreased from 31,695 in 1993 to 28,526 in 2003. According to Jeanne Goldberg, senior attorney adviser for the EEOC, this is due to changes in the composition of the workforce. "Changing immigration patterns are boosting the number of people from parts of the world with less familiar religious beliefs and practices. For example, immigration from Asia represented 26 percent of the total in 2002 compared with just 9 percent in 1970. European immigration, meanwhile, dropped to 14 percent in 2002 from 62 percent in 1970. The workforce also is aging," she adds. "The older people get, the more important religion becomes to them."[120]

The nature of religious bias incidents varies widely. In one instance, a woman who was a practicing Jehovah's Witness sued a restaurant chain because she could not wait tables unless she agreed to join in the singing of "Happy Birthday," a practice that would conflict with her religious beliefs. She settled for $53,000 and a new religious accommodation policy. In two other cases, a restaurant did not have to relax its grooming policy to allow a Sikh man to keep his beard, and a public school did not have to allow a Muslim teacher to wear religious garb. Future lawsuits are certain to break new ground as companies, the courts, and Congress determine how to deal with religious discrimination in the workplace.[121]

The Workplace Religious Freedom Act has been introduced each year for the past five years and is still under consideration by the U.S. Congress. Its purpose is to disallow arbitrary and unfair refusal to tolerate religious expression in the workplace. According to one of the act's cosponsors, John Kerry (D–Massachusetts), "No worker should have to choose between keeping a job and keeping faith with their cherished religious beliefs."[122] Opposition to the act comes mainly from business groups who fear it will be burdensome.[123] Backed by a broad-based coalition of religious groups, this legislation is designed to respond to the increase in incidents of religious bias by requiring employers to do more to accommodate religious beliefs. The act would allow religious expression such as taking a particular day off or dressing in a particular manner, as long as safety and health considerations were not jeopardized. According to the Title VII law, employers must make reasonable accommodations unless doing so represents an undue hardship. In 1977, the Supreme Court ruled that anything more than minimal effort or expense could be considered undue hardship. The proposed legislation would raise the definition of undue hardship to "significant difficulty or expense."[124]

Color Bias.

Color bias is another issue raising new challenges for the workplace. As part of the Civil Rights Act of 1964, discrimination based on color has been illegal for a long period of time. As a practical matter, however, color bias has been largely ignored until recently.

Color bias refers to the shade of a person's skin rather than a person's race. Federal law has already determined color bias to be illegal. The Civil Rights Act of 1964 prohibits discrimination based on "race, color, religion, sex or national origin."[125] Most people do not realize that race and color are considered to be separate by law and both are covered by law, so many cases go unreported.[126] For example, a person who favors light-skinned African-Americans over those with darker skin is guilty of color bias, not racial bias. Color bias can occur among people of the same race and, according to the EEOC, the number of intrarace color bias cases is on the rise.[127] EEOC Chairwoman Cari Dominguez says we are now in the "mélange millennium." She notes, "We have a lot of racial blends, and we're trying to work out at way to determine what kind of adverse employment decisions can occur as a result."[128]

Sexual Orientation and Transgender Discrimination.

When Wal-Mart extended its antidiscrimination policy to gay and lesbian employees, it signaled that workplaces are becoming less hostile to gay employees.[129] Some consider Wal-Mart to be a laggard because so many companies now include sexual orientation in their categories of protected workers. By the end of 2003, 360 of the Fortune 500 and 49 of the *Fortune* 50 had policies that ban discrimination based on sexual orientation. Two hundred of the Fortune 500 firms, and 34 of the Fortune 50 firms, offered health insurance benefits to domestic partners.[130] More than two thousand private companies, colleges and universities explicitly prohibited discrimination based on sexual orientation. Many of these organizations have domestic partner benefits as well. There is no federal antidiscrimination statute, although 14 states, the District of Columbia, and numerous municipalities have one.[131]

Another issue that presents special challenges for business is the treatment of transgender and transsexual employees. "Transgender" refers to a person who identifies with his or her opposite sex and acts accordingly. "Transsexual" refers to a person who is undergoing or has undergone sex change surgery.[132] This is not a new workplace issue. In 1993, the Washington State Supreme Court upheld Boeing Co.'s 1985 firing of a male software engineer who dressed in women's clothes and insisted on using the women's restroom while the sex-change operation was pending. The court ruled that discomfort with one's biological sex was not a handicap.[133] What is new is the opinion of the courts and the stance that corporations have begun to take since that day. From 2001 to 2004, 26 *Fortune* 500 companies banned discrimination based on "gender identity and expression." Similar protections are offered by 67 cities and counties.[134] Fifteen states have either laws or administrative rulings that prohibit gender stereotypes and discrimination.[135] In June 2004, the Sixth U.S. Circuit Court of Appeals (which covers Michigan, Ohio, Kentucky, and Tennessee) heard the case of a transsexual Ohio firefighter who had been fired. In the first such action by a federal court, the court ruled that Title VII of the Civil Rights Act of 1964 protects transsexuals and that the sex-stereotyping doctrine covers people who change their sex.[136]

AFFIRMATIVE ACTION IN THE WORKPLACE

Affirmative action is the taking of positive steps to hire and promote people from groups previously discriminated against. The concept of affirmative action was formally introduced to the business world in 1965, when President Lyndon B. Johnson signed Executive Order 11246, the purpose of which was to require all firms doing business with the federal government to engage in affirmative actions to accelerate the movement of minorities into the workforce. Few people realize, however, that the federal government did not make a real commitment to affirmative action until the administration of President Richard M. Nixon, who revived the practice of racial hiring preferences.[137] Companies today have affirmative action programs because they do business with the government, have begun the plans voluntarily, or have entered into them through collective bargaining agreements with labor unions.

The Range of Affirmative Action Postures

The meaning of affirmative action has changed since it was first introduced. It originally referred only to special efforts to ensure equal opportunity for members of groups that had been subject to discrimination. More recently, the term has come to refer to programs in which members of such groups are given some degree of definite preference in determining access to positions from which they were formerly excluded.[138]

Daniel Seligman identified four postures in two groupings that define the range that affirmative action may take.[139] He categorized the following affirmative action postures as "soft" or "weak":

1. *Passive nondiscrimination.* This posture involves a willingness in hiring, promotion, and pay decisions to treat the races and the sexes alike. This stance fails to recognize that past discrimination leaves many prospective employees unaware of or unprepared for present opportunities.
2. *Pure affirmative action.* This posture involves a concerted effort to enlarge the pool of applicants so that no one is excluded because of past or present discrimination. At the point of decision to hire or promote, however, the company selects the most qualified applicant without regard to sex or race.

Postures that Seligman termed "hard" or "strong" were as follows:

3. *Affirmative action with preferential hiring.* Here, the company not only enlarges the labor pool but systematically favors minorities and women in the actual decisions, as well. This could be thought of as a "soft" quota system.
4. *Hard quotas.* In this posture, the company specifies numbers or proportions of minority group members that must be hired.

Over the past 30 years, much confusion has surrounded the concept of affirmative action, because it was never clear which of the aforementioned views was being advocated by the government. In hindsight, we can now see that the government was advocating positions based on whichever posture it thought would work, or based on the particular candidate and political party in office at the time. Early on, "soft" or "weak" affirmative action (Postures 1 and 2) was advocated. It became apparent, however, that these postures were not as effective in getting the results desired. Therefore, "hard" or "strong" affirmative action (Postures 3 and 4) was later advocated. The real controversy over affirmative action began with the use of soft quotas and "preferential hiring" (Posture 3) and "hard quotas" (Posture 4). Today, when people speak of affirmative action, they are typically referring to some degree of preferential hiring, as in Postures 3 and 4. Figure 18-7 summarizes the key Supreme Court decisions on affirmative action.

The Concept of Preferential Treatment

Let us briefly consider some of the arguments that have been set forth both for and against the concept of **preferential treatment**, which undergirds affirmative action. The underlying rationale for preferential treatment is the principle of **compensatory justice**, which holds that whenever an injustice is done, just compensation or reparation is owed to the injured party or parties.[140] Many people believe that groups discriminated against in the past (for example, women, blacks, Native North Americans, and Mexican Americans) should be recompensed for these injustices by positive affirmative action. Over the years, deliberate barriers were placed on opportunities for minorities—especially blacks. These groups were prevented from participating in business, law, universities, and other desirable professions and institutions. Additionally, when official barriers were finally dropped, matters frequently did not improve. Inequalities became built into the system, and although mechanisms for screening and promotion did not intentionally discriminate against certain groups, they did favor other groups. Thus, the view that we can and should restore the balance of justice by showing preferential treatment became established as a viable option for moving more quickly toward economic equality in the workplace and in our society.[141]

The Concept of Reverse Discrimination

The principal objection to affirmative action and the reason it has become and remained controversial is that it leads to **reverse discrimination**. This concept holds that when any sort of preference is given to minorities and women, discrimination may occur against those in the majority—often, but not always, white males. For well over a decade now, white males who feel passed over because of preferences for minorities or women have been filing reverse discrimination suits.[142] They argue that Title VII prohibits discrimination based on race, color, or sex and that this includes reverse discrimination as well. All of this has created an intensely controversial public policy dilemma: How can we show

FIGURE 18-7

Key Supreme Court Decisions on Affirmative Action

Date	Case	Setting	General Finding
1978	Bakke	Admission to university medical school	Mildly supportive affirmative action (AA)
1979	Weber	Quota-based training program of private employer (Kaiser)	Supportive of AA
1984	Shotts	City fire department (Memphis)	Minor setback for AA; qualified seniority plans OK for layoffs
1986	Wygant	Jackson, Michigan, Board of Education—school teachers	Mixed finding; seniority system upheld, preferential treatment not always wrong
1986	Firefighters	Municipality (City of Cleveland Fire Department)	Supportive of AA; minorities may be given hiring preferences
1986	Sheet Metal Workers	Labor union	Strongly supportive of AA; court can order AA for those who were not specific victims of discrimination
1987	Alabama State Police	State police force	Strongly supportive of AA; court can order promotion quotas
1987	Johnson	County transportation department (Santa Clara)	Strongly supportive of AA; AA can promote women to remedy their historical exclusion from certain job categories
1989	*Richmond v. Crosen*	City government	Mild limitation of AA
1989	*Martin v. Wilkes*	Setting unknown	Supportive of reverse discrimination charges
1995	Adarand Constructors	Federal contractors	Instituted strict scrutiny standards; set-asides did not pass test
2003	*Grutter v. Bollinger et al.*	University admissions	Upholds affirmative action policy of law school but rejects policy that automatically gives 20 points to people of color; says race can be one of many factors considered

preferential treatment for minorities and women and at the same time not discriminate against white males? This is very difficult, if not impossible, to do. The next question then becomes a matter of public priority: Should we as a nation pursue affirmative action, even if it means that some opportunities for white males will have to be sacrificed in the process? There are strong opinions on both sides.

Minority Opposition to Affirmative Action

Although it is clear that affirmative action is one of the major pillars of the mainstream civil rights agenda, during the past decade a growing and more visible number of blacks have begun to speak out against such policies.

Two prominent African-American critics of affirmative action are Dr. Thomas Sowell and Professor Stephen L. Carter. Dr. Sowell has argued that blacks would be better served in the long run if affirmative action programs as we now know them were abolished.[143] Stephen L. Carter, a law professor at Yale University, who admits that his race helped him get into college, wrote a widely read and reported book titled *Reflections of an Affirmative*

Action Baby.[144] Professor Carter's concern seems to be with the effects of affirmative action on those whom the policy was intended to help. According to Carter, affirmative action sets up a dichotomy between "best" and "best black." Carter recalls how, over and over, his teachers told him he was the "best black" they had enrolled. The "best black" syndrome holds that, however accomplished a black person might be, she or he is likely to be categorized as "first black," "only black," or "best black" or measured by a different, most likely inferior, standard.[145] Carter does not want to eliminate all types of affirmative action immediately. He supports some degree of racial consciousness, particularly in admissions to colleges and professional schools, but thinks that at some point the preferences must fall away entirely. He is against turning affirmative action into a tool for representing the "points of view" of excluded groups.[146]

The Adarand Decision and Strict Scrutiny

The 1995 case of *Adarand Constructors Inc. v. Pena* (115 S. Ct. 2097) was a turning point in affirmative action. In it, the Supreme Court ruled 5 to 4 that all government action based on race must meet the **strict scrutiny** standard of judicial review. Strict scrutiny has two components: (1) The program or policy must meet a compelling government interest, and (2) the program or policy must be tailored narrowly to meet the program or policy objectives. Although the ruling does not declare affirmative action to be unconstitutional, it sets extremely tough standards for any program to pass.[147]

The effects of the Adarand decision are still being felt. An intense round of court cases followed the decision, as affirmative action programs were put to the strict scrutiny test. These cases resulted in some landmark decisions, such as *Hopwood v. the State of Texas*, in which the Fifth Circuit Court held that using race as a consideration in University of Texas Law School admissions did not pass the strict scrutiny test. In June 1995, former President Clinton issued a memorandum to all programs that use race, ethnicity, or gender as a consideration in decisions. The directive said that any program must be eliminated if it creates a quota or a preference, causes reverse discrimination, or continues after the goal of equal opportunity has been achieved. Although the Adarand decision applies to federal programs only, its effect is being felt in the private sector, because it sheds light on the actions the courts may take.[148]

The Corporate View

It is not easy to generalize on how the corporate community feels about affirmative action. Initially, business was opposed to the idea. As time passed, however, and as business leaders gained experience with affirmative action programs, their views changed somewhat. The corporate sector does not appear to be adamantly opposed to affirmative action. However, it is also clear that business would prefer to be free of government mandates.

A recent survey of 3,200 employers in Atlanta, Boston, Detroit, and Los Angeles showed that affirmative action has little if any negative effect on worker productivity. The results indicated that when companies stress affirmative action in their recruiting, they are more likely to follow it with appropriate training and careful evaluation. Proactive companies have found that the qualifications and work performances of the female and minority employees they hire through these efforts equal those of their other workers. Firms that put no effort into outreach tend to hire less qualified female and minority candidates. However, the study found that even these workers' performances did not suffer.[149]

The business community seems to have accepted affirmative action programs as good business policy. Some executives see goals and timetables simply as good ways of measuring progress, and others see them as ways to stave off expensive discrimination suits. For some employers, affirmative action has practical business value in customer relations, especially for makers of consumer goods and providers of consumer services. Most large companies have entrenched affirmative action programs, and they think that tinkering with these programs now might draw wrath from women and minorities. Many executives think that if affirmative action is necessary and government requires it, a systematic program that has the government's approval is an effective way of going about it.[150]

The Future of Affirmative Action

An important affirmative action battleground has been university campuses, because much of the recent activity for and against affirmative action has been directed at college admissions. When California voters approved Proposition 209 in 1996, affirmative action in state programs and state schools ended. That same year, the Fifth Circuit Court of Appeals ruled that the University of Texas could not use race as a factor in admissions. In May 1998, the House defeated an amendment that would eliminate race- or gender-based preferences in admission to colleges that receive federal funds, but that fight has moved to the voting booth. In 1998, Washington state voters approved Initiative-200 (I-200), which is modeled after California's Proposition 209 and is a measure that ends affirmative action programs in state and local government hiring and contracting and in college and university admissions. Interestingly, university admissions are one area where, for many years, white males have benefited from affirmative action. A female applicant successfully sued the University of Georgia for gender bias after being denied admission when she found that they added points to the total student index score of applicants if they were male. In 2001, the *Christian Science Monitor* analyzed admission data and interviewed admissions officers at colleges and universities across the nation. They found evidence of a bias toward white males in college admissions and recruitment. A spokesman for the Office of Civil Rights in the U.S. Department of Education told the *Monitor* that they are averaging 20 complaints each year about gender bias in college admissions.[151]

The 2003 Supreme Court ruling in the University of Michigan affirmative action case was widely held as a victory for affirmative action and in many ways it was. However, the impact on subsequent university actions has been more ambiguous. The Court found that race could be one of many factors given consideration in university admissions because it furthers a "compelling interest in obtaining the educational benefits that flow from a diverse student body."[152] The Court, however, also struck down an undergraduate admissions policy that automatically gave 20 points to a person of color, saying that applicants must receive "truly individualized consideration."[153] In response to the ruling, many universities are now retooling their scholarship and orientation programs that are geared specifically to minorities. They are opening these up to students of other races who might qualify for them due to other factors such as socioeconomic background.[154]

The Shape of the River by William Bowen, former president of Princeton, and Derek Bok, former president of Harvard, addresses the issue of race and college admissions.[155] In this book, Bowen and Bok present a major study that analyzes the performance of 45,000 students at 28 selective colleges and universities over 20 years. The authors draw on student data and lengthy follow-up questionnaires to chart the progress of white and black students (they focus on black because of the wealth of data available). Compared to whites, blacks entered with lower grades and lower test scores and subsequently had lower degree-completion rates. However, 20 years later, more blacks had obtained professional or doctoral degrees. In addition, blacks were more active in community service and more likely to lead civic groups. According to Bowen and Bok, blacks became the backbone of the middle class. Black and white students felt that the diversity they experienced on campus improved their college experience and subsequently helped them adjust to the workplace.[156]

Of course, as the authors allow, statistics do not tell the whole story. No statistics were available about the white students who were not admitted because of affirmative action and the opportunities they may have lost. Whatever the subsequent decisions regarding affirmative action in university admissions, there will be a reaction. In the wake of Proposition 209, minority enrollment at the University of California has dropped sharply, creating a "brain drain" in graduate programs. The problem is that fewer minority students are applying: Schools have taken advantage of Proposition 209 to recruit bright minority students away from California campuses.[157]

The future of affirmative action in the United States is more uncertain than it has ever been. Business must wait until the dust settles on this issue before committing to any radical positions. In the meantime, it is expected that businesses will continue their diversity programs as demographic changes in workforce composition continue and as they realize their ongoing responsibility—both legally and ethically—to address race, gender, age, disability, and family issues in a socially responsible manner.

Companies are increasingly recognizing that their diversity programs may constitute a competitive advantage or may be used as competitive weapons and that this strategic incentive is an added reason for them to stay on track. It is somewhat ironic to note that some firms are realizing that the civil rights laws cover white males as well as minorities and women and that some companies are even taking special care to be sure they reach out to white males and gain their support as part of their diversity programs.[158]

■ SUMMARY

This chapter addresses several subgroups of employee stakeholders whose job rights are protected by law. The United States got serious about the problem of discrimination by enacting the Civil Rights Act of 1964, which prohibited discrimination on the basis of race, color, religion, sex, or national origin. Laws covering age and disabilities were passed later. The EEOC was created to assume the major responsibility for enforcing the discrimination laws. Like other federal agencies, the EEOC has had problems. However, on balance it has done a reasonable job of monitoring the two major forms of discrimination: disparate treatment and disparate impact. Discrimination issues discussed in this chapter include the movement from civil rights to social benefits; the plights of African-Americans, Asian-Americans, Hispanics, and women moving into professional/managerial positions; comparable worth; sexual harassment;

fetal protection policies; and religious discrimination. In addition, new and evolving discrimination issues such as sexual orientation, gender identity, and color bias as separate from race were discussed.

Affirmative action was one of the government's answers to the problem of discrimination. Considerable controversy has surrounded the question of how far affirmative action should go. There is evidence that opposition to affirmative action is growing. However, corporations have undertaken affirmative action by building their human resource management policies on affirmative action principles, and they will likely continue these practices in the future. To do otherwise at this point might evoke criticism from minorities, women, and others. Furthermore, sound stakeholder management requires companies to continue to be fair in their employment practices.

▪ KEY TERMS

Age Discrimination in Employment Act (ADEA) (page 572)

affirmative action (page 595)

Americans with Disabilities Act (ADA) (page 573)

bona fide occupational qualification (BFOQ) (page 572)

Civil Rights Act of 1991 (page 576)

color bias (page 594)

comparable worth (page 586)

compensatory justice (page 596)

disparate impact (page 579)

disparate treatment (page 578)

Equal Employment Opportunity Commission (EEOC) (page 576)

Equal Pay Act of 1963 (page 573)

fetal protection policies (page 590)

four-fifths rule (page 579)

major life activities (page 575)

preferential treatment (page 596)

Pregnancy Discrimination Act of 1978 (page 590)

protected groups (page 567)

reverse discrimination (page 596)

sexual harassment (page 586)

strict scrutiny (page 598)

Title VII of the Civil Rights Act of 1964 (page 571)

▪ DISCUSSION QUESTIONS

1. List the major federal discrimination laws and indicate what they prohibit. Which agency is primarily responsible for enforcing these laws?

2. Give two different definitions of discrimination, and provide an example of each.

3. What effect do you think the Americans with Disabilities Act (ADA) is having on businesses? Explain your answer.

4. Explain the dilemma of affirmative action versus reverse discrimination. Do you think the Supreme Court is headed in the right direction for handling this issue? Explain.

5. To whom do you think preferential treatment should be given in university admissions? Explain your answer.

▪ RECOMMENDED CASES

Many of the end-of-text cases may be related to Chapter 18. You may wish to consider studying the following cases with Chapter 18.

Case 16. "GLOBAL (IN)EQUALITY?: THE MERRILL LYNCH SEX BIAS CASE." This case highlights the difficulty of determining whether discrimination exists when pay scales are opaque and bonuses are the primary form of compensation. Stephanie Villalba had a high-flying career at Merrill Lynch (ML), but when she received a new line manager it all began to go downhill, ending in her dismissal. Villalba sued ML for sex discrimination, victimization, unfair dismissal, and unequal pay. ML countered that her dismissal was due to poor perform-

ance. How can one determine who is correct? What would you do if you were either of the parties in the suit?

Case 37. "IS HIRING ON THE BASIS OF "LOOKS" UNFAIR OR DISCRIMINATORY?" This case addresses the practice of hiring employees based on their appearance. Abercrombie & Fitch (A&F) has made a practice of hiring their employees based on their having a certain "look" that reflects the store's image. A&F became the target of a lawsuit from four organizations that charge that practice is discriminatory. Is hiring on the basis of looks discriminatory? Would it ever be appropriate? Where should the line be drawn?

Case 38. "WHEN MANAGEMENT CROSSES THE LINE."
This case is written from the perspective of a college student who is a server in a local restaurant. Her manager singles certain female employees out for his "sick humor and cruelty" when no witnesses are around. He is in charge of the schedule and is known for firing employees for any infraction. Jobs are scarce and she could be easily replaced. What should she do?

■ WEB RESOURCES

The URLs listed here are current at the time of publication. Should any of these Web sites change, please search under the company's or organization's name for an updated address.

American Civil Liberties Union
http://www.aclu.org

Catalyst
http://www.catalystwomen.org

Committee of 100
http://www.committee100.org

Employment Law Alliance
http://www.employmentlawalliance.com

Equal Employment Opportunity Commission
http://www.eeoc.gov

Execunet
http://www.execunet.com

Freedom Center
http://www.freedomcenter.org

Human Rights Campaign
http://www.hrc.org

NAACP
http://www.naacp.org

National Organization for Women
http://www.now.org

Ontario Consultants on Religious Tolerance
http://www.religioustolerance.org

Project Implicit
https://implicit.harvard.edu/implicit

World Conference on Racism
http://www.un.org/WCAR

InfoTrac® College Edition   http://www.infotrac-college.com

Additional information on the topics discussed in the chapter can be researched by logging onto the InfoTrac College Edition Web site.

■ ENDNOTES

1. Charles J. Sykes, *A Nation of Victims: The Decay of the American Character* (New York: St. Martin's Press, 1992).

2. Paul Hollander, "We Are All (Sniffle, Sniffle) Victims Now," *The Wall Street Journal* (January 18, 1995), A14.

3. William F. Glueck and James Ledvinka, "Equal Employment Opportunity Programs," in William F. Glueck, *Personnel: A Diagnostic Approach*, rev. ed. (Dallas, TX: Business Publications, 1978), 593–633.

4. *Ibid.*, 597–599.

5. "Equal Opportunity: A Scorecard," *Dun's Review* (November 1979), 107.

6. *Ibid.*, 108.

7. The World Almanac and Book of Facts 1987 (New York: World Almanac, 1986), 129.

8. McKay Jenkins, "Despite Education Gains, Blacks Still Trailing Whites in Income," *The Atlanta Journal* (September 20, 1991), A16.

9. Isabelle dePomereau, "United States: Why Black Financial Progress Is Running into Speed Bumps," *The Christian Science Monitor* (February 4, 1998), 5.

10. "Black Hole," *The Economist* (November 16, 1996), 67–68.

11. Roy S. Johnson, "The New Black Power," *Fortune* (August 4, 1997), 47.

12. *Ibid.*

13. Eileen P. Gunn, "The Money Men," *Fortune* (August 4, 1997), 75.

14. Cora Daniels, "Too Diverse for Our Own Good," *Fortune* (July 9, 2001), 116.

15. Aaron Bernstein, "Racism in the Workplace," *Business Week* (July 30, 2001) 64–67.

16. EEOC, "Title VII: Enforces Job Rights" (Washington, DC: The U.S. Equal Employment Opportunity Commission, Office of Communications, October 1988), 1.

17. EEOC, "Age Discrimination Is Against the Law" (Washington, DC: The U.S. Equal Employment Opportunity Commission, Office of Communications, April 1988), 1.

18. EEOC, "Equal Work, Equal Pay" (Washington, DC: The U.S. Equal Employment Opportunity Commission, Office of Communications, October 1988), 1.

19. EEOC, "Equal Employment Opportunity Is . . . the Law" (Washington, DC: The U.S. Equal Employment Opportunity Commission, Office of Communications 1986), 1.

20. Henry H. Perritt, Jr., *Americans with Disabilities Act Handbook* (New York: John Wiley & Sons, 1990), vii.

21. U.S. Department of Justice, Office on the Americans with Disabilities Act, *The Americans with Disabilities Act: Questions and Answers* (Washington, DC: Government Printing Office, 1991), 1. Also see "Disabilities Act to Cover 500,000 More Firms," *The Atlanta Journal* (July 25, 1994), E1.

22. *Ibid.*

23. Ron Lent, "Employers Usually Win Disability Cases," *Journal of Commerce* (July 9, 1998), 5A.

24. Karen E. Saul, "EEOC Issues ADA Guidance," *Credit Union Magazine* (August 2003), 82.

25. *Ibid.*

26. Warren Richey, "Court Boosts Civil Rights Law for Disabled," *The Christian Science Monitor* (May 18, 2004), 1.

27. Kathi Wolfe, "Handicapped by a Law That Helps," *The Washington Post* (July 26, 1998), C1.

28. John Hockenberry, "A Just Cause; Americans with Disabilities Act Helped Disabled People Get Fair Treatment, Despite Rumors of Frivolous Lawsuits," *NBC News Transcripts: Dateline NBC* (August 24, 1998).

29. Lent, 5A.

30. Jay Matthews, "Most Corporate Leaders Support Disabilities Act; Poll Reveals Little Increase in Actual Hiring," *The Washington Post* (July 14, 1995), B3.

31. Daily Record Staff, "Survey Finds Employers Prevail 94.5 Percent of Time in Discrimination Cases." *Daily Record* (July 3, 2003), 1.

32. *Ibid.*

33. John D. Rapoport and Brian L. P. Zevnik, *The Employee Strikes Back* (New York: Collier Books, 1994), 233–234.

34. EEOC, "Commission Enforces EEO Laws" (Washington, DC: The U.S. Equal Employment Opportunity Commission, Office of Communications, November 1988), 1.

35. "Job Discrimination Complaints Against Private Employers Fall," *The Wall Street Journal* (March 9, 2004), D5.

36. *Ibid.*

37. Bob Tarmarkin, "Is Equal Opportunity Turning into a Witch Hunt?" *Forbes* (May 29, 1978), 29–31.

38. Bill McAllister, "Civil Rights: What Happened at the EEOC When Thomas Was There?" *The Washington Post Weekly Edition* (September 16–22, 1991), 31.

39. "Quiet Crackdown: The Quarry—Corporate Civil Rights Violators," *Business Week* (September 26, 1994), 52.

40. This and other information about the EEOC is available on the EEOC's Web site at http://www.eeoc.gov.

41. Ryan Johnson, "Leading with the Power of One," *Workspan* (October 2002), 34–38.

42. James Ledvinka, *Federal Regulation of Personnel and Human Resource Management* (Boston: Kent, 1982), 37. Also see W. N. Outten, R. J. Rabin, and L. R. Lipman, *The Rights of Employees and Union Members* (Carbondale, IL: Southern Illinois University Press, 1994), chapter VIII, 154–156.

43. Glueck and Ledvinka, 304.

44. Ledvinka, 37–38.

45. *Griggs v. Duke Power Company*, 401 U.S. 424, 1971.

46. Theodore Purcell, "Minorities, Management of and Equal Employment Opportunity," in L. R. Bittel (ed.), *Encyclopedia of Professional Management* (New York: McGraw-Hill, 1978), 744–745.

47. *Smith v. City of East Cleveland*, 502 F. 2d 492, 1975.

48. *Wallace v. Debron Corp.*, 494 F. 2d 674, 8th Cir., 1974.

49. Mary-Kathryn Zachary, J.D., "Discrimination Without Intent," *Supervision* (May 2003), 23–26.

50. *Ibid.*

51. Henry Louis Gates, Jr., "The Two Nations of Black America," *Brookings Review* (Spring 1998), 4–7.

52. Shelley Branch, "What Blacks Think of Corporate America," *Fortune* (July 6, 1998), 140–143.

53. Eisenhower Foundation, "Kerner Commission's Separate and Unequal Societies Exist Today: Report," *Jet* (March 23, 1998), 4–6.

54. "Blacks: A Cheerier Picture," *The Economist* (July 8, 1995), 27.

55. Diane Stafford, "Despite 50 Years of Desegregation, Blacks Still Lag in Economic Factors," *Kansas City Star* (May 16, 2004), 1.

56. *Ibid.*

57. Martin Gilens, "Race and Poverty in America: Public Misconceptions and the American News Media," *Public Opinion Quarterly* (Winter 1996), 515–541. See also Mark Fitzgerald, "Media Perpetuate a Myth," Editor and Publisher (August 16, 1977); and Abigail Thernstrom and Stephan Thernstrom, "Black Progress: How Far We've Come—and How Far We Have to Go," *Brookings Review* (Spring 1998), 12–16.

58. Randy Cohen, "The Ethicist, You Name It," New York *Times Magazine* (May 30, 2004), 16.

59. Gates, 4–7.

60. "Race Relations Better, But Bias Persists, Poll Finds," *Jet* (May 3, 2004), 10.

61. Colbert I. King, "Fix It Brother," *The Washington Post* (May 22, 2004), A27.

62. Marie Arana, "The Elusive Hispanic/Latino Identity," *Nieman Reports* (Summer 2001), 8–9.

63. Michael Barone, "The Many Faces of America," *U.S. News & World Report* (March 19, 2001),18. See also Thomas P. Edsall, "Census a Clarion Call for Democrats, GOP," *The Washington Post* (July 8, 2001), A5.

64. *Ibid.*

65. Steve Bates, "Hispanics See Discrimination in the Workplace," *HR Magazine* (February 2003), 16.

66. Anthony Ramirez, "America's Super Minority," *Fortune* (November 24, 1986), 148–164.

67. Cliff Cheng, "Are Asian-American Employees a Model Minority or Just a Minority?" *Journal of Applied Behavioral Science* (September 1997), 277–290. See also Joyce Taing, "The Model Minority Revisited," *Journal of Applied Behavioral Science* (September 1997), 291–315. Some popular press articles have also questioned the Model Minority characterization of Asian-Americans. For examples, see James Walsh, "The Perils of Success," *Time* (Fall 1993), 55–56; and Chris Peacock, "The Asian-American Success Myth," *Utne Reader* (March 1988), 22–23.

68. "A Superminority Tops Out," *Newsweek* (May 11, 1987), 48.

69. Arthur S. Hayes, "Asian-Americans Go to Court to Fight Bias," *The Wall Street Journal* (September 3, 1991), B5.

70. Karl Schoenberger, "Asian Americans Underrepresented on Corporate Boards, Group Says," *San Jose Mercury News* (April 1, 2004), 1.

71. David Leonhardt, "Women Closing the Pay Gap," *The New York Times Upfront* (April 18, 2003), 6.

72. http: www.catalystwomen.org

73. Regina Fazio Maruca, "Says Who?" *Harvard Business Review* (November/December 1997), 15–17.

74. Victor D. Infante, "Why Woman Still Earn Less Than Men," *WorkForce* (April 2001), 31.

75. "Women Earn 20% Less Than Men, GAO Finds; Decision to Leave Jobs for Longer Periods Does Not Account for Disparity," *The Washington Post* (November 21, 2003), E4.

76. Rosemary Batt, Susan Christopherson, Ned Rightor, and Danielle Van Jaarsveld, "Net Working: Work Patterns and Workforce Policies for the New Media Industry," *Economic Policy Institute* (February 2001), 1–57. Quoted in *Infante.*

77. Linda Babcock, Sara Laschever, Michele Gelfand, and Deborah Small, "Nice Girls Don't Ask," *Harvard Business Review* (October 2003), 14–16.

78. *Ibid.*

79. *Ibid.*

80. *Ibid.*

81. Cheri Ostroff and Leanne E. Atwater, "Does Who You Work with Matter? Effects of Referent Group Gender and Age Composition on Managers' Compensation," *Journal of Applied Psychology* (August 2003), 725–740.

82. Colin Allen, "Office Gender Balance Can Influence Your Paycheck," *Psychology Today* (November/December 2003), 17.

83. *Ibid.*

84. Laura Pincus and Bill Shaw, "Comparable Worth: An Economic and Ethical Analysis," *Journal of Business Ethics* (April 1998), 455–470.

85. Cathy Trost, "Pay Equity, Born in Public Sector, Emerges as an Issue in Private Firms," *The Wall Street Journal* (July 8, 1985), 15.

86. E. Jane Arnault, Louis Gordon, Douglas H. Jones, and G. Michael Phillips, "An Experimental Study of Job Evaluation and Comparable Worth," *Industrial and Labor Relations Review* (July 2001), 806–815.

87. Joel P. Rudin and Kimble Byrd, "U.S. Pay Equity Legislation: Sheep in Wolves' Clothing," *Employee Responsibilities and Rights Journal* (December 2003), 183–190.

88. "One-Fifth of Women Are Harassed Sexually," *HR Focus* (April 2002), 2.

89. http://www.eeoc.gov

90. *Ibid.*

91. *Ibid.*

92. Marilyn Machlowitz and David Machlowitz, "Hug by the Boss Could Lead to a Slap from the Judge," *The Wall Street Journal* (September 25, 1986), 20.

93. "Ruling to Define Sex Harassment in the Workplace," *The Atlanta Journal* (March 2, 1993), A4.

94. Lisa Genasci, "What Does High Court's Harassment Ruling Mean?" *Athens Banner-Herald* (November 10, 1993), 21.

95. Quoted in *Genasci.*

96. Erik Brady, "Colorado Scandal Could Hit Home to Other Colleges," USA Today (May 26, 2004), http://www.usatoday.com.

97. *Ibid.*

98. "Mitsubishi Harassment Settlement Approved," *The New York Times* (June 26, 1998), D20.

99. Dan Lonkevich, "Demand Growing for Harassment Coverage," *National Underwriter* (Property and Casualty/Risk and Benefits Management) (August 10, 1998), 26.

100. Susan B. Garland, "Finally, a Corporate Tip Sheet on Sexual Harassment," *Business Week* (July 13, 1998), 39.

101. Anita Cava, "Sexual Harassment Claims: New Framework for Employers," *Business and Economic Review* (Jul–Sept.

2001), 13–16; Ted Meyer and Linda Schoonmaker, "Employers Must Think Outside the Sexual Harassment Box," *Texas Lawyer* (February 12, 2001), 36.

102. Beth Brophy, "Supreme Court Gives Motherhood Its Legal Due," *U.S. News & World Report* (January 26, 1987), 12.

103. Isabel Wilkerson, "AT&T Settles Bias Suit for $66 Million," *The New York Times* (July 18, 1991), A16.

104. Gillian Flynn, "Watch Out for Pregnancy Discrimination," *Workforce* (November 2002), 84.

105. http://www.eeoc.gov.

106. Mary Lord, "Pregnant—And Now Without a Job," *U.S. News & World Report* (January 23, 1995), 66.

107. "Under a Civil Rights Cloud, Fetal Protection Looks Dismal," *Insight* (April 15, 1991), 40–41.

108. *Ibid.*

109. http://www.now.org

110. *Ibid.*

111. Michael Barbaro, "Wal-Mart Promises to Do Better; Retailer Ties Bonuses to Diversity Goals," *The Washington Post* (June 4, 2004), E1.

112. *Ibid.*

113. *Ibid.*

114. Sheldon Steinhauser, "Age Bias: Is Your Corporate Culture in Need of an Overhaul?" *HR Magazine* (July 1998), 86–88.

115. George J. Church, "Unmasking Age Bias," *Time* (September 7, 1998), H3.

116. Steinhauser, 86–88.

117. Anne Fisher, "Older, Wiser, Job-Hunting," *Fortune* (February 9, 2004), 46.

118. Jeffrey J. Kros, "Age Discrimination Law Narrowed," *Workspan* (May 2004), 78–80.

119. Neal Lerner, "Employers Attempt to Balance Work and Religion; Complaints Alleging Religious Discrimination Have Jumped 75 Percent in the Past Decade," *The Christian Science Monitor* (April 12, 2004), 14.

120. *Ibid.*

121. Mark Hansen, "Suing Bosses over Beliefs," *ABA Journal* (April 1998), 30–32.

122. John Elvin, "Does Religion Belong in the Workplace?" *Insight on the News* (October 28–November 10, 2003), 16.

123. *Ibid.*

124. Hansen, 30–32.

125. Marjorie Valbrun, "EEOC Sees Rise in Intrarace Complaints of Color Bias," *The Wall Street Journal* (August 7, 2003), B1.

126. *Ibid.*

127. *Ibid.*

128. *Ibid.*

129. Matt Murray, "Wal-Mart Shift Shows Job Sites Welcome Gays," *The Wall Street Journal* (July 7, 2003), A9.

130. http://www.hrc.org

131. *Ibid.*

132. Jennifer Hamilton, "Supreme Court to Hear Transgender, Transsexual Case," *Pacific Business News* (February 27, 2004), 5.

133. "Labor Letter: Transexual Employees," *The Wall Street Journal* (April 13, 1993), A1.

134. http://www.hrc.org

135. *Ibid.*

136. "HRC Lauds Federal Court Ruling Asserting Protection for Transsexual Employees Under Existing Law," Human Rights Campaign Press Release (June 1, 2004), http://www.hrc.org.

137. David L. Chappell, "If Affirmative Action Fails . . . What Then?" *The New York Times* (May 8, 2004), B7; Terry H. Anderson, *The Pursuit of Fairness: A History of Affirmative Action* (New York: Oxford University Press, May 2004).

138. Thomas Nagel, "A Defense of Affirmative Action," Report from the Center for Philosophy and Public Policy (College Park, MD: University of Maryland, Fall 1981), 6–9.

139. Daniel Seligman, "How 'Equal Opportunity' Turned into Employment Quotas," *Fortune* (March, 1973), 160–168.

140. Tom L. Beauchamp and Norman E. Bowie (eds.), *Ethical Theory and Business*, 2d ed. (Englewood Cliffs, NJ: Prentice Hall, 1983), 477–478.

141. *Ibid.*, 478.

142. "White, Male and Worried," *Business Week* (January 31, 1994), 50–55.

143. Tony Mecia, "Sowell Blasts Affirmative Action's Harmful Effects," *Campus* (Fall 1991), 6–7.

144. Stephen L. Carter, *Reflections of an Affirmative Action Baby* (New York: Basic Books, 1991).

145. Ernest Holsendolph, "Affirmative Action: Books Take a Hard Look," *The Atlanta Journal* (September 20, 1991), 1G, book review.

146. Linda Chavez, "An Insider's Account of Affirmative Action," *The Wall Street Journal* (September 6, 1991), A7, book review. See also James E. Ellis, "Up from Affirmative Action," *Business Week* (September 23, 1997), 20.

147. Mitchell F. Rice and Maurice Mongkuo, "Did Adarand Kill Minority Set-Asides?" *Public Administration Review* (January/February 1998), 82–86.

148. *Ibid.*

149. "Does Hiring Minorities Hurt?" *Business Week* (September 14, 1998), 26.

150. "Business Week/Harris Executive Poll: Corporate America Grades Its Efforts," *Business Week* (July 8, 1991), 26–30.

151. Clayton, Mark, "Admissions Officers Walk a Fine Line in Gender-Balancing Act," *The Christian Science Monitor* (May 22, 2001), 11.

152. Linda Armstrong, "The Ebb and Flow of Affirmative Action; Landmark Decisions of the Past Decade," *Network Journal* (October 31, 2003), 30.

153. Daniel Golden, "Not Black and White: Colleges Cut Back Minority Programs After Court Rulings; They're Wary of Scholarships Based on Race in Wake of the Michigan Cases; New Ways to Define Diversity," *The Wall Street Journal* (December 30, 2003), A1.

154. *Ibid.*

155. William G. Bowen and Derek C. Bok, *The Shape of the River: Long-Term Consequences of Considering Race in College and University Admissions* (Princeton: Princeton University Press, 1998).

156. Ethan Bronner, "Study Strongly Supports Affirmative Action in Admissions to Elite Colleges," *The New York Times* (September 9, 1998), B10.

157. Laura Hamburg, "UC Graduate Programs See Fewer Blacks," *San Francisco Chronicle* (September 18, 1998), A19.

158. "Taking Adversity out of Diversity," *Business Week* (January 31, 1994), 54–55.

Chapter 19

■ OWNER STAKEHOLDERS *and* CORPORATE GOVERNANCE

CHAPTER LEARNING OUTCOMES

After studying this chapter, you should be able to:

1 Link the issue of legitimacy to corporate governance.
2 Identify the best practices that boards of directors can follow.
3 Identify the major changes in boards of directors that have been employed to improve corporate governance.
4 Discuss the principal ways in which shareholder activism exerted pressure on corporate management groups to improve governance.
5 Summarize the issues surrounding compensation of the CEO.
6 Discuss the problems that have led to the recent spate of corporate scandals and the efforts that are currently underway to keep them from happening again.

The bankruptcy of Enron, once the seventh largest company in the United States, sent shockwaves through corporate America. Then the bankruptcies of corporate giants WorldCom and Global Crossing followed, leaving investors wondering where they could place their trust. The subsequent stock market collapse cost investors approximately $6 trillion.[1] When about 250 companies in the United States had to restate their earnings in 2002 (compared to 92 in 1997 and 3 in 1981), it became clear that more effective corporate governance was sorely needed.[2] SEC chairman William McDonough had the following comment on the impact of the scandals: "I firmly do believe that the whole American system of life, government and the management of our economy were in jeopardy as the American people were losing faith in the system."[3] These scandals threatened more than the individual companies involved—the legitimacy of business as a whole had been called into question.

In this chapter, we will explore corporate governance and the ways in which it has evolved. First, we will examine the concept of legitimacy and the part that corporate governance plays in establishing the legitimacy of business. We will explore how good corporate governance can mitigate the problems created by the separation of ownership and control and examine some of the specific challenges facing board members today.

LEGITIMACY AND CORPORATE GOVERNANCE

To understand corporate governance, it is useful to understand the idea of **legitimacy**. Legitimacy is a somewhat abstract concept, but it is vital in that it helps explain the importance of the relative roles of a corporation's charter, shareholders, board of directors, management, and employees—all of which are components of the modern corporate governance system.

Let us start with a slightly modified version of Talcott Parsons's definition of legitimacy. He argued that "organizations are legitimate to the extent that their activities are congruent with the goals and values of the social system within which they function."[4] From this definition, we may see legitimacy as a condition that prevails when there is congruence between the organization's activities and society's expectations. Thus, whereas legitimacy is a condition, **legitimation** is a dynamic process by which business seeks to perpetuate its acceptance. The dynamic process aspect should be emphasized, because society's norms and values change, and business must change if its legitimacy is to continue. It is also useful to consider legitimacy at both the micro, or company, level and the macro, or business institution, level.

At the *micro level of legitimacy*, we refer to individual business firms achieving and maintaining legitimacy by conforming with societal expectations. According to Epstein and Votaw, companies seek legitimacy in several ways. First, a company may adapt its methods of operating to conform to what it perceives to be the prevailing standard. For example, a company may discontinue door-to-door selling if that marketing approach comes to be viewed in the public mind as a shoddy sales technique,[5] or a pharmaceutical company may discontinue offering free drug samples to medical students if this practice begins to take on the aura of a bribe. Second, a company may try to change the public's values and norms to conform to its own practices by advertising and other techniques.[6] Amazon.com was successful at this when it began marketing through the Internet.

Finally, an organization may seek to enhance its legitimacy by identifying itself with other organizations, people, values, or symbols that have a powerful legitimate base in society.[7] This occurs at several levels. At the national level, companies proudly announce appointments of celebrities, former politicians, or other famous people to managerial positions or board directorships. At the community level, the winning local football coach may be asked to endorse a company by sitting on its board or promoting its products.[8]

The *macro level of legitimacy* is the level with which we are most concerned in this chapter. The macro level refers to the corporate system—the totality of business enterprises. It is difficult to talk about the legitimacy of business in pragmatic terms at this level. American business is such a potpourri of institutions of different shapes, sizes, and industries that saying anything conclusive about it is difficult. Yet this is an important level at which business needs to be concerned about its legitimacy. What is at stake is the existence, acceptance, and form of business as an institution in our society. William Dill has suggested that business's social (or societal) legitimacy is a fragile thing:

Business has evolved by initiative and experiment. It never had an overwhelmingly clear endorsement as a social institution. The idea of allowing individuals to joust with one another in pursuit of personal profit was an exciting and romantic one when it was first proposed as a way of correcting other problems in society; but over time, its ugly side and potential for abuse became apparent.[9]

Quite a bit of the excitement and romanticism has long since worn off; business must accept that it has a fragile mandate.[10] It must realize that its legitimacy is constantly subject to ratification. And it must realize that it has no inherent right to exist: It exists solely because society has given it that right.[11]

In comparing the micro view of legitimacy with the macro view, one may observe that, although specific business organizations try to perpetuate their own legitimacy, the corporate or business system as a whole rarely addresses the issue at all. This is unfortunate because the spectrum of powerful issues regarding business conduct clearly indicates that such institutional introspection is needed if business is to survive and prosper. If business is to continue to justify its right to exist, the question of legitimacy and its operational ramifications must be remembered.

The Issue of Corporate Governance

The issue of corporate governance is a direct outgrowth of the question of legitimacy. The word *governance* comes from the Greek word for steering.[12] Shareholders count on boards to steer the company in their absence. For business to be legitimate and to maintain its legitimacy in the eyes of the public, it must be steered in a way that corresponds to the will of the people.

Corporate governance refers to the method by which a firm is being governed, directed, administered, or controlled and to the goals for which it is being governed. Corporate governance is concerned with the relative roles, rights, and accountability of such stakeholder groups as owners, boards of directors, managers, employees, and others who assert to be stakeholders.

Components of Corporate Governance

To appreciate fully the legitimacy and corporate governance issues, it is important that we understand the major groups that make up the corporate form of business organization, because it is only by so doing that we can appreciate how the system has failed to work according to its intended design.

Roles of Four Major Groups. The four major groups we need to mention in setting the stage are the shareholders (owners/stakeholders), the board of directors, the managers, and the employees. Overarching these groups is the **charter** issued by the state, giving the corporation the right to exist and stipulating the basic terms of its existence. Figure 19-1 on page 610 presents these four groups, along with the state charter, in a hierarchy of corporate governance authority.

Under American corporate law, **shareholders** are the owners of a corporation. As owners, they should have ultimate control over the corporation. This control is manifested primarily in the right to select the board of directors of the company. Generally, the degree of each shareholder's right is determined by the number of shares of stock owned.

FIGURE 19-1

The Corporation's Hierarchy of Authority

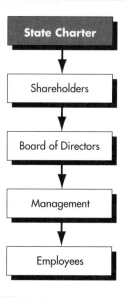

The individual who owns 100 shares of Apple Computer, for example, has 100 "votes" when electing the board of directors. By contrast, the large public pension fund that owns 10 million shares has 10 million "votes."

Because large organizations may have hundreds of thousands of shareholders, they elect a smaller group, known as the **board of directors**, to govern and oversee the management of the business. The board is responsible for ascertaining that the manager puts the interests of the owners (i.e., shareholders) first. The third major group in the authority hierarchy is **management**—the group of individuals hired by the board to run the company and manage it on a daily basis. Along with the board, top management establishes overall policy. Middle- and lower-level managers carry out this policy and conduct the daily supervision of the operative employees. **Employees** are those hired by the company to perform the actual operational work. Managers are employees, too, but in this discussion we use the term *employees* to refer to nonmanagerial employees.

Separation of Ownership from Control.
The social and ethical issues that have evolved in recent years focus on the *intended* versus *actual* roles, rights, responsibilities, and accountability of these four major groups. The major condition embedded in the structure of modern corporations that has contributed to the corporate governance problem has been the **separation of ownership from control**. In the precorporate period, owners were typically the managers themselves. Thus, the system worked the way it was intended; the owners also controlled the business. Even when firms grew larger and managers were hired, the owners often were on the scene to hold the management group accountable. For example, if a company got in trouble, the Carnegies or Mellons or Morgans were always there to fire the president.[13]

As the public corporation grew and stock ownership became widely dispersed, a separation of ownership from control became the prevalent condition. Figure 19-2 illustrates the precorporate and corporate periods. The dispersion of ownership into hundreds of thousands or millions of shares meant that essentially no one or no one group owned enough shares to exercise control. This being the case, the most effective control that owners could exercise was the election of the board of directors to serve as their representative and watch over management.

The problem with this evolution was that authority, power, and control rested with the group that had the most concentrated interest at stake—management. The corporation did not function according to its designed plan with effective authority, power, and control flowing downward from the owners. The shareholders were owners in a technical sense, but most of them perceived themselves as investors rather than owners. If you owned 100 shares of Walt Disney Co. and there were 10 million shares outstanding, you likely would see yourself as an investor rather than an owner. With just a telephone call issuing a sell order to your stockbroker, your "ownership" stake could be gone. Furthermore, with stock ownership so dispersed, no conscious, intended supervision of corporate boards was possible.

The other factors that added to management's power were the corporate laws and traditions that gave the management group control over the **proxy process**—the method by which the shareholders elected boards of directors. Over time, it was not difficult for management groups to create boards of directors of like-minded executives who would simply collect their fees and defer to management on whatever it wanted. The result of this process was that power, authority, and control began to flow upward from management

---

FIGURE 19-2

Precorporate Versus Corporate Ownership and Control

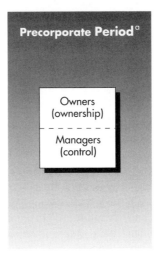
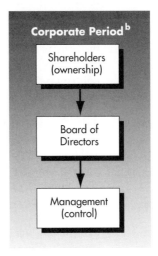

---

[a] In the precorporate period, the owners were also the managers, and therefore ownership and control were combined. Later, large companies hired managers, but the owners were always there to exercise control.

[b] In the corporate period, ownership was separated from control by the intervention of a board of directors. Theoretically, the board should have kept control on behalf of owners, but it did not always turn out that way.

rather than downward from the shareholders (owners). **Agency problems** developed when the interests of the shareholders were not aligned with the interests of the manager, and the manager (who is simply a hired *agent* with the responsibility of representing the owner's best interest) began to pursue self-interest instead.

The Role of the Board of Directors

It is clear from the preceding discussion that a potential governance problem is built into the corporate system because of the separation of ownership from control. It is equally clear that the board of directors is intended to oversee management on behalf of the shareholders. However, this is where the system had once broken down. For corporate governance to function as it was originally intended, the board of directors must be an effective, potent body carrying out its roles and responsibilities in ascertaining that management pursue the shareholders' best interests.

Are boards doing what they are supposed to be doing? In fairness, boards have improved in many ways. James Heard is the CEO of Proxy Monitor, a leading proxy voting advisor to institutional investors. He has seen many positive changes resulting from the pressures institutional investors imposed: More directors are independent, more directors own stock in the company, and boards are more likely to demand change.[14] In a 2003 survey of corporate directors, 75 percent of respondents said they were spending more time on board matters each month, and 67 percent said full board meetings are now longer.[15]

If corporate governance has improved, how could debacles like Enron and WorldCom still occur? Much of the blame was placed on the auditors: Arthur Andersen was the auditor for Enron, WorldCom, and Global Crossing. Andersen had a built-in conflict of interest from doing both consulting and auditing for the same company. For example, in 2000 Andersen earned $25 million from auditing Enron and $27 million from providing Enron with consulting services.[16] Lavish CEO paychecks and the boards who approved them also drew the ire of investors. Enron's Ken Lay made about $220 million, and Global Crossing's Gary Winnick made over $500 million prior to the bankruptcies, which left many investors with nothing.[17] Surprisingly, most of the behavior that led to these bankruptcies fell within the letter of the law. And so the response to them was geared toward changing the law, making it more difficult for firms to mislead investors. The Sarbanes–Oxley Act, designed to tighten up the auditing process, is discussed later in this chapter.

The Need for Board Independence.   Board independence from management is a crucial aspect of good governance. It is here that the difference between **inside directors** and **outside directors** becomes most pronounced. Outside directors are independent from the firm and its top managers. In contrast, inside directors have some sort of ties to the firm. Sometimes they are top managers in the firm; other times, insiders are family members or others with close ties to the firm or the CEO. To varying degrees, each of these parties is "beholden" to the CEO and, therefore, might be hesitant to speak out when necessary. Courtney Brown, an experienced director who served on many boards, said that he never saw a subordinate officer serving on a board dissent from the position taken by the CEO.[18] Insiders might also be professionals such as lawyers under contract to the firm or bankers whose bank does business with the firm: This can create conflict-of-interest situations.[19] For example, a commercial banker/director may expect the company on whose board she or he is serving to restrict itself to using the services of her or his own firm and be willing to support the CEO in return for the business provided.

Another problem is managerial control of the board processes. CEOs often can control board perks such as director compensation and committee assignments. Board members who rock the boat might find they are left out in the cold. As one corporate board member told *Fortune*, under conditions of anonymity, "This stuff is wrong. . . . What people understand they have to do is go along with management, because if they don't they won't be part of the club. . . . What it comes down to is that directors aren't really independent. CEOs don't want independent directors."[20]

Issues Surrounding Compensation

CEO Compensation.
The issue of executive pay was a lightning rod for the concern that managers place their own interests over those of their shareholders. Two issues are at the heart of the CEO pay controversy: (1) the extent to which CEO pay is tied to firm performance, and (2) the overall level of CEO pay.

The move to tie CEO pay more closely to firm performance grew in momentum when shareholders observed CEO pay rising as firm performance fell. Many executives had gotten staggering salaries, even while profits were falling, workers were being laid off, and shareholder return was dropping. Shareholders were assisted in their effort to monitor CEO pay by stricter disclosure requirements from the Securities and Exchange Commission (SEC). The revised compensation disclosure rule, adopted by the SEC in 1992, was designed to provide shareholders with more information about the relationship between firm performance and CEO compensation.[21] According to the results of one study, it seems to have worked. Since the rule's implementation, compensation committees have met more frequently, lessened the number of insiders as members, and become more moderate in size. More importantly, largely through the use of stock options, CEO pay became more closely aligned with accounting and market performance measures than it was before the rule's implementation.[22] There was some evidence that boards of directors were becoming the watchdogs they were always supposed to be.[23]

Tying firm pay to performance is only one issue surrounding CEO pay. The other is the level of pay that CEOs receive. This issue has taken on increasing meaning as CEO salaries have skyrocketed. Executive Excess 2003, the annual CEO compensation survey by the Institute for Policy Studies and United for a Fair Economy, reports that the ratio of CEO pay to the average work is 282 to 1. That is seven times as large as the 42-to-1 ratio found in 1982.[24] Admittedly, this represents a decline from 2000, when the gap between CEO pay and average worker pay had risen to a staggering 531 to 1.[25] However, median CEO pay is still on the rise—up 5.9 percent in 2002.[26] Had the minimum wage risen at the same rate as CEO pay from 1990 to 2003, the federal minimum wage would be $14.40.[27]

Some of the money being paid to CEOs is money that could be going to the government to support federal, state, and local programs. The nonpartisan organization, Citizen Works, compiled a list of corporations with the most subsidiaries located in tax havens: The median pay of the CEOs was 87 percent higher than that of the CEOs who do not

SEARCH THE WEB

CEO PayWatch

The AFL-CIO sponsors CEO PayWatch (**http://www.aflcio.org/paywatch**), a Web site that is an "online center for learning about the excessive salaries, bonuses and perks of the CEOs of major corporations." Visitors to the Web site can enter their 1996 pay and find out what they would be making today if their pay had grown at the same rate as the typical CEO's or they can play "Greed: The Executive PayWatch Board Game." On a more serious note, the Web site provides instructions for assessing the pay of CEOs at public corporations and determining the relationship of that pay to the firm's performance. Instructions are also given for beginning a campaign of shareholder activism in any company.

In an article for *Time* (31 May 2004 v163 i22 p62), Daren Fonda poses the $64,000 question: "Just how much is a CEO worth?" The article focuses on New York Attorney General Eliot Spitzer's efforts to reform financial practices on Wall Street and then explores the knotty issue of CEO compensation. Fonda points out that CEOs are like sports free agents who are likely to go where the cash is greenest. To read more about CEO compensation in the post-Enron world, log on to InfoTrac College Edition at **http://www.infotrac-college.com** and keying record number A117031551.

utilize tax havens.[28] Tax havens aren't the only way that corporations avoid paying taxes. Corporations are not required to report executive stock options as expenses. By not expensing CEO stock options, 350 leading firms saved an estimated $3.6 billion from 1997 to 2002. That figure represents the combined 2003 budget deficits of seven of the largest states (Florida, Illinois, Pennsylvania, Ohio, Michigan, New Jersey, and Georgia). It also is equivalent to the 2003 Medicaid funding shortfall for all 50 states.[29]

Executive Retirement Plans.   Executive retirement packages have traditionally flown under the radar, escaping the notice of shareholders, employees, and the public. However, as details of some retirement packages have become public, those packages have come under increased scrutiny. Former General Electric chairman and CEO Jack Welch's retirement package was disclosed during his divorce proceedings. Country club memberships, wine and laundry services, luxurious housing, and access to corporate jets were but a few of the perks that Welch has enjoyed.[30] The disclosure that the New York Stock Exchange had awarded its former chairman and CEO Richard Grasso a $139.5 million retirement package, amid slumping stocks and cost pressures, also raised the ire of shareholders and their advocates.[31] Part of the public's frustration is that these CEO retirement packages stand in stark contrast to the retirement packages that workers will receive. Less than half of today's workers have retirement packages, and those that do usually have the less lucrative defined contribution rather than the defined benefit plans.[32]

Outside Director Compensation.   It was suggested earlier that there may be some link between CEO and executive compensation and board members. Therefore, it should not be surprising that directors' pay is becoming an issue, too. Paying board members is a relatively recent idea. Eighty years ago, it was illegal to pay nonexecutive board members. The logic was that because board members represented the shareholders, paying them out of the company's (i.e., shareholders') funds would be self-dealing.[33] A 1992 Korn/Ferry survey showed that board members typically spent 95 hours a year on the board. By 2000, that figure had increased to 173 hours. The average director received a 23 percent increase in pay for the 82 percent increase in time spent on the job.[34] Not surprisingly, a 2003 survey by *Corporate Board Member* magazine found that 80 percent of board members felt directors should be paid more in light of the "added responsibility of recent board governance reforms."[35]

Consequences of the Mergers, Acquisitions, and Takeovers

Mergers and acquisitions are another form of corporate governance, one that comes from outside the corporation. The expectation is that the threat of a possible takeover will motivate top managers to pursue shareholder, rather than self, interest. The merger, acquisition, and hostile takeover craze of the 1980s brought out many new issues related to corporate governance. The economic prosperity of the 1980s, coupled with the rise of junk bonds and other creative methods of financing, made it possible for small firms and individuals to buy large corporations. Many corporate CEOs and boards went to great lengths to protect themselves from these takeovers. A major criticism of CEOs and boards during this period was that they were overly obsessed with self-preservation rather than making optimal decisions on behalf of their owners/stakeholders. Two of the most questionable top management practices to emerge from the hostile takeover wave were poison pills and golden parachutes. We will briefly consider each of these and see how they fit into the corporate governance problem we have been discussing. Then, we will examine the issue of insider trading.

Poison Pill.

A **poison pill** is a shareholder rights plan aimed at discouraging or preventing a hostile takeover. Typically, when a hostile suitor acquires more than a certain percentage of a company's stock, the poison pill provides that other shareholders receive share purchase rights designed to dilute the suitor's holdings and make the acquisition prohibitively expensive. Some poison pills adopted by companies have been ruled illegal by the courts.[36] However, efforts to adopt poison pills continue. In 2001, Yahoo!'s board of directors adopted a poison pill that would make a hostile takeover prohibitively expensive. The plan gave Yahoo! shareholders the right to buy one unit of a share of preferred stock for $250 if a person or group acquired at least 15 percent of Yahoo!'s stock. According to the company, the poison pill was not instituted in response to any specific acquisition threat but instead to "deter coercive takeover tactics."[37] In 2003, the pace of poison pill adoption seemed to be slowing as the efforts by shareholders to dismantle them increased.[38]

Golden Parachutes.

A **golden parachute** is a contract in which a corporation agrees to make payments to key officers in the event of a change in the control of the corporation.[39] The original intent of golden parachutes was to provide top executives involved in takeover battles with an incentive for not putting themselves before their shareholders. However, Buchholtz and Ribbens conducted a study of over 400 tender offers (i.e., takeover attempts in which the acquirers offered shareholders premiums to sell their shares) and found that golden parachutes had no effect on takeover resistance. Neither the existence of the parachute, nor the magnitude of the potential parachute payout, influenced CEO reactions to takeover attempts.[40]

Cochran and Wartick offer several arguments against golden parachutes. They argue that executives are already being paid well to represent their companies and that their getting additional rewards constitutes "double dipping." They also argue that these executives are, in essence, being rewarded for failure. The logic here is that if the executives have managed their companies in such a way that the companies' stock prices are low enough to make the firms attractive to takeover specialists, the executives are being rewarded for failure. Another argument is that executives, to the extent that they control their own boards, are giving themselves the golden parachutes. This represents a conflict of interest.[41]

Insider Trading Scandals.

Insider trading is the practice of obtaining critical information from inside a company and then using that information for one's own personal financial gain. A scandal began in 1986 when the Securities and Exchange Commission (SEC) filed a civil complaint against Dennis B. Levine, a former managing partner of the Drexel Burnham Lambert investment banking firm, and charged him with illegally trading in 54 stocks. Levine then pleaded guilty to four criminal charges and gave up $10.6 million in illegal profits—the biggest insider trading penalty up to that point.[42] He also spent 17 months in prison.

Levine's downfall set off a chain reaction on Wall Street. His testimony led directly to the SEC's $100 million judgment against Ivan Boesky, one of Wall Street's most frenetically active individual speculators. In a consent decree, Boesky agreed to pay $100 million, which was then described as by far the largest settlement ever obtained by the SEC in an insider trading case. Boesky, it turns out, had made a career of the high-rolling financial game known as **risk arbitrage**—the opportunistic buying and selling of companies that appear on the verge of being taken over by other firms.[43] The Boesky settlement set off a flurry of litigation as dozens of private and corporate lawsuits were filed in response to these disclosures.[44] Ivan Boesky then fingered Martin Siegel, one of America's most respected investment bankers, at Kidder Peabody. Apparently Siegel and Boesky began conspiring in 1982, and over the next 2 years Siegel leaked information about upcoming takeovers to Boesky in exchange for $700,000 cash. Siegel pleaded guilty and began cooperating with investigators, and then he himself proceeded to finger two former executives at Kidder Peabody and one at Goldman Sachs.[45]

The insider trading scandals rocked Wall Street as accusations reached the upper levels of the financial industry's power and salary structure. New arrests seemed to occur weekly, and one of the most frequently asked questions was "Who's next?"[46] In 1987, Ivan Boesky was sentenced to 3 years in prison. However, Boesky helped prosecutors reel in the biggest fish of all—junk bond king Michael Milkin. The Securities and Exchange Commission accused Milkin and his employer, Drexel Burnham, of insider trading, stock manipulation, and other violations of federal securities laws. Drexel Burnham agreed in 1988 to plead guilty to six felonies, settle SEC charges, and pay a record fine of $650 million. A year later, the junk bond market crashed and Drexel Burnham filed for bankruptcy. In 1990, Milkin agreed to plead guilty to six felony counts of securities fraud, market manipulation, and tax fraud. He agreed to pay a personal fine of $600 million and later was sentenced to 10 years in prison.[47] He served only 2 years in prison before being released. Insider trading concerns continue today. In 2003, Martha Stewart was found guilty on four counts of making false statements and obstruction of justice regarding a controversial sale of ImClone Systems stock. This brought the topic of insider trading back into the daily news.

Insider trading allegations cause the general public to lose faith in what they thought was the stable and secure financial industry. If large investors can act on information that smaller investors do not have, the playing field is not level. In 2001, to prop up investor confidence, the SEC instituted new disclosure rules designed to aid the small investor who historically has not had access to the information large investors hold. Regulation FD (fair disclosure) set limits on the common company practice of selective disclosure. When companies disclose meaningful information to shareholders and securities professionals, they must now do so publicly so that small investors can enjoy a more level playing field.[48]

Board Member Liability

Concerned about increasing legal hassles emanating from stockholder, customer, and employee lawsuits, directors have been quitting board positions or refusing to accept them in the first place. Although courts rarely hold directors personally liable in the hundreds of shareholder suits filed every year, over the past several years there have been a few cases in which directors have been held personally and financially liable for their decisions. The Trans Union Corporation case involved an agreement among the directors to sell the company for a price the owners later decided was too low. A suit was filed, and the court ordered that the board members be held personally responsible for the difference between the price the company was sold for and a later-determined "fair value" for the deal.[49] In addition to the Trans Union case, Cincinnati Gas and Electric reached a $14 million settlement in a shareholder suit that charged directors and officers with improper disclosure concerning a nuclear power plant.[50]

The Caremark case further heightened directors' concerns about **personal liability**. Caremark, a home health care company, paid substantial civil and criminal fines for submitting false claims and making illegal payments to doctors and other health care providers. The Caremark board of directors was then sued for breach of fiduciary duties because the board members had failed in their responsibility to monitor effectively the Caremark employees who violated various state and federal laws. The Delaware Chancery Court ruled that it is the duty of the board of directors to ensure that a company has an effective reporting and monitoring system in place. If the board fails to do this, individual directors can be held personally liable for losses that are caused by their failure to meet appropriate standards.[51]

IMPROVING CORPORATE GOVERNANCE

We first discuss a landmark legislative effort to improve corporate governance, the Sarbanes–Oxley Act of 2002. We then proceed to other efforts to improve corporate governance, which may be classified into two major categories for discussion purposes. First, changes could be made in the composition, structure, and functioning of boards of directors. Second, shareholders—on their own initiative or on the initiative of management or the board—could assume a more active role in governance. Each of these possibilities deserves closer examination.

Sarbanes–Oxley

One downside to Sarbanes–Oxley is the cost required to meet the act's regulations, a burden that can be intolerable for small companies. Two articles in *Business Week* (24 May 2004 i3884 p74 and p120) detail the growing trend toward deregistration—delisting a company so that its stock can no longer be traded publicly. The "little guys" are deciding that they might be better off in private hands, because they are generally overlooked by institutional investors and because they find compliance with Sarbanes-Oxley too expensive. Read what happens when a company "goes dark" by logging on to InfoTrac College Edition at **http://www.infotrac-college. com** and keying record number A116864763 or A116864810.

On July 30, 2002, the **Accounting Reform and Investor Protection Act of 2002** was signed into law. Also known as the **Sarbanes–Oxley Act (SOA)**, it amends the securities laws to provide better protection for investors in public companies by improving the financial reporting of companies. According to the Senate Committee report, "the issue of auditor independence is at the center of (the SOA)."[52] Some of the ways the act endeavors to ensure auditor independence are by limiting the nonauditing services an auditor can provide, requiring auditing firms to rotate the auditors who work with a specific company, and making it unlawful for accounting firms to provide auditing services where conflicts of interest (as defined by the act) exist. In addition, the act enhances financial disclosure with requirements such as the reporting of off-balance-sheet transactions, the prohibiting of personal loans to executives and directors, and the requirement that auditors assess and report upon the internal controls employed by the company. Other key provisions include the requirement that audit committees have at least one financial expert, that CEOs and CFOs certify and be held responsible for financial representations of the company, and that whistle-blowers are afforded protection. Corporations must also disclose whether they have adopted a code of ethics for senior financial officers and, if they haven't, provide an explanation for why they haven't.[53] The penalties for noncompliance with SOA are severe: A CEO or CFO who misrepresents company finances may be fined up to $1 million and imprisoned for up to 10 years. If that misrepresentation is willful, the fine may go up to $5 million with up to 20 years imprisonment.[54]

In 2003, one year after the passage of the SOA, critics pointed to significant successes, while expressing concern over work that has yet to be accomplished. Some saw evidence that executives and directors were being more diligent in their reporting to shareholders but expressed concern that executives were becoming too risk-averse.[55] Others felt that there was an increase in firms turning private to avoid the regulations: The cost of compliance can be as much as three times the cost prior to the act's implementation.[56] John Castellani, president of the Business Roundtable, said that members of the Business Roundtable expect to pay from $1 million to $10 million for SOA compliance. Castellani noted, however, that the improvement in corporate governance and investor confidence is worth the pain.[57] Most observers agree that more time must pass before the impact of the SOA can be fully assessed.

Changes in Boards of Directors

In the past decade or so, changes have begun to be made in boards of directors. These changes have occurred because of the growing belief that CEOs and executive teams need to be made more accountable to shareholders and other stakeholders. Here we will discuss several of these changes and some other recommendations that have been set forth for improving board functioning.

Composition of the Board. Prior to the 1960s, boards were composed primarily of white, male inside directors. It was not until the 1960s that pressure from Washington, Wall Street, and various stakeholder groups began to emphasize the concept of board diversity. Forty years later, their efforts were beginning to pay off: 78 percent of U.S. board members were outsiders.[58] Of the S&P 500 companies, 93 percent had at least one female director. Although most firms still only have one token female director, the tide seems to be shifting: 21 percent of new board members were women, and 25 percent of the nation's largest companies had more than one female director.[59] Ethnic minorities are making inroads, too. Sixty percent of U.S. corporate boards now have ethnic minority directors, with African-Americans comprising 39 percent, Latinos comprising 12 percent, and Asians comprising 9 percent of the positions. The world seems to be awakening to the importance of diverse and independent boards. The problem is that good candidates are increasingly hard to find.[60]

Part of the problem is an increase in demand for good independent directors. Institutional investors value good corporate governance so highly that they are willing to pay a premium for firms with outside directors. A recent study by the McKinsey Company found that the premium was as high as 28 percent in Venezuela. Although it varied, each country's premium was well above 15 percent.[61] South Korea passed a law requiring that outside directors occupy at least one-fourth of the positions on large company boards.[62] This increase in demand for outside directors is part of the reason they are in increasingly short supply.

Another factor limiting the supply of directors is the greater level of expectations placed on board members. Board committees and subcommittees are now given more to do than ever before. Furthermore, the globalization of business has placed new demands on board members for travel. Last, firms realize the time demands placed on outside directors, and so they limit the number of outside boards on which their own executives may sit. For example, former GE CEO Jack Welch would not allow his senior managers to sit on the boards of other companies.[63]

The difficulty in finding outside board members is exacerbated when searching for members of minority groups or women to bring diversity to the board. In the past, many candidates were excluded because they never had the title of CEO. A new trend in board recruitment, focusing more on experience than title, is helping to bring more independence and diversity to the boardroom. This broadens the pool of candidates available.[64]

Today, advocates of strong, independent, and diverse boards have largely succeeded in convincing corporations of the importance of board composition. The difficulty now is in putting those recommendations into effect.

Use of Board Committees.

The **audit committee** is typically responsible for assessing the adequacy of internal control systems and the integrity of financial statements. Recent scandals, like Enron and WorldCom, and the many companies that have subsequently needed to restate earnings underscore the importance of a strong audit committee. Commenting on the Cendant Corporation's class action suit for securities fraud, *The Wall Street Journal* opined, "Too many audit committees are turning out to be toothless tigers."[65] In a 2003 survey, 81 percent of board members felt that audit committee chairs should be paid more than chairs of other committees because of their added responsibilities.[66] To lessen the occurrence of such scandals, the Securities and Exchange Commission has placed much emphasis on audit committees, and the New York Stock Exchange mandates such committees, composed of independent outside directors, for the firms listed with it. Charles Anderson and Robert Anthony, authors of *The New Corporate Directors: Insights for Board Members and Executives,*[67] argue that the principal responsibilities of an audit committee are as follows:

1. To ensure that published financial statements are not misleading
2. To ensure that internal controls are adequate
3. To follow up on allegations of material, financial, ethical, and legal irregularities
4. To ratify the selection of the external auditor

According to Arjay Miller, a board member and former president of Ford Motor Company, there should be at least one meeting per year between the audit committee and the firm's internal auditor.[68] The internal auditor should be scheduled to meet alone with the committee and always be instructed to speak out whenever she or he believes something should be brought to the committee's attention. The committee should also meet with the outside auditor in a setting in which members of management are not present. Three major questions should be asked of the outside auditor by the audit committee:

1. Is there anything more that you think we should know?
2. What is your biggest area of concern?
3. In what area did you have the largest difference of opinion with company accounting personnel?

The **nominating committee**, which should be composed of outside directors, or at least a majority of outside directors, has the responsibility of ensuring that competent, objective board members are selected. The American Assembly recommended that this committee be composed entirely of independent outside directors. The function of the nominating committee is to nominate candidates for the board and for senior management positions. In spite of the suggested role and responsibility of this committee, in most companies the CEO continues to exercise a powerful role in the selection of board members.

The **compensation committee** has the responsibility of evaluating executive performance and recommending terms and conditions of employment. This committee should be composed of outside directors. Both the New York Stock Exchange (NYSE) and NASDAQ require that the compensation committee be composed of independent board members. One might ask, however, how objective these board members are when the CEO has played a significant role in their being elected to the board.

Finally, each board has a **public issues committee**, or **public policy committee**. Although it is recognized that most management structures have some sort of formal mechanism for responding to public or social issues, this area is important enough to warrant a board committee that would become sensitive to these issues, provide policy leadership, and monitor management's performance on these issues. Most major companies today have public issues committees that typically deal with such issues as affirmative action, equal employment opportunity, environmental affairs, employee health and safety, consumer affairs, political action, and other areas in which public or ethical issues are present. Debate continues over the extent to which large firms really use such committees, but the fact that they have institutionalized such concerns by way of formal corporate committees is encouraging. The American Assembly recommends that firms develop evaluation systems to help them monitor the social performance of their corporate executives, but the evidence does not show that companies are doing this.[69]

Getting Tough with CEOs.

It has always been a major responsibility of board directors to monitor CEO performance and to get tough if the situation dictates. Historically, chief executives were protected from the axe that hit other employees when times got rough. Changes are now occurring that are resulting in CEOs being taken to task, or even fired, for reasons that heretofore did not create a stir in the boardroom. These changes include the tough, competitive economic times; the rising vigilance of outside directors; and the increasing power of large institutional investors.

Since 2000, CEOs have been "dropping like flies."[70] From 1995 through 2000, two-thirds of major companies worldwide replaced their CEO at least once. By 2003, CEOs had come to know that their tenure was uncertain at best.[71] Looking back on 2003, the *Christian Science Monitor* commented, "While the perks of sitting in a corner office are great, job security isn't one of them."[72]

Some analysts see the increasing turnover in CEOs as a positive thing. "I take it as a good sign, because it says boards of directors are tougher on CEOs than they used to be," says Donald P. Jacobs, former dean of the Kellogg School of Business at Northwestern University. Still others express their concern. Rakhesh Kurana of Harvard Business School opines, "We've made this a superhero job. Boards look at the CEO as a panacea and get fixated on the idea that one single individual will solve all the company's problems." One thing is clear: Boards in general cannot now be accused of giving CEOs a free ride.[73]

Other suggestions have been proposed for creating effective boards of directors and for improving board members' abilities to monitor executive teams to ensure that crises do not occur undetected. Figure 19-3 summarizes some of these recommendations.

SEARCH THE WEB

U.S. SEC EDGAR DATABASE

The U.S. SEC has made it possible for shareholders and other interested parties to retrieve publicly available filings through its Web site (**http://www.sec.gov**). Filings submitted to the SEC from January 1994 to the present are available 24 hours after they are received. The Web site also offers news and other investor information to enable shareholders to be more active and informed participants in the corporate governance process.

FIGURE 19-3

Improving Boards and Board Members

Building a Better Board[a]

- Define the role the board intends to undertake.
- Be explicit about their financial goals.
- Widen the talent pool for directors, and seek the skills and experience that fit the future needs of the firm.
- Encourage constructive dissent.
- Divide and delegate work to promote deeper analysis.

Being a Better Board Member[b]

- Be willing to challenge management.
- Be willing to do lots of homework.
- Control the flow of information.
- Meet outside of the CEO's sphere—both with other board members and lower level managers.
- Don't sacrifice performance for collegiality.

SOURCES: [a]Colin B.Carter and Jay W. Lorsch, "Director, Heal Thyself," *The Wall Street Journal* (January 6, 2004), B2. [b]Carol Hymowitz, "How to Be a Good Director," *The Wall Street Journal* (October 27, 2003), R1, R4.

Increased Role of Shareholders

Prior to the 1980s, civil rights activists, consumer groups, and other social activist pressure groups insisted that companies join their causes. Today, companies increasingly understand the stakeholder perspective. However, it has created a new dilemma for companies as they deal with two broad types of shareholders. First, there are the traditional shareholder groups that are primarily interested in the firm's financial performance. Examples of such groups include the large institutional investors, such as pension funds. Second, there are growing numbers of social activist shareholders. These groups are typically pressuring firms to adopt their desired postures on social causes, such as Third World employment practices, animal testing, affirmative action, and environmental protection.

A major problem seems to be that both groups of shareholders feel like neglected constituencies. They are attempting to rectify this condition through a variety of means. They are demanding effective power. They want to hold management groups accountable. They want to make changes, including changes in management if necessary. Like companies' earlier responses to other stakeholder activist groups, many companies are resisting. The result is a battle between managers and shareholders for corporate control.[74]

A recent example of this battle between managers and shareholders is the effort by the Living Wage, an antisweatshop group, to use shareholder resolutions to raise wages for workers in Indonesia. A shareholder must own $2,000 of Nike stock for a minimum of one year to propose a resolution that would change company policy. Jim Keady and Leslie Kredu, directors of the group, traveled the country, speaking at colleges in an effort to find individuals and organizations to donate to their cause. Among other demands, the group wanted Nike to disclose all factory locations, remove language that prohibits athletes who wear Nike gear from criticizing Nike, allow monitoring of factories by a worker rights consortium, and only work with factories that pay a wage sufficient to support a small family and still allow savings. Nike spokeswoman Vada Manager questioned the group's claims, stating that Nike has strict wage, labor, and environmental codes in its factories that are monitored and enforced.[75] In September 2002, Keady addressed the annual meeting of Nike to question the closing of a factory in Indonesia: He was escorted from the meeting by security officials and a Portland police officer.[76]

Our discussion of an increased role for shareholders centers around two perspectives: (1) the perspective of shareholders themselves asserting their rights on their own initiative, and (2) initiatives being taken by companies to make shareholders a true constituency. The shareholder initiatives will dominate our discussion, because they clearly constitute the bulk of the activity underway.

Shareholder Initiatives.
These initiatives may be classified into three major, overlapping areas: (1) the rise of shareholder activist groups, (2) the filing of shareholder resolutions and activism at annual meetings, and (3) the filing of shareholder lawsuits.

SEARCH THE WEB

AN INVESTOR'S GUIDE

In December 1972, the Investor Responsibility Research Center (IRRC) was formed "to provide timely and impartial analysis concerning corporate social responsibility issues." The IRRC (http://www.irrc.org) became a central organization that serves as a resource center for shareholder activism. The IRRC is unique in this arena in that it is nonpartisan and strives to not advocate any particular side of an issue it covers.

Rise of Shareholder Activist Groups. One major reason that relations between management groups and shareholders have heated up is that shareholders have discovered the benefits of organizing and wielding power. **Shareholder activism** is not a new phenomenon. It goes back over 60 years to 1932, when Lewis Gilbert, then a young owner of 10 shares, was appalled by the absence of communication between New York-based Consolidated Gas Company's management and its owners. Supported by a family inheritance, Gilbert decided to quit his job as a newspaper reporter and "fight this silent dictatorship over other people's money." He resolved to devote himself "to the cause of the public shareholder."[77]

The history of shareholder activism is too detailed to report fully here, but Gilbert's efforts planted a seed that grew, albeit slowly. The major impetus for the movement came in the 1960s and early 1970s. The early shareholder activists were an unlikely conglomeration—corporate gadflies, political radicals, young lawyers, an assortment of church groups, and a group of physicians.[78] The movement grew out of a period of political and social upheaval—civil rights, the Vietnam War, pollution, and consumerism.

The watershed event for shareholder activism was Campaign GM in the early 1970s, also known as the Campaign to Make General Motors Responsible. Among those involved with this effort was, not surprisingly, Ralph Nader. The shareholder group did not achieve all its objectives, but it won enough to demonstrate that shareholder groups could wield power if they worked hard enough at it. Two of Campaign GM's most notable early accomplishments were that (1) the company created a public policy committee of the board, composed of five outside directors, to monitor social performance, and (2) GM appointed the Reverend Leon Sullivan as its first black director.[79]

One direct consequence of the success of Campaign GM was the growth of church activism. Church groups were the early mainstay of the corporate social responsibility movement and were among the first shareholder groups to adopt Campaign GM's strategy of raising social issues with corporations. Church groups began examining the relationship between their portfolios and corporate practices, such as minority hiring and companies' presence in South Africa. Church groups remain among the largest groups of institutional stockholders willing to take on management and press for what they think is right. Many churches' activist efforts are coordinated by the Interfaith Center on Corporate Responsibility (ICCR), which coordinates the shareholder advocacy of about 275 religious orders with about $90 billion in investments. The ICCR was instrumental in convincing Kimberly-Clark to divest the cigarette paper business and pressuring PepsiCo to move out of Burma. It is now taking on such issues as global warming, environmental pollution, and the practice of using sweatshops to manufacture garments and shoes.[80]

Institutional investors (pension funds, church groups, foundations) now dominate the marketplace and thus wield considerable power because of their enormous stock holdings. They now serve as lead plaintiffs in securities class action suits, often with groundbreaking results.[81] This influence continues to grow. Recently, a new spurt in the growth of shareholder activism became apparent. Analysts attribute this increase directly to the Internet. According to Damon A. Silvers, associate general counsel of the AFL-CIO, "Think about the cost of doing a mailing to all of a company's shareholders. On a Web site, you can gain access to everybody."[82]

Filing of Shareholder Resolutions and Activism at Annual Meetings. One of the major vehicles by which shareholder activists communicate their concerns to management groups is through the filing of **shareholder resolutions**, or shareholder proposals. An example of such a resolution is, "The company should name women and minorities to the board of directors." To file a resolution, a shareholder or a shareholder group must obtain a stated number of signatures to require management to place the resolution on the proxy statement so that it can be voted on by all the shareholders. Resolutions that are defeated (fail to get majority votes) may be resubmitted provided that they meet certain SEC requirements for such resubmission.

The shareholder groups behind these shareholder proposals are usually socially oriented—that is, they want to exert pressure to make the companies in which they own stock more socially responsive. Although an individual could initiate a shareholder resolution, she or he probably would not have the resources or means to obtain the required signatures to have the resolution placed on the proxy. Thus, most resolutions are initiated by large institutional investors that own large blocks of stock or by other activist groups that own few shares of stock but have financial backing. Foundations, religious groups, universities, and other such large shareholders are in an ideal position to initiate resolutions. Religious groups prominent in this endeavor include the Episcopal Church, the United Church of Christ, the Lutheran Church in America, the United Methodists, the United Presbyterian Church, and the American Jewish Congress.

The issues on which shareholder resolutions are filed vary widely, but they typically concern some aspect of a firm's social performance. For example, Mobil, Pfizer, and Union Camp were asked to study the safety of tobacco additives produced and sold by them and combusted and inhaled by humans. Several firms, including American Brands, Kimberly-Clark, Philip Morris, and RJR Nabisco, were asked to spin off their tobacco units from the rest of their operations. Wendy's and PepsiCo (Kentucky Fried Chicken, Taco Bell, Pizza Hut) were asked again to make all their restaurants smoke-free. Other popular resolutions have dealt with environmental issues, use of the McBride Principles in doing business in Northern Ireland, and board diversity (naming more women and minorities to corporate boards).[83]

Because most shareholder resolutions never pass, one might ask why groups pursue them. The main reason is that they gain national publicity, which is part of what protesting groups are out to achieve. Increasingly, companies are negotiating with groups to settle issues before resolutions ever come up for a vote. Several years ago, in a rare reversal of attitude, Exxon Corporation's management recommended that shareholders vote in favor of a resolution calling for the company to provide reams of data on its strip-mining operations. Exxon had agreed ahead of time to the request of the United Presbyterian Church and several Catholic groups, which sponsored the resolution, but the groups wanted the resolution to go all the way to a vote, and the company acquiesced. What happened at Exxon reflects subtle changes as management groups, increasingly sensitive to public criticism, are more willing to sit down before annual meetings and work out agreements on shareholder resolutions. In other instances, resolution requests were withdrawn from Pfizer, Inc., and Union Camp after Pfizer agreed to draft a written policy banning sales of its products to tobacco makers, and Union Camp agreed to cease promoting flavors it generates for tobacco products.[84]

Closely related to the surge in shareholder resolutions has been the increased activism at corporate annual meetings in the past decade. Professional "corporate gadflies" purchase small numbers of shares of a company's stock and then attend its annual meetings to put pressure on managers to explain themselves. An example of the kind of social activism that can occur during an annual meeting was the case in which GM shareholders sought explanations for a series of embarrassing controversies surrounding the automaker. Some shareholders wanted to know why the company substituted Chevrolet engines in cars sold by some of its other divisions, a move that infuriated many consumers who were not notified of the changes.[85] More recently, corporate executives have been asked to explain high executive compensation packages, positions on hostile takeover attempts, plant closings, golden parachutes, and environmental issues.

The motives for bringing up these issues at annual meetings are similar to those for filing shareholder resolutions: to put management on the spot and publicly demand some explanation or corrective action. Activism at annual meetings is one of the few methods shareholders have of demanding explanations and obtaining accountability from top management.

Defending a company at annual meetings has become such an important task of top management that several consulting firms now publish annual booklets of shareholder questions that are likely to be asked. These booklets are intended to help management and directors anticipate and plan for what they might be quizzed on at annual meetings.

The SEC proposed amendments to its rules on shareholder proposals in 1997. Some of these amendments would have made it more difficult for shareholders to resubmit proposals after they had been voted down. A 340-group coalition, including the Episcopal Church, the Methodist Church Pension Fund, the National Association for the Advancement of Colored People (NAACP), the Sierra Club, and the AFL-CIO, converged on Washington to protest the proposal. A study by the Social Investment Forum showed that 80 percent of past resolutions would have been barred after their third year if the original proposals had been accepted. Bowing to "considerable public controversy," the SEC took only one action—reversing the "Cracker Barrel" decision. In 1991, when Cracker Barrel Old Country Store decided to fire, and no longer hire, gay employees, shareholders sought to have that policy overturned. The SEC ruled that hiring falls under the category of **ordinary business decisions** and thus was entirely the province of corporate directors and officers. In 1998, the SEC reversed that ruling and returned to its earlier policy of deciding on a case-by-case basis.[86]

Filing of Shareholder Lawsuits.   We earlier made reference to the **shareholder lawsuit** in the Trans Union case. Shareholders sued the board of directors for approving a buy-out offer that the shareholders argued should have had a higher price tag. Their suit charged that the directors had been negligent in failing to secure a third-party opinion from experienced investment bankers. The case went to trial and resulted in a $23.5 million judgment against the directors.[87] The Trans Union case may have been one of the largest successful shareholder suits, but it was dwarfed by the Cendant suit, which resulted in a $2.83 billion class action settlement.[88] A 2003 study from Stanford University found that the number of securities class action suits filed in 2002 increased by 31 percent over the number of such suits in 2001, from 171 to 224 filings.[89] As these suits proliferate, many wonder whose interests are really being served. Quite often, the shareholders' attorneys walk away with more money than the protesting shareholders receive.

Shareholder suits are easy to file but difficult to defend. One study estimated that 70 percent of the suits are settled out of court. Therefore, charges of corporate wrongdoing are seldom resolved. Quite often, these lawsuits are seen as legitimate protests by shareholders against management actions, and the threat of litigation does deter corporate misbehavior. From the company's viewpoint, however, such lawsuits are an expensive nuisance. Some experts argue that management's quick willingness to settle before going to trial invites more suits. In spite of this, companies give in because the downside risks of trials and adverse publicity are too great.[90]

In 1995, Congress sought to stem the growing tide of shareholder lawsuits by passing the **Private Securities Litigation Reform Act of 1995**. The law made it more difficult for companies to bring class action lawsuits to federal court.[91] However, rather than stemming the tide of lawsuits, the act simply prompted shareholders to change their venue. Suits filed in federal court decreased, while suits filed in state courts increased. The Securities Litigation Uniform Standards Act of 1998 was designed to plug that loophole. It says that "Any covered class action brought into any state courts shall be removable to the federal district courts for the district in which the action is pending."[92]

Company Initiatives.

The need for companies to reestablish a relationship with their owners/stakeholders is somewhat akin to parents having to reestablish relations with their children once the children have grown up. Over the years, the evidence suggests that corporate managements have neglected their owners rather than making them a genuine part of the family. As share ownership has dispersed, there are several legitimate reasons why this separation has taken place. But there is also evidence that management groups have been too preoccupied with their own self-interests. In either case, corporations are beginning to realize that they have a responsibility to their shareholders that cannot be further neglected. Owners are demanding accountability, and it appears that they will be tenacious until they get it.

Public corporations have obligations to their shareholders and to potential shareholders. **Full disclosure** (also known as **transparency**) is one of these responsibilities. Disclosure should be made at regular and frequent intervals and should contain information that might affect the investment decisions of shareholders. This information might include the nature and activities of the business, financial and policy matters, tender offers, and special problems and opportunities in the near future and in the longer term.[93] Of paramount importance are the interests of the investing public, not the interests of the incumbent management team. Board members should avoid conflicts between personal interests and the interests of shareholders. Company executives and directors have an obligation to avoid taking personal advantage of information that is not disclosed to the investing public and to avoid any personal use of corporation assets and influence.

With regard to corporate takeovers, fair treatment of shareholders necessitates special safeguards, including (1) candor in public statements on the offer made, (2) full disclosure of all information, (3) absence of undue pressure, and (4) sufficient time for shareholders to make considered decisions. A constructive purpose, not a predatory one, should be served by takeovers. The firm's major stakeholders are its owners. They are interdependent with other stakeholders, and, therefore, management should carry out its obligations to other constituency groups within the context of shareholder concern.[94] Successful shareholder programs do exist. Berkshire Hathaway Inc. is a company known for attending to its shareholders, and CEO Warren Buffett is praised by shareholders in return.[95] One indication of Berkshire Hathaway's relationship with shareholders is the annual meeting. Buffett calls the annual shareholders' meeting "Woodstock weekend for capitalists." It's not unusual for shareholders to attend a minor league baseball game decked out in their forest green Berkshire Hathaway t-shirts and caps. Many wait in line to have a picture taken with Buffett or get his autograph.[96]

Shareholder programs are not a substitute for keeping shareholders foremost in the minds of managements and boards when economic decisions are being made. However, they do demonstrate an attempt by managements to give serious consideration to corporate/shareholder relations. These types of programs help the corporate governance problem because they show the shareholders that they matter and that they are important to the firm.

■ SUMMARY

Recent events in corporate America have served to underscore the importance of good corporate governance. Although they are the firms' owners, shareholders are too diffuse and removed from the corporation to effectively monitor the activities of the corporation and its managers. For that reason, they must rely on the board to represent their interests by advising and monitoring corporate management. To protect their interests and ascertain that corporate governance is effective, shareholders have grouped together to regain their ownership power. Institutional shareholders own sufficient blocks of stock to gain the ear of the firm's boards and executives. They have been using this access to effect change.

In many ways, corporate governance has improved. CEOs no longer enjoy job security when firm performance suffers. Corporations can no longer release false or misleading reports without threat of consequences. The growth in CEO pay has tapered off, although it remains at extremely high levels. These improvements are worthy of note, but they are insufficient to protect the legitimacy of business.

To remain legitimate, corporations must be governed according to the intended and legal pattern. Governance debacles such as Enron threaten not only the legitimacy of the company in question, but also of business as a whole. Steps are being taken to lessen the likelihood of another Enron occurring, but continual vigilance must be maintained if corporate governance is to fully realize its promise and its purpose, that of representing shareholder interests and being responsive to the needs of the many individuals and groups who have a stake in the firm.

■ KEY TERMS

Accounting Reform and Investor Protection Act of 2002 (page 617)
agency problems (page 612)
audit committee (page 619)

board of directors (page 610)
charter (page 609)
compensation committee (page 620)
corporate governance (page 609)

▪ DISCUSSION QUESTIONS

1. Explain the evolution of corporate governance. What problems developed? What are the current trends?

2. What are the major criticisms of boards of directors? Which single criticism do you find to be the most important? Why?

3. Explain how governance failures such as Enron could happen. How might they be avoided?

4. Outline the major suggestions that have been set forth for improving corporate governance. In your opinion, which suggestions are most important? Why?

5. In what ways have companies taken the initiative in becoming more responsive to owners/stakeholders? Where would you like to see more improvement? Discuss.

▪ RECOMMENDED CASES

Many of the end-of-text cases may be related to Chapter 19. You may wish to consider studying the following cases with Chapter 19.

Case 5. "MARTHA STEWART: FREE TRADING OR INSIDER TRADING?" This case is about Martha Stewart, who was chairman and CEO of the company she founded until an indictment for lying to investigators about possible insider trading brought about her resignation. In addition to the issue of insider trading, this case explores the impact of a company's highly visible figurehead running afoul of the law. Was Martha Stewart a scapegoat, as many believe, or did she receive just punishment for crimes she committed?

Case 41. "DICK GRASSO AND THE NYSE: IS IT A CRIME TO BE PAID WELL?" This case explores the issue of CEO compensation at the New York Stock Exchange (NYSE). When the details of NYSE chairman Dick Grasso's compensation package were announced, a public uproar ensued. In the 4-year contract approved by NYSE directors, Grasso would receive a lump sum of $139.5 million

in deferred compensation and pension benefits. He was subsequently fired on charges that he manipulated the board into providing such high compensation. Is the level of compensation appropriate? If not, who is responsible for the excess? Is it the board or is it Grasso?

Case 42. "SOCIAL REFORM OR SELF-INTEREST?" This case chronicles the efforts of Frank Blethen, publisher of the family-owned *Seattle Times*, to eliminate the federal inheritance tax. Although it is not unusual for newspapers to support various causes, the support usually remains on the editorial page. Critics fault Blethen's campaign for including ads in the news pages and on a Web site. They also charge Blethen with pursuing self-interest due to the windfall that repeal would provide him and for having slanted coverage of the issues. What are the rights of a newspaper publisher in the pages of a newspaper that he or she owns? Are there limits to the types of causes that can be promoted or to the ways in which those causes can be promoted?

■ WEB RESOURCES

The URLs listed here are current at the time of publication. Should any of these Web sites change, please search under the company's or organization's name for an updated address.

Business Roundtable
  http://www.brt.org

Citizen Works
  http://www.citizenworks.org

Corporate Governance
  http://www.corpgov.net

The Economist
  http://www.economist.com

Investor Responsibility Research Center
  http://www.irrc.org

Interfaith Center on Corporate Responsibility
  http://www.iccr.org

Living Wage
  http://www.livingwagecampaign.org

Martha Stewart
  http://www.marthatalks.com

OMB Watch (citizen's group)
  http://www.ombwatch.org

Pay Watch
  http://www.aflcio.org/paywatch

Securities and Exchange Commission
  http://www.sec.gov

United for a Fair Economy
  http://www.ufenet.org

InfoTrac® College Edition   http://www.infotrac-college.com

Additional information on the topics discussed in the chapter can be researched by logging onto the InfoTrac College Edition Web site.

■ ENDNOTES

1. "Special Report: Corporate America's Woes, Continued—Enron: One Year On," *The Economist* (November 30, 2002).
2. *Ibid.*
3. James Toedtman, "Lawmakers Commemorate One-Year Anniversary of Corporate Governance Legislation," *Knight Ridder Tribune Business News* (July 31, 2003), 1.
4. Cited in Edwin M. Epstein and Dow Votaw (eds.) *Rationality, Legitimacy, Responsibility: Search for New Directions in Business and Society* (Santa Monica, CA: Goodyear Publishing Co., 1978), 72.
5. *Ibid.*, 73.
6. *Ibid.*
7. *Ibid.*
8. *Ibid.*
9. William R. Dill (ed.), *Running the American Corporation* (Englewood Cliffs, NJ: Prentice Hall, 1978), 11.
10. *Ibid.*
11. *Ibid.*
12. "Special Report: Corporate America's Woes, Continued—Enron: One Year On," *The Economist* (November 30, 2002).
13. Carl Icahn, "What Ails Corporate America—And What Should Be Done," *Business Week* (October 17, 1986), 101.

14. John A. Byrne, "The Best and Worst Boards," *Business Week* (January 24, 2000), 142.
15. "What Directors Think Study 2003," Corporate Board Member, http://www.boardmember.com.
16. "Special Report: Corporate America's Woes, Continued—Enron: One Year On," *The Economist* (November 30, 2002).
17. *Ibid.*
18. Murray L. Weidenbaum, *Strengthening the Corporate Board: A Constructive Response to Hostile Takeovers* (St. Louis: Washington University, Center for the Study of American Business, September 1985), 4–5.
19. Linda Himelstein, "Boardrooms: The Ties That Blind," *Business Week* (May 2, 1994), 112–114.
20. Carol J. Loomis, "This Stuff Is Wrong," *Fortune* (June 25, 2001), 72–84.
21. John A. Byrne, "Executive Pay: Deliver—Or Else," *Business Week* (March 27, 1995), 36–38.
22. Nikos Vafeas and Zaharoulla Afxentiou, "The Association Between the SEC's 1992 Compensation Disclosure Rule and Executive Compensation Policy Changes," *Journal of Accounting and Public Policy* (Spring 1998), 27–54.
23. Ann Buchholtz, Michael Young, and Gary Powell, "Are Board Members Pawns or Watchdogs? The Link Between

CEO Pay and Firm Performance," *Group and Organization Management* (March 1998), 6–26.

24. Sarah Anderson, John Cavanaugh, Chris Hartman, and Scott Klinger, "Executive Excess 2003: CEOs Win, Workers and Taxpayers Lose" (Washington, DC: Institute for Policy Studies and United for a Fair Economy). http://www.faireconomy.org/press/2003/EE2003_pr.html

25. Sarah Anderson and John Cavanaugh, "Executive Excess 2001" (Washington, DC: Institute for Policy Studies and United for a Fair Economy), http://www.ips-dc.org/projects/execexcess2001.htm.

26. Sarah Anderson, John Cavanaugh, Chris Hartman and Scott Klinger, "Executive Excess 2003: CEOs Win, Workers and Taxpayers Lose" (Washington, DC: Institute for Policy Studies and United for a Fair Economy). http://www.faireconomy.org/press/2003/EE2003_pr.html

27. *Ibid.*

28. *Ibid.*

29. *Ibid.*

30. John J. Sweeney, "Commentary: The Foxes Are Still Guarding the Henhouse," *Los Angeles Times* (September 19, 2003), B13.

31. *Ibid.*

32. *Ibid.*

33. Geoffrey Colvin, "Is the Board Too Cushy?" *Director* (February 1997), 64–65.

34. "The Fading Appeal of the Boardroom," *The Economist* (February 10, 2001), 67.

35. "What Directors Think Study 2003," Corporate Board Member, http://www.boardmember.com.

36. *Ibid.*

37. Verne Kopytoff, "Yahoo's Not an Attractive Target for a Takeover, Analysts Say," *San Francisco Chronicle* (March 3, 2001), D1.

38. Andrew Countryman, "More Resolutions Appear Asking U.S. Firms to Remove Anti-Takeover Policies," *Knight Ridder TribuneBusiness News* (August 4, 2003), 1.

39. Philip L. Cochran and Steven L. Wartick, "Golden Parachutes: Good for Management and Society?" in S. Prakash Sethi and Cecilia M. Falbe (eds.) *Business and Society: Dimensions of Conflict and Cooperation* (Lexington, MA: Lexington Books, 1987), 321.

40. Ann K. Buchholtz and Barbara A. Ribbens, "Role of Chief Executive Officers in Takeover Resistance: Effects of CEO Incentives and Individual Characteristics," *Academy of Management Journal* (June 1994), 554–579.

41. Cochran and Wartick, 325–326.

42. George Russell, "The Fall of a Wall Street Superstar," *Time* (November 24, 1986), 71.

43. *Ibid.*

44. Donald Baer, "Getting Even with Ivan and Company," *U.S. News & World Report* (March 2, 1987), 46.

45. Anthony Bianco and Gary Weiss, "Suddenly the Fish Get Bigger," *Business Week* (March 2, 1987), 29–30.

46. "New Arrests on Wall Street: Who's Next in the Insider Trading Scandal?" *Newsweek* (February 23, 1987), 48–50.

47. James B. Stewart, "Scenes from a Scandal: The Secret World of Michael Milkin and Ivan Boesky," *The Wall Street Journal* (October 2, 1991), B1.

48. Christopher H. Schmitt, "The SEC Lifts the Curtain on Company Info," *Business Week* (August 11, 2000).

49. "A Landmark Ruling That Puts Board Members in Peril," *Business Week* (March 18, 1985), 56–57.

50. Laurie Baum and John A. Byrne, "The Job Nobody Wants: Outside Directors Find That the Risks and Hassles Just Aren't Worth It," *Business Week* (September 8, 1986), 57.

51. Paul E. Fiorella, "Why Comply? Directors Face Heightened Personal Liability After Caremark," *Business Horizons* (July/August 1998), 49–52.

52. Michael Schlesinger, "2002 Sarbanes–Oxley Act," *Business Entities* (November/December 2002), 42–49.

53. *Ibid.*

54. Jonathon A. Segal, "The Joy of Uncooking," *HR Magazine* (November 2002), 52–57.

55. "Leaders: Sox It to Them; American Corporate Reform," *The Economist* (August 2, 2003), 14.

56. Tom McGhee, "Public Firms Turn Private to Avoid SEC Regulations," *Knight Ridder Tribune Business News* (October 26, 2003) 1.

57. *Ibid.*

58. "The Fading Appeal of the Boardroom," *The Economist* (February 10, 2001), 67.

59. Toddi Gutner, "Wanted: More Diverse Directors," *Business Week* (April 30, 2001), 134.

60. "Board Diversity Increases," *Association Management* (January 2000), 25.

61. Paul Coombes and Mark Watson, "Three Surveys on Corporate Governance," McKinsey Quarterly (No. 4, 2000), cited in "The Fading Appeal of the Boardroom," *The Economist* (February 10, 2001), 67–69.

62. "The Fading Appeal of the Boardroom," *The Economist* (February 10, 2001), 67.

63. *Ibid.*

64. Gutner, 134.

65. Joann S. Lublin and Elizabeth MacDonald, "Scandals Signal Laxity of Audit Panels," *The Wall Street Journal* (July 17, 1998), B1.

66. "What Directors Think Study 2003," Corporate Board Member, http://www.boardmember.com.

67. Charles A. Anderson and Robert N. Anthony, *The New Corporate Directors: Insights for Board Members and Executives* (New York: John Wiley & Sons, 1986), 141.

68. Arjay Miller, "A Director's Questions," *The Wall Street Journal* (August 18, 1980), 10.

69. Donald E. Schwartz, "Corporate Governance," in Thornton Bradshaw and David Vogel (eds.) *Corporations and Their Critics* (New York: McGraw-Hill, 1981), 227–228.

70. Anthony Bianco and Louis Lavelle, "The CEO Trap," *Business Week* (December 11, 2000), 86–92.

71. Jeffrey D. Sonnenfeld, "The CEO Blues," *The Wall Street Journal* (December 9, 2003), A20.

72. David R. Francis and Seth Stern, "Era of Shaky Job Security for the CEO," *Christian Science Monitor* (December 4, 2003), Web edition. http://www.christiansciencemonitor.com/2003/1204/p01s01-usec.html?related

73. *Ibid.*

74. Bruce Nussbaum and Judith Dobrzynski, "The Battle for Corporate Control," *Business Week* (May 18, 1987), 102–109

75. Andy Dworkin, "Critic Aims to Change Nike from Within," *The Oregonian* (March 9, 2001).

76. Edward D. Murphy, "Nike Holds Annual Meeting in Portland, Maine," *Knight Ridder Tribune Business News* (September 19, 2002), 1.

77. Lauren Tainer, *The Origins of Shareholder Activism* (Washington, DC: Investor Responsibility Research Center, July 1983), 2.

78. *Ibid.*, 1.

79. *Ibid.*, 12–22.

80. "Religious Activists Raise Cain with Corporations," Chicago Tribune (June 7, 1998), *Business Section*, 8.

81. Max W. Berger, John P. Coffey, and Gerald H. Silk, "Institutional Investors as Lead Plaintiffs: Is There a New and Changing Landscape?" *St. John's Law Review* (Winter 2001), 31–48.

82. "Analysts Seize Control of Corporate Purse Strings over the Internet," *PR News* (June 26, 2000). Insights were excerpted from "2000 Best Practices in Corporate Communications" prepared by the Public Affairs Group/Best Practices in Corporate Communications, http://www.bpincc.com.

83. Dale Kurschner, "Tobacco Taboo: How Affirmative Action Are You?" *Business Ethics* (March/April 1995), 14–15. Also see Robert C. Pozen, "Institutional Investors: The Reluctant Activists," *Harvard Business Review* (January–February 1994), 140–149.

84. John A. Byrne, "How Much Should It Take to Keep the Board on Board?" *Business Week* (April 17, 1995), 41.

85. Leonard Apcar and Terry Brown, "GM Reputation Is Defended by Chairman Under Barrage of Shareholder Questions," *The Wall Street Journal* (May 23, 1977), 17.

86. "Shareholders and Corporate Hiring," *The New York Times* (May 23, 1998), A14. Information is also available on the SEC Web site at http://www.sec.gov and the Social Investment Forum Web site http://www.socialinvest.org.

87. Thomas J. Neff, "Liability Panic in the Board Room," *The Wall Street Journal* (November 10, 1986), 22.

88. "Shareholders Force Cendant to Change Corporate Governance by Court Order," *Investor Relations Business* (January 24, 2000), 1.

89. "Thirty-One Percent More Securities Class Action Suits Filed in 2002 Than in 2001," *Securities Class Action Clearinghouse* (March 13, 2003), Press Release.

90. Richard B. Schmitt, "Attorneys Are Often Big Winners When Shareholders Sue Companies," *The Wall Street Journal* (June 12, 1986), 31.

91. Steven M. Schatz and Douglas J. Clark, "Securities Litigation," *International Financial Law Review* (June 1998), 27.

92. "Securities Litigation Reform Revisited," *Journal of Accountancy* (January 1999), 20–21.

93. "The Responsibility of a Corporation to Its Shareholders," *Criteria for Decision Making* (C.W. Post Center, Long Island University, 1979), 14.

94. *Ibid.*, 14–15.

95. Mel Duvall and Kim S. Nash, "Auditing an Oracle: Shareholders Nearly Deify Warren Buffett for the Way He Manages His Diverse Holding Company, Bershire Hathaway of Omaha," *Baseline* (August 1, 2003) 30.

96. Amy Kover, "Warren Buffett: Revivalist," *Fortune* (May 29, 2000), 58–60.

■ CASES

CASE ANALYSIS GUIDELINES

The guidelines presented below have been designed to help the student analyze the cases. They are not intended to be a rigid format. Each question is intended to bring out information that will be helpful in analyzing and resolving the case. Each case is different, and some parts of the guidelines may not apply in every case. Also, the student should be attentive to the questions for discussion at the end of each case. These questions should be answered in any complete case analysis. The heart of any case analysis is the recommendations that are made. The Issue/Problem Identification and Analysis/Evaluation steps should be focused on generating and defending the most effective set of recommendations possible. In all stages of the case analysis, the stakeholder, ethics and CSR concepts presented in the text should be used. The guidelines are presented in three stages:

ISSUE/PROBLEM IDENTIFICATION

1. **Facts and Assumptions.** What are the *central facts* of the case and the *assumptions* you are making on the basis of these facts?
2. **Major Overriding Issues/Problems.** What are the *major overriding issues* in this case? (What major questions/issues does this case address that merit(s) their/its study in this course and in connection with the chapter/material you are now covering?)
3. **Sub-issues and Related Issues.** What *sub-issues* or *related issues* are present in the case that merit consideration, discussion, and action?

ANALYSIS/EVALUATION

4. **Stakeholder Analysis.** Who are the *stakeholders* in this case, and what are their stakes? (Create a stakeholder map to depict relationships.) What *challenges/threats/opportunities* are posed by these stakeholders? What stakeholder characteristics are at work (legitimacy, power, urgency)?
5. **CSR Analysis.** What Corporate Social Responsibilities (CSR) *economic/legal/ethical/philanthropic* does the company have, and what exactly are the nature and extent of these responsibilities to the various stakeholders?
6. **Evaluations.** If the case involves a company's or manager's actions, evaluate what the company or manager did or did not do correctly in handling the issue affecting it. How should actions have been handled?

RECOMMENDATIONS

7. **Recommendations and Implementation.** What *recommendations* would you make in this case? If a company's or a manager's strategies or actions are involved, should they have acted the way they did? What actions *should* they have taken? What actions should the company or manager take now, and why? Be specific and include a discussion of alternatives (*short-term* and *long-term*). Identify and discuss any important *implementation considerations*.

WAL-MART: THE MAIN STREET MERCHANT OF DOOM

The small town was in need of a hired gun. The people were tired of dealing with the local price-fixing merchant scum who ran the town like a company store. This low-life bunch held the people of the town in a death grip and were perceived by the townspeople to overcharge on every purchase. In spite of what appeared to be a case of collusion, the law was powerless to do anything. What competition there was had been effectively eliminated.

Suddenly, coming over the rise and wearing white, their hired man came riding. The women and children buzzed with excitement. The men were happy. Although his methods of getting the job done turned some people's stomachs, the local watering hole buzzed with tales of how this hired gun would change their world for the better, how someday soon they would have the benefits long afforded the big city. But, others asked, at what price?

THE MODERN VERSION OF THE "HIRED GUN"

In his final days, the man appeared to be somewhat too frail to handle the enormous job. Yet, the courage and self-confidence that he instilled in his associates radiated a belief in low prices and good value for all to see. As his associates rode into town, that radiance put to rest the people's fears that things had changed. Sam's spirit, the Wal-Mart Way, had come to town.

Sam Walton, founder, owner, and mastermind of Wal-Mart, passed away on April 5, 1992, leaving behind his spirit to ride herd on the colossal Wal-Mart organization. To the consumer in the small community, his store, Wal-Mart, was seen as a friend. On the flip side, many a small-town merchant had been the victim of Sam's blazing merchandising tactics. So what is Wal-Mart to the communities it serves? Is Wal-Mart the consumer's best friend, the purveyor of the free-enterprise system, the "Mother of All Discount Stores," or, conversely, is it really "The Main Street Merchant of Doom"?

THE MAN NAMED SAM

Samuel Moore Walton was born March 29, 1918, near Kingfisher, Kansas. His father was a salesman in the insurance, real estate, and mortgage businesses. The family moved often. Sam was a strong, lean boy who learned to work hard in order to help the family. He attended the University of Missouri starting in the fall of 1936 and graduated with a degree in busi-

ness administration. During his time there, he was a member of the Beta Theta Phi fraternity, was president of the senior class, played various sports, and taught what was believed to be the largest Sunday school class in the world, numbering over 1,200 Missouri students.[1]

At age 22, Sam joined J. C. Penney. One of his first tasks was to memorize and practice the "Penney Idea." Adopted in 1913, this credo exhorts the associate to serve the public; not to demand all the profit the traffic will bear; to pack the customer's dollar full of value, quality, and satisfaction; to continue to be trained; to reward men and women in the organization through participation in what the business produces; and to test every policy, method, and act against the question: "Does it square with what is right and just?"[2]

Sam's First Store. In 1962, at age 44, Sam Walton opened his first Wal-Mart store. He took all the money and expertise he could gather and applied the J. C. Penney Idea to Middle America. Sam first targeted small, underserved rural towns with populations of no more than 10,000 people. The people responded, and Wal-Mart soon developed a core of loyal customers who loved the fast, friendly service coupled with consistently low prices. Later, Sam expanded his company into the large cities, often with numerous Wal-Marts spread throughout every part of the city.

THE STORE THAT SAM BUILT

By 1981, Wal-Mart's rapid growth was evident to all and especially disturbing to Sears, J. C. Penney, Target, and Kmart, because Wal-Mart had become America's largest retailer. The most telling figures are those of overhead expenses and sales per employee. The overhead expenses of Sears and Kmart ran 29 and 23 percent of sales, respectively, whereas Wal-Mart's overhead expenses ran 16 percent of sales. At this time, the average Sears employee generated $85,000 in sales per year, whereas the average Wal-Mart employee generated $95,000.[3]

By 2001, Wal-Mart Stores, Inc., had become the world's largest retailer with $191 billion in sales. The company employed 1 million associates worldwide through nearly 3,500 facilities in the United States and more than 1,000 stores throughout nine other countries. Wal-Mart claimed that more than 100 million customers per week visited Wal-Mart stores. The company had four major retail divisions—Wal-Mart Supercenters, Discount Stores, Neighborhood Markets, and Sam's Club warehouses. As it entered the 2000s, Wal-Mart had been named "Retailer of the Century" by *Discount Store News*, made *Fortune* magazine's lists

This case, originally prepared by William T. Rupp, Robert Morris University, was revised and updated by Archie B. Carroll, University of Georgia, in 2004.

of the "Most Admired Companies in America" and the "100 Best Companies to Work For," and was ranked on *Financial Times'* "Most Respected in the World" list.[4] By 2004, Wal-Mart's sales had grown to $256.3 billion and it had 3,200 nationwide facilities. Wal-Mart also had 1.2 million workers in the U.S.[5]

Sam the motivational genius. He promoted the associate—the hourly employee—to a new level of participation within the organization. He offered profit sharing, incentive bonuses, and stock options in an effort to have his Wal-Mart associates share in the wealth. Sam, as the head cheerleader, saw his job as the chief proponent of the "Wal-Mart Way." The Wal-Mart Way reflected Sam's idea of the essential Wal-Mart culture that was needed for success. Sam felt that when a customer entered Wal-Mart in any part of the country, he or she should feel at home. Examples of the culture included "exceeding customer expectations" and "helping people make a difference." He was a proponent of the "Ten-Foot Rule," which meant that if a customer came within 10 feet of an associate, the associate would look the customer in the eye, greet him or her, and ask if the customer needed help.[6]

As he was growing the business, Sam, the courageous, borrowed and borrowed, sometimes just to pay other creditors. Arkansas banks that at one time had turned him down later competed with banks that Sam himself owned. Sam, the CEO, hired the best managers he could find. He let them talk him into buying an extensive computer network system. This network corporate satellite system enabled Sam to use round-the-clock inventory control and credit card sales control and provided him with information on total sales of which products where and when. This computer control center was about the size of a football field and used a Hughes satellite for uplinking and downlinking to each store.

Sam the Mortal. In 1992, Sam, the mortal, died of incurable bone cancer. At age 73, Sam Walton said that if he had to do it over again he would not change a thing. He said, "This is still the most important thing I do, going around to the stores, and I'd rather do it than anything I know of. I know I'm helping our folks when I get out to the stores. I learn a lot about who's doing good things in the office, and I also see things that need fixing, and I help fix them. Any good management person in retail has got to do what I do in order to keep his finger on what's going on. You've got to have the right chemistry and the right attitude on the part of the folks who deal with the customers."[7]

Sam, the innovator, developed the "store within a store" concept by training people to be merchants, not just employees. These "store within a store" managers have all the numbers for their departments—breakdowns of how they are doing in relation to the store and the company as a whole. This concept provides big opportunities by providing big responsibilities. Sam set the goal of visiting every Wal-Mart store every year. To do this, he flew his own twin-prop Cessna and visited up to five or six stores per day. Two early social responsibility innovations were Wal-Mart's "Buy American" plan and its "Environmental Awareness" campaign.

SAM AND SOCIAL AWARENESS: THE "BUY AMERICAN" PLAN

Wal-Mart's "Buy American" program was a result of a 1984 telephone conversation with then-Arkansas Governor Bill Clinton. The program was a response to Sam's own enlightenment: He learned that Wal-Mart was adding to the loss of American jobs by buying cheaper foreign goods. Everything Sam stood for came out of his heartfelt obligation to supply the customer with low-cost quality goods, but running counter to this inner driving force was the realization that he was responsible for the loss of American jobs. This contradiction and dilemma drove him to find a solution. His conversation with Governor Clinton inspired Sam to do something about the problem.

The goal of the Buy American plan was to support American-based manufacturers by doing business with them so that they would not go out of business. His primary method for doing this was to give the manufacturers large orders or contracts so that they could stay in business.[8]

Sam wanted other manufacturers to join him in the Buy American plan. He wrote to 3,000 American manufacturers and solicited them to sell to Wal-Mart items that Wal-Mart was currently buying from overseas suppliers. Wal-Mart's competitors did not meet the challenge to "Buy American." Kmart stated that it would rather buy American-made goods but that it was looking for the best deal for the customer. Target said it was for free trade and that as the customer's representative it just wanted the best deal for the customer. Wall Street analysts responded positively, saying that Wal-Mart's plan was possibly the beginning of a change of direction for American retailers.[9]

In February 1986, about 12 months after the Buy American plan had begun, Sam held a press conference. He showed off all the merchandise Wal-Mart was now buying domestically. He estimated that Wal-Mart's Buy American plan had restored 4,538 jobs to the American economy and its people.[10] The Buy American plan was one of Wal-Mart's early efforts at corporate social responsibility.

The Buy American Plan morphed over the years into the well-publicized "Made in the U.S.A." campaign in which Wal-Mart called customers' attention to these local products with special labels. At some point in time, Wal-Mart eventually abandoned this emphasis and became one of the largest purchasers of products made overseas. In fact, the company in time became the country's largest purchaser of Chinese goods in any industry. Some say that by taking its orders abroad, Wal-Mart forced many U. S. manufacturers out of business.[11]

SAM AND SOCIAL CONCERNS: THE "ENVIRONMENTAL AWARENESS" CAMPAIGN

As awareness of the environment was on the rise, Sam looked for a way to involve Wal-Mart in the environmental movement. In August 1989, an ad in *The Wall Street Journal* proclaimed

Wal-Mart's "commitment to our land, air and water." Sam envisioned Wal-Mart as a leader among American companies in the struggle to clean up the environment. John Lowne, corporate vice president and division manager for Reynolds Metals Company, stated, "Wal-Mart's move will indeed set a precedent for the entire retail industry. I'm surprised it has taken other retailers this long to follow suit."[12]

Wal-Mart wanted to use its tremendous buying power to aid in the implementation of the campaign. Wal-Mart sent a booklet to manufacturers stating the following:

> At Wal-Mart we're committed to help improve our environment. Our customers are concerned about the quality of our land, air and water, and want the opportunity to do something positive. We believe it is our responsibility to step up to their challenge.[13]

In the stores, shelf tags made from 100 percent recycled paper informed customers as to the environmental friendliness of the highlighted product. As a result of these shelf tags and Wal-Mart's advertising, customer awareness has increased, and some environmentally safe product manufacturers are reaping the rewards of increased Wal-Mart orders. Linda Downs, administrative manager of Duraflame/California, said that Duraflame logs had been proven to burn cleaner than wood and that Wal-Mart's campaign had helped Duraflame to deliver this message. She went on to say, "Wal-Mart has helped drive home the message we have been trying to promote for years. They have really given us great publicity."[14]

In the *Wal-Mart Associates Handbook*, new associates were indoctrinated with the "Wal-Mart spirit." The section on the environment said:

> As a responsible member of the community, Wal-Mart's commitments go beyond simply selling merchandise. With environmental concerns mounting world-wide, Wal-Mart has taken action. Home office and store associates are taking decisive steps to help the environment by making community recycling bins available on our facility parking lots. Other action plans include "Adopt-a-Highway" and "Adopt-a-Beach" programs, tree planting and community clean up and beautification. By forming a partnership with our associates, our manufacturers and our customers, we're convinced we can make the world a better place to live.[15, 16]

SAM AND THE MERCHANTS OF MAIN STREET

Not everyone has been excited to see Sam and his mechanized Wal-Mart army arrive and succeed. Small merchants across America shudder when the winds of the "Wal-Mart Way" begin to blow. Kennedy Smith of the National Main Street Center in Washington, DC, says, "The first thing towns usually do is panic." Once Wal-Mart comes to town, Smith says, "Downtowns will never again be the providers of basic consumer goods and services they once were."[17]

Steamboat Springs. Some towns learned to "just say 'no'" to Wal-Mart's overtures. Steamboat Springs, Colorado, is one such city. Colorado newspapers called it the "Shootout at Steamboat Springs." Wal-Mart was denied permission to build on a 9-acre parcel along U.S. Route 40. Owners of upscale shops and condos were very concerned with the image of their resort community, and Wal-Mart, with its low-cost reputation, just did not fit. The shootout lasted for 2 years, and finally Wal-Mart filed a damage suit against the city. Countersuits followed. A petition was circulated to hold a referendum on the matter. This was the shot that made Wal-Mart blink and back down. Just before the vote, Don Shinkle, corporate affairs vice president, said, "A vote would not be good for Steamboat Springs, and it would not be good for Wal-Mart. I truly believe Wal-Mart is a kinder, gentler company, and, while we have the votes to win, an election would only split the town more."[18]

Iowa City. In Iowa City, Iowa (population 50,000+), Wal-Mart was planning an 87,000-square-foot store on the outskirts of town. A group of citizens gathered enough signatures during a petition drive to put a referendum on the ballot to block Wal-Mart and the city council from building the new store (the city council had approved the rezoning of the land Wal-Mart wanted). Jim Clayton, a downtown merchant, said, "Wal-Mart is a freight train going full steam in the opposite direction of this town's philosophy." If businesses wind up going down, Clayton says, "you lose their involvement in the community, involvement I promise you won't get with some assistant manager over at Wal-Mart."[19] Wal-Mart spokesperson Brenda Lockhart commented that downtown merchants can only benefit from the increase in customer traffic provided "they offer superior service and aren't gouging their customers."[20] Efforts to stop Wal-Mart and the Iowa City Council were not successful. Wal-Mart opened its Iowa City store on November 5, 1991.

Pawhuska, Oklahoma. Meanwhile, in Pawhuska, Oklahoma, as a result of Wal-Mart's entry in 1983 and other local factors, the local "five-and-dime," J. C. Penney, Western Auto, and a whole block of other stores closed their doors. Four years later, Dave Story, general manager of the local *Pawhuska Daily Journal Capital*, wrote that Wal-Mart was a "billion-dollar parasite" and a "national retail ogre."[21]

Wal-Mart managers have become very active in Pawhuska and surrounding communities since that time. A conversation with the editor of the Pawhuska paper, Jody Smith, and her advertising editor, Suzy Burns, revealed that Wal-Mart sponsored the local rodeo, gave gloves to the local coat drive, and was involved with the local cerebral palsy and multiple sclerosis fund-raisers. On the other hand, Fred Wright, former owner of a TV and record store, said, "Wal-Mart really craters a little town's downtown."[22]

Kinder, Louisiana.

Shift to Kinder, Louisiana (population 2,608). Wal-Mart moved into this small Louisiana town in 1981. On December 31, 1990, the store was closed. During the time Wal-Mart operated in Kinder, one-third of the downtown stores closed. The downtown became three blocks of mostly run-down, red-brick buildings. The closest place to buy shoes or sewing thread was 30 miles away in Oakdale, Louisiana—at another Wal-Mart. Moreover, Kinder lost $5,500 in annual tax revenues, which represented 10 percent of the total revenues for the city.

The tactics Wal-Mart employed during its 10 years in Kinder left a bad taste in the mouths of some small retailers. Soon after Wal-Mart's arrival, a price war broke out between Wal-Mart and the downtown retailers. The retailers told *The Atlanta Journal-Constitution* in November 1990, "Wal-Mart sent employees, wearing name tags and smocks, into their stores to scribble down prices and list merchandise." Lou Pearl, owner of Kinder Jewelry and Gifts, stated that Wal-Mart associates came to her store and noted the type of art supplies she was carrying. Shortly thereafter, Wal-Mart began carrying the same merchandise at discount prices. Sales at Kinder Jewelry and Gifts dropped drastically, and Pearl dropped the merchandise line. Within several weeks, so did Wal-Mart.[23] Perhaps Troy Marcantel, a 29-year-old downtown clothing merchant, said it best: "What really rankled me was that they used people we have known all our lives. I still don't understand how our own people could do that to us."[24]

THE MAIN STREET MERCHANTS ORGANIZE WELCOMING COMMITTEES

By the 1990s, there were dozens of organized groups actively opposing Wal-Mart's expansion.[25] Some of these groups were and still are run by social activists left over from the 1960s and 1970s. Instead of protesting the Vietnam War, nuclear proliferation, or the destruction of the environment, they have turned their efforts to Wal-Mart specifically and capitalism in general. One of these activists, Paul Glover, who was an antiwar organizer, defined Wal-Mart as the epitome of capitalism, which he despises. For Mr. Glover and others, Wal-Mart stands for "everything they dislike about American society—mindless consumerism, paved landscapes, and homogenization of community identity."[26]

Boulder, Colorado.

In Boulder, Colorado, Wal-Mart tried to counter these allegations by proposing a "green" store. Steven Lane, Wal-Mart's real estate manager, said that a "green store" would be built that would be environmentally friendly, with a solar-powered sign out front and everything. His efforts were trumped by Spencer Havlick, an organizer of the first

Earth Day in 1970, suggesting that the entire store be powered by solar energy. Mr. Lane did not respond.[27]

Protest organizers united against the spread of the "Wal-Mart Way" differ from the downtown merchants in that these protesters have no financial stake. Hence, these activists are attacking on a higher plane, a philosophical plane. The accusations ring with a tone of argument that was made by other activists protesting polluting industries (e.g., the coal, nuclear, and chemical industries). These activists accuse Wal-Mart of "strip-mining" towns and communities of their culture and values.

One possible root of this culture clash may be attributed to the unique facets of the internal corporate culture at Wal-Mart's headquarters. This is a place where competition for the reputation as the "cheapest" is practiced. An example is the competition among employees in procuring the cheapest haircut, shoes, or necktie. Wal-Mart is a place where playacting as a backwoods "hick" has been an acceptable behavior within the organization. Consequently, as a result of the internal culture of Wal-Mart and the external environment, some analysts believe that a clash of priorities was inevitable as Wal-Mart moved into larger, more urban settings.

New England Opposition.

Some of the greatest opposition to Wal-Mart's growth came from the New England area. This area holds great promise for Wal-Mart because of the large population and the many underserved towns. These towns are typically underserved in three ways: in variety of product choices, in value, and in convenience. The opposition to Wal-Mart entering these New England markets includes some high-profile names, such as Jerry Greenfield, cofounder of Ben & Jerry's Homemade ice cream, and Arthur Frommer, a well-known travel writer.[28] In addition to New England, other areas, such as resort areas, opposed Wal-Marts because they wanted to insulate their unique cultures from what they considered to be the offensive consumerism that is usually generated by Wal-Mart's presence.

Sprawl-Busters.

Al Norman, a lobbyist and media consultant, has turned opposition to Wal-Mart into a cottage industry. Mr. Norman publishes a monthly newsletter called *Sprawl-Busters Alert*. He has also developed a Web site (http://www.sprawl-busters.com/) that has vast information for citizens who are fighting to prevent Wal-Mart or other "big box" stores from locating in their cities or neighborhoods. Norman achieved national attention in 1993, when he stopped Wal-Mart from locating in his hometown of Greenfield, Massachusetts. Since then, he has appeared on *60 Minutes*, which called him "the guru of the anti-Wal-Mart movement," and has gained widespread media attention. Today Norman continues to serve as a consultant and travels throughout the United States helping dozens of coalitions fight Wal-Mart. Norman has published two books: *Slam-Dunking Wal-Mart: How You Can Stop Superstore Sprawl in Your Hometown* and

The Case Against Wal-Mart. In his books, he lays out the arguments against urban "sprawl."

On the Sprawl-Busters Web page, consumers around the country are given the opportunity to write in the details of their fights with Wal-Mart. Examples in 2004 included Thornton, Colorado; Titusville, Florida; Greenwood, Indiana; and Jackson, Michigan.[29]

Sprawl-Busters is not alone in its focused criticism of Wal-Mart's presence in communities. Another organization, Wal-Mart Watch, has an active Web page (http://www.walmartwatch.com/) that details what it believes to be Wal-Mart's threat to America. On its Web site, the organization details what it considers to be the "Top 10 Wal-Mart Worst Actions."

AGGRESSIVE GROWTH AND CONTINUING CHALLENGES

For its part, Wal-Mart has continued its aggressive diversification and growth pattern. At a retail industry convention in 2004, Lee Scott, Wal-Mart's current CEO, was asked whether Wal-Mart was trying to take over the world. Scott replied, "I don't think so. All we want to do is grow." But, as *The Economist* magazine has asked, "How *big* can it grow?"[30] Sales of Wal-Mart as of fiscal year 2004 were $256 billion and the company is already the world's biggest company by that measure. It is estimated that eight out of ten households shop at Wal-Mart at least once a year, and more than 100 million customers worldwide visit Wal-Mart every week of every year. As a humorous aside, photos circulating over the Internet, supposedly coming from the *Exploration Rover*, show NASA's recent discovery of a Wal-Mart on Mars.[31]

A Nation Unto Itself.
The *New York Times* argued in 2004 that Wal-Mart is becoming a nation unto itself. In fact, the newspaper stated that if Wal-Mart were an independent nation, it would be China's eighth-largest trading partner. In terms of its low prices and impact, some economists say that the company has single-handedly cut inflation by 1 percent in recent years as it has saved customers billions of dollars annually.[32] It is little wonder the newspaper is talking about "The Wal-Martization of America."[33] Figure 1 on page 638 provides some recent statistics about Wal-Mart.

As of 2004, Wal-Mart was continuing to experience mixed reception in cities and towns across America. Many welcomed Wal-Mart with great enthusiasm. But, opposition to Wal-Mart is fierce in some places. The biggest plum Wal-Mart has been seeking recently has been growth in the State of California. Though it already has 133 Discount Stores in California, it desires to open at least 40 Supercenters in California in the next three to five years. Wal-Mart's troubles are best depicted in the opposition met in suburban Los Angeles. Citizens in Inglewood, California, a suburb of LA voted in Spring 2004 to block the company's proposed 60-acre development. The company spent $1 million on a ballot initiative, but hit a wall as the vote went 60% against them.[34] Interestingly, the opposition in California has not focused as much on urban sprawl, traffic congestion, and its impact on local retailers, as much as on Wal-Mart's low wages and employee benefits.[35]

Global Growth.
In addition to domestic growth, Wal-Mart continues its aggressive growth internationally. According to its *2004 Annual Report*, Wal-Mart has 982 Discount Stores, 257 Supercenters, 80 Sam's Clubs, and 36 Neighborhood Markets in international markets worldwide. Mexico and Canada have the most Wal-Mart stores, followed by the United Kingdom, China, Germany, Brazil, and Argentina.[36] In the longer term, the bulk of Wal-Mart's growth will come overseas. Just as Wal-Mart has met resistance in many communities in America, it has also met some resistance and challenges overseas. It has been quite successful in Canada and Mexico, but has struggled elsewhere, often with laws or cultural practices of other countries.

Germany.
Wal-Mart entered Germany in 1997–98 by purchasing two local retail chains, Wertkauf and Interspar. The company has lost money ever since it entered Germany. Challenges have included price controls, which limit below-cost selling, rigid labor laws, and demanding zoning regulations. The company also faced well-entrenched rivals there, such as Metro and discounters such as Aldi and Lidl. According to a study conducted in Germany, Wal-Mart's entry there was "nothing short of a fiasco."[37] In the beginning, Wal-Mart's expatriate managers experienced a massive culture clash. This was not helped by their refusal to learn the German language. Wal-Mart has come to be seen in Germany as an unattractive employer, in part because of low wages and also because of a frugal policy on managers' business expenses.[38]

United Kingdom.
Wal-Mart had a smoother entry into the United Kingdom (UK). Its strategy was the same as in Germany, buying out an established firm. In June 1999, it took over the Asda chain and now has stores and depots all over the U.K. This was a perfect match as the Asda culture was modeled after that of Wal-Mart. Wal-Mart plans 10 to 12 new stores per year in the U.K. where Friends of the Earth has criticized the company for planning to put mezzanine floor extensions in stores around the country. These would be internal second floors suspended above the existing floor, giving added floor space without the requirement of planning department permission. Privately, it is said Wal-Mart plans to become the largest food retailer in the U.K. by 2005.[39]

China.
Difficulties in South Korea have not stopped Wal-Mart's quest in Asia and China. In July 2003 it opened its first store in Beijing, after having already opened some 22 stores elsewhere in China. Wal-Mart, which is already the largest buyer of Chinese products is striving to become the biggest seller to the Chinese as well. Some observers say Wal-Mart is doing well and starting to change the culture. Instead of Chinese shoppers

FIGURE 1

Recent Statistics About Wal-Mart

$256.3 Billion in Net Sales in 2004

$4 billion paid in U. S. federal income taxes in fiscal year 2004

1,478 Domestic Discount Stores
1,471 Domestic Supercenters
538 Domestic SAM'S CLUBS
64 Domestic Neighborhood Markets
1,355 International Stores
2,460 Grand total of all stores Domestic and International[1]

335,000 Shareholders of record

1.2 Million Employees in the U. S.
1 in 23 U. S. employees Wal-Mart employs
1 in 20 retail employees Wal-Mart employs[2]

Feature Story on the cover of *Business Week*: "Is Wal-Mart Too Powerful?"[3]

Feature story on the cover of *The Economist*: "Wal-Mart: Learning to Love It"[4]

25% of the U. S. economy's productivity gains from 1995-1999 came from efficiencies at Wal-Mart

Sales are more than four times those of Home Depot

800,000 new jobs are expected to be created by Wal-Mart in the U. S. over the next five years.[5]

Market Share: Wal-Mart's U. S. Market Share of Selected Products:[6]

Dog food	36%
Disposable diapers	32%
Photo film	30%
Toothpaste	26%
Pain remedies	21%

Percentage of U.S. households that made a Wal-Mart purchase in 2003: 82%[7]

Supermarkets closed since Wal-Mart saturated Oklahoma City: 30[8]

Lawsuits: Just about every other hour of every day of every year, Wal-Mart gets sued. Wal-Mart is considered to be the "most sued" company in America.[9]

"Topic A" in Business Schools—Wal-Mart has displaced perennial powerhouses General Motors and Sears and the company most studied in business schools.[10]

---

[1] *2004 Wal-Mart Annual Report.* Also see http://www.walmartstores/com
[2] "Wal-Mart by the numbers," *USA Today*, June 23, 2004, 1A.
[3] *Business Week*, October 6, 2003.
[4] *The Economist*, April 17–23, 2004.
[5] Bill Saporito, "Can Wal-Mart Get Any Bigger?" *Time*, January 13, 2003, 38–43.
[6] Jerry Useem, "One Nation Under Wal-Mart," *Fortune*, March 3, 2003, 66.
[7] Anthony Bianco and Wendy Zellner, "Is Wal-Mart Too Powerful?" *Business Week*, October 6, 2003, 108.
[8] *Ibid.*
[9] James K. Glassman, "Wal-Mart's Ugly Suit," *Wall Street Journal*, May 30, 2002, A14.
[10] Constance L. Hayes, "The Wal-Mart Way Becomes Topic A in Business Schools," *The New York Times*, July 27, 2003, 10 BU.

---

making a daily trip to the fish market, they are beginning to make a weekly visit to Wal-Mart. Al Norman, Wal-Mart critic, is troubled deeply by Wal-Mart's global expansion. Says he: "Wal-Mart is Americanizing retailing around the world. It is a really undesirable outcome both culturally and economically for a U.S. company to be exercising so much power."[40]

Japan. One of Wal-Mart's most recent battlefields is Japan where it is finding expensive real estate and cramped space a challenge. Its "everyday low price" strategy is befuddling shoppers who are accustomed to poring through newspapers looking for discounts. Employees are balking at the "ten foot rule" because in their culture clerks typically wait for a customer to ask a question before speaking.[41] Wal-Mart saw the need to acquire a stake in supermarket chain Seiyu, Ltd. and is gradually remodeling Seiyu's 400 food and apparel stores into the Wal-Mart image. Discount stores are fairly new in Japan and long-protected mom-and-pop stores make up close to 60% of all retailers. U. S. firms

such as Gateway, Office Max, Foot Locker, and Burger King all failed in Japan. As Wal-Mart proceeds to grow in Japan, its chief competitor, Aeon, which operates 368 supermakets tries to respond. Aeon recently sent hundreds of employees to visit Wal-Marts in the United States, South Korea, and China, to analyze the competition.[42]

Becoming Politically Active. It was Wal-Mart's desire to grow globally that caused the company to ramp up its efforts at lobbying in Washington, D.C. The precipitating event was Wal-Mart's realization that U.S. negotiators had agreed upon a 30-store limit on retailers operating in China when it agreed to support China's entry into the World Trade Organization in the late 1990s. As a result of this realization, the company recently decided it had to get into lobbying even though it went against founder Sam Walton's policy of staying out of politics. Today, Wal-Mart has five lobbyists on its payroll and a number of other hired political consultants to help it. In 2003, the company's political action committee was the biggest corporate donor to federal parties and candidates, with more than $1 million in contributions.[43]

Millions of Supporters.

In spite of its challenges, Wal-Mart has millions of supporters, 100 million of them weekly are customers. Many consider the company to be socially responsible in addition to being a provider of thousands of jobs, low prices, and high value and service. As we progress through the first decade of the new millennium, Wal-Mart has numerous corporate citizenship initiatives at the local and national levels. Locally, Wal-Mart stores underwrite college scholarships for high school seniors, raise funds for children's hospitals through The Children's Miracle Network Telethon, provide local fund-raisers money and manpower, and educate the public about recycling and other environmental topics with the help of "Green Coordinators."[44] On October 6, 1998, the Walton Family Charitable Support Foundation, the charitable program created by Sam Walton's family, announced the largest ever single gift made to an American business school: $50 million to the College of Business Administration of the University of Arkansas. Helen R. Walton, the "first lady" of Wal-Mart, said that she and her husband established the Foundation to support specific charities, including the University.[45]

Achievements.

On its own Web page, Wal-Mart touts in detail its achievements. It says the American public appreciates Wal-Mart's community-involvement efforts:

- In 2003 and 2004, Wal-Mart was named by *Fortune* magazine as the most admired company in the United States.
- In 2002, Wal-Mart was presented with the Ron Brown Award for Corporate Leadership, a presidential award that recognizes companies for outstanding achievement in employee and community relations.
- *Forbes* magazine recognized Wal-Mart in 2002 as being one of the most philanthropic companies in America.
- In 1999 and 2000, Americans named Wal-Mart as the company they think of first in supporting local causes and issues, according to Cone, Inc.
- Wal-Mart ranked among the top five corporate foundations by giving in 1999 and 2000, according to the Foundation Center.

More information about Wal-Mart can be located on-line at http://www.walmartstores.com and http://www.walmart.com. The SAM'S CLUB Web site can be accessed at http://www.samsclub.com.[46]

In spite of its achievements, article titles from recent newspapers and magazines raise questions about Wal-Mart's power and impact. Some of these include the following:

"The Wal-Martization of America"[47]

"Is Wal-Mart Too Powerful?"[48]

"Is Wal-Mart Good for America?"[49]

"One Nation Under Wal-Mart"[50]

"Wal-Mart Gives Globalization a Bad Name"[51]

EPILOGUE

Sam, the hired gun, learned his lessons well. The people who bought at his stores were well satisfied. The downtown merchants who survived learned to coexist with the hired gun's associates. But things would never be the same. The changes had come rapidly. The social fabric of the small town was changed forever. The larger cities continued to fight.

The hired gun rode on, searching for that next town that needed to be liberated from the downtown price-fixing bad guys. The search has become more complicated as the opposition has risen, but the spirit of Sam rides on.

THE WAR ON WAL-MART: OTHER ISSUES FACING THE COMPANY

The primary issues in the above case are Wal-Mart's size and impact on local communities. This includes the threat of putting other merchants out of business, the creation of urban sprawl, and the traffic congestion created when the company decides to locate in a particular site. In short, the negative and positive impacts on communities have been considered. In the past few years, Wal-Mart has begun to face other issues that merit consideration. In addition to anti-sprawl activists and merchants, Wal-Mart is now facing new opposition from labor unions, other activist organizations, and lawsuits. Its labor practices are being increasingly questioned. The company has been accused of paying wages so low that workers cannot live off of them, making employees work "off the clock" without overtime pay, paying few or low benefits, and taking advantage of illegal immigrants. In 2004, the company was hit with a class-action lawsuit on gender discrimination against women. This class action lawsuit covers 1.6 million current and former employees, making it the largest private civil rights case ever.

Because these issues are so expansive and important, we do not address them in the present case. Another case, focusing primarily on Wal-Mart's labor practices and the issues outlined above, has been prepared for separate discussion. Case 31, titled "Wal-Mart and Its Associates: Efficient Operator or Neglectful Employer?" may be discussed following this case or deferred until a more in-depth consideration of employee stakeholders is undertaken.

Questions for Discussion

1. What are the major issues in this case? Assess Wal-Mart's corporate social responsibility using the four-part CSR model. Is Wal-Mart socially responsible for its devastating impact on small merchants? What about its impact on communities in terms of sprawl, traffic congestion, and impact on the appearance of the environment? What responsibility, if any, does the company have to these merchants or to the communities it enters?

2. Most of Wal-Mart's success has come at the expense of the small merchant. What should Wal-Mart do, if anything, to help other vital businesses in the community survive? Why?

3. Sam Walton has been called a motivational genius. After reading this case and with what you have observed at your local Wal-Mart store, explain how this motivational genius empowered the employee. What is the "Wal-Mart Way"? Explain its impact on the associate and on the community. What will happen now that Sam is no longer the motivational leader?

4. Some regard Wal-Mart as a leader in the area of corporate social responsibility. How do the "Buy American" program and the "Environmental Awareness" campaign illustrate this? Are these programs really examples of corporate social responsibility or are they gimmicks to entice customers into the stores? Are the benefits of its more recent corporate citizenship programs offset by the company's harmful impact on merchants?

5. Wal-Mart has closed five stores in its short history. What responsibility, if any, does Wal-Mart have to the employees who are let go? What about its loyal customers and the community?

6. Wal-Mart is finding severe resistance to its expansion into New England and California. From Wal-Mart's perspective, draw the stakeholder map. Define the true goals of the opponents of Wal-Mart. Include a consideration of the following: (a) stopping Wal-Mart's expansion, (b) preserving the status quo (e.g., downtown community, social fabric), (c) developing a cause that will pay their bills, (d) fighting for an ideology, or (e) something else. What should Wal-Mart do?

7. As Wal-Mart expands into the international arena, what problems or issues do you anticipate it will face? In general, what should Wal-Mart's approach be in these other countries? Is it unethical to change another country's culture?

Case Endnotes

1. Vance H. Trimble, Sam Walton: *The Inside Story of America's Richest Man* (New York: Penguin Books, 1990), 30. Also see Bob Ortega, *In Sam We Trust* (New York: Times Business, 1998).
2. *Ibid.*, 34.
3. Janice Castro, "Mr. Sam Stuns Goliath," *Time* (February 25, 1991), 62.
4. Wal-Mart's Web page (http://www.walmartstores.com), "Wall Mart at a Glance."
5. Stephanie Armour, "Wal-Mart in Record Sex-Bias Lawsuit," *USA Today*, June 23, 2004, 1A.
6. For up-to-date information on the Wal-Mart culture, see http://www.walmartstores/com
7. John Huey, "America's Most Successful Merchant," *Fortune* (September 23, 1991), 50.
8. Wal-Mart's Web page, *ibid.*
9. Trimble, 260.
10. Trimble, 261.
11. "Made in the U.S.A.," http://www.pbs.org/itvs/storewars/stores3.html.
12. Richard Turcsik, "A New Environment Evolves at Wal-Mart," *Supermarket News* (January 15, 1990), 10.
13. *Ibid.*, 10.
14. *Ibid.*, 11.
15. Wal-Mart Corporation, *Wal-Mart Associates Handbook* (July 1991), 14.
16. *Ibid.*, 14.
17. Dan Koeppel, "Wal-Mart Finds New Rivals on Main Street," *Adweek's Marketing Week* (November 10, 1990), 5.
18. Trimble, 255.
19. "Just Saying No to Wal-Mart," *Newsweek* (November 13, 1989), 65.
20. *Ibid.*, 65.
21. Karen Blumenthal, "Arrival of Discounter Tears the Civic Fabric of Small-Town Life," *The Wall Street Journal* (April 14, 1987), 1, 23.
22. *Ibid.*, 23.
23. Charles Haddad, "Wal-Mart Leaves Town 'High, Dry,'" *The Atlanta Journal-Constitution* (November 26, 1990), A4.
24. *Ibid.*, A4.
25. Bob Ortega, "Aging Activists Turn, Turn, Turn Attention to Wal-Mart Protests," *The Wall Street Journal* (October 11, 1994), A1, A8.
26. *Ibid.*, A1.
27. *Ibid.*, A8.
28. Joseph Pereira and Bob Ortega, "Once Easily Turned Away by Local Foes, Wal-Mart Gets Tough in New England," *The Wall Street Journal* (September 7, 1994), B1.
29. Hometown America Fights Back, http://www.sprawl-busters.com/search.php?SRCHrecent=1
30. "Special Report on Wal-Mart: How big can it grow?" *The Economist*, April 17, 2004., 67–69.
31. *Ibid.*
32. Steven Greehouse, "Wal-Mart, a Nationa Unto Itself," *The New York Times*, April 17, 2004, A15.
33. "The Wal-Martization of America," *The New York Times*, November 15, 2003, A26.
34. "In California, Wal-Mart Hits a Wall," *New York Times*, April 11, 2004, 10WK; Also see Ann Zimmerman, "Wal-Mart Loses Supercenter Vote," *Wall Street Journal*, April 8, 2004, B7.
35. Ann Zimmerman, 2004. *Ibid.*
36. Wal-Mart *2004 Annual Report*, 55.
37. "Special Report Wal-Mart: How big can it grow," *The Economist*, April 17, 2004, 68.
38. *Ibid.*
39. Andy Rowell, "Welcome to Wal-World: Wal-Mart's Inexhaustible March to Conquer the Globe," *Multinational Monitor*, October 2003, 13–16.
40. *Ibid.*, 16.
41. Ann Zimmerman and Martin Fackler, "Wal-Mart's Foray into Japan Spurs a Retail Upheaval," *Wall Street Journal*, September 19, 2003.
42. *Ibid.*
43. Jeanne Cummings, "Wal-Mart Opens for Business in Tough Market: Washington," *Wall Street Journal*, March 24, 2004, A1.
44. Wal-Mart Web page, http://www.walmartstores.com.
45. University of Arkansas Web page, http://www.uark.edu (October 6, 1998), press release.
46. http://www.walmartstores.com
47. *The New York Times*, November 15, 2003, A26.
48. *Business Week*, October 6, 2003, 100–110.
49. *The New York Times*, December 7, 2003, 1WK.
50. *Fortune*, March 3, 2003, 66–78.
51. Jeffrey E. Garten, "Wal-Mart Gives Globalization a Bad Name, *Business Week*, March 8, 2004, 24.

| THE BODY SHOP INTERNATIONAL PLC

When North American consumers have been asked to describe the cosmetics industry, they often respond with words such as "glamour" and "beauty." Beginning in 1976, The Body Shop provided a contrast to this image by selling a range of 400 products designed to "cleanse and polish the skin and hair." The product line included such items as "Honeyed Beeswax, Almond, and Jojoba Oil Cleanser" and "Carrot Facial Oil." Women's cosmetics and men's toiletries were also available. They were all produced without the use of animal testing and were packaged in plain-looking, recyclable packages.[1] The primary channel of distribution was a network of over 600 franchised retail outlets in Europe, Australia, Asia, and North America.[2] The company enjoyed annual growth rates of approximately 50 percent until 1990, when net income began to level off. Few questions were raised in the media about this decline in performance, because the firm's social agenda and exotic product line captured most of the public's interest. Indeed, at this point in time, The Body Shop was the poster-child company for the burgeoning corporate social responsibility movement.

ANITA RODDICK: FOUNDER

Managing director and founder Anita Roddick was responsible for creating and maintaining much of the company's marketing strategy and product development.[3] Roddick believed that The Body Shop was fundamentally different from other firms in the cosmetics industry because "we don't claim that our products will make you look younger, we say they will only help you look your best."[4] She regularly assailed her competitors: "We loathe the cosmetics industry with a passion. It's run by men who create needs that don't exist."[5] During the 1980s, Anita Roddick became one of the richest women in the United Kingdom by challenging the well-established firms and rewriting the rules of the cosmetics industry.

Honors and Awards. Anita Roddick became admired within the business community for the conviction of her beliefs and the success of her company. She received many honors and awards, including U.K. Businesswoman of the Year in 1985, British Retailer of the Year in 1989, and the Order of the British Empire.[6] The firm's customers included several celebrities, including Diana, Princess of Wales, Sting, and Bob Weir of the Grateful Dead. Ben Cohen, cofounder and chairman of Ben and Jerry's,

described her as an incredibly dynamic, passionate, humorous and intelligent individual who believes it's the responsibility of a business to give back to the community . . . she understands that a business has the power to influence the world in a positive way.[7]

Mrs. Roddick opened the first Body Shop store in Brighton, England, as a means of supporting her family while her husband was taking a year-long sabbatical in America. Her husband, Gordon Roddick, a chartered accountant by trade, was using much of their savings to finance his trip. Anita Roddick had little money to open a store, much less to develop products or purchase packaging materials.[8]

Field Expeditions. She called upon her previous experience as a resource. Having been a United Nations researcher for several years in the 1960s, she had had many opportunities during field expeditions to see how men and women in Africa, Asia, and Australia used locally grown plants and extracts, such as beeswax, rice grains, almonds, bananas, and jojoba, as grooming products. Roddick knew that these materials were inexpensive and readily obtainable. With some library research, she found several recipes, some of which were centuries old, that used these same ingredients to make cosmetics and skin cleansers. With the addition of inexpensive bottles and handwritten labels, Roddick quickly developed a line of products for sale in her first Body Shop. She soon opened a second store in a nearby town. When Gordon Roddick returned to the United Kingdom in 1977, The Body Shop was recording sizable profits. At Anita's request, he joined the company as its chief executive officer.[9]

The Body Shop's strategy grew out of the company's early reliance on cost containment. Roddick was able to afford only 600 bottles when she opened her first store. Since she was looking for the cheapest packaging option, she chose urine sample bottles. Customers were offered a small discount to encourage the return of empty bottles for product refills. This offer was extended to both retail and mail-order customers.[10] The Body Shop could not afford advertising, so Roddick resolved to succeed without it.[11]

The Body Shop's retail stores were somewhat different from the cosmetic salons and counters familiar to shoppers in highly industrialized nations. The typical retail sales counter relied on high-pressure tactics that included promotions, makeovers, and an unspoken contract with the customer that virtually required a purchase in order for the customer to receive any advice or consultation from a sales counter employee.[12] Body Shop employees were taught to wait for the customer to ask questions, be forthright and helpful, and not to press for sales.[13]

This case was prepared by William A. Sodeman using publicly available information.

Employees. Store employees were paid a half-day's wages every week to perform community service activities. At the company headquarters in Littlehampton, England, The Body Shop employed an anthropologist, six herbalists, and a variety of others in similar fields. There was nothing that resembled a marketing department. Husbands and wives frequently worked together and could visit their children during the workday at the on-site day-care center.[14] The company's hiring procedures included questions about the applicant's personal heroes and literary tastes, as well as their individual beliefs on certain social issues. At one time, Roddick was ready to hire a retail director, but refused to do so when he professed his fondness for hunting, a sport that Roddick despised because of her support for animal rights.[15]

PROSPERITY AND SOCIAL ACTIVISM

As the company prospered, Anita Roddick used her enthusiasm and growing influence on her suppliers and customers. The Body Shop began to produce products in the country of origin when it was feasible and paid the workers wages that were comparable to those in the European Community.[16] Customers were asked to sign petitions and join activist groups that The Body Shop endorsed, mostly in the areas of animal rights and environmental causes. The Body Shop contributed significant portions of its earnings to these groups, including Amnesty International and People for the Ethical Treatment of Animals (PETA). Roddick was careful to choose causes that were "easy to understand"[17] and could be communicated quickly to a customer during a visit to a Body Shop store.

Animal Testing. An example of this corporate activism was The Body Shop's opposition to a practice that had become common in the cosmetics industry. Cosmetics firms were not required to perform animal testing of their products to comply with product safety and health regulations. Rather, companies voluntarily adopted animal-based testing procedures to guard against product liability lawsuits.[18]

The Body Shop was not worried about such lawsuits, because the product ingredients Roddick chose had been used safely for centuries. In addition, the older recipes had been used for many decades without incident. These circumstances led to the company's rejection of animal-based product testing. Any supplier wishing to do business with The Body Shop had to sign a statement guaranteeing that it had done no animal testing for the previous 5 years and would never do such testing in the future. The Body Shop used human volunteers from its own staff and the University Hospital of Wales to test new and current products under normal use. The Body Shop also volunteered to share the results of its tests on individual ingredients with other cosmetics manufacturers.[19]

The Draize Test. Most other cosmetics firms used a variety of procedures to determine the safety of cosmetics

products, with two animal-based tests becoming the standard procedures. The Draize test involved dripping the substance in question, such as shampoo or a detergent paste, into the eyes of conscious, restrained rabbits and measuring the resultant damage over the course of several days. Rabbits cannot cry, which allowed researchers to complete the tests quickly. Another test required researchers to force-feed large quantities of a substance to a sample of laboratory animals. The substance could be a solid (such as lipstick or shaving cream), a paste, or a liquid. The lethal dose of a substance was determined by the amount that had been ingested by an individual surviving animal when 50 percent of the sample had died, hence the name of the test, LD50.[20] Beginning in the 1970s, animal rights groups such as the Humane Society and PETA began protesting the use of these tests by the cosmetics industry. The Body Shop lent its support to these groups' efforts, labeling all animal testing as "cruel and unnecessary." By 1991, alternative procedures that involved far less cruelty to animals had already been developed but were yet to be approved for industry use.[21]

THE BODY SHOP IN THE U. S.

In the United States, The Body Shop's market share was limited by two factors. First, its prices were significantly higher than those charged for mass-marketed products in drugstores, although they were generally comparable to the prices charged for cosmetics and cleansers at department store sales counters. Second, The Body Shop was constrained by the number of stores it had opened in the United States. By 1991, only 40 stores had been opened in a dozen metropolitan areas across the country. A mail-order catalog and a telephone order line were used to supplement the American retail stores, but they were inadequate substitutes for the product sampling and advice that were readily available at The Body Shop's stores. Roddick maintained that those consumers who sampled Body Shop products became loyal customers: "Once they walk into one of our stores or buy from our catalogue, they're hooked."[22]

Going Public. The Body Shop was taken public in London in 1984, with the Roddicks owning a combined 30 percent of the outstanding stock. The firm's subsequent sales and net income figures grew during 1985 to 1990 from sales revenue of $15.3 and net income of $1.4 million to $137.7 and $14.7 million.[23] Without The Body Shop's monetary donations to various social causes, all of these net income figures would be higher than reported in the financial statements. Estimates of the company's annual contributions to outside organizations varied from several hundred thousand to several million dollars.

Industry analysts considered The Body Shop to be a strong performer with the potential to prosper even in an economic downturn. The exotic nature of its products, such as hair conditioner made with 10 percent real bananas and a peppermint foot lotion, would attract consumers who desired affordable luxuries. Analysts regarded the public's desire for personal care products as "insatiable," especially in North America.[24] The addition of the strong emotional appeal of social issues formed the basis for one of the most successful marketing and promotional concepts in the cosmetics industry in decades.

The twentieth anniversary of Earth Day, celebrated in 1990, focused media attention on many of the environmental issues that Roddick and The Body Shop regularly addressed. Further, it spurred interest in environmental issues in the commercial sector.

Competition.
Several new entrants and existing competitors challenged The Body Shop in the United States and Europe. Among the largest of these firms were Estee Lauder and Revlon. The Limited had opened 50 Bath & Body Works stores, patterned after The Body Shop's outlets and located in shopping malls across the United States. In addition, an English competitor, Crabtree & Evelyn, had held a significant presence in North America and Europe since the mid-1970s.

By 1991, The Body Shop was a successful and profitable firm that had attracted a variety of well-financed competitors. The company faced a real threat from these firms because they were all well financed and had a broad range of experience in marketing cosmetics. Each of these firms was well established in the United States, yet no one firm dominated the new product segment that The Body Shop had helped create.

In addition, there were indications that the environmental concerns that attracted customers to The Body Shop might not have permanent drawing power. Roddick had vowed never to sell anything but environmentally friendly cosmetics and grooming products in her stores, but the industry was growing and changing faster than anyone had anticipated. It seemed that The Body Shop needed to take action to ensure its long-term survival.

Roddick's Role.
When asked about her role in the company, Anita Roddick stated:

> The purpose of a business isn't just to generate profits to create an ever-larger empire. It's to have the power to affect social change, to make the world a better place. I have always been an activist, I have always been incredibly impassioned about human rights and environmental issues. The Body Shop is simply my stage.[25]

Questions for Discussion

1. How does The Body Shop address the four components of corporate social responsibility? In The Body Shop, what tensions among these components are at work?

2. Anita Roddick claims that her firm does not advertise, yet it receives free media exposure and publicity through the social causes it champions and her personal appearances. Is this an appropriate approach for a business to follow?

3. Analyze The Body Shop's power using both levels and spheres of power discussed in Chapter 1.

4. What is your assessment of Anita Roddick's philosophy regarding the "purpose of a business"?

5. What are Anita Roddick's strengths and weaknesses as a leader? Should she stay on in a managing role or step aside and allow a more experienced person to run the marketing operations?

6. The Body Shop asks potential employees questions about "personal heroes" and individual beliefs. Is it ethical to ask such questions of applicants? Are these questions legitimate ones to ask in the first place? Are such questions fair to the applicants?

Case Endnotes

1. Catalog, The Body Shop (Fall 1990).
2. Laura Zinn, "Whales, Human Rights, Rain Forests—and the Heady Smell of Profits," *Business Week* (July 15, 1991), 114.
3. *Ibid.*, 114.
4. Samuel Greengard, "Face Values," *USAir Magazine* (November 1990), 89.
5. Zinn, 114.
6. Greengard, 93.
7. Greengard, 97.
8. Zinn, 115.
9. Greengard, 94.
10. Greengard, 94.
11. Zinn, 114.
12. Greengard, 90.
13. Maria Koklanaris, "Trio of Retailers Finds Soap and Social Concern an Easy Sell," *The Washington Post* (April 27, 1991).
14. Greengard, 90.
15. Zinn, 115.
16. The Body Shop promotional literature, 1991.
17. Zinn, 115.
18. The Body Shop promotional literature, 1991.
19. The Body Shop promotional literature, 1991.
20. Peter Singer, *Animal Liberation: A New Ethics for Treatment of Animals* (New York: Avon Books, 1975), 48.
21. The Body Shop promotional literature, 1991.
22. Greengard, 89.
23. Compact Disclosure database, 1991.
24. Koklanaris.
25. Greengard, 97.

THE BODY SHOP'S ADVERTISING CAMPAIGN

The first appearance by Anita Roddick in a U.S. television commercial was seen in 1993. This came as something of a surprise to long-time Body Shop (BSI) customers and her competitors in the cosmetics industry. These people believed that Roddick abhorred advertising as a wasteful practice that created needs. The company did promote certain nonprofit groups in its stores and catalogs, including Greenpeace, People for the Ethical Treatment of Animals, and Amnesty International. However, The Body Shop had a policy of not advertising directly to consumers.[1]

AMERICAN EXPRESS

Roddick agreed to lend her endorsement to an American Express marketing campaign that featured founders of fast-growing retail firms such as BSI and Crate & Barrel. Not coincidentally, all of the firms featured in the campaign accepted the American Express charge card as a payment method. The main message of the campaign was that customers of these stores preferred to use the American Express card and that the store founders also found the card useful in their day-to-day business.

Roddick appeared in three commercials and a series of print advertisements as part of this advertising campaign. The advertisements included Roddick's brief description of the company's purpose and sourcing practices and used film footage and photographs of her travels in search of exotic new ingredients.

SELLING OUT

Although the Roddick commercials received a positive response from advertising industry professionals, some long-time BSI customers accused Roddick of "selling out" and breaking her promise never to advertise BSI products. Roddick responded

This case was prepared by William A. Sodeman, Hawaii Pacific University, using publicly available information.

that the commercials promoted American Express and did not specifically promote Body Shop products. The advertisements gave The Body Shop valuable publicity in much the same way that Roddick's social activism and personal appearances had done in the past.

RUBY

In 1997, The Body Shop unveiled Ruby, a voluptuous size 18 doll created to counter media images of thin women.[2]

Questions for Discussion

1. What is your opinion on The Body Shop/American Express advertising campaign? Was it a sound business decision on Roddick's part?

2. What does the American Express campaign imply about The Body Shop and its customers? Is this different from the image of the nonprofit organizations that The Body Shop endorses?

3. What (if any) conflicts exist between the images and public reputations of The Body Shop and American Express?

4. Did Roddick commit an ethics transgression by advertising through the American Express ad that contravened her earlier statements and policy, or was this different? How should she explain herself?

5. Though "Ruby" seemed to be an isolated advertising event, what is your appraisal of this?

Case Endnotes

1. The materials used in this case are based on Jennifer Conlin, "Survival of the Fittest," *Working Woman* (February 1994).
2. "History," The Body Shop International PLC, *Hoover's Online*, July 7, 2004.

THE BODY SHOP'S REPUTATION IS TARNISHED

Between 1991 and 1995, The Body Shop continued to expand its operations. The Body Shop had opened 1,200 stores by early 1995.[1] Over 100 company-owned and franchised stores were operating in U.S. shopping malls and downtown shopping districts. During the period 1991 to 1994, sales and net income grew from $231 million and $41 million to $330 million and $47 million, respectively.

The Body Shop had moved its U.S. headquarters from Cedar Knolls, New Jersey, to a less expensive and more central location—Raleigh, North Carolina. The original location worked well when The Body Shop opened its first U.S. stores in New York City and Washington, DC, but soon proved to be a logistical problem. Roddick was frustrated that the New Jersey hires did not seem as creative or impulsive as her English staff. In retrospect, she realized that having some of her U.K. staff help train the first U.S. managers and employees or even setting up her headquarters in a college town such as Boulder, Colorado, or a city such as San Francisco would have been a better choice than starting from scratch in New Jersey.[2]

PROBLEMS ARISE

The Body Shop had bigger problems to deal with than the location of its national headquarters. The Limited continued to open its chain of Bath & Body Works stores on a nationwide scale. Placement of a Bath & Body Works store in a mall usually precluded The Body Shop from entering the same mall. (There were some exceptions, most notably very large shopping malls such as the Mall of America in Bloomington, Minnesota.) All of The Limited's stores, from Express and Victoria's Secret to Structure and Lerner's, were company owned. This allowed a greater degree of flexibility and speed than The Body Shop's franchising system. Further, The Limited had started grouping its stores in malls to create its own version of the department store. During the holidays, Express and Structure stores carried special selections of Bath & Body Works products to induce customer trial and develop brand awareness. The Limited's size and power as one of the major retailers in the United States made the company a strong threat to The Body Shop's continued presence in the U.S. retail market. In an alarming move, The Limited began opening Bath & Body Works stores in the United Kingdom, which presented a direct threat to The Body Shop on the company's home soil.

This case was prepared by William A. Sodeman, Hawaii Pacific University, using publicly available information.

Confusion. The similarities between The Body Shop and Bath & Body Works stores also created some confusion. Some less-observant customers of The Body Shop were bringing empty Bath & Body Works bottles to The Body Shop to be refilled because Bath & Body Works did not have its own refill policy and the products often seemed similar. The Body Shop protected its slogans, territory, and franchises with an aggressive legal strategy that included an out-of-court settlement with The Limited in 1993.[3]

Competition. Other companies had successfully introduced organic or natural beauty products in discount and drugstores, a market segment that The Body Shop had completely ignored in its global operations. Traditional retailers including Woolworth's and Kmart had also entered what had come to be known as the minimalist segment of the personal care products industry. Woolworth's entry was an expanded selection of organic bath and body case products in its deep discount Rx Place chain. Kmart's line of Naturalistic cosmetics was sold in over 1,800 stores.[4] Other new companies included H2O Plus, which sold its products in its own retail stores but did not make claims about animal testing as had The Body Shop and Bath & Body Works.

GOOD PRESS

The Body Shop continued to receive new accolades and to hit new heights of prosperity. Anita Roddick published her autobiography, Body and Soul, in late 1991. Roddick donated her portion of the royalties to several groups, including the Unrepresented Nations and Peoples Organization, a self-governing group that spoke for Kurds, Tibetans, and Native Americans; the Medical Foundation, which treated victims of torture; and a variety of individual political prisoners. The 256-page book, which was written and designed by Roddick, Body Shop staff, and an outside group, resembled a mixture of catalog and personal memoir. Hundreds of pictures and headlines were used throughout to emphasize and clarify particular points of interest. On the final page of the book, where one would expect to see the last page of the index, is the coda of the final chapter. The last line of text, printed in large boldface letters, reads "Make no mistake about it—I'm doing this for me."[5]

Media Attention. Partly as a result of the book's publication, The Body Shop received a great deal of flattering media attention. Inc.[6] and Working Woman[7] ran cover stories featuring

645

Anita Roddick. *Fortune*[8] and *Business Week*[9] published shorter articles that focused on Anita Roddick and the company's performance. *Time* began its article with a story on Anita's fact-finding mission to Oman, where she obtained a perfume recipe from a local tribe only after dropping her pants and showing the Bedouin women her pubic hair. Bedouin women pluck theirs every day.[10]

BAD PRESS

In 1992, some members of the media began to criticize The Body Shop and the Roddicks. The *Financial Times* gave The Body Shop the dubious honor of headlining its 1992 list of top 10 corporate losers after the price of Body Shop stock dipped from $5.20 to $2.70 during September.[11] Stock analysts had reacted to a disappointing earnings report, and the news set some minds to wondering if the company could indeed grow quickly enough to capture a leadership position in the minimalist market, or if there was a minimalist market at all.

Millennium Project. Around this time, The Body Shop invested $5 million in a 10-part documentary series called *Millennium*. This series, which was shown around the world on television networks including PBS and the BBC, was meant to celebrate the wisdom and history of native cultures. The director quit the project during filming, accusing the Roddicks of distorting the tribal rituals depicted in the film to suit various new-age ideals.[12] The Body Shop sold a book version of *Millennium* in its stores to help promote the series and raise funds for donations.

In 1993, a British television news magazine telecast a report on The Body Shop. The show alleged that The Body Shop knowingly sourced materials from suppliers that had recently performed animal testing. The Body Shop sued the TV station and the production company for libel and won a significant financial award after a 6-week court battle. Anita Roddick sat in the courtroom every day and compared the experience to confinement in a "mahogany coffin." The Body Shop won the suit and a £276,000 settlement by proving to the British court that the company had never intentionally misled consumers about the animal-testing policy, which encouraged manufacturers to give up animal testing but did not claim that ingredients had never been tested on animals.[13]

Jon Entine's Exposé. In 1994, *Business Ethics* magazine, a well-respected U.S. publication, published a cover story on The Body Shop that built upon many of the allegations that others had presented over the years. The resulting controversy engulfed the journalist, the magazine, and The Body Shop in a new wave of controversy that threatened The Body Shop's already slow expansion into the U.S. market.

In June 1993, journalist Jon Entine had first been approached by disgruntled current and former Body Shop staffers about several of the company's practices. After overcoming his initial skepticism and doing some preliminary investigations in Littlehampton,

The Body Shop's headquarters, Entine was convinced he had a sound basis on which to develop a story for his current employer, the ABC news magazine "Primetime Live." When ABC decided not to renew the contract and to drop The Body Shop story, Entine began his own investigation, which eventually resulted in the *Business Ethics* article.[14] In the preface to the article, magazine editor and publisher Marjorie Kelly wrote:

> *Long-time readers will note that the following article represents a distinct departure from our typical editorial style. It has not been part of our mission to publish the exploits of companies that fall short of their stated social goals. But we believe the story of The Body Shop must be told, chiefly for the lessons it provides those of us who seek to promote ethical business practices. Still, we bring this story to you with mixed emotions. We have been ardent admirers of Anita Roddick and her company for many years; two years ago this month [September 1992] we featured her on our cover. But, after weeks of debate, including several conversations with Body Shop representatives, we concluded the greater good would be served by raising these issues in print. We earnestly hope this dialogue will be a constructive one.*

Entine's Allegations. In the article, Entine made several claims:

- Anita Roddick had stolen the concept of The Body Shop, including the store name, recycling of bottles, store design, catalogs, and products, from a similar store she had visited in Berkeley, California, in 1971, several years before she opened her first Body Shop in Brighton in 1976.
- Roddick had not discovered exotic recipes for some of her products as she had previously claimed: Some were outdated, off-the-shelf formulas that had been used by other manufacturers, whereas others featured unusual ingredients, around which Roddick and company employees had woven fanciful tales of her travels of discovery.
- Many Body Shop products were full of petrochemicals, artificial colors and fragrances, and synthetic preservatives and contained only small amounts of naturally sourced ingredients.
- Quality control was a continuing problem with instances of mold, formaldehyde, and E. coli contamination reported around the world, thus requiring the use of large amounts of preservatives to give the products stable shelf lives.
- The U.S. Federal Trade Commission had launched a probe into The Body Shop's franchising practices, including deceptive financial data, unfair competition, and misleading company representation. One husband-and-wife franchising team compared the company to the Gambino crime family.
- The Body Shop's "Trade Not Aid" program was a sham, providing only a small portion of The Body Shop's raw

materials while failing to fulfill the company's promises to suppliers.

- Between 1986 and 1993, The Body Shop contributed far less than the average annual pretax charitable donations for U.S. companies, according to the Council on Economic Priorities.

Entine published a similar article in a trade magazine, *Drug and Cosmetic Industry*, in February 1995.[15] In this article, he discussed The Body Shop's policies regarding animal testing, citing an internal memo from May 1992. At that time, 46.5 percent of The Body Shop's ingredients had been tested on animals by the ingredients' manufacturers, which was an increase from 34 percent the previous year. This and other practices raised new concerns about the company's slogan "Against Animal Testing" and tainted the company's 1993 victory in its libel suit against the TV program.[16]

Response to Entine's Article.

The response to Entine's *Business Ethics* article was swift and furious. In June, well before the article's publication, Franklin Development and Consulting, a leading U.S.-based provider of social investment services, had sold 50,000 shares of The Body Shop because of "financial concerns."[17] With rumors spreading about the article in early August, the stock fell from $3.75 to $3.33 per share. Ben Cohen, cofounder of Ben & Jerry's and a *Business Ethics* advisory board member, severed his ties with the magazine. The U.S. and British press ran numerous pieces on the article and its allegations. These articles appeared in newspapers and magazines such as *USA Today*,[18] *The Economist*,[19] *The New York Post*,[20] and *The San Francisco Chronicle*.[21] *The London Daily Mail* secured an exclusive interview with one of the founders of the California Body Shop, who described the company's early years and how they eventually came to legal terms with the Roddicks over the rights to The Body Shop trademark.[22]

Entine was interviewed by a small newsletter, the *Corporate Crime Reporter*, in which he defended and explained his research and the article.[23] One point of interest was Entine's claim that Body Shop products were of "drugstore quality," which he based on the company's use of obsolete ingredients and formulas and a *Consumer Reports* ranking that placed Body Shop Dewberry perfume last out of 66 tested.[24] Dewberry is The Body Shop's trademark scent and is used in all of its stores as part of the "atmosphere." *Corporate Crime Reporter* also noted that another reporter, David Moberg, had brought similar allegations against The Body Shop in a separate article published the same month as Entine's.[25]

Rift in Progressive Community.

In January 1995, *Utne Reader* published a forum including commentaries by Anita Roddick, Entine, Moberg, and Franklin Research founder Joan Bavaria. The forum was remarkable in the sense that it presented a structured set of responses to the charges. Editor Eric Utne noted the rift that the article had caused in the progressive business community and described how the Roddicks, Marjorie Kelly, and other parties had begun holding face-to-face meetings to mend their relationships.[26] Entine described the same meetings as "a family gathering a few days after everyone's favorite uncle was found molesting a neighbor's child. The scandal was on everyone's mind, few would openly talk about it, and most hoped that ignoring it would make it fade away. It didn't."[27] Moberg encouraged consumer watchdog groups to do their jobs more carefully, citing the case of the British group New Consumer, which had previously given The Body Shop high ratings.[28] Roddick maintained that the truth had been sacrificed in a rush to judgment but that she had managed to cope with and learn from the experience.[29]

GORDON RODDICK: DEFENDER OF THE REALM

Anita Roddick has been known to ask her employees what irritates them about their store.[30] Gordon, Anita's husband, is a bit more philosophical in his approach, yet he also speaks out on issues that concern him. After their entry into the U.S. market, the Roddicks became frustrated with the regulatory barriers they encountered. Most of the problems that The Body Shop encountered were small. However, The Body Shop had two full-time employees and one lawyer devoted exclusively to regulatory compliance in the United States. Gordon Roddick estimated that it cost The Body Shop an additional 5 percent of its revenues to do business in the United States, thus supporting his claim that the American free market economy was anything but free.[31]

Entine's *Business Ethics* article aroused Gordon to new heights of anger according to those who knew him. Body Shop lawyers had successfully persuaded *Vanity Fair* to refrain from publishing a different version of the article earlier in the year. *Vanity Fair* compensated Entine for his work, paying him $15,000 plus an additional $18,000 to cover his expenses in writing and researching the article. Entine was paid only $750 by *Business Ethics* magazine for the article.[32]

Counterattack.

Early in Entine's investigation, The Body Shop had hired the international public relations firm of Hill & Knowlton (H&K) to launch a counterattack on Entine's credibility and motives. H&K vice president Frank Mankiewicz, who was a former president of National Public Radio (NPR), sent letters to ABC requesting that it drop its Body Shop story.[33] He also used his contacts at NPR to place an interview with Entine and a follow-up story that included comments from Body Shop supporters on NPR news programs such as "All Things Considered." Further attempts to intimidate *Business Ethics* magazine failed. The editor and publisher, Marjorie Kelly, knew that publishing the article was a risk, but she had checked and rechecked Entine's sources and was satisfied that his charges were sound. However, if The Body Shop chose to sue the magazine, she also knew that the cost of getting to the summary/judgment phase of the trial could put the small magazine out of business.[34]

Gordon Roddick responded to the *Business Ethics* article within a month of its publication by sending a 10-page letter on Body Shop letterhead to all *Business Ethics* subscribers. In this letter, he denied many of the charges made in the article. The letter offered statements by several people that appeared to contradict their own quotations in the article.

Decoys Get Letter. Several staff members at *Business Ethics* magazine were not pleased with the letter, which they had received in the mail because they were included as decoys on the subscriber mailing list. This is a common practice in the mailing-list industry to help prevent the misuse of subscriber addresses. The publisher of *Business Ethics* magazine could not recall authorizing the magazine's mailing-list service to rent the list to The Body Shop. It did not take long for the mailing-list company to discover that The Body Shop had obtained the magazine's subscriber list through a third party. Said Ralph Stevens, president of the mailing-list firm, "The Body Shop duped a prominent and legitimate list-brokerage company, a respected magazine, and they duped us . . . . If this is any indication of the way [The Body Stop does] business, of their regard for honesty and integrity, I give them a failing mark on all counts."[35] In late 1994, The Body Shop hired a business ethics expert to lead a social audit of the company.[36]

THE SITUATION AS OF 1995

By July 1995, Anita Roddick was already considering the possibility of opening Body Shop stores in Cuba, hoping to beat her competitors to that market and at the same time convert the Cubans' social revolution into a profitable yet honorable business revolution.[37] The company was also considering opening retail stores in Eastern European countries. At the same time, the media attention on the company had raised serious concerns among customers, among Body Shop supporters, and within the financial community. Since August 1994, the company's stock price had plummeted by almost 50 percent to 120p, an all-time low.

Losses. The Roddicks took millions of dollars in paper losses on their holdings, despite having sold a portion of their stock in July 1994.[38] The company faced increased competition from several larger firms, including Procter & Gamble, Avon, Kmart, The Limited, L'Oreal, Crabtree & Evelyn, and Marks & Spencer. Other companies, such as H2O Plus, were making progress in their efforts to open retail stores that featured products similar to those of The Body Shop. The company had hired Chiat/Day to develop advertising campaigns for worldwide use and conduct a marketing study in the United States.[39] There was at least one report that the company was looking for a U.S. advertising agency.[40] The questions that had been raised as a result of media investigations and The Body Shop's responses left some observers wondering what principles the company espoused and if the company could regain its earlier level of success.

Questions for Discussion

1. How has The Body Shop continued to address the four components of corporate social responsibility?

2. What is your assessment of The Body Shop's response to the Business Ethics article? Has The Body Shop misrepresented itself to stakeholders, and if so, how?

3. Jon Entine and others have accused The Body Shop of using intimidation to stifle critics. Does this appear to be a valid criticism? Was The Body Shop justified in hiring Hill & Knowlton to conduct a public relations campaign?

4. Has The Body Shop's reputation been damaged by the incidents in this case? How might the company improve its reputation? Do you believe the steps described in this case, including the hiring of an advertising agency, will help or hinder these efforts?

5. Describe the roles you believe Gordon and Anita Roddick should play in The Body Shop's operations. How might a stockholder, a customer, a supplier, and an employee assess the roles that the Roddicks should play?

Case Endnotes

1. Body Language—The Body Shop, World Wide Web site http://www.the-body-shop.com (May 1995).
2. Anita Roddick, *Body and Soul: Profits with Principles, The Amazing Success Story of Anita Roddick & The Body Shop* (New York: Crown, 1991), 135–136.
3. Jennifer Conlin, "Survival of the Fittest," *Working Woman* (February 1994).
4. Faye Brookman, "Prototypes Debut," *Stores* (April 1994), 20–22.
5. Roddick, 1991.
6. Bo Burlingame, "This Woman Has Changed Business Forever," *Inc.* (June 1990).
7. Conlin, 29.
8. Andrew Erdman, "Body Shop Gets into Ink," *Fortune* (October 7, 1991), 166.
9. Laura Zinn, "Whales, Human Rights, Rain Forests—And the Heady Smell of Profits," *Business Week* (July 15, 1991), 114–115.
10. Philip Elmer-Dewitt, "Anita the Agitator," *Times* (January 25, 1993), 52–54.
11. *Ibid.*, 54.
12. *Ibid.*, 54.
13. Conlin, 30–31.
14. Jon Entine, "Shattered Image," *Business Ethics* (October 1994), 23–28.
15. Jon Entine, "The Body Shop: Truth & Consequences," *Drug and Cosmetic Industry* (February 1995), 54–64.
16. Entine, 1995, 62.
17. Judith Valente, "Body Shop Shares Plunge on Reports of Sales by Funds and FTC Inquiry," *The Wall Street Journal* (August 24, 1994).
18. Ellen Neuborne, "Body Shop in a Lather over Ethics Criticism," *USA Today* (August 29, 1995), B1.
19. "Storm in a Bubble Bath," *The Economist* (September 3, 1994), 56.
20. Martin Peers, "Journalist's Probe Hits Body Shop," *New York Post* (August 25, 1994), 33.
21. Dirk Beveridge, "Uproar Threatens Body Shop Stock," *The San Francisco Chronicle* (August 25, 1994), D1.

22. Rebecca Hardy, "American Woman Recalls the Heady Days of Her Hippy Perfume Store . . . And a £2.3m Deal with the Roddicks," *London Daily Mail* (August 28, 1994).
23. "Interview with Jon Entine," *Corporate Crime Reporter* (September 19, 1994), 13–18.
24. "Interview with Jon Entine," 17.
25. David Moberg, "The Beauty Myth," *In These Times* (September 19–October 2, 1994).
26. Eric Utne, "Beyond the Body Shop Brouhaha," *Utne Reader* (January–February 1995), 101–102.
27. Jon Entine, "Exploiting Idealism," *Utne Reader* (January–February 1995), 108–109.
28. David Moberg, "Call in the Watchdogs!" *Utne Reader* (January–February 1995), 101–102.
29. Anita Roddick, "Who Judges the Judges?" *Utne Reader* (January–February 1995), 104.
30. Elmer-Dewitt, 52.
31. "Regulation Time: 60 Seconds with . . . Gordon Roddick," *Inc.* (June, 1993), 16.
32. Ruth G. Davis, "The Body Shop Plays Hardball," *New York Magazine* (September 19, 1994), 16.
33. *Ibid.*
34. Maureen Clark, "Socially Responsible Business Brawl," *The Progressive* (March 1995), 14.
35. *Ibid.*
36. "Ethics Study for Body Shop," *The New York Times* (October 31, 1994), C7.
37. Conlin, 73.
38. "Stake Reduced in Body Shop," *The New York Times* (July 11, 1994), C7.
39. James Fallon, "Body Shop Regroups to Meet Competition in Crowded U.S. Arena," *Women's Wear Daily* (October 21, 1994), 1.
40. Anthony Ramirez, "Body Shop Seeks Its First U.S. Agency," *The New York Times* (June 27, 1995), D7.

Case 3B

| THE BODY SHOP INTERNATIONAL PLC (1998–2004)

By 1998, The Body Shop International had grown into a multinational enterprise with almost 1,600 stores and 5,000 employees in 47 countries.[1] That year, after several years of lackluster financial performance, Anita Roddick gave the company's CEO post to a professional manager and became executive cochairman with her husband, Gordon. Anita maintained that job titles were meaningless, anyway.[2]

Despite the change, the company's financial performance between 1995 and 1997 continued to be unimpressive:[3] Worldwide sales revenue and operating profits grew from $303 million and $21 million in 1995 to $377 million and $19 million, respectively, in 1997.

More Advertising.

In 1995 to 1996, The Body Shop began to experiment with advertising in North American markets. According to one observer, The Body Shop originally thought that its brands and human-rights agenda would create valuable word-of-mouth promotion among socially conscious consumers and that advertising would not be needed. The Body Shop's anti-advertising strategy largely paid off in the United Kingdom and other European nations, where human rights activism and commerce blended more seamlessly and consumers had fewer brands and retailers than in the United States. The strategy did not work effectively in the United States, where brand differentiation was crucial. In 1997, for example, The Body Shop's same-stores sales in the United States dropped 6 percent, the company's worst performance since entering the U.S. market 10 years earlier.[4]

This case was prepared by Archie B. Carroll, University of Georgia, using publicly available information.

Since it has begun, U.S. advertising has been piecemeal, often targeted toward the Christmastime holiday sales push. In addition, it has been quirky. For example, Anita Roddick taped a radio spot that slammed the cosmetics industry. In the radio spot, Roddick said, "If more men and more women understood what really makes people beautiful, most cosmetic companies would be out of business."[5]

Getting its Act Together.

The Body Shop seemed to be trying hard to get its act together in the U.S. market. It hired a new CEO in fall 1998 and created the position of vice president for promotions. These were significant moves for the company, but it would take more than advertising to turn things around. The Body Shop typically plays down product efficacy in favor of hyping product ethicality. A case in point is its Mango Body Butter, whose ingredients the company promotes as from a "woman's cooperative in Ghana." Sean Mehegan, a writer for *Brandweek*, summarized the company's dilemma this way: "How much American consumers care about such claims lies at the heart of whether The Body Shop can turn itself around here."[6]

THE BODY SHOP'S SOCIAL AUDITS

In 1994, perhaps in response to the *Business Ethics* magazine article by Jon Entine calling its integrity into question and perhaps on its own initiative, The Body Shop began an elaborate program of annual social audits examining, in particular, its environmental, social, and animal protection initiatives. Through the social audit program, which the company based on mission statements and goals in numerous social performance categories, the company established detailed social and ecological milestones for 1995–1997. In its 218-page *Values Report 1997*, the company reported its progress.[7]

The Body Shop set policies in three areas: human and civil rights, environmental sustainability, and animal protection. In each category, the company set forth a conceptual framework for the auditing process. The auditing process in each category depended heavily on stakeholder interviews. The stakeholders who were interviewed included employees, international franchisees, customers, suppliers, shareholders, and local community/campaigning groups. The company identified the media as a potential stakeholder group for inclusion in future social auditing cycles.[8]

ALLEGATIONS CONTINUE

In 1998, The Body Shop continued to face charges that could threaten its future. The company faced a possible flood of allegations and lawsuits by franchisees charging fraudulent presentations by the company when they bought their franchises. Many U.S. franchisees had been angry at what they saw as unfair buyback terms if they wanted to get out of the business. There was talk of group action that could involve claims in the hundreds of millions of dollars.[9]

An example of the kind of lawsuit being filed was that of Jim White, who was asking for $32 million in damages. He was suing The Body Shop for fraud, fraudulent inducement, and inequitable treatment of franchisees. White claimed that the company offered rock-bottom buyback prices to franchisees caught in a 5-year spiral of declining U.S. sales. White claimed he was offered only 20 cents on the dollar and that others were offered as low as 5 cents on the dollar.[10]

INTO THE NEW MILLENNIUM

The early 2000s continued to be tumultuous for The Body Shop. The company continued to grow, but sales and profits were not good. As a result of poor Christmas sales in 2000, its annual profits were down 55 percent as it entered 2001. In the United Kingdom, the company found itself operating in a much more competitive marketplace than its beginnings 25 years prior. Most high street retail chains now are fielding their own "natural" cosmetics and toiletries, and price and promotional battles left the company's products more expensive than its rivals'.[11]

Legal Difficulties. In September 2001, a major *Fortune* magazine article featured some of the legal difficulties The Body Shop was facing because of conflicts with franchisees. It was reported that eight U.S. Body Shop franchisees, who owned 13 locations, were accusing the parent company of impeding their business. In December 2000, this group filed a lawsuit against the company asking for damages in the neighborhood of $2 million. One major complaint was that the company-owned stores were getting much better treatment than the franchisee-owned stores. Franchisee owners complained of the company failing to deliver them products while the company-owned stores had no

problem getting products. Some franchisee owners saw this chronic out-of-stock problem as a ploy to force them to sell their franchises back for a fraction on the dollar.[12]

Roddicks Step Aside. In 2002, Anita and Gordon Roddick stepped down from their positions as co-chairs of the board of directors. Along with their friend, and early investor, Ian McGlinn, they maintained control of more than 50% of the company's voting rights. Anita Roddick was to remain involved in a "defined consultant role." At about this same time, the company had been in discussions with potential buyers of the company but these talks were abandoned when offers were below what the company expected.[13] Peter Saunders, former president and CEO of the The Body Shop in North America became CEO of the company.

Financials. Annual Sales and Net Income slumped in 2001 and 2002 but snapped back in 2003 and 2004:[14]

	2004	2003	2002	2001
Annual Sales ($Millions)	711.9	602.0	538.8	539.7
Annual Net Income ($Millions)	40.5	21.5	7.7	13.7

As of 2003, sales percentages for various regions of the world were as follows:[15]

UK/Ireland	63%
Americas	26%
Europe, Middle East, And Africa	8%
Asia Pacific	3%

Growth & Competiton. By 2004, The Body Shop was operating more than 2,000 stores in 50 countries worldwide and about 70% of them were franchised. On the competition front, the company has been surpassed by Bath & Body Works and receives significant competition from Boots, the UK drugstore chain. With profitability on the rise, the company plans to open 300 new shops, mostly in Central Europe, Japan, the UK, and the U.S. It is forming a joint venture with its franchisee, Mighty Ocean, to do business in China and it is in discussions to purchase The Body Shop Canada (108 stores) from its franchisees there.

Though Anita Roddick is no longer at the helm, the Body Shop has continued its emphases on environmental and social values. In 2004, the company's Web site http://www.usa.thebodyshop.com/ summarized its important values as follows:[16]

- Against Animal Testing
- Support of Community Trade
- Activating Self Esteem
- Defending Human Rights
- Protecting Our Planet

CEO Peter Saunders is striving to get the company back on a sound, financial footing. Saunders message is posted on the company's Web site:[17]

My challenge as CEO is to revitalize our retail outlets, grow composite store sales, improve our product offer and brand communications, and invest in employee development and customer service. In delivering this plan, we will consistently apply our social and environmental principles and demonstrate integrity and transparency in our relationships with our stakeholders.

Status of Company Criticism. Much of the criticism of The Body Shop for the issues raised earlier, still led in part by Jon Entine, has subsided. A review of Jon Entine's Web site, however, shows that he continues to critique The Body Shop and continues to write periodic articles and newspaper columns about the company. Entine's Web site may be accessed at: http://www.jonentine.com/index.htm.

Anita Roddick Now. What about Anita Roddick now? She published her second book, *Business As Unusual: The Triumph of Anita Roddick and the Body Shop*, in 2001. Also in 2001 she published *Take it Personally: How to Make Conscious Choices to Change the World*. One of her first priorities is now writing. She explained, "I'm at the point in my life where I want to be heard." She adds, "I have knowledge and I want to pass it on."[18] In an interview with *Across the Board* magazine published in 2001, Anita commented on her experiences with professional consultants and executives who are not as concerned as she is about preserving The Body Shop's values. She stated: "The hardest thing for me are the marketing people, because they focus on us as a brand and our customers as consumers. We've never called it a brand; we call it The Body Shop. In 20 years, we've never, ever, ever called a customer a consumer. Customers aren't there to consume. They're there to live, love, die, get married, have friendships—they're not put on this planet to bloody consume."[19]

In 2003 Roddick published *A Revolution in Kindness*, her most recent book. She continues to speak and write and raise money for social causes. In 2004, she was attempting to raise £100,000 over two years for The Body Shop Foundations "Protect the Child" program that fights child sex abuse.[20]

The Future. The future is uncertain for The Body Shop but trends seem to be upward in terms of its projected growth and finances. Journalists like Jon Entine continue to write articles that are critical of The Body Shop.[21] Despite the criticism, the company continues to make management and strategic changes and to pursue social programs and social and sustainability audits. In the hard, cold world of global competition, founder Anita Roddick learned some tough lessons in the past decade. Although she may still believe that the purpose of a business is not just to generate profits, it has become increasingly apparent that the tension between financial and social performance requires delicate balancing of, and careful attention to, both. At stake is nothing less than the firm's survival and Roddick's stage for bringing about social change.

Questions for Discussion

1. Has Anita Roddick betrayed her philosophy about advertising by beginning to advertise in U.S. markets? Does this decision have ethical implications? Or, is it just a business decision?

2. Would you invest in The Body Shop in North America? Why or why not?

3. Will The Body Shop's social auditing program save the firm's reputation? Has the firm "snapped back" from the damage done to its reputation in the mid-1990s?

4. Do the low buyback prices offered to U.S. franchisees reflect poor Body Shop ethics or just the economic reality of risky investments?

5. Is The Body Shop regarded today as a socially responsible and ethical firm? Research the answer to this question and be prepared to report your findings.

6. At the end of these cases, what is your impression of Anita Roddick? Comment on her strengths and weaknesses and a businessperson and leader.

7. By the end of the case, does it appear that The Body Shop has finally figured out how to balance its financial and social interests? Why has the criticism subsided?

Case Endnotes

1. "Capitalism and Cocoa Butter," *The Economist* (May 16, 1998), 66–67.
2. *Ibid*. Also see Ernest Beck, "Body Shop Founder Roddick Steps Aside as CEO," *The Wall Street Journal* (May 13, 1998), B14.
3. *Values Report 1997*, The Body Shop (October 1997), 150.
4. Sean Mehegan, "Not Tested on Humans," *Brandweek* (May 19, 1997), 54.
5. *Ibid.*
6. *Ibid.*
7. *Values Report 1997*, 7–12.
8. *Ibid.*, 10–12.
9. Jan Spooner, "Body Shop Faces U.S. Legal Fights," *Financial Mail* (London) (February 22, 1998).
10. *Ibid.*
11. Harriet Marsh, "Has the Body Shop Lost Its Direction for Good?" *Marketing* (London) (May 10, 2001), 19.
12. Carlye Adler, "The Disenfranchised," *Fortune* (September 2001), 66–72.
13. Sarah Ellison, "Body Shop's Two Founders to Step Aside; Sale Talks End, *Wall Street Journal*, February 13, 2002, A15.
14. The Body Shop International PLC, "Financial Overview," *Hoover's Online*, July 7, 2004, http://www.hoovers.com/body-shop
15. The Body Shop International PLC, "Products/Operations," *Hoover's Online*, July 7, 2004, http://www.hoovers.com/body-shop/
16. "Values Reporting," http://www.thebodyshop.com/web/tbsgl/values_rep.jsp, July 7, 2004.
17. Quoted in "Values Reporting," http://www.thebodyshop.com/
18. Mike Hofman, "Anita Roddick: The Body Shop International, Established in 1976," *Inc.* (April 30, 2001), 61.
19. Matthew Budman, "Questioning Authority," *Across the Board* (January 2001), 15–16.
20. "Body Shop Appeal Aims to Raise £100K," *Third Sector*, February 25, 2004, 7.
21. Jon Entine, "Vivisecting the Anti-Vivisectionist Movement," *Drug & Cosmetic Industry* (January 1997), 38–41.

Case 4

FACING A FIRE

Hermann Singer was returning home from his surprise 70th birthday party when a "not-so-welcome" second surprise occurred. A boiler at his textile firm exploded, injuring 27 people and destroying three buildings. The devastating fire made national news. Suddenly, the future of HFS Corp., the 90-year-old business that his grandfather built, was in doubt.

THE COMPANY

The HFS Corporation was located in a small New England town. Because it employed 2,400 people, it was the one bright light in an economically depressed area. If the plant were to close or move, the impact on the community would be devastating. Furthermore, many of the current workers were the sons, daughters, and even grandchildren of other factory workers: They did high-quality work for which they were well paid. Singer considered his workers to be a part of his extended family, and he considered the community to be his home. While other New England textile manufacturers moved South to find lower wages, HFS Corporation stayed in New England and continued to pay one of the highest wage scales in the business.

THE DECISION

Singer had some difficult decisions to make. At 70, he had the option of using the insurance money to retire to Florida. The stock market seemed to be anticipating such a move because, the day after the fire, the price of his main competitor's stock rose sharply. Nevertheless, rebuilding remained an option.

This case was prepared by Ann K. Buchholtz, University of Georgia.

Several of HFS's main customers pledged their support of rebuilding and sent checks totaling over $300,000 along with their verbal pledges. Other individuals, moved by the huge loss, sent checks intended to help the now-jobless HFS employees. The money was a help, but nowhere near the estimated $1.5 million per week that would be needed to pay employee salaries. In total, it would cost an estimated $15 million to continue to pay the workforce during the rebuilding. Although Singer's personal wealth was sufficient to cover this expense, the potential expenditure was significant.

THE CHOICE

Singer had two main options: (1) rebuild the factory or (2) retire on the insurance proceeds. If he opted to rebuild, other decisions awaited him. Should he stay in New England or relocate where wages are lower? During rebuilding, should he pay his workers some or all of the wages they would have received, or should he wait until the factory was again operational?

Questions for Discussion

1. What should Hermann Singer do? Why?
2. Should he rebuild the factory or begin retirement?
3. If he rebuilds, should he relocate the firm to an area where wages are lower?
4. What provisions, if any, should Singer make for his employees? For the community?
5. What would you do if you were Singer?

Case 5

MARTHA STEWART: FREE TRADING OR INSIDER TRADING?

A blowing gust of wind moved the trees in the courtyard where the ImClone emblem stands in front of the company's headquarters in New York. ImClone Systems Incorporated, founded in 1984, "is a biopharmaceutical company dedicated to developing

This case was prepared by Kareem M. Shabana, University of Georgia

breakthrough biologic medicines in the area of oncology. The Company has utilized the many advances made in the fields of molecular biology, oncology, genomics and antibody engineering to build a novel pipeline of product candidates designed to address specific genetic mechanisms involved in cancer growth and development."[1] The company's main focus is "the development of therapeutic products for the treatment of cancer and cancer-related disorders."[2]

Twenty stories above the courtyard, Dr. Samuel Waksal, chief executive officer and founder of Imclone, stood behind his office window watching a sunny day turn into a gloomy afternoon as the somber clouds formed at the horizon. He had just received information that the "Food & Drug Administration refused to accept an approval application for ImClone's promising new Erbitux cancer drug."[3] The FDA was planning to make a public announcement of its decision the next day. Now, Dr. Waksal is pondering the future of his company and his investment. Expectations about Erbitux had been a prime reason for ImClone's soaring stock prices. Indeed, once the FDA's decision was made public, ImClone's stock prices would likely suffer.

THE DILEMMA

While there was no escape for ImClone itself from this unfortunate development, Dr. Waksal considered the alternatives available to him to minimize his losses, and maybe the losses of some family members and close friends. Dr. Waksal, his father Jack, his daughter Aliza, and a number of close friends had significant investments in ImClone. All of them would surely incur substantial losses at the start of the trading day tomorrow. Of course, selling his stock and advising his father, daughter, and friends to sell their stock would reduce their losses. However, since these sales would be based on information not available to the public, these transactions may be deemed illegal. Dr. Waksal was faced with a tough decision. On one hand, Dr. Waksal could refrain from engaging in questionable trading practices and therefore incur a significant amount of losses in his investment. On the other hand, he could choose to sell his stock based on the information he received reducing his investment losses, but violating the law and ethics of fair trade.

The Decision and Its Consequences. Soon Dr. Waksal reached a decision. Before the day was over he was on the phone trying to sell "$5 million of ImClone stock through brokerage accounts at Merrill Lynch & Co. and Bank of America Corp. But the brokers wouldn't execute the order because his shares were 'restricted,' which prevented him as an ImClone insider from selling them."[4]

Before long, on Wednesday, December 12, 2002 four FBI agents visited Dr. Waksal's house at 6:30 A.M. in the morning and took him into custody after charging him with insider trading.[5] It had been found that Dr. Waksal's father had dumped $8.2 million in ImClone Stock before the FDA announcement. Also, his daughter is believed to have dumped $2.4 million worth of ImClone stock. A close friend of Dr. Waksal's, Ms. Martha Stewart, herself the founder and chief executive officer of Martha Stewart Living Omnimedia Inc., had also sold 4,000 shares just before the bad news broke.[6] In addition, Dr. Waksal himself had been found to have bought "put" options that allowed him to profit from ImClone's stock decline.[7]

A PLEA BARGAIN

The government and Dr. Waksal reached a plea agreement wherein Dr. Waksal pleaded guilty to securities fraud and other charges.[8] Also, Dr. Waksal agreed to admit that he had tipped undisclosed individuals to dump their stock before the FDA decision was made public. Dr. Waksal's attorney, Lewis Liman, "said in a statement, 'we are glad that we have been able to reach this settlement with the SEC, and that Dr. Waksal will be able to put this part of the legal issue behind him.'"[9] In return, his father and daughter were spared facing charges.

Concerns about the effect of Dr. Waksal's work history on the plea bargain were raised. Dr. Waksal had been "asked to leave Stanford University, the National Cancer Institute of the National Institutes of Health, Tufts University School of Medicine and Mount Sinai School of Medicine for what supervisors and others said was misleading, and in one case, falsified research."[10] Dr. Waksal is now serving a seven-year prison sentence.[11]

ImClone Stock Takes a Nose Dive. It was the sharp decline in ImClone stock the day after the FDA made its announcement that caught the attention of compliance officers at Merrill Lynch. The ImClone stock had dropped 16%.[12] Later the stock reached a low of $7.55 down from $62.80 on December 24.[13]

A CHAIN REACTION

The government was also suspicious of Ms. Stewart's sale of her ImClone stock. It was believed that she had sold her shares after she received information about the FDA's decision regarding Erbitux before this information was made public. A spokesperson for Ms. Stewart denied the allegations and insisted that Ms. Stewart had a prearranged agreement with her broker, Mr. Bacanovic, to sell ImClone stock if it fell below $60. Her assistant broker, Mr. Douglas Faneuil, however, claimed that such an agreement never existed, and that Ms. Stewart sold her 4000 shares of ImClone after she learned that Dr. Waksal and other family members had dumped their stock.[14] Apparently, the government had enough reason to believe that Ms. Stewart had indeed used insider information in her sale of the ImClone stock just before the FDA decision was made public. Eventually, charges of insider trading and were brought up against Ms. Stewart.

In the wake of the government's accusation of Ms. Stewart's insider trading in ImClone stock, an investor in Martha Stewart's own company, Martha Stewart Living Omnimedia Inc., filed a lawsuit accusing her of insider trading in her own stock.[15] It was believed that after information about the government's intention of charging Ms. Stewart with insider trading in her ImClone stock, Ms. Stewart and a number of top executives at Martha Stewart Living Omnimedia Inc. sold significant amounts of their stock to avoid the losses that they would incur when the government publicly announced charges against Ms. Stewart. Since Martha Stewart's company is built around her personal identity and achievements, it was expected that the stock would take a big hit once charges against Ms. Stewart were made public. Sure thing, stock of Martha Stewart Living Omnimedia Inc. plummeted by 60% after the charges were made public.

In response to the allegations, a spokesperson for Martha Stewart Living Omnimedia Inc. claimed that these charges were baseless. Her spokesperson said that Martha Stewart had sold her stock before she knew she was under investigation. As for the other executives, their sales were unrelated to Martha Stewart. The executives were simply cashing in their options, the spokesperson asserted.[16]

IN COURT

After the plea negotiations failed, as Ms. Stewart would not agree to any plea that required jail time, Martha Stewart appeared in the Manhattan courtroom to be charged.[17] "The nine count indictment alleges that Stewart altered evidence that she traded on inside information about the biotech company ImClone Systems, conspired with her stockbroker to lie to federal officials investigating the trade and defrauded shareholders in her company, Martha Stewart Living Omnimedia, by misleading them about why she had sold the stock."[18] In response to these charges, Ms. Stewart's voice clearly echoed in the courtroom "Not Guilty."[19]

A Court Verdict. Judge Miriam Goldman Cedarbaum announced that Martha Stewart was guilty on four counts: obstruction of justice, conspiracy, and two counts of making false statements.[20] The most serious charge of securities fraud was dropped, however. The main reason is believed to be that the plea bargain of Mr. Douglas Faneuil, Martha Stewart's assistant broker, shed doubt on his testimony, which was a key part to Ms. Stewart's indictment.

The verdict made a clear impression on Ms. Stewart's daughter Alexis who had accompanied Ms. Stewart in the courtroom throughout the trial. Martha Stewart, on the other hand, maintained her resolve. The public opinion about the verdict was mixed. While some believed that Ms. Stewart was justly tried and convicted, others insisted that Martha Stewart was a victim of a frustrated government and a scapegoat for the big corporate scandals like Enron and WorldCom.

Was Stewart a Scapegoat? Earlier, after the charges had been brought up against Ms. Stewart, James Comey, U.S. Attorney for the southern district of New York, asserted "Martha Stewart is being prosecuted not for who she is but what she did."[21] In contrast, Martha Stewart fans and supporters display their support in different ways. Some stood outside the courthouse against police barricades chanting "we love you

Martha."[22] Others conveyed their message through reports. Rosie O'Donnell, a friend of Martha Stewart's expressed her disappointment to *Newsweek*: "I am outraged and beside myself. This is a travesty. Shame on the federal government."[23] Martha Stewart's retired secretary also expressed her feelings to *Newsweek*: "This is all about the need to make an example of a powerful woman. . . . Martha Stewart is not Enron."[24]

While the conviction of Ms. Stewart is supposed to be grounded on evidence, the effect of the public image of Martha Stewart may have played a role as well. Juror Hartridge expressed her perception of Martha Stewart to a *Newsweek* reporter: "She seemed to say: 'I don't have anything to worry about. I fooled the jury. I don't have anything to prove.'"[25] Even the support that Martha got from friends like Rosie O'Donnell and Bill Cosby seemed to have worked against her. Juror Hartridge seemed to have taken celebrities' appearance in court as a tactic to sway the jury. She asserted, "Like that was supposed to sway our decision."[26]

Martha is Sentenced. On July 16, 2004, Ms. Stewart was sentenced to 5 months in prison and 5 months in home confinement. This was the minimum sentence. In announcing the sentence, Judge Cedarbaum said that she had received more than 1,500 letters written on behalf of Ms. Stewart. The judge stated that it is "apparent that you have helped many people outside of your own family and that you have a supportive family and hundreds of admirers."[27] Ms. Stewart reiterated at that time that she would appeal her conviction. The judge decided that Ms. Stewart could remain free during her appeal and some experts predicted this could take as long as a year.[28]

When Ms. Stewart received the minimum sentence, the stock price of her company rose immediately in response to the minimum sentence. As word spread about her relatively light sentence, her company's stock rose by 37%.[29]

THE FUTURE OF TWO COMPANIES

After further development of Erbitux and resubmission for FDA approval, ImClone received approval for its promising drug, and its stock soared again. Unfortunately for Dr. Waksal, he ended up losing his position as chief executive officer of ImClone, paying a hefty fine to the SEC, and receiving maximum sentence from the court. His daughter and father, however, are spared facing charges based on the plea-agreement that Dr. Waksal made with the government.

Martha Stewart Living Omnimedia Inc.

Throughout the process of Martha Stewart's investigation, indictment, and trial, speculations about the future of her company and its future seemed to get the attention of the business news. Some believed that the loyalty to the Martha Stewart brand would endure these tough times. Others, like Mr. Jeff Swystun, a brand consultant with Interbrand had different expectations. He asserted, "The parent company has got to distance itself from Martha Stewart the person pretty quickly." He then added, "They have to drop her name from everything that hits the customer."[30]

While the passage of time will tell how Martha Stewart Living Omnimedia Inc. will be affected by this crisis, present indicators show that Ms. Stewart is far from accepting defeat. Regarding the legal issues, she has explicitly said that she plans to appeal her verdict. As for her business career, while she had to step down as chief executive officer of Martha Stewart Living Omnimedia Inc., for a brief period she assumed the new position of chief creative officer.[31]

Martha Stewart seems to have a determination to stay close to her company. Her new title of chief creative officer did not send the message that she was moving away from her company any time soon. However, in March of 2004 she resigned as chief creative officer and a director of the company. Ms. Stewart still owns 61% of the company's shares.[32]

Public Support.
The public support that she got from the fans that stood outside the courthouse, or those who visited her Web site http://www.marthatalks.com clearly have indicated that she has a loyal customer base. Moreover, she received support from the business community as well. Kmart Holding Corp. continues to carry Martha Stewart products. *The Wall Street Journal* writes: "Kmart Holding Corp. chose to stand by Martha Stewart's embattled company, extending its license agreement for two years and dropping a lawsuit over royalty payments."[33] In the end, the future of Martha Stewart Living Omnimedia Inc. lies in the hands of the American customer. Her challenge is well depicted in the words of Jeffrey Sonnenfeld of Yale University: "Americans love to forgive. . . . But this is going to be pretty damn hard for her to get past."[34]

Lengthy Appeal.
With Judge Cedarbaum's decision to permit Ms. Stewart to remain free during her appeal, which could take a year or longer, considerable uncertainty regarding her company's future remains. It has even been speculated that her freedom may work against her company's stock because closure is not being reached on the case, and the stock market dislikes uncertainty. And, with Ms. Stewart free for some undetermined length of time, the company's board will now have to address a very important strategic decision regarding the extent of her involvement in the company during the appeals process.[35]

Questions for Discussion

1. What are the ethical issues in this case?
2. Was Martha Stewart guilty of a serious crime or was she a scapegoat for other, more serious, CEO malfeasants, who had not yet been brought to justice?
3. Has the media attention given to the Martha Stewart case been excessive? Has this helped or hurt her case?
4. Does Ms. Stewart's sentence seem appropriate given the magnitude of her offense? Is a prison sentence the appropriate penalty for her offenses?
5. If you were on the Board of Directors of Ms. Stewart's company, what role would you say she should play after this case has been settled? Should she be kept away or kept close to her company? Why?
6. Do current research on this case and update Ms. Stewart's personal situation and that of her company.

Case Endnotes

1. http://www.imclone.com/content.php?pg=company_overview.html.
2. http://www.biospace.com/company_profile.cfm?companyID=1046.
3. Catherine Arnst in New York, with John Carey in Washington and Jack Ewing in Frankfurt. *Business Week*, February 10, 2002.
4. Kara Scannell. *Wall Street Journal*. (Eastern Edition). New York, N.Y.: Mar. 12, 2003. pg. C.1.
5. Jayne O'Donnelle and Julie Appleby, *USA Today*. http://www.usatoday.com/money/health/2002-06-11-imclone.htm.
6. Greg Smith. *Knight Rider Tribune Business News*. Washington: Oct. 15, 2002 pg. 1.
7. Kara Scannell. *Wall Street Journal*. (Eastern Edition). New York, N.Y.: Mar. 12, 2003. pg. C.1.
8. Daniel Kadlec. *Time*, Mar. 15 2004. pg. 64.
9. Kara Scannell. *Wall Street Journal*. (Eastern Edition). New York, N.Y.: Mar. 12, 2003. pg. C.1.
10. Jerry Markon, Joann S. Lubin and Geeta Anand. *Wall Street Journal*. (East edition). New York, N.Y.: Sep. 30, 2002. pg. A.6.
11. Daniel Kadlec. *Time*, Mar. 15 2004. pg. 64.
12. Daniel Kadlec. *Time*, Mar. 15 2004. pg. 64.
13. Jayne O'Donnell and Julie Appleby, *USA Today*. http://www.usatoday.com/money/health/2002-06-11-imclone.htm.
14. Greg B. Smith. *Knight Rider Tribune Business News*. Washington: Oct. 22, 2002 pg. 1.
15. Greg B. Smith. *Knight Rider Tribune Business News*. Washington: Aug. 22, 2002 pg. 1.
16. Tom Hamburger and Jerry Markon. *Wall Street Journal*. (Eastern Edition). New York, N.Y.: Aug. 22, 2002. pg. A.6.
17. Jyoti Thottam. *Time*, Mar. 16 2003. pg.44.
18. Jyoti Thottam. *Time*, Mar. 16 2003. pg.44.
19. Jyoti Thottam. *Time*, Mar. 16 2003. pg.44.
20. Daniel Kadlec. *Time*, Mar. 15 2004. pg. 64.
21. Jyoti Thottam. *Time*, Mar. 16 2003. pg.44.
22. Keith Naughton and Barney Gimbel. *Newsweek*, Mar. 15, 2004. pg. 28.
23. Keith Naughton and Barney Gimbel. *Newsweek*, Mar. 15, 2004. pg. 28.
24. Keith Naughton and Barney Gimbel. *Newsweek*, Mar. 15, 2004. pg. 28.
25. Keith Naughton and Barney Gimbel. *Newsweek*, Mar. 15, 2004. pg. 28.
26. Keith Naughton and Barney Gimbel. *Newsweek*, Mar. 15, 2004. pg. 28.
27. Constance L. Hays, "5 Months in Jail, and Stewart Vows, 'I'll be Back,' " *The New York Times*, July 17, 2004, A1.
28. Andrew Ross Sorkin, "Will a Short Sentence Prove Sweet for a Stock?" *The New York Times*, July 18, 2004, BU6.
29. *Ibid.*
30. Keith Naughton and Barney Gimbel. *Newsweek*, Mar. 15, 2004. pg 28
31. Jyoti Thottam. *Time*, Mar. 16 2003. pg.44.
32. Sorkin, 2004, *ibid.*
33. Amy Merrick, *Wall Street Journal*. (Eastern Edition). New York, N.Y.: Apr. 27, 2004. pg. B.4.
34. Keith Naughton and Barney Gimbel. *Newsweek*, Mar. 15, 2004. pg. 28.
35. Sorkin, 2004, *ibid.*

| THE CASE OF THE KILLER PHRASES (A)

As the students of Class 35 of the Marberry Executive MBA program straggled into the classroom for their one-day workshop on business ethics, they stopped by the front set of seats to drop off their written assignments. Professor Stevens chatted with a couple of the members of the group while lining up his stack of cases and videos for the day's work. Just as the clock reached 8:00 a.m., the appointed time for the workshop to begin, Max Snell stopped and casually asked, "Gee, Professor Stevens, our study group did the case write-ups as a group effort. We weren't sure that was correct, was it?" Taken a bit by surprise, because the written assignment was to be done by each student individually, Professor Stevens replied, "Just drop your paper on the pile and I'll look at it later."

The workshop day was filled with lectures, discussions, videos, and case discussions. Professor Stevens forgot about Max's comment, but, as he got into his car to drive home after the 8-hour workshop, he realized he would have to deal with the group's nonconforming actions carefully.

BUSINESS ETHICS WORKSHOP

The Business Ethics Workshop had been taught by a variety of people over the years. Recently a retired professor of philosophy from New York had come in to teach it. The reviews had been mixed, so the Marberry Executive MBA (MEMBA) Academic Committee asked Bob Stevens, a tenured senior professor at Marberry State University and Past President of the American Business Ethics Academic Association, to give the workshop in addition to continuing to teach the Program's Business Policy course. The Academic Committee's hope was that Professor Stevens, a past winner of the Program's "Best Instructor" Award, would be able to strike the proper balance between theory and managerial practice.

The Marberry Executive MBA program was similar in conception to most executive MBA programs. Students were expected to be promising mid-level and senior-level executives from local and regional organizations. Each student must have an executive sponsor who commits to helping the student deal with the pressures inherent in having to continue working full-time while completing the MEMBA in two years going alternative weeks Friday/Saturday. Sponsors were expected to be informal liaisons between their firms (which were paying over double what the local

This case was contributed by Steven N. Brenner, Portland State University. Used with permission.

university charged for its MBA program). The financial realities of executive MBA programs include the need to generate demand from large organizations and to maintain cordial and positive relationships so that large numbers of their employees are sent to these more expensive programs.

GRADING THE PAPER

When Professor Stevens got home around 5:45 p.m. that day, he was bushed and decided to wait until the next day to tackle the grading of the Workshop's Pass/Fail assignment. The next morning he went straight to the paper turned in by Max Snell, a member of the "Five Aces" study group (see Exhibit 1). The content was certainly well within the "Pass" range. It seemed odd to him that the list of his study group members was handwritten at the top of the first page of Max's paper. If this was truly a group paper, why hadn't the group's names been part of the printed material?

Bob took a moment and went to a copy of the Workshop assignment that read, "You are to prepare an analysis of each case consisting of . . . ." Why had the other 37 students in the Business Ethics Workshop seen this as an individual assignment, while the Five Aces concluded it was a group assignment? For group assignments, Professor Stevens had always included language such as, "Your group is to . . . ." as a way of signaling only one version of the work need be submitted. There had never been this situation before.

Leafing through the pile of 42 papers, Bob selected the Five Aces' other four papers and gave them a quick look. It seemed strange that each of the five papers had both significant similarities and obvious differences. As he thought about the group's actions, he realized that each member of the Five Aces had submitted his/her own slightly modified "version" of the various assigned case analyses.

CONCLUSIONS

More careful examination of the group members' papers led to the following conclusions:

1. Only Max's paper listed the other group members. The other group members had listed themselves as the sole author of their submitted paper.
2. Each of the five papers was slightly different. For example, the ordering of the five case analyses varied among

the group's set of papers. The wording of each paper's introduction was different, some had added their own analytical points, and some presented differential or supplemental recommendations.

3. There were a few phrases that seemed to be in four or all five of the papers. These phrases were essential to the communication of some key point or conclusion. Professor Stevens saw these as "killer phrases"—elements of the group's analysis that none could bring themselves to leave out of their own papers.

Reflecting on what he had just read, Professor Stevens drew some tentative conclusions. First, some or all members of the Five Aces had worked together on the five case analyses (the "killer phrases" were substantial evidence of this). Second, they had planned to submit individual papers under their own names without telling the instructor (evidence for this was that only one had handwritten the other group members' names on his paper). Third, the group may not have been "confused" about the nature of the assignment (evidence for this was the apparent attempt at individualizing each person's paper). Fourth, a potential claim that they thought this was a group assignment was contradicted by their submitting five individual papers instead of only one group paper.

CONSIDERING ALTERNATIVES

Professor Stevens thought about what he had found and considered alternatives, but decided that he had better get the other papers graded given the MEMBA's expectation that grades would be ready within two days of a workshop. As he

proceeded to grade the other students' papers, he settled into a comfortable routine—reading the situation/issue description section quickly, pondering the level of analysis provided, and determining whether the recommendations were persuasive. About two-thirds of the way through the seemingly never-ending pile, Bob came upon a paper with the same "killer phrases" found in the Five Aces group's papers. William Marshall's paper was nearly identical to the work of five who had worked together. Looking at Class 35's team roster showed that Marshall was not a member of the Five Aces, but was part of the "Fearsome Foursome."

The situation had just gotten extremely complex. How had Marshall gotten the Five Aces work? Had he been an active participant or just found their work and used it as his own? Why hadn't his name been placed on the paper Max Snell had submitted? Was that an oversight or a signal that he had really done nothing more than copy (with minor cosmetic changes) the work of one of the Five Aces members? Perhaps, even more improbably, the Five Aces could have used his paper as the basis of their work.

Bob Stevens was dumbfounded at the picture that had just emerged. Five or six members of the Executive MBA Program might have committed plagiarism (Max's decision to provide the full list of contributors might reduce his behavior below "plagiarism" as he had provided an accurate picture of who had done work on his submitted paper). One (the individual from the other study group) may or may not have done any work on his paper beyond a modest attempt at concealment or may have had

---

his paper used, with or without his knowledge, as the basis of the Five Aces' papers. The situation seemed to demand action, but Professor Stevens realized that any explicit action on his part bringing up plagiarism could lead to a lot of work for him and serious consequences for those involved.

How to Proceed?

After completing the grading of 36 other Business Ethics Workshop papers, Professor Stevens sat back in his home office chair and thought about how to proceed. A variety of questions raced through his brain.

- Who should he contact first (the students; Professor Tim James, the Program's academic committee chair; or Marjorie Washburn, the Program's executive director)?

- What evidence, if any, should he develop?
- Should a student's motive or circumstances matter?
- What definition of "plagiarism" did the students have?
- Did they do something worthy of formal action?
- What impact would a formal accusation and/or determination of plagiarism have on an EMBA student or on the MEMBA program itself?
- Was any action required given that the "course" was a workshop and the grading, pass/fail?
- What time and effort might be required to resolve any issues raised about these papers?

Question for Discussion

1. If you were Bob Stevens what would you do and why?

Case 7

TO HIRE OR NOT TO HIRE

As a manager in human resources, part of my job is to guide the process by which my company selects new employees. Recently, we selected an applicant to fill a computer analyst position. The supervising manager and a selection panel selected this applicant over a number of others based on her superior qualifications and interview.

Background Check

However, a routine background check indicated that the applicant had been convicted 18 years earlier for false check writing. The application form has a section where the applicant is asked if he or she has ever been convicted of anything other than a traffic violation. In response to that question, this applicant wrote "no." When informed of this, the supervising manager stated that she would still like to hire the applicant, but asked me for my recommendation. The job does not involve money handling.

This case was prepared by Tim Timmons.

Questions for Discussion

1. If the applicant mistakenly thought that her record had been cleared over time and therefore did not lie intentionally, would that make any difference?

2. Should the fact that the applicant did not tell the truth on one part of the application automatically disqualify her from further consideration?

3. Should the supervising manager be allowed to hire this applicant despite the fact that the applicant lied on her application, provided the manager is willing to take the risk and assume responsibility for the applicant?

4. If the applicant freely admitted the conviction, should she still be considered for the position? Should a minor offense committed 18 years ago, when the applicant was in her early 20's, disqualify her when she is overall the most qualified applicant? What types of convictions, and how recent, should disqualify potential new hires?

DOES CHEATING IN GOLF PREDICT CHEATING IN BUSINESS?

In 2004, David Callahan published a new book titled *The Cheating Culture: Why More Americans are Doing Wrong to Get Ahead*. In this book, Callahan documents how cheating has been on the rise the past two decades. It has been evident in business scandals, doping in sports, plagiarism by journalists, and cheating by students.[1]

Callahan blames the dog-eat-dog economic climate of the past two decades for much of the cheating that is going on. He points to four reasons why we have more cheating today. *New pressures* are part of it. *Bigger rewards for winning* is also a key factor. *Temptation* is ever present. Finally, he believes *trickle down corruption* has been at work. With this fourth point, he is referring to the tendency for everyone to start cheating because they perceive the system is stacked against them and so people start making up their own rules to justify their actions.[2] In short, he argues that we live in a cheating culture.

CAN ONE HOLD TWO STANDARDS?

One issue that frequently comes up in discussions of cheating and ethics is whether people can hold one set of standards or ethics in their personal lives and another set of standards or ethics in their business lives. This question is often raised about our political leaders as well. Often the discussion juxtaposes one's personal ethics in specific spheres of life such as dealing with family, friends, or playing sports with one's ethics in business or some other profession of which one is a part. Debate is often continuous on this topic and both sides are well represented in the dialog.

A Personal Experience. Years ago, the author of this case used to play golf with a man who held impeccable golf ethics. He meticulously followed every detailed rule of the game and made sure all around him did also. Over the years, however, this man always bragged about how much he was cheating the federal government out of taxes. He proclaimed often that he had not paid his taxes in five years. It was interesting that the man never saw the disconnect between his golf ethics and his personal ethics.

To think about this topic further, it is interesting to consider the findings from a recent survey of CEOs regarding the extent to which they cheat, or bend the rules, in the game of golf —a game typically associated with business executives.

This case was prepared by Archie B. Carroll, University of Georgia.

THE SURVEY AND OTHER OPINIONS

A survey of prominent corporate executives commissioned by Starwood Hotels and Resorts generated some interesting findings. According to their study of 401 high-ranking corporate executives, 82% admit to being less than honest on the golf course. When asked whether they wager on golf, 87% said they did. When asked what was the largest bet they ever made on a golf game, the average high was $589. For executives making over $250,000 per year, the average high was $1,947.[3] So, money is often at stake in the games they play. A summary of findings to come out of the Starwood study were the following:

* 99% consider themselves honest in business
* 87% have played with someone who cheats at golf
* 82% say they cheat at golf
* 82% hate others who cheat at golf
* 72% believe business and golf behavior parallel each other.[4]

Others Are Doing It. Do executives cheat at golf more frequently than other golfers? GolfDigest.com asked this question of golfers and nearly half said they believe that fewer than 40% of golfers fudge at the game. *USA Today* interviewed a dozen CEOs and they said they personally bend the rules sometimes. They also report, however, that they observe other CEOs bending the rules constantly. Behaviors often witnessed is the "other guy" improving their lies, hitting do-over shots (mulligans), forgetting a whiff (missed swing), forgetting to count a missed 3-foot putt, and kicking their balls out of the rough or their opponent's balls into the sand.[5]

IS GOLF ETHICS RELATED TO BUSINESS ETHICS?

One former bank president interviewed said he has declined a loan or two after witnessing a CEO cheat on the golf course. The bank president was dumbfounded when CEOs would cheat during the same time that he is judging their honesty with respect to a possible loan. The bank president concluded: "When you see what they'll do for a $10 bet, it makes you wonder what they'd do on a million dollar loan."[6]

It's a Social Thing. The CEO of Starwood is also a golfer. According to him, he doesn't see the survey as an indictment of the character of executives. "This is a social thing, not a corporate report card," he says. But, the former CEO of Chipshot.com says that "cheating is very much a part of the journey of golf." Another CEO goes on: "I suspect that CEOs as a class of people have a need to appear competent at a lot of things."[7]

In commenting further on the study's findings, the CEO of Starwood noticed the disconnect between some of the findings. He noted that 82% say they under-count strokes, improve their lie, or some other rules violation, but when asked whether they are honest at business, 99% of them say they are.[8]

An organizational psychologist who has been interviewing business executives for decades observed that executives who lie do not consider themselves to be liars. It is similar to their reporting that their outstanding strength is working with people, but when you speak to their subordinates they call that their biggest weakness. The consultant went on to say that "They lose their ability to distinguish what is honest and what is not." The lies get bigger and bigger and "we're seeing this played out everywhere now, from Tyco to Enron."[9]

Confirming this same point, another consultant observed an executive cheat by kicking his opponent's ball twice, sending it into the bushes. The opponent could not find the ball and had to take a one-stroke penalty never imagining his opponent had done this. The consultant was with the ball-kicker later and confronted him about his action. The executive-golfer humorously rationalized: "That was worth about $75,000 per kick. That's probably more than the top kickers in the NFL make." The consultant was quite surprised that the executive would look him in the eye and try to make this clever comment, especially when the executive knew he did speaking and writing on ethics in management."[10]

Insights into Character. Interestingly, the CEOs differ about whether golf cheaters are business cheaters, but they almost all agree that the way executives handle the frustration of the game gives them insights into the executive's character. Another CEO observed that he really gets concerned with his golfing partners start blaming their poor shots on the sun or on some other distraction. He said you need to watch out for golfers like that. But, he said that he is unconcerned about routine cheating. He concluded: "I would be suspicious of a CEO who didn't cheat. If they have a good golf game, they should be spending more time running the company."[11]

Questions for Discussion

1. What are the ethical issues in this case?
2. Do we live today in a "cheating culture?" Do you agree with Callahan's analysis of the situation?
3. Is cheating outside of work in one's personal life directly or indirectly related to cheating at work?
4. How can a person hold two sets of ethics and behave consistently in either venture? Give examples from your own personal life.
5. Could flawed ethics in golf just be considered "part of the game" and unrelated to ethics at work?
6. What insights into executive behavior and thinking do you get from this case?
7. Are there parallels between the experiences of executives described in this case and the lives of students? How are they similar or different?

Case Endnotes

1. Daniel Callahan, *The Cheating Culture: Why More Americans are Doing Wrong to Get Ahead.* New York: Harcourt, Inc., 2004.
2. *Ibid*, 20-23.
3. Del Jones, "Many CEOs Bend the Rules (of Golf)" *USA Today*, June 26, 2002, 1A.
4. *Ibid.*
5. *Ibid.*, 2A.
6. *Ibid.*
7. *Ibid.*
8. *Ibid.*
9. *Ibid.*
10. *Ibid.*
11. *Ibid.*

Case 9

| THE TRAVEL EXPENSE BILLING CONTROVERSY

Early in 2000, Neal A. Roberts, an employee of Pricewaterhouse-Coopers LLP, the major accounting firm, learned that his employer was earning millions of dollars a year by way of a billing practice that he thought was questionable. PricewaterhouseCoopers (PwC), the accounting Goliath, had been collecting large rebates on airline tickets and other travel expenses being charged as expenses to clients of the firm. It turns out that these rebates were not being returned to the firm's clients in the form of savings, but rather, the firm was keeping these rebates for itself. In short, travel expenses had become a source of profits for the firm and their unknowing clients were footing the bill.[1]

This case was prepared by Archie B. Carroll, University of Georgia.

The way this was working was that the firm would bill the clients for the full price of airline tickets and other travel-related expenses, but privately, the firm negotiated discounts and rebates that they then got at the end of the year based upon total amounts spent. The clients, of course, were unaware of the back-end discounts and rebates the firm was getting; therefore, they were being charged more than the firm's true out-of-pocket expenses for the items.

Mr. Roberts apparently made a number of attempts to object to his firm's practice, but had little or mixed success. His efforts did help to generate several private lawsuits and a government investigation into PwC's rebate scheme. One case, in particular, was taking place in Texarkana, Arkansas, and it resulted in the public disclosure of numerous company documents upon which the facts of the case are being publicly established. The documents have been revealing how a number of professional firms in accounting, consulting, and law, have been turning reimburseable expenses such as airfare and hotel rooms into profit centers for themselves.[2]

SEVERAL FIRMS INVOLVED

The lead plaintiff in this and several other cases was Warmack-Muskogee LP. Warmack-Muskogee's lawsuits were against PwC, KPMG and Ernst & Young, so it wasn't just PwC that had been accused of these practices. These three firms had been charged with billing their clients for the full face amount of certain travel expenses, such as airline tickets, hotel rooms, and car-rental expenses, while pocketing undisclosed rebates and volume discounts they received under various contracts they had with airline, car-rental, lodging, and other travel expense related vendors.[3] One defense these firms has frequently set forth is that everyone else is also doing it.

PwC AGREES TO SETTLEMENT

Though not admitting guilt, PwC agreed in December 2003 to a settlement estimated to be worth $54.5 million. PwC had once provided litigation-consulting services for Warmack-Muskogee. One third of the settlement will go to the plaintiff's attorneys and the balance will be available to current and former PwC clients in the form of cash or credits for future services.[4]

DETAILS OF THE PRICEWATERHOUSECOOPERS CASE

When Neal Roberts inadvertently discovered his firm's travel billing practices, he made an effort to address the problem while working within the confines of his firm. Roberts raised objections to the practice. One person responding to Robert's concerns was Barbara Kipp, the partner in charge of PwC's ethics department. Kipp wrote an email in April 2000 to another top partner in which she said "Al, while I appreciate the importance of managing as tight a fiscal ship as we can, I somehow feel that we are

being a bit greedy here." Kipp was addressing Albert Thiess, the New York-based partner responsible for oversight of the firm's travel department.[5] Kipp also said in her email that she thought the rebate policy looked like the firm was "double dipping."[6]

Complaint to Ethics Hotline.
Roberts was not the only partner in the firm to raise questions about the travel expense rebates. Jean Joslyn, at the time a director of the firm's health-care consulting group in Chicago, earlier wrote an email in February 1999 to James F. Lennon, the firm's global-travel director. Joslyn said in her email: "My question is how this rebate will be allocated back to our clients?" Lennon's reply was similar to Thiess' opinion, "We negotiate these deals, not our clients." A couple days later Joslyn, who was disturbed by the response, called the firm's ethics hotline and left a message of concern about the practice.[7]

According to the firm's documents, the ethics complaint filed by Joslyn led to a meeting in New York on March 19, 1999 in which the 14 attendees, which included members of the firm's management committee, decided that the firm would reinstate a 12.5% front-end discount that would lower the ticket prices to clients. What the committee did not tell Joslyn was that the total discounts, including the back-end rebates, would continue to exist and in some instances would be as high as 40 percent. This meant that PwC would continue to pocket substantial amounts on many of their expenditures.[8]

Roberts Continues to Push.
Upon learning of the discounts and rebates the firm was keeping, Roberts sent an email to a partner he was working with in Dallas on litigation-consulting for the Federal Deposit Insurance Corporation. He said: "I cannot believe that such discounts exist since that would leave us open to billing fraud accusations on most government contracts and others as well."[9] Next, Roberts contacted Hilary Krane, an in-house PwC lawyer and she recommended he contact the firm's ethics department. In addition, Krane sent Roberts a copy of an earlier email she had written to one of the firm's lawyers in Washington, DC in which she expressed her own concern about the practice. In her email she expressed unease that the firm was billing government clients for plane tickets without telling them about the back-end discounts and rebates her firm was collecting.[10]

Policy is Revised.
By October 2000, a working group including Kipp, Krane, Theiss, and several others met and made the decision to do something. They decided to shift most of the discounts up front so their clients could benefit from the reduced prices. Under their revised policy, PwC would seek front-end discounts of 28% with 8% rebates remaining to "cover our costs." Under this policy, the firm would still get to keep 8% savings. The group announced its new policy to be effective January 1, 2001, but decided there was no need to reimburse their clients for the millions they had collected previously on the earlier rebates.[11]

ROBERTS AND THE FALSE CLAIMS ACT

Roberts was still not satisfied with the firm's decision and he continued to press it to refund previous clients an amount equal to the back-end rebates the firm had received. By late 2000, Roberts engaged a law firm, Packard, Packard, & Johnson, of Salt Lake City, that specialized in filing False Claims lawsuits against federal contractors, such as his firm.[12]

False Claims Act. The False Claims Act is a piece of federal legislation that is designed to help the government ferret out fraud on the part of firms with which it does business. Under the Federal False Claims Act, private citizens who know of people or companies that are defrauding the government may sue on the government's behalf and share in the proceeds of the suit. Citizens who bring these causes of actions do so under the qui tam provisions of the Act.[13] The *qui tam* provisions allow an individual, frequently acting in the role of a whistleblower, to bring suit and share in the damages recovered as a result of the lawsuit. Over the past decade or more, hundreds of *qui tam* lawsuits have been filed and these have resulted in four billion dollars in recoveries for the United States Treasury. The whistleblowers who filed these suits may collect between 15% to 30% of the recovered taxes and penalties and this has resulted in more than $100 million for their efforts over this time span.[14] In 2003 alone, the lawsuits filed under this act recovered $1.5 billion.[15]

Back to Robert's Situation. From this point on, Roberts had a financial interest in his lawsuit against his own firm. He started cooperating with investigators who began looking into the activities of his firm. During this period, Roberts reported that his pay and status at the firm were declining and he complained that he was being urged to retire early. His annual pay was cut by 50%, but a spokesman for the firm said that the pay cut started before his first complaints in early 2000. He was told by partners that he was not producing enough business for the firm.

Mr. Roberts retired from PwC in May 2001. On October 1, 2001, the firm stopped taking airline rebates completely. The company started structuring all discounts as front-end price reductions that would be passed on to the clients. They also decided to charge clients $25 to $60 per ticket for "transaction" fees which are disclosed to the clients.[16]

Questions for Discussion

1. Identify the ethical issues in this case.
2. Who are the stakeholders and what are their stakes?
3. What is your appraisal of the ethics of the travel expense billing practices described in the case? What are the ethical arguments for and against them?
4. Did Roberts' complaint to the ethics department help or not? Did his firm seem receptive to his concerns?
5. What does the travel billing practice tell you about the *culture* of professional firms such as accountants, consultants, lawyers? Does it make you wonder what other practices are being used in which the clients are not being informed?
6. The case ended with the company paying a huge settlement and eventually providing the discounts to the clients that Roberts and others were calling for. Is this a case of a firm's greed and self-interest getting in the way of their sense of fairness to their customers?
7. What is your assessment of the *qui tam* provisions of the False Claims Act? Does this provide a financial incentive for employees to want to gather "dirt" on their employers and use it for their own financial gain? What are the strengths and weaknesses of such a law?

Case Endnotes

1. Jonathan Weil, "Court Files Offer Inside Look at Pricewaterhouse Billing Clash," *Wall Street Journal*, January 5, 2004, A1.
2. *Ibid.*
3. LuAnn Bean, "Rebates: Do the big four need an ethics audit?" *Journal of Corporate Accounting & Finance*, May/June 2004, 37.
4. Weil, A1.
5. Jonathan Weil, "PricewaterhouseCoopers Partners Criticized Travel Billing," *Wall Street Journal*, September 30, 2003, C1.
6. Weil, January 5, 2004, A10.
7. Weil, January 5, 2004, A10.
8. *Ibid.*
9. *Ibid.*
10. *Ibid.*
11. *Ibid.*
12. *Ibid.*
13. The False Claims Act Resource Center, http://www.falseclaims act.com/
14. Ibid. "Qui Tam Provisions of the False Claims Act."
15. "IRS May Offer Co Whistle-Blowers Share of Recovered Taxes," *Wall Street Journal Online*, June 19, 2004, http://www.wsj.com/.
16. Weil, January 5, 2004, A10.

Case 10

PHANTOM EXPENSES

Jane Adams had just completed a sales training course with her new employer, a major small appliance manufacturer. She was assigned to work as a trainee under Ann Green, one of the firm's most productive sales reps on the East Coast. At the end of the first week, Jane and Ann were sitting in a motel room filling out their expense vouchers for the week.

INFLATING EXPENSES

Jane casually remarked to Ann that the training course had stressed the importance of filling out expense vouchers accurately. Ann immediately launched into a long explanation of how the company's expense reporting resulted in underpayment of actual costs. She claimed that all the sales reps on the East Coast made up the difference by padding their expenses under $25, which did not require receipts. A rule of thumb used was to inflate total expenses by 25 percent. When Jane questioned whether this was honest, Ann said that even if the reported expenses exceeded actual expenses, the company owed them the extra money, given the long hours and hard work they put in.

This case was written by David J. Fritzsche, Penn State Great Valley. Permission to reprint granted by Arthur Andersen & Co., SC.

FOLLOW THE AGREED-UPON PRACTICE

Jane said that she did not believe that reporting fictitious expenses was the correct thing to do and that she would simply report her actual expenses. Ann responded in an angry tone, saying that to do so would expose all the sales reps. As long as everyone cooperated, the company would not question the expense vouchers. However, if one person reported only actual expenses, the company would be likely to investigate the discrepancy and all the sales reps could lose their jobs. She appealed to Jane to follow the agreed-upon practice, stating that they would all be better off, that no one would lose his or her job, and that the company did not really need the money because it was very profitable.

Questions for Discussion

1. What are the ethical issues in this case?
2. Given all the factors, what should Jane have done?
3. What would have been the consequences for Jane and the company if she had accurately reported her expenses? What would the consequences have been if she had inflated her expense account as Ann had urged her to do?
4. What ethical principles would be useful here?

Case 11

FAMILY BUSINESS

Jane had just been hired as the head of the payroll department at R&S Electronic Service Company, a firm of 75 employees. She had been hired by Eddie, the general manager, who had informed her of the need for maintaining strict confidentiality regarding employee salaries and pay scales. He had also told her that he had fired the previous payroll department head for breaking that confidentiality by discussing employee salaries. She had also been formally introduced to Brad, the owner, who

This case was written by Dr. Marilyn M. Helms, Associate Professor of Management, University of Tennessee at Chattanooga. Permission to reprint granted by Arthur Andersen & Co., SC.

had told her to see him if she had any questions or problems. Both Brad and Eddie had made her feel welcome.

GREG'S HIGH COMMISSIONS

After 3 months of employment, Jane began to wonder why Greg, a service technician and Eddie's brother, made so much more in commissions than the other service technicians. She assumed that he must be highly qualified and must work rapidly because she had overheard Brad commending Greg on his performance on several occasions. She had also noticed Brad, Eddie, and Greg having lunch together frequently.

One day, Eddie gave Jane the stack of work tickets for the service technicians for the upcoming week. The technicians were to take whatever ticket was on top when they finished the job they were working on. After putting the tickets where they belonged, Jane remembered that she had a doctor's appointment the next morning and returned to Eddie's office to tell him she would be reporting late for work.

EDDIE SHOWS FAVORITISM

When she entered Eddie's office, she saw Eddie give Greg a separate stack of work tickets. As she stood there, Eddie told her that if she mentioned this to anyone, he would fire her. Jane was upset because she understood that Eddie was giving the easier, high-commission work to his brother. Jane also realized that Eddie had the authority to hire and fire her. Because she had been at the company for only a short time, she was still on probation. This was her first job since college. She wondered what she should do.

Questions for Discussion

1. What are the ethical issues in this case?
2. Is a family business different from other types of businesses with respect to employee treatment?
3. What was Jane's ethical dilemma?
4. What should Jane have done? Why?

Case 12

|JUST BETWEEN FRIENDS? P2P VS. IP

In 1999, Shawn Fanning, a freshman at Northeastern University, founded Napster. Fanning's brainchild was the beginning of an explosion in peer-to-peer file sharing (P2P), allowing users to trade music over the Internet without sacrificing quality. Two years later, Napster had grown to 58 million registered users.[1] The success of Napster prompted a flurry of lawsuits charging that Napster's file-sharing service breached copyright law and violated intellectual property (IP) rights. After losing in court, Napster began to convert its formerly free service to a subscription base. Roxio, a software maker bought the Napster brand name and operated it as a legitimate service.[2]

REPLAYTV

Although the Napster case may have been resolved, the genie is out of the proverbial bottle. Many industries have already been "Napsterized" with more to follow. This peer-to-peer (P2P) revolution has raised questions about the ethics of sharing other people's IP (intellectual property). For example, in 2001, a variety of entertainment industry leaders, including Disney, Showtime, NBC, ABC, CBS, and Paramount, filed a joint lawsuit against ReplayTV and its parent company SonicBlue. This product, which won an Emmy for technological innovation, allowed users to make perfect digital copies of programs, replay them without commercials, and e-mail them to friends over the Internet.[3] The litigation eventually prompted ReplayTV to drop the commercial skipping and file sharing attributes of the product.

This case was written by Ann K. Buchholtz, University of Georgia.

PEGASUS ORIGINALS

Adam Cohen of *Time* tells the story of Pegasus Originals, a stitching pattern company.[4] Pegasus Originals sells patterns for needlework of various types. Jim Hedgepath, the president of Pegasus, was vacationing in the Rockies when he heard that a new Web site was allowing people to download his artists' copyrighted works for free. Although Hedgepath was able to close down that site by threatening to sue, another underground Web site soon opened. One of these outfits, Pattern Piggies, questioned Hedgepath's right to fight their actions. As one user declared defiantly, "Ladies, this is war, and I'm out for blood." The ease with which his patterns could be copied caused Hedgepath to question the future of not only his business but also the stitching pattern industry. "Many artists have gone, and many more will go," says Hedgepath. "I've talked to a lot who are looking for something else to do."[5]

The ability of customers to exchange content over the Internet has caused a drastic shift in firm strategies. Hedgepath decided that file sharing was an opportunity rather than a threat. He began Web design and worked on creating encrypted stitching patterns that can be downloaded for a fee and cannot be e-mailed to others. The Internet opens Pegasus to a much broader market, and so it is possible that Pegasus will be more profitable than it would otherwise have been. Similarly, book publishers and music distributors are setting up their own Web sites to distribute their digitalized materials. In the words of Hedgepath, "I used to tell pattern sellers to think about where the Internet was going to fit in their lives," he says. "Now I tell them to think about where they are going to fit in the

Internet." Of course, not everyone has weathered the change. Hedgepath's Australian distributor went bankrupt.[6]

THE QUESTION

There are two sides in the P2P versus IP debate. On the P2P side, users argue that technology must advance to deliver what customers want. They say they represent the economic welfare of society at large rather than just the copyright holders when they push the envelope. They point to the new technologies companies have employed in response to their actions as proof they are having a positive impact. On the IP side, proponents point to the loss of more than $10 billion in software piracy. They say that content creators have no reason to be creative if their IP is not protected, and that represents a loss for consumers and society.[7] In 2004, Sen. Orrin Hatch (R-Utah), sponsored the Inducing of Copyright Infringement Act of 2004 which, according to Senator Hatch, is designed to "simply confirm that existing law would allow artists to bring civil actions against parties who intend to induce others to infringe copyrights."[8]

Questions for Discussion

1. What are the ethical issues involved in this case?

2. Do you think that P2P services are ethically justified in their actions? On what do you base your arguments?

3. As a consumer, where do you draw the line? Would you use (or have you used) free P2P file-sharing services? When do you feel that P2P users are justified in receiving free content? When are they not?

4. If you were able to write the law on copyright protection in the digital age, what would it say? What IP protections and/or P2P freedoms would you uphold?

Case Endnotes

1. http://www.cnn.com/SPECIALS/2001/napster/timeline.html.
2. Ron Harris, "Judge Refuses to Dismiss Suit Against Napster Funders," *San Diego Union Tribune* (July 15, 2004), http://www.signonsandiego.com.
3. "Video Lawsuit to Rival Napster Row," *Electronic Times* (November 5, 2001), 3.
4. Adam Cohen, "Napster the Revolution" (September 25, 2000), http://www.cnn.com/ALLPOLITICS/time/2000/10/02/revolution.html.
5. *Ibid.*
6. *Ibid.*
7. Nicholas Imparato, "The Great Chess Game," *Intelligent Enterprise* (December 5, 2001), 18.
8. Joanna Glaser, "File Trading Bill Stokes Fury," *Wired* (June 24, 2004), http://www.wired.com.

Case 13

THIS LITTLE PIGGY:
SHOULD THE XENO-PIG MAKE IT TO MARKET?

Xenotransplantation is the transfer of living cells, tissue, and organs from one species to another, such as from a pig to a human for medical purposes. The transplanted material is called a *xenotransplant* and is the technological base upon which the xenotransplant industry is built.

The history of xenotransplantation dates back to the first transplant of a pig kidney into a human in 1906. Other experiments have included kidneys transplanted from goats, sheep and chimpanzees, livers and bone marrow from baboons, and hearts and skin from pigs. In 1982, a California baby lived for 3 weeks on a baboon's heart transplant.[1]

BENEFITS TO ORGAN FARMING

There are many anticipated benefits to organ and tissue transplants, including extended life expectancy and improvement of

This case was written by Joseph G. Gerard, SUNY Institute of Technology and Ann K. Buchholtz, University of Georgia.

the quality of life. A severe shortage of human organs and tissue, however, provides for a keen interest in those alternatives that might meet this shortage. This makes xenotransplantation, with its potentially "unlimited source" of organs and tissue, a very attractive alternative indeed.[2] Currently, there are more than 70,000 Americans on waiting lists for new hearts, livers, or kidneys, and fewer than 20,000 will receive them. Any disease currently treated by human-to-human transplants (e.g., diabetes, liver failure, Parkinson's disease, cancer, and AIDS) could potentially be treated by xenotransplantation, even though xenotransplantation, particularly the whole organ transplants involving baboon and chimpanzee hearts, has met with limited success.

In May 2004, researchers in New Zealand found that a technique they developed to transplant pig cells into diabetics also may hold promise for people who suffer from brain injuries or strokes. While still in the experimental stage, the research showed that transplanting brain cells into stroke-injured rats reduced their brain damage by forty percent.[3]

WHY PIGS?

Pigs make a good choice because their organs are an appropriate size for adult patients. Plus, pigs have large litters, grow to adulthood quickly, are relatively easy to breed, and can be raised in sterile environments.

Although organs from animals closest to human beings are less susceptible to immune system rejection, nonhuman primates like apes and monkey are limited in number, costly to raise, and are relatively slow to mature. Another problem with primates is that they may harbor unknown viruses that do them no harm but that are devastating diseases in humans. This happens because viruses can cross the species barrier and is especially risky with nonhuman primates. It can happen with other species as well, however, and it is made more likely when living organs are placed directly into the human body. Pathogens (organisms that cause disease, such as viruses or bacteria) bypass skin and gastrointestinal tract defenses, which, in turn, trigger a response from the immune system.

PROBLEMS AND CONCERNS

Immune suppressant drugs manage the immune system reaction fairly well in human-to-human transplants, but this rejection becomes increasingly violent in more distantly related species and requires higher strength immunosuppressant drugs. PERV (Porcine Endogenous Retro-Virus) can infect human cells in the laboratory, supporting the belief that the same may occur with transplant recipients. Parts of pig retroviruses may also recombine with parts of human viruses to create a new virus. This effect has also been observed in the lab.[4] One suggested solution to the PERV problem is the use of cloning technology. This would provide consistent groups of donor organs that prevent rejection while providing a known retrovirus-free organ to the donor; this approach may take several years to develop.

Primates. One of the biggest issues surrounds the fact that "to get to the point where surgeons will be good at transferring organs from pigs into humans, they will need to trial on primates. And the use of primates is rightly considered a last resort," Michael Banner, chair of the British government's animal procedures committee, told The London Times. One of the reasons for this, says Banner, is the rich social and mental life primates possess "and because they are our cousins, people rightly feel that the use of primates is of more concern than the use of other species." In 1997, researchers in the United Kingdom conducted more than 3,900 experiments on 3,425 primates.[5]

Mass Production. Genetic engineering would increase the number of animals used because they would be cloned specifically for research. "Scientists are sometimes too willing to overlook these issues' ethical implications," says Banner. "To suppose that how the public reacts to these new technologies is simply a matter of unfamiliarity is patronizing. Often, people's unease can be spelt out perfectly coherently."[6] In 2000, Akira Onishi from the National Institute of Animal Industry in Japan, successfully cloned a pig named "Xena" using a DNA removal and injection procedure previously used on mice. However, to get one successful transplant, they had to transplant 110 cloned embryos. In 2004, South Korea announced plans to spend $60.5 billion over the next ten years to mass produce pig organs for human transplantation.[7]

SOME OTHER OPTIONS

An alternative to using living cells is to design and build devices like the artificial heart, pancreas, liver, and kidneys currently under development by a number of companies. However, research, design, and construction of this type of machinery, with its various sensors and chemical pumps, is costly. Living cells may also be combined with more typical machinery to produce a type of hybrid. Circe Biomedical of Lexington, Massachusetts, for example, is testing a "bio-artificial" pancreas that contains living pancreatic cells taken from pigs. A patient's blood first flows through a graft into a membranous tube surrounded by the pig pancreatic tissue. The pig cells detect the level of glucose in the human bloodstream through the membrane and release insulin as required. The patient's immune system never detects the presence of the pig cell because they are encased in plastic. The immune system attack that xenotransplant biotech firms are trying to engineer around never takes place. Although this does avoid the cross-species gene-sharing issue, the pig cell manufacture does still require animal cloning and production for harvest and, thus, does not sidestep other ethical issues.[8]

CONCLUSION

For some companies, the future of xenotransplantation still seems bright and its rewards not so distant. For instance, a joint venture between BioTransplant and Novartis to form Immerge BioTherapeutics Inc. appeared to signal an optimistic view of the industry. The newly formed Boston-based company would focus solely on the development and therapeutic applications of xenotransplantation of cells, tissues, and organs.[9]

Other companies, like Scottish PPL, Geron, and the Roslin Institute near Edinburgh, creator of Dolly the sheep, appear to shy away from work and investment in xenotransplantation. Grahame Bulfield, director of the Roslin Institute, denies that new safety issues have arisen stating, "We've not found any new problems—they're the same as they've always been." The move, he says, is purely commercial—a shifting of focus toward the cloning of new tissues.

Questions for Discussion

1. Should companies be allowed to continue research and development in xenotransplantation? Do the benefits outweigh the risks?

2. Does xenotransplantation threaten the quality of human life? If so, what threats exist? Do similar threats exist for other species? Are quality of life issues less important for some species than for others? What, if anything, makes animal rights different from human rights?

3. What threats does xenotransplantation hold for the environment as a whole? Who are the different stakeholders involved? What are their stakes?

4. Given that many countries do not restrict human xenotransplantation, what threats exist globally with xenotransplant technology?

5. Is the issue more or less complicated than other bioethical topics like cloning or stem cell research? How can one make the argument that therapeutic cloning, such as that used in xenotransplantation, should be permitted while reproductive cloning, like that advocated by groups like the Raelians (see Chapter 8), should not?

Case Endnotes

1. Anthony Browne, "When Science Makes a Pig's Ear of It; You Think There Should Be a Big Public Debate About Transplanting Animal Organs into Humans? Don't Be Silly; Profits Are at Stake," *The New Statesman* (November 15, 1999).
2. Canadian Corporate Newswire, "Canadian Public Health Association Seeks Opinions of Canadians on Xenotransplantation: Xeno Web Site Launched at http://www.xeno.cpha.ca" (December 13, 2000).
3. Simon Collins, "Cell Transplants Offer Stroke Victims Hope," *The New Zealand Herald* (July 19, 2004), biotech.com.
4. "The Regeneration Game," *Chemist & Druggist* (March 4, 2000).
5. Alison Goddard, interview with Michael Banner, "The Heart of the Debate," *The Times Higher Education Supplement* (September 18, 1998).
6. *Ibid.*
7. "Korea to Mass Produce Pig Organs for Human Transplants," *Sydney Morning Herald* (June 1, 2004), http://www.biotech.com.
8. "The New Organ Grinders," *The Economist* (June 23, 2001).
9. "Joint Venture Tackles Xenotransplantation," *Drug Discovery & Development* (April 2001).

Case 14

|TOXIC TACOS? THE CASE OF GENETICALLY MODIFIED FOODS

In September 2000, the Genetically Engineered Food Alert Coalition, a coalition of environmental and consumer groups, accused Taco Bell of using StarLink genetically modified (GM) corn in their taco shells. The FDA had approved the StarLink gene for animal (but not human) consumption. The incident prompted the recall of 300 corn-based foods and alarmed the public about the possible dangers of genetically modified foods.[1]

The debates surrounding genetically modified food have continued to grow since the StarLink incident. According to David Roy of the Centre for Bioethics at the Clinical Research Institute of Montreal, the debates often produce "more heat than light." They are more emotional in nature than they are intellectual. One of the main dangers of the GM food debate is that neither side is listening to the other: Involved parties "tend to let debates become excessively polarized."[2]

SOME OF THE CURRENT ARGUMENTS

Proponents for GM foods argue that their potential risks should be judged once scientific consensus has been reached. In the meantime, they say these GM crops will feed a hungry world by multiplying per-acre yields and at the same time

This case was prepared by Joseph G. Gerard, SUNY Institute of Technology, and Ann K. Buchholtz, University of Georgia.

reduce the need for herbicides and pesticides. GMs detractors, on the other hand, claim that possible future benefits of the technology should not outweigh present dangers. They recommend a slowdown in order that society may digest innovations of past years. They want long-term outcomes to be "clearer" before anything else is done.

Scientific Evidence. Science-based arguments contrast for both parties as well. Governments, often citing company studies, make the claim that GM crops are similar to non-GM ones and, therefore, do not pose a threat to consumers. Environmental watchdog groups, like the U.S. Public Interest Research Group, a member of the Genetically Engineered Food Alert Coalition, disagrees. Studies claiming similarity between GM and non-GM crops, they say, are flawed and conclude nontoxicity without sufficient evidence.[3]

GOING TO EXTREMES?

Neither pole is exempt from accusations of extremist thinking. Anti-"GMers" believe that researchers and developers of new technology promise too much. In recent years, a variety of plants that produce their own pesticide—as well as herbicide-resistant seed and plants, and others with more "exotic" features—have made it to the marketplace where their benefits are lauded and their deficits seem nonexistent. But, ask GM food opponents, has testing been sufficiently long term to really test environmental impact? Have possible dangers for wildlife and plants that consume or ingest GM food been tested? What is the effect of that food as it moves through the food chain? Has gene flow been controlled? Some say that new reports provide evidence that studies are often too limited in both space and time to reach a conclusion.[4]

Industry's Response. GM proponents respond that their detractors often exaggerate environmental hazards, do not substantiate their claims with scientific evidence, and are simply reacting out of fear. Those who stand by GM technology then point to examinations by government agencies "so long and rigorous that many standard foods wouldn't pass." Their field research never uncovers even a slight headache. Some even say it would be wrong to try to replicate the research.[5]

SOME OF THE CURRENT ARGUMENTS

The difficulty the European Union has had in making decisions regarding GM foods is emblematic of the divisiveness the issue creates. Nine EU countries—Latvia, Denmark, Cyprus, Malta, Italy, Greece, Austria, Portugal and Luxembourg—voted against the license. Nine others—Czech Republic, Slovakia, Belgium, France, Ireland, Netherlands, France, Sweden and

Britain—voted in favor. Hungary, Slovenia, Greece and Spain abstained, while Estonia and Poland expressed no view.[6]

Questions for Discussion

1. What are the ethical issues in this case?
2. Do you think that either group, pro-GM or anti-GM foods, is correct while the other group is wrong? If so, what reasoning do you give for supporting the position of one group over the other? Is it possible for both to be right? What ethical concepts help you decide?
3. Is there any way to bridge the gap between these groups? If so, what would the advantages and disadvantages be?
4. If you were crafting GMO (genetically modified organism) public policy, what would you recommend?

Case Endnotes

1. "The StarLink Fallout," *Successful Farming* (January 2001), 33–39.
2. "Biotechnology and Bioethics," *MacLean's* (November 5, 2001), 38.
3. Geoffrey Lean, "Ask No Questions, Hear No Truths; Geoffrey Lean on the Scandalous Treatment of a Scientist Who Dared to Cast Doubt on the Safety of GM Foods," *The New Statesman* (September 24, 2001).
4. *Ibid.*
5. "Biotechnology and Bioethics," *ibid.*
6. Paul Gietner, 'EU Governments Deadlocked Over Monsanto Genetically Modified Corn Product," *San Jose Mercury News* (July 19, 2004), http://www.mercurynews.com.

Case 15

| SOMETHING'S ROTTEN IN HONDO

George Mackee thought of himself as bright, energetic, and with lots of potential. "So why is this happening to me?" he thought. George, with his wife Mary and his two children, had moved to Hondo, Texas, from El Paso 4 years earlier and was now the manager of the Ardnak Plastics plant in Hondo, a small plant that manufactured plastic parts for small equipment. The plant employed several hundred workers, which was a substantial portion of the population of Hondo. Ardnak Plastics Inc. had several other small plants the size of Hondo's. George had a good relationship with Bill, his boss, in Austin, Texas.

THE EMISSSIONS PROBLEM

One of the problems George's plant had was that the smokestack emissions were consistently above EPA guidelines. Several

This case was written by Geoffrey P. Lantos, Stonehill College. Permission to reprint granted by Arthur Andersen & Co. SC.

months ago, George got a call from Bill, stating that the EPA had contacted him about the problem and fines would be levied. George admitted the situation was a continual problem, but because headquarters would not invest in new smokestack scrubbers, he didn't know what to do. Bill replied by saying that margins were at their limits and there was no money for new scrubbers. Besides, Bill commented, other plants were in worse shape than his and they were passing EPA standards.

A QUESTIONABLE SOLUTION

George ended the conversation by assuring Bill that he would look into the matter. He immediately started calling his contemporaries at other Ardnak plants. He found they were scheduling their heavy emissions work at night so that during the day when the EPA took their sporadic readings they were within standards. George contemplated this option even though it would result in increasing air contamination levels.

THE DOUBLE BIND

A month went by, and George still had not found a solution. The phone rang; it was Bill. Bill expressed his displeasure with the new fines for the month and reminded George that there were very few jobs out in the industry. That's when Bill dropped the whole thing into George's lap. Bill had been speaking to the Mexican government and had received assurances that no such clean air restrictions would be imposed on Ardnak if they relocated 15 miles south of Hondo in Mexico. However, Ardnak must hire Mexican workers. Bill explained that the reason for relocating would be to eliminate the EPA problems. Bill told George he had one week to decide whether to eliminate the fines by correcting the current problems or by relocating.

George knew that relocating the plant on the Mexican side would devastate the infrastructure of the city of Hondo and would continue to put contaminants into the air on the U.S. side. When he mentioned the possibility to Mary, she reinforced other concerns. She did not want him to be responsible for the loss of the jobs of their friends and extended families.

Questions for Discussion

1. Who are the stakeholders in this situation, and what are their stakes?
2. What social responsibility, if any, does Ardnak Plastics Inc. have to the city of Hondo?
3. What are the ethical issues in this case?
4. What should George do? Why?

Case 16

| GLOBAL (IN)EQUALITY?: THE MERRILL LYNCH SEX BIAS CASE

Stephanie Villalba's career was in high gear. In May 2002, after sixteen successful years with Merrill Lynch, she was promoted to the position of first vice-president and appointed head of the European private client business. Villalba was made responsible for more than 250 financial advisors in continental Europe and the United Kingdom division.

THE PROBLEMS BEGIN

According to Villalba, things began to go downhill five months later when she received a new line manager, Ausaf Abbas. She claimed that Abbas "bullied, belittled and undermined" her. As an example she cited a trip on an executive jet to a business meeting, where Abbas instructed her to sit in the stewardess's seat and serve drinks to Abbas and other male colleagues.[1]

Villalba earned about $700,000 in salary and bonuses in 2001. In 2002, she earned a little less than $550,000 ($150,000 was base salary and the rest was bonus), while the people she recruited to work for her were offered $600,000 to $800,000.[2] Her four peers who ran similar operations in other regions earned 33 to 50 percent more. In February 2003, Villalba was given another post; she considered it a "clear demotion" and rejected the offer. After a three month sabbatical, she was dismissed in July and subsequently sued the investment bank for $13.8 million.[3] Villalba charged Merrill Lynch with sex discrimination, victimization, unfair dismissal and unequal pay.[4]

This case was prepared for the 6th Edition by Ann K. Buchholtz, University of Georgia.

REACTIONS TO THE CLAIM

Merrill Lynch argued that the dismissal had nothing to do with gender but was a response to poor performance. Her region recorded higher post-9/11 losses than any of the other regions. The company also notes that she was replaced by a woman. In testimony before a three-person tribunal, Merrill acknowledged that Villalba was paid less than comparable executives in other regions, "but not dramatically so," adding "it is practically inevitable that employees doing comparable work in different parts of ML will receive different levels of total compensation."[5]

The Industry. However, an article in the Economist indicates that people who work in London have no doubt that there is substantial discrimination against women. They cite a former business manager of one of the large investment firms who said that women are paid salaries about 25 percent lower than those that men receive. The gender difference in bonuses is even greater: Opaque pay structures involving huge bonuses make it easy to discriminate without repercussions.[6]

The Possible Precedent. The case has drawn world-wide attention because of a new question it raises—should executives working in different parts of the world be paid equally? According to Sue Ashtiany, an employment lawyer not involved in the case, "The case could be precedent setting. This case is shining a torch on the issue of what global businesses are paying employees doing like work, or work of equal value, in different countries. The big question mark is whether she can compare herself to someone in Japan or New York or anywhere outside the EU. That is what everyone is watching."[7]

Questions for Discussion

1. What are the ethical issues involved in this case?

2. What is your assessment of the incident on the executive jet? Does it affect your outlook on the charges brought by Villalba?

3. Does the size of Villalba's pay affect your outlook on the case? Why or why not?

4. Should executives working in different parts of the world be paid equally? Should executives working in different parts of the same country (with different costs of living) be paid differently? Why or why not?

5. Does your answer to question #3 hold true for lower level workers too? Why or why not?

6. If you were a member of the tribunal hearing the case, how would you rule on the various charges?

Case Endnotes

1. "Sexism and the City," *Economist* (June 12, 2004), 53–54.
2. Sara Calian, "Merrill Sex-Bias Suit Highlights the Issue Of Global Pay Scales," *Wall Street Journal* (June 16, 2004), C1.
3. "Sexism and the City," 53.
4. Calian, C1.
5. *Ibid.*, C1.
6. "Sexism and the City," 53–54.
7. Calian, C1.

Case 17

NIKE, INC.

In January 2001, Jonah Peretti decided to customize his Nike shoes and visited the Nike iD Web site. The company allows customers to personalize their Nikes with the colors of their choice and their own personal 16-character message. Peretti chose the word "sweatshop" for his Nikes.

After receiving his order, Nike informed Peretti via e-mail that the term "sweatshop" represents "inappropriate slang" and is not considered viable for print on a Nike shoe. Thus, his order was summarily rejected. Peretti e-mailed Nike, arguing that the term "sweatshop" is present in Webster's dictionary and could not possibly be considered inappropriate slang. Nike responded by quoting the company's rules, which state that the company can refuse to print anything on its shoes that it does not deem appropriate. Peretti replied that he was changing his previous order and would instead like to order a pair of shoes with a "color snapshot of the 10-year-old Vietnamese girl who makes my shoes." He never received a response.[1]

THE PR NIGHTMARE BEGINS

Before Nike could blink an eye, the situation turned into a public relations nightmare. Peretti forwarded the e-mail exchange to a few friends, who forwarded it to a few friends, and so forth. Within 6 weeks of his initial order, the story appeared in *The Wall Street Journal*, *USA Today*, and *The Village Voice*. Peretti

This case was written by Bryan S. Dennis, Idaho State University.

himself appeared on "The Today Show" and he estimates that 2 million people have seen the e-mail. At the height of the incident, Peretti was receiving 500 e-mails a day from people who had read the e-mail from as far away as Asia, Australia, Europe, and South America.[2,3]

Nike refused to admit any wrongdoing in the incident and stated that they reserve the right to refuse any order for whatever reason. Beth Gourney, a spokesperson for Nike, had the following to say regarding the incident:

> Clearly, he [Peretti] was attempting to stir up trouble; he has admitted it. He's not an activist. Mr. Peretti does not understand our labor policy. If he did, he would know that we do not hire children; our minimum age for hiring is 18 . . . and we don't apologize for not putting the word "sweatshop" because our policy clearly states: "We reserve the right to cancel any order up to 24 hours after it has been submitted."[4]

Nike, Inc. is no stranger to sweatshop allegations. Ever since the mid-1990s, the company has been subject to negative press, lawsuits, and demonstrations on college campuses alleging that firm's overseas contractors subject employees to work in inhumane conditions for low wages. As Philip Knight, the CEO and founder of Nike, once lamented, "The Nike product has become synonymous with slave wages, forced overtime, and arbitrary abuse."[5]

History of Nike, Inc.

Philip Knight started his own athletic shoe distribution company in 1964. Using his Plymouth Reliant as a warehouse, he began importing and distributing track shoes from Onitsuka Company, Ltd., a Japanese manufacturer. First-year sales of $8,000 resulted in a profit of $254. After 8 years, annual sales reached $2 million, and the firm employed 45 people. However, Onitsuka saw the huge potential of the American shoe market and dropped Knight's relatively small company in favor of larger, more experienced distributors. Knight was forced to start anew. However, instead of importing and distributing another firm's track shoes, he decided to design his own shoes and create his own company. The name he chose for his new company was "Nike."[6]

Nike's Use of Contract Labor.
When the company began operations, Knight contracted the manufacture of Nike's shoes to two firms in Japan. Shortly thereafter, Nike began to contract with firms in Taiwan and Korea. In 1977, Nike purchased two shoe manufacturing facilities in the United States—one in Maine, the other in New Hampshire. Eventually, the two plants became so unprofitable that the firm was forced to close them. The loss due to the write-off of the plants was approximately $10 million in a year in which the firm's total profit was $15 million. The firm had a successful IPO in 1980, 8 years after the company was founded. Currently, Nike is the largest athletic shoe company in the world.[7]

Nike does not own a single shoe or apparel factory. Instead, the firm contracts the production of its products to independently owned manufacturers. Today, practically all Nike subcontracted factories are in countries such as Indonesia, Vietnam, China, and Thailand, where the labor costs are significantly less than those in the United States. Worldwide, roughly 530,000 people are employed in factories that manufacture Nike products. The company gives the following as a rough breakdown of the costs per shoe:

Consumer pays: $65
Retailer pays: $32.50 to Nike, and then doubles the price for retail
Nike pays: $16.25 and then doubles the price to retailers for shipping, insurance, duties, R&D, marketing, sales, administration, and profits

The $16.25 price paid the factory includes:

Materials:	$10.75
Labor:	$2.43
Overhead + Depreciation:	$2.10
Factory Profit:	$0.97
Total Costs:	$16.25[8]

Even in today's hi-tech environment, the production of athletic shoes is still a labor-intensive process. For example, for practically all athletic shoes, the upper portion of the shoe must be sewn together with the lower portion by hand. The soles must be manually glued together. Although most leaders in the industry are confident that practically the entire production process will someday be automated, it will still be many years before the industry will not have to rely upon human labor.

Other Firms In the Industry.
Nike's use of overseas contractors is not unique in the athletic shoe and apparel industry. All other major athletic shoe manufacturers also contract with overseas manufacturers, albeit to various degrees. However, one athletic shoe firm, New Balance Inc., is somewhat of an anomaly and operates six factories in the United States.[9]

Nike spends heavily on endorsements and advertising and pays several top athletes well over a million dollars a year in endorsement contracts. In contrast, New Balance has developed a different strategy. They do not use professional athletes to market their products. According to their "Endorsed by No One" policy, New Balance instead chooses to invest in product research and development and foregoes expensive endorsement contracts.[10]

The Sweatshop Movement Versus Nike

There is one pivotal event that is largely responsible for introducing the term "sweatshop" to the American public. In 1996, Kathie Lee Gifford, cohost of the nationally syndicated talk show "Live with Regis and Kathie Lee," endorsed her own line of clothing for Wal-Mart. During that same year, labor rights activists disclosed that her "Kathie Lee Collection" was made in Honduras by seamstresses who earn 31 cents an hour and are sometimes required to work 20 hour days. Traditionally known for her pleasant, jovial demeanor and her love of children, Kathie Lee was outraged. She tearfully informed the public that she was unaware that her clothes were being made in so-called "sweatshops" and vowed to do whatever she could to promote the antisweatshop cause.[11]

Nike Is Accused.
In a national press conference, Gifford named Michael Jordan as another celebrity who, like herself, endorses products without knowing under what conditions the products are made. At the time, Michael Jordan was Nike's premier endorser and was reportedly under a $20 million per year contract with the firm.[12] Nike, the number-one athletic shoe brand in the world, soon found itself under attack by the rapidly growing antisweatshop movement.

Shortly after the Gifford story broke, Joel Joseph, chairman of the Made in the USA Foundation, accused Nike of paying underage Indonesian workers 14 cents an hour to make the company's line of Air Jordan Shoes. He also claimed that the total payroll of Nike's six Indonesian subcontracted factories is less that the reported $20 million per year that Jordan receives from his endorsement contract with Nike. The Made in the USA Foundation is one of the organizations that ignited the Gifford controversy and is largely financed by labor unions and U.S. apparel manufacturers that are against free trade with low-wage countries.[13]

Nike quickly pointed out that Air Jordan shoes are made in Taiwan, not Indonesia. Additionally, the company maintained that employee wages are fair and higher than the government-mandated minimum wage in all of the countries where the firm has contracted factories. The company released the following data about its wages:

Country	Minimum Monthly Wage	Average Monthly Wage at Nike Factories
Taiwan	14,124 NT$	25,609 NT$
South Korea	Won 306,030	Won 640,000
Indonesia	115,000 rupiah	239,800 rupiah
China	RMB 276	RMB 636
Thailand	2,950-3,150 baht	4,435 baht
Vietnam	331.050 VND$	640.030 VND$

Nike asserted that the entry-level income of an Indonesian factory is five times that of a farmer. The firm also claimed that an assistant line supervisor in a Chinese subcontracted factory earns more than a surgeon with 20 years of experience.[14] In response to the allegations regarding Michael Jordan's endorsement contract, Nike stated that the total wages in Indonesia are $50 million a year, which is well over what the firm pays Jordan.[15]

Nike soon faced more negative publicity. Michael Moore, the movie director whose 1989 documentary *Roger and Me* shed light on the plight of laid-off auto workers in Flint, Michigan, and damaged the reputation of General Motors chairman Roger Smith, interviewed Philip Knight for his 1997 movie *The Big One*. On camera, Knight referred to some employees at subcontracted factories as "poor little Indonesian workers." Moore's cameras also recorded the following exchange between Moore and Knight:

Moore: Twelve-year-olds working in [Indonesian] factories? That's OK with you?

Knight: They're not 12-year-olds working in factories . . . the minimum age is 14.

Moore: How about 14, then? Doesn't that bother you?

Knight: No.[16]

Knight, the only CEO interviewed in the movie, received harsh criticism for his comments. Nike alleged that the comments were taken out of context and were deceitful because Moore failed to include Knight's pledge to make a transition from a 14- to a 16-year-old minimum age labor force. Nike prepared its own video that includes the entire interview.[17]

In early 1998, Thomas Nguyen, founder of Vietnam Labor Watch, inspected several of Nike's plants in Vietnam and reported cases of worker abuse. At one factory that manufactures Nike products, a supervisor punished 56 women for wearing inappropriate work shoes by forcing them to run around the factory in the hot sun. Twelve workers fainted and were taken to the hospital. Nguyen also reported that workers were only allowed one bathroom break and two drinks of water during each 8-hour shift. Nike

responded that the supervisor who was involved in the fainting incident has been suspended and that the firm had hired an independent accounting firm to look into the matters further.[18]

Nike Responds. In early 1997, Nike hired former Atlanta mayor Andrew Young, a vocal opponent of sweatshops and child labor, to review the firm's overseas labor practices. Neither party has disclosed the fee that Young received for his services. Young toured 12 factories in Vietnam, Indonesia, and China and was reportedly given unlimited access. However, he was constantly accompanied by Nike representatives during all factory tours. Furthermore, Young relied upon Nike translators when communicating with factory workers.[19]

In his 75-page report, Young concluded that "Nike is doing a good job, but it can do better." He provided Nike with six recommendations for improving the working conditions at subcontracted factories. Nike immediately responded to the report and agreed to implement all six recommendations. Young did not address the issue of wages and standards of living because he felt he lacks the "academic credentials" for such a judgment.[20]

Public reaction to Young's report is mixed. Some praise Nike. However, many of Nike's opponents disregarded Young's report as biased and incomplete. One went so far as to state the report could not have been better if Nike had written it themselves and questioned Young's independence.[21,22]

In 1998, Nike hired Maria Eitel to the newly created position of vice president for corporate and social responsibility. Eitel was formerly a public relations executive for Microsoft. Her responsibilities are to oversee Nike's labor practices, environmental affairs, and involvement in the global community. Although this move is applauded by some, others are skeptical and claim that Nike's move is nothing more than a publicity stunt.[23]

Later that same year, Philip Knight gave a speech at the National Press Club in Washington, DC, and announced six initiatives that are intended to improve the working conditions in its overseas factories. The firm chose to raise the minimum hiring age from 16 to 18 years of age. Nike also decided to expand its worker education program so that all workers in Nike factories will have the option to take middle and high school equivalency tests.[24] The director of Global Exchange, one of Nike's staunchest opponents, called the initiatives "significant and very positive." He also added that "we feel that the measures—if implemented—could be exciting."[25]

COLLEGE STUDENTS, ORGANIZED LABOR, AND NIKE

Colleges and universities have direct ties to the many athletic shoe and apparel companies (such as Nike, Champion, and Reebok) that contract with overseas manufacturers. Most universities receive money from athletic shoe and apparel corporations in return for outfitting the university's sports teams with the firm's products. In 1997, Nike gave $7.1 million to the

University of North Carolina for the right to outfit all of UNC's sports teams with products bearing the Nike Swoosh logo.[26] Additionally, academic institutions allow firms to manufacture apparel bearing the university's official name, colors, and insignias in return for a fee. In 1998, the University of Michigan received $5.7 million dollars in licensing fees.[27] Most of these contract and licensing fees are allocated toward scholarships and other academic programs.

Organized Labor.
In 1995, the Union of Needletrades, Industrial and Textile Employees (UNITE) was founded. The union, a member of the AFL-CIO, is formed by the merger of The International Ladies' Garment Workers' Union and the Amalgamated Clothing and Textile Workers Union and represents 250,000 workers in North America and Puerto Rico. Most of the union members work in the textile and apparel industry. In 1996, UNITE launched a "Stop Sweatshops" campaign after the Kathy Lee Gifford story broke to "link union, consumers, student, civil rights and women's groups in the fight against sweatshops at home and abroad."[28]

In 1997, UNITE, along with the AFL-CIO, recruited dozens of college students for summer internships. Many of the students referred to that summer as "Union Summer and it had a similar impact as Freedom Summer did for students during the civil rights movement."[29] The United Students Against Sweatshops (USAS) organization was formed the following year. The USAS was founded and is led by former UNITE summer interns.[30]

University Organizations.
The USAS has chapters at over 50 universities across the United States. Since its inception, the organization has staged a large number of campus demonstrations that are reminiscent of the 1960s. One notable demonstration occurred on the campus of UNC in 1997. Students of the Nike Awareness Campaign protested against the university's contract with Nike due to the firm's alleged sweatshop abuses. More than 100 students demanded that the university not renew its contract with Nike and rallied outside the office of the university's chancellor. More than 50 other universities, such as the University of Wisconsin and Duke, staged similar protests and sit-ins.[31]

In response to the protests at UNC, Nike invited the editor of the university's student newspaper to tour Nike's overseas contractors to examine the working conditions firsthand. Nike offered to fund the trip by pledging $15,000 toward the students' travel and accommodations costs. Ironically, Michael Jordan is an alumnus of UNC.[32]

Critics of the USAS contend that the student organization is merely a puppet of UNITE and organized labor. They cite the fact that the AFL-CIO has spent more than $3 million dollars on internships and outreach programs with the alleged intent of interesting students in careers as union activists. The founders of the USAS are former UNITE interns. The USAS admits that UNITE has tipped off the student movement as to the whereabouts of alleged sweatshop factories. Also, in an attempt to spur campus interest in the sweatshop cause, UNITE sent two sweatshop workers on a five-campus tour. They have also coached students via phone during sit-ins and paid for regularly scheduled teleconferences between antisweatshop student leaders on different campuses. According to Allan Ryan, a Harvard University lawyer who has negotiated with the USAS, "[T]he students are vocal, but it's hard to get a viewpoint from them that does not reflect that of UNITE."[33]

Many students have denied allegations that they are being manipulated by organized labor and claim that they discovered the sweatshop issues on their own. Others acknowledge the assistance of organized labor but claim it is "no different from [student] civil rights activists using the NAACP in the 1960s."[34] John Sweeney, president of the AFL-CIO, claims the role of organized labor is not one of manipulation but of motivation. Others assert that the union merely provides moral support.[35]

Regardless of the AFL-CIO's intentions, the students have had a positive impact upon the promotion of organized labor's antisweatshop agenda. According to the director of one of the several human rights groups that are providing assistance to the students:

> *At this moment, the sweatshop protest is definitely being carried on the backs of university students. If a hundred students hold a protest, they get a page in The New York Times. If a hundred union people did that, they'd be locked up.*[36]

THE FAIR LABOR ASSOCIATION AND THE WORKER RIGHTS CONSORTIUM

In 1996, a presidential task force of industry and human rights representatives was given the job of addressing the sweatshop issue. The key purpose of this task force was to develop a workplace code of conduct and a system for monitoring factories to ensure compliance. In 1998, the task force created the Fair Labor Association (FLA) to accomplish these goals. This organization is made up of consumer and human rights groups as well as footwear and apparel manufacturers. Nike is one of the first companies to join the FLA. Many other major manufacturers (Levi Strauss & Co., Liz Claiborne, Patagonia, Polo Ralph Lauren, Reebok, Eddie Bauer, and Phillips-Van Heusen) along with 157 colleges and universities have also joined the FLA.[37]

FLA Requirements.
Members of the FLA must follow the principles set forth in the organization's Workplace Code of Conduct. Member organizations that license or contract with overseas manufacturers or suppliers are responsible for ensuring that factory employees are paid either the minimum wage as required by law or the average industry wage, whichever is higher. Additionally, the code of conduct sets limits on the number of hours employees can work, allows workers the right to collective bargaining, and forbids discrimination.[38]

Each member firm must conduct an internal audit of every manufacturing facility on a yearly basis. Further-more, members of the FLA must disclose to the FLA the location of all subcontracted factories. This information will not be made public. The FLA uses a team of external auditors to monitor the compliance of these factories with the FLA's code of conduct. For the first year of a firm's membership, 30 percent of the total number of factories will be examined by the FLA. After the first year, 5 to 15 percent will be monitored. These monitoring activities consist of a combination of announced and unannounced factory visits, and results are made available to the public.[39]

The WRC Alternative.

The USAS opposed several of the FLA's key components and created the Worker Rights Consortium (WRC) as an alternative to the FLA. The WRC asserts that the prevailing industry or legal minimum wage in some countries is too low and does not provide employees with the basic human needs they require. They propose that factories should instead pay a higher "living wage" that takes into account the wage required to provide factory employees with enough income to afford housing, energy, nutrition, clothing, health care, education, potable water, child care, transportation, and savings. Additionally, the WRC supports public disclosure of all factory locations and the right to monitor any factory at any time. As of July 2001, 80 colleges and universities have joined the WRC and agreed to adhere to its policies. UNITE and the AFL-CIO support the WRC and are opposed to the FLA.[40]

Nike, a member and supporter of the FLA, opposes the Worker Rights Consortium. The firm states that a concept of a living wage is impractical as "there is no common, agreed-upon definition of the living wage. Definitions range from complex mathematical formulas to vague philosophical notions." Additionally, Nike is opposed to the WRC's proposal that the location of all factories be publicly disclosed. The firm states that this is classified information that may divulge trade secrets to its competitors. Nike also claims that the monitoring provisions set out by the WRC are unrealistic and biased towards organized labor.[41]

In 2000, the University of Oregon joined the WRC. Philip Knight, an alumnus of the university, had previously contributed over $50 million to the university—$30 million for academics and $20 million for athletics. Upon hearing that his alma mater had joined the WRC, Knight was shocked. He withdrew a proposed $30 million donation and stated that the "the bonds of trust, which allowed me to give at a high level, have been shredded" and "there will be no further donations of any kind to the University of Oregon."[42,43]

EPILOGUE

In May 2001, Harsh Saini, Nike's corporate and social responsibility manager, acknowledged that the firm may not have handled the sweatshop issue as well as they could have and stated that Nike had not been adequately monitoring its subcontractors in overseas operations until the media and other organizations revealed the presence of sweatshops.

We were a bunch of shoe geeks who expanded so much without thinking of being socially responsible that we went from being a very big sexy brand name to suddenly becoming the poster boy for everything bad in manufacturing.

She added, "We realized that if we still want to be the brand of choice in 20 years, we had certain responsibilities to fulfill."[44]

Some Positive Developments.

In early 2001, Oregon's state board of higher education cast doubt on the legality of the University of Oregon's WRC membership, and the university dissolved its ties with the labor organization.[45] In September of the same year, Phil Knight renewed his financial support. Although the exact amount of Knight's donation was kept confidential, it is sufficient enough to ensure that the $85 million dollar expansion of the university's football stadium will go through as originally planned. In 2000, the stadium expansion plans suffered a significant setback when Knight withdrew his funding. Many of the proposed additions, such as a 12,000-seat capacity increase and 32 brand new skyboxes, were able to happen, largely due to Knight's pledge of financial support.[46,47]

Nike released its first corporate social responsibility report in October 2001. According to Phil Knight, "[I]n this report, Nike for the first time has assembled a comprehensive public review of our corporate responsibility practices."[48] The report cites several areas in which the firm could do better, such as worker conditions in Indonesia and Mexico. The report, compiled by both internal auditors and outside monitors, also notes that Nike is one of only four companies that has joined a World Wildlife Fund program to reduce greenhouse admissions. Jason Mark, a spokesman for Global Exchange, one of Nike's chief critics, praised the report and stated that Nike is "obviously responding to consumer concerns."[49]

Kasky v. Nike, Inc.

Nike's problems with fair labor issues still continued. Labor activist, Mark Kasky had sued Nike in 1998, arguing that Nike had engaged in false advertising when it denied that there was mistreatment of workers in Southeastern Asian factories. At issue was the question of whether Nike's defense of its practices was commercial speech, for which there are laws against making misleading claims or political speech, for which free speech protections apply. The California Supreme Court ruled that Nike's statements about labor conditions could be construed as false advertising. Nike appealed this ruling to the U.S. Supreme Court which sent it back to the California court, without making a judgment on the free speech issue. In September 2003, Kasky and Nike settled the case for a $1.5 million donation to the Fair Labor Association.[50] The settlement, however, left many questions unanswered. Many feared that the risk of lawsuit would have a chilling effect, causing firms to no longer release social responsibility reports which, unlike the SEC financial reports, are all voluntary. They may be right. Nike's 2001 corporate social responsibility report turned out to be its last. The company announced that, due to the California decision, they would not release a corporate social responsibility report in 2002–2003. Nike released a "Community Investment" report detailing its philanthropic efforts instead.[51]

Questions for Discussion

1. What are the ethical and social issues in this case?

2. Why should Nike be held responsible for what happens in factories that it does not own? Does Nike have a responsibility to ensure that factory workers receive a "living wage"?

3. Is it ethical for Nike to pay endorsers millions while its factory employees receive a few dollars a day?

4. Is Nike's responsibility to monitor its subcontracted factories a legal, economic, social, or philanthropic responsibility? What was it 15 years ago? What will it be 15 years from now?

5. What could Nike have done, if anything, to prevent the damage to its corporate reputation? What steps should Nike take in the future? Is it "good business" for Nike to acknowledge its past errors and become more socially responsible?

6. What are the goals of the AFL-CIO? Does the campus anti-sweatshop movement help or hinder the AFL-CIO's goals? Are the students being "used" by the AFL-CIO?

7. Is Nike's defense of its practices commercial speech or political speech? What are the long-term implications of your decision, not only for Nike but for business in general?

Case Endnotes

1. Copy of e-mail exchange found at Department of Personal Freedom Web site, http://www.shey.net/niked.html.
2. *Ibid.*
3. ABC News Web site, http://abcnews.go.com/sections/business/DailyNews/nike010402.html.
4. *Ibid.*
5. Bien Hoa, "Job Opportunity or Exploitation," *Los Angeles Times*, (April 18, 1999).
6. Philip Knight, "Global Manufacturing: The Nike Story Is Just Good Business," *Vital Speeches of the Day*, 64(20): 637–640.
7. *Ibid*, 637–640.
8. Nike Web site, http://www.nikebiz.com/labor/faq.shtml.
9. New Balance Web site, http://www.newbalance.com/.
10. New Balance Web site, http://www.newbalance.com/.
11. David Bauman, "After the Tears, Gifford Testifies on Sweatshops—She Turns Lights, Cameras on Issue," *Seattle Times* (July 16,1996), A3.
12. Del Jones, "Critics Tie Sweatshop Sneakers to 'Air' Jordan," *USA Today* (June 6, 1996), 1B.
13. *Ibid.*
14. Nike Press Release (June 6, 1996).
15. Del Jones, 1B.
16. Garry Trudeau, "Sneakers in Tinseltown," *Time* (April 20,1998), 84.
17. William J. Holstein, "Casting Nike as the Bad Guy," *U.S. News & World Report*, (September 22, 1997), 49.
18. Verena Dobnik, "Nike Shoe Contractor Abuses Alleged," *The Atlanta Journal-Constitution* (March 18, 1997), A14.
19. Simon Beck, "Nike in Sweat over Heat Raised by Claims of Biases Assessment," *South China Morning Post* (July 6, 1997), 2.
20. Matthew C. Quinn, "Footwear Maker's Labor Pledge Unlikely to Stamp Out Criticism," *The Atlanta Journal-Constitution* (June 25, 1997), F8.
21. G. Pascal Zachary, "Nike Tries to Quell Exploitation Charges," *The Wall Street Journal* (June 15, 1997).
22. Simon Beck, 2.
23. Bill Richards, "Nike Hires an Executive from Microsoft for New Post Focusing on Labor Policies," *The Wall Street Journal* (January 15, 1998), B14.
24. Philip Knight, 640.
25. Patti Bond, "Nike Promises to Improve Factory Worker Conditions," *The Atlanta Journal-Constitution* (May 13, 1998), 3B.
26. Allan Wolper, "Nike's Newspaper Temptation," Editor & Publisher (January 10, 1998), 8–10.
27. Gregg Krupa, "Antisweatshop Activists Score in Campaign Targeting Athletic Retailers," Boston Globe (April 18, 1999), F1.
28. UNITE Web page, http://www.uniteunion.org/research/history/unionisborn.html.
29. Krupa, F1.
30. UNITE Web page.
31. Wolper, 8–10.
32. Wolper, 8.
33. Jodie Morse, "Campus Awakening," *Time* (April 12, 1999), 77–78.
34. Krupa, F1.
35. Morse, 77–78.
36. *Ibid.*
37. Fair Labor Association Web site, http://www.fairlabor.org.
38. *Ibid.*
39. *Ibid.*
40. Worker's Rights Consortium Web site, http://www.workersrights.org/.
41. Nike Web site, http://www.nikebiz.com/labor/index.shtml.
42. Philip Knight Press Release (April 24, 1000) Found at: http://www.nike-biz.com/media/n_uofo.shtml.
43. Louise Lee and Aaron Bernstein, "Who Says Student Protests Don't Matter?" *Business Week* (June 12, 1000), 96.
44. Ravina Shamdasani, "Soul Searching by 'Shoe Geeks' Led to Social Responsibility," *South China Morning Post* (May 17, 2001), 2.
45. Greg Bolt, "University of Oregon Ends Relationship with Antisweatshop Group," *The Register Guard* (March 6, 2001).
46. Hank Hager, "Frohnmayer: It's a Very Happy Day for Us," *Oregon Daily Emerald* (September 27, 2001).
47. Bellamy, Ron, "Nike CEO to Resume Donations to University of Oregon," *The Register Guard* (September 26, 2001).
48. McCall, William, "Nike Releases First Corporate Responsibility Report," *Associated Press State & Local Wire* (October 9, 2001).
49. *Ibid.*
50. Adam Liptak, "Nike Move Ends Case Over Firm's Free Speech," *New York Times* (September 13, 2003)
51. http://www.srimedia.com; For detailed coverage of this case and its implications, see http://www.reclaimdemocracy.org/nike/.

TELEPHONE DEREGULATION: THE PRICING CONTROVERSY

The Telecommunications Act of 1996 was the first major overhaul of telecommunications law in nearly 62 years.[1] It mandated that states allow competition in local telephone service, and it required local telephone providers to lease any or all of their network components to their new competitors at prices to be set by the Federal Communications Commission (FCC). The FCC decided to pursue one national pricing policy, with some state variations to accommodate regional differences in costs. It ruled that the local telephone providers could charge a price for the use of their network components that would just cover the costs that an efficient provider would incur to provide those components for rent. A series of court challenges followed the FCC's decision, but on January 25, 1999, the Supreme Court issued a ruling that the FCC did have the authority to set the pricing.

ARGUMENTS FOR FCC-SET PRICING

Reaction to the ruling was decidedly mixed. Proponents of the FCC ruling argued that deregulation would never happen if the local Bells were able to set their own prices. Given that freedom, they would likely overcharge for their networks and possibly deny access to important network components. This seemed particularly unfair because, as long-distance telephone companies were driving hard to enter local markets, local providers were pushing to enter nationwide long-distance service. Gene Kimmelman of Consumer's Union said, "This decision will help small companies to come into the local market and take on the reigning monopolist."[2]

ARGUMENTS AGAINST FCC-SET PRICING

Opponents of the ruling were less optimistic. They questioned the fairness of charging today's efficiency-based prices for networks that were built at a time of efficiency-suppressing regulation. They also expressed concern that local Bells would not be motivated to upgrade their technologies. Robert W. Crandall of

This case was written by Ann K. Buchholtz, University of Georgia.

the Brookings Institute opined, "Why should these firms be required to invest in new, often risky technology for delivering advanced high-speed services if they are to be required to offer any such new facilities to their rivals at cost?"[3]

THE PLACE OF REGULATION IN DEREGULATION

The Telecommunications Act, its implementation and consequences continue to be heavily debated. At issue is the extent to which it is necessary to regulate the process of deregulation. In the words of the CATO Institute, "Congress wanted market competition but did not trust the free market enough to tell regulators to step aside and allow markets to function on their own."[4] Still others contend that the major players were too powerful to allow competition if they were given too free a hand to operate. The U.S. Senate Committee on Commerce, Science, and Transportation planned to revisit the legislation following the 2004 elections.[5]

Questions for Discussion

1. How do you balance the property rights of the local Bells against the entry barrier that those networks present?
2. Which is more important: opening a monopoly to competition or encouraging the development of new technology? Do you agree with Mr. Crandall that the pricing procedure designed by the FCC will limit investment in new technology?
3. If you were an FCC commissioner, what would you do?

Case Endnotes

1. http://www.fcc.com/telecom.html
2. Michael M. Weinstein, "Economic Scene: It's Hard to Tell Who Won in the High Court Phone Ruling," *The New York Times* (January 28, 1999), C2.
3. Robert W. Crandall, "The Telecom Act's Phone-y Deregulation," *The Wall Street Journal* (January 27, 1999), A22.
4. http://www.cato.org
5. Doug Mohney, "Open Season On Telecommunications Act of 1996," *Von Magazine* (April 26, 2004). http://www.vonmag.com.

| THE CALA REPORT: LOBBYING ETHICS

"Citizens Against Lawsuit Abuse" and "People for a Fair Legal System"—the names of these organizations would lead one to believe they are composed of individual people who have organized at the grassroots level to solve a problem about which they feel deeply. However, according to a report prepared by Public Citizen and the Center for Justice and Democracy, Citizens Against Lawsuit Abuse (CALA) organizations are part of a "national corporate-backed network of front groups that receive substantial financial and strategic assistance from some of America's biggest corporations."[1] In The CALA Files: The Secret Campaign by Big Tobacco and Other Major Industries to Take Away Your Rights, they argue that the goal of these organizations is to insulate corporations from having to pay a price for their reckless behavior.

THE CALA STUDY

Public Citizen and the Center for Justice and Democracy studied dozens of CALA groups in 18 states and found among other things that:

1. Although they claim to be supported by individual donations, they are funded mostly by large corporate donors and representatives of industries that want to be shielded from lawsuits. Central to this effort is the American Tort Reform Association, a coalition of major corporations and trade associations.

2. They hide their pro-business agenda behind friendly consumer-oriented names. The intent to deceive is shown in a memo from the Tobacco Institute, "In order to be totally effective, the grassroots effort must appear to be spontaneous rather than a coordinated effort."[2]

3. According to documents made public during the tobacco litigations, tobacco companies spend millions each year to weaken tort laws through forming and funding groups such as these.

4. The CALA efforts have been successful. They have achieved passage of legislation designed to limit consumer rights to sue manufacturers, and they have conducted successful "voter education" campaigns to unseat judges who favor expanded consumer rights and elect judges who favor limits on liability.

This case was written by Ann K. Buchholtz, University of Georgia.

The CALAs are just one example of the practice of forming fake "grassroots" organizations, sometimes called "shell groups," to further corporate interests. According to The Washington Post, groups such as "Citizens for a Sound Economy" provide analyses that add an air of authority to corporate arguments—while often maintaining the corporate donors' anonymity."[3] Public Interest has also cited "Citizens for a Better Medicare" as being created and funded by the pharmaceutical industry.[4]

NOT IN MY BACKYARD

According to a report prepared by Public Citizen and Citizen Action, another leading consumer group, corporations only seek tort reform when they are the defendants. "The National Association of Manufacturers: A Study in Hypocrisy," documents a variety of cases where corporations are the plaintiffs and charges, "the same companies lobbying to restrict the legal rights of people injured or killed by defective products have unfettered access to our nation's courts as their own private playground."[5] Examples of frivolous corporate cases include the time when Exxon sued the Georgia minor league baseball team, Columbus Redstixx, for violating their trademark by having two Xs in their name and the time when Gillette sued Norelco for ads depicting nonelectric razors as "ferocious creatures."

The View From CALA. For their part, CALA groups say that they are not against the legal system, but that tort reform is needed to corral an out-of-control civil justice system. They don't oppose needed lawsuits, simply the frivolous excesses that abuse the system. They point to the Business Week article that said tort litigation is costing the United States nearly 2 percent of its gross domestic product, which is twice as much as litigation costs in Europe.[6] The issue of tort reform became a centerpiece of the 2004 elections when John Edwards, a trial lawyer, was named the Democratic candidate for vice-president. The issue is one that will continue for some time.

Questions for Discussion

1. By searching on the term "CALA," you can find the Web sites of a variety of CALA organizations. Search their Web sites and decide whether you agree with the assessments of the CALA report. Do you find their practices to be deceptive or defensible? Do the various CALAs differ in that regard?

2. Where do you draw the line? What limits should be placed on corporate lobbying under shell grassroots organizations? Does your attitude toward "shell" lobbying groups vary with the extent to which you agree with the causes they are promoting?

3. What, if any, public policy recommendations would you make?

Case Endnotes

1. An overview of the CALA report and information on purchasing the full report are available at the Public Citizen Web site, http://www.citizen.org.
2. Robert Weissman, "The 'Lawsuit Abuse' Scam," *Multinational Monitor* (September 2000), 7.
3. "Think Tanks: Corporations' Secret Weapon," *The Washington Post* (January 29, 2000), 1.
4. http://www.citizen.org.
5. *Ibid.*
6. "Putting Brakes on the Litigation Machine," *Business Week* (January 29, 2001), 144.

Case 20

| DTC: THE PILL-PUSHING DEBATE

What do Vioxx,® Claritin,® Prilosec,® Viagra,® and Paxil® have in common? They are the five most highly advertised drugs in the United States.[1] Although their brand-name recognition does not rival that of Coca-Cola, their names are familiar to consumers across the nation. They are the flag bearers of the direct-to-consumer (DTC) advertising efforts of the pharmaceutical industry, and that places them in the forefront of the DTC debate. A 2003 AC Nielsen study found that 17 percent of new prescriptions filled were the result of DTC advertising.[2] Furthermore, patients were significantly more likely to refill a prescription that arose from DTC advertising.[3]

THE PROBLEM

Why debate DTC advertising? In his testimony before the Senate Commerce Subcommittee on Consumer Affairs, Dr. Sidney Wolfe, director of the Public Citizen's Health Research Group, expressed the following concern: "There is little doubt that false and misleading advertising to patients and physicians can result in prescriptions being written for drugs that are more dangerous and/or less effective than perceived by either the doctor or the patient. This can then lead to a subsequent toll of deaths and injuries that would not have occurred had safer, more effective drugs been prescribed."[4] Dr. Wolfe cites the following findings from medical studies as cause for concern:

1. Consumers rate drugs significantly more positively when ads have incomplete risk statements.
2. Consumers believe that there is prior scrutiny of DTC ads by the FTC and that DTC ads are held to a higher standard than other ads. Both of those beliefs are wrong.

3. DTC ads provide only a minimal amount of educational information
4. When a study asked what patients would do if a doctor refused to prescribe a drug that a patient wanted because of a DTC ad, 25 percent said they would seek a prescription elsewhere; 15 percent said they would terminate their relationship with the physician.[5]

THE DEBATE

Consumer groups claim that one cause of the increase in health care costs is the explosion of DTC ads and the unnecessary medication that results. The advertising seems to work. The sales of the heavily advertised drugs increased by 32 percent compared to 14 percent for other drugs. However, proponents of DTC ads argue that they help patients. Dr. Richard Dolinar, an endocrinologist, says that the ads empower consumers, "Direct-to-consumer advertising is getting patients with diabetes into my office sooner so they can be treated."[6]

Other doctors complain about drugs being advertised directly to consumers. These doctors claim it makes it very difficult to prescribe the appropriate medication when a patient comes to your office already committed to the drug he or she wants the doctor to prescribe. This takes much of the diagnosis and prescribing freedom and authority out of the hands of the professionals who should be making these judgments.

Questions for Discussion

1. What are the ethical issues in this case?
2. Should DTC advertising be permitted? If so, should DTC advertising be judged by the same criteria as other advertising? If not, how should it be judged differently?

This case was written by Ann K. Buchholtz, University of Georgia.

3. What public policy changes would you advocate regarding DTC?

Case Endnotes

1. Diane West, "DTC Ads Subject of FDA and FTC Reviews," *Drug Store News* (October 22, 2001), 11-12.
2. http://www.acnielsen.com (2004).
3. *Ibid.*
4. Sidney M. Wolfe, "Direct-to-Consumer (DTC) Ads: Illegal, Unethical, or Both," *Public Citizen's Health Research Group Health Letter* (September 2001), 3-4.
5. *Ibid.*
6. Ira Teinowitz, "DTC Regulation by FDA Debated," *Advertising Age* (July 30, 2001), 6.

Case 21

| WHEN SPIRITS COLLIDE: LIQUOR VS. BEER

An epic battle of wills has been brewing in the world of spirits. Diageo, the U.S. liquor market leader with 27 percent of the market,[1] has taken on Anheuser-Busch, U.S. beer industry leader with 56 percent of the market,[2] in a no-holds-barred battle of titans. At issue are the two industry's comparative tax treatment and the different restrictions they face in sales, advertising and promotion in the United States.

THE BEVERAGE ALCOHOL BUSINESS

The Beer Industry. Since Prohibition was repealed in the United States in 1933, the beer industry has worked to cultivate an image of "sports, fun and patriotism."[3] The slogan of a 1940s ad campaign was "America's Beverage of Moderation." In most states, beer can be sold in convenience stores. The television airwaves are filled with beer commercials, making beer one of the largest consumer-goods advertisers.[4]

The Liquor Industry. While beer has enjoyed an upbeat, sport-oriented image in the United States, liquor has been associated historically with seedy characters and smoky bars. Because of its higher alcohol content, liquor had been treated differently from beer. Liquor's federal excise taxes are more than double those of beer and almost three times those on wine. The age limit for drinking beer is lower than the age limit for drinking liquor in some states. State laws regarding when and where liquor can be sold are usually considerably more stringent than the restrictions placed on beer. Despite their relative disadvantage, the liquor industry accepted its position for years. According to Chuck Phillips, former chief executive of Diageo North America, "The spirits industry had lived for years with this feeling that we don't want to stick our heads above the parapet because the beer people would get upset."[5]

This case was prepared by Ann K. Buchholtz, University of Georgia.

THE BATTLE BEGINS

Although the liquor industry had often complained of having an unfair playing field, they did little to level it until 1985, when Seagram launched a campaign entitled "A drink is a drink is a drink." Based on the idea that a standard serving of beer, wine or liquor has the same alcohol content, Seagram argued that the liquor and beer industry should be treated the same in taxation, distribution and advertising. Unable to get the U.S. networks to break a self-imposed ban on liquor advertising, Seagram's took out a magazine ad with the tagline, "What the networks do not want you to know about alcohol." Seagram was able to buy a few ads on cable and local TV stations but not enough to have much impact. In 1996, Seagram sold most of its assets to Diageo.

Diageo Enters the Fray. With the purchase of Seagram, Diageo became the global leader in the liquor industry. In 2001, the company launched a direct attack on the beer industry by marketing Smirnoff Ice, a malt beverage brewed like beer with spirits flavoring. The product contained no vodka and so it could employ the same marketing and distribution options available to beer. Smirnoff Ice was a huge success, taking one percent of the beer market by late 2001. This prompted Anheuser-Busch to get into the malt beverage business by introducing Bacardi Silver in 2003.[6]

Diageo became the force behind the strengthening of industry lobbying group DISCUS, the Distilled Spirits Council of the United States. To help the group improve its lobbying efforts, they hired Guy Smith, who served as a lobbyist for Philip Morris and as public relations advertiser to President Clinton during the impeachment hearings. DISCUS sided with Mothers Against Drunk Driving (MADD), and against the beer industry, in supporting the legislation that lowered the blood alcohol limit to .08 in virtually all states. DISCUS also helped defeat tax increases on liquor in 26 states, losing in only four.[7]

Diageo lobbied the broadcast networks to allow liquor advertisements on their programs. In late 2001, NBC agreed to air the advertisements. Diageo worked with MADD to develop the advertising campaign. They agreed to air only anti-drunk-driving ads in the first four months, to only air ads where a minimum of 80 percent of the viewers were of legal drinking age, and to avoid any youth-oriented programs such as concerts. Although NBC subsequently dropped its plans to allow liquor advertisement, liquor ads appeared on 500 local broadcast stations in 2004. That's a sevenfold increase over the 70 on which they appeared in 2001. These efforts to promote liquor have met with some success. In 2003, liquor volume rose 3.2% while beer volume fell .2%. Liquor's share of the beverage alcohol market rose from 27.9% in 1998 to 29% in 2003, while beer's share fell from 59.6% in 2003 to 57.4% in 1998.[8] Even more worrisome for the beer industry is the fact that the highly valued 21 to 24 year old demographic group's drinking patterns have changed, with beer playing a less prominent role.[9]

The Beer Industry Responds. Anheuser-Busch circulated a rival booklet called "A drink is not a drink" among legislators to counter the liquor industry's argument that liquor, wine and beer were equivalent. *The Wall Street Journal* described a meeting between Augustus Busch III, then Anheuser-Busch chief executive, and a congressman at a Washington restaurant. Mr. Busch asked the waitress to bring three martinis and three light beers to the table and then suggested that the congressman drink the three martinis while he drank the three light beers. After that, they could discuss equalization of the restrictions on beer and liquor. The congressman declined the offer and dropped the subject.[10]

In 2002, NBC cancelled its agreement with Diageo to air liquor ads, saying that pressure from advocacy groups and members of Congress convinced them to make the move. Executives at Diageo and other industry insiders privately attributed NBC's move to their not wanting to lose the $53 million in advertising that Anheuser-Busch spent on NBC that year. The beer industry also successfully lobbied the Treasury Department's Alcohol and Tobacco Tax and Trade Bureau (TTB) to change the rules for the formulation of malt beverages to allow no more than .5% of its alcohol to come from spirits flavoring if the beverage is to fall into the beer category. Because the majority of Smirnoff Ice's flavor comes from spirit flavorings, these changes would require Diageo to undergo the enormous expense of completely changing its formula and production systems. The final decision on the rule change is expected in late 2004.

THE FIGHT CONTINUES

Both sides continue to argue their positions with no sign of abatement. "They want to be us, but they're not us," said August Busch IV, president of Anheuser-Busch's North American business.[11] Diageo Chief Executive Paul Walsh said, "I admire Anheuser-Busch. They have a great business and maybe if I were in their position I would try to protect these barriers as well." Walsh concedes that that company may have underestimated Anheuser-Busch's political influences but said that Diageo would still work to level the playing field. "We're not targeting Anheuser-Busch here. We're targeting the consumer," said Paul Walsh. "And those lines (between liquor and beer) are going to get blurred whether Anheuser-Busch likes it or not, because that's what the consumer wants."[12]

Questions for Discussion

1. What are the major ethical issues in this case?
2. Who are the stakeholders in this situation? How would you prioritize their claims?
3. Do you agree with the arguments made by Diageo and DISCUS? Is "a drink a drink" or is there a substantive difference between liquor and beer? Should the two beverages have differing treatments with taxes, distribution and advertising?
4. Is it ethical of DISCUS to lobby for equal treatment? Is it ethical for the beer industry to resist?
5. What is your reaction to DISCUS's interaction with MADD? Is DISCUS being socially responsible or manipulative or both?

Case Endnotes

1. Deborah Ball and Christopher Lawton, "Lifting Spirits: In Its Long War With Brewers, Liquor Industry Gets Aggressive," *The Wall Street Journal* (May 24, 2004) A1.
2. BevExpo 2004 Industry Fact Sheet, http://www.bevexpo.com
3. Ball and Lawton, A1.
4. *Ibid.*
5. *Ibid.*
6. *Ibid.*
7. *Ibid.*
8. *Ibid.*
9. James B. Arndorfer, "New Drinkers Don't Belly Up To The Beer Bar," *Advertising Age* (June 21, 2004), S4.
10. Ball and Lawton, A1.
11. *Ibid.*
12. *Ibid.*

| THE NEW TOBACCO FIGHT

The advertising industry is concerned about a proposal for curbing tobacco advertising that just won't go away. It was first proposed in 1996 by former FDA commissioner David Kessler. That proposal was struck down, but in 2004 even more restrictive curbs reappeared as part of a legislative package which, among other things, would put severe curbs on the ability of tobacco companies to advertise their products.

THE PROPOSAL

The legislation would give the FDA broad authority to regulate tobacco. Of primary concern to the advertising industry are the constraints that it would place on the tobacco industry's ability to market and distribute tobacco. The proposal includes the following mandates:[1]

1. Ads must be composed of only black and white text, unless the readership is at least 85% adult and there would be fewer than 2 million readers under 18.
2. All ads and labels must refer to the product as "a nicotine delivery device."
3. A brief government statement must be on the product (in addition to the surgeon general's warning).
4. T-shirts, hats and any other promotional items are prohibited.
5. Giveaways, rebates and refunds are banned.
6. Only the corporate name can appear on any event sponsored.

In July 2004, the Senate approved the package by a 78 to 15 vote.[2]

THE ADVERTISING INDUSTRY'S RESPONSE

The precedent that could be set by this proposal troubles the advertising industry: If tobacco can be so sharply curbed, could fatty food and/or alcohol be next? Advertising groups sent a letter to legislators arguing that marketers have the right to market legal products as long as they do so honestly, without misleading claims. The letter said, "While the government has a legitimate interest in fighting the use of tobacco products by minors, the proposed regulations sweep far too broadly and result in massive censorship of truthful speech aimed at adults."[3]

When the advertising industry fought these restrictions in 1996, they argued that the restrictions on advertising were unconstitutional. The restrictions were overturned by the Supreme Court

This case was prepared by Ann K. Buchholtz, University of Georgia.

but not for the reasons the advertising industry argued. Instead, the Supreme Court ruled that the FDA lacked the authority to regulate tobacco. The legislation now proposed would give the FDA the legal authority they previously lacked.[4]

When the American Association of Advertising Agencies (Four As) and the Association of National Advertisers (ANA) joined forces to fight the restrictions in 1996, the entire tobacco industry fought alongside them. The curbs suggested in the 2004 proposal were more restrictive than the curbs planned in 1996. However, Altria, the parent of Philip Morris USA, endorsed the new legislation. Brown & Williamson Tobacco Co. and R.J. Reynolds Tobacco Co. continued to oppose the proposed restrictions.[5] According to R.J. Reynolds, the legislation "fails to make U.S. tobacco farmers more competitive and would be financially disastrous for tobacco manufacturers, their employees, their business partners and adult smokers, many of whom are lower- and middle-income wage earners."[6] Advertising industry groups are contemplating embarking upon another expensive legal battle to fight the proposed restrictions. Dan Jaffe, executive VP of the ANA, said, "We have sued against it in the past and would consider doing it again."[7]

Questions for Discussion

1. What are the ethical issues raised by this case?
2. Who are the stakeholders impacted by this situation? How would you prioritize their claims?
3. Do you agree with any or all of the tobacco advertising restrictions proposed? Would you agree if they were proposed for fatty foods or alcohol? Explain your answer.
4. Is it ethical for the advertising industry groups to lobby against the proposed restrictions on tobacco advertising? Would it be ethical to lobby against similar restrictions on fatty foods or alcohol? What limits, if any, would you place on the issues for which lobbyists should fight?

Case Endnotes

1. Ira Teinowitz, "Ad Groups Prep For New Tobacco Fight," *Advertising Age* (June 7, 2004), 12.
2. Helen Dewar, "Senate Backs Compromise on Tobacco," *Washington Post* (July 16, 2004), A1.
3. Teinowitz, 12.
4. *Ibid.*
5. *Ibid.*
6. Dewar, A1.
7. Teinowitz, 12.

BIG PHARMA'S MARKETING TACTICS

"Big Pharma" is the name the business press uses for the gargantuan pharmaceutical industry. Most of us are familiar with Big Business and Big Government. Now, Big Pharma is in the news and has been for several years regarding its marketing, advertising, and sales tactics. As *Time* magazine recently stated, it's hard to empathize with the drug industry these days because of the high cost of our prescriptions. We either just emptied our wallets in paying for our latest prescription or just returned on a Greyhound bus from Canada where we bought our prescriptions for less.[1]

Big Pharma, itself, is aware it is in for challenges to its marketing and sales tactics. In the summer of 2004, a major conference was held in Boston where industry representatives discussed the sale and illegal marketing of drugs for "off label" uses that were not approved by the Food and Drug Administration. A lawyer from one of the law firms that sponsored the conference said "Rarely has a conference been more timely."[2]

It is hard to visualize Big Pharma cowering before FDA regulators because the industry has built up an army of lobbyists in Washington, DC to protect its interests. Public Citizen recently reported that the industry had 526 lobbyists - almost one for every member of Congress.

THE INDUSTRY

The pharmaceutical industry is one of the healthiest in America. In 2003, prescription drug sales in the U. S. were up almost 12% to $216 billion. Among the top ten companies, they booked combined profits of approximately $50 billion. This represents average profit margins of 14%, which is among the highest of any industry in the U.S.[3]

The top ten U. S. pharmaceutical companies, according to the 2004 *Fortune* magazine annual rankings, include the familiar names, with higher sales at the top of the list:[4]

1. Pfizer
2. Johnson & Johnson
3. Merck
4. Bristol-Myers Squibb
5. Abbott Laboratories
6. Wyeth
7. Eli Lilly
8. Amgen

9. Schering-Plough
10. Forest Laboratories

Among this group, only Johnson & Johnson ranked (#7) among *Fortune*'s "most admired companies."

The pharmaceutical industy spends between $15-$20 billion a year on promotional spending. This includes both professional and direct-to-consumer spending by the drug makers.[5] In spite of its size and success, Big Pharma has been called into question for a number of years now for its questionable marketing, advertising or sales techniques. The charges have included questionable advertising to consumers and charges of dubious ethics and a number of them have resulted in lawsuits. It seems quite amazing, actually, that the pharmaceutical industry has not been more in the spotlight.

PROMOTION TO MED STUDENTS

Big Pharma starts its promotional techniques while the doctors are still students in medical school. There the med students have in the past received free lunches, pens, notepads, and other gifts that are given by the companies. The companies start early trying to persuade the young doctors to prescribe their products by inundating them with logo-infested products and other gifts. A number of medical students have become fed up with the practice and have resisted the free gifts and have started movements to stop the practice from occurring in the first place.

One med student, Jaya Agrawal, helped to launch a national campaign calling on students to sign a pledge saying they would not accept drug-industry gifts. Medical students on other campuses have organized seminars and lectures on the issue. Ms. Agrawal was reminded of how difficult it would be to get everyone to think like her when she moved into an apartment she was planning to share with two other students and noticed a Big Pharma logo on a clock in three rooms of the apartment.[6]

LAWSUITS

The attorneys general in Ohio and Pennsylvania filed lawsuits in March 2004 charging fraud or deceptive sales practices against a number of companies. The State of Ohio claims five companies provided false wholesale pricing data that led their Medicaid program to pay more than it should have for drugs. The State of Pennsylvania filed suits against Pfizer and twelve other drugmakers claiming problems with pricing. They also questioned the free samples and free trips for doctors that the companies allegedly have been providing.[7]

This case was written by Archie B. Carroll, University of Georgia.

In recent years, the objectivity of clinical trials that have been used in the process of developing new drugs has been criticized. In addition, companies have been reportedly illegally promoting drugs for uses for which they were not approved. The result of this is that doctors may be prescribing, and patients may be using, drugs for conditions for which those medicines are not needed, are not appropriate, or might hurt them.[8] A consideration of specific cases and specific companies reveals some of the details.

Prescribing of Neurontin.
Pfizer Inc.'s Warner-Lambert unit recently agreed to pay $430 million to settle civil and criminal charges that it illegally marketed the prescription drug Neurontin, an anti-seizure drug. It is legal for doctors to prescribe FDA-approved drugs for whatever uses they see fit. However, according to the law, the drug companies are not permitted to encourage or promote their drugs for uses for which they have not been approved.[9]

Government officials claim that Warner-Lambert pushed doctors to prescribe Neurontin for maladies ranging from migraines to social disorders even though it was not approved for such uses. The company's tactics, it was claimed, involved sending doctors on lavish trips to Florida or to the Olympics when they were held in Atlanta, where they received presentations on unapproved uses of the drug. Among the one-on-one sales tactics later used included sales pitches to doctors, the dispatching of "medical liaisons" who falsely presented themselves to be experts, and teleconferences in which the sales reps would recruit physicians to talks about off-label uses.[10]

Sales of Neurontin were $2.4 billion in the U. S. during 2003, and off-label sales were estimated to be 90% of overall Neurontin sales. This information came from a lawyer who was representing David Franklin, the whistle-blower who brought this information to light. According to Franklin, "Patients every day are still taking this drug hoping it's effective, and there's really no evidence for that. That, to this day, keeps me up at night."[11]

Promoting Paxil.
In June 2004, Eliot Spitzer, the combative attorney-general of New York, filed a lawsuit alleging that GlaxoSmithKline (GSK), the world's second largest drug firm, had covered up results from clinical trials of its drug, Paxil, an antidepressant. Spitzer alleged that the drug was at best ineffective in children and at worst could increase suicidal thoughts. GSK has denied the charges. Spitzer charged the company with "repeated and persistent fraud" in promoting the drug.[12]

IMPROPER PAYMENTS

Sometimes the questionable marketing of drugs entails improper payments or bribes. In June 2004, the Securities and Exchange Commission announced that the drugmaker Schering-Plough Corporation would pay a $500,000 penalty to settle claims that one of its subsidiaries made improper payments to a Polish charity in a quest to get a Polish government health official to buy the company's products.[13]

The SEC claimed that Schering-Plough Poland donated about $76,000 to a Polish charity, over a three year period, ending in 2002. Chudnow Castle Foundation, the charity, was headed up by a health official in the Polish government. Apparently, this information came to light while regulators were investigating several pharmaceutical companies for compliance with the U. S. Foreign Corrupt Practices Act. The SEC charged that the payments were not accurately shown on the company's books and that the company's internal controls failed to prevent or detect them. The SEC said that the charity was legitimate, but that the company made the contributions with the expectation of boosting drug sales. In addition to paying the fine, the company also agreed to hire an independent consultant to review the company's internal control system and to ensure the firm's compliance with the Foreign Corrupt Practices Act.[14]

THE CASE OF SCHERING-PLOUGH

Few cases more vividly illustrate the questionable marketing tactics of Big Pharma than that of the allegations against Schering-Plough. According to an investigation by the *New York Times*, Schering-Plough has been using the marketing tactic of making payments to doctors in exchange for their commitment to exclusively prescribe the company's medications. One doctor reported receiving an unsolicited check for $10,000 in the mail. He said it had been made out to him personally in exchange for an enclosed "consulting" agreement in which all he had to do was prescribe the company's medicines.[15]

Financial Lures.
Interviews with 20 doctors, industry executives, and observers close to the investigation of Schering-Plough and other drug companies revealed a "shadowy system of financial lures" that the companies have been using to convince the physicians to favor their drugs. In the case of Schering-Plough, the tactics included paying doctors large sums of money to prescribe its drug for hepatitis C and to participate in the company's clinical trials that turned out to be thinly disguised marketing ploys that required very little on the part of the doctors. The company even barred doctors from participating in the program if they did not exhibit loyalty to the company's drugs.[16]

One doctor, a liver specialist, and eight others who were interviewed, said that the company would pay them $1,000 to $1,500 per patient for prescribing Intron A, the company's hepatitis C medicine. The doctors were supposed to gather data, in exchange for the fees, and pass it on to the company. Apparently, many doctors were not diligent in recordkeeping but the company did little. Another liver disease specialist said that the trials were "merely marketing gimmicks."[17] According to some doctors, the company would even shut off the money if one of the doctors wrote prescriptions for competing drugs, or even spoke favorably about other competing drugs. Other doctors reported being signed up for consulting services and being paid $10,000 and the only purpose was to keep them loyal to the company's products.[18]

In another case, Schering-Plough had been charged with and was expected to plead guilty to federal charges that it had not provided Medicaid with the lowest drug prices and would pay a fine.[19]

Management Reactions. In response to the allegations against it, Schering-Plough CEO Fred Hassan indicated that the violations took place before he took office in 2003. He went on to outline steps he was taking to get the company on track. This included instituting an "integrity hotline" for employees to report wrongdoing and the creation of a chief compliance officer to report directly to the CEO and the board. Hassan said that compliance has to become "part of the DNA" of a drug company.[20] Another company official said that the company has been "undergoing a company-wide transformation since the arrival of new leadership in mid 2003," which is a "commitment to quality compliance and business integrity."[21]

A TITANIC SITUATION

Pharmaceutical companies have paid the U. S. government more than $2 billion since 2001 to resolve charges of fraudulent sales and marketing tactics. A record payment of $875 million was made by TAP Pharmaceutical Products as a settlement in 2001 over a kickback schedule to get doctors to prescribe its prostate-cancer drug, Lupron. A former federal prosecutor said that almost every major firm is under investigation now. He concluded "We've got a Titanic situation here. What we don't see is the rest of the iceberg."[22]

Questions for Discussion

1. What are the ethical issues in this case?

2. Who are the primary stakeholders in these incidents?

3. Is there any justification for the marketing tactics described in the case?

4. What is your evaluation of giving free promotional items to med students? What are the arguments for and against such practices?

5. What ethical principles may be violated by the marketing tactics? Do any of these ethical principles *support* the companies' actions?

6. Big Pharma needs enormous sums of money to conduct R & D and to advance its industry. Do the ends justify the means because our health is at stake?

7. What response do you think physicians should take when approached regarding some of the schemes presented in this case?

8. Schering-Plough seems to be back on track upon the appointment of Fred Hassan as CEO. What is your evaluation of the steps the company is taking?

9. What does your personal research indicate is the status of the above cases or that of Big Pharma?

Case Endnotes

1. Daren Fonda and Barbara Kiviat, "Curbing the Drug Marketers," *Time*, July 5, 2004, 40-42.
2. *Ibid.*, 40.
3. *Ibid.*, 41.
4. "America's Most Admired Companies," *Fortune*, March 8, 2004.
5. Chris Adams, "Student Doctors Protest Largess of Drug Makers, *Wall Street Journal*, June 24, 2002, B1.
6. *Ibid.*
7. Monica Roman, "Pointing at Big Pharma," *Business Week*, March 22, 2004, 56.
8. Carolyn Susman, "False Marketing of Drugs Raises Red Flags," *Cox News Service*, May 25, 2004.
9. *Ibid.*
10. Lewis Krauskopf, "Pfizer Fined $430M; Guilty of Illegal Marketing of Drug," *The Record* (Bergen County, NJ), May 14, 2004, B01.
11. *Ibid.*
12. "Business: Trials and Tribulations; Pharmaceuticals," *The Economist*, June 19, 2004, 74.
13. Judith Burns, "SEC Settles Bribery Case VS. Schering-Plough Corp." *Wall Street Journal*, June 9, 2004.
14. *Ibid.*
15. Gardiner Harris, "As Doctor Writes Prescription, Drug Company Writes a Check," *The New York Times*, June 27, 2004, 1YT.
16. *Ibid.*
17. *Ibid.*
18. *Ibid.*
19. Reuters news service, "Schering-Plough could plead guilty on pricing— NYT," June 28, 2004.
20. Fonda and Kiviat, 2004, 41.
21. Reuters, June 28, 2004.
22. Fonda and Kiviat, 2004, 41.

FIRESTONE AND FORD:
THE TIRE TREAD SEPARATION TRAGEDY

It is often tricky to know when an ethical or social issue really begins. Does it begin before it is "recognized" or "identified" as an issue? Does it begin when an isolated manager recognizes an incident or a trend and reports it via a memo to his superiors? Does it begin once the media get hold of information and the frenzy begins? Such questions are raised in the case with the Firestone-Ford tire tread separation debacle that began dominating business news in the fall of 2000 and continues today.

Ask any consumer about the two most critical features of safety on their automobiles, and most will quickly respond—brakes and tires. It is not surprising, then, that the tire tread separations that began appearing on certain categories of Firestone tires, especially those associated with the Ford Explorer, caught the public's attention like no other recent product safety issue. Was this a tire problem or an SUV problem? Was this Firestone's problem or Ford's problem? Were both companies responsible for what happened? Were government regulations administered through the National Highway Traffic Safety Administration (NHTSA) adequate to protect the public? These questions are simple to ask but difficult to answer as new information about these issues comes to light with the passage of time.

Let's start where the "public" knowledge of the product dangers began to surface—with a couple of accidents reported since 1998.

TWO KEY ACCIDENTS

Jessica LeAnn Taylor was a 14-year-old junior high school cheerleader on the way to a homecoming football game near her hometown of Mexia, Texas, on October 16, 1998. She was in a Ford Explorer SUV, driven by a friend of her mother's, when the tread on the left-rear Firestone ATX tire allegedly "peeled off like a banana," leading the Explorer to veer left and roll over. Jessica died in this accident.[1] In another incident, two years later, Victor Rodriguez and his family piled into the family's Ford Explorer over Labor Day weekend and prepared to visit a sick aunt at a hospital in Laredo, Texas. As Rodriguez started down Interstate 35, he was startled by a thumping sound and looked in his rearview mirror to see the tread shredding off one of his Firestone Wilderness AT tires. Rodriguez was unable to control his vehicle. It flipped, ejecting five of its passengers. Among the passengers was his 10-year-old son, Mark Anthony, who died instantly.[2]

This case was written by Archie B. Carroll, University of Georgia.

Jessica LeAnn Taylor and Mark Anthony Rodriguez were just two of many victims in a broadening safety crisis that, according to some accounts, had taken the lives of close to 90 Americans by fall 2000 and had "driven fear into the hearts of motorists" who had begun to think of the sport utility vehicle as the ideal family car.

A KEY COURT VICTORY

Though the tribute for bringing the tire safety/SUV tragedy to a head may have begun in a number of different places, one account attributes the tenacity of Jessica Taylor's family lawyer, Randy Roberts, with much of the credit. Roberts was a small-town lawyer, and when he took the case he realized there was not much hope in taking on a corporate giant such as Firestone, a unit of Japan's Bridgestone Corporation. As many other tire companies have successfully done in the past, Firestone ruled out a tire problem at the very outset. It and other companies have been successful in keeping lawsuits and consumer complaint data confidential, or private, saying the Taylor accident was similar to only one other with which they were familiar. Randy Roberts did not buy this argument, and in November 1999 he won a crucial victory from state judge Sam Bournias, who ordered Firestone to turn over any information on complaints or other lawsuits as well as employee depositions associated with these lawsuits concerning its ATX and Wilderness tires. The judge also permitted Roberts to share this information with other lawyers who were involved in similar lawsuits.[3]

Other Lawsuits. Roberts discovered that other attorneys, for example, Bruce Kaster of Ocala, Florida, and Tab Turner of Little Rock, Arkansas, had been suing Firestone for much of the decade over the same type of issue. Though a trial date for his case had not been set, Roberts was one of the first to sense the broad scope of potential tire defects. At that time, he reported that there had been more than 1,100 incident reports and 57 lawsuits by February 2000.[4]

THE NHTSA GETS INVOLVED

By February 2000, the National Highway Traffic Safety Administration (NHTSA) had received fewer than 50 complaints over the better part of the previous decade about the suspect tires. It began to receive tips from State Farm Insurance that it was experiencing an unusually high number of insurance claims in which these tires were associated. After a report on tread separation accidents by Houston's TV station KHOU,

30 to 40 more complaints came in. At this point, NHTSA got interested. They contacted Randy Roberts, and Roberts was quite willing to help them do their work. He reported his findings about widespread complaints, and it is believed to have been a significant factor leading up to Firestone's voluntary recall of 6.5 million possibly defective tires. The voluntary recall began August 9, 2000, and it included the Radial ATX, Radial ATXII, and certain Wilderness AT tires.[5]

By September 2000, the recall had only replaced about 2 million tires. One reason was due to a tire shortage of replacement tires. At about the same time, the NHTSA reported that possibly 1.4 million more tires, especially those manufactured at the Decatur, Illinois, plant, may be susceptible to the same type of tread separations.[6]

THE FINGER-POINTING BEGINS

As the bad news spread and in the absence of any good news, the finger-pointing between Bridgestone/Firestone and Ford began and continued unabated. Ford's position was best articulated by then-CEO Jacques Nasser, who stated that "this is a tire issue, not a vehicle issue." Nasser was trying to distance Ford from responsibility for the tire failures. For its part, Firestone argued that Ford's recommended lower air pressure for the tires may have contributed to the problem. Firestone said it recommended 30 PSI for the tires whereas Ford was recommending 26 PSI for the tires.[7] It would later come out that Firestone believed the lower air pressure may have been an important contributory factor in the tire separations.

Investigations. The finger-pointing and squabbling between Firestone and Ford created a very unclear picture of what was going on and why. The result was that both companies began to be investigated by the media and government, and the situation got worse for them both. The confusion caused Congress to begin hearings in September 2000 as top executives of both companies were summoned to Washington for testimony. At about the same time, it got worse for both as Venezuelan consumer protection officials were expected to recommend that both Ford and Firestone be charged with criminal negligence after investigating more than 60 deaths in that country that had been linked to accidents involving Ford Explorers equipped with Firestone tires.[8]

CONGRESSIONAL HEARINGS AND THE UNFOLDING STORY

In congressional hearings in early September 2000, Congress began grilling Bridgestone/Firestone and Ford executives about problems with their tires in the United States and abroad.[9] Congressional investigators reported on internal documents from both Firestone and Ford that the two companies were aware of the tread separation problem. The documents revealed that the companies knew something was amiss. In the unfolding paper trail, it was suggested that Firestone should have understood it had glitches at its Decatur, Illinois, plant, where some of the damaged tires had been identified as having been manufactured. A chart circulated inside the company by Firestone analysts earlier in the year had shown that nearly 60 percent of claims against the company in 1999 were for tires made during a strike that was taking place at the Decatur plant. Also, Firestone knew that two-thirds of the dollar payments it had made to settle claims involving tire separations came from the Decatur plant. On top of this, a March 12, 1999, Ford memo was disclosed that suggested that Firestone was reluctant to recall suspect tires in Saudi Arabia because doing so would require the company to notify the U.S. Department of Transportation.[10] So, evidence that there was trouble was available to both the companies.

Another Accident Victim. After another accident victim, Lori Lazarus, heard about the big Firestone tire recall, she was very upset but not surprised. Back on Labor Day 1996, while driving home from Disney World, a Firestone tire on her Ford Explorer had shredded. Her SUV flipped into a drainage ditch, leaving her trapped. She was finally saved by passing motorists, who pulled her from the submerged vehicle. She still suffers from headaches and balance problems. The 31-year-old teacher was bitter that Ford and Firestone were just beginning to own up to their problems. She said, "They've known something was wrong for years."[11]

DAMAGE CONTROL CONTINUES

With the allegations spinning out of control, Ford and Firestone began full-blown damage control. Pressure was mounting to widen the recall. Critics wanted to know if the companies were guilty of a cover-up or just dragging their feet. Evidence continued to unfold that both companies had known about the problem for years. Lawsuits first started occurring in 1991. Documents from those lawsuits showed that Firestone had begun reimbursing some consumers for faulty ATX tires as early as 1989. By 1997, insurance adjustors at State Farm began noticing a pattern of problems with ATX and Wilderness tires. In a few cases, they sought and received reimbursements from Firestone. State Farm said it shared its data with federal safety regulators in 1998, but an investigation into the tires was not opened up until 2 years later. In 1998, Ford also noticed Firestone treads unraveling on Explorers in Saudi Arabia, Asia, and South America, and in 1999 began replacing tires on nearly 50,000 foreign vehicles. Ford did not reveal to U.S. regulators its foreign recall until May 2000.[12]

Previous Lawsuits. Through the judicious use of its lawyers, Firestone was able to conceal the fact that it had been sued many times before due to tire problems. How was this possible? An investigation by *U.S. News and World Report* found that Bridgestone/Firestone routinely used legal protective orders to conceal crucial data that was generated when consumers filed warranty claims with the company. The head of Trial Lawyers for Public Justice, Arthur Bryant, observed, "Deaths and serious injuries could have been prevented with these tires if manufacturers had not been able to use protective orders and court secrecy to hide the dangers." It took months for federal investigators to get access to the warranty data from Firestone. It finally became public only after Congress demanded it at the hearings in early September, 2000.[13]

Reporting Not Required. Apparently, tire makers are not legally required to share potentially damaging reports with the government as other industries must do when public safety issues arise. For example, manufacturers and hospitals are required to notify the Food and Drug Administration every time a medical device such as a pacemaker is involved in an injury or death. The NHTSA has no such clout with the tire makers. The companies are required to report on themselves only if they discover a defect. Clarence Ditlow of the Center for Auto Safety, a consumer advocacy organization, says the federal government requires manufacturers to surrender adjustment data "only in the aftermath of a tragedy." Lawmakers have been angry about this. Transportation Secretary Rodney Slater wants this loophole closed. He admits the NHTSA does not have the authority to get the critical safety numbers, but it appears Congress is now ready to do something about this.[14] The NHTSA also claims that it has not received adequate funding from Congress to do its work effectively.

THE CRISIS WOULD NOT GO AWAY

Throughout the fall of 2000 and early 2001, both Ford and Firestone scrambled to contain the crisis that would not go away. It is not clear which company was catching the greatest amount of heat. *Fortune* magazine called it Jacques Nasser's, Ford's CEO, "biggest test"—a crisis that jolts customers, suppliers, employees and sends the company's stock reeling as it threatens the company's good name.[15] *Business Week* referred to it as "a crisis of confidence" for Ford, as Nasser scrambled to contain the problem at Ford.[16] Throughout most of this time, Ford was able to deflect the blame and pin most of the responsibility on the tire maker, but as investigations continued, Bridgestone/Firestone fired back. Then-Firestone executive vice president John Lampe said the problem is that Ford Explorers have a tendency to roll over. He pointed out that Explorers had been involved in 16,000 rollovers since the model was introduced a decade earlier, and that less than 10 percent of those accidents involved tread separations of Firestone tires. Critics had been concerned about the stability of the Explorer well before Firestone announced its tire recall.[17]

FIRESTONE'S HANDLING OF THE CRISIS

For Bridgestone/Firestone, its apparent lack of savvy in handling the tire crisis seemed to make matters worse. Bridgestone president Yoichiro Kaizaki is a star in Japan. He is credited with globalizing operations and doubling profits during an earlier period. His performance in the tire crisis left a lot to be desired. His strategy was to lie low and not make public appearances. One consultant said, "This is a huge crisis, but Bridgestone and Kaizaki are handling it terribly." A former company executive said, "They just don't have a clue how to handle this." Bridgestone's apparent strategy had been to hunker down and wait for this thing to blow over. This seems to be the normal approach used in Japan. There, few managers are comfortable dealing with the press and investors. The former company executive said, "The Japanese don't understand the value of PR." Masatoshi Ono, CEO of Firestone in the United States, apparently did not perform any better than Kaizaki.[18]

OTHER FACTORS

In late 2000, representatives from Bridgestone/Firestone went into action and engaged in a lot of finger-pointing. Much of their action was to blame Ford and other factors for many of the tire problems. Some of these "other factors" included the weight of the Ford Explorer, the SUV that had figured into so many of the reported accidents and deaths. Other factors mentioned by Firestone executives were the "uneven weight distribution" on the Explorer's back axle. Firestone officials said that more weight is distributed on the left side of the Explorer, making the vehicle potentially unstable and more susceptible to a serious accident when the tires fail. Related to the weight issue, Firestone claimed that Ford recommended a tire inflation level of 26 PSI when it was calling for an inflation level of 30 PSI.[19] Ford disputes that the weight of the Explorer contributed to the tire failures.[20]

Three Other Factors. Firestone identified three other factors contributing to the deadly accidents. These included unspecified "manufacturing problems" at their Decatur, Illinois, plant, the design of the tire in the shoulder area, and "customer usage." This last factor referred to the company's belief that motorists driving their vehicles at high speeds and the great amount of use to which they put the tires were contributing factors.[21]

THE LITIGATION PACKET

By early 2001, the tread separation controversy had assumed its rightful place in the long history of product litigation. In a featured article entitled "The Litigation Machine," published in *Business Week*, lawyers could read about the "Firestone Tire

Tread Separation" litigation packet that could be purchased from the Association of Trial Lawyers of America (ATLA). The ATLA is the powerful Washington trade group that serves as the tort bar's central brain trust. The litigation packet, all 689 pages of it, is distributed only to plaintiff's lawyers. It provides a step-by-step guide to suing Bridgestone/Firestone and Ford Motor Company. After a breezy synopsis of the tire debacle, the manual proceeds to offer its lawyer-readers with everything they need to get a lawsuit started.[22]

Included in the manual are 59 complaints from previously filed tread separation cases that, with a few minor changes to reflect local laws, can be recycled to be used anywhere in the country. Also included are a list of documents to request from Firestone, a package of useful National Highway Traffic Safety Administration documents, and a directory of informative Web sites.[23]

FIRESTONE'S NEW CEO

By April 2001, Firestone had a new face at the helm—John Lampe, its new CEO. The company's reputation had been badly damaged and the company continued to fight lawsuits, but the new CEO was determined to restore credibility to the embattled company. Over the previous 9 months, Firestone had recalled 6.5 million tires from Ford Explorers after some tires shredded on the highway, leading to rollovers that the NHTSA said had killed 174 people and injured 700 more. Lampe ordered Firestone's Decatur plant to change its manufacturing process and spent $50 million to upgrade several different facilities.[24]

Lampe Defends His Company. Lampe also went on the attack to defend his company against Ford Motor Company. Since the recall had begun, Ford placed all the blame for the Explorer rollovers on Firestone. Lampe had testified earlier that Ford had made its new Explorers too heavy to drive safely at the tire air pressure it recommended. Questions continued to be raised whether the design of the Explorer could have contributed to the crashes. According to Joan Claybrook, executive director of Public Citizen, a public advocacy group, Lampe went after Ford relentlessly. She said, "That took some guts. Very few suppliers go after the auto companies." At that time Ford was still buying one-third of its tires from Firestone and was its biggest customer, though business between the two companies was diminishing.[25]

THE CORPORATE DIVORCE

Criticism and escalating mistrust of each other led to a divorce between Firestone and Ford in May 2001. In a May 21 meeting, it was clear the two companies were continuing to point fingers at one another and blame each other for the tire separation problems. At that emotional meeting, Lampe dropped a bombshell. He severed all ties with Ford, its largest customer.

He handed Ford executives a prepared letter that said, in essence, that they would no longer do business with Ford, and then they asked to be excused from the meeting. The letter caught Ford by surprise. Jacques Nasser recalled: "I've been around for a long time, and that's the first time I've heard anyone say they didn't want to do business with the Ford Motor Company."[26] The next day, Ford announced that it would replace 13 million Firestone tires, at a cost of $3 billion.

Magnitude of Divorce. To appreciate the magnitude of this corporate divorce, it should be noted that the two companies had had a 100-year relationship with one another. It was one of the oldest partnerships in U. S. business history, initially forged through the personal friendships of Harvey S. Firestone and Henry Ford. Further, it was cemented by the marriage of their grandchildren William Clay Ford and Martha Parke Firestone. Lampe later stated, "The decision I had to make to terminate our relationship with Ford was the most difficult, the most painful, decision I've ever made. But it was the only decision we could take." Ford's Nasser remained resolute. "This is a tire issue and only a tire issue," Nasser said before a congressional subcommittee. "We do not get any satisfaction from this dispute with Firestone. But we cannot and will not let them dictate when Ford Motor Company can and will act to protect our customer's safety."[27]

CLOSING OF THE DECATUR PLANT

In late June 2001, Bridgestone/Firestone announced plans to close its troubled factory in Decatur, Illinois. In terms of capacity, it was the company's third largest plant. The company decided to close the plant as it faced almost a 50 percent plunge in sales of its flagship Firestone-brand tires. The company also hoped the closure would help the company regain its financial footing and help put the tire-recall crisis behind it. Firestone also said that the Decatur plant was operating at half its capacity and was targeted because of its age and the expected cost of modernization. The Decatur facility had been originally built as a tank factory in World War II and was converted to tire manufacturing when the company bought it in 1963.[28]

LAWSUITS CONTINUED

On the lawsuit front, in August 2001, Firestone settled the first trial to come out of the Firestone tire debacle. The company agreed to pay $7.5 million to the family of a 40-year-old woman who was paralyzed and suffered brain damage in the rollover crash of a Ford Explorer. In making this settlement, the company wrapped up the first of hundreds of defective-tire lawsuits to go to trial since the recall of 6.5 million tires in August 2000. The plaintiff in this case, Dr. Joel Rodriguez, whose wife, Marisa, had suffered the injuries during a rollover crash in a Ford Explorer SUV, initially had named the Ford

Motor Company as a defendant. However, Ford settled out of court before the trial for $6 million.[29] Bridgestone/Firestone had blamed the accident on the Explorer, saying that design flaws made it prone to rolling over. In settling the case, Bridgestone/Firestone admitted no liability.[30]

To add to its troubles, in September 2001, Ford paid $15 million to a Florida family whose daughter had been seriously injured and left in a vegetative state when a Ford Econoline van rolled on top of her. The couple was awarded $30 million, but the amount was cut in half because the girl was not wearing a seatbelt. The jury found Ford guilty of manufacturing a defect in the tire valve on the vehicle, which caused the tire to explode and the van to roll over.[31]

NASSER'S DOWNFALL

By fall 2001, Ford was continuing to flounder and the tire-SUV controversy was only part of the problem. The company's brand name had been sullied by the Firestone scandal, its vehicle quality ranking had plummeted, and dealers and employees had become fed up with Jacques Nasser. Though Nasser had great visions for the company, he and the company got ensnarled in events that brought them both down. In early November 2001, chairman William Clay Ford, Jr., great-grandson of the founder and part-time chairman for the previous 3 years, fired Nasser. Bill Ford himself took over as CEO. This was a turnabout for Nasser. Just 15 months prior, he was the auto industry's rising star. Some observers had compared him to a young Jack Welch. Some of his bold management innovations, however, did not endear him to his workers. One of his management initiatives was that 10 percent of all workers would receive a "C" grade on their performance evaluations; that could lead to their termination. This Darwinian HR initiative resulted in employee lawsuits. The new CEO was seen to be a healer.[32]

According to Brock Yates, editor-at-large of *Car and Driver* magazine, Mr. Nasser was a hero until the Ford Explorer/Firestone rollover squabble. From that moment on, Nasser and the company began a downward spiral that resulted in his dismissal. When you added in the severed relationship with Firestone, slipped Ford quality, and the recession, Nasser was finished.[33]

ANOTHER RECALL AND CLASS-ACTION STATUS

In October 2001, Firestone recalled an additional 3.5 million tires. It had fought the NHTSA over this additional recall for a year, but finally capitulated and agreed not to fight the recall. These tires were the Wilderness AT tires mounted on SUVs. Most of these tires were manufactured prior to 1998 and placed as original equipment on vehicles. According to Firestone, there were only about 768,000 of these tires still on the market.[34]

In late November 2001, Ford and Firestone suffered another crushing blow when U. S. District Judge Sarah Evans Barker ruled

in Indianapolis that more than 500 individual lawsuits related to Explorers and Firestone and its private brand tires would be combined into a single, massive class-action lawsuit. Class-action status opens the door for millions more to join those already suing. This came as disturbing news for the automaker and tire company, both financially strapped by problems to date. According to this ruling, anyone who ever owned or leased a Ford Explorer, or had Firestone-made tires during the past 12 years, could qualify for reimbursement for economic losses from Ford or Bridgestone/Firestone. Both companies said they plan to appeal the decision.[35]

By December 2001, federal highway regulators had connected 271 deaths and hundreds of additional injuries to Firestone-Explorer accidents.[36]

MORE RECENT EVENTS

In 2004, a Texas judge approved a $149 million settlement of class-action lawsuits stemming from the huge recall.[37] This settlement was only for those who were not injured or suffered property damage from the tires. The unfriendly relationship between Ford and Firestone has warmed somewhat in the past three years. However, Firestone does not think Ford is likely to become a customer in its U. S. market again soon. John Lampe, the CEO, said he believes that eventually Firestone will return as one of Ford's major tire suppliers at some point in time but he wouldn't specify when.[38]

Does Firestone Still Owe Ford? In 2001, Ford spent nearly $3 billion of its own money replacing almost 13 million Firestone tires that it said could not be trusted. To this day, some are saying that a reasonable argument could be made that Firestone owes that money to Ford. At a minimum, it has been argued that Bridgestone/Firestone owes Ford $600 million which represents the 2.7 million Ford-replaced tires that the NHTSA formally ruled were unsafe.[39] As things currently stand, it is not likely that such a payment would be made. John Lampe, in an interview in January 2004 said "Ford's decision to do their replacement program in 2001 was their decision. They did it on their own. We were not in favor of it. Everybody knows that. We took the responsibility in 2000. They took the responsibility in 2001."[40]

In 2003, Bridgestone/Firestone had a net profit of $83 million on sales of $7.6 billion. Ford lost $559 million on sales of $94 billion in North American operations. Both companies have improved over their 2001 disastrous results.[41] Many experts thought Bridgestone/Firestone would never recover from the tread separation tragedy, but they apparently have.

Worth a Movie? In 2004, it was announced that a feature film was being made showing the many sides of the Ford-Firestone tire calamity. It was reported that Michael Douglas would produce and star in the film based on Adam Penenberg's book, *Tragic Indifference*. The film is expected to be released in 2005.[42]

Questions for Discussion

1. What are the major and minor ethical issues involved in this case?

2. Who are the stakeholders and what are their stakes? How do legitimacy, power, and urgency factor in? Do these companies care about consumers? Discuss.

3. Conduct a CSR analysis of both Firestone and Ford. How do they measure up in fulfilling their various social responsibilities?

4. Who is at fault in the tire separation controversy? Bridgestone/Firestone? Ford Motor Company? The NHSTA?

5. Is the Firestone brand name ruined or do you think it has been saved? Will the Ford Explorer maintain its status as a popular SUV? Does the public have a short memory?

6. Do you think Firestone has an ethical responsibility to pay Ford $3 billion (or $600 million) for the tires it replaced on its own because the company did not think they were safe?

7. Research the current status of both Bridgestone/Firestone and Ford. What has happened since the end of the case?

Case Endnotes

1. Daniel Eisenberg, "Anatomy of a Recall," *Time* (September 11, 2000), 29.
2. Keith Nauthton and Mark Hosenball, "Ford vs. Firestone," *Newsweek* (September 18, 2000), 27–28.
3. Eisenberg, 29–30.
4. Eisenberg, 30.
5. "Bridgestone/Firestone Voluntary Tire Recall," Bridgestone/Firestone Web page: http://mirror.bridgestone-firestone.com/news/corporate/news/00809b.htm.
6. Eisenberg, 31.
7. Eisenberg, 31.
8. Joann Muller, Jeff Green, Nicole St. Pierre, and Pamela Moore, "Firestone and Ford: The Ride Gets Bumpier," *Business Week* (September 11, 2000), 42.
9. David Kiley, Earle Eldridge and Thomas Fogarty, "Congress Seeks Details on Tire Recall Situation," *USA Today* (September 5, 2000), 8B.
10. Marianne Lavelle, "Apologies Will Not Be Accepted: Firestone Clearly Knew Something Was Amiss," *U. S. News & World Report* (September 18, 2000), 62.
11. Keith Naughton, "Spinning Out of Control," *Newsweek* (September 11, 2000), 58.
12. *Ibid.*
13. Jim Morris and Marianne Lavelle, "Secret Data Reveal Why Tires Went Bad," *U. S. News & World Report* (September 25, 2000), 42–43.
14. *Ibid.*
15. Soo-Min Oh, "Jac Nasser's Biggest Test," *Fortune* (September 18, 2000), 123–128.
16. "A Crisis of Confidence," *Business Week* (September 18, 2000), 40–42.
17. Joann Muller, David Welch, and Jeff Green, "Crisis Management: Would You Buy One? *Business Week* (September 25, 2000), 46.
18. Irene Kunii and Dean Foust, "They Just Don't Know How to Handle This," *Business Week* (September 18, 2000), 43.
19. Stephen Power and Timothy Aeppel, "Firestone Cites Explorer's Weight as Contributor to Tire Accidents," *The Wall Street Journal* (December 19, 2000), A4.
20. Todd Zaun, "Bridgestone Chief Repeats: Others Share Blame on Tires," *The Wall Street Journal* (December 21, 2000), A15.
21. Power and Aeppel, *ibid.*
22. Mike France, "The Litigation Machine," *Business Week* (January 29, 2001), 114–123.
23. *Ibid.*
24. David Welch, "Meet the New Face of Firestone," *Business Week* (April 30, 2001), 64–66.
25. *Ibid.*, 66.
26. Caroline Mayer and Frank Swoboda, "Anatomy of a Divorce," *The Washington Post Weekly Edition* (June 25–July 1, 2001), 17.
27. *Ibid.*
28. Timothy Aeppel and Todd Zaun, "Firestone Plans to Close Troubled Decatur Factory," *The Wall Street Journal* (June 28, 2001), A3.
29. Richard Oppel, "Bridgestone Agrees to Pay $7.5 Million in Explorer Crash," *The New York Times* (August 25, 2001).
30. "Family Settles with Firestone for $7.5 Million," *The Atlanta Journal-Constitution* (August 25, 2001), E4.
31. "Ford to Pay $15 Million in Van Rollover Incident," *The Atlanta Journal-Constitution* (September 21, 2001), F3..
32. Keith Naughton, "Hit the Road, Jacques," *Newsweek* (November 12, 2001), 44.
33. Brock Yates, "It's Curtains for Jac the Knife," *The Wall Street Journal* (October 31, 2001), A24.
34. Nedra Pickler, "Firestone Recalls 3.5 Million More Tires," *The Washington Post* (October 4, 2001).
35. David Kiley, "Judge Expands Lawsuit vs. Ford, Firestone," *USA Today* (November 29, 2001), 3B. Also see Joseph B. White, "Suits Against Ford, Firestone Are Given Class-Action Status," *The Wall Street Journal* (November 29, 2001), B14.
36. White, *ibid.*
37. "Judge OKs $149 million Firestone Settlement," *Automotive News*, March 22, 2004, 30.
38. Richard Truett, "BFS, Ford warm up to each other," *Rubber & Plastic News*, March 15, 2004.
39. Harry Stoffer, "Ford Should Collect from Firestone," *Automotive News*, April 21, 2003, 14.
40. Quoted in *Ibid*, 14.
41. *Ibid.*
42. Jason Stein, "Feature film will tell Ford-Firestone story," *Automotive News*, April 26, 2004, 1.

THE COFFEE SPILL HEARD 'ROUND THE WORLD

Stella Liebeck and her grandson, Chris Tiano, drove her son, Jim, to the airport 60 miles away in Albuquerque, New Mexico, on the morning of February 27, 1992. Because she had to leave home early, she and Chris missed having breakfast. Upon dropping Jim off at the airport, they proceeded to a McDonald's drive-through for breakfast. Stella, a spry, 79-year-old, retired department-store clerk, ordered a McBreakfast, and Chris parked the car so she could add cream and sugar to her coffee.[1]

What occurred next was the coffee spill that has been heard 'round the world. A coffee spill, serious burns, a lawsuit, and an eventual settlement made Stella Liebeck the "poster lady" for the bitter tort reform discussions that dominated Congress during 1995. Over ten years later this lawsuit is still in the news and subject to continuing debate.

THIRD-DEGREE BURNS

According to Liebeck's testimony, she tried to get the coffee lid off. She could not find any flat surface in the car, so she put the cup between her knees and tried to get it off that way. As she tugged at the lid, scalding coffee spilled into her lap. Chris jumped from the car and tried to help her. She pulled at her sweat suit, squirming as the 170-degree coffee burned her groin, inner thigh, and buttocks. Third-degree burns were evident as she reached an emergency room.

Hospitalization.
Following the spill, Liebeck spent a week in the hospital and about 3 weeks at home recuperating with her daughter, Nancy Tiano. She was then hospitalized again for skin grafts. Liebeck lost 20 pounds during the ordeal and at times was practically immobilized. Another daughter, Judy Allen, recalled that her mother was in tremendous pain both after the accident and during the skin grafts.[2]

According to a *Newsweek* report, Liebeck wrote to McDonald's in August 1994, asking them to turn down the coffee temperature. Though she was not planning to sue, her family thought she was due about $2,000 for out-of-pocket expenses, plus the lost wages of her daughter who stayed at home with her. The family reported that McDonald's offered her $800.[3]

STELLA FILES A LAWSUIT

After this, the family went looking for a lawyer and retained Reed Morgan, a Houston attorney, who had won a $30,000

settlement against McDonald's in 1988 for a woman whose spilled coffee had caused her third-degree burns. Morgan filed a lawsuit on behalf of Liebeck, charging McDonald's with "gross negligence" for selling coffee that was "unreasonably dangerous" and "defectively manufactured." Morgan asked for no less than $100,000 in compensatory damages, including pain and suffering, and triple that amount in punitive damages.

McDonald's Motion Rejected.
McDonald's moved for summary dismissal of the case, defending the coffee's heat and blaming Liebeck for spilling it. According to the company, she was the "proximate cause" of the injury. With McDonald's motion rejected, a trial date was set for August 1994.

As the trial date approached, no out-of-court settlement occurred. Morgan, the attorney, said that at one point he offered to drop the case for $300,000 and was willing to settle for half that amount, but McDonald's would not budge. Days before the trial, the judge ordered the two parties to attend a mediation session. The mediator, a retired judge, recommended McDonald's settle for $225,000 using the argument that a jury would likely award that amount. Again, McDonald's resisted settlement.[4]

THE TRIAL

The trial lasted 7 days, with expert witnesses dueling over technical issues, such as the temperature at which coffee causes burns. Initially, the jury was annoyed at having to hear a case about spilled coffee, but the evidence presented by the prosecution grabbed its attention. Photos of Liebeck's charred skin were introduced. A renowned burn expert testified that coffee at 170 degrees would cause second-degree burns within 3.5 seconds of hitting the skin.

The Defense Helped Liebeck.
Defense witnesses inadvertently helped the prosecution. A quality-assurance supervisor at McDonald's testified that the company did not lower its coffee heat despite 700 burn complaints over 10 years. A safety consultant argued that 700 complaints—about one in every 24 million cups sold—was basically trivial. This comment was apparently interpreted that McDonald's cared more about statistics than people. An executive for McDonald's testified that the company knew its coffee sometimes caused serious burns, but it was not planning to go beyond the tiny print warning on the cup that said, "Caution: Contents Hot!" The executive went on to say that McDonald's did not intend to

This case was written by Archie B. Carroll, University of Georgia.

change any of its coffee policies or procedures, saying, "There are more serious dangers in restaurants."

In the closing arguments, one of the defense attorneys acknowledged that the coffee was hot and that that is how customers wanted it. She went on to insist that Liebeck had only herself to blame as she was unwise to put the cup between her knees. She also noted that Liebeck failed to leap out of the bucket seat in the car after the spill, thus preventing the hot coffee from falling off her. The attorney concluded by saying that the real question in the case is how far society should go to restrict what most of us enjoy and accept.[5]

THE JURY DECIDES

The jury deliberated about 4 hours and reached a verdict for Liebeck. The jury decided on compensatory damages of $200,000, which it reduced to $160,000 after judging that 20 percent of the fault belonged to Mrs. Liebeck for spilling the coffee. The jury concluded that McDonald's had engaged in willful, reckless, malicious, or wanton conduct, which is the basis for punitive damages. The jury decided upon a figure of $2.7 million in punitive damages.

Company Was Neglecting Customers. One juror later said that the facts were overwhelmingly against the company and that the company just was not taking care of its customers. Another juror felt the huge punitive damages were intended to be a stern warning for McDonald's to wake up and realize its customers were getting burned. Another juror said he began to realize that the case was really about the callous disregard for the safety of customers.

Public opinion polls after the jury verdict were squarely on the side of McDonald's. Polls showed that a large majority of Americans—including many who usually support the little guy—were outraged at the verdict.[6]

JUDGE REDUCES AWARD

The judge later slashed the jury award by more than 75 percent to $640,000. Liebeck appealed the reduction, and McDonald's continued fighting the award as excessive. In December 1994, it was announced that McDonald's had reached an out-of-court settlement with Liebeck, but the terms of the settlement were not disclosed due to a confidentiality provision. The settlement was reached to end appeals in the case.

Debate Over Temperature. Coffee temperature suddenly became a hot topic in the industry. The Specialty Coffee Association of America put coffee safety on its agenda for discussion. A spokesperson for the National Coffee Association said that McDonald's coffee conforms to industry tempera-

ture standards. A spokesman for Mr. Coffee, the coffee-machine maker, said that if customer complaints are any indication, industry settings may be too low. Some customers like it hotter. A coffee connoisseur who imported and wholesaled coffee said that 175 degrees is probably the optimum temperature for coffee because that's when aromatics are being released. McDonald's continues to say that it is serving its coffee the way customers like it. As one writer noted, the temperature of McDonald's coffee helps to explain why it sells a billion cups a year.[7]

LATER INCIDENTS

In August 2000, a Vallejo, California, woman sued McDonald's, saying she suffered second-degree burns when a handicapped employee at a drive-through window dropped a large cup of coffee in her lap. The suit charged that the handicapped employee could not grip the cardboard tray and was instead trying to balance it on top of her hands and forearms when the accident occurred in August 1999. The victim, Karen Muth, said she wanted at least $10,000 for her medical bills, pain and suffering, and "humiliation." But, her lawyer, Dan Ryan, told the local newspaper that she was entitled to between $400,000 and $500,000. Attorney Ryan went on to say, "We recognize that there's an Americans with Disabilities Act, but that doesn't give them (McDonald's) the right to sacrifice the safety of their customers." It is not known how this lawsuit was settled.

Suits Go Global. It was also announced in August 2000 that British solicitors have organized 26 spill complainants into a group suit against McDonald's over the piping hot nature of its beverages. One London lawyer said, "Hot coffee, hot tea, and hot water are at the center of this case. We are alleging they are too hot."

From Coffee to Pickles. In a related turn of events, a Knoxville, Tennessee, woman, Veronica Martin, filed a lawsuit in 2000 claiming that she was permanently scarred when a hot pickle from a McDonald's hamburger fell on her chin. She claimed the burn caused her physical and mental harm. Martin sued for $110,000. Martin's husband, Darrin, also sought $15,000 because he "has been deprived of the services and consortium of his wife." According to Veronica Martin's lawsuit, the hamburger "was in a defective condition or unreasonably dangerous to the general consumer and, in particular, to her." The lawsuit went on to say "while attempting to eat the hamburger, the pickle dropped from the hamburger onto her chin. The pickle was extremely hot and burned the chin of Veronica Martin." Martin had second-degree burns and was permanently scarred, according to the lawsuit. One report was that the McDonald's owner settled this case out of court.[8]

ISSUE WON'T GO AWAY

The Stella Awards. For over ten years now, the coffee spill heard 'round the world continues to be a subject of heated debate. The coffee spill and subsequent trial, publicity, and resolution "prompted a tort reform storm that has barely abated."[9] One school of thought held that it represents the most frivolous lawsuit of all time. In fact, a program called the "Stella Awards" was begun to recognize each year's most outrageous lawsuit. The awards were the creation of humorist Randy Cassingham, and his summaries of award winning cases may be found at http://www.stellaawards.com.[10] In actuality, most of the lawsuits he chronicles are far more outrageous than the coffee spill in which an elderly lady did get seriously injured. On the other hand, consumer groups are still concerned about victims of what they see as dangerous products and they continue to assail McDonald's callous unconcern for Stella Liebeck.

In the ensuing decade, lawsuits over spilt beverages have continued to come and go, but most of them have been resolved with less fanfare than Stella's case. As for S. Reed Morgan, the lawyer who successfully represented Stella Liebeck, he has handled only three cases involving beverages since Liebeck's suit. Morgan has turned down many plaintiffs, but said he is only interested in such cases if they involve third-degree burns.

Another Scalded-Granny Case?

There is a possibility, however, that Morgan may soon move back to stage center, as it was reported in summer 2004 that he has a new McDonald's coffee case that resembles the Liebeck case. This case involves Maxine Villegas, a grandmother in her 70s, who was a passenger in a car stopped at a drive-through, where coffee splashed on her legs and resulted in third-degree burns. In a deposition, Villegas testified coffee spilled on her legs when her sister was passing her the cup of coffee.[11]

Whether the Villegas case will turn out to be another Liebeck case or not remains to be seen. Matt Fleischer-Black, writing in *The American Lawyer*, perhaps summarized its potential well:

> *Villegas' complaint against McDonald's may generate nothing more than jokes for Jay Leno and David Letterman. Yet in light of the influence of the earlier suit, this scalded-granny case may keep a 90 million-cup-a-day industry on alert for another decade to come.*[12]

Questions for Discussion

1. What are the major issues in the Liebeck case and in the following incidents?

2. What are McDonald's social (economic, legal, and ethical) responsibilities toward consumers in the Liebeck case and the other cases? What are consumers' responsibilities when they buy a product such as hot coffee or hot hamburgers? How does a company give consumers what they want and yet protect them at the same time?

3. What are the arguments supporting McDonald's position in the Liebeck case? What are the arguments supporting Liebeck's position?

4. If you had been a juror in the Liebeck case, which position would you most likely have supported? Why? What if you had been a juror in the pickle burn case?

5. What are the similarities and differences between the coffee burn cases and the pickle burn case? Does one represent a more serious threat to consumer harm? What should McDonald's, and other fast food restaurants, do about hot food, such as hamburgers?

6. What is your assessment of the "Stella Awards?" Is this making light of a too serious problem?

7. What are the implications of these cases for future product-related lawsuits? Do we now live in a society where businesses are responsible for customers' accidents or carelessness in using products?

Case Endnotes

1. Andrea Gerlin, "A Matter of Degree: How a Jury Decided That a Coffee Spill Is Worth $2.9 Million," *The Wall Street Journal* (September 1, 1994), A1, A4.
2. Theresa Howard, "McDonald's Settles Coffee Suit in Out-of-Court Agreement," *Nation's Restaurant News* (December 12, 1994), 1
3. Aric Press and Ginny Carroll, "Are Lawyers Burning America?" *Newsweek* (March 20, 1995), 30-35.
4. Howard, 1994, 1.
5. "Coffee-spill Suits Meet ADA," Overlawyered.com, http://www.overlawyered.com/archives/00aug1.html.
6. Gerlin, A4.
7. *Ibid.*
8. Associated Press, "Couple Seeks $125,000 for Pickle Burn on Chin," *Athens Banner Herald* (October 8, 2000), 6A. Also see Associated Press, "Couple Sues over Hot Pickle Burn," (October 7, 2000), http://www.washingtonpost.com.
9. Matt Fleisher-Black, "One Lump or Two?" *The American Lawyer*, June 4, 2004.
10. "The Stella Awards for 2003," *Business Insurance*, February 16, 2004, 16. Also see "See the funny side of tort," *Reactions*, December 2003, 46.
11. Fleisher-Black, 2004, *ibid.*
12. *Ibid.*

THE HUDSON RIVER CLEANUP AND GE

One of the major challenges businesses face with respect to government regulations is that often compliance with existing regulations during an earlier period does not protect them against expensive problems that occur or come to light later. The plight of General Electric (GE) with respect to its dumping of PCBs over 30 years ago is a classic case in point.

For decades, GE had electrical equipment-making plants along the Hudson River in New York. During the period prior to 1977, GE discharged more than 1.3 million pounds of PCBs (polychlorinated biphenyls) into a 40-mile stretch of the Hudson before the chemicals were banned in 1977. In 2001, the PCB-contaminated upper Hudson River had become the largest EPA Superfund site in the nation and is about to become the most expensive to clean up.[1] In August 2001, the Environmental Protection Agency (EPA) circulated a draft proposal informing General Electric that it would have to spend hundreds of millions of dollars to clean up the PCBs that were legally dumped over a 30-year period that ended in 1977.[2]

According to *Business Week*, the Bush administration and the EPA, under fire for its environmental policies, have ordered GE to clean up the Hudson in what has been called the biggest environmental dredging project in U. S. history. The decision would reaffirm a plan developed in the waning days of the Clinton administration. A GE representative has stated that the company is "disappointed in the EPA's decision," which it says "will cause more harm than good." Environmentalists, predictably, have praised the decision, and the Sierra Club executive director called the decision a "monumental step toward protecting New Yorkers from cancer-causing PCBs."[3]

The cleanup plan has become a heated and politically-charged debate in fall 2001, as an investigative report has detailed how environmentalists (the Greens) have claimed that GE and the EPA have used the recent terrorists' attacks on the World Trade Center and Pentagon as a distraction from the priority of the planned cleanup. The Greens have charged that GE and the EPA, under the leadership of EPA administrator Christine Todd Whitman, have been delaying and "negotiating in the shadow of September 11." The executive director of the Clearwater advocacy groups and spokesperson for the coalition said regarding the recent meetings between GE and EPA— "It smells really bad."[4]

USE OF PERFORMANCE STANDARDS

The Greens have charged that a modification of the cleanup plan is in the works that would favor GE. This would be the

This case was prepared by Archie B. Carroll, University of Georgia.

establishment of "performance standards" to measure the effectiveness of dredging to remove the PCBs. In a change from the original Clinton administration plan, the revised goal of the EPA would be to roll out the dredging project in stages with periodic testing for PCBs. EPA stated: "The performance indicators being considered will include measuring PCB levels in the soil and the water column, as well as measuring the percentage of dredged material that gets re-suspended." The agency adds: "Based on these objective scientific indicators, EPA will determine at each stage of the project whether it is scientifically justified to continue the cleanup. PCB levels in fish will be monitored throughout the project as well."[5]

Would GE Be Favored?
Environmentalists believe that the performance standards would be weighted in ways that would favor GE's position and would put an early lid on the project. They have communicated to EPA that they do not want any standards built into the project that will offer GE an "out." Environmentalists who have met with the EPA have claimed they were talking to a brick wall—that their arguments were brushed off. One stated: "That office (EPA), with all due respect, seems to get its information from G.E. It's a political process being handled inside the [Washington] beltway; it's inappropriate and possibly illegal." The Greens have stated they plan to start an advertising blitz hammering on its claim that terrorism has been used as a cover while EPA and GE scheme a way to dilute the plan.[6]

THE HUDSON RIVER

Close to 40 miles of the half-mile wide Hudson River is involved in the possible cleanup. It is a pastoral and wooded stretch of the river that winds in the shadows of the Adirondacks, which serve recreational activities of numerous towns and villages. At one time, these villages were thriving examples of American industrial power. Today, most of the factories, mills, and plants are closed. Like in many other industries, jobs headed south, west, across borders, or across oceans as companies tried to extricate themselves from what they saw as devastating taxes and regulations. Though not obvious to the eye, the hidden problem of hazardous waste pollution has been a significant barrier to redevelopment of the area.[7]

SUPERFUND SITE

In 1983, the upper Hudson was named a Superfund site by the EPA. This meant that GE would be held responsible by law for cleaning up the pollution resulting from years of disposal of pollutants, regardless of whether the disposal was legal at the time. John Elvin, an investigative reporter, claimed that the Hudson River is just one of 77 alleged sites to be in need of cleanup under the EPA's Superfund program. Also, it is believed that there are numerous other sites in addition to the upper Hudson River where PCBs were dumped. In addition to the Hudson River area, the chemicals were used at plants throughout the New England area.[8]

PCBs

PCBs are a large family of fire-retardant chemicals that GE once used in the production of electrical products. There are over 200 variations of the chemical and they were, for the most part, dumped legally in the years before it was determined they posed a possible cancer risk. The PCBs were oily and tarry and were disposed of as fill for roadbeds, housing developments, and other such uses. It was reported that GE often dispensed the material free to residents surrounding its factories. In various forms, the company sold or gave away what is now considered a contaminated waste product to be used as a wood preservative, fertilizer, termite inhibitor, and as a component in house paints. As for directly dumped wastes, the PCBs are now said to be leaking into groundwater from landfills that GE had put caps on.[9]

PCBs Are Dangerous. According to the EPA, PCBs have been found to cause cancer and can also harm the immune, nervous, and reproductive systems of humans, fish, and wildlife. They think the chemicals are especially risky for children.[10] A critic of GE has been David Carpenter of the State University of New York's School of Public Health. According to Carpenter, all experts except those allied with GE believe PCBs to be a "probable" cause of cancer in humans. Carpenter has lashed out at GE for "deceitful and unscientific" claims that are "preposterous." Carpenter claims that PCBs are linked to reduced IQs in children, attention deficit disorder, suppressed immune systems, diabetes, and heart disease.[11]

Controversy. There is some controversy over whether PCBs are dangerous or not. Like the EPA, environmental groups believe they are dangerous. A handout from the Friends of a Clean Hudson coalition states strongly: "PCBs are a class of synthetic toxic chemicals universally recognized as among the world's most potent and persistent threats to human health." On the other hand, a former GE employee who worked intimately with PCBs for 25 to 30 years states differently. To put it in layman's terms, he said, "You're talking about a big, fat, slippery, stable molecule that doesn't break down. That's why it was used in lubrication and cooling in the manufacturing process. It's just plain sludge, that's all."[12] Another hazardous-waste-management expert was reported as saying: "I've been in PCBs up to my armpits. So have any num-

ber of engineers and scientists working with GE and other firms. I drank a half glass of the stuff accidentally 25 years ago. The fact is there are no reported cases of cancer traced to PCBs. This controversy is 25 percent an environmental concern and 75 percent politics in a state and towns abandoned by GE, left with no industry and a lot of trash." In spite of his views, the expert does think that GE should clean up the "hot spots" where dumping was most severe and the rest of the river should be left to heal on its own.[13]

GE's Position

GE has not accepted EPA's cleanup plan as a done deal. The huge, wealthy company, one of the largest in the world, has cranked up a barrage of TV infomercials, radio and TV ads, and initiatives by top-tier Washington lobbyists to sway the public, media, and government. The company has fielded an imposing cadre of Washington lobbyists. Among these lobbyists have been former senator George Mitchell, former House speaker-designate Bob Livingston, and several other prominent people.[14]

Jack Welch Chimes In. Recently retired former chief executive officer of GE, the legendary Jack Welch, was negotiating with regulators over this issue as far back as the 1970s. Welch summarized the company's position in a statement he made to GE stockholders while he was CEO: "We simply do not believe that there are any adverse health effects from PCBs."[15] Today, one estimate is that GE has already spent millions of dollars fighting the proposal to clean up the river. The company contends that the proposed dredging would actually be more destructive because it will stir up PCBs buried in the mud and recontaminate the river. Supporting GE's position, Rep. John Sweeney has said that he would continue to fight the dredging plan because it will have an adverse impact on local residents.[16]

One journalist estimated that GE may end up spending as much fighting the EPA plan as it would if they just went ahead with the cleanup. This raises the obvious question as to why GE would fight the plan. According to John Elvin, investigative reporter, it is because the company thinks it is a precedent-setting case that could leave the company open to a tobacco-sized settlement claim. As it turns out, this is only one of the many sites GE used legally to dispose of manufacturing by-products, and PCBs are just one of the many possibly hazardous wastes that the company had to deal with over the years. Apparently, GE used as many as 77 sites alleged to be in need of cleanup under the Superfund program.[17]

CITIZEN'S AND ENVIRONMENTAL GROUP'S VIEWS

Many of the residents of the upstate area that would be most affected by a GE cleanup prefer to just leave the situation alone and let the river heal itself. A poll commissioned by GE and handled by Zogby International found that 59 percent of the residents in the region favor letting the river deal with the pollutants naturally. Another poll done by Siena College Research Institute found that 50 percent of all the residents along the entire length of the Hudson want the river left alone. On the other side, polls have shown that a large majority of the citizens want a cleanup.[18] The survey results seem to depend on which citizens are chosen to be polled.

Grassroots Opposition.
There is even some grassroots opposition to EPA's dredging plan. An example is found in Citizen Environmentalists Against Sludge Encapsulation (CEASE) and Farmers Against Irresponsible Remediation (FAIR). CEASE has proposed acts of civil disobedience to prevent the government from coming onto private property. According to one CEASE activist, "the downstate enviros are only interested in punishing GE at the expense of agriculture, recreation, and other economic interests in our community."[19] FAIR, for its part, asked a federal district court in Albany, New York, for a preliminary injunction blocking EPA from issuing a final decision until it provided additional information on the impact of the dredging project. But, the U.S. District Court for the Northern District of New York ruled that it did not have jurisdiction over the case because the Superfund Amendments and Reauthorization Act of 1986 prohibits judicial review at this point in the case.[20]

Supporters of the Cleanup.
For their part, environmental groups continue to think that the cleanup is the right thing to do. Advocates of the cleanup say that the project would be a "gift from heaven" to the rustbelt towns along the Hudson River. Friends of a Clean Hudson, a coalition of 11 major environmental groups, commissioned a study in which they concluded that thousands of jobs and hundreds of millions of dollars would come into the area once the project was underway. The coalition claims benefits that could include the creation of close to 9,000 new jobs with annual payrolls of up to $346 million. In a reaction to this report, Rep. Maurice Hinchey, whose district includes a downstate portion of the river, claims that as a result of the dredging "tourism will increase, the fishing industry will be revived, thousands of jobs will be created and property values will rise."[21]

According to reporter John Elvin, there are many festering grudges still held against GE. GE was once the centerpiece of the bustling and prosperous area. He contends that GE eventually left the region because of New York's antibusiness environment and that, in recent years, legislators have felt free to tax the company to their heart's content, but the company expressed its own right to pack up and leave. He maintains that many state and local officials, and some citizens, just want a last piece of GE's hide—a last chance to make GE pay.[22]

Only time will tell fully what will happen to GE and the contaminated Hudson River. It is obvious from all the interests involved and opinions expressed, however, that it is less than clear what should take place in the PCB-tainted Hudson River.

PROGRESS TO DATE

Companies may resist, but government agencies do not go away. Such is the case in the continuing saga of the Hudson River cleanup. In 2001, the Bush administration ordered a full-scale dredging of a 40 mile stretch of the river. It was to be the largest environmental dredging project in history. GE has to pay the estimated $490 million charge for the cleanup and the project is expected to take about a decade, with dredging beginning in 2005. In 2003, it was reported that the Hudson River cleanup was moving on schedule although at the time GE was withholding payments, according to environmental groups. A spokesman for Environmental Advocates, one of 13 concerned groups that formed the Friends of a Clean Hudson coalition, "contrary to dire predictions of two or three years ago, the project is on track." Critics say that GE has not been cooperative but the company denies this evaluation of their efforts. At that time, the environmental groups graded the key players in the cleanup. The U. S. Environmental Protection Agency got a "B" and GE got a "D."[23]

Performance Standards Finalized.
In May 2004, the EPA finally released its final quality of life performance standards for the Hudson River cleanup.[24] By March 2004, an environmental progress report was released in which it was stated that more than 290,000 pounds of PCBs had been removed from the Hudson Falls Plant site. GE installed a comprehensive network of collection and monitoring wells to capture PCBs in the bedrock and prevent them from reaching the river. Also in March 2004, the New York State Department of Environmental Conservation (DEC) had approved GE's plan to build innovative under-the-river tunnels to capture the final few ounces a day of PCBs that are thought to trickle out of the river bottom near the Hudson Falls plant.[25]

Progress on the Hudson River cleanup may be monitored on the EPA's Web site: http://www.epa.gov/hudson/.

Questions for Discussion

1. What are the social and ethical issues in this case? Which are major and which are minor?

2. Who are the stakeholders and what are their stakes? Assess their legitimacy, power, and urgency.

3. Do research on PCBs. Do your findings clarify their status as being so hazardous they must be removed? Or, are they best left where they have settled?

4. Who is now responsible for the contaminated Hudson River? GE? EPA? State of New York? Local citizens? What ethical principles help to answer this question?

5. Do research on the Superfund. Does it appear to be fair environmental legislation?

6. What action should take place on the contaminated Hudson River? Who should pay?

7. Do research on this case and update the case facts. Has anything changed since the facts were presented that affects its resolution?

Case Endnotes

1. James L. Nash, "Compliance Not Good Enough, GE Finds Out," *Occupational Hazards* (September 2001), 47ff.
2. "Hudson River Cleanup," *Business Insurance* (August 6, 2001), 2.
3. Monica Roman, "GE's Hudson River Blues," *Business Week* (August 13, 2001), 40.
4. John Elvin, "Greens Exploit Terror Against GE," *Insight* (November 19 2001), 22-25.
5. Glenn Hess, "Hudson River Cleanup Could Cost GE About $460 Million," *Chemical Market Reporter* (August 6, 2001), 1, 29.
6. *Ibid.*, 23.
7. *Ibid.*
8. *Ibid.*, 24.
9. *Ibid.*
10. Hess, *Ibid.*, 1;29.
11. Elvin, *Ibid.*, 25.
12. Elvin, *Ibid.*, 24.
13. *Ibid.*
14. *Ibid.*, 23.
15. *Ibid.*, 25.
16. Hess, *Ibid.*, 29.
17. *Ibid.*, 24.
18. *Ibid.*, 24.
19. *Ibid.*
20. "New York Attacks Push Back Decision on Hudson Dredging," *Chemical Market Reporter* (October 1, 2001), 18.
21. Elvin, *ibid.*, 25.
22. *Ibid.*, 22.
23. Yancey Roy, "Environmental Groups Check on Hudson River Cleanup," *Rochester Democrat and Chronicle*, February 7, 2003.
24. http://www.epa.gov/hudson/quality_life.htm#draft
25. "New York State Approves GE Plan for Hudson River Tunnel Project," (press release), March 16, 2004, http://www.ge.com/en/company/news/hudson_tunnel.htm.

Case 27

| SAFETY? WHAT SAFETY?

KIRK'S FIRST YEAR

Kirk was a bright individual who was being groomed for the controller's position in a medium-sized manufacturing firm. After Kirk's first year as assistant controller, the officers of the firm started to include him in major company functions. One day, for instance, he was asked to attend the monthly financial statement summary at a prestigious consulting firm. During the meeting, Kirk was intrigued at how the financial data he had accumulated had been transformed by the consultant into revealing charts and graphs.

NEW MANUFACTURING PLANT

Kirk was generally optimistic about the session and the company's future until the consultant started talking about the new manufacturing plant the company was adding to the current location and the per-unit costs of the chemically plated products it would produce. At that time, Bob, the president, and John, the chemical engineer, started talking about waste treatment and disposal problems. John mentioned that the current

This case was written by Donald E. Tidrick, University of Texas at Austin. Permission to reprint granted by Arthur Andersen & Co., SC.

waste treatment facilities could not handle the waste products of the "ultramodern" new plant in a manner that would meet the industry's fairly high standards, although the plant would still comply with federal standards.

Cost Increases. Kirk's boss, Henry, noted that the estimated per-unit costs would increase if the waste treatment facilities were upgraded according to recent industry standards. Industry standards were presently more stringent than federal regulations, and environmentalists were pressuring strongly for stricter regulations at the federal level. Bob mentioned that since their closest competitor did not have the waste treatment facilities that already existed at their firm, he was not in favor of any more expenditures in that area. Most managers at the meeting resoundingly agreed with Bob, and the business of the meeting proceeded to other topics.

Kirk's Dilemma. Kirk did not hear a word during the rest of the meeting. He kept wondering how the company could possibly have such a casual attitude toward the environment. Yet he did not know if, how, when, or with whom he should share his opinion. Soon he started reflecting on whether this firm was the right one for him.

Questions for Discussion

1. Who are the stakeholders in this case, and what are their stakes?

2. What social responsibility does the firm have for the environment? How would you assess the firm's CSR using the four-part CSR definition presented in Chapter 2?

3. How should Kirk reconcile his own personal thinking with the thinking being presented by the firm's management?

4. What should Kirk do? Why?

Case 28

| LITTLE ENOUGH OR TOO MUCH?

Bryan is Hired

Bryan was recently hired by a large chemical company to oversee the construction of production facilities to produce a new product. X Chemical Company developed a new industrial lubricant that it felt it could produce at a price close to those of its competitors. The plant to manufacture the lubricant was built on land adjacent to the East River. X Chemical had already applied for and received the necessary permit to dump waste materials from the process into the river. Several other chemical plants in the near vicinity are also releasing waste materials into the river.

Bryan's Concern. Bryan is concerned because the government agency that oversees the permit process granted X Chemical a permit to release more waste into the river than previously anticipated. An additional stage in the production process that would have reduced the waste and recycled some materials became unnecessary due to the regulatory agency's decision. Because the additional process would have added capital and production costs, it was not built as part of the existing plant. Yet, X Chemical has always stated publicly that it would do all that it could to protect the environment from harmful materials.

The Company

The company has had mediocre performance for several quarters, and everyone is anxious to see the new product do well. Tests have shown it to be a top-quality industrial lubricant that can now be produced at a cost significantly below those of their

competitors. Orders have been flowing in, and the plant is selling everything it can produce. Morale in the company has increased significantly because of the success of the new product. Due to the success of the new product, all employees are looking forward to sizable bonuses from the company's profit sharing plan.

Bryan's Decision

Bryan is upset that the company failed to build the additional stage on the plant and fears that the excess waste released today will cause problems for the company tomorrow. Bryan approaches Bill Gates, the plant supervisor, with his concerns. Bill replies, "It's up to the government agency to protect the river from excess waste, and the company only had to meet the agency's standards. The amount of waste being released poses no threat to the environment, according to the agency. The engineers and chemists who originally designed the production process must have been too conservative in their estimates. Even if the agency made a mistake, the additional recycling and waste reduction process can be added later when it becomes necessary.

Implications. At this point, building the additional process would require costly interruptions in the production process and might cause customers to switch to our competitors. Heck, environmental groups might become suspicious if production was stopped to add the additional process—they might see it as an admission of wrongdoing. No one in the company wants to attract any unwarranted attention from the environmental groups. They give us enough trouble as it is. The best thing we can do is make money while the company can and deal with issues as they come up. Don't go trying to cause trouble without any proof. The company doesn't like troublemakers, so watch your step. You're new here, and you wouldn't want to have to find a new job."

This case was originally developed by Eric Heist, graduate student at Washington University, as a class project in "Ethical Decision Making." Edited and submitted by Raymond L. Hilgert, Professor of Management and Industrial Relations, Washington University. Permission granted to reprint by Arthur Andersen & Co., SC.

Bryan is Unsure. Bryan is frustrated and upset. He can see all the benefits of the new product, but inside he is sure the company is making a short-sighted decision that will hurt them in the long run. The vice president of operations will tour the plant next week, and Bryan is considering approaching the officer with his concerns. It might also be possible to contact the government agency and request that the permit be reviewed. Bryan is unsure what to do, but he feels he should do something.

Questions for Discussion

1. What are the social or ethical issues in this case?
2. Are the ethical issues in this case those of the firm or of Bryan? Discuss.
3. Assess the corporate social responsibility of the firm based on the comments of Bill Gates, the plant supervisor.
4. What ethical responsibility, if any, does Bryan have in this case? What should he do? Why?

Case 29

| THE BETASERON® DECISION (A)

The United States Food and Drug Administration's (FDA) approval of interferon beta-1b (brand name Betaseron®), made it the first multiple sclerosis (MS) treatment to get FDA approval in 25 years. Betaseron was developed by Berlex Laboratories, a U.S. unit of Schering AG, the German pharmaceutical company. Berlex handled the clinical development, trials, and marketing of the drug, while Chiron Corporation, a biotechnology firm based in California, manufactured it. The groundbreaking approval of Betaseron represented not only a great opportunity for Berlex but a dilemma. Supplies were insufficient to meet initial demand, and shortages were forecast for three years. With insufficient supplies and staggering development costs, how would Berlex allocate and price the drug?

THE CHALLENGE OF MULTIPLE SCLEROSIS

MS is a disease of the central nervous system that interferes with the brain's ability to control such functions as seeing, walking, and talking. The nerve fibers in the brain and spinal cord are surrounded by myelin, a fatty substance that protects the nerve fibers in the same way that insulation protects electrical wires. When the myelin insulation becomes damaged, the ability of the central nervous system to transmit nerve impulses to and from the brain becomes impaired. With MS, there are sclerosed (i.e., scarred or hardened) areas in multiple parts of

This case was written by Ann K. Buchholtz, University of Georgia. It was written from public sources, solely for the purpose of stimulating class discussion. All events are real. The author thanks Dr. Stephen Reingold, Vice President Research and Medical Programs at the National Multiple Sclerosis Society, and Avery Rockwell, Chapter Services Associate of the Greater Connecticut Chapter of the Multiple Sclerosis Society, for their helpful comments. All rights reserved jointly to the author and the North American Case Research Association (NACRA). Used with permission.

the brain and spinal cord when the immune system mistakenly attacks the myelin sheath.

The Impact of MS. The symptoms of MS depend to some extent on the location and size of the sclerosis. Symptoms may include numbness, slurred speech, blurred vision, poor coordination, muscle weakness, bladder dysfunction, extreme fatigue, and paralysis. There is no way to know how the disease will progress for any individual, because the nature of the disease can change. Some people will have a relatively benign course of MS with only one or two mild attacks, nearly complete remission, and no permanent disability. Others will have a chronic progressive course resulting in severe disability. A third group displays the most typical pattern, which is periods of exacerbations, when the disease is active, and periods of remission, when the symptoms recede yet generally leave some damage. People with MS live with an exceptionally high degree of uncertainty, because their disease can change from one day to the next. Dramatic downturns as well as dramatic recoveries are not uncommon.

THE PROMISE OF BETASERON

Interferon beta is a naturally occurring protein that regulates the body's immune system. Betaseron is composed of interferon beta-1b that has been genetically engineered and laboratory manufactured as a recombinant product. Although other interferons (i.e., alpha and gamma) had been tested, only beta interferon had been shown, through large-scale trials, to affect MS. Because it is an immunoregulatory agent, Betaseron was believed to combat the immune problems that make MS worse. However, the exact way in which it works was yet to be determined.

Research. In clinical studies, Betaseron was shown to reduce the frequency and severity of exacerbations in ambulatory MS patients with a relapsing-remitting form of the disease. It did not reverse damage nor did it completely prevent exacerbations. However, Betaseron could dramatically improve the quality of life for the person with MS. For example, people taking Betaseron were shown to have fewer and shorter hospitalizations. Betaseron represented the first and only drug to have an effect on the frequency of exacerbations.

Administration. Betaseron is administered subcutaneously (under the skin) every other day by self-injection. To derive the most benefits from the therapy, it was important that the MS patient maintain a regular schedule of the injections. Some flu-like side-effects, as well as swelling and irritation around the injection, had been noted. However, these side-effects tended to decrease with time on treatment. In addition, one person who received Betaseron committed suicide while three others attempted it. Because MS often leads to depression, there was no way to know whether the administration of Betaseron was a factor. Last, Betaseron was not recommended for use during pregnancy.

THE BETASERON DILEMMA

FDA approval for Betaseron allowed physicians to prescribe the drug to MS patients who were ambulatory and had a relapsing-remitting course of MS. An estimated one-third of the 300,000 people with MS in the United States fell into that category, resulting in a potential client base of 100,000. The expedited FDA approval process for Betaseron took only 1 year instead of the customary 3. As a result, Berlex was unprepared to manufacture and distribute the treatment. Chiron Corporation had been making the drug in small quantities for experimental use and did not have the manufacturing facilities to handle the expected explosion in demand. Chiron estimated that it would have enough of the drug for about 12,000 to 20,000 people by the end of the year. By the end of the second year, Chiron expected to be able to provide the drug to 40,000 patients. Depending on demand, it might take about three years to provide the drug to all patients who requested it. Chiron's expanded manufacturing represented the only option for Berlex, because the process required for another company to get FDA approval to manufacture the drug would take even longer.

Pricing. In addition to availability, price was a concern, because successes must fund the failures that precede them. Betaseron represented years of expensive, risky research by highly trained scientists in modern research facilities. Furthermore, genetically engineered drugs were extremely expensive to manufacture. In the case of Betaseron, a human interferon gene is inserted into bacteria, resulting in a genetically engineered molecule. The stringent quality controls on the procedure take time and are expensive. As a result, the price of Betaseron was expected to be about $10,000 per year for each patient.

Betaseron brought great hope to people with MS and a great quandary to Berlex. How should Berlex handle the supply limitations, the distribution, and the pricing of this drug?

Questions for Discussion

1. What are the ethical issues in this situation? Which issues must Berlex consider first when determining how to distribute Betaseron?
2. Given the shortage of the drug, how should Berlex decide who receives it and who waits? Give a specific plan.
3. How should Berlex handle the logistics of distribution?
4. How should Berlex determine the drug's relative pricing (assume the drug costs about $12,000 per year)?
5. Who, if anyone, should be involved in the decision making?

Case 30

| A MORAL DILEMMA: HEAD VERSUS HEART

SITUATION

A 42-year-old male suddenly and unexpectedly died of a brain tumor, leaving behind a wife and small child. During a review of his employee benefits, it was noted that although he was eligible for an additional company-sponsored life insurance plan used for plant decommissioning purposes, his name was not identified on the insurance rolls.

Evaluation. It was determined that when the employee was promoted to supervisor 3 years before his death, his paperwork had been submitted to the corporate office for inclusion in the

This case was prepared by David A. Levigne.

program. Coincidentally, the program was under review at the time, and the employee was not entered into the program due to administrative oversight.

Legal Review. A legal department review determined that the program was offered to certain supervisory employees at the discretion of the company. Therefore, there was no legal obligation to pay.

DILEMMA

The death benefit was twice the employee's salary. Because the employee was not enrolled in the life insurance program, if the company were to pay any benefit, it would have to come from the general fund (paid from the business unit's annual operating budget).

To pay or not to pay? The company could argue that it must start acting like a business and use its head, not its heart.

Existing company programs adequately compensate the individual's family; no additional dollars should be paid. On the other hand, it was an administrative oversight that failed to enter the employee into the program. What would you want the company to do for you if you were the one who suddenly died?

Questions for Discussion

1. As a manager, you are steward of the company's funds. Are you willing to forego departmental improvements and potential salary increases to honor this claim? Remember, there is no legal obligation to pay.
2. Would you feel an ethical obligated to pay? Would you be perceived as a weak manager if you do?
3. What are the ethical issues in this case?
4. What would you do? Why?

Case 31

| WAL-MART AND ITS ASSOCIATES: EFFICIENT OPERATOR OR NEGLECTFUL EMPLOYER?

In the past decade, the primary criticism of Wal-Mart, one of the world's largest companies, has been its impact on communities and small merchants. Anti-sprawl activists and small-town merchants, in particular, have taken issue with the company moving into their communities. In *Case 1—Wal-Mart: The Main Street Merchant of Doom*, these issues along with Wal-Mart's international growth and impact, were presented in some detail.

In the past few years, however, other issues concerning the company have become important as well and have begun dominating the news. In particular, Wal-Mart's treatment of its employees has raised many issues in public and business discussions. Paradoxically, Wal-Mart refers to its employees as "associates," a term intended to bestow a more lofty status than the term employees.

Many people do view Wal-Mart to be an excellent provider of jobs in communities, and in spite of criticisms that have been raised by many, people continue to seek out employment with Wal-Mart. Though it has high turnover, it is viewed by many as a stable place to work and some individuals have sought to establish careers at the company. In 2004, Wal-Mart was named America's Most Admired company for the second time in a row in the annual *Fortune* magazine rankings.[1] In spite of this, *Fortune* writer Jerry

Useem asks "Should we admire Wal-Mart?" He goes on to say "Some say it's evil. Others insist it's a model of all that's right with America. Who are we to believe?"[2]

Employee Allegations and Issues. Many different employee-related issues with respect to Wal-Mart have been the focus of much news coverage in the past few years. The company has been accused of hiring too many part-time workers, offering jobs that are actually dead-end jobs, paying low wages and poor benefits, forcing workers to work "off the clock," that is, to work overtime without overtime pay, and taking advantage of illegal immigrants. Over the years, the company has also been accused of gender discrimination against women, who occupy most jobs at the company. Coupled with these allegations of employee treatment, the company, which is currently not unionized, has fought unions and unionization everywhere it locates.

LOW PAY, HARD WORK, QUESTIONABLE TREATMENT

Wal-Mart is the nation's largest employer. As such, it is not surprising that it has a large number of interactions with employees

This case was prepared by Archie B. Carroll, University of Georgia.

and these interactions will be both positive and negative. Wal-Mart claims to offer "good jobs, (and) good careers," but a growing number of employees have become vocal in recent years about their working conditions at the company. As with many retailers and service industries, in general, Wal-Mart is accused of offering low pay and few benefits. One report was that the average, full-time hourly worker at Wal-Mart earned barely $18,000 a year and that forty percent of employees opt not to receive coverage under the company's medical insurance plan because it costs up to $2,844 a year plus a deductible. Many of these employees are angered by the disparity between their low wages and the company's high profits.[3]

One Person's Experience.

Journalist Barbara Ehrenreich, author of the best-seller *Nickel and Dimed: On (Not) Getting By in America*," spent three weeks working at a Wal-Mart to get insights into whether many of the claims she had heard about Wal-Mart's treatment of employees was true. Ehrenreich had claimed she'd heard stories about Wal-Mart workers being locked in stores overnight and being asked to work extra hours without overtime pay. During her three weeks there, she said she saw a side of the mega-retailer that most people who shop there never get to see. She remembered workers having to crouch behind racks of clothing to chat with co-workers because her department head forbade talking among workers during work hours.[4] Ehrenreich complained that it was undignified for women in their 50s to have to resort to such behavior on the job.

Further, she observed that many of the store's cheapest items were often unaffordable to the workers who sold them because of their low pay. She observed: "when you work for a company who you can't afford to buy their product, you're in trouble." She went on, "Here is this store that's oriented toward the lower end of the economic spectrum, but not low enough [for its own workers]." She said on one occasion she had to go to the local food bank and she was mistaken for another Wal-Mart worker who had just been there.[5]

Of course, some people would say that there is nothing wrong with low pay and few benefits if a business can still find workers willing to work there. After all, in a free market, this is the way the economic system works. And, indeed, one reason Wal-Mart has been so efficient and has contributed to nationwide productivity increases is precisely because of its tight controls on labor costs. The McKinsey consulting group has said that Wal-Mart was responsible for roughly 25 percent of the nation's productivity gains in the 1990s. Their low prices have also contributed significantly to low inflation. Financial guru Warren Buffett has expressed the opinion that Wal-Mart has contributed more than any other company to the economic vigor that is found in America.[6]

Working Off the Clock.

One of the most serious allegations of unfair treatment reported by some Wal-Mart employees is that of being asked to "work *off* the clock." This means that employees are pressured to do overtime work for which they do not get paid. One employee reported that he was asked to work off the clock by both the store manager and the assistant manager. The allegation is that managers would wait until an employee has clocked out and then say something like, "Do me a favor. I don't have anyone coming in—could you stay here?" Before you knew it, four to five hours passed before you got away.[7] According to Wal-Mart's *2004 Annual Report*, the company is, indeed, the defendant in numerous cases containing allegations the company forced employees to work "off the clock" or failed to provide work breaks.[8]

The Pressure Is On.

The company blames individual store and department managers for any unpaid overtime. They claim it is against company policy to not pay for overtime. However, there is evidence that managers are under significant pressure from corporate headquarters to get more work done than can be done with the number of employees allowed. One attorney for an employee said that headquarters collects reams of data on every store and every employee and uses sales figures to determine how many hours of labor it wants to allocate to each store. Then, the store managers are required to schedule fewer hours than allotted and their store performance is closely monitored on a daily basis. The store managers, in turn, put pressure on lower managers, and employees start feeling the pressure to work hours without pay. In another case, a former Wal-Mart manager claimed that supervisors had been known to regularly delete hours from time records and even to reprimand employees who claimed overtime hours so the store could keep its labor costs under control.[9]

LABOR UNION RESISTANCE

Because of employee complaints and desires to have higher wages and more generous benefits, Wal-Mart employees have been targeted by union organizers for decades, especially recently. Wal-Mart's huge size and number of employees allows the firm to increasingly "set the standard for wages and benefits throughout the U. S. economy."[10]

A Typical "Associate."

The experience of Jennifer McLaughlin, age 22, an employee at the Paris, Texas Wal-Mart is typical of many of the company's employees. Jennifer lives in a modest apartment complex with her one-year-old son and drives to the store five days a week and slips on her blue vest with "How May I Help You?" inscribed on the back. She works at a frenzied pace, often feeling there aren't enough workers to do all that has to be done. She feels stressed out as she says "They push you to the limit. They just want to see how much they can get away with without having to hire someone else." According to McLaughlin, she has been three years with the firm, earns just $16,800 a year and says "I'm considered high paid." She continues: "The way they pay you, you cannot make it by yourself without having a second job or someone helping you, unless you've been there for 20 years or you're a manager."[11] Jennifer is the type worker the union organizers try to get to sign a card indicating their willingness to vote for a union should a representation vote be held.

Unionization Attempts.

Across the country, workers in many states have tried to get unions organized but so far they have not had very much success. According to one report, employees at more than 100 stores in 25 states, including the store in Paris, Texas, are currently trying to get union representation. Wal-Mart has tried in various ways to fight the union organizing efforts. The company has engaged in actions that have been judged to be in violation of federal labor laws. Wal-Mart has been held to be in violation of the law in 10 separate cases in which the National Labor Relations Board has ruled that it has engaged in illegal activities such as confiscating union literature, interrogating workers, and discharging union sympathizers.[12] According to one management consultant, Wal-Mart will go to great lengths to keep unions out.

At the time of writing (July 2004), there are no unions in any part of Wal-Mart. Back in 2000, the meat-cutting department at a Wal-Mart in Jacksonville, Texas, voted to join the United Food and Commercial Workers (UFCW) union, becoming the only Wal-Mart store that had successfully unionized. The company responded quickly. Within two weeks, Wal-Mart totally eliminated its meat-cutting departments throughout the company nationwide.[13] The company claimed it took this action as part of a strategy to have meat cut by outside vendors and supplied differently rather than as a decision to eliminate the union.

The UFCW is the union that has been most aggressively trying to unionize Wal-Mart across the country. Several full time union organizers travel the country trying to convince employees to agree to a union vote in their store. The UFCW, which represents 1.4 million workers in the grocery and retail industry, has representatives in many different cities attempting to convince workers to sign a card indicating they want a union vote held at their store. According to the National Labor Relations Board, a workplace needs 30% of its workers to sign cards calling for a union election to have one held. Unions often try to get 50% of the employees to sign a card, because they want to increase their chances of winning.[14]

Success in Union Resistance.

There are several reasons why the unions have not been successful in unionizing Wal-Mart. First, many employees feel intimidated by the company and fear signing on with a union. They fear retaliation of some kind and many of the employees cannot afford to lose their jobs. Second, Wal-Mart has mastered the art and science of fighting unionization. At one point, the company had a "union avoidance program." In this program, the company, with its vast resources, will wear people down and even destroy their spirit.

One consultant said that each Wal-Mart manager is taught to take attempts at union organizing personally and to consider that supporting a union is like slapping the supervisor in the face.[15] Wal-

Mart is considered to be a very sophisticated adversary when it comes to fighting unionization. Managers are asked to call a 24-hour hotline if they ever see a hint of unionization taking place, and a labor team can be dispatched to a store under threat at a moment's notice.[16] Third, many Wal-Marts are located in Southern states that do not have a history and tradition of unionization.[17]

For its part, a Wal-Mart spokesman says that the company is not anti-union, it is "pro-associate."[18] According to writer Karen Olsson, "Wal-Mart has made it clear that keeping its stores union-free is as much a part of the culture as door greeters and blue aprons."[19]

USING ILLEGAL IMMIGRANTS

In late 2003, a series of predawn raids by federal agents were conducted in which they rounded up 250 illegal immigrants working as cleaning crews in 61 Wal-Marts across 21 states. Though not technically employees of the company, the company is being accused by federal officials of knowing that its contractors were using the illegal immigrants as employees. The Immigration and Customs Enforcement program claims it has wiretaps revealing that Wal-Mart knew contractors were using illegals in their cleaning crews.[20]

Wal-Mart is fighting against the charges, because it reports that the company was cooperating with the government for as long as three years in federal investigations in Chicago and Pennsylvania. Wal-Mart reports that it was led to believe that it was not a target of the investigation and that it did not sever its ties with the contractors because federal officials had asked them to leave the relationships in place during their investigations. Wal-Mart claims that it was told it would be given a heads-up before any arrests were made in its stores, but that did not happen.[21]

Wal-Mart claims that it did what it could to insure that its contractors were hiring legal workers, both before and after the raid. Antidiscrimination provisions of the immigration code limits an employer's ability to investigate an employee's legal status, the company claimed. In fact, in 1996, the Immigration and Naturalization Service (INS) filed a complaint against Wal-Mart for requiring prospective hires who were not U. S. citizens to show more verification than that required by law. The company paid a $60,000 fine and became very hesitant to ask for more assurances about the status of its contractors' employees, the company claims.[22]

Ending Relationships.

Wal-Mart claimed it began to end its relationships with outside cleaning contractors beginning in 2002. The company concluded it could typically save money by having its own crews cleaning and polishing the floors. By October 2003, when the raid occurred, fewer than 700 stores (18%) were still using contractors. This was down almost half of the stores that were using outside contractors in 2000. The company said it adopted a new written contract in 2002 that included stronger contractual commitment by the outside contractors that they were complying with all federal, state, and local employment laws. The company admitted it unwittingly may have still been doing business with some of the contractors that were in violation and that their own investigations revealed that they were dealing with companies with different corporate identities and names that made it difficult to eliminate suspected violators.[23]

SEX DISCRIMINATION

The most serious issue Wal-Mart now faces is accusations of gender discrimination against women. In 2001, six women filed a gender bias lawsuit against Wal-Mart claiming they were discriminated against. The case, *Dukes v. Wal-Mart*, started as an EEOC complaint by Betty Dukes, the lead plaintiff, who claimed she had been trying to get promoted from the cashier ranks for nine years.[24] In a landmark decision in June of 2004, a federal judge in San Francisco ruled that the sex discrimination lawsuit could proceed as a class-action lawsuit, affecting as many as 1.6 million current and former female employees who have worked for the company since December 26, 1998.[25] The lawsuit, which has been called the "largest private civil rights case ever,"[26] has the potential to go on for years and doubtless will have significant repercussions for Wal-Mart and other companies in the retail and other industries.

The Allegations. Lawyers for the plaintiffs presented various statistical analyses supporting their allegations of sex discrimination. They presented detailed statistical models documenting that Wal-Mart paid their full-time female workers 5%-15% less than full-time males doing the same jobs. The lawyers also contended that the disparities between females and males increased as employees moved up in the management ranks.[27] Plaintiffs also claim that Wal-Mart's 2001 payroll statistics, the year the lawsuit was filed, also revealed discriminatory patterns such as the following:

- Female workers in hourly jobs earned $1,100 less than men
- Women managers earned $14,500 less than their male counterparts
- 65% of Wal-Mart's hourly employees were female, but two-thirds of the company's managers were men
- On average, it took men just 2.86 years to get promoted to assistant manager but it took women 4.38 years, despite better performance ratings.[28]

Individual cases also documented allegations of sex discrimination against the company. The case of Gretchen Adams is illustrative. Adams, the mother of four, took an hourly job at the Wal-Mart in Stillwater, Oklahoma in 1993. Adams was quickly promoted to manager of the deli department where she supervised 60 workers and flew around the country training hundreds of other workers. She learned that a man she had trained was now making $3,500 more than she was and she was told it was "a fluke." She witnessed other men leapfrog past her and she never landed the job of store manager she says she was promised. Adams claimed

she complained and "they told me where to go." She quit the company at the end of 2001.[29]

Figure 1 presents a summary of the major lawsuits that are underway against the company as presented in the "Litigation" section of its 2004 Annual Report.

Other women made sworn statements that Wal-Mart had denied them requests to be placed in a management training position leading to a salaried position, denied them jobs as support managers in favor of men who had less seniority or qualifications, gave promotions to men with less experience, and were fired for not going along with alleged acts of sexual harassment.[30]

A summary of the major allegations against Wal-Mart includes three major areas. First, women claim they are denied equal promotions. Second, women claim they are paid less for the same jobs, even whey they have more experience. Third, women claim they are subjected to sexist actions and gender stereotyping.[31]

Did Top Management Know? Lawyers for the plaintiffs are developing the argument that top managers at Wal-Mart knew about the sex bias that was taking place in the company. The lawyers are preparing to argue that women complained to corporate executives, including CEO Lee Scott, about pay dis-

FIGURE 1

Lawsuits Underway Against Wal-Mart

Wal-Mart is defendant in a number of legal proceedings. Wal-Mart has been charged with:

- Forcing employees to "work off the clock" or without adequate work breaks.
- Sex discrimination in *Dukes v. Wal-Mart*. The suit alleges that the company engaged in a pattern and practice of discriminating against women in promotions, pay, training, and job assignments. The suit seeks injunctive relief, compensatory damages, punitive damages, and attorney's fees.
- Purchasing Corporate-Owned Life Insurance (COLI) in which the policies lacked an insurable interest in the lives of the employees who were the insured under the policies. The suit seeks to recover the proceeds of the policies under theories of unjust enrichment and constructive trust.
- Not paying for prescription contraceptives for female employees. This class action lawsuit (*Mauldin v. Wal-Mart Stores, Inc*) is composed of female Wal-Mart Associates who were participants in the company's health and welfare plan from 2001 to the present. The class seeks amendments to the plan to include coverage and back pay for all members of the class in the form of reimbursements of the cost of prescriptions. The complaint alleges gender discrimination under Title VII of the Civil Rights Act.
- Failure to hire or make transfer requests to women who were not hired or transferred into positions for which they applied. The class seeks back pay and injunctive relief.

Source: Summarized from "Litigation" section of Wal-Mart's *2004 Annual Report*, 48–49.

parities or sexism and received very little response. They are also arguing that information was shared with board members and that outsiders complained and got little or no response from corporate offices.[32]

The Company's Defense.

Wal-Mart has long argued that it treats its female employees fairly. The company has said that women do not apply for promotion as often as men and this accounts for the under-representation of women.[33] The main argument by the company has been its opposition to the lawsuit being ruled a class action lawsuit. The company argues that decisions about employees are made at the individual store level and that a class action lawsuit is too unwieldy because it thinks it should be able to present evidence defending itself against each individual plaintiff's claims and that this would not be possible in a class action trial. Wal-Mart claims that in a class action of this size it means that store managers will not be given the opportunity to explain how they made individual compensation and promotion decisions.

The company is also expected to argue in its appeal of the class action judgment that the class was certified under laws intended to provide injunctive relief, that is, to stop a particular practice, but that the judge ruled that the class can also seek monetary damages which the company does not think applies to the case. Part of the monetary relief could be punitive damages, but for these to apply, it has to be proven that Wal-Mart management "fostered or recklessly ignored discriminatory practices." The judge concluded that whereas the individual decisions were made at specific store locations, there was some evidence of a corporate culture of gender stereotyping that may have affected the decisions made at the store level.[34] Judge Martin Jenkins was not ruling on the merits of the case, but was simply saying there was some evidence of a corporate culture permeating the organization that may be related to the discrimination, and thus he allowed the case to move forward as a class action.

Lawyers who are not a part of the case have said that Wal-Mart should continue to appeal that since employment decisions are not made centrally, but at individual stores, the class action suit is based on an erroneous concept. The company should argue that each plaintiff would have to sue the individual store in which the alleged practice took place, and the company would then be able to defend itself against each claim.[35]

Dragging On for Years.

Based on other huge class action discrimination lawsuits, the lawsuit against Wal-Mart for sex discrimination could drag on for years and could have ramifications for the retail industry in which the company is the dominant leader. The retail industry is ranked among the top 20 occupations for women in the U. S., according to the Department of Labor, and about 42% of retail sales staffs are women, according to 2003 annual averages. The lawsuit, which is the largest private civil rights case ever, will surely be watched by many for years to come.[36]

CHANGES IN LABOR PRACTICES AT WAL-MART

Partially as a result of criticism and bad publicity Wal-Mart has been receiving in recent years, the company announced at its 2004 annual meeting some changes that were planned to improve conditions for its workers. CEO Lee Scott outlined the changes at its annual shareholders' meeting in Fayetteville, Arkansas, but it may take several years before the true impact of the changes take place and are felt throughout the company.[37]

One change will include the creation of a compliance group to oversee workers' pay, hours, and their breaks. The company is also testing a new program that will alert cashiers when it is time for them to take a meal break. Another change is the implementation of a new system that will require employees to sign off on any changes that are made to their time cards. The company also plans to implement software that will force managers to adhere to state employment rules regarding areas such as how late teenagers can work. While announcing these new policies, Scott mentioned several times that he was tired of the adverse publicity that the company was getting.[38]

New Pay Scheme.

One of the most sweeping changes that the company announced was a new pay scheme for its employees. Though the details and ramifications of the new pay plan were sketchy when publicly announced, it was apparent they were partially in response to the bad publicity the company has gotten over its pay policies. As a part of the new pay plan, workers would be divided into pay classes with clearly defined starting and ceiling rates, and workers below a certain minimum would be given a raise. Changes would also take place in how annual pay is calculated, changing from a percentage of salary to a flat dollar amount. In addition, merit raises would be limited to about 5% of the store's employees. As one writer observed, "Wal-Mart seems to be shaking up its pay structure. But like nearly everything this giant does, that's sure to spark new firestorms."[39]

Following the annual meeting, one Wal-Mart director, John Opie, indicated that the company was very concerned about its image and that it was "working very hard" to improve it. He added, "you'll continue to see excellent progress on it."[40]

Questions for Discussion

1. Identify and describe the major ethical issues facing Wal-Mart and the likely stakeholders to be affected.

2. Wal-Mart has been said to have excessive power in its relationship with communities. How is its manifestation of power with employees similar or different than with communities? Which is the most serious issue? Why?

3. Are many of the allegations by employees at Wal-Mart just reflections of the changing social contract between companies and their workers? Are many of the so-called problems just the free-enterprise system at work? Discuss.

4. Regarding the various labor practices discussed in this case, do they reflect immoral or just amoral management actions?

5. Is the practice of being required to "work off the clock" an unethical practice or just "to be expected" in the modern world of work? After all, many salaried employees are expected to work "until the job is done" no matter how many hours it takes.

6. Is it wrong for Wal-Mart to fight unionization? Sam Walton always felt the company should function as one big happy family and that unions were to be resisted. What is your evaluation of the union opposition?

7. Regarding the allegations of sex discrimination, does it sound like the company has been guilty of systemic discrimination? Should Dukes v. Wal-Mart proceed as a class action suit, or should Wal-Mart be permitted to defend itself against each charge at the store level?

8. If Wal-Mart can effectively argue that women are contributors to their plight by not applying for promotions or for seeking fewer responsibilities to accommodate family priorities, should the company be held to be in violation of sex discrimination laws because the statistics reveal differences between women and men?

9. Do you think the changes in labor practices at Wal-Mart will effectively address the issues that have been raised concerning the company?

10. Conduct Web-based research on Wal-Mart and update allegations and lawsuits against the company.

Case Endnotes

1. Ann Harrington, "America's Most Admired Companies," *Fortune*, March 8, 2004, 80.
2. Jerry Useem, "Should we Admire Wal-Mart?" *Fortune*, March 8, 2004, 118–120.
3. Karen Olsson, "Up Against Wal-Mart," *Mother Jones*, March/April 2003, 54–59.
4. Tammy Joyner, "Author had eyes opened at work," *Atlanta Journal Constitution*, June 27, 2004, Q1.
5. *Ibid.*
6. George F. Will, "Waging War on Wal-Mart," *Newsweek*, July 5, 2004, 64.
7. Olsson, 58.
8. Wal-Mart's 2004 Annual Report, 48.
9. Olsson, 58.
10. Olsson, *Ibid.*, 55.
11. *Ibid.*
12. *Ibid.*
13. *Ibid.*
14. Cora Daniels, "Up Against the Wal-Mart," *Fortune*, May 17, 2004, 112–120.
15. Olsson, 56.
16. Daniels, 116.
17. Daniels, 116.
18. *Ibid.*
19. Olsson, 58.
20. Ann Zimmerman, "After Huge Raid on Illegals, Wal-Mart Fires Back at U.S.," *Wall Street Journal*, December 19, 2003.
21. *Ibid.*
22. *Ibid.*
23. *Ibid.*
24. Cora Daniels, "Women vs. Wal-Mart," *Fortune*, July 21, 2003, 79–82.
25. Ann Zimmerman, "Judge Certifies Wal-Mart Suit as Class Action," *Wall Street Journal*, June 23, 2004, A1.
26. Stephanie Armour and Lorrie Grant, "Wal-Mart Suit Could Ripple Through Industry," *USA Today*, June 23, 2004, 4B.
27. Ann Zimmerman, "Wal-Mart Adds to Legal Team," *Wall Street Journal*, July 1, 2004, B2.
28. Lisa Takeuchi Cullen Wilson, "Wal-Mart's Gender Gap," *Time*, July 5, 2004, 44.
29. *Ibid.*
30. Stephanie Armour, "Rife with Discrimination: Plaintiffs describe their lives at Wal-Mart," *USA Today*, June 24, 2004, 3B.
31. *Ibid.*
32. Stephanie Armour, "Women say Wal-Mart execs knew of sex bias," *USA Today*, June 25, 2004, 1B.
33. "Wal-Mart: Trial by Checkout," *The Economist*, June 26, 2004, 64.
34. Zimmerman, 2004, B2.
35. Jonathan D. Glater, "Attention Wal-Mart Plaintiffs: Hurdles Ahead, *The New York Times*, June 27, 2004, BU5.
36. Stephanie Armour and Lorrie Grant, "Wal-Mart suit could ripple through industry," *USA Today*, June 23, 2004, 4B.
37. Constance L. Hays, "Wal-Mart Plans Changes to Some Labor Practices," *The New York Times*, June 5, 2004, B2.
38. *Ibid.*
39. Wendy Zellner, "A New Pay Scheme for Wal-Mart Workers," *Business Week*, June 14, 2004, 39.
40. Hays, 2004, B2.

Case 32

| DEAD PEASANT LIFE INSURANCE: SMART BUSINESS OR POOR ETHICAL PRACTICE?

Caroline Murray was mourning the death of her husband, Mike, when she received a call from the employee benefits division of his company requesting a copy of the death certificate.* After asking why they needed the certificate, Caroline was surprised to learn that her husband's company had purchased a life insurance policy on her husband. Especially surprising was the fact that Caroline had no record of the policy, and apparently, neither did her husband. This particular policy listed only the company as

This case was written by Jill Brown, University of Georgia.

beneficiary and allowed the company to borrow against Mike's policy, write-off the loan's interest on its taxes, and receive a tax-free payout upon Mike's death. Mike's position at the company was not an executive one; he was the security guard at a local manufacturing company, and his company received $80,000, tax-free, upon his death. His family received nothing. How did this happen? Through the company's purchase of a life insurance policy nicknamed "dead-peasant's" life insurance.

CORPORATE-OWNED LIFE INSURANCE POLICIES

The Prevalence of COLIs. Corporate-owned life insurance policies (COLI) have been around for years. They are used as funding mechanisms for protecting businesses against the loss of its "human capital," however until recently most states required that an employer have an "insurable interest" in the lives of the employees that they insured. In the 1980's many states relaxed this requirement, and businesses began taking life insurance policies out on hourly workers. Articles in *The Wall Street Journal* in early 2002 drew newfound attention to the large corporations who purchased a considerable number of these policies, including AT & T, Dow Chemical, Nestle, Pitney Bowes, Procter & Gamble, Enron, and more.[1] A 2002 *San Francisco Chronicle* article cited the fact that Wal-Mart took out COLI policies on over 350,000 of its workers in the 1990's.[2] According to a 2003 *The Wall Street Journal* article, COLI policies like these cost taxpayers $1.9 billion in revenue a year on a federal basis.[3] While some regulation by Congress has limited the amount that companies might deduct in interest on loans to $50,000 from each of these policies, the popularity of these policies continues to grow with the incentives of cash value build-up and the result-ant tax-free investment. In 2001, it was estimated that premiums on these policies had grown to $2.8 billion.[4]

The Laws Regarding COLIs. How is it that companies are able to take life insurance out on employees without their knowledge? Part of the confusion lies with the different state laws. Some state laws, like those in Texas, require that employees "consent" to having their lives insured while other states, like Georgia, do not require consent. Additionally, some employees "consent" without knowing it. In one Texas lawsuit, Wal-Mart employees alleged that they consented without knowing it when they were offered a special $5,000 death ben-efit when Wal-Mart launched the program from 1994-1996. Wal-Mart disputed the claim by stating that the policies were signed in Georgia with an insurance management company located in Georgia, and therefore the more lenient Georgia law applied, regardless of the consent issue.[5] Wal-Mart ended up settling the suit after the 5th US Circuit Court of Appeals upheld a ruling that Wal-Mart lacked sufficient financial inter-est in the lives of its rank-and-file employees.[6]

CRITICS

The COLI Debate. Critics of peasant insurance policies point to the disincentives for employee safety; after all, if a company is going to collect money on an employee's death, what incentives do they really have to protect that employee? Additionally, critics point to the comparison to slaveholders' policies, the loss of tax revenues, and the use of these policies to fund exorbitant executive compen-sation programs. Supporters of these insurance policies cite the fact that it is no different than insuring a business asset and it is perfect-ly legal. For years, companies have protected their interests with life insurance policies on their CEOs, top management team members and executives whose deaths could seriously impact a company's bottom line. Finally, many supporters point out that these insurance policies provide a nice vehicle for funding the growing costs of retiree benefits, so there is financial soundness to these policies that offer benefit to all employees of the companies.

The Current Situation. While different states continue to set the parameters for the legalities of these policies, some companies have decided to cancel these COLI policies to avoid the risk of lawsuits from family members of the deceased who say that they are the rightful owners of the policies. In January, 2002, Wal-Mart canceled most of these policies after several lawsuits with similar companies resulted in stiff penalties and settlements. However, despite the risk, the *Houston Chronicle* reported that an attorney for the Hartford Life Insurance Company estimated that one-fourth of the Fortune 500 companies still have these "dead peasant" policies.[7] As a result, widows and widowers of the employees of these companies may continue to receive surprise calls from their benefits divisions, even as they mourn the death of their loved ones.

Questions for Discussion

1. What are the major ethical issues involved in this case?
2. How does the idea that these policies fund executive com-pensation and/or retiree benefits affect your answer to #1?
3. Should Congress create more stringent guidelines for the administration and use of these types of COLI policies?

Case Endnotes

* Fictional characters based on a true story.
1. Schultz, E.E. & Francis, T. "Valued Employees: Worker Dies, Firm Profits—Why?," *The Wall Street Journal*, 4/19/02.
2. Sixel, L. "Executives Benefit from Works' Demise. 'Dead Peasant' Policies Pay Out to Bosses When Employees Die," *San Francisco Chronicle*, 4/28/02.
3. Francis, T. "'Janitors Insurance'—Profiting When Employees Die," *The Wall Street Journal*, 2/19/03
4. A. Etzioni, "'Peasant Insurance' A Corporate Shame," *The Atlanta Journal and Constitution*, January 30, 2003, 3.
5. Sixel, L. "Profiting from Death? Lawsuit Filed in Wal-Mart Life Insurance Case," *The Houston Chronicle*, April 25, 2002,1.
6. G. Gonzalez, "Wal-Mart Settles Suit Over COLI Policies," *Business Insurance Daily News*, January 9, 2004,1. Additional sources: http://www.socialistviewpoint@pacbell.net; http://www.laborresearch.org.
7. *The Houston Chronicle*, 1.

THE CASE OF THE FIRED WAITRESS

Ruth Hatton, a waitress for a Red Lobster restaurant in Pleasant Hills, Pennsylvania, was fired from her job because she was accused of stealing a guest-comment card that had been deposited in the customer comment box by a disgruntled couple.[1] The couple, who happened to be black, had been served by Ms. Hatton and were unhappy with the treatment they perceived they got from her. At the time of her firing, Ms. Hatton, age 53, had been a 19-year veteran employee. She said, "It felt like a knife going through me."

THE INCIDENT

The couple had gone to the Red Lobster restaurant for dinner. According to Hatton, the woman had requested a well-done piece of prime rib. After she was served, she complained that the meat was fatty and undercooked. Hatton then said she politely suggested to the woman that "prime rib always has fat on it." Hatton later explained that, based on her experience with black customers in the working-class area in which the restaurant was located, the customer might have gotten prime rib confused with spare rib.

Upset Customer Leaves. Upon receiving the complaint, Hatton explained that she returned the meat to the kitchen to be cooked further. When the customer continued to be displeased, Hatton offered the couple a free dessert. The customer continued to be unhappy, doused the prime rib with steak sauce, then pushed it away from her plate. The customer then filled out a restaurant comment card, deposited it in the customer comment box, paid her bill, and left with her husband.

Inadvertently Thrown Out. Ms. Hatton explained that she was very curious as to what the woman had written on the comment card, so she went to the hostess and asked for the key to the comment box. She said she then read the card and put it in her pocket with the intention of showing it to her supervisor, Diane Canant, later. Hatton said that Canant, the restaurant's general manager, had commented earlier that the prime rib was overcooked, not undercooked. Apparently, the restaurant had had a problem that day with the cooking equipment and was serving meat that had been cooked the previous day and then was being reheated before being served. Later, Ms. Hatton said that she had forgotten about the comment

This case was prepared by Archie B. Carroll, University of Georgia.

card and had inadvertently thrown it out. It also came out that it is against Red Lobster's policy to serve reheated meat, and the chain no longer serves prime rib.[2]

HATTON'S FIRING

Canant said that she fired Ms. Hatton after the angry customer complained to her and to her supervisor. Somehow, the customer had learned later that Ms. Hatton had removed the comment card from the box. Ms. Canant recalled, "The customer felt violated because her card was taken from the box and she felt that her complaint about the food had been ignored." Referring to the company's policy manual, Canant said Ms. Hatton was fired because she violated the restaurant's rule forbidding the removal of company property.

Not a Big Deal. Another person to comment on the incident was the hostess, Dawn Brown, then a 17-year-old student, who had been employed by the restaurant for the summer. Dawn stated, "I didn't think it was a big deal to give her the key (to the comment box). A lot of people would come and get the key from her."[3]

THE PEER REVIEW PROCESS

Ms. Hatton felt she had been unjustly fired for this incident. Rather than filing suit against the restaurant, however, she decided to take advantage of the store's peer review process. The parent company of Red Lobster, Darden Restaurants, had 4 years earlier adopted a peer review program as an alternative dispute resolution mechanism. Many companies across the country have adopted the peer review method as an alternative to lengthy lawsuits and as an avenue of easing workplace tensions.

Success of Peer Review Program. Executives at Red Lobster observed that the peer review program had been "tremendously successful." It helped to keep valuable employees from unfair dismissals and it had reduced the company's legal bills for employee disputes by $1 million annually. Close to 100 cases have been heard through the peer review process, with only 10 resulting in lawsuits. Executives at the company also said that the process has reduced racial tensions. In some cases, the peer review panels have reversed decisions made by managers who had overreacted to complaints from minority customers and employees.[4]

HATTON'S PEER REVIEW PANEL

The peer review panel chosen to handle Ruth Hatton's case was a small group of Red Lobster employees from the surrounding area. The panel included a general manager, an assistant manager, a hostess, a server, and a bartender, all of whom had volunteered to serve on the panel. The peer review panel members had undergone special peer review training and were being paid their regular wages and travel expenses. The peer review panel was convened about 3 weeks after Hatton's firing. According to Red Lobster policy, the panel was empowered to hear testimony and to even overturn management decisions and award damages.

Testimony Heard. The panel met in a conference room at a hotel near Pittsburgh and proceeded to hear testimony from Ruth Hatton, store manager Diane Canant, and hostess Dawn Brown. The three testified as to what had happened in the incident.

Through careful deliberations, the panelists tried to balance the customer's hurt feelings with what Hatton had done and why, and with the fact that a company policy may have been violated. Initially, the panel was split along job category lines, with the hourly workers supporting Ms. Hatton and the managers supporting store management. After an hour and a half of deliberations, however, everyone was finally moving in the same direction and, the panel finally came to a unanimous opinion as to what should be done.[5]

Questions for Discussion

1. What are the ethical issues in this case from an employee's point of view? From management's point of view? From a consumer's point of view?
2. Who are the stakeholders, and what are their stakes?
3. As a peer review panel member, how would you judge this case? Do you think Ms. Hatton stole company property? Do you think the discharge should be upheld?
4. Do you think the peer review method of resolving work complaints is a desirable substitute for lawsuits? What are its strengths and weaknesses?
5. If you had been Ms. Hatton, would you be willing to turn your case over to a peer review panel like this and then be willing to live with the results?

Case Endnotes

1. Margaret A. Jacobs, "Red Lobster Tale: Peers Decide Fired Waitress's Fate," *The Wall Street Journal* (January 20, 1998), B1, B4.
2. *Ibid.*
3. *Ibid.*
4. *Ibid.*
5. *Ibid.*

Case 34

| VIOLENCE IN THE WORKPLACE: WHO IS TO BLAME?

Michael Rahming, age 50, worked as a painter at Fairview Developmental Center. Fairview is a Costa Mesa California organization that serves people with developmental disabilities. Rahming had difficulty getting along in the workplace. He claimed that he was mistreated and often ended up in confrontations with people. In an effort to help him, Fairview sent him for psychiatric evaluations.[1]

The Attack. In July of 1991, Rahming went on a shooting rampage. He shot and killed one supervisor after shooting and wounding another. He then drove his truck across campus searching for executive director Hugh Kohler. He found Kohler in a hall and shot him in the head. The bullet went about a quarter of an inch into Kohler's skull and then ricocheted back. Kohler fought with Rahming who shot him across the skull for a second time, creating a furrow at the top of

This case was prepared by Ann K. Buchholtz, University of Georgia.

Kohler's head. As Rahming began to choke Kohler with his hands, Kohler pushed him back and closed the office door between them. He then was forced to alternate between holding the door shut and jumping back when shots came through the wood. The fight continued until police arrived and subdued Rahming.

The Aftermath. Rahming received a sentence of sixty years in jail. The attack caused nerve damage to Kohler's head and spine, leaving him in chronic pain. In spite of the pain, Kohler continued in his position for twelve years. The damage took its toll and so in 2003 Kohler's doctors told him that he could no longer work. At the age of 55, he went into disability retirement.

Rahming's defense lawyer, Michael Naughton, said that Fairview should have done more to prevent the attack. He suggested that Fairview could have forced Rahming into therapy. He said his history of confrontations should have served as an indicator. His previous psychiatric evaluations said he had paranoid tendencies.

Kohler counters that he did send Rahming out for three psychiatric evaluations. They concluded that he was fit to work in spite of the fact that he was probably paranoid. Kohler said, "My mistake was that I never saw him as a time bomb that would explode."[2]

One week after the shooting, the final psychiatrist's report arrived. It said that Rahming was fit for work.

Questions for Discussion

1. What are the ethical issues in this case?
2. Who are the stakeholders and how would you prioritize their claims?

3. Do you agree with Mr. Naughton that Fairview should have done more?
4. How would you determine responsibility following an incident of workplace violence? What could and should organizations do to avoid these incidents?

Case Endnotes

1. This case is based on information in the following article: Stephanie Armour, "Managers Not Prepared for Today's Violence," *USA Today* (July 15, 2004), http://www.usatoday.com.
2. *Ibid.*

Case 35

| PIZZA REDLINING: EMPLOYEE SAFETY OR DISCRIMINATION?

The issue came to a head in March 1996 when William Fobbs, father of three, wanted to order a pepperoni-and-mushroom pizza for his family one night. Much to his surprise, Domino's refused to deliver to his home. Mr. Fobbs then called Mr. Pizza Man, a local restaurant. It also refused to deliver.

Mr. Fobbs, a security guard, lives in a tough, predominantly black neighborhood near Candlestick Park in San Francisco. He was outraged and ended up feeding his kids tuna-fish sandwiches that night instead of the pizza they wanted.

GRANDMOTHER GETS INVOLVED

Exasperated, Mr. Fobbs called his grandmother, Willie Kennedy, then a 72-year-old champion of minority rights who also happened to be a member of San Francisco's Board of Supervisors. Ms. Kennedy's reaction was that her grandson had experienced racism. She said, "It can only be because we are black people." Ms. Kennedy got her friends at City Hall involved, and the result was that San Francisco passed the first law that makes it illegal for a pizza restaurant, or any business, to refuse to deliver to a particular neighborhood that is within its normal delivery area.

Some observers think that a law on pizza redlining is just one more example of the city's propensity to excess. Mr. Fobbs, however, takes the issue seriously. He said, "I felt like I was in Vietnam, somewhere in the far-off jungle."[1]

ACLU SPEAKS OUT

Dorothy Ehrlich, executive director of the American Civil Liberties Union (ACLU) in Northern California, supports the

This case was written by Archie B. Carroll, University of Georgia.

law.[2] She says that it is a blow against discrimination and ought to serve as a model for other communities. Pizza-chain owners and others in the restaurant delivery business say the issue is about *crime* and *safety*, not discrimination or race. They point to the fact that several pizza deliverers have been murdered on the job in the past few years. They say that obeying this law puts their employees' safety and lives at risk. Someone pointed out that a Domino's pizza deliveryman was murdered in San Francisco in 1994 in an area designated safe, a so-called "green" zone.[3]

OWNER DEFENDS HIMSELF

Wally Wilcox owns the Domino's restaurant that refused to deliver to Mr. Fobbs. Wilcox owns three restaurants that, like most Domino's restaurants across the country, use a computer system that categorizes neighborhoods as green, yellow, or red. Customers in "green" neighborhoods get delivery without questions. In "yellow" areas, customers must come out to the delivery car to pick up their pizzas. Customers in "red" zones do not get delivery. They are considered dangerous.

No Discrimination. Wilcox, who is white, declares that he is not racist and does not discriminate. He pointed out that the Fobbs incident was ironic because it occurred due to error. Mr. Fobbs's street had not been entered into the computer, and restaurant workers did not know his address was in their territory. Despite the mistake, Wilcox defends his restaurant's policy of not delivering to dangerous areas, like public housing projects. Wilcox pointed out that the person ordering the pizza could be a good person but that when the deliverer arrives at the address he or she could be attacked by others in the area. Wilcox also pointed out that it was one of his drivers who was shot and killed in 1994 in San Francisco's Excelsior district, which is not far from where Mr. Fobbs lives. Wilcox said that street toughs "own the area."

THE POSITION OF HEADQUARTERS

Tom McIntyre, spokesman for Domino's Pizza, Inc., which is headquartered in Ann Arbor, Michigan, said that his company has hundreds of outlets with bulletproof glass because of the threat and the experience of being robbed. The headquarter's office distributes the area classification software the restaurants use to categorize areas as green, yellow, or red. However, the categorization is up to the store owner's discretion.[4]

Other national pizza chains, like Little Caesar Enterprises, Inc., and Pizza Hut, say they have policies similar to Domino's. Pizza Hut, the nation's largest chain, says it uses local crime statistics in each delivery area to determine which areas are safe and which are off limits.

DANGEROUS JOBS

Crime statistics support the conclusion that pizza deliverers are frequently assaulted, robbed, and sometimes killed on the job. The National Institute for Occupational Safety and Health released a study that showed that the riskiest jobs are those in which workers deal with the public, exchange money, and deliver goods and services. In San Francisco, where the Fobbs incident occurred, it has been reported that many pizza drivers, some of them minorities themselves, have been known to carry guns to protect themselves from assaults.

Law Denounced. The California Restaurant Association denounced the law in a letter to the Board of Supervisors, pointing out that the requirement violates federal occupational safety and health laws. These laws bar employers from forcing workers into hazardous situations. The association also pointed out that worker's compensation premiums may escalate due to the new law.

Defenders of the law say it lacks real authority. According to the law, violation is a civil offense that imposes no fines. However, it does make it easier for those who are snubbed to sue for damages.

THE KANSAS CITY EPISODE

A year later, an episode occurred in Kansas City, Missouri, which was related to the San Francisco case. In this case, Pizza Hut was involved. Paseo Academy in Kansas City phoned in a $450 pizza order 4 days in advance. The pizza was to be for a midday party for honor-roll students. Much to the school's surprise, the Pizza Hut in the area refused to take the order, saying the area was unsafe. A local chain, Westport Pizza, was more than happy to fill the order.

A few days later, Dorothy Shepherd, principal of Paseo Academy, learned that Pizza Hut had recently won a $170,000 contract to deliver pizzas twice a week to 21 Kansas City high schools and junior high schools, including Paseo, a $34 million state-of-the-art school that serves a 70 percent minority student body. Shepherd was outraged. She said, "I respect their wanting to protect their drivers. But how could it be unsafe one day but safe enough for them when it came to that contract? We didn't move the school."

Pizza Hut Asserts Safety Is Issue. Rob Doughty, a spokesman at Pizza Hut's Dallas headquarters, accused school officials of "reacting to emotion" when they talked about canceling the contract with Pizza Hut. Doughty said, "The sole issue is the safety of our employees." He said that the company works out its "trade area restrictions" based on crime statistics. He pointed out that two Pizza Hut drivers had been killed in the preceding 6 weeks, both in presumably safe areas. One murder occurred in Sacramento, California, and the other in Salt Lake City, Utah.

Is a Boycott Appropriate? Doughty claimed that regularly scheduled deliveries, like those called for in the school system contract in Kansas City, can be done safely with more than one driver but that the firm does not and cannot afford to do that with spot orders in which one driver is involved, like the order at Paseo Academy. The company may not get a chance to make any deliveries to Paseo on the contract, however, because students were agitating for a Pizza Hut boycott, and the school board was tempted to spruce up menus with pizza from local firms.[5]

DOMINO'S CHANGES POLICY

In June 2000, it was announced that Domino's Pizza, Inc., would no longer limit delivery service in minority neighborhoods without hard evidence that its drivers are at risk. The company reached an agreement with the Justice Department that its managers will consult crime reports and talk to community groups and local businesses before shutting off an area. The decision came following an incident in Washington, DC, wherein several residents of a black neighborhood sued Domino's for refusing to deliver to customers' doors. The plaintiffs pointed out that their neighborhood actually had a lower crime rate than other areas where Domino's not only delivers, but actually has stores.[6]

Is Pizza an Entitlement? Not everyone agreed with Domino's being forced to change. Sarah McCarthy, a writer asked: Is pizza the newest entitlement?[7] According to McCarthy, the Justice Department bullied Domino's into compliance even though the company could point to 24 of its drivers who had been killed on the job. Apparently, the Justice Department stated that all people, regardless of race or creed, had a right to pizza and that Domino's was essentially guilty of racial profiling because of its policies. In response, *Investor's Business Daily* said "What about the right of all people," regardless of race or creed, "to avoid getting killed?" "Call us crazy, but that right would seem to trump the Justice Department's newly pronounced right to pizza.[8]

EPILOG

Incidents, debates and differences of opinion continue between those who think pizza must be delivered to dangerous neighborhoods and the pizza companies that continue to maintain that it is an issue of employee safety and that they have a responsibility not to place their employees in places where they may get injured or killed.[9] Is pizza redlining discrimination or employee safety?

Questions for Discussion

1. What are the ethical issues involved in pizza deliveries to dangerous neighborhoods that are often predominantly inhabited by minorities? What tensions exist between economic and ethical issues? Whose interests are dominant—consumer stakeholders or employee stakeholders?

2. Are pizza companies genuinely protecting their employees, for which they should be applauded, or discriminating against minorities because they "redline" and are unwilling to deliver to areas they consider dangerous?

3. Should San Francisco law, which makes it illegal for a pizza restaurant or any other business to refuse to deliver to a neighborhood that is within its normal service range, be rescinded? What are the ethical as well as the legal issues?

4. Is Pizza Hut in Kansas City engaging in an unethical practice by refusing spot deliveries but agreeing to large-dollar contract deliveries in areas it considers dangerous to its drivers? Is its two-driver versus one-driver explanation reasonable?

Case Endnotes

1. Sewell Chan, "Pizza Redlining: Hot Issue Becomes Law in San Francisco," *The Wall Street Journal*, July 10, 1996, A1.
2. American Civil Liberties Union, "With Liberty and Pizza for All," (July 10, 1996). http://archive.aclu.org/news/w071096c.html
3. "The Politics of Pizza Delivery," *Time* (July 22, 1996), 38.
4. Chan, A1.
5. James L. Graff, "The Perils of Pizza Hut," *Time* (January 27, 1997).
6. "Domino's Delivers," *USA Today* (June 7, 2000), 14A.
7. Sarah J. McCarthy, "Pizza, the newest entitlement," *WorldNet Daily*, June 24, 2000, http://www.worldnetdaily.com
8. Quoted in *Ibid*.
9. These incidents have repeated themselves in many places including Tarpon Springs, Florida. For more information, read "Redlined residents say racism is behind delivery denial," August 19, 2002, Pizza marketplace.com, http://www.pizzamarketplace.com/news; "Florida operator ends 7-year redlining policy," September 3, 2002, Pizza Marketplce.com, http://www.pizzamarketplace.com/news; "Pizza Hut to cease redlining in Tarpon Springs on Nov. 1," October 7, 2002, http://www.pizzamarketplace.com/news

Case 36

AFTER-EFFECTS OF AFTER-HOURS ACTIVITIES: THE CASE OF PETER OILER

Few people question an employer's right to control an employee's behavior on the job. However, when an employer takes action based on an employee's off-duty conduct, questions of ethics arise. More than half of all states prohibit firing based on various types of after-hours conduct.[1] Federal law prohibits firing that is discriminatory. Some cases, however, fall through those cracks. If you were the judge in the Peter Oiler lawsuit, how would you rule?

Work History. By all accounts, Peter Oiler was a good worker. Hired in 1979 to drive a truck for Winn-Dixie, his responsibilities included driving a 50-foot truck, loading supplies from the company warehouse, driving them to Winn-

This case was prepared by Ann K. Buchholtz, University of Georgia.

Dixie stores throughout southeastern Louisiana, and unloading them. Oiler received above average performance ratings and was promoted three times during his tenure at Winn-Dixie. He adhered to company policies in all ways, including his attire and his presentation.[2] In his private time, Oiler liked to take on the persona of "Donna" at home, donning women's clothing, accessories, makeup, wigs and fake breasts. Though he usually stayed home, Oiler would sometimes go out as Donna with his wife and friends to restaurants, the shopping mall, or church.[3]

The Situation Arises. In 1999, Oiler had a meeting with his supervisor Greg Miles. A year earlier, Oiler had been bothered by a rumor that had been circulating that Oiler was gay and so he asked Miles to take action against it. At the meeting, Miles asked if the rumors had subsided and Oiler said that they had. Miles asked Oiler why the rumors bothered him and Oiler said it was because he is transgender instead of gay. When Miles asked what transgender was, Oiler explained that it refers to people who have feelings about their gender that are sometimes inconsistent with their anatomical sex. Oiler added that he had no intention of ever changing his sex or living as a woman full-time.[4] He was a happily married, heterosexual man, about to celebrate his 25th wedding anniversary.

Winn-Dixie Responds. Miles said he would have to check the company policy about transgender employees. On November 1, 1999, Miles informed Oiler that a supervisor had seen Oiler dressed as a woman off-duty. Oiler said that he did sometimes dress as a woman but never on-duty. Miles responded that Oiler's activities could harm Winn-Dixie's image and so the company was asking him to resign. He recommended that Oiler look for another job. Oiler said he did not want another job because he was happy at Winn-Dixie. He continued to work in his position. From November 4, 1999 to January 5, 2000, Winn-Dixie managers had five meetings with Oiler. They told him to find another job because he was about to be terminated. They said they had no problem with his work performance but his off-duty dressing as a woman could hurt Winn-Dixie's public image. Oiler reiterated that he would not wear women's clothing at work. At the January 5, 2000 meeting, Oiler was terminated.[5]

The Aftermath. Oiler sued Winn-Dixie for gender discrimination. He argued that the company fired him because he did not fit the company's gender stereotype of a man. Ken Choe, an American Civil Liberties Union attorney who represented Oiler, said, "Everyone agrees he was not terminated for anything related to his job performance. All of the cross dressing behavior occurred off the job." In September 2002, a federal judge in New Orleans ruled that transgendered people are not a protected class and so laws against sex discrimination do not apply to them.[6]

Although Oiler lost in court, he may have won the battle for public opinion. According to Oiler, "Quite a few people told me, "You're not hurting anybody. You do your job extremely well. How can they do this?" Oiler adds that Winn-Dixie's reaction has made other workers feel less secure. "The common theme (among former coworkers) was, "If they can get away with this, what can they do to me? It's got a lot of people saying, "Where's the limit?""[7]

Questions for Discussion

1. What are the ethical issues in this case?
2. Who are the stakeholders and how are they impacted by this situation?
3. Do you agree with the federal judge's decision? If you were the judge what would you do?
4. A recently passed ordinance in New Orleans prohibited discrimination against off-the-job cross-dressing. However, the Winn-Dixie branch that fired Oiler is located just outside that jurisdiction. Does this affect your answer to #2?
5. For what after-hours behavior do you feel it is appropriate to terminate an employee? For what after-hours behavior is it not appropriate? Where do you draw the line and how would you describe that line if you were developing a policy to put into an employee manual?

Case Endnotes

1. Carolyn Hirschman, "Off Duty, Out of Work," *HR Magazine* (February 2003), 50-56.
2. http://www.aclu.org
3. Hirschman, 50-56.
4. http://www.aclu.org
5. *Ibid.*
6. Hirschman, 52.
7. *Ibid.*, 52.

Case 37

IS HIRING ON THE BASIS OF "LOOKS" UNFAIR OR DISCRIMINATORY?

According to an attractive young woman, a student at Northwestern University in 2003, the same thing happens to her every time she goes shopping at Abercrombie & Fitch. On at least three occasions, store managers have approached her and offered

This case was written by Archie B. Carroll, University of Georgia.

her a job. This young woman, Elizabeth, measures in at 5' 6" and has long blond hair. She has an attractive, stylish appearance. Elizabeth looks like she belongs in an A & F catalog.[1]

Does this happen by coincidence to her? Apparently not. A former assistant manager for A&F said that it is, in fact, company policy that managers approach attractive people and ask them if they wanted a job. The store philosophy has been that if you have the best-looking college kids working for you, everyone would want to shop there.[2]

Nothing New? Hiring on the basis of "looks," appearance, or physical attractiveness is nothing new. Certain industries have been doing it for years. In recent years, however, it has become part of a growing trend on the part of merchants who want to project a particular image. A&F is not the only store to engage in this practice. Retail chains, such as the Gap, and Benetton, take pleasure in employing attractive people, often from different backgrounds and races. Allegations against A&F, however, have been that their classic American look is narrowly defined by such traits as blond, blue-eyed, and preppy. A&F finds these workers by recruiting on certain college campuses, sororities, and fraternities.[3]

According to a CBS News report, the image of A&F is "party-loving jocks and bare-naked ladies living fantasy lives." A&F wants its sales reps to reflect what is up on its walls—cool and seductive. Elizabeth, mentioned before, says that "the skirts are getting shorter. The tops are getting smaller. That seems to be the trend and Abercrombie is going with that."[4] A&F once had a reputation for the classical, classic look, but that is apparently gone now. In its place is a provocative new strategy targeted towards teens and twenties. Apparently, the more parents get outraged by their approach, the larger their sales. With more than 600 stores and annual sales in excess of $1 billion, the company has become the leading teen retailer.[5]

LAWSUITS ALLEGE DISCRIMINATION

In recent years, some discrimination experts, as well as individuals who believe they have been excluded because of looks, have been raising the question of whether hiring employees on the basis of their "looks" is discrimination of some kind. In fact, in June 2003, a coalition of four organizations filed an employment discrimination lawsuit against A&F. The coalition filing the lawsuit included the Mexican American Legal Defense Fund, the Asian Pacific American Legal Center, the NAACP Legal Defense and Educational Fund, and the law firm of Lieff Cabraser Heimann & Bernstein, LLP. The nine Hispanic and Asian plaintiffs to the lawsuit claim that A&F discriminates against people of color, including Latinos, Asian Americans, and African Americans, in its hiring practices, job assignments once hired, compensation, termination, and conditions of employment.[6]

Allegations. The young adults who comprise the plaintiff group have alleged that they were qualified to work at A&F but were either not hired or terminated because of their race, color, and/or national origin. The lawsuit asserts that A&F enforces a national, corporate policy of showing preference to white people for sales positions, desirable assignments and favorable work schedules. The lawsuit details some of the practices claimed to be illegal, including recruiting, hiring, and maintaining a dispro-

portionately white workforce, systematically discouraging minority applicants, and refusing to hire qualified minorities for positions working on the sales floor. The lawsuit alleges that when minorities are hired, they are channeled into less prominent positions—the stockroom, overnight shift positions, and out of the public eye.[7]

The "A&F Look." The grievance goes on to claim that the company implements its discrimination in part through a detailed and meticulous "Appearance Policy," that requires all Brand Representatives to exhibit the "A&F Look." The lawsuit maintains that the company rigorously maintains the "A&F Look" by vigilant scrutiny and monitoring of its stores by managers from the region, district, and national office. In addition, as part of the monitoring policy, stores have to submit a picture of their Brand Representatives who fit the "look" to the corporate office each quarter. Then, the corporate office selects about 15 stores' pictures and holds them up as exemplary models and distributes them throughout their national network of stores. The pictures, it alleges, are almost invariably of white, young people.[8]

Specific Complaints. A representative for the Mexican American Legal Defense and Educational Fund said "If you look at the material they put out, they are cultivating an all-white look." He went on "It is difficult to understand why, given that their target age demographic is even more heavily minority than the rest of the population."[9] One recent graduate of Stanford University, a Filipino-American, said he applied for a position at a store at which he previously worked, but was told "We're sorry, but we can't rehire you because there's already too many Filipinos working here."[10]

Second Lawsuit. A&F was named in a second lawsuit alleging discriminatory practices in November 2003. This lawsuit, which is seeking class-action status, was filed on behalf of a woman who alleged that her application was denied because she is an African-American. This suit was filed by Jesse Jackson's Rainbow/Push Coalition and three Philadelphia-area law firms.[11] According to AbercrombieLawsuit.com, a new consolidated class action lawsuit was formed bringing the previous two lawsuits into one consolidated suit.[12]

THE A&F POSITION HAS SUPPORTERS

Representatives from A&F say that the company does not discriminate. A&F's director of communications said that the company likes hiring sales assistants, who they call "brand representatives" who look great. He said that the brand representatives are ambassadors to the brand and the company wants them to look great, project individuality, project enthusiasm, and make the store a warm and inviting place to shop.[13]

Related Opinions. Some retailers defend the approach to hiring used by A&F insofar as it attempts to identify and use brand enhancers. For example, one senior industry analyst said "Being able to find a brand enhancer, or what I call a walking billboard, is critical. It's really important to create an environment that's enticing to the community, particularly with the younger, fashionable market. A guy wants to go hang out in a store where he can see good-looking gals."[14] A New Orleans lawyer who represents many hotels and restaurants said: "Hiring someone who is attractive isn't illegal per se. But people's views on what's attractive may be influenced by their race, their religion, their age."[15] One former sales manager for L'Oreal said that she had perceived intense pressure to hire attractive saleswomen, even if they were not competent. She said that company managers tried to force her out when she ignored a directive to fire a woman that her top manager believed was not "hot" enough.[16]

RELEVANT LAWS

There are no federal laws that say you cannot discriminate on the basis of appearance. It is also acceptable for employers to have certain "grooming" (appearance) guidelines. However, it is against the law to discriminate based on a number of different features such as gender, race, age, color, disability, and other legally protected characteristics. The debate arises when someone suspects they were discriminated against because of a "protected characteristic," such as color, age, national origin, and so on, but the employer claims that this was not the case. Therefore, a plaintiff wishing to challenge the legality of "appearance" discrimination somehow has to link or associate appearance to discrimination on the basis of gender, race, age, disability, or some other legally protected characteristic.[17]

The two most likely laws someone might find relevant to "appearance" discrimination would be Title VII of the Civil Rights Act, and the Americans with Disabilities Act. It should be added, however, that at least one state law (District of Columbia Human Rights Act) does make it unlawful to hire on the basis of personal appearance.[18] Therefore, a careful study of federal, state, and local laws is necessary to help judge these cases.

After considering the practices of A&F, we are left with several questions: Is it legal to make employment decisions based on "looks" or appearance? If so, under what circumstances? Is it ethical to take such actions? If so, under what circumstances?

Questions for Discussion

1. What are the legal and ethical issues in this case?
2. What is your evaluation of the concept of the "A&F look?" Have you personally observed this concept in practice?
3. Are the employment practices of A&F discriminatory? Are they unfair? What ethical principles or precepts guide your analysis?
4. What could A&F be doing, that it is not doing, that would make its practices less controversial?
5. Carefully read up on relevant laws and other cases to decide how you think a judge or jury would decide in the A&F case.

Case Endnotes

1. Steven Greenhouse, "Going for the Look, but Risking Discrimination," *The New York Times*, July 13, 2003, 10YT.
2. *Ibid.*
3. *Ibid.*
4. "The Look of Abercrombie & Fitch," CBSNews.com, December 5, 2003.
5. *Ibid.*
6. "Discrimination Lawsuit Filed Against Abercrombie & Fitch Co." Afjustice.com, 2003-2004.
7. *Ibid.*
8. *Ibid.*
9. "Abercrombie & Fitch Faces Discrimination Lawsuit," *USA Today*, July 14, 2004.
10. *Ibid.*
11. "Business Brief—Abercrombie & Fitch Co: Discriminatory Hiring Practices Are Alleged in a Second Lawsuit," *Wall Street Journal*, November 20, 2003, 1.
12. AbercrombieLawsuit.com, January 6, 2004.
13. Greenhouse, 10YT.
14. *Ibid.*
15. *Ibid.*
16. *Ibid.*
17. Gerard Panaro, "Is Hiring on the Basis of Appearance Illegal?" BankersOnline.com, July 8, 2004.
18. *Ibid.*

Case 38

| WHEN MANAGEMENT CROSSES THE LINE

While working at a very popular corporate restaurant as a server, questionable practices often occur between managers and employees. It is a well-known fact that restaurants are hot beds

Contributed by Julia E. Merren.

for sexual harassment among coworkers. Sexual harassment is problematic enough among peers, but even more disturbing when the abuse comes from management. One of my managers has had a tendency to single out several female servers, including me, for his sick humor and cruelty. On a number of occasions, he has made disparaging remarks to my friends and me. Unfortunately, he does it when no one else is within earshot. Once he told me that my only way to advance in life was to "work" my assets. He never touches us. He just makes comments that make us feel uncomfortable. Many of us are tempted to mention our grievances to him but fear retribution. Intimidation is his method of managing.

This particular manager is in charge of our schedule and has a history of firing employees for the slightest infractions. He is not a dumb man; he knows that what he is doing is against the law, but he does it in such a way that his victims have no witnesses. My fellow coworkers and I have talked at length about what to do and feel that we have no recourse without evidence. We desire to work in an environment free of abuse but we also need to work. Our manager knows this and uses it to his advantage.

Questions for Discussion

1. What are the legal and ethical issues raised in this case?
2. Has sexual harassment occurred in this case, or just typical, flirtatious talk among fellow workers?
3. What should people like me do in situations like this?
4. What steps should be taken to prevent problems like this in the future?

Case 39

| CRACKER BARREL OLD COUNTRY STORES

Cracker Barrel Old Country Stores is a popular restaurant chain operating in the southeastern United States. It was founded in 1969 in Lebanon, Tennessee. Travelers on interstate highways are familiar with the stores, which operate in large buildings that look like rural general stores and serve southern-style meals featuring such foods as country ham, turnip greens, fried chicken, cornbread, and grits. Cracker Barrel restaurants are popular with families traveling by car and groups traveling by bus who want quick service and low prices but wish to avoid fast-food franchises. Local residents also enjoy dining at Cracker Barrel after Sunday church services.

Cracker Barrel restaurants are company-owned by CBRL Group and feature table service, gift shops, and clean restrooms. Management and employees concentrate on providing the best possible food and service. High-quality ingredients are used; for example, pancakes are served with real maple syrup and butter. "We don't skimp, because you can skimp yourself out of business," says the company's chief financial officer. Employees can be tested on their duties: Even servers and dishwashers have their own sets of tests on sanitation, food preparation, and dish stacking. Those who pass are given raises, cash incentives, and enhanced benefits as they move up the management ranks. Managers can double their incomes by meeting profitability goals.[1]

THE NEW EMPLOYMENT POLICY

In February 1991, Cracker Barrel management developed a new employment policy. Local managers were sent a memo

This case was initially prepared by William A. Sodeman, Hawaii Pacific University, and revised and updated by Archie B. Carroll, University of Georgia.

instructing them to terminate any employee "whose sexual preferences fail to demonstrate normal heterosexual values." In a press release, the company explained that the new practice was justified because Cracker Barrel was "founded upon a concept of traditional American values."[2] Such employment practices are legal in most states.[3] At least 11 employees were fired as a result of this memo.[4] Some managers noted in the employee files that the terminations were made because the employees were homosexual.[5]

The new policy was notable because the restaurant industry employs higher-than-average numbers of gays and lesbians. The flexible schedules, creative atmosphere, easy mobility, and social opportunities that are common in restaurant work are attractive to gays and compatible with the gay lifestyle. According to Wharton School entrepreneurship professor Edward Moldt, "There's a heavy preponderance of homosexuals in the restaurant business, and what [Cracker Barrel is] doing is losing a lot of people who could be very good in the jobs they're in. They're missing the business aspect of this."[6]

THE PROTESTS BEGIN

After 10 days, the termination policy was rescinded by corporate headquarters. Some fired employees claimed that store managers were instructed to hire new employees and to avoid rehiring any employee who had been terminated under the policy.[7]

Over the following 2 years, several external stakeholder groups applied pressure on the company. Queer Nation, a civil disobedience group that advocates gay and lesbian rights, began to picket Cracker Barrel stores in the Atlanta area. Some members staged sit-ins on Sunday afternoons, ordering only beverages as the "after-church crowd" was descending on Cracker Barrel stores. Protesters cooperated with the police and the local media, and when the eventual trespassing arrests were made, Queer Nation members were videotaped by local media and the ABC news magazine "20/20" as they were handcuffed and hauled off to jail.[8]

Protests in Northern States.

By this time, Cracker Barrel was expanding its operations to northern, pro-union states including Michigan, Ohio, and Wisconsin. The protests in these states were wilder, as they were run by unions and a different gay organization, ACT UP. Both groups became more militant, chanting slogans such as "Shut down the Bigot Barrel" and accusing the company of selling racist merchandise, including Confederate souvenirs and "mammy dolls," in its gift shops. These groups also organized protests on Wall Street to raise awareness of the publicly-traded firm within the investment community.[9]

THE RESOLUTIONS

Investors from various religious organizations and government pension funds filed proxy resolutions with Cracker Barrel to renounce their employment policies that discriminated against homosexuals. This was done because the groups felt the company was continuing its former policies. Cracker Barrel appealed to the Securities and Exchange Commission (SEC), which granted the company permission to exclude these resolutions from its annual meeting. The SEC concluded that employment policies did not require shareholder approval because they were "ordinary business decisions." In early 1998, the SEC reversed its decision, saying that it would review shareholder resolutions on a case-by-case basis.[10]

Success and Expansion.

Cracker Barrel has continued to expand from its southeastern base, opening new facilities in the Midwest and Northeast United States while forming a parent company, CBRL Group, Inc., to make acquisitions, like of the Logan's Roadhouse chain, which it purchased for $179 million in 1998.[11] By 1998, Cracker Barrel Old Country Store had been named "Best Family Dining" by Restaurants and Institutions magazine for the eighth year in a row and "Best Restaurant Chain" by Destinations magazine for 5 consecutive years.[12] Nevertheless, the controversy continued. In 1998, New York City Comptroller, Alan Hevesi, used the city retirement system's 200,000 shares of stock to propose that Cracker Barrel link executive pay to its ability to recruit new employees "without regard to race, color, creed, gender, age, or sexual orientation."[13] That same year, a protest group picketed the Culinary Institute of America's award dinner because it honored Cracker Barrel president, Ronald N. Magruder.[14] Last, "Out at Work" (an HBO documentary about discrimination in the workplace) featured the story of Cheryl Summerville, a Cracker Barrel cook who had been fired because of her sexual orientation.[15]

Resolution Eventually Passes.

It was not until 2002 that a shareholder resolution to bar sexual orientation discrimination passed. The resolution received 58 percent support from voting shareholders at CBRL Group's Nov. 26, 2002 annual meeting. After this vote, the company's board of directors voted immediately and unanimously to amend its Equal Employment Opportunity policy to include protection against sexual orientation discrimination.[16]

RACE DISCRIMINATION ENTERS PICTURE

In 1999, Cracker Barrel was hit with racial discrimination charges by current and former black employees who claimed they were discriminated against in pay and promotions. In March 2003, a U. S. District Court judge denied class action status to this lawsuit.[17] These lawsuits are still ongoing.

Customer Discrimination.

In December 2001, the company was sued for $100 million by a group of 21 black customers from 10 states claiming they were denied service and segregated in the smoking section. The group's attorney alleged that "These are not isolated incidents, but part of an overall corporate policy." The company's senior vice president of human resources disputed the charges, calling them "totally inaccurate." He went on to say that this "flies against the way our company operates and this case is without merit. They're way out on the limb on this one." He said the company has an antidiscrimination policy based on race, age, and gender. One of the black customers who said she and several others were denied service cited an experience at a Chattanooga, Tennessee, restaurant where the manager said the restaurant was closed. However, she said a group of whites, who arrived after them, was seated and served.[18]

Civil Lawsuits Expand.

By 2004, the civil lawsuits against Cracker Barrel covered 100 plaintiffs. The company has said that the lawsuits are baseless and contain false claims that the company has discredited under cross examination. Further, the company claims that attorneys have waged a multiyear media campaign to recruit plaintiffs and win financial settlements against the restaurant chain. A spokeswoman for Cracker Barrel, which has been named "Best Family Dining Chain in America" for 13 years by the industry's R&I magazine, said "We are vigorously defending ourselves."[19]

The civil lawsuits against the company are seeking more than $100 million. According to the NAACP, one of the plaintiffs in these lawsuits, the company must compensate the victims.[20]

Justice Department Settlement.

On its behalf, in May 2004, the U. S. Department of Justice announced the settlement of a lawsuit alleging racial discrimination against

African-American customers by Cracker Barrel. The Justice Department's complaint alleged that Cracker Barrel had violated Title II of the Civil Rights Act of 1964 by engaging in a pattern or practice of discrimination against black customers and prospective customers on the basis of their race or color. The specific charges were that the company:[21]

- Allowed white servers to refuse to wait on African-American customers
- Segregated customer seating by race
- Seated white customers before African-American customers who arrived earlier
- Provided inferior service to African-American customers after they were seated, and
- Treated African-American customers less favorably than white customers when they complained about the quality of food or service.

Steps Company Must Take.
The Justice Department entered into a five-year agreement with the company that requires Cracker Barrel restaurants nationwide to take the following steps to remedy the problem:[22]

- Adopt and implement effective nondiscrimination policies and procedures
- Implement new and enhanced training programs to ensure compliance with Title II and the consent order
- Develop and implement an improved system for investigating, tracking, and resulting discrimination complaints
- Retain an outside contractor to test the compliance of the restaurant with Title II and the consent order.

Unlike the civil lawsuits that are seeking monetary damages, the Justice Department settlement did not impose fines. And, as part of the settlement with the Justice Department, the company admitted no wrongdoing. The company maintains that it has long had policies banning discrimination.[23]

Company Update.
In 2004, CBRL operated 502 company-owned Cracker Barrel Restaurants in 41 states and 107 Logan's Roadhouse Restaurants in 17 states. The company employs over 50,000 employees and has annual revenues exceeding $1.9 billion.

Questions for Discussion

1. Given Cracker Barrel's strategy, which focuses on family dining, could its policy regarding homosexual employees be justified? What ethical principles and concepts support your thinking? Could Cracker Barrel have more effectively implemented its new policy? How?
2. Are special-interest groups justified in holding protests against company policy? How might Cracker Barrel have handled the Queer Nation and ACT UP protests besides calling in the police to arrest the trespassers?

3. How much authority and power should employers have in developing employment policies? What is the proper role of shareholders in defining these policies? What is the proper role of the courts?
4. Despite the controversy described in this case, Cracker Barrel has continued to perform well in a highly competitive environment. Has this performance been achieved in spite of or because of Cracker Barrel's foundation on "traditional American values"?
5. What is your assessment of the racial discrimination charges being leveled against the company? Is the company guilty, or is it too early to tell?
6. Does it seem appropriate that customers who have been discriminated against should be able to file lawsuits for $100 million? What ethical principles justify this demand?
7. Does the company have a public relations fiasco on its hands? How should it respond to this crisis?

Case Endnotes

1. Toddi Gutner, "Nostalgia Sells," *Forbes* (April 27, 1992), 102-103.
2. Marlene Givant Star, "SEC Policy Reversal Riles Activist Groups," *Pensions & Investments* (October 2, 1992), 33.
3. Joan Oleck, "Bad Politics," *Restaurant Business* (June 10, 1992), 80, 84, 89.
4. Givant Star, 33.
5. "20/20: Whom Do You Sleep With?" (November 29, 1991).
6. Oleck, 89.
7. Oleck, 84.
8. Oleck, 84; "20/20."
9. Oleck, 84, 89.
10. Abbott A. Leban and Frederick D. Lipman, "Excludability of Shareholder 'Social Responsibility' Proposals from Proxy Statements," *Securities Regulation Law Journal* (Spring 1994), 78-86.
11. Bill Carlino, "Cracker Barrel to Acquire Logan's Roadhouse in $179M Deal," *Nation's Restaurant News* (December 21, 1998), 3, 141.
12. "Cracker Barrel Old Country Stores Consistently Honored Nationwide as 'Best Family Dining' Restaurant and 'Best Restaurant Chain,'" *PR Newswire* (March 4, 1998).
13. Katia Hetter, "Focus on Cracker Barrel Hiring/Hevesi Opposes Anti-Gay Policy," *Newsday* (October 16, 1998), A67.
14. "Protest over Culinary Group's Guest of Honor," *The New York Times* (October 15, 1998), B3.
15. Joanne Ostrow, "Out at Work, An Eye-Opener" *Denver Post* (January 6, 1999), F5.
16. William Baue, "Record Shareowner Vote Prompts Cracker Barrel to Bar Sexual Orientation Discrimination," December 12, 2002, http://www.socialfunds.com
17. "Cracker Barrel Discrimination Suit Denied Class Action Status," *Nashville Business Journal*, March 10, 2003.
18. Shelia M. Poole, "Cracker Barrel Faces Racial Bias Lawsuit," *Atlanta Journal-Constitution* (December 14, 2001), G2.
19. Julie Schmit and Larry Copeland, "Cracker Barrel Customer Bias was Flagrant," *USA Today*, May 7, 2004.
20. *Ibid.*
21. Department of Justice, "Justice Department Settles Race Discrimination Lawsuit Against Cracker Barrel Restaurant Chain," press release, May 3, 2004, http://www.usdoj.gov/usao/gan/press/05-03-04.html.
22. *Ibid.*
23. Schmit and Copeland, 2004, *ibid.*

THE CASE OF JUDY

Judy was paralyzed from the neck down. She must have help getting out of bed, getting dressed, and getting into a motorized wheelchair. Judy says that she still has the greatest ability of all: her mind, which is as sound as ever. She says if she can find a way to attend the university, she will get a degree in public administration and she wants to have a career in that field.

JUDY COMES TO YOU

She has come to you, a vocational counselor at the state Department of Rehabilitation, as the first step in getting the funding she needs from the state in order to pursue this educational and career goal. Your responsibilities are

This case was reprinted from Norma Carr-Ruffino, Managing Diversity, 4th ed., Needham Heights, MA: Pearson Custom Publishing, 2001. Used with permission.

- *Regarding education:* to predict the possibility and probability that an applicant will actually complete the educational program he or she enters
- *Regarding occupation:* to predict the possibility and probability that an applicant will actually get and retain a job in the proposed field
- *Regarding funds:* to allocate scarce state funds for rehabilitation in a manner that produces the best results for persons with disabilities and for society

Questions for Discussion

1. Considering Judy's situation and your responsibilities, what will your decisions be? What are the potential ethical challenges in this situation?
2. What will you say to Judy?

DICK GRASSO AND THE NYSE: IS IT A CRIME TO BE PAID WELL?

The former New York Stock Exchange (NYSE) Chairman Richard A. (Dick) Grasso has a personal story that is well known in Wall Street circles. His father left his family when Grasso was an infant, and so he was raised in a blue-collar neighborhood by a single mother and two unmarried aunts. After dropping out of Pace University and then serving two years in the Army, Grasso joined the NYSE as a clerk in the stock lists department. Rising through the ranks, Grasso eventually became the NYSE Chairman and CEO in 1995.[1]

THE PAY PACKAGE

On August 27, 2003, the details of Dick Grasso's compensation package were made public. In the 4-year contract approved by NYSE directors, Grasso would receive a lump sum of $139.5 million in deferred compensation and pension benefits. Two weeks later on September 9, the NYSE revealed that

This case was prepared by Ann K. Buchholtz, University of Georgia

Grasso had also been promised $48 million more that did not include his base pay or his $2.4 million annual bonus.[2] The disclosure of the package created an instant uproar. In addition to NYSE directors and seat holders, large institutional investors expressed their dismay. The Securities and Exchange Commission (SEC) began an investigation as individual investors expressed outrage.

THE CRITICS

When critics compared Grasso's pay to that of other executives who are responsible for regulation of the securities industry, they found it excessive. Robert Glauber is chairman and chief executive of the National Association of Securities Dealers, which is responsible for regulating NASDAQ as well as many brokerage firms. His compensation package was about $2 million. SEC Chairman William Donaldson makes $142,000 annually. Furthermore, when Donaldson headed the NYSE he earned $1.5 million (1991) and $1.65 million (1992).[3]

Critics point out that Grasso's 2001 pay package of $30.5 million was nearly equal to the NYSE's net income that year. They also found Grasso's one-time bonus of $5 million for leadership on September 11 to be inappropriate. From the mayor of the city to firefighters and police officers, many exhibited leadership but he was the only one to receive a bonus in compensation.[4] Others point to Grasso's failure to reform the internal governance at NYSE. The board members are hand-picked in a time when independence has become valued.[5] Phil Angelides, head of the California Public Employees' Retirement System (Calpers), found it "particularly troubling" that Grasso received his largest payouts at a time when corporate scandals were rocking the markets.[6]

THE DEFENDERS

Those who defend Grasso's compensation point to the success of the NYSE, 1,549 of its 2,800 companies were added under his watch.[7] Kenneth Langone, who chaired the NYSE compensation committee from June 1999 to June 2003 declared, "The guy earned every penny we paid him."[8] He pointed to Grasso's successful handling of the Y2K concerns and the September 11 terrorist attacks and praised Grasso for helping increase the value of the NYSE's seats. During Grasso's tenure, the price of a seat rose from $810,000 to $1.9 million, reaching $2.65 million at one point in 1999.[9] Others have noted Grasso's success at expanding the NYSE's global listings and securing the NYSE's position as the world's leading stock market.[10] A *Wall Street Journal* editorial opined that Grasso should not be faulted for taking compensation awarded him by the board: The compensation committee was filled with financial services executives who knew what they were awarding him.[11] In his own defense, Grasso wrote:

My record at the NYSE speaks for itself. The value of a membership seat nearly tripled during my tenure as chairman, soaring to more than $2 million from $700,000. The income to seat owners leasing their seats to others likewise jumped to $300,000 from $100,000. Under my leadership, the NYSE significantly increased its market share. It nearly doubled the number of listed companies, and the great majority of the near-500 non-U.S. companies now on the NYSE were listed during my tenure. I proudly oversaw the implementation of the Big Board's technology platform, widely regarded as one of the most sophisticated in the world. Even in the late 1990s, when the dot-com craze gave the technology-laden NASDAQ the edge, the NYSE reigned supreme.[12]

THE FALLOUT

On September 17, 2003, less than a month after the pay package was disclosed, Grasso was ousted from his position. A NYSE press release explained Grasso's firing by saying that the pay deal had inflicted "serious damage" on the stock exchange's reputation.[13] In January 2004, the NYSE asked New York Attorney General Elliott Spitzer to investigate. In February 2004, the NYSE demanded that Grasso return $120 million which they felt Grasso had manipulated the board into providing. Two weeks later, Grasso responded that he would not return any of the compensation in question. In May 2004, Spitzer filed a lawsuit against Grasso, the NYSE, and former NYSE compensation committee chairman, Kenneth Langone, claiming that the size of the pay package violated the laws regarding compensation in not-for-profit organizations.[14] The suit charges that the pay package resulted from Grasso's manipulation and intimidation of an unaware board of directors and that Langone helped mislead the directors into voting for a package that appeared smaller than it was.[15] The suit also demands that Grasso return more than $100 million and forego any future payments.[16] Arguing that the NYSE is not a charity and that the compensation committee members are all high level financial executives who are not easily duped, Grasso has vowed to fight the lawsuit.[17] *The Wall Street Journal* notes that his choice of Brendan Sullivan, who successfully defended Oliver North, as his attorney is indicative of a plan to fight rather than settle.[18]

Questions for Discussion

1. What are the ethical issues in this case?
2. Who are the stakeholders impacted by this situation? How would you rank their claims?
3. What is your reaction to Richard Grasso's compensation package? What criteria are bringing you to your conclusion?
4. Do you agree with the firing of Richard Grasso? Do you agree with Attorney General Spitzer's lawsuit? Who is to blame for this situation? Who are the victims? Irrespective of what the courts decide, who do you think is in the wrong?
5. What changes would you make so that this problem would not happen again?

Case Endnotes

1. Gary Weiss, "The $140,000,000 Man," *Business Week* (September 15, 2003), 84–90.
2. Kate Kelly, "Langone Says NYSE Wasn't Misled on Pay Of Ex-Chief Grasso," *Wall Street Journal* (June 15, 2004), C1.
3. Suzanne Craig and Kate Kelly, "Large Investors Call for Grasso to Leave NYSE," *Wall Street Journal* (September 17, 2003), C1.
4. *Ibid.*
5. Weiss, 84–90.
6. Craig and Kelly, C1.
7. Weiss, 84–90.
8. Kelly, C1.
9. *Ibid.*
10. Weiss, 84–90.
11. "Spitzer v. Grasso," *Wall Street Journal* (May 25, 2004), A16.

12. Richard A. Grasso, "My Vindication Will Come in a Courtroom," *Wall Street Journal* (May 25, 2004), A16.
13. Charles Gasparino, "Dick Grasso Defending the Exchange Rate," *Newsweek* (July 26, 2004), 8.
14. Kara Scannell, "Grasso's Millions: Spitzer's Winning Streak Heads for Court," *Wall Street Journal* (May 25, 2004), C6.
15. Kate Kelly, "Money Brawl: Grasso v. Spitzer," *Wall Street Journal* (July 21, 2004), C1.
16. Kelly (June 15, 2004), C1.
17. Gasparino, 8.
18. Scannell, C6.

Case 42

SOCIAL REFORM OR SELF-INTEREST?

Raise Hell and Sell Newspapers is the biography of Alden J. Blethen, the man who bought *The Seattle Times* in 1896. It chronicles the ups and downs of Alden's rise from extreme hardship to great success. After a string of business failures, Alden borrowed money from family members to buy a failing newspaper, *The Seattle Daily Times*. When he died in 1915, his wish was that his now-successful newspaper remain in family hands.[1]

FRANK BLETHEN

Although Frank Blethen became publisher in 1985, he did not know much about Alden until the biography was published as part of the centennial celebration of Blethen family ownership of *The Seattle Times*. Moved by the book's account of the fiercely independent Alden, Frank Blethen took some family members and *Times* staffers on a pilgrimage to trace Alden's path from Maine to Seattle. Frank returned from the trip saying that it had given him and his family a touchstone they did not have before, as well as a renewed commitment to family ownership. Since Frank took over as publisher, *The Seattle Times* has won numerous awards, including three Pulitzer Prizes. Frank has rejected numerous offers to buy the paper out.[2]

THE CAMPAIGN

In the late 1980s and through the 1990s, Frank Blethen took a more active and visible leadership role in promoting issues he felt were important to the community. The paper ran ads supporting the United Way; honoring Dr. Martin Luther King, Jr.; and opposing a ballot measure that would end affirmative action. None of these initiatives, however, caused the kind of controversy that arose when Blethen began a campaign to eliminate the federal inheritance tax. Referred to as the "death tax" by opponents, the inheritance tax rate was as high as 5 percent on estates valued at over $3 million. Proponents of the tax said it brought the federal government $19.8 billion in revenue and

This case was prepared by Ann K. Buchholtz, University of Georgia.

that cutting it represents a tax break for the rich. Opponents of the tax point to inheritors who have had to sell off family businesses, like farms and newspapers, to be able to pay their taxes.[3]

The campaign Blethen waged against the inheritance tax was both impassioned and unprecedented. Rather than just writing editorials, the paper published an ad against the tax on its news pages. Larger than a half-page, the ad urged readers to ask their Congresspeople to support the tax's repeal. The ad said that it was sponsored by the "Committee to Repeal the Death Tax," a lobbying group formed by Blethen and Seattle Chamber of Commerce president, George Duff. In small print, the ad said it was "brought to you courtesy of *The Seattle Times*." Readers were referred to a Web site (http://www.deathtax.com) that was created and maintained by *The Seattle Times*.[4]

BLETHEN'S CRITICS

Critics of Blethen's campaign against the inheritance tax faulted it on several grounds. They argued that creating a public interest group, placing ads in news pages, and maintaining a Web site all went beyond the measures a business like a newspaper should take when supporting a cause. Critics also raised concerns about the role of Blethen's self-interest, citing the millions of dollars that would accrue to Blethen's family if his campaign were successful. They also faulted the Web site for slanted coverage of the issue. For example, the site stated that repeal of the tax would not add to the national deficit and would spur the economy; however, it failed to mention that this view is not supported by Congress's tax estimators. In a 1999 letter to the editor of *The Seattle Times*, Fred Flickinger referred to 1998 as the year journalistic integrity died at *The Seattle Times*.[5]

THE CURRENT SITUATION

President George W. Bush signed a $1.35 trillion tax cut into law in 2001, included in it was a gradual phase-out of the inheritance tax over ten years. By the end of 2010, the inheritance tax would be fully repealed. However in what Newsweek's Jane Bryant Quinn refers to as "a contemptible piece of consumer fraud," the tax rates revert back to their pre-legislation levels after only one year.[6] For the estate tax, having its total repeal last only one year effectively masks what the true cost of a permanent repeal would be. Although this helped to get the legislation passed, it did not totally satisfy the advocates nor did it silence the critics. Critics are trying to end the gradual phase-out, while advocates are striving to make the bill permanent.[7] As of mid-2004, mounting federal deficits made permanent repeal seem unlikely and so some advocates were seeking a compromise. As of this writing, no movement had occurred and the battle wages on.

Questions for Discussion

1. What are Frank Blethen's rights and responsibilities as the publisher of a major regional newspaper?

2. Is Blethen exercising a publisher's right to advance editorial opinion, or is he using the newspaper to promote his own self-interests?

3. Frank Blethen has espoused four core values that guide the activities of the newspaper. The first two are "Remain family-owned, private, and independent" and "Serve the community through quality journalism." Are these two core values in conflict in this situation? If so, can they be prioritized?

4. If you were advising Blethen, what would you recommend that he do?

Case Endnotes

1. Sherry Boswell and Lorraine McConaghy, *Raise Hell and Sell Newspapers* (Pullman, WA: Washington State University Press, 1996).
2. Michael R. Fancher, "Family Makes Visits to Roots, Reaffirms Commitment to the Times," *The Seattle Times* (October 19, 1997), A27.
3. Danny Westneat, "Publisher Promoting His Causes in Times Ads: Blethen May Launch Effort Against I-200," *The Seattle Times* (August 25, 1998), A1.
4. Howard Kurtz, "A Publisher Presses His Point," *The Seattle Times* (August 31, 1998), C1.
5. Fred Flickinger, "Estate Tax Pulled Plug on Journalistic Integrity with Tax Editorial," *The Seattle Times* (January 11, 1999), B5.
6. Jane Bryant Quinn, "Yes Indeed - The Rich Do Well While Those In Lower Brackets Are Left With The Scraps," *Newsweek* (June 11, 2001), 30.
7. http://www.dollarsandsense.org/archives/2003/0103hunter.html

ONLINE RESOURCES

All government information   http://www.firstgov.gov
America's Promise   http://www.americaspromise.org
American Civil Liberties Union   http://www.aclu.org
American Psychological Association   http://www.apa.org
American Society for Bioethics & Humanities   http://www.asbh.org
The American Society for Quality (ASQ)   http://www.asq.org
Arts and Business Council, Inc.   http://www.artsandbusiness.org
Association of Trial Lawyers of America (ATLA)   http://www.atlanet.org
The Aspen Institute   http://www.aspenbsp.org
Association for Practical and Professional Ethics   http://www.indiana.edu
Beard Center for Leadership in Ethics   http://www.bus.duq.edu/Beard
Better Business Bureau (BBB)   http://www.bbb.org
Beyond Grey Pinstripes   http:// www.beyondgreypinstripes.org
Bhopal Express   http://www.bhopalexpress.com/facts.html
Bhopal Web sites   http://www.bhopal.org   http://www.bhopal.net
          http://www.bhopal.com
Bioethics   http://www.bioethics.net
BSR Resources   http://www.bsr.org
Budget watchers   http://www.ombwatch.org
Business Committee for the Arts, Inc.   http://www.bcainc.org
Business Community Connections   http://www.bcconnections.org.uk
Business for Social Responsibility   http://www.bsr.org
Business Roundtable   http://www.brtable.org
The Conference Board   http://www.conference-board.org
Catalyst   http://www.catalystwomen.org
Cato Institute   http://www.cato.org
Caux Roundtable   http://www.cauxroundtable.org
CDC Business Responds to AIDS   http://www.hivatwork.org
Center for Corporate Citizenship   http://www.bc.edu/centers
Center for Public Integrity   http://www.publicintegrity.org
Center for Responsive Politics   http://www.opensecrets.org
CEO PayWatch   http://www.aflcio.org/paywatch
CERES   http://www.ceres.org
Children's Advertising Review Unit   http://www.caru.org
Choose Climate   http://www.chooseclimate.org
Citizen Works   http://www.citizenworks.org
Citizens for Tax Justice   http://www.ctj.org
ClimateStar   http://www.climatestar.org
The Coalition of Americans for Research Ethics   http://www.stemcellresearch.org

Co-op America Sweatshops   http://www.sweatshops.org
Commercial Alert   http://www.commercialalert.org
Committee of 100   http://www.committee100.org
Committee to Encourage Corporate Philanthropy
     http://www.corphilanthropy.org
Common Cause   http://www.commoncause.org
Common Good   http://www.cgood.org
Computer Ethics Institute   http://www.cpsr.org
Consumer.gov   http://www.consumer.gov
Consumer Product Safety Commission   http://www.cpsc.gov
Consumer Reports   http://www.consumerreports.org
Corporate Accountability Project   http://www.corporation.org
Corporate Communication Institute   http://www.corporatecomm.org
Corporate Governance   http://www.corpgov.net
CorpWatch   http://www.corpwatch.org
Council for Responsible Genetics   http://www.gene-watch.org
Council of Public Relations Firms   http://www.prfirms.org
Crisis Management: A Leadership Imperative   http://www.pfdf.org
Crisis Management Food Safety   http://www.foodsafetynetwork.ca/crisis.htm
Crisis Management Institute   http://www.cmionline.org
CSR Europe   http://www.csreurope.org
Electronic Privacy Information Center   http://www.epic.org
Employee Assistance Program Association   http://www.eap-association.org
EnviroLink Network   http://www.envirolink.org
Environmental Protection Agency (EPA)   http://www.epa.gov
Ethics Officer Association (EOA)   http://www.eoa.org.
Ethics Resource Center   http://www.ethics.org
European Crisis Management Academy   http://www.ecm-academy.nl
Fair Labor Association (FLA)   http://www.fairlabor.org
Federal Election Commission   http://www.fec.gov
Federal Trade Commission   http://www.ftc.gov
Food and Drug Administration   http://www.fda.gov
FirstGov.gov   http://www.FirstGov.gov
The Foundation Center   http://www.fdncenter.org
Freedom Center   http://www.freedomcenter.org
Global Policy Forum   http://www.globalpolicy.org
Global Reporting Initiative   http://www.globalreporting.org
Global Sullivan Principles   http://globalsullivanprinciples.org
Good Money, Inc.   http://www.goodmoney.com
Government Accountability Project   http://www.whistleblower.org
Greenpeace   http://www.greenpeace.org
Human Rights Campaign   http://www.hrc.org
Human Rights Watch   http://www.hrw.org
Infact   http://www.infact.org
Infact Canada   http://www.infactcanada.ca
Institute for Business, Technology & Ethics   http://www.ethix.org
Interfaith Center on Corporate Responsibility   http://www.iccr.org
International Campaign for Justice in Bhopal   http://www.bhopal.net

International Labour Organization   http://www.ilo.org

International Society for Ethics and Information Technology
      http://csethics.uis.edu

Investor Responsibility Research Center (IRRC)   http://www.irrc.org

Living Wage   http://www.livingwagecampaign.org

Markkula Center for Applied Ethics at Santa Clara University
      http://www.scu.edu/ethics

NAACP   http://www.naacp.org

National AIDS Fund   http://www.aidsfund.org

National Association of Manufacturers   http://www.nam.org

National Association of Working Women (9 to 5)   http://www.9to5.org

National Coalition for Patient Rights   http://www.nationalcpr.org

National Committee for Responsive Philanthropy   http://www.ncrp.org

National Federation of Independent Business   http://www.nfib.org

National Human Genome Research Institute   http://www.genome.gov

National Organization for Women   http://www.now.org

National Park Foundation   http://www.nationalparks.org

National Parks Conservation Association   http://www.npca.org

National Reference Center for Bioethics   http://www.georgetown.edu/research

National Whistleblower Center   http://www.whistleblowers.org

National Workrights Institute   http://www.workrights.org

NIH Bioethics Resources on the Web   http://www.nih.gov

Nonprofit Risk Management Center   http://www.nonprofitrisk.org

Occupational Safety and Health Administration (OSHA)   http://www.osha.gov

OECD Guidelines Multinational Enterprises   http://www.oecd.org

Olsson Center for Applied Ethics, University of Virginia
      http://www.darden.virginia.edu

OMB Watch   http://www.ombwatch.org

The Ombudsman Association   http://www.ombuds-toa.org

Online Privacy Alliance   http://www.privacyalliance.org

Ontario Consultants on Religious Tolerance   http://www.religioustolerance.org

Points of Light Foundation   http://www.pointsoflight.org

President's Council on Bioethics   http://www.bioethics.gov

Privacy.Org   http://www.privacy.org

Privacy Rights Clearinghouse   http://www.privacyrights.org

Privatization Web site   http://www.privatization.org

Project Implicit   https://implicit.harvard.edu

Public Affairs Council   http://www.pac.org

Public Citizen   http://www.citizen.org

Public Interest Groups   http://www.pirg.org

Public Relations Society of America   http://www.prsa.org

Rainforest Action Network   http://www.ran.org

Reason Public Policy Institute (RPPI)   http://www.privatization.org

Regulations Web site   http://www.regulations.gov

Ronald McDonald House   http://www.rmhc.org

Science Controversies On-Line Partnerships in Education (SCOPE)
      http://scope.educ.washington.edu

Securities and Exchange Commission (SEC)   http://www.sec.gov

Sierra Club   http://www.sierraclub.org
Social Accountability International   http://www.sa-intl.org
Social Auditing   http://www.neweconomics.org
Society for Business Ethics   http://www.societyforbusinessethics.org
Students Against Sweatshops Canada   http://opirg.sa.utoronto.ca
Sweatshop Watch Web site at   http://www.sweatshopwatch.org
Transparency International   http://www.transparency.org
United for a Fair Economy   http://www.ufenet.org
United Nations Environment Programme   http://www.unep.org
United Nations Global Compact   http://www.unglobalcompact.org
U.S. Chamber of Commerce   http://www.uschamber.com
U.S. Consumer Product Safety Commission   http://www.cpsc.gov
U.S. Department of Justice,   http://www.osec.doc.gov
U.S. Department of Labor   http://www.dol.gov
U.S. Food and Drug Administration   http://www.fda.gov
U.S. Public Interest Research Group   http://www.uspirg.org
U. S. Sentencing Commission Guidelines   http://www.ussc.gov
U.S. Equal Employment Opportunity Commission (EEOC)
    http://www.eeoc.gov
United Students Against Sweatshops (USAS)
    http://www.studentsagainstsweatshops.org
United Students Against Sweatshopshttp://www.studentsagainstsweatshops.org
Wharton Ethics Program   http://www.wharton.upenn.edu
Worker Rights Consortium   http://www.workersrights.org
Workplace Fairness   http://www.workplacefairness.org
World Conference on Racism   http://www.un.org/WCAR
World Trade Organization   http://www.wto.org

NAME INDEX

SUBJECT INDEX